This book is dedicated to our Mothers whose self denial, courage and love helped to save our lives.

The cover depicts one of the wheels
of the Sun God chariot in a 13th century temple
at Konarak, Orissa, India.

SECOND WORLD WAR STORY

POLES IN INDIA 1942-1948

based on archive documents
and personal reminiscences

Collective Work

ASSOCIATION OF POLES IN INDIA 1942-1948

Published with the assistance of the Association's
publication fund and Polonia Aid Foundation Trust.
Copyright © of the Association of Poles in India 1942-1948.
Copyright of the English text belongs to the translator,
but the original story to the author.

ISBN 978-0-9538928-2-2

Summaries from copyright documents
in Oriental and India Office Collections of the British Library
appear by permission of Her Majesty's Stationary Office.

1st Polish Edition ISBN 0-9538928-0-8 in 2000 (London)
2nd Polish Edition ISBN 0-9538928-1-6 in 2002 (Warsaw)

Printed and bound by T. J. International Ltd, Padstow UK

Book production in association with "Amolibros", Milverton UK

EDITORIAL BOARD
    Teresa Glazer
    Jan K. Siedlecki
    Danuta Pniewska
    Wiesława Kleszko
    Joanna Chmielowska

GRAPHIC LAYOUT
    Jan K. Siedlecki
    Joanna Chmielowska

BOOK COVER
    Alexander Werner
    Jan K. Siedlecki

TYPESETTING
    John Young (Jan Chrząszczewski)
    Sally Young

Editorial Board would like to thank B. Siedlecka for her sketches from India, Institutions and Archives which made their collections available and all Members of the Association who helped with this publication and who sent their memoirs and photographs.

Apart from the chapters translated by the authors, we wish to express our gratitude to all others translators: J. Wadoń, S. & W. Harasymów, B. & M. Trella, Z. Reynolds, K. Borucka, A. Brzozowski, P. Jones, M. Paluch also to B. Pająk for her editorial help and all those who contributed to the index.

Most photographs were made by B. B. Bage of Kolhapur and remainder by J. Dobrostanski, Jan K. Siedlecki, Z. Peszkowski and Z. Kaptur.

TABLE OF CONTENTS

Map of Poland in Europe		viii
Historical Preamble		ix
Editorial Note		x
Foreword: Msgr. Z. J. Peszkowski		xi

PART I   1

1. How and why several thousand Poles came to India	Leszek Bełdowski	3
Reminiscences of individual journeys to India	Teresa Glazer	21
	Danuta Pniewska	24
	Skrzat Anna	27
	Mila Brzozowska	28
2. British Rule in India (an outline)	Leszek Bełdowski	30

PART II   35

3. Resume of Polish Centres & Settlements Outline of Financial Considerations	Jan K. Siedlecki	37
4. Bombay: The Centre of Polish Government Agencies	Eugenia Maresch	39
Stefan Norblin	Jan K. Siedlecki	67
5. Children's Camp in Balachadi - Jamnagar	Wiesław Stypuła	69
6. Panchgani: The Health Resort	Wiesława Kleszko	130
Travelling with Hanka Ordonówna	Alicja Walczowska	131
St. Joseph's Convent	Teresa Mamnicka	140
7. Transit & Temporary Camps:	Isabella Wolff	146
Country Club & Malir nr. Karachi	Wiesława Kleszko	155

PART III   163

8. Kolhapur and Panhala	Leszek Bełdowski Jan K. Siedlecki	165
Impressions from a trip to Kolhapur	Marian Berch	170
9. Valivade: The Main Polish Refugee Camp	Jan K. Siedlecki	173
10. Administration of the Valivade Camp	Jan K. Siedlecki & Janina Pająk	183
11. Law and Order	Jan K. Siedlecki	192
12. Works Department and the Co-operative Society	Jan K. Siedlecki & Helena Tutak	199
13. Social Welfare	Jan K. Siedlecki	209
14. The Food Supply	Jan K. Siedlecki	215
15. Health Services	Wiesława Kleszko	223
16. Orphanages	Wiesława Kleszko	239
In Valivade	Maria Juralewicz	242
Memories of one member of the Orphanage	Janina Małkowska	251
17. Pastoral Care & Religious Organisations (Polish Catholic Mission in India)	Zofia Zawidzka	260
18. The Cultural Section	Ela Słowikowska	280
The Theatre	Janina Mineyko	286
19. Education	Danuta Pniewska & R. Tomaszewska	292
The School as we remember it	collective work	332

20. Physical Education & Development of Sport	A. Błach & S. Ucinek	344
Scouts take to water - at a price	Jurek Kowalski	348
21. Polish Scouting Movement in India	Danuta Pniewska	351
Engraved in our memory	collective work	386
22. Everyday life in the Camp	collective work	415
23. An Outline of Polish – Indian contacts	Wiesław Stypula	438
Our contacts with the Indians	collective work	439
24. A Tour of Southern India	Irena Dziewulak	466

PART IV   479

25. The end of the War and registration with UNRRA	Teresa Glazer	480
26. Repatriation	Teresa Glazer	487
27. From Exiles to Emigrants	Teresa Glazer	496
28. Places of Settlement after India		504
Great Britain	Teresa Glazer	
Poland	Jagoda Lempke	518
Difficult beginnings	Anna Kajak	523
Early recollections	Bronka Rozkuszko	526
Jerzy Krzysztoń	Halina Krzysztoń	529
Africa	Zofia Evershed	530
Australia	U. Paszkowska	534
Canada	Maria Solecka	544
USA	Irena Metelica	550
Others in USA	Teresa Glazer	553
Argentina	M. Poplawska	555
Europe (Belgium, France and Italy)	Teresa Glazer	556
Central Asia & India	Teresa Glazer	559
29. Friendly Gatherings, Formal Organisation and Reunions	K. Skorupińska	560
30. India Revisited: Early Encounters	J. Kowalski	574
Jamnagar Club Excursion (1986)	W. Stypuła	576
Touring India (1994)	I. Mahorowska	577
The Polish Eagle in Kolhapur (1998)	D. Pniewska	579
Excursion to the South (1998)	J. K. Siedlecki	582
Present day impressions of Valivade (1994/98)	K. Koziełł	583
Maharaja Son's Wedding (1999)	Jan K. Siedlecki	584
The Third Visit to Kolhapur/Valivade	A. Chendyński	585
Abbreviations		588
Glossary		589
Indo-Polish Library Publications	E. Maresch	591
Index of names		597
List of Polish Refugees in India 1942-1948		616

Nearly 400 (395) photographs, 21 maps and plans, 32 documents (or their fragments), 18 drawings and numerous vignettes illustrate the book contents.

MAP OF MID 18TH CENTURY EUROPE
SHOWING POLAND BEFORE THE PARTITIONS

HISTORICAL PREAMBLE

Poland as a State, emerged on the European scene in the 10th century and not long ago celebrated 1000 years of its Christian tradition. Important in its development was a voluntary union with Lithuania in 1569, creating a powerful kingdom in Central Europe. Another significant event was the defeat of the aggressive Knights of the Teutonic Order, who under the guise of spreading Christianity were acquiring lands in Eastern Prussia. The hostilities ended with a treaty, which gave Poland access to the Baltic Sea through the port of Gdańsk (Danzig) at the estuary of the river Vistula, and direct trade route with Western Europe.

Sixteenth century was a 'golden age' in Poland's history. In spite of class system and serfdom, so prevalent in the whole of Europe, there was a widespread religious toleration and marked prosperity. Learning increased and arts prospered. Landed gentry called 'szlachta' recognised by their family crest, were gaining more power in the Assembly known as 'Sejm' against the power of the magnates who were sitting in the 'Senat'.

In 1506, the last hereditary monarch of Jagiellonian dynasty died leaving no heirs and from then on, kings were elected by the General Assembly. The most outstanding elected king of Poland was Jan Sobieski, who came to the rescue of Vienna, besieged by the Turks and crushed the invading hordes in 1683, saving Europe for Christianity against enslavement by Islam.

In time, the misuse of the 'liberum veto' based on the conception that resolutions of the 'Sejm' must be passed unanimously, resulted in frustration of parliamentary sessions and no work done. (Originally it was meant to be a safeguard against tyranny.) Internal weakness encouraged Poland's aggressive neighbours to interfere in her affairs. In 1772, Frederick II of Prussia colluded with Catherine II of Russia, to usurp the lands nearest to their borders. Austria joined in the partition of Polish territories. So sharp was the shock, that in 1791, the Polish patriots inspired by the ideas of the French Revolution met at a 'Sejm' in Warsaw and agreed on a new constitution: crown was to be hereditary, the 'liberum veto' removed, merchants were to have equal rights with 'szlachta' and peasants were granted some improvements in their life, as well as a promise to be freed from serfdom.

But it was too late. Impending foreign domination was imminent. An uprising of Polish patriots led by Kościuszko, eventually failed. In 1795 the final partition of Poland's territory was executed by Austria, Russia and Prussia. Even though Poland disappeared from the map of Europe, the Poles retained a strong sense of nationality and revolts against the oppressors continued in 1831 and 1863. Both were failures, and as a result, thousands deported to Siberia – a place of exile and death.

In the First World War (1914-1918), Poles were forced to fight on all fronts. Józef Piłsudski succeeded in raising an independent military force 'Legiony' (Polish Legions), which in 1918 freed Poland from foreign occupation. The Armistice Day 11th November became Poland's Independence Day. Treaty of Versailles in 1919 confirmed re-creation of independent Poland and established new boundaries. It was threatened the following year by Soviet Russia, but a significant victory over the Soviet armies in August 1920 thwarted their attempt to spread communism to Western Europe.

In twenty years between the two World Wars, Poland had rebuilt itself into a modern European state, only to be annihilated by the Germans and the Soviets, subjugated to the communist regime till 1990. Presently, Poland is once again sovereign and independent. In May 2004 she took her inherent place among the European nations, by joining the European Community.

EDITORIAL NOTE

...History can be well written only in a free country - Voltaire
*...I take delight in history, even its most prosaic details,
because they become poetical as they recede into the past.*
George Macaulay Trevelyan

Our Indian adventure is intrinsically linked to World War II: after the deportations to the Soviet Union we found safe refuge in India, where we could stay until the end of the War and return to our own Country. Unfortunately the Yalta Agreements made that impossible. Very few people went back to Communist Poland; the great majority scattered throughout the Western World. But the bonds of friendships formed in India survived and we occasionally had reunions in different parts of the world until we formally organised ourselves into the Association of Poles in India 1942-1948.

As children or teenagers, more than half a century ago, we did not realize just how unique was our stay in India. As mature adults we decided to research the archives, camp chronicles and our own diaries, to preserve that small, but unique part of the history of the Polish Refugee Odyssey during and after the War. It was only after the majority of the authors of this collective work reached retirement age, that we found time for research and writing. To our advantage was the fact that many documents, previously unobtainable in Poland and only available after a fifty year gap in England, became now accessible. We often quote the original documents in order to better convey the spirit of those days and maybe help future researchers, enlivening the text with personal reminiscences and entries from our youthful diaries.

The first Polish edition of this book sold out among the people whose story it told, the second found its way to many universities and libraries in Poland, as research of the deportations to Russia, had until recently been forbidden, and all the material found in the London Public Record Office, British Library, or the Polish Institute and Sikorski Museum, was new to them. The English edition will be of interest to our children and grandchildren for whom English became the first language, also our friends in India, and hopefully all students of the period of the Second World War.

As it is a collective work, we have retained the individual style of different authors so our English may seem rather unconventional.

<u>The late L. Bełdowski,</u> *a former member of the Editorial Board, made an enormous contribution to the Polish edition of this book. He was the first to start collecting relevant documents, always paying great attention to historical detail. Sadly he is no longer with us to help with the English edition.*

Explanatory note: In Polish we do not address strangers as "you", but use a different form (like the French "vous") Pan (gentleman) and Pani (lady). Hence Pani Wanda Dynowska etc.

FOREWORD
by Monsignor Z. Peszkowski, Scoutmaster

Whoever picks up this unusual book to read, should know, that it contains an integral part of the story of the Polish nation. We were born during the short period of independence of our Country 1918-1939, brutally ended by the aggression of Hitler's Germany and Bolshevik Russia. Those of us, who found ourselves in India, were the victims of Bolshevik hatred. We were torn from our homes, removed from fighting lines, or work places. Mothers with small children, aged parents, were given 15 minutes to half an hour to pack the bare necessities, leave everything else behind and in the midst of one of the severest winters in 1940, be bundled into cattle trucks, which would take them into exile. It is hard to describe how terrible and inhumane the whole experience was, but it did happen to us simply because we were Polish. We had not committed any crimes or broken any laws.

Before we arrived in India, the country of our salvation, we suffered hunger, cold, humiliation and bondage in our exile. Many thousands or our countrymen had perished. By a miracle of Providence our lives were spared and we were freed from this inhuman land. The exodus of Poles from the USSR was a most unusual event. Not many people realize that in the history of Tsarist Russia or Soviet Union, release of any nation from captivity had never occurred. This miracle can be compared to the exodus of the Chosen people from Egyptian slavery. The civilians left under the wings of General Anders' Army.

The inhabitants of the Polish settlements in Jamnagar and Valivade constituted a unique community. I experienced this every day as a Scout instructor sent by Army Command to work with the Polish youth. The major part of the refugee community consisted of youth and children, whose childhood had been stolen. We tried to come to terms with the past traumas and prepare ourselves for a normal life in the future, in Poland. The Scout adventure helped us in this. We felt the closeness of God in our lives. When we think back to those days, we remember so many people: friends, relatives, colleagues, instructors, teachers, and the administrators of our settlements.

Today I am writing these words as a priest and I am grateful to God for the wonderful gift of those Indian days. During our stay in India we witnessed the day when on 15th August in 1947 India gained independence. It was a meaningful celebration for all of us; we thanked God for the joy of their freedom, as we ourselves knew what it meant to be deprived of it. The date also coincided with a Polish anniversary of "The Miracle of the Vistula" (victory over the Soviet Army in 1920), and a feast day of Our Lady.

History of the Polish refugees in India is recorded on the pages of this book. May it help the Reader to reflect upon the strange fate of the Poles, who had been condemned to be annihilated by the enemies of mankind: (fascism and bolshevism), yet who survived. Unpredictable are God's ways...

PART I

   HOW AND WHY SEVERAL THOUSAND POLES CAME TO INDIA
   REMINISCENCES OF JOURNEYS TO INDIA
   BRITISH RULE IN INDIA

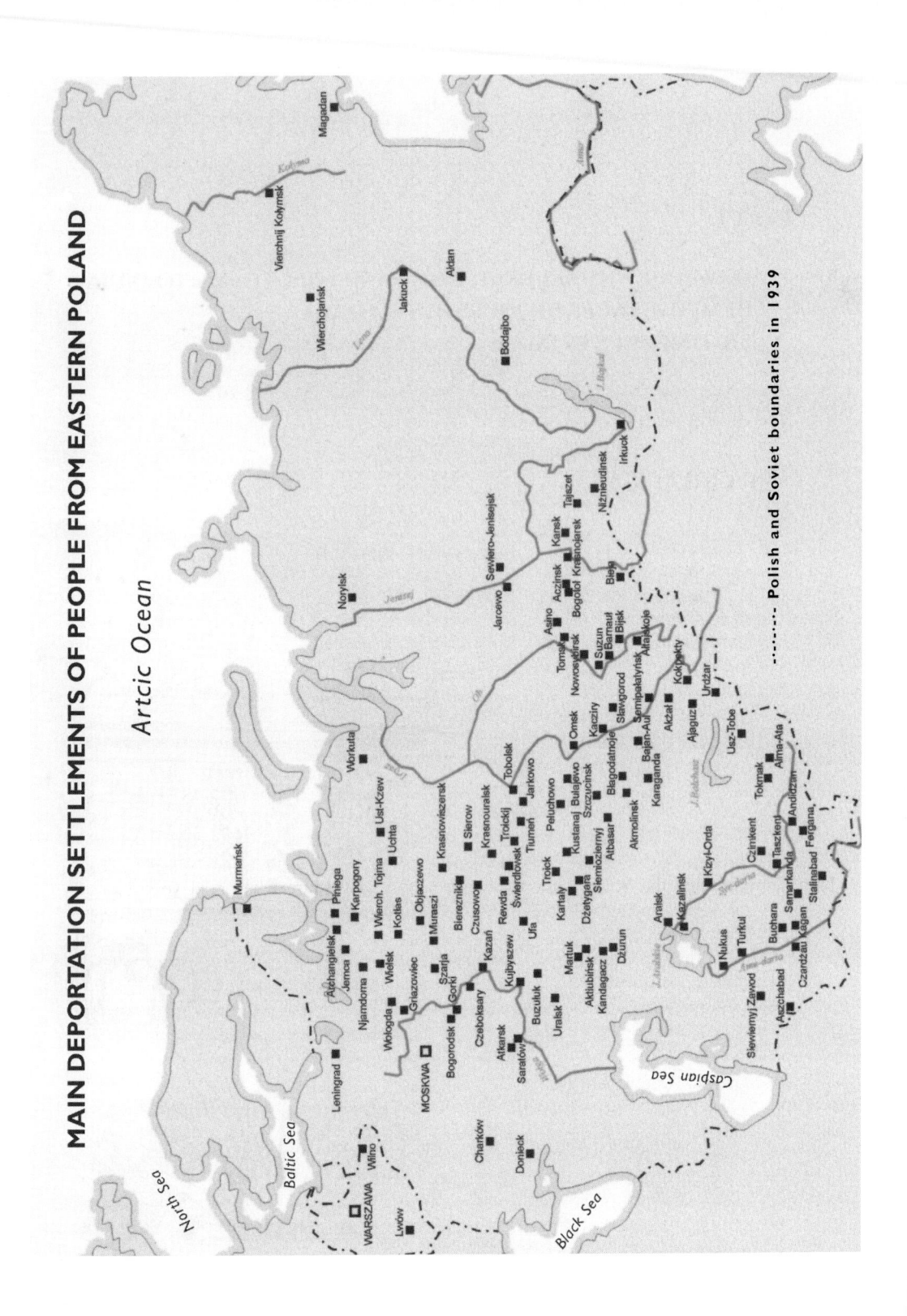

MAIN DEPORTATION SETTLEMENTS OF PEOPLE FROM EASTERN POLAND

Arctic Ocean

------- Polish and Soviet boundaries in 1939

HOW AND WHY SEVERAL THOUSAND POLES CAME TO INDIA
Leszek Bełdowski

Although the authors of this book and their contemporaries were born in independent Poland, the shadow of war threatened their childhood without them being aware of it at the time. The Treaty of Versailles 1919, which was responsible for the post first world war settlement of Europe, aimed to weaken Germany. She was forced to return to Poland territories acquired in the 18th century partitions of Poland, Alsace-Lorraine to France and her army was drastically reduced. The Germans complained bitterly that it was a 'dictat' and that they were forced to accept these conditions. These grievances, exploited later by Hitler were a contributory factor for the outbreak of the WWII.

In the fourth year of the World War II, several thousand Poles found themselves in India and many more passed through its transit camp on their way to Africa, Mexico and New Zealand. In order to answer how and why this happened one has to go back to 1918.

German-Soviet Relations

From the moment of regaining independence in 1918, Poland's existence was threatened by both Germany and the Soviet Union. This became real warfare when next year the Red Army moving westwards faced the Polish Forces. Germany was keenly watching this conflict expecting to exploit the defeat of the Poles. The *Reichswehr*, a professional German Army limited to 100,000 men by the Treaty of Versailles, was like a state within a state and could afford to carry out its own foreign policy[1] which was initiated by the Head of the Army Board and its chief organiser, a pro-Russian Gen. Hans von Seect.[2] In a letter on 31st January 1920 he wrote: "...only in strict cooperation with Russia will Germany have a chance to regain its world power..."[3] Officially Germany had to be neutral, but it tended to sympathise with Russia.[4]

These sentiments were noted by the Russians, but not reciprocated at the time. In 1920, Russia was expecting to win and did not feel like sharing the spoils of war. She intended to press westwards and spread the communist revolution. The Soviet Gen. Tukhachevsky was urging his army to 'march over the corpse of Poland to kindle the worldwide fire of revolution'.[5] After their defeats on the outskirts of Warsaw and the river Niemen (Nemunas), on 2nd October 1920 Lenin said: "...Such was the position that had the Red Army advanced victoriously another few days, not only would Warsaw have been captured (that would not have mattered so much), but the peace of Versailles would have been destroyed. Therein lies the international significance of this Polish war."[6]

The German expectations and Russian plans came to nothing. The Red Army was decisively beaten and forced to retreat. The deadly threat passed away. Germany and Russia whilst remaining on the periphery of the European political scene reached an understanding because their aim was to by-pass the resolutions of the Treaty of Versailles. When invited to an Inter-Allied conference in Genoa in April 1922, the German and Soviet delegates without informing their hosts, moved to nearby Rapallo. There the Treaty of Rapallo was signed, ostensibly formalizing Soviet-German diplomatic and trade relations but secretly consolidating military collaboration discussed in earlier negotiations, i.e. production of arms and aeroplanes in Russia by the German industry,[7] the very thing forbidden by the treaty of Versailles. Even more important for Germany was the chance of military collaboration. In Russia they could train their officers in the use of arms which was prohibited in Germany. In the Russian air force German officers were employed as flying instructors and Soviet officers were being trained in Germany.[8] In Russia, the Germans had secret training centres specialising in armour, aircraft and poison gas, the production of which came to an end in 1927. Both countries derived long term benefits from this contact between the General Staff and mutual training of the Officer Corps. The twelve year long cooperation was very beneficial to both armies. From 1933-1939 Germany was able to create in six years the most powerful air force and armoured units in the world.[9] The Red Army also learned a lot from the Germans, making use of their technical planning.

The military understanding between Germany and Russia, directed against Poland, had a long-standing tradition dating back to the partitions of Poland in the XVIII century by both states. After the Treaty of Locarno in 1925 in which the Germans guaranteed the *status quo* of their borders with France and Belgium, but not with Poland, the Polish Ambassador in Berlin saw the outbreak of war in 5 or 8 years' time. The Russo-German military collaboration was noted by Polish counterintelligence and was known to the Polish General Staff.[10]

When Hitler came to power in January 1933, he could begin to realize his plans concerning the position of Germany in Europe. From that moment the friendly relationship between the two countries (Germany and Russia) began to deteriorate. Some historians believe the fault was with Germany[11] and others blame Russia.[12]

In November 1937, at the conference of the heads of all armed forces, war and foreign affairs ministers, Hitler presented his long term plans. He believed in the necessity of acquiring *lebensraum (living space)* as being the key issue shaping German foreign policy. To safeguard the nation's future, Germany had to achieve self-sufficiency in food production and it had to increase its supply of raw materials.

In order to carry out these aims Germany would have to conquer new territories in Europe to enlarge the 'living space' for its people. He insisted that the conquered people must not outnumber the Germans. It was then that Hitler outlined his policy of genocide and proposed the annexation of Austria, occupation of Czechoslovakia and invasion of Poland. He claimed that in this part of Europe Germany can achieve most for the lowest cost.[13]

Beginning from October 1933, the Soviets tried to find a *rapprochement* with the new government of Germany, despite Hitler's anti-communist stance and propaganda abuse on both sides. As the German pressure on Poland increased, the not so cordial relations between Germany and the USSR improved. This time it was Russia hoping to take advantage of the German-Polish conflict and on 23 August 1939, a none aggression and mutual cooperation pact was signed by the two countries. In the additional secret protocol a new partition of Poland was planned.

The day before in his speech, Hitler said to his commanders: "...I have given orders to shoot anyone who dares to say one word of criticism, because the aim of this war is not to reach a certain objective, but a total annihilation of the enemy. For the time being therefore, I have placed in the East my units with the death skull insignia, ordering them to shoot without mercy, many women and children of Polish origin and language. Only in this way and manner we shall be able to acquire 'living space'... Poland will be depleted of its people and populated by Germans." He was afraid that at the last minute, Chamberlain or some other 'dirty pig' *(saukerl)* would put forward proposals changing those plans.[14]

The Outbreak of World War II and the Partition of Poland

Having obtained Stalin's cooperation, Hitler invaded Poland on 1st September 1939. While the Polish Army desperately fought numerically and technically superior German forces in the West, the Red Army invaded from the East on 17th of the same month, breaking the non-aggression pact signed with Poland in 1933 and extended in 1934. It occupied the Eastern provinces of Poland making further resistance by the Poles impossible, although the defence of Warsaw did not end until 27th September and the Hel peninsula up to 2nd October. The last battle was fought by Gen. Kleeberg outside Kock from 2nd to 5th October 1939.

In order to escape the invading Soviet Army, the Polish Government, General Staff, some units of the Polish Army and civilians crossed the border into Romania and Hungary where they were interned. Among them were politicians, scientists, engineers and high government officials. In accordance with article 24 of the Polish Constitution of 1935, President I. Mościcki resigned and nominated Władysław Raczkiewicz as his successor, who was sworn in on 30th October 1939. Gen. Władysław Sikorski who was Commander in Chief of the Polish Forces from 28th September, was now asked to form a new Polish Government in France. The new Government started re-establishing the Polish Forces by recruiting men from migrant Poles in France and soldiers who had escaped the internment camps in Romania and Hungary. These men were arriving in France with the help of Polish diplomatic missions, by land through the Balkans and Italy or by sea routes from ports in Romania, Yugoslavia and Greece.

When fighting ceased in Poland and all resistance was broken, von Seect's dream of a common frontier with Russia was realized, although later events did not bring the expected benefits to Germany.

The two invaders almost immediately began to implement their genocide policy regarding the conquered nation. Stalin was anxious to alter irrevocably the structure of the ethnic population in the part of Poland under Soviet occupation. Even though the Soviet Union did not declare war on Poland and the Red Army in their propaganda leaflets talked about their friendly intentions, the prisoners of war were treated with exceptional brutality. Terror was introduced behind the smoke screen of 'fraternal aid', saving the people from the catastrophe of war and the yoke of capitalism. Nikita Krushchev and Commander Siemion Timoshenko ordered the Red Army to liquidate 'the enemies of the people'. In a number of cases some prisoners of war, policemen, land owners, Catholic and Orthodox clergy were murdered on the spot. On the heels of the Red Army came the infamous political secret police, the NKVD, who were willingly aided by local communists recruited mainly from ethnic minorities. They also served as prison guards, militiamen and informers. Soon there were mass arrests of state officials, professors and teachers, active members of political parties and social and religious organisations. Next came the turn of clergy, entrepreneurs, shopkeepers, farmers and land owners. They were condemned to death or imprisonment in labour camps without trial by the haphazardly constituted tribunals, because they were arbitrarily proclaimed to be a socially dangerous element.

In addition to these acts of lawlessness, they also organised pseudo-elections to the Western Ukrainian and Western Belorussia Assemblies. People were pressurised to vote on 22nd October 1939 for one list of candidates. The elected Deputies were mostly native Russians and a few

Polish communists, who immediately asked the Supreme Soviet Assembly to incorporate these 'states' into the Soviet Union, which was carried out on 1st and 2nd November 1939. In consequence the Polish citizens of these territories automatically became Soviet citizens.[15] How it looked locally is described by Jan K. Siedlecki, who as a child witnessed the following: "In the village of Rumno near Komarno, the polling station was situated in the vicarage where we were billeted. The room where the votes were being counted, was separated from our quarters by a thin door. Consequently throughout the night we could hear the swearing of the Soviet Officials counting the votes which were obviously not to their liking. Nevertheless the next morning when the results were announced, it was proclaimed that nearly 100% of votes were for their candidates...".

Deportations and Places of Exile

At the end of 1939, the Soviet Authorities already decided on 'ethnic cleansing' by means of mass deportations. The first one in February 1940 was carried out in freezing temperatures. It consisted of farmers, ex-army settlers, foresters and civil servants, all deported to the northern territories of the USSR. The second wave of deportations, comprising the families of prisoners of war, army personnel that did not return home after the September campaign, families of those previously arrested, businessmen, merchants, land owners, wealthy farmers, social activists, all went to Kazakhstan in April 1940. The third deportation in June 1940 consisted mainly of families who were evacuated to Eastern Poland at the start of the war. The fourth one in June 1941 spread into the Vilnius region and included professional classes and remnants of the previous categories as well as people from the Baltic States.

Accurate numbers of those deported are largely unknown. Polish sources estimates vary between 1.6 and 2.2 million. These figures include the above mentioned categories, but in addition it should be said that some people were forcibly recruited into the Red Army as well as labour units. It must also be pointed out that the Polish Government in Exile as well as the Polish authors counted all those who lived in Poland in 1939 as Polish nationals, whereas the Soviets excluded the ethnic minorities such as Jews, Ukrainians and Belarussians.

In this book we are mainly concerned with those people in all four deportation because they made up the Polish communities in the refugee camps in India. According to Polish estimates there were between 980,000-1,080,000 of civilian deportees whilst Sudoplatov, an official in the Soviet Intelligence Service, quotes a figure of 1.2 million in his recently published book.[16]

Deportations were carried out brutally and ruthlessly. The NKVD official, assisted by armed soldiers and militia would come, mostly between midnight and dawn, to arrest people on their list, irrespective of their health and age. Babies, children, old and sick, people who could not possibly be considered as a potential work force or being actively hostile to the Soviet invader, were all being deported. Many of them were to die during transportation, especially the first one in February 1940.

To illustrate the point, let me quote Maria Solecka: "I was 13 when they came to arrest us. The family consisted of my parents, older sister and my younger brother. This first deportation was a total surprise and shock to all of us... We lived in a settlement called Weteranówka not far from Krzemieniec in the Wolhynia region. We were not wealthy. They came after midnight, an officer of the Red Army and a couple of civilians... They read the order of deportation and told us to dress and pack. The officer turned out to be rather humane... He advised us what to pack and what would be useful for the winter... It was dawn when we were leaving. The frightened neighbours were peering through the windows. It was very cold and the snow lay deep on the ground..."[17]

Halina Werpachowska wrote about the second deportation: "It was early morning on the

13th April 1940. Silence enveloped the house and the children were asleep. Suddenly the stillness was broken by dogs barking and a moment later by loud knocking on the door. The nanny, Hela, went to open it. A few Russian soldiers and civilians of Polish origin burst in. 'Does the family of a Polish officer live here?' Was the first question. My mother half paralysed with fear did not answer. We were allowed two hours to pack. In a while two horse drawn carts drew up in front of the house. My mother dressed my four year old sister and then me, while nanny was throwing all sorts of things into a trunk and packing some food into a sack together with other items that may be useful for the journey ahead. This is how our exile started..."[18]

The next deportation is remembered by Andrzej Bałaban: "They came at night as usual, between 1 and 2 a.m. Again the loud hammering on the front door. They told us to get dressed and follow them... My mother who spoke Russian fluently swore and ordered them out of the room, so that she could get dressed. Obediently they trooped out... Initially they would not let us take anything insisting that the place we were going to would have everything for us, but mother would not listen and hurriedly started to pack..."[19]

Some transports were going to European Russia and some to Kazakhstan and Siberia. The deportees were scattered from Arkhangelsk on the White Sea to Lake Balkhash in Kazakhstan and from Stalingrad (now Volgograd) on the river Volga, to Irkutsk in eastern Siberia. These railway transports consisted of cattle trucks converted to carry people by the construction of lower and upper deck at each end of the wagon. Above the upper deck, there was a small window with iron bars. It was impossible for the elderly to climb on the upper deck and not all the people could be accommodated on these two decks. The remainder had to make do lying on the floor of the centre section, which had an iron stove and a hole serving as a toilet. According to the instructions of Beria, the Head of NKVD, each train was to consist of 55 carriages including a passenger one for the guards and medical personnel; 53 goods trucks for the deportees and one for the sick. There were also 4 luggage trucks, one truck-stall (of unknown designation).[20] To the best of my knowledge there were no medical personnel nor a carriage for the sick, but I do remember the following scene: an elderly woman with a heart condition suddenly felt faint at one of the stations. After persistent hammering on the door, the guard opened it and on learning what the trouble was advised to 'take pepper' for a weak heart. The deportees were to receive one hot meal a day 'free of charge' and 800 grams of bread. These 'hot meals' were given out mostly at night near larger stations and consisted usually of gruel. The rail journeys lasted anything from a few days to a few weeks. Especially hard were the conditions of those who had to travel by cart or sledge from the railway station to the final place of their destination, sometimes many miles away.[21] The elderly and small children mostly, could not cope and died on the way.

On arrival at their destinations people were employed felling trees, in the brick-yards and on the construction of railway lines, digging peat and quite a few in various types of collective farms. They were required to fulfil the 'norm' as their pay depended on it. These prescribed 'quotas' were usually beyond the physical capability of the deportees. Out of their meagre earnings, many women had to maintain and feed their children and elderly parents. Of great assistance were the parcels from Poland and the sale of clothing brought with them, but not all people had relatives in Poland. Often whole families were being deported and not all of them had anything to sell. Sending parcels from a country impoverished by the invader was not always easy. Right from the beginning people were suffering from hunger. The bitterly cold climate, undernourishment and hard labour beyond human endurance were taking its toll on the health of the exiles. Vitamin deficiency resulting in sores, frost bite, night blindness and malaria were beginning to be a common occurrence. Many of the places were without medical assistance and even if it existed there was a definite lack of medicines or dressings. A number of kolkhoz farms were tens or even hundreds of miles away from doctors' help, which with primitive transport was virtually inaccessible.[22] The substandard and inadequate accommodation was also a contributing factor to the state of health of the exiles. In the previously quoted reminiscences of Maria Solecka, one can read how "...the hunger was ever present and nobody now would believe that during my two year exile in the Soviet Union, I never had a single egg or drank a glass of milk. At night I dreamt of food and on waking up I was cross that I did not eat enough..."[23]

Andrzej Bałaban unfortunately fell ill at the turn of 1940/1941 and wrote later: "...I had a temperature of 41°C. Losing consciousness, I was sometimes delirious. After a few days of this unspecified illness, when the only medicine my mother was able to obtain for me were a few aspirin pills, she asked the director of the collective farm for a horse drawn sledge to take me to a paramedic in the next settlement some 20 miles away. He categorically refused, saying that he cannot endanger the horses as wolves were in the neighbourhood, for a Polish child, even if it were to die... he will not release the horses. Our hopeless struggle with the illness lasted over a month. Visiting friends thought it to be typhoid fever and maybe it was, but eventually the temperature subsided..."[24] It is not surprising therefore that the death rate amongst the Polish exiles was high, reaching tens of thousands and so in a way the exile was a kind of slow extermination.

The Sikorski-Majski Agreement

The outbreak of war between Germany and Russia on 22nd June 1941 ignited a vague hope for the surviving Polish prisoners and exiles. News from the front was scarce. From the loudspeakers in major settlements one either heard of Red Army withdrawals onto strategically prepared positions or the cursing of treacherous behaviour by their former ally. Soviet propaganda made much of the German perfidious breach of faith, as if the breaking of international treaties and agreements was totally alien to the USSR.

On 13th July 1941 Great Britain signed a mutual aid treaty with Russia where no preconditions were attached to the former ally of Hitler. In the face of the easy victories made by the German Armies, the British were afraid of a complete breakdown of Soviet defences and decided immediately to help them in the diplomatic field and from August by the supply of provisions and munitions by sea.

Gen. Sikorski saw a possibility of rescuing Polish prisoners and deportees from Russia since we now became allies fighting against Germany, a common enemy, and of strengthening the Polish army abroad. Negotiations initiated by the British Foreign Ministry were difficult. The Soviets were talking of creating a new Polish State strictly within Polish ethnic boundaries and establishing a National Polish Committee in Moscow, which would then help to create a Polish Army in the Soviet Union to fight the Germans. This was totally ignoring the existence of a Polish state since 1918, which had an internationally recognised Government and an Army fighting Germany since September 1939. In his negotiations with Ivan Majski, the Soviet ambassador in London, Gen. Sikorski was demanding an annulment of the previous German-Soviet agreement concerning the partition of Poland, permission to install in Moscow a Polish Embassy and the creation of an organisation that would aid the Poles in the USSR. By insisting on the release of all prisoners of war, political prisoners and other civilian deportees, an independent Polish Army could be recruited. The Army was to be under the authority of the Polish Government in London. In the face of Soviet intransigence and under pressure from the British the question of Polish eastern boundaries, as established at the conference in Riga in 1921, was omitted from the Agreement signed by Gen. W. Sikorski and the Soviet Ambassador I. Majski, on 30th July 1941. However, bearing in mind past and later experiences of treaties with the Soviets, one can be fairly certain that no formula could be binding on them and would only be adhered to if advantageous to them and strictly enforced. In the protocol of the Agreement it states that from the moment diplomatic relations between the two countries are resumed, the Soviet Government will grant "...an amnesty to all Polish citizens deprived of their freedom in the territories of the USSR, whether as prisoners of war, or as a result of other valid reasons...". By signing this document, the Polish Government was forced to accept the acts of lawlessness on the part of the Soviet Union".[25]

With the worsening situation in the middle of the war, the Polish Government was in an invidious position. Resisting Soviet territorial demands and aspirations of dominance, the Government was losing its support from the alliance with Great Britain for whom the prime ally in Europe was now the Soviet Union. Furthermore the Governments of the Western Allies (including the USA which entered the war in December 1942) and their press, were infiltrated by Soviet agents and enthusiastically supported by left wing biased intellectuals duped by the Soviet propaganda machine. Meanwhile in the West the press and radio were competing in their admiration of the Soviet Union and its spurious achievements while Stalin's Russia continued its anti-British and anti-American propaganda.[26]

Teresa Burek with Gen. Anders

From the 'Amnesty' to the Evacuation

On the 12th August 1941, the Soviet Presidium issued an 'amnesty' repeating the false accusations made as a basis of deportations[27], but not all prisons and *gulags* (forced labour camps) complied. The Polish Ambassador, prof. S. Kot arrived in Russia on 4th September. It was not a particularly good choice, for he seemed to lack political and diplomatic skills.[28] The principal task of the new embassy was to cooperate in the creation of the Polish Army under the leadership of Gen. W. Anders, just released from an NKVD prison. The deported Polish nationals scattered throughout the vast territory of Soviet Russia also needed help.

It was at this time that major discrepancies in the actual number of Poles arrested, deported or taken prisoner of war came to light. In April 1941, Molotov was talking of just over 300,000, whereas Beria (chief of NKVD) in his report in August of the same year quoted 391,575 including 26,197 POWs.[29] However, according to the Polish accounts the number of Poles in the USSR was 1.5 million, and 15,000 army officers remained unaccounted for. (Later found murdered in Katyń forest.)[30]

At the end of 1941 soon after the meeting with Gen. Sikorski, Stalin during discussions with the British Foreign Secretary, Anthony Eden stated that the Polish eastern boundaries should be along the Curzon line as proposed after WWI. When asked if he had conveyed this to the Poles Stalin replied, "No, but you can tell them it is imperative.(31)

All this was happening at the time when, although the battle for Moscow was being slowly won by the Red Army, the overall war situation was still critical. The Polish Embassy originally in Moscow moved to Kuybyshev and with approval of the Soviet Authorities, 20 offices were set up with some 400 Delegates where a larger concentration of deportees existed. Registration centres for Polish citizens began directing the men to Army call up points in Buzułuk, Tatishchev and Totskoye, at the same time organising distribution of food, medicines and other necessities. Despite huge transport and communication difficulties this system functioned successfully until July 1942, when the Soviet Authorities under the pretext of espionage began closing these offices, arresting many of the staff and confiscating the office files. It was then that Ambassador Kot, apparently due to illness, left his post and retired to Tehran. Despite difficulties of war, communist rule and obstacles being created by the Soviet Authorities, the Embassy managed to establish 807 agencies by the end of 1942, including orphanages, schools, soup kitchens and medical aid centres. All at the cost of 7 million roubles per month excluding supplies purchased directly by the Polish Government in London and imported within the framework of Lend-Lease or donated by charitable organisations.

At the beginning of 1943, some 271,000 people, including 80,000 children under 16 years of age (of which 19,000 were orphans) received aid from the Embassy.(32) An additional 51,000 Poles, who were deported farther north, had no contact with the Embassy and received no help. Information from the released prisoners of war showed a complete disregard for the agreements reached, when another 125,000 were still detained by the Soviets despite interventions of the Polish Embassy.(33)

The creation of a strong army controlled by the Polish Government in London was contrary to the long term Soviet policy of securing domination over Poland. It is not surprising therefore that the Soviet Union did not adhere to the agreement of 30th July 1941, or the military pact of 14th August 1941, nor the subsequent stipulations of the Kremlin conferences.

Initially thousands of emaciated Polish prisoners, sometimes with their families, came to the Army assembly points. They came from the Northern part of European Russia, from Siberia and Kazakhstan. From the vast territory of Soviet Russia, people travelled for weeks, dying of hunger and disease, arriving at their destination in a state of utter exhaustion. Later, difficulties were being created to stop them from joining the Army. They were forbidden to disembark on arrival and were sent further south where there was no food or accommodation for them. As a result even more people died.(34)

The Army was being formed in extremely harsh weather conditions, under canvas, with temperatures of -52°C. Food was inadequate for the physical condition of the ex-prisoners in the course of the military training. In addition rations were being curtailed so as to limit the number of men in the Army. There were also shortages of military equipment and armaments but despite this and contrary to the agreement it was demanded that one division, only partially equipped and trained, must be sent to the front.

From January 1942 the Army was moved south where climatic conditions were better. In the warmer climate epidemics of dysentery and typhoid were rife. Malaria was later encountered[35] and in the course of a few months some 90,000 soldiers and civilians were dead.[36]

At the same time, the British War Office was instructing its Military Mission in the USSR to press for a speedy evacuation of the Polish Forces to the Middle East.[37] The Soviet Authorities precipitated the crisis by reducing the food rations for a 75,000-77,000 strong Army to supplies sufficient for 26,000 and later temporarily for 40,000. During talks with Stalin regarding food and armaments supplies, Gen. W. Anders received his consent for the evacuation of airmen, navy personnel and part of the army, which incidentally was already agreed during Gen. Sikorski's visit to Moscow the previous December. Gen. Anders also obtained permission to evacuate women and children.

According to the report of Col. A. Ross for March and April 1942, there were 31,189 military and 12,408 civilians evacuated from the Soviet Union.[38]

During his visit to Great Britain in the Spring of 1942, Gen. W. Anders acquainted the Premier and Commander in Chief Gen. W. Sikorski with the overall situation in the USSR and was urging the evacuation of Polish people from the Soviet Union.[39] However Gen. Sikorski considered that the Army should remain in the USSR This concept was based on the premise of having three separate Polish Army groups: in Great Britain, in the Middle East and in the Soviet Union, all of the same strength. The rationale for this was, that should Allies suffer a defeat in one theatre of war, not all Polish Forces would be lost. The Polish Council of Ministers in London considered and approved this plan at their meeting on 30th April and 19th May 1942.[40]

During Molotov's visit to London in May-June 1942, the evacuation of the Polish Forces from the Soviet Union was raised by the British Government.[41] Soon afterwards the Polish side drastically changed its position. On 2nd July 1942 Gen. Sikorski sent a telegram to Gen. Anders informing him that as suggested by the Poles, Stalin consented to the evacuation of the whole Polish Army, under pressure from the British and American Governments. The Polish Government accepted this proposal on condition that the Polish children and civilians living in the vicinity of the Army bases will also be released.[42] In his communiqué No. 4, Gen. Sikorski, as the supreme commander, gives the following reason for the evacuation: "...because of the Soviet Union not fulfilling its obligation..."[43] and on 31st August in his telegram to the Polish Embassy in the USSR he further elaborates the reason: "...it became obvious that the Soviets will not allow an independent Polish Army on its territory".[44]

The British were eager to welcome the Polish Army, but were reluctant to accept the civilian population. At the end of the first phase of the evacuation, this view could perhaps be illustrated by quoting extracts from the British Minister of State in Cairo to the Foreign Office in London on 22nd June 1942. He was concerned about the arrival in the Middle East of

Gen. Anders saluting civilians

From Krasnovodsk to Pahlewi on a ship

the Polish civilians without prior agreement of the British Government. He wrote: "...if the Poles die in Russia, the war effort will not be affected. If they were to pass to Persia we, unlike the Russians, will not be able to allow them to die and our war effort will be gravely impaired. Action must be taken to stop these people from leaving the USSR before we are ready to receive them (and then only at the rate we are able to receive and ship them away from the head of the Persian Gulf) however many die in consequence."[46]

Despite such objection, in August 1942, alongside 43,476 military personnel, 26,094 civilians came out of Russia by sea, from Krasnovodsk to Pahlevi in Persia.[47] Departures were carried out in very difficult conditions as described by Andrzej Bałaban, then nine years old: "I remember the last days in the Soviet Union as one big nightmare. Especially our two day ordeal in sweltering heat in Krasnovodsk. There was no drinking water and we had to walk the last 4 km between the train and the boat. Totally exhausted we were dropping parts of our luggage not knowing if we can make it in time and whether the boat will take us. Alongside the road we saw dead and dying people. When at last we reached the shore there, in front of the boat *Kaganovich* there was a whole heaving mass of humanity disorderly and noisy. I would not say that the boarding was haphazard, but it seemed impossible for us to get on. An NKVD officer who was standing by the gangway, started calling names from his list. The crowd went silent. Eventually we heard "...let the Bałaban woman and her child come" but still the people would not let us through so the officer pulled out his gun, fired in the air and shouted "let the Bałaban woman and child go" and so we arrived on the boat. We were on the threshold of freedom. Here on the deck there was indescribable congestion with everybody trying to find a place. During the night of 20th August 1942 there were permanent queues for the only four available toilets. People were relieving themselves over the side resulting in three children from the orphanage falling overboard and drowning in the Caspian Sea. By the time we anchored the deck was covered in human excrement. Together with the others I added to this held tightly by my mother. There was no other way. When we landed, for the first time we felt really free and happy having left behind the suffering of our 2½ years in the USSR"[48]

Iran and India

On his return journey from Russia to England, Gen. Sikorski wrote a letter to Mr. Winston Churchill informing him of the results of his talks with Stalin, in which he managed to obtain an agreement to transfer part of the Polish Army from Russia to the Middle East. On receipt of this information the British Army created a Polish Evacuation Staff (PES) under the command of Col. Alexander Ross of the 10th Army. His task was to organise the reception of these Polish units and their transport to Iran and Palestine. They were to come across the Caspian Sea by boat from Krasnovodsk.

Iran was occupied by the British and Russian forces since August 1941. The port of Pahlevi on the shore of the Caspian Sea was in the Soviet zone and it required the consent of Soviet Authorities to set up camps there capable of receiving the Poles after disembarkation. The camps were staffed by British, Polish and Indian forces. Permission was given on 24th March 1942, one day before the arrival of the first contingent. Hurriedly a building was hired by PES, where the airmen and navy personnel from that transport were to be located. The Russians stipulated the whole evacuation would take no more than eight days. This not only created difficulties for the PES, but put additional strain and discomfort on the evacuees.

In Tehran awaiting the arrival of the first evacuees, the PES requisitioned a large machine gun factory, capable of accommodating about 5,000 men. They were then surprised to learn that 'up to 10,000 civilians of both sexes and mixed ages' are likely to accompany the soldiers. In fact 12,408 came and accommodation had to be found for them without delay. Permission was obtained from the Iranian Government for the lease of land and some buildings next to the military airfield, called Dosha Tappeh located a few miles east of the town. Here camp No. 2 was organised on 8th April 1942 and camp No. 1 was set up on 31st December 1942. Each was capable of accommodating about 8,000 people. The first civilian transport by land from Pahlevi arrived in Tehran on 30th March 1942.

The Shah of Persia lent an unfinished orphanage building which the British Army adapted as a hospital for the Polish evacuees. From about May 1942 there were unconfirmed rumours concerning additional transports of Polish refugees. British Authorities therefore made ready an area under the canvas in the woodland of Yusufabad, some 5 miles north of Tehran. This was camp No. 3, established at the end of June 1942 and camp No. 4 was for the Army. Camp No. 5, mainly for the orphans and their carers, was located in a large building with a garden. In March, to extradite them from the crowded camps in Tehran and secure better living conditions for the children, an orphanage was started in Isfahan. At its peak it had 2,600 inhabitants living in rented accommodation in different parts of the town.

As from July 1942, all questions connected with the stay of Polish refugees in Iran and their onward transportation was dealt with by the British organisation called 'Middle East Relief and Refugee Administration' (MERRA) with its headquarters in Cairo. Col. A. Ross was in charge of it in Iran.

Leaving "Paradise"

1. Field Bakery
2+3. Disinfectant Points
4. Polish Command
5. Governor's Location
6. Quartermaster
7. Shah's Palace
8. Russian Military Barracks
9. Russian Command
10. Shore Line
11. British Command
12. Food Store
13. Polish Food Store
14. Russian Petrol Storage Tanks
15. Bathhouses
16. General Supplies Warehouse
17. Fish Processing Plant

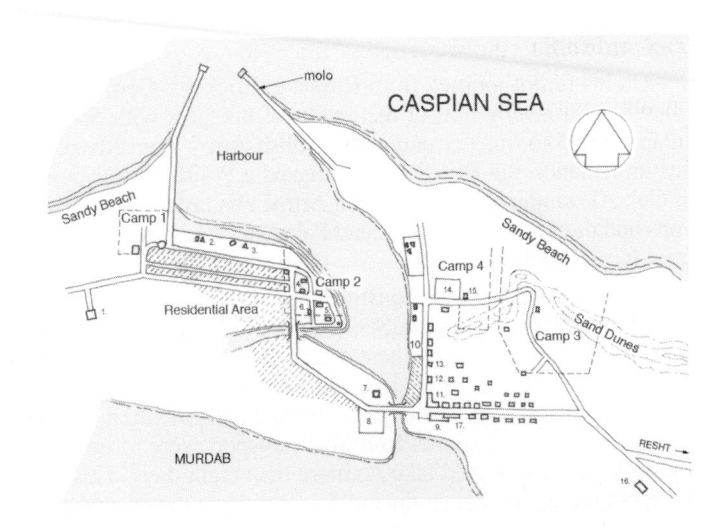

After the first phase of the evacuation the Soviet Authorities maintained that it was completed and insisted on the removal of Polish staff from the camps in Pahlevi. Fortunately this did not happen because in July 1942 came the news of further arrivals. Col. Ross, now an official of MERRA, returned to Pahlevi to receive them. There were 5 camps in Pahlevi capable of housing about 40,000 people. Camps No. 1 and 2 were for civilians, No. 3 and 5 for the military, whilst No. 4 was for the women's auxiliary forces (PSWK). Upon arrival the civilians were first put in camp No. 1 and after disinfection transferred to camp No. 2. Similarly the soldiers went to No. 3 and then to No. 5.

The first transport of the second evacuation phase arrived in Pahlevi on 10th August 1942. Subsequent boats loaded with the military and civilians were coming day and night for the next 21 days, each carrying between 4,000 and 5,000 people. People with infectious diseases were mixed up with the healthy ones. There was unbelievable congestion. Some days 2-3 boatloads would arrive almost simultaneously bringing anything between a few hundred and a few thousand people.

Polish military personnel here, consisted at its peak of 181 officers and 2,336 non-commissioned staff and soldiers. At the same time there were 19 British and 11 Indian officers plus 25 British and 328 Indian non-commissioned officers and soldiers.

Camp in Pahlevi

Just before the second evacuation the greater part of the 1,200 bed Polish hospital in Tehran was transferred to Pahlevi. Almost immediately it became apparent that it was not big enough. The physical condition of the new arrivals was terrible. It was five times worse than the first, mainly because they were starving that much longer. Their weakened bodies were easily susceptible to all sorts of illnesses like typhoid fever. Malaria brought from the USSR accounted for 40% of illnesses. Even soldiers were too weak to walk to the shore carrying personal equipment. Of all the arrivals of 113,437 during March, April and August 1942, 568 mainly civilians died on arrival in Pahlevi. At its zenith, on 8th September 1942, there were 838 people in hospital with about 2,000 convalescing. Moreover, there were sick people in the camp afraid to report their illness for fear of being left behind in the USSR. Their state of health reflected the conditions under which they existed.

The cost of the Pahlevi operation for the month of September 1942 was 5,144,589 rials which was about 11 shillings and 6 pence per person. This did not include provisions purchased locally nor the transportation provided by the United Kingdom Commercial Corporation.

Along the route from Krasnovodsk to Pahlevi 74,935 military personnel and 38,502 civilians were evacuated. An additional 2,694 came by road from Ashkhabad in Russia to Meshed in Persia. The first ones along this route were the children. In March 1942 the Polish Red Cross (PCK) sent from India 6 lorry loads of provisions for the Poles in the USSR. On their return journey, over 160 orphans and their guardians came through Meshed and Zahedan in Persia, then by special train to Bombay in India. The next expedition consisting of 24 army lorries brought back nearly 240 children with their carers, again to Bombay while their camp in the state of Navanagar was being built. The last transport went to Karachi from where they travelled by boat to Jamnagar. This way some 675 children with their wardens came to the Balachadi camp.[49]

Despite the breakdown of diplomatic relations between the Soviet and Polish Government in exile, after the discovery of mass graves of 4,500 murdered Polish officers in Katyń forest near Smoleńsk in April 1943, small groups of up to 200 Poles were still allowed to leave USSR. Their number eventually reached about 2,020 arriving in Tehran by land in army lorries.

The total number of Polish civilians evacuated by the Caspian Sea route from the Soviet Union to Persia was 38,502 and 2,694 that came by land through Ashkhabad and Meshed plus 675 children taken directly to India. Out of those numbers 6,123 were called to serve in the Women's Auxiliary Service, and some 1,005 girls went to Cadet schools, whereas 1,653 Polish Jews left for Palestine by sea. Thus 31,740 people remained to be re-located till the end of the war.

The organisation and administration of the refugee camps came under the jurisdiction of the British and Polish Armies. In Tehran however it was in the hands of the representatives of the Polish Government's Ministry of Social Welfare in London, whose Delegate Mr. W. Styburski began his duties on 1st April 1942 and was later transferred to India in the same capacity.

Every civilian refugee camp in Tehran had its own Polish staff comprising the quartermaster, administration officers, police guards and sanitary personnel. At its peak in camp No. 1 there were 7,985 people, 4,727 in camp No. 2 and 360 in the 3rd. In the town itself lived 1,920 people in private accommodation. The majority of them were employed in Polish, British and American offices or institutions.

In Persia the Polish refugees received the best care possible in wartime circumstances although the living quarters were crowded and noisy. Sometimes the barracks had leaking roofs and were damp if made of mud bricks.

Provisions for the underfed Polish refugees, who also suffered lack of vitamins, were a priority. The daily menu consisted of meat, fish or sausages, oats, milk, eggs, potatoes, rice or beans, vegetables and fresh or dry fruit, butter, jam, bread, tea, coffee or cocoa. Special care was being taken of children and pregnant women. At the beginning people were given vitamin C and the food was good and plentiful.

In addition people were receiving clothing or 3 yards of material, blankets, sheets and towels. The monthly cost of maintenance of Polish refugees in Persia was £7.5 per person.

The health of those arriving in Tehran was still poor. The Polish Red Cross Hospital with 800 beds was inadequate, so part of the British hospital was made available for the Poles. Slowly the number of sick people was reduced. At the beginning of 1943 there were 991 patients, but at the end of the year only a third remained sick. That year 2,119 people died, which was 5% of the total number of evacuees.

The stay of Polish refugees in Persia had to be relatively short, not only because of the uncertain political situation and difficulties of food provision but also because the Poles were unjustly blamed for the general food shortages resulting from incompetent local administration. The Iranian Government therefore was demanding that the British should evacuate the Poles.[50]

(from the left, front row): Karol Bader, the Shah Reza, Lt. Col. Antoni Szymański and Delegate of the Welfare Ministry Wiktor Styburski (later in India) (standing behind): Councilor Witold Okoński, Zbigniew Ubysz and 1st. Secretary of the Legation Bohdan Kościałkowski.

At the conference of Governors in Nairobi in June 1942, the British Government together with the Governments of their colonies in East Africa, decided to relocate the Polish refugees in Kenya, Uganda, Tanganyika and Nyasaland. The two Rhodesias and the Union of South Africa also acceded to this resolution. Initially the Government of India also agreed to accept 5,000 Polish children from the USSR and in December 1942 consented to an additional 6,000. In February 1943 an agreement was reached with Mexico to receive 4,000 Polish refugees. The Authorities of various African colonies as well as the Government of India agreed to accept the Poles with some reluctance. India was mindful that it had to bear the brunt of the burden of the war with Japan. Since May 1942 Burma was occupied by the Japanese forces and India felt threatened. It must also be remembered that the Government of India was troubled by the independence movement under Gandhi's leadership which was demanding immediate self determination and so did not want to help the British war effort.

The route from Iran to Africa was along the Persian Gulf. As it was impossible to guarantee a direct shipment from Khorramshahr, MERRA set up a transit camp in Ahwaz some 90 miles inland. It consisted of one storey buildings and a few large camel stables, all belonging to the Iranian army. The camp was capable of housing up to 3,000 people in the winter but only 2,000 in the summer when the temperatures could reach +48°C in the shade. From 2nd August 1942 every few days, according to the available accommodation in Ahwaz, there was a special train running from Tehran. Initially it carried 800 people per journey, but later only half of that number in a goods train because of a rail accident. Shipment in war time was very irregular with the route and departure time kept secret, so that rational planning was virtually impossible. In May 1943 some 4,000 people were still awaiting departure.

Between 10th August 1942 and December 1943 there were 26 shipments totalling 22,135 passengers. Unfortunately the total cost of this operation is unknown, but to quote an example, on 18th August 1942 a boat sailed from Khorramshahr to Karachi with 779 passengers at a cost of £471.19.3 for a 5 day journey.[51]

The sea routes in the Persian Gulf were under constant threat of attack from German and Japanese submarines. In October and November alone, 40 boats were sunk by the Germans and 4 by the Japanese. The success of the German U-boats was mainly due to the effectiveness of Indian spies hostile to British rule who were employed in the offices of shipping lines. Information regarding departures and destinations was passed to the German agent residing in the neutral territory of Portuguese Goa. One Italian and three German boats were interned in the port of Marmagoa from the beginning of the war. One of them had a powerful radio station through which the German Resident would communicate with the U-boat captains.

British counterintelligence first abducted the German Resident and then arrested other agents operating between the ports of Goa. Finally to remove the U-boat threat altogether it was decided to destroy the radio station. This was executed by a special force recruited from the Calcutta Light Horse reserve regiment, which on 9th February 1943 sunk all the Axis ships without a single loss of life. From then on the enemy submarines were operating blind without much success.[52]

In August 1942 the Country Club transit camp was established near Karachi, where the Polish refugees awaited transport to Africa and Mexico. Another temporary camp was organised in Malir for people who were to remain in India. From there they later travelled to Bombay and thence to Valivade near Kolhapur.

The original idea of placing Poles in India came in August 1942 from Barbara Vere-Hodges of the Women's Voluntary Services (WVS). In the face of the systematic annihilation of the Polish nation by the Germans and after talking to Generals Haller and Januszajtis, recently returned from the USSR she concluded that everything possible should be done to save the Poles deported to the Soviet Union. Her proposal was to evacuate them to India and she informed the India Office accordingly. This was then passed to the Viceroy of India who gave a noncommittal reply, but perhaps her impractical proposal was the basis of subsequent decisions.[53]

The Government of India urged by the British Government finally agreed to receive the Poles but imposed hard conditions, expressed in unnecessarily harsh terms, more appropriate to the enemy than an allied population. For example, the standard of accommodation was to be lower than previously provided for prisoners of war and interned personnel of the Axis. There would now be no electricity and camps would not be built in places of tolerable climate. Furthermore the Government of India reserved the right to control the finances, distribution of maintenance and giving 'advice' (without appeal) to Delegates of the Polish Authorities.

It was in such circumstances that Poles, deported from their Soviet occupied homeland to the forced labour camps in Siberia and the steppes of Kazakhstan, now found freedom in India.

Translated by Jan K. and Barbara Siedlecki

NOTES

1. Sebastian Haffner: *Diabelski pakt z dziejów stosunków niemiecko-rosyjskich 1917-1941*. Lublin, Oficyna historii XIX i XX wieku, 1994, p.78
2. F.L. Karsten: *The Reichswehr and the Red Army, 1920-1933*. Survey No. 44-45, Oct 1962, p.114
3. ibid: p.115
4. A. Albert (W. Roszkowski): *Najnowsza historia Polski 1918-1980*. Londyn, Polonia, second edition 1989, p.64
5. F.W. Reddaway: *Marshal Pilsudski*. London, Routledge, 1939, p.133
6. V.I Lenin: *Collected Works*. 4th edition 1966, vol. 31, pp.305-306
7. Haffner op. cit. p.87, Carsten op. cit. pp.18-19
8. Carsten op. cit. p.123
9. Haffner op. cit. p.91
10. Michael Laffan: *Weimar and Versailles: German Foreign Policy, 1919-1933*. In: The Burden of German History 1919-1945: Essays for the Goethe Institute, London, Methuen. 1989 p.86
11. Carsten op. cit. p.131
12. Haffner op. cit. p.104
13. Documents on German foreign policy 1918-1945. Series D. vol.I, pp.29-39
14. Documents on British foreign policy, 1919-1939, 3rd series vol.7, document No.314, pp.257-260. Another version of this speech is in Documents on German foreign policy, 1918-1939. Series D (1937-1945), vol.7, document No.192, pp.200-206

15. W. Frazik: *Polacy w ZSSR w Latach 1939-1945*. Słownik historii Polski. Kraków, Księgarnia Akademicka, 1944, p.99

16. Główny Urząd Statystyczny: *Historia Polski w Liczbach,* Warszawa, GUS, 1994, p.195
    A. Albert op. cit. p.323
    Neal Acherson: *The Struggles for Poland*. London. Michael Joseph, 1987, p.93
    Czesław Łuczak: *Polska i Polacy w Drugiej Wojnie Światowej*. Poznań, UAM, 1993, p.514
    P. Sudopłatow: *Special Tasks: the Memoirs of an Unwanted Witness, a Soviet Spymaster*. London, p.277
    Krystyna Kersten: *Ilu Polaków Naprawdę Wywieziono do ZSSR?* Ewidencja Berii. Polityka No.2, 8.1.1994, p.25
    Albin Głowacki: *Widmo Berii w Statystyce?* Polityka, No.6, 5.X.1994
    Aleksander Gurianow: *Cztery Deportacje 1940-1941*. Karta No.12, 1994, pp.114-136

17. Maria Solecka: *Polski 'Element'. 56 Rocznica Zsyłek Polaków w Głąb ZSRS (sic)*. Toronto, Gazeta, No.33, 16-18 Lutego 1996, p.16 (Photocopy in the archives of the 'Association of Poles from India 1942-1948)'

18. Halina Werpachowska: *Moje Wspomnienia z Dalekiej Tułaczki* p.1 (in the archives of the 'Association of Poles from India 1942-1948)'

19. Andrzej Bałaban: *W Stepach Kazachstanu - (Wspomnienia z Lat Dzieciństwa 1939-1948)*, (in the archives of the 'Association of Poles from India 1942-1948)'

20. Nikołaj F. Bugaj: *Specjalna Teczka Stalina - Deportacja i Reemigracja Polaków*. Zeszyty Historyczne 107, 1994, pp.76-151

21. Grażyna Strumiłło-Miłosz: *Znad Świtezi w Głąb Tajgi (Rozmowy z Moją Matką)*. Olsztyn. Wydawnictwo 'Pojezierze'. 1990, pp.53-57

22. A. Albert op. cit. p.323
    N. Acherson op. cit. p.93
    Wojciech Frazik op. cit. p.101

23. M. Solecka op cit. p.16

24. A. Bałaban op. cit. pp.18-19

25. Document on Polish-Soviet relations. 1939-1945, vol.1 1939-1943. London. Heinemann, 1961, pp.108, 142
    A. Albert op. cit. pp.354-356

26. Andrew Rothstein Obituary. *The Times* 29.9.1994
    Andrew Boyle: *The Climate of Treason*. London. Hodder and Stoughton, rev. edition 1980 John Costello and Oleg Tsarew: *Deadly Illusions*. London, Century, 1993
    Edward Jay Epstein: *Dossier: the Secret History of Armand Hammer*. New York, Random House, 1996
    John Cairncross Obituary. *The Times*, 11.10.1995
    Stephen Koch: *Double Lives: Stalin, Willi Muenzberger and the Seduction of the Intellectuals*. London, Harper Collins, 1995
    Bernard Levin: *Blind Eye to Murder;* Andrew Rothstein... *The Times* 30.9.1994
    Bernard Levin: *The Traitor's Traitor;* John Cairncross... *The Times* 13.10.1995
    Ruaridh Nicoll: *McCarthy Came Close to Truth*. *The Observer* 12.5.1996 p.22
    Barrie Penrose and Simon Freeman: *The Tory and the Traitor (John Cairncross)*. *The Observer Review*, 15.10.1995, p.4
    Chapman Pincher: *Their Trade Is Treachery*. London, Sidgwick & Jackson, repr. 1981

27. Document on Polish-Soviet relations, vol.1 document No.110, p.145

28. Władysław Anders: *Bez Ostatniego Rozdziału*. 3 wyd. 1959, pp.68-69, 84, 121, 123

29. Beria's Report: *'Karta'* No.11, p.128 and W. Frazik *'Poles in the USSR'* p.100.
    The numbers quoted were unknown to the Polish Authorities at the time. According to the NKVD documents made public in 1990, they held 130,242 Polish POWs. Out of this 86,536 were released home, conveyed to

Germany and escaped. However, 43,706 remained in the USSR and out of which 25,115 joined the Polish Army, but there was a shortfall of 18,591 men.

30. Tomasz Pieszkowski: *The Fate of Poles in the USSR 1939-1989*. London, Gryf Publications. 1990, p.51

    Julian Siedlecki: *Losy Polaków w ZSSR w Latach 1939-1989*. Londyn, Gryf Publications, 1987, pp.329-341

    Jan Sałkowski: *Deportacje Obywateli Polskich z Kresów Wschodnich RP do ZSSR, 1939-41. Encyklopedia Historii Polski: Dzieje Polityczne*. Warszawa, Morex, 1994. Vol.1, pp.137-138

31. Passages concerning Poland in the record of the Secretary's of State Moscow conversations from December 16th to 20th, 1941, p.128. Public Records Office (PRO): FO 371/31077

32. Alexander Ross: *The Report on Polish Refugees in Persia, April 1942-December 1943*. Tehran, Middle East Relief and Refugee Administration, 1st May 1944. PRO: WO 371/42781, pp.3-4

33. A. Ross op. cit. p.4

    W. Anders op. cit. p.108

34. W. Anders op. cit. p.76

    G. Strumiłło-Miłosz op.cit. p.77

35. W. Anders op. cit. pp.96, 108-110

36. W Frazik op. cit. p.101

37. India Office Records (IRO): L/WS/1/961, p.216

38. W. Anders op. cit. pp.112-123

    A. Ross op. cit. p.7

39. W Anders op. cit. pp.127, 130

40. Documents on Polish-Soviet Relations op. cit. Document No.213, pp.342, 597-598, (IPiMS), coll. PRM 73/1 - III

41. Document on Polish-Soviet Relations op. cit. Document No.233, p.600

42. ibid Document No.233, p.375

43. IP&MS (Polish Institute & Sikorski Museum) coll. PRM 73/1 p.144

44. IP&MS (Polish Institute & Sikorski Museum) coll. PRM 73/1 pp.145-149

45. (omitted when the text was shortened)

46. From Minister of State. Cairo to Foreign Office. 2.Vi.1942. PRO: FO 371 32630 W 9035

47. A. Ross op. cit. p.7. Additional description of the evacuation of Poles from the USSR, their stay in Iran and further travels are based on two reports in PRO: FO/371/42781 and PRO: WO 204/8711

48. A. Bałaban op. cit. pp.34-35

49. (omitted when the text was shortened)

50. IP&MS (Polish Institute & Sikorski Museum). Dr. E. Banasiński coll. 129

51. IOR: L/WS/1/961, p.56 "Persian Minister recently informed Sir A. Cadogan that his government were disturbed at the influx of Polish troops and civilians into Persia. They were at a loss to know how these persons could be accommodated and feared that their presence in Persia might accentuate food difficulties and endanger public health."

52. IP&MS: coll. NP & OS A18 file 15

53. IOR: L/P&J/8/412, coll. 110/N1, 110/N2

INDIVIDUAL REMINISCENCES OF THE JOURNEY TO INDIA

Warsaw - Novosibirsk - Valivade
by Teresa Glazer (Kurowska)

I was seven years old and living in Warsaw when the Second World War broke out. I was equipped with a gas-mask and well used to the sound of air-raid sirens announcing practice alarms. Yet when the Germans started their strategic bombing raids on the capital on 1st September 1939 without any warning, nobody made for the air-raid shelters, people stopped in their tracks and looked up in disbelief at the clear September sky from which a shower of bombs fell.

We lived in the Żoliborz part of Warsaw, next to the Citadel, flanked by a railway bridge on the left and the Gdański railway station on the right. In the first days of the war we saw families evacuated from the west of the country in overcrowded trains which used to stop outside the station to make room for regular trains and our mothers passed on hot drinks and words of encouragement to them, but as the raids on Warsaw intensified our turn came to be evacuated from the city. Our train was hit by a passing German plane a few miles outside Warsaw.

My father was in the army and mother had to look after my two year old brother Andrzej, my elderly granny and me as well as a small suitcase with just a change of clothing, since nobody doubted that the war was going to end quickly in German defeat as our Allies, Great Britain and France declared war on Germany on 3rd September.

In the meantime we were moving away from the capital in a horse-drawn cart, driving through small towns like Ryki with all the houses along the main road burning as the result of German incendiary bombs, or other ones where human and horse corpses lay on both sides of the road. When German planes on the way to or from a specific bombing raid flew low shooting at people thronging the road, my mother hid us in roadside ditches sheltering our heads by her hands saying: 'if they get us let it be together'. My Gran however never descended from the cart but waved her umbrella fiercely at the planes muttering awesome curses. Somehow we got safely to the country house of the Parysiewicz family near Kowel where it looked as if the war had not yet reached. But after a few days on 17th September the Bolshevik armies marched in occupying the whole of Eastern Poland. Our friends' country estate was confiscated and we all moved to the nearby town of Kowel, where my father in civilian clothing, after the fall of Warsaw, managed to join us. We tried to return to Warsaw but it was not easy as it meant crossing the new Russo-German border. We tried to do it openly and applied for permission to travel from the new authorities.

But the third wave of mass deportations of the Polish population into Russia was on its way. It consisted mainly of people who had been evacuated from western Poland at the start of the war and of refugees. They came for us at 2 a.m. on 29th June 1940 and told us to pack our belongings within half an hour. The NKVD man in charge said sarcastically, 'You wanted to travel to Warsaw, didn't you?' We were packed into cattle wagons without any windows. The train rushed without any stops till it crossed the Russian-Polish border. Later, on Russian territory, it would often stop in the middle of nowhere outside railway stations and people would get out to stretch their legs, try and boil some water on a primus stove, boil eggs, etc. It was rather hazardous because without any warning the train would start moving slowly and it was necessary to get back on in a hurry. After crossing the Polish border nobody tried to run away. From time to time we were herded to communal baths to wash and have our clothes 'deloused'. Lice were the first of the plagues visited upon us. Later came others namely hunger, frost (temperatures of -40°C) and bed-bugs. We left the train in a small town called Teguldet in the district of Novosibirsk. From there we were taken by a steam boat along a river to a settlement in the midst of huge forests. In the autumn those forests provided us with edible mushrooms and all kinds of berries but in the winter there was only the daily ration of clay-like, black yet the best in the world-tasting bread. Andrew and I just talked about food nonstop. He was only two when the war started so he did not remember much. I used to describe cakes, butter, cocoa, chocolate to him like objects beyond one's reach in a fairy tale. My Grandmother often gave him her ration saying 'I can't eat this clay'. She soon died and we buried her in the hard, frozen earth in a primitive box made of a few rough boards.

After amnesty was declared in 1941 my father wanted to join the Polish army being formed in southern Russia. We started our journey down the river on a raft trying to reach the nearest town with a railway station. Unfortunately our primitive raft was tossed from one bank of the river to the next and we had to stop at the nearest settlement of Polish deportees. My father got a job looking after the horses working for the local *kolkhoz (collective farm)*. My mother had to chop wood, clean and generally look after a dormitory for 30 single young working women, who used to bring their precious portions of bread, wrapped in white cloth to our family shack, which was more private, to prevent them being stolen. Two year old Andrew would kneel down and inhale the tempting aroma of newly baked bread but he knew it was not ours and he must not touch it. However one time, after I returned from an expedition to obtain some potatoes, which would sometimes surface during the spring ploughing of the fields, I noticed that one of the pieces of bread entrusted to us had some regular holes in it. Could it be cockroaches? Seeing how worried we were, Andrew owned up that he was responsible for the damage.

Next door to us lived a family with 4 children whose father tried to commit suicide several times until he succeeded. All the neighbours tried to help since the prevailing philosophy at that time in Russia was: 'He who does not work does not eat'. My father told the eldest boy to come to the stables and he gave him a small bag of oats meant for the horses. Unfortunately the boy was apprehended and the marked bag was identified. At night my parents talked long into the night that it was not safe for father to stay, since in spite of the political amnesty he might never be able to reach the Polish army if they accused him of giving away fodder meant for working animals. Father disappeared that night and we had no contact with him for some time until a Polish Jew who managed to conduct some commerce between the different settlements brought the letter. It was decided that I would travel with this enterprising man on his next journey down the river in a steam boat in order to arrange a family reunion and continuation of our interrupted journey to the Polish army. Mother gave me some money for the ticket in a string bag which I put round my neck and hid inside my jumper. After we boarded the boat my guardian placed me on a top berth and went about his business. I waited for him a long time and then decided to try and buy my ticket by myself. Since the woman selling tickets could just about see the top of my head she told me that my mother should get my ticket. I stretched my hands up pressing my fare on her and explained that my mother was not with me, but it was no use.

When we arrived at our destination people were leaving the boat through a wobbly plank thrown onto the land and handing their tickets to a big woman standing by the exit. I took my money out and tried to explain why I did not have a ticket but the woman pushed me aside like a tiresome insect. The boat was emptying and the engine made a fearsome noise. What was going to happen to me? This was the worst experience in my 8-year old existence because for the first time I found myself without any grown ups in charge. I took advantage of some important woman carrying a baby being made a fuss of and scarpered onto the dry land. I found my guardian talking to a group of people and he dismissed my concern with a simple statement that I saved my ticket money so what was there to talk about? Later we found my father who had managed to contact some Polish authorities and arrange our journey to southern Russia.

After we reached Yangiyul where my father joined the army the last transport of civilians was being organised to Persia through the mountains in army trucks. The list of people included in this transport was being read out in alphabetical order and since there were many more people waiting to get out of Russia than it was possible to include in that transport you could hear people crying when their letter of the alphabet was finished and the list went on to the next letter.

We travelled through dangerous mountain serpentines in army trucks, from Ashkhabad through Mashhad to Tehran. Here we were housed in temporary barracks where every family was allocated as much space as was required for a mattress for each member, in our case, three. We received some second hand clothing from American charities and primary schools were organised for the children who had missed so much schooling during our exile in Russia.

We only stayed a short while in Tehran. Polish officials together with the British authorities prepared more permanent settlements in Africa and in India where we were to await the end of the war. We chose India. Having travelled through Ahvaz where we lived in royal stables for a time, then a transit camp, then a transit camp in Karachi, we reached Valivade.

View of the Camp in Tehran

Nowogródek - Bożenówka - Achinsk - Dzhalal-Abad - Krasnowodsk - Pahlevi - Tehran - Valivade
by Danuta Pniewska, translated Y. Ryszkowska

Memory is a selective feature of human beings: individuals retain vastly different emotions, feelings and impressions from the very same occurrences. The deepest mark left on my mind by the events of the war years was of the unexpected humanity and compassion we came across in so many instances. I also realized then, that human beings can find the strength to make music, laugh and joke and show concern for others, even in the most desperate circumstances.

The NKVD came knocking on our door on the night of the 20th June 1941. Their arrival was not wholly unexpected as the previous evening we had noticed horse carts of Belarussian peasants gathering in the town centre. This was usually a sign that another deportation of Poles to Russia was planned for that night. We considered spending the night with neighbours, but this was no guarantee of escape, so decided to stay put. I heard my father being taken to the kitchen still in his nightclothes, and my mother pleading with the policemen not to enter my bedroom and frighten the child. 'The child' was myself – a 15 years old teenager, for the last couple of months worrying, why we had not been deported, like other Polish patriots. (I did not yet realize that Soviet authorities carried out their ethnic cleansing using well tried methods, social standing not individual character being the criterion; and father, being merely a civil servant, did not qualify until now.) Now I sat on my bed, tying my hair with a red-and-white ribbon, to demonstrate my patriotism. Emerging from my room, I found a Russian soldier, who had accompanied the NKWD, barring the door to the kitchen with the bayonet of his rifle. He was only a young chap, obviously unsure how to act and did not protest when I pushed him aside to hug my father before he was taken away. Some people were very roughly treated when deported. We were lucky to have a decent group of men, who did their unpleasant job efficiently, but without unnecessary brutality.

My mother, having packed a small valise which father was allowed to take with him to prison, flatly refused to pack our belongings, professing through tears that we were going to a certain death. Translating for the NKWD was a Polish Jew, whose name I do not know, but whom I mention in my prayers to this very day. He took me aside, urging: "Your mother is not capable of doing anything right now, you must pack, take everything you can..." Then he proceeded to help me bundle up food, bedding, ours and father's warm clothes, photographs taken out of family albums and even the crucifix from the wall. Those things helped us to survive the Siberian winter.

On that beautiful June day I walked behind the cart loaded with our belongings through the familiar streets. Nowogrodek had fairly recently become the administrative centre for the county, but had no proper railway station yet, only a narrow gauge track. We therefore had to be taken to Nowojelnia, where we were loaded onto the train made out of what looked like cattle trucks. These had two tier racks constructed, on which we were to sleep, and a hole in the floor for a toilet. Initially, family members would hold up a blanket as a screen whenever the toilet was being used. However, as time passed, it became commonplace to indicate to fellow travellers that they should look away.

Our deportation differed from earlier ones in that it took place just two days before hostilities broke out between the USSR and Germany. News of that reached us as the train was crossing the Polish border. In Minsk we learned that German planes were bombing Nowogrodek. Our escorts, made anxious by this turn of events, paid little attention to us. They let us out at stations to get 'kipiatok' (boiled water – a drink freely available to all travellers in Russia) and sometimes we were able to buy some food from local people. It would probably have been possible to escape – except there was nowhere to go.

My geography teacher, Karol Łoziński, was in our wagon. He woke us one morning at sunrise, to catch sight of the Urals, which form the border between Europe and Asia. Also with us were the families of the Delatycki brothers, well-known Jews from Nowogrodek. On the 17th September 1939 they had greeted the Red Army with red banners and flowers, as it marched into our town, but this had not saved them from imprisonment nor their wives and children from deportation.

Our desperate situation only came home to me when at the end of a few weeks journey we arrived in Achinsk in Krasnoyarski Kray, in Siberia. We were held there for a few days in a huge empty hall that was surrounded by a tall perimeter fence. Two days later a transport from Latvia arrived. Those people had been deported after the outbreak of war. They had been taken in tremendous haste, had not been able to pack their belongings and had had no food on the journey. We heard many tragic stories: of the mother who had killed her two children, because they were crying for bread; of the old lady whose sons were arrested during the transport, and who wandered endlessly along the fence, calling their names. At night, we tried to sleep, curled up on our baggage, while an old man prayed out loudly: "O Lord, forgive them, for they know not what they do." My mother shouted that she had no intention of forgiving them.

At last the horse carts arrived that were to take us to our final destinations. Mother and I were taken with four other families to the kolkhoz called Bożenówka. We travelled for two days, stopping for a few hours during the night, which we spent huddled by a campfire, to keep the mosquitoes at bay. Arriving at the kolkhoz the following evening, we were surprised to be treated to a hot supper by its manager. Two empty cottages were allocated to us, furnished only with few wooden racks which acted as beds and an iron stove. The majority of the local menfolk had been called up into the army, so we were welcomed as a badly needed workforce. Almost all the inhabitants of the village were descendants of the tsar's exiles, which perhaps explains why they felt compassion for us. Desperately poor themselves, they could not help us much, but they were friendly. We laboured alongside them, although to little effect.

My mother, who came from a land owning family, only had a theoretical knowledge of farm work. She received only half a day's wage for her full day's labour in the fields. I, on the other hand, managed to get a more profitable position as an assistant to the warehouse manager. This involved opening and closing the gates, as the carts brought in the farm produce, shovelling grain, and keeping the fire going in the hut where drivers came to warm their hands and gaze in amazement at the primitive caricatures I drew on the whitewashed walls using charcoal from the fire. The full day's wage I received for these tasks was supplemented by additional half-day's pay for patching up sacks. My good fortune in obtaining this lucrative position probably stemmed from the fact that I resembled the elderly warehouse manager's deceased granddaughter. We were paid in grain, mostly oats, which we had to carry on our backs to the mill. Our contacts with other inhabitants of the village were sporadic. They came to us occasionally - singularly, never in groups – to beg for holy pictures and medals, to hear our accounts of life in Poland or to barter some meagre handful of food for our clothes.

About the so called 'amnesty' declared for the Polish prisoners and deportees, we learned by chance. Newspapers in the kolkhoz were worth their weight in gold, as they were used for rolling cigarettes. One day, during the interval in haymaking, an elderly man called Sikorskij, pulled an old newspaper out of his pocket, read it and laughed out loud. "Look, aunties" (cietuszka – popular Russian way of addressing elderly women). "They are writing about me in the papers". In the newspaper there was a photograph of the Polish general Władysław Sikorski and the Russian minister W. Mołotov, with a detachment of soldiers, at the Moscow airport. All Polish women dropped their rakes and ran to the kolkhoz manager. He promised to investigate, and after some time an official arrived with documents that would give us permission to leave the kolkhoz. And then the early Siberian winter arrived.

My mother suddenly discovered untapped sources of energy. She travelled to the nearest town, Achinsk, and managed to find lodgings and obtained permission to live there – no small achievement in the bureaucratic Soviet Union. Our kind kolkhoz manager had by then been called up into the army, but whoever replaced him provided a horse driven sledge to get us and our belongings to the town. Although there was no electricity in our new quarters and the water had to be carried from the air hole in the nearby river, by then frozen solid, life was easier in town. To pay for the lodgings I had to look after the landlady's baby, while my mother tried to sell remnants of our clothes at the market, or barter them for food. The main advantage was the presence of other Poles, with whom we could freely meet, and the existence of the tiny office of the Delegate (a person nominated by the Polish Embassy in the USSR to look after the former deportees). Although it was not readily accepted by many local Soviet officials, we were no longer prisoners and the Polish Government in Exile was recognized by the Allies as a partner. This office could not provide much help, but dispensed advice and newspapers. The Polish newspapers, produced by the newly organised Polish Army in USSR, were manna from heaven to us, being read and passed on from hand to hand. As there was a limited supply of them, I spent hours copying articles and poems using diluted green eczema lotion, as there was no ink available, to be sent to less fortunate friends still living in a distant kolkhoz.

My father, who joined General Anders' army upon his release from prison, managed to trace us and sent a document requesting us, the wife and daughter of a Polish Soldier, to join him in Dzhalal-Abad in Uzbekistan. My resourceful mother promptly endowed him with another daughter, adding the name of my friend, Irka Łozińska, to this document, and organised a group of fifteen people eager to join the army. The aforementioned Delatycki brothers were also released from prison. Unable to join the Polish Army, since they had earlier renounced Polish citizenship in favour of the Soviet one, they traced their families with the help of the Red Cross and arrived in Atchinsk. My mother visited them, eager to hear news of friends and relatives, whether they were dead or alive. The Delatycki brothers assisted us by bribing the stationmaster to sell us tickets and secure two compartments in a carriage for our party.

It was a long and eventful journey from snow-covered Siberia to springtime in Uzbekistan, where the 5th 'Kresowa' Division of the Polish Army was stationed. We sold the remains of our garments to buy some food and dried our last rations of bread, so that we had sustenance. About halfway through the journey, a case of typhoid was discovered in our carriage. With other passengers we were taken off the train for the disinfecting bath, thereby losing our reserved seats. We had to force our way onto another train, into the carriage full of Soviet soldiers.

Young boys – in wartime, probably separated from their families and friends for a long time were eager to talk with the few young women among us. But our mothers immediately forbade any fraternisation (talking with Russians, communists, enemies who invaded our country!) and relegated us to the top shelves in the sleeper, from where we could only watch the soldiers singing and even trying to dance between the seats. Only Lydia, the only Belarussian girl among us, who spoke Russian well, talked with the soldiers. Then the train stopped - a frequent occurrence, caused by engine troubles - in the middle of a large field of wild tulips. The boys jumped out to collect them, returning with huge bunches of brilliant red flowers. Of course we climbed down, and sat demurely on the seats, awaiting the flowers. But they were all for Lydia. Another incident happened when the train stopped at a station. One of the soldiers jumped onto the platform and returned holding something behind his back. "Linoczka", he said, "I got a present for you". "Chocolates? Flowers?", I wondered. But it was half a loaf of bread. I still find it very moving, that a young man, in a country that claimed to be a paradise for its citizens, would buy bread as a present for a girl.

Dzhalal-Abad was a paradise for us. The town was full of Polish soldiers, since the 5th 'Kresowa' Division was billeted there and in surrounding neighbouring villages. We attended open air Holy Masses and concerts given for the soldiers by popular Polish performers, such as Renata Bogdańska, Ruszała and Borucki. A makeshift school was opened for the children and the surplus from the Army kitchens was distributed among the civilians.

However summer was coming to a close. The Polish Army was being moved to Persia and Iraq, and their families – if they were lucky enough to reach them in time - were being evacuated from USSR. So we went by train to Krasnowodsk – the Russian port on the Caspian Sea, where an anxious wait began. Every ship that arrived was said to be the last one, nobody knew whether we really be allowed to leave. We sat on the hot sand in the searing heat, with no shade available and no water. Eventually an enterprising Russian woman from a nearby settlement appeared with a bucket of water. My mother bought a bottle of this water in exchange for her gold wedding ring, which she had managed to retain up to that time. She rationed out this water carefully, a few drops at a time. On board the ship however, water was plentiful. It was so overcrowded, that the only place we could find to lie down was on the deck beside the water barrel with a broken tap. During the daytime, a stream of thirsty people would step over us to get the water and at night the barrel would overflow.

We arrived at Pahlevi (now Bandar-e-Anzali) in Persia, when the tide was out, and had to be transferred to a smaller vessel in order to reach the shore. This was so overcrowded that, squeezed under the deck, we were short of air and prayed that we would not die now, when freedom was so close at hand. I do not know how long this journey lasted – was it fifteen minutes, one or two hours? However long it was, it seemed like the most desperate time of my life.

Some years of further travelling followed, now in a free, but still very strange world: the few weeks on the sandy beach in Pahlevi; the crazy coach ride along the serpentine mountain roads to Tehran, Persians coming out of their mountain huts with trays of peaches, pomegranates and apricots; a few restful months in the Third Civilian Camp in Yusuf Abad; the unrelenting heat in Ahvaz, (a port in the south of Persia); another sea voyage, this time a little more comfortable on board of an English ship, singing Scout songs between the bouts of sea sickness; and at long last India… There, in the Valivade Camp, which was to remain our home from home for the next five years, for the first time since leaving Poland we had our own front door. True, it consisted of a bamboo mat, but it had a padlock and to us was a symbol of regained privacy and freedom. We also had friends, sunshine and flowers, and an ardent happy hope for the future which, as it turned out, would not be fulfilled.

From Siberia to the Polish Army *by Anna Skrzat*

When the news of an amnesty for the Polish prisoners in hard-labour camps reached us in Siberia, a group of Poles managed with the aid of bribes to board two wagons on a goods train and we started our journey south. We travelled for nearly a month. Our train used to stop 1 or 2 km outside a railway station. We never knew for how long we would stop: a few hours?, a few days? We were cold and hungry so people organised expeditions to the stations in order to obtain some hot water and food. Once, when the train stopped a few kilometres outside the town, my 11-year old son Staszek joined two men who decided to walk to the railway station to bring back some provisions. When he turned round he noticed that the train had started moving. He alerted his companions who jumped onto the first truck but left him behind. The train was gathering speed. My son got hold of the floor of our wagon and a 16-year old boy tried to haul him in but shouted that he would not be able to manage it. I threw myself on the floor. Other people were holding my legs and I managed to grab his clothing and by some supernatural strength bring him inside the moving train. Staszek fainted and his legs were bleeding but he was alive.

Three Generations of Exiles *by Mila Brzozowska (Balawender)*

Deportations to Siberia were not invented by the Communists but had been practised under the Tsarist Russian regime. My great-grandfather was exiled to Siberia after the collapse of the 1863 uprising to a hard labour camp. His wife later joined him and their son was born there. When he grew up he married a daughter of another Polish exile and their daughter Marta, my mother, was born there. During the First World War 1914-1918 my father who served in *Legiony (Polish Legion)* became a prisoner of war in Russia and was sent to Siberia. He met and married my mother there. In 1929 through the exchange of prisoners of war my parents returned to independent Poland. Like many other *Legioniści (ex members of Legiony)* my father received some land in eastern Poland and settled happily with his family, a wife and three daughters.

But 20 years later on 10th February 1940 our whole family followed in my great-grandfather's footsteps..... to the same regions of Siberia.

Translated and edited by Teresa Glazer

We were deported in similar wagons

AYSHA
by Zofia Zawidzka

The 'buran' - a terrible Siberian snow storm had broken loose soon after Christmas burying our sloppily constructed barrack in snow drifts - the authorities were compelled to billet us in the huts of the local Kazakhs. It was winter 1941.

She sat on the ground
Eyes fixed on the leaping flames.
Her dark face
All aglow with firelight,
Was framed
By a white linen yashmak.
Glistening tears
Flowed silently
Down her cheeks
Carved by years of weeping.
"My children -
She whispered -
My children
Starved to death.
All of them.
Ten of them"...
Slowly, distinctly
She counted
Her fingers
To make sure
That we understood.
"All of them.
Ten.
My husband was killed.
Herds of cattle,
Sheep, camels
Perished...
Herds as vast
As the steppes of Kazakhstan...
Gold, jewels...
They took everything"...
Helplessly she opened
Her empty iron strongbox:
"It was full
And my children...
Starved to death"...

❀

That was why...
That was why
She secretly fed us
At night.
Her present husband
And stepdaughter
Would not pardon
Such extravagance.
That was why
She had left us
A pot of wheat and milk
The night before.
Our first meal in three days.
And my brother was only
Six years old...
I promised
Never to forget
Her compassion,
Her tears.
I promised to send her tea
When we were free again,
When we returned home.
"You will be freed
And you will forget".
She whispered
Staring into the fire,
Into her past
Which was contained in
Three words.
Three words!
"They all died".

❀

I have not sent her tea.
But I have not forgotten.

❀

I have not forgotten you,
Aysha...
The time will come
When the whole universe
Will witness
The fulfilment
Of Christ's words
Upon your soul:
"Come ye blessed
Of my Father,
Possess you the Kingdom
Prepared for you
From the foundation
Of the world,
For I was hungry,
And you gave me to eat"...

BRITISH RULE IN INDIA
by Leszek Bełdowski

This can be best illustrated by the way India entered the second World War. In September 1939 the Viceroy, Lord Linlithgow, declared that India was in a state of war with Germany without any consultation with political leaders or other representatives of public opinion. Although this autocratic decision was in line with the Indian constitution, formulated and established by an Act of Parliament in 1935, the subsequent political consequences proved to be very damaging.

As the Government of India is often quoted in this book let us look at what and how it governed and evolved. According to the 1941 census its territory consisted of 1,581,410 sq. miles with a population of 388,997,955. That government ruled directly over 865,44 sq. miles with 295,808,722 population. This was called British India. The Maharajas ruled over the Princely states which consisted of 715,964 sq. miles with 93,189,233 people.[1] English influence began with commercial contacts. Up to the anti-British uprising in 1857, generally known as the Great Mutiny, the British East India Company held sway over India. Only after the disintegration of Moghul power, local wars between its rulers and rivalry with the French East India Company led the British into territorial conquest thus reducing the number of native states. Having dislodged the French and assuming a dominant role after the Moghuls, the Company acquired huge territories which it continued to enlarge. It was then that the British Government turned its attention to the activities of the Company. Control over it was tightened in 1773 by an act of Parliament which nominated a Governor General.

In 1784, a Supervisory Board was created which in 1813 took away from the Company its trading monopoly whereupon it was transformed into an administrative branch of the Government. 1857 marked the end of territorial expansion and in the following year India became a subject of the British Crown. The territories governed by the Company have become British India. During the 1857 uprising the majority of the maharajas declared their support for the British therefore it was decided their present rule should be supported and maintained.

The system of government in India established by an Act of Parliament in 1858 was described by C. E. Carrington as absolute despotism, but an American historian called it benevolent absolutism.[2] The power vested in one man, who was both Governor General and Viceroy, was enormous. His superior in London was a minister in the Government responsible for Indian affairs, answerable to Parliament and the Monarch. The Governor General was at the head of the Executive Council and the law establishment. He had the power to veto any acts of law passed by the Central Government and in the provinces. In critical situations he could issue decrees after prior consultations with the British Government and the Monarch.

Long before that, British political circles were aware that India is not and never will be a colony and that increased participation of local people would eventually lead to self government. In 1885 one of the founders of the Indian National Congress was an Englishman, A. O. Hume and George Yule was the chairman in 1888-89. Between the wars (1918-1939) it was understood by the governing circles in London and Delhi that the army could keep peace at no great cost to the British taxpayer, but the maintenance of law and order would require participation of Indians in the Administration and Judiciary. Having decided on this approach, the British Government reserved the right to decide the scope and timing of constitutional changes. This was understandable in view of the contradictory political aims and economic interests between London and Delhi. In addition there was a highly complicated political, religious and social interaction in India itself. Frustration and irritation grew among Indian political and social leaders who observed the Dominion Status of Canada, Australia, New Zealand and South Africa. They regarded the successive reforms too limited and too late. In addition racial arrogance of civil and military British officials was increasing political tension and anti-British attitudes.

Political reforms were progressing in a number of directions and very unevenly. These were: loosening the Parliamentary power over the Government of India, replacing the British with Indians in central and local Governments, introducing democracy and curtailing the Governor General's power.[3]

During the first World War India reinforced the British Imperial Army with over a million soldiers and its treasury paid £30 million annually to the war chest, not counting generous donations to the Red Cross or subscription to war bonds. In return the Indian National Congress was expecting constitutional reforms.[4] The Act of 1919 was anticipating a gradual introduction of representative government in India. What is worse, the Rowlat's Act of the same year directed against revolutionary communist movements, gave power to the authorities of arrest and imprisonment. This provoked spontaneous demonstrations, attacks and arson against the British. The organisers of the general strike and passive resistance movements did not have control of the demonstrating masses which led to bloody repressions in Amritsar, Lahore and Gujranwala. Here planes armed with bombs and machine guns were used.[5] Events of 1919 worsened the already strained relations between the governing and the governed.

In 1935 Parliament voted the next and last constitutional reform. India was to become a federation of all the provinces of British India and those princely states choosing to participate. The British provinces were to receive autonomy.

This did not happen because the maharajas did not want to join the federation, although the 1935 reforms did not upset the administrative structure of the states that were to join. With the collapse of this plan the chance to create a united India after gaining independence in 1947 was lost.

Despite negative attitudes these reforms were being slowly introduced in the provinces of British India. Their governors became quasi constitutional rulers who had the power to dismiss inefficient governments and assume executive power. The elected ministers were responsible to the legislative body which was also elected and which controlled the

Jhansi Fort siege

governments of each province. The number of those qualified to vote was increased from 7 million in 1920 to 36 million, of which 6 million were women and 3 million pariah (lowest caste).

The Viceroy was still responsible for the defence of the country, religious matters, foreign affairs and tribal questions.

Due to these reforms a number of Indian officials and politicians gained administrative experience and were able to assume power in 1947. It is also worth remembering that despite the original sharp criticism, many of its clauses were later incorporated in the constitution of independent India.[6]

It is difficult now to enumerate the total number of states. Between 562 and 629 were quoted. They varied in size and population as well as degree of economic, political and social development. Some were comparable with such European states as Austria or Belgium as far as their territories or population were concerned. Others were no bigger than aristocratic country estates in Europe. The British were classifying them according to their wealth, size and position held by their ruler. This was expressed by the privileges granted and their autonomy. The most important were those who had the right to between a 21 and 11 gun salute with a further six subgroups. The next category were those who had no gun salute and whose power was more limited. In the lowest category were those of hereditary country estates whose owners had no civil or criminal jurisdiction over its subjects. The Maharaja of Kolhapur, where the Polish Refugee Camp was located, was honoured with a 19 gun salute and was placed in the first group. The Maharaja of Navanagar, where the Polish children were in Balachadi Camp, would be greeted with a 13 gun salute.

By the Act of 1858 British Government was obliged to honour the treaties made by the East India Company with the Maharajas, so there were no further territorial changes. Maharajas could be temporarily removed for criminal offences, for acting against the British Government and for an incompetent rule. Those states then would come, for the time being, under direct British administration. For example the state of Mysore remained under such administration from 1831 until 1881. Sooner or later candidates from other ruling houses were brought in to fill the vacant seats and the number of states remained unaffected.

Compliance with those Acts however did not mean that the autonomy of these states remained unchanged because it was being gradually reduced by the Government of India. The British India monetary system and imperial system of post and telegraph was imposed. Jurisdiction over railway lines crossing their territories was withdrawn. Arming of the

by the British Forces in 1857

police was also curtailed. From 1900 the maharajas had to obtain permits to travel abroad. The Resident or political agents liaised between the maharajas and the Viceroy and their advice had to be followed.

In the case of under age maharajas, their states were governed by British guardians and administrators. After coming of age the young rulers were obliged to uphold the reforms introduced by those administrators and to follow the directives given by the Residents.

The Maharajas could not declare wars or sign peace treaties. They could not send ambassadors to other princely states or foreign countries. They could not employ certain categories of Europeans without prior permission of the Viceroy. Some states were paying a levy to the British Crown, which then was at the disposal of the Government of India.

Those states were not British territories and their people were not British subjects, but they were under the British protectorate. They were not governed by the laws of British India and remained outside the jurisdiction of their courts.[7]

In the years 1921-1947 there was Princes' Chamber which acted in an advisory capacity to the Viceroy and his Council.[8]

Political parties seeking independence of India regarded the Maharajas' rule as an anachronism which only served British interest. By August 1947 almost all the Princely States had acceded to either Indian or Pakistan Union and in the next two years the resistance of the remaining Princes was broken. In the same year (1947) Princely status was abolished by the Republic of India which gained independence under the spiritual leadership of Mahatma Gandhi.

The British East India Company had found India divided and weakened by domestic wars. The country was then known not only for its great literature, magnificent art and architecture and spirituality, but also for its practice of burning widows on their husbands' funeral pyres, of sacrificing children in the Ganges river, of killing baby daughters to avoid future dowries, of human sacrifices for good harvests and of burying lepers alive.[9]

The British were fighting these cruel customs, gradually bringing peace instead of wars, incorruptible administration, rule of law in place of oriental despotism and defence of the country against outside invasion. One of the most important common factors in the face of the diversity of local or native languages was the use of English in law and interstate communication. They introduced and built railways which served economic development and unified this huge country. Up to 1870 they built 6,400 km of track. At the end of British Rule the railway system had grown to 65,217 km which transported some

622 million people annually. By comparison China, which is three times the size of India, had only 14,082 km of railway lines in 1951.[10]

Even at the time of the Great Uprising (the Mutiny of 1857) the British founded universities in Calcutta, Madras and Bombay. Students there became familiar with English literature and history from which later they extracted the ideas of freedom and progress to reinforce their opposition to the British Rule. It is thanks to these enlightened people that the principles of democratic government, being introduced toward the end of the British Rule, developed into full democracy, which exists to this day.

Translated by Jan and Barbara Siedlecki

NOTES

1. *The Statesman's Year-Book, 1947*, p.110.
2. C.E. Carrington: *The British Overseas: exploits of a nation of shopkeepers.* p.940.
   P. Knaplund: *The British Empire, 1815-1939.* p.499
3. C.E. Carrington: op. cit., p.941
4. R.P. Massani: *Britain in India: An Account of British Rule in the Indian Subcontinent.* p.90
5. A. Read & D. Fisher: *The Proudest Day: India's Long Road to Independence.* p.163-178.
   P. Knaplund: op. cit., p.763-4
6. A. Read & D. Fisher: op. cit., p.254-9
7. *Whitaker's Almanac*, 1942, p.730-1
   I. Copland: *The Princes of India.* p.20-1
   The Statesman's Year-Book, 1947, p.109
   Whitaker's Almanac, 1940, p.867
8. A. Palmer: *Dictionary of British Empire & Commonwealth.* p. 282-3
9. R.P. Massani: op. cit.
10. *Encyclopaedia Britannica*, 1947 and 1967

PART II

    POLISH CENTRES AND OUTLINE OF THEIR FINANCES
    BOMBAY: THE CENTRE OF POLISH GOVERNMENT AGENCIES
    CHILDREN'S CAMP IN BALACHADI-JAMNAGAR
    PANCHGANI: HEALTH RESORT AND CONVENT
    TRANSIT CAMPS: COUNTRY CLUB & MALIR

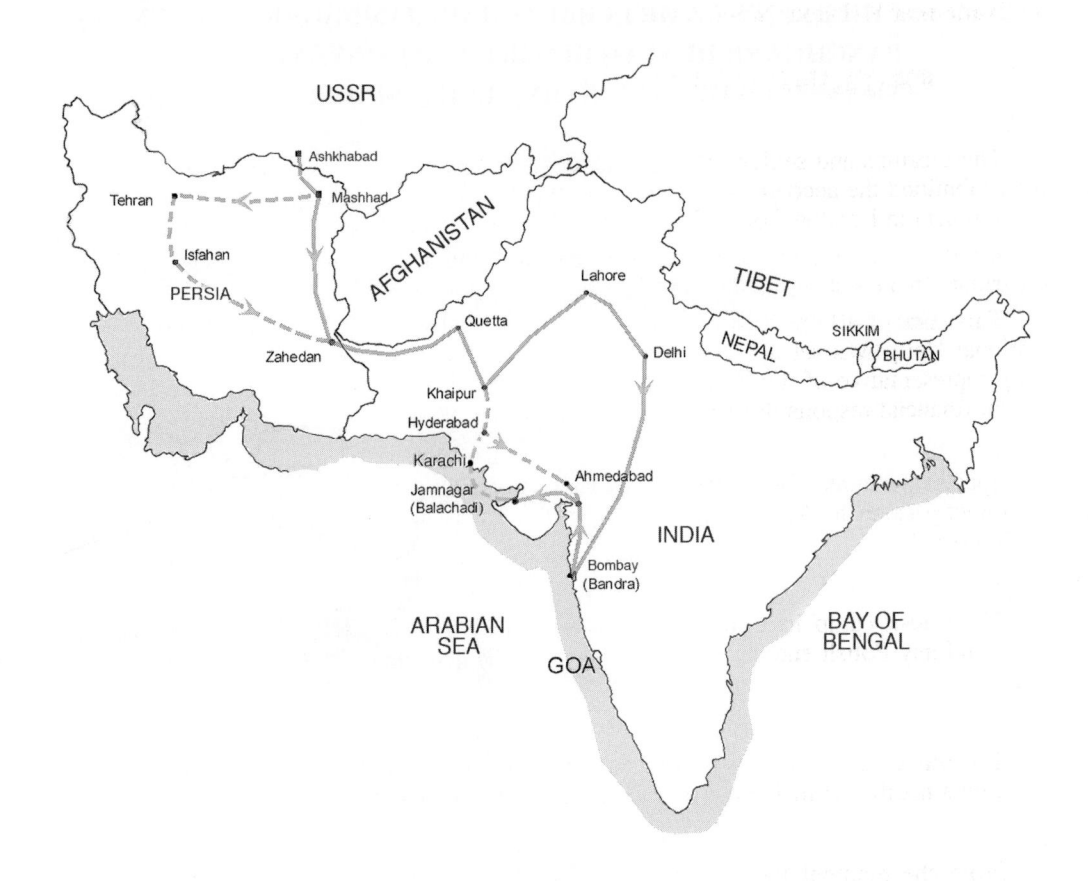

ROUTE TO BALACHADI

RESUME OF POLISH CENTRES AND SETTLEMENTS
by Jan K. Siedlecki

Bombay *(the Consulate & other Authorities)*	2 Dec 1933	-	12 Oct 1946
Bandra in Bombay *(temporary orphanage bungalows)*	2 Apr 1942	-	15 Jul 1942
Panchgani *(rest centre)*	Aug 1942	-	Nov 1946
Balachadi near Jamnagar *(children's camp)*	16 Jul 1942	-	1 Nov 1946
Country Club near Karachi *(transit camp)*	4 Sep 1942	-	2 Oct 1945
Malir near Karachi *(temporary camp)*	29 Mar 1943	-	18 Aug 1943
Valivade near Kolhapur *(family settlement)*	23 Jul 1943	-	22 Feb 1948

OUTLINE OF FINANCIAL CONSIDERATIONS

1.(i)

These camps and settlements were initially paid for by the Government of India, who then submitted the accounts to the Polish Consulate in Bombay for payment by the Polish Government in London from credits obtained from the British Government.

It must be remembered that the Government of India repeatedly stated that it will "not contribute to the upkeep of the Poles".

This state of affairs existed up to 5th July 1945 when the Provisional Government of National Unity was set up in Warsaw by the Russians and recognised internationally as truly representative of the Polish nation. Unfortunately that Government did not want to accept financial responsibilities for its citizens abroad.[1]

1.(ii)

Special accounts for certain aspects of education and cultural activity were paid for directly from the Ministry in London to the Social Welfare and Education Delegates in Bombay.[2]

1.(iii)

The transit camp in Country Club was financed by British Military Authorities in India and any Polish enquiries were met with a standard war phrase as being a "military secret".

1.(iv)

The Balachadi Camp was maintained by charitable donations to the Polish Children's Fund by a number of maharajas, commercial enterprises and other wealthy individuals.

2.

From the moment the Polish Government in London ceased to be internationally recognised, an Interim Treasury Committee for Polish Questions was set up, which was represented in India by the ex-consul Dr. J. Litewski as the head of the Polish Welfare Committee there.

This enabled the Government of India to curtail Polish expenditure and change the Camp Commandant in Valivade. In addition all the Poles in the Administration of the Camp were now directly employed by the Government of India. This Welfare Committee ceased to exist on 12th Oct 1946.[3]

3.
As from Aug 1946 until July 1947, Valivade Camp was paid for from UNRRA funds and later, until the departure of the Poles from India at the beginning of 1948, by IRO. The method of financing the expenditure was similar to that established before, i.e. the Government of India paid initially and then submitted the accounts to these organisations.

It should also be pointed out that UNRRA had taken over "the financial and administrative responsibilities, reserving the right of removing anybody for undesirable political activity or obstructing the repatriation *(to Poland)*.[2]

More detailed descriptions will be continued in later chapters, although it must be said that it was easier to get this information from English sources, because the Polish records tend to get obscured by minute details from which it was impossible to obtain an overall picture.

REFERENCES AND NOTES
1. IOR: L/AG/40/1/131 (RRO A-5)
2. AAN: file No. 84
3. as No. 1
4. ibid

BOMBAY
THE CENTRE OF THE POLISH GOVERNMENT'S AGENCIES
by Eugenia Maresch (Polnik)

The Refugees

By June 1940, France had capitulated and the Polish Government in exile had to be evacuated to Britain, together with a much-depleted army of some 20,000 men; The majority, estimated at 50,000 who fought alongside the French, were either killed, injured (4,000) or taken as prisoner of war by the Germans. The rest were castigated by the neutral Switzerland, who kept the Poles in permanent detention camps until the end of the war. After settling down in London, the Polish Government and particularly Gen. Władysław Sikorski, the Prime Minister, faced a difficult political decision, which ultimately enabled him to recover the bulk of the Polish Army and their dependants who were imprisoned or forcibly deported on Stalin's orders to the depth of the Soviet Union in 1939-1940-1941. Their release was only possible after an agreement, which was signed by Maisky and Sikorski in London on 30 July 1941, whereby Stalin agreed to the formation of a Polish army within the Soviet Union to fight against Germany.

With the release of Polish soldiers from imprisonment, their dependants also started to arrive at the military camps looking for shelter. These refugees had to be looked after by other designated bodies. The relief work for the civilians was going to be administered by a newly created Ministry of Labour and Social Services headed by Jan Stańczyk, a Socialist, with L. Grosfeld deputising. The needs of the Polish refugees scattered throughout the Soviet Union, which was vast, were urgent, and the Ministry had to set up twenty so-called provincial delegations (Delegaturas), under the supervision of the Polish Ambassador. Their aim was to keep track of the Polish citizens, to register them and bring immediate help of clothing, medicine and food. However, the Russians were suspicious and accused the delegates of 'engaging in activities hostile to the Soviet Government'. They confiscated the documents and closed their offices with the tragic consequence that thousands of refugees were left behind, unable to be evacuated until 1954, back to Poland.

The Refugees Desk at the Foreign Office (FO) controlled the relief work and all matters were dealt with through the Polish Ambassador to Britain, Edward Raczynski and his Councillors J. Ruciński, A. Baliński, M. Marlewski, rather than the Ministry of Social Services and its 'Delegaturas'. The Central Department of the Foreign Office, headed by First Secretary

Frank K. Roberts, dealt with the political aspect of the refugees. Roberts was in the diplomatic service since 1930 and had served in Paris and Cairo. Other names that frequently appear in the FO documents are those of A.W.G. Randall, P. Mason and E.A. Walker. The Central Department worked closely with the Secretary of State for India, Mr. Leo Amery, who, in turn, communicated matters to the Viceroy of India residing in New Delhi. The India Office in Whitehall was run by Mr. R. N. Gilchrist, who kept in close contact with the Government of India Home Department also in Delhi, under Capt. A.W.T. Webb, Principal Refugee Officer. The FO considered his opinions paramount. Capt. Webb informed London regularly by sending them quarterly reports. One, dated 20 May 1943 stated:

"The period under review may conveniently be referred to as that of the Polish invasion of India. True, as yet only a bridge-head has been established and the main body of the Home Department during the last four months have been directed to preparing to meet the expected landing of 11,000 Poles"[1]

The newly appointed Polish Ambassador to Russia, Prof. Stanisław Kot had sent his first report from Kuibyshev to the Polish Government in London, describing the beleaguered state of the Poles recently released from Soviet prisons and slave labour camps. Russia herself was on the brink of starvation and the barest necessities of life could not be obtained, unless sent from the West. Councillor M. Marlewski of the Polish Embassy presented the report to A.W.G. Randall at the FO with the proposition that the Polish Consul General in Bombay together with his wife, would undertake relief work. Documents reveal that in early 1941, the Polish Relief Fund in London took up the offer of an Englishman, Mr. Foster Anderson and his wife, to arrange a relief trip via India to Uzbekistan, but later changed their mind and preferred to use the Polish Consular staff in Bombay. The expedition was to be organised under the auspices of the Polish Red Cross and financed by the Polish Refugee Fund as well as governmental grants. Tentative consultations with the Delhi office ensued, with a view to obtaining visas and free passage for the refugees through Afghanistan and Iran. To this effect, a telegram was dispatched to the British Ambassador Sir Stafford Cripps in Kuibyshev, to find out if the Russians would approve this route.[2]

The FO officials knew that such was the magnitude of the undertaking that it was difficult to see how a charity alone could cope. Furthermore, there were political implications and financial matters to be considered by authorities, particularly the British Treasury. Some diplomats considered the relief to be symbolic as there was little chance of getting supplies distributed in Russia on a sufficiently large scale before winter. Additionally, the road routes, which were busy with the military traffic, were bound to be a problem.

The Government of India had already expressed anxiety about a relatively small influx of Poles, who as early as 1940-1941 had arrived in India. Further studies of documents reveal that in fact, it was the Consul General himself, who cabled London with a proposition of taking a group of stranded Polish refugees from the Balkans, provided the Polish Government would support them and obtain permission from the Government of India and the British. They were the first group of 330 Polish citizens, part of the 'emergency quota' for whom Ambassador Raczyński, was instrumental in acquiring visas and funding. Described as intellectuals, civil servants and their dependants, they were stranded in Romania and Yugoslavia after fleeing Poland in 1939. The refugee escape routes were long and arduous; some came through Russia and Japan, others via Istanbul, Aleppo, and Baghdad to Basra, then carried on by sea to Karachi and Bombay - their last port of call.

The Polish Consulate in Bombay was a safe haven for the refugees. Consul General Eugeniusz Banasiński and his wife Kira took care of their 'Polish Colony'. Most of them settled near the Consular premises and found employment; others depended entirely on the Relief Fund and social help. At the outbreak of war, there were over 33,000 Poles (military personnel and civilians) stranded in Romania and 20,000 in Hungary. The authorities of these countries were afraid of repercussions from the Germans who prohibited them to issue visas and demanded the Poles be deported back to Poland. Certain categories of Polish internees were removed from Palestine, Cyprus and Iraq and sent to East Africa. The same rules applied to all the refugees: that responsibility for financing and maintaining the Poles be entirely that of the Polish Government in exile.

The question of Polish deportees from the Soviet Union was a different matter. Their number was estimated at a staggering 1.5 million and in order to evacuate any of them from southern regions of Uzbekistan, where most of the Polish Army was assembled, permission had to be sought for transit through neighbouring Iran. The Iranians were alarmed at the prospect, despite assurances that the first 25,000 civilians would be accepted without significant burden to the Iranians. Nevertheless, a diplomatic telegram from the Foreign Ministry in Tehran to the Iranian Legation in London, was intercepted by British Intelligence, which revealed a written order to insist upon the Foreign Office to use their power to expel the Poles from Tehran as soon as possible, regardless of whether they were soldiers or civilians, adding "we have neither accommodation nor provisions for them and that there is a great risk of their spreading various diseases".[3] The alternative solution which was presented by F. Roberts at the FO, meant helping the Poles with medical supplies only and give up the idea of mass evacuation altogether. However, he approved a plan to bring out individual Poles who would be useful to the war effort, or those, who were particularly requested by the Polish Government.

For the British, the question of accommodating the refugees was an additional problem. A ciphered telegram from the War Office to the State Department in Washington informed, that, in September 1942, Great Britain had in their care 99,114 refugees (including 40,368 Germans, 5,584 Austrians, 12,255 Belgians and 8,437 Poles) and 37,407 Italian prisoners of war.[4] It was assumed that America would help by taking a quota of 26,000 Polish civilians, but the Americans would not agree, suggesting south of Iran was a suitable location in which to establish settlement camps and promised financial help.[5] Similar reactions were received from the Canadian and Australian governments. As for the Union of South Africa, its government cited its domestic situation as a deplorable excuse. They did offer to accept 2000 Greek refugees, but only 186 Poles were taken by the city of Durban, and no more were wanted. With this negative response, the British authorities looked towards the Dominions to disseminate the refugees.

The FO was reluctant to proceed with evacuation plans without the co-operation of the Russian authorities. There was strong pro-Russian feeling among the British people, and a massive war relief for the Russian army was being prepared. However, the Polish appeal for help such as finding the supply source, the evacuation routes and finances to cover the expense, were eventually resolved. A series of meetings was arranged involving the Treasury, Sir F. Humphrys, head of the British Relief Fund and Mrs. Barbara Vere-Hodges from the Women's Voluntary Service WVS, who, as an experienced refugee worker, had been approached by Maj. Victor Cazalet (a Liaison Officer to Gen. Sikorski) to prepare a scheme for the evacuation and care of the Polish exiles from Russia, and their final resettlement in India.[6] The administration had been moving very slowly, until Gen. Sikorski's poignant letter of 3 June 1942, to Prime Minister Churchill, which, for historical purposes is quoted in its entirety.

My Dear Prime Minister,

I would like to bring to your knowledge a question, which is of great importance to my country. It concerns the fate of 50,000 Polish children in Russia who are in danger of starvation. I am enclosing some photographs, which will, I am sure, justify the appeal I am making directly to you. Its urgency is even more pressing on account of critical food situation in Russia. This alarming situation is rapidly deteriorating and many children have been taken ill with oedema due to starvation.

The Polish Government has approached the Governments of countries, who might be of help to us in this matter, (the United States, Canada, South Africa, Egypt etc.) So far we have received information that thanks to the personal interests shown by President Roosevelt, the American Government with the help of the American Red Cross is willing to assume responsibility for a batch of 10,000 of these children who will perhaps find temporary shelter on South African soil.

There remains however, the extremely urgent problem of evacuation of all these children from Russia to Persia and then finding temporary accommodation for them in healthy climatic conditions. It occurs to me that besides the territory of the Union of South Africa, accommodation might be found in Kenya, Uganda, Tanganyika, Rhodesia and India. It may be that Syria and Palestine could receive some of the children. I do not expect that the Soviet Government will raise any objections provided the matter is dealt with in a discreet manner and does not involve great expense on their part. Conscious of your warm sentiments towards the Poles I feel sure that you will understand my great anxiety and desire to save those children who for so many reasons are especially treasured by the Polish nation.

Yours very sincerely, W. Sikorski[7]

The Foreign Office made it clear that the problem of Polish civilians in the Soviet Union was for the Poles to sort out with the Russians. Sikorski's official plea to evacuate 50,000 children was not strictly true as the number included whole families of all ages. However, the request made an impact on Anthony Eden, the Minister of Foreign Affairs who interpreted Sikorski's letter as an argument that between the German extermination policy and the fate of the people in the USSR, the basis of Poland's national life was being systematically destroyed. The ill treatment of the Poles by Stalin was an important obstacle

Polish Col. St. Lechner, Lt. Col. Kireiew and Lt. Col. Alex Ross

to future Polish-Russian relations. The German propaganda machine was particularly interested in obtaining information on the harsh treatment of Poles in the Soviet Union. It was exemplified by a German telegram intercepted by the British: a warning was sent to New Delhi and passed on to the Bombay censorship section to maintain a strict watch on all refugee's correspondence.[8] On account of these political considerations, Eden asked the Secretary of State for India to consult with the Viceroy to give sympathetic consideration to receive as large a number of Polish children to India as possible. He also promised to examine the existing arrangements with African countries.

The evacuation of the Polish Army from the USSR between April and September 1942 amounted to a total of 69,917 persons, among them 41,103 military and 28,814 civilians, of whom 1400 were hospitalised and 239 had died in transit.[9] A report dated 14 April 1942 by T.H. Preston, Chief Repatriation Officer of the British Embassy in Cairo, who visited the Polish refugees in Tehran, describes their conditions as deplorable. The elderly and young children were near exhaustion, obviously caused by starvation. Many of them lay huddled together, day and night, too weak to move or to speak. There were 600 of women and children in hospital, all lying in close proximity: 250 typhus patients, and the rest suffering from dysentery, cholera, smallpox and meningitis. Conditions in the latrines were even worse. T.H. Preston accompanied by Brigadier Crampton, found dead bodies lying in excrement, while corpses were left uncollected in the mortuary. They protested to Gen. Zając (C in C Polish Forces in the Middle East 1941-42), which resulted in a salutary tightening of discipline in the camp hospital and a severe reprimand for the Senior Camp Officer. Slowly things improved and the daily death toll dropped from 30 to 12.[10]

With each day, life in the camp became more orderly. On a subsequent visit, T.H. Preston compiled a very interesting report on the professions and qualifications of some 2718 adults (out of 5,903 refugees 3185 were children); 46% came from farming or small holdings, approximately 17% were in dressmaking and tailoring, and 17% had teaching diplomas or clerical qualifications. The remaining 19% consisted of carpenters, nurses, shoemakers, bakers and butchers, electricians, mechanics, hairdressers and members of the legal profession. All the men were too old for military service and only a few spoke English.[11]

The administration of the refugees in Iran was nominally controlled by the Middle East Relief and Rehabilitation Administration (MERRA) based in Cairo. The principal financial arrangement, under which the Polish refugees in Iran and other countries were maintained, was an agreement, signed in April 1942, between the Polish Government and HM Treasury. Under the terms of the agreement, Polish Delegates of the Ministry of Labour and Social Services, were allocated a sum of £115,000 per month for the upkeep of camps in Tehran, Ahwaz, Isfahan and Meshed. Prior to this, an advance was allocated from the British military funds to pay for personnel engaged in the evacuation, for local transport (Pahlevi evacuations cost 6 million Rials) and for purchase of goods, equipment, etc. The total expenditure known by MERRA to have been incurred up to the end of 1943 was £2,428,500 advanced by the Financial Councillor and £39,662 extended under Army Impress accounts, making a total of £2,468,162. The average cost of maintaining one refugee was £7 and 10 shillings per month. These payments were consolidated by the British financial authorities and eventually charged as a debt to the Polish Government.

In the case of refugees in India, the Home Department in New Delhi, under Capt. A.W.T. Webb, acted as agent in control of expenditure, payments and supplies. Initially, the First Delegate, Wiktor Styburski, in consultation with the Consulate and Capt. Webb's Home Department, formulated a monthly budget. However, in one of Webb's reports, he clearly makes a distinction: "It was the Government of India that set the budgets following unofficial consultation with the Delegate, who in turn had to concur with the Consul". Either way, the budgets had to be approved by both sides and the amount consolidated with the Treasury. Eventually a sum would be placed into the Imperial Bank of India, to the credit of the Polish Consul and Delegates' offices, i.e. the 'Delegaturas'. As a rule, the Delegates resented financial control measures and would have preferred a system of lump sums, with complete liberty on expenditure and accounts. The upkeep of the Poles in India was between £22,000 and £23,000 per month.

For the Foreign Office, the problem of finding overseas placements for some of the refugees was of the greatest urgency. India, East and South Africa, even Canada, were considered. The refugees had to agree that their domicile, wherever it might be, would be temporary, and would terminate at the end of the hostilities.[12] Such requirements were strongly criticised by the Minister of State in Cairo, Mr. Casey, who demanded clarification as to how this policy could be implemented. It all depended on a number of factors, such as the possibility of returning to their country of origin, the immigration policies of H.M. Government, the whole question of the resettlement of the population in Europe after the war, the problem of stateless persons etc.

These problems were still facing the officials towards the end of the war in 1945, who had the task of resettling the Polish refugees once more, this time permanently. Documents show that, in addition to the 4,800 refugees settled in India, there were still 3,800 persons in Iran awaiting evacuation, 1000 in Lebanon while Syria, and East Africa (Kenya, Uganda, Tanganyika, Nyassaland) had 18,500. South Africa had given temporarily asylum to about 500 youngsters and orphans, who were accommodated at a place called Outdshoorn. Mexico had given refuge to 500 children and New Zealand had taken 840 (mainly orphans) on a permanent basis.

At the end of the war, those who were dependants or relations of soldiers of the Polish Army were allowed to join them in Great Britain. Those who wanted to return to Poland (a relatively small number of 473 took up the offer) were repatriated. Others were left with a forlorn hope of ever reaching the shores of the most prosperous and generous of all countries, namely, the United States of America and Canada. This was resolved much later, when the policy of uniting the families took effect and many migrated across the ocean. A vast country of Australia with a population of only 7 million eventually agreed (in 1947) to take 19 Poles; in 1950 it was barely augmented by 1,179. The Union of South Africa with its huge resources, under much pressure, admitted just 140 families in February 1948.

Jewish refugees were in a real predicament, as nobody wanted them. Faced with this dilemma, Mr. Robert Hankey (FO and Commonwealth Relations Office) in charge of the resettlement of refugees seriously considered sending them to Argentina or "to sell them to IRO" (International Refugee Organisation).[13] Similar humiliation of not being wanted befell all the refugees, who were simply thankful to God for being alive. (See chapter on UNRRA, repatriation and resettlement.)

Some Poles in India Before Wold War II

Rare history books, which mention the subject, indicate that individual Poles travelled to India for religious or cultural inspiration, seldom for trade. The most prominent was patriarch Władysław Michał Zaleski, the Apostolic Delegate who spent 25 years building up the Catholic Episcopate in India and Ceylon (now Sri Lanka). Consecrated Archbishop in 1892, he set up two Seminars, one in Candy (Ampitiya), which he chose as his residence. He worked tirelessly until 1916 and on returning to Rome published his memoirs in French "Voyage a Ceylon et aux Indes 1887". After his death and burial in Campo Verano in Rome in 1925, it was revealed that he had expressed the wish to be buried in the Polish Chapel (funded by Countess Ogińska) of Our Lady of Ostrabrama in Candy. Archbishop Zaleski's ashes were taken to India as late as 1957; yet again, they were not interned according to his wishes. The church of Central Seminar in Poona (a pre-war garrison town lying between Kolhapur and Bombay) became his place of rest.[14]

There were other Polish clergy who followed the patriarch's mission. Rev. August Dehlert worked among the Tamils and later as a teacher in Bombay; Rev. Jerzy Piesur had chosen Bengal and Madras where he worked in publishing. Another was Rev. Leon Piasecki who at the outbreak of WWII worked in Calcutta as an editor of a popular English language paper *The Herald*. He and another newcomer to India, Dr. Maryla Falk, who lectured at the University, wrote articles to the press about Poland.

Dr. Falk was a prolific contributor to the literary periodicals such as the Calcutta Geographical Society in 1939. At least three are worthy of note: The King of the Himalayas, Kopernik (Copernicus) and Poland and its Frontiers. Her friend and colleague R.H. Kinvig wrote a booklet entitled *Poland*, which was admired and often quoted by a writer Chatterjee. At that time, Calcutta University was the centre of learning and, remarkably, had a Polish Department of Oriental Studies, where Maryla Falk lectured. She was also the secretary of the Indo-Polish Association in Calcutta, with the great poet Rabindranath Tagore (1861-1941) as president.

There were other Polish traveller-writers who visited India before the war: Hanna Skarbek

Peretiatkowicz who, in 1935, wrote a book 'Indie bez retuszu' (India undisguised); Ferdynand Goetel and Aleksander Janta-Połczyński, who acted as an impresario for the famous Indian dancer Ram Gopal, with whom he travelled to America, Australia and Europe, including Poland, spreading the Indian culture worldwide.

In 1933, Maurycy Frydman, a Polish engineer, arrived in India. He was instrumental in setting up an electrical factory in Mysore (southern India). In 1936 he met Gandhi with whom he developed a lifelong friendship, was inspired by him and admired his 'passive resistance movement' towards the British rule. He designed a simple weaving tool to be used at home by the poorest of the poor to weave their traditional 'khaddar'. During Gandhi's imprisonment, Frydman returned to Mysore and befriended the Maharaja of Aundh's son and started to dabble in politics. He wrote a new penal law, and was instrumental in influencing the Maharaja to create the first open prison in Mysore (which apparently still exists), envisaging the eventual abolition of the death penalty. Frydman understood the psychology of the Indian people; he once said that 'Hindus kill almost exclusively after a dispute over the land or through jealousy'. A spiritual man, born a Jew, he followed the teachings of the Hindu teacher Shri Raman Maharishi and the philosopher Krishnamurti. He fell under their spell and simply went 'native'.[15] Through their Indian connections Frydman met an extraordinary Polish woman by the name of Wanda Dynowska. Their circle of friends came from the Anglo-Polish Association in Bombay, with its president Lord Mayor M.R. Massani, a Socialist, writer and member of the Legislative Council; he was a great man and a fearless advocate of beleaguered Poland. Time was ripe for Frydman and Dynowska to start publishing. It was to be the beginning of a business partnership and lifelong friendship, which lasted until 1971.

Wanda Dynowska was born in St. Petersburg of Polish parentage. She spent her childhood in the hauntingly charming countryside that lies in present day Latvia. She worshiped nature, and her love of mysticism was apparent. Writers, painters, poets, bards and thinkers frequented her parents' house. She became seriously involved with the Theosophical Society as early as 1914 and edited two periodicals 'Myśl Teozoficzna' (Theosophical Thinking) and Biuletyn (The Bulletin). Under the influence an English woman Annie Besant and India's Krishnamurti, she devoted much time and energy to her newly found religion. Whatever she undertook, she executed with great passion. She was much influenced by Krishnamurti's An Esoteric Philosophy of India and translated his book *At the feet of the Master*. In 1935 she was invited to India to attend a Theosophical Conference. Her visit was meant to be short but she actually stayed in India until her death in 1971.

While in India, Dynowska followed the trend created by the Maharishi and Gandhi, at whose side she was constantly present, a devoted listener and pupil until his assassination in 1947. Gandhi called her 'Umadevi' (bright soul), a name she cherished and used all the time. When, in 1939, the news reached her of the invasion of Poland by Hitler's army, she wanted to return home. However, on reaching Bucharest and seeing the Polish troops trying to reach France, she decided to return to Bombay and involve herself in helping the refugees in any way she could. The Polish Consulate offered her a place in the press and cultural section, which she accepted. In fact it created a new outlet for her work in publishing.

The Polish Consulate

When Poland regained its independence in 1918, the country's foreign trade had to be rebuilt anew, first with Europe then with the Far East. According to British Colonial rule, Consulates dealing with trade were allowed to be established at seaports only, such as Calcutta or Bombay, which became the venue rather than Delhi. The Polish Consulate in Bombay opened in 1933, carrying great hopes for the future. It had a full compliment of staff headed by Dr. Eugeniusz

Banasiński. The official reception was held at the elegant Consular residence in Malabar Hill.

Hanna Skarbek-Peretiatkowicz (1892-1968), who visited her married sister in India at that time, wrote an account of this event: "It was attended by 100 guests, mainly diplomats and staff of other Consulates, local dignitaries, society members and intellectuals, both Hindu and Mohammedans. The dress of the Hindu servants was decorated with Polish emblems and colours. The furniture, although local, was upholstered with Polish fabrics. There were tapestries and cushions, ceramics, sculptures (one of Piłsudski's head, for example) and pictures imported from Poland. The whole ambience was unusual and was commented upon by the guests who, unlike the Poles, had more conventional version of decorations."[16]

After settling in, Banasiński was invited by the Bombay International Fellowship, to give a talk on Poland and her turbulent association with her neighbours. Soon an academic link was established between the Polish Society of Orientalists and the Bengali Economic Institution, interested in the achievements of Polish economists and sociologists alike. Others followed. Prof. Helena Willman-Grabowska from the Jagiellonian University in Kraków (Cracow) gave lectures on Polish literature and history, while Rev. Monsignor Andrzej Krzesiński started the pioneering work of organising a 'Catholic Action' in Southern Ceylon (Sri Lanka).[17]

Banasiński had studied science at Fryburg University in Switzerland. At the time of the Russian Revolution in 1917, he found himself in the Ural region, where he was employed as a tutor to the children of the wealthy Poklewski family (friends of the Duke of Kent and the late Princess Marina). He escaped to Harbin in Manchuria, where a colony of Poles, mostly civil engineers, was employed on the construction of infrastructure of mines, bridges and railways. With a good command of three languages, he was engaged to teach at the local Polish Grammar School in Harbin, as well as working for the Anglo-Russian Assurance Company (probably a cover for intelligence work). While in Harbin, he met Consul Jerzy Litewski who some years later was to take over the Consulate in Bombay.

In 1921 Banasiński married Kira Ćwirko-Godycka, a lady of great strength of character, under whose influence he joined the diplomatic service. After completing his studies in Warsaw, he was employed as a Trade Counsellor in the Polish Embassy in Moscow and later in Tokyo. In 1933, he was appointed Consul for the newly created post in Bombay. In 1939 he became Consul General with overall responsibility for outposts in Calcutta, Colombo, Burma, the Malay Peninsula and as far as Aden, which were run by Honorary Consuls.[18]

In 1939, the Consulate increased its staff to 13. The oldest and most experienced was Vice-Consul Tadeusz Lisiecki whose duties, among others, were to inspect two Polish ships, "Kościuszko" and "Batory", when they were in port. He had a reputation as a good organiser and was instrumental in arranging and leading the first land expedition to Soviet Russia with supplies for the refugees. The Consulate had a radio and cipher operator, Zygmunt Żerdzicki, three trade Counsellors, and two secretaries. Three additional persons were employed to deal with Polish-Indian matters: Wanda Dynowska, already a resident and spoke the language, was responsible for Press and Propaganda; Dr. Maryla Falk dealt with academic matters in Calcutta and Harishandra Bhatt, the only local person to be employed by the Consulate, was extremely useful in dealings with the local matters.

Limited documentary evidence on the living conditions in Bombay can be found in a report sent to London by the former Polish Ambassador in China, Count Alfred Poniński, who happened to be passing through Bombay in February 1943. He was surprised at such a small number of staff, in view of the wartime demands. By then, Bombay had become a transit port for heavy military traffic. Accommodation was scarce and very expensive, as was the cost of living (£1 = 13 Rs). Two rooms to let would cost Rs 500 per month; European food for a month at least Rs 170; a light tropical suit (no doubt tailor made), Rs 175 and a pair of shoes Rs 45.

Putting aside such mundane matters, Poniński's report reflects the mood of political atmosphere in India at the time. He was very critical of Wanda Dynowska and her support for the Indian National Congress, and feared the potential consequences for the Polish Consulate. It is true, that being close to Mahatma Gandhi, Dynowska publicly supported the movement for India's independence. She was his 'disciple' and followed his teachings. By nature, her sympathies were ideological rather than political, and she identified India with Poland's recent struggle for freedom. It was obvious that Poniński did not want Dynowska to demonstrate her feelings openly in front of the British. Banasiński had to defend her against these accusations before the Polish Foreign Minister in London.[19]

With the outbreak of war, the role of the Consulate changed dramatically. Dr. Banasiński, supported by his wife Kira, worked tirelessly to draw attention to the plight of the Poles who found themselves homeless and destitute. For a short while, Banasiński acted on behalf of the Polish Red Cross, but, having other obligations, soon made Kira its official representative. This was not, by any means, the only work she undertook. As soon as the Polish Government in exile was formed, she was to act as a Delegate for the Polish Ministry of Labour and Social Services. The two functions complimented each other and the work ran smoothly. Kira, by nature a very energetic person, took on the challenge. Soon, contacts were established with the Indian Red Cross. In practical terms, the Consulate followed London's example by launching a 'Relief Fund for Refugees' with the support and help of Lord Linlithgow, the British Viceroy for India, who donated Rs 10,000. (This donation should not be confused with the 'Polish Children's Fund', a public appeal launched by the Viceroy, for funds to support the first 500 orphans to come to India. The fund's yearly receipts were quoted as Rs 360,000, the exchange rate being £1= Rs 13.)[20]

The 'Polish Relief Committee' was set up on 17 October 1939, headed by the Archbishop of Bombay His Grace Thomas Roberts, supported by Consul Banasiński as deputy, invited Mr. A. G. Gray, a Bank Manager to act as treasurer. Under the patronage of Lady Lumley, wife of the Governor, Kira worked independently chairing the 'Ladies Auxiliary Committee'. A bulletin was published under the title *Polish Relief Work*, which carried general news and listed donations as well as cultural events. In a short time, similar committees were set up by the local societies in Calcutta, Rangoon and Colombo; they had their own bulletin under the appropriate title *Poland Today*. On the first anniversary of war, a brochure was issued 'Resurrecturis, to those who will rise again', with a moving foreword, by Arch. Roberts. It was full of uplifting articles written by prominent people, among them the poet Rabindranath Tagore. In support of the Relief Committee, the Polish Ministry of Social Welfare in London assigned an additional sum of £150,000 (of which only £60,000 was spent) from the 'Polish Civil Credit' for the purchase of food and medicine.[21]

For propaganda purposes, aimed primarily at the US Government, the FO was keen to publicise the British Government's actions in providing practical and financial assistance for Polish refugee children. With this in mind, Mr. E.A. Walker, Director of the FO Refugee Department, suggested a broadcast of the news on radio. However, he made a reservation, that the true reason for help should not be disclosed. Russia was on the brink of starvation herself. The FO was adamant that nothing should jeopardize Anglo-Russian relations.[22]

This huge enterprise, considered by the British to be unachievable, proved to be a salvation for many Poles. The expedition to Soviet Russia with material help for the Polish children eventually triggered off the possibility of mass evacuation of Polish civilians. Children in particular were a priority as they were a great potential for regeneration of the Polish nation.

New Delhi Authorities

The Home Department of the Government of India (later renamed the Department of Commonwealth Relations) was ultimately involved in running the business of accommodation and maintenance of the refugees. It had executive powers from the FO in London via the India Office. In charge of the Home Department was the Principal Refugee Officer, Capt. A.W.T. Webb, a strict disciplinarian, who dispatched obligatory periodical reports to London. At least nine of these can be found in The National Archives in Kew, London. They are comprehensive, running into eight or more foolscap pages, written in standard military format. From these reports one gathers precisely what camp life was like, how the Department worked, with constant changes in notification on the number and category of refugees, they were supposed to be dealing with. Intense activity was reported in securing selected sites, loaned by the Indian State for building the camps, purchasing equipment, setting up hospitals and schools, arranging food suppliers and clothing, all of which was arduous to administer in wartime.[23]

Problems of a different nature arose when Consul Banasiński, with his wife as a 'Civil Delegate', arrived in Chela to inspect a newly constructed camp, which was intended for, but never used by Royal Air Force personnel. Webb managed to secure it for half the original purchase price. Unfortunately, the Consular couple were of the opinion that, without expensive adaptation, the camp would be unsuitable for children. Their criticism exasperated Webb, who sarcastically blamed everything on the dust and dirt, which blew into Consul's ears and onto his new shoes.[24]

Polish Consulate, Malabar Hill, Bombay

Leaving these comments aside, both Banasiński and his wife Kira were genuinely concerned about the unhealthy surroundings of Chela and Balachadi camps, where malaria was reported. Although denied by both Capt. Webb and Lt. Gen. Sir Gordon Jolly, Director General of India Medical Service, who visited both camps and gave them the 'all clear', there were instances of people suffering from both: malaria and other diseases such as typhoid, which unfortunately killed 31 year old Ms. Cathie Clarke, Liaison Officer for the Polish Children's camp in Balachadi. Curiously, in 2004 while visiting Holbeach cemetery in Lincolnshire, a grave stone dedicated to her was found, written in Polish. It reads: *'In remembrance to Cathie Clarke, a Liaison officer at the Polish Children's Home in Balachadi, who died before her time on 19th July 1943 age 33. Grateful for her care and noble heart. Polish Children'*. Underneath there is a short, just as tragic inscription: *'To Rosemary Elizabeth infant daughter of Colonel Geoffrey Clarke MBE and Cathie Clarke [parents]. Died in Jamnagar India on September 15th 1939 aged 11 months.'*

In July and August 1943, when all 'the dust' had settled, Minister Stańczyk paid a visit to India. He had a meeting with Webb and a number of problems were cleared up, with one exception. Webb had objected of having a Pole as a camp Commandant. In his third report to London on 13 September 1943, he wrote confidentially: "I am driven more and more to the conviction that the time is not far distant when we shall have to take the administration of camps into our own hands".[25]

On 14 February 1943, Delegate Styburski sent a telegram to MERRA giving precise instructions for the evacuation procedure to start on 1 March 1943. The British Ambassador in Tehran, Sir R. Bullard was to carry out the selection of those to be evacuated to India. All persons were to be issued with visas. Quotas fixed for other countries would have to be strictly observed. There was to be an advance party from Tehran, composed of the camp superintendent, amenities officer, quartermaster, accounts officer, police officer with an assistant and 3 civilian policemen, 2 clerks, chief physician, 2 medical officers, 2 dentists, 2 security officers, a hospital matron and 9 qualified nurses, 15 probation nurses, 7 hygienists for sanitary duties and 4 helpers. This personnel was to be paid a similar scale to that in Tehran. Each party of 1000 refugees was to be accompanied by the following staff: one superintendent, one trained teacher per 30 children and one clerk. It was envisaged that only two priests for 5,000 persons evacuated were to be assigned. This was hardly adequate for the pastoral and counselling needs of these distressed persons.[26]

Webb's attitude towards the newly appointed Delegates was passive, if not negative. There was a personality clash between them based on hidden rivalry – as to who has more influence over decisions made in London. Webb did not see the need to consult people like Darlewski, whom he saw as "a youngish man who knows less about more subjects than anyone has a right to, and nothing at all about tact". In his opinion, the only credible person representing the Polish Foreign Office was the Consul General in Bombay.

The Consulate had good connections with the Indian authorities, while the Delegates had yet to establish themselves. English was not their forte and having to represent a Ministry abroad under wartime conditions was proving difficult. The Consulate was responsible for all dealings with the Indian authorities. Matters came to a head when the London Poles proposed a 25% increase in the subsistence allowance (from the Polish Funds) for all refugees in the Valivade Camp. At Webb's instigation, a reply from Mr. Mason of the Foreign Office arrived indicating two 'fundamental principles' to be adhered to. The first sounds diplomatically familiar in today's terms: "were the expenditure in Valivade to exceed that prevailing in camps of other nationalities, the Government of India would be exposed to considerable embarrassment - even to charges of racial discrimination". The second principle was, in fact, a reiteration of a policy of the British and Indian Governments that the subsistence allowance was only for the destitute and, emphatically, not for women who had husbands or brothers in the Forces who could help. It was also stressed that the current funding was adequate for the Polish refugees in Valivade while spending more money would only cause local inflation.[27]

The lack of harmony among the Poles in Bombay created further problems. Darlewski refused to hand over some correspondence files to Banasiński for scrutiny. They, allegedly, contained derogatory remarks about the Polish Government who wanted to stop the flow of refugees. More precisely, it was Ambassador Kot who wanted to stop further exodus of Poles, after Stalin's complaints. Banasiński considered the refusal an act of insubordination. Darlewski, on his part, thought that Banasiński was an inept and powerless Consul, who had a tendency to submit to the British authorities (Capt. Webb) in New Delhi.

Budgets were always a sensitive matter. Prepared by the Delegates, they were sent to London for approval and back to Delhi, with instructions from the Treasury to release the money to the Poles in Bombay. A bone of contention was the expenditure called the 'Cultural Uplift'. Written into the 1943 budget, it included a one-off payment of Rs 10,000, to set up playgrounds and branch libraries in common rooms, known as 'świetlice'. These were to be staffed by 17 people for whom a recurring sum of Rs 6,640 was requested. Webb's comments were devastating: "these grants are far in excess of anything of the kind provided in British evacuee camps (Greek and Maltese). While India has to find charitable funds the Polish Government can find money to expend on what many will regard as unessential frills in time of stress and financial stringency". In spite of these objections £2,000 was assigned from the Polish Relief Fund in London.[28]

Curiously, the Greek and Maltese refugees were also assigned a similar 'Cultural Uplift' from other sources with different consequences. Lectures and films on child welfare and hygiene, after a short trial, had to be discontinued for lack of interest. Even sightseeing tours paid for by the Indian States were not taken up and Webb thought it "a total waste of money, a complete failure".[29]

There were also light hearted problems which Webb describes as: "The disinclination of the Polish men in Kolhapur to be trained as members of the Camp Fire Brigade, might have been classed perhaps as indiscipline, were it not for the naïve explanation given. The men had to be replaced by a band of young women and in extenuation of what appeared to be a sad reflection on Polish manhood, it was explained that the relative 'paucity' of men among so many grass-widows, required the former to conserve their strength". Webb's sarcastic remarks on the sexual prowess of Polish men, illustrates why, indeed, the 'Cultural Uplift' was a necessity!

The unfortunate disaster of a fire that devastated a large district of Bombay, affected the Poles profoundly. There was a shortage of premises and Webb's Home Department suggested that the 'Delegaturas' with all the offices and departments, occupying a rented and very spacious place at 15/17 Nepean Sea Road, should vacate it. Banasiński's personal intervention in Delhi, on behalf of Darlewski, made Webb's resolve go further. The 'Delegaturas' were to be moved out of Bombay to Valivade, a more convenient place, near the people for whom they were responsible. There were strong objections by all concerned and New Delhi had to concede by moving the 'Delegaturas' to less prestigious premises, but still in Bombay, at 7 Pedder Road.

Additional problems had arisen with the Resident, Col. Harvey who lived in Kolhapur and observed the camp life, feeding Webb with his derogatory comments about discipline and the morality of some Valivade women who frequented the Recreation Centre for the Allied Forces near Kolhapur as a "holiday resort". The Resident and other British officers blamed the camp Commandant Capt. W. Jagiełłowicz whom they considered "inefficient" and pressed strongly for his dismissal by putting Col. Neat, a British Officer, in his place. After further consultations London agreed. Another matter, that concerned Capt. Webb, was the introduction of a ration scheme for none local foodstuffs (see J. Siedlecki's chapter on the Food Supply). Above all,

Webb advocated strongly the repatriation of the refugees to Poland. This matter has been on his mind for some time, and he forcefully presented this case on behalf of the Government of India to the FO in London in 1946.[30]

The Federation of Poles in Bombay

As already mentioned, the first trickle of Polish refugees and their families escaping the ravages of war, reached Bombay in the fall of 1940-1941. They took two possible routes of escape: one through the north-east of Poland from Wilno (Vilnus), travelling east through the Soviet Union and China to reach the waters of Japan; the other south-east through Romania, Turkey and Iraq to Basra port, from there by sea routes to Bombay. Documents reveal that initially, not more than 300 Polish nationals, many of them Jews, were seeking asylum in Bombay. In general, they were people of means, entrepreneurs, whose aim was eventually to reach America. The Polish Consulate was very generous in arranging suitable housing and financial help. Those of independent means and skills took on suitable employment or established small businesses. In July 1941 at least 14 families were receiving financial assistance: Rs 60 per person, and Rs 260 for a family.[31]

This Polish colony of different professions and faiths formed an integrated community, calling themselves the 'Federation of Poles in India'. Its chairman was an academician from Kraków University, Dr. Leon Sternbach. In reality, the Federation's aim was to consolidate and communicate with other European refugees in India, in particular, the Czechs. At that time in London, the Polish Government led by its Premier Władysław Sikorski, started serious negotiations with the Czech Government with a view to form a Federation of Central European Leagues, which would be involved in the post-war reconstruction of Europe. Both groups co-operated in this field and, for a time, jointly published a brochure 'Czechoslovak - Polish Relations' edited by F.M. Baranek, which was distributed in Calcutta, Bombay and Lahore. The proceeds went to the relief fund for Polish children in the Soviet Union.

The Laufer family and others on the river Tigris from Turkey to Iraq "Rafting to Bombay"

The Federation had its official publication - *The Polish News*. An illustrated monthly newspaper appeared in January 1942, with a print run of 200, eventually increasing to 1200. Its first editor, for a short while, was Wanda Dynowska. The periodical dealt mainly with cultural and political matters.[32] Much later, in 1946, when the organisation moved from Bombay to Valivade, a short news Bulletin (for members only) was printed, dealing mainly with official regulations of UNRRA (United Nations Relief and Rehabilitation Administration). The sentimental poetry of Marian Hemar, an extremely popular artist and songwriter, before the war and after, was regularly included to provide light relief. Only fragments of these publications can be traced, making it difficult to describe fully life in Bombay during the war.

The Federation also undertook charity work in aid of the Polish civilian refugees. A group of women devoted their time to sewing garments and packing clothes. A committee was formed which worked closely with the Consulate and the Polish Red Cross in India. There was time for cultural pursuits. The most talked about exhibition of Polish culture was the 'United Nations Fete' in Bombay. Some members organised events of a patriotic nature, to sustain their morale. The colony was fortunate to have artists and actors in their midst. The paintings of Norblin, for example, enriched the Maharajah's palace in Jodhpur (see the end of the chapter). Actresses and singers like Żelichowska and Ordonówna gave concerts and visitors, such as painter Feliks Topolski, sketched beautiful Indian temples and the empire architecture of New Delhi. Ram Gopal, the famous Indian dancer, took part in a concert in aid of the refugees. Life of the colony seemed bearable and busy.

The 'Delegaturas'
The Offices of Representatives for:
The Ministry of Labour and Social Welfare
The Ministry for Religious Affairs and Education.

A document dated 1 June 1943, written by Mr. R. N. Gilchrist of the India Office in London, informed the Polish Government in Exile that India was willing to receive 11,000 refugees on condition, that the Polish Government would take total responsibility to maintain them. In expectation of such a large number of refugees, it had become clear to the Polish Government that Madame Banasińska, a temporary Delegate for the Red Cross, as well as a Delegate for Social Services, would not be able to cope alone. Consequently, a separate and permanent post was to be established. Minister Stańczyk, who was in charge of the Ministry of Labour and Social Services, wanted to visit India to see for himself what arrangements needed to be made. He aimed at setting up a Central Office for Delegates, who would represent him and other Ministries.

The role of a Delegate was to act as a liaison person between the local authorities in India and the British administration located in New Delhi. Capt. Webb, the Principal Officer for Refugees within the Government of India took on the role of a trustee for the Polish Government in London, and assumed full responsibility for the refugees. To him, 'Delegatura' had an advisory function without executive powers, and he resented any interference. This created constant conflict, as the Polish Government rightfully wanted to be in charge of their nationals.[33]

At the conference in Bombay on 29 May 1943, Minister Stańczyk already had a person in mind, who had previous experience of setting up a Delegate's offices in Tehran.[34] Mr. Wiktor Styburski was a civil servant, deputy director of the Polish Bank (Bank Polski). He and his staff had been charged with ensuring the safe delivery of a consignment of Polish gold (valued at 340 million zlotys) into the hands of the Polish Government in exile who resided in Paris at that time. They were transporting it through Romania to the port of Constantsa, then by sea to Marseilles and eventually to Paris. The latter part of the plan had to be abandoned as France fell and the gold was redirected to Dakar, in French West Africa, where it remained stranded for some years. Styburski like Kira Banasinska was a temporary Delegate, until a permanent replacement was found.

His successor, Dudryk-Darlewski, endowed with a stiff upper lip manner, was not the easiest person with whom the Consulate or New Delhi could work harmoniously. To start with, he got off on the wrong foot with the Consul's wife Kira, with whom his predecessor had had an affair. In fact Styburski admired her greatly for another reason: she was hard working and had experience in welfare work. For this reason he had made her deputy with responsibility for liaison with the British, a post she held until her husband's resignation in 1944.

The Polish coalition government in London was also at loggerheads. Political and personal contentions were rife. Minister Kot, by now acting as a plenipotentiary of the Polish Government in the Middle East, objected to Minister Stańczyk coming over for an inspection of the refugee camps. Eventually Ambassador Raczyński intervened in condemning this party bickering.[35]

In mid-summer of 1943 Minister Stańczyk made an arduous trip to New Delhi, where he met and talked with Capt. Webb. Documents reveal that on his return journey he called on Gen. Anders in Beirut and reported on the "dreadful condition" of the refugees in India (which was a gross exaggeration). It was in Stańczyk's nature to dramatise the issue, to give the impression that his Ministry was extremely important and overworked dealing with refugee problems. Documents reveal that Col. Hopkinson of the British General Staff had sent a report to the FO about his meeting with General Anders and Minister Stańczyk while in Beirut. The General had brought up the subject of 25,000 Polish civilians, the families of his soldiers, who were still in the Soviet Union awaiting evacuation. He criticised the Government for not being firmer with Stalin, and stressed that it was Stańczyk's responsibility as the Minister for Welfare to press this subject home in London. Stańczyk, however, was preoccupied with the politics and rumours circulating in the Middle East concerning the strained relations between Sikorski and Anders, and this was of great interest to him.[36]

The Central Office

Saying farewell to the delegates:
(sitting) M. Goławski, Łukasiewicz, W. Styburski, K. Banasińska, S. Dudryk-Darlewski, ..., (standing): S. Śliwińska, ..., ..., M. Berch, H. Kozielska, ..., S. Małaczyńska, ..., (3rd row): ..., J. Sułkowski, Lt. Cz. Gulczyński, ..., Dr. Goshal, (last row: M. Chmielowiec, ..., Krawczyk, Małaczyński, J. Dajek, ..., ..., Opolska, Mgr. Kościukiewicz, Z. Łopiński

The Central Office was housed at numbers 15-17 Nepean Street in Bombay and consisted of five departments: Secretariat, Accounts, Supply and Employment, Health Service, Cultural and Education, with a total monthly budget of Rs 446,000 (£34,000).

It had to work according to the rules and regulations prescribed by their refugee status, which strictly regulated every aspect of camp life. There were endless problems facing the Central Office. At the beginning, there was a shortage of qualified staff, such as doctors, nurses, teachers or administrators and the Delegate searched among the Polish exiles to fill the gaps. The New Delhi authorities that had set rules on procedure, resented this 'bypass'. Employees receiving Rs 100 required special approval and justification from the British authorities. This ridiculous red tape slowed down the process of running the camp and in fact was unnecessary.

India could not, or would not designate better climatic regions such as the hillside stations for the erection the refugee camps. For a temporary stay, the land had to be bought cheaply on the market. There were additional difficulties in purchasing building materials, so the accommodation was not of European standard, with no electricity, running water or indoor toilets. All this was acceptable to the 'Delegaturas', bar one issue; while acknowledging the rights of the Poles to administer themselves inside the camps, the Indian Government insisted on retaining control of finances.[37]

The 'Delegaturas' were responsible for looking after four camps and one health retreat in Panchgani. Jamnagar was the first camp to be set up in 1942, while Banasińska was still a Delegate. It eventually housed 586 persons, mostly children and staff. Karachi Country Club was a primitive transit camp with a grand name, located about 10 miles from Karachi; it was opened on 4 September 1942. Because of the distance from Bombay, a mini 'Delegatura' was set up with Mr. J. Gruja at its head. He was helped by Zygmunt Rosada, Hieronim Serwacki, Józef Zalewski, Zofia Kiełbinska and Irena Szatkowska. Malir Camp, which accommodated 2239 people, was a large site leased from the American Forces. It was solidly built and had no water restriction. Panchgani was a complex of English style houses, situated among five hills of moderate climate. It was used as a holiday retreat for employees of the 'Delegaturas' and as a recuperation centre for ailing children from the camps. Valivade Camp was the last and the largest camp to be constructed (towards the end of 1943) and accommodated over 5000 people.

The Secretariat

One of the first tasks of the Secretariat was to prepare the formal status formalities and rules for Polish refugees, which defined the rights and responsibilities of the refugees and specified the terms of conduct while on Indian Territory. The Secretariat also compiled an accurate list of refugees, created a personal record for each person, kept track of the refugees in transit between camps, dealt with British requests for the adoption of orphans, and arranged placements for young people in English speaking boarding schools. All disciplinary matters were dealt with by the Secretariat. A very able man, Marian Berch, ran it.[38]

Accounts

The Accounts department, under the direction of Mr. Jan Sułkowski, was responsible for preparing the monthly budgets and sending them to London and New Delhi. The department administered two sources of accounts. The first source was the Polish Ministry of Finance in London, which transferred a total of Rs 40,000 (£3,000) per month into the Bombay branch of the Imperial Bank of India. It covered all expenses of Consular staff, 'Delegaturas' and other staff working in administration of camps, subsistence grants and room allowances for people living independently in Panchgani or Bombay. It also covered any dental treatment or maternity allowances.

The second main source of income consisted of credits paid out by the British Treasury to the Polish Government in exile, according to a signed agreement, that after the war this credit would be repaid using the gold reserves stranded at the time in Dakar. Credits for all the refugees, over the war years, amounted to £32 millions. These credits were to be used to enable the refugees to run their own households by giving them allowances for food and clothing. All budgets which passed through the Central Office, had to be approved by Capt. Webb, Principal Refugee Officer in New Delhi, on whose recommendation London credits were released. Monthly budgets for Valivade camp, Jamnagar and Panchgani totalled Rs 406,000 (£31,000). It was prepared by the camp account clerks, with the assistance of a British liaison officer otherwise known as 'Resident' representing Capt Webb, and sent to him for approval.[39]

Supplies and Employment

This department was considered to be the most difficult to run, mainly due to the lack of skilled staff. It fell upon Styburski and Berch to manage it. They were convinced that the morale of people in the camps was low due to the unemployment situation and this had to be addressed. Setting up self-help projects, co-operatives and small workshops was the obvious answer. A plan was devised to purchase machinery for sawing, woodwork and shoe repairs. Much time was wasted as Webb kept delaying his decision to go ahead. In his reports to London, Styburski was concerned that, unless able-bodied men and women in the camp were gainfully employed, criminal elements would prevail. He had already noticed incidents of pilfering, lying, false accusations, trivial intrigues and often laziness to do any work at all. This caused him great embarrassment each time he had to deal with the local authorities. It took some time for the Central Office to function properly and, in the meantime, the good offices of the Consulate were used for negotiations and wholesale purchases, which according to Dudryk-Darlewski were prone to abuse. The life of central stores was short-lived; it was closed down on 16 September 1944.

Health Service Department

This particular department was responsible for assessing and supplying the needs of camp hospitals, from furniture to medical equipment, as well as dental surgeries, drug stores, first aid posts and the like. It prepared leaflets on general health problems, nutrition, infectious diseases, and arranged inoculations. It was also responsible for training nurses and sanitation staff. At first there were shortages of qualified staff, which was of particular concern to Styburski as there was an outbreak of malaria in Malir camp. Out of 418 sick patients, only 233 regained their health permanently. The department had to arrange regular inspection of camps, especially public places. It also ran the sanatoria for tuberculosis patients in Panchgani. In overall charge of the Health Service, was the Chief Medical Officer for Western India States, Rajkot, Col. Atkinson. It was his duty to inspect all health service outposts and produce regular reports to New Delhi.

Education Department

Prior to setting up a separate 'Delegatura' for education in India, an agency was run from Tehran under the auspices of the Ministry of Works and Education. Mrs. Halina Bruner ran such an agency in Bombay. With the sudden influx of children arriving in Karachi en route to Valivade, a newly formed 'Delegatura' took control of educational and cultural needs. By September 1943, Michał Goławski[40] took on the upgraded post of Delegate representing the then Minister of Education, Prof. Folkierski. Goławski had studied history and taught in a grammar school. At the outbreak of war he was employed by the Education Department of Białystok Council. Like thousands of Poles in 1940 he was imprisoned and deported to Soviet Russia. In 1942 he joined the newly formed Polish Army and was evacuated to Iran with hundreds of civilians. Shortages of qualified staff allowed Goławski to be seconded from the Army and involved once more in education.

His task as a fully-fledged Delegate was vast and varied; it encompassed not only the prime subject of education, but also cultural and religious departments. The latter was the domain of the Rev. Kazimierz Bobrowski, who had to present regular reports to Goławski on issues concerning the religious welfare of refugees, which he often ignored. In the Delegate's care were primary and secondary grammar schools known as 'Gimnazia,' as well as adult education classes. Much time was devoted to re-creating the pre-war teaching programme. Books were scarce.

Lady Dow, wife of the British Governor General of Sindh Province, was gracious enough to cover the cost of the construction of Polish printing typesets (at Rs 10 each) so that printing could begin in earnest, starting with a formal Register of refugees. Four lists in all were printed, the last one indicating that there were a total of 4475 people in India. It was useful (especially for the Red Cross) in tracing missing members of families who had become separated or lost. Rev. Antoni Jankowski was able to reprint small missals, extracts of the New Testament and other religious printing matters so necessary for the soul and moral upkeep of the Catholic faith. These were followed by reprints of school texts, to supplement inadequate supply from Polish publishers in United Kingdom and the Middle East, namely Jerusalem and Beirut, where the Cultural Section of the Polish Army was stationed during the war. English books were usually purchased in Bombay. There was a newly formed Literary Circle in Malir and Valivade Camps, which started to produce a bulletin in a poster form, intended for school children, called *Na Etapie (On Course)*. Goławski was also responsible for extra curricular activities, such as setting up reading rooms ('świetlice'), arranging trips, lectures and funding amateur theatre groups and choirs. A separate advisory team was set up to keep track of teachers' qualifications, supply of books and school aids. Additional duties involved the upkeep of school buildings, as well as the welfare and management of all teaching staff.[41]

As he was stationed in Bombay, over 400 kilometres from Valivade, Goławski nominated Maj. Ludwik Naimski as his representative to reside in, and take care of immediate problems at Valivade camp. Zdzisław Żerebecki, acted as a school Inspector. A full compliment of staff, among them Janina Grochocka, Władysław Rayman, Janina Sułkowska, Eugenia Duszynska and Krystyna Biskupska, who in effect was employed as a censor, helped out on a regular basis. On the whole it was a self-sufficient, inwardly orientated 'Delegatura' whose aim was to preserve all that was dear to Polish hearts, namely, its language and traditions; to nurture and sustain them until the time would came to return home to Poland.

Cultural Department

POLAK w INDIACH
Organ Delegatury Minist. Pracy i Op. Społecz. w Bombaju

Rok II. Nr. 18-19 (28-29)   BOMBAJ, 15 WRZEŚNIA—1 PAŹDZIERNIKA, 1944   Cena : an. 4

While the Department's prime activity was education, other cultural interests were pursued. In February 1943 a two weekly periodical *Polak w Indiach (A Pole in India)* was born. It was the official organ of the 'Delegaturas', and thereby, of the Polish Government. It was printed by Shree Laxmi Narayan Press in Bombay, with Polish typesets constructed by the Polish engineer Maurycy Frydman. There were 50 editions up to 1945. After the war, when the British refused to recognise the legitimacy of the Polish Government in Exile, the publishing of *Polak w Indiach* was taken over by the oldest organisation in India, the Federation of Poles. This fortnightly periodical first appeared in February 1943 and lasted till 1945 when Delegatura was liquidated in Bombay and the publication was done in Valivade, printed on a press donated by Lady Dow. The last issue (No.117) appeared in February 1948 and was dedicated to Gandhi and his life. Curiously, it included an editorial note that the paper had been prepared by a Hindu who was deaf and blind! Needless to say he had no knowledge of the Polish language. In its 'heyday' the issue of *Polak w Indiach* reached 2000; half of it was for the local readers, while the other half was sent abroad to 17 countries that had Polish settlements. Reuters were the chief supplier of news, as well as PAP (Polish Agency Press) in London. It was supplemented with news of local events, letters, an advice column, children's corner and literary articles. Its chief editor was an engineer Franciszek Sarnowiec, but in fact the *spiritus movens* (mainspring) of the paper was Michał Chmielowiec, a literary man who, before the war had studied philosophy and literature at the Jagiellonian University in Kraków. He wrote good articles for *Kurier Poranny (The Morning Courier), Sygnały (Signals) and Kultura (Culture)*. He contributed to an avant-garde magazine *Nasz Wyraz (Our expression)*. This fascination with avant-garde literature stayed with him for the rest of his life. Chmielowiec was an exceptionally talented writer and gifted editor, much too good for a mediocre periodical aimed at general readership. He suffered the same fate of deportation into Russia and his health suffered as a result. This left him unfit to serve in the armed forces, which was rather fortunate for 'Delegatura', to have him as an editor.

Editorial staff and guests (from top left)
M. Chmielowiec, A. Kisielnicka, L. Sternbach,
J. Grochocka, J. Zanoziński (Consul),
I. Chmielowcowa, L. Litawska, F. Sarnowiec

The 'propaganda section', probably better described today as public relations, was headed by a literary minded Alicja Kisielnicka. She wrote poems, plays and most prolifically, articles to *Polak w Indiach*, illustrated by another talented graphic designer Krystyna Biskupska (also employed in the censorship department.) The two ladies met in Tehran and their friendship lasted well into their late years. While in the Central Office, they started a daily newspaper *Żywy Dziennik (Living Daily)*.

There were other young women in the Central Office with literary talents who contributed to the cultural life of the Poles. Janina Sułkowska edited the children's supplement of the *Polak w Indiach* called *Słoniątko Indyjskie (Little Indian Elephant)*, while Irena Świątkowska wrote short stories, one of them *Śnieżka (Snow Queen)* acquired fame by being staged in the camps; it also mesmerised an Indian audience at the Maharajah's palace in Kolhapur. She delighted the Bombay colony with her wartime marriage to Michał Chmielowiec.[42]

'The Polish Scouting Association in India' also printed a lot of aids for internal use, usually on primitive duplicating machinery. Two unusual titles come to the fore: *W Kręgu Pracy* and *W Kręgu Wodzów*, both circular periodicals, one intended as a guide for work with the Brownies and Cubs, the other more of a task booklet for the company leaders. Only three books went to print: *Zarys geografi Indii (A short geography of India), Praca Wędrownikow i Skautów (Scouting Activity)* in 1947, *Kalendarz Harcerstwa w Indiach (A Calendar of Polish Scouting in India)* 1947.

Polonica

There were also independent publications, which did not fall into official agencies' category. Among others, several academic papers, written by Dr. Ludwik Sternbach of Jan Kazimierz University in Lwów (Lviv). The Polish Consulate employed Sternbach as a chief censor, but above all he was a scholar and was invited to lecture at the Bharatiya Vidya Institute in Bombay on a subject he knew well – the ancient culture of India. He had written several papers in English, which were published in learned societies' periodicals such as Bharatiya Vidya, the Poona Orientalist and Journal of Annamalai University.[43] The subjects covered were:

Medieval European Travellers 1946, Judicial Studies in Ancient Indian Law 1946; Vesya – synonyms and aphorisms, dealing with prostitution, 1945; Judicial Aspects of the Gandharva form of marriage, 1945; India as known to medieval Europe, 1944; Some form of marriage in ancient India, 1944.

The Indo-Polish Library

Of all the Polish publishing organisations in India, the most prolific and creative was the Indo-Polish Library in Bombay, which was founded in March 1944 at the initiative of two Poles, Wanda Dynowska and Maurycy Frydman. With the immediate hunger for religious and school books being satisfied and other books available from publishers in Britain or the Middle East (Jerusalem), there was a need for other types of literary books in both Polish and English, on Indian and Polish subjects. W. Dynowska and Frydman who knew the languages, religions, history and culture of the Indian Continent, were ideal candidates for the publication endeavour. W. Dynowska concentrated on editorial matters, Frydman on technical problems. I could only trace one joint venture as authors, when they published under the title *Dwugłos z Indii (Two Voices from India)*. Otherwise, it was W. Dynowska who wrote or edited the works. Their books reached public and University libraries, laying the foundation for a better understanding of the political situation of Poland, by the intellectuals in India. The first 28 issues were later reprinted in English, books such as: F.A. Voigt's *Great Britain, Poland and Russia*; P. Jordan's *First to fight*; or B. Boswell's *The Eastern Boundaries of Poland*.

W. Dynowska's creative writings started with a book, which sounded like a tourist's guide: *Z Pielgrzymką hinduską w głąb Himalajów (A Hindu pilgrimage deep into the Himalayas)*, published in 1944. Others were to follow: *Underground Poland*, 1945; *The Heart of the Nation*, 1945;

TRZY DROGOWSKAZY
ANTOLOGIA INDYJSKA
BHAGAWAD GITA
PIEŚŃ PANA
CZŁOWIEK WE WSZECHSWIECIE
ANTOLOGIA INDYJSKA
PIELGRZYMKA HINDUSKA
KASZMIR
NAUKA SZRI RAMANA MAHARISZI
RAZEM POD WIATR
PODSTAWY HINDUSKIEJ KULTURY
PRAWO OFIARY I NAUKA SERCA
ANTOLOGIA INDYJSKA
UWAGI O
ANTOLOGIA INDYJSKA

India fighting for Freedom, 1947; *Razem pod wiatr (Together against the wind - Indian poetry)*; *Pożegnanie Polski (Farewell to Poland)* and many others. Perhaps the most prominent were the editorial translations such as: the anthology of Polish poetry *The Scarlet Muse*; the holy book Bhagawad Gita reprinted in 1947, 1956, 1960 and 1972; a voluminous Polish translation of *The Sacred Songs of Tamilland*; seven volumes of *Anthology of Songs* from all centuries and provinces, translated from Tamil, Hindi, Gujurati, Marati and Bengali languages. Even today, W. Dynowska's translations are considered to be a unique understanding of eloquent Sanskrit verses.[44]

With the closure of the Polish Consulate in October 1945, the Indo-Polish Library had lost its guardian and benefactor. W. Dynowska had to turn to her generous Hindu friends to help her out. Much later, help was forthcoming from the Indian Government in the form of a grant; no doubt it was in their interest to promote Anglo-Polish literature to the Western world. Following the death of Wanda Dynowska in 1971, the library significantly reduced its output; only six reprints were done over the next five years, until the death of her lifelong friend and literary partner Maurycy Frydman in 1976. After thirty years of hard work and having published a total of 132 books, the life of The Indo-Polish Library finally came to an end.

During the war, the Polish Government set up a mobile archive within the Polish Armed Forces, under the odd name of 'Archiwum i Muzeum Polowe' (Field Archives and Museum), headed by Dr. Leon Koczy. It had a subsidiary institution in Beirut, Lebanon, where all bibliographic data was collected, including that from India. Regretfully, the Beirut bibliography, which was published after the Poles left India, is incomplete with only 131 registered items. This figure is moderate when compared with bibliographies compiled for Polish settlements in other countries: Iran 275, Lebanon 331, Iraq 70, and the African Continent 51. During the Poles' stay in India, 96 books were printed (35 in the Polish language, 57 in English, 3 in Hindi and one in Tamil). There were 12 periodicals, 7 academic theses and 16 ephemeral publications such as bulletins, fliers, posters, cards etc.[45] Perhaps the most important source of information about the life and times of the Poles' stay in India is a handwritten Chronicle of Valivade Camp, now at the Polish Institute and Sikorski Museum in London.

'Delegatura' of the Polish Red Cross

The Bombay agency of the Polish Red Cross was established relatively late. In February 1941 Consul General took on the responsibility, but soon passed it on to his wife Kira. She was in her element. With her diplomatic connections and efficiency, she worked tirelessly until October 1944 when she relinquished the post to Michał Goławski who managed it until its liquidation in April 1946. Oddly enough, in his ultimate report to London he was very critical of Madame Banasińska's formal attitude.[46]

It can be assumed that Banasińska relied on help and assistance from the consular staff, while Goławski employed new people: S. Śliwinska as secretary, Edwin Citron as Chief Accountant, A Mrozowa - book keeper and M. Kotlarczyk in charge of Catering. The first major undertaking by Kira Banasińska was to organise two expeditions to Soviet Russia; the first to deliver food, clothing and medicines, and the second to bring 160 children to India. The 'Delegatura' of the Red Cross was responsible for relocating children in the camps. This experience proved to be invaluable for later transportations of hundreds of civilians by sea and land from Tehran to Karachi. It also continued its traditional work of locating missing relatives. Here, too, Kira Banasińska was criticised by Eustachy Sapieha, a Delegate of the Red Cross in Nairobi, who stated that she allowed a large number of families to be broken up at the sorting points in Tehran and Karachi in 1942.

From that time the 'Delegatura' had its own administration for the distribution of medicines to all field hospitals, and arranged admissions of patients to the local hospital. Much later, in June 1944 through a generous donation, mainly from War Relief Service (WRS) part of a large American charity called National Catholic Welfare Conference (NCWC), it was possible for the Polish Red Cross to open its own hospital.

Documents reveal that the 'Delegatura' of the Ministry of Labour and Social Services was not very keen on the project, but eventually accepted the argument that after the war, when time was right to return to Poland, a small, well-equipped hospital might be a big asset. War time Defence rules made it possible to lease buildings by compulsory means. This is what happened with large premises at 15-17 Queens Road leased for a sum of Rs 57,000. It accommodated consulting rooms, wards, one operating theatre, living quarters and offices. All the hospital equipment was bought with money donated by the WRS (62%) as well as the Central Office of the Polish Red Cross in London and donations from local people in Bombay, among them: Sir Dorabji Tata Trust, Rs 2,500; Navy ratings from a Polish ship Białystok, Rs 244; Ciba Ltd, Rs 350; Mrs. S. Miranda, Rs 500; War Gift Fund, Rs 10,000. In total Rs 84,972 was collected. In addition, an assortment of goods was gratefully received. Legally, The Polish Red Cross Hospital belonged to the Association of the Polish Red Cross while the 'Delegatura' was responsible for its running and administration.[47]

POLISH RED CROSS HOSPITAL
(by Wiesława Klepacka Kleszko)

The opening ceremony was performed in June 1944. His Grace Arch. Thomas Roberts blessed it in the presence of many British, Indian and Polish guests. In her inaugural speech, Kira Banasińska thanked all the benefactors for their generosity. The hospital was designated primarily for Polish patients, but admitted other nationalities when beds were available. The premises were adequate. It housed 6 wards, operating theatre, surgery, emergency, rest room, dining room, storeroom, living quarters for a doctor and 5 nurses. Additional rooms were set aside for offices and the Rector of the Polish Catholic Mission who acted on behalf of the 'War Relief Services', the main benefactor.

A hospital Committee and 'Delegatura' administered the hospital.

Sitting: M. Widmańska, K. Banasińska, Dr. Jalal Bazergan, W. Łaguna, Dr. Konarski (standing): W. Kobuz, R. Wojciechowska, K. Kisiówna

They had rules for admission of patients. If camp hospitals did not have proper facilities or lacked experienced staff, patients were transferred to Bombay through a Central Office of 'Delegatura' (Health Service department). The daily charge for meals was Rs 3, 6 or 8 according to the patient's means. The Welfare Service 'Delegatura' paid for treatment and other services such as dentures, glasses, X-rays etc. Medicines were paid for by 'War Relief Services' and bought in local pharmaceutical establishments. Infectious diseases were treated in specialised hospitals like Maharatta Plage Hospital (for cholera and smallpox) or the Arthur Road Infectious Hospital for plague.

The Senior Registrar was Dr. Jalal Bazergan, an Iranian with a fair command of the Polish language. He was assisted by Matron M. Widmańska, Theatre sister H. Górska, Ward Sisters: W. Czogało, Z. Gawroń, J. Góral, A. Malcharek, J. Siewierska, Cz. Ciążyńska, E. Goślinowska, nurses G. Haracz, R. Jędrzejewska, K. Kiś and others.[48] In addition, Indian doctors helped out on a voluntary basis, which was very much appreciated. Key medical personnel were: General Internal Illnesses – Drs. F. Moose, A. Masina, and J. Patel; Respiratory Problems – Dr. R. Bilimoria; Surgery – Dr. R. Cooper; Paediatrics – Drs. A. Major and A. Pullar; Ophthalmology - Dr. Banaji; Ear, Nose and Throat – Dr. J. Damany; Dermatology and Venereology – Dr. S. Horohna; Dentistry – Dr. J. Naegemvala; Gynaecology – Dr. H. Waters; Clinical Analysis – Drs. S. Noronham and H. Bilimoria.

Over a period of almost three years 318 patients were treated and 58 surgical operations were performed. Over 360 patients were seen at the surgery and emergency departments. With the liquidation of all Polish organisations in India, the hospital was given over for Indian patients. In the spring of 1947 the building, leased for the duration of war, was returned by the "Delegatura" to the Sanatorium of the Muslim Council and the hospital sold to Dr. Jalal Bazergan, who ran it as a private clinic until 1956. For sentimental reasons it was called Polish hospital.[49]

Polish Catholic Mission

The deportation of over 200 Polish priests to the Soviet Union had dire consequences. Of the 53 who were released from prison, 44 were engaged as army chaplains and only 9 ministered to the civilian population.[50] When Rev. Kazimierz Bobrowski was made Rector of the Polish Catholic Mission for India in October 1943, three Polish priests were already working with the first wave of refugees. Rev. F. Pluta was in charge of the orphanage in Balachadi. Revs. L. Dallinger and A. Jankowski at first worked in Karachi transit camp and then in Valivade. Rev. Bobrowski's responsibility was to assist and alleviate any administrative problems with the Polish and British authorities. He also ministered to the needs of members of the Polish Air Force with the British Forces in Burma and the officers and men of the Polish Navy whose ships happened to arrive in Bombay.

The three organisations, namely, the Ministry of Religious Affairs and Education, the Polish Catholic Mission and the National Catholic Welfare Conference, were closely connected by the very nature of their work. However, organisationally, they were totally independent, hence frictions were evident among the Delegates and the Rector, caused by the interference in one another's affairs. In a number of reports written by Goławski, he complains about Bobrowski's unreasonable attitude and lack of co-operation.[51]

Complaints must have gone much higher as, in the second half of 1945, Bobrowski was released from his duties and sent with a group of boys to a seminary (theological school) in Orchard Lake Michigan USA.[52] A controversial figure, he had been evacuated to Romania at the outbreak of the war, where he taught in a Polish school for a year. He was fluent in French, German and English, became an assistant to the Papal Nuncio N. Cortesi, moved to Tel-Aviv, where he set up the first Catholic parish and then onto Beirut to teach in the College Francais. Eventually he was sent by Bishop Józef Gawlina, Chief Army Chaplain, to India to take charge of the Polish Mission there. The running of it was based on the model of the French Catholic Mission.

The National Catholic Welfare Conference (War Relief Services)

The NCWC was an umbrella organisation bringing together the American Catholic charities run by its Episcopate, clergy and parishes. It operated nationally, but with the outbreak of the war in Europe in 1939, the Conference acted magnanimously by enlarging its services abroad and assisted in helping those in need. A new Section was created, the 'War Relief Service', under the directorship of Rev. O'Boyle, who liberally helped the people of 41 nations in need. The Americans, following a visit to USA by Bishop Gawlina gave a generous help. A separate Polish Section, Służba Pomocy Katolickiej Polakom (SPKP, the Catholic Relief Service for Poles) was created under the direction of Rev. Alojzy Wycislo, an American of Polish descent.[53]

The first aid to reach Polish refugees in India was in the second half of 1943. Money was sent via His Grace Archbishop of Bombay J. E. Thomas Roberts, to be passed on to Rev. Bobrowski for disposal according to need. After Bobrowski's departure to America, Rev. Jankowski who had experience and the drive, for publishing religious material such as prayer books, small missals, catechisms and other religious ephemera, ran the Polish Section. The NCWC also printed the bulletin *Informator Prasowy*, (Press Information) intended for internal use.

SPKP's financial help was directed towards existing organisations as well as setting up of new, independent ones. In the first instance, help was given to all primary and secondary schools in Karachi, Valivade, Jamnagar and Panchgani. Science equipment, musical instruments and other school aids were bought with SPKP's money. The Polish Red Cross received the most generous donation, to purchase vital equipment for the Polish Hospital in Bombay. Help was also given to the Polish Scout and Girl Guide Association to cover expenses for camp equipment, bivouacs, publications and instruction courses.

Few people living in the camps, who frequented the 'świetlice', realized what 'SPKP' meant, or that the American people funded the common rooms. The previously mentioned study group of Polish boys who travelled to America was also funded wholly by SPKP.[54] At the end of the war in 1945, this charitable work continued in Poland. Rev. Alojzy Wycisło managed to get permission to work in cooperation with the Polish charity, 'Caritas', which still operates to the present day.

Liquidation of Polish Agencies in Bombay

With the Allied invasion of Normandy and the inexorable push of the Russians towards Warsaw and Berlin, the end of the war was fast approaching. The policy of the British Government towards Poland had been settled a long time ago at the Tehran Conference in November 1943. It was deplorable that, without consulting their Polish ally, Churchill and Roosevelt agreed to Stalin annexing the eastern half of Poland and making the Curzon Line the post-war frontier. As a consequence of these tragic decisions, the refugees were denied the care and protection of their legitimate government. In Bombay everyone felt uncertainty about the future. Ominous news arrived from London that the refugees' problems were being taken over by UNRRA (United Nations Relief & Rehabilitation Administration).

Rumours were rife and the stakes were high. Faced with an unwelcome decision of the Polish Foreign Ministry to employ a non-diplomat Wiktor Styburski at the Embassy, Banasiński resigned. In August 1944 in a farewell speech to his staff, Banasiński expressed grief at leaving his diplomatic post after 12 years of unswerving duty.[55] Capt. Webb's praise for the Consul's wife was exceptional: "Madame Banasińska is a grand worker, patriot, and a delightful colleague. I miss her greatly and so, I think, do all who worked with her in India". For these glowing, fully justified achievements, in 1948 she was awarded the King's Medal for Courage in the Cause of Freedom (KMC) from King George VI.

As a postscript, after eight months' stay in England and out of work, the couple decided independently to return to India. They tried to make a living from a business of which Kira was the instigator and driving force; her husband had no aptitude for it. He was a sensitive man, a keen collector of antiquities. His collection of Chinese, Japanese and Indian Art was donated to a museum in Poland in the early sixties. This unique collection, admired by many Poles, is the only testimony to his hard work. In 1961, they took Indian nationality. Regretfully Banasiński died suddenly in 1964 and was buried in a Catholic cemetery at Haines Road in Bombay.[56] Kira lived to a glowing old age of 102 in Hyderabad. She died in 2001 and is buried with her husband in Bombay.

Towards the end of 1944, the Consulate welcomed new arrivals from Harbin, Consul Jerzy Litewski and Counsellor Jan Zanoziński. In effect, these were temporary appointments, and the task of the new Consul was essentially the liquidation of a familiar set up, in readiness for a new regime to take over. Litewski was an officer of the Polish Intelligence Service II Bureau who, from 1934-37, served in its Eastern Section in Istanbul. The Polish Colony in Bombay was not aware of his secret past or the intentions of the British Secret Intelligence Service (SIS) to acquire his expertise. Litewski was very well acquainted with the methods of internal and external activity of the Soviets, in which the British were very interested. Much later, SIS was to give him a glowing reference as a superior colleague and excellent officer who dealt with firmness in his relations with the Japanese while in Harbin.[57]

According to the instructions of the Polish Government in exile residing in London, the Bombay Consulate was to be closed at the end of September 1945. Consul Litewski, after relinquishing his post, was to head the Committee for the Polish Refugees. The residence was to be cleared, furniture sold and the proceeds of Rs 60,000 sent to London, together with personal files and silver. A list of Poles residing in India was given to Rev. Kozłowski, by now Rector of the Catholic Mission, who later dispatched it to Archbishop Gawlina.[58]

The liquidation of the Central Office of 'Delegaturas' occurred almost simultaneously. In March 1945, The Welfare Delegate Dudryk-Darlewski was sending urgent letters to London requesting instructions as to what to do with documents and money, whether to pass them on to the Polish Red Cross, UNRRA, or the newly formed Committee for the Polish Refugees. Also who should take on the inventory, perhaps to the committee members of the Federation of Poles, who were transferred from Bombay to Valivade. Darlewski was rightly worried as he was still responsible for 3779 refugees in Valivade, 1250 in Karachi, 322 in Jamnagar, 114 in Panchgani and 112 still residing in Bombay; a total of 5577 persons. An additional concern was the attitude of Capt. Webb and the Resident Col. Harvey, who were pressing Darlewski to install a British Commandant, Col. Neat, in Valivade camp.[59]

By July 1945 all Polish Agencies in Bombay were closed down. Some members of the Federation of Poles and the editorial staff of Polak w Indiach were moved to Valivade to be with the rest of the refugees. The Federation was still active and grew to a sizeable number of 1500 members. They also had a fair sum of money (Rs 17,000) which enabled them to support further publication of the popular *Polak w Indiach*, this time printed on their own printing machine. They donated money to schools, paid for printing courses, and supported the activities of the Scouts and Girl Guides. The Federation represented the refugees and spoke on their behalf in meetings with the authorities regarding the destinations of those who were not dependants of members of the Polish Forces, (category E), who had nowhere to go. With the subsequent transportations of the refugees to Poland, United Kingdom, Africa, Lebanon, Brazil and Argentina, the life of the Federation of Poles, once an active colony in Bombay, irrevocably ground to a halt.[60]

NOTES

1. The National Archives London (TNAL) FO 371/36712 ref. W10537, Capt. A.T.W. Webb's report 20 May 1943
2. TNAL FO 371/29214 ref. W 11380/324/48 report of a visit to FO by M. Marlewski, notes by A.W. Randall, Sir Alexander Cadogan, G.E. Millard and F.K. Roberts, September 1941.
3. TNAL HW 12/275 ref. 102922 cipher telegram from Ministry of Foreign Affairs Tehran to the Iranian Legation in London, intercepted by the British Intelligence 3 April 1942.
4. TNALFO 371/36709 War Cabinet Office telegrams to Washington January 1943.
5. TNAL T 160/1204, W 10996/87/48 note from A.G.Randal FO to the Treasury 21 August 1942
6. TNAL FO 371/29214 ref. W 11880 note by Mr. M. Clouson (India Office) to Mr. V.G.Lawford (FO) on 4 October 1941.
7. TNAL FO 371/32629 ref. W 8236/87/48 letter from PM Gen. Sikorski to PM Churchill 3 June 1942.
8. TNAL HW 12/295 no 126414, diplomatic telegram from Ministry of Foreign Affairs Berlin by Braun von Strumm to German Consulate in Lourenco Marques 22 December 1943. It reads: According to a declaration of Eden in the House of Commons another 40,000 Polish refugees are to be sent shortly from Persia to East and South Africa, India, Palestine and Mexico. Transport arrangements are almost completed. We are particularly interested in receiving as soon as possible descriptions of these Polish refugees, their experiences and conditions in the Soviet Union. We would be glad if you make an effort to obtain by every possible means the reports in question".
9. Armia Polska w ZSSR 1941-1942 (The Polish Army in USSR 1941-1942) Cipher telegram from Consul General M. Koptielov in Pahlevi to Stalin, from the Soviet Archives, Institute of Political Studies PAN, edited and translated by Prof. Wojciech Materski, II vol. Warsaw 1992.
10. TNAL T 160/1204 ref. W 7317/87/48, report by T.H. Preston to Ambassador Sir Miles Lampton Cairo, 26 April 1942.
11. Ibid, Appendix to W 7317/87/48 dated 28 April 1942.
12. TNAL T160/1204 ref. W 10996/87/48 note by A.W. Randall FO to W.L. Fraser Treasury dated 21 August 1942.
13. TNAL FO 371/71528 ref. N 451/11/55 & N 1409, note from R.M.A. Hankey FO to J.G. Ward in Rome regarding emigration of some Poles to Argentina, 20 January 1948.
14. Żychiewicz T. Ludzkie drogi (Human crossroads), Znak, 1981, s.79
15. Budrewicz Olgierd, Spotkania z Polakami (Meetings with Poles), Interpress, Warsaw 1969.
16. H. Skarbek-Peretiatkowicz Indie bez retuszu (India without disguise), Poland 1935?
17. Archiwum Akt Nowych, further AAN (The National Archives Warsaw), Teki Archiwalne T II, W. Zmysłowski Źródła do dziejów Indii i stosunków polsko-indyjskich (The source of Indian history and the Polish-Indian relations)
18. Instytut Polski I Muzeum gen. Sikorskiego (The Polish Institute and Sikorski Museum) further PISM, KOL 129/1
19. PISM, A11 E 615
20. TNAL T.160/1204 ref. W 10/42/8168/48 22 July 1943
21. TNAL FO 371 32628
22. Ibid
23. TNAL FO 371/36736 Capt. Webb's 3 report 20 May 1943
24. Ibid

25. TNAL FO 371/36712 Capt. Webb's 4 report 13 September 1943
26. TNAL FO 371/36712 ref. W 2699 14 February 1943
27. TNAL FO 371/42882, ref. WR 908/657/48 Mr. Mason to Mr. Budny London 22 September 1944
28. TNAL FO 371/36736 Capt. Webb's 3 report 20 May 1943
29. TNAL FO 371/42882 appendix B, Webb's 7 report 1 November 1944
30. TNAL FO 371/51153 Webb's 8 report 16 June 1945
31. AAN, 83 / 2-6
32. Polak w Indiach (A Pole in India) No.8 (66) 1946, article on the Federation of Poles in India
33. PISM, A 11 E 536
34. AAN, 88 138-141
35. Edward Raczyński: In Allied London, the wartime diaries of the Polish Ambassador, London 1962
36. TNAL FO 371 34593
37. TNAL FO 371 36712
38. AAN, 83 / 205
39. PISM, A 11 E 536
40. Biblioteka Polska w Londynie, further PBL, (Polish Library in London) Jeżewski's Archives
41. PISM, A 23 / 16
42. BPL, Jeżewski's Archives; Irena Chmielowiec's reminiscences
43. Teka Bejrucka,(Cahiers de Beyrouth), bibliographic material, The Polish Institute, Beirut 1949.
44. Ibidem
45. Ibidem
46. PISM, A 23 / 14
47. PISM, A 11 E 385
48. Ward Sisters: Czesława Ciążyńska, Wanda Czogało, Zbigniewa Gawroń, Eugenia Goślinowska, Jadwiga Góral, Halina Górska, Adela Malcharek, Jadwiga Siewierska, Maria Widmańska; Nurses Genowefa Haracz, Regina Jędrzewska, Władysława Kobuz, Katarzyna Kiś and Rozalia Wojciechowska.
49. PISM, KOL 129; AAN, 83 97/101; IOR, L/AG/40/131; Polak w Indiach No. 11 1944
50. Stanisław Kot: Listy z Rosji do gen. Sikorskiego (Letters from Russia to Gen. Sikorski) London 1956 p.315
51. PISM, A 23 / 16
52. Archiwa Polonii Orchard Lake (Polonia Archives in Orchard Lake) Michigan USA, Syg. 1 / 145 / 852
53. Duszpasterz za Granicą (Clergyman abroad) Rome 1995 p.82 Roman Nir Rev.:Duszpasterstwo w polskim obozie przejściowym w Karachi 1942-1945 (Religious care in the Polish transit camp in Karachi 942-1945).
54. Polak w Indiach (A Pole in India) No.116, 1948, L. Mikuszewski: Z działalności SPKP (The proceedings of SPKP)
55. Autobiography of Ms Kira Banasińska, authorised by her and co-authored by Ms Geeta Verghese, Bombay 1999?
56. Ibid
57. Intelligence Co-operation between Poland and Great Britain 1939-1945, Report of the Anglo-Polish Historical Committee, London 2005.
58. PISM, A 11 E 753
59. PISM, A 11 539
60. Polak w Indiach (A Pole in India) No.1 (116), 1948, Antoni Jankowski Rev.: Z działalności Zjednoczenia Polskiego w Indiach (The proceedings of the Federation of Poles in India).

STEFAN NORBLIN
(by Jan K. Siedlecki)

Norblin had an extraordinary ancestry; he descended from the French royal painters who came to Poland in 1772 at the invitation of Count Czartoryski to set up a painting school at the court of the Polish King Stanislaw August. Although most of the family returned to Paris in 1804, Stanislaw Ignacy Norblin remained in Warsaw, where his son Stefan was born in 1892.

He had a privileged childhood, with good education, culminating with commercial studies in Antwerp in 1910. During this time he started to copy the paintings by Rubens and Rembrandt. In Amsterdam he was enticed to pick up art as a profession. His first exhibition of paintings was shown in Amsterdam in 1913. He then moved to London and Paris where he was employed as an illustrator. Much wiser and more experienced, he returned to Poland in 1915 and settled in Warsaw. During the Soviet-Polish war of 1920, Norblin joined the army as a volunteer. Knowing several languages, he acted as a translator to the Polish adjutancy at the Riga Conference.

Back in Warsaw, his career truly flourished among the elite, as a leading graphic illustrator and portrait painter, especially in the 1930's after his second marriage to Lena Zelichowska an actress and singer. He established himself not only in the commercial field, fashion, costume and stage design, but became known for his travel posters and book illustrations. The best being the "Life of Columbine" in Art Deco style influenced by Audrey Beardsley. His forte, however, were portraits of beautiful women, the military like Marshal J. Pilsudski and people from well to do establishment or trade. For example the chocolate magnate A. Wedel family. By 1925 Norblin was a well known painter and was invited to join the "Zachęta" – equivalent to the Royal Academy of Arts and in 1935 he became its honorary member.

When the war broke out in 1939 he and his wife, had to abandon their unfinished villa and like thousands of fleeing Poles became homeless. His path of refuge was through Romania, Turkey and Baghdad, where he painted the royal Ghazi family in Iraq. The Norblins eventually arrived in Bombay in 1940, where their son Andrzej-Piotr was born in 1944. Here he was commissioned to paint scenes from Ramayana in palaces of Morvi and Ramgarh. In February of that year, he held an exhibition in Jehangir Hall in Bombay of portrait paintings of several Maharajas. Amongst them of Kumarsaheb and other Raja Sahebs.

He was lucky to have met Maharaja Umaid Singh, who commissioned him to design the interiors of his new palace Umaid Bahwan in Jodhpur, which was designed by the English establishment architect, Henry Vaughan Lanchester. Its construction started in 1928 and although costly, provided employment for a number of people during the time of famine. The furniture in the Art Deco style was designed by the sculptor named Roslyn and made by the firm of Maples in London. This style was favoured by a large section of the Indian society, for being European rather than British in its origin. It also synthesised with the romanticism of ancient India. Unfortunately the shipment of the furniture in 1942 was torpedoed by a German U Boat.

Wild boar hunt in the sitting room by Norblin with chrome and marquetry table lamp in Art Deco Style

The task that the Maharaja placed upon Norblin was extremely challenging - to recreate all the furniture (which was then to be executed by local craftsmen) together with murals and general décor. Norblin tackled the project with his usual enthusiasm and the result of his artistic achievement was unique if not magnificent. However his inexperience let him down for the oil paint on concrete white washed walls eventually failed and these murals are now the subject of extensive restoration.

After the war, in 1946, Norblin decided to resettle in America. His son's health needed the Californian sun rather than New York where he was being invited to join the graphic activities of the Polish artistic community. In San Francisco, despite joining the Society of Western Artists, Norblin failed to make a living as a painter. His wife Lena, did not fare any better by being employed as a manicurist. Life was hard for them and after trading the jewellery and fur coats to make ends meet, Norblin plunged into depression. What was tragic, was that his eyesight was fading and with the onset of his own health problems, not wishing to be a burden to her, he committed suicide in 1952.

A sad ending to a talented artist, whose work was almost forgotten, but can still be traced in far away places.

(based on: Art Deco Exhibition catalogue in London, The Association Bulletin No.27, Deco Luxury – "Indian Style" book, TVPolonia film and Dictionary of Polish Artists, Vol. VI, Warsaw.

CHILDREN'S CAMP IN BALACHADI, JAMNAGAR
by Wiesław Stypuła
Translated and edited by Janina Wadoń (Łochowska)

The Declaration of the Government of India

Negotiations for the evacuation of Polish children from the Soviet Union dragged on, having to take place out of necessity, on the sidelines of the war. The fate of these children was not of primary concern for the key players of World War II, as most diplomatic efforts focused on the escalating military operations. Since no solutions could be found, the initial negotiations conducted between the Government of India and the Polish Authorities in the fall of 1941, stalled and reached an impasse.

The crucial event which ended this standstill, was the declaration of the Government of India that they would accept 500 Polish children into India.[1] The declaration was announced on 3rd January, 1942, ten days after Soviet permission had been obtained for the first evacuation. It is interesting to note that this declaration did not come from one of the more prosperous countries, nor from any of the larger Polish émigré communities, but from a country considered at that time to be among the poorest in the world.

India's declaration, although very important, on its own could not determine whether the evacuation and relocation operations could take place, or be successful. Aside from whether it would even be possible to bring the children to India, as intended, a number of other questions still had to be answered, such as: when could the children be brought in, for how long, and at whose expense.

The Sponsorship of Polish Children by Maharajah Jam Saheb

This subsequent impasse was brought to an end by a hospitable gesture from Maharajah Jam Saheb's offer to accept 500 Polish children into his Nawanagar principality.

Maharajah Jam Saheb Digvijay Sinhji was at that time chairman of the council of Indian princes, and one of the two delegates from India at the war cabinet of Great Britain, where among others, he met General W. Sikorski, Commander in Chief of the Polish army and Prime Minister of the Polish government in exile, based in London.

During an interview with an editor of the weekly magazine *Poland* the Maharajah explained his motives:[2]

"Deeply moved and distressed by the suffering of the Polish nation, and especially of those who are spending their childhood and youth in the tragic circumstances of this most terrible of wars, I wanted to contribute, and, in some way, improve their lot by offering them refuge in a country which is far away from the ravages of war. Maybe there, in the beautiful hills beside the seashore, the children will be able to recover their health and to forget the ordeal they went through... I am extremely pleased that I have the opportunity to alleviate the suffering of these children, as I sympathise with the Polish nation and its relentless struggle against oppression, a nation which has produced such magnificent sons. My father was very interested in the Polish situation. He learned about it from Ignacy Paderewski, the great Polish pianist and statesman with whom he used to meet at the League of Nations in Geneva. I myself remember one of these meetings. My father brought me with him to Geneva, when I was a young boy, and introduced me to his great friend. During the conversation, the master drew attention to my hands, and remarked that my fingers were slim and well suited for the piano. But, to my great disappointment, my father expressed the opinion that, although I had good fingers, I was tone deaf. The friendship between my father and Paderewski was, to a great extent, instrumental in creating my interest in Poland. Now, when the Polish nation is fighting so heroically, when Polish soldiers take part in battles on all fronts, when more than a million Poles have been dispersed throughout the world, I am trying to do whatever I can to save the children; as they must regain their health and strength after these dreadful trials, so that in the future they will be able to cope with the tasks that await them in a liberated Poland."

Maharajah Jam Saheb's offer put an end to any previous discussions of placing individual children with wealthy families, or sending small groups of children to convents, monasteries, or schools in India. His proposal met with the endeavours of the Polish Authorities in exile to bring exiled children together for the duration of the war, rather than disperse them.

After the Maharajah's offer, arrangements to accommodate the children in India moved along very quickly. At the initiative of the Polish Consulate General in Bombay, and with the support of the Government of India, the Committee of Relief for Polish Children was established in Delhi. It consisted of the British representative of the Government of India, Deputy Minister Capt. Archibald Webb; Polish Consul General Dr. Eugeniusz Banasiński; the Catholic Archbishop of Delhi; and the representatives from the Chamber of Indian princes. A Polish Children's Fund was opened with a Rs 50,000 (or about £3,500) grant from the Viceroy of India, and Rs 8,500 (or about £600) collected by the Polish Red Cross. The Fund was managed by its Secretary, Capt. Webb, acting as the Principal Refugee Officer.

In addition, the Relief Fund for Polish Children was set up with contributions from private individuals, as well as sums pledged by several Maharajahs, who offered to sponsor a specified number of children until the end of the war. The initiator and most passionate advocate of this idea among the Indian princes was Maharajah Jam Saheb. At one of the meetings of the Committee of Relief for Polish Children, a proposal was made that specific children be assigned to particular sponsors. The Polish Authorities circumvented this awkward situation by providing the children's names to sponsors through the drawing of lots, and then giving them the photographs of the children they had sponsored.

Thus two fundamental problems were resolved: finding a location for the camp for the first 500 children, and the funding to maintain it. The Polish Government in Exile gave a guarantee to cover the difference between the charitable contributions and the actual expenses.

The First Evacuation of Polish Children from the Soviet Union to India

J. Dajek (transport manager), T. Lisiecki (vice-consul), Dr. S. Konarski and Fr. Pluta

Ever since the amnesty had been announced in August 1941, the Polish Embassy in the Soviet Union made countless attempts to obtain Soviet permission for the evacuation of the children, but for some time the prospects of getting it did not look hopeful. From a political and propaganda standpoint, the evacuation of Polish civilians from the Soviet Union was not to the advantage of the Soviet central authorities (since this would expose to the rest of the world the fact that the Soviets were using Poles as forced labour). Likewise, local Soviet authorities, openly hostile towards Poles, were obviously not partial to the idea of an evacuation. However, in spite of the obstacles encountered on its way, the Polish Embassy went ahead with organising relief for Poles dispersed in the vast expanse of the Soviet empire. Several hundred Embassy representatives, known as 'delegates' were dispatched across the huge country in search of Polish exiles, and especially in search of orphaned and lost children. Out of necessity, these delegates had to act in isolation, and could rely only on their own wits and resourcefulness.

Despite their extremely modest means, the Delegates had managed to set up various assembly points and small temporary orphanages, to which they steered the children with the intent of evacuating them across the Soviet-Iranian border, should such an opportunity arise. To facilitate swift evacuations, the Delegates had initially considered opening two large transient orphanages, in Ashkhabad and in Samarkand. However, due to the protracted negotiations for Soviet permission and host countries, they had not managed to arrange this until the Polish Red Cross expedition arrived from India in the latter part of 1941.

The expedition, under the leadership of Vice-Consul Tadeusz Lisiecki, with chief driver Jan Dajek supervising the convoy of trucks, brought supplies of food, clothing, and medicine to Poles in the southern regions of the Soviet Union, and, on its way back to India, was planning to evacuate Polish children from the temporary orphanages.

The Soviet agreement for the evacuation of the first group of Polish children was finally announced on 24th December, 1941, by the Commissioner for External Affairs of the Soviet Union, A. Wyszynski. On 3rd January, 1942 the Polish Authorities were informed that the expedition from Bombay could take the children with them to India. At that moment, the evacuation became a reality and members of the expedition were finally able to deal with outstanding organisational and technical preparations.

The most important task was to assemble the children in one location, as close to the Iranian border as possible, as originally planned. Ashkhabad, where the expedition was stopping over, was still considered the most appropriate for that purpose, but finding accommodation for the children was not easy because all hotels had been converted into military hospitals. After much effort, the children were housed in a workmen's hotel, the 'Kolkhoz'. This long, one-storey building, with nineteen rooms, kitchen and laundry, was suitable for conversion into an orphanage. A significant role in arranging this accommodation was played by Michał Tyszkiewicz, with the help of Councillor Żmigrodzki, the official representative of the Polish Embassy in Kuybyshev, stationed in Ashkhabad.

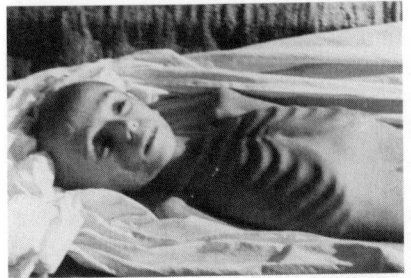

The next task was to transport the children from temporary orphanages to Ashkhabad. This was extremely difficult because there was no direct transportation or lines of communication with remote Uzbek, Turkic and Tadzhik towns and settlements - hundreds or even thousands of kilometres from Ashkhabad. All members of the expedition from India joined in to help in finding and transporting the children.

The first to arrive in Ashkhabad were children from the orphanage in Wrevskoy, near Tashkent, who were brought under the care of Hanka Ordonówna, a very popular singer, wife of Michał Tyszkiewicz. Later, she gave a detailed account of her experiences from that period in her autobiography *Tułacze Dzieci* (The Exiled Children):

"The state of the children's health was catastrophic. Apart from general exhaustion, almost all had fever; many suffered from scurvy and whooping cough, and a few even fell ill with typhus. Henio, who was three years old, looked rather pathetic in pants meant for a five-year-old child. With his legs - skin and bones - his sunken chest wrapped in a tight sweater, his shaved head swaying on a gaunt neck, and his arms like toothpicks, Henio was a typical example of a Polish child in Russia. His body and the skin on his head were covered with scurvy sores and insect bites. 'These are not children', the doctor was saying, wringing her hands, 'these are ruins'.

Having won his battle with the Soviet state police (NKVD) for the buildings, my husband Michał started his war on lice. The stubborn bugs were resistant to the fumigation of children's clothes and multiplied with frightening speed. In desperation, Michał covered his clothes with an apron, his head with a towel, and started throwing the heap of infested rags, one by one, into the fire, watching them burn into ashes. The fire glowed bright deep into the night, burning in its flames the last traces of wretched poverty, and its symbol - lice."

Another group of children was brought to Ashkhabad from the orphanage in Kattakurgan by Jadwiga Tarnogórska: a courageous woman, who, in order to contact the Polish delegate in Samarkand, had travelled in a freight train, hidden on a fuel tank. Later she wrote in her memoirs:

"After a number of trying experiences, most of which had ended up as public prosecution cases, I was spared from another arrest thanks to the goodwill and kindness of the people I met in this foreign land. At the beginning of 1942, I finally arrived at the Polish orphanage at Kattakurgan in Uzbekistan, where I was eagerly received. I then devoted all my time and energy to my work in this sad and abject environment. The children looked like skeletons wrapped in rags, covered with lice and wounds, and sad like death itself. I cooked soups for them from pigweed and sorrel, which they ate with a piece of rationed bread. In all the time I spent with them, I didn't see even a trace of a smile on their faces, not even for a second. I encouraged them to play ball, but they looked at me with surprise, and turned their little heads away, as if to let me know that this was not what mattered to them. They were sad, and so was I, but I could not see any possibility of improving their dreary existence at the time."

One of the next groups was brought to Ashkhabad by a Delegate. It was a small group of just a few children from the local Uzbek orphanage in Kasansay, a distant small town in the

Fergana valley, close to the Chinese border. The children had to cross dozens of kilometres through the desert - partly on foot and partly on a two-wheeled cart - before they reached the district town of Namangan where they were to board a train for their 1,500-kilometre journey to Ashkhabad.

Apart from the children who were in these groups, most other children arrived in Ashkhabad with guardians met by chance.

There were a few exceptional instances of children arriving at the assembly points entirely on their own, after overcoming incredible difficulties in order to reach their destination. The best known example was a seven-year-old boy who, after the death of his parents from typhus, was left with his 18-month-old sister - alone on the Uzbek farm. When news reached him that evacuations were being organised somewhere in town, the boy set out on foot on a dozen-kilometre journey to Samarkand, with his little sister on his back. Walking with bare feet through marshes and fields covered with snow, he managed to scrounge some food for both of them to eat along the way. The boy's perseverance was all the more remarkable considering that the members of the Red Cross expedition from India had not managed to get through to that particular farm because of the disastrous state of the road.

There was one adult who arrived in Ashkhabad without any children in tow, and not of his own choice, but at the order of his superior, the Chief Army Chaplain, W. Cieński. Years later, he recalled their conversation:[3]

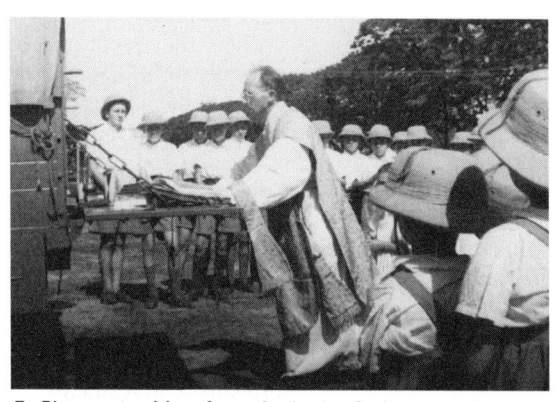

"Why me? I asked... and Fr. Cieński replied: 'because the expedition from India has arrived and they need a priest and a leader'... 'Fr. Chaplain' I said, 'you know very well that I don't like regimentation, that I am like a cat who follows its own path, but now at the time of war, when the Polish army is being assembled to fight on the front, my duty is to be a soldier. However, if God wishes otherwise, and if it is true that God speaks through you, then, there is no other way but to agree, even though I have a different opinion and some doubts."

Fr. Pluta saying Mass from the back of a lorry on the way to Balachadi

Thus, Capt. Franciszek Pluta, the army chaplain, tied his fate to a group of Polish orphans for many years to come.

After several weeks of exhausting work involving many people, contacts had been made with distant orphanages awaiting their turn for transports, and 200 children and over a dozen guardians were assembled in Ashkhabad for the first evacuation.

On 12th March, 1942, the evacuation to the Iranian city of Meshed began. At first, 92 children departed with five guardians, and a week later, the next 74. In Meshed, the two groups were accommodated in quarters rented from the local orphanage and were put under quarantine. Dr. Konarski was very busy at that time because, apart from his regular duties of caring for the sick, he had to examine all the children before their long journey.

Other members of the expedition were also quite busy. Under the supervision of the chief driver all vehicles were thoroughly checked and fine-tuned. Taking into consideration their limited resources and the delay due to the sudden illness of their leader, one of the members of the expedition, Henryk Hadała offered their vehicles for hire in local transportation. This brought substantial income which was allocated to better food supplies for their stay in Meshed, and for the journey. The Iranian market had shortages of such basic staples as bread, milk and vegetables. Even if it was possible to get these, prices were extremely high.

The British consul and the American Mission in Meshed, showed considerable interest in the Polish children and offered assistance. Taking advantage of these favourable circumstances, and of British outposts along the route of the expedition, Consul Lisiecki arranged stops for shelter and food in Birjand and Zahedan, and even a medical post, in case of an emergency - a real possibility when travelling with a large group through such difficult terrain.

On 4th April 1942, after a three-week stay in Meshed, during which the children's physical condition improved somewhat, the expedition set out on its journey to India. Excellent organisation, good reconnaissance of the route, and meticulous preparation of the vehicles made it possible to cross the Iranian mountain terrain without major difficulties, in spite of terrible sandstorms. There was however, a shortage of outposts with accommodation and eating facilities. Because of that, most overnight stops were in sheds, in large garages, or in the trucks in which they were travelling. Their diet consisted mainly of dry provisions and fruits. In spite of these difficulties, the atmosphere within the group was very calm and friendly, and Dr. Konarski's patients did not keep him very busy.

On 10th April, the expedition crossed the Iranian border to India, and arrived safely in Nok Kundi. The next day, they boarded a special train to Quetta, where they were met by the Delegate of the Polish Red Cross in India - Kira Banasińska, wife of Consul General in Bombay. They were to have a six hour stopover for bathing, and then tea in the gardens of the official residence of the administrator of Baluchistan, but a four hour delay in arriving, limited their stop in Quetta to a brief welcome at the station by local authorities and community organisations. The children sang a few songs, and the people at the station treated them with various sweets and colourful books. After this friendly welcome, the group continued its journey to Delhi, and then to Bombay, stirring great interest and compassion in the local population throughout the entire several thousand kilometre route.

Mrs. Banasińska, who had been guiding that transport, described their journey in her report to the headquarters of the Polish Red Cross in London:

"In spite of their shaved heads and ill-fitting, tattered clothes, the children made a good impression, arousing genuine sympathy. At many stops on the way to Bombay, local people greeted the children at the stations, treating them with sweets, fruits, cold drinks and toys. The warmest welcome was at the station in Rohra, and in New Delhi, where the children were greeted by the Deputy Secretary of State from the Home Department, Mr. Conran Smith. Feeding the children during the journey had been assigned to Spencer and Co., who fulfilled their duties very well, preparing four meals per day, strictly according to the menu I had planned. A large section of the last car in the train was set apart for the ill: three cases of measles and four of whopping cough. According to the local custom, bins with ice were placed in each car to cool off the air.

On 15th April 1942 at 5 p.m. the children arrived in Bombay, where they were welcomed at the station by Consul General Dr. E. Banasiński, and representatives of the Polish Colony and of the Polish Committee of Relief for Victims of War.

Thus Consul Banasiński's idea became a reality, after a several thousand kilometre journey, the Polish orphans from the Soviet Union found shelter and hospitality in India. It was not the end of their journey yet, because Bandra centre was organised for a temporary stay, while waiting for the completion of the permanent camp."

Considering the negligible resources available to the Polish Red Cross, its evacuation of the first group of Polish children from the Soviet Union to India was an unparalleled success.

The cost of delivery of a ton of merchandise, was approximately £15 on this 5,500 kilometre route from Bombay to Ashkhabad; whereas the cost of the evacuation of one child, or a guardian, from any of the southern republics of the Soviet Union to the borders of India, on an approximately 4,000 kilometre route, was only £6, counting all expenses: transportation, food, clothing, supervision and a three week quarantine in Meshed.

Temporary Centre in Bandra

After welcoming ceremonies at the station in Bombay the children were transferred to Bandra, a seaside district of Bombay, where they were accommodated in rented villas, with twenty-eight rooms.

Since there were no other suitable candidates, the leadership of the orphanage was undertaken by Mrs. Banasińska herself. The positions in the management of the kitchen, clothing, and the infirmary, were assigned by her to three of the children's guardians: Jadwiga Tarnogórska, Anna Mróz, and Wanda Ruszczyc, respectively. They were paid for their work in accordance with the budgets allocated for Polish refugees by Indian authorities.

Children in Bandra

Within just a few days after their arrival, various diseases and deficiencies surfaced, all sorts of skin problems, many cases of whooping cough, etc.

At the request of the Polish Consulate General, a specialist from the military hospital in Bombay, Dr. Templeton, was assigned to examine the children in order to decide which of them required hospital care. Extensive physical examination revealed the children's health to be very poor. There were ten cases of ear inflammation, twenty of lung disease (seven of them requiring treatment in a tuberculosis sanatorium), one case of tuberculosis of the bone, and forty cases of tonsillitis. Seventy children had eczema or infectious skin ulcers. The state of the children's teeth was also alarming, seven hundred teeth required urgent care or removal.

Because of the danger of rapid spread of communicable diseases, and possible outbreak of an epidemic as a result of the children's weakened immune system, it became absolutely necessary to reorganise the orphanage. The children ranged in age from two year old toddlers to sixteen year old adolescents, but they were divided into groups according to the state of their health rather than age. Eight children were transferred to the civilian section of the military hospital in Bombay. The children in better condition were divided into two groups, regardless of sex: one for those under the age of twelve, and one for those over twelve. The third group was placed in a house designated as the infirmary, which was equipped only with basic indispensable medicines, first aid supplies and surgical instruments. The care of the sick children was entrusted to a local physician, Dr. Jamnadas Patel, and the duties of nurse were performed by Wanda Ruszczyc.

A boy with an eye disease was successfully operated on at the municipal hospital. The children with tonsillitis were operated on by one of the best local surgeons Maj. Puller, and an American physician Dr. Pool. There were also three operations on the children with appendicitis.

Apart from treating the children who required immediate medical attention, preventive measures were undertaken: all children were inoculated against small pox, typhus and whooping cough. This was very important because they arrived in Bandra during the season of extreme heat, when the body's natural resistance was lower.

A few days after their arrival, the children encountered language difficulties, especially at the hospital and out-patient clinic. None of them, and hardly anyone among the adults, could speak English, which was then the official language of India. To solve this problem, Mrs. Banasińska made an arrangement with the French Catholic Mission of the Salezians for the temporary transfer of Brother Eustachy to the orphanage. Brother Eustachy, a Slovakian monk, was fluent not only in English but also in local dialects. Besides his work as a translator, he was very attentive in care giving, helping with shopping, etc.

Polish Boys in Bandra

In addition, an English language teacher was hired, who immediately started her work with the children, and later with the guardians. The children's diligence and progress was quite remarkable, and Capt. Webb, who had visited the orphanage, made a point of mentioning this with satisfaction in his report to the government.

It was not possible however, to organise a regular school yet, because of the transient status of the Bandra centre, a lack of suitable quarters, books, curriculum, and above all, a complete lack of qualified Polish teachers. The most important thing at that time, was to improve the state of the children's health, both physical and psychological.

The role of spiritual leader was fulfilled from the beginning by Fr. Franciszek Pluta. The religious upbringing undertaken by him at the orphanage was not easy at this early stage, because many children were displaying various behavioural problems. Deprived of parental care, the children had been living, until very recently in an environment in which a tough and often brutal fight for survival dominated. It was difficult for them to adjust to the totally different conditions, and to change their acquired habits.

From time to time, deep psychological wounds erupted. An extreme example was a boy rescued from a Soviet orphanage, in

Bungalows in Bandra

which Polish children had been treated with merciless cruelty. The effect of his trauma was so great, that when he noticed two children whose appearance reminded him of his tormentors, overwhelmed by an urge to retaliate, he tried to drown them while bathing in the sea.

The children's life at the orphanage was governed by a routine adapted to their health. The days began with a wake-up call at 6 a.m., followed by getting dressed, prayer and breakfast, and then various informal talks and lessons. After a 12 o'clock lunch, and a compulsory two-hour rest, groups of children went for walks, played ball, bathed in the sea, or rehearsed for artistic performances.

In spite of being in fragile health, Hanka Ordonówna continued and expanded the cultural activities which she had initiated during the children's brief stay in Ashkhabad. Apart from teaching the children singing, dancing, group games and proper stage conduct, she also introduced them to basic acting.

An important occasion in the life of the orphanage in Bandra, was the annual celebration of the Polish Constitution on the 3rd May in 1791, four years after the US Constitution. The celebrations started with a mass during which Fr. Pluta delivered a patriotic sermon. Among the guests of honour were: the Archbishop of Bombay, Thomas T. Roberts; members of the Diplomatic Corps; representatives from various community centres and organisations; and a large group of local friends of the Poles. The festivities continued at the local high school. After the Polish national anthem, Consul Banasiński delivered a passionate speech about the enormous effort of the Polish nation in its fight for freedom and independence, and then Fr. Pluta spoke about the meaning and role of the Polish Constitution. After the children's performance of folk dances and songs, and a highly applauded solo performance by Hanka Ordonówna, the festivities closed with the British national anthem, sung by a choir.

In June 1942, after just a few weeks of intensive preparation by Fr. Pluta, the first group of children received the Sacrament of Confirmation, and two weeks later another group received First Communion. Both occasions were celebrated with festivities.

Guests and Patrons in Bandra: Arch. T. Roberts, Consul E. Banasiński, Vice-consul T. Lisiecki, Polish Red Cross Delegate K. Banasińska, Fr. Pluta, F. Sarnowiec, Z Rozwadowska, J. Tarnowska and Hanka Ordonówna (in uniform)

The people of Bombay, both native and English, were exceptionally friendly towards the Polish children. Almost every day someone visited the orphanage, bringing gifts of fruit, sweets, toys and books. There were also parcels coming in with footwear, clothing, and fabrics, as well as donations to the Polish Red Cross, totalling Rs 4,000.

Distinguished local dignitaries were frequent guests at the centre, undoubtedly thanks to the personnel of the Consulate and of the Polish Red Cross, who were very successful in drawing public attention to the situation of the Polish children.

Archbishop Roberts, who was very well disposed towards the Poles, visited the orphanage several times, and in May, Lady Lumley, wife of the Governor General of Bombay, came for a visit with her daughter. The children welcomed their guests with song and dance performances under the direction of Hanka Ordonówna. There was extensive coverage of these visits in the Indian press.

As the health of the children improved, life at the orphanage became more lively and recreational activities increased. There were various events specially organised for the children, such as: a film of Gulliver's Travels; a picnic arranged by Sir Alvyn Ezra on the famous Bombay beaches of Juhu, where the children arrived in ten coaches; and a reception for all children, arranged by Mrs. Donald Hill in one of the sports clubs of Bombay.

The children also enjoyed visits from English sailors stationed in Bandra, and very emotional visits from the crew of the Polish ship *Kościuszko*, which had arrived in Bombay at that time. Besides sweets, the Polish sailors gave the children two priceless gifts: a wireless set, and a large Polish national flag, which later fluttered in the breeze on a high flag pole in the children's camp in Balachadi.

BALACHADI, THE FIRST POLISH REFUGEE CAMP IN INDIA

Location

Having invited the Polish children, Maharajah Jam Saheb proposed building a camp for them near his seaside summer residence. which was close to the village of Balachadi, and twenty five kilometres from Jamnagar - the capital of his Navanagar state on the Kathiawar Peninsula (now Gujarat state) in north-west India.

The history of the Kathiawar Peninsula, formerly known as Saurashtra, stretches to legendary times, when gods, people and nature existed in a close relationship. The religious and ethical

Maharaja's Residence

influence of Hinduism and Buddhism, which is based on the principle of non-injury to any living being, and on the belief of achieving perfection of the soul through the cumulative effect of one's actions has undoubtedly contributed to the fact that the peninsula was also popularly called 'The Good Land'. The people living there were known for their great sense of dignity, kindness and tolerance, in spite of the fact that their land was a meeting of two very different cultures and religions, Hindu and Muslim.

The village of Balachadi was a small, but very old settlement. It was situated on an ancient pilgrimage route to Dwarka, the capital of the kingdom of Krishna, one of the most celebrated of the Hindu gods, who, according to Indian mythology, descended to earth to rid the world of evil demons.[4] Apart from a few dozen dwellings, there were the ruins of a fortified wall in the village, and an observation tower. Close to the village was a seasonal shallow lake in which fresh water collected during the summer monsoons. It fed the wells of the neighbourhood for many months after. The farming population of the village cultivated the land and raised cattle, goats and sheep.

The Maharajah's summer residence sat on the top of a cliff by the sea, hidden in the rich flora of a small orchard park.

Banian Tree

On the flat sand dunes along the beach ran a narrow strip of dwarf acacias, low desert plants, small cactuses and sharp seashore grass. Amidst this green strip were well maintained golf courses. Beyond the dunes stretched a semi-desert landscape, typical for this part of India. It was interspersed with many rocky hills covered in parts with short grass and in other parts with thorny shrubs or tangled masses of cactuses. Near the well and fresh water reservoirs grew date palms and huge fig trees known as banyans. During high tide, the water flooded lower terrains and the shallow flood water sometimes reached the foot of the hills. One of these hillocks had been chosen as the site of the future camp for the Polish children. It was located about a mile from the Maharajah's residence and the village of Balachadi.

Construction of the Camp

After the approval of the site for the camp by the Government of India, the Maharajah started the project by assigning the preparation of technical specifications to his chief engineer J. O. Jagus, and by appointing his secretary Maj. Geoffrey Clarke as chief construction coordinator.[5] The technical and organisational aspects of the project were quite difficult, because the site chosen for the camp lacked services and was far away from any larger settlements.

In India however, the deciding factor for the suitability of a given site for the construction of habitable dwellings, was the possibility of obtaining drinking water. The location chosen for the Camp met this requirement. The existing well, cut in rock near the village of Balachadi, ensured plenty of fresh water for the camp. To provide a continuous supply of fresh water to the residents, two closed concrete reservoirs were built on the rim of the hill, between the well and the pumps in the camp, each with a 20,000 gallon water inflow regulating capacity. These reservoirs also made it possible to store water for the critical pre-monsoon periods of drought.

Another important factor in the choice of the site for the camp was its accessibility. There was already an asphalt road from Jamnagar to the Maharajah's summer residence, and a gravel road was built between his residence and the future camp. The telephone line was extended along this road, providing direct connection between the camp and Jamnagar. Many farmers from the neighbourhood found employment during the construction of the camp.

BALACHADI CAMP

1. school
2. common room
3. offices
4. chapel
5. dining halls
6. assembly ground
7. hospital
8. stores
9. living accommodation
10. staff quarters
11. washing facilities
12. servants quarters

sports grounds

The camp was built on two levels. The living and administration quarters were on an irregular 90 x 250-metre-long plateau, which had been created by levelling off the peak of the hill. The bathhouses, washrooms, toilets, laundry rooms, workshops, storage rooms, garage and living quarters for the Indian labourers, were all located around the slope and at the foot of the hill.

In spite of limited space, about fifty buildings of various sizes were built on the hill. The total number of the buildings in the camp was over sixty. The buildings, known as barracks, were grouped into three areas, according to their function. The children's living quarters were located on the central and south part of the hill, the camp office, kitchens with dining rooms, chapel and community centre were in the south, the hospital, walk in clinic, pharmacy, doctor's cottage, and nurses' living quarters were all on the east end of the hill. The main entrance to the camp, as well as the central square, were also in this area.

The one storey barracks were of very basic brick and wood construction, covered with red tiles. Other building materials were crushed stone, logs and matting.

The children's barracks were 5.2 x 39.6 metres one-room dormitories, each accommodating twenty to thirty children. There were no ceilings, and the floors consisted of compacted earth. The doors were made of wooden frames covered with matting, and the unglazed window openings had vertical strips, on which mosquito nets were installed during the monsoon periods. Each child had a bed made of wood with a jute net base, a small table or shelf, and a metal trunk for personal belongings. There were four extra tables in each barrack for general use. The barracks for the adults were divided into small double occupancy units, each with two separate rooms and one shared bathroom.

The other barracks were similar, but the floors in the hospital, kitchen and bathhouses were made of concrete. There were four bathhouses in the camp, equipped with showers and taps for filling wash basins, each designed to accommodate eighty people at any given time. Although certainly not built to a high standard, the camp met the children's basic needs.

In spite of the limited funds allocated for the project, the construction of the camp took only a few months, including design and outfitting with basic equipment. Accomplishing such an undertaking, under conditions in India at that time, required not only great organisational skills, but also an enormous effort from all parties involved in the project. A very prominent role was played by the Maharajah himself, who personally supervised the construction, and even provided financial assistance when needed.

All essential work was done according to schedule, making it possible for the children to move from the temporary centre to their permanent camp. The preparations for the transfer of the orphanage from Bandra to Balachadi began in the middle of June, after the inspection of the camp by Capt. Webb and Mrs. Banasińska, who in addition to being a Delegate of the Polish Red Cross, was at that time also a Delegate of the Ministry of Social Welfare in the Polish Government in London. The transfer date was set for mid July, at which time the construction was expected to be completed.

In the meantime preparations were being made for subsequent transports of children awaiting their evacuation from the Soviet Union. On 1st June 1942, a telegram was sent to the Government of India with an official request for India's agreement to accept an additional 500 Polish children, this time with the guarantee from the Polish Government in Exile, to cover the children's total cost of living. After obtaining the agreement from the Government of India, a decision was made to expand the camp in Balachadi with facilities for up to 800 children. Instructions were given to start construction, which was expected to be finished at the end of October.[6]

Main Square

Transfer from Bandra to Balachadi

The temporary centre in Bandra was closed down within the time agreed upon with the Indian authorities. The work started a week earlier with the transport of the newly purchased furniture, mattresses and kitchen equipment sent in three cars on the train from Bombay to Jamnagar. Thanks to the attentive supervision of Brother Eustachy, the goods reached their destination in undamaged condition.

The train with the children left for Jamnagar on 16th July 1942.[7] Seven children were left behind in Bombay, three of them recovering after surgery. The same day, four girls were sent to a tuberculosis sanatorium in the health resort district of Panchgani, where the Polish Rest Centre was later established. The girls were sent there under the care of Mrs. Van Damme, wife

Main Square with Polish Flag

of the Consul of Luxembourg, and a very active member in the Polish Red Cross in India.

Mrs. Banasińska supervised the journey with the help of Mrs. Dubash, another active member in the Polish Red Cross, who had collected Rs 2,000 for the Polish children from the local Parsee community.

Upon their arrival in Jamnagar on 17th July 1942, the children were greeted at the station by local dignitaries, but the Maharajah was unable to welcome them personally because the train had been delayed by a few hours. From the station, the children were transported to the Balachadi Camp in ten buses and a special coach for the sick. After their arrival, the group was treated with lunch prepared by the Maharajah's kitchen staff, who continued preparing meals for them until the camp's kitchen was put into service two days later.

During the festive celebration of the group's arrival, the flag, which the children had received from the Polish sailors in Bandra, was raised at the flag pole in the central square. From that day on, it was saluted every day as a symbol of Poland's existence in this remote, but very hospitable land. From that moment, the small Balachadi hill was transformed into little Poland for the children.

The same day, Mrs. Banasińska assigned the role of a temporary Camp Commandant to Fr. Pluta, while still searching for a qualified civilian candidate in India and abroad.

The next day, Catherine Clarke, wife of the Maharajah's secretary, Maj. Clarke, arrived at the camp in her role as a liaison officer between the camp and the Indian Authorities. Mrs. Clarke delivered the camp budget, which had been established by the Government of India, and outlined the general principles of cooperation. The administration of the camp was to stay in Polish hands, and the bank account for the monthly deposits of funds was to be held in the name of the Camp Commandant.

The following day, the representatives of the camp administration paid a courtesy visit to their sponsor, Maharajah Jam Saheb and on 20th July the Maharajah visited the camp. During his visit, the Maharajah told the children how glad he was to be able to host them in his land, and urged them to work hard on self improvement, because the future of Poland depended on them. His friendly personality and fatherly attitude won the children's hearts. This warm and pleasant atmosphere was the beginning of a great mutual friendship, and since then every visit of the Maharajah was a very special event for the children.

The first days in the camp were spent on assigning barracks to the children, organising treatment of the sick, and making preparations for the arrival of the second transport.

Second Transport

On the 3rd and 14th July 1942, two groups of Polish children were evacuated from Ashkhabad to Meshed,[8] where they were put under quarantine. At the beginning of August, a total of 220 children and seventeen guardians left Meshed on their journey to India, in a convoy of numerous trucks. The organisation and supervision of this transport was in the hands of the members of the first Red Cross expedition, who followed almost the same route as before.

Passing through this terrain during the summer was very difficult. The worst problem was the heat and dust which was blown by strong winds from the desert and stirred up by the trucks. After a few minutes on sandy roads, the canvas-covered trucks were coated inside with an enormous amount of dust and fine sand, which permeated the clothing and hair, and forced its way into the eyes and nostrils. Another problem was an insufficient supply of water for drinking on the road, as well as for washing at stops.

Dr. Konarski had to watch the children very carefully to prevent poisoning or infection. Any kind of epidemic would have had grave consequences, as getting help in these remote regions would have been impossible.

Still another problem was the question of safety. On the first stretch of the route various groups of warring tribes from the borderland of Iran and Afghanistan were conducting their operations, allegedly at the instigation of German intelligence. And in Northwest India, armed bands of local Hurs were prowling through the countryside, attacking mainly at night, and stealing as much as they managed to carry with them. Because of that, the leaders of the convoy and the Indian drivers were equipped with firearms, and the children were instructed on how to behave in the face of danger. Along the most dangerous stretches of the route, local authorities provided special military escorts for extra protection. There were a few instances of attempted extortion by armed individuals, but the security measures prevented any major disturbances.

Arriving in India from Persia

Driving on the narrow mountain roads, especially on the borderline between Turkmenistan and Iran, required exceptional mechanical reliability of the vehicles and great skill on the part of the drivers. These roads were known for car accidents.[9] Fortunately, apart from stirred emotions, the journey on that stretch of the route ended successfully.

After a few days the convoy crossed the border between Iran and India, and headed towards Quetta and Hyderabad, where the children were to board the train to their destination.

The mood of the whole group changed dramatically after crossing the border to India, as both the children and the adults began to feel safe. In Iran, especially in Meshed, due to the presence of Soviet soldiers in the streets, everyone had lived in fear that someone might suddenly send the whole transport back to the Soviet Union.

In India the children were greeted very warmly. Local committees practically competed with each other in their hospitality. One of the most unforgettable experiences for the children was their visit to the estate of the local Rajah in the Nok-Kundi region. The contrast between the primitive surroundings during their journey, and the lavish setting of the Rajah's residence was so great that, at first, the awe stricken children were speaking in whispers and walking on tip-toes. But after a few hours they started behaving more naturally, and the usually quiet paths in the beautiful orchard garden resounded with their singing and cries of joy. The owner observed his guests with great understanding and kindness, treating them with fruit and sweets, and even allowing the boys to frolic in his garden pool, which glittered with an illuminated fountain and a multitude of tiny gold fish.

This idyllic atmosphere was suddenly interrupted by the news that the extremely heavy summer monsoon in the Himalayan mountains had flooded the Indus valley. The flood water, up to five metres deep, had spread over several dozen kilometres, flooding villages, roads and railway tracks. The rushing current of the river carried thousands of trees, parts of houses, furnishings, and drowned animals. The north west regions from the Himalayas to the Indian Ocean, were completely cut off from the rest of the country.

Mrs. Banasińska, who had left Balachadi after having taken care of the camp's basic organisational needs upon the arrival of the first transport of children, was desperately trying to get to Quetta with the intention of navigating the second transport. But in spite of her persistent attempts to get there and to find a way of transporting the children to Balachadi, she did not manage to get through to them. Her courage, however, was commendable, as she travelled by public transport over a stretch of several thousand kilometres, through regions which were flooded and plundered by armed Hur insurgents. Travelling alone, in an environment controlled by rebellious Islamic ethnic groups, was quite an undertaking for a young white woman.

The meticulous plans, prepared by the Polish Consulate and the Indian authorities for the convoy's journey through the territory of India, had to be completely changed. Several alternative possibilities were considered, but only two of them were feasible. The first one was to transfer the children from Quetta to Karachi in three or four army transport planes promised by the command of the American garrison stationed in Hyderabad. From Karachi the children were to continue their journey to Jamnagar either by train or by sea. The second option was to keep the children in Quetta until the flood conditions improved; at which time they were to travel by ferry across the flood waters of the Indus river. After long negotiations, the second plan was adopted, and the transport was sent to Quetta for a temporary stay.

Initially, the exhausted children did not accept this decision with enthusiasm, but later they were sorry to part with this hospitable town. Within just a few weeks of their stay in Quetta, without fear of what the next day might bring, and without having to fight for survival, most of the children not only regained some physical strength but also started recovering psychologically after their recent traumatic experiences and long, exhausting journey.

Quetta served significant strategic functions at that time; there was a large army garrison stationed there, with an airport at its disposal. The town was situated in a picturesque valley, surrounded by mountains. The favourable climatic conditions attracted many English officers and higher government officials, who lived there, in most cases, with their families.

Since no official documentation had been found concerning the children's stay in Quetta and their journey to Balachadi, the author of this narrative had to rely on his personal reminiscences of this interesting and important time in their long journey.

I remember that our group was accommodated in brick barracks assembled in a series of sections, each with a small courtyard surrounded by a high wall. The dormitories assigned to us were equipped with about a dozen evenly spaced beds covered with army blankets. Above the beds were neatly rolled blue mosquito nets, and in between the beds were small tables with place mats and little packages of sweets. Best of all was the amazing whiteness of the sheets!

Entering these dormitories for the first time had a great impact on us, as we were coming into a completely different world. Overwhelmed, we stood still, not knowing how to behave in this sanctuary of cleanliness and order. Feeling uneasy and unsure of ourselves, we started speaking to each other in whispers, just in case.

Timidly, I walked to the bed assigned to me, and at that moment I felt that I had found my place in the world once again. I had my own bed! Mine, and mine alone! Large, comfortable and beautifully made. With that mysterious mosquito net above it.

This quiet time of wonder was interrupted by a loud voice from the courtyard, calling us all to a meeting, and informing us that we were going to stay in these barracks, previously occupied by an army unit, until we could cross the Indus river. Next, we all went to the bathhouse, and then to the army warehouse to collect personal items assigned to us. Apart from the shorts which were a bit too long for me, I received white trousers, a khaki shirt, sandals, a handkerchief, a towel, soap, a toothbrush and a cork helmet.

At 2 p.m., lunch, and after that... rest in the dreamlike bed. This was the beginning of our orderly life. The first few days were spent in getting used to the daily routine, and exploring our new surroundings. For the boys the greatest attraction was a large city square, where various activities took place every day: army drills, band rehearsals and sports events. Our favourite were the drills of the Sikh and Gurkha units. The tall Sikhs were very impressive with their long beards and large turbans. When marching, they raised their arms, and before stopping, minced their steps and raised their knees almost to their beards.

In contrast to the Sikhs, the Gurkhas, with their short bow legs, looked rather funny at first glance, but we were quite impressed with their broad bladed 'Kukri' swords, and their stern willful faces. Later, we learned that these highlanders of Nepal were among the best fighters in the world, especially unequalled in hand to hand combat. Fearless and uncompromising, they spread panic in enemy lines. We used to watch their drills with breathless excitement.

A different kind of attraction for us was an army band of pipers rehearsing parade marches. At the front, the drum major was waving his large baton in all directions. Behind him, several dozen musicians, dressed in knee length plaid skirts and huge berets with dangling pompoms, carried strange instruments adorned with ribbons. We were fascinated with their music, which we had never heard before. Original in its sound, loud and rhythmic, it invited one to march or dance.

After a few days, we felt very much at home in our new environment. Plenty of activity, a good diet, and many attractions made us feel well, both physically and psychologically. The only thing difficult to bear was the heat. Everyone had to wear a helmet, and, of course, this met with our disapproval. The helmets fell off whenever we ran, interfered with playing, and were constantly disappearing somewhere, but during the noon hours we were not allowed to appear outside without one.

The arrival of such a large group of children, and Polish children at that, created a certain sensation in Quetta. There were many visits at the orphanage, bringing new surprises every day. Meeting the orphans, treating them with sweets, and making a group photograph was considered the proper thing to do. The distinguished wives of the local dignitaries were also looking us over to find whether we would be appropriate guests at future events in their bungalows. As a rule, these initial meetings were successful, and after each of them, a small group of children was invited for a Saturday or Sunday picnic.

There was a bit of commotion associated with the preparations for such occasions. First, the children were selected as a reward for good conduct. Later, after a medical examination, there was bathing, the choosing of appropriate clothes, a brief lesson in proper behaviour, last minute instructions, and the candidates were ready for a visit.

One day, it was my lucky turn for such a privilege. There were six of us, and a guardian who could speak English. Two black limousines arrived to pick us up. The smartly uniformed Indian drivers courteously invited us to enter. Unsure of myself, I sat on the edge of the seat, for I had never travelled in such a grand vehicle before.

We all remained silent during the entire trip through the town. Everything there was new and elegant, with lots of gardens. After a while, the guardian translated the information, offered by the driver, that about ten years ago this town had been totally destroyed by a powerful earthquake.

By then, our idyllic life in Quetta was in its third week. The first part of September passed by. The swollen waters of the Indus river were gradually subsiding, and the ferry boats on the river were back in service. It was time for us to set out on our further journey.

The day before our departure, we had two, emotionally very intense, experiences. In the morning there was an announcement that our drivers had received an order to return to their army units, and were going to leave us. When they came to say goodbye, it was difficult to recognize them in their uniforms. After offering them our small gifts, and expressing our heartfelt thanks, we gathered for a group photograph, and, after the last handshakes and friendly backslapping the drivers left, followed by our loud good-byes. It was a sad moment for us, as we had grown very attached to them, and with their departure we felt as if a part of our mobile homes was gone. But there was no time for such reflections, as something strange was happening outside.

The bright, and usually distinct orb of the sun started clouding over with a dense mist. The sunlight was cutting through this strange curtain with more and more difficulty. The diffused light acquired a mysterious glow. There was complete silence, a disturbing, distressing silence. Then, a short whistle of wind came from afar. It rapidly increased in volume, and, in a few seconds, exploded in a violent thunderclap. The storm was heading in our direction. It whirled around the courtyard and dashed forward in its wild fury. The whole world started spinning. Enormous masses of dust, mixed with sand, were swirling around in the air, with various objects, branches, newspapers and rugs flying about. It all dropped down to the ground at one moment, and then was instantly picked up back into the air. Tiles were falling down from the roof tops, creating a dreadful clatter. Screams of terror were coming from all directions.

At first we watched quietly, but, when the storm reached us, we fled in panic and fear. Someone was shouting instructions not to hide inside, because the buildings could collapse! Better to remain outside! There was a lot of confusion, running and screaming. When everything calmed down a bit, and we began to gather in the middle of the courtyard, a dark ridge appeared on the mountains. It was moving very quickly, changing its direction frequently. Everything that was in its way was sucked in and raised higher and higher.

I was watching with real dread as the spinning funnel-shaped twist headed towards our courtyard. In an instant, the mattresses, blankets, pillows and sheets drying on the stone-wall were invited into this infernal dance. Some were raised high up and then dropped down near us, and some flew into the air like huge kites, and disappeared from our sight. It all happened quite quickly, but, to us, it seemed to drag forever. When the wind calmed down, and the sun appeared again, everything started coming back to normal. Although still in a bit of a shock, we started counting our losses and profits. For the wild whirlwind provided us with a few 'gifts'. Among them, the most valuable was an army belt with large, shiny metal buckles, an object of pride for the lucky finder, and the envy of his colleagues.

In the evening, long hours were spent on sharing our impressions of the day. We were told later that we had witnessed a known phenomenon, which occurred in those regions regularly. As it turned out, we were lucky, since there had been much more powerful storms than that one. Supposedly, there were incidents when people and animals were swept by the raging whirlwind. Sometimes, whole houses had been destroyed, and their torn roofs were found several hundred metres away. The best known was the destruction of the army base at the seaside in the vicinity of Karachi.

The following morning, after the storm, there was a lot of activity as we were getting ready for our journey. This time, when the trucks with the new drivers arrived to pick us up, we behaved like experienced tourists, taking our seats without any rush or excitement, and placing our baggage underneath the benches.

Good-bye hospitable Quetta! In spite of the turmoil of that eventful day, you remain in my memory as one of the nicest places in the world - to which my thoughts still go back with pleasure.

Our next destination was Hyderabad, about 500 kilometres away. Even though the road was reasonably good, our convoy moved slowly. The traffic was heavy, full of army trucks and various two-wheeled carts pulled by buffaloes or camels. The little towns on our route were full of people on bicycles. The narrow streets were crowded and noisy; voices of shouting people blended with street music, the roar of animals, and continuous honking of motor vehicles. Everyone in this ants nest was trying to mark his existence. Finally we turned into a side road, and arrived at the flood waters which, due to their immensity, had the appearance of a gigantic lake. As far as we could see, there was water.

Our overnight stay in the trucks was quite tiring. The last three weeks, spent almost in comfort, somehow made us less hardy. In the morning, a large wooden ferry pulled up towards the shore, several dozen metres from dry land. Crossing to the ferry through muddy overflow arm of the river was not easy, but we managed; a tow line had to be used only once. For sanitary reasons, we were not allowed to step down from the trucks, because of all the debris in the sludgy flood waters. After driving us to the ferry, the trucks returned to the shore; there was no room for them on the narrow deck.

As we were crossing the river and its flood waters, the shore disappeared from the horizon after a few hours, but the other shore was nowhere in sight. The further we were getting away from land, the less secure we felt, the creaking ferry did not inspire confidence.

In the middle of the river, the water was a little cleaner, but there were still various things floating on it, clumps of cane and hay, various boards, branches, and occasionally even dead animals.

Our attention however, was drawn to something quite different. From time to time, some strange ridges appeared and disappeared in the water beside our ferry. At times the water spun turbulently around them. What were they? We wondered. Fish? Or what? The mystery was finally solved by one of the adults, these were crocodiles, beasts of prey!

The news spread like lightning. The rather monotonous crossing of the river, suddenly burst with excitement, as we started scaring each other with stories of what would happen if... The younger, and more fearful children, started moving quietly to the middle of the ferry, while the bolder ones, in order to impress the others, moved towards the railing, and even tried to lean over. Someone took out a small penknife; it might become handy. Everyone was watching the water carefully, and as soon as any of these strange shapes appeared, a loud cry would pierce the air, "There! There it is!" And so, the next few hours were spent on looking out for crocodiles.

In the late afternoon, we finally reached land. This time the ferry pulled up to a wooden dock. After the last look at the crocodile river, we stepped down onto the shore. "It's good to feel the hard ground under my feet," I thought with relief. After roll call, we quickly took our seats in the trucks and were driven to an overnight stop near a small railroad station. This was the end of our travel in trucks. The remaining distance of 1,500 kilometres was to be covered by train.

Thanks to a few small monkeys romping on the roof, our first encounter with the train was very pleasant. Each of us wanted to touch, or pat them, or give them some food, but the monkeys, cheerful and gentle in appearance, were more aggressive at closer contact.

In the train we occupied three third-class cars, with six to eight children in each small compartment. The hard benches did not bother us since we were used to that, but there was a very unpleasant smell. Apparently, someone had given instructions for a thorough disinfection of all compartments, and unfortunately, this sweet, nauseating smell was with us until the end of our journey. It was more bearable when the train was moving and we could open the windows, but during our overnight stops, the windows had to be closed to keep out unwanted intruders.

Another exasperating problem during our journey was the extreme heat. The train cars, built of wood and sheet metal, were like sauna baths when overheated in the sun, especially when we entered the south rim of the Thar desert, where, to protect ourselves from its hot breath, full of dust mixed with fine sand, we had to keep the windows tightly closed.

The landscape outside the windows of the moving train was quite monotonous at first. As far as we could see there was a scarcely populated sandy desert with areas of rocky terrain. From time to time, the camel caravans appeared on the horizon. When we changed our direction from the west to the south after Morwar, the landscape suddenly changed with the appearance of the mountains of Aravalli, which separated the Deccan plateau from the Thar desert. These rather low mountains, covered with shrubs, stretched along several hundred kilometres of our route, but by then we were too exhausted to appreciate this more interesting scenery and were looking forward to the end of our journey.

At last, after two days, we arrived at the small town of Rajkot. The people greeting us at the station appeared to have been expecting us. While looking around, we wondered whether this was our destination. The first impression was very pleasant; the town was full of gardens and nice small houses. We felt that we could stay there for good, but we had to move on.

After two hours, we arrived at the next town, bigger, but less interesting than the first one, at least near the station. One of the dilapidated one storey buildings had a large sign: **JAMNAGAR**. We were not aware at that time, on 27th September, 1942, that this exotic name would engrave itself so deeply into the story of our lives. The trucks were waiting for us at the station, and, after one more hour, our transport arrived at its destination: Polish Children's Camp in Balachadi.

There were 232 children and 19 guardians at the time of our arrival.[10] This number differs slightly from the numbers on the evacuation lists from Ashkhabad. The difference might have resulted from inaccuracies in reporting.

Subsequent Transports of Polish Children to India by Land

According to several participants, the third large transport with 250 children travelled from the Soviet Union by land through Meshed and Zahedan in Iran, and then in India through Hyderabad to the port of Karachi; from where, on 8th December 1942, part of the group travelled by sea to Jamnagar.

According to the 6th June 1942 report from the Office of the Delegate in Bombay, about 680 children were brought from the Soviet Union to India by land.[11] This number roughly corresponds with the approximate number of children from the three main transports.

According to the accounts from other sources, there was also an indirect route to India by land through Meshed and Tehran, and then through Isfahan and Khorramshahr to Karachi.

One of the transports, consisting of a group of about a hundred girls, was organised under the leadership of Lieut. A. Olszewski, who had been assigned the task of transporting them to India from the Polish orphanages, which had been initially set up in Iran.[12] These children were sent to India at the invitation of Maharajah Boekwad from Baroda, and were to remain under his care until the end of the war.

Equipped with nine field trucks and a passenger jeep, Lieut. A. Olszewski's convoy was accompanied by nine uniformed guardians, two soldiers and two cooks. The servicing of the trucks was assigned to Indians from British transport companies. Planned in detail by the British command, the convoy followed the route of army transports delivering equipment and munitions to the allied forces in the Middle East. It was the shortest route to India from Isfahan, across the southern regions of Afghanistan, and then, through Hyderabad and Ahmadabad to Baroda.

Heavy traffic and the poor condition of the narrow road, as well as the tremendous heat, seriously slowed down the convoy.

The second overnight stop, in a sparsely populated territory of Afghanistan, had a bad effect on the children's morale. The snarling of hungry desert jackals viciously fighting for garbage, and the shots to scare them away from the tents, caused panic among the children and made it impossible for them to sleep. The same night, one of the children was bitten by a snake, and a little girl, Ania Wadecka, was stung by a scorpion. In spite of an anti venom injection and various antiseptic compresses, the girl's condition deteriorated rapidly. Her weakened system was unable to fight the poison, especially since the sting was close to the lymph nodes.

It was impossible to get immediate medical help in this desolate mountain terrain, and the traffic congestion on the narrow winding road prevented the convoy from going faster. At one point, a prolonged delay was caused by an accident involving two local cars which rolled down a thirty metre precipice, and the wounded required help.

Notwithstanding these difficult road conditions, the leader of the convoy instructed the drivers to speed up, in order to bring Ania to the hospital as quickly as possible. But in spite of all the efforts to save her life, Ania died an hour after arriving at the military hospital in Jacobabad.

Lieut. A. Olszewski described the final journey of this little girl from the distant Polish city of Poznań, who died in India in such tragic circumstances:

"The funeral procession moved slowly, with Sister Kozłowska, myself, and the sergeant behind an open two-wheeled cart with Ania's coffin and garlands of flowers beside it. The girls followed us in a column four abreast, and, at the end, Indian soldiers carried a wooden cross, the inscription plate, and two shovels. The road stretched across the town and when I turned around at one moment, I noticed that we were followed by several dozen local people, whose curiosity was aroused by the sight of a foreign funeral.

The burial plot was in the cemetery for soldiers and foreigners. On behalf of all of us, and of our homeland, I bid farewell to this child, the daughter of a nation which, although conquered by the enemy, continues its fight for independence."[13]

Shortly after the funeral, the convoy moved on in a mournful mood in the direction of Hyderabad. The overnight stop in the suburbs of that city also proved to be unlucky. During an extremely powerful monsoon storm, six out of twelve tents collapsed, in spite of all the precautions taken. Part of the blame for this was attributed to the older girls who inadvertently had unfastened the tents in the midst of the storm. The storm lasted only forty minutes, but its effect was quite visible. With the exception of only eleven children who did not sustain any injuries, the rest suffered bruises, scrapes, scratches, as well as strained muscles or tendons on arms and legs. Fortunately, nobody was more seriously hurt. In the morning, the convoy continued its journey on a peaceful route to Ahmadabad, and then to Baroda.

Polish Children in their 'Little Town'

Because the Balachadi Camp was meant exclusively as a children custodial care centre, the children sent to the Camp were either orphans or had only one parent, or their parents or older siblings were missing, or had joined the Polish Army, which was being assembled in the Soviet Union.

The number of children living at the camp was continuously changing because of: transfers of children to medical and therapeutic centres, departures of older teenagers to English schools in India, missing and found family members and subsequent endeavours to reunite them in other refugee camps, and also departures to other countries.

According to various reports from the Office of the Delegate in Bombay, and the accounts of the camp Commandant, there were between 300 and 700 refugees living in the Camp at any one time; eighty to ninety percent of them were children. During the four and a half years of its existence, a total of about 1,000 children lived at the camp, at one time or another. The highest number was reached at the end of 1942, after the arrival of the third transport. In subsequent years, after the border between Iran and the Soviet Union had been closed, the number of children arriving at the camp decreased, while the number of children leaving the camp, after reaching the age of adolescence, continued. There were about 300 children living in the camp at the time of closing it down in November 1946.

The social cross-section of children in the camp was approximately the same as the cross-section of Poles exiled to the Soviet Union. Most of them were children of military settlers, professional soldiers, civil servants, teachers, etc., who

Boys in front of living quarters: J. Urban and Cz. Lichodziejewski (in field caps)

On the roof of a school building in 1944 (T. Dobrostański 3rd from left)

had been living in Eastern Poland until the outbreak of the war. There were only a few children from other regions.

Almost all the children were Polish and Roman Catholic. A few were of Ukrainian or Belarussian origin, or from mixed marriages. This situation resulted from an adverse position taken by the Soviet authorities with regard to evacuating Polish citizens of non-Polish origin. Consequently, placing such individuals on the evacuation lists was very difficult for the organisers of the transports, and often required such measures as falsifying personal data. In spite of these difficulties, a certain percentage of the evacuated children were of Jewish origin.[14] At first they were sent to Polish refugee centres, but later some of them were taken into the care of various Jewish organisations or individuals.

The children from the first three transports ranged in age from two years old to sixteen; 28% were between thirteen and fourteen, and 16% were over fifteen.

The health of most children, arriving at the Balachadi Camp with subsequent transports was similar to that of the children from the first transport at the end of their temporary stay in Bandra. A fragment from an article published in the Indian press, after Lady Fitzherbert's visit at the camp, described the children's situation as follows:

"A tragic example of the children's physical condition was two and a half year old Czesia Grula, whose starved body weighed as little as that of a four month old baby. In spite of the abundance of food in the camp, the children remember the days of hunger during the war, and, unable to get rid of their fear that there might be no food the next day, they often hide bread or fruit under their pillows."[15]

Intellectually, the children were at very different levels. Some were exceptionally talented, and displayed a high degree of intelligence, and some were slow and delayed in their intellectual growth. This could be explained not only by their unequal start before the war, but also by the interruption of their development during the exile, especially of those who lost their parents or guardians at an early age.

In spite of their exposure to the negative conditioning of a tough fight for survival during their exile in the Soviet Union, the children came out of this traumatic trial victorious, without having lost either their national identity or the moral principles which had been implanted in them by family and school.

It does not mean that the inhuman conditions of their forced exile in the Soviet Union did not leave any mark on them. Certain characteristics in their behaviour became more pronounced, such as insubordination, excitability, or drowsiness. But there were also positive qualities which developed in them, such as self-reliance, resourcefulness and perseverance. In the long run, living in a group had a balancing effect on the children's behaviour. The restless calmed down and grew gentler, and the apathetic ones became more active.

Adults in the Camp

Some of the Teaching Staff: standing from the left: M. Janas, F. Wronko, W. Tyszkiewicz, J. Ptakowa, J. Masiewicz and I. Styczyńska; Sitting: W. Woronowicz, H. Krzętowska, Fr. Pluta, and E. Pokrzywka

To organise a camp with several hundred children, and to enable it to function properly, it was necessary to devise a structure, and to set up special services, but initially there was no one with adequate experience to undertake the role of a leader. Most adults arriving at the camp as guardians did not have qualifications for the roles assigned to them. Only a few had any professional training and hardly anyone knew English. Many of the adults were not only in poor physical health, but their psychological state was not the best after the ordeal they had gone through. Nonetheless, there was an urgent need to arrange life for themselves and for the children in their care.

Most of the children were recovering from the trauma of their recent experiences relatively quickly, and with their natural inclination for activity, enthusiasm, and, by then, revived joy of life, they somehow inspired the adults into action. And so, these exhausted and emotionally traumatized adults, quite unprepared for life in a tropical climate, undertook the enormous task of organising the whole of the community life in the camp from scratch.

It would be impossible to overstate the commitment and effort of this rather small group of Polish refugees, and of the devoted local people who assisted them. Although it would not be feasible to name all of about a hundred adults who lived at the camp at one time or another, those who exerted essential influence on the camp's life ought to be mentioned, as it was thanks to them that in this far-away country, on the shores of the Indian ocean, a little Poland was brought to life.

Undoubtedly, the key role was played by Fr. Pluta, who was officially appointed by Mrs. Banasińska as Camp Commandant, after her search for a civilian candidate ended

Bogdan Czaykowski greets the Consul J. Litewski in 1945

unsuccessfully. Although reluctant to accept such a responsible role, in addition to his duties as the pastor of the church, he fulfilled this role with great dedication. Fr. Pluta was a very interesting person: a priest, a soldier, and a passionate patriot. He was full of energy and imagination, bold in expressing his thoughts, and courageous in his endeavours. Putting a lot of heart into his undertakings, he always strove to bring them to a successful completion.

Jadwiga Tarnogórska's contribution to the community life in the camp was manifold. In addition to managing the kitchen, she was also active in the camp's cultural life: running one of the community centres, and participating in the preparations for various festive occasions and children's artistic performances. She remained with the children from the time she had taken care of them at the orphanage in Uzbekistan, before bringing them to Ashkhabad for the first evacuation, to the last day of the camp. Mrs. Tarnogórska had left her own child behind in Poland (like many other mothers who left their babies with relatives in a desperate effort to save them from an almost certain death in exile).

Maria Skórzyna was the first headmistress of the camp school. It was thanks to her that, with the help of just a few other teachers, in less than a month after their arrival with the second transport, fifteen primary-school classes were organised, and later, a secondary-school class was set up. All this was accomplished in very difficult conditions, without textbooks or other school aids, and with many children requiring individual tutoring.

Janina Dobrostanska contributed to the life of the community by organising , directing and stimulating cultural activities, into which she managed to draw almost all the residents. She was an experienced pre-war actress from Bydgoszcz Theatre.

Antoni Maniak was sent from the army to undertake the children's physical education. The arrival of this young and athletic man at the camp with the predominantly female adult population, was a great event. Everyone was impressed by his strength, dexterity and sense of humour. A former member of the Lvov Sports Team, *Pogoń*, Mr. Maniak was adept at all sports, although he used to describe himself as just a street-smart boy from Lvov. Strict and demanding on the field, he did not have to wait long to see the results of his efforts.

Janina Ptak was a young teacher who arrived at the camp in the role of a guardian in the second transport, shortly after experiencing the tragedy of the death of her second child. Apart from taking care of the youngest children, and teaching catechism she immersed herself with great passion into organising Scouting - almost as if to stifle the pain of her personal loss.

J. Dobrostańska (lst on left: head teacher with her nursery class. Amongst them E. Styczyńska, M. Bożek, Cz. Bartosz and J. Jaiko (1943)

One of the most admired adults in the camp, Mrs. Ptak managed to captivate many 'wild souls'. Her winning manner and profound kindness had a tremendous effect on the children's morale and attitude towards life. In her speech at their reunion forty years later, Mrs. Ptak explained what had motivated her to stay with the orphans:

"On the second or third day after the death of my child, I spoke to Bishop Gawlina who visited our orphanage in the Soviet Union. 'What should I do?' I asked, and he answered, 'Go to Tehran, to the army. Join your husband. You are both young, you can start a new life'. But one night, as I was walking along the hall and looking at you lying on blankets spread on the floor. I heard one of the children crying, "Mummy! Mummy!" I was only beginning my life and could not understand many things, but, brought up in an idealistic spirit at home, Scouting and school, I decided that I must stay with you. You were the orphans. You needed care and love."

And she stayed with them for the whole five long years.

Local People Associated with the Camp

The existence and proper functioning of such a large children's refugee camp required the help and co-operation of the local community. Apart from Maharajah Jam Saheb, there were many other local people involved in the life of the camp. Depending on their duties, they can be divided into three categories: official clerks, educated specialists and physical workers.

In the first group, the most important role was played by Principal Refugee Officer, Capt. A. Webb, who worked in close co-operation with his subordinate liaison officers, and with the Polish Consulate in Bombay. All refugee centres were under his management, especially in matters pertaining to the budget. The Commandant described his co-operation with Capt. Webb quite favourably. In spite of budget limitations, in most cases Capt. Webb took into account the Commandant's proposals.[16]

School Band: (from the left standing): Janusz Pokrzywa - saxophone, two Indian Instructors, Tadek Sidoryk - saxophone, Staszek Polak and Wiesiek Stypuła - cornets, Stefan Kłosowski - trombone, (sitting): Stefan Bukowski - accordion, Stasia Szymańska - bass, Staszek Kempa and Zygmunt Kordas - violins, Janek Płusa - mandolin

The role of liaison officer was performed at first by Catherine Clarke, who was a nurse by profession, and a person of great personal refinement and kindness. She was very caring towards the Polish children, but died of typhoid fever a year later. Her duties were taken over by her husband, Maj. Clarke, the Maharajah's secretary, who was also very well disposed towards the children, but due to his many other responsibilities, visited the camp very rarely. His duties in the camp were performed by Narry Marshall, one of the Parsee followers of the ancient religion of Zoroastrianism. Being a single person,

Mr. Marshall had become so attached to the camp that he almost treated it as his home - and its residents as his extended family. He was an exceptionally obliging man, always ready and able to help. It was his responsibility to find reliable contractors, negotiate and sign contracts, and keep records of all financial accounts between the camp and the Indian authorities.

Among the educated specialists, who made their mark in the history of the camp, were two Indian doctors, Dr. Kirit Ashani and Dr. Anant Joshi, both assigned to work in the camp by the Maharajah. The role of the chief physician was performed for quite a long time by Dr. Ashani, while Dr. Joshi took care of the camp's pharmaceutical supplies, and made contacts with local medical services. Thanks to the dedicated work of these two doctors, and of the medical personnel assisting them, most diseases and health problems with which the children had arrived, were totally or partially cured, and there were no serious cases of tropical diseases. The commitment and amicable disposition of both doctors was so great that their friendship with those who had been in their care withstood the test of several decades.

Two army musicians were sent to the camp at the Maharajah's invitation, soon after the discovery of a large set of musical instruments which had been donated to the orphanage some time ago by the American charitable organisation - National Catholic Welfare Conference[17] - but were still kept at the warehouse because none of the camp personnel could play them. Assigned to the school to teach music and to set up a band, both musicians fulfilled their duties remarkably well. Under their direction, the band became an attraction at all the children's performances.

Among Indian physical workers was a group of a dozen cooks, who were brought to the camp from Goa, a small Portuguese colony in India. These young, cheerful Indians, always ready for a joke, were very much liked by the children. They learned to speak Polish quite quickly, and in their free time often accompanied the children on various hikes in the vicinity of the camp.

Most physical work and special services were provided by a few local craftsmen, who were engaged in shoe making, tailoring, roof repair, carpentry, stretching jute-nets on beds, etc. This was a very busy group of workers, who could barely keep up with the constantly increasing needs of the growing children.

Fr. Pluta, with his beloved dog Abu and Chowkidar - Bahan

In the last group of Indian physical workers were the inhabitants of the neighbouring villages who were cleaning the camp's streets, hospital, and sanitary quarters, as well as laundering bed linen, fumigating living quarters and exterminating insects. Thanks to their rather unrewarding, but most indispensable daily work, the camp was always clean and tidy, and there was never any danger of an epidemic due to unsanitary conditions.

In conclusion, it would be impossible not to mention one of the most popular Indians in the camp, who was known as *Chowkidar* (guard). A rather short man with bushy moustache, he performed his role as the Commandant's orderly with great earnestness and commitment, qualities which he also displayed in his care of the dog 'Abu', and of other animals constantly brought to the camp. The children adored Abu.

In his report from 1945, the new Polish Consul General in Bombay, Jerzy Litewski, wrote about the relationship between the local people and the Polish children:

"I would like to mention the exceptionally friendly attitude of Maj. G. Clarke, a liaison officer, who treats the children's welfare almost as a matter of honour. He continues the work started by his departed wife, who truly loved our children. The Maharajah, with his warm personality and kind hearted attitude towards the children, has created an atmosphere of cheerfulness and trust. His relationship with adults is also cordial. He visits the camp with his family quite often, and attends most of the shows organised by the children. His hospitable attitude towards the children has been manifested by providing for many of their material needs. There had never been an occasion when, after his visit, the Maharajah would not offer a certain sum to the camp. Once, when I attended the Nativity Play, Fr. Pluta thanked the Maharajah for his fatherly attitude towards the children, and quoted what the Maharajah had said to him earlier, "Please tell the children that they are no longer orphans because I am their father."

Quite characteristic of the Maharajah was his view on children's eventual departure from India:

"I anticipate and believe that Poland will be truly independent, but, if that should not happen right away, then I think that you will not be returning to Poland within the next few years. In such an event, I will support you, and, after two years, we would have to decide what should be done next."[18]

Unfortunately, these proved to be prophetic words, since, as it turned out, the children could not return to an independent Poland. The Maharajah had not only kept his promise of support, but also prevented the threatened deportation of the children to Communist-ruled Poland.

Nursery class with an Indian carer (2nd from left: R. Gutowski, 3rd. M. Bożek, 4th. Cz. Bartosz and 5th. E. Styczyńska

Organisational Structure of the Camp

The Balachadi camp was organised, for the most part, without the constraints of external interference. Certain restrictions, especially those pertaining to the number of the employed personnel, resulted solely from the limitations of the budget.

The strongest influence on the organisation was exerted by the Commandant, who, being an army chaplain, had implemented certain para-military structures within the camp.

The children were divided into groups of twenty to thirty for each barrack. The main factor in the division was the children's intellectual level; the second criterion was their age. As a result of this division, the children living in the same barrack might have differed in their physical development, but attended the same or parallel classes. The barracks with the youngest children had full-time guardians, and the older children were taken care of by adults who fulfilled this role on a part-time basis, in addition to their other work.

To assist in the day to day life in the barracks, children were elected or assigned to perform such duties as: representing their barrack, maintaining order within, assigning duties for the daily cleaning, organising help for sick children, bringing their group to meals and meetings, keeping record of children leaving the camp, etc. In the absence of a guardian, these young assistants took care of all the children in their barracks. In the barracks occupied by small children, the duties of the assistants were performed by teenagers. This system of peer help created a feeling of security, solidarity and trust, and a bond comparable to family ties. The bonds which developed among the children in the course of time were so strong that several decades later, after living apart in different parts of the world, many still keep contact with each other.

In the spring of 1943, after gaining some experience, and taking into account the budget allocated to the camp, the Commandant submitted the following organisational structure for the approval of the Bombay Office of the Delegate of the Polish Ministry of Social Welfare:

1. Headquarters
2. School, including nursery classes
3. Guardianship
4. Cultural activities and sports
5. Health and Sanitary Services
6. Food Management
7. Supply and Services, including warehousing.

The organisational structure introduced by the Commandant stayed in place, with some small changes, throughout the existence of the camp.

The Headquarters, or the chief administration of the camp, consisted of a team of only three people: the Commandant, his assistant and a secretary. The first two functions were performed from the beginning to the end by Fr. Pluta and Zofia Rozwadowska. The position of secretary was usually vacant, and, only periodically, various individuals from the camp's personnel were recruited for more urgent office work. *Chowkidar* was unofficially employed at the Headquarters. In addition to his role as the Commandant's orderly, he was also performing duties of a janitor, messenger, watchman, etc.

The Commandant's authority in the camp was comparable to that of the commander of an army unit. This similarity was further accentuated by his officer's uniform with which he rarely parted, in spite of the intense heat. His Polish uniform was complemented by a cork helmet and a long flexible cane, modelled on those used by English officers - a symbol of authority in India at that time.

Hand wash before meals

The Commandant was to coordinate more important matters with the Office of the Delegate in Bombay, and was to consult with the Community Council composed of all official employees of the camp, but his was the decisive voice.

The Food Management Section was the largest. Apart from the manager, Jadwiga Tarnogórska, and a few other Polish employees, the rest of the total of about forty workers were Indians, employed as cooks, cook helpers, and *hamals* who did most of the menial kitchen work. The task of managing the kitchen, which had been first assigned to Mrs. Tarnogórska in Bandra, expanded in the Balachadi Camp to include such duties as: organising food supplies through local distributors, inspecting all food on delivery, planning daily menus, and managing all kitchen workers who were preparing meals for the entire camp and the hospital. During the meals, the older girls helped by serving food and feeding the youngest children. They were compensated for their work with a small payment. Working in the kitchen was one of the hardest jobs, because of inadequate equipment, the oppressive heat during summer, and problems with lighting and keeping the fire on during the monsoon. In spite of these difficulties, this section functioned very efficiently, and delays in the preparation of meals were extremely rare. During the four and a half years of the camp's existence, there were no incidents of food poisoning or epidemic from gastric causes. To achieve this was not easy as food spoiled rapidly in the tropical climate, and there was no refrigeration.

The Health and Sanitary Section was also quite large. Apart from two, and periodically three doctors, and a few nurses, it employed a large number of local people in cleaning jobs, and in the battle against mosquitoes and other troublesome insects.

The Supply and Services Section employed only six to eight workers, in the warehouses and in technical services. It was a very hard and unrewarding work, especially during the long monsoon periods, when the excessive dampness caused mildew in stored clothing, bed linen, mattresses, etc.. The older teenagers helped in airing and drying the contents of the warehouses. The amount of work in technical services was illustrated in the monthly reports from this section. For example, during the month of May, in 1944:[19]

Dining Hall

324 pairs of children's sandals were repaired,

186 items of bed linen and mosquito nets were mended,

488 items of kitchen and bed linen were laundered, including those from the hospital and from the personnel.

All workers employed in the camp received remuneration in accordance with the budget established by the Government of India. In the beginning this pay was rather low, having been affected, to some extent, by India's inflation at that time. Monthly pay ranged from Rs 150 (or about £11) for the Commandant's work, to Rs 15 (or about £1) for the job of a street sweeper. Although Rs 15 was obviously a low pay, it was a large sum for these very poor people.

Because of their refugee status, Polish workers in the camp were not entitled either to regular wages, or to a pension. Instead, they received an allowance for their duties performed within the camp. The amount of allowance for work in lower positions was determined by the Commandant, in accordance with the budget, individual qualifications, and work performance.

Since the Balachadi camp was intended exclusively for children, the only adults permitted to live in it were those working for the camp. If an adult refugee refused to work, or was unable to work for health reasons, the Commandant would arrange for his transfer to another refugee camp.

Girls' Dormitory

Climate

There was no hesitation regarding the decision to locate the camp for Polish children on the Kathiawar peninsula. In comparison with the extreme climate in the rest of the Indian subcontinent, the climate on the peninsula was considered by both Indian and Polish Authorities as quite suitable for Europeans.

The Kathiawar peninsula lies between three geographic and climatic regions: to the north it reaches the lowlands of the Great Indian Desert, to the south and west it is surrounded by the Indian Ocean, and to the east lies the vast expanse of the Deccan Plateau. The interaction of these regions created a micro-climate on the peninsula, comparable to steppe conditions. The hot breath of the desert and of the sun-heated plateau was moderated by the moist sea air; while, during the summer monsoon, the strong south-west winds blowing very humid air from the ocean, on contact with dry air of the desert, had difficulty penetrating the peninsula. As a result of these interactions, the monsoon season on the Kathiawar peninsula lasted only a few weeks, during which the precipitation ranged from 300 to 400 mm, which was much lower than in Bombay. The periods of heat were also shorter and milder than in other parts of India. As a rule, they lasted ten to twelve weeks in the pre-monsoon period between April and June, and two to three weeks after the monsoon, usually in November. The temperature during these periods, even in the shade, reached above 38°C. In the periods of summer monsoon, and from November to April, the temperature during the day fluctuated between 15 to 30°C, and at night fell to about 12°C. During the cold season, there were sporadic dips in temperature, close to 0°C.

Nevertheless, in these generally favourable climatic conditions, there were considerable deviations from time to time. One of them occurred in the summer of 1942, when unusually heavy and prolonged rains in north-west India resulted in catastrophic flooding of the Indus river, greatly delaying the second transport on its way to Balachadi.

Malaria Epidemic

The heavy monsoon rains, which also extended over the whole Jamnagar region, filled the lower terrain surrounding the Balachadi Camp with water, creating huge breeding grounds for malaria carrying mosquitos. The sudden outbreak of the malaria epidemic took the camp by surprise. Its effect was escalated by the fact that, after their very recent arrival from the Soviet Union, the children were still in poor physical condition.

During the post-monsoon period in November 1942, soon after the arrival of the second transport, the epidemic reached alarming proportions. Over eighty percent of the residents fell ill with malaria, and the camp changed into a huge hospital. Since this occurred during the early organisational stage of the camp, it made the situation even more difficult. There were no doctors specialising in tropical diseases, and no auxiliary personnel or adequate supply of medicine. The overworked Dr. Ashani, and a few nurses, stayed up day and night, either at the hospital or at the living quarters of the sick.

Dr. A. Joshi (standing at the back) with medical staff and Dr. Ashani with Fr. Pluta 1943/44

The alarmed Polish and Indian authorities launched strong action in an effort to wipe out the epidemic. It was a very difficult undertaking, because the epidemic had spread throughout the vast regions of India, with its population of several hundred million. There was a shortage of doctors and also of quinine, the essential medicine. Since the demand for quinine was far greater than the means of production, its distribution was strictly regulated by the Government of India, and the Indian authorities were required to send it to the army as a first priority.

During the early stages of the epidemic, in the understandable uncertainty and confusion arising out of the concern for the children's health, various representatives of the Polish Authorities tried to find whom and what to blame for this situation. A lot of controversy was created because of different opinions as to the suitability of the location of the camp, and the efficiency of handling the epidemic.

The following reports, from the Office of the Delegate in Bombay to the Polish Ministry of Social Welfare in the Polish Government in London, illustrate this situation:

"Jamnagar is a known malaria region" - reported Henryk Hadała. "The proof of this is the fact that, during the months of October and November in 1942, out of 341 children there were 320 cases of malaria. Lack of essential medical treatment resulted in a situation where, in most cases, the malaria went into a state of relapse, recurring from six to twelve times. As a result, the children are very anaemic, weak, and unable to do any work. The high wartime cost of living, and the limited budget, has not provided for the proper diet required in the treatment of severe anaemia."

Kira Banasińska, who, in her role as the delegate of the Polish Ministry of Social Welfare at that time, had inspected the Balachadi Camp before the transfer of the children from Bandra, defended the suitability of the camp's location and the efficiency of anti-malaria action:

"Mr. Hadała's allegation that Jamnagar is a known malaria region is unfounded. The site chosen for the camp by the Government of India is next to the summer residence of the prince of Navanagar. It is located on a hill, half a mile from the sea, open to the breeze from every direction. High ranking English officials from the Kathiawar states come to the village of Balachadi for their vacations. That, in itself, indicates that this location is healthy.

I don't deny that the malaria epidemic had caused a lot of hardship in the camp, and my comments, in a report to the Minister of Social Welfare in London, drew his attention to that. At my request, the Indian Government immediately delegated the Director of the Malaria Institute, Dr. Jaswant Singh, to explore what could be done to prevent the spread of the epidemic. Appropriate amounts of quinine, Atabrine and plasma-quinine were delivered to the camp. Sewers and neighbouring villages were disinfected, and yet the epidemic retreated very slowly, though, fortunately, without even one case of death. In January, the camp was inspected by the English military Chief of the Sanitary Service in India, Sir Gordon Jolly, and presently the situation can be considered under control. There are still thirty children in the hospital suffering from recurring malaria attacks, but there are no new cases. From the third transport of 250 children, only forty fell ill with malaria."[20]

In front of the hospital during the malaria epidemic 1942/43 (W. Stypuła with bandaged head)

In this heated atmosphere, all sorts of hasty decisions were made, including an ultimatum concerning the future of the camp. W. Styburski, the new delegate for India from the Ministry of Social Welfare in the Polish Government in London, reported:

"During Minister Stańczyk's visit to Delhi, the Indian authorities assured us that the health of the Polish children and refugees in Jamnagar would be their responsibility. They declared that, to the best of their ability, they would help us to take the malaria and bed-bug situation under control. It has been decided that an anti-malaria crew will immediately start disinfection of all mosquito breeding grounds in the vicinity of the camp, and if the sanitary conditions will not be brought under control within four weeks, the camp will be closed down, and both the children and adults will be transferred to Chela."[21] (Another camp in India, which was meant for Polish refugees but was never used.)

While such reports were being circulated between various official departments, the real battle for the children's health continued in the camp. The Commandant persistently dispatched his requests to Bombay for a doctor, quinine and Atabrine. The medicine was sent by the Indian authorities soon after, but the physician designated by the Polish Authorities, Dr. Józef Rubinsztein, arrived after a considerable delay.

Nevertheless, upon his arrival in the camp, the doctor started his work very energetically, concentrating mainly on preventive measures. Strict rules were introduced with regard to putting the mosquito nets in place; wearing long trousers and shirts with long sleeves in the morning and evening, and applying eucalyptus ointment on the face and other exposed parts of the body. Older Scouts and Guides were recruited into action. A special course was organised, at the completion of which the participants could earn a proficiency badge. Apart from theory, a number of field activities were conducted, such as: observing and describing the main paths of insect flight into the camp, and locating the breeding sites, to which the sanitary crews were later sent. The insects were examined under a microscope for the presence of the malaria microbe.

India imported a special antiseptic substance, called pyrethrum, and, out of 180 tons purchased, eighteen tons, or ten percent was allocated to the camp. This was an undeniable proof of the great concern of the Government of India for the well being of the Polish children.[22]

The role of the camp's sanitary inspector was assigned to Dr. Tavinder. All living quarters were fumigated, and all open water reservoirs were disinfected. Fumigation of living quarters stirred up objections among the residents, because the pyrethrum, although quite effective on mosquitoes, had a peculiar irritating smell. The anti-malaria rules, especially sleeping in closed and, therefore, stuffy quarters, did not meet with the children's approval either. This made the work of the guardians very difficult, because it was their responsibility to enforce the rules.

The success of the preventive action depended not only on the co-operation of the residents of the camp, but also of the inhabitants of the neighbouring villages. But the resistance there was even stronger than in the camp, due to the distrust of local people towards doctors and medicine. When the sanitary crews started disinfecting open water reservoirs in the neighbourhood, the villagers strongly objected, because the stored monsoon water was their main source of fresh water during periods of drought. Health service workers had to use various methods, at first even paying villagers to make them co-operate with preventive measures and the malaria treatment. This situation gradually changed, in time, the villagers eagerly accepted treatment, and co-operated with the health inspector in disinfecting the area. The outcome was quite impressive, the percentage of the disease among the local population dropped from eighty percent in 1943 to forty percent in 1944.

The results of the enormous effort in fighting the malaria epidemic in the camp were even more remarkable. After his visit to the camp at the beginning of 1945, Consul General Jerzy Litewski described the malaria situation in his report to the Ministry of Foreign Affairs in the Polish Government in London:

"According to the doctor's report, eighty percent fell ill in 1942, forty percent in 1943 and twenty percent in 1944. There were only two cases of first attacks of malaria during the entire year of 1944. Therefore, in the opinion of the doctor, the malaria has been brought under control. In answer to my question, whether in these circumstances the number of children at the camp could be increased to six or seven hundred, both Dr. Rubinsztein and Commandant Fr. Pluta, gave a positive answer, on condition that continued medical care would be assured.

During my visit to Jamnagar, the nights and days were very cool, but there was not even one child suffering from a cold, a fact which, in the doctor's opinion, proves that the children's immune system has been restored. Taking into consideration our general effort to provide the best possible conditions for the Polish refugees in India, which could never be achieved without our co-operation with local authorities, I declare that the Balachadi camp in the Jamnagar region should not be closed down, and that the number of residents can be increased by bringing children from the orphanage in Isfahan."[23]

Similar opinions were expressed in Indian circles. After his visit to the camp, Archbishop T. Roberts stated:

"The same way as on the Burman front, a great victory was achieved in Jamnagar in fighting disease with medical science, especially in view of the fact that the Polish children had arrived in India in a lamentable state of health, and were susceptible to all sorts of diseases. If the reader were ever to go there, he could see the records depicting this amazing victory of science and medical care."[24]

Education

Regular education was organised in the Balachadi Camp after the arrival of several qualified teachers with the second transport, at the end of September 1942. The earlier casual lessons at the temporary centres in Bandra and Quetta, as well as in the Balachadi Camp, were more a case of occupying the children's time and preparing them for school, rather than actual teaching.

After the initial classification, based on the children's intellectual level, and their psychological state, the difference in the children's age within the same classes was often three to four years. In the beginning, many frightened children withheld information about themselves, in an effort to be assigned to lower classes. The traumatic experiences of life in exile in the Soviet Union had left a definite mark on their minds. The guardians and teachers had to patiently break through many stumbling blocks, not so much to encourage these children to school work, as to help them overcome the reluctance to expose their inadequacies to other children. For these reasons, the children from lower classes were much more frequently transferred to higher classes than the other way around. Those who had not managed to start their education before deportation from Poland, were in the most

Summer 1945: children in front of the school (Maharaja's Guest House)

difficult situation. Some of the youngest, who had problems with the Polish language, were interposing Russian or Uzbek words. Even many older children had difficulties, not only in reading, but also in expressing themselves verbally.

After the introduction of a regular education, the administration encountered problems in their efforts to convert some of the barracks into a school, which by then comprised fifteen classes in a primary school (age 7 to 13, one in secondary, and two in a nursery school. The long, one-room barracks were not suitable for the division into smaller classrooms, because they were built to serve as bedrooms, and had inadequate lighting.

Lesson with Helena Krzętowska Class IVa in 1944

As usual, the help came from Maharajah Jam Saheb, who offered his guest house for the school's use. Since this large brick building, at the foot of the hill, did not quite solve the problem, the Maharajah very generously assigned additional buildings to the camp, but there was still insufficient room for the school's needs. The problem was finally solved by introducing a rotation system of lessons within the existing classrooms, with some classes held out-doors.

Lack of text books necessitated a memory system of teaching and learning. Often the hand written notes, which had been laboriously taken by students during the lessons, were later used by other students as text books. In time, regular text books were reprinted by Arab printers in the Near East, and sent to the camp, but their supply was so limited that there were long periods when one book was shared by several, or even by more than a dozen students.

It was only at the end of 1942 that the school received the first outline of the curriculum from the Polish Board of Education in Tehran.

The problem with the shortage of fully qualified teachers was never solved. On 31st July 1943, out of the seventeen staff members only ten had teaching qualifications. Even the two missionaries, Brother Stanislaus, and Brother Oscar (a Czech and a Slovak respectively), who were teaching English and knew their subject well, had no training in education. They both escaped from Burma before the impending Japanese invasion, and having found shelter at the camp, became engaged in teaching and other duties.

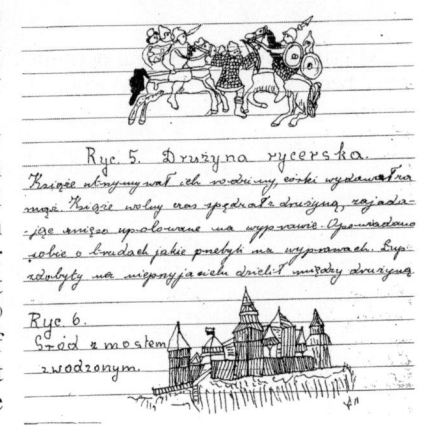

As a rule, there was one teacher for thirty students. Their teaching hours fluctuated between twenty to twenty eight per week, with additional hours spent on tutoring the children whose education was delayed, and on supervising and helping younger children with homework. Apart from teaching, most teachers also participated in community work.[25] In spite of such difficult beginnings, the results of the hard work and dedication of the school's first Headmistress, Maria Skórzyna, and her Staff, were quite impressive. The percentage of the children who failed to pass to the next grade at the end of the school year, was minimal.

In January 1943, a group of ten more gifted girls, who had reached the age of fifteen, were sent to a Catholic school at St. Joseph's Convent in Karachi, where they were to learn English, sewing, typing and home economics. Those who were more advanced in the English language were assigned to classes with academic courses.[26] At about the same time, fifteen older boys were sent to high school in Mount Abu, in the scenic mountains of Aravalli.[27] Subsequently, seven students were sent to a technical school in Bombay and twelve to high school in Panchgani. Six older boys were enlisted as sailors-in-training on the Polish ship *Kościuszko*.

In time, the teaching personnel began to leave the camp for Valivade - a much larger Polish refugee camp in India, near Kolhapur - primarily because of the more difficult living conditions, and more rigid rules in the Balachadi Camp, in comparison with those in Valivade. Another reason was the camp's location, away from large cities or any larger settlements.

A great loss to the camp school was the transfer of Headmistress Maria Skórzyna to Valivade, where she became Head of a teacher training college.

In spite of the decreased personnel and several changes of headmistress, the school at the Balachadi Camp functioned efficiently. In March 1944, it gained the designation of a recognised school and was officially named, St. Andrzej Bobola Primary School Third Grade. At the completion of that school year, the children received their first official school certificate. The school's standard of teaching came to a test after the eventual transfer of the children to Valivade, in November 1946. Although the educational system in Valivade was on quite a high level, the children and teenagers from the Balachadi Camp did not have academic difficulties.

History Lesson in Class V

Cultural Activities

Participation in cultural activities was strongly promoted by the camp administration, not only because homework did not fully occupy the children's free time, and did not satisfy their various interests, but also because these activities were an excellent way of representing the camp. A fact which was acknowledged by all visiting guests. A positive picture of the camp was very important, especially in Indo-English circles, because the essential source of funds for the camp were voluntary contributions from various organisations and several Indian Maharajahs.

Even though, for health reasons, Hanka Ordonówna had not been able to continue her journey with the children to Balachadi - as she had been sent to a tuberculosis sanatorium in Panchgani - her dedicated pioneer work was not in vain. The cultural activities, initiated by her during the children's brief stay in Ashkhabad, and at the temporary centre in Bandra, were carried on in the Balachadi Camp by Jadwiga Tarnogórska, and Jadwiga Masewicz, a teacher and the first head of the Cultural Section. Most children, especially the girls, eagerly participated in cultural activities, and collaborated in creating new programs. A number of groups representing various interests were organised and, after a brief period of rehearsal, were ready to face an audience.

The expanding cultural activities created the need for a community centre, which was organised in one of the barracks. Although very modestly equipped at first, it soon became the main meeting place for all residents.

The adults came there to listen to the only radio in the camp, and to read newspapers or outdated Polish magazines left behind by guests. The older children and teenagers had a choice of several sets of draughts, chess, skittles, and an American game, called 'The Millionaire', which, after having been duplicated by them, became their favourite pastime. The youngest children had their own little corner, where they could play with various toys donated by charitable organisations. The oldest boys took charge of the table tennis.

Chess tournament 1945: on the left Marian Różański - A. Maniak supervises

A strong attraction for the teenagers was an old fashioned record player, with its impressive large trumpet, and several pre-war records. The piano, a very valuable gift from the Maharani, was used by the children for choir and dance rehearsals.

Equipped with a newly built stage, the Centre became a place for all festive occasions. The first of them was held on 24th May 1943 in celebration of the quadri-centennial anniversary of Polish astronomer, Nicolaus Copernicus, founder of the theory of a sun-centred system of planetary motion. The festivities continued in the evening with the Polish dance and song performance in the camp square.

In the meantime, preparations were made for the traditional celebration of the equinox, and for a table tennis tournament.[28]

A great sensation was created in the camp by the arrival of an Indian film crew, who were making a film about Polish children. The film was later shown throughout India on the 'News of India'. After the success of this first film, the Indian authorities planned to make subsequent episodes with the intention of showing them periodically in the cinemas of India.[29]

The turning point in cultural activities was the arrival of Janina Dobrostańska. Since the budget had not anticipated regular positions for

Cinderella with leading actors: Bożena Sito and Marian Różański. Guests: Jam Saheb, Fr. Pluta and Z. Rozwadowska

this kind of work, she was officially hired by the Commandant as the Headmistress of the Nursery School, but her main responsibility was the direction of the Cultural Section. The professional expertise, enthusiasm and creative inventiveness of this hard working former actress had an enormous impact on the cultural life of the camp, and placed it on a very high level, despite limited resources. The work of her extensive programs was distributed among ten groups headed by teachers, whom she recruited as volunteers. The groups comprised: political and historical reviews, camp news, press reports, bulletins, library, theatre, decorative and fine art, choir, music and sports.

In addition, a Cultural Education Committee was set up to serve as an advisory body co-operating with all groups. The committee consisted of: Camp Commandant, Fr. Pluta, Headmistress of the school, Waleria Tyszkiewicz, Head of Guardianship Section, Rozalia Skarzeńska and Guider Janina Ptak.[30]

The cultural activities were based on the concept of competition and reward. Competing with each other were not only various groups, but also classes, barracks, and individuals. To excel became 'fashionable'. The children, who were so frightened and full of complexes not long ago, began to discover their dormant talents and interests. The leaders of the groups tried to draw as many children as possible into team work. Practically every child belonged to a team, and most participated in the activities of several groups. In some of these after-school activities, such as sports and music, the Administration had to cool off the teenagers' excessive involvement.

Children in National Costumes for the "Poland in Song and Dance" show in Sept. 1944

As the camp's monthly reports to the Office of the Delegate in Bombay illustrate, the programs of the activities at the Community Centre included: Saturday evening dances for the teenagers, table tennis tournaments, weekly reviews of current events for adults and older teenagers, weekly briefings for guardians, teachers' meetings, publication of Camp News, including children's creative writings, weekly briefings for the personnel of the Guardianship section, teachers' meetings, etc.[31]

In time, the range of cultural activities expanded and a more ambitious repertoire developed. The achievements of the particular groups were displayed during festive celebrations of national and historical events, at ceremonies of folk traditions, and on such occasions as, beginning and end of the school year, Scout Promise, blessing of the camp's flag, the children's First Communion, Confirmation, etc.

Special concerts and shows were prepared for guests. One of them: *Poland in Song and Dance* was performed on 9th September 1944 for the Maharajah, his family and the whole local elite. The concert was so popular that it was repeated twice for the local people, with one performance held in the reception hall at the Maharajah's palace in Jamnagar.

One of the most enthusiastic members of the audience was the Maharajah himself. After one of the first performances, the Maharajah offered Rs 1,001 to the camp. The one extra rupee, he explained, was a deposit for the next successful show. The Maharajah accepted most invitations, and, if he was not able to attend the performance, he delegated one of the local dignitaries, who, being aware of the established custom, also felt obliged to offer a gratuity. The funds raised at these concerts replenished the camp's bank account considerably.

The main goal of the cultural activities was to cultivate the national, folk and religious traditions, but in time, a number of more current elements were introduced. For instance, Hitler or Stalin would appear among the negative characters in the Nativity Play, a Siberian exile, or a soldier from Monte Cassino, would bring gifts to the manger, and St. Nicholas would arrive on a camel with gifts for the children. The wreaths, traditionally thrown into the river during the equinox, would, of course, be thrown into the nearby gulf.

Among the many shows and various theatre productions, some earned special distinction with their exuberance, beautiful staging and high artistic standard. The themes, drawn from Polish literature, were an inspiration for all. Great effects were created by imaginatively designed stage settings, and by elaborate costumes, which required many weeks of laborious effort, as most were handmade. Stage settings were assembled by the older boys, with the help of an adult skilled in carpentry. The plays were performed to a large audience of camp residents and guests from Jamnagar. The youthful actors delighted the audience. Among the most talented were Bogdan Czaykowski, Bożena Sito and Marian Różański.

Within a short time, after the arrival of the two Indian army musicians, several dozen children learned to play various instruments. From a group of the most talented and persevering, an orchestra was assembled and, after a few months of strenuous practice and rehearsal, was ready to display its accomplishment. The first performance, at the end of 1944, was received enthusiastically, even though the

St. Nicholas

musical standard of the presentation was not yet very high. Since then however, the orchestra added lustre to every festive occasion, not only in the camp but also at various local festivities. One of them was the celebration of the fifth birthday of the Maharajah's son, the heir to the prince's throne. At the end of the performance by Polish groups, the little prince was presented with the gift of a beautifully embroidered Kraków regional costume, with a hat adorned with real peacock feathers.

In the middle of 1945, Head of the Cultural Section, Janina Dobrostańska, was transferred to Valivade, and was replaced by Czesława Ciążyńska, who introduced courses in decorative and fine arts, and undertook the leadership of the Music Group.

In time, the orchestra attained a more ambitious repertoire, including Lehar and Strauss. After the eventual closing of the camp, at the end of November 1946, the members of the orchestra were transferred, in a slightly reduced number, to Valivade, where they continued to perform. Their last performance there was on 3rd January 1948, during an evening of music and song: 'Welcome New Year 1948 - Farewell Valivade.'

Sports and Recreation

Morning Exercises

Although the Camp Administration was quite aware of the importance of physical education for the proper development of the children, at first there was no one qualified to undertake this task. Out of necessity, physical activities were conducted on a casual basis by the School, Cultural Section, Guardianship Section, and various spontaneously created sports teams.

This situation changed radically with the arrival of Antoni Maniak, who started his work by preparing an extensive program, which included: compulsory morning gymnastics, compulsory exercises at school, voluntary afternoon exercises, and training of sports teams.

Morning exercises, supervised by the person on duty, or by Mr. Maniak himself, were followed by a strenuous march-run, which was a nightmare for most of the girls and less fit boys. Mr. Maniak carefully observed each group, and, if he noticed any slacking, he would prolong the workout by one more round of running. After the workout, the groups marched back to the camp to the rhythm of a song.

Much less rigorous were the exercises with individual classes at school which were training for gymnastic displays, usually in the school yard. These exercises were liked by the younger children, especially by the girls. The boys preferred to play football (soccer) or to climb the lianas of huge banyan trees, which grew next to the school building.

Basic sports training was conducted in the afternoon, and it was then that Mr. Maniak fully demonstrated his skills. Apart from football, in which he was an unequalled master, he was also excellent in volleyball, basketball and swimming, and he knew the secrets of all the track and field disciplines, including pole vaulting. Sport was the passion of his life, which he tried to instil into everybody. Strong and muscular, Mr. Maniak had many eager followers among the boys. He was their idol, whose level they aspired to reach.

To enable the teams to practice, it became necessary to build sports fields. Since no expenses for such purposes had been anticipated in the budget, all the work of levelling the surface of this rocky terrain had to be done manually with picks and shovels. In spite of that, after a few months of very hard physical labour, the young sports enthusiasts produced: a sports ground with a running track for athletics, a court for basketball and volleyball, and a track and field plain for training and tournaments. The fields were almost as hard as pavements. Each contact with the surface was painful and caused sores and bruises, which left many football enthusiasts constantly wearing bandages on their arms and legs.

The work accomplished by the boys aroused the most sincere admiration of Maharajah Jam Saheb, who, not only outfitted the courts with additional equipment and installations, but also became the Polish team's most loyal fan.

With professional coaching, youthful enthusiasm and systematic hard work, the teams quickly improved their skills, greatly motivated by the introduction of rivalry. To put their skills to the test, after a few months of training and practice, contact was made with students from a local school, to initiate team games.

The camp teams, although quite excited, faced the first games with some anxiety. However, their concerns proved to be unfounded, as the first confrontation with Indian students from the neighbouring village of Hadiana ended in their victory. Although the rival teams turned out to be rather weak, the victory of the Polish teams was achieved not so much by better skills, as by much stronger determination and will to win.

Their next opponents were older cadets from Jamnagar. In the first game, the Polish football players won 6:0 on their home ground; the return game in Jamnagar was 0:0 tie.

After these initial successes, the camp teams started looking around for more challenging rivals. An offer to play a series of matches with an Indian team from the OKHA Navy unit, under British command, was received simultaneously with excitement and apprehension. The Indians approached the match very seriously, treating it as an international event. Basic rules of the game were agreed upon, admitting the coaches as players. Two British officers from the command unit for the Indian team, and for the Polish team, naturally, Mr. Maniak. The role of referee was assigned to an English officer from the visiting team. It was agreed that the players would wear their national colours and the match would start with the singing of the anthems of the participating teams.

Thus the teenage boys from the Balachadi Camp had the honour of representing their country in this football match which took place in the spring of 1944.

On the day of the match, the start of the game was greatly delayed by waiting for the arrival of the Maharajah. Finally, well into the afternoon, after two or three warm-up games, a cavalcade of cars arrived with the Maharajah in the first car. After a brief greeting, the Maharajah took his seat beside the Commandant, in a large wicker chair from the Camp's office. Beside him sat the guests he had brought from the neighbourhood, and next to them, the camp's personnel. The children, and a large group of locals, enticed by the spectacle, sat around the ground.

After the official welcome and introduction of the players by the team captains, everyone joined in singing the anthems: *Jay, Jay Mahara... God Save the King...* and *Jeszcze Polska nie zginęła* (Poland has not

Volleyball Team with Trainer A. Maniak

yet perished...) And then, the referee's whistle started the battle on the field. The first minutes were very tense. There were many imprecise passes, throws and kicks on the uneven field. The game got off to a slow start, even though no one was holding back. The presence of the distinguished guests, as well as stage fright before the first match, had an intimidating effect on the players.

Part way through the first half, the moment everyone was waiting for finally arrived! After Mr. Maniak's terrific solo rally and pass from Jurek, a boy known as 'Dedena' scored the first goal. The frenzy of released joy swept throughout the whole field. The screaming was so loud that it drew crowds of local people. There was no end to the cheering. After rounds of hugging and backslapping, 'Dedena' was beaming with joy. Even the Maharajah stood up, smiling and clapping for the longest time.

The captain of the visiting team appealed to the referee, but the referee pointed decisively to the middle of the field, ending any further discussion. Although his heart must have been on the side of his team, he maintained his objectivity as a referee.

Then the real match began. The battle for each ball was fought with unrelenting determination, especially between the two captains. Although they were equal in skill, the Englishman was somewhat superior in speed, while Mr. Maniak was physically stronger. It was quite clear that they were fighting with each other for prestige. Both were aware that the final outcome of the match depended on them.

Finally, half-time. The children rushed to pour water over the boys, from the containers brought for that purpose. In the heat well above thirty degrees, this had a reviving effect. It was only then that all sorts of scratches, scrapes, bruises and bumps were discovered. The hard, uneven field had taken its toll. Everybody washed, applied iodine, and bandaged his wounds, but no one complained.

Mr. Maniak gathered his players to assess the situation. "It's not bad" - he said. "If we use our heads, we'll have a chance to win the final battle. But we mustn't allow the opponent to impose his style upon us."

On the other side of the field, the equally tired Indian players listened to their coach, who appeared extremely agitated. It was clear that his emotions took the upper hand. He had intended to show the opposing team how to play, and, now his honour was being threatened. He reprimanded his players with a shrill, sharp voice, while they listened attentively, silently nodding, as they could not contradict their officer - and a white man at that - an Englishman.

The second part of the match started with an aggressive attack by the visiting team. Every few minutes a scuffle broke out near the camp's goal. Great excitement mounted in the stands. Young fans shouted so loud that it was impossible to hear the whistle, but the decisive and unmistakable wave of the referee's hand made the Camp team embarrassed. A penalty kick. Fouling the opponent on their own ground had been so obvious that none of the players of the camp's penalized team even tried to argue with the referee.

The opponents' coach then placed the ball eleven steps from the goal, and... confidently kicked it into the top corner, way above the camp goalie, who dove to the ground. And so: a tie. There were only minutes left in the game.

From that moment of levelling, the situation changed radically. The players of the visiting team started playing worse every minute. They appeared to have completely lost their strength. One could clearly see great exertion on their tired, sweaty faces. Even the best of them, the long-legged Mehta, would have welcomed the referee's whistle with relief.

In contrast, the boys from the Camp team were imbued with new spirit. There were no missed balls. Everyone fought to the last gasp - no matter that the legs refused to obey, that the lungs were short of breath, that every fall was so painful. Resolution appeared on their stubborn faces: "We must win! Win!" Every few minutes Mr. Maniak shouted with a hoarse voice: "Boys, fifteen minutes left; ten minutes left to go; five minutes more; we must win! They are more tired than we are."

And then, when it seemed that the match would end in a tie, the infallible 'Dedena' started his dance at the opponents goal. After dodging two players, he launched a fierce battle with the third one. With his strength visibly ebbing, he still managed to pass the ball to Mr. Maniak, who was running up the field, and then Mr. Maniak, after dodging the last defence player, kicked the ball with such force that the goalie did not even manage to react.

There were no nets on the goals, so the ball soared up far away, and landed next to the school building. Before it was brought back, the referee blew the whistle signalling the end of the match.

The overjoyed players of the camp team started running around the field as if possessed. There was no end to hugging and backslapping. One of the players, known as the 'Bear', grabbed the coach into his powerful arms and, together with other team mates, threw him into the air. Once more, and once again. When finally Mr. Maniak stood on his feet and regained his balance, at first, overwhelmed with emotion, he could not utter even one word. After a long while, he spoke with a choking voice: "Thank you boys. Thank you very much. This was the most important match of my life. Thanks again."

In the flush of excitement, the children screaming at the top of their lungs, stormed into the playing field and surrounded the players. Everyone wanted at least to touch their hero. Gesticulating excitedly, the Commandant sprung up from his seat. Even the most composed guardians, who barely tolerated this chasing after a ball, and who had watched with horror the tough fight of their dirt streaked and bruised children, let themselves get carried away by this wave of enthusiasm.

The Maharajah rose up from his armchair, and stood smiling and clapping bravo, almost as if it mattered more to him that the match had ended in a victory for these newcomers from a distant country, than for his own countrymen.

Finally, the contestants made their way in front of the distinguished guests, and, standing abreast, cheered the defeated team with three rounds of Hip! Hip! Hurrah! And then someone broke in with 'Poland has not yet perished...'. At first only the players, but in no time the others picked up the song, at first falteringly, but after a while several hundred voices joined in a rousing rendition of the Polish anthem.

For the camp community, the victory won by their teenage boys in this first international match with the Indian team of OKHA Navy,[32] was an affirmation that Poland had persevered as a nation. Leaving the field, everyone moved slowly, as if to prolong this elated mood.

Since then, football, which had not been viewed by everyone at the camp in a favourable light before, became an established sport. The victory won in this tough fight started a two-year sports battle, waged by both sides with alternating luck. The stake was not small, since it was a fight for the state primacy. All matches between the Indian navy and the Polish boys from the Balachadi Camp were great events, attended by almost all the residents of the camp and a large number of local fans, including the Maharajah who, without exception, always rooted for the Polish teams.

In time, the range of competition expanded, and eventually included volleyball and field hockey, which was very popular in India. While in volleyball both sides were matched in strength, in field hockey the Indians were decidedly stronger. In spite of that, several Polish players were invited to join the Jamnagar hockey teams which were competing in state matches.

Apart from team games, the camp sports ground was used for training short and long distance races, and all kinds of throws and jumps, including pole vaulting with bamboo poles. The achievements in these athletics were displayed from time to time during tournaments, with most of the teenagers and children participating. The winners received token awards, such as books or souvenir albums.

Another location for sports activities was the nearby gulf, where Mr. Maniak conducted swimming lessons. Bathing in the exceptionally warm sea was a favourite pastime for all residents of the camp. Because of a certain degree of danger involved, strict rules were introduced, especially for the younger children. During the receding tide, the rapid fall of water transformed the usually calm gulf into a rushing torrent, which exposed many sharp rocks.

Some of the older boys, looking for greater excitement, were practising diving into the large village wells cut in rock. This, of course, was strictly forbidden, but they could not resist the temptation of these challenging jumps into cool water.

Among the various recreational activities were excursions in the vicinity of the camp. At first glance, it was a rather monotonous landscape, but on closer exploration, very interesting, with lots of surprises.

For the older boys, most mysterious and intriguing were the rocky hillocks full of huge cactuses, intertwining in places into gigantic masses and providing safe shelter for jackals, lizards and snakes. The purpose of their excursions to the hills was to see the animals living there, and to pick tasty red berries from the thorny bushes. It was also possible to detect wild peacocks there, whose feathers were treasured by the boys as priceless trophies of each excursion.

Another purpose the older boys had for their excursions to the hills was experimenting with so-called 'fireworks' - very carefully hidden from the guardians, far away from the camp. Of course, both practising with, and possession of these dangerous explosives was strictly forbidden, but many 'dare devils' did not obey these rules.

There were also excursions to the nearby villages, Kira and Hadiana, and to small groves full of date and other palms, especially nice at the time of the ripening of the fruits.

The younger children liked the 'Big Forest' with huge fig trees, which provided a pleasant cooling effect, and a nesting sanctuary for colourful parrots, wild doves, and many small squirrels, some of which had become tame and settled permanently at the camp. Unfortunately, this location became associated with one of the camp's greatest tragedies. On 17th July 1945, fourteen year old Bolesław Jarosz drowned in a seasonal lake beside this forest. The circumstances of his death were never determined, since practically no one had ever swum in this shallow lake. Bolek, however, had been known to spend time at the lakeside alone.

After a quiet funeral at a small church cemetery in Jamnagar, Bolek was buried beside the grave of Piotr Mojsiewicz, a younger boy, who died of a serious illness in 1943, a few months after arriving at the camp. Bolek's tragic death shook everyone and plunged the camp into deep mourning for many months. After this accident, leaving the camp by oneself was strictly forbidden.

In time, the older teenagers, especially the more daring boys from the senior class, again began exploring. Searching for new interesting places, they reached further terrains beyond the ten kilometre radius already explored. The most exciting for them was a few days expedition along the seashore. Another outlet for the more active teenagers was cycling on old bicycles rented from Jamnagar.

All these activities, both in sports and recreation, transformed the emaciated frail children into strong, healthy and impressively athletic adolescents. A fact which, to the great satisfaction of the administration, and of the Maharajah, was emphasized by all guests visiting the camp. The most valuable contribution involved in this achievement was, of course, made by Mr. Maniak.

After School Care

The upbringing and after school care of the children was undertaken by the Guardianship Section and the Church. The Guardianship Section was one of the most neglected organisational structures in the camp because of insufficient financing and the lack of qualified personnel. The budget estimated only six positions as guardians. Obviously this handful of guardians could not manage to take care of several hundred children of both sexes and quite diversified age. In these circumstances, the full-time guardians were assigned to take care of the youngest children, and the role of the guardians of the older children and teenagers was performed on a part time basis by teachers and other employees of the camp. For instance, the role of guardian in the barrack with the oldest boys was performed first by the sports trainer, and later by the Camp Commandant.

The full-time guardians, recruited mostly from among individuals who had been taking care of the children during the evacuation from the Soviet Union, did not, as a rule, have any training. Their work was based more on intuition than on professional knowledge, and their attention was focused on establishing and keeping order. The main stress was put on observing rules, maintaining the routine of personal hygiene, and keeping the barracks tidy. In camp conditions this was essential, especially with younger children.

In the periods of heat and during the monsoon seasons, the guardians had the additional responsibility of enforcing the rules pertaining to wearing proper clothing, protective sun helmets, refraining from staying outside in the afternoon, etc. Although disliked by both the guardians and the children, the routine night inspections to ensure that all mosquito nets were properly tucked in, were essential in preventing malaria epidemics. For the guardians on duty, these night inspections of such a large number of beds were tedious, and the children were disturbed by the guardians' flashlight, which often woke them up.

The work of the guardians was not easy, because the children did not eagerly comply with instructions from adults. Especially in the beginning each restraint of freedom met with resistance. For instance, following the example of their Indian peers, many children, mainly the boys, preferred to walk with bare feet rather than to wear sandals, which rubbed their feet, interfered with running and were often falling apart. The fact that the children were walking with bare feet was not only upsetting to the guests visiting the camp, especially to Polish officials, but was creating other problems as well. Apart from the aesthetic aspect, it did not cause much harm within the camp, but, the moment the children stepped outside the camp grounds, there was an increased risk of scorpion stings, of injuries to the toes on rocky terrain, and of stepping on thorns.

Visiting Bishop and Fr. Pluta (standing at the back): W. Wronowicz, F. Głodkowa and J. Ptakowa

First Communion with Local Bishop and Priests

With persistent effort, the administration and guardians managed to enforce wearing sandals at official functions, church services, and festive celebrations, but as soon as these occasions ended, the children threw off their sandals, and somehow made them disappear mysteriously. In the end, the administration became reconciled with this state of affairs, especially since the shoddy sandals were falling apart at such a rate that the Camp shoemaker could not keep up with repairing them.

Despite all the efforts to teach the children to obey the established rules, this process went on for quite a long time, and it actually never really ended. An example of this was the practice of setting aside part of a slice of bread and hiding it under the pillow for later, a habit which obviously had begun out of fear that there might be no food 'later'. Of course, taking bread from the dining room and keeping it in the living quarters was not allowed for health reasons, but some children were unable to get rid of this habit for many years. What a pleasure it was for them to lie in bed at night and pull out a piece of bread from under the pillow, or, better still, a piece of crust, and chew on it leisurely, as slowly as possible.

An interesting, but ineffective experiment, initiated by the Guardianship Section, was a peer court. This project of having the court of fellow students investigate and judge violations of rules or norms of community life, ended in failure because of the severe sentences passed by the children. A striking example was a case concerning a boy who had committed a few minor thefts, and for that was sentenced to: a total boycott by fellow students, one week of strict isolation, an injunction forbidding him to attend the daily morning and evening flag salute in the camp square, and wearing a sign on his back 'I am a thief'.[33] The Commandant revoked this sentence in the latter part of the week, and in time the practice of peer court was discontinued. But that did not stop the children from this type of activity. The only difference was that it became more covert.

Chapel's Interior

In general, the Guardianship Section fulfilled the responsibilities of supervision, protection and discipline very well. But the Church had a much stronger influence on the children. The circumstances were very favourable. The Camp Commandant was a clergyman, a substantial number of guardians and teachers were very religious, and almost all residents of the camp were practising Roman Catholics. It did not mean that life at the camp revolved exclusively around the Church. Although Fr. Pluta was quite strict as the Commandant of the Camp, as a pastor of the Church, he left a considerable margin of latitude to the residents. The daily practice of religion began from glorifying the splendour of God's creation in a hymn sung during the morning flag salute at the camp square, and continued with brief thanksgiving prayers before meals. On Sundays and holidays all the children were obliged to attend mass. Attending the May services, joining the Rosary devotion, serving as altar boys, and participating in the choir, was voluntary. The choir, under the direction of Irena Styczyńska, performed at both church and other festive occasions.

Fr. Pluta was a great enthusiast of the choir and singing. He himself had an excellent voice and liked to sing at every opportunity. Often, even during the religious instruction, or Latin class, in order to relax the students, he would interrupt the lesson and start singing his favourite song, known as 'Pularda', together with the whole class. There were even rumours that 'little sinners' with good voices received lighter penance at confession. The younger children were prepared for their First Confession and First Communion at catechism lessons given by Mrs. Ptak.

During the periods preceding the religious holidays, when the overworked Commandant could not keep up with his duties as a pastor of the Church, a Catholic priest from a small parish in the town of Rajkot, assisted him. 'Hardened sinners' made sure to go to confession to the visiting priest, well aware that his knowledge of the Polish language was limited to a few words of absolution.

Before Christmas and Easter all entertainment was suspended and superseded by preparations for performances associated with the approaching religious holidays. In Advent, before Christmas, apart from a brief retreat, most teenagers took part in setting up the Nativity scene at the church and

Prayers in the Chapel

attended rehearsals for the traditional Nativity Play. During Lent, before Easter, while all teenagers participated in a retreat, Christ's tomb was set up at the church, in accordance with a Polish Easter custom, and preparations were made for the Passion Play. Palm Sunday was celebrated in the folk tradition of greeting each other with palm fronds. Many boys treated this a bit too zealously, leaving visible marks on each other for days to come. During Holy Week, attendance at the church increased greatly. Besides liturgical services, confessions and quiet prayer, on Good Friday groups of Scouts and Altar Boys stood guard at Christ's tomb. The Sunday Resurrection mass, and Easter breakfast, brought the official period of Easter celebrations to an end.

The informal ending took place a day later, when, in keeping up with the 'Wet Monday' custom of pouring water over each other, the excited teenagers created a virtual flood in the Camp. No one was spared, neither the personnel, nor the Commandant. The children had complete freedom on that day, because the guardians were afraid to leave their quarters.

Many Church festivities in the camp were attended by local clergy. After one of his visits, Archbishop Roberts wrote: "One of the most moving ceremonies I have ever witnessed is a ceremony conducted daily at the camp square. Twice a day, at dawn and sunset, the boys and girls march to the square, say their prayers, sing hymns, and salute the flag..."[34]

There is ample evidence that the religious teaching in the camp did not fall on barren ground. Following a vocation to serve God, a few boys completed studies at theological seminaries, and some girls entered convents. For several decades, even though dispersed around the world, a large number of the Camp's former students kept regular contact with Fr. Pluta, and with their catechism teacher, Mrs. Janina Ptak.

Resolving Differences Within the Camp Community

As in most large communities, people in the Balachadi Camp did not always get along with each other. Considering that they were a random assemblage of individuals who, by a strange turn of fate, found themselves all thrust together, there were many reasons for conflicts. Each of them came burdened with their own traumatic experiences. There wasn't a person who had not lost at least one member of their immediate family.

As a rule, the adult community divided itself into groups, which formed according to such criteria as: functions performed at the camp, educational level, personal interests, and family social status. Some lived in harmony and some were at odds with each other. One major area of disagreement among the adults was caused by the three conflicting views with regard to the upbringing of the children, and, in particular, by the very different approaches to discipline.

The dominant approach was, of course, the one championed by the Commandant, Fr. Pluta, and also supported by the Czech missionary, Brother Stanislaus, who taught English in senior classes. This approach was based on obedience, order and strict observance of established rules. Any insubordination was subject to specific punishments such as: a tough talk or a public reprimand; an order prohibiting one from leaving the barrack or the camp; and even spanking, which was more humiliating for the children than painful. The Commandant's cane was often put to use on such occasions. This, of course, met with the guardians' disapproval. The Commandant's impulsiveness, and at times dictatorial manner, triggered strong objections among the people working with him. At first, there were even attempts to replace him, but, due to the lack of another suitable candidate, and thanks to strong support from Capt. Webb and the Maharajah, Fr. Pluta was never replaced as Camp Commandant. He earned the respect of higher authorities with his determination and earnestness whenever acting in the interests of the Camp, or for the welfare of the children.

Although the Commandant was a strong advocate of bringing up children with military discipline, he also believed and practised a system of rewards. Good behaviour, progress in school work and achievements in various teams or community organisations, were rewarded with public praise, small gifts, trips to the cinema in Jamnagar, or delightful visits to the Maharajah's residence. This system of rewarding achievements had, to some extent, a balancing effect on the use of punishment by the Commandant. In time, even the children, who originally had resented the strict discipline, grew to appreciate him.

Forty years later, Fr. Pluta explained the goal of his work in the Balachadi Camp to those who had been in his care in the past, and with whom he kept contact throughout these years: "I did everything I could to help you grow into young eagles and not into ordinary ducklings."

A totally different approach to the upbringing was used by Mrs. Ptak, who transferred all the love she had for her own tragically lost children onto the children entrusted to her care. Her method was a reflection of her idealistic outlook. She did not believe in punishment, gentle persuasion and a one-to-one talk were her style. There were no bounds to her unconditional love and compassion, as she tried to reach to the most sensitive depths of the children's souls. Almost all the girls and boys fell under her spell, and, since she also happened to be an attractive young woman, some of the older boys became infatuated with her.

The third approach was represented by Mr. Maniak. On the one hand, he treated the older boys almost like colleagues, in spite of a difference in age of more than ten years, but at the same time he was quite demanding, and worked his students to a heavy sweat during gymnastic exercises. He did not tolerate shirking. If he noticed any student loitering about, or trying to evade compulsory exercises, then, this otherwise very cheerful and robust young man, would deal with that student strictly. His methods were quite straightforward, sometimes it was just a strong word of reproof, and sometimes an extra 'dose' of workout. After such 'therapy', the children swore 'never again'... particularly the girls, who dreaded the strenuous march-runs and jumping over the 'horse'. Witnessing the sweat and toil of her children, Mrs. Ptak often intervened on their behalf before the Commandant, although he did not always agree with her arguments.

Disagreements among the adults, of course, had different underlying causes than between the children. Some of them were easy for the children to grasp, while others were more difficult to understand. As a rule, the disputes at the 'top' did not hold much interest for the children, and the adults also tried to hide their discords from the children. In time, there were fewer and fewer rifts among the adults and after a few years they practically disappeared.

Of much more importance to the children were frictions which concerned them and occurred among them. Spending time constantly together helped them to get to know each other better, and naturally, not only new friendships evolved, but also various conflicts erupted. A certain rift between the children was caused by the mere fact that some of the guardians and teachers in the camp had their own children living together with them in the Camp. Perceived by other children as privileged for having mothers, they were not very popular, and with the exception of a couple of polite and cheerful boys, they were beaten up occasionally. This problem was soon noticed by the Commandant, and, much to the consternation of the mothers, and despite their complaints, he decided that all the children should live together, and stood firm in his position that all children were equal and should be treated accordingly. In spite of this effort to treat all children equally, the children of the personnel continued to stand out from the rest. Generally, they were more neatly dressed, more restrained verbally, and seemed to be protected by a sort of impenetrable screen.

A noticeable split occurred between the teenagers when Mrs. Ptak, also known as Guider Janina, organised Scouting. Although strongly encouraged by the administration, it was not compulsory to join in. Taking advantage of this situation, the more rebellious boys formed an independent group, with Felek as its self-appointed leader. There were some clashes between Felek's group and the Scouts, but the Scouts' definite majority and conciliatory spirit averted more serious conflicts.

One day Felek, Ciura and Mazur led their 'gang' on one of their hikes in the vicinity of the camp and ended up on the farmers' fields, where they dug up some peanuts. The villagers, who observed them, decided to complain. Since the Commandant was away at that time, they made it clear that they would see him upon his return. Realizing that they were in trouble, the young 'peanut harvesters' met secretly for a consultation to decide what could be done to reduce the punishment, in the event the complaint was made. After long deliberations, two plans of action were adopted: first, no one would admit who was responsible for organising the excursion; second, the entire group would appeal to Guider Janina to let them join Scouting.

It was a known fact that belonging to Scouting, apart from being promoted as an interesting and useful way of spending one's free time, had other advantages, such as more lenient punishments, thanks to Guider Janina's interventions before the Commandant. The boys went out of their way to make a good impression on her and she was delighted with their decision to join Scouting. There was quite a surprise the next day, when, with the speed of light, the news spread throughout the Camp that these well-known 'trouble-makers' had made such a reversal in their attitude to Scouting.

Upon the Commandant's return, a few of the bolder villagers arrived with their complaint. Taken in by the boys, and still unaware of the peanut incident, Guider Janina came to the Commandant at the same time to share the pride of her new success in Scouting. Although not at all convinced about the sincerity of such a sudden transformation by Felek's group, the Commandant's fury was tempered by Guider Janina's fervent pleading on the boys' behalf. To the pleasant surprise of the villagers, the Commandant gave them some clothing in compensation for their trampled field, and to the boys a stern warning: "If anything like this happens again, then...." Thus, Guider Janina's great advocacy skills became even more renown but, to her great disappointment, the boys, one by one, lost interest in Scouting, and in the end only two remained.

A fundamental division between the sexes was not a problem as far as the children were concerned, because the boys and girls were attracted to each other, particularly when they reached the age of adolescence. But, despite the fact that the camp was co-educational, the Commandant did whatever he could to prevent friendships among teenagers from becoming more intimate. This, of course, did not stop the more ardent teenagers, but forced them to meet beyond the Camp grounds.

Włodzio, a hot-blooded youth, was caught twice on a date with the attractive and amiable Stasia. His punishment became a public example and a warning to all other potential candidates for romantic escapades. Even though the Commandant gave Włodzio his caning behind closed doors, he did it in the barrack of the oldest boys. The official reason for the punishment was leaving the camp in the evening without permission, but the real reason was obvious to all concerned.

Sometime later, the Commandant drove his point home one last time, when he tested Włodzio's proficiency in Latin grammar in front of the class. Although Włodzio did not do well, the Commandant, who was in a good mood that day, did not give him a failing mark.

Instead, on leaving the class, he looked at Włodzio with a twinkle in his eye, and recited a simple student verse about a young man being reproved by his father for spending time on paying complements to a pretty girl instead of doing his work.

From time to time, conflicts of a more serious nature erupted between the older teenagers, especially among the boys. These were usually triggered by the rivalry over a pretty girl, or a struggle for esteem within the group. There was once such a confrontation between Stasio and Maciek, who had been at odds with each other for some time. Their fight started after the discovery of food under Stasio's pillow. Since Maciek had been on duty in their barrack at that time, Stasio accused him of 'helping' he guardian in finding the hidden food. Usually quiet and composed, Maciek flared up with anger at this insult hurled at him in front of all the other boys. Sharp words were exchanged, followed by name-calling and punching. Since this happened to be during their barrack's compulsory afternoon rest, it was decided, with the approval of all, that the quarrelling boys would resolve their conflict in the evening, with a duel. Four judges were appointed to select the site for the duel, and to make sure that the rules of the fight were complied with. It was agreed that no knives, clubs, sticks or stones should be used, just bare fists. The first to fall to the ground would acknowledge the victory of his opponent.

The chances of both boys were more or less equal. Stasio had agility, speed and gumption to his advantage, while Maciek had great physical strength. The fight started at 8:15 p.m., with neither one nor the other having the upper hand. At one moment both charged simultaneously at each other and ended up in a head-on collision. Maciek's forehead hit Stasio's face, and Stasio's nose spouted a fountain of blood, covering the faces of both boys. The sight of blood cooled off the excitement among the spectators. The judges rushed to pull the boys apart. Smeared with blood, and only half conscious, the boys were taken to the bathhouse. The cold water cooled off their heated blood, and cleansed their wounds and scratches. After a few days, when the bump on Maciek's forehead disappeared, and Stasio's bruise under the eye faded away, the boys made peace with each other, and declared that, although their fight had not been resolved, their strength was equal. In time, they became good friends.

Fredek's Enterprise

One day, thirteen year old Fredek Burdzy acquired two little chicks from a nearby village, and, in a very short time, raised a flock of chicken which supplied eggs for the whole camp.

Maharajah Jam Saheb noticed the chicken during one of his visits, and wanted to know where they had come from. When Fredek was introduced to him, the Maharajah, impressed with his initiative, found the boy very much to his liking. On his next visit, the Maharajah brought two ducklings for Fredek, so that he could also raise ducks. On another occasion, gave Fredek five turkey eggs, which the boy soon turned into a flock of thirty turkeys. In response to Fredek's question, why pigs were black in India and not pink - as he remembered them from Poland, the Maharajah procured for him three little European pink pigs.

Ruin of Tower in Balachadi

Once Fr. Pluta brought two white pigeons to the Camp. With the help of a friend, Fredek took care of them and, pretty soon, there were 300 pigeons in the pigeon houses in the village tower. Among other animals in this menagerie were: five peacocks, three parrots, fifteen rabbits, and a tamed mongoose.

Scouting in the Balachadi Camp

Polish Scouting in India began at the Balachadi Camp, shortly after the transfer of the first transport of children from Bandra, in July 1942. It was initiated spontaneously by a group of ten boys who formed the Patrol of Eagles, and by a group of older girls who organised a Girl Guide patrol. At that early stage, there were only two Scouts who had already made their Scout Promise.

The Scouting movement, as such, developed in the camp after the arrival of Guider Janina Ptak with the second transport of children, at the end of September 1942. Thanks to her hard work and passion for Scouting, within a short time the Girl Guide patrol expanded into the Romuald Traugutt Troop,[35] and shortly after other Girl Guide troops were organised. Meanwhile, the Patrol of Eagles also expanded into a troop, and most of the younger children were recruited into Cubs and Brownies.

The early stage of Scouting at the camp coincided with the difficult challenges of fighting the malaria epidemic and introducing the children to life in the organised community. Guider Janina initiated several educational aspects in her Scouting program, and involved Scouts in various functions, essential to the well being of the children, and to the camp as a whole.

An important part of the Scouting program was the training of the children in personal hygiene, and in the prevention of venomous stings by refraining from walking barefoot on wet ground, or picking up stones underneath which scorpions nested. Equally essential was checking all nooks and crannies in the barracks and in beds before nightfall, because venomous scorpions, arthropods and centipedes crawled into the camp, and even into the beds, in search of dry places during the monsoon periods. Sometimes snakes crawled into the barracks through cracks in the roofs. The job of locating and eliminating them was done by the older boys, or by Indian cooks' boys. Occasionally, the Commandant's shot gun was used for this purpose, while, at other times, the tamed mongoose, known for its ability to kill snakes, was put to work.

Preventive measures and first aid became compulsory topics at all Scouts' meetings. Each troop, patrol or pack leader conducting Scout camp activities outside the camp grounds, was required to be equipped with a kit containing antiseptic and disinfecting remedies, a tourniquet, etc., in case of an emergency. The outcome of this ongoing, long term training, and the implementation of preventive measures was most evident in the children's developed skills in avoiding the risks of potential venomous stings, as well as in overcoming the paralysing fear, which impeded getting help quickly. The incidents of stings were rare, but when they had occurred, immediate first-aid was administered. This was one of very important achievements of the camp, particularly when compared with the frequent complications, or even deaths, caused by venomous stings or bites among the local population. The Scouts' contribution in implementing preventive measures in everyday life of the camp was indispensable. For their participation in fighting the malaria epidemic, they earned the proficiency badge of Anti-Malaria Scout, created specially for them.

The first Scout investiture was celebrated at the camp with the festive ceremony of the Scout Promise on 15th August, 1943. Guider Janina then registered her Group with the Polish Scouting Association in the East, and reported that it consisted of: three Girl Guide troops, two Boy Scout troops, three packs of Brownies, and one pack of Cubs. The teenagers, who had been transferred from the camp to English schools in India, were included in Guider Janina's Group as independent patrols: two Girl Guide patrols from Karachi, one Boy Scout patrol from Mount Abu, and one Girl Guide patrol from Panchgani. Altogether, there were 239 members in the Group on 1st September, 1943.[36] After the registration, Guider Janina Ptak (Chodorowska), was officially appointed as leader of the Polish Scout Group in the Jamnagar region.

Scout Camp in 1944

Although not an athletic person herself, Guider Janina favoured outdoor activities in her Scouting programs. Since there were no locations with shade trees in the vicinity of the Camp, most Scout activities were conducted during the morning or evening hours. The most enjoyable were those conducted at night. The pleasant cool air, the sky lit with stars, the mysterious moonlight, the chirping of crickets and cicadas, the haunting wailing of jackals, and a distinct scent of the earth - aroused a feeling of wonder. Most of these night activities started with a wake-up alarm and ended with a campfire. For days and days afterwards, the participants re-lived the adventures of their trail hikes, orienteering, searches for hidden treasures, etc..

During the school vacation in October 1943, one of the hottest months of the year, Guider Janina organised a two-week Scout Camp at Oinjerk, thirty kilometres from Jamnagar. Assisting her in running the camp were: two quartermasters, a hygienist, a secretary, a guardian, and troop leaders. The main goal of camping was to enable the participants to get to know each other better, to improve the skills required for earning proficiency badges, and to select potential candidates for future Scout leaders. An important part of the program was to familiarize the participants with the surrounding natural environment, which was similar to the environment around the Balachadi Camp and to acquaint them with the difficult conditions of the wilderness and its various dangers and threats. The aim of the camping activities was to develop courage, self-reliance and resourcefulness, all essential in the life of the orphaned children, who would have to depend on their own strength and decisions in the future. At the conclusion of the Scout camp program, thirty five girls and twenty five boys had earned Scout badges.[37] The ending of the Scout camp activities was celebrated with a giant campfire, to which all residents of the Balachadi Camp were invited.

The activities conducted during the difficult year of 1943 enhanced the organisational growth

Girl Guides - Camping

of Guider Janina's Group, in spite of regular transfers of older teenagers to other schools. Two-thirds of the Group members earned various Scout badges,[38] and on 22nd December 1943, Guider Janina was promoted to the position of Assistant Scoutmaster.[39] In January 1944, there were three meetings of the whole Group, fourteen meetings of troops, several dozen meetings of patrols, and sixteen meetings of cub packs. The independent troop of Girl Guides in Karachi took part in the Indian Jamboree, during which they performed duties of translators. At the end of 1944, Guider Janina's Group expanded into the Fourth Independent Scout Tribe in India.[40]

Official visit of the Scoutmasters (seconded from the army) Hm. B. Pancewicz (on the left) and Hm. Z. Peszkowski, between them J. Dobrostańska (on the left) and J. Ptakowa. Standing in front (2nd from right) T. Dobrostański: Jan 1945.

During the year of 1945, two interesting events made their mark in the history of Scouting at the Balachadi Camp. One of them was the arrival of two Scout instructors from Valivade: Scoutmaster Bronisław Pancewicz and Scoutmaster Zdzisław Peszkowski. The purpose of their eleven-day visit was to conduct a one-week course for teachers and guardians, a course for Scout leaders, and practical training during the Scout meetings, campfires, etc.

The course for teachers and guardians focused on the ideology of Scouting and methods of working with adolescents and children. Impressed with the Scouting ideology, high level of instruction, and the enthusiasm of the instructors, the participants of the course evaluated it very favourably.[41] The courses and training ended with a campfire, with all the residents of the camp, and other guests invited for the occasion.

Another memorable event was described in a Polish publication *Skaut:*

The ceremony of blessing the Scout flag, which took place on 12th May 1945, can be considered one of the most festive occasions in the life of the camp. The celebrations started with a morning mass, dedicated to Scouting. The blessing of the flag, nails being driven into the flag pole, and the procession, were all conducted in the afternoon. The occasion was honoured by the presence of a great friend of Poland, Maharajah Jam Saheb. Handing over the flag to Guider Janina, the Maharajah delivered a moving speech:

"It is a great honour for me and my wife to be godparents of this flag of Polish Scouting. Let the nails, which are being hammered into this flag pole, be the nails in the coffins of the enemies of freedom and of your homeland. I will always remain faithful and loyal

Maharaja Jam Saheb Digvijay Sinhji - "Godfather" of the Scout Banner (12.5.45)

towards Poland, and will always sympathize with the future of your country. I am certain that Poland will be independent, and you will return to your homes in a country free from oppression. As long as the Polish spirit, which is known to the whole world, will remain the same as it is now, it will win freedom for your country. Protect this flag, even with your life, if need be, because imbued with such spirit, you will conquer all adversities. In the history of Jamnagar, today's occasion will remain as one of the most beautiful events that have ever taken place here. May God bless you and let you return to a truly free and happy Poland."[42]

Unfortunately, the Maharajah's heartfelt wishes did not come true, even though the war had ended.

Having no place to go, the children continued to benefit from the hospitality of their sponsor, but the camp experienced increasing financial difficulties, which also affected Scouting. To raise additional funds for Scouting, a Scout Supply Store was organised with operating capital from the Headquarters of Polish Scouting in India, based in Valivade. Managed by a special committee, with Guider Janina as one of its four members, the store replenished the almost empty Scout account.

In the Spring of 1946, in view of the anticipated closing down of the Balachadi Camp, Guider Janina was delegated for a reconnaissance visit to Valivade. During her visit there, she camped with the Valivade Scouts in the most charming recesses of the borderland of the Deccan jungle. In her reply to a letter from the author of this narrative, who was a teenager at that time and the leader of the newly formed Patrol of Falcons, Guider Janina wrote:

"Dear Wiesio! Thank you and your Patrol for the greetings. I am so glad that the boys work eagerly, and behave well. You couldn't have given me a more pleasant surprise, boys. But you will give me even greater joy, and will prove that you really have been looking forward to my return, if I would be able to award you with the Pioneer Scout badge. I was thinking of you when I was camping with the Valivade Scouts, and I felt sorry that I had not been able to take you to such a beautiful and easily accessible terrain as theirs. Indeed, having such conditions for growth, they should be perfect Scouts. But never mind! It's not that difficult to be perfect in favourable conditions, isn't it so, Wiesio? Convey my greetings to Stefan and to the whole troop. To you and the Patrol, I send a cordial 'Be prepared', and wish you successful hunting.

Guider Janina, 22nd May, 1946."[43]

Fr. Pluta and the Maharaja reviewing the march past of the Girl Guides after "dedication" of the banners.

Writing these words, Guider Janina was not aware yet that it was just a few months before she would be organising a farewell Campfire for her whole Tribe, and that upon their transfer to Valivade, all her Scouts would be integrated into its various organisations.

Farewell Time

The war in Europe had come to an end, although the Americans were still fighting their final battles with the Japanese, and the International Red Cross was working in high gear. People, who had been lost in the turmoil of the war, were searching for their loved ones. Families, separated by the war, were reuniting. The time to return home had arrived, creating joy and euphoria around the world.

Unfortunately, in the lives of the people in the Balachadi Camp, the end of the war did not bring change for the better. Naturally, they were happy to hear about the triumphant march of the allied armies into Berlin, but the news that the Polish army, which had fought for freedom together with the allied armies, had not been invited to participate in the Victory Parade, filled them with deep disappointment and sorrow.

The newspapers and magazines were full of photographs of soldiers of various nationalities returning triumphantly to their countries, enthusiastically welcomed by their people. But Polish soldiers were not there, although not long ago much had been written about them and their bravery.

'What happened?' The children were asking, but no one could give them a clear answer. Their minds filled with bewilderment, and anxiety crept into their hearts. From the chaos of fragmented news, three very painful questions arose. Since the war had ended, why were Polish soldiers not returning to their country, armed and triumphant? Why did Polish native lands no longer belong to Poland? What was going to happen to the Polish children who had nowhere and no one to return to?

View of the Camp and School

Other complicated matters emerged at the same time, making the situation of the Camp even more difficult. While India's struggle for independence intensified after the war, the social status of most Indian princes rapidly diminished. The position of Maharajah Jam Saheb was still relatively strong because he belonged to a group of the most progressive Rajahs, who were in favour of gaining independence as quickly as possible. Nevertheless, the economic situation of the camp and its future existence became problematic.

During the countless meetings at the Commandant's office, two vital concerns were discussed over and over. Where to accommodate several hundred children and adolescents? How to provide some security for their future? Many letters and petitions were sent to world powers, but the world at that time had far more important problems to deal with.

As a result of the Commandant's overseas journeys in search of a new shelter, several dozen older teenagers were placed in Catholic schools and seminaries in the United States, but his persistent efforts to find a place for the whole camp did not end in success.

In the meantime, a representative from communist-ruled Poland arrived in Valivade, attempting to convince people to return to their homeland. The news of this reached the

Children on the beach at low tide: 1st on the right J. Dobrostańska two boys in front T. Dobrostański and L. Pietrzykowski 1942/43

Balachadi Camp, but was received with strong resistance from both the guardians and the children. Most children were orphaned, and their native lands in Eastern Poland were no longer within the Polish state. The probability of forced deportation of the orphans created a complicated situation. The British authorities seemed to be in favour of the children's return to Poland, and, although from the legal point of view, this might have been the correct solution, it did not take into account the children's feelings at that time. Many of the orphaned children had no family in Poland, and did not want to return to a homeland controlled by the same hostile country which had deported them at the beginning of the war, and was responsible for the death of their parents and for their own suffering. Also, a number of children had close or extended family members abroad, who had legal rights to decide about their future.

The camp administration was confronted with a difficult dilemma. A conference was called at the Maharajah's palace, with the Commandant and liaison officer, Major Clarke. After long deliberations, it was decided that none of the children should be sent anywhere against their or their guardian's will. To prevent such an eventuality, a plan was conceived for a group adoption of the orphans, including those who, in the absence of reliable data, were considered to be orphans. The Commandant, as the chief administrator of the camp and the pastor of the church, was to provide moral and spiritual guidance for the children, the Maharajah was to assure material assistance, and Major Clarke was to obtain consent from the Government of India.

The names of the children were placed on two separate lists: one with those who had a parent or adult siblings in Poland or abroad, and the other one with those who did not have any legitimate guardian. The act of adoption was prepared in Jamnagar by a lawyer from Bombay, and was approved by the Court of Justice of the Navanagar state. One of the clauses of the Act included a statement that the individuals mentioned in the Act were proxies for the legal parents of the adopted children. Thus, an Indian prince, a British officer and a Polish priest became the substitute adoptive parents of a group of several hundred Polish children.

The final episode of this matter was both unexpected and sensational. On his return journey from the United States, the Commandant stopped in Cairo in an effort to get some assistance for the camp from UNRRA, the United Nations Relief and Rehabilitation Administration. To his astonishment, he learned that there was a warrant for his arrest, issued by the Russian deputy director of UNRRA, who described the Commandant as an 'International Kidnapper.' In the end, the matter was cleared up, and the Commandant, spared arrest and internment, returned safely to the camp.

The departures of people from the camp began gradually. At first, a few guardians and teachers left with their children. Later, a number of children, who had family members in the Polish army in the West, or among Polish émigrés, joined them in England, France, and Italy. Most people were making arrangements to emigrate to the United States and Canada, and some to Australia and New Zealand. A few individuals went to Polish refugee camps in Africa.

In the middle of 1946, the final decision was made to close down the Balachadi Camp. This was a very difficult time for the children. Having been one of them, the author recounts:

I remember how hard it was for us to part with this place to which we had grown so deeply attached, and how sad it was to bid farewell to so many wonderful and charming people, who had become so close to our hearts.

Farewell - Good Man from the Good Land: 'Polish' Maharajah Jam Saheb. Your tears and your voice trembling with deep emotion, when you spoke to us for the last time at the station in Jamnagar, said it all.

Farewell - Fr. Chaplain, Commandant of our Camp, who steered the vessel of our life in exile with such great commitment and dedication.

Farewell - Teachers and Guardians, who not only taught us how to live and work, but also tried to create a family home for us in such difficult conditions.

Farewell - kind hearted Dr. Ashani, thoughtful Dr. Joshi, and indispensable Narry Marshall. Your hard work and devotion will forever retain you in our grateful hearts.

Farewell - affable, delightful people: You Bathiwal, Mr. Flic, Bhati, Chakidar and Bajban, with whom we shared so many pleasant experiences.

Farewell - Cooks, Technical Workers and Sweepers. It was thanks to your hard work that the camp functioned so efficiently.

Farewell - Land of Jamnagar, so dear to our hearts.

The last festive, but very sad ceremony of removing our national flag from the flag pole at the camp square, at the end of November 1946, was accompanied by an outburst of weeping. One more stage of our refugee life had ended.

The remaining group of several hundred children moved on to the south, to find temporary shelter in Valivade, the other Polish Camp in India.

Within less than two years they all had left India and settled in various countries around the world.

NOTES

1. AAN: Zespół 88, pages 37-43.
2. *Dzieci polskie gośćmi Indii*. Wywiad dla tygodnika *POLSKA*, number 17, 25 November, 1942 (Interview for weekly magazine Poland)
3. K. Franciszek Pluta: fragment of speech at the reunion of former students, USA 1981
4. Arthur L. Basham: *INDIE*, page 68, number 375-6
5. AAN: Zespół 88, pages 6-9
6. Ibid: pages 37-43.
7. Ibid: pages 2-4
8. *Dzieci Polskie w Indiach* (evacuation lists) *Polska Walcząca* appendix to number 31 1942 page 1
9. A. Olszewski: *Tropikalnym szlakiem 2 Korpusu*. pages 25-26
10. AAN: Zespół 84, page 57
11. AAN: Zespół 83 page 213
12. A. Olszewski: *Tropikalnym szlakiem 2 Korpusu*. page 41
13. Ibid
14. *Dzieci Polskie w Indiach.* (evacuation lists) *Polska Walcząca,* appendix to number 1, 1942 page 1-3
15. Polish Children's Haven. Sad memories. *Times of India* 1942
16. Franciszek Pluta: Letter to former students October 3, 1983
17. PwI: rok 4, number 2, (60), 1946, *Kronika Osiedla Jamnagar*
18. AAN: Zespół 89: page 3 number 4
19. AAN: Zespół 86 page 279
20. AAN: Zespól 88 page 131
21. AAN: Zespół *Skaut* 85 pages 9-10
22. AAN: Zespół 89 page 42
23. Ibid:
24. Arcybiskup Bombaju o uchodżctwie polskim w Indiach. *Polak w Indiach,* December 1, 1944 (Translation of an article from The Examiner November 25, 1944)
25. AAN: Zespół 85 page 61
26. AAN: Zespół 88 page 135
27. Ibid: page 97
28. AAN: Zespół 85 page 61
29. AAN: Zespół 88 page 134
30. AAN: Zespół 86 page 31
31. Ibid: pages 98-9
32. AAN: Zespół 86 page 98
33. Ibid: page 94
34. PwI: rok 2, page 23 (33)
35. Bronisław Pancewicz: *Harcerstwo w Indiach,* 1977, page 5
36. *Skaut*, number 13/14, 1943, page 38
37. *Skaut*, number 15/16, 1943, page 35
38. AAN: Zespół 86, page 34
39. *Skaut*, number 13/14, 1943, page 43
40. Bronisław Pancewicz: *Harcerstwo w Indiach*; 1977, page 6
41. Ibid: *Skaut*, number 8/9, pages 43-45 1945
42. *Skaut*, number 8/9, 1945
43. Janina Ptak: letter to the author, 22 May, 1946.

OUTLINE OF THE CAMP'S FINANCES
compiled by Jan K. Siedlecki

History of 500 Polish orphans in Balachadi is unique for they were maintained by the *Polish Children Fund* from charitable donations of some Maharajas, Indian organisations and industrial enterprises. The outlay can be divided under three separate headings:-

1. The cost of bringing the children to Balachadi is difficult to account for because some of it was tied up with the general aid to Poles in southern Russia. For that the Polish Consulate in Bombay received in 1941 £20,000 plus £6,000 to buy material help, medical supplies and transport (6 lorries + 14 from the army supplies and one bus) i.e. £26,000 x Rs 13.25 = Rs 344,500.[a]

2. Purchase of fitting out needed for the children in transit, supply of food, transportation and temporary accommodation in Bandra up to 20 Oct. 1942, came to Rs 131,950, out of which Rs 58,226 was to be covered by the Viceroy and other charities and the remainder of Rs 73,224 was owing from the Polish Government in London.[b]

3. The cost of building the Camp on the ground leased by the State Council was Rs 600,000 and equipping the same was Rs 150,000 (the Camp was wound up by Nov. 1946).[c]

4. Capt. AWT Webb (Principal Refugee Officer in the Govt. of India and Secretary of Polish Children Fund) reported that from 1st Jan. to 1st Aug. 1946, the Fund paid for the childrens' maintenance Rs 1,450,000.[d]

It should be noted that in accordance with the Agreement, any shortfall in the expenditure was to be covered by the Polish Government in Exile. In addition this Govt. was paying for the education of children in English Schools (e.g. Rs 26,660 in Jan.1944) and other costs, like Rs 463 for musical instruments (8 Sep. 1944).[e]

Moreover, I have to mention the subsidies the Camp was receiving for schooling; according to the report for the third quarter of 1944, the Polish Ministry of Education donated Rs 1,335 and Rs 6,530 was assigned from the Govt. of India budget for the Polish Refugees.[f]

NOTES
- (a) Polish Institute & Gen Sikorski Museum in London: Banasinski file 129/5
- (b) ibid
- (c) India Office Record (British Library) L/AG/40/1/131 (RRO A-5) 11th Report of 6.1.47
- (d) ibid
- (e) Polish Institute A23/21
- (f) ibid A23/18

PANCHGANI - THE HEALTH RESORT
by Wiesława Kleszko (Klepacka)

In the second half of the nineteenth century Dr. Tytus Chałubiński discovered the health giving properties of the, as yet unknown, Polish resort of Zakopane. At the opposite end of Eurasia, the British discovered Panchgani. It was John Chesson who in 1850 realized its value in the treatment of lung disease;[1] and thirteen years later, thanks to Sir Hartley Frer, president of Bombay, Panchgani was established as a resort.

Who would have predicted, that in the long distant future, Panchgani would be so important in treating Polish TB patients!

Panchgani, 1380 metres above sea level, lies about 300 km south of Bombay, some 100 km from Poona. It is surrounded by the Krishna valley in the north and in the south by the Yenna valley which is part of the Sahyadri mountain range. Above Panchgani lies Tableland - a virtually flat topped mountain covered with grass - ideal for sports activities. Stach Harasymów recalls 'we would accompany our mothers to Tableland, where we would watch hockey or golf - games which were unfamiliar to us. We were also fascinated by the little lake.'[2]

The journey from Bombay to Panchgani took 8 hours in total - 4 hrs by train to Poona from where a bus weaved its way along narrow mountain roads for a further 4 hours. The roads were barely separated from precipitous falls by chain link fencing.[3]

'...The climate in Panchgani was dry, relatively cool and completely free of mosquitoes. The temperature never peaked above 36.6°C and the vegetation was lush due to monsoon rainfall. The villas dotted on the mountainside amongst the greenery were a striking sight.'

Panchgani developed from the humble beginnings of just two hundred inhabitants to a town of 3,000 population both Indian and European. Most villas were their summer retreats. They spent the summer months in Panchgani leaving just before the monsoon season. The town expanded with the years accommodating exclusive boarding schools for both sexes, but most important, sanatoria - the climate being ideal for the treatment of tuberculosis.

'...About half an hour's bus ride from Panchgani lies the town of Mahableshwar on the perimeter of the jungle, with its rich intertwining foliage. Local guides claimed there were wild orchids but we did not see any, neither the tigers, cobras nor deadly snakes. In the night we could hear the cries of the hyenas and jackals but mostly we slept soundly oblivious to everything, lulled by the fresh mountain air.'

I couldn't compare these mountains around Panchgani to our Tatra mountains, but they had their own particular charm enticing even people with weak hearts to walk in them. I won't forget the sharp bracken which scratched my legs on our expeditions! At night the cool, rustling wind would come down the mountain into our homes, just as in Poland.'[4]

Travelling with Hanka Ordonówna (*a famous Polish singer in the 1920s & 1930s*)
- by A. Walczowska

I first saw Hanka in Ashkhabad, with her handsome husband, Count Tyszkiewicz welcoming transports of children arriving from various orphanages in Uzbekistan to await departure for India.

She looked young and pretty with her shoulder-length blond hair tied with a wide black ribbon. She was quite tall, slim, with a beautiful figure and skin. She was always smiling, even though, we knew, that she was not well.

The building in which we were stationed seemed like a palace after the conditions we left in the USSR. We were given soft blankets, which made sleeping comfortable even without beds.

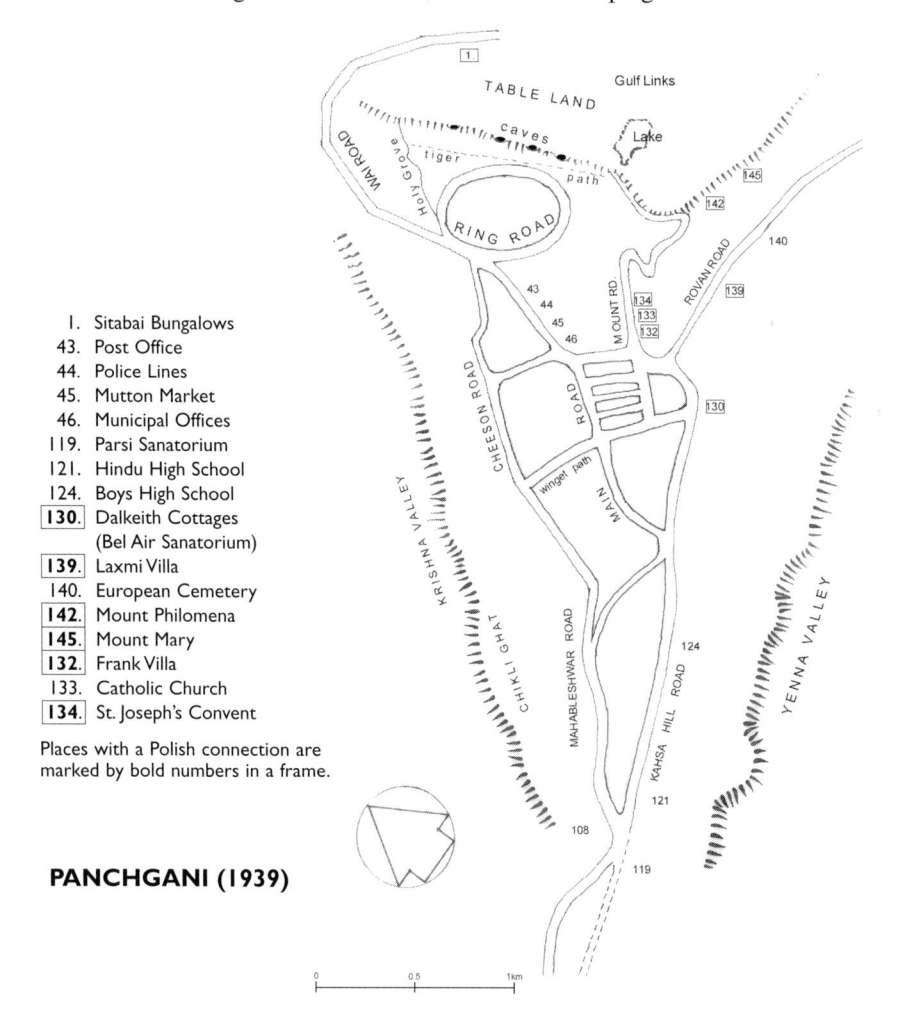

1. Sitabai Bungalows
43. Post Office
44. Police Lines
45. Mutton Market
46. Municipal Offices
119. Parsi Sanatorium
121. Hindu High School
124. Boys High School
130. Dalkeith Cottages (Bel Air Sanatorium)
139. Laxmi Villa
140. European Cemetery
142. Mount Philomena
145. Mount Mary
132. Frank Villa
133. Catholic Church
134. St. Joseph's Convent

Places with a Polish connection are marked by bold numbers in a frame.

PANCHGANI (1939)

Ordonka liked telling us stories to cheer us up, e.g. how one day she answered a knock on her door and there was a little 4-year old standing there sobbing, because 'the bastards had taken her bread away'. It turned out that she had been storing bread under her pillow, in case hunger returned, but it had gone mouldy and was thrown away.

The next day after our arrival, our lice-ridden clothes were burned and we had medical inspection. My temperature was higher than normal, so the doctor asked me if there had been any history of tuberculosis in my family? I did not think so, but in the USSR I lived with a family, who all had TB. The doctor said, that there was no treatment available in the local hospital and I would certainly die, unless she passed me fit for travel to India. I had to promise to report my condition as soon as we arrived in Bombay and in the meantime to keep it a secret. I know that I owe her my life.

When I left hospital I was given clean clothes: flannel trousers, a shirt and a cap to cover my shorn hair. Tadek Herzog slapped me on the back and called me mate. I was promised a dress and did get one just before our journey, but they forgot about the underwear. I was too shy to mention it to Pani Hanka and regretted it later as it was a constant cause of embarrassment: I was always last to get on to the lorry and when we travelled by train I had to wait till everyone fell asleep before climbing on to my berth. I shall never forget the joy of receiving 3 pairs of knickers on arrival in Bombay. It was only then that I told my friends my concerns during the journey, which resulted in endless teasing!

We stayed in 3 villas in Bandra, an elegant suburb of Bombay by the sea. The rooms were spacious and light, several bathrooms, toys. There were 10 members of staff, who looked after us. Hanka Ordonówna did not stay with us, but she visited frequently. She organised the festivities to celebrate a Polish national holiday on 3rd May. She brought some regional costumes which she had managed to save during her exile in Russia. Some children danced, then she herself sang and recited poetry. A Polish ship *Kościuszko* docked in Bombay at that time, so the crew joined us. It was her last public appearance before she started her TB treatment in a sanatorium in Panchgani where I joined her soon. We were all mentioned in a book she published later, called *Tułacze Dzieci (Homeless Children)*.

We were well looked after by the doctors in Panchgani. Pani Hanka, in spite of her illness, was full of energy and plans for the future. She decided to enter an international festival, where she was to present dolls dressed in Polish regional dress. She brought a lot of fabrics, ribbons, beads and we were all helping to make her Polish stall in Bombay a success. We heard later that the dolls were very popular.

During the Christmas holidays she dressed a leafy tree so artistically, that it almost looked like a traditional one. She left the sanatorium to join her husband, who had an important position at one of the diplomatic missions. She sent for her things, so we did not get a chance to say goodbye properly.

Polish patients in Bel-Air - the TB sanatorium in Panchgani

During the period 1941-42, the Polish orphans who arrived in India from the USSR via Persia and needed medical attention, were sent after a short stay in Bandra-Bombay, to Panchgani.

Ala Król remembers: '...at first there were six of us - Janina Puk, Władzia Dobolewicz, Mila Kot, Jadzia Misiur, Hanka Ordonówna and I. However, the number of people who needed treatment gradually increased.'

In one case a small number of children needing treatment in the mountain climate were sent to a sanatorium in Ootacamund in the south of India.

At the health resort

Our doctors in Bel-Air were Dr. H. Jacoby and Dr. F.C. DaCunha who used all the knowledge available to them to help both the Polish children and adults fight TB. Some patients were treated in closed sanatoria, others required open air treatment.[5]

The presence of many TB sufferers in the camps led the MPiOS to open a Social Welfare Centre in Panchgani where they had a good chance of recovery. This took place in August 1943.[6]

It was also planned to open a purely Polish sanatorium because of the language and dietetic differences between the Poles and the Hindus. This is illustrated by the example that feeding beef to the Polish patients by the Hindu directors was forbidden because the Hindus do not eat beef. Lamb had to be served instead. Also the cultural differences and lack of hygiene, spurred on action for a separate Polish sanatorium.[7]

From the moment the Social Welfare Centre was open, the Poles started their own kitchen in the sanatorium, which provided nutritious and appetising meals much to the delight of the patients. These meals were certified by a doctor as reaching a required standard. The Social Services kept in regular contact with the residents by post, also providing books and newspapers. A cosy common room did much to make life tolerable for the inmates whose numbers could reach 200 at times.

The sanatorium was comfortable and well equipped. Some of the children learned the local dialect, whilst the Hindus learned Polish! Our girls taught the Hindu women to embroider Polish designs, supplied by a Polish teacher.[8]

The children cured of TB lived in a villa named Laxmi, in the grounds of the sanatorium under the supervision of a doctor and a governess. In other villas they carried out open-air treatment for both adult and child convalescents.[9]

For Ala Król and many other children like her, Panchgani remained their home throughout their stay in India.

The Social Welfare Centre in Panchgani

This centre came into existence in August 1943. The ultimate achievement was the purchase of a villa and the setting up of an administration system. The details are related in the report of the MPiOS in October 1944 as well as in the account of the last director of the centre - Kazimierz Łęczyński.

The villas were called Mount Mary, Mount Philomena, Laxmi, Villa Frank and included the head office of the Centre, food store, kitchen, dining room, schoolrooms and dormitories. There was also a first aid centre and living quarters of the nurse teachers, and bedrooms for the convalescents, holiday-makers and guests.

The villa Sithabai was situated away from the above mentioned ones and could only be reached by car which the Mother Superior of the Convent gladly provided. Many of our girls were educated at the Convent. Two bungalows were occupied by children in the 10-16 age group and the third by the employees of the Centre and holiday-makers.[10]

Life in the Centre was based on a strict routine, described in one of the contemporary memoirs:

'The dormitories were clean and tidy - at Christmas the girls decorated them to their individual tastes and tried to make them as homely as possible. At Easter each dormitory held its own Easter breakfast which again re-enacted the togetherness of home.

On the whole one could not fault the conditions. Food was served five times a day and the portions were ample. The living conditions were excellent - almost luxurious. The surrounding countryside was beautiful. The Polish children in English schools were in constant touch with the Centre and made full use of the library. Their exemplary behaviour served as good publicity for the good name of the Polish people.'[11]

W. Styburski, J. Stańczyk, K. Banasińska among children

The Centre was also famous for its Sunday afternoon teas to which the Convent girls were invited together with their Indian colleagues.

There was only one unpleasant incident in this quiet and pleasant spa town - the arrival of a Polish sailor from Bombay, who got some Polish patients drunk on vodka and one of them threatened the Indian staff with a knife. Such behaviour from a white person was regarded with distaste and astonishment by the locals. Although the culprit was suitably punished and promised good behaviour in the future, this incident caused the Polish authorities a lot of trouble.[12]

Data analysed in November 1944, showed the inhabitants of the Centre to be mostly women and children - there were ten men at the most.

Monthly cash allowances at the end of November 1944 were greatest for the girls in the convent @ Rs 220, than for patients in the sanatorium @ Rs 175. For other teenagers studying at the Centre Rs 35 and was allowed Rs 20 pocket money for adults.[13]

Medical care in the Centre

The medical director of the sanatorium was Dr. F.C. DaCunha, a world specialist in lung disease, shared his expertise and goodwill with our surgery at the Centre.

In 1944 doctors from the Polish army arrived at the Centre. Three names spring to mind - Dr. Samuel Wieselberg, Dr. Rosenthal and Dr. Grażyna Miklaszewska who remained until the end. The nursing staff were: Loda Gawron, Waleria Zawadowska and Wanda Łagunowa who had completed her nursing training in Poland. She was a delightful person who was staying in Panchgani in a

Villa Laxmi: I. Harbuz, J. Pacak, ..., K. Łęczyński, W. Łaguna and W. Zawadowska

small elegant villa, together with her two children. Once, when she invited a group of older girls to tea, they were much impressed by the presence of a real English butler.[15]

Apart from patients with lung problems Panchgani also served as a convalescent home for people needing a rest from everyday stresses. A fair number of young students found their way here. One could also, money permitting, pay to stay in Panchgani as a holiday resort, open to everybody. Short passage from *Polak w Indiach* about Panchgani:

'Children already cured of TB stay in the villa *Laxmi* where they convalesce. Their faces fill out, although still pale from the illness. After only a few weeks it is difficult to control their eagerness to explore the mountains denied them for fear of a relapse.'[16]

In 1946, treatment for TB of the bones was embarked on, as well as treatment for premature babies.

Schoolwork in Panchgani

All the children sent to the sanatorium were wrenched away from their schoolwork in 1940-1941 and as a result of this had a two year gap in their studies. In Panchgani they cured ailing bodies. In the Bel-Air sanatorium Jan Sytnik became the main teacher who busied himself with their education. He was later joined by Maria Mitro, another qualified teacher sent by the Ministry of Education.

Ala Król remembers her:

'She arrived with us on the first train from Russia and from the beginning she was my favourite teacher. Our friendship lasted for years and when she later got married to Aleksander Milker both were frequent guests at our house.'[17]

Initially in Panchgani the children were taught in groups, as it was impossible to form classes with such a diverse age group - both from a medical as well as IQ point of view.

As more children arrived education had to be organised properly. In the year 1944/45 the school roll totalled 56. They were following the primary school curriculum, taught by Antonina Dzięgielewska (Head), Apolonia Najdzicz and Jan Sytnik.[18]

By 1946 children of secondary school age were taught separately. There were 6 groups of primary school pupils totalling 45 and 11 teenagers following a secondary school curriculum.

The secondary school was run by Mgr. Urszula Pacak.[19] In the words of Ala Król 'she worked miracles in passing on as much of her knowledge as possible - in history, the Polish language and especially literature which she loved. She also gave us a good grounding in Latin grammar. We owed it to her that we were able to continue our secondary education in Valivade without interruption.' Other temporary teachers we came into contact with were Helena Asłanowicz and Maria Wierzbicka.

Teaching the children in the sanatorium was far removed from a normal school life and called for special qualities as the teachers had to cooperate with the doctors and the medical regimes. The children were taught in short sessions to allow for their short attention span due to illness and this method achieved great success. In April 1947 the Centre was closed down and thus ended the era of schooling in Panchgani. The children returned to Valivade and resumed mainstream schooling there.

Cultural life in Panchgani

Neither the patients nor convalescents in Panchgani could contribute much to the cultural life, but the girl students from the Convent were very keen to show off Polish folklore to the other nationalities.

For the depature of Dr. Rosenthal

In 1944, Jan Pacak arrived in Panchgani and during his stay wrote a play *A Cracow Wedding* based on folk songs. When he eventually came to settle here, he was nominated cultural/educational director.[20] He ran the choir at the Convent, produced anniversary celebrations and practised nonstop with the group performing *A Cracow Wedding*. This was staged in Bombay, Kolhapur, Valivade, Poona and Mahableshwar. It was specially adapted for foreign audiences. Both military and civilian personnel enjoyed the twenty two folk songs, dances and tableaus performed in colourful national costumes. The duration of the show is one and three quarter hours.[21]

J. Pacak left Panchgani for a private post and only visited at weekends, but even then he helped organise shows such as the arts festival at the Convent held on 30th May 1946, the programme for 11th November in commemoration of regaining of Polish independence in 1918 and the artistic programme accompanying the unveiling of a commemorative plaque at the Convent in 1945.[22]

Other shows which were put on were: *Cinderella* and *The Gondoliers* - in which the airmen from the camp at Mahableshwar also took part - 'real' men were needed for this! Otherwise, in the case of the dances the tall girls dressed up as men. Rehearsals took place in the Convent, with the kind permission of the nuns. However, after the premiere of *A Cracow Wedding*, Mother Superior, from her front seat which was slightly lower than the stage, decided that too many white knickers were on show and ordered the girls to wear their longer, gym ones in future performances! And there was no arguing with the decision! The beautiful garland of the bride, plus the marriage coif were made in the cooperative *Zgoda* in Valivade and carefully transported by the bride's mother to Panchgani.

The title roles were played in *A Cracow Wedding:* Maria Wawrzynowicz - the bride,

Teresa Orzechowska - the groom. In *Cinderella* Alina Suchecka played Cinderella and Teresa Orzechowska the Prince. Dr. Maks Rosenthal played the violin accompaniment in *A Cracow Wedding* and also performed solo *Ave Maria* at the nuns' request in the Convent chapel.

The Polish girls always received standing ovations.

The festival on 30th May 1946 saw the joining of forces of the Centre and the Convent. 'The festival took place in the beautifully situated Sithabai - dancing was performed by the female students and there was a lottery, lucky dip as well as an exhibition of handicrafts.

The following day at the Convent under the auspices of Mother Superior and the head of the Centre Mgr. Łęczyński there was a theatrical performance arranged and rehearsed by J. Pacak. The proceeds of the show went to help the families in Poland.

The artistic contents of the show were greatly enhanced by the piano recital of a well known Indian pianist - Olga Craen - playing Chopin's Revolutionary Elude, Ballad in C minor, Polonaise in A Flat major and the Waltz in F minor on a very small and hastily organised piano *(the only musical instrument available in Panchgani).*

Apart from the piano recital the programme also included a female choir directed by J. Pacak, two sentimental songs by Stasia Miluska from Valivade, a tableau of the Warsaw uprising of 1944 accompanied by a recital of the poem *We demand arms* by the young and promising Renia Płocka who also performed a dance from *A Sieradz Wedding*.

The entire programme was repeated on a Saturday night and was attended enthusiastically by both Poles, English and Indians staying at the sanatorium.[23]

Closing down of the Centre

The Poles left Panchgani in 1947. The winding up of the settlement in Valivade followed as the families were going to join their menfolk in England - and others were returning to Poland.

Panchgani was closed first. The patients came to Valivade with their carers to continue their treatment. The healthy children were enrolled in schools before moving on. We left two graves behind: Mrs. Świeżawska was buried in Panchgani, while a patient of the sanatorium, a Polish Jew, was laid to rest in the nearest Jewish cemetery at Poona.

Translated by Krystyna Borucka

NOTES
1. I Nicholson and F. Kusy: India, 1993 p.318
2. arch. KPI S. Harasymów's written description
3. ibid: Antonina Dzięglewska's written contribution
4. PwI year II, No. 13-14 (23-24) 1944 & I. Nicholson and F. Kusy: India 1993, p.318
5. ibid: report No.3 , July 1943, p.14 by the delegate of MPiOS (Ministry of Works and Social Welfare
6. AAN: File 86, page 130, 183
7. ibid:
8. PwI: year IV, No. 8 (66) 1946
9. AAN: File 87 p.423-425 & Mgr. K. Łęczyński's oral contribution
10. ibid: File 87 p.243-245
11. PwI: year II, No.13-14 (23-24) 1944
12. AAN: File 87 p.149
13. ibid: File 87 p.138-146

14. (omitted when the text was shortened)
15. arch.KPI: Alicja Walczowska (Król) written contribution

    F. Kalinowski (Lotnictwo Polskie w Wielkiej Brytanii (Polish Air Force in Great Britain) 1940-1945 p.100 - 'Pilot Mjr. Piotr Łaguna was killed in action on German airfield near Calais in France. He was Commander of the Polish Fighter Wing'.

16. PwI: year II, No. 13-14 (23-24) 1944
17. arch.KPI: Alicja Walczowska - written contribution
18. AAN: File 87 p.423-425
19. arch.KPI: Alicja Walczowska - written contribution
20. ibid: Ewa Gruszka (Pacak) - written contribution
21. ibid: Mrs. J. Grochocka's letter to the Camp Commandant
22. ibid: Panchgani - a cut out from *Polak w Indiach (Poles in India)* (no number)
23. PwI: year IV, No.11-12 (69-70) 1946

Reminiscences of Panchgani - *by S. Harasymów*

My mother took my cousin Anek Cwetsch and myself to Panchgani during the school holidays. We boarded a train in Kolhapur late in the afternoon and shared a sleeping compartment with Mrs. M. Borońska and her son Witek, my friend. The top bunk was the most appealing place for us youngsters. Witek got there first, crossed his legs, turned his right arm into an elephant's trunk and made his eyes squint, pretending to be an Indian divinity - Ganesha. We all burst out laughing. But our mums quickly realized that the locals seeing this 'profanation' could be offended, so we were scolded and told to behave. Our train journey to Poona (about 225 km) took the whole night.

Early in the morning we arrived in Poona, made our way to the nearby bus station and soon found our bus. It was subdivided into at least 3 compartments. The seats close to the driver were the most expensive and this was reflected in the passengers' attire. The other seats graduated to the very cheap and affordable by the poor. Those people carried a lot of luggage stacked high on the roof. The bus had a large cylinder at the back, where the burning charcoal emitted gas. This fuelled the engine. On this early and cool morning the bonnet flaps were up and the engine block was being heated by burning kerosene on a tray-like ledge. At first I thought the engine was on fire and I nearly jumped out of the window.

Eventually we departed on the 100 km long journey to Panchgani. Just outside Poona the road took us across a plain but soon afterwards it started to climb up a mountain range. I don't remember the speed we travelled at or the number of charcoal bags we used but we covered the whole distance in four hours. At noon we reached Panchgani. The health resorts I had visited in the Polish highlands like Iwonicz or Krynica flashed into my mind and I looked forward to finding their similarity in India. Instead I found vast differences: exotic flora, Indians dressed in colourful saris and flowing white garments and signboards in English and Hindu. There were no majestic spruce trees, dark forests, no Polish Highlanders in their regional costumes and none of the richly decorated architecture.

Despite all these nostalgic reminiscences, as soon as we moved into our quarters in the Villa Frank set in a beautiful garden, we liked the place. The standard of living here was much higher than in the Valivade Camp. The walls were made of bricks, the windows and doors were real - not made of matting. There were proper finishes to walls, floors and ceilings. Other bonuses were the electric lights and running water. We enjoyed the park-like garden with its old shady trees, almost waiting to be climbed. A group of small, mischievous monkeys frequently visited the garden. It all seemed like great fun. Really tasty meals were served in the nearby Mount Mary Villa and second helpings were the order of the day.

One of our great enjoyments there, was cycling on hired bikes. There was a stretch of a few kilometres of bitumen road. For the cyclists it was heaven. There were no such roads near Valivade. We could now ride fast and in comfort on a smooth surface. Here I learned to ride with hands off handlebars. Other roads there had a gravel surface. I will never forget the ride with my cousin down the road near our villa. I was his passenger sitting on the cross bar. At the bottom of the hill there was a sharp bend. This is where he lost control and we both hit the gravel. The little rounded stones cut into our knees, elbows and hands. Oh, the pain was terrible! But next day we were cycling again.

We also organised many excursions. We walked the 'Tiger' footpaths around the Tableland, explored the caves where tigers had their dens long ago. On the way there we noticed little chicken-like birds. According to our older friends, they were partridges. The next day we bought some horse tail hairs and under our friends supervision we made noose-like snares. We set them up many times and in different locations but we didn't catch a single partridge.

The Archbishop of Bombay - about the Polish refugees in India
(Polak w Indiach -1.12.1944)

The Archbishop Thomas Roberts describes his visit to Panchgani in the Catholic periodical *The Examiner*:

"The cool climate in Panchgani suits the Poles well, as after years in Siberia they do not tolerate heat well. There are a few villas for children and adults who come here for a holiday. I am astonished at how these children have blossomed from their sad state on arrival in Panchgani after a tortuous land trek from Russia. It is true to say that the Poles in India are the victims of Russian barbarism and not, as previously quoted, victims of the Nazis.

The Poles are indebted to the Daughters of the Holy Cross for their care of the many Polish children. It is indeed an act of great love and wisdom to absorb so many foreign children and to educate them successfully.

The Polish girls in return have achieved great results in English, the arts and handicrafts as well as Polish language and literature. They show a great ability and willingness to learn. I hope that soon the public in Bombay and other places will enjoy, as I had, the visual feast from Polish childrens' activities and performances in Panchgani.

Many, but sadly not all, who need treatment for TB live in the sanatorium at Panchgani. The Indian doctors and nurses give their best in the treatment - others donate radios, books and puzzles to help pass the time."

Polish pupils at St. Joseph's Convent - *by Urszula Pacak*
(Polak w Indiach year IV, No.2 (60) 1946)

The Convent run by the Daughters of the Holy Cross was situated in a picturesque location in the mountains around Panchgani. The sisters' lives revolved around teaching, nursing, and care of orphans and prisoners.

The building was light and airy, recently (1936) decorated and provided an excellent environment for education. The convent numbered spacious and comfortable classrooms, workshops, a music hall, ten pianos, a well equipped library and a dining room. The atmosphere was conducive to study.

The large gymnasium doubled as a classroom, also as a theatre hall for school productions, or again as a cinema for the occasional black and white silent film. Children adored the movies and reacted noisily showing sympathy for oppressed heroines or outrage at the deplorable behaviour of the villains. Sisters only smiled at this show of youthful enthusiasm but did not try to stop it. They were so understanding, calm and caring, so different from those remembered at the Ursuline or Sacre Coeur convents back home.

The Polish Authorities paid all the bills for the Polish students at the convent and the girls rewarded them with a willingness to learn. They claimed top positions in class despite English being their second language.

The Polish government after the war will be well rewarded by such highly educated citizens helping to rebuild their country - all thanks to the Daughters of the Holy Cross.

St. Joseph's Convent - *by Teresa Mamnicka (Orzechowska)*

There were 12 of us who set off from the orphanage in Balachadi-Jamnagar on 27.8.1943 to study at the convent in Panchgani. It was quite traumatic parting from our families and embarking on the 3-day journey broken only by a stop in Bombay. We were delighted to experience the excellent standards of health and education in Panchgani.

The first 3 months were spent with Sister Gemma on a crash course in English. One of the first things I remember learning was the Lord's Prayer. We found the language quite difficult but buckled down to our studies and passed the entrance exams. We were then allocated to our various classes. Bogusia and I were placed in Class 5.

Our daily routine started at 7 a.m. with the rising bell which saw us up and dressing quickly. After daily Mass we walked silently in pairs to the refectory. Conversation was only allowed after Mother Superior's greeting 'Blessed be Jesus Christ'. After breakfast we made our beds and changed into our school uniforms ready for the 10 o'clock assembly in the school hall. Lessons followed till 1 p.m. when we had a break for lunch. After lunch we said rosary in the chapel and then half an hour's free time. After this, lessons resumed till tea time. I must admit I had a healthy appetite and was happy to relieve Iwona Rutkiewicz of some of her food as she was very figure conscious. One of my favourites was bread and butter with bananas!

After tea we would go for a walk even in the monsoon rains and always in pairs! We then did homework for a couple of hours in the large hall before going up to our dormitories in silence! We also took part in gymnastics, volleyball, hockey and team games on 'Tableland'. During the monsoon, when it rained incessantly for weeks, if the rain stopped and the sun came out, Mother Superior gave us half a day off to play hockey or go for walks. We especially liked our excursions to the mountains with Sister Gemma - we would buy sweets from her tuck shop and set off briskly. Sister Gemma also enjoyed our company because we sang a lot - something which reminded her of her childhood in Germany.

Group of girls with Mother Superior.

Reminiscences of school life

The school year in the convent commenced in February and ended in December. We were keen to learn, sometimes skipping a year through sheer hard work. In 1945 B. Wojewódka, B. Szołkowska, U. Korzeniowska, B. Sibińska and I went to class 7.

I. Rutkiewicz and I were the only Polish girls there, the rest were English and Indian. I had a friend, Pamela Brindley, whose mother taught in the lower school - she and another teacher were very understanding of our plight in exile, as was Mrs. de Souza, who was particularly kind to us. It was thanks to her that we all passed the 'Junior Cambridge' exams with flying colours. In 1946, having skipped a class, we sat and passed 'Senior Cambridge' exams which enabled us to apply for university. Bogusia Mukosiej remembers her time at the convent as 'hard, difficult and sometimes disagreeable, but on the whole rather wonderful'. There was a lot of humour in our lives. I remember how, on the first day, Sister Gemma asked us after tea in sign language to say grace and one of us - in her consternation, said the grace for after lessons instead of after tea.

There were also other misunderstandings. For Christmas 1943, when our fellow boarders had left for home, the Sisters organised a surprise feast for us after midnight mass. They were disappointed when we could not eat any food as we were so full after our Christmas Eve celebrations at the Polish Centre and had to fast from midnight as we wanted to go to communion the next day.

Sister Gemma was hurt the most because she put a lot of heart and effort into the preparations. She even made a fake Christmas tree for us and had presents under it. The tree was made by first soaking thick ropes in the starch, then tying pieces of it on the sticks (branches) and combing them out into shape. Then they were dyed green, dried and put into the stick on the base which had holes for these branches. It looked beautiful. We had a present for Sister Gemma also. We gave her cushions which we made and embroidered by ourselves. She was a lovely nun. She taught us English when we did not know a word of it, taught us about the customs and life in the convent and was always ready to defend us when we were in trouble. Later on we also learned from her a little about cooking and sewing. She took us for walks and picnics on sunny days and she loved our singing. We became friends for ever and stayed in contact with her until she died in Germany.

Sister Ludberga (beautiful and gifted nun), who taught us history was not always a fair teacher. I was very afraid of her. For some reason she disliked me. She was German and perhaps was jealous of my friendship with Biddy von Dingelage (also German), whose father was a count and was interned like all German subjects who lived then in India. Once, during our silent walk, someone else was talking and Sister Ludberga implying that it was me, hit me hard on the back. I could not forget that for a long time and kept out of her way as much as I could. (Biddy is in Australia now.)

Other Sisters were great, pleasant and loving: Sister Cecilia taught singing, Sister Helen Mary with a beautiful smile was tiny and very friendly, Sister Margaret Clair loved nature, flowers and all beautiful things. Sister Mary Alban, Mother Superior of our school was good, understanding and loving, just like a mother. An old Sister Mary Haldin was frail and had to be carried to church for Mass in a sedan chair.

Consul J. Litewski with Dr. G. Finkler (and on the left) K. Łęczyński

While the other girls were taught French, our group was taught Polish language, literature and history by Mgr. Urszula Pacak. We were inspected regularly by Mgr. Michał Goławski who seemed impressed by our progress.

In 1945 we welcomed three new arrivals from Valivade and in February 1946 a large group of Polish girls came to learn English - among them Irena Idkowiak, Halina Szafranek, Zosia Dudek and Renia Płocka.

After the first three months of intensive study of English, we were placed in regular classes where we had to put an inordinate amount of effort into every subject. The most difficult class exams were those in English language - which even the native girls found difficult! I would often get 0% in my dictation for making 10 mistakes! The timed essays too we found difficult - compressing the contents and accuracy into the required time.

In the higher classes English literature encompassed Shakespeare and the English Romantic poets which we found quite difficult. In history - apart from British history we also had to study the American and French Revolutions and the British Empire. Sister Ludberga taught history which probably explains why I was not too fond of the subject!

Maths on the other hand, was my favourite subject and thanks to Miss de Souza and another Indian teacher we all gained top marks. Geography was another subject I enjoyed and did well in it, thanks to my good memory.

The Convent courtyard

We also studied Religious Knowledge which comprised not only the Catechism but also reading and interpreting the Gospels and the Acts of the Apostles.

The fine arts were taught to a very high standard. Leśka Korzeniowska passed with distinction and went on to become a professor in the USA. I myself also passed despite having limited talent; I just enjoyed sketching.

Sister Cecilia taught singing - mostly hymns - but the only exams taken in music were grades for the piano.

In our final year Sister Gemma taught us practical subjects such as cleaning and cooking. I do not know where we found the time for all this but it was very relaxing.

The Sisters' method of preparing us for the exams was to take away our textbooks a fortnight prior to them - thus hoping our minds would relax. At those times my mind would focus on all sorts of recipes - especially cakes, which we baked under Sister Gemma's watchful eye and which everybody loved. She had an endearing habit of calling us *'dziewczynki' (girls)* in Polish.

During the foreign language exams, we Polish girls sat Polish language, literature and history - the other girls sitting French and Hindi.

I was interested in botany and anatomy but sadly these were not taught. Chemistry I was very wary of, especially the practical experiments! Physical Education was taught with enthusiasm and vigour and some of the younger girls achieved very high standards. Our school had a great reputation and was known throughout the whole of India.

We had an unfortunate brush with typhus in 1945-46 after two pupils Iwona Rutkiewicz and Barbara Szołkowska sneaked out to the market in Panchgani to buy some Indian sweetmeats. The girls were placed in quarantine for three months while we fervently prayed for their recovery. It all ended well: Mother Superior forgave them and no more was said about it.

One wonderful experience for us was meeting Mahatma Gandhi in 1945 in Panchgani when he came for a rest there.

Encouraged by Mrs. Pacak, our Polish teacher, we started corresponding with Polish soldiers, like many friends in the Camp. I remember how we would sit by the window on moonlit evenings and share the news from these letters. Renia Płocka's letters from her soldier, the professor, were especially interesting. She read them so beautifully that we all fell in love with Mr. Łempicki. Renia married him later and settled down in Mansfield, England. She devoted her artistic talents to the children of the Polish Saturday School. Today she is already a widow but Bogusia Wojewódka is still spending her senior years in the USA with her 'soldier'.

After Senior Cambridge examinations we left the convent and went to the Polish Camp in Valivade-Kolhapur, taking with us very pleasant memories of our stay with the Sisters of the Holy Cross.

My thoughts always go back with fond feelings and gratitude to the place where we spent our carefree young years under the care of the loving sisters.

Commemorative Plaque in the Convent - *by Zofia Kiełbińska*
(Polak w Indiach No.1 (59) - 1946)

11th November 1945 was a day of double celebration for Poles in Panchgani. Firstly, it was the anniversary of Polish Independence and secondly, unveiling of the commemorative plaque in the convent - inscribed both in Polish and English.

In the morning we went to mass celebrated by Father Jankowski after which the Delegate S. T. Darlewski gave a speech outlining the Poles' gratitude to their Indian hosts, with special mention of the Sisters of the Holy Cross. Mother Superior replied in kind, saying how the standard of the school had improved with the presence of the Polish girls.

After these formalities the whole school put on a gymnastic display, after which the Poles hosted a breakfast in the halls of the convent.

In the evening there was a commemorative celebration including speeches, poetry readings, singing both in Polish and English and ending with Polish national dances. Our English counterparts put on the play *Cinderella*. The high standard of the whole production - costumes, lighting and content, gave us all a much needed morale boost in these trying times.

NA PAMIĄTKĘ POBYTU DZIECI
POLSKICH KTÓRE WYGNANE ZE SWEJ
OJCZYZNY KSZTAŁCIŁY SIĘ W TEJ SZKOLE W
ATMOSFERZE ŻYCZLIWOŚCI
I SERDECZNOŚCI - PŁYTĘ TĘ
UFUNDOWALI WDZIĘCZNI POLACY

THIS PLATE IS GIVEN BY THE
GRATEFUL POLES WHOSE CHILDREN
BEING EXILED FROM THEIR COUNTRY
WERE EDUCATED IN THIS CONVENT
IN AN ATMOSPHERE OF FRIENDLINESS
AND CORDIALITY

PANCHGANI 11TH NOVEMBER 1945

The finances of the Centre

The only accounts available to us were for the year 1943-44 and these can be summarised as follows:

Initial Expenditure:
1. Equipping the accommodation for TB patients (Rs 1,200) and other sick children (Rs 2,400)
2. Clothing and re-equipment of the 82 TB children (Rs 9,840)
3. Childrens' travel expenses (Rs 4,500) and the initial medical diagnoses (Rs 1,250)

Recurring Expenditure:
1. Monthly cost of sanatorium for TB patients (Rs 103,320) for rent and maintenance of their accommodation (Rs 1,221) + two villas for other sick children (Rs 67, 200)
2. Annual salary for two guardians (Rs 2,400) and the cook (Rs 1,704)
3. Additional cost for dietary meals (Rs 3,600 p.a.)

Expenditure for other sanatoriums in Miraj and Ootecamund was covered by the Panchgani budget.[14]

Panchgani Personnel

The heads of the Centre were as follows: Amelia Kotlarczyk, Stanisław Dzięgielewski and Mgr. Kazimierz Łęczyński.

Office staff included:
Łucja Tabaczyńska - Secretary
Magdalena Stelmach - Head
Waleria Płocka - Accountant/Bursar
Wanda Łęczyńska - Head of the Polish section of the kitchen

Teaching staff:
Franciszka Dubicka
Zofia Mamniak
Stefania Wojakowska and
Mieczysław Pałys

We were occasionally helped by the graduates of the secondary school:
Eliza Harbuz
Janina Sipika and
Jadwiga Wałdoch

Polish Girls in St. Joseph's Convent were:

Eleonora Korzeniowska
Urszula Korzeniowska
Władysława Mikulicka
Henryka Okoń
Iwona Rutkiewicz
Bożena Sibińska
Maria Skórzanka
Alina Suchecka
Barbara Szołkowska,
Bogumiła Wojewódka
Teresa Orzechowska
Maria Kłosowska
Irena Tatarczuk
Maria Wawrzynowicz
Helena Weindling

TRANSIT CAMPS

I. COUNTRY CLUB near KARACHI
by Izabella Wolff

General information

After a short stay in Iran, at the request of the Persian Government, Polish refugees were transferred to transit camps: Country Club and Malir, both near Karachi, India. The more permanent settlements in Africa and India, where they were to spend the rest of the war years, were not yet ready. At the end of the summer in 1942 large numbers of refugees, around 21,000, moved through the international port in Karachi on the way to more permanent settlements. The largest number - 12,642 went to Africa, 4,356 settled elsewhere in India, some 1,403 went to Mexico. A group of 1,600 Polish Jews after being evacuated from the USSR, were given permission to go to Palestine, but Iraq refused them transit by land so they had to wait for transport by sea. On average there were about 2,000 people staying in the transit camp at any given time. All new arrivals were issued with tropical helmets and towels. Those who needed it were also supplied with clothing.

The camp was administered by British military authorities in cooperation with Polish staff numbering 200. The British administration under Capt. S. Allan the camp's Commandant, was responsible for law and order, allocation of accommodation and equipment, supplies of food, public health and hygiene, the postal services and censorship. S/Lt. K. Ingram was Transport and Information officer, S/Lt. Palin - Finance Officer, Capt. H. Lewett in charge of the clinic. Various other office duties were carried out by British non-commissioned officers.

General view of the camp

The Poles were responsible for education and other cultural activities, provision of clothing, payment of salaries of the Polish employees in the administration, and for compiling lists of transports leaving the camp as well as liaising with other camps. The Polish camp Commandant was A. Terlecki in 1943, later S. Dziadowicz; the interpreter was - J. Banasz. A lawyer, Z. Rosada who acted as a representative of the Polish Ministry of Social Welfare used to travel to the camp every other day.

Funds needed for the running of the camp as well as Rs 3 per person weekly pocket money came from the British military. Details of the amounts spent were not available as they were considered 'military secrets'. The Polish sources reveal that the cost of education was approximately Rs 12,000 per quarter. All those who were fit were obliged to work. Some people worked outside the camp in an American military camp folding up parachutes. There was a small co-operative dealing in groceries, (the profits from which later helped to purchase a printing press in Valivade). In a separate tent there were eight sewing machines for use by dress makers and some women did embroidery.

Capt. S. Allan and girls in Cracovian dress

Catering

Food rations for the inhabitants of the Country Club were the same as those for the European army personnel, with additional items for children and those prescribed special diets by the doctor. There were 3 canteens in the camp: the largest employed 27 staff and served around 1,000 adults, next came the children's one which served over 500 and employed 9 people in the kitchens and 8 in the dining room. Lastly, there was a mess for the 53 camp personnel served by 4 staff.

In the kitchen

Meals were served 3 times a day: breakfast (tea, bread and margarine, marmalade, cheese); lunch (meat, vegetables and pudding) and a light supper. Cooking and most of the more strenuous jobs were carried out by the Indian staff. Polish women prepared meals for children under 6 years of age and served meals in the canteen. The children's kitchen and canteen were in a separate tent, supervised by the camp doctor, Capt. Lewett. Some additional items for the children were purchased from a special fund of Gen. Hind of about Rs 1,000 per week.

The canteen

It was possible to supplement the diet with fresh fruit available locally, and the occasional purchase of American army rations of 'ham & eggs', chocolate and biscuits - which were luxuries at that time. Food rations were satisfactory, but some items like Christmas pudding or dried bananas, were not always to the taste of Polish palates and a butt of many jokes.

Unlike the living quarters, both kitchens and dining rooms had cement floors. Sanitary regulations were strictly adhered to: kitchen staff had to wear overalls, head covers, use nets to cover food and fly-flaps.

Health Care

Mjr. S. Allan with hospital staff

We learn from the Polish fortnightly newspaper *Polak w Indiach* that both the British and Polish authorities were anxious to provide sound sanitary conditions in the camp. Strict rules were imposed concerning sleeping under mosquito-nets, spraying the tents with insecticide, using anti-malaria cream, drinking chlorinated water, taking extra doses of salt, all in order to prevent tropical diseases.

Statistics from May 1945 show that there were more cases of eye infection due to the desert dust and glare, (451) than those of malaria - 203.

The camp hospital was situated in a cluster of separate tents consisting of a large one with hospital beds, an adjoining smaller one for the use of nursing staff, a wooden hut housing a dispensary, open between 10.00-12.00 and 15.00-17.00 for out-patients, pharmacy and dental surgery open twice a day.

In case of an emergency patients could visit the doctor on duty at any time. Between the years 1942-45 hospital staff often changed. Dr. H. Lewes was in charge, assisted by Dr. Kalisz - a Pole in the British army - and Dr. Tiachow, later transferred to Valivade, and 6 nurses. The camp hospital had its own laboratory, where blood and urine tests could be carried out. More serious cases, and those needing x-rays were sent to the Military Hospital in Karachi. In the month of November 1942 for example 152 were sent there of whom six people died.

Hospital staff with Dr. Tiachow

Most common were skin diseases, eye infection, dysentery and malaria. Patients with contagious diseases were kept in separate tents. The most common children's diseases were whooping cough and mumps.

Inside the hospital tent

Pastoral Care

A wooden Chapel was a pleasant landmark in the stony desert. It was officially inaugurated on 14th February 1944 by Monsignor Alcuin van Milterburg OFM. Initially the Franciscan monks from Karachi used to come to the camp and say Mass on Sundays and holidays of obligation. The inhabitants of the camp, however, felt a need for a Polish priest and petitioned the Consul General. As a result Father A. Jankowski was sent and started his pastoral work in August 1943. He remained there until the closure of the camp.

Camp Chapel

Education and cultural life

Many difficulties had to be overcome before adequate schooling could be organised in the camp: a shortage of qualified teachers, no textbooks. There were 520 children between the ages of 7-14, who missed school during their exile in the USSR and therefore could not be classed in age groups but rather according to ability. Primary school of 4 levels was opened in several tents with very primitive equipment: a table and some beds instead of desks. The largest was the group of 7-10 years old.

Level I	183 children	7-10 years old	5 forms
Level II	105 children	8-12 years old	3 forms
Level III	118 children	9-13 years old	3 forms
Level IV	114 children	10-14 years old	3 forms

The headmistress Mrs. A. Ryżewska and staff

Mrs. Anna Ryżewska became Headmistress and she had 16 staff to help her to devise a suitable syllabus and run the school. Levels I and II did little more than the 3 R's and listening to stories. Levels III and IV besides reading and writing in Polish, also did some history, geography and the beginnings of English as a foreign language taught by Mr. Jan Mołdzyński. Since there were no textbooks, children took dictated notes. In the afternoon children and teenagers gathered in the communal room where one person read aloud stories from Polish literature. Lessons took place from 10 a.m. to 12 noon. Gymnastics and any sports like volleyball, netball or football had to be played at 7 a.m., before breakfast, because of the heat later on in the day. Three boys and 12 girls attended British schools.

Nursery school children with toys from Lady Dow Renia Zelichowska in front and Andrew Kurowski on the left

There were 59 children aged 3-7 for whom a nursery was opened. They had no toys until owing to the initiative of the Governor's wife Lady Dow and Mrs. Dubash on behalf of the Delegate of the Polish Red Cross in Bombay, a special tent with a carpet, toys and books was opened in November 1942.

In the evenings both adults and teenagers frequented community rooms, where press reports were read out, some books were available in the library section, gramophone records and radio could be listened to, chess and other games played. The library was rather limited so books were often read aloud. It was difficult to organise longer courses in a transit camp, but some inhabitants gave interesting talks.

"*Polak w Indiach*" reports chess tournaments, table-tennis competitions with the Americans, some Polish youngsters competing with the English and Indian youth in athletics, volleyball and football.

During a festival in Karachi there was a Polish stand showing examples of handicrafts of the inhabitants of the Country Club and giving information about Polish culture and history.

From the right: H. Chrystowska and J. Kurowska

Personal reminiscences: *by Izabella Wolff (Nieczykowska)*

On the 1st of December 1943 we sailed in as part of the contingent of 1366 refugees from the port of Khorramshar in the Persian Gulf to Karachi, then in India now in Pakistan.

It was a surprise and a real pleasure to see the passenger liner M/S Batory under the Polish ensign awaiting us in the Port of Khorramshar. After 2 years as deportees in the Soviet Union and then as refugees exiled from our Country, it was nice to see the welcoming crew of the Polish ship and to be able to communicate with them in our native tongue. We were very well looked after all through the voyage. But the passage was not uneventful. The Arabian Sea was still full of German U-boats. When one day the alarm sounded, and we heard explosions, the answer to our questions "what was going on?", was only a quiet and confident reply, "just a few depth charges that we have sent on their way!"

I arrived in Karachi with my mother, Maria Nieczykowska and younger sister Krystyna on 8th December 1943. The transit camp known as "The Country Club" in which we found ourselves was to be our home for the next 2 years. We were housed in army tropical tents, joined together to form accommodation for 50 people. The tents were equipped with bedding and, very importantly, with mosquito nets. A short distance from the tents were rows of shower cubicles, laundry and toilets; rudimentary, but quite adequate for the needs of the people on the move. Hurricane lamps provided light. The staff of the Camp enjoyed a little more comfort and privacy, having single family tents, and an adjacent smaller one with washing facilities.

The mess provided meals for all of us, as there were no provisions for self catering. The canteen which was open on all sides encouraged uninvited guests such as vultures. At times they swooped in and out with someone's dinner! Our nearest neighbours were two air force bases - British RAF and American A.F. The constant flights over our Camp provided some diversion in an otherwise very monotonous life.

The stony Sind desert, where only cacti and few thorny bushes grew, was inhabited by wild mules, hyenas and friendly reptiles. The mules serenaded us at night keeping people awake, hyenas were always on the prowl dragging all sorts of equipment from the tents and creating a dreadful noise during the night.

There was very little variation in the night and day temperatures (25-34°C), only during the monsoon season did the temperature fall a little at night. The rainfall was very low, only about 20 cm per year. Exceptionally in 1944 it rained for three weeks without stop for the first time in living memory. The desert did not provide any outlet for the flood waters, so the surplus water washed away the surface soil and formed a stream right across our Camp; many heavy, drenched tents lay flat on the ground.

The tornado that touched the Camp was very frightening. I was on the way to the canteen, when suddenly the sky darkened, while the air was very still and calm. From a distance I could see a rising column of dust, and in no time at all the tornado passed close by, fortunately not damaging the Camp area, except for a few flattened tents. The local villages suffered most. The tornado then moved on to the coast and the sea, where it created huge waves and flooded the coastal settlements and small islands around Karachi.

We were often invited to many religious and civic festivities by the local population.

At the invitation of the Bishop of Karachi we celebrated the Feast of Christ the King on 26th November in the Cathedral of St. Patrick in Karachi.

At the City festival, which was held at the Government House, the Polish stand gave the local population some insight into our history and culture in pictures. There were many exhibits of Polish craft created by the ladies and the school children of the Country Club.

After the reception in the gardens with its beautifully kept lawns, there was regional dancing performed by groups of Indian, English and Polish dancers. The finale of the show were the mazurka and polonaise dances, for which we received a huge ovation.

Scouting

The young people enjoyed all sorts of activities organised by the Scout Movement. Scouting gave us many new interests and we learned new skills with the help of the English Rover Scouts who visited our Camp once a week. In spite of language difficulties, we managed to communicate and learn all about ropes and knots and how to make leather book marks, purses, book covers etc.

We were grateful for their interest in us and looked forward to their next visits. To this day we keep in touch with Leslie Wright, one of the Rover Scouts, an airman in the RAF who served in India during the war. He has attended a few of our functions in London, and we were glad to renew our friendship.

Younger children joined Cubs and Brownies who also were very busy learning how to be a good citizen in the future.

Jamboree in the Mango Grove

The Polish Scouts and Guides kept in contact with British and Indian Troops, attending conferences and meetings. The highlight of this cooperation was a Jamboree a few miles from Country Club in the Mango Grove. It took several days to prepare the Camp and 150 Scouts and Guides took part. The Senior Guides and Scouts on parade greeted Mjr. W. Allen, the Camp Commandant of the Country Club and the Polish Consular official from Bombay, Mr. Z. Rosada, who opened the Jamboree. There followed a church service, and the raising of the flag and the march-past. The tea party and the dancing were a great success and everybody enjoyed themselves. The Polish Scouts received a special greeting from the Governor and Lady Dow, the Commissioner of the local Troop. To commemorate the Jamboree, badges made out of fabric with Scout insignia and wording "Miniature Jamboree - Karachi 1943/44" were issued.

Field exercises; first on the left Helenka Tomaszewska

To celebrate the end of World War II in Europe in 1945, Polish members of the Karachi Scouts and Girl Guides joined in the festivities and took part in the Victory Parade in Karachi.

Theatre

Creation of the theatre was achieved by a dedicated group of people who managed to keep it going, in spite of enormous difficulties. In one of her articles, Polish journalist Krystyna Chociej described her impressions; she wrote "the theatre is a symbol of Polish culture and traditions. The drama group arrived in Karachi from Ahvaz, Iran where it flourished, but because of resettlement of people, only a small group of them remained and had to take over the work. They worked very hard to entertain the Camp population and many visitors."

How true were her words. There were no printed scripts, no music sheets. Everything had to be written from memory by people who had some training before the war and remembered the plays, music scores and choreography of the Polish regional dances. Background scenery and props were another problem; they had to be improvised, on many occasions using just white sheets. The Camp Commandant Mjr. Allan managed to provide a covered area, which served as 'dressing rooms' for the artists, a curtain and our own generator to give lighting effects on stage. Oh, what a luxury!

In 1943 the American Red Cross in Karachi invited the Troupe to organise a Concert. The programme consisted of dances and songs, solo and quartet, fragments of plays and poetry. It was a very successful evening and there were more invitations from YMCA, British RAF and American Hospitals.

The Camp often entertained British and American Forces. The programme had to break a language barrier, therefore it mainly consisted of songs and regional Polish dances. A pair of gypsies who lived in the Camp sang and danced *Czardasz* beautifully. On one occasion, the British Personnel took part in the show with their own original numbers. The most memorable of these was a number when a man dressed in a pink organza dress complete with attached wings, and wearing a blond wig, sang 'Oh, if I were a little bird...'. That in itself was funny enough, but hilariously, from under the dress, you could see his black army boots and hairy legs, which of course created hoots of laughter and sent the audience into hysterics.

Theatre troupe

Our mother Mrs. M. Nieczykowska and Mr. S. Tarasiewicz composed music and wrote lyrics to the musical entitled *Krakowskie Wesele (Cracow Wedding)*. It was beautifully staged, there were colourful costumes, designed and made by the ladies in the craft department, tuneful songs, and regional dances of Cracow. Many actors and school children took part in the musical and the show was very popular with the British and American audience. The Americans showed their appreciation by whistling. This to us was a little confusing, we thought they did not like the show, as Polish audiences only whistle when they are unhappy, but the misunderstanding was explained to us afterwards.

The staging of the musical was such a great success, that there were many invitations to visit Army Camps in the Karachi region. We tried to give our people some joy and hope for the future by constantly reminding ourselves of our culture and inheritance and by doing so, we were also spreading a little propaganda about Poland.

Baśka, the white goat

Baśka, an intelligent goat, was a great attraction in the Camp; it was probably the mascot of a British army regiment. The goat with its habits was unique. Every morning, when the chapel bell tolled, she was the first to lead us to Mass, although, I must stress, that she never reacted to the sound of midday Angelus Bell. On Sundays she actually took part in the service, kneeling at the appropriate time, her usual place being with the school choir. At one time, during the visit of the Bishop of Karachi, she led the procession, not allowing anyone to drive her away.

Most goats can be very spiteful and she was

no exception, she regularly ate documents from the priest's desk and created havoc in the ladies' workshop, where she devoured finished dresses and craftwork. She often invaded bathrooms and was very fond of soap; which must have been a tasty addition to her poor desert diet.

During the last year of our stay in the Country Club, she produced two black and white kids; she must have found a black mate. The kids inherited their mother's ways. Unfortunately we do not know the fate of the goats after we left for Valivade.

Manora

The Island of Manora in the Bay of Karachi, in Arabian Sea, was a holiday destination for the Staff of the Country Club, where for a small payment one could stay for a week or so. We called the Island 'Our Paradise', with its rich flora, sandy beaches and open sea. The sea was not without dangers; strong currents claimed many careless victims who ventured too far out. An English soldier convalescing here after service in Burma lost his life trying to rescue a drowning Polish girl. Another menace were dangerous sea creatures like jellyfish and blue devils with their long stinging tails. In spite of all that, we had good time there. The fresh food, mainly - fish from the local fisherman, fruit and vegetables from the vendors, were wonderful and a real treat, since they were not available in the Camp. We were sad to leave this heaven and return to the stony desert and tents in Country Club.

The transfer to Valivade

In February 1945 it was decided that the Transit Camp would be closed as there were no more transports of refugees coming from Iran or other countries. The Camp personnel were transported by train down to Kolhapur-Valivade, the Polish settlement for 5,000 people. The last days of the Transit Camp were described in the *Daily Gazette Karachi* edition of 25th September, 1945 and in the Polish translation in the *Polak w Indiach* no.20 (54) under the title *The last days of the Transit Camp*. "On Sunday in the Refugee Camp the day started with the Mass celebrating the 3rd Anniversary of the founding of the Camp and its imminent closure. After the service Polish Administration Personnel and Mr. Z. Rosada, a representative from the Polish Ministry in Bombay, thanked the British Commandant Mjr. A. S. Allan for the care that he and his Staff had provided for all the refugees who passed through the Camp during its existence. Mjr. A. S. Allan addressed the gathered guests and people of the Camp in their native Polish language, wishing everyone the best of luck for the future. The unexpected speech in Polish moved the people, and resulted in an ovation for Mjr. A. S. Allan."

In the evening Scouts, Guides, Cubs and Brownies were on parade before the Brig. L. R. Burrows, Commander in Chief of the Region. A special vote of thanks was given to him for his sympathetic approach and understanding. In his reply, Brig. Burrows said that it had been a pleasure and a privilege to look after 22,000 refugees who were in transit to other continents including Africa and Australasia and he hoped that it had forged a permanent friendship and understanding between us.

After the speeches there was a banquet at which Brig. Burrows and his wife, together with the officers from the Sind Province and their wives, were entertained by Mr. Z. Rosada. To end the first part of the festivities, Scouts, Guides, Brownies and Cubs paraded in front of the guests. Finally, there was a concert given by the Polish amateur dramatic society. This was interrupted by torrential rain but thankfully the stage was big enough to accommodate all who took shelter there and the concert continued.

The last days were full of goodbyes. Lady Dow and the ladies from the WVS (Women's

Voluntary Service), who often visited the Camp, came to see us. In her speech she said that she had been very happy to help Polish refugees, but that the people of Sind Province had also helped by providing clothing, books etc., so that the thanks should also go to them. Thanks were expressed to Lady Dow and the WVS with gifts, songs and Polish dances.

I cannot say that we were sorry to leave 'Country Club'. Constant partings with friends who left for distant parts of the world hardened us. We never knew what the future held for us. Unfortunately this is the refugees' lot. But we were young, idealistic and believed that one day we would see our home country again.

II. MALIR near Karachi
by Wiesława Kleszko (Klepacka)

A. Klecki, J. Chmielowska and J. Pacholski

A habitable but unoccupied American site in Malir was a godsend to the Polish Authorities at the time, when the Country Club transit camp proved inadequate. Mrs. Kira Banasińska, the wife of the Polish Consul General in Bombay, reached an agreement with Gen. Brady that Polish refugees might occupy this camp for about 4 months, before going to Valivade, where a more permanent settlement was in the last stage of construction.

The delegate of the Polish Ministry of Social Welfare (MPiOS) took care to establish an administration, which would run this camp in Malir, and later be transferred to Valivade. Capt. Władysław Jagiełłowicz was appointed Camp Commandant and he appointed the personnel to fill the departmental posts.

After the desert like sands of the Country Club, the sight of some green vegetation in Malir lit a smile on the faces of those arriving, and the living conditions raised exclamations of pure delight! After life in tents, where everything was covered in sand, bungalow-style blocks built of bricks, with concrete floors were a luxury. It was a temporary camp en route to Valivade near Kolhapur where we, and the people still arriving from Persia, were to live till the end of the war, and then hoped to return to free Poland.

Malir offered excellent facilities in blocks with 6-9 rooms, containing 14 beds with mattresses, pillows, blankets and mosquito nets, housing 90-125 people. There were also some double rooms. One bathroom per 3 blocks was provided with 16 showers, 1 laundry with 8 taps and 1 toilet for 16 people. Two steel rubbish bins with lids, and fire fighting sand-filled buckets completed the household needs. Drinking water was chlorinated. In order to maintain general cleanliness and hygiene inside and around the blocks, the occupants were made responsible for it. As the meals came from the communal kitchen, a rota of helpers was appointed by the block managers. Coupons were issued for meals. The menu agreed with the contractor on a ten days' rota was displayed in the dining rooms. The daily cost of feeding a child was Rs 1.11.0 and 2-3 rupees per adult. The monthly pocket money amounted to 10 rupees per adult; clothing was obtained from the camp stores, as well as $1/8$ litre of paraffin daily for lighting. The appeal to save water was repeated daily. The inhabitants washed their clothes receiving a bar of washing soap and 4 oz (100 g) washing soda per week. In addition to this there was a bar of red carbolic toilet soap for personal use. An Indian contractor was employed to wash clothes for children in the two orphanages: the isfahan one from Tehran, with headmaster Z. Ejchorszt, teaching staff and guardians (which eventually went to Santa Rosa, Mexico), and the other orphanage which together with the rest of the Camp's population was to be sent to Valivade.

Our spiritual needs were met by the chaplains Rev. Leopold Dallinger and Rev. Zygmunt Jagielnicki. Sunday Masses were said in the camp chapel in block 125. Both clergymen held a teaching position in the camp's school.

For general camp safety, **Camp Security Services** had to be established with 44 security guards working on a shift basis. Only a few minor infringements occurred. On one occasion an American soldier together with two Indian soldiers tried to enter one of the blocks, as well as two Muslim kidnappers who tried to gain access to the orphanage dormitory. They were frightened off by the raised alarm and dealt with by the British Authorities. For some time then each block had its own night watchman, but this post was soon abolished; the vigilance of the Security Services was sufficient.

T. Kurowska and small Renia Żelichowska with Poles in the American Army

The Record Office kept a card index with full particulars of all inhabitants, to be able to give an accurate summary of peoples' whereabouts i.e. as the *Camp Chronicle (Kronika)* noted on 3rd March 1943: 1,602 inhabitants of whom 165 were staying in hospital. A list of professionals helped the Camp Commandant to call to action in time of need.

The Department of Employment did not have much to do in Malir due to our brief stay there, but the organisational rhythm was fast. Already on the 19th April a tailor's workshop was opened, equipped with 6 sewing machines, 24 machinists and one cutter. It produced overalls, Scout and camp security uniforms, theatrical costumes and curtains for the Community Hall. The cobblers' workshop employed 6 cobblers and one cashier. The charge for repairs depended on the type of repair as well as the price of leather on the market. All workers were paid on a daily basis. A concession for watch repairs was granted to a Hindu.

A Polish Musical ('Crackovians' and 'Mountaineers')

Using his initiative, Jan Pacak, an engineer, organised ladies to embroider and weave, opened a shop, also a toy shop. Dolls dressed in Polish regional costumes were a huge success in Bombay and Kolhapur. Mr. Pacak took over the chair of this department after Witold Bidakowski left with an advanced party for Valivade-Kolhapur in June 1942.

Sports enthusiasts rallied quickly, and a Sports Club came into existence. Two teams of netball and football were formed and matches played, to the satisfaction of players and onlookers alike.

Postal Services with Army Field Post in the Middle East, and with the rest of the war-free world worked very efficiently. The small camp post room processed 483 letters in April 1943, our first month in Malir. The servicemens' families were in contact again.

***

Education

The first priority in organising daily life in the Camp was the establishment of a primary school for the 300 children, who enrolled, forming school No. 1 with 9 classes under the headmistress Blanka Potocka. The school was equipped with desks and chairs, but there were not enough of them. The only textbooks available were those that the teachers themselves had managed to save throughout exile. School No. 2 consisted of Isfahan Orphanage children, and had 14 classes, 17 staff 2nd 2 classes of grammar school pupils. This, as previously noted, was an independent unit, en route to... somewhere.

According to the May 1943 census there were then 1,098 children in the Camp, including 575 orphans. The ages of the children ranged from 3-19, of which $1/5$ were boys. These were either partly or fully orphaned, rescued from the USSR. The nurseries cared for the toddlers. In both orphanages, apart from the appointed guardians, older children also helped to look after the young ones to create as much a family atmosphere as possible.

The great shortage of grammar school teachers prevented the opening of a grammar school. To break the monotony in the life of the youngsters, who had already started secondary education before the outbreak of the war, the Cultural Sectiont (RKO) launched a series of lectures, covering literature, history, art, geography, science and various other general knowledge themes. This task was undertaken by: Michał Chmielowiec, Witold Bidakowski, Zygmunt Łopiński, Rev. Leopold Dallinger, Rev. Zygmunt Jagielnicki, Dr. Leon Koziełkowski, J. Banasz.

June 22nd 1943 saw the most welcome arrival of some grammar school teachers from Persia. Under the headship of Zdzisław Żerebecki a school was opened for 285 enrolled pupils, in 10 classes with 12 teachers. They experienced the same acute shortage of educational material, but both the teachers and pupils worked hard, happy that education had been resumed and a supply of books promised by the Polish Legation in Bombay.

Scout-master Witold Bidakowski and Irena Świątkowska started a branch of the Scout patrols movement, thus 3 girls' units (42 Girl Guides) and 2 boys' units (28 Scouts) were formed. The Camp administration provided a Scout Hut for their activities, also supplying maps, games etc.

This was the nucleus of the education system, following the programme set down by the Polish Ministry of Education (MWRiOP).

***

The Cultural Department

The inhabitants were provided with a daily bulletin with news from all fronts of the war, international and political events and local camp news and orders. The only sources for the world news were BBC Radio from London, *The Voice of America, The Polish Daily* from London, The Times of India (Bombay edition) and various publications in Polish from the Middle East where the Polish Army was currently training.

The Community Centre (świetlica) was visited by about 250 people daily. A radio set was the first main purchase, followed by a piano, thanks to the efforts of our liaison officer Mrs. Mabel Button. The piano was not only a teaching instrument to those who wanted to study music or to continue their studies, but it was also a wonderful support to the theatrical shows and concerts.

Children who had been deprived of the world of fables and fairy tales were the primary concern of the theatrical group. Alicja Kisielnicka and Irena Świątkowska wrote and produced *Cinderella* and *Hansel and Gretel*. Adults were delighted to see shows featuring scenes from life in the camp. At each performance the 400-seat hall was full.

There was also a gramophone and 49 records, a fledgling library, cards and games. In a separate reading room one could find Polish papers and it did not matter if they were out of date, also the illustrated English press, easy to 'read' with our almost non-existent knowledge of English at this stage of our stay in India.

Hospital - facts and memories

Every human settlement requires a hospital. The Polish Camp in Malir needed one too, even though it was only to be for a few months. Now, well over 50 years later since the first entry in the Camp Chronicle I can vividly recall life in our camp hospital.

The two blocks designated to the hospital stood quite a distance apart from each other and housed 100 beds. The pharmacy and outpatients department stood nearby. The doctors on duty were Dr. Maria Wysocka, Dr. Barbara Brunnee, as well as the hospital administrator Dr. Leon Koziełkowski. Apart from Sister Holland, already a war widow, who worked as a volunteer to help her compatriots, there were 6 of us sisters, 8 orderlies and also some sanitary inspectors working throughout the camp with the Indian workers.

Each hospital block consisted of two airy, long wards with rows of beds along the wall, and a wide passage in the middle. A small room was provided for the staff in the middle of the ward with a residual small buffet, where it was possible to brew tea. In the side rooms of the block the housekeeping sister reigned with her bed linen chest. Next to her was the administrator and the matron. The patients' food was provided by the camp kitchen.

The second block like the one described, was occupied by both women and children, and also by men. Showers and toilets were outside.

The pace of work was tremendous. Adults and children filled the beds - and sometimes children had to be put top to tail in bed. Malaria was rife. There were case of 'nerves', 'livers', 'women's complaints', but the worst of them all were skin complaints caused by two years of hunger, malnutrition and vitamin deficiency while in exile in the USSR, also tropical rashes which made treatment so much harder for us and the suffering patients. In this tropical climate no traditional European way of applying ointments and dressings worked successfully even with a proper rich-in-vitamins diet - but avoiding water.

It is generally thought that each doctor knows best what he is doing. In Malir there was an element of rivalry in skin treatment. Dr. Wysocka ordered a twice daily change of dressings with a local wash down only - no showers - it was made all the more difficult as sometimes one could not see a clear patch of skin amongst the rashes. For some children even a loose cotton nightgown and boys pyjamas made of slightly thicker material, irritated the skin.

Dr. Brunnee who took a keen interest in the treatment of tropical medicine, had other ideas. Firstly, the patients luxuriated under twice daily showers, using copious amounts of red carbolic soap, which we named 'toilet soap', next came the application of the then newly-discovered antiseptic solution Eusol for external use, whereas other ulcerations were individually dressed. The oral medication and diet prescribed by both doctors was identical. The result? Healing was much faster in 'division two', but alas not in mine.

Just how quickly people wanted to get better brings back to mind the following episode. A discharged patient received a bottle of American concentrated cod liver oil, of which she had to take a few drops daily over the next month. Some days later she returned covered in greasy cod liver oil sweats and smelling unpleasant. Irritated by her slow recovery and maybe even by the stinginess of the prescribing doctor, she took the extremely concentrated cod liver oil much too fast with such unfortunate results.

The records in the Camp Chronicle show a few details from the hospital work. In April 1943, our first month in Malir, 430 people attended the hospital of which 67 serious cases were sent to the Military Hospital in Karachi. The outpatients' department dealt with 1,373 cases and 487 consultations were made. In May, the worst month for skin diseases, 3,466 people were treated, 288 received consultation and 314 were hospitalised.[1]

In June the Typhoid Fever Vaccination programme started, followed by two more at monthly intervals (concluded in Valivade). It was obligatory for every inhabitant of the Camp.

Regular visits to the dentist in the Country Club were organised twice a week for tooth extractions and once a week to Karachi for oral treatment and fillings. The cost of fillings (5 rupees each) was covered by the Ministry of Social Security (MPiOS).

To help the children to catch up with healthy development, it was agreed to hand out food, supplementary to the daily rations: 100g of bread, 20g of sugar, 5g of butter, 2 lemons and 100g of green vegetables.[2]

The announced visit of Lord Wavell, the Viceroy of India electrified the Camp. As he was to visit the hospital, the wards shone with an extra brilliance, the glass in the windows was like crystal, the blankets on the beds were made up in the most elegant and efficient way, the patients 'dressed up' in clean linen, the nursing staff rattled about in starched aprons. We expected the Viceroy to walk along the wards to see these people who through no fault of their own were stranded in India. Unfortunately all he did was to stand in the doorway and glance in. Did we make any impression on him? The Viceroy and Field Marshal, and also a poet? He was visiting the Camp with an English and Polish retinue of course!

From July the hospital became slowly deserted due to the transfer to our new Camp. My turn to say goodbye to Malir arrived. A temporary hospital block had to be set up in Valivade as the Camp hospital was not yet ready. The four months spent in Malir remain in my memory as a typical daily journey from the living accommodation block to the Hospital, for a whole day's duty and the return at nightfall. Sometimes to take advantage of a day off duty, we were able to go to Karachi (always with an escort), and by studying various tempting menus were able to afford banana fritters as they were the cheapest. The aim of my shopping was a pair of elegant ladies sandals (we wore 'unisex' type in the Camp), whose colourful and thin straps badly hurt my toes while walking! I also saw a cobra and a fakir performance on the pavement, a sacred cow halting the cars, trams and tongas, the statue of the Empress of India who was also Queen Victoria of England (very similar to the one in front of Buckingham Palace in London of which I was not then aware). Such a picture remains in my mind to the pre-war tune: 'India, woven with legends, India, country of my dreams, India'.

From the hot province of Sind (now in Pakistan), we moved to the monsoon season in Valivade in the State of Kolhapur. The crossing of the Arabian Sea to Bombay was very stormy, but the scenery on the train journey to Valivade was fascinating. This was hopefully the last stage of our wanderings.

***

How we lived...

Living in Malir meant waiting for transfer to Valivade, but in spite of that we made ourselves at home.

Within a few weeks of our arrival, Easter came in April. The first remembrance of Christ's Resurrection outside the USSR to be celebrated in freedom. Apart from the religious festivities, a traditional Easter breakfast - *święcone* - was served: hard-boiled eggs, previously blessed by the priest and then shared with one another - the symbol of Life. Best wishes were exchanged, but the mood was sad. The words of the Camp Commandant Capt. Władysław Jagiełłowicz: 'let us be together in thoughts with those whom we cannot have beside us', dominated this Easter celebration. No brightly coloured painted eggs, no rolling them in the open. However due to this festive day, the Delegate from Bombay donated 125 rupees for sweets to be distributed to children at school and orphanage in place of chocolate Easter Eggs.

Next came the national holiday, commemorating the Polish Constitution of 3 May 1791, one of the first in Europe. The open air Mass and the Scout march-past in front of the Camp Commandant and the Liaison Officer uplifted our hearts.

The 8th anniversary of the death of Marshal Józef Piłsudski was passed in silent prayers on 12th May. Also in May, the Minister of Social Welfare, Jan Stańczyk, arrived from London. He was pleased to note that the signs of hunger and physical debility acquired in the USSR were wearing off. He appealed to the Polish youth to work hard taking advantage of schooling, acquire new skills, for every pair of hands will be needed to raise our homeland from the ruins.

June brought a name day of the four Władysławs: the President of the Polish Republic - Raczkiewicz, the generals Anders and Sikorski and our much loved Camp Commandant - Captain Jagiełłowicz.

On a blistering hot and sunny morning of 6th July, we received the news of the tragic death of Gen. Sikorski in Gibraltar. All Poles felt this loss very deeply, as it was thanks to him and Gen. Anders that we owed our exodus from the USSR. Mourning flags were hung at half mast and many people wore black armbands. The requiem Mass was said mingled with tears. Nobody could have predicted such a blow.

The Allied victory over Gen. Rommel in Tunisia was celebrated with a thanksgiving Mass in Karachi's Anglican cathedral followed by a parade through the town. Our uniformed Girl Guides and Scouts, also children dressed in folk costumes took part, gathering the applause of the onlookers.

The children from primary school No. 1 put on a performance for the American hospital patients in Karachi, to which our own sick were also referred; it was greatly appreciated and the performers invited to come again.

The Camp office received an official letter from the Viceroy of India with thanks for our contribution to the English Wings Fund. Those arriving on the ship *Ronna* from Persia to India collected 755 rupees.

The American soldiers donated 86 rupees for the needs of the Camp youth, by way of thanks for the show.

Women aged 19-43 could apply to join the Womens Auxiliary Air Force.

The dry hot season was on, the winds blew far less sand than in the Country Club scorpions appeared from time to time and refreshing evenings were very much welcomed. Slowly the time of our departure to Valivade drew near. The advance party consisting of 21 people with the Camp Commandant left on 8th June 1943. This set in motion apprehensive discussions: What is it going to be like there? Will it be worse? The walls of the blocks are made of matting, dirt floors, non-stop rain, mildew everywhere... But the people who had already left wrote that it was not bad despite the rainy season in this part of India and the climate is infinitely better, with lush vegetation. In Malir an extraordinary thing happened, - as the Camp chronicler Alicja Kisielnicka wrote: a thorny bush, next to the block housing the hospital personnel, burst into bloom as if to say farewell. The beautiful small flowers drew attention to themselves. Every few moments people would stop, look at the bush and leave not touching the flower. Long may it decorate this desert!

Trains and lorries were organised one by one and finally 2,384 people, including 575 orphans left for Valivade. The Isfahan Orphanage returned to Karachi Country Club, together with the WAAF volunteers and 9 people with father Antoni Jankowski.

Malir became deserted, Valivade became populated, but nobody thought that it would be for five long years.

Translated by Zofia Reynolds

REFERENCES AND NOTES

Based on the following sources:
IPiMS Banasiński's collection 129
ibid C811A Camp Chronicle
AAN88, 72/88

EVACUATION ROUTE FROM RUSSIA TO INDIA

PART III

- **KOLHAPUR AND PANHALA**
- **VALIVADE**
- **ADMINISTRATION OF THE VALIVADE CAMP**
- **LAW & ORDER**
- **WORKS DEPARTMENT & THE COOP SOCIETY**
- **SOCIAL WELFARE**
- **THE FOOD SUPPLY**
- **HEALTH SERVICES**
- **ORPHANAGES**
- **PASTORAL CARE & RELIGIOUS ORGANISATIONS**
- **THE CULTURAL SECTION & THEATRE**
- **EDUCATION & REMINISCENCES**
- **PHYSICAL EDUCATION & SPORT**
- **POLISH SCOUTING IN INDIA**
- **EVERYDAY LIFE IN THE CAMP**
- **AN OUTLINE OF POLISH – INDIAN CONTACTS**
- **TOUR OF SOUTHERN INDIA (1946)**

1. Shalini Palace Hotel
2. Mahalakshmi Temple
3. The Old Palace
4. Town Hall
5. Hospital
6. Gardens
7. St. Xaviers School
8. Christian Cemetery
9. Maharaja's Palace
10. Villas

KOLHAPUR CITY 1946

KOLHAPUR AND PANHALA
by Leszek Bełdowski and Jan K. Siedlecki

Kolhapur probably derives its name from its geographical position because 'Koll' means a depression between the hills which translates into Kollapur, eventually becoming Kolhapur in the Maratha language.

There are four stages in the development of the town. The oldest part uncovered by the excavations of 1946/47 were on the hill of Brhamapuri, on the eastern bank of the Panchganga river. This area goes back to the Satavahana dynasty of the Ist to IVth century. Kolhapur's importance grew because of its situation at the meeting place of several trade routes and the proximity of the Panhala fort. Then for some unknown reason it went into decline until the VIIIth or IXth century when it started developing as a place of worship to the goddess Ambabai (Mahalaxmi). The first written history of Kolhapur dates back to the XIth century and afterwards the town belonged to various kingdoms. For a while it was ruled by the cruel Mahommedan dynasty of Bahmani. By the XVth century it was part of another Muslim rule, that of Adil Shah of Bijapur.

It was only in the XVIIth century that the Marathas led by Shivaji Bhonsale, later called 'the Great', fought to free themselves from the Mahommedan yoke creating the Maratha kingdom in the middle of India. In 1674 Shivaji was crowned king of Raigad and assumed the title of Chhatrapati (Lord of the Canopy).

Mahalaxmi Temple

He was tolerant in religious matters and supportive of economic development. He had a strong army and a fleet of several hundred ships, plus over two hundred forts.

When the capital was moved from Panhala to Kolhapur in 1782 the town entered its third stage with the building of the royal palace behind the temple. The town defences were strengthened and with the establishment of British Superintendence in 1845 the fourth stage of development began and lasted until Indian independence.

The Princely State of Kolhapur was over 3,200 sq. miles. According to the 1941 census the population was over a million, 93,000 of whom lived in the town itself. Situated half way between Pune and Goa, it lies on the plateau nearly 1,800 ft. above sea level on the Panchganga river, a tributary of Krishna. The State was stretching from the Western Ghats covered with evergreen monsoon forests to the fertile Deccan plains in the East. Its main products were rice and sugar cane from which the popular molasses was made.

"Stambha", obelisks for holding torches

Villagers were weaving rough cloth and making clay pots. The town was famed throughout India for its soft leather shoes and sandals (chappals). In our time, Kolhapur was also an important centre of the film industry and in Panhala one could encounter film crews engaged in making historical and mythological films.

When relating the history of Kolhapur it is impossible not to write about the fort of Panhala, previously known as Panhalagad or watery mountain, one of the most interesting places in Western India. It is situated some 12 miles NW of Kolhapur, nearly 3,000 ft above sea level. The history of these two places is inextricably linked. Panhala first came into prominence under the Shilahar dynasty and then in the XIVth century it was under Mahommedan rule. By 1489 the king of Bijapur had built up its defences to what we see today.

Panhala is surrounded by 15-30 ft thick walls 30-35 ft high, some built on a natural escarpment. It has a quadruple gate, *Char Darwaja* on the eastern side, damaged by the British cannonade in 1844. The handsomely sculpted *Tin Darwaja* on the western side had charming Persian inscriptions.

Drumgate "Nagarkhana" (1834)

Tin Darwaja - detail

" In the name of God, the Compassionate, the merciful. This sentence is the key of the gate of the treasury of the Ruler (God). The rebuilding anew of the fortress of the seat of government of Panhala, took place in the days of the rule of my Emperor, the Protector of the World in the kingdom of Panhala, Ibrahim Adil Shah. May God preserve his kingdom. In the date of the year AH (Anno Hagirae) 954. In the administration of Malik Daud Aka who was deputy governor during the absence of the Emperor. Inscribed by Salarson of Ahmed the minister."

and on the surrounding border:-

"Such a building there is not anywhere on the face of the earth. The water which is in this well is not inferior to the water Paradise, whoever drinketh of it saith this. May the mercy of God rest on the builder of this structure for nothing can be better than it. The world will not keep faith. Be thou happy. You should not plant the tree of grief in your heart and always read thou the book of pleasant meaning. You must eat and carry on affairs. It is clear how few days we can stay in this world. The builder and digger of this water supply was Daud Aka."

We called it the 'wet gate' because of its fresh water spring. On the northern side was *Wagh Darwaja* which we renamed 'tiger's gate'. The most ancient buildings there were the stone built granaries within the walls of Balekilla. Panhala now is a charming holiday resort.

The history of Panhala and Kolhapur is also connected with the Great Shivaji. It is impossible here to recount all the wars and history of succession, but a few choice episodes might be interesting.

When Shivaji started establishing his Hindu kingdom, he captured Panhala in 1659 by bribery. Other forts surrendered and Maratha rule was established. Aurangzeb, the last of the Great Moghuls, together with the king of Bijapur tried to recapture it. While Shivaji was defending it, he soon realized the hopelessness of the situation and began negotiating with the enemy. By leaving the defence in the hands of his faithful Col. Bhaji Prabhu, who fell in the Panharpian pass, Shivaji was able to escape. This episode became known as the Thermopylae of the Deccan.

Another colourful incident was the case of the three Ghoparde brothers who led a raid against the Aurangzeb camp when the ropes of his gold decorated tent were cut causing it to collapse. The raiders disappeared into the monsoon night thinking they had killed the Great Moghul but he was visiting another tent.

Tin Darwaja - with the lions motif

Enthronement of the newly adopted Maharja Shahaji (1947)

After Shivaji's death in 1680 the fight for succession broke out between his two sons, Sambhaji and Rajaram and their descendants, culminating in the meeting between the two cousins in 1731 below the fort walls of Panhala. A truce supposedly securing peace and tranquillity was signed. It was a great occasion, the splendour of which purportedly outshone the meeting of Henry VIII and Francis I on 'the field of the cloth of gold' in France, but the martial people of Kolhapur soon found an outlet in piracy and warfare.

Later Rani Jijabai ruled with talent and decision on behalf of her son, but her reputation was tarnished by human sacrifices before the goddess in Panhala. Soon after the prince was persuaded to move the capital to Kolhapur, but the wars continued virtually until 1800.

Subsequently in 1821 Maharaj Absaheb was murdered in his own palace in Kolhapur. The assassins were caught and condemned to be trampled to death by elephants in Panhala's courtyard, which we called 'the elephants' yard'. Relative peace followed the nascent of British rule after the 1857 uprising which the Kolhapur Marathas did not join.

Thus we reach the beginning of the 20th century when the Kolhapur Chhatrapatis received from the British the hereditary title of Maharaj. Shahu was decorated with GCSI, GCVO, GCIE and Cambridge university gave him an honorary law degree. He was also awarded the 19 gun salute.

He was succeeded by Rajaram II who continued the enlightened policy of his father and started democratic innovations. The town Council responsible for education, health care and communication became electable from 1927. Two years later the High Court and Appeal Law Court was established. He also modernised the drainage and established free education for women. In 1933 an office of the Resident to Kolhapur was created to have a direct link with the Central Government and the Viceroy.

When he died in 1940 without male issue the elder of his two wives Dowager Maharani Tarabai had to adopt an heir, the one year old Pratapsingh, Shivaji V who unfortunately died in 1946 and a new maharaja had to be adopted. This time she chose a 37 year old close relative of the Kolhapur Chhatrapatis, Vicramsinharao Puar (grandson of the Maharaj Shahu) who was then the Maharaj of

Temple columns that inspired our monument

Dewas Senior. Her choice was generally approved by the citizens of Kolhapur and his adoption as Shahaji Chhatrapati was celebrated in March 1947.

At the beginning of World War II he volunteered for the army and served in the 4th Indian Division in North Africa. At that time Kolhapur State contributed a Motor Transport Company and an infantry battalion of Rajaram Rifles. The British gave him the order of GCSI and in 1962 he was promoted to general by the President of India.

His rule was short because when India gained independence on 15th August 1947, the Kolhapur State was integrated into the Indian Union in March 1949. He was interested in wild life and warfare, especially Maratha history. Due to his support and financial aid many books were published on this neglected subject.

In 1962 he adopted his heir and successor, for his son remained as Maharaja in Dewas. He chose Dilipsingh of Bhosale family of Nagbur born in 1948, thereafter named Shahu. Half a century later in 1998 as Maharaja Chhatrapati of Kolhapur he presided over the unveiling of our monument and hosted in his palace representatives of the Polish Government and the Association of Poles from India.

Translated and abridged by Jan and Barbara Siedlecki

NOTES

This chapter was based on the following:

The *Columbia cyclopaedia* 3rd edition, (1963)

Ian Copeland: *The British Raj and the Indian Princess*, paramountcy in Western India 1857-1930, (1982)

Encyclopaedia Brittanica Vol. 13, (1947)

Louis Frederic: *Słownik cywilizacji indyjskiej (Dictionary of the Indian Civilisation)*, (1998)

Manokar Malgonkar: *Chhatrapatis of Kolhapur*, (1971)

N. V. Sovani: *Social Survey of Kolhapur City*, vol 2, (1951)

IOR:T 12699-*Panhala*: Rao Bahadur & D. B. Parasnis

IOR:R2 (1021/1060) *Inscriptions at Panhala*, by Col. Watson 1885/86

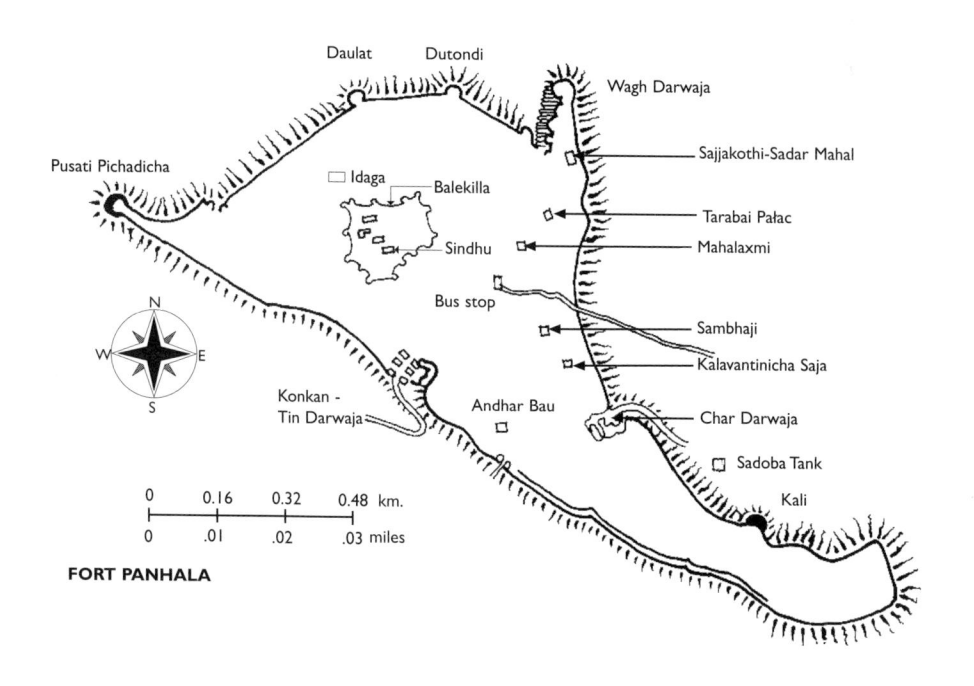

FORT PANHALA

IMPRESSIONS FROM A TRIP TO KOLHAPUR
Excerpts from an article printed in 'Polak w Indiach' 15.10.1943
by Marian Berch (Secretary to the Welfare Ministry Delegate in Bombay)

The town of Kolhapur is situated about 300 miles south of Bombay, measured along the railroad and nearly 100 miles inland from the Indian Ocean. It takes 3 hours to get from Bombay to Poona on an electric train and 14 hours from then on to Kolhapur on a narrow gauge steam train. The whole route runs across a beautiful and fertile country diversified by mountains and rivers. The most attractive section is from Bombay to Poona, where the railroad cuts across scores of kilometres of mountain ranges. There are many tunnels cut in solid rock and in between them one can see dark rocky mountains where, during the monsoon season cascading waters form pretty waterfalls. There are also deep ravines filled with vigorous vegetation, typical of the season, and the sky above is adorned with delicate, almost translucent clouds. The jungle below has its rich fauna well hidden from the passing train. The route also passes several rivers and their tributaries. The water is well utilized by the locals for irrigation of rice fields. In addition there can be seen wide cornfields, sugar cane plantations and market gardens meticulously cultivated despite the very primitive tools used.

Past Poona, the train enters a fertile plain with rich vegetation, clusters of trees and bushes and pastures with cattle. The dark skin of the Indians, loads carried on their heads, two-wheeled carts pulled by bullocks, cactuses and palms and colourful birds remind the stranger that this is an exotic country. Because of the varied and beautiful landscapes the train trip to Kolhapur is a real pleasure.

Closer to Kolhapur the terrain is more undulating with scattered flattened hills. About 6 miles before the town, our settlement *(Valivade Camp)* can be seen from the train windows. It is situated on a hillock surrounded by cultivated fields and clumps of trees. Rows of single storey residential and utility blocks on stone foundations and covered with a uniform red tile - a rare sight in this region - signify that we are approaching the settlement of our displaced people. I am getting excited and curious realizing that I will soon set foot in the Polish settlement. Distant ranges and a river flowing nearby enrich the panorama. The pleasant feeling of the journey continues after arrival in the settlement.

The climatic conditions in India depend mainly on the altitude above sea level. It may sound strange that places only 2 or 3 hours of train journey apart, can have entirely different climates. Kolhapur is luckily 700 metres above sea level so it is almost at the same altitude as Zakopane *(Poland)*. In Kolhapur there are no extreme hot or cold days, consequently our refugees feel comfortable in this climate.

Close to the administrative section of the settlement there is a large, round flower bed, with Polish and British coats of arms and three flagpoles. The centre one flies the Polish flag every day and the other two - the British and Kolhapur State flags on special occasions.

Lanes separate the rows of residential blocks which have continuous verandahs on both sides. Along these verandahs there are flower beds creating a pleasant village atmosphere. Early in the morning before work and after office and workshop hours, one can see residents busily watering and weeding their little gardens. I notice that people are proud of them and there seems to be a kind of competition in making best use of the garden space.

I remember the cramped conditions of the refugees in the Tehran camps. It is quite the opposite here - peace and tranquillity. One has to look for the residents. Some of them work in offices, shops and workshops. Children and their teachers are in the schools. The medical staff is in the hospital and the rest - mainly women - are at home cooking, washing and cleaning. During some hours there is an increase in activity on the streets: housewives going shopping, workers going to or back from work and children running to school. In the evening the settlement comes to life again. In the community reading rooms people gather to share the papers and listen to radio programmes. Young people stroll along the main street.

Perhaps the most positive impression of the place is its cleanliness - the cleanliness in the streets and squares and inside the offices and living quarters. All public areas are well swept with no papers, cigarette butts or even match sticks to be seen. Everything is absolutely clean.

I visit a few private homes. The tables are covered with tablecloths or napkins, on the walls there are rugs, kilims or hand-embroidered wall hangings. There are curtains at every window, flowers on the tables, chests of drawers and shelves. These homes are pleasant to look at. They do not resemble any barracks or a cheap hotel. They are furnished alike but arranged differently, creating an individual and cosy atmosphere. The general feeling of the place is welcoming. There are many calm and satisfied faces and cheerful children. There is no nagging and one can see no ill effects of camp life. The people are well dressed. Even during weekdays ladies and girls are dressed tastefully in pretty and clean frocks and smart shoes. It looks like an unending holiday. I remember seeing these people in Russia and on their arrival in Pahlevi. The difference is really tremendous.

Unlike in the other camps the people here are happy to receive a monthly food allowance so that they can buy provisions and cook and eat meals of their own choice. There is also room for small savings. This system gives an opportunity for housewives to demonstrate their cooking, shopping and housekeeping skills. It also has a psychological advantage over a system with a communal kitchen and canteen. It gives self-confidence to the refugees who suffered so much harm and injustice and also has an educational value.

I would like to sum up in a few words what this settlement in Kolhapur *(Valivade)* is. It is definitely not a camp. It is a pleasant settlement where people can satisfactorily get through the time of war until our return to Poland is possible. With a clear conscience I can wish all Polish refugees in Africa, Mexico and other countries around the world as good a life as that of our people living in Kolhapur.

Translated by Stanisław and Wanda Harasymów

VALIVADE CAMP

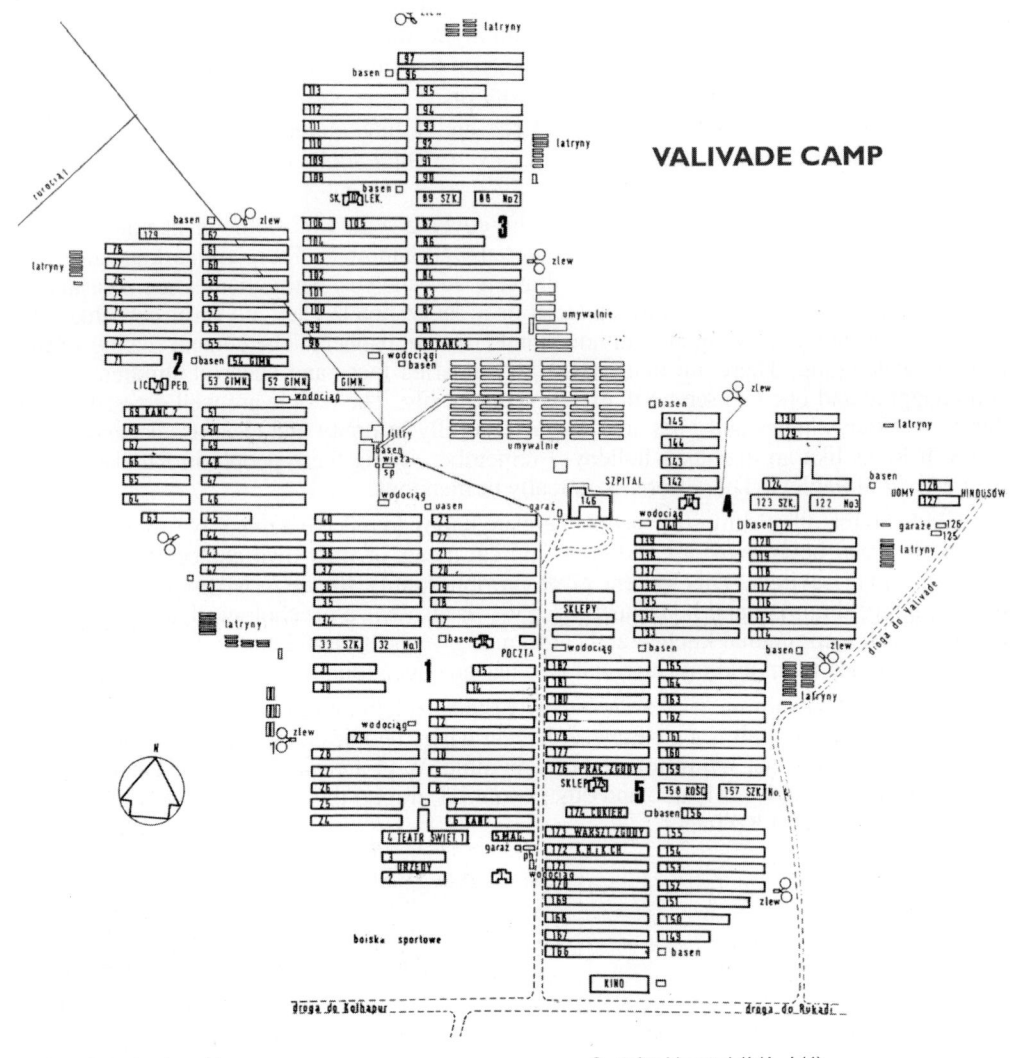

1. Commandants House
2-3. Urzędy = Offices
4. Teatr/Swietlica = Theatre/Common room
5. Mag(azyn) = Warehouse
6. Kancelaria = Administration
   P(olicja) h (Induska) = Indian Police
   Poczta = Post Office

   Dzielnice Osiedla = Camp Zones
No. 1. Barracks 1-40
No. 2. Barracks 41-75
No. 3. Barracks 80-113
No. 4. Barracks 116 -130 + 138 - 144
No. 5. Barracks 114 - 145 + 133 - 137 + 149 - 182

   Sklepy = Shops
   (176) Prac, (173) Warszt = Co-op Workshops
   (174) Kośc (ioł) = Church
   Kino = Cinema

Szpital = Hospital (141 -146)
Sk(lep)lek(arski) = Chemist Store
Orphanage = Zone 4

Szk-nr = School No. 1, 2, 3, 4
Gim-& Lic Ped. = High Schools

Garaż = Garage
Basen = Fire Brigade Cistern
Filtry = Water treatment Reservoir
Umylwanie = Washing Facilities
Latryny = Latrines
Wodociąg = Stand Pipes
Weża = Watch Tower
Zlew = Soakaway

Boiska sportowe = Sports Ground
Droga do = road to Kolhapur
              road to Rukadi

VALIVADE
THE MAIN POLISH REFUGEE CAMP
by Jan K. Siedlecki

As early as December 1941, Dr. E. Banasiński, the Polish Consul in Bombay, was seeking authorisation from his Government in London to discuss with the Government of India the question of acceptance of Polish refugees. The cost of their maintenance would be covered by the Polish Government from a British Government loan. This was agreed in September 1942 and in November the British Secretary of State formally asked the Viceroy of India to receive 5,000 Polish refugees.[1]

Shortly afterwards the Viceroy agreed in a secret telegram to "...take this number despite difficulties. No guarantee in good all year climates. Old buildings e.g. disused barracks may be available, but if new required, because of materials shortage, we can guarantee only mud huts or tents or other accommodation below standard previously provided for prisoners of war, internees and evacuees... this foreign group... subject to acceptance of these conditions, although this might cause dissatisfaction among the British people in India whose wives cannot come to India."[2]

Unable to find any original documentation regarding the building of the camp, I was obliged to use Dr. E. Banasiński's prompt and detailed reply of July 1944 to the questionnaire from the (Polish) National Audit Office. Some of these questions could be called inappropriate or even naive in the circumstances but the more relevant ones can be summarised as follows: who chose the site, prepared the plans and agreed the budget? On whose behalf was the building contract executed and who supervised the work? Who checked and accepted it? Did the Polish authorities have any say in these matters? Have they issued any instructions or accepted any proposals? Has the Consul inspected the premises? Has any opinion been sought from either Polish or other consultants?[3]

Political and financial considerations

Regarding the question of settlement and life of the Polish refugees in India, it was pointed out to us that the Government of India was a Trustee of His Majesty's Government in London and by the same token an Agent of the Polish Government in exile.

The Polish Authorities were aware of this situation and in general did not interfere in the choice of the site nor the workings of the Public Works Department. The Government of India, whilst prepared to listen and consider the views of the Delegate of the Polish Ministry of Social Welfare, reserved the power to make decisions, having the ultimate responsibility for the welfare of the Polish refugees in India.

View of the camp

In view of the above it is perhaps understandable why the Polish Minister, J. Stańczyk, who was visiting India at the time, was reluctant to take a stand on financial considerations like supplying additional funds. These would come directly from his Ministry in London but would have been outside the budgets agreed by the Government of India. Although the Minister requested cement floors in all the camp barracks cement was considered a military priority, as was glass for the windows and also drainage pipes. So the Minister had to accept the Government's of India point of view.[4]

Choice of the site

General view of the Camp

Polish Authorities were anxious about their people whose health suffered because of their deportation and deprivations in Russia. The outbreak of malaria in the first camp near Jamnagar was also causing concern. The British were well aware of the situation since they used to send their families during the hottest months to the hill stations at higher altitudes. Consideration had to be given to the food and water supply but the railway connection was also important. Towards the end of November 1942 Capt. A. W. Webb, Principal Refugee Officer in the Government of India, requested the Kolhapur State to "receive several thousand Polish refugees as it was impossible to place them in the hill stations and the Deccan plateau was the second best. The Camp should be of simple construction like mud huts or tents and Kolhapur would appear to be the most suitable."[5]

In January 1943 Capt. Webb went there to investigate possible locations with Mr. Perry, premier of the Kolhapur State. Sonthali, between Kolhapur and Panhala was found to be unsuitable as it would have only 10,000 gallons of water daily when 50,000 was required.

Then Bapat Camp was rejected due to its proximity to the municipal water supply and the danger of contamination or even shortage to the town in the hot season. Finally, Valivade Park about 4 miles east of Kolhapur was chosen. It was 250 acres of land belonging to the council, fenced off and close to the road and railway. Adjacent were several hundred acres of excellent arable land which could be used for growing vegetables under irrigation with surplus water from the Camp. The site was less than half a mile from the river and capable of providing ample water supply in all seasons.

The formal request for building the Camp in Valivade was made on 11th February 1943 and the Kolhapur Durbar *(Council)* gave permission on 19th March. The planned inspection of the site on 20th March by Dr. Banasiński and his wife together with the Prime Minister of Kolhapur was postponed until 9th of April.

Presumably as a result of this visit, W. Styburski, the Delegate of the Ministry of Social Welfare in Bombay was able to write on 16th May to London confirming that representatives of the Government of India and the Polish Consul had unanimously agreed that this place, 220 miles south of Bombay, at an altitude of 700 metres, with a healthy climate and minimal malaria hazard was most suitable for the proposed camp.

Entrance to the Camp

Planning of the camp and its construction

The Department of Public Works drew up the plans for the site having regard to the availability of building materials. These were then submitted for approval by the Department of Internal Affairs which in this case suggested slight modifications: Firstly, that in lieu of 'single tiles' the roofs should be covered in 'double country tiles'. Secondly, that instead of 'chatai' walls from floor to ceiling, the first two feet should be in rubble stone set in lime mortar. Thirdly, that instead of 'balies' for uprights, bamboos should be used which would be cheaper and more easily available. According to the wishes of the Polish Authorities life in the Camp should resemble that in a normal properly organised settlement with separate accommodation and cooking facilities for individual families.

Tender stage & pre-contract phase

Despite the usual procedure of going out to competitive tender in the case of public buildings, Capt. Webb on 2nd January 1943, went to the Hindustan Construction Co. in Ballard Estate, to ascertain if they would be prepared to

On a verandah

CROSS SECTION

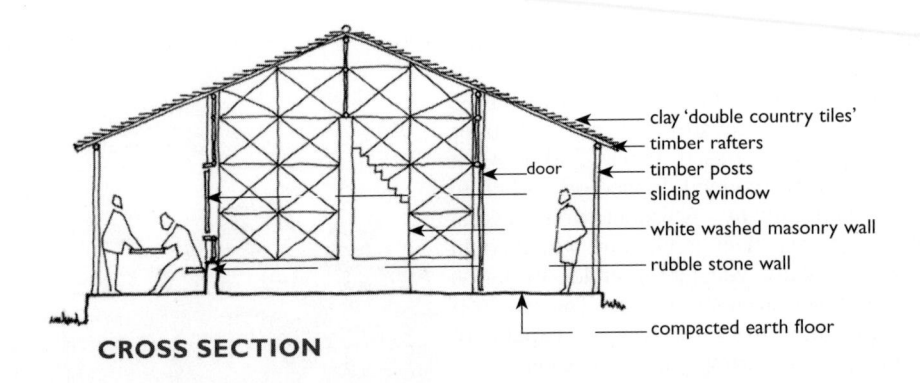

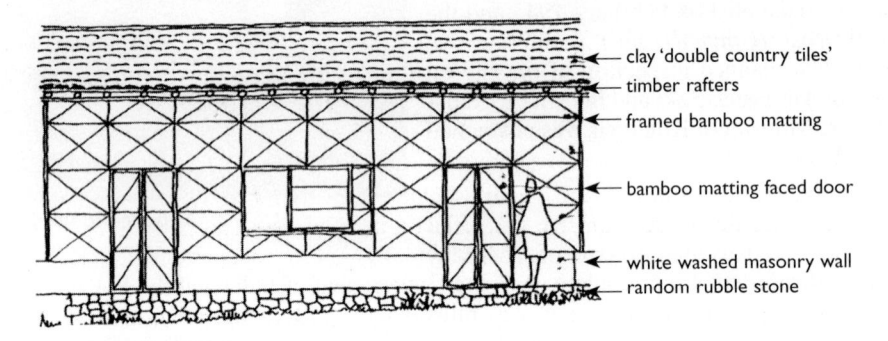

- clay 'double country tiles'
- timber rafters
- timber posts
- door
- sliding window
- white washed masonry wall
- rubble stone wall
- compacted earth floor

ELEVATION

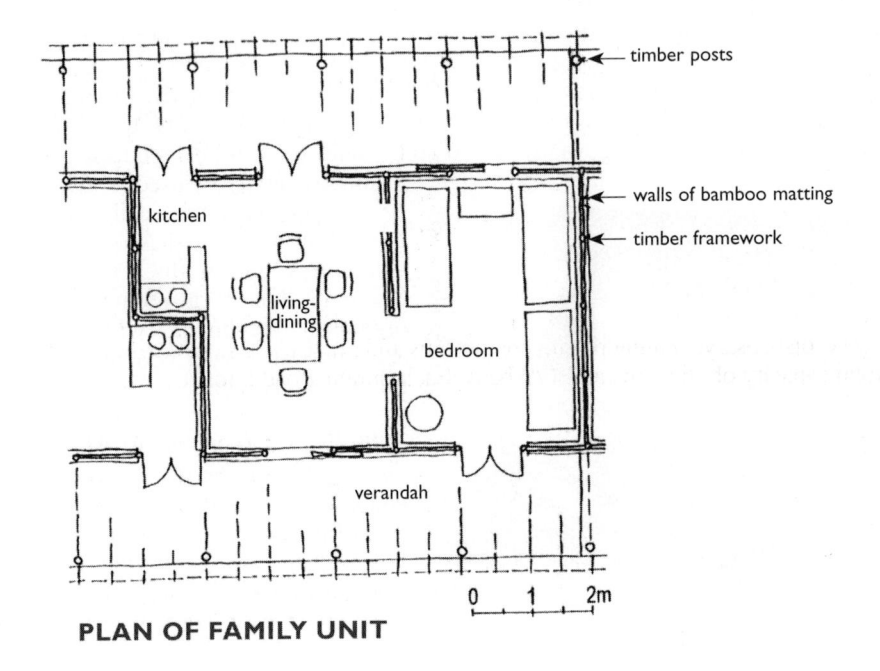

- clay 'double country tiles'
- timber rafters
- framed bamboo matting
- bamboo matting faced door
- white washed masonry wall
- random rubble stone

PLAN OF FAMILY UNIT

- timber posts
- walls of bamboo matting
- timber framework
- kitchen
- living-dining
- bedroom
- verandah

0 1 2m

tender for this contract. He showed them the plans prepared by the Public Works Department and gave a rough idea of the type of buildings required. He was then told that the company could have the camp ready by the end of April.

On 16th February Capt. Webb reported to the Secretary of State that the tender from Hindustan Construction was being checked by the Works Department and although some alternative details of construction were made and the cost of family quarters questioned, the overall building rates were approved. The total cost of the Camp would be approximately Rs 30 lakhs (Rs 300,000) and after the preliminaries were completed he proposed to go to Kolhapur to finalise with the Contractor the camp layout with special reference to the water supply.[6] Dr. E. Banasiński was satisfied that the proper procedure was observed and the contract approved by the relevant authorities, which given the circumstances and the shortage of time was no doubt understandable.

Building the camp and its supervision

According to the same letter of July 1944, the supervision of this type of contract was usually undertaken by the Central Public Works Department, the cost of which could amount to Rs 55,000 recoverable from the Polish Government Treasury. It was therefore decided that Lt. Col. J. D. Condie, an evacuee from Burma who had built and organised settlements for 50,000 people, would be employed as a supervising engineer at a monthly salary of Rs 750.

Starting date of the contract must have been at the end of March 1943 because the Consul wrote in April about his site inspection. Likewise, the Camp Commandant Capt. W. Jagiełłowicz, mentioned in his report for August that when he arrived in Valivade at the beginning of June, he found the Camp still under construction.

The 3,000 local workmen employed were housed in primitive sheds around the perimeter of the Camp. He was then informed by the Supervising Officer that the building of the camp should be finished in 3-4 months, but on 23rd July only one zone was handed over.[7] It can only be assumed that the camp was virtually completed at the departure of J. D. Condie on 13th November 1943 - approximately 7 months after the work commenced.

The most comprehensive picture of the actual buildings can be found in the monthly report dated 1st January 1944, prepared by the Camp management for the Polish Authorities in Bombay. The whole Camp was divided into 5 zones of approximately 28 barracks each containing 10 family units of two rooms and a kitchen. For single persons there were individual rooms with communal kitchens. On each side of the barrack was a verandah under the same roof, with dirt floors same as the rest of the living accommodation except the kitchen which had sand and cement screed. The end walls were of random rubble stone. The side walls, doors and windows were of framed bamboo matting.

The communal buildings were constructed in the same manner but in the main building of the hospital all floors were screeded and windows glazed. The building included outpatients, dental surgery, dispensary, waiting room, 3 bathrooms and toilets. The sick occupied 4 barracks with the total capacity of 16 wards and 170 beds. Each building had 5 toilets. There was also a mortuary and a garage, both built in stone.

The orphanage occupied 14 barracks, each with two communal bedrooms of 35 beds with a warden's room in the middle. The staff was accommodated in two barracks of 14 rooms each and containing a communal kitchen. In addition two barracks were designated as a school with a total of 12 classrooms. In one of them there was a dining hall and a kitchen which had 9 hearths, 7 cauldrons, 3 ovens including one for bread.

There were 9 school buildings of 6 classrooms each of the same construction with dirt floors and partition walls of bamboo mats between classes. The lack of soundproofing was a constant source of irritation. The sliding windows however had stretched cotton sheets instead of bamboo matting. Some schools had common rooms for the general public. School no.1 for example had a room for 100 people and school no. 2 for 40. Later more such rooms were created.

One of the school buildings was converted into a church by the removal of internal partitions and the addition of a small spire and a choir balcony. The floors had cement screed. The theatre was originally located in the lecture room used by the Cultural & Educational Department, but later it used the cinema built by the Camp's Supply Syndicate.

The Cooperative ran a cafeteria as well as workshops, stores and offices which were located in 5 family barracks. All had sand and cement floors.

Other buildings in the Camp which were built of stone were: the Post Office, the Indian Police hut, and the Camp Central Store. In addition there were two barracks totalling 29 rooms which were taken over by the Camp Administration including the Education Inspectorate, the Refugee Council and the Liaison Officer. In one of these buildings there were 4 guest rooms with masonry shower cubicles, but there were also 12 more guest rooms scattered throughout the Camp. The lighting in all the buildings was by means of paraffin lamps.

With regard to hygiene and sanitary accommodation, there were 75 buildings comprising 750 washrooms and laundry, which meant 150 such facilities for each zone of the Camp. In 50 toilets showers were also installed, all with cement floors. Apart from that, some 69 latrines were provided with 5 cubicles in each block. These were fitted with galvanised boxes which were emptied twice a day. The water from the nearby river was pumped into two main tanks of 13,200 gallons capacity, located at the highest level in the centre of the Camp. It was then distributed to 6 local tanks as drinking water and 2 tanks for washing purposes totalling some 114 taps dispersed throughout the Camp.[8]

It was also noted in the Camp Chronicles that as from 19th April 1944 a stop called VALIVADE HALT was established on the railway line, which would facilitate travel to Kolhapur, Poona and Bombay.

The end of building contract

The manner of the handover of completed works caused most of the misunderstandings between the Polish and British Authorities.

The Consul in his reply of July 1944 stated that neither he nor the Polish Delegate were authorised by the Polish Government to 'interfere' in the building contract of the camp. If they were to appoint independent consultants or 'experts' to inspect the premises this could have been misconstrued as a vote of censure or mistrust which would upset our relations with the British Government. Bearing this in mind, the Consul felt reluctant to take any steps to safeguard Polish interests which might intrude upon responsibilities undertaken by the Government of India. This was also highlighted when the Polish Delegate W. Styburski suggested the appointment of a committee to inspect the buildings before they were taken over by the Polish Authorities. Capt.

Main street

Webb objected because, as previously pointed out, the Government of India was acting on behalf of the British Government and therefore could not agree for the Polish Government to question its competence.

It is worth considering the realities of the situation at the local level. Capt. Jagiełłowicz, the designated Camp Commandant, arrived in Valivade on 11th June 1943 at the head of a small spearhead group at the instigation of Capt. Webb. He was to prepare the camp to receive the Polish refugees temporarily located in Malir. As the Liaison Officer was not yet appointed, he was to communicate directly with Lt. Col. Condie who, apart from imparting some general information, was not prepared to discuss any method of building or construction details which were already approved by the Government in Delhi. Clearly it was not in the prerogative of the Polish Commandant and so he waited for the official handover which never happened.[9]

Another sore point raised by the Polish Audit office in Bombay was the question of the missing furniture to which Capt. Jagiełłowicz replied on 11th February 1944. The barracks in which it was stored were secured with padlocks. The windows and doors were nailed down and the zones were patrolled daily. Inferior quality of the furniture eaten away by termites contributed to the fact that a lot of it was awaiting repair in the joinery workshops under the control of the Polish Works Department. It would have been impossible to comply with the suggestion of putting all the furniture into a secure store as there was not one big enough. The Contractor had left three streets piled high with furniture and it took several weeks and many workmen to sort it all out.

In conclusion Capt. Jagiełłowicz complained that he did not receive any reply from the Supervising Engineer Lt. Col. Condie to his request for proper handover documentation.[10]

As it was pointed out before, the National Audit Office showed a complete lack of understanding of local conditions and the accepted procedures for a building contract. Despite war conditions and the need for speed an absence of any official handover indicates a total disregard for the eventual user whose Government was to foot the bill.

The official opening of the Camp

Originally it was thought that this ceremony would be performed by the Maharani of Kolhapur, but if unable to do it due to the illness of her adopted son, the future Maharaja could do it. However, she was convalescing at the time in Bombay and the British Authorities did not even want to inform her of these plans in case she would use it as an excuse for returning to Kolhapur.[11]

It was therefore decided that the ceremony should be performed by the Prime Minister of the Kolhapur State, E. W. L. Perry, CIE, ICS. Unfortunately even though the programme and list of invitations was approved at the end of December 1943, the event was cancelled because at the beginning of January 1944 the Camp suffered a diphtheria epidemic. Instead it was proposed that Dr. N. B. Khare BA, MD, a member of the Commonwealth Relations Department in the Governor's General Council would visit Valivade on 27th April 1944 during his tour of India.

Despite the cancellation of the opening ceremony the Minister of Social Welfare in London, Jan Stańczyk sent this telegram on 17th January 1944: ... "to all concerned, c/o Mr. G. S. Bozman, Secretary to the Government of India Overseas Department - ... may I convey on behalf of the Polish Government our warmest gratitude to the Delhi Government who were the first ... in receiving Polish evacuees from Russia ... special thanks are due to the organisers of the Kolhapur settlement, where the Polish refugees have been enabled to enjoy conditions similar to their normal family life. Not only those ... benefiting from such hospitality, but the whole Polish nation now enduring such terrible *(war)* ordeals, will always remember the generosity of India ... the friendship engendered by our two peoples ... *(during)* the hardships of war, corresponds to the friendship uniting our two countries."[12]

Capt. W Jagiełłowicza welcomes Dr. N. B. Khare

Repairs & maintenance

It was obvious right from the beginning that the buildings were of cheap construction and some of the timber affected by termites. Even as early as August 1943 a roof had collapsed during a storm, but it was impossible or inappropriate to set up an enquiry. As from January 1944 repair work of all damaged windows, doors and roofs started under the supervision of an English engineer.[13]

A month later a Building Works Department was set up in the Administration Offices of the Camp. Timber pillars eaten away by termites were replaced in 29 family barracks and screed floors repaired in 370 kitchens. At the end of the month a whirlwind smashed roof tiles in 5 barracks. Later on in the summer a storm damaged roofs in 75 barracks. These were repaired by using tiles from the latrines.[14] In 1946 the Camp Chronicles described a hurricane which caused considerable damage, but luckily there were no fatalities. In his final report of 1947 Capt. Webb summarised the picture as follows: ..."The Camp had to be constructed in a great hurry and a special Engineer Officer was employed to ensure the work was done in time. ... The Camp was designed for 3 years occupation which expired at the end of 1946. Early in 1947 when our efforts to be rid of the Poles by the end of this year failed and it looked as if they might remain here for up to 2 years so we ordered a survey of the buildings. Central Public Works Department reported that to make it safe for the monsoon season only Rs 150,000 would be required for immediate repairs. But where was the money to come from? At the time we thought of the most urgent repairs, up to Rs 100,000 (could be) money from UNRRA savings, from 1st November 1946 to March 1947 to avoid collapse of the roofs and causing casualties among the refugees. Even if the Poles were to leave by the end of the year, this expenditure is unavoidable. If these funds are not enough we might get another Rs 40,000 from April and May accounts".[15]

The Kurowski family bedroom

Planned liquidation of the Polish Camps

As early as in the Autumn of 1943 the Foreign Office in London wrote to the Polish Ambassador, Count Raczyński, suggesting that an understanding should be reached between the Polish Government and the Government of India regarding the eventual disposal of all the camps constructed for the Polish refugees in India. Balachadi and Chela in Navanagar State and Valivade in Kolhapur were built on sites lent by the Rulers of these States. The Polish Government should not expect more than a breakup value of these camps whether existing or constructed later. But if any camp be sold as it stands and fetch a price higher than 'breakup' the Polish Government will receive the benefit.[16]

In his report of July 1947 Capt. Webb states that the Kolhapur Durbar is anxious to purchase the camp and much of its equipment. A valuation committee of Central Public Works Department and State Officers is to be appointed. Any equipment left over, will have to be auctioned and proceeds of sales credited to His Majesty's Government (Polish Account). Experience from other camps shows that it works out at 15% for the cost of buildings and 12% for the equipment.

It must be remembered that when these camps were built at the height of the war, costs were high and materials available, especially wood, were of the poorest quality.[17] When we last revisited Valivade in 1998, a great many barracks, though some in altered form, were still standing and occupied. Again I could not find any papers regarding the financial transactions concerning the sale of the Camp and its equipment after our departure and the arrival of the Indian refugees from the Sind province, which after the partition of India is now in Pakistan. This is the province where our first transit camps of Country Club and Malir near Karachi were located.

Kitchen with Z. Grużewska

NOTES

1. IP&MS: coll Banasiński 129/5
2. IOR: L/P&J/8/412 (coll. 110/N/1)
3. As no. 1
4. As no. 1
5. IOR: R2(952/76)
6. Final cost according to Capt. Webb was Rs 32 lakhs (the Consul quotes 33 lakhs)
7. JAG: coll Reply to the letter of 30th June 1944 from the Audit Office in Bombay (JAG?)
8. ANN: file no. 85 (report for December 1943)
9. As no. 7
10. JAG: private files)
11. As no. 5
12. ANN: file no. 83
13. IP&MS: Camp Chronicles C811/a
14. ANN: file no. 85
15. IOR: L/AG/40/1/131 (RRO/A-5)
16. IOR: L/P&J//8/413 (coll.110/N/2)
17. As no. 15

Main street 50 years later

ADMINISTRATION OF THE VALIVADE CAMP
by Janina Pająk & Jan K. Siedlecki

In January 1943 K. Banasińska as a Delegate of the Ministry of Social Welfare, wrote to the Minister J. Stańczyk in London that "Capt. A.W.T. Webb *(the Principal Refugee Officer in the Government of India)* is of the opinion that the Camp Commandant should be a Pole. He thinks that to appoint an Englishman could be unfavourably interpreted as an inability to govern ourselves. He emphasises that the whole administration should be in Polish hands. At the same time he advises against full autonomy which was tried in camps of other nationalities and it did not work due to local intrigues and quarrels... He is also against any presence of a Consular representative, as this might encourage a split in the proper functioning of the administration."[1]

At the end of February 1943 the Foreign Office notified the Polish Embassy in London that the Camp will be ready in March, which was an impossibility if one takes into account that the permission for its construction was given only a few days previously. It then asked the Polish Authorities to send ahead an administrative nucleus, which should not be difficult bearing in mind that such an apparatus was already established in the temporary Camp n Malir.[2]

The Administration consisted of the following Departments:

Administration Office	Financial & Management
Building & Technical	Cultural & Educational (*)
Voluntary Fire Brigade	Camp Security Guards (*)
The Post Office	Army Families Register
Refugee Records Office	Health Service (*)
Sports Section	(Departments marked (*) are described in other chapters)

Their work was based on the Statute of the Polish Refugees in India dated 25th June 1943, which was replaced with minor amendments six months later by the Rules and Regulations.[3]

From the very beginning, until his removal caused by his negative attitude during the registration by UNRRA, the Camp Commandant was Capt. W. Jagiełłowicz, at a salary of Rs 500 per month.[*] He had overall control of the Camp administration and represented the Camp to outside Authorities. He was responsible for the management of the approved

Camp Budget. He also endeavoured to convey the needs and desires of its inhabitants to the Delegate of the Social Welfare Ministry in Bombay. He was very popular and generally respected as "father figure" of the Camp.

Staff of the camp before the departure of Capt. W. Jagiełłowicza 16.9.1945. (sitting from left): K. Kowalewska, J. Dąbrowska, J. Brażuk, Z. Łopiński, ..., Z. Żerebecki, Fr. J. Przybysz, Mrs. M. Button, R. Dusza, Fr. L. Dallinger, O. Grabianka, J. Dobrostańska, B. Tijewski, (standing mid row): W. Melnarowicz, W. Górska, J. Jerzykowska, ..., E. Szczucińska, ..., ..., L. Turowiczowa, ..., O. Ostrihanska, J. Kossowska, W. Czekierska, Z. Saplisowa, ..., ..., H. Skrzeczkowska, H. Hajdulowa, ..., F. Pietrulewicz, H. Chrystowska, S. Żołądkiewicz, F. Żogał, W. Feń, W. Klepacka, T. Pawłowska, I. Magnuszewska, A. Dzierżek, W. Oszmiański, F. Wałdoch, (standing top row): L. Wawrzynowicz,, W. Bidakowski, E. Latawcowa, W. Chojno, E. Zimińska, ..., ..., ..., H. Jędrychowska, R. Fałdrowicz, H. Gromadzka, J. Gurgul, ..., W. Pitura

M. Wirth, O. Grabianka, E. Latawiec and W. Melnerowicz

To help him in this task he had a deputy, O. Grabianka and a quartermaster Z. Łopiński (@ Rs 300 each, monthly). The rest of the administration consisted of secretaries, interpreters and messengers with remuneration of Rs 40-50 monthly.

When the Polish Government in London was no longer internationally recognised and our maintenance was paid by UNRRA, Capt. Jagiełłowicz was replaced in October 1945 by Lt. Col. A.C.B. Neate, at a salary of Rs 1,000 monthly (as an Englishman he was deemed to be impartial regarding the possible split between pro-Warsaw or pro-London Government supporters). His deputy was then R. Dusza, whilst M. Button was responsible for the finances of the Camp and S. N. Rishi joined them as quartermaster.

Lt. Col. Neate in turn was replaced in January

Welcoming the new Col. Neate

1947 by Lt. Col. D. S. Bhalla, IMS, IAMC, who stayed until September of that year and afterwards it was Mrs. Button who became the Commandant with M. Goławski as her deputy.

The Camp was divided into five districts, each with its own manager (@ Rs 120 monthly):

(1). S. Laskowska, (2). L. Wawrzynowicz, (3). W. Walczak, (4). W. Walles, (5). E. Ziemińska *(all as of November 1944)*. Each manager had two deputies (Rs 80 each, monthly).

Each barrack had its own representative responsible for communicating the inhabitants' needs to the manager who in turn conveyed them to the Camp Commandant. Instructions from the HQ came in reverse through the same channels.

Besides the above mentioned personnel the management of each district included leaders from the Security Guards, Fire Brigade and Health Service, as well as representatives from the Cultural Department. Such management was also responsible for accommodation, taking care of the inventory, aesthetic appearance of the barracks and their surroundings.

Lt. Col. D. S. Bhalla, I.M.S, I.A.M.C.

Financial and Management Department

Z. Łopiński, J. Jerzykowska, H. Hajdul, E. Haczewska, J. Dąbrowska and I. Kasprowicz

This was headed by I. Kasprowicz (@ Rs 170 monthly) with B. Zawojska (@ Rs 120 monthly) as deputy, plus another dozen or so people. They were dealing with family allowances and were responsible for apportioning the Welfare Ministry's approved budget between the camps of Valivade, Balachadi and Panchgani Rest Centre. In addition this Department included the Supply Department, which was originally in charge of the allocation of furniture and other household items. Later it was supposed to be promoting the Co-operative Society's activity in the Camp.[4]

Building and Technical Department

At the beginning there was an engineer, Gune, (@ Rs150 monthly), representing the general contractor. The Polish Head of this Department was W. Bidakowski (@ Rs 120 monthly) and his deputy, R. Fałdrowicz.

Towards the end of 1944, the monthly report lists numerous repairs that were required: internal and external matting walls, doors and windows in the barracks, a number of chairs and tables, toilet lid covers and doors, hospital beds, toilet seats and the addition of window bars in some wards, blackboards and school desks, also a number of cement floors were added.

By December 1943 some of this work was taken over by the Co-op *(see later chapter on the Works Department)* but the report does not say who actually carried it out and we can only guess that local labour was employed.

The pumps supplied nearly 600,000 gal. of chemically treated water and almost 1,000,000 gal. of untreated water.[5]

Voluntary Fire Brigade

Bearing in mind the timber and bamboo matting construction of the Camp barracks, it is amazing that there is so little about the Brigade's activities in the Camp Chronicles, for if these buildings caught fire it would have been a disaster.

According to an early Camp Management report for September 1943 it was difficult to recruit 30 volunteers for this service out of 1,484 adults. At the beginning the Chief Officer was paid out of the budget for Security Guards but already in December 1943 we read about the Chief and 24 men with a British instructor.

Towards the end of 1944 there was a company of some 20 men (@ Rs 55 monthly) with 6 section leaders (@ Rs 70 monthly) and J. Błaszczak as the commander (@ Rs 125 monthly) and his deputy M. Kacera (@ Rs 70 monthly).[6]

In one of the monthly reports we read that the Brigade was practising an 8 hrs drill almost everyday. Once a week there was an inventory control of water pumps and checking up on water level in the tanks. Every barrack was equipped with 8 buckets and 4 hand pumps. They would also have to make sure that people knew how to use kitchen stoves - 'sigris'.

A case was recorded in February 1944 when the curtain caught fire in one of the barracks but by the time the fire patrol arrived in 3 minutes the fire was already put out by the family.[7]

The Post Office

The Indian Sub-Post Office in Valivade was established in August 1943 at the request of the Government of India.[8]

The Polish Post Office, according to the November 1944 report, was operating in accordance with a relevant Polish Army Standing Order, for its head, L. Budnik (Rs 100 monthly) was familiar with it. His deputy was S. Żołądkiewicz (Rs 80 monthly).[9] They were responsible for collecting ordinary and registered letter deliveries from the Camp's inhabitants and passing them to the Indian Sub Post Office. At the same time it would collect the post from the Indians for Camp addresses.

Polish Post Master L. Budnik and S. Żołądkiewicz

To have some idea of the postal volume the following excerpts might give some indication: in December 1943 - 3,999 letters, i.e. 154 daily and in March the following year there were 7,123 letters, i.e. 274 daily. Parcel post was limited until contact was established with families in Poland and Russia. In June 1944, the Audit Office records between 10,000 and 18,000 letters monthly.[10]

The Post Office function would not be complete without mention of the Board of Censors in Bombay which is dealt with in another chapter.

Records Office

J. Dąbrowska, J. Jerzykowska, and I. Magnuszewska

This Office in the last days of 1943 consisted of J. Dąbrowska (at a salary of Rs 120 monthly) with two deputies. Apart from registering the inhabitants and keeping record of their allowances, they were also responsible for allocating the accommodation to the new arrivals and visitors. The Register listing the Polish refugees in India was eventually published by the Ministry of Social Welfare in Bombay. At the time it was hoped that the Register would return to Poland, but in the meantime it served as a means of finding and uniting dispersed families. It must be remembered that the Polish Camp in Karachi (Country Club) served as a transit centre on the way to East Africa and other places.[11]

On the basis of this Register at the end of 1944 we can calculate that in Valivade alone there were 353 men, 1,957 women and 1,422 children of whom 630 were boys and 792 girls totalling 3,732 people.

Capt. Webb in his final report of April 1947 quotes the following numbers:
- (a). receiving maintenance in Kolhapur Camp   4,482
- (b). residing in the Camp but not receiving maintenance   77
- (c). living outside the Camp   195

                           4,754 [12]

Army Families Register

It would appear that it was set up in Valivade at the beginning of 1944 and it began registering families at the request of the Polish Army HQ[13] The Department was headed by W. Górska (@ Rs 100 monthly) who had three helpers. Most of the Camp inhabitants had someone in the Army. Apart from the initial registration there was also a need for the verification of the benefits for claimants, widows and orphans.

According to the reports of S. Dudryk-Darlewski, Delegate of the Social Welfare Ministry, such a Register originated in Tehran. This was before we came to India when it was agreed that a wife would receive £1 monthly and each dependant 10 shillings from voluntary donations of members of the Polish Forces. At the beginning the British Authorities forced the Polish Delegate to deduct this amount from the allowance due to each Polish refugee. This 'rule' was cancelled in 1944 and the agreed procedure was as follows: the money orders from the Army were posted to the British Army in India, which was given to the Polish Consulate in Bombay and then transferred to each individual family c/o the Delegate for Social Welfare.

Thus we find that a backlog of Rs 24,274 was paid to the families in India (between January 1943 to the end of February 1944) for the dead, lost or interned Army personnel. This was in addition to Rs 61,360 from the living family members (from September 1943 to the beginning of January 1944).

At that time also the Army Verification Section received enquiries from Valivade questioning 40 cases. Worthy of note is that in Valivade an Aid for Polish Soldiers Committee collected in July 1944 a sum of Rs 2,523 and organised 1,494 letters to servicemen.

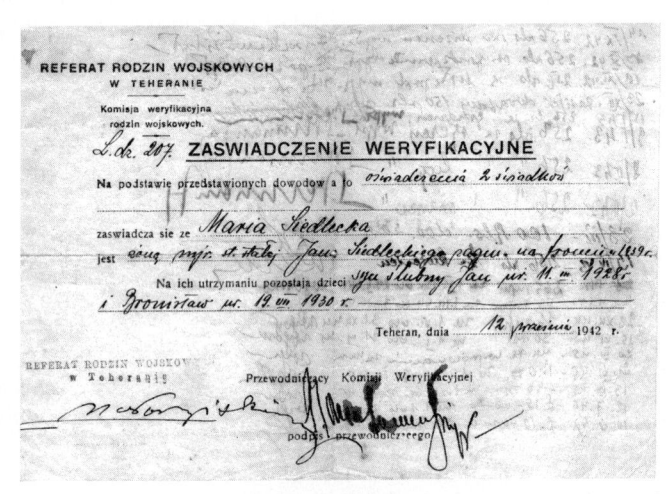

POLISH REFUGEE COUNCIL

"The Council is to represent the inhabitants, their desires and complaints *versus* the Administration of the Camp and at the same time through its own Audit Office would supervise and control the activities of various Departments. It would also have an influence on public opinion when acting as an intermediary" in accordance with the Polish Refugee Statute as described in the Polish newspaper in India.[14]

At the inaugural meeting of the Council in November 1943, the following were also established: The Disciplinary Board *(described in the chapter Law and Order)* and the Audit Office. At the same meeting the membership of the Council was established as follows: Z. Żerebecki *(Schools Inspector)*, Grabianka *(Camp Commandant's Deputy)* and J. Latawiec *(High School teacher)*.

A puzzling question is why or how the people from the Administration were involved in setting up the workings of this body when the Council was supposed to be an independent intermediary between the executive powers of the Camp and its population. The only plausible explanation is that there were so few professional men available that they were used on both sides.

At the Council meeting in December 1943, the *Camp Chronicles* record the following subjects on the agenda: the question of useful employment for some of the inhabitants, the problem of adequate food supply, charitable action on behalf of the local Indian population (e.g. a collection of spare clothing to be organised) and a souvenir badge of our stay in India.[15]

Subsequent elections to the Council in May 1944 resulted in the Rev. Fr. J. Przybysz becoming chairman for a brief period. He was succeeded by Mjr. L. Naimski who however resigned in March 1945. He was replaced by his deputy Mgr. J. Pawłowski, who remained as chairman after the next election in September 1946 despite the fact that Fr. J. Przybysz obtained more votes and stayed as his deputy.

When the elections to the Council were held on 17th August 1947 there appears to be no record in the *Chronicles* or in the press. However, in the *Polak w Indiach* newspaper an article was published by the Federation of Poles in India listing a number of accusations against the Council stating that despite a two year lapse since the last election *(?)* nobody noticed the absence of their activity... that the Federation is of the opinion that the Council should act as a consultative body to the Administration... that it should watch over the sale of rationed bread *(see later chapter on Food Supply)* and check its quality... that it should control the supply of sugar, flour and kerosene... that it should adjudicate in any quarrels between the refugees. Finally it states that the Federation disagreed with the new Rules proposed by the Council and therefore a new set was being proposed.

It is difficult to understand this outburst in view of the regular elections recorded and the Council's involvement in the food negotiations in the autumn 1945 and later in February and September 1946 *(see subsequent chapter on Food Supply)* which are documented in the India Office Records in The British Library. It is curious that so little information on the subject seems to have survived in the Polish records.

Audit Office of the Council

The Rules for its function were discussed at a conference in April 1943 between the Delegates of the Ministry of Social Welfare W. Styburski, K. Banasińska and Capt. W. Jagiełłowicz in connection with setting up the temporary camp in Malir as a precursor to Valivade. It was proposed that the Audit Office should consist of three people with appropriate qualifications to scrutinise and control the performance of the various Departments of the Administration. They were to cooperate with the Commandant and also be responsible for everything that happens in the Camp.[16] This situation contradicts the Rules and Regulations *(for Polish refugees in India)* because it cannot check and be responsible for a particular Department at the same time. For example the Audit Office however was not empowered to establish the budget for the camp which was the responsibility of the Delegate of the Social Welfare in Bombay.

Again we seem to have the controversy regarding the establishment of the Audit Office Rules for which Z. Łopiński was responsible.[17] He was the quartermaster of the Camp and directly answerable to the Commandant. Perhaps, once more, the shortage of qualified people was the reason. After the first formative months, in May 1944 new members of the Office were voted in: E. Szczucińska (as the chairperson @ Rs 170 monthly) and W. Chojno and S. Zubrzycki (@ Rs 130 monthly each). They later issued a general report covering the period November 1944 to August 1945 from which some excerpts are quoted here.

"The Audit Office has carried out repeated checks in various Sections of the Administration... the Orphanage, the Central Storage block, Sanitation Department and the Health Service... It found a few irregularities, worked out a price list for the butchers' shops, generally checking up on the food price increases. Details of these investigations were scrupulously submitted to the Camp Commandant.

From its inception the Office never came across any abuse of power, malfunction or spitefulness. Shortcomings were generally caused by the lack of professionalism or working instructions, but they were gradually eliminated as people acquired the necessary skills. Some of the trouble was prompted by the unfamiliar weights and measures of British India. Inferior quality of the materials used in furniture, fire buckets in the orphanage and hospital were causing problems, but none of this was due to negligence or embezzlement.

More serious investigations were referred to either the Security Guards or the Indian Police. If a monetary shortfall was discovered the guilty party had to make up the difference. On the whole this Office was satisfied that the economic management of the Camp was conducted properly and in accordance with the Rules laid down by the Ministry of Social Welfare."[18]

Translated by Jan and Barbara Siedlecki

Staff of the Camp with guests: (sitting from left) Mr. Sen, Olgierd Grabianka, F. Grabiankowa, Maria Jagiełłowicz, Michał Goławski, Mrs. Litewska, Consul Jerzy Litewski, Mrs. Mabel Button, delegate Stanisław Dudryk-Darlewski, Military advisor to the Maharaja, Napasaheb Ingle, Mr. Kittur, Vijaysingh B. Mahagaonkar, Roman Dusza, Czesław Gulczyński and Khanderao B. Gaikwad, (standing): Mjr. Ludwik Naimski, Fr. Leopold Dallinger, Zygmunt Łopiński, Bronisław Tijewski, inspector Zdzisław Żerebecki, ..., Witold Bidakowski, Halina Hajdulowa, Capt. Władysław Jagiełłowicz, Tadeusz Szul, Wanda Górska, ..., Capt. T. Wilczewski, Helena Małachowska and Zdzisław Sikorski

NOTES

To a large extent the contents of this chapter, unless otherwise stated, are based on the article by A. Kisielnicka in the paper *Polak w Indiach* no.18/19 dated 15.IX - 1.X.1944

1. IP&MS: Dr. E Banasiński (coll. 129)
2. IOR: L/P&J/8/412 (coll 110/N/1)
3. AAN: file no. 85 (pp 19-22)
4. KPI: archives
5. JAG: archives
6. KPI: archives
7. KPI: archives
8. IOR: R2 (953/82)
9. JAG: archives
10. KPI: archives
11. IP&MS: List of Polish Refugees in India
12. IOR: L/AG/40/1/131 (RRO/A-5)
13. IP&MS: Chronicles C 811/a, b & c
14. AAN: file no. 84
15. IP&MS: Chronicles C 811/a, b & c
16. AAN: file no. 88 (pp 18-19)
17. AAN: file no. 85 (pp 164-192)
18. KPI: archives

ADDITIONAL NAMES OF PERSONNEL NOT MENTIONED IN TEXT

General Administration
Melnerowicz Władysława
Tomaszewska Stanisława
Kowalewska Kazia
Małachowska Helena
Marczyńska Stefania
Baranowski Franciszek
Warawa Anna
Bodura Zofia
Gaweł Władysława

District Administration
Jadwiga Brażuk
Felicja Żogal
Maria Kijanowska
Antonina Puchalska
Antonina Strycharz
Maria Majewska
Blumska Maria
Serednicka Karolina
Chrystowska Halina

Financial and Management
Turowicz Leontyna
Haczewska Elżbieta
Oszmiański Wawrzyniec
Zbyszewska Bronisława
Magnuszewska Irena
Tobianka Artur
Wałdoch Franciszek
Hajdul Halina
Jerzykowska Janina
Wesołowska Jadwiga
Czarniawska Wanda
Piskorski Stefan
Ziarkiewicz Józef

Fire Brigade
Dymicki Jan
Tyski Karol
Mikulicki Józef
Szczęsnowicz Wiktor
Abol Aleksander
Bronowicka Zofia
Gurgul Józef
Węgrzyn Józef
Kwiecień Marcin
Szczypek Stanisław
Bagińska Zofia
Baryluk Michał
Bielecka Kazimiera
Chomko Konstanty
Dragosz Zofia
Wilczyński Antoni
Gałka Stanisław
Ignatowicz Józefa
Jadziewicz Jan
Józefczyk Stanisława
Marchewka Józef
Michalak Stanisława
Misuno Władysław

Records Office
Bratkowska J
Wilczyńska Maria
Latawiec Eugenia
Wirth Maria

LAW AND ORDER
by Jan K. Siedlecki

Apart from the purely humanitarian side of our rescue from the Soviet Union at the time, there was also an agreement by the British in November 1942 "to evacuate wives and children of Polish soldiers so as not to demoralise or undermine their morale". As European refugees and citizens of an allied state, our arrival in India presented certain problems to the Authorities. Our legal status was later further complicated by the international recognition of the Polish Government in London being transferred to the Government installed by the Soviets in Warsaw.

Initially the Authorities were concerned with problems of law and order inside and outside the Camp. The basis of criminal and civil order amongst Polish refugees was discussed by the Polish Authorities right from the beginning of our arrival in India. At a conference in Karachi in April 1943, it was suggested that "a substitute of the criminal justice system be created in the form of citizens' courts to deal with any conflicts among the refugees, or any offences against existing regulations."[1]

Even before that, in January 1943 Mrs. K. Banasińska wrote to the Ministry of Social Welfare in London, that "criminal offences or transgressions within the Camp, should be dealt with by local jurisdiction in the same manner as in the refugee camps of other nationalities. Cases occurring outside the Camp boundaries should be taken care of by the special justice office that functions alongside of the Resident's court.[2]

At the conference in May 1943 the Polish Minister, J. Stańczyk agreed with these proposals.[3]

Disciplinary Board

The Board was set up at a meeting of the Camp Refugee Council in November 1943, with O. Grabianka as its chairman, who was soon replaced by Mr. F. Podsoński. The function of the Board was described in the Polish paper *Polak w Indiach* as adjudicating any disputes between the residents of the Camp, as well as disciplining cases submitted by the Camp Security Guards. According to the Camp Management report for February 1944, the Board sorted out 25 disputes and disciplinary cases in the previous six months.[4]

Camp Security Guards

Capt. Webb advised that these guards, or 'Civilian Police' as he called them, should be made up from residents of the Camp invalided out of the army rather than anybody who had been a professional policeman. According to the report for November 1943, these guards comprised the commander, Mr. B. Tijewski (at a salary of Rs 120 monthly), his deputy Mr. J. Sieczko (Rs 100 monthly), five district leaders (at Rs 85 each, monthly) and 40 guards (at Rs 60 each, monthly). They were between 20 and 66 years old and included 7 women.

In February 1944, the Guards reported 3 cases of theft, 7 cases of insulting behaviour and 3 cases of disturbances including some damage to public property and 16 cases of misbehaviour contrary to the Camp regulations. Some of these were perpetrated by teenagers; 9 were reported to the Disciplinary Board and 23 cases to the Camp Commandant. I could not find much more after that. Whether this was due to the shrinking of Polish authority because of the political circumstances it is difficult to ascertain.[5]

Camp security guards

At the same time the Camp Chronicles noted that 'according to the Law in India arrest leading to imprisonment can only be made by the Indian Police. Therefore if an arrest is to be made, the Camp Commandant is to hand over the case to the local police. This is a warning and it is hoped that it will not have to be used. Penalties for petty thefts, property damage and breaking Camp Regulations are to be dealt with by the Disciplinary Board. Any of these perpetrated by school children will be referred to the School Authorities".[6]

Detention Centre

Quite a separate problem was created by the existence of a large number of women and girls, who due to the scarcity of male company in the Camp were seeking it elsewhere. They became a magnet for visits from British and other soldiers. Because of this the Polish Delegate proposed in July 1944 the creation of a detention centre to control the situation. The Ministry in London however, objected to it not only because it was impractical, but also 'politically' incorrect.

However the Camp Management reported in November of the same year that such a centre had already been set up for single young women and girls and that they had by now designated a special barrack for about 14 difficult boys and a detention centre for 29 girls. Nothing more could be gleaned from Polish sources.

Reverting to British documentation, it would appear that in May 1944 there were complaints against soldiers of the British Forces visiting the Camp 'for obvious reasons'. According to the Police inspector from Belgaum (February 1945) those visits were reciprocal. The women paid visits to the town not only for shopping, but also to meet the soldiers. The inspector visited Valivade in January 1945 to make enquiries and had a meeting with the Camp Commandant and the senior doctor to check up on the VD situation. The Liaison Officer, Mrs. M. Button confirmed that there were only a small number of such visits to the Camp, despite the fact that it is only 2 miles away from the convoy personnel Military Camp. The problem was however that the British soldiers were not taking any notice either of the Camp Security Guards or the Indian Police and refused to leave by the prescribed 7 p.m.. Finally Brig. Forbes was approached with a request to move the Military Camp further away from the Polish Refugee Camp, which should be made 'out of bounds'.[7]

Poles from the British Army visiting the Camp

We also find a mention in the Camp Chronicles dated 28th September 1946 that "the Authorities issued an order according to which the Valivade Camp was to be closed to other nationalities and only Polish soldiers could visit the Camp providing they had a permit from the Liaison Officer'.

British Jurisdiction

As our Government in London formally ceased to exist we could be treated as stateless refugees. Even up to July 1945 disciplinary procedures were not resolved as demonstrated by the letter in May 1945 from the Camp Commandant to the Social Welfare Delegate in Bombay asking for help. He explained that because there was no prison in the Camp, nor did the management have the legal status of a proper police force, some criminal elements in the Camp felt free to act with impunity. Referring these cases to the local Indian Police did not bring the required results as the procedure took too long and sentencing was light.[8]

This matter was also discussed on 9th July 1945 at a meeting of Kolhapur Municipal Authorities with Capt. Webb representing the Government in New Delhi, when the change of Camp Commandant was anticipated. Their proposals tended to be largely in line with those suggested before by the Polish Authorities.

Two days later the Resident wrote to New Delhi, pointing out the difficulties in this regard: "...these people are mainly uneducated peasants *(Editor's note: To generalise like this, showed an arrogant and ill-informed attitude, because in reality there was a cross-section of Polish society, from intelligentsia to the illiterate peasants)* with a large proportion of women from whom one cannot expect the same standard of behaviour as is usual of that class of Europeans who normally come to India. This causes trouble to Indian Police who make arrest and the trial of such case is beyond the normal scope of State Magistrate, especially when women are concerned. The state has no suitable jail. ...The Poles are not permanent State Subjects, nor Subjects of any declared Government, but refugees granted temporary haven of rest in their search for homes. ...Their language and customs are different to those in India and present difficulties."[9]

It was only in October 1945 that there was a reply from the Political Department in New Delhi, stating that: "...the State jurisdiction over Europeans is exercisable by or under the authority of the Crown Representative's Court to try any of the Polish refugees ...for criminal offences ...also if a state subject or other Indian resident is charged with crime against one of these refugees, the State Court will have jurisdiction... But all other cases involving the Poles should be tried in the Residency Courts. Regarding the appointment of a Polish judge as a magistrate to try the cases exclusively... between the Poles, there are no objections *(but)* the practicality is that such a magistrate would have no knowledge of the State or British Indian Law, (and should it come to an appeal it would lead to considerable difficulties)... *(Finally)* procedural law is to be followed in investigation and trial laid down in the Code of Criminal Procedure and the Indian Evidence Act applied to Kolhapur Residency Area..."[10]

According to the Camp Chronicles in December 1945 "the Court from Kolhapur comes to Valivade to preside over criminal cases, and that it lately sentenced a Polish resident to 3 weeks imprisonment"[11]

Almost a year later on 18th October 1946 the Kolhapur Resident in a letter to Capt. Webb regarding savings in the Camp maintenance, points out that "...at present the Durbar, at its own expense, keeps a nominal police force in the Camp (a non-commissioned officer and three men). The actual policing of the Camp is carried out by the Polish Security Guards (about 40 in number). If they were not paid now, they might refuse working. If the Poles kick up rough or even create a demonstration, who was to deal with it? Local police have no experience in dealing with agitated Europeans, especially women... But on the whole the camp behaved very well in the past, which must be due to being gently policed by their own. Therefore money should be found to continue payment to these policemen."[12]

From these documents it would appear that the British and the local authorities did not really know how to deal with us and eventually in 1947, a 'SPECIAL KOLHAPUR STATE (ORDER) TO COVER CRIMINAL CASES AND CIVIL SUITS CONCERNING POLES IN VALIVADE' was issued by H. H. Chhatrapati of Kolhapur. This was in exercise of his powers under section 6 of the Kolhapur Legislative Assembly Regulation 1942. The preamble states that 'it was expedient to make provision for better administration of the Civil and Criminal Justice in the Polish Refugee camp at Valivade in the Kolhapur State! It is to be called Valivade (Polish) Camp Maintenance Order Act 1947 and it extends to the boundaries of the Camp area and half a mile outside. It applies to all Polish Nationals. Its Board shall consist of 5-7 members elected from the Polish inhabitants of the Camp. It can appoint special Camp Police and deal with offences as described under the Kolhapur penal code 1945. Some of these are as follows: spreading infection, fouling the water, obstruction of public way, theft and trespass. It considers various penalties, like Rs 50 fine and/or detention, but "male offenders could be liable to whipping in accordance with 1884 Act adopted by the State."[13]

In the event I do not think its provisions came into being as the Camp began to disband towards the end of 1947.

The prison problem

One of the main problems was that the jail in Kolhapur had no separate accommodation for European prisoners. There appears to be lack of documentation for the earlier years, but in June 1945, the Liaison Officer Mrs. M. Button agreed that the two female Polish inmates convicted of assault, could be incarcerated in the lower flat of her house in Kolhapur.

Later on during a July conference in town, it was proposed that a detention centre be created in one of the existing barracks, the cost of which was submitted in September. However the *Camp Chronicles* notes that it was only at the beginning of 1947 that the barracks 186 and 187 were erected in the third District of the Camp for this purpose.

Any prisoner serving more than one month, should be transferred to the Central European jail in Yervada nr. Poona. Then came the question of who pays for the jail and transport there. The Kolhapur Durbar was under the impression that as it accepted the Poles in its territory, the cost incurred should be covered by the Government of India, which in turn would recover this debt from the Polish Government in London. Capt. Webb however considered that acceptance of the Poles by Kolhapur carried certain obligations. By the middle of September 1945, the Secretary of State in Bombay proposed that the Kolhapur Durbar would bear the maintenance and transport charges. Polish prisoners however, could only be admitted in Yervada if accommodation was available. Eventually it was agreed by the Chief Accountant of the Government of India that any expenses accrued by the Polish prisoners would be treated like any other expenditure connected with the Polish refugees.

At the beginning of December 1945 an interesting correspondence ensued between the Polish Camp Commandant, Lt. Col. Neate and the Kolhapur Resident concerning Antoni M. who stayed in Kolhapur prison for the whole of his sentence. He was freed before the responsibility for payment was finally decided. The same happened in February 1946 regarding the case of Edward Sz., who served his two week sentence in Kolhapur before accommodation was found for him in Yervada.[14]

Examples of offences

There are not many, especially in the Polish records. However those noted in the British documentation seem fairly characteristic. The majority of them come from the period when the Polish Government in London ceased to function and we were under direct care of the British through the Interim Treasury Committee. From available research it would appear that residents of the Camp were basically law abiding.

In June 1945 we find some 10 criminal cases dealt with by the Kolhapur Magistrate. They were mainly brawling offences. It was also recorded that Jadwiga G. was sending gold coins in a tobacco tin to her husband in the Army and that Zofia J. was doing the same, but concealing them in a bar of soap.[15]

In August Capt. Webb wrote to Mrs. Button that he was informed that Poles were investing their savings in gold (which was relatively cheap in India). It was common knowledge apparently that they buy silver and gold jewellery at inflated prices and she was asked to warn them that to take it out of India was illegal.

At the beginning of December 1945 before a Railway Magistrate Court was a case no. 92/4 where Baburao Bhalla was beaten up by Zofia T., Antonina N., Adam Sz. and Gulab M. M.. The last one was sent to jail for 2 months and the remainder for one month and each had to pay Rs 10. An interesting example of the prevailing atmosphere was the case of Marian O. who was imprisoned in Yervada. On 11th September 1946 the Resident of Kolhapur wrote to Lt. Col. Neate requesting assurance that the prisoner will not be repatriated to Poland against his wishes.

Registration of Foreigners Rules 1939

Generally we were unaware of legal restrictions imposed on our Scout camps, travels, excursions and attendance at English schools. It could be that such permission as was required was sought collectively on our behalf by our guardians, school or camp authorities.

It is not surprising that the British were dealing with such issues cautiously, bearing in mind that Japan, having conquered Burma had formed an army from their Indian prisoners of war. India was on the road to independence but its Congress leaders were being imprisoned for opposing a unilateral declaration of war in their name.

Even the Polish Consul at the beginning of 1943 had to obtain permission to visit Kolhapur to see and approve the chosen Camp site. The same permission was extended later the same year to cover the Polish Minister J. Stańczyk and then to W. Styburski, M. Goławski and eventually S. Dudryk-Darlewski, Delegates of the Ministry of Social Welfare and Ministry of Education respectively.[16]

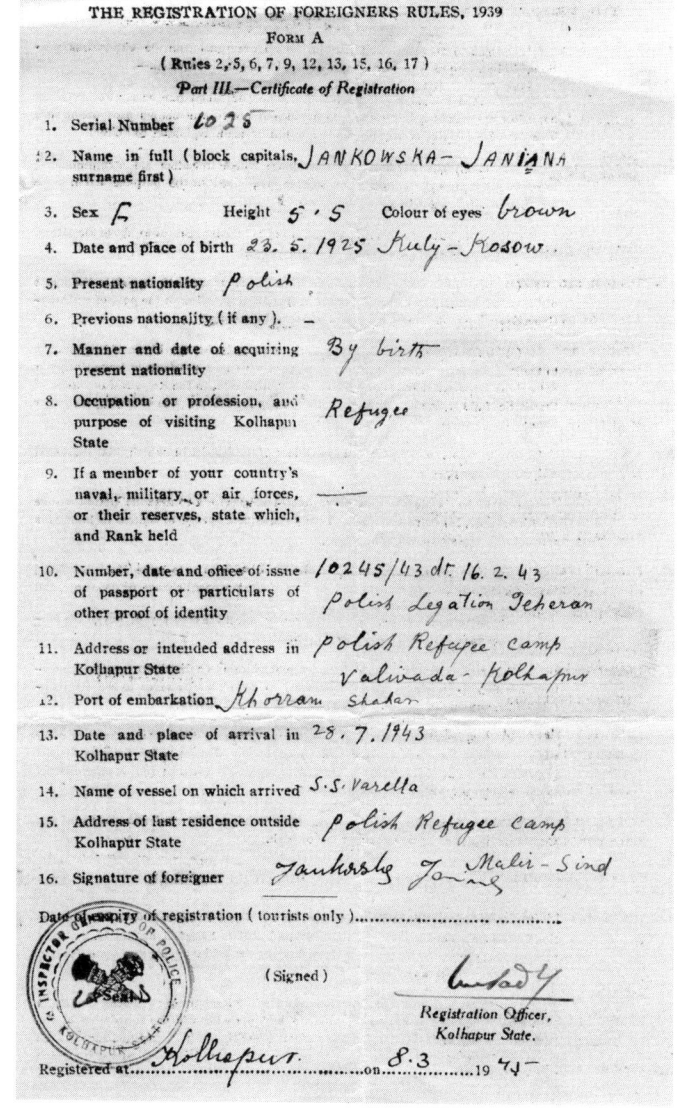

From the examined documents it appears that there was no restriction on our movement outside the Camp or going to the town provided that one was back by 10 p.m.. It was however recommended that we should register in accordance with the Rules of 1939. There were nevertheless language difficulties in translating the 'Certificate of Registration' form and because the British Authorities did not trust a Polish interpreter employed in the Administration Offices, it was proposed that a Chinese working for British Intelligence should be used.

Between January and May 1945, from the Camp of about 4,000 people, 1,761 had registered from the eligible 2,311. Those that did could travel freely providing that they reported to the police upon arrival at their destination.

As the Poles were accepted in India on the basis of a group transit visa it was understood that they would remain within the Camp therefore they should not expect the same treatment as other Europeans who had a full or normal visa. It was deemed 'undesirable for them to roam at will all over India' but the Authorities could not find any precise regulation forbidding it.[17]

In the meantime a few Poles left the Camp seeking employment, all with the full knowledge of the Polish Commandant, who was not supposed to condone it. It was therefore suggested that the right of issuing such work permits be transferred to the Liaison Officer. Mrs. Button was supposed to issue travel permits for hospital treatment and education in schools outside the Camp or for leave. This was to be done in conjunction with the Inspector General of Police in Kolhapur. It was also hoped that these restrictions would reduce the number of railway and town incidents.

A year later in November 1946 we read in the *Camp Chronicles* that there were frequent occurrences of people travelling without permits. Lt. Col. Neate forbade this, warning that any future cases would be treated seriously and punished.[18]

It was only in April 1947 that a regulation was published in the *Chronicles* allowing employment outside the camp, provided that the employee would return when recalled. It was also stated that the workplace could be changed if the Camp Commandant was notified.[19]

It could be that the British Authorities were afraid that due to the political situation in Europe, some of us might want to remain in India. There was also talk of Wanda Nowicka and Katarzyna Kowalska, who having married Indians could remain in India if they so desired. It should also be remembered that the British, at that time masters of India, felt responsible for us, especially after India's declaration of independence in August 1947.

Translated and abridged by Jan & Barbara Siedlecki

NOTES

1. IOR: L/P&J/8/413 coll. 110/N/2
2. AAN: file no. 88 (present - W. Styburski, K. Banasińska & W. Jagiełłowicz)
3. IP&MS: Dr. E. Banasiński collection (file no. 129)
4. AAN: report of the Camp Management for February 1944
5. PwI: 15 IX - 1 X 1944 A. Kisielnicka
6. IP&MS: Camp Chronicles C 811/A
7. IOR: R2 (952/76)
8. KPI: arch. Camp Com. letter to the Delegate MPiOS in India (May 1945)
9. IOR: R2 (952/76) present - Capt. C.W.L. Harvey, Capt. A.W.T. Webb, Rao Saheb G.B. Deshmukh, Khan Bahadur N.N. Sadri and Capt. E.W.M. Magor
10. IOR: R2 (952/76) 11th July 1945
11. IP&MS: Camp Chronicles C 811/B
12. IOR: R2 (953/82)
13. IOR: L/AG/40/1/131 file RRO/A-5 enclosure 'G' Capt. Webb memo of July 1947
14. IOR: R2 (953/82) Kol. & Deccan Agency
15. IOR: R2 (953/82) Kol. & Deccan Agency
16. IOR: R2 (953/82) Kol. & Deccan Agency
17. IOR: R2 (952/76) letter from Dist. Suptd. of Police (Belgaum)
18. IOR: L/AG/40/1/131 file RRO/A-5 enclosure 'D' Capt. Webb memo of July 1947
19. IP&MS: Camp Chronicles C 811/A+B

WORKS DEPARTMENT AND THE COOPERATIVE SOCIETY
by Helena Tutak (Masiulanis) and Jan K. Siedlecki

When in August 1943 the co-op was set up, it soon took over virtually all the activities of the Works Department, which was responsible for the maintenance and repair of the Camp. By December this Department became known as 'Building Works'.

At the same time, the Polish Authorities' concern was somewhat different as noted in the writings of W. Styburski, Delegate of the Employment and Social Welfare Ministry, from which these excerpts are quoted: "...one has to pay particular attention to the question of employment if we are to avoid a slow demoralisation of these people... the majority of them are women and teenagers and employment has to suit these groups. Already in Tehran we found that it was relatively easy to organise sewing groups or workshops where women can earn additional money... It should be possible to establish workshops on the Cooperative principle, where young people could learn various skills to enable them to work professionally upon their return to Poland. The workshops could be handicrafts, embroidery or toy making, shoecraft, metalwork, hairdressing, fruit and vegetable growing skills... Funds or loans should be made available to create workshops equipped with machines and materials... These, as well as the funds for training courses, should be included in the Camp budgets, initially paid for by the Government of India, while the salaries of the administration or tutors should be paid directly by the Polish Government in London..."[1]

It was also stated that the aim of the Polish Authorities was "...to create a normal life in a perfectly run township...". This would have been difficult to achieve as the traditional family units at that time were without their 'bread winners', who were mostly in the Army. Apart from that, the limited employment available was mainly in the running and service of the Camp, i.e. administration, security, or teaching, health service etc. There was no other viable work as we could not compete with Indian labour. Nevertheless it was thought that instead of spending part of our refugee allowance on the profit of local shopkeepers or workers, it should remain in Polish hands. However the Camp Management report for December 1943 pointed out that: "...an Indian worker can produce a shirt for 1-3 annas. Our Co-op will charge for it 20-24 annas. An Indian worker will earn Rs 15-18 per month, but the Polish one will require Rs 30-40. Laundry, shoe repairs, etc. are cheaper by 50% from local craftsmen. The same goes for shop assistants, so that a cake in the Indian shop cost 1 anna, in the Polish one it will cost 2 or even 4 annas."[2]

The state of employment

According to the Delegate's report for August 1943 employment was as follows:

1. Number of people employed in the Camp Administration	210
2. Number employed in the Co-op workshops (*)	131
3. Number of pre-school children	95
4. Number of school children	1,148
5. Number of children not in schools	58
6. Number of patients in hospital	28
7. Number of people absent from the Camp	21
8. Number of unemployed	835
	2,526 [3]

(*) In December 1943 the number of people working in the administration of the Coop was 9, in the workshops there were 96 and 13 trainees (total 118).[4] Almost a year later in November 1944 there were 63 trainees in the apprentice courses, 70 trainees for the course in pattern cutting and sewing, 68 hosiery apprentices and 51 in tailoring courses - totalling 252 + admin staff.[5]

Presumably the additional number of people employed by the Co-op was due to the increase of Camp's inhabitants to 3,732 at that time. Unfortunately there were no more reports on this, due to the formal closure of the Polish Government in exile. We do know that the final population of the Camp was just over 5,000 but the number of people working for the Co-op is not reported.

Staff of the Co-op: (sitting) ..., A. Lipiński, Z. Sikorski, Mgr. J. Szymańska, President L.T. Skrzypek, Fr. A. Jankowski, I. Kasprowicz, ..., (standing) W. Pitura, ..., ..., M. Antolik, J. Klepacki, ..., ..., ..., ..., ..., ..., S. Królikowska, ..., ..., ..., P. Masiulanis, ..., (and last but one) M. Kapuścińska

The Cooperative Society

The beginnings of the Polish Co-op in India was described in the *Polak w Indiach (Poles in India)* newspaper in 1944 by its founder Mr. Jan Pacak. He recalled three phases beginning with its inception in the Malir Camp, when the professional instructors were sought, availability of materials investigated, prices checked and the viability of dressmaking, shoe and toy workshops researched. Later in Valivade the second phase began investigating how many people were willing to invest in the Society. Family barracks were converted into workshops and equipped with machines and materials, finally entering into the proper work and development phase. The aim was to create a number of workshops, employing a maximum number of Camp inhabitants to train a future generation of master craftsmen, to propagate Polish folk art and secure funds for continuity of the work.

Certificate of course completion for Co-op managers and accountants

He acknowledged the difficult position of the Society abroad lacking master craftsmen and professional apprentice schools, but fortunate that its employees do not have to earn a living and pay taxes. Because equipment was supplied by the Ministry, the Society in return, apart from its normal commercial activity, felt obliged to provide vocational training and also serve some cultural propaganda.

The majority of the employees were either amateurs or complete novices. The younger ones usually still attended school but it was hoped that they would join the Co-op and get professionally qualified. The apprentices in the dressmaking, hairdressing and joinery workshops were mostly from the orphanage. The fact that the Co-op was good for our publicity was evident by the popularity of our folklore at a recent exhibition in Bombay where British, Indian and Czech customers bought our products. This was followed by orders for the folk costumes, dolls and embroidery despite relatively high prices.

Pacak also recollected that at the beginning they had to borrow Rs 50 from the Commandant, which after two months turned Rs 1,700 profit. Initially there was a lack of understanding on the part of the inhabitants, which changed when the Society employed 124 people earning between Rs 40 and 100 in addition to their monthly allowance of Rs 53.

In the second year of its existence in Valivade, the management of the

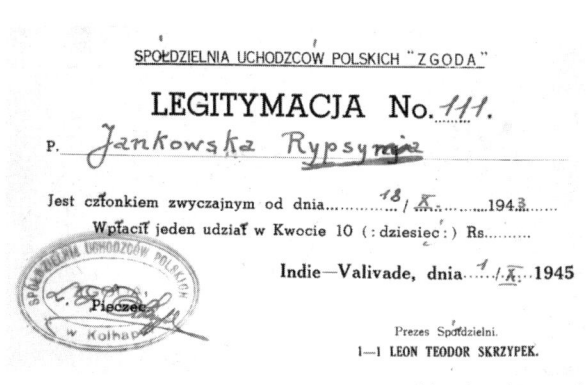

Membership card

Co-op was as follows: M. Ogibiński @ Rs 120 per month - Director of the Co-op, P. Masiulanis @ Rs 90 per month - his deputy and J. Klepacki - the Accountant @ Rs 40 per month.[6]

The article expressed hope that the trainees, despite being unable to compete with the local market, will learn some professional skills with which to return to Poland together with all the acquired equipment.[7]

The workshops

Mrs. A. Szarejko - seamstress school

Unable to find specific documentation relating to the workshops we were obliged to base this part of the chapter wholly on the article by Mrs. A. Kisielnicka in the Polish newspaper in India of Sep./Oct. 1944 entitled *The Achievements of One Year*:

"The clothing workshop started with 10 workers and now employs 52. Work consists of not only private orders but also orders from the Welfare Ministry and from other Camps as well as Valivade; theatre costumes, Scout and Fire Brigade uniforms. Anticipating orders from the British Army for uniform repairs, this workshop will require a larger number of employees.

Dolls and craft workshop employed 12-17 people. From its inception until March 1944 they produced embroidery, but chiefly dolls, which did not prove popular apart from one bulk purchase by Bata. Production then changed to much smaller, more artistic dolls, with moveable arms and legs. Ladies handbags and belts were made to order and dolls in Polish costumes were a good public relations ploy at the Bombay and Kolhapur exhibitions.

The weavers' workshop was set up for promotion of Polish Folk Art but it was also used for training pupils from 'The Village Husbandry Instructors' School'. It employed three instructors. Their tapestries and floor mats were becoming popular even amongst the Indians.

The shoe repair shop employed only 3-7 workers who dealt mainly with repairs. They also made 100 pairs of boots for the Security Guards and the Fire Brigade. There was little demand for made to measure, because people preferred to buy ready made shoes or sandals in Kolhapur, for which the town was famous. Although of inferior quality, they were inexpensive.

The shoe shop was created in March on the basis of a contract signed by the Delegate of the Ministry and the Bata Shoe Company. It was to supply shoes to be sold in the camp. The Co-op would receive 25%

Mrs. Klar - Dolls shop

Weaving workshop

of the sale price. In April they sold shoes to the value of Rs 1,030. In May for Rs 322, in June for Rs 811 and July for Rs 566. The explanation for such meagre sales was that Bata sent small quantities of quality shoes for which there was no demand.

The General Store was opened in August 1943. At the beginning its sales were limited to cakes, sweets, cigarettes and fruit, but later the shop was selling metal suitcases, raincoats and galoshes. It also increased its sales of products brought from Bombay, such as conserves, jam, etc. which were being sold cheaper than in the Syndicate shops. Soon they were also hoping to sell fats at competitive prices to stimulate healthy competition.

The canteen was created mainly for single people, for the workshop personnel and for visitors. It had 7 employees including two Indians. One could eat there for about Rs 50 per month, which was approximately the monthly allowance. There were about 80 regular customers. In May 1944, they undertook catering for the Scout and Girl Guide camps, for which they employed 4 Polish cooks and 4 Indian helpers to feed 130 people at a cost of Rs 20 per head. Although this action did not make profit, it did help in running the camps.

As soda water manufacture started in June this year just before the monsoon, it is too early to assess its development.

The joinery workshop served mainly the Camp Administration for repair of buildings school tables and benches. It employed 3-7 people.

A small metal workshop was virtually a repair shop consisting of 1-3 people who undertook private orders for domestic and kitchen use.

The masonry workshop had a Polish leader and 10 Indian workmen, who dealt with cement floors in common rooms and private kitchens, stone steps by the barracks and masonry work in the church, hospital and orphanage kitchen.

The barber's shop fulfilled the limited needs of the Camp.

The Co-op turnover for this period could be summarised as follows: from 1st August 1943 to the end of December was Rs 97,948 and for the next 6 months it was Rs 58,227. Altogether the turnover was Rs 356,275, which meant Rs 6,761 for the first month of its existence but in July 1944 it was Rs 46,073. This encouraging result proved

Shoe repairs

that the Co-op fulfilled the aspirations of its founders and the needs of the Camp providing employment and training to so many people. It also bears positive witness in the eyes of foreigners visiting the Camp."[8]

The reality was perhaps somewhat different if one was to read the reports of the Audit Office dated 1st October to 31st December 1943: "The barber's shop works at a loss because it has to pay an Indian professional barber, but any work for the orphanage remains unpaid by the Liaison Officer's order... There is a problem with the shoe repair shop because in its accounts it does not record the leather it receives free of charge from the Ministry. Likewise, when the Co-op shows its profit or earnings, the equipment or materials received are never listed; neither did it show the earnings of its staff (Rs 2,830 up to October 1943) because it was paid by the Employment Department of the Camp Administration."[9]

Resume of the Co-op enterprises

Lacking any subsequent documentation, it was difficult to follow Coop's further development and activity. But in June 1946 a note in the *Camp Chronicles* that: "...by the decree of an Indian Court of Kolhapur State the former director of the Co-op Society was condemned to one year of imprisonment with enforced labour and payment of Rs 200 back to the Society."[10] *(Not to be confused with J. Pacak, founder of the Camp Co-op.)*

We then learn from the same source that at the next AGM in September 1946 a new management was elected, with L. Skrzypek as the chairman, C. Polechowicz his deputy and I. Kasprowicz as financial director.[11]

Wł. Bidakowski - Joinery shop

Later, in June 1947 there is an article in the Polish newspaper entitled 'Rebirth of a useful institution" from which we learn that "...in September 1945, the Co-op was facing complete ruin with losses of Rs 2,500. They owed its employees Rs 4,500, but had only Rs 5 in the account..." How this came about we can only guess for the paper says that "...we do not want to go back to the distressing events generally known to all..." It then goes on to say that any sums owing were written off and earnings are now regularly paid, although shareholders cannot expect any profit for the time being. The employees earned Rs 50,000 in the meantime, which was considered best proof of the social usefulness of this enterprise![12]

Virtually at the end of the Camp's existence the Society was dissolved. The Chairman of the Supervisory Board, Mr. J. Sułkowski, who presided over its closure, confirmed that the Co-op in the final stage was very active, being lead very skillfully and energetically. The goods in their shops were cheaper than elsewhere which influenced the market prices of its competitors. All the shareholders shares increased by 20% profit. The final dissolution was to be carried out by representatives of the Federation of Poles in India and the Refugee Council. It was anticipated that Rs 2,000 would be left over, of which Rs 200 should be donated for the use of the Cultural Department and of the remainder 50% should go for warm clothing for children in the orphanage, 40% to schools and 10% for social aid to be administered by the Federation. Final liquidation was envisaged for January 1948.[13]

As we could not find full documentation relating to the Co-op enterprises, we are unable to give a balanced picture. For example we do not know its starting capital nor the value of its subsidies in the form of equipment and materials. We do know however that the salaries of its personnel were paid out of the Camp's budget, but we did not find accounts of its running costs and earnings.

Commercial considerations aside, it could be said that the Co-op's activity was a success for it gave employment to a number of people, provided vocational training to some and undoubtedly had the desired propaganda effect.

But even if the quoted events show divergence between intentions and reality it must be said that our 5 year stay in India showed that we did not passively await our fate and the outcome of the war.

The Polish printing press

(sitting): L. Benal, Fr. A. Jankowski, A. Świergoń, Z. Żerebecki, Mrs. Piórkowska, M. Chmielowiec, ..., ...

The history of this press was described in some detail in the Polish newspaper by Mrs. A. Kisielnicka: "... When at the end of 1945 the Country Club was being liquidated, Mr. L. Benal and the management of the Co-op, *Społem (Together)* decided to purchase a printing press from the proceeds of the sale. Thus Rs 5,000 was donated by the Co-op and Rs 1,500 by the *NCWC (National Catholic Welfare Conference)* to purchase a printing press which was then installed in Valivade in May 1946. Some sets of type were borrowed from Bombay but nobody knew how to operate the machine. A volunteer was found and sent to Kolhapur for training. There they had to use sign language because naturally nobody spoke Polish and only a few managed some English. Upon his return he had to train his assistants with the help of an English technical manual.

The work began with the orders for circulars and office forms for the Camp Administration. This was followed by the 200 page manual on teacher training with other booklets and brochures later.

In October of the same year the press was transferred into the ownership of the *NCWC* in the belief that this will guarantee its existence in this uncertain period, before being shipped to Poland. As the Interim Treasury Committee was being wound up, a sum of Rs 1,157/9 was donated for the training of typesetters. The course was completed by about 40 young people which later on enabled the Polish newspaper *Polak w Indiach* to be printed in the Camp every Saturday despite the fact that within a few months its very existence was questionable. At the same time more type was purchased to facilitate the paper's production."[14]

In addition to the printing shop there was also a bookbinding workshop, managed by Bronisław Janowski and funded by the Cultural and Educational

Mr. A. Świergoń at printing press

Department. The workshop was of great importance as Polish books were scarce and those used in schools and libraries were in constant use requiring frequent repair.

For an epilogue let me quote from the last edition of the Polish paper dated 20th February 1948: "Because of the disposal of our printing press, we had no choice but to entrust it to the Indian printers in Kolhapur. This firm had only just been established and the printing of our newspaper was to them of considerable importance, but its main typesetter did not speak Polish or English, and could not read or write in any language. He was also deaf. We hope therefore that our readers will forgive numerous printers errors..."

Translated and abridged by Jan and Barbara Siedlecki

NOTES

1. AAN: file no 88 (Styburski writings of 16 and 21 May 1943)
2. AAN: monthly report for December 1943 from the Camp Management
3. AAN: monthly report for August 1943 from the Delegate of the Ministry
4. AAN as no. 2
5. JAG/KPI archives
6. PwI: 15.III-1.IV.1944
7. JAG/KPI archives
8. PwI: 15.III-1.IV.1944
9. JAG/KPI: report no 6 of the Board of Control (1.X-31.XII.1943)
10. IP&MS: (Polish Institute and Sikorski Museum) Camp Chronicles C811/b & c
11. ibid
12. PwI: no 7 (7.VI.1947)
13. PwI: no 35/36 24.XII.1947
14. PwI: no 6 (8.V.1947)

Private Enterprise

Mr. M. Bereźnicki with son Józef and other employees

Apart from 'official' employment in the Co-op, etc. there also eventually developed some private enterprise, of which some examples are quoted.

Typical were the products of a pork butcher Mr. Ławniczek. The second butcher's shop was established by Mr. M. Bereźnicki where our school friend Feliks Zając worked. The premises were by the river and they worked during the night manufacturing continental meat sausages. They had to work fast because the meat was not yet minced in the evening but by the morning it had to be delivered to the shops in the market. For his night's work Feliks would receive 1 rupee and a ring of sausage. The third butcher was Mr. Romaniuk who had been a game keeper employed in the forests of Count Kaszycki. His speciality was sausages made from small black pigs reminiscent of wild boar in Poland. How was it that in a country where they do not eat pork, where cows are 'sacred', where refrigerators were unheard of, nobody suffered from food poisoning?

Apart from these men there were quite a number of women engaged in cooking dinners on their little stoves for those who could not spare the time. These precooked meals were sold much in the manner as present day 'take away' food.

Some of our ladies were gainfully employed in making dresses and children's wear. Mrs. P. Wilczyńska had a draper's shop and frequently travelled to Bombay for her purchases.

There was also the photographic shop of Messrs Pitura & Zajkowski and freelance photographers Mr. Klimsiak and Mr. Bachrynowski.

A cosmetic salon provided skin care with the aid of various creams and at Mr. Skrzydlewski's hair salon one could get a permanent wave.

Opposite the main entrance to the Camp Mr. Szustek had a cafe with most excellent cakes where one could socialise with friends.

Mr. Wróblewski released from the Army, made shoes to measure, but Mr. Zawistowicz, previously employed on the railways could only manage repairs.

Just outside the perimeter of the Camp was an Indian bazaar or market where one could buy all the fruit and vegetables needed, also ground nuts in molasses. Some Polish shops were also there: Mr. Tysko was selling 'poteen' a home made vodka from bananas. There were other shops with dress making material brought over from Bombay or Poona by our enterprising compatriots.

LIST OF NAMES OF EMPLOYEES OF THE WORKS DEPARTMENT
(according to the report for November 1944 of the Camp Commandants Office to the Ministry of Social Welfare)

Ogibiński Marian	Klepacki Józef	Adamczak Wojciech
Masiulanis Piotr	Górska Maria	Świergoń Antoni
Krajewska Wincentyna	Wojciechowska Elżbieta	Pobereźniczenko Tadeusz
Adamek Maria	Lipiński Andrzej	Stępniewska Leokadia
Bidakowski Witold	Grobel Lucyna	Latawiec Marcin
Czekaj Ignacy	Pelc Jan	Tkaczyk Franciszek
Ziubrzycki Bronisław	Królikowska Stanisława	

JAN PACAK (1900-1982)
by W. Kleszko

His personality embodied two passions of land surveying as a profession and his love of music. As a student of Lwów Polytechnic he was in the internationally famous choir. Later he established and led choirs in the catholic organisations. Then came the war and deportation to the Soviet Union.[1]

Shortly after the "amnesty" in 1941, he arrived in Kazakhstan and as the official representative of the Polish Embassy was helping to organise the gathering of deportees from various labour camps in Russia. He helped to establish school classes, an orphanage, even a club room and some work places. These consisted of dressmaking, knitting, shoe repairs and hairdressing, working for the local population on a barter basis.[2] He also developed a social life, organising commemorative meetings for the national days and gatherings for Sunday mass in the club until the final evacuation to Persia.

Coming to Tehran he was a deputy commander for the part of the Camp No. 2 from October 1942 to January 1943. For the Cultural Department he organised a Polish Peoples' Theatre, which gave many performances in various camps and in the town itself. The show which had a good propaganda value was called: "Polish children for the children of Iran". He also built a loom and experimented with hand woven and knitted fabrics employing women in the camp.[3]

Later in the camps Country Club and Malir, in India, he continued his work directing the Peoples' Theatre. In May 1943 at a farewell performance for the departing crew of the Polish ship *Kościuszko*, Rs 80 was collected for parcels for Polish POWs in Germany.[4]

In July 1943 Pacak arrived with his family in Valivade where he headed the Works Department from August 1943 to April 1944 and established the co-op. In time the Pacak family moved to Panchgani where his wife Urszula worked as a guardian for the sick children and from February 1945 she was a teacher for the High School courses[5] while Mr. Pacak was the head of Social Activities. There he led a choir in the Convent of St. Joseph and organised the Polish amateur dramatic show *Cracovian Wedding* which went on tour. Unfortunately misunderstandings connected with the proposed show in Belgaum resulted in his resignation. After taking professional employment outside the Centre.[6] He would then visit his family at weekends until the end of November 1946 when the Centre was closed.

In 1950 he left India to settle in Perth, Western Australia, where he worked as a surveyor in the Land Department. In his leisure time he enthused some 70 Polish children and organised a song and dance group. With the financial backing of the Polish Combatants Association (SPK) the troupe developed, eventually acquiring its own costumes. In time it became known as *Young Mazowsze* (alluding to famous Polish State song and dance company).[7]

In 1980 Mr. and Mrs. Pacak joined their daughter Ewa in Adelaide, where he died in 1982.

Translated by Jan K. Siedlecki

NOTES
1. Catholic Weekly
2. Polish Weekly
3. Commandant of Camp No. 2 Report dated 8.3.1943
4. Formal Handover Report
5. Appointment's letter
6. Department of Social Welfare letter
7. Catholic Weekly

SOCIAL WELFARE
by Jan K. Siedlecki

To describe the care provided for the refugees I refer to the series of articles entitled *Polish Social Welfare in India - Development of its Institutions and Care Centres*. These were published in a Polish paper *Polak w Indiach* in April 1946, in which a summary is made of their activities up to the end of existence of the Polish Government in London in July 1945, the previous year when it ceased to be internationally recognised and could no longer provide assistance to its citizens. The Polish Consulate in Bombay, the Delegates of the Ministry of Social Welfare and the Ministry of Education also ceased to function. In their place, a Polish Welfare Committee in India was set up, representing the Interim Treasury Committee for Polish Questions, in London. Our social care continued, but in a changed form.

The problems of looking after its refugees was already recognised by the Polish Government in March 1942, when it established a separate Agency inside its Legation in Teheran. This Agency created by the Foreign Office was of a political nature and in August 1943 it was changed into the Ministry of Social Welfare initially incorporating an Educational Section. It was noted how difficult it was to find suitably qualified personnel, bearing in mind that most of the men were either in the Army or were left behind in Russia (murdered in Katyń). It must be remembered that at the time most of the women did not work professionally.

The last article in the series entitled *The Bright and Dark Side of Exile (Blaski i Cienie Uchodźstwa)* is probably most interesting because it sheds some light on our stay in India: "The happiness that we feel for not being left behind in Russia and our lives not being dictated by the NKVD (later known as KGB) is perhaps difficult to describe... In India we have regained a sense of stability. Individual living accommodation with its own cooking facilities gave the women an impression of domestic independence although husbands, the usual breadwinners were missing. For a few, life was even better than before the war. Every woman was able to take care of her family. Her children were clothed and were being educated. In addition some women were able to acquire further education or vocational skills.

At the same time as a result of not being able or rather not having to work, some people acquired an unhealthy attitude to work and money. This does not show us in a favourable light in the eyes of the British Authorities in India who then demand a reduction in our allowance... On the whole however we do not intend to stay, not only because of the climate and our inability to work here, but even if India was to agree for us to remain, we could not compete with the local labour. Besides people have faith in the Authorities to enable them to join their husbands in whatever countries of the Commonwealth would have them."[1]

Maintenance

In the same series of articles we found information on how we were cared for: "...the initial supply of clothing was distributed from the camp stores. But according to the survey carried out at the beginning of 1944, people expressed their preference for receiving money to purchase clothing. This was set at Rs 60 per person per year. It has also to be mentioned that a special agency in the Delegate's Welfare Section in Bombay had considerable problems with obtaining these supplies, as during the war, the market was very limited. Bulk purchases had to be made through a special Polish Commission or through local Government Supplies. Such a Department or even a War Department would indicate where and how the purchases are to be made. Furthermore such departments would check and control the price and quality of the goods. This was little known to our refugees, causing some unpleasant suspicions. The market was also curtailed because of priority exercised by the Military".

Having started with the 1946 newspaper articles I would now like to go back to describe the beginnings and quote from the Welfare Office report for June-August 1943 that "the Agency dealing with supplies exists only in theory because of the lack of suitably qualified personnel. It would appear that such a nucleus existed in the Consulate which had been there for some years and therefore had more knowledge in this field. It could therefore carry out the most immediate purchases. What was needed however was a long term purchasing plan. The purchases were being sent directly to the camps from firms which were then paid by the Welfare Office.

The Polish refugees coming out of Persia were very unevenly clothed, but now they are more or less fully equipped. Although they came out of Russia with nothing, they should have enough basic belongings to take with them upon their return to Poland."[2]

As stated before, the people preferred receiving money to make their own purchases instead of being supplied by the Authorities who seemed unable to cope with the situation. Nevertheless, before the vote was taken, people were provided for in the first months of their arrival in the camp. According to the same series of articles referred to before, some of the quotas allocated to each person were as follows:

2 men's shirts	3 shirts	1 mattress and pillow
3 boy's shirts	3 skirts	4 bedsheets
2 pairs of men's shorts	3 blouses	4 pillow cases
3 pairs of boy's shorts	2 brassieres	1 blanket or eiderdown
2 pairs of pyjamas	3 pairs of drawers	2 towels and bath towel
3 pairs of underpants	8 yds of dress material	1 toothbrush
2 vests	2 night shirts	1 night pot
1 pith helmet (m/f)	3 sanitary towels	1 washing-up bowl
1 pair of sandals (m/f)	1 comb (m/f)	1 paraffin lamp

Plus a tea kettle - a mug and milk jug - two plates - knife, fork and spoon - two cooking pots - two buckets -a washing-up bowl - two charcoal stoves - two tea towels one floor broom. In addition each domestic unit was equipped with 1 dining + 1 kitchen table, 3 chairs, 3 beds and 3 mosquito nets with frames, 1 dressing table with mirror and 1 shelf.

With regard to the clothing allowance mentioned before, the following prices should be noted as recorded in the Camp management report for December 1943: "...Rs 12 for one pair of shoes, Rs 12-20 for a woman's dress, Rs 1-2 per yard for underwear material, Rs 20 for a man's khaki shorts with one bush jacket and Rs 200 for a woollen suit".[3]

Cost of living

During the visit to Delhi of the Polish Welfare Minister Jan Stańczyk in April 1943, a divergence of views became apparent between the Government of India and the Polish Authorities, especially regarding the so called 'cultural uplift'. This was extra or additional money being spent on education or other cultural activities. At this conference a *pro memoria* entitled *Problems concerning Polish Refugees* was discussed and presented as follows: "... the Government of India shall be asked to provide sufficient funds to cover the cost of any expenditure for the Polish Camps. This should not only be for the refugee maintenance and administration of the Camps, but also for their education and cultural expenses, together with health services and other expenses deemed appropriate by the Delegate."[4]

The Polish newspaper in India wrote on the same subject in April 1946: "the Delegate for Social Welfare was receiving funds directly from its Ministry in London for previously agreed purposes, such as maternity allowance for women released from the Army, anti-malaria clothing in Jamnagar (boots and long sleeve shirts) monsoon clothing (raincoats and rubber boots) and special equipment for orphans, including tin suitcases. Out of this fund the Army Families Association in Valivade was financed and an additional supplement for the orphanage, expenditure on culture and education, like the Polish newspaper *Polak w Indiach* and other books, papers and magazines, payment for another representative's office in Karachi, Polish doctors and some personnel in the camp there. In addition there was a 'Central Budget' for all the Polish Refugee Camps which were administered by the Government of India. Out of these, funds were allocated for purposes previously agreed with the Polish Authorities. The Social Welfare Office also paid for the Camp's priests, cultural and educational work and for specific supplements to the maintenance allowance."

At the same conference in April 1943, we find a confidential note referring to an understanding in the Government of India circles, that funds advanced to the Polish Government will be written off after the war like other debts of this kind. In his report of October 1942 Capt. Webb writes: "...that it would be unfair to have the Polish refugees maintained in better conditions than the British tax payer, who is already paying for them (irrespective of the final outcome) and will continue to pay for some years..."[5]

This sentiment was prevalent at the time and it was influencing the attitude of the Government of India, which insisted on the greatest possible savings and control over expenditure, so that it does not exceed basic requirements. They were against excessive administration, and extras such as children's pocket money, which was considered unjustifiable in war time. Concern was also expressed regarding the repayment of funds spent on the Polish refugees by their own government, basing it on the same principle as applied to British refugees.

On 23rd September 1943 Capt. Webb wrote to the Polish Delegate: "...referring to the misunderstanding between your office and the Government of India, which came about due to a different viewpoint. We do not oppose individual items which have already been approved in the Camp budget, but we would object to the 'inflation supplement' which could in fact create the inflation. If there is a difference of opinion, I trust we can settle it on the spot, without referring to London, but let us hope we will not have many such incidents. We want to keep the expenditure on the Polish refugees at the lowest possible level, but within the bounds of acceptability. This outlay is higher than for any other nationality of refugees. In the circumstances, without jumping on your duties, I hope you will understand our position."[6] To which Mr. Styburski replied: "...we understand perfectly the war conditions we live in and have no intention to press demands that would diminish local supplies. With regard to the Camp budgets, we consider them adequate for our needs. But it must be pointed out that our refugees who lived through Soviet deprivations, have a greater than average claim because their health and general wellbeing needs rebuilding. We value friendly relations with local population and we hope for a better understanding in the future."[7]

It is also of interest to quote a paragraph from the Polish Consul Dr. Banasiński's report dated 9th July 1944 in which he states that: "...any plans, estimates and accounts for building the Camp which would concern our treasury regarding repayment of the debt... these documents are in the archives of the Government of India and will be submitted to the Polish Government c/o British Government for repayment, together with any expenditure connected with their *(Polish refugees)* stay in India. All this to be finalised and presented after their departure and when all accounts are closed"[8] Unfortunately we were unable to find any such documents in the India Office Records.

Going back to the visit of Mr. J. Stańczyk (Minister of Social Welfare) to India in May 1943, his Delegate in Bombay wrote at the time: "...the whole expenditure connected with the maintenance of refugees in the Camps, must be included in the budget financed by the Government of India. This should include not only provision of food, accommodation, clothing and health service, but also anything to do with education, vocational training and the creation of workshops etc. On the other hand the cost of the administration should be paid directly by our Government in London, but within the framework of agreed budgets."[9] Unfortunately his advice was not followed or the administration apparatus would have had more freedom.

Food allowance

As the great majority of the Camp inhabitants were self catering, the expenditure for food was by far the biggest part of the general allowance. It is therefore useful to note prices (in rupees) for some products, as quoted by the Office of Social Welfare in Bombay in their report for December 1943:[10]

1 lb of bread	= 0/5/0	1 lb of mutton	= 0/8/0
1 lb of flour	= 0/4/6	1 lb of olive oil	= 0/7/6
1 lb of rice	= 0/5/6	1 lb of coffee	= 2/0/0
1 lb of milk	= 1/0/0	1 lb of tea	= 1/4/0
1 lb of butter	= 1/10/0	1 lb of potatoes	= 0/5/0 to 0/7/0
1 dozen eggs	= 1/4/0	1 lb of onions	= 0/1/0 to 0/4/6
1 lb of molasses	= 0/6/0	24 lbs of charcoal	= 1/8/0
2 lbs of sugar	= 0/7/0	1 lb of cooking fat	= 2/0/0

Estimated daily cost at the time was Rs 2/3/0 per adult and Rs 1/10/0 per child.

According to the Delegate's report for July 1943, people arriving at the Camp were fed for the first two days from a communal kitchen before catering for themselves.

Their monthly allowance was as follows:
adults (over 16 years) Rs 43/12/0 + pocket money of Rs 10/0/0	= Rs 53/12/0
teenagers (over 12 years) Rs 40/0/0 + pocket money of Rs 5/0/0	= Rs 45/00/0
children (over 6 years) Rs 28/0/0 and no pocket money	= Rs 28/00/0
children (below 6 years) Rs 25/00/0 and no pocket money	= Rs 25/00/0

The allowance for older children was adequate, but the situation of the younger ones was worse because the British insisted that they ate less. The Polish Authorities did not agree with this and wanted it to be increased.[11]

In the Camp management report for December 1943 we read that (for the time being) salaried refugees, or those receiving financial help from the relatives in the Army were not entitled to the pocket money.[12]

The last table from which we can draw comparisons was quoted in the UNRRA Camp budget dated September 1947. Although the totals remain the same for adults and teenagers the composition of the monthly allowance is altered by reducing money for the food and adding some for inflation. At the same time by allowing inflation and pocket money for the children, their monthly allowance was increased from Rs 28 to 45 and from Rs 25 to 35.[13]

It must be pointed out that the 'allowance' was mainly for food, whilst the 'pocket money' was for all other expenses like soap, etc. This money and the 'inflation supplement' were a bone of contention between the British and Polish authorities in 1944 described in the chapter on Polish Offices in Bombay. It is interesting to read what Lt. Col. C.W.L. Harvey (Kolhapur Resident) wrote to Lt. Col. Neate (Polish Camp Commandant) on 10th October 1946: "Europeans, (even the lower Polish classes) could hardly exist on Rs 70 per month... even if Poles are given extra for clothing, but this has also risen in price considerably. Then there are such items as household utensils, bed linen, lighting, fuel, soap, cosmetics and occasional cinema... One has to be very frugal to live for less than Rs 100... perhaps reduced by 10% or 15% for other members of the same family... How they manage to live on the miserable pittance they receive at present, I cannot understand and can only think they must have financial help from outside... For the really poor, I feel Rs 100 per month is a minimum..."[14]

It is interesting to see the difference in assessment of our needs between Capt. Webb - Principal Refugee Officer (Sep. 1943) and Lt. Col. Harvey (the man 'on the spot' 3 years later). But it also contradicts his statement in Feb. 1946 when he wrote about 'spending power of the Poles (see chapter on the Food Supply).

In support of his argument he then quotes the following examples: his 'messenger boy' was earning Rs 24 in 1943, but now earns Rs 37/12/0, i.e. 50% more. According to S. M. Pardeshi (Syndicate Contractor) inflation was 50% in the last two years, whilst the Resident claimed it to be 75%. He also pointed out that Kolhapur was not a cheap place to live in. It was dearer than Poona, but cheaper than Bombay.

In conclusion it must be said that our allowances did not keep pace with inflation and it must have been hard for our mothers, especially those not working or those without a husband in the Army, to keep us properly clothed and fed. It is also difficult to draw an accurate picture of the situation, because with the collapse of our Government in London, its sources of information ceased and when we passed into the care of UNRRA the documentation is primarily British and therefore one-sided.

Comparison of Camp budgets

1. Valivade Camp was built and furnished to receive 5,000 Polish refugees on the ground leased by the Kolhapur Durbar [15] Rs 3,200,000
2. Monthly budget for the maintenance of its inhabitants (approved in August 1943) [16] 236,871
   Initial outlay for equipping the Camp Rs 60,750
3. April-May 1944 budget (with amendments) increased [17] 336,152
4. Monthly budget from October 1944 increased [18] 351,138
   Plus one off additions Rs 22,850
5. Average monthly budget financed by the Interim Treasury Committee, as from 1st October 1945 [19] 213,235

6. Monthly budget of the Camp, including the refugees from Balachadi and Panchgani (1 Aug - 31 Dec 1946) [20] 304,664

7. As of September 1947 monthly budget was reduced due to its inhabitants dispersal [21] 244,323

It is difficult to give a full picture of the expenditure when dealing only with the available fragments. Maintenance for the Camp and its inhabitants was paid for by the Government of India, which was then reimbursed by our Government in London. All these transactions are properly documented. But any direct grants from the Polish Ministries to their Delegates in Bombay are very confusing because in their accounts for Welfare or Education, it is almost impossible to find which funds were allocated in the Camp budget by the Government of India and which came from London.

Finally as an example of British distrust, it might be interesting to quote from Capt. Webb's memorandum dated July 1943: "Polish officials are apt to oppose any detailed financial control. They would prefer to have global sums of money which they could dispose of as they wish. This would save a lot of work for the Government of India, but it is not what is understood to be our responsibility to the British Government. Therefore we would gladly undertake such a task if it be the wish of HMG. There are ongoing discussions on the subject between the Government of India and the Polish Authorities."[22]

Whilst it is understandable that the Polish officials wanted to have control over details of the expenditure, especially as it was a loan, it must be said that their approach tended to be rather bureaucratic.

Translated and abridged by the Author

NOTES

1. *Polak w Indiach:* no.8/66 April 1946
2. AAN: file no. 85 pp 167-168
3. ibid
4. IP&MS.: Dr. E. Banasiński (coll. 129)
5. IP&MS: Dr. E. Banasiński (coll. 129) no.126/L42 Poll. Evn.
6. IP&MS: Dr. E. Banasiński (coll. 129)
7. ibid
8. ibid
9. AAN: file no. 88
10. AAN: file no. 85
11. ibid
12. ibid
13. IOR: L/AG/40/1/131 (RRO/A-5)
14. IOR: R2 (953/82)
15. IOR: as no. 13
16. IOR: L/P&J/8/413 (coll. 110/N/2)
17-19. IOR: L/AG/40/1/169 ('A' ring file)
20. IOR: L/P&J/8/414 (coll. 110/N/3)
21. IOR: L/AG/40/1/131 (RRO/A-5)
22. IOR: L/P&J/8/412 (coll. 110/N/1)

THE FOOD SUPPLY
by Jan K. Siedlecki

How many of us, growing up in India can truthfully recollect what was the food situation then? We were more interested in Scouting and school exams. Food was for our mothers to worry about. We had the impression that food was plentiful and prepared mainly in the traditional Polish way. We were unaware of any shortages, which must have been to the credit of the Authorities and our mothers who are no longer here to correct that memory. We still recall our stay in India as one of the most memorable periods in our lives. If it was not for the war, its consequences and our uncertain future, we could almost have been happy. This would be a natural reaction after the deprivations suffered in Russia. It could also be argued that we were simply oblivious of the reality, as reading contemporary documents the situation was far from rosy.

To start at the beginning, I quote from the report of the Delegate for the Social Welfare Ministry for August 1943 which was only in the second month of our arrival in Valivade. Initially there were some problems with the food supply and some inconvenience in purchasing due to the inadequate number of shops. These difficulties were overcome when the Supply Syndicate became acquainted with the quantity and the type of food required. The situation also improved when individual private shops were established at the perimeter of the Camp. The inhabitants were warned however not to buy eggs or meat there because it could be unhygienic due to the hot climate. The Camp security guards were to make sure that this regulation is strictly adhered to. Cleanliness in the Syndicate shops is good and the people are pleased with this state of affairs, which will further improve once the Cooperative will establish shops. I am not sure that the Coop ever intended to compete with the Syndicate. A few months later in December 1943, the Camp management stated that apart from sugar, there did not appear to be any system of rationing for the local European population and our refugees were treated in the same manner.

General food situation in India

The British and Indian point of view can best be illustrated by documents found in the India Office Records on which most of the material in this chapter is based. It should also be noted that after the withdrawal of international recognition of our Government in London, reports from its Delegates abroad ceased and I had to rely on British documentation only.

At that time the food situation in India was very much influenced by the war and food was mostly reserved for the Military.

In the initial stages of the camp's existence there was also famine in Bengal which was kept secret by the British Authorities. Food distribution was controlled in every state and the sudden influx of Polish refugees with different dietary demands must have caused problems for the Local Authorities. This was not generally appreciated by the Camp inhabitants.

Two years after setting up of the Camp, the Resident of Kolhapur wrote to the Government in Delhi in July 1945 ..."no difficulty is envisaged in respect of the food grains or sugar, but fuel, eggs, vegetables and dairy produce are barely sufficient for the local population. Because of these shortages, the Syndicate has to pay above the controlled prices to ensure supplies to the Camp... Also there are no restrictions on the Poles to go farther afield to obtain supplies"... This will be further aggravated by the increase of the Camp population from 3,000 to 4,700.

When the situation deteriorated six months later, the Prime Minister of Kolhapur wrote to the Resident in January 1946: "Food and civil supplies were expected to be the responsibility of the Central Government. This has not happened causing hardship to the people of Kolhapur and owing to the local crops failure the situation became worse. Difficulty is encountered in negotiating the wheat quota from the Punjab Government... so the Kolhapur Durbar finds it almost impossible to feed the Camp from day to day."

This was confirmed on 13th March, the political department in New Delhi wrote to the Resident that ..."Kolhapur State is one of the areas in South India badly affected by drought and the State is finding it difficult to feed its own population".[1]

Misunderstanding

Apart from the general food situation in India and the Deccan States in particular, one has to look also at the misunderstanding which arose when the Central Government asked the Kolhapur Durbar in February 1943 to accept the Polish refugee camp. Just before that in January there was a telegram directing the Durbar "to ensure import of food supplies e.g. flour and wheat for feeding the Poles and not to endanger local supplies",[2] but in May of the same year there is a note from the Food Department written to the Home Department "... not withstanding any undertaking which may have been given to Kolhapur Durbar (*of which there was no record*) it is regretted that at present it is impossible that allotment of foodstuffs for Polish refugees can be made."

Later in 1945 according to the Resident, the problems that caused most inconvenience were "...the inroads made by the Poles on very limited resources of foods..." The Kolhapur Durbar confronted the Central Government in Delhi to fulfil its commitment. This perhaps was the reason for the outburst of the Kolhapur Minister of Education Rao Saheb G.B. Deshmukh (*he was also in charge of Civic Supplies and Rationing*) who wrote in February 1945 to the Central Authorities in Delhi that: "...complete rationing has been introduced in the city... but the Polish Camp, which is practically a suburb of Kolhapur does not have any... In addition to the uncontrolled supplies they get from the Syndicate and bazaar outside... the Poles flock to the city in great numbers... At the beginning it was expected that the Authorities of the Camp would observe orderliness in respect of purchases of the controlled articles, but it is apparent that the Poles perhaps due to the impression that they have immunity from punishment... not only resort to continuous black marketeering, but are also in perpetual imposition of the limited supplies of the State. Therefore rationing should be extended to the Camp... and *(we)* propose isolation of the Camp..."

Two days later, the Kolhapur Prime Minister's Office comments about the extremely poor Poles "being prepared to pay very high prices for food, but that a month ago when the

Poles tried to pay controlled prices, the rascally locals would not sell them any and for some days after they nearly starved." Months later in July, Capt. Webb pointed out that "local shopkeepers were beneficiaries but the State acceptance of the Camp brought with it certain responsibilities." The Government of India assured the Kolhapur Durbar that they will supply grain to the Polish Camp... and suggested that supplies be made available... on the same basis of rationing as supplied to the Army.

The Supply Syndicate

Before moving to the actual problems of supply and rationing we must look at the role played by the 'Syndicate'. Presumably it was created not just for monopolistic commercial reason but also to relieve the Local Authority of the responsibility of maintaining the Polish Refugee Camp. The 'Supply Syndicate to the Polish Refugee Waliwada Camp was established on 20th May 1943 "...to erect and maintain on site, or several sites *(shops)* in the Camp Waliwada Park... to supply goods at rates not higher than market prices... subject to the approval of... an officer of the Government of India, an officer of Kolhapur State and two Polish officials... The Syndicate shall consist of two parties... The first one being the Governor General in Council and the second being the four named persons: Col. N. D. Ingle, Shirmant B. A. Mahagonakar, Shankarlal Pardeshi and R. A. Kittur, who as security will be required to deposit Rs 25,000 each in the initial account of the Syndicate... The management of this enterprise to be entrusted to Mr. Pardeshi."

All this was perfectly satisfactory before local competition materialised and before shortcomings in the foodstuffs' supply manifested themselves. The situation changed when in May 1945 Capt. Webb felt obliged to write to the Liaison Officer, Mrs. M. Button that the food difficulties were caused by obtaining the supplies within the State limits. He proposed therefore that in future all foodstuffs be obtained outside the State and to prohibit their purchase within, either by the Syndicate or the Poles themselves. He insisted also that the Syndicate must become the sole source of supply. When in July Capt. Webb met the Kolhapur Authorities it was agreed that "the food shortages have arisen due to the Poles". Furthermore it was proposed to prohibit the local merchants or shopkeepers from trading in the Camp and ways of making the Poles buy only from the Syndicate was also discussed.

A few days later the Kolhapur Residency wrote to New Delhi: "...as there is *(food)* shortage, the Syndicate has to pay above controlled prices to ensure supplies to the Camp... also there are no restrictions on the Poles to go farther afield to obtain supplies... This will be further aggravated by increase in the Camp population from 3,000 to 4,700... Therefore the Kolhapur Regency Council is now asking the Government of India to implement its undertaking and provide supplies to the camp... and as the Civil Government has no organisation for this, it was suggested that the supplies be provided through the Military... and that the monthly requirements be provided to the Syndicate, which is licensed by Durbar to open shops in the Camp."

In January 1946 there was a shortage of bread in the Camp. So it was suggested that if the bread baking facilities in Kolhapur were inadequate, the Syndicate could bake it in the Camp. Almost simultaneously, in March, there seemed to be shortage of eggs and it was proposed that purchases should be made from 15 adjoining villages. The Syndicate expressed readiness to undertake this but was awaiting price agreement.

An incident illustrating the atmosphere at the time is given by quoting from a letter of September 1946, written by the Chairman of the Polish Refugee Council Mgr. J. Pawłowski to the Camp Commandant. He complained that although Mr. A. Klecki *(the quartermaster of the Valivade orphanage)* was granted permission to purchase food 'outside' the State with the full knowledge of the Syndicate managers, the local police prevented him doing so at the request of the Syndicate. The Council therefore asked for the 'free market to be reinstated for all foodstuffs because by granting a monopoly to the Syndicate costs had escalated above the *(monetary)* allowance received by the Refugees'... and as this episode illustrates 'the Syndicate is terrorising the Poles.'

The question of rationing

We can recollect no rationing in the Camp but it is interesting to recall the general background. It could be that because of Minister Rao Saheb's letter of 12th February 1945, Capt. Webb when writing in May to the Liaison Officer of the Camp, suggests that the current difficulties were caused by purchases made inside the Kolhapur State. He proposes that the Syndicate and the Poles should be prohibited from shopping inside the State boundaries. At the same time he is asking where at present does the Syndicate buy its supplies and points out, that if there is rationing in Kolhapur, the Camp should conform to the same principle.

Later on our Delegate for the Social Welfare Ministry, at a meeting with Capt. Webb in June, suggests that if the purchases are made outside the State, rationing should be adapted to the Polish diet and also advises that additional food be allocated to the Camp.

According to the Minister's request a list of Camp requirements was prepared in June 1945, but when sending it to Capt. Webb, Mrs. Button admits to having no knowledge of where the present purchases are made, because they are not carried out centrally and her guess would be within 60-70 miles radius. She also reported that rationing is definitely in force in Kolhapur for particular items like kerosene, sugar and basic corn and that the Authorities intend to introduce it in the Camp although Polish needs would be totally different. Poles require meat, eggs, butter, milk, potatoes, fruit and vegetables, which are precisely the items in short supply in Kolhapur. If the Government of India was to take responsibility for supplying the Camp, Local Authorities would implement rationing there.

In the same letter, referring to the 'token money' suggested by Capt. Webb some time ago, Mrs. Button thought it best if it only related to purchases inside the Camp. However, this could create difficulties when shopping 'outside' for items not supplied by the Syndicate and provided the Durbar was not against Poles shopping in the City. To implement this, part of the refugee allowance would have to be paid in 'real' money.

Six months later the Premier of Kolhapur suggested to the Resident that the Camp should be isolated, i.e. the Poles should be forbidden to shop in Kolhapur and outside the perimeter of the Camp for such products as milk, eggs, fruit, bread and butter ...at the same time offering to distribute such commodities as soon as the Central Government supplies them from outside.

Although the question of rationing in the Camp was previously discussed, it was not introduced, but the cost of its implementation was given in a letter dated 13th March 1946, from the Minister Rao Saheb G. B. Deshmukh to the Director of Food Supplies in the Deccan States: "...it is estimated at Rs 5,000 per annum, but also Rs 1,000 would be required for the initial set (cards, forms, permits) and employment of staff: one assistant rationing officer, one assistant inspector, two clerks and two peons salaries of Rs 4,300 per annum."

The problem with food supplies

A special conference was called on 28th January 1946 attended by Lt. Col. C.W.C. Harvey (the Resident), Capt. E.W.M. Magor (secretary), E. Perry (Premier of Kolhapur), Rao Saheb G.B. Deshmukh (Minister of Education and Food Supplies), Lt. Col. A.C.B. Neate (Polish Camp Commandant) and S.M. Pardeshi (General Manager for the Syndicate).

Condensed minutes of the meeting, together with a resume of extracts from the letter written by the Resident on 12th February 1946 to the Department of Food in New Delhi is given below:

1. "The Kolhapur Regency Council tried their best, but with scarcity of food and spending power of the Poles, it is obliged to ask for help as it was forced to provide 'large quantities of non-indigenous foodstuffs to a voracious alien population".

2. On the understanding that the food will be forthcoming from elsewhere, the Kolhapur Durbar accepted the Polish Camp. The Food Department then asked the Durbar to supply the Camp with 2 tons of rice and 50 tons of wheat per annum. It was established at the time that the Camp will require on a monthly basis:

60 tons of bread	60 tons of meat or fish	30 tons of fresh vegetables
26 tons of milk	13 tons of sugar	8 tons of onions
4.5 tons of cooking oil	200 tons of firewood	30 tons of potatoes
and 150,000 eggs		

3. At this Conference the following agenda was discussed:

(a). Supply of foodstuffs under a Basic Plan, i.e. wheat, flour, rice, etc. Prior to 1945 Kolhapur Durbar asked for 1,500 tons per annum for the Camp. This was included in the overall demand for the State from the Food Department. If that quota was received it would have been at the expense of others.

(b). Eggs and milk. It was admitted that they are not sold at controlled prices. The main reason being that the Poles were buying them (independently) as eggs are a necessity for the Europeans. It was decided that a depot should be set up for both eggs and milk where they would be sold at controlled prices at specific hours and any surplus should then go to the City of Kolhapur. It would be an offence to buy these products outside the Depot. *(I do not think this ever happened.)*

(c). Vegetables. Here is a similar problem but it is not practicable to take any steps to ameliorate the situation. Potatoes however are an important food for the Poles of lower classes. In Poland they normally consume 1 ton per annum per head. This would mean 4,500 tons per annum for the Camp. A reasonable offer would be 2,000 tons per annum.

(d). Meat is not causing any problems at the moment because the Poles eat buffalo meat for which there is no local demand.

4. If the Central Government intends to keep these people in India, it must make proper arrangements to feed them. The only organisation in the Deccan States capable of doing so is the Military Supply Directorate. The other alternative is that quotas be made available to the Polish Camp separately from the Deccan States Food Unit by the Department of Commonwealth Relations."

The situation must have been critical because later on in February 1946, Lt. Col. Neate asked the Resident for information concerning the food supply and instructions regarding security measures in case of disturbances in the Polish Camp.

The Polish point of view

This is best illustrated by quoting from the Polish petition dated 11th February 1946, signed by Mgr. J. Pawłowski, Chairman of the Refugee Council to the Resident with added comment(s) from Lt. Col. Neate.

Listing shortages of flour, groats and rice, also milk and eggs and requests:

1. To increase the bread rations - (not possible and bread is not rationed)
2. To grant sporadic supply of flour - (Syndicate should occasionally run an extra issue)

3. To open a dairy store for milk and eggs - (already decided a few days ago)
4. To stop restrictions on dealer competition - (such liberty makes for healthy competition but it violates the terms of the Syndicate agreement)

The Resident replied on 19th February: "In all India the food situation has become worse since last October. Countries both in Asia and in Europe are facing famine conditions... Decisions were taken for the whole of India and these must also apply to the Camp." Hoping that the Poles will take note of the situation he lists the following recommendations:

1. Basic rations per head per day to be reduced to 75% of the existing.
2. Children below the age of 8 years will have half of the adult ration.
3. Supplementary rations of food grains for manual workers to be reduced by half or eliminated.
4. All food grains will be included in the cereal group.
5. Issue of extra quantities of rationed foodstuffs for religious and other festivals (including marriages) will stop.
6. An investigation is being made into allocations of food for certain catering establishments.

Nevertheless, one month after the Military deliveries started, the misunderstandings and accusations from the Polish side continued. The main cause was an inadequate food supply and the monopolistic attitude of the Syndicate. Another meeting on 30th September 1946 was convened between the Resident and those representing the Camp: Mrs. Button, the Commandant and Mr. R. Dusza and Mgr. J. Pawłowski for the Poles, plus Mr. Pardeshi from the Syndicate. A shortened version of the minutes of the meeting highlights Polish complaints and the attempts to satisfy them:

1. An agreement has been signed between the Kolhapur Durbar and the Syndicate, granting them exclusive rights to supply the Polish Camp.
2. Complaints about the inferior quality of charcoal which contains 30% of powder and shortchange in weight - 'it should be supplied in smaller bags'.
3. Short measures of kerosene: - 'the Syndicate agreed to rectify it'.
4. Eggs are very small, often bad and expensive: - 'the Syndicate to be permitted to buy not more than 400 eggs daily and the Poles to be allowed to buy them outside the State'.
5. Supply of vegetables: some initial 'teething problems' experienced by the Army.
6. Meat: - The Syndicate complains that their sales of 1,500 lbs daily have fallen to 600-700 lbs as the Poles were illicitly buying it from outside. This was admitted but blamed on the Syndicate being unable to supply Polish demand. It was agreed that the Poles will buy 1,500 lbs from the Syndicate and sell it among themselves *(the practicality of this is questionable)*.
7. Native employees (130 of them): the Syndicate was supplying them with foodstuffs but as the Army had taken over this responsibility they were excluded from certain items like sugar. 'It was suggested that *fair price shops* be established for these people and operated by the Syndicate'.
8. Sugar: 'The Poles agreed not to complain about the price of 5 annas for 1 lb'.
9. Sausages: - 'It was agreed that the manufacture for their own consumption should be allowed as the Syndicate was not interested and the Poles could obtain the pigs themselves'.

10. Meetings should be held fortnightly between the Polish representatives and the Syndicate to review the situation.
11. Polish objection about searches of their luggage and dwellings by members of the Syndicate looking for illicit purchases of goods: - 'in future complaints should be directed to the Minister of Education (and Supply), but the Poles must desist taking the law into their own hands'.

Army supplies

The only organisation capable of supplying food to the camp was the Army. Negotiations started in July 1945 when it became apparent that the local authorities had no means of dealing with the situation. It was also suggested at the time that the supplies should be organised from the Army depot in Belgaum and that the distribution, at an agreed price be carried out by the Syndicate.

After four months the Local Authorities were still unable to persuade RIASC *(Royal Indian Army Supply Corps)* to undertake the supplies. It was also thought that the food situation had improved slightly and at the same time it was expected that in view of the cessation of war in Europe, the Polish population will be leaving shortly.

By January 1946 the HQ of 110 South Command (Poona Area) proposed to place a reserve of 10-15 days supply for emergency use at the Camp. This would eliminate the necessary turnover of stock for which there was no outlet. A few days later an order was given to HQ 170 (Belgaum) Sub-area, to issue immediately to the Resident for the Polish refugee Camp: 15 days reserve stock of flour, sugar and wood. Unfortunately at the end of February they still had not established when and what foodstuffs were to be supplied and who is paying for them. As the Camp did not have its own storeroom to receive these supplies, it was proposed that the Syndicate should take care of them but the Kolhapur Authorities were requesting that the foodstuffs be delivered to the Camp directly.

It was only on 13th April that Capt. Webb formulated the monthly requirements for the camp (based on 4,000 adults and 320 children below 8 years of age):

1. Cereals (maida-a local cereal)	41.5 tons	6. Vegetables	29 tons
2. Potatoes (fresh)	21.5 tons	7. Milk	58,000 lbs
3. Sugar	4 tons	8. Butter	1,700 lbs
4. Eggs	3,000 dozen	9. Firewood	25 tons
5. Meat	27 tons	10. Charcoal	55 tons

The purchases were to be made through the Syndicate, which could deposit a sum of money with RIASC Depot against which orders would be placed.

He then notes that as the Camp has its own slaughterhouse *(although none of us can remember its existence)* and adds that camel meat is too expensive for the Poles, who prefer buffalo meat to beef or mutton. In Rao Saheb's 'requirement' formulated a fortnight earlier, one can read that although the slaughter of *(venerated)* cows is prohibited in Kolhapur about ten buffaloes are butchered daily for the camp's consumption.

On 18th April 1946 the Resident sent a telegram to the War Department QMG *(Quartermaster General)* in New Delhi regarding the promised foodstuffs for the Camp " ...In view of the famine conditions here - urgently advise which Military authorities will commence the supply..." To which he had a reply dated 8th of May: "Separate indents not required as the quantities are so small. These will be issued from the stock. It applies to food grains, 'other items' to be obtained from local supplies by RIASC".

The following month the Resident responded questioning "...other items like potatoes, vegetables, milk, butter, eggs, firewood and charcoal - and what is to be 'local supply' as it was shortages of these commodities that prompted the request in the first place... but there are no difficulties with sugar as Kolhapur Mills are only 3 miles from the Camp and the Refugees already receive 9 lbs per head per annum."

Within days on 5th June the War Department is "considering the proposal that the Army should take over the maintenance of the Camp" and RIASC was asking "...to allot storage accommodation in one of the disused palace buildings for Polish Camp supplies... as the present place has insufficient space and does not provide protection from rain."

At the end of June it was agreed that as of 1st July 1946 "the Army will be responsible for the supplies to the Polish camp... and issues will be made to and on demand by the Supply Syndicate... at the current issue rates and will be paid for in cash at the time of issue..."

Three days later the Army was still questioning "...will the Syndicate draw direct from the Supply Depot in Poona or Belgaum? and will they employ their own transport? How frequently will they draw the supplies? Is their payment to be in cash on the spot or monthly? If the supplies are to be by train will the Syndicate pay for the freight? Also confirming that fresh supplies of potatoes, onions and fresh vegetables as well as butter, meat and eggs are to be drawn daily from the Supply Depot in Belgaum." Eventually it was on 1st September 1946, more than a year after the negotiations started, that the Army commenced their supplies. This is hardly an example of suggested food dumping, but more probably illustrates the famous Indian bureaucracy or shows that the food shortages might have been exaggerated.

Epilogue

During my research in the India Office Records I accidentally came across the information contained in this chapter. I thought this topic relevant as there appears to be nothing on the subject in *Kronika Osiedla (Camp Chronicles)*, nor any comment in the Polish press in India. Either the problem did not exist or was not serious enough to bring it to the Polish Authorities' attention. They in turn might have wished to conceal it and not cause concern among its Military whose families were in India.

However, it would appear from the quoted documentation that most of the difficulties with food supplies occurred in the second half of our stay in India which coincided with the official cessation of the workings of our Government in London. The British sources could perhaps be suspected of unilateral presentation of the food situation, but for the presence of a Polish representative at some of the meetings in Kolhapur. I cannot even add a personal assessment of the food situation because in those latter stages I was living away from the Camp at a boarding school in Bombay, eating curry twice a day, everyday and being more concerned with our future than the present.

Translated and abridged by Jan and Barbara Siedlecki

NOTE

Apart from the first two quotations from the report of the Delegate's Office of Social Welfare (AAN file no. 85) the remainder is based on IOR Kolhapur and Deccan State Agency files R2 (952/76) and R2 (953/83).

HEALTH SERVICES
by Wiesława Kleszko (Klepacka)

The Hospital in the Laxmi Villas

From July 1943, the newly erected Valivade Camp began to accept its new residents into the recently completed buildings, with the exception of the hospital which was still under construction. The increase in the population made the makeshift hospital block inadequate, especially for the critically ill. The State Hospital in Kolhapur would not accept all of our seriously ill patients. On top of that, their operating theatre charges would have been quite a burden on the Camp's budget.

Luckily a solution was found. The Kolhapur Town Council offered Laxmi Villas to be utilised as a hospital for a period of one year. The complex was situated outside the town in a park setting. It had running water, electric lighting and ceiling fans, and consisted of several brick buildings, including staff quarters. In the park there were old mango trees with pale green flowers, pomegranate trees, beautiful when in bloom, various bushes, and tuberose plants with fragrant flowers, the scent of which could cause headaches. During the night duties, in the still of the night, the sugar cane plantations outside the garden sounded just like the waves of the sea.

The road to Laxmi Villas bypassed Kolhapur. It crossed the green fields and its verges were planted with rows of 'jungle flame' trees. When in bloom they looked like they were literally ablaze. On entering hospital grounds, the place resembled an oasis of green tranquillity and quietness. Even though patients transferred from the makeshift hospital in Valivade Camp found themselves here in similar timber-framed beds with coconut fibre netting and with identical bed linen, they were in uncluttered, cool and tidy wards. There were 52 beds.

The doctor-in-charge of the two hospitals was Edmund Rosenbaum who lived in the Laxmi Villa complex with his family. How strangely intertwined are peoples' lives! Dr. Rosenbaum was Jewish of German descent. His wife was born in Szczecin. They both left Nazi Germany. He completed his medical studies in Italy, where he found himself out of the frying pan and into the fire, so he left for Palestine. After a short stay there he went to India. He was then over thirty, full of energy, highly qualified and without any prejudice towards any human beings. But when Britain became involved in the Second World War, he was interned as a German citizen. The internees were kept in a camp in Lahore, Kashmir, where the 'enemies' had better living conditions than we, as allies. At least that was his opinion after he joined us.

Despite his relatively comfortable but idle life, he volunteered, when English Authorities were looking for a doctor, to take care of us. He was warned that Poles were his enemies and might lack confidence in him because of his German origin. But Dr. Rosenbaum took the risk and came to Valivade with his family to treat the sick. He spoke English and German but not Polish. This problem was solved because Dr. Leon Koziełkowski as well as Franciszka Baryła and Wiesława Klepacka knew the German language. These two and Irena Rządzińska, who could also speak English were sent to the Laxmi Villas. The rule was that during every shift there would always be one interpreter sister present. Despite this language barrier patients' confidence grew in Dr. Rosenbaum, in Laxmi Villas and in Valivade Camp.

At first I. Rządzińska was the liaison officer between us and the elderly matron, Mrs. Loveday and then the Doctor's wife Zenta replaced her. Two Indian sisters - Ada Power and tiny Mrs. Daman joined the four Polish nurses. They both had more experience than we had. They lived in the same Laxmi complex and wore saris. Because of our poor command of the English language, social contact with them was not possible.

In spite of such unusual conditions, care of the patients' did not suffer. Only the surgical cases were sent to the State or the American Hospital in Kolhapur. Our hospital in Laxmi Villas provided an excellent opportunity for convalescence. Patients could relax by lying in deck chairs on the verandah or in the garden. Polish patients from the English hospitals were also sent to Laxmi Villas.

Laxmi Hospital - W. Klepacka, E. Goślinowska, F. Baryła and E. Bezdel

One of the early convalescents was an eight year old Czesia Górska who was seriously ill and was sent from Jamnagar to Bombay for treatment. After spending a year in an English hospital, in Laxmi she played in bed for hours with the Doctor's daughter Ellen, because they both could speak fluent English. No interpreter was required for her during the Doctor's visits. She was in India by herself (her father and her siblings in Lebanon) so all the Polish sisters became her aunts and she soon was able to speak her native Polish again thus becoming one of the first bilingual persons. But her greatest happiness came from the Doctor's new diagnosis and successful treatment that put her on her feet. Although we had many comforts, we had no wheelchairs in the hospital and the younger children had to be carried for a walk in the garden.

At the hospital a small laboratory was run by the Doctor's wife, the pharmacy by Maria Widmańska and the kitchen by the ladies Nowakowa and Tybura.

Report No. 8 dated 26.02.1944 of the Audit Committee in Valivade, which scrutinised all the institutions and hospitals, stated that the average patient's stay in the Laxmi hospital was 17 days. The staff, apart from those mentioned before, consisted of: two kitchen hands, Indian cleaners in the wards and latrines, gardeners, an electrical technician, one laundryman and four guards. The Committee recommended keeping detailed written records of the patients' medical cards, an inventory of kitchen equipment and of transport expenses.

We had generally successful results of our medical treatments, but unfortunately we also had some fatalities. The first to die was our school friend - Bogusław Kołodyński.

In January 1944 all the people suspected of diphtheria in Valivade Camp were sent to Laxmi. They were mainly from the orphanage. Immediately an isolation ward was opened in a bright and spacious room. Luckily it was a false alarm. Before they were returned to the camp they were able for a short time at least to enjoy the beauty and space of Laxmi. After this scare all children up to the age of ten in Valivade were inoculated against diphtheria.

There was a lot of work and it was very demanding, both in a medical and psychological sense. The majority of the patients were women of different age groups. The continuing war and participation in it of their loved ones also had an influence on the patients' health. It required a lot of understanding and sensitivity on the part of the staff and the doctor when dealing with various illnesses which included some cases of venereal disease, well camouflaged by frequent 'liver attacks'. There was bitterness and anger when the illness was diagnosed but the happiness from a successful treatment was shared by both doctor and patient.

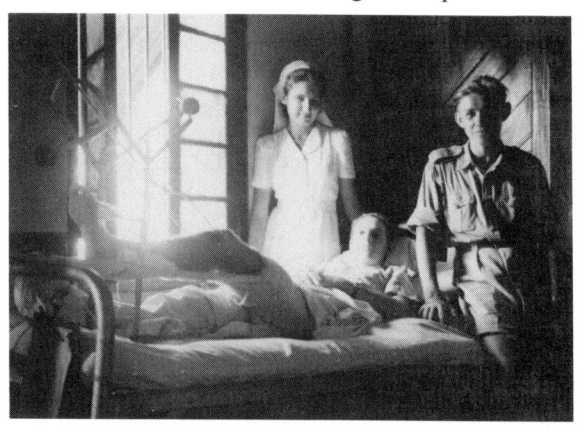

Romek Blumski, Zbyszek Nowicki and Irka Adamczyk

The Laxmi patients were visited by their friends and families from the Camp. From time to time Fr. Leopold Dallinger celebrated Mass there and at Christmas time Girl Guides came along with him to sing carols during and after the service. The whole hospital staff, the doctor with his family and the matron attended such festivities.

During the Christmas and Easter celebrations the kitchen staff prepared at least one traditional Polish meal.

Meanwhile the hospital in Valivade Camp moved into the newly completed buildings. The hospital's term in Laxmi had come to an end and we all returned to the Camp Hospital.

THE HOSPITAL IN VALIVADE CAMP

In the middle of July 1943 the first transport of Polish refugees arrived in Valivade and on 16th of July a temporary hospital was opened in a building designated for the Primary School No. 1 located in the first district of the Camp.

A residential block accommodated only 20 beds because it was assumed that the seriously ill patients would be transferred to the State Hospital in Kolhapur. The hospital beds were the same as in the living quarters. The bed was timber framed with coconut fibre netting and had a mattress and pillow stuffed with kapok, bed linen, a blanket and a mosquito net. There was kerosene lighting. Water for patients was carried in buckets from the banks of water taps situated in the square. There were latrines in the hospital grounds. They were kept clean by an Indian pariah. This was the main job he was allowed to do according to the Indian caste law at the time. The family members supplied meals for the patients because the temporary nature of the hospital did not allow for a kitchen.

The first two serious cases - a pregnant woman and a man requiring surgical treatment were taken to Kolhapur. Among the other early patients admitted to the hospital were two boys under the age of ten, who had eaten some unknown berries growing outside the Camp and suffered food poisoning. Dr. Rosenbaum (then the only doctor) and nurses on duty went through several stressful hours trying to keep them alive with the limited number of medications and instruments. Luckily the young boys survived. Because of this incident the Camp Commandant Captain W. Jagiełłowicz appealed to the parents, guardians and children not to eat unknown berries or fruit. Large, coloured warning posters were displayed all over the residential quarters.[1]

The hospital staff consisted of a Medical Director - Dr. Rosenbaum, sisters and nurses, and two pharmacists. The pharmacy, when established, was well stocked with medicines, dressings and bandages but the storage space was inadequate.

There were 4 hospital blocks. Each of them had two or three wards staffed with the on-duty sisters, nurses and cleaners and later on students of the nursing courses on their work experience. There were also: a laboratory and dental outpatients department.

The day duties on wards were of 6 hours' duration and the night duties of 12 hours. The night duties occurred every third day.[2]

Hospital personnel

The hospital kitchen was opened on 16th February 1944.

As a consequence of the increase in the Camp's population and the closure of the hospital in Laxmi Villas, a number of doctors from the Polish Army in the Middle East joined the new hospital staff.

In May 1944 Dr. Rosenbaum, who had been medical director, was called to join the British Army. The next few months were rather 'fluid' to the hospital medical staff until matters settled in November 1944.

Dental Surgery

Dr. Maks Rosenthal was in charge of the dental surgery and Mr. Patel, a technician, worked in the laboratory. Later on Bogusław Szczurowski joined the team. Cecylia Szymel[3] was the first and for many years the only Dr. Rosenthal's assistant. Later there were also other assistants who had attended a Dental Course. In accordance with the instructions given by the Ministry of Social Welfare there was a need to promote mouth hygiene and regular dental visits. Special emphasis was put on dental care among the children and the young people.

After the hunger and lack of dental care experienced in Russia, the general condition of the refugees' teeth was rather poor. Technical help in the form of dentures, crowns etc. was only considered as a last resort for people in real need.

Dr. Alfred Tomanek - in charge of Health Services at the Ministry of Social Welfare in its Bombay office, found it necessary to organise a Technical Dental Course in Valivade Camp. His statement was as follows:

"In 1944, in accordance with the Health Services Act, private dental surgeons were paid a large sum of money for dentures. The Health Services Office in Bombay proposed setting up its own dental laboratory at the Dental Surgery in Valivade Camp Hospital. The laboratory would be able to produce all sorts of dental technical work at a cost 40% lower than that on the open market."

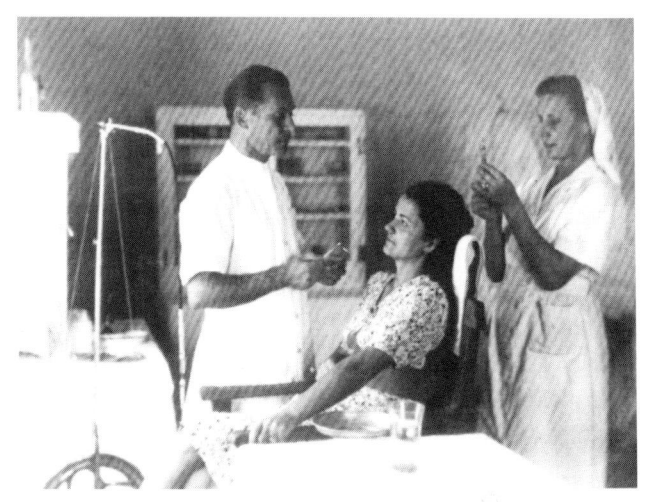

Dental Surgery - Dr. M. Rosenthal with assistant C. Szymel

The laboratory equipment was bought for about Rs 4,000 with the money saved in the Autumn of 1944 on dentures, fees for which would otherwise have been paid to a private dental surgeon. At the same time there was a proposal to utilise the dental laboratory as a Dental Technicians' School for young candidates.

From 18 candidates only 11 were admitted because of size limitations of the laboratory and of the instruments available.

The Health Services Office proposed the course to be in two parts:

a). A 3-month course for the assistants to dental surgeons and mouth hygienists to span over 326 hours of theory and practice in the dental laboratory

b). A 9-month proper course in technical dentistry to span over 1,281 hours of theory and practice in the dental laboratory

The first part of the course was completed in May 1945 and the second in October.

Completion of the Dental Technician's course did not entitle the graduate to set up an independent practice. Only an additional two years of practical experience under the supervision of a qualified dental technician or a dental surgeon entitled the graduate to participate in a practice with a dental surgeon.

Technical and Dental Course with Dr. A. Tomanek, 1946

This course was a very interesting experiment because it was the only one which, apart from the loan from the Ministry's Office in Bombay, was able to pay for all the running expenses from its earnings. It also became an independent place of work employing 11 students together with 6 lecturers and instructors.

Profits from the Dental Laboratory were turned into scholarships for students studying there (Rs 30-50), fees for lecturers, instructors and an accountant, loan repayments and the purchase of laboratory materials.

The Dental Laboratory also employed two Indian dental surgeons. One of them taught English as well.

On completion of the course and after the loan was fully repaid the Dental Surgery was to become a Cooperative Work Place.[4]

The Infant Health Clinic

It was established on 1st January 1944 and was run by Dr. Grażyna Miklaszewska-Czekańska 3 times a week. The Clinic cared for 40 infants who were weighed every fortnight, examined and their overall development monitored. The mothers received free advice about feeding and other aspects of infant care. Sick infants were directed from the Clinic to a special child care ward.

The average number of consultations varied from 80-120 a month. According to the doctor in charge of the Clinic, the infants coped well with the summer heat and the number of illnesses was low. But during the monsoon period the situation worsened - it was easy to catch a cold. This season required special home care. To make sure that the infants received this special care and their mothers followed the doctor's instructions, the Clinic organised doctor's home visits. The nursing mothers were also cared for and advised by the Clinic. The Medical Director - Dr. R. Żarnower reported that in October 1944 there were 65 consultations and in November there were many cases of respiratory tract infections and one case of recurrent malaria among the infants. Inoculation against smallpox was carried out but no actual cases of smallpox were recorded. These early inoculations were considered necessary because the disease was endemic locally. In November there were 132 consultations at the Clinic and the hygienists visited 60 homes with infants.[5]

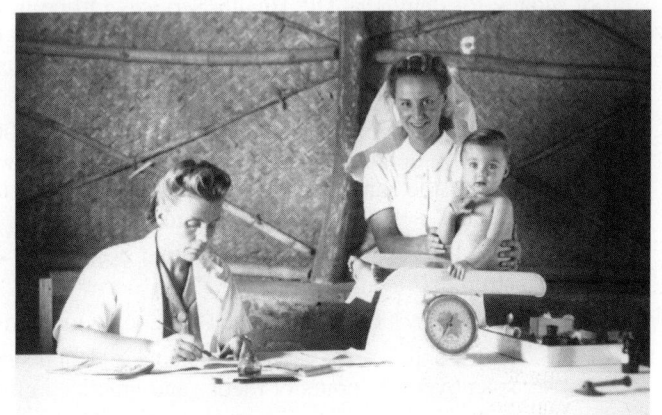

Dr. G. Miklaszewska-Czekańska and J. Chronowska

The Running of the Hospital

From the available reports of the Audit Committee, we can trace the running of the Valivade Camp Hospital. Consecutive hospital visits by the Committee, from 1943, kept track of bed occupancy, sometimes showing up to 90 hospitalized patients depending on climatic and seasonal conditions. The Committee also took notice of some shortcomings, e.g. the cauldron of scalding water for debugging beds was set too high above the open fire resulting

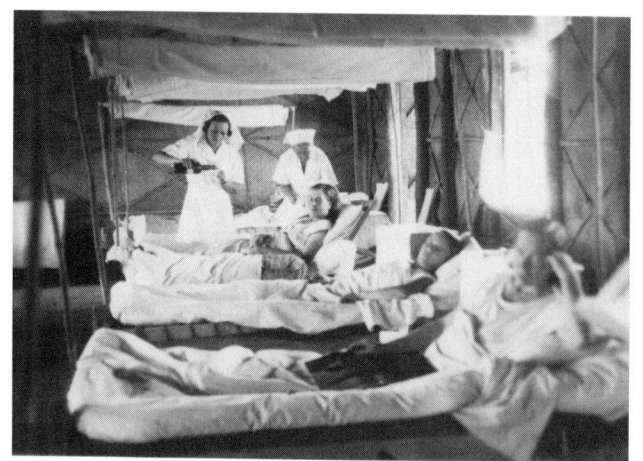

Inside the hospital

in wastage of fuel which was difficult to get at the government controlled prices. The Auditors scrupulously controlled the hospital inventory, cooking and table utensils, as well as bed-linen stores, finding them almost every time consistent with the Inventory Book.[6]

From the few incomplete Medical Reports for October 1944 the number of consultations totalled 6,801, the most numerous of which were children (5,171). This was in the early period when people were coming back to normality and began to nurse their illnesses caused by the abnormal living conditions during the war and deportation. These diseases were as follows: internal, tropical, infectious, eye, ear, skin, neurological, venereal and a few surgical cases. Many were sent to the Polish Red Cross Hospital in Bombay, which was quite modern and better equipped. In time the health of the adults and children improved. The number of cases of malaria and other tropical diseases (Maltese fever and amoebic dysentery) decreased and 21 tuberculosis cases were directed to the TB sanatorium in Panchgani.

All vaccinations were of a preventative nature because in the region[7] there were sporadic outbreaks of various diseases like smallpox in the neighbouring village and Kolhapur, cholera in the district or a case of an oriental plague in Kolhapur. The Chronicle of the Camp and the Vaccination Book published by Health Service Section of the Ministry of Social Welfare Office in Bombay state when the following vaccinations took place:

Vaccinations for:

Enteric (fever)	01.08.1944	25.06.1945		
Smallpox	21.03.1944	21.08.1944	Nov. 1945	
Cholera	23.07.1945	30.07.1945	03.08.1945	Oct. 1945
Plague	14.03.1945	21.03.1945	12.11.1945	

The sanitation team in the Camp in October and November 1944 arranged scalding of 2,652 beds, disinfection of 182 beds, 376 dwellings and 936 items of household effects.

It was necessary to open on 20th October 1944 a Marriage Counselling Centre to prevent undesirable marriages to avoid hereditary illnesses.

A separate health service was organised for the Orphanage. Dr. Gustaw Finkler and nursing staff were appointed to care for the children. An isolation ward was opened for 30 chronic trachoma cases. Two courses - a Sanitary Hygiene and Anti-Malaria Treatment were organised for the children and conducted by Dr. Finkler.

We found no mention in available records about the laundry workers serving the hospital. They picked up the dirty linen and returned it cleaned and ironed. It was quite tricky to do the laundry especially during the monsoon. They worked efficiently and had a pleasant appearance.

Excerpts from the Chronicle of the Camp about unusual events [8],[9]

An epidemic of diphtheria

It broke out in January 1944 and although mild, it was necessary to isolate the children. For this reason they were transferred to Laxmi Villas.

British authorities supplied the vaccine. All children up to 16 years of age were to undergo mandatory vaccination. There was a financial penalty for those who abstained.

No person was permitted to leave the Camp.

But pathological examinations in Kolhapur proved that it was a false alarm.

Food poisoning

"Cold meats, which appeared in clandestine sales, found a wide clientele among the camp residents. Unfortunately these products caused many cases of food poisoning. In this climate such poisoning is severe and difficult to treat.

Purchase of suspected cold meats was banned."

Venereal diseases

"Because of the emergence of venereal diseases, the Camp Commandant asked the Medical Director to introduce strict prophylactic control inside and outside the Camp. At the same time the doctors were asked to conduct public lectures among the adolescents and the adults about these diseases".

An incident of rabies

"In the third week of July 1945 a grievous incident happened, when a dog bit several people. Because the examination of the dog's head performed in Bombay proved that he was rabid, an order was given to poison all stray dogs in the camp. All persons bitten by this dog were vaccinated to prevent the development of rabies.

All dog owners who wanted to keep dogs, had to get them registered at the Administration Office of the camp and had to purchase a metal disc to be worn by the dog on its collar."

The Team of Hygienists

This team came into being during the setting up of the camp in the summer of 1943. Two hygienists were responsible for each sector. Their duties included inspections of the dwellings as well as control of personal hygiene and cleanliness of bed linen. Because of the daily reports presented to the team leader, any shortcomings were quickly rectified. The incidents of messy dwellings and any neglect in personal hygiene were quite rare. The residents were aware of the value of hygiene in the collective type of living.

The Sanitation - Maintenance Team

Since the early days of the Camp's existence there was a crew of Poles and Indians working under an Indian doctor, responsible for the sanitation in the Camp. In due course the final make up of the Sanitation-Maintenance Team took shape. It consisted of: "1 Indian inspector, 1 Indian manager, 3 sector leaders, 3 hygienists and 1 interpreter. Also Indian staff of

Disinfection of beds

20 workers to maintain clean lavatories, 19 street sweepers, 7 bathroom cleaners, 7 workers engaged in the scalding of beds, 7 workers for spraying of insecticide in buildings, open drains and bushes, 3 workers to disinfect waste waters and gullies.

The Sanitation Inspector himself directed all sanitation - maintenance actions, prepared disinfectants, controls cleanliness of shops, public squares and lavatories as well as scalding of beds. The Committee confirmed some improvement in the maintenance of lavatories but recommended further refinement in efficiency. The anti-malaria laboratory indicated further reduction in mosquito numbers. Not all samples of water taken from the local ponds show some presence of mosquitoes".

Educational Courses[10]

Standing: P. Benal, M. Błach, Dr. G. Finkler, J. Pniewska, K. Goślinowska, M. Audykowska, G. Klimowiecka, sitting: E. Maciejewska and J. Chronowska

The *Chronicle of the Camp* states that when the Camp achieved its full capacity of inhabitants in July 1944, enrolments were announced for the first **3-month Medical Emergency Course of the Polish Red Cross**. It was organised by the hospital doctors who were also lecturers and financed by the Cultural Department. Its aim was to increase the small hospital staff. Candidates up to the age of 40 were accepted. They had 6 hours per day of lectures including practical training. After completion of this course the graduates could continue with a 12-month course of the same name and specialize in midwifery, laboratory work or dental laboratory work. The students visited the X-ray Department in the State Hospital in Kolhapur, where they familiarized themselves with the equipment and the method used in taking X-rays. There were 17 graduates on this course.

In association with the appointment of the newly qualified sisters, the Polish Red Cross carried out verification of all working Polish nursing staff in India and presented them with appropriate Certificates.

The second **Medical Emergency Course of the Polish Red Cross**, under the same patronage, opened in January 1945 for 20 candidates from the Orphanage.

On the request of Health Services Authority and the Polish Red Cross in Bombay, the Medical Director in Valivade organised, for the sisters employed at the hospital, an **8-month Medical Laboratory Course** at the Analytical Chemistry Laboratory in the camp Hospital. The course began in October 1945 and 10 graduated. Having such a laboratory in the Camp gave a degree of independence from the use of the laboratories in Kolhapur and provided some savings in the hospital budget.

The **Dental Laboratory Course** described earlier in the Dental Surgery section, was very successful in every way.

Graduates from the secondary school were eligible to attend a *6-month Nursing Course organised for them by the Polish Red Cross*. The course ended in August 1947 and was repeated once more thanks to the financial support of NCWC. Dr. Gustaw Finkler conducted both courses with the cooperation of the hospital staff. After 3 months of practical experience 20 young people received Diplomas.

For the sisters with a long experience a *6-months Proficiency Nursing Course* was made available with special emphasis on infection and tropical diseases, as well as midwifery. The course was financed with the help of Fr. Antoni Jankowski, vicar of our parish, who was also representative of NCWC in India. The course was completed on 23.08.1947.

The last of the courses, a 4-month *Cosmetic and Hygiene Course* concluded with an examination on 16.08.1947. It was financed

Health or Sanitation course for the High School leavers - August 1946

by the Cultural Department and conducted by Dr. Alfred Tomanek. Other lecturers were S. Królikowska, a graduate from the *Institut de Beaute CEDIB* in Paris and J. Kościukiewicz M.Sc. The students spent 170 hours on theory and practice covering a wide programme of cosmetics and hygiene, such as the status of cosmetics in medical science, anatomy, histology, cosmetic resources plus practical exercises in cosmetic treatments.

The doctors also supervised Scouting proficiencies by lecturing in speciality courses and participated in Scouting camps. Girl Guides had practical nursing experience in the hospital and the laboratory. Those who attained a badge of *Samaritan Proficiency* provided first aid service at the Scout and Cub Camps not only to the participants but also to the local Indians who, especially in Chandoli, besieged the First Aid Post early in the mornings.

Probably every one of us was a patient at the camp hospital in Valivade, seeking help in sickness. Lavish attention and generous care in regaining full health was offered, despite some shortcomings.

Transportation of the Sick to Great Britain

The population of the Camp was constantly decreasing as the families of military personnel were leaving for England and others were repatriated to Poland. Closure of the Camp was imminent and the hospital waited for special transport for the hospitalized patients who would not be able to travel otherwise.

Finally instructions came to take action. This is what the *Chronicle of the Camp* states:

"25 patients from the Valivade Camp, the Health Centre in Panchgani and the Vanlasvade Sanatorium sailed (on 16.11.1947) from Madras to England aboard a hospital ship. The sisters who accompanied them were Eugenia Maciejewska and Stefania Sudoł. All Polish patients were relatives of military personnel who had served in the Polish Army under British command and were eligible to settle in England.

The first stage of the journey was by the Red Cross hospital train from Kolhapur to Madras, where transfer to an English ship took place".[11]

Now Stefania Ryszkowska (Sudoł) completes this laconic report:

The hospital ship named *Somerset* was destined to sail to Southampton, a port on the southwest shore of England. Aboard the ship were sick British: civilians and military personnel who had to leave because of political changes which occurred on 15th August 1947, the year when India regained its independence.

During the four-week long voyage a normal hospital routine was maintained.

Sister Stefania took care of the tuberculosis patients, while sister Eugenia cared for the other patients and the geriatrics.

After disembarkation in Southampton S. Sudoł accompanied the tuberculosis patients to the IV Polish Hospital in Whitchurch and E. Maciejewska handed over her patients to the Polish Hospital in Penley in Wales. Later both of them were employed in the Polish hospitals in Great Britain.

Translated by Stanisław and Wanda Harasymów

NOTES
1. IPiMS: Camp Chronicle C811A, page 52
2. arch. JAG
3. IPiMS: Camp Chronicle C811A, page 102
4. PwI: year 3 No.19(63) 1945
5. ibid: year 2 No. 18-19 (27-28) 1944
6. arch. KPI:Audit Commission Report No. 13, 25.9.1943
7. IPiMS: Camp Chronicle C811A, page 11 & 26, C811C, page 6 & 25 & Innoculation Card - S. Harasymów
8. ibid: Camp Chronicle C811A, page 118, 121, 124
9. ibid: Camp Chronicle C811B, page 26
10. ibid: Camp Chronicle C811B, page 175
11. ibid: Camp Chronicle C811C, page 32

List of people also employed by The Health Service who are not mentioned in the text

Dr. Erika Rosenthal	Gynaecology Department	(up to May 44)
Dr. Maria Wysocka	Internal Diseases	(up to May 44)
Karolina Krajewska	Matron	(up to May 44)
Józef Pawłowski M.Sc.	Pharmacy Directors	(up to May 44)
Jadwiga Suchocka M.Sc.		(up to May 44)
Anna Szyszkin	Pharmacy Employees	(up to May 44)
Anna Stankiewicz	Pharmacy Office	(up to May 44)
	Sisters, Nurses, Cleaners	
Dr. Marcus Tajchner	Deputy Director	
Dr. Józef Feier	Medical Practitioners	
Dr. Samuel Wieselberg		
Dr. Jerzy Tiachow		
Jadwiga Suchocka M.Sc.	Chief Pharmacist	
Józef Pawłowski M.Sc.	Pharmacists	
Mieczysława Łossowska		
Anna Szyszkin		

Romualda Łoś Pharmacy Trainees
Maria Cisiewicz
Anna Stankiewicz Pharmacy Clerk
Janina Mueck Housekeeping Sister
Helena Kucharska Matron

Kitchen:
Lidia Snastin Chef
Zofia Rak Cooks
Franciszka Kopeć
Olga Jurczyńska
Aleksandra Szewczyk
Teofila Kupczyńska

Sanitation Team:
Dr. Ramish Inspector
Antoni Kokociński Team Leader
Antoni Duda + 4 persons Section Leaders
Helena Zator Debugging of Beds
2 persons Fighting Malaria

a). Sisters of the Polish Red Cross:

Aniołkowska Alicja	Głębicka Helena	Materek Jadwiga
Audykowska Maria	Goślinowska Eugenia	Michalska Aleksandra
Bargiełowska Kazimiera	Greczyło Danuta	Mickiewicz Leokadia
Jarmułowicz Melania	Mularczyk Lidia	Benal Paulina
Jędrzejewska Oktawia	Narolska Mieczysława	Bernsztain Renata
Kirchner Zofia	Pniewska Jadwiga	Bezdel Ewalda
Błachowa Maria	Klimowiecka Genowefa	Szabłowska Wiktoria
Chmielowska Zofia	Krajewska Karolina	Szpadowska Aleksandra
Chołąckiewicz Jadwiga	Kudlicka Olga	Tarasiewicz Aleksandra
Chronowska Janina	Wcisło Stanisława	Dembińska Janina
Masiulanis Pelagia	Zawadowska Waleria	

b). Nurses:

Baran Stanisława	Kamińska Zofia	Skrzypek Bronisława
Bielska Pelagia	Piórkowska Emilia	Świątek Maria
Biedrońska Józefa	Ryciak Anna	Szymel Cecylia
Czachor Wanda	Romanowska Bogumiła	(dental assistant)
Hryczyszyn Helena	Szczepańska Władysława	

c). Hygienists:

Adamek Bronisława	Piotrowska Filipina	Zagórska Irena
Dudko Wanda	Serocińska Helena	

Oh, Precious Health! *by Stanisław Harasymów (personal reminiscences)*

Our Valivade Camp was situated in the wide valley of the Panchganga River on the Deccan Plateau. The climate was tropical, hot, dry summers and wet, monsoon winters. It was regarded as reasonably healthy for the locals. But for the displaced people from a much cooler climate of central Europe, it could be considered dangerous. As a preventive measure, the Polish Authorities supplied every resident with a cork helmet for the summer and a rain cape for the winter, as well as a mosquito net. The water pumped from the river had to be boiled before consumption. We were also warned of scorpions, poisonous spiders and snakes. All health services were free of charge.

As far as personal hygiene goes, there were some problems and difficulties. We lived in a very primitive environment. The latrines, due to the stench, were located on the outskirts of the Camp. For some the walking distance was considerable and chamber pots were in use. Hand and face washing was done in a wash bowl. The water was carried in buckets from the banks of water taps located at several points of the camp. The bathrooms with showers only and the laundries with cement troughs were centrally positioned, making it hard for some people to walk there, especially in the wet season.

Living close to the main hospital building we sometimes witnessed injured boys with broken arms, cuts and bruises walking to the casualty department. I was there too with a thorn in my foot and a scorpion sting to my toe. There was also a delivery ward nearby. On one occasion the screams coming out from there turned the blood in my veins to ice. And at the back of the hospital stood a small mortuary. Every time I went near it, I felt a shiver of fear. There was a lot of open space around it, yet we kept our soccer or baseball games away from the place.

Despite all warnings and precautions taken, there was no shortage of patients. The most common sickness was malaria and not so common amoeba, sunstroke, tropical illnesses, infectious diseases and even colds. The ladies were frequent visitors at the outpatients department. According to gossip some women pretended to be ill. Injections of aqua pura (pure water) were very effective. One of the doctors was quoted as saying that these ladies lacked vitamin 'M', meaning man, i.e. husband. Gossip spread fast through walls of bamboo matting.

I myself spent some time in the Camp hospital. It started with jaundice, then there were complications: blood tests showed malaria although I never suffered an attack of that illness, later amoebic dysentery. Our doctors knew very little about tropical diseases. Several doctors held a consultation in order to diagnose my condition and prescribe a cure. I had to follow a strict diet for a month and suffered very high temperature. I wrote in my diary that in time I got used to the hospital routine and made new friends. When I left I was very weak and had a lot of catching up to do with my school work. I had to have private tuition.

My God! How primitive our living conditions were, and how far medicine and health services have since progressed? But that was more than half a century ago. Then we were displaced persons after the horrors of war and the hell of communism in Russia. The financial capabilities of the Polish Government in Exile were limited. But the health services provided were sufficient and much better than those available to the poor Indians. I wish to stress that the health care in Valivade Camp was well organised, effective and efficient. All those responsible for taking care of our 'precious' health in this little Polish enclave should be commended. They did a tremendous job.

GENERAL PARSEE HOSPITAL - BOMBAY
by Irena Metelica (Hajduk)

Many graduates from the secondary school in Valivade completed the Polish Red Cross Nursing Courses and gained practical experience in the Camp's hospital. However, there was a lack of vacancies on the hospital roll in 1946-7 during the closing-down period.

Then unexpectedly Dr. Mistry arrived in Valivade looking for a few sisters to undertake employment in the Parsee Hospital in Bombay. After several interviews with Dr. Mistry and his wife who made the final choice, 9 candidates were offered employment. The salary offered was Rs 75 per month plus living quarters, board and laundry.

In connection with acceptance of this employment there were a lot of formalities to take care of, such as obtaining permission from the Government in Delhi to leave the Camp and to work. The Camp Commandant took care of this and Wanda Dynowska gave us some practical advice for the journey and promised to meet us at the railway station.

We were surprised and fascinated by this beautiful, huge hospital. We went through a glazed covered way joining two buildings and into the nurses' quarters which had a glazed verandah running around the building. There were clean beds, each with an electric fan and cupboards - for us a real luxury! The dining room was in the same building.

Helena Kojder in Pola Kojder's book *Marynia, Don't Cry* described the hospital as follows: "... the building was divided into three levels. The ground floor was for the poor and was free of charge. It was the most difficult ward to look after because the patients there were usually seriously ill. The middle class patients in the general and surgical wards, occupied the first floor. The second floor was reserved for the very rich and had only a few patients."

After showing us around the hospital, we were acquainted with the local rules and regulations. Our shifts would alternate every two weeks. After the morning shift ending at 3 p.m. we were allowed to leave the hospital but had to return by 8 p.m. After the afternoon shift we had to obtain special permission to leave the place. But after the night shift we were only allowed to take a few short walks because the management was concerned about our rest.

For the night shift there were special bedrooms upstairs, yet they woke us up to drink hot chocolate! We were too sleepy to drink so we told the servant to take it back. In turn he became upset and begged us on his knees to accept it because he feared the matron!

We also had a lovely middle-aged *ayah* who looked after us, made up our beds, tidied up the rooms and delivered our clean linen. Our uniforms were so starched that it was not easy to put them on and in the afternoon they were 'withered' and crumpled because of the hot weather.

Mr. and Mrs. Mistry with M. Goławski, Eugenia Bień, Irena Hajduk, Irena Idkowiak, Irena Magnuszewska, Stella Kaptur, Janina Nawój, Helena Kojder, Adela Malcharek and Helena Siewerska.

I shall never forget the early days of our nursing job. First of all we were told that we were on 3-month trial and if anyone of us was not able to cope she would be send back to the Camp.

We were sent to different wards so we would not speak Polish. Generally the local sisters were quite nice but at the same time they watched and observed our every move to spot any mistakes. Our English was not very good so our questions were limited. Dr. Mistry was very friendly and helpful and Mrs. Mistry organised evening lectures on hospital procedures. Unfortunately our girls did not show much enthusiasm and frequently missed them.

However Irena Idkowiak wrote: "I love the nursing job in the hospital and work diligently. A patient's smile is my best reward but I get distressed when a patient dies." The impression of her first night duty is not to be forgotten: "...it is dark in the ward, there is a light on my table. This is my first night duty, I am solely responsible for all the patients but it is a positive feeling. I have already been employed in this hospital for two months and I am satisfied, because for the first time I am earning my living. I never dreamed of such a job in Bortnica *(in Poland)* when I was 12. How many thousands of miles is my beloved village?..."

Doctors' rounds were terrifying. The tradition of this hospital was such that when a doctor's car arrived, an Indian, in a beautiful turban, struck a brass gong. The number of strikes indicated a doctor's status, e.g. three strikes for a surgeon. Immediately we stopped our window-gazing and ran to his patient to make sure everything was prepared for the visit. Those 'important' doctors were always in a hurry and all changes or corrections in the patient's treatment were dictated very quickly. I still wonder how we managed not to poison anyone.

The very rich patients had their own servants at the bedside as well as private nurses who were subordinate to us. If a patient demanded a particular nurse, then she was transferred to that floor. Sometimes the whole family came to visit the patient just to have a good look at the Polish nurses.

Members of the staff were not allowed to accept any presents other than chocolates. Once an awkward situation arose when a mother of a small child bought us some silk cloth for frocks. After long negotiations we were allowed to keep it.

In spite of the fact that English was generally used we had to learn a little Gujarati to communicate with some of the patients. Obviously, in many cases, we had to communicate using sign language.

The ward sister was always an Indian of a higher rank but during the night we were left alone with the servants. They sat on the verandah in the on-duty sister's field of vision, otherwise they would hide in the corners and sleep. Twice during the night shift we had to write a report which was picked up by a special messenger.

Twice a day we had to provide our patients with a treatment called 'backs', which meant rub-down their backs with alcohol and powder with talcum powder to prevent bedsores. Every patient wore a light undershirt belted with a cord containing many knots, similar to a rosary. This cord was very much in our way so we pulled up the undershirt leaving the cord on the naked flesh. Eventually someone told us that after morning prayer the cord should remain on top of the undershirt.

When a patient died a screen was placed around the bed and a light was turned on. Accustomed to saving energy we would turn the light off, but then we found out that the light had to be left on so that the soul could find its way to heaven.

Other countries, other laws; one always learns something new. Helena Kojder remembers: "Prevailing social segregation in the hospital was also imposed on aspects of nursing and collaboration among the staff. For example, the nurses did not handle bedpans. Segregation was in force even in the canteen - students and nurses had to be seated separately and the doctors ate in another place."

In our free time we would go shopping in the city but never alone. Our first move towards emancipation was to cut off our plaits and get our hair permed and set in a smart style in the Taj-Mahal Hotel. This was an expensive outlay but our mothers were not aware of this.

We tried to do some sightseeing in Bombay and it's environs but we had to rely on our friends, because for a white woman to travel alone by bus was a rarity. Mrs. Mistry was very kind and drove us around or invited us to her place for tea and once we attended a ball organised by the medics.

Opposite the hospital, right on the shore of the Arabian Sea, was the Breach Candy Club, for Europeans only, where one could spend time after work. Sailors of various nationalities and English inhabitants of Bombay went there regularly. "Especially on Sunday - Helena Kojder remembers - the orchestra played, and under shady umbrellas on a manicured lawn sat the British clientele, in service to the Crown in India."

We Poles preferred to gather on a balcony next to our quarters to talk, read letters and sing together.

There were 9 candidates for the positions offered in the Parsee Hospital: Eugenia Bień, Irena Hajduk, Irena Idkowiak, Irena Magnuszewska, Stella Kaptur, Janina Nawój, Helena Kojder, Adela Malcharek and Helena Siewerska.

Thus the months of work went by and we were offered 3-year contracts, but due to the closing down of the Valivade Camp the offer was not viable.

Janka Nawój got married to Gordon - an officer in the British Navy. We were leaving one by one to go to England as families of the military personnel. They bade us farewell very sincerely, especially Dr. Mistry and his wife, with whom I was in contact for many years in the USA, because they too left India and settled in Los Angeles. It is a pity that in the USA instead of practising medicine, the doctor had to make a living as an insurance agent, as his medical qualifications were not recognised.

Translated by Stanisław and Wanda Harasymów

Dr. Erika Rosenthal with Nurses

ORPHANAGES

DEVELOPMENT OF ORPHANAGES *by Wiesława Kleszko (Klepacka)*

Amongst thousands of Polish families deported in 1940-41 from the annexed Polish territories to the USSR, were large numbers of children. Apart from those deported with the families there were instances of children on their own meeting the same fate. For example, 176 workers' children attending a summer camp at Druskienniki were removed to a *'dyet-dom'* (State Institution for Children) in Udmurtskij Republic at the outbreak of the Soviet-German war.[1] Author Irena Wasilewska who after the 'amnesty' worked as a child welfare officer for the Polish Mission in the USSR, describes her experiences in a book *Za Winy Niepopełnione*. She met and remained in contact with many children orphaned during the exile, separated from their families during the train journey into exile, or later, while on the way south, where the new Polish Army was being created. Polish children who lost their parents or carers were often placed in Soviet *'dyet-doms'*. Whilst there, usually because of their poor knowledge of the Russian language, they were bullied and mocked by the other children.

Twelve year old Janka wrote: "Russian children bullied us terribly. Called us names: 'You Polish narks, Polish ladies, white bourgeois. You lived well in Poland so now you have to suffer.' We would just sit down in a corner and cry. We were not allowed to pray, so we would pray under cover of our blankets. They mocked us, saying that there is no God and that Poland would never exist again, yet we believed that we would return to Poland, in another year or two, but return we would. They kept telling us, that we had as much chance of seeing Poland again, as of 'seeing one's ear without a mirror'.[2] We had our clothes and food stolen, some children were jailed by the NKVD for thefts in town. At school we were taught that humans descended from monkeys. We did not believe this and laughed at the idea and the teacher was angry with us for not believing'.

The children were kept in *'dyet-doms'* till the age of fourteen. On reaching that age they were sent to work on collective farms *(kolkhoz)*. It was fortunate that following the 'amnesty', Polish child welfare workers began to seek out orphans scattered throughout the region, remove them all from *'dyet-doms'* and send them to Ashkhabad.

Following the 'amnesty', the first task of the Polish Authorities was to provide care and assistance to the children. Thanks to the initiative of the Polish community and the Polish Army, 83 orphanages were established throughout the USSR.[3] The orphanages were often housed in wooden, or earthen sheds. Lacking beds, the children slept on the floors. There was a shortage of bedding, underwear, kitchen utensils. None the less, each orphanage, even the most poorly equipped, was fulfilling two most important functions - to prevent children starving and to give them shelter. Often little children were left at orphanage doors by despairing mothers unable to feed them. Some children walked many kilometres to seek shelter and protection in the orphanages. Financial support for the orphanages came from the Polish Government Agencies. Bread, sometimes cereals and cooking oils were supplied by the local authorities at government controlled prices; vegetables had to be purchased from bazaars at high prices. The main support towards their existence came from aid arriving from England, the USA, New Zealand, Australia and other countries, as gifts for the Polish exiles. These included items of clothing, footwear, blankets, medicines, sugar, jams, condensed milk, biscuits, cocoa and fats. Polish soldiers, as a rule, shared their rations with children in the orphanages attached to their units. The numbers of these children were substantial. Children often reached Polish army units having escaped from Soviet orphanages. Sometimes partly Russified, often not even knowing their names, the ability to say *Our Father...* in Polish was the only proof of their nationality.[4] The soldiers were themselves active in rescuing children from Soviet institutions. Thousands of these children never reached their desired destination; hundreds reached the Army posts too late, only to die amongst their own.

The Polish Embassy in Kuybyshev and the Polish Army Command organised orphanages, schools and nursery schools at each military base.[5] In accordance with the Soviet law, children of 14 years and older could not remain in orphanages. To solve this problem, the Army established cadet schools for girls and boys. A school for the girl cadets was set up at Karkin-Batash in May 1942 and accommodated 691 girls. By July the number rose to 1,036 girls. This locality, known as the 'death valley', had an appalling climate, hot, dry and unhealthy, which led to an outbreak of typhoid. To escape the epidemic the school was moved to Guzar and to kolkhoz Molotov near Shacurisjabs. On the 25th August 1942, the schools for boy and girl army cadets left the USSR, crossing the Caspian Sea, to eventually reach Teheran in Persia. This was the largest group of children to leave the Soviet Union.

At the initiative of Polish exile communities, 43 schools were established in the Soviet Union. One of these was opened in Bukhara during the spring of 1942. To house the school the Soviet authorities provided an old Synagogue building, which was previously used as a grain store. Officially opened on the 3rd of May, the Polish National Holiday, it was blessed by a priest and a rabbi, while local Authority representatives spoke about tolerance for various nationalities in the USSR. Thus came into existence a proper school, staffed by enthusiastic teachers with 200 pupils, the majority of whom were Jewish children from Poland.[6]

Evacuation to Persia was also to embrace all orphanages under the care of Polish Social Welfare. To facilitate the evacuation, a transit orphanage was established with the help of the Polish Red Cross at Ashkhabad near the Persian border. At this stage an invitation was received from Maharaja Jam Saheb for the children to stay in his Principality of Nawanagar for the duration of the war. The invitation was gratefully accepted and steps were taken to assemble the children in Ashkhabad in preparation for an overland journey to India. Other children gathered, were waiting for transport to Teheran. During a long stay at Ashkhabad there were moments of disquiet and tension, when the Soviet authorities began to harass the orphanage staff by periodic visits and even arrests. In Irena Wasilewska's book one boy, named Israel, describes the unexpected visits by the NKVD and their attempts to remove boys to collective farms. Night searches also took place. Attempts were made to persuade older children to accept Soviet passports.

All Jewish children registered themselves as Christians, convinced that otherwise they would not be allowed to leave the Soviet Union.[7] On reaching Meshed in Persia the transport commander, vice-consul Dr. Tadeusz Lisiecki, was approached by a special envoy from the Jewish Agency in Palestine with a request to re-direct the Jewish children to Teheran, where they would be cared for by the Jewish Committee. During their stay in Meshed, it was proposed that the local Jewish Community would look after them. Dr. T. Lisiecki noted that on the 18th August 1942 he despatched two lorries, part of his Indian convoy, to take Jewish children to Teheran. He stresses that this happened at the express wish of the Jewish Agency and the Jewish Community representatives.[8]

Based on statistical information from Col. Ross of the Middle East Relief & Refugee Administration, approximately 20,000 children and youths were evacuated from USSR in two moves, in April and August 1942. Children transported across the Caspian Sea were lodged in a temporary camp in the Persian port of Pahlevi. There they were issued with clean clothing and were given the chance of a short rest under medical supervision. From Pahlevi they were sent to existing camps for Polish civilians in Teheran. As recorded by Stanisława Synowiec-Tobis, on 7th November 1942, the children were transferred from Teheran to Isfahan, which was referred to as a 'town of Polish children', and it already accommodated more than 3,000 children. It was also a destination for the girl Army Cadet schools.[9] Another member of this 'children's town', Jadzia Mieczkowska, confirms: "Our orphanage was an assembly of various organisations, beginning with an orphanage from Karakul in Uzbekistan and orphans from Teheran - it kept increasing in size like a snowball rolling down a hill. In February 1943 we were joined by girl Army Cadets, girl Guides and girls from No.2 Institution under the care of Sisters of Charity.[10] As can be gathered from the above, it was in Isfahan that the children were regrouped to enable them to settle down in some place for the duration of the war. Younger girl Army Cadets were 'demobilised' and joined the civilian orphanages whilst older girls were sent to Palestine, and became the responsibility of the army."

Stanisława Synowiec-Tobis further notes, that she had been sent with a group of children to Kuma City. There they joined another 1,000 orphans under the care of Zygmunt Ejchorszt, preparing to leave for India. The group then moved to Ahwaz. From there they finally sailed for India after receiving entry visas. They landed in Karachi and were initially accommodated in a transit camp near Karachi called 'Country Club'. Later, as a group named 'Isfahan Orphanage', they were transferred to a holding camp, Malir, in the same locality. When Malir Camp closed down, the civilians and orphans from Teheran left for Valivade Camp near the Indian City of Kolhapur. The 'Isfahan Orphanage' had returned to the 'Country Club' and eventually departed on the 2nd November 1943 to settle in Santa Rosa, Mexico.

In 1944 the New Zealand Government offered asylum to Polish orphans and half-orphans whose parents died in Russia and Teheran. A group of 733 children and personnel left Isfahan reaching Wellington in New Zealand after a 44 days journey. They were accommodated in a camp in Pahiatua, 150 kilometres from Wellington.

In 1943, following an agreement between the Polish Government and Marshal Smuts of South Africa, a former army camp at Oudtshoorn in Cape Province was offered as accommodation for Polish children. The camp became known as the 'Polish Children's Home'. This well equipped and well organised centre was a home to a group of Polish children until its closure in 1947.

The orphanages, also known as 'institutions for bringing up children', stressing the most tender and loving essence of the expression 'bringing up', were a substitute home and family for the children until their closure some years after the end of the war. Following are the reminiscences of two of the former wards.

NOTES

1. arch. KPI: *Za winy niepopełnione (For Sins Not Committed)* Irena Wasilewska, page 40, Rome 1945
2. Ibid: page 73-4
3. Ibid: page 54
4. Ibid: page 55
5. *Isfahan Miasto Polskich Dzieci (Isfahan, the Town of Polish Children)* Koło Wychowanków Szkół Polskich Isfahan and Lebanon, page 15-16
6. arch. KPI: vide 1. page 62
7. Ibid: ibid page 75-76
8. IPiMS: A73-67 Report of Manager of Polish Transport to USSR. Meshed 18.August 1942, no. 109-II/42
9. arch. KPI: *Poles of Santa Rosa: Our 50th Anniversary 1946-1996.*
10. Ibid: *Wspomnienia z Sierocińca w Malir.* Jadwiga Mieczkowska (Przychodzeń)

THE VALIVADE ORPHANAGE NAMED AFTER GENERAL W. SIKORSKI
by Maria Juralewicz (Sztela)

The Orphanage *(Zakład Wychowawczy Im. Gen. Władysława Sikorskiego)* was so named on the 14th August 1943, while still located at Malir near Karachi. When its Director Mr. Z. Ejchorszt had left with a group of children for Mexico, Mrs. Olga Sasadeusz became the new Director and under her supervision 181 children and 10 staff were moved from Karachi camps to a newly constructed Valivade Camp. Not all the children were orphans, some were separated from their parents or had only one parent living, usually a father serving in the Army or stationed in England, or still living in Poland. According to statistics of 1st November 1944, out of the total of 359 wards: 119 were orphans, 143 had one parent living and 97 had both parents living.[1]

Staff with Sasadeusz (J. Figula with flowers) and Zerebecki

The Orphanage was accommodated in 14 buildings, each having two dormitories separated by a house-mistress's or house-master's room in the centre. Each dormitory contained 35 beds. The buildings were constructed on stone foundations. Walls, doors and window shutters were of bamboo matting, roofs were covered with red tiles and there were no ceilings. Floors were of clay, periodically treated with an application of cow manure to guard against ants. Furniture consisted of timber frame beds with jute rope netting, a mattress and a mosquito net, a chair, a steel trunk that also served as a table and two hanging kerosene lamps. Buildings had verandas running along two sides, shaded in greenery and bordered by flower beds that were looked after by the children. Two buildings of 14 rooms each with a shared kitchen were reserved for the teachers' living quarters. Two further buildings housed 12 school classrooms. One building accommodated a messroom with built-in kitchen. The kitchen was equipped with a 9 burner cooking range, 2 large built-in stock pots, 2 ovens and a bread oven. Both the kitchen and food store had concrete floors.

Canteen

The girls and the boys were housed in separate dormitories. Furthermore, the aim was to group the children of the same age and school levels close together. Attempts were made to keep siblings together, unless age differences were too great.

Each building had its house-mistress or house-master (there was always a shortage of the latter). Those caring for the very young were provided with extra assistants. The older children were responsible for keeping their quarters tidy, the younger ones had cleaners doing it for them. Bedclothes were sent away for washing, personal items had to be washed by the children themselves - with the exception of the younger ones. The older girls helped their brothers and younger sisters. Some older girls assisted the dormitory staff with the care of the younger children. In cases where checks by a hygienist found lice in the hair of young children, the older children assisted in an effort to eradicate the infestation without the need to have the heads of youngsters shaved.

Bed-bug infestation was another problem. Beds were dipped in boiling water by Indian workers, but children themselves had to carry the heavy beds back to the dormitories. Here again the older children assisted the younger ones. Twenty nine young women and senior girls were accommodated in separate quarters within the complex. A group of 14 difficult to control boys was placed in an isolation block. This group consisted of one boy in 7-11 age range, twelve in 12-15 and one above 16. Thirteen of them attended the junior school and one did not study or work. Two staff members looked after young women and senior girls and 1 was assigned to the boys' isolation block.[2]

Provision of clothing:

The children were provided with following items of clothing and items of personal use:-

Girls received 4 skirts, 4 blouses, 4 sets of underwear, 4 nightdresses, 2 pairs of footwear, 2 towels, 4 bed sheets, 2 pillow cases, 2 combs, 1 tooth brush and soap. Boys received 4 pairs of shorts, 4 shirts, 2 pairs of pyjamas and 1 Scout uniform. At the end of 1946 the girls were issued with dress fabric, which they could use to make their own dresses in the camp's Co-op sewing workshop. Additionally, girl Guides were provided with uniforms.

Children below the age of 16 received Rs 5 as pocket money, at the age of 16 it went up to Rs 10. The representative of the Polish Ministry of Social Welfare was involved in a lengthy argument with Capt. Webb concerning the children's allowance.

Letters addressed to the children were distributed during the main meals. Letters for very young children would be picked up by house-mistresses, who later assisted children in reading them.

The age of the children:

The ages of children in December 1944 were recorded as follows:[3]

    6   children aged 4 to 6 years,
   43   children aged 7 to 11 years,
 129   children aged 12 to 15 years,
 181   children aged 16 years and above.

The age of some of the very young children could not be ascertained as they did not remember how old they were, had no personal papers and there was no one else to provide this information. I remember, while in Isfahan, each child had to give her/his date and place of birth and names and whereabouts of parents. When a child was unable to give the required details, an interviewer would estimate the child's age, so that he/she could be placed in an appropriate age group.

The Kitchen

Children's information about their fathers' employment prior to year 1939:

Farmers, ex-army land settlers	250
Lower rank state employees, police, postal services	25
Government officers	17
Local government officers	6
Tradesmen and traders	9
Teachers	6
Professional soldiers and other professions	46

Parents' whereabouts:

Both parents in the USSR	55
Father P.O.W. in Germany, mother in the USSR	5
Parents in Poland or refugees in other countries	19
Father in the Army, mother in the USSR	17
The sole living parent in the USSR	51
Father P.O.W. in Germany	5
The sole living parent in Poland or a refugee in other countries	88

The Personnel (end of 1944)

    1. Orphanage Director
    2. Deputy Director
    3. 12 house-mistresses (depending on requirement at a particular time)
    4. Physical education instructor
    5. Assistants to the house-mistresses
    6. Recreation room supervisor
    7. Tutors
    8. Janitor
    9. Administrator
   10. Office clerks

11. Kitchen supervisor
12. Cooks
13. Kitchen help
14. 18 Indian employees: 11 water carriers, kitchen help, translator
15. Dressmaker
16. Nurse and hygienist (seconded from the camp hospital)

The personnel was financed partly from the Orphanage's budget and partly by other Sections, such as: Fire Service, Security, Education; and from funds of the Office of the Delegate in Bombay.

In 1943-1944, the number of children rose to 398 through an influx of children of various ages from other locations.

To ensure an efficient functioning of the Orphanage, in 1944 the Camp Commandant prepared a set of rules. The adherence to these rules was controlled by an Audit Committee, which conducted regular audits in the presence of the Orphanage Director and the Administrator.

Director of the Orphanage
O. Sasadeusz, Quartermaster
A. Klecki amongst their charges

Education

According to the records, on the 12th July 1944 out of the 398 wards, 352 attended schools and 8 kindergarten, 8 girls did not engage in studies and 1 boy was mentally deficient. The older girls, who lived separately from younger children, worked in dressmaking workshop or health services. The 8 difficult to control boys were separated under the supervision of a special carer. They were taught bookbinding skills and eventually employed in this trade at a small wage. Later on many other boys attended bookbinding courses or found some form of employment.

We have to realize that many children were over 16 years old. They found themselves in the Orphanage because of young siblings they looked after. They were often behind with their education and it was difficult to place them in schools. However, every effort was made to find a place for them in the education system suited to their age, abilities and aims. Initially the, majority of the children attended Primary School

School No. 3

attached to the Orphanage and under the charge of Mrs. Sasadeusz. Later on a large group attended General Education High School. A smaller number studied at Commercial High School, Teacher Training Lycee, School for Rural Instructors or Technical School.

Problems arose when children completed their schooling and reached maturity. What to do with them? Where to find them employment? A number of boys left for the Naval School in

England, another group were recruited for physical work in Australia. Some of the girls found employment in the Orphanage kitchen, others were left to fend for themselves within the camp community.

The children did their homework in the dormitories or in the recreation room where the lighting was better and tutorial help was available.

The house-mistresses attended regular interviews with teachers to discuss the progress and problems of each student and to ascertain what individual help was needed. This event was always a cause of high anxiety for the children.

Activities outside the school

Apart from their school work, the children were involved in Scouting and in religious organisations. The majority belonged to Scouts or Girl Guides organisations, which were highly developed in the Camp and had a great influence on the formation of their characters, moral attitudes and patriotism as can be gathered from their contemporary diaries. They attended camps, excursions and participated in other activities. The No.5 Girl Guides Company had its own room where they met regularly.

Older girls attended courses in dressmaking, typing, embroidery, knitting, mechanics and many other useful skills.

Boys played soccer, volley ball, palant (a type of baseball), rode bicycles, read books and skylarked.

The girls found diversion in needlework, embroidery, crocheting and sewing. They read a lot, trying to make up for the initial lack of books. It was their ambition to become familiar with the best of our writers. The heroes of the books were talked about and subjects raised in the books were later discussed. Some girls loved sport, ball games, bicycle riding. Bicycles from Indian hire shops were often mechanically unreliable, but this had never put off the enthusiasts.

Company of Guides with Mrs. Sasadeusz, her son Witold & Mr. Bidakowski (in the middle)

The Camp cinema was a great attraction. It screened English and American films. The difficulty in understanding the English dialogues did not stop children from joining the queues and pushing and shoving to obtain the best cheap tickets to get in to see a film. Children who were sent money by their parents in the Army, often shared with those who had none. Older children used to attend theatre performances by Camp artists. The Orphanage had a choir and an artistic group which took part in National and Religious celebrations held in the recreation hall.

Religious Celebrations and Holidays

First Communion for children from all the schools

The First Communion for the young children was followed by a dinner attended by Fr. Dallinger and Fr. Przybysz. The children participating in the First Communion were dressed in white and the hall was beautifully decorated. When on a visit to administer the Sacrament of Confirmation, the Bishop of Bombay also visited the Orphanage. Care was taken to celebrate Christmas in a manner that would at least partly compensate for the absence of parents and a home atmosphere. Marysia Woźniak in her diary gives the following description of 1945 Christmas Eve and Easter.

"...From the morning of the Christmas Eve there was a rush of activities: thorough cleaning, dressing the Christmas tree with hand-made decorations and coloured candles. Cooks, with the girls' help, preparing Christmas Eve meal. Like in a large family, every one was busy with the preparations.

The sound of a bell at 6 p.m. announced that the supper was ready. All children dressed in their best waited for their dormitory house-mistresses and house-masters to lead them to the dining room festively decorated. On the way we glimpsed our guests: Fr. Dallinger and Fr. Przybysz, Delegate Mr. Goławski, School Inspector Mr. Żerebecki, High School Headmistress Mrs. Borońska, Captain and sailors from the Polish ship *m.v. Batory* and others. The tables were covered with white tablecloths and wafers placed on top. After prayer Mr. Goławski wished everyone a happy Christmas. Other guests shared *opłatek* (traditional wafer) with each child, while wishing them all the best. Everyone was moved - hoping for the next Christmas in free Poland - there were tears in many eyes. Older children helped with serving the traditional Christmas Eve food: beetroot soup, dumplings and compote. Fr. Przybysz handed us hymn books and we all sang carols. Next, the Christmas presents placed under the Christmas tree were handed out, mostly sweets, fruit, nuts and cakes. The midnight Mass was attended by older children. Everyone went to the Mass on Christmas Day and Boxing Day, marching in pairs to the Church. The meals on these Holy Days fitted the occasion. The free time was for the children to use as they chose.

Another popular event was the carnival ball held in the recreation hall, with boys and girls

Weddings of the wards: K. Kisiówna with Edward Searles, H. Hryczyszyn with George Fiddell and M. Świątek with Jim Nottman

dancing to the gramophone music under the eye of their carers. Even those who could not dance tried their best.

Easter had its own charm. There was the obligatory Easter confession, the traditional vigil at the Lord's Tomb and attendance at the Easter Mass, followed by the dinner during which all participated in the customary sharing of eggs - a symbol of new life, but the events of Easter Monday, the custom of *Śmigus Dyngus* were most eagerly awaited. From early morning everyone was rushing around with water filled containers and poured water over anyone they came across. Boys stripped to their shorts, ran around throwing buckets of water over girls' heads and dresses".

In the life of the Orphanage, tragic events had also occurred, such as the death of Henryk Grzybowski who collided with a lorry while riding a bicycle, or the drowning of Hania Badura in Panchganga river. Officially children were not allowed to go outside the Camp without permission, but this rule was never strictly observed.

Of a different and happy nature was the wedding of Gienia Kotlarz with Klemens Siałkowski, a soldier on leave from the Army. They met by correspondence. Many girls corresponded with the soldiers at the battle front. This way the soldiers had a chance to share their thoughts, dreams and longings with a young and sensitive person. Following an exchange of letters, friendships developed leading to romances and betrothals and even marriages. Youth has its privileges, the exchange of letters made for a diversion in an otherwise monotonous life and gave hope of meeting in future in free Poland.

At the end of 1946 the Orphanage's population had swelled to 603 by the arrival of children from Jamnagar. Places had to be found for them in the dormitories and importantly, the size of the kitchen had to be increased. Marysia Wylot noted in her diary: "A great confusion arose in our institution. We set up portable beds for the youngest children and placed their belongings in allocated places. Meals had to be split into two seatings. The kitchen could hardly cope with such a large number of children. The dormitories were crammed, but cosy. Our family has grown".

Nutrition and Staff Changes

The Orphanage wards were well nourished. Menus were prepared by the Director in cooperation with a doctor. On an average 40 to 60 children were on a supplementary diet of additional fruit and eggs. The Audit Committee made sure that the food value was adequate (about 2,940 calories daily per child). They also kept a watchful eye on living conditions, cleanliness and generally on the children's well being. Children with lung problems would be sent to a sanatorium in Panchgani, where the good climate and excellent food led to a speedy improvement in health and return to Valivade.

Mrs. Sasadeusz was the Orphanage's Director and at the same time Head of No. 3 Primary School. Performing these two functions proved to be too onerous for one person. This led to the appointment of Mrs. Felicja Wierzchowska as the Director who held this position from 1944 until her return to Poland in 1947. She was succeeded by Mr. Kazimierz Łęczyński, who remained the Director until the closure of the Orphanage in 1948. In 1944 the position of Administrator was taken over from Mrs. Zofia Grużewska by Mr. Aleksander Klecki, who held it until the end. All the above mentioned officers were responsible to the Audit Committee for the proper functioning of the Orphanage.

The Case of Children's Adoption

A directive of the Polish Ministry of Welfare Services of the 10th March 1944 was issued in response to many applications to adopt Polish children by the citizens of Great Britain, USA, Canada and other Western countries, warning that there was a danger that those children might lose their national identity. The directive emphasised, that the aim of the authorities responsible

1947 - group of children with Director K. Łęczyński, A. Klecki and M. Pałys

for the orphans saved from Russia was to assure the return of the children to their country after the war, as valuable well educated and well brought up citizens of Poland.[4]

When at the end of the war the Allies ceased to recognise the Polish Government in London, the attitude of the Polish Authorities in exile towards the return of orphans to Poland changed radically. The Communist regime in Poland had the legal right to demand the return to Poland of all orphans under the age of 17. To stop the compulsory repatriation of orphans, an action was begun to have all orphans in this category adopted by their carers, teachers or families in the Camp. The legal adoption procedures were completed in Kolhapur court on 27th November 1945. Children with parents in Poland returned to their country at the parents' request. Children with fathers, or other close relatives in England, left to join them. The last transport for England left in February 1948. The remaining children under the care of Mr. A. Klecki were transferred to an Orphanage in Tangeru, East Africa.[5] How close were the ties developed between the children could be judged by the scenes of affectionate farewells when parting. There were promises of keeping in touch as small presents were offered to those departing. The promises of remaining in touch with each other were often kept and contacts were maintained even after years of separation. The meeting of children and their parents was another emotional event. Fathers, who had spent the war years as soldiers, were often surprised at how their children had grown up. They themselves, trying to adapt to a civilian life, were often at a loss as how to start living with their children again. At times awkward moments occurred when meeting again after

Younger boys with Mrs. O Sasadeusz & their form mistress

years of separation, neither the parents nor the children knew how to react to each other. A ten year old girl, who met her parents in England, wrote later that she did not recognise them. She was at a loss how to behave - should she curtsey or kiss them? So she just stood there and the parents remarked 'hasn't she grown'.

To give a short appraisal of the Orphanage and its function it must be concluded that having gathered parentless children it had given them care, education, moral upbringing and inculcated discipline and spirit of patriotism. It organised their every day, satisfying all the material needs. The aim was to give them a chance to develop to their maximum potential. That this was achieved is proved by the wards' successes in their future life. Many achieved high positions and many also became active in their communities, always understanding the needs of others and ready to offer help.

To conclude, let us quote Marysia Woźniak again:

..."In the Orphanage we formed a large family supporting each other. Older children cared for the younger ones and offered them help. When need arose we helped with the general work, including kitchen duties. Whenever, as sometimes happened, there occurred a shortage of cooks senior girls helped with the cooking. Perhaps this is the reason why we still want to be useful, happy to assist the needy, preferring to 'give' rather than to 'take'. The feeling of satisfaction at having carried out our duties well, good deeds performed and services rendered to others, were to us a source of great happiness.

Today we realize and value the effort put into our upbringing by our teachers and carers and feel gratitude towards them. Scattered around the world, whenever we happen to meet we greet each other with great joy like long separated members of a family."

Having spent years together in circumstances where lifelong friendships had been formed, we are happy to meet again whenever there is an occasion. Today, when most of us have reached the retirement age, we realize how much toil and effort it took our teachers and carers to ensure that our lives would not be wasted. But even at that time we appreciated their labours and had been thankful.

Allow me to say sorry for all the worries, disobediences, tactlessness and many a grey hair we caused them and express deep gratitude and sincere thanks for their toil and love. We know very well how difficult it is to bring up and educate other people's children.

NOTES
1. arch. Jag: Report on Orphanage 1.XI.1944
2. AAN: file 87, page 356-7
3. arch. Jag: Report dated 1.XII.1944
4. IPiMS: Camp Chronicle C811A, page 149-50
5. Interview with Mgr. K. Łęczyński and Maria Lode

Translated by Bogusław Trella

NAMES OF THE ORPHANAGE PERSONNEL NOT INCLUDED IN THE TEXT

Aniołkowska Janina	Jeleński Aleksander	Rytlewska Maria
Bałaban Łucja	Kalinowska Eufrozyna	Rymarkiewicz Władysława
Belbot Agata	Klecki Aleksander	Socha Maria
Bronowicz Jadwiga	Kochanowska Eugenia	Szczawińska Stanisława
Cichocka Jadwiga	Kuchcicka Wanda	Sztengel Helena
Chomczenowska Zofia	Lech Aniela	Szemis Wirginia
Dacz Irena	Lotarewicz Władysław	Szyk Helena
Golinowska Helena	Łoszowska Antonina	Topolnicka Janina
Grochola Zofia	Maleńczyk Maria	Topolnicki Aleksander
Gryzel Franciszka	Ostaszewska Maria	Wolniewicz Maria
Gutkowski Kazimierz	Piotrowicz Józef	Wierzchowska Felicja

MEMORIES OF ONE MEMBER OF THE ORPHANAGE
by Janina Małkowska (Zbróg)

The former British minister of education, Mrs. Gillian Shephard, writing an article for a book about her school in Norfolk begins thus: "When you look back to school days after more than 30 years, it is difficult to disentangle what is memory and what is enduring effect." For Polish children childhood, school days, adolescent years and the war are all woven together. Memories, by force of fact are both collective and personal. In recalling events of 50 years ago one has to go back to a certain moment in time.

I left the Soviet Union as an army cadet with the newly formed Polish Army. Our ages varied between 12-16 years. We carried backpacks, wore khaki uniforms with forage caps. These travelled mostly in our pockets as they would not stay put on a shaved head. As the months passed, the older girls joined the army.

Immediately after boarding the packed train I had an attack of malaria. The first one occurred in Tashkent, and its re-occurrences dogged me for years. Somehow room was found for me to lie down, medicine was given, then I lapsed into unconsciousness. I have no recollection of this journey, which took the same route as the one described by Jurek Krzysztoń in his book *Wielbłąd na Stepie*.

In Krasnovodsk we were housed in barracks and slept on folded blankets on a cement floor, girls at one end boys at the other. The barracks stood on the outskirts of town. To one side on the horizon was Krasnovodsk and the port with huge cranes, behind us slopes and large old trees, in front of us sand and the Caspian Sea. The sand quickly changed into grey dust and an oily sludge. We were forbidden to go there, and we didn't. While in the cadets we were initially well fed, as due to our experiences in Siberia and Uzbekistan we were pitifully emaciated. A daily ration of chocolate was a 'must'. At first it was a treat but later, especially when one was thirsty, less so, but we would be in trouble if we rejected it. Once, when I went for a walk along the beach with a friend, we saw a Gypsy woman with a baby. We gave her our chocolate. She grabbed my hand, looked into my eyes and started talking very quickly in Russian. We listened in bewilderment. Maybe it is just as well that I did not believe any of the things she told me then, because half a century later, I must admit that all she said came true. We never met her again, although we often walked the same way.

The day of our departure from the Soviet Union finally arrived. We walked in twos in long lines to the pier, treading upon a variety of things dropped from open suitcases and torn bundles. The civilians could not cope with carrying all their possessions aboard the ship. On the pier was a multitude of women with children of various ages. Polish and Russian soldiers kept order. As we boarded, the gangplank over the dark brown water swayed underfoot.

Someone in uniform took my hand firmly, led up and hustled me on to the deck, then reached hurriedly towards the next pair of hands. We were told to move toward the edge of the deck. With relief I took off my backpack and sat on it. Immediately someone grabbed my shoulders and shouted loudly 'Child you'll drown yourself'. Being held fast by a soldier, I looked behind - no barrier - half a step and I would have been overboard. From the pier rose up the cries of children and lamentations of women unwilling to leave their meagre possessions behind. Above all that noise, the loud voice of a soldier was urging them to board the ship.

Mess kits in hand we stood in a long queue for soup and bread, and an even longer one to the toilets. Many people were sick. At last we were allocated our spaces and told to lie down on the deck on folded blankets. The ship sailed, darkness fell but there were no stars. The Caspian Sea was calm, somewhere people sang a devotional song. At last the singing stopped, - someone muttered a prayer. We fell into an uneasy sleep. Suddenly a terrible cry pierced the night. I opened my eyes in time to see a dark shape pass behind the railing and hear a sharp splash. The alarm siren sounded, the ship stopped, lifeboat was lowered, but the body was not found. We sailed on to Persia, today's Iran.

Pahlevi, was a forest of tents and sand, sand everywhere - in the blankets, in the clothes, in the mess kits and on the beach, where the Persian traders had their stalls with small trifles but mostly with halva. We used to buy small amounts of it and ate it from a piece of paper. It tasted wonderful.

Then through the massive mountains of Elbruz we drove to Teheran in a long convoy of lorries, each one carrying twelve girls and one adult seated on benches on either side of the lorry. The road hewn from the mountain was rough, with no barrier on the side of the sheer drop. We moved slowly. Rounding the sharp ends in the road, the back of the lorry hung over the precipice. We climbed higher and higher. On one side were overhanging cliffs, on the other was the loud rustling sound of the windswept tops of trees below. After almost a day's journey we began to descend.

In Teheran we lived in army barracks outside the town. Daily routine consisted of morning exercises, drill and an inspection of the barracks. We slept on cement floors, showers were nearby. For meals we lined up with our mess kits and cutlery, cups were kept in the dining area. Lessons were held in the open, under a shady tree. Apart from the teacher's notebook in which he recorded our progress, there were no exercise books or pencils. We wrote on slates which were cleaned and left for the next class. We accepted our strange situation as a matter of course, nothing surprised us anymore. In our free time we visited the town's places of interest. A family friend now a sergeant, in the Polish Army, found me, arranged a pass and used to invite me for tea and cakes. My favourite were profiteroles. I still remember their delicious taste today. A few months later we were segregated: older girls were sent to Palestine, the younger army cadets, myself included, travelled to Isfahan, where there was a large centre for Polish adolescents and young children, among whom were many orphans, some very young. Here we were housed in various town buildings. Polish personnel ministered to and cared for us. As girl cadets we were housed in a large convent building. The rooms had beds and tables; bathrooms, the dining hall, the chapel and the school were within the same building.

Skipping a year, I was enrolled in second year of high school. In Isfahan exercise books were provided and the hours of study were regular. Extra curricular activities involved learning poems and folk dancing in preparation for the celebration of national holidays. Excursions were organised to old historic places, especially to the well known and beautiful mosques.

We still wore our army cadet uniform. Every afternoon, as a part of our drill, we marched stamping our feet along the suburban footpaths, singing loudly. I don't know how the residents reacted to this, but we enjoyed ourselves, joked and laughed, yet still managed to maintain the tempo of the march. Many of us joined the girl Guides.

In Isfahan we were often hungry. I remember queueing for supper and being handed a cup of sweetened tea and a thick slice of white bread smeared with a teaspoon of honey. Some older girls protested loudly and things did change later. The convent with its complex of large buildings and its garden of colourful flowerbeds in front was surrounded by a high wall, the huge gate locked with a key. We were shut in, and outings were undertaken only under strict adult supervision.

After some months we were again segregated: an older group of girls went to Palestine, the rest of us were joined by children from other Polish schools in Isfahan and told that our destination was India. But first we were transported to Ahwaz on the Persian Gulf. Here the authorities housed us in army barracks which had narrow windows for coolness. We slept on a cement floor. Some way further on was the British Army base, housing soldiers of English, Indian and Australian nationality. Still further on was the American base.

There was no escape from the heat in Ahwaz. The sun hung like a big copper plate in a brown-grey sky. It was hot, very hot, even in the shade and in the barracks. Daily routine was easier - care was taken that we kept ourselves and our surroundings tidy, attended meals and had a good night's sleep. In this climate numerous children and adults fell ill, and as everywhere else, when we left Ahwaz, we left some graves behind us.

A short train trip took us to the port, where American soldiers helped us to board a ship A smiling soldier came up to me, took my backpack, my hand and led me aboard. He gave me a handful of sweets for which I thanked him, but I needed a drink, not sweets. For several days while sailing, we were escorted by two naval vessels, as there was the danger from U-boats and mines. Both sides engaged in the war had great interest in this area, because of the oil resources. Once we passed the mouth of the Gulf, the escorts left us and we sailed safely to Karachi.

After disembarking we rode through the town in open lorries. We saw houses with flat roofs and wide green lawns often surrounded by creepers whose flowers of every colour contrasted sharply with white walls. We passed shops, then the poor quarter, where houses resembled flimsy sheds constructed from anything and with everything. Among these milled a mass of adults and children. Here and there, dressed in tropical uniforms strolled English soldiers walking always in pairs. We stopped a short distance past the town. Only the English sense of humour could have given the name of 'Country Club' to the number of large tents spread among the sandy scrub.

Here everything was well organised and our daily routine normalised. The nights were

Young performers (artistes) in their costumes

interrupted by the howling of the prowling jackals, which streaked through our tent like a lightning, but still managed to pick up some object. Soap always went missing after their visit.

In Karachi my body finally rebelled against the heat. I developed a high temperature and boils all over my body and landed in the camp Sick Bay. An English army doctor - a wonderful man, tall, broad shouldered but somewhat comical looking, with his rotund torso overhanging his army regulation shorts - examined me. He knew two Polish words, I knew two English ones, but between his slow nods, wide smiles and my tears of pain, we came to an understanding. I had full faith in his capacity to cure me, and he did.

The hospital tent was dug into the ground making it slightly cooler, its floor was moistened daily so the air was free from dust. Following injections, medicines and baths, my temperature subsided after a few days and my appetite slowly returned. A couple of weeks later I returned to my group and joined in the normal daily occupations.

Some time later, girls from the camp, who had younger siblings but no parents, joined us and together we became known as the Gen. W. Sikorski Orphanage.

Performance of a Fairy Tale

Accompanied by our Staff we were moved to Malir where an American army base was situated, but as there was some distance between us, we seldom saw the soldiers.

Here we were housed in army barracks which were divided into small rooms with large windows. Outside were wide terraces shaded by extended roofs. There was an Administration block, the first aid room, the kitchen and the dining room, hygienic amenities and the school block. Past the Orphanage and past the sandy scrub ran an asphalt road devoid of any traffic except for an occasional army truck heading towards the base and the loud motorcycles at night. We wore white blouses with grey skirts. Clothes were made for us on site by dressmakers. Normal schooling was quickly organised.

The fully equipped American Army Base Hospital stood on the edge of the base. After a few weeks I developed a severe attack of malaria and found myself in the Base Hospital in a six-bed ward. Despite the medical treatment the temperature did not subside. In a semi-conscious state I was indifferent as to what was being done to me and by whom. But with time, good care, medicines and a lot of fluids I slowly improved and began to eat.

At long last I could return to the Orphanage and its daily routine. But after one month we were taken to the port and boarded a ship for Bombay. As it happened, the Polish ship *Batory* was berthed in the port and its Polish crew quickly made themselves known to us. To us they were an exciting novelty. Judging by their enthusiastic greetings we also meant something special to them. An officer, Jan T., took me under his protection and in the next few years corresponded with me. Whenever *Batory* was in Bombay he visited me, brought me small gifts and left some pocket money. In a fatherly manner he was pleased with my progress in school and was ever ready with good advice. His wife and daughter remained in Gdynia. I hope that the good Lord allowed him to return to them.

From Bombay a long journey by train took us to Kolhapur and the nearby Valivade.

The Camp was still in the process of being built. Our group, 180 children of various ages and 10 adult personnel were placed in a temporary accommodation until our own quarters were completed. Nearby was the kitchen and the dining block. On the other side was a large recreation hall, further on a dental surgery and a small first aid clinic. The shower arrangements provided some privacy. Medical examinations and checks by a hygienist were carried out regularly. Boys were housed separately. Older girls with small brothers - (the older boys were sent to Palestine from Teheran and Isfahan) - had full and easy access to them and could take care of their small personal needs. This left the carers more time for those who were all alone. I myself was alone - my two brothers had already been in the army in 1939 and both were taken prisoners by the Germans.

We were 30 in a dormitory. Beds were arranged heads against the wall between the windows. There was sufficient space in between the beds for individual belongings and a tin trunk, which was covered with a small tablecloth and doilies and served as a table for books, letters, etc. We hung small tapestries, mats, over the bedheads, so the overall effect was nice and neat. Bed linen was changed regularly and the place was cleaned in our absence. At each end of the hall was a table on which were placed drinking water, cups, a washing bowl and an iron. Outside ran a shady terrace, with a narrow bed of greenery then a wide space and the next block.

Although the Orphanage had an independent administration, it was an integral part of the Camp. As a group we differed in family backgrounds and origins. Some of us were from the Eastern, some from other parts of Poland. I myself came from central Poland. Private matters, such as dates of exile into Siberia, one's experiences while there, were seldom talked about and never asked about unless someone volunteered, mostly after the receipt of sad news about a near relative. We were fully engrossed in daily living, yet still fully conscious that the bloody struggle in Europe and nearer to India, in Burma, still continued. Family bonds also differed. Among us were girls who had lost both parents and were with younger siblings, girls who were all alone and girls whose parents still remained in the Soviet Union. Some may have had a father, an older brother or a sister in the army, but may have had left their mother in a grave on the Kazakhstan steppe.

We differed also in characters and talents. Among us were girls good at sport, dancing or singing. Some had a good sense of humour and always saw the lighter side of every situation. They made us laugh. There was lots of laughter, lots of singing. We simply absorbed songs of every kind: army, Scout, folk, patriotic, not to mention the hymns. There were always girls with good voices who remembered many popular Polish songs and Ukrainian 'dumkas'.

The Orphanage personnel treated us well and fairly in all respects. In turn, we respected them and turned to them with trust for an advice or an explanation of a given situation. Over the months our house mistresses changed, but each one in her own way was pleasant and caring. Each night they saw to it that our mosquito nets were properly tucked in, exchanged a few words with those awake, turned the lamps down and quietly left the room. We fell asleep feeling that everything around us was safe and good.

But we did not always laugh. I recall one of the earlier years during which the office of All Souls' Day was celebrated very solemnly - prayers in the church, candles, dirges. We returned to our dormitory sad and thoughtful. Then one of us began to sob. In the space of a couple of minutes we were all sobbing loudly and inconsolably, as if each one of us in her soul evoked the terrible and tragic images seen and experienced from the beginning of the war. We could not be consoled for a long time. In the following years All Souls' Days were celebrated with less solemnity.

Celebrations, whether a Church feast day or a national holiday began with an after breakfast Mass. At lunch time, official and non-official guests mixed with us, talked, joked and joined us at the table. In the afternoon, if it was a national holiday, we all went to the Recreation Room to take part in the celebration. The warm words of Father Dallinger, his eyes full of understanding and compassion when he approached us with the Christmas Eve wafer, or the kind smile of the Delegate, Michał Goławski, were remembered for a long time.

When by 1943 the camp became fully established, shops also appeared. We were given pocket money, a few rupees for small personal needs such as hairpins, needle and thread, sweets or perhaps a visit to the cinema. With a fixed address we now began to receive letters - sometimes money - from relatives or friends in the army. When we became older, we could obtain permission to go shopping in Kolhapur. But Kolhapur as a shopping place we found to be unpleasant. The streets were packed with every type of contraption that could be pulled, pushed or driven - carts, motorcycles, ramshackle cars, bicycles and prams. On the footpath were beggars standing or lying down, sometimes with lame children beside them. The crowd just passed them by. Around all that, the strong scent of various spices sold in the open stalls wafted into the air, and of course, the unavoidable aroma of 'curry'. What we found more pleasant were the organised trips to the ancient relics, temples and to the maharajah's palace surrounded by extensive gardens.

Inspector Żerebecki with the children

The daily routine in the Orphanage did not change over the three years: reveille, folding of mosquito nets, morning toilet, breakfast. Anyone feeling unwell stayed in bed and was looked after. After breakfast we walked to school, having first tidied up our beds and belongings. Nobody checked up on us, we ourselves were responsible for taking the necessary books and materials to school. After school and lunch in the early afternoon there was a period of silence or more properly, of rest. It was a pleasure to take one's shoes off and lie down on the bed. But not everyone took a nap; some sewed, some read some talked quietly. After our rest, came afternoon tea and free time, then supper and again free time - used perhaps for doing homework, letter-writing or visiting a friend in the camp. In the pre-monsoon time, when the heat increased, the greenery turned brown and the strong wind raised the fine sand into the air, every spare moment was spent under a shower.

The Scouting movement blossomed. Never before and never afterwards were there such favourable conditions for its existence. Religious, patriotic and willing youth and children were on the spot. The necessary equipment for all Scouting activities e.g. excursions, camping etc. was at hand. Apart from the Scouting movement, religious and sporting organisations also existed. If anyone did not wish to join any one of these organisations, their wishes were respected. Freedom of choice prevailed.

Our Scout campfires held on a hill outside the camp were wonderful events. We sat in a large circle on the still warm grass, we told stories and played games. In the dusk of the evening the flames rose upwards, above us was the huge dark blue sky and the emerging stars. Our Scout songs, the happy, the sad and the religious ones also flowed upwards. Sometimes down below a train passed, the chuff-chuffing locomotive with a long string of palely lighted carriages behind it, stopped briefly at the Valivade Halt, then moved on. We knew that a similar train would take us out of here, but we did not know when. When at the end of the night we stood with our arms linked and sang softly '...*God is near...*', we really felt Him very near.

News from the European fronts reached us regularly. After its heroic struggle, the Warsaw Uprising collapsed, with tragic consequences for the city and the nation. The Red Army moved towards the west and Berlin, the British and American Forces moved from west to east, also towards Berlin. Our Polish soldiers fought and died on every front.

Wolf Cubs and Girl Guides

Two Scoutmasters arrived in Valivade, sent from the army. Uniformed, they looked healthy and energetic. One of them, Zdzisław Peszkowski, whom we called 'Ryś', liked to stroll through the camp streets carrying a horsehair switch, which he waved about as if driving away invisible flies. He was a fair game for our comedians and mimics. But when on a camp in Panhala I developed malaria with accompanying high temperature, it was 'Ryś' who sat with me, talked to me, restrained my flailing arms and gave me drinks of water until I was taken back to Valivade.

Schooling proceeded along its normal course. Some teachers we liked more, others less, some had a sense of humour, others lacked it, but all were very demanding - for the educational standard was high. We respected all of them. The day of the intermediate exams arrived. Most passed well, students who had problems with the required school program, fell away. The rest of us had to decide our future course of study. I enrolled in a Teachers' Training Lycee.

The war in Europe finished, the peace treaty was signed in May 1945. In Asia and in the Pacific the war continued until America - for the first time in human history - used an atomic bomb on two Japanese cities. But the end of the war did not bring joy to Polish people, neither those in Poland itself, nor to those scattered around the whole world. At that time we did not understand the cynical politicking which considered only the great powers and their advantages, not the fate of small nations, but we learned fast. In Valivade fear and suspicions took hold and alarming gossip buzzed around: "Russia is demanding the return of people born in the eastern region *(Kresy)*", "Russia wants to take Polish children" and many more such conjectures sprang up from sources unknown. A 'paper adoption' of children from the Orphanage by the women from the camp was organised, as if that had any meaning. The numbers in the Orphanage increased. Youths from hospitals, schools and sanatoria in different parts of India, alone or in twos or threes, joined us.

In January 1946, in order to improve our English, a group of us was sent to Panchgani, to St. Joseph's Convent for a few months. Segregated according to our ages we took part in all the normal studies even though we did not always comprehend all. Homework was done at individual tables under the eye of the teacher on duty. The other pupils, English and the few Indian girls, were nice and friendly. Everyday uniform was a cream coloured dress with a red tie, for Sunday, a light green tie. An English 'boater' with a ribbon matching the colours of the ties was a part of the uniform and compulsory attire when outside the convent.

Soon after our arrival at the Convent, news spread around the school of the arrival of two maharajahs' daughters. One, older than we were, always serious and rather sad, wore a flowing sari and was as beautiful as the pictures of the Indian goddesses. The other one wore a light summer dress, was plump and jolly. She was in our class and her name was Rupina. Jerking her dark fringe about, she used to point out the funny side of everything. We laughed with her. A couple of weeks later as I was walking along the corridor I was stopped by a beautiful, unknown to me melody, coming from one of the classrooms. Opening the door I was surprised to see Rupina sitting at the piano, lightly playing and singing. When she saw me, she stopped and informed me that the melody was *Danny Boy*. I begged her to continue. She went on playing and later taught me the lyrics of the song. The ancient Irish melody is even to-day among the ones that I enjoy the most and when sometimes I hear it on the radio, I am again a schoolgirl in Panchgani and see Rupina at the piano.

Mixed class room with O Sasadeusz and J. Figuła (last on the right, sitting is A. Chendynski)

On returning to Valivade I began to study at the Teachers' Lycee. The classmates were very pleasant, the tutors very demanding. In the dormitory no big changes. But a mood of impending departures was in the air. We all knew it had to happen, but did not know when. A small group of girls and boys departed for America. Every letter received held the information that the Polish Forces (under the British command) were being moved to England, where family re-unions were to take place. The demobilised soldiers had to face a change to a civilian life, the need to search for work and lodgings or to try for resettlement in other countries. Polish people rightly felt betrayed by their allies - Polish politicians deluded themselves with the belief that America and England would soon declare war on Russia.

In the meantime the UNRRA was organising a transport to Poland. Girls who had contact with their parents there, taking their advice, put their names down for repatriation. The girls studying for matriculation moved from the dormitory to a block with double-rooms. Daily routine remained the same, except that the lamp remained burning much longer. Often, when finishing an essay, I heard the rustle of a huge, hairy, brown spider making his way along the wall matting. Without disturbing him I watched his progress, which always ended behind the window frame. I made sure my own and my room-mate's mosquito nets were well tucked in, put away my homework, turned off the lamp and soon fell asleep.

One late evening, while writing letters, I heard muttering and what sounded like a loud scuffle outside my window. Surprised, I ventured outside, walked around the block and saw that right under our window an Indian night watchman was killing a cobra with a stick. Stretched out, the reptile looked long, perhaps longer than when alive. I thanked the night watchman and asked him to remove it before the morning. On the whole the evenings were quiet. From afar could often be heard a male voice singing a haunting Indian melody and the drawn out creaking of a cart pulled slowly by oxen and heading for the morning market. I liked the far off singing in the stillness of the night.

The administration office received lists of names for departure to England. As we already knew, the first to depart were the immediate family members: wives and children. Extended family members would join them later. These departures affected our Orphanage as the personnel changed frequently. The last director, Mr. Kazimierz Łęczyński, was understanding and pleasant; among ourselves we called him 'Kaziczek'.

At the end of 1946 the Jamnagar Orphanage joined us. Some of the children were already listed for departure to England. The last transport left at the beginning of 1948. I was on that list. A small number of youth who remained in the Orphanage left soon after for East Africa. After nearly five years of existence, the Gen. W. Sikorski Orphanage was wound up.

The Orphanage was not what the name would suggest. It was not quite an orphanage, as many of us had at least one parent living. It was not a school, as its staff did not include teachers. We attended the Camp schools which embraced all the children and youth in Valivade. Was it an enclosed institution? Definitely not - completely open, we were always free to move around the Camp.

The Orphanage in Valivade was something unique during the war and after the war. It was not called 'home', as we all knew that once the war was over we would all go our separate ways. We were cared for as far as our health, upbringing and education was concerned. Were we closely knit? It could not have been otherwise.

Years passed, children grew up, youth matured. We left Valivade sure of ourselves, with faith in our future and in life.

Translated by Maryla Trella

Orphanage with their carers

PASTORAL CARE AND RELIGIOUS ORGANISATIONS POLISH CATHOLIC MISSION IN INDIA (PCM)
by Zofia Zawidzka

Origins

The Polish Catholic Mission (PCM) for the civilian population in India was established in October 1943 by Fr. Kazimierz Bober-Bobrowski - appointed Rector of the Mission by the Office of the Polish Army Field Bishop (Ep. Józef Gawlina). The Mission ceased to exist when the last rector, Fr. Kazimierz Kozłowski, SJ left India in 1948.[1]

PCM Function and Activities

Duties of the PCM during the 1942-1948 period consisted mainly of providing pastoral care for the Polish population living in India (in camps and settlements), and for employees of the Polish diplomatic agencies as well as the Red Cross hospital founded by the WRS NCWC. Care was also extended to members of the British Armed Forces and sailors serving on various ships harboured temporarily in Bombay, who were of Polish origin. Furthermore, the PCM was responsible for establishing several Catholic associations and organisations, supervising religious education in the schools, visiting them as well as Scout and Girl Guide units active in the Polish Camps.

Orchard Lake (USA) Archives

After the death of Fr. Bobrowski archival records concerning PCM pastoral care in India were transferred to the Orchard Lake Polonia Archives. The records consist of about 500 documents covering the 2-year period of diverse and problematic subject matter such as the collaboration between the PCM and both the Polish Consul General and the Polish Red Cross Delegate in India. The records include: (1) documentation of religious education and school visitations; (2) periodical reports concerning contacts with Boy Scout and Girl Guide units; (3) Wanda Dynowska's lectures on Hinduism for adults and youth (considered 'controversial' by the Rector); (4) discussions of problems related to religious, moral and patriotic education;

(5) records of equipment purchases for school science laboratories financed by the NCWC; (6) records of the distribution of Field Bishop Office Catholic Press Centre publications and of the delivery of Polish books from London, England. Since the Pastoral Care budget was taken over by the Ministry of Education, these documents also include statements of pastoral requirements, as well as, those of the PCM Rector's Office.

Pastoral Care

A separate and voluminous section of the Archives includes documents, letters and pastoral reports from various Polish Camps. Most of these documents originated in the Valivade Kolhapur Camp, mainly dating from the 1943-45 period. These include: Fr. Leopold Dallinger's reports on general descriptions of the settlement, detailed description of the church construction, consecration and functional quality. Documents also include financial, organisational and managerial reports concerning food supply, employment and statistics pertaining to the population, denominations, celebration of Sacraments (baptisms, communions, confirmation, marriages, last rites) and funerals. There are also descriptions of retreats, missions, devotions, church fairs, as well as celebrations of religious and national holidays. There are lists of religious education teachers, questionnaires for teachers and curricula of religious education.

A separate part of the section includes rules, regulations and activities for youth religious organisations, *Dom Katolicki* (Community Centre), the church choir and Catholic Action.

This section of the Archive also includes correspondence relating to various topics such as: mixed marriages, statements regarding missing and/or dead persons, school religious education, teaching permits granted to lay teachers, lists of subscriptions to Polish catholic periodicals, purchased books, book store catalogues, questionnaires, discussions of personal matters, correspondence *(in some cases controversial)* between the Rector and the Delegate of MP&OS, as well as documents containing criticisms by the Rector, often unfounded, directed at various aspects of religious education and youth organisations in the Valivade Camp. These accessible documents suggest that the attitude of the Rector showed no evidence of honouring previously negotiated agreements of mutual cooperation or observing basic rules of Christian tolerance.[2]

On the other hand, relationships with local civil and church authorities (e.g. Archbishop Dr. Henry Doering SJ, Bishop of the diocese of Poona which included Valivade), as revealed by the preserved documentation, evolved in a harmonious way.[3]

In addition to the pastoral activities in Valivade, the above described Archives also contain documentation relating to the transit Camp in Karachi (Country Club), as well as the Polish Children's Camp (orphanage) in Balachadi-Jamnagar, and the Rest Centre in Panchgani.[4]

One of the major PCM achievements was sending a group of potential candidates for the priesthood to the Orchard Lake Seminary in USA.

PASTORS

Fr. Kazimierz Bober-Bobrowski (1905-1991)

Appointed senior chaplain of the Polish Forces in the Far East, with his permanent seat in Bombay *(see chapter on Bombay)*.

Msgr. Leopold Dallinger (1884-1965)

Fr. Dallinger received Holy Orders in 1908 and served in several parishes in the diocese of Lwów until World War I (1914-1918). During the war he served as a chaplain in the

Austrian Army. After the war, from 1919 to 1939, he taught religion in local high schools. In April 1940 his family, as well as other people, were rounded up for deportation, he joined them of his own accord and was deported to the Soviet Union. In December 1941, he joined the Polish Army being formed in the Soviet Union by Gen. Anders, and served as a chaplain. In 1943 he was appointed parish priest in Valivade Camp (India)[5] and remained there until 1947. During the years spent in Valivade he won people's hearts, esteem and respect. The farewell speech delivered by Alicja Kisielnicka bears witness to his accomplishments:

"As everybody knows, Fr. Dallinger has been appointed transport commander of the group leaving for the Middle East in the near future. There is a rumour going around that nobody would be surprised if, by mistake, this transport would arrive in heaven instead, because this holy priest could easily transform all his subordinates into angels. There is no malice in this joke, - she added, 'it really is based on a firm conviction that travelling in Fr. Dallinger's company is quite a privilege.

It was generally accepted by the people of Valivade where Fr. Dallinger lived and worked, that he unquestionably possessed a rare and precious gift of moral authority. Perhaps Fr. Dallinger was held in such high regard because he always tried to avoid the limelight: he was practically invisible, and was truly the most modest man in Valivade. People also knew that although he never imposed his opinions on others, in questions demanding a clear and uncompromising decision, he was always outspoken. For months on end he was the only priest working in Valivade, yet he always had time for troubled or unhappy people. His days were work-filled, beginning with early morning mass celebration, followed by teaching at schools and spending long evening hours in the confessional. His sermons were short and to the point but touched hearts because they were so simple, yet displayed deep understanding of human nature. It is significant that the last few minutes before his departure, the crowd became very silent."[6]

Having arrived in England, Fr. Dallinger returned to the work of service and never stopped teaching and sharing his life with others. He spent his last years teaching at a girls' school in Pitsford. The school was run by the Sisters of the Holy Family of Nazareth. During the weeks, months and years of his last illness, he became totally dependent on his kind carers. It must have been a very difficult time for this priest, who never wanted others to bother about him. Obviously it was not easy for him to accept help, but accept it he did, submitting to the will of God and meeting His demands wholeheartedly. He never left Pitsford, died there and was buried on the school grounds and thus remained amongst the youngsters he loved and who loved him.[7]

Fr. Jan Przybysz, Congregation of Marians, 1909-2008

As a young boy he attended a high school run by the Marian Fathers, entered their novitiate and continued his studies at the Major Seminary and Stefan Batory University in Wilno. In January 1940, soon after the invasion of Poland by the Soviet Army, he was ordained a priest. In June 1941 he was deported to the labour camp in Krasnoyarsk, where he worked in the forest felling trees, and where, in secrecy, exercised his priestly duties. After the amnesty proclamation for the Polish prisoners, Fr. Jan joined the Polish Army and served as a chaplain until 1942, when he was transferred to the Camp No.1 in Teheran, next (in 1943), to Karachi and ultimately, in December 1943, to Valivade, where he taught religion and Latin in high schools. He was also in charge of the church choir. In the summer 1947 Fr. Jan left for England and later moved to a newly opened Marian Centre in the USA. Fr. Jan returned to England in 1951 and was instrumental in purchasing Fawley Court, in Henley-on-Thames and converting it into a Boarding High School for boys. Until 1971, he served as Pastoral Carer for Poles living in Wales. Then in 1971, Fr. Jan returned to Fawley Court, where he lived until his death in 2008. Fr. Jan was a member of the Association of Poles in India, he attended several reunions, and he celebrated his 90th birthday in their company.[8]

Fr. Antoni Jankowski (1914-1972)

Born in 1914 in the Archdiocese of Lvov, he studied philosophy and theology at the Jan Kazimierz University of Lvov. Fr. Antoni was arrested twice in the course of the year 1939-1940 by Soviet authorities and deported to the northern Ural mountains. In 1941 he joined the Polish Army under the command of General Anders. Fr. Antoni was ordained in Yangi-Yul by Ep. Józef Gawlina, the Polish Army Field Bishop, and was originally designated to work with Poles left behind in the Soviet Union. However this plan had to be abandoned later as any pastoral work within the borders of the Soviet Union was forbidden. Having arrived in Persia, Fr. Antoni worked in the Polish camp in Ahwaz from August 1943 to June 1945, when he became a permanent chaplain in the Karachi transit camp. He remained there until its closure and then moved to Valivade. During his stay in Karachi and subsequently in Valivade, he managed WRS-NCWC funds that enriched and diversified the cultural and educational lives of the inhabitants. He was the co-founder-manager of the printing press in Valivade - responsible for publishing 20 books as well as printing (as of April 1947) *Polak w Indiach*. He was the last president of the Federation of Poles in India.[9] Fr. Antoni left India with the last group of 150 Poles and arrived in England via Lebanon. Having settled in England he served Poles as their parish priest in Hiltingbury and Southampton. He died suddenly in July 1972.

Fr. Kazimierz Kozłowski SJ, Scoutmaster (1902-1966)

Born in July 1902, he entered the Jesuit Order at the age of 15 and was ordained in 1930. He held the office of Superior in the Kołomyja Jesuit House when the Second World War broke out. During the formation stage of the Polish Army in the Soviet Union he was appointed assistant chaplain of the Polish Armed Forces and, later on, chaplain of the Polish Embassy in the Soviet Union. He held this position until his departure from the Soviet Union in August 1942. After a short stay in Teheran he was appointed the PCM Rector in India.[10] He worked in Valivade until January 1948, when he left for Great Britain, and very soon after, joined Jesuit Missions in Zambia. He was described by his superiors as a 100% wandering missionary - he thoroughly enjoyed visiting native villages, evangelizing people and spreading the Good News. In 1966 he became a chaplain in a local hospital. In 1967 he visited Poland and England and returned to Africa with bold building plans. He enthusiastically started and completed his construction of a chapel with a parish hall in suburban Lusaka. Soon after, he fell seriously ill, and was transferred to Salisbury (today Harare), where he died on 14th August 1968 and was buried in the English sector of the Mission cemetery in Chishawasha.

Cardinal Adam Kozłowiecki S J, his boyhood friend, wrote the following lines: I knew him since my early days in Chyrów, later we both shared the novitiate and finally we both shared the missionary work in Kasisi (Zambia). I had a high opinion of him as a priest and a missionary. He was totally dedicated to his work. I was told that heart failure had been the ultimate cause of his death.'[11]

Msgr. Franciszek Jan Pluta (1905-1990)

Msgr. Pluta was born in December 1905 in Cleveland USA. His parents sent him to Poland to study theology. He graduated from the Seminary in Równe and was ordained in Łuck in 1933. He started his pastoral care duties with the elementary and high school children. Later, Msgr. Pluta engaged in parish work and eventually became a parish priest in a newly organised parish in Janowa Dolina, shortly before the start of the World War II. Imprisoned by the Soviet authorities, he was sent to several different prisons and ended up in Kiev, where he was sentenced to death. The sentence was fortunately reduced to 15 years of hard labour in a labour camp. After the proclamation of the amnesty, Fr. Pluta reached Buzułuk, where the Polish Second Corps was in the initial stages of organisation under the command of General W. Anders. Very soon afterwards, he was sent on a special assignment to take care of the Polish Children as future commandant of the camp to be located in India. He left for India with the first group of over 100 persons (orphans and teachers) in April 1942. The destination was Jamnagar-Balachadi, where the land for the camp was offered by a great friend of Poles, Maharaja Jam Saheb Digvijay Sinhji. After the war, there was a serious threat that the children would be deported back to Poland, and educated in Communist ideology. However, thanks to the Maharaja's unique position of influence, a very unusual procedure of adoption of the minors was successfully carried out. The children's legal representatives were: Fr. Pluta (moral protection), Maharaja Jam Saheb Digvijay Sinhji (financial support) and Jeffrey Clark, (representing the British authorities). In 1946 Fr. Pluta travelled to the United States, where he secured support of Polish organisations in the States and founded, in Chicago, an 'Association of Protection for the Polish Children in India' and this ensured for Polish orphans an upbringing in a Polish environment.

During the gradual liquidation of the Polish camps in India, Fr. Pluta managed to send to the US two groups of young people with a tentative vocation to religious life. He liked to recall a touching incident: one of the boys called him years later and reminded him how once, after some major trouble making - he had been threatened by the exasperated Father: 'I'll kill you or make a human being out of you', then there was silence followed by the words: 'Thank you, Father, for making me into a human being.'

In 1953 Fr. Pluta moved to Canada and founded a Polish parish in London, Ontario. He was active not only in his parish but throughout the diocese and eventually became a synodal judge. In the same year Pius XII appointed him a House Prelate.

In 1957 he led the first postwar pilgrimage from the American continent to Poland and delivered a new therapeutic instrument, so-called 'cobalt bomb', a gift from the Canadian Polonia. Two years later he initiated a second pilgrimage to Częstochowa led by Bishop John Cody.

Fr. Pluta retired at the age of 70, but he never stopped his pastoral activities or forgot his friends from Jamnagar.[12] He kept in touch with them and supported them for many years. Fr. Pluta died in Toronto on January 23, 1990.[13]

Brother Jan Orysiuk Salesian (1915-1993)

Born in 1915, Jan entered the Salesian Order in 1937. Soon after the invasion of Poland by the Soviet Union Br. Jan landed in Siberia, sharing the fate of thousands of Poles. Following the route of other Polish exiles, he reached Persia, and eventually arrived in India. Like thousands of others he and his parents stayed in Valivade camp. He was responsible for the altar servers, taught religion in the elementary school, was an active Scout. Always helpful, appreciated and popular, Br. Jan won everyone's respect and trust. One of his former altar boys, Franciscan Fr. Błażej Edward Karaś, remembers how the first group of the altar boys was trained: 'I lived with my sisters and a younger brother in block No. 64. Providentially, our closest neighbours were Br. Orysiuk and his parents. Soon after we got to know each other Br. Jan asked me (I was 12 at the time) if I'd like to learn serving at mass. I thought - why not! I did not have the slightest idea how to go about it. Br. Jan immediately offered to teach me, starting with lesson number one and lent me a service booklet with all the proper responses which I copied without delay. And so my training began. Soon after, and under Br. Jan's careful supervision, I assumed my duties as an altar boy, serving during Fr. Dallinger's early morning mass. After my friends found me out, all of them wanted to join the ranks of the altar servers. So my next task was to teach them all the responses. I spoke the priest's words, performing liturgical motions to test them. In this way the first group of altars servers was trained and took up their duties at the altar.'[14]

W. Kleszko who prepared an obituary notice after Brother Jan's death, wrote:

'To be able to move to England and join his parents, Br. Orysiuk had to pass through the DP (displaced persons) camp in Germany. After his parents' death he settled with the Salesian Fathers in Gloucester. He truly was a master of all trades, particularly in the field of mechanics. Sent off to a Salesian Mission in Zimbabwe he performed nothing short of miracles restoring old vehicles. He participated in the first Polish Scouts Jamboree in England and attended three of our reunions. In early March 1993 I came across him on the stairway of the POSK building in London. He looked surprisingly well and quite fit despite a recent illness. We spoke about our forthcoming annual general meeting which he intended to attend. He seemed to be full of renewed enthusiasm. Unfortunately he suffered another relapse and died in April 1993.'[15]

Czesław Kowalewski was a well known and respected church sexton. In addition to his church duties, he made candles for church use and at Christmas time he baked wafers for Christmas Eve, which he used to sell to the parishioners.

Józef Król was an ever-present and faithful organ player at all the church services and accompanied the church choir.[16]

THE VALIVADE CHURCH

Construction and Description.

St. Andrew Bobola church, consecrated in February 1944 by the Archbishop of Poona, Dr. Henry Doering, was the heart of the Valivade Camp. The Building Committee started the reconstruction works in October 1943. Formerly nothing more but a barrack, the church was reconstructed according to the plans prepared by Jan Pacak and under his supervision. Jan Pacak worked free of charge in spite of his many other responsibilities. The church had a small pinnacle with a bell and a large clock. It rose above the roofs of the Camp and was visible from all points. The following invocation was inscribed above the main entrance: *God save Poland*.[17]

The suspended ceiling was made of a linen-like grey cloth. The main altar was elevated and separated from the rest of the church by the altar rail.[18] There was a painting of St. Andrew Bobola above the altar and a beautiful reproduction of Murillo's Florentine Madonna with the Child Jesus in the right side altar. The altars were always decked with fresh flowers. Here, young people gathered for celebrations, couples vowed love until death, infants were baptized, and children received their First Holy Communion and the Sacrament of Confirmation. Here also, people gathered to bid the final farewell to their loved ones.

Here, at the feet of the Madonna, women spent hours in silent prayer for their husbands and sons, for brothers and fathers entering new battlefields of the raging war. Here, they thanked God for every sign of life and bent down in sorrow when their letters were returned with a short message written across the familiar envelope: 'Died in action'. Here many young people made choices that often had a life-long and irrevocable significance.

Canonical Visits

His Grace Archbishop Dr. Henry Doering, SJ Titular Bishop of Poona, visited Valivade twice. The first visit took place in February 1944.[19] Having learnt about the forthcoming closure of the camp, the Archbishop decided to make a second canonical visit to Valivade Camp in October 1947. The Archbishop emphasized the significance of Divine Providence in the history of man and enjoined the faithful to seek its protection in the forthcoming stages of our seemingly unending migration. He expressed hope that it would soon come to an end. Despite his advanced age (he was 88 years old) the Archbishop visited the hospital, blessed each patient and asked many questions pertaining to their illnesses. The following day, after the mass, the Archbishop visited the cemetery where he prayed at each of the Polish graves.[20]

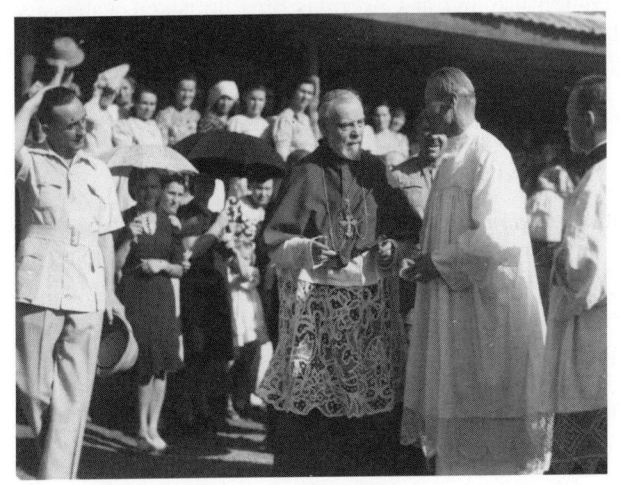

The Parish Council, (from the left): W. Bidakowski, J. Nowicki, Z. Grużewska, Fr. L. Dallinger, Fr. J. Przybysz, A. Świergoń and Br. J. Orysiuk

Visit of Arch. Dr. H. Doering with Fr. Dallinger and Fr. J. Przybysz, on the left Mr. Grabianka - 19 March 1944

Archbishop T. D. Roberts SJ, Titular Archbishop of Bombay, also visited the Camp in 1944. Later he described all his visits to the Polish Camps in India in the November issue of *The Examiner*. Referring to Valivade, he wrote as follows: 'I heard prayers in many languages but never and nowhere, neither in Europe nor in Asia, did I hear prayer so unified and full of zeal as in hymns and prayers in St. Andrew Bobola Church in Valivade Kolhapur. The crowd of two thousand faithful reminded me of Our Lord's Blessings, 'Blessed are the sorrowful. There were practically no men present amongst the faithful except for young boys, seniors and invalids. Men of Poland either died or were still fighting to save what was still possible to save.'

Other interesting visits were paid by the Anglican Bishop in 1946 and the Bishop of the Greek Orthodox Church.[21]

Visit of Arch. T. D. Roberts (from left) W. Jagiełłowicz, ..., H. Małachowska, M. Goławski, S. Dudryk-Darlewski, Z. Żerebecki, ..., B. Tijewski and Fr. L. Dallinger

Initial Attempts Toward Interfaith Dialogue

Wanda Dynowska had lived in India since before the war and was quite well known there (see Bombay chapter in this book). She used to visit her relatives in Valivade and frequently lectured on Hinduism and Buddhism. Her controversial talks resulted in lively discussions and caused quite a lot of resentment. Nobody ever thought in Valivade in 1945/47 that, in a way, she represented the first stirrings of future interfaith dialogue, one of the many fruits of Vatican II. There is no doubt Wanda Dynowska contributed to breaking down the walls of resistance and distrust towards other faiths, which then characterized Christianity. In a way, she was ahead of her own time. She followed her deeply intuitive, untrodden and obscure spiritual path into darkness and as far as I understand she had no support whatsoever from the official Christian Churches. She probably never even guessed how close she was to the path leading to understanding the underlying unity in faith that all the people are children of God regardless of their beliefs. Her life's journey towards finding a common language, despite all the differences, for Christianity, Hinduism and Buddhism had not been totally utopian. Who could have foreseen in Valivade that a couple of dozen years later the Pope would invite representatives of all great religions to pray for peace at the tomb of St. Francis of Assisi?

It is fitting to quote here the words of Fr. Marian Batogowski, who was present at her death, considered her 'precursor of the universal ecumenism' and wrote later the following lines: 'If we, the priests and the faithful *(Catholics)*, who without any reservations receive and distribute the Holy Sacraments, had an attitude and disposition similar to hers, we would have been a holy and beautiful community. I said mass in her modest room. She was sitting peaceful, attentive, silent. It was one of the most touching masses I ever celebrated. Many Tibetan children were present and we prayed together. Here was a life coming to an end, a life that was dedicated to building bridges between the East and the West, not for tanks, guns and exploitation but for genuine friendliness and brotherhood.'[22] She risked everything and remained faithful to the path that she believed was her path to God. 'The wind blows where it pleases; but you do not know whence it comes and whither it goes; such is every man who is born of the Spirit' (J3, 8).

THE LITURGICAL YEAR

Advent and Christmas

Observing our ancient tradition meant attending a pre-dawn mass celebrated in honour of Our Lady during the four weeks of Advent. In the darkness barely illuminated by the altar candles, we listened to the prophecy of Isaiah: 'Behold a virgin shall conceive and bear a son, and shall call his name Immanuel, God with us.' (Is.7, 10).

Advent was also a time of retreats and waiting for Christmas, which was always celebrated in the solemn and emotional atmosphere of home and family love. When the first stars twinkled in the sky, the families gathered around the table for the traditional Christmas Vigil, a meatless meal. The wafer was broken and shared, Christmas wishes were exchanged, carols were sung and Christmas presents were opened. When, after the war, contacts were again resumed with relatives in Poland, many people received the wafer by mail and it made Christmas Eve very special. And Christmas wishes always included that one great wish: to persevere and endure our exile, to keep faith and hope that Peace for all people of goodwill will reign in the end, and that we will return to our free homeland. After the traditional Christmas Eve meal, Midnight Mass was celebrated outside the church, under starry skies. The thoughts of all those gathered went back in time to the Poland of their early childhood.

During the Christmas season, people gathered to sing carols, share gifts, eat all the goodies, watch the Nativity play performed by children, and kept wishing one another that they might spend future Christmas holidays in a liberated Poland.[23],[24]

The Christmas season ended on February 2, the Feast of Purification (now Presentation of Jesus in the Temple), also known as Candlemas Day.

Inside the Church

Lent and Easter

Lent was once again a time of retreats, 40-hour devotions, the Way of the Cross and the specific Polish Lenten devotions of 'Bitter Laments'.[25]

During Holy Week most of the young people were actively engaged in celebrations of the Triduum (Holy Thursday, Good Friday and Holy Saturday). Scouts usually kept guard at the symbolic Tomb and the members of the Sodality of Our Lady participated in the adoration of the Blessed Sacrament. One of the girls described the hours of adoration in her diary:

'For a moment my thoughts went back to my early childhood. The joyful but serious atmosphere at home, Holy Week was always serious but I knew that in a couple of days all would be Joy because of Jesus' Resurrection. My thoughts tear away from memories and are again lost in silent prayer: Oh, Lord grant us a free homeland and a safe return.'[26]

On Holy Saturday samples of festive foods were brought to the church to be blessed.[27] And then, after weeks of waiting, Easter, the Feast of Resurrection arrives, always joyous, always filled with hope, peeling bells, singing voices.

Patronal Feasts, May and June Devotions

May 16, feast of St. Andrew Bobola, a Polish 17th century martyr celebrated annually in the spirit of thanksgiving for the graces received. It was also a day of prayer for the fallen in action, killed in prisons and concentration camps during the World War II. It ended by praying for our safe return to free Poland.[28]

During the month of May many people attended charming evening devotions in honour of Our Lady[29] followed by the month of June devotions in honour of the Sacred Heart of Jesus.[30]

Pentecost Sunday or 'Green Holidays'

According to our tradition, churches and homes are richly decorated with greenery for the Pentecost Sunday (hence the popular name). Pentecost is preceded by a nine day Novena in honour of the Holy Spirit.

Corpus Christi

The Feast of Corpus Christi was celebrated with an impressive and beautiful procession. The Blessed Sacrament was carried to four altars, constructed in four different sites around the camp. At each altar the beginning of one of the four Gospels was read. This was followed by a solemn benediction with the Blessed Sacrament. During the procession, little girls in white, lavishly sprinkled flower petals walking immediately before the priest, who carried the monstrance with the Blessed Sacrament. Usually the four altars and the route of the procession were richly decked with flowers, decorative hangings and holy pictures. The bells rang, clouds of incense mixed with the scent of flowers, the people sang and banners flapped in the wind.[31],[32]

Corpus Christi procession

October - a month dedicated to the Rosary and the Solemnity of Christ the King

October is usually associated with autumn, falling leaves, ripened fruit, with nature silently preparing for hibernation. Not in India! October in India is still one of the hot months of the year. The monsoons are over and there is an abundance of life everywhere. Grasses, flowers and fruit are at the peak of their beauty. Even schools are closed for the whole month. But hot weather did not prevent people from participating in the daily evening devotions of the Rosary. Every evening the church was full.

The last Sunday of October was dedicated to Christ the King (since Vatican II the Feast of Christ the King is celebrated on the Sunday before the first Sunday of Advent). The Eucharistic Crusade, with the help of other religious organisations, was responsible for the festive celebrations. And it was always a great success.

Solemnity of All Saints and All Souls Day

The prayers for the dead commenced on All Saints Day (November 1), with Vespers for the dead celebrated at the Kolhapur cemetery (Polish section). Candles placed on all the graves burned brightly. Prayers at the site of the symbolic tomb in the Camp were dedicated to the fallen during Warsaw Uprising and ended with the painful ritual of 'the roll call of the fallen'. Wiesia Kleszko remembers:

"We, the graduating class of 1945, tended to the special grave, where one of our class colleagues was buried. He was 29 and rather lonely. He wanted to complete his education, but his heart, exhausted by the deportation and all that went with it, simply failed him and he died six months after his final exams. So there we were standing over his grave. Another young man, only 20 years old, died of bone TB, despite all available treatment and surgery. For both of them we were the only 'family'. So, mourning them both, we thought about their mothers, who probably would never know that their young sons had been buried in India, and that their school friends had mourned them and kept candles burning on their graves. There were no forgotten graves on that day. Girl Guides placed flowers and lit candles on all unattended graves."

A shrine in the Camp

According to the Polish newspaper *Polak w Indiach*, dated October 8, 1947, there were about 80 graves in the Christian cemetery of Kolhapur; all of them were marked by gravestone and commemorative plaques.

Pilgrimage to St. Francis Xavier's Tomb in Goa

In May 1947, Fr. A. Jankowski joined a bicycle pilgrimage consisting of the Boy Scouts, to Goa, and later published the story of this interesting trip in the newspaper *Polak w Indiach*.[34] The following are the excerpts from his article:

"The idea of the bicycle pilgrimage was first suggested by the Boy Scouts of Valivade. The round trip was supposed to take no more than 10-14 days. Twenty four boys decided to participate in the pilgrimage. The average age of the participants was about 15. The whole undertaking of cycling 250 miles appeared to me somewhat risky, to say the least! Today I must admit with pleasure that my fears were unfounded. The boys, including the youngest ones, passed the test with flying colours.

In 1510 Alfonso da Albuquerque arrived in Goa, occupied it and then permanently bound it to Portugal. At the time, the population was entirely Hindu. Alfonso built churches and palaces, founded judicial and legal systems, developed commerce and, to strengthen the relationship with Portugal, he encouraged mixed marriages. The arriving Portuguese ships brought Franciscans, the first Roman Catholic priests who started Evangelization of Goa. Soon after, they were joined by Dominicans, Jesuits, Teatins, Lazarists and others. The religious life of Goa came to full bloom. In 1537, the Pope appointed the first bishop of Goa. Today (1947), there are over 60,000 Catholics in about 150 parishes and over 400 churches. Since 1886, the Archbishop of Goa also acts as Primate of India and Patriarch of East India.

We reached Panjim, the capital of Goa, in the afternoon, Saturday, May 8. It was a tidy town of 20,000, similar to European towns of this size. Surprisingly we came across another Pole there (where on earth are no Poles present???), Mr. Kronenberg. Thanks to his knowledge of Portuguese and local connections, he rendered us many invaluable services throughout our stay in Goa. Next day, being Sunday, we were guests of Portuguese youth and attended mass celebrated by a Polish priest, with the sermon preached by a local priest. In the evening we paid a visit to the vice Governor, don Vasco da Gama (yes, a direct descendant of his famous forefather!) On the following Monday we fulfilled our intended pilgrimage to the tomb of St. Francis Xavier, where I celebrated mass and the boys sang Polish hymns. After the mass we remained immersed in silent prayer. St. Francis ceased to be a remote saint. His life seemed to take shape right before our eyes: his youth, his university studies, his prospects for an academic career, the meeting with Ignatius Loyola, and sudden decision to become a Jesuit priest, his missionary work in India and Japan, his lonely death on Sancian island, near Japan. Two years after his death his body was brought back to Goa and has been venerated there ever since.

Poles sometimes have crazy ideas. The boys came up with such an impossible idea. They wanted to get a relic of St. Francis for our church in Valivade. Of course it was out of the question but as a token of consolation we were offered a white ribbon which had been used as a seal on the Saint's tomb from 1932 to 1942. Later in the day we toured Velha Goa, the ancient capital.

On the following Tuesday, invited by the members of an organisation somewhat similar to the Scouts, we went camping in Bamboline. To reach our destination we had to travel by bus, by boat and on foot. It was my first camping experience and I was impressed by the speed with which the boys skillfully pitched the two tents and constructed a tiny chapel decorating everything with sea shells.

We spent two days there in a friendly atmosphere surprising our hosts with a tale of a Pole that had preceded Portuguese in discovering Goa. We found that piece of information in the library of Msgr. Scudera in an old book on the history of Goa. According to the story, when Vasco da Gama landed in Goa for the first time, he was so discouraged by all the difficulties he had to deal with, that he would have returned to Portugal but for an accidental meeting with a Polish Jew. This man was serving as Prime Minister for the Goan King Zabajo, and offered, in the king's name, to negotiate an alliance between da Gama and the king. It was he who was truly instrumental in bringing Vasco da Gama to Goa. History further relates that the Pole converted to Catholicism during a visit to Portugal, and out of his gratitude to Vasco da Gama, assumed the name of Gaspar da Gama.

Besides all of our enriching experiences, the satisfaction of learning so much and achieving such an athletic feat, the pilgrimage had quite a remarkable additional significance: by publicizing our presence we made Poland much better known in Goa. Many people had heard nothing or very little about Poland, and nobody seemed to have the foggiest idea how unjustly Poland had been treated after the war that had just ended. The boys conquered the hearts of the people of Goa and, what is more important, made Poland a better known and appreciated country by inspiring several articles in the local press on that topic." *(For the detailed diary of the pilgrimage trip to Goa see Chapter on Scouting.)*

RELIGIOUS ORGANISATIONS, GROWTH AND ACTIVITIES

The Religious life in various Polish camps in India was not only centred on the church building, traditional devotions and private paths of piety. There were several religious organisations which evolved amongst both young and more mature people: the Marian Sodality consisting of two branches: one for girls and one for boys; Eucharistic Crusade; Rosary Society; Altar Servers, and Catholic Action.

Sodality (Girls) was organised in 1945 with 44 initial members. Training of the members and preparation for their solemn pledge started without delay. The work included organising members in groups (each group with a different assignment e.g. embroidering the banner and making badges). In addition to the groups, the girls also worked in sections which had specific goals and engaged in specific types of action. These were: Apologetic, Marian, Eucharistic, Missionary, Charities and Choir. All the work was pointed in two definitive directions: a. Self-discipline and b. The practical dimension of the spiritual maturing expressed in the context of daily life (relationships with others at school, at home, with neighbours and the sick, especially with those who required some assistance). Other types of action consisted of preparing celebrations for specific occasions, day trips to the neighbouring countryside, contacting other Sodality units (e.g. in Syria) to share common experiences pertaining to the work of the organisation, and preparing a one-page newsletter. Editing a commemorative booklet about our history and work in Valivade was one of the greater achievements of the boy and girl Sodalities.

3 May 1947 - Sodality Parade led by Z. Zawidzka

The Boys Branch of the Sodality was organised much later (in 1947), probably because of relatively small numbers of candidates, as most older boys were in the Cadets. However, despite its short life-span, the members deepened their faith as well as awareness of the Eucharistic mystery. They opened up to the needs of others to a remarkable degree and tried their best to overcome bad habits with goodness.

In spite of the generation gap between the youthful members of both Sodality branches and the older people, misunderstandings and differences in attitudes were overcome and basic harmony prevailed.[35]

Other difficulties confronting Sodality members were serious life problems and the necessity of making decision at a crucial period of their lives. Often it meant assuming responsibilities that surpassed their capabilities. It was clear, however, that the members of Sodality demonstrated a degree of maturity, did not shun responsibilities, and eventually found their proper place among their peers; this resulted in harmonious cooperation, reciprocal support and respect.

Writing about the members of Sodality, I can't omit a reflection that the perspective of about 50 years brings to mind. After years of unbroken or renewed contact I am deeply impressed by their truly Christian attitude toward life. To what extent (if at all) the Sodality movement played a role in their lives, only they can answer. No doubt they still remember with warm affection the 'mother' Sodality unit. It seems that even belonging to this movement involved a beautiful and authentic experience of God.

The Children Eucharistic Crusade unit dates back to 1944 when Fr. Bobrowski organised it. There were about 200 'Crusaders', including both boys and girls aged 9-14. Those who had already participated in the movement before the war now became natural leaders. The main purpose of the Eucharistic Crusade was practising devotion to Our Lord in the Blessed Sacrament. It meant frequently receiving Holy Communion and observing monthly confession. The children also attended a monthly meeting which included a talk about the Eucharist, usually delivered by a priest. The children were grouped in so-called troops and units. On the first Sunday of the month they attended mass carrying their banner and pennons present. The Crusade participated in the Corpus Christi procession and other religious celebrations.

Marian Sodality

When most of the Valivade inhabitants, including Eucharistic Crusade leaders, left for England, one of them took the banners to London and handed them over to the Rector of the Polish Catholic Mission for England and Wales.[36]

Altar Servers *(as of May 1947 Altar Servers Scout Troop No. 4)*[37]

Touching memories were found in the diaries the boys kept. One of them Edward Karaś, today a Franciscan, Fr. Błażej wrote:

... "The boys were very interested in the Altar Service. They were almost ready to fight with one another to be accepted. It seemed that handling bells and thurible attracted them most. But they also found kindling embers most fascinating and thoroughly enjoyed swinging the thurible to the point of spilling embers. Once, during the service, it happened to me too. The priest was at the altar placing the Host in the monstrance when I, swinging the thurible (slowly!), scraped its bottom against the rough carpet, and spilled the embers. It could have ended in a disaster. But not for nothing was I a son of a blacksmith! Quickly, with bare fingers I picked up the glowing embers, placed them in the thurible and, by the time the priest turned around and came down the steps, I was ready with the thurible opened to receive the incense.

Serving at the altar during the holidays, particularly during the Holy Week, was by far most interesting. Fr. Kozłowski spent a lot of time teaching us the Gregorian chant.

I am quite sure that it is true for all of us maintaining that no member of the altar servers and/or Schola Cantorum ever regretted the happy times spent in practice or service at the altar. Personally I'd love to relive those moments again".

Another Altar Server, Stach Harasymów, remembers:

"My decision to join the ranks of altar boys was influenced by Fr. Kozłowski, our Scoutmaster, who maintained that every Scout should serve at the altar. Considering it my duty I started to learn the server's responses. The first response in the Latin Mass, which was then the norm in the Roman Catholic Church was: *'Ad Deum qui laetificat juventutem meam'*. The beginners usually served in the second or third pair of altar boys on the missal or the wine side. There were also vespers and other church services where the altar boys required some additional skills, e.g. at the blessing of the palms on Palm Sunday. The celebrant would walk the aisles with an aspergillum sprinkling the holy water on the palms held by the congregation. My duty was to hold back the priest's cope so he could take a better swing with the aspergillum. Every time he took a swing back, my face and hair were drenched with the holy water. The priest was not aware of this. I tried unsuccessfully to avoid the downpour, but I had to hang on to the celebrant's cope. When we finally arrived back at the altar my partner, carrying the holy water on the other side of the priest, burst out laughing when he saw me dripping wet.

I do not remember when I said *Deo gratias* for the last time at the end of a Mass. It was probably just after we left India. I have fond memories of my service as an altar boy. The years went by. When my son, who was born in Australia, joined the ranks of the altar boys, I felt very happy and in some way rewarded'.

Several Scout servers grew into prominent people: e.g. Archbishop Marian Oleś who was appointed Apostolic Nuncio for Turkmenistan, Uzbekistan and Kazakhstan (N. B. the first Pole appointed to such a post in 95 years).[38]

Alter boys with Fr. J. Przybysz and Br. Orysiuk (15 May 1944)

Celebrations, spectacles and shows were set up and performed by religious youth organisations to commemorate or celebrate holidays and anniversaries of special events.

A solemn celebration was staged with the combined effort of several religious youth organisations to commemorate the liberation of the Primate of Poland, Cardinal A. Hlond, imprisoned by the Germans in 1942.[39]

A fairy tale spectacle 'Three Gifts Offered to God' was produced (including artistic lighting) and performed by the Sodality members.[40] Celebrations in honour of Christ the King and Mary Mother of God were staged on the appropriate feast days.[40],[41] The World Mission Sunday was commemorated in 1947. The Altar Servers troop staged a show about St. Stanisław Kostka, directed by Br. Orysiuk on All Saints Day. It was a great success rewarded by long lasting applause.[42]

Rosary Association (Children and Adults)

Br. Orysiuk led the children Rosary group of 150 members. Three hundred and sixty adult members were grouped in 24 'roses'. All members of the Rosary Association were engaged in some charity works.[43]

Catholic Action

Founded by Fr. Bobrowski in 1945, this group consisted of 75-100 members. Their main achievement was mailing 81 parcels in 1946 to orphanages in Poland. All the parcels reached their destination, as confirmed in 1947. Catholic Action participated in raising funds for renovations of one Station of the Cross in Jerusalem. The total amount of the collection was 4,633 rupees and 6 annas.[44]

RELIGIOUS VOCATIONS

Departure to Orchard Lake Seminary

Candidates for the Seminary in Orchard Lake

Sending off young boys with a tentative religious vocation to USA was one of the major achievements of the PCM in India. As a result of correspondence between Archbishop E. Mooney, president of WRS-NCWC, and Bishop Józef Gawlina, regarding the possibility of future studies at a Seminary in USA, the inhabitants of the Polish camps in India were polled, and 31 young men were selected as possible candidates for priesthood.[45] All the candidates were granted US entry visas. Their travel expenses to the US were financed by the Central Office of the NCWC in Washington. The voyage was possible only thanks to Col. H. C. Halgerson (American Army Commander for India and Burma), who agreed to include the boys in the nearest transport of American soldiers, returning home after completing tours of duty in the Far East. Some of the boys' expenses, incurred while staying in Bombay to handle all the formalities, were covered by a Spanish Jesuit resident in Bombay. The 'Supply Department' Director provided all the necessary materials for clothes appropriate for the more moderate climate of America. The boys finally boarded the ship Gen. M. B. Steward-AP-140 on October 3, 1945 in Calcutta, and arrived in New York on November 24. The very next day they were in Orchard Lake.[46]

The boys were enthusiastically welcomed in the States by the organisers of their journey. The Polish Daily News published their photograph with the following caption: 'Saved from the Bolshevik hell'. The newspaper included an appeal by the Rector of the Polish Seminary to the American Polonia for funds to help Polish youth.[47] When the boys got off the ship, entered the passengers' area and sang the Polish national Anthem, tears flowed freely. Thirty one boys eventually completed their high school studies and graduated. A few became priests.[48]

The girls enter the Bernardine Convent

Three congregations (Bernardines, Felicians and Franciscans) in the States were interested in accepting possible candidates.[49] Thanks to Fr. Pluta's efforts, 50 girls with potential vocations were sponsored by the Bernardine Sisters (Reading, Pa.) They left for the States in 1947 by boat *Marina Addar*.

In search of vocations

Mother Clemenza Mancini, Provincial Superior of an Italian teaching Congregation (St. Ann of the Providence), visited Valivade in search of vocations. She spent only a few days in Valivade and did not find any definitive vocations, but those few days were enough for the bonds of friendship to sprout and flower until her death in October 1964. She died of cancer after 52 years of missionary life. She was a very simple and quiet woman. One felt comfortable in her presence. According to several letters received after her death, she was well loved and respected by her sisters. Although she did not find any prospective candidates for her congregation, I am devoting a few lines to her memory because her attitude to missionary work was rather typical of the post Vatican II era, years before the convocation of the Council by Pope John XXIII. She told me then, that missionary work means above all implanting and fostering Christian values rather than producing ever greater numbers of converts to Catholicism. I never forgot her wisdom.

Candidates for the Convent on their way to USA

Polish Catholic publishing activity in India, in addition to newspapers, periodicals and schoolbooks, consisted of printing 250 copies of The *Small Prayer Book*, 1,000 copies of prayer books, and 500 copies of the *Way of the Cross and Lenten Lamentations*. These were printed in a printing shop equipped with Polish fonts in Karachi. In Valivade, a one page Newsletter entitled *Ave Maria* was published for a short period of time by the Girls Sodality, and a commemorative booklet, entitled *Cześć Marii*, was published by both Sodalities, and printed by the NCWC printing shop in Valivade - Kolhapur.

Closing down the Valivade Camp

With the Camp closing down, the Pastoral Centre, unique in the Diocese of Poona, ceased to exist. Though the graves of many loved ones were left behind there, it was also a site of many marriages and many births of new Poles, in whose documents the country of birth was marked for ever: INDIA.

Translated by the author

Zofia Nowicka, the author

NOTES

1. APOL Archives of Polish Catholic Mission (PCM) in India, pp.1, 15, 8, 18, 17-18, 19, 20-24
2. New Archives, Warsaw, 87/11 (87 p.213-14)
3. APOL Archves of PCM in India, p.22, 8, 24, 6, 25, 8
4. PwI: 1.X.1944 p.5
5. APOL: Archives of PCM in India, p.7
6. PwI: 1.XII.1944 p.5
7. Arch. KPI: *Młodzi w Valivade* 1943-1948, Album of Reunions in London 1971 and 1973, publ. in 1975 p.17
8. Ibid: Jubilee celebrations at Fawley Court 23.I.1999, speech by Eugenia Krajewska.
9. APOL: Archives of PCM in India, p. 23
10. Ludwik Grzebień SJ, Adam Kozłowiecki SJ: *Wśród ludów Zambii*, T. I, p.238, 355
11. Author's own correspondence.
12. Organiaers of Fr. Pluta's golden jubilee p.20-27
13. Obituary in *Głos Polski* 10th Feb. 1990
14. Fr. B. E. Karaś ofmConv:- *Spotkanie serc*, Reunion of 'Indians', 1987, p. 39
15. Arch.KPI Bulletin No.7,1987, p.20,
16. Ibid: Letter from T. Ignasiuk (Kowalewska), dated 20-09-1998 20.9.1998
17. APOL: Archives of PCM in India, p.10
18. PwI: 15.IX - 1.X.1944 p.2
19. Ibid: year II, No.5, 1944 p.3
20. Ibid: year V, No.26, 1947 p.3
21. IPiMS: *Kronika*, C811B s.57
22. Arch. KPI Bulletin No.4 1992, p.12
23. IPiMS: *Kronika*, C811B p.57
24. Sodality in India, 1948 p.24-25
25. APOL: Archives of PCM in India, pp.10 and 20
26. Sodality in India, 1948, p. 21
27. IPiMS: *Kronika*, C 811B, p.11
28. PwI: year III, No.1, 1945
29. Ibid: year IV, No.18, 1946
30. Sodality in India, 1948 p.27
31. IPiMS: *Kronika*, C811C, p.17
32. PwI: year V, No. 8, 1947, p. 5
33. IPiMS: *Kronika*, C811B, p.76, 83, 84
34. PwI: no 6, 1947 p. 4 and no 7, 1947, p. 4
35. Sodality in India 1948 pp.7, 15, 39, 51
36. Arch.KPI Woch (Rubczewska) Wanda, letter dated 4th July 1994
37. Pancewicz B. M. - *Harcerstwo w Indiach*, 1947, p. 109
38. *Zbiegli się żurawie z daleka*, Colective work p 60, Reunion in Warsaw 1992
39. PwI: year III, No.11, 1945
40. Sodality in India, 1948 pp.7 and 8
41. IPiMS: *Kronika*, C811B, p.83
42. Ibid: *Kronika*, C811C, p.29, 31
43. APOL: *Archives of PCM in India*, p.11
44. IPiMS: *Kronika*, C811B, p.24, 90
45. APOL: *Archives of PCM in India*, p.13-14
46. IPiMS: *Kronika*, C811B, p.38
47. PwI: year IV, No.2, 1947
48. *Duszpasterz polski za granicą*, 1996, No. 2/199
49. APOL: *Archives of PCM in India*, pp.5, 26, 13, 8

Part of the cemetery in 1946

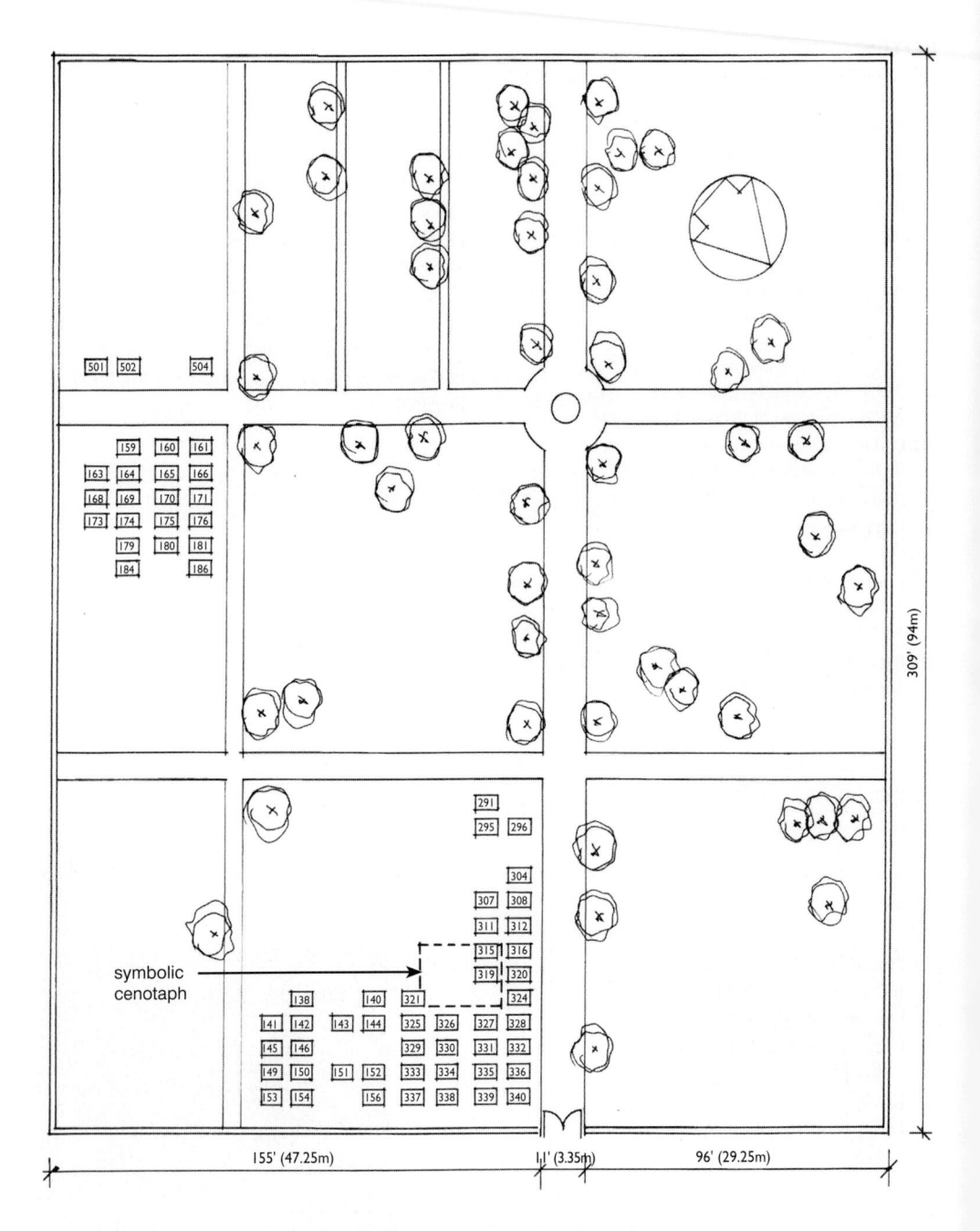

KOLHAPUR CEMETERY

(plan of Polish graves according to PMC in India)

Liber Moratorium Vol.1, List of people that died in Valivade-Kolhapur
(The no grave precede the name of deceased, but a number of names were missing)

1943
1. JANKOWSKI Józef
2. KOŁODYŃSKI Bogusław 140
3. SZUL Zdzisław
4. KATKIEWICZ Marta Ewa 143

1944
5. ANTOSZEWICZ Maria 144
6. IWANEJKO Katarzyna 132
7. BANIOWSKI Stanisław 141
8. GODLEWSKI Józef 142
9. CZAJKA Maria 145
10. BIELECKIE Jadwiga i Barbara
11. CIECHANOWICZ Mikołaj 150
12. PORONIONY PŁÓD xx
13. ORZEŁ Władysław Wiktor
14. GODLEWSKA Danuta Halina
15. MAZUREK Franciszka 153
16-17. WĘGRZYN Józef i Anna 154
18. BANBUŁA Waldemar 146
19. WALENIA Antoni 156
20. ANDRIJEWSKA Zofia 151
21. ORZECHOWSKA Maria

xx patrz pod-rozdział 'Tragiczne Wypadki'

1945
22. WLIZŁO-WILIŃSKA Aniela 152
23. KURKOWSKI Waldemar 337
24. GRZYBOWSKI Henryk xx 325
25. OTTO Magdalena 321
26. BUŁAKOWSKA Anna 329
27. WALCZAK Władysława xx 333
28. GODLEWSKI Adam Sylw. 338
29. GWÓŹDŹ Leokadia 326
30. DAJEK Jan 330
31. ŚLUSARCZYK Salomea 334
32. HUDYGA Danuta 320
33. JODŁOWSKI Marian 319
34. LATAWIEC Joanna 327
35. SZUMCZYK Aleksander 331
36. JADZIEWICZ Jan 324
37. FORMANKIEWICZ Wład. xx 315
38. MICHALSKA Danuta 335
39. TUBIELEWICZ Ludwika 316
40. SUSZYŃSKI Bogdan S. G. 328
41. PARZYCH Ryszard 332
42. KURKOWSKI Adam 336
43. MĘDRALA Andrzej 312
44. PLATTA Jan 307
45. JUTRZENKA Antoni 308
46. STARUSZKIEWICZ Andrzej 340
47. MAŁACHOWSKA Helena A. 339

1946
48. OSTROWSKI Waldemar Józef 304
49. DUBOWIK Zofia 296
50. PALIWODA Julia 311
51. KWIATKOWSKA Zofia 295
52. KAISER Maria 291
53. SIECZKO Jan 161
54. MASIULANIS Nadzieja 160
55. NOWAKOWSKI Jan 166
56. ŻÓŁTAŃSKA Teresa 159
57. WÓJCICKI Stanisław 504
58. KRUK Krystyna Maria 164
59. LATAWIEC Marcin 165
60. PIEŚLAK Tomasz 171
61. BABIS Teresa Zofia 169
62. CZARNY Józef 163
63. BUC Aniela 170
bez nazwiska 178 - (nie ma w książce)

1947
64. DZIUBATY Jan 168
65. KOSTECKI Piotr 176
66. CHMIELOWSKA Zofia M. 175
67. BODURA Anna xx 174
68. CHRONOWSKA Julia Zofia 173
69. DOBOLEWICZ Władysław 181
70. JAKUBIK Władysław 180
71. KOWAL Piotr 502
72. STRUPCZEWSKA Jadwiga 179
73. CZEKIERSKA Wanda 186
74. BRYCKI Bolesław 184
75. MASIULANIS Antonina 501
76. WIŚNIEWSKI Andrzej
77. DZIADURA Maria 149

List of Marriages (Liberum Copularum), Births and Christenings (Liberum Natorum) and Deaths (Liberum Mortuorum) are to be found in the Polish Edition of the same book or in the archives of Polish Mission in Devonia Road, London GB.

Kolhapur Cemetery "the Cenotaph" erected by the Polish War Graves Commission in 1986/7, renovated in 1994

THE CULTURAL SECTION
by Ela Słowikowska (Woyniłłowicz)

This was one of the most important sections in the administration of the Valivade Camp.

The facilities of this Camp provided a welcome respite to its inhabitants after the horrors of their deportation to the Soviet Union. But "men don't live by bread alone". The religious support was provided by the Fr. Leopold Dallinger and other priests at the St. Andrew Bobola Church in the Camp. The cultural and educational needs of the inhabitants were catered for by the Culture and Education Section, with the support of the Ministry of Social Welfare of the Polish Government in London.

It was a very difficult task requiring a breadth of knowledge, as well as the ability to work with very limited resources in order to bring various aspects of Polish culture to the inhabitants of Valivade, far away from their homeland.

The first director of this Section was Michał Chmielowiec, a well known journalist, followed by other dedicated people and a host of helpers, too numerous to mention here.

The work of this section included the following activities:
1. Adult education
2. Organising lectures and talks
3. Group reading of Polish literature in order to overcome the shortage of Polish books and periodicals
4. Lending library activities
5. Providing information on a range of current topics, such as:
   a) aspects of daily life in the Camp
   b) daily radio news
   c) local news bulletins, giving political commentary
6. Amateur theatre
7. Music lessons
8. Organising a number of common rooms and arranging activities for children
9. Running various competitions
10. Specialised courses

Further education courses for adults were very popular right from their inception, with 165 students (64 of whom were over 55). They included teaching of reading and writing to the illiterate. To those a new world became open: A. Kisielnicka gave examples in *Polak w Indiach*. "A woman in her 70s, born in Eastern Poland under the Russian rule, never attended school. She had learned to speak Polish at home, but could neither read nor write. She was rather embarrassed to enrol at her age, but longed to be able to write letters to her son in the Army and be able to read his, as well as sign her name on official forms. After she completed the course, she would often sit on the verandah with a book in her hand."

Lectures and talks on a wide range of subjects were run either as single 40 min. lectures or series of 3-4 talks delivered by teachers and by a wide range of specialists. It should be noted, that all teachers and specialists were themselves the deported people, who experienced the same hardships as their students. Therefore their enthusiasm for teaching and the hunger for knowledge were mutual. Group reading sessions took place in the common rooms and attracted up to 100 listeners at a time.

Staff of the Cultural Section: T. Pawłowska, W. Tyszko, A. Kisielnicka, H. Hajnowa, (sitting): W. Stankiewicz, A. Sahanek, A. Brzezińska, J. Michalska (standing) Director Mjr. L. Naimski, K. Cariuk, K. Karasiewicz and J. Rymar

A daily bulletin giving news summary and a commentary was initially issued in 26 copies, using antiquated equipment and was publicly displayed in various areas of the Camp and in the common rooms. Later, for a small payment, these bulletins were delivered to individual homes.

The sources of information were Polish radio programmes from the BBC and the Voice of America in New York. Because of difficult reception due to atmospheric conditions, but also to interference by enemy stations, at least two people at any time were involved in collecting it. This was later correlated and delivered on the next morning to the Cultural Section. Editing of the radio news, as well as of the information from the *Times of India* in Bombay and from *Dziennik Polski i Dziennik Żołnierza* (The Polish Daily and Soldiers' Daily) from London was the responsibility of Antoni Birar.

After the withdrawal by the British Government in 1945 of the recognition of the

Common room assistants - (standing): J. Kotlicka, H. Brzezińska, W. Klepacka, K. Cariuk, St. Parafińska, H. Jędrychowska, H. Gromadzka, C. Naglik, K. Karasiewicz, Maruti, (sitting): J. Krzysztoń, R. Dusza, J. Dobrostańska, Director RKO J. Michalska

Polish Government in London in favour of the "Provisional Government of National Unity" in Poland, the Polish radio transmissions from London were discontinued. The Section then introduced regular 30 minute sessions of 'Live Radio'. This involved daily reading of bulletins issued by the Bombay Office of the Polish Ministry of Social Welfare in London, which at that time was the only factual source of information about Poland, both internally and internationally. 'Live News' was a presentation for the public. It included a detailed political commentary, information about events in Poland, topical local news items, light entertainment and poetry readings. The Section also organised a series of lectures on the current political situation in Poland and on the partition of Poland, resulting from the Yalta Agreement by Roosevelt, Churchill and Stalin.

Common room No. 1

Other more serious events included the commemoration of the tragic death in Gibraltar of the Polish Premier, Gen. W. Sikorski and of important national holidays.

The Common Rooms

With time, a number of Common Rooms were established serving adults and young people. They were used for the purpose of meetings, social life, as reading rooms and lending a growing number of some 3,000 books managed by J. Kotlicka. This also included Polish and English papers and periodicals sent to Valivade from Britain, USA, the Middle East and Italy.

In 1944 the Camp had 5 such Common Rooms: the Central, No..1 was the most popular as it had a gramophone, 138 records, a radio, 12 sets of chess, 8 of draughts, 12 sets of playing cards for the bridge enthusiasts and a separate room for table tennis. It also had a stage for concerts and live theatre performances.

No.2 Common Room was equipped with collections of games and toys for the use of children. The Orphanage had their own (No..4) Common Room with a separate space for homework. It was there that the *Society of Friends of Polish Soldiers* was started. Children were in regular contact by correspondence with soldiers at the front or in the military hospitals for the wounded.

Standard opening hours were from 3.00 p.m to 9.00 p.m. or as late as midnight because there were BBC and Voice of America broadcasts late.

3rd of May Celebrations

Group reading of classical Polish literature, such as historical works by Sienkiewicz for adults and children's stories became very popular. Reading Polish books to patients in the local hospital provided tremendous help in speeding up their recovery, proving once again that "man does not live by bread alone".

Common Rooms were furnished with tables and chairs, bookshelves and chests for games and toys, with Polish folk decorations and photographs and pictures illustrating life in Poland, on the walls.

In the Common Rooms there were held monthly lectures on topical subjects such as the Polish-Soviet and the Polish-German relations, commemorating historical events and talks by visiting Polish sailors and airmen. There were also series of lectures by Wanda Dynowska about India, its culture, religion and customs in order to improve the understanding of the generous hosts of the Poles in the Valivade Camp. A great emphasis was put on Polish folk customs, particularly relating to Christmas and Easter.

The fighting involving Polish forces in all theatres of war and especially in Italy and during the Warsaw uprising in 1944 had a deep effect on the school children. They agreed to devote, for a number of days, 15 minutes daily to bring them emotionally closer to the Polish soldiers through suitable readings. One of the most successful spectacles was devoted to the beauty of Poland, through short sketches, songs, dances and poems, depicting various Polish regions.

Valivade Camp Chronicle and the Polish Press

The regular preparation of a chronicle recording the life in Valivade, on the exotic background of India and incorporating topical photographs and extracts from the paper *Polak w Indiach*, was started by Alicja Kisielnicka and later continued by Wiesława Klepacka. Extracts from the Chronicle appeared regularly in the paper.

Cultural Section was receiving copies of local Polish papers from East Africa describing the life of Polish refugees there. They were *Poles in Africa* and later *Voice of Poland*, both from Nairobi. In one of the issues, there was a list of Polish refugees brought by sea from Karachi to East Africa, which helped a number of people in Valivade to find lost relatives and friends. Through the Polish paper in China, *Echo of Shanghai*, the Poles in Valivade learned of the existence of a large Polish community there. This mainly consisted of Poles, who escaped from the Germans and the Soviet Union.

After the end of the war, arrived the Polish paper ***Nowiny***, issued in Germany by the Polish forces.

It is very satisfying to find these issues of the Valivade Chronicle in the Gen. W. Sikorski Institute and Museum in London, providing a record of the life of the Polish refugees in India.

Exhibitions

The administration of the Camp organised a number of major exhibitions:

At the beginning of 1944 there was an exhibition illustrating the life in pre-war Poland, opened by

Polish stand at Kolhapur - W. Feń, ..., B. Królikowska, ..., H. Hajdul, W. Klepacka, H. Krupińska, J. Dobrostańska, A. Skomorowski, Lt. L. T. Skrzypek

the Rt. Rev. Henryk Doering, the Archbishop of Poona.

It included examples of Polish folk art, regional dresses and handicrafts as well as 650 photographs of the architecture, history and beauty of Poland, together with appropriate statistical information. The exhibition was well attended by Indian, British and other foreign visitors.

As part of the Victory Day celebrations in 1945, the City of Kolhapur organised an exhibition, in which the inhabitants of the Valivade Camp were invited to participate with a number of stands, showing life in Poland and the input of Polish forces in the war.

One more exhibition

During the same year a group of young people gave a show of Polish folk dancing and ballet in the Maharaja's palace, for invited dignitaries of the principality.

In June 1947, another major exhibition was organised in the Camp. It included examples of Polish regional and other handicrafts produced by the students of the various courses such as printing, art, dress making, secretarial, health care, leather goods, woodwork, shoemaking, toys, map making, photography, philately, archaeology and engineering design. It included illustrations of the activities of Scouts and Girl Guides and performances by two local orchestras and a choir. All this work was carried out with a very minimum of resources.

The enthusiasm and the tremendous effort by teachers and students alike was aimed at the preparation for work on return to free Poland.

Concerts

Two teachers gave piano lessons, including teaching of the theory and the history of music.

There were regular concerts organised in the Camp with the support of the local schools. From 1944 there were regular music sessions for the schools based on the work of individual composers with a commentary.

All these events were well attended by Indian and British visitors from Kolhapur and the region.

Competitions

A number of competitions, on a wide range of subjects, such as for the most attractive living quarter, the best garden, the best theatrical sketches, plays, or games such as chess were organised and well attended.

Summing up, the people in the Camp in spite of the hot climate did not want to waste a single day after the horrors of their earlier experience in the Soviet Union.

Exhibition in the Camp

Woodwork: J. Kowalski, J. Siedlecki, W. Matulewicz, H. Wądołkowski, J. Pacholski, J. Abramowicz, R. Blumski, J. Liszka and S. Kaszuba

NOTE

Based on PwI year 2 no 18/19 (28-29) 1944
4 no 8 (66) 1946
5 no 21/22 (101/102) 1947
Camp Chrinicals IP i MS C811B
JAG, AKPI Enc 7 to Cultural Section Report verbal & written reports from Common Rm Assistants

Workshop: J. Kaśków, J. Pacak and J. Abramowicz, ...

NAMES OF THE PEOPLE NOT MENTIONED IN THE TEXT WHO PARTICIPATED IN THE WORK OF THIS SECTION

Birar Antoni	Biskupska Krystyna	Cariuk Kleopatra
Dudek Zofia	Fechter Władysław	Gurgul Janina
Harbuz Eliza	Jankowska Rypsyma	Jankowski Tadeusz
Katkiewicz Henryk	Kuchcicki Władysław	Kaliszek Irena
Koziełkowski Leon Dr.	Klepacki Józef	Kurzeja Janusz
Krzysztoń Janina	Koczan Ewa	Kaśków Jan
Mückowa Janina	Mikuszewski Leonard	Martusewicz Helena
Nowosielska Lucyna	Orysiuk Jan	Poczobut-Odlanicka Zofia
Rokicka Dobrosława	Skrzat Anna	Skrzypek Leon
Szczyrska Maria	Suszyński Mikołaj	Szymańska Janina
Siedmiograj Wanda	Szarejko Józef	Szarejko Anna
Świątkowska Irena	Szczanowski Stanisław	Topolnicka Jadwiga
Wolski Józef	Wilczyńska Zofia	Wróblewska Jadwiga
Woyniłłowicz Ela	Wiktorowicz Krystyna	Zagórska Zofia
Żerebecki Zdzisław		

Translated by M. Brzozowski

THEATRE
by Janina Mineyko (Niezabytowska)

As soon as we were out of Russia after all the harrowing times in often degrading conditions and totally deprived of any cultural activities, we were eagerly trying to fill that gap by organising all sorts of shows, revues and even forming amateur theatres where possible.

As a result of being deprived of Polish cultural activities during the deportation to the Soviet Union, we felt a great need for the Polish theatre.

And so - already during our stay in the Transit Camp - Country Club near Karachi (then in India) - some of us, High School pupils, prepared sort of a revue, in which dressed in turbans and flowing white robes, bowing low, we recited petitions and thanks to Allah - a scene which at the present time would probably be considered politically incorrect.

3rd of May 1943 - Ahwaz

Subsequently, high school pupils A. Klecki and R. Płocka organised a small youth theatre which staged sketches illustrating life in the camp, as well as extracts from Polish classics by Mickiewicz, Żeromski and Wyspiański. They also presented folk dances and a duet of Polish Gypsies, who performed in their traditional costumes gypsy songs and dances. These shows were often attended by the British camp employees or the personnel of the neighbouring American and British military camps, who showed their appreciation by enthusiastic whistling and stamping of their feet, which caused some consternation as according to our custom it signified disapproval.

In the temporary Camp in Malir, there were theatre performances for adults and children, organised by Irena Świątkowska, Irena Paulikowa and Eugenia Korzeniowska together with a number of dedicated amateur performers.

When two more permanent camps were established in Balachadi near Jamnagar for children mainly orphans, and Valivade near Kolhapur for some 5,000 adults and children, the Polish refugees settled there.

On the way to Balachadi Camp, the children were driven through Baluchistan and had to stop for 9 weeks in Quetta because of floods. During this time, they produced an open air show with performances of folk dancing and songs, using specially made make-shift costumes. It was difficult to communicate with the cloth merchants - mime had to be used. Somebody had an ingenious

Regional show in Balachadi

idea to use metallic bottle caps for jingling chains for belts in boys' costumes from the Cracow region. Girls whose heads had been previously shaved because of typhus, wore head-dresses made of ribbons and flowers to cover their lack of hair. The profit from this show was donated for British war orphans.

On arrival in Balachadi Camp, a theatre group was organised and run by Janina Dobrostańska, a professional actress from Poland. As part of a cultural and educational programme of activities, a library, a common room, a choir, dance and theatre groups and an orchestra were organised. The main performers in the group were B. Czaykowski, S. Bukowski, Jurek and Tadek Dobrostańscy, Bronka Czerniawska, Zosia Bolanowska, Zosia Kowalec, Freda Mordak, Marian Różański, Bożena Sito, Ela Respondowska, Halina Rutkowska, Wiesiek Stypuła and Jan Bielecki.

M. Chmielowiec with the performers of the Eastern Fairy Tale

The first performance was a Nativity Play by Leon Schiller, later modified every year to reflect changes of our current life. This and other spectacles at the Camp were often attended by Indian and British visitors and even by Jam Saheb, Maharaja of Navanagar. During one performance it was necessary to make a special screen for visiting Moslem ladies, with openings for their eyes only - according to their religious principles.

Other shows included the staging of Polish classics, such as a very demanding presentation of *Kordian* by Słowacki (in which young Bogdan Czaykowski distinguished himself), folk dancing in colourful regional Polish costumes accompanied by own orchestra, choral performances, shows based on fairy tales, etc.

One of the most memorable occasions was a show organised in the palace of Maharaja Jam Saheb, who was a special friend of Poles and whose father was a friend of the famous Polish composer and patriot Ignacy Paderewski. The Indian palace orchestra took part in the performance playing Polish folk tunes. At the end of the performance, besides the British and Polish national anthems children sang the anthem of Navanagar State, which greatly moved the Maharaja.

Song and dance troupe from Valivade in Bombaju

In addition there were many regular cultural evenings in the Cultural Activities Rooms, organised by adults and children.

The amateur theatre activities in Valivade date from mid 1943, organised by Alicja Kisielnicka. *The Eastern Fairy Tale,* written by her was first performed in the Camp and later in the Maharaja's palace in Kolhapur, attended by Maharaja's young son and other Indian children. In November 1943 a school group staged performances of Polish folk dancing in Bombay, as part of the Polish Culture Days.

The theatre developed further under Ludwik Naimski with the aid of Antoni Skomorowski, a professional actor and director of one of the theatres in pre-war Warsaw, presenting a number of shows including Polish classics, such as *Śluby Panieńskie* by A. Fredro, followed by other performances of the works by Fredro and Bałucki, as well as children's stories. The troupe consisted mainly of High School pupils and people of goodwill, who loved theatre, music and song. They enjoyed themselves immensely while performing in spite of primitive conditions and audiences responded enthusiastically, warmly applauding. In due course the stage conditions improved thanks to S. Pardeshi, a local Indian contractor and a fluent Polish speaker, who provided a cinema with a large stage/screen and a proper amphitheatre seating. The repertoire depended on the availability of texts, on the mood to express a patriotic uplifting of spirits as well as light entertainment.

Maj. Naimski with Mrs. Tetmajer wearing the original Cracovian bodice, and sister-in-law

One of the highlights was the staging in 1944 of "The Wedding", a classical drama by Stanisław Wyspiański. Although concerned with serious political and historical problems, it caused a sensation when first staged in 1900 in Cracow, because it was based on a real wedding of a Polish poet, Lucjan Rydel with a peasant girl and many characters were based on the

The Wedding

contemporary members of the Cracow elite. The elder sister of the heroine of this play, Mrs. Tetmajer, in whose house the wedding took place, lived in the Camp as a mature lady and still had the original Cracovian bodice, (part of the folk dress in which she was married), saved throughout her period of deportation to the Soviet Union, which she lent to the Bride in our production.

At the end of 1945, the theatre presented the New Year's Review commenting on the topical events during the past year in the Camp and internationally, in poems, songs and sketches. In December 1946 the theatre staged a production by Janina Dobrostańska, newly arrived from Balachadi, of a traditional Polish Nativity Play. The play was based on the classical texts by Polish poet Lucjan Rydel and the book *Polish Customs* by Maria Dynowska. This involved the folk dancing group, the choir and the Camp orchestra, as well as young and old amateur actors.

In February 1946 there was a *Chopin Matinee* with solo performances of piano music, song and poems by a number of performers.

Later that year, to commemorate a centenary of the birth of H. Sienkiewicz, a famous 19th century writer of historical novels and a Nobel prize winner, an ambitious adaptation of one of his novels, *Pan Wołodyjowski* describing the Turkish and Tartar invasions of Poland in the 17th century, was staged under the title *Hajduczek*.

During 1946 and 1947 several performances in a lighter mood were performed. These included comedies like *Charley's Aunt* by Brandon Thomas, others like *Zemsta* by A. Fredro, *Teatr Amatorski* by Bałucki and *Sublokatorka* by Grzymała-Siedlecki. Also with the help of by Hanka Sahanek there was a fairy-tale staged,

Nativity play

Charley's Aunt

written by one of the younger pupils of the High School.

The Literary Circle at the secondary school presented two Polish classics, *The November Night* by S. Wyspiański, about a Polish uprising against the Russians in 1831 and an allegorical play, *Lilla Weneda* by J. Słowacki. In both of these Szczęsna-Orzeł (later a star of the *Pro Arte Theatre* in London) distinguished herself.

Members of the theatre group who took part in most of the performances were: L. Naimski, J. Niezabytowska, T. Pawłowska, A. Skomorowski, T. Herzog, H. Sahanek, A. Szwaglis, A. Birar, A. Klecki, H. Wądołkowski, J. Tiachow, J. Kucharski, J. Dobrostańska. Others who took part in some plays were: Z. Nowicka, M. Leśniak, Z. Peszkowski, R. Jagiełłowicz, W. Ostrowski, W. Lotarewicz, J. Dzikowski, Cz. Gulczyński, B. Szczurowski, W. Fechter, J. Augustyn, W. Kozłowski, I. Krajewska.

In January 1948 the Valivade Camp was closed and the inhabitants were taken either to

The Tenant

Great Britain, to Tangeru in Tanganyika or Koja in Uganda. Some of the members of the theatre in Valivade ended up in Koja and staged there some of the performances previously shown in India. However, the previous enthusiasm faded away - the world political scene was not propitious for us - and it was time to plan how to rebuild more or less normal life in difficult circumstances.

Nevertheless, in the hearts of our audiences - and us - 'the actors' there still remained the fond memories of live Polish word and music from the stage, which could not be replaced by, and compared to, cinema films or television.

"Grube Ryby" (Fat Cats) - (standing from the left): K. Gutkowski, W. Latawiec, ..., J. Dobrostańska, ..., H. Sztrom, T. Pawłowska, A. Birar, (sitting): H. Sahanek and J. Niezabytowska

Translated by A. Brzozowski in collaboration with the Author

NAMES OF PEOPLE, WHO TOOK PART IN THE ACTIVITIES OF THE AMATEUR THEATRE, NOT MENTIONED IN THE CHAPTER

Biskupska Krysia	Bujanowska Irka	Czarnecka Maria (Mgr.)
Chmielowska Halina	Chmielowska Joanna	Frydel Radosław
Goławska Maria	Gutowski Kazimierz	Korzeniowska Eugenia
Kolischer Roma	Kurzeja janusz	Kucharski Józef
Marcinkiewicz Zuzia	Narkiewicz Felicja	Nowicka zofia
Pacholski Jasiek	Paulikowska Irena	Sztorn Helena
Styczyńska Irena	Światkowska Irena	Stankiewicz Wanda
Tiachow Jerzy (Dr.)	Ternogórska Jadwiga	Trella Lila

EDUCATION

by Danuta Pniewska with initial input of R. Tomaszewska (Loszek)

From our school desks and books,
Playgrounds and games
In Kraków, Lwów and Warszawa
We were snatched by the shadow of Messerschmitts

Scattered throughout the world
By the merciless hand of War
We, the exiled Polish children,
Yearn for our old schools

    And we long to return to
    Our dear Poland
    To offer her our young
    Vigorous strength

We simply want to be taught
In our Polish tongue
And grow up to be Poles
Brave and good

We want our fathers
Fighting in the Polish flanks
To embrace us proudly
Like their younger troops

by Krystyna Kernberg – Tehran 1943[1]
(Translated by Adam Lewis)

    The young author of this naive poem has highlighted two important aspects of our childhood in exile: the hunger for a Polish school and the aims and quality of that school. Polish schools over the centuries, even in the dark years of the 19th century when Poland lost its independence to three invaders, were not only the sources of knowledge, but also places where strong characters were formed and patriotism instilled. These two aims, and the hope of a return to Poland at the end of the war, were the factors, which had a big impact on the programmes and teaching methods employed in the Polish schools in exile.

    Two years of Soviet occupation influenced the education of Polish children in various ways. In localities with large ethnic minorities the Polish schools were closed and all children had to attend Belarusian or Ukrainian ones. In towns with a large Polish population the schools worked in the native language but used the Soviet system. Our six years of Primary and six years of Secondary School were combined into their ten years school called 'Dziesięciolatka'. Russian, Belarusian or Ukrainian languages were taught, as well as political (read communist) indoctrination. Those Polish teachers, who were not arrested or deported, were allowed to keep their jobs. Religious training was discontinued, so was Latin, and a lot of our Polish textbooks for History, Literature etc., were confiscated, as - what we would call today - 'politically incorrect'. Science subjects, however, were taught at a good level. The atmosphere at the school depended on the people in charge. At my school in Nowogródek, the head teacher was a decent Russian - it was the teacher of political science we were afraid of!

Those of us who were deported to Russia in the last transports in June 1941, had two years of that Soviet school behind us, and therefore not such a long interruption of our formal education. Those deported in 1940 were worse off. For various reasons not many of them attended schools in Russia. Joanna Chmielowska recalls: - "At our first place of deportation, Pryiszynskij Owczyj Sowchoz, only my younger brother Jurek and I attended school. My mother insisted that my older sister, Halina, aged 14 was also entitled to study, so we were allowed to move to Kolkhoz Spasowka, which had a six-class school. However, when the winter came, our education ended due to the lack of suitable footwear. The only advantage of the move were the slightly better living conditions in the 'kolkhoz'." (There were two kinds of collective farms in the USSR: sowhoz and kolkhoz.)

In the labour camps, or at the timber camps, even the 4-grade schools seldom existed.. Where they did, few children attended. They had no suitable clothes and had to look after their younger siblings while their mothers worked. Also, their parents were afraid of political indoctrination and provocation: "In our 'posiolek' (hamlet) - writes Teresa Kurowska - "children of Polish and Russian inmates had to go to school. But on the third school day the Russian teacher asked the kids whether their parents held old religious superstitions, or preserved holy pictures etcetera. One Russian boy admitted that his mother kept an icon hidden at the bottom of her trunk. When I told this to my parents, they decided it was safer to keep me away from school."

When the so-called 'amnesty' was declared, wherever the news reached Polish deportees, the mass exodus started towards the south of the Soviet Union where the newly formed units of the Polish Army were offering

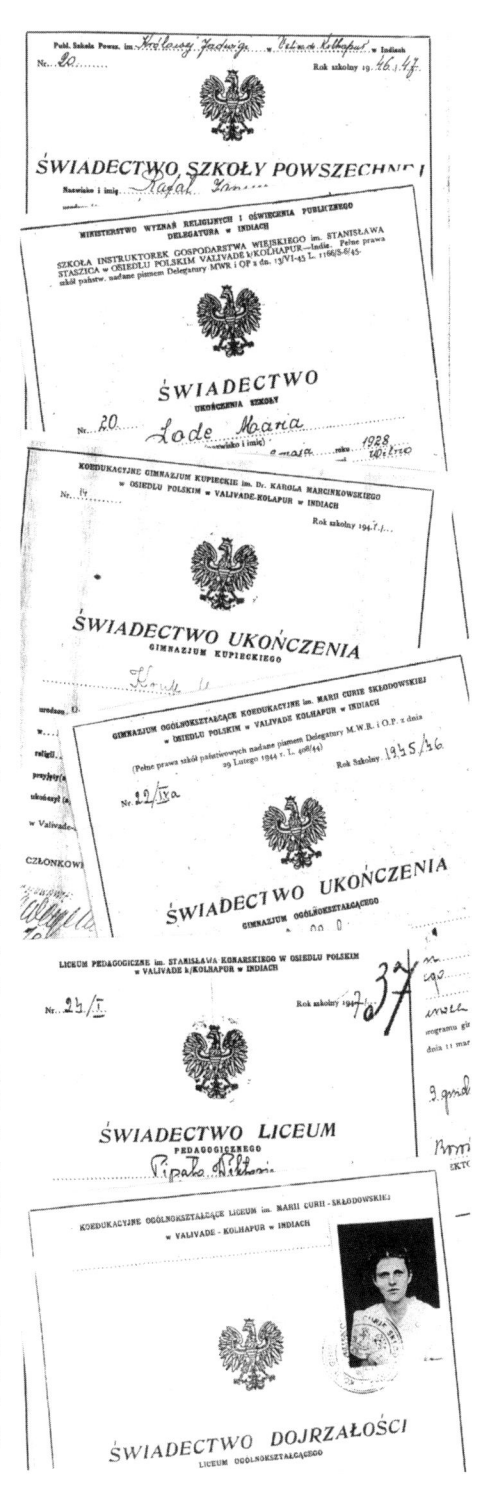

293

some care and help. Straightaway little Polish schools mushroomed. With no textbooks, exercise books or premises, and just an enthusiastic teacher sitting on a bed in a barrack, or on a stone in the open air, with a haphazard assembly of pupils, these first ephemeral creations were from the beginning condemned to closure at short notice, and offered neither exams nor certificates. Yet they fulfilled an important role. After the merciless years when survival was the main issue, they were introducing the children of exiles to the world of culture and knowledge and were giving them the semblance of a normal life.

Morning PT in front of the High School, Valivade

At last the time of departure from the USSR arrived. The lucky ones, who had managed to reach the army, sped off by train to Krasnowodsk to be evacuated to Persia. In the three civilian camps in beautiful Tehran, the schools were nearly normal, even though some of us in camp No. 2 had to sit on piles of bricks and there were still no textbooks, except the odd ones brought by some people into exile, but we had tables, blackboards, pencils and teachers! There were problems with allocating children to correct classes - many had no Birth Certificates, some even did not remember their birth dates - and the long gap in schooling resulted in placing children well below their normal age group levels. Those, who like myself, had completed two years of Soviet school in occupied Poland, had to pass exams in Polish language, literature and history, which was not easy with the shortage of suitable books. But weren't we happy!

It was 1943. The war was going on somewhere around us, but we were too young to join the army and so our war effort went into studying hard - and with joy!

Tehran was only one of frequent stops in our wanderings - further journeys awaited us, to refugee camps in Africa, India, Mexico, New Zealand. Those schools, so painfully and busily assembled, planned to move as units with the teachers, pupils and their families, to wherever we were sent next. But the English authorities, which by then assumed responsibility for us, were not very sympathetic towards such ambitions. Was it not enough that we had survived? That we had food, and clothes (second-hand ones, mostly donated by people in the USA), and a promise of some sort of housing, medical help and possibly, at some later date, a job? The most urgent problem was to move us from Persia. Ships and trains were wanted for army transports and the enemy's boats patrolled the seas. Why did we want education? And who was going to pay for it?

These problems occupied the adults. Young people were oblivious of them - for wherever a group of them arrived, a Polish school would open.

PROGRAMMES AND AIMS

The Polish Government in Exile was enormously concerned with the problems of education for the generations of young Poles dispersed around the world. Among them were those destined to spend the rest of the war years in India. So, as early as May 1942, telegrams flew between the Polish Ministry of Foreign Affairs in London and the Polish Consulate in Bombay, discussing plans for our future.

One of these plans was to place small groups of Polish children in Anglo-Indian convent schools, to help them learn English. Some English and Indian families volunteered to adopt Polish orphans, or to employ older girls as nannies and domestic helps. In a telegram, dated 10.06.1942, Consul E. Banasiński opposed those plans. His objections were that the educational level in those convent schools was not very high, that the Indian food served might not agree with children still suffering from the results of malnutrition in Russia, and that dispersing them over such a large area would make any control by Polish authorities extremely difficult. The Ministry accepted his arguments. There were also patriotic reasons: keeping the children in larger settlements ensured they would attend a Polish school, which would give them a Polish upbringing and enable them to resume education in the Homeland, to which we all still believed, we would soon return.[2]

This concern with not allowing us to lose our national identity became the main theme in planning school curricula. The pre-war Polish system of Primary School for ages 7-12 and Secondary School for ages 13-18 was kept; pre-war textbooks, miraculously found, were reprinted by the Polish Army in the Middle East and all national and religious holidays were duly observed, as were Polish traditions and folklore. The grades 'very good', 'good', 'satisfactory' and 'unsatisfactory' appeared on our annual school reports, instead of the percentage system of marking used by English and Indian schools. Even the school reports themselves were facsimiles of the pre-war ones. Books (sometimes hand-copied), pictures and photographs, were obtained with great difficulty, to help us learn about the geography and history of our country; the country whose future frontiers were uncertain, and subject to negotiations among our Allies.

Of course, this continuation of the pre-war system was not only a question of ideology but also of practical possibilities. The war still raged. Nobody was writing new textbooks. Use of the English ones was difficult because both pupils and teachers had a limited knowledge of the language, as French or German had been the foreign languages taught in the majority of schools in pre-war Poland. However, the predominant factor was nostalgia - we were still pining for our country, longing for Polish books, Polish poems, Polish songs....

So, we were writing essays about the towns and villages from which we were deported; even though surrounded by exotic Indian vegetation, we were drawing Polish poppies and marigolds, or snowy winter scenes. Polish plays were staged and Polish songs and dances learned. Since every Pole abroad considers himself to be an ambassador of his country, we organised exhibitions and shows to which the Indian community was cordially invited. And of course, the political situation being what it was, those of us old enough to take part, indulged in lengthy political discussions.

Incidentally, this preoccupation with Poland and things Polish did not always serve well those, who after the war decided to return to Poland. The following examples, although amusing to us, in a country under communist rule could have resulted in serious repercussions. One of our friends, Jurek Szczawiński, on returning to the People's Republic, enrolled in school. When asked by the teacher to name the Polish President (then pro-soviet Bolesław Bierut) replied with the name of the President of the Polish Government in Exile, Mr. Władysław Raczkiewicz. This was taken for deliberate insolence and his mother was summoned to the school. Told by the headmaster that Jurek did not know the name of his country's president, she screamed at her son "Surely you know? It's Raczkiewicz of course!"[3]

The second incident happened to Halina Strycharz. Soon after her return to Poland her teacher asked for volunteers to write an essay about the Polish Army in Russia. The class decided that Halina, who had spent a few years in Russia, was the best person to do it. The young teenager knew only of our saviour, Gen. Anders, whose 2nd Corps (part of the British 8th Army) had rescued us and enabled us to escape from the Soviet Union. She found some old papers brought from India and wrote an emotional essay, which concluded with her own opinions of life in the USSR and of the Soviet atrocities in Katyń. Unfortunately, the army her professor had in mind was General Berling's army, created by the Russians to fight alongside their forces against the Germans. This was the only one you could mention at that time in Poland, and the class listened to the essay with amazement. The poor teacher hastily called it a misunderstanding, and Halina escaped any unpleasant consequences. A few years later when sitting for her matriculation exam, the same teacher drew her aside and warned her: "Please don't compromise me by writing anything dangerous!"[4]

It seems strange that among all our essays and pictures, there were none referring to our war and deportation experiences. Perhaps it was due to excessive care for our psychological well being - a sort of therapy - allowing us to forget hardships and tragedies sustained while in the USSR. But children are resilient and placed in a friendly environment they recover easily and forget past problems. Sadly, that excessive caution caused the loss of many potentially priceless documents that could have been written by the young witnesses to history.

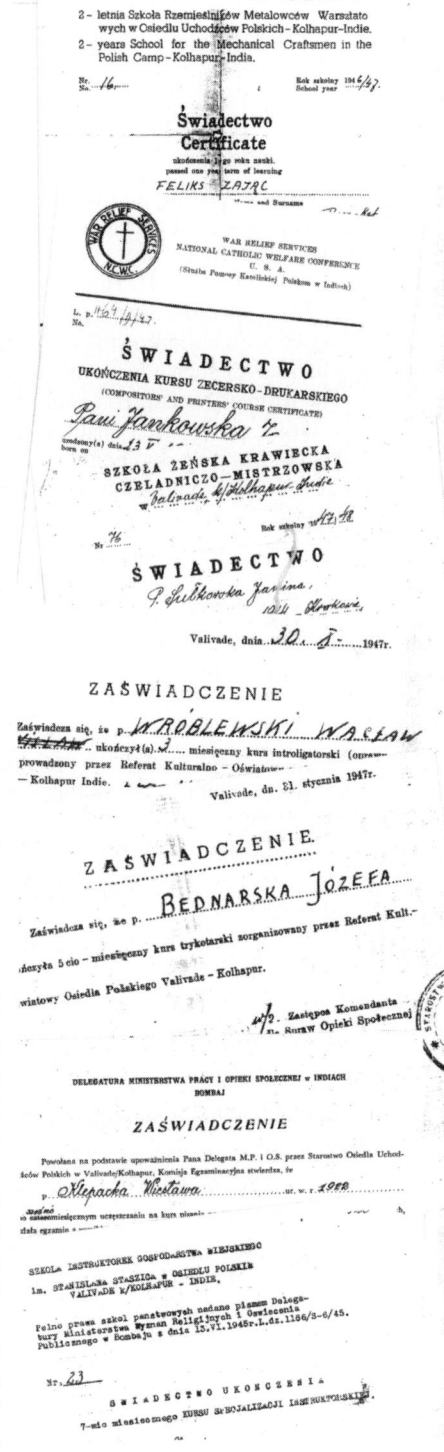

With the passage of time, with the disastrous Tehran and Yalta agreements signed and the return to our homeland still problematical, there came a new approach to education. Whether we chose to return or stay abroad, we needed some practical skills and qualifications. Learning English also became recognized as a great asset. So, on the 16th May 1945, the Ministry of Education issued a letter to Delegates in Jerusalem, Nairobi and Bombay, recommending the urgent training of teachers of English, who could not only help their pupils learn the language, but also make contacts with local British and Indian communities, use English and American educational publications, and provide an additional skill should they return home to Poland. This met with an enthusiastic response from our Delegate, Mr. M. Gołcawski, who from the beginning was an ardent advocate of sending our young people to English schools. Our Schools Inspector, Mr. Z. Żerebecki, who had learnt English in pre-war Poland, personally conducted the first course of English for 60 teachers. His proposals to employ the best of our Indian teachers of English, Mr. B. Appadurai and Miss A. DeSouza, to run an additional evening course, did not meet with the Delegate's approval due to the lack of funds, but he sent some badly needed textbooks - McCallum's and Epstein's, popular at that time.[5]

For the pupils, English was even more of a problem. In March 1946 a suggestion came from Bombay that our schools should change to bi-lingual lectures. This was rejected as impractical due to the poor knowledge of English among the teachers, and the lack of textbooks. Instead, the number of English lessons was increased, some English terminology was introduced in certain subjects, and pupils destined for English schools had to do their revision in English of the material learned in Polish.[6]

During our last years in Valivade great emphasis was put on all sorts of technical and occupational courses. The calls for changes in our curriculum came too late. The last school year had to be shortened and exams taken earlier to ensure that all students left India with some sort of certificate or diploma.

ORGANISATION & FINANCES

Polish settlements in India, separated by considerable distances, enjoyed a certain amount of autonomy in running their internal affairs. However, when it came to dealings with authorities, whether the British in Delhi or the Polish in London, a central approach was required.

In July 1943 the Polish Ministry of Education in London created in Bombay, alongside the existing office of the Delegate of the Ministry of Labour and Social Welfare, a temporary section to deal with all aspects of education and schooling in the camps and settlements in India. While co-operating with the Delegate in matters concerning schools, it answered directly to the Polish Office of Education and Schools, at that time existing in Tehran. Mr. M. Gołcawski, who arrived in Bombay from Tehran on 27th May 1943, became its Director. By September 1943 the rapid development of many schools and courses made it necessary to convert this section into an independent "Delegatura" (Department of the London Ministry of Education).

After the end of the war, with the creation of a new People's Republic of Poland - officially free but actually subjugated to the Soviet Union - Western countries withdrew their recognition of the Polish Government in Exile, and in 1945 both "Delegaturas" ceased to operate. Mr. Gołcawski remained in Bombay supervising and helping the schools, at first as vice president of the Committee for the Care of Refugees formed by Interim Committee for Polish Questions in London, and when that shut down, as Representative of the Polish Red Cross. All these institutions are described more fully in other chapters.

As soon as the Valivade Camp started functioning, school became compulsory for all children over seven years old. Schools, some of which had already existed in the temporary camps, were reopening one after another, as the number of inhabitants grew. The commitment of the Camp Authorities may be judged by the fact that in less than two months some school facilities were ready to be used by the children arriving from temporary camps in Karachi.

Valivade was created as a more permanent place of residence, and the school buildings were prepared with that in mind. They were spacious and comfortable, although constructed, like the rest of the camp buildings, from flimsy materials: bamboo mat walls on wooden supports, earthen floors, roofs of clay tiles without ceilings. Only the windows were different - instead of the bamboo mat shutters they had frames covered with linen, allowing the children some light and privacy. Long blocks were divided into classrooms with bamboo mat partitions, somewhat inconvenient, as the more unruly and noisy classes could interrupt lessons going on next door. Long verandahs shaded by overhanging roofs, and the climbers planted alongside them, were useful during the breaks, as the hot Indian sun stopped us from going outside and we had not yet learned the benefits of a midday siesta. Only early in the morning could some physical training take place - due to the lack of a communal hall, in front of our classrooms. Infrequent school assemblies also were held in the open. Plain wooden tables with a hole for the ink pot but without drawers (books had to be kept on the floor), blackboards and map stands, were a great improvement on the furnishing (or lack of it) in our previous schools. The more ambitious schools took great care of the long, narrow flower beds along the walls, growing shade-giving climbers, cannas with flame-like flowers, and sometimes even a small papaya tree.

Although the schools curriculum was planned on the pre-war Polish model, the calendar division of the year was dictated by the climate. The school year started on the 15th June, often with the beginning of the monsoon bringing a welcome respite from the hot weather, and ended on the 31st March. Most of the young people spent the long vacations, when temperatures reached 40°C, camping in hill resorts, Panhala or Chandoli, where it was cooler. However, the walk to church for the Mass celebrating the beginning of the school year, invariably ended with a drenching downpour. There was also a short break of two weeks in October, when the weather was cooler.

The problems besieging the schools in transit camps were slowly solved in Valivade. Greater stability in the movement of pupils and teachers allowed for more systematic studies. There was still a shortage of qualified teachers (many of them perished in Russia, or joined the Polish Forces), books were in short supply and other teaching aids non-existent. In the first months, pages of the few existing books were duplicated on a primitive Gestetner machine or even copied by hand. Later on Polish pre-war textbooks started arriving, reprinted by the Polish firms in England or the Editorial Committee of the Polish Army in the Middle East in Jerusalem. A few books were reprinted in India as early as 1943, thanks to the commitment of Lady Dow, wife of the British Governor of Karachi, who purchased the first set of Polish characters for the local printer. Later the Bombay Delegate followed suit. Gradually the situation improved - library stocks increased, books could be taken home instead of listened to in the common rooms, and pupils could study from textbooks instead of handwritten notes. But until the end of our stay some books, like English Dictionaries, had to be shared by several pupils and the arrival of new volumes in the library caused a sensation, long queues and fervent discussions.

Contrary to the views of both British and Indian Authorities who often questioned "the cultural whims" of refugees, Polish institutions in London appreciated the need not only of schools for children, but also means of further education, job training and cultural entertainment for grownups, bored with enforced leisure caused by shortage of jobs. They encouraged the camp authorities to provide them. However this difference of opinion, especially when financial outlay was involved, led to many misunderstandings.

A good example of this was a problem concerning religious teaching. When the Rector of the Polish Catholic Mission in India, Fr. K. Bobrowski, left for the USA in October 1945, his job was temporarily taken over by one of the other three priests who were already burdened with sharing their pastoral duties with teaching in camp's schools and participating in social activities. So, as early as October 1945, the Field Bishop of the Polish Army, J Gawlina, obtained leave from the Polish Army in the Middle East for one of the Army chaplains, Fr. K. Kozłowski, to take over the duties of the Rector in India. However, the application for an Indian visa met with the following reply from Delhi: - "The Government of India does not require the services of Fr. Kozłowski. In future, any such requests should only come from the Indian Government."[7] It took a whole year of negotiations by the Committee for the Care of Refugees in Bombay, the Bishop's Curia of the Polish Army in the Middle East, and the Schools section of ITC (Interim Treasury Committee for Polish Questions) in London, to persuade the Indian authorities that our need was real and urgent. Finally, after giving an undertaking that his arrival would not require any financial outlay, as he would still receive his army pay, permission was granted and Fr. Kozłowski arrived in October 1946 to relieve Fr. Przybysz, who returned to his school duties.

Financing the needs of Polish refugees in India was rather complicated and is described more fully in other chapters. As far as education was concerned, the premises, furniture and basic salaries of the teachers were covered in the camp's budget and therefore had to be approved by the British officials at the Government of India. On the other hand, any overtime, textbooks, library books and extra curricular activities, were paid for with donations received directly from the Polish Government in London, and when it was no longer recognized by the Allies, from the ITC.

The sums spent on educational needs were extensive. In the first years the cost of material outlay, equipment, furniture, books, etc., was great. Large and constant expense were staff salaries. In one monthly budget for the year 1944/45, we found the following figures for salaries:

Secondary School Head – Rs 220, teacher – Rs 120, teacher of English – Rs 150,
Primary School Headmistress – Rs 120, teacher – Rs 100,
Instructor in Agricultural College – Rs 100, Trainee – Rs 80,
Secretary – Rs 80, Nurse – Rs 50, Caretaker – Rs 50,

With two head teachers, 126 teachers, six secretaries, seventeen caretakers and some additional employees, plus the outlay for books and other equipment, the maintenance of the experimental farm and other outgoings, the whole figure came to over Rs 23 000. This equaled roughly the monthly allowance for 436 refugees. So perhaps it is not so surprising that these cultural requirements, so natural for us, met with the disapproval of our foreign patrons.[8]

The situation worsened considerably when the care of Polish refugees was taken over first by UNRRA and later by the IRO. As part of an extensive savings program, salaries were cut, overtime abolished and the number of teaching posts reduced. Extra funds from London no longer came. On October 18th 1946, in their last letter, Mr. Jerzy Litewski, head of the closing Polish Committee for Refugees, and his deputy M. Goławski, warned that the reductions in funding to be implemented from 1st of November by UNRRA "...would reduce life in the settlement to the level of primitive vegetation." Apparently, only the English and Indian employees were to retain their salaries, while the Poles were expected to work for merely their meagre monthly allowance, a sum hardly sufficient for two weeks' expenses. The most alarming prospect was that "...studies of our youngsters (118 girls and boys) in English schools would cease at the end of October, a month before the examinations, causing them to lose the whole years' work."[9]

Fortunately this did not happen. Desperate endeavours to find the necessary funds resulted in money coming from the London based I. Paderewski School Fund. Some of this money was used for additional pay for the teachers, the rest for the pupils, especially those in English schools. The last occupational courses in the camp were financed by the Federation of Poles in India, or by fees paid by the students themselves.

Due to the great goodwill of all participants, these problems were somehow resolved. The greatest difficulty and cause of stress was the unstable political situation; the frequent switching of the institutions which governed our lives, and the uncertainty of various plans for our future. The last two years were spent in the shadow of constantly changing dates for leaving India, which created in the settlement an atmosphere of fear and worry. Only the determination of our teachers and the willingness of pupils allowed the majority of us to leave India with qualifications enabling us to resume studies or find employment in our new places of residence.

INSPECTORATE

An important role in our Educational System was played by the Schools Inspector. He inspected schools, ensuring their work reached the required standard, discussing problems and needs with the head teachers and representing them to the London and Bombay Authorities. While the Delegate of the Ministry of Education had to concentrate his efforts on obtaining finance and supplies, and negotiate terms with ever changing patron organisations, the Inspectorate which was situated locally, was easily accessible and it understood the needs and problems inside the camp.

Former director of our Grammar school, Zdzisław Żerebecki, accepted the appointment of Inspector on 1.9.1943, but retained his post of maths teacher in higher classes. Being also the Deputy Delegate of Min. of Education, he had lively contacts both with the Bombay authorities and the teaching staff in Valivade. Extremely active and energetic, he not only found time to write an instruction manual for teachers, organise lectures and English lessons for them, but also to take active part in all cultural activities in the camp. His staff consisted of two secretaries: Mrs. Zofia Saplis and Janina Kossowska, with temporary help from a former pupil, Janina Niezabytowska.[10]

Z. Żerebecki and his secretaries J. Kossowska and Z. Saplisowa

To ease the inspector's considerable work load, in April 1945 the Delegate of the Ministry of Education wrote to his Head Office in London, requesting permission to create a new post of Deputy Inspector. In fact, the Headmistress of one of the schools, Mrs. Harasymów, had already started inspecting primary schools. Her salary was to be covered partly from the budget of the camp, partly from the funds of the Delegate's Office. However, this suggestion was not accepted, so Mrs. Harasymów unofficially combined the two functions until the end of the school year, and then resigned and accepted the position of lecturer in Methods of Education in the newly opened Teacher Training College.[11]

The English and Indian officers, civil servants and other officials, often visited the camp and invariably inspected our schools, accompanied by our Inspector, who was pleased with the interest shown. Their opinions, as a rule, were positive, and even enthusiastic, but there was one unpleasant visit. At the end of January 1946 Col. A.C.B. Neate, then the Camp Commandant of Valivade, told Mr. Żerebecki that his friend, the Indian Schools Inspector in Poona, Mr. L. R. Desai, would like to see our schools. This visit turned into a 3 days long, very thorough inspection, with only one aim – to find ways of reducing spending on education. In March, the Committee for the Care of Refugees received a rather critical report. Inspector Desai thought that Polish teachers' salaries were "too liberal"; their weekly working hours (22) were 8 hours shorter than those in Indian schools, and the extra curricular instructors for woodwork etc. were unnecessary. The harshest criticism he bestowed on the teachers of English – both Polish and Indian. They were – he said - inexperienced, and using old-fashioned methods. His final recommendations were to cut 30 Polish teachers' posts, reduce the salaries of the rest, do away with all nursery school helpers, nurses and secretaries, and liquidate the Special Fund for books, as he considered there were already too many held. The only expense he considered necessary was for replacement of all textbooks for English with more up to date ones. Also teachers of English should have their salaries increased and the new ones should be sought by advertising in Indian Press.

In his reply, Inspector Żerebecki explained, that the Polish teachers, unused to the Indian climate and whose health was badly affected by the deportation, could not work longer hours. The number of posts in nurseries and lower classes of primary schools was automatically decreasing each year, as there were no new pupils, but the older children needed every support to keep up the good results they were now achieving.[12]

In October 1946 UNRRA took over the care of Polish refugees. As the Bombay offices closed one by one, Mr. J. Litewski, Director of the Refugee Committee and his deputy, Mr. Goławski wrote to inspector Żerebecki, asking him -"to continue his care of Valivade schools and to extend it over schools in Jamnagar and Panchgani". They also informed London authorities of the change, adding: -"all Polish teachers in India will now be dependant on the English Commandants of the Camps and their Polish deputies, while their actual employer, acting through those English Commandants, will be in fact UNRRA".[13]

The first move by this "new employer" was to abolish the post of an Inspector. Protests from teachers, the Polish Camp Commandant and Prof. Sulimirski from School Section of ITC brought no results. Finally, Mrs. Button, the English Deputy Commandant for Financial Affairs, agreed that after two months of unpaid work, the Inspector could continue doing his job unofficially, paid as if he were a teacher of English. However, the odd oversight by UNRRA - when the post of inspector was abolished, they forgot to abolish his two secretaries - enabled the inspector's office to continue operating. The last months were spent concentrating on ensuring that majority of older students could leave India with some certificates, even if it meant accelerating the dates of exams. Mr. Żerebecki was also fighting English and Polish authorities to obtain the three months' compensation, to which the teachers were entitled on the termination of their contracts.

Leaving Valivade for Poland on 1.7.1947 he handed over his duties to the Headmistress of the Grammar School, Mrs. Borońska, who performed them, unofficially and without extra pay, until the liquidation of the camp.

PRIMARY SCHOOLS

Nursery Schools. Although the majority of mothers in the camp had no jobs, there were some with full time employment in offices, the hospital, schools etc. while others were unable to look after their kids for other reasons. The newspaper "Polak w Indiach" in April 1946 stated that in the school year 1943/44 each of the camp's five Districts had its own nursery, together accommodating 150 children under the age of seven, which was starting age for primary education in Poland. These were treated as part of the primary schools, and their staff were paid at the same rate as school teachers. In 1946 only three nurseries remained. Older children progressed up the school system and for obvious reasons, there were no new pupils.[14]

Primary Schools in Valivade were organised progressively, as the number of children in the settlement grew. The first transport arrived from Malir on 16.7.1943, and School No.1 opened on the 21st of the same month, a mere five days later. The first 103 pupils were divided into six forms, under the Headmistress, Blanka Potocka, Parish Priest Fr. Dallinger and four teachers. Their classrooms had simple tables and chairs, but only one blackboard. School No.2 opened on the arrival of the second transport on 28.7.43. In the Camp Chronicle a note appeared: "there are still 100 children unable to attend school, due to the shortage of furniture…" But this problem must have been solved speedily, for in November 1943 School No.3 was opened, for the orphanage. In the school year 1943/44 1028 children attended those three schools. Initially the conditions were difficult – there was a shortage of blackboards, textbooks and other equipment. Pupils were too young to learn by making notes or just listening. So old cardboard boxes were turned into substitute blackboards, pages of the few existing textbooks were hand copied for pupils and other educational aids were made from available bits and pieces. But the work progressed at a normal or sometimes even quicker pace, as there were two years of lost education to catch up with. The pupils were mostly willing and hardworking. They had been bored by 2 years of forced inactivity, and appreciated the pleasure of learning in their native tongue with friendly and helpful teachers.

The nursery at School No. 2

Staff on School No. 1:
R. Jankowska, …,
I. Laniewska,
Z. Chrząszczewska, …,
J. Katkiewicz,
M. Ściborska,
Standing: Z. Nowicka,
M. Leśniak,
Z. Zagórowska,
A. Skrzat, …,
W. Borzemska,
brother Orysiuk,
M. Bobolska and
J. Abramowicz

By the end of that school year the school equipment was more or less completed, small supplies of maps, atlases, pictures etc. arrived, and though each textbook still had to be shared by 3 or 4 pupils, the total situation was improving steadily.

Eventually each District had its own Primary School. Those were:

Queen Jadwiga's School No.1, in District 1 – first Headmistress Blanka Potocka, then Zofia Chrząszczewska.

Adam Mickiewicz School No.2, in District 2 – Headmistress Antonina Harasymów

Gen. Sikorski's School No.3, in the orphanage – Headmistress Olga Sasadeusz

Henryk Sienkiewicz School No.4, opened in 1944/45 – first Headmistresses Anna Chylowa then Helena Kurzeja.

School No.5, opened in November 1946, when the children from Balachadi Camp were finally transferred to Valivade - headmistress Helena Asłanowicz.

Fluctuations in the camp's population caused frequent changes in school staff, but over the five years of their existence, eighty one men and women taught in those schools and six trainee teachers, recruited from among the school leavers. Their names appear at the end of this chapter.

We were unable to trace all statistical rapports, but from the archival materials available we give, as an example, figures for the first school year – 1943/44[15]

School No. 1		School No. 2		School No. 3	
Form	Pupils	Form	Pupils	Form	Pupils
1a & 1b	56	1a & 1b	68	1a & 1b	51
2a,b,c	99	2a & 2b	57	2	45
3a & 3b	73	3a & 3b	58	3	42
4a & 4b	65	4a & 4b	65	4a & 4b	50
5a & 5b	66	5	46	5	42
6	33	6a & 6Ib	47	6a & 6b	57
	392		**341**		**287**

Some of the classes were quite large, due to the shortage of teachers and accommodation, but that was long before the 'one to one' method favoured in some modern schools was even

Staff of School No. 2:
sitting: M. Gimza, J. Wróblewska, A. Harasymów, K. Kamińska, M. Kowalczyk, Z. Alberti,
standing: A. Szwaglis, R. Kolischer, ..., ..., brother J. Orysiuk, M. Bobolska and J. Abramowicz

heard of. Kids were supposed to keep quiet and listen, and this gave good results. The Camp Chronicle for that year states "...In the beginning of April, the school year, which for some pupils started in Tehran, ended with the campfire, at which the 300 Scouts and Guides received their badges, and the best pupils from all schools received prizes. (At that time, the Delegate of the Min. of Education, Mr. M. Goławski, an old Scout himself, had to help Mr. W. Bidakowski, the only Scoutmaster in Valivade, hence the educational and Scouting celebrations often took place together).

Form 5 of School No. 4 with the Head Mrs. A. Chylową, M. Wróblewski, D. Kruszyńska, Zając, A. Kardasiński, Romanowska, B. Twarowska, Miss W. Kirdzik and J. Bernatowicz

The same Camp Chronicle tells us, that many pupils spent that year's long holiday preparing for a special exam that would enable them to skip one year at their school.

Harrowing war experiences, interrupted studies often resulting in diminished knowledge of their own language, split families or no family able to offer home help – all that caused a large number of pupils studying in classes a year or two behind their age level, and afraid to attempt the move forward. With some pupils this problem remained for many years. As late as 1946, in the report of Delegate M. Goławski we find figures referring to all Polish primary schools in India (in Valivade, Balachadi & Panchgani) showing the numbers of those studying at the right age level, and those behind.[16]

Form	Girls	Boys	G+B	Normal age	Late
1	27	18	45	45	-
2	46	53	99	96	3
3	73	89	162	142	20
4	125	139	264	228	36
5	182	160	342	205	137
6	164	136	300	128	172
Total	**617**	**595**	**1212**	**844**	**368**

As we can see, after three years of extensive studies, $1/4$ of the pupils were still behind their age level, despite the great efforts made by the pupils and teachers. Only a few of them managed to complete two years' material during the one school year. There is very little discrepancy between boys and girls in primary schools (unlike the secondary school level), as these children were too young to be admitted to military schools.

There were many extra-mural activities. Each school organised excursions, performed school plays and encouraged its pupils to work in the small school gardens. Most pupils were members of the Girl Guides and Boy Scouts units, or of the religious organisation "Krucjata" (The Childrens Eucharistic Crusade). The most active in arranging exhibitions and shows for the whole settlement was School No. 3. A possible reason could be that without adult family members to take care of their free time and provide them with entertainment, the orphanage children had more time and inclination to take part in those activities.

Apart from the five Primary schools in Valivade Camp, some efforts were made to provide education for the children temporarily residing in the Health Centre in Panchgani. At the beginning lessons were held in small groups. In December 1944 an attempt was made to organise a normal six-form Primary school for 56 pupils. Yet the constant turnover of the pupils and their poor health made normal schooling impossible, and the name was changed back to Primary Courses. Their teachers were treated as the employees of Valivade Camp.

Form 5 of School No. 5: Drawing lesson

SECONDARY SCHOOLS

In Valivade there was a comparatively small number of very young children due to the high mortality rate in Russia and the absence of fathers. There were few young people, especially men, as those who survived, were in the Polish Forces or Military Schools. There were however a lot of teenagers, for whom education and leisure programmes had to be found. Quite a number of the younger "teens" had to attend the primary schools due to the interruptions in their education. For the others, Secondary Schools were organised.

Morning break at the Grammar School

The largest was the **"Maria Curie-Skłodowska Gimnazjum and Liceum Ogólnokształcące"** - the four-year Grammar School and two-year Lycee (equivalent to the English two year 6th Form), preparing students for the ordinary and advanced School Leaving Certificates called "Matura" (matriculation). It opened on 19th August 1943. Its beginnings came from a similar school in Civilian Camp No.1 in Tehran. Due to the great efforts of its Director, Zdzisław Żerebecki, it was supposed to go to British Colonies in East Africa in one transport, with all its staff, pupils and their families. This journey which started in March 1943 was interrupted at Ahvaz transit camp where, in insufferably hot climate (apparently "Ahvaz" in Persian means "hell" and it is one of the hottest places on earth) the school resumed lessons, while awaiting for a suitable shipment. However, as the enemy submarines increased their activity in the Indian Ocean, instead of East Africa, this transport was directed to another transit camp, in Karachi, India (now Pakistan). There it reopened again in the temporary Camp Malir, before moving to its more permanent home, Valivade Camp. It arrived there at the end of July and finally began the more or less regular and stable work, which lasted for the next five years. Besides the Director Żerebecki this group included his secretary, Mrs. Joanna Kowalska and our favourite History teacher, Miss Hanka Handerek.

However, soon afterwards, another group of teachers arrived, led by Dr. Maria Borońska, who in Tehran was designated as the Head of Valivade High School. This caused some consternation. She agreed to work as the Polish Language and Literature lecturer, but on the 1st of September, a new position of School Inspector was created, and taken over by Mr. Zerebecki, as well as a position of Deputy Delegate of Min. of Education, leaving Dr. Borońska in charge of the High School.

The High School started working in 9 groups – three First Year Forms, two Second Year Forms and one each of Third and Fourth Year Forms in Grammar School and two Forms of Lycee. Soon additional First Year Form had to be opened on arrival of the orphanage. The Headmistress, her deputy and twelve teachers formed the staff at the beginning. At the end of school year 43/44, the number of pupils was as follows:[17]

Form 1a, 1b, 1c, & 1d	173
Form 2a & 2b	92
Form 3	33
Form 4	19
Lycee 1st year	11
Lycee 2nd year	11
Total	**339**

In September 1944 our newspaper, *"Polak w Indiach"*, quoted the number of students as 453, and when the older pupils from Balachadi Camp arrived in Valivade, the number reached 800.

"Gimnazjum and Liceum" - the two schools, under joint directorship, occupied four buildings, only one of which was built of stone. It contained the Physics and Biology laboratories, the Scouts room and a small room for use of the school Red Cross Circle. The other buildings made of coconut mating, contained classrooms, offices, staff rooms and Girl Guides room. In June 1945 another building was erected, containing more classrooms and the Physical Training Hall. The buildings were surrounded by greenery, each Form looking after their own little garden.

The Camp Chronicle tells us that the buildings were furnished with simple tables, benches and blackboards. In the beginning there was an acute shortage of textbooks, but unlike the Primary Schools, here students were able to take notes. They also copied poems and fragments of prose from the inadequate library stocks. But the following year the school started with 4687 books borrowed from Delegatura, plus their own 1654. There were also 50 maps, many botanical and scientific tables mostly made by students, models of geometric figures and finally even a small but very useful science Laboratory, equipped with the aid of money provided by the NCWC (National Catholic Welfare Conference) from USA.[18] Now, in the modern 21st Century, when schools are equipped with computers and every possible gadget, how pitiful our meagre resources would look, but how happy and proud we felt then on receiving them.

In February 1944 The Polish Ministry of Education in London conferred on the school full State School status and acknowledged its name.

The staff: (sitting): F Wray, M. Borońska, Fr. L. Dallinger, M. Skórzyna, (standing): ..., E. Karwowska, J. Kowalska, Z. Sikorski, J. Szymańska, J. Latawiec, A. Handerek, H. Katkiewicz, M. Czarnecka, F. Podsoński, J. Latawcowa and J. Kłosowska

Five matriculation exams were conducted in which ninety eight students received School Leaving Certificates (Matura), enabling them to enter university.

March 1944	11
March 1945	11 + 3 extern
October 1945	26
March 1947	26
December 1947	21

The matriculation at the end of the school year 1945/46 was taken in October 45, because the very hard working and determined class managed to do a two-year programme in a year and a half which enabled them to start further studies at the English institutions in Bombay and Panchgani in November of that year. The final school year 1947/48 was, by special permission of the Ministry, shortened in all Valivade schools to enable students to leave India with a finishing Certificate.

Great problems faced those who wanted to enter Higher Education. Some efforts were made to obtain places at Indian Universities, but the unsympathetic attitude of the British Authorities, our student's limited knowledge of English, and the constant financial shortages put paid to all those plans. The same fate met plans to send some students for veterinary and dental studies in Edinburgh. Most of the 1944 graduates were employed as teachers in Primary Schools. Another group found employment in the camp administration. Only the group taking the

"Lycee" Form

exam in October 1945 took advantage of Art and Commercial Colleges in Bombay, or the special Commercial Course organised for them at the Panchgani Convent. In 1946 the Camp Authorities organised Nursing Training in Valivade, and several graduates obtained the Polish Red Cross Diploma, enabling them to work in hospitals. The March 1947 graduates were promised places at the University of Madras, but the volatile political situation, the imminent independence of India and resulting departure of the British, changed those plans as well.

Mr. A. Nigelszporn amongst his pupils, K. Siara, S. Kalawajtis, Z. Nowicki, Cz. Cwajna, I. Łosowska, A. Kurzawska, L. Truksa, A. Gębski, S. Ucinek, T. Kozłowski, W. Kopiec and A. Błach

Liceum Pedagogiczne im. Stanisława Konarskiego (Stanislaus Konarski Teacher Training College) opened on 15th June 1945, at the suggestion of the Delegate of Min. of Education. It admitted students who had completed four years of Grammar School. Mrs. Maria Skórzyna became its Principal; teaching staff were shared with other schools. The original three year programme was shortened to two years; two Final exams took place in March and December 1947. Among the twenty nine students who obtained Primary School Teachers' Diplomas were two post-matriculation students who were allowed to take only the specific teaching subjects, and took the shortened exam only a few hours before boarding the train for further emigration.

Gimnazjum Handlowe im. Karola Marcinkiewicza (Secondary School with Commercial bias) was created with the similar idea of giving the dispersing students some professional training. At the start of the 1945/46 school year, thirty eight students enrolled; in the next school year two more First year classes were opened. The graduates were expected to work in commercial or cooperative establishments. Headmaster Zdzisław Sikorski had to share staff with other schools or obtain help in specialist subjects from the administration of the Camp. Three sets of students completed the school.

All the above schools worked in close cooperation, sharing not only

First Year of the Teacher Training College: (sitting) K. Karasiewicz, K. Kuchcicka, Teachers: H. Katkiewicz, M. Skórzyna, A. Harasymów, H. Zakrzewska, M. Rycerz, (middle row standing) D. Urbaniec, M. Bojarska, S. Krupa, H. Syberyjska, K. Nowakowska, J. Siwek, C. Naplocha, (top row standing) W. Tomas, J. Rolczewska, W. Ostrowska, H. Polańska, A. Chyla, J. Wojniłowicz and A. Panek

equipment but also teachers. Maria Skórzyna shared the duties of the Teacher Training College Principal with those of the lecturer in Propaedeutic of Philosophy and Psychology at the Lycee; our popular and overworked historian Anna Handerek delivered lectures on the History of Education in the Teacher Training College, and Inspector Żerebecki, already a Jack of all trades, terrorised pupils with his maths lessons in all three schools. When the older students from the Country Club, Malir and Balachadi started arriving in Valivade, some Primary School teachers had to be promoted to Secondary School level.

Commercial Secondary School with its Headmaster Z. Sikorski and Mrs. Spława-Neuman

The already quoted Delegate's Report of October 1946 gives us some idea of the composition of the High Schools population (gimnazjum & lyceum in Valivade and gimnnazjum in Balachadi)

Form	Girls	Boys	G+B	Normal age	Late
1 Gim.	95	84	179	83	96
2 Gim.	83	69	152	77	75
3 Gim	102	31	133	37	96
4 Gim.	131	12	143	38	105
1 Lyc.	49	5	54	5	49
2 Lyc.	27	3	30	2	28
Total	**487**	**204**	**691**	**242**	**449**

It is evident that at the Secondary School level there were twice as many girls as boys, especially in the higher forms, because more boys than girls joined Cadets Schools or Polish Forces. Also, nearly half the students were in the class below their normal age group. One possible explanation is that there was much more material to be assimilated than in Primary schools, if one wanted to work through two years' curriculum in one school year and holidays. This is even more evident in the occupational schools, Teacher Training College and Commerce College:

Form	Girls	Boys	G+B	Normal age	Late
1 CC	35	5	40	2	38
2 CC	45	1	46	4	42
3 CC	40	1	41	-	41
1 TTC	31	-	31	2	29
2 TTC	20	-	20	1	19
Total	**171**	**7**	**178**	**9**	**169**

The older boys who preferred to attend vocational courses, were not included in the above figures. But the overwhelming majority of girls in Secondary Schools gave those schools specific characteristics - there was, for example, less interest in the sciences, more in humanities, languages, literature or theatre. The enormous number of young people who were behind in their studies shows how difficult it was to catch up on those few years lost through war and deportations.[19]

TECHNICAL SCHOOLS AND VOCATIONAL COURSES

Even before the Second World War ended so disastrously for us in May 1945, when we were still hoping to return to free Poland, the plans for introducing vocational training courses were being considered. It was obvious that in the war-ravaged Poland there would not be enough places at universities and colleges for all returning deportees, and also that our country would require workmen skilled in all sorts of trades. When, after the infamous Yalta Conference, it became clear that the majority of Polish Refugees would refuse to return to Poland given over to our communist neighbours, and that they would have to find the means to live in foreign countries, the necessity of vocational training became urgent, especially for those without inclination towards higher education.

In November 1945 an offer of 250 apprenticeship places for Polish boys aged 15-18 was received from an Indian factory Bata. On the advice of Mr. L. Wieniawski of the Welfare Section of the Interim Committee for Poles in London, it was refused, because starting very young, unqualified boys on the factory floor might prejudice their future careers. Instead, efforts were made to provide occupational training inside Valivade Camp. This was not an easy option. With the lack of suitable buildings, equipment and materials (shortages of practically everything caused by the military requirements having priority), few suitably qualified teachers and both climatic and social conditions so different, it was a brave, if not foolhardy undertaking, but it met with some success.

Szkola Instruktorek Gospodarstwa Wiejskiego (Stanislaus Staszic College of Rural Management). The Soviet Authorities carried out their policy of pacification and sovietisation in Poland mainly by imprisoning and murdering the Polish Intelligentsia: officers, judges, professors, civil servants etc, but they also deported to the Soviet Union a great number of country folk. Many of them came from the families of so called "borderland settlers" – army volunteers, who after fighting in the First World War were given small parcels of land in the under populated Eastern Poland, called "Kresy" (Borderland). Ordinary villagers, who opposed collectivisation or simply were known for their unwillingness to accept the communist way of life were also deported. Many girls in the Valivade orphanage came from such backgrounds and were expected to return to their farms, or take up similar employment in the future.

The Staff: M. Wasilewska, M. Bielawska, Head M. Suszyński, K. Peszyńska, W. Walles, Cz. Polechowicz and J. Latawiec

From the initiative of Prof. Mikołaj Suszyński and under his headship, a two year college for seventy five girls was opened in May 1944. The aim of the college was to prepare and qualify the group of future Regional Advisers. In pre-war Poland it was a popular job for women qualified to help farmers' wives to improve the quality of village life, not only by carrying out efficient and prosperous farming but also by encouraging cultural activities among the villagers. The curriculum of the college apart from the general educational

College of Rural Management, amongst the pupils are: Head M. Suszyński, M. Wasilewska and sitting: Cz. Polechowicz

subjects, (Religious Studies, Polish Language, History and Maths) and the occupational subjects, included also the organising of social and cultural activities. There were theoretical and practical lessons in cooking and dressmaking, very important for the girls from the orphanage, who could not learn those simple skills from their mothers. The school had poor facilities for many of those subjects – e.g. all the cooking had to be done on the small, one pot charcoal stoves, popular in India, but totally unknown in Poland. But the meals cooked were eaten together, with additional instructions about etiquette, laying the table and so on.[20]

Even more crucial was the lack of farm machinery and tools - the state of Maharasthra being greatly overpopulated and poor, its agriculture was mainly carried out manually. So the teachers were compelled to explain the use of mechanical help with pictures and descriptions rather than practical demonstrations. With the lack of suitable textbooks, scripts had to be prepared by the teachers from the available English publications. The local climate, so different from the European, made the cultivation of many crops impossible. With all those problems in mind, the Rector of Polish Catholic Mission, Father K. Bobrowski and the School Headmaster, M. Suszyński, attempted - with the help of The American War Relief Service - to transfer the whole College to the USA or Canada. When he was taking to the USA a group of Polish boys, candidates for the clerical Seminary, Father Bobrowski took also the detailed program of the College and personal data of its students, hoping to get help from American bishops to realize the project. But the war was reaching its end, the Allies no longer required Polish Forces.

They had the rebuilding of their economies to think about and the ambitious plans of small groups of Polish refugees were irrelevant and met with no encouragement.

The Farm. An Experimental Farm belonging to the school was created with great difficulty on three hectares of stony ground. The stones had to be excavated, poor soil improved, and the field crisscrossed with canals, to bring the water in the dry seasons and take it away during the monsoon. The three buildings were adapted to house six cows, four goats, fifty chickens and twenty rabbits.

Marysia Lode, one of the students who completed the first two year course, wrote: - "Apart from the common fields, each student had a small plot for individual cultivation. The Indian worker supervised the watering. We were growing tomatoes, cucumbers, many other vegetables and flowers, as well as bananas and papaya trees. The crops were delivered to the Orphanage kitchen or were sold to inhabitants of the camp. The money earned was used to pay the Indian workers and other expenses. Mrs. Wincentyna Krajewska taught us dressmaking and cutting, Mrs. Maria Dąbek typing, and Scoutmaster, B. Pancewicz gave us driving lessons. Some of the pupils helped in the orphanage, teaching younger girls knitting, and those who belonged to Girl Guides movement, willingly helped in the summer camps kitchens".

Work on the farm

When the school closed, the farm was handed over to the Scouts and Guides. The official hand over was on the 1st March 1947. Each company of Guides or Scouts was to be responsible for cultivating and watering a segment. They started with a lot of enthusiasm, but hard work was time consuming and became rather sporadic. Mr. Polechowicz managed the farm as before, with the help of a committee (M. Kwiatkowska, B. Zbyszewska, H. Handerek) and the paid Indian workers. Yet its main crop – beautiful white tuberoses with a wonderful aroma, bloomed there until the closure of Valivade.

Dwuletnia Szkola Rzemieślników Metalowców Warsztatowych (Two year Metalwork School) opened in June 1946, directed by two officers seconded from Polish Forces, J. Szwajnoch and B. Gwieździński. It was intended for the boys, who were not too happy in mainstream education. One of them, Feliks Zając, describes the school: - "It was situated in the 5th District. From 8.00a.m. till noon we had practical training in the workshops as locksmiths, lathe turners, car mechanics and blacksmiths. Theory was taught in the afternoon: parts of the machinery, tools etc. We were also given lessons in Mathematics, Polish and English, and Religious instruction. We spent breaks in a local café, where I made friends with some Indian boys. Driving tests for cars and motorcycles we had to pass in front of Kolhapur police."

The September 1947 issue of *POLAK W INDIACH* No.23 (103) warned that once again financial problems threatened the closure of the school, and once again it was saved by Federation of Poles in India increasing its monthly subsidy to Rs 142 and Refugee Committee,

School of Metalwork

which agreed to provide another Rs 100 from the Social Fund created by the Polish businessmen in the settlement – on top of the money provided by the school budget. After J. Szwajnoch's departure for Australia, Józef Abramowicz took over the Headship. He introduced draughtsmanship and made efforts to increase the speed of work so that the boys could complete their training before leaving Valivade. On 4.10.1947 the school also started a draughtsmanship course for adults, with the help of C. Kolendo.

Czeladniczo-Mistrzowska Szkoła Krawiecka (The School of Dressmaking and Tailoring) opened originally in Isfahan, Persia. After arriving in India, a group of former pupils with their teacher, Józef Szarejko, reopened it in Valivade. Learning cutting and dressmaking was accompanied by all sorts of handiwork, for which the pupils often won prizes in competitions organised by the School of Artistic Craftsmanship in Kolhapur. In the February 1947 exams, three of the participants received the Master Dressmaker Certificates and forty others Certificates of Apprentice Dressmaker. One of the three fully qualified women remained in the school as an instructor; another opened her own course, while a third found employment in the secondary school in Kolhapur, run by the American Catholic mission.

Various occupational courses were organised from the first months of Valivade's existence, but their number grew as the closure of the Camp was approaching. In the beginning they were run by the Cultural Section with the

School Exhibition with Headmaster J. Szarejko

encouragement of both the Delegates' offices in Bombay. When those were closed, the Refugee Committee took over. Some courses were organised and many helped financially by the War Relief Services NCWC from the USA. Nursing courses were organised by the Polish Red Cross and Refugee Committee and staffed by the personnel of the Valivade hospital. ZHP (Polish Boy Scouts and Girl Guides Association) ran many courses - Driving, Office Work and First Aid - mainly for their members. Towards the end of the Camp's existence, even some private small professional courses were started, so great was the demand for practical training. Those were financed from various sources, and partially paid for by the participants, especially the cost of materials required for practice. Certificates and diplomas, originally issued in Polish, were later verified in English or issued bilingually.

Information about the courses mentioned in this chapter was obtained from incomplete sets of reports and articles in the Camp Chronicle and Polish newspapers, and from various certificates sent by our members, so it may not cover everything, but it gives a picture of the

Graduation day at the school

variety of interests, and the eagerness to gain knowledge and skills by the inhabitants of the camp, as well as the invention and industry of those who organised them.

The first vocational courses, organised by the Cultural Section (RKO) were as follows: in September 1943 a course for apprentice surveyors; in February 1944 a **Bookkeeping Course**; in April 1944 fourteen people learned bee-keeping under H. Korzeniowski. The dressmaking course led by Mrs. W. Krajewska was so popular, she had to repeat it four times. We read in the RKO report for June 1946 that the then, current one, had 126 participants who, working twelve hours weekly, produced from own materials 126 male shirts, drawers, pyjamas, aprons and dresses. Attached to the course was a small workshop repairing uniforms for the British Army; it employed ladies eager to earn a few rupees to supplement the meagre refugee allowances. Mrs. W. Łosoś and J. Juzwin ran the **Knitting Course**, where different forms of knitting, as well as making patterns for cardigans and pullovers, was taught.

Knitting Course Exhibition at the Dressmaking School

Very popular were the eight-monthly **Courses for Cooperative Workers**, led by Z. Sikorski. The first of them had forty members, twenty two of whom sat for the initial economics exam. It covered bookkeeping, economic, geography, some legal and fiscal problems and citizenship. It was accompanied by shorter courses in typing, both for its members and other people; one of them was a **six-monthly Typing Course** in 1946 for the school leavers.

NCWC organised four **Printing Courses**, followed by a few months' practice in the camp printing works, on which Mr. F. Andrzejowski trained over twenty printers. A two-monthly telegraphic course, repeated three times, was run by F. Skrzydlewski. S. Królikowska organised four-monthly courses of cosmetic and hygiene, with medical help from Dr. Tomanek. F. Skrzydlewski opened a private hairdressing salon, in which trainee hairdressers were instructed, and B. Janowski ran bookbinding courses.

Several **Driving Courses** included knowledge of the engine and electrical parts, finding and repairing small defects, repairing tyres, car maintenance, the Polish and English road codes. But the actual driving was severely restricted due to small number of available cars and the shortage of petrol caused by war restrictions. The popular instructor on those courses was the Scoutmaster, B. Pancewicz. There were many Health and First Aid courses, described in the Chapter "Health Service."

Accountancy Course with Headmaster J. Sułkowski (in middle)

Besides the courses of decidedly vocational profile, in very great demand were English

Typing Course

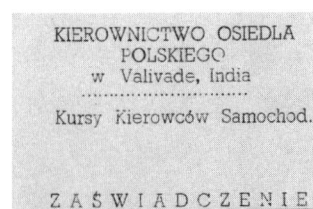

lessons. They were run practically all the time, in different groups and on different levels. At the beginning these were organised mainly for the Camp's employees, with fees paid by the students. In November 1944 the first free courses, organised by RKO, with B. Romanowska as teacher, were attended by eighty eight people. Gradually the number of courses and pupils grew. Some of the Indians employed in the Camp also gave personal tuition.

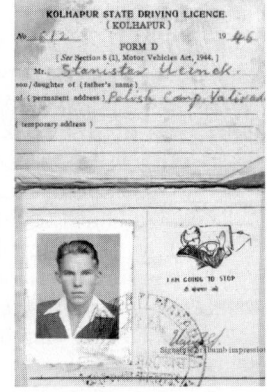

EXTRA-CURRICULAR ACTIVITIES

All schools try to supplement their programmes by additional voluntary activities, in which the pupils may take part, according to their interests and inclinations. In Valivade, such activities were organised with the same aim as the school curriculum – forming ties with our distant, nearly forgotten but still beloved, country.

Most of the pupils belonged to the Girl Guides and Boy Scouts Association and to religious organisations: Sodality and Eucharistic Crusade, described fully in other chapters. Here we concern ourselves with the clubs and association run by the teachers on the school premises.

The Literary Club recruited its members from higher forms of the Grammar School and Lyceum. Its aim – as its organiser, Mrs. M. Czarnecka wrote later in our book *"Młodzi w Valivade"* was: "...enlarging the knowledge and understanding of Polish literature and language, and performing for the inhabitants of Valivade excerpts from the masterpieces of Polish drama, poetry and music... Young club members brought a lot of enthusiasm to its work, especially that concerning drama. They themselves suggested projects of plays, concerts, poetry evenings and demanded more initiatives... The moving spirit of the club was Szczęsna Orzeł..."

The Club members met for talks, lectures and discussions followed by preparation of artistic evenings. Among the most successful performances was the drama by S. Wyspiański, *Noc Listopadowa* ("November Night" – the story of the night of 29th of November 1830, during which Cadets of the Warsaw Military College launched an insurrection against the Russian occupants by an attack on Belvedere, the residence of the hateful Grand Duke Constantine). Directed by Mrs. M. Czarnecka, with magnificent costumes made by the pupils themselves and their mothers under the supervision of the art teacher, Mrs. Goławska, and with the real rifles and sabres borrowed from the local army unit, it so delighted the young performers, that... "during the enchanting Indian night, they marched, armed, through the whole settlement, letting their thoughts run to that night in Warsaw, over a hundred years ago"... (M. Cz. again) Olek Klecki had the role of uprising's leader Lieut. Wysocki, while the goddess Pallas Atene was played by Hanka Sahanek. The performance on 16.2.1945 was attended by the new consul, Jerzy Litewski, paying his first visit to the camp. Other performances included J. Słowacki's drama *"Lilla Weneda"* with Szczęsna Orzeł in the title role, and a shortened version of Moniuszko's opera *"Halka"*, directed by H. Katkiewicz and performed against the background of beautiful scenery, created by M. Goławska and one of her pupils, Halina Kamińska. In most of the performances the school choir took part, with the piano accompaniment of Mrs. Maria Sahanek. Outstanding among the many actors and reciters were Wanda Ostrowska, Marysia Szczyrska and Janusz Kurzeja.

The club also produced a school news-sheet, which displayed articles written by pupils, on the literary or contemporary themes: the war situation, political news, letters from the Polish soldiers, poems, occasionally a heated exchange of views. The mainstay of the paper was Freda Studzińska, who spent many nights, copying the articles in her beautiful handwriting. Arts teacher, M. Goławska oversaw the layout while Olek Klecki contributed many illustrations. Unfortunately no copies survived.

The Geographic Club was organised by K. Łęczyński, when he returned to Valivade from Panchgani and became our teacher of geography in the Grammar School. Its main attraction were frequent excursions into the surrounding country. For a short time there also existed a Botanical Club, run by M. Suszyński.

Poor as we were, all sorts of charity initiatives were eagerly supported. In July 1945 all schools collected presents for the children of the former Polish forced labour workers and prisoners of war, stranded in Germany. According to the newspaper *"Polak w Indiach"* the individually wrapped small parcels were packed into eleven large containers – presents for Polish children from their friends who had themselves suffered hunger, extreme poverty and deprivation and were now willing to share everything they possessed . We were also collecting money for Christmas presents for the Polish soldiers, many of whom had no families; for the victims of the floods in Poland and for poor children in India. These spontaneous collections, especially in the period of constantly reduced wages and continuous complaints about insufficient allowances, must have been puzzling to our English carers, and their excess probably worried some of the inhabitants – because in November 1945 the Commandant of the camp, Col. Neate, forbade organising any collections without permission.

Polish Red Cross Clubs existed in all the schools. Some of them ran First Aid Courses. The Grammar School Club was supervised by Mrs. J. Hardy. In the management group, among others were Janka Jankowska and Freda Studzińska, who described their activities for us. They participated in the First Aid courses run by the Scouting organisation, carried on correspondence with the members of the Indian Red Cross in Kolhapur (first attempts at correspondence in English!), embroidered handkerchiefs for the Polish soldiers. Janka Jankowska remembers that those who took part in the trip to Southern India in 1946 were met with friendly reception during the Congress of Indian Red Cross which was then taking place in Mysore.

Youth section of the Red Cross

Letter Writing to the Polish Forces. - All schools responded to the appeal from the Polish Red Cross in Bombay, to write letters to the Polish soldiers, many of whom were unable to trace members of their families and felt lonely. As reported in "Polak w Indiach" in September 1944, of 2000 letters sent to Delegatura, 1500 were written by children and young people. Writing letters, originally introduced in school lessons, was beneficial to both sides. Children, who were missing their fathers and elder brothers, wrote simply, from the heart, often attaching small presents. An earlier issue of that newspaper printed a letter written by the eight years old Tommy S: …"Dear Mister Soldier. I am going to say a prayer for your health every evening, together with prayers for my mother and father. I will pray that no bullet kills you. When mama tells me about the war, I get scared of the shooting… What would you like me to send you? I have a lot of nice postage stamps, some from Poland, and other… Boys wanted to buy them, but I didn't want to sell them. But I can give some to you. And don't laugh at me for being afraid of the war, because I am still a little boy, that is why."

Wiesia Kleszko, who was then in the top class of Liceum, remembers: . "…So we wrote that letter as our home work, put it into the envelope addressed to the Unknown Polish Soldier … and waited for the reply. Sometime it did not arrive, and it was necessary to write again; sometimes you ended with two correspondents. That is what happened to me. My first soldier, elderly corporal Marian Zieliński received my letter during the landing in Italy, where he became seriously ill and was sent back to Egypt; his reply came, when I was already corresponding with someone else. Marian was slowly dying with tuberculosis, but we were corresponding till his death. He sent me some personal belongings, which - as he wished - I was able to send to his family in Poland after the war".

Some girls were not keen to correspond with strangers, but got in touch with lonely soldiers through family members or friends in the Forces. My father worked in the staff records office of the Fifth "Kresowa" Infantry Division and dealt with the papers of soldiers joining this unit. He sent to me names of the boys from our town, Nowogródek, or of some of his lonely colleagues, which I distributed among my friends. Also the friends, whom we left in Russia, after tracing our addresses via Red Cross, often wrote begging us to trace their male relatives in the army, with whom they had lost contact. Some of us keep to this day crumbling, yellow letters and photos.

Karolina Bilińska-Jurecka, in her book "Dzienniczek Karolinki" (Karolina's Diary) quotes a fragment of her letter, written as an eleven years old primary school pupil to private Karol Batis on 27.12.1944; …"Christmas in the orphanage was sad, even though spent with my sisters and many friends; I missed my mother, father and brother. I felt great pain in my heart for all those Polish soldiers, who could not share "opłatek" with their nearest" And she adds: "I am so pleased, that you have the same name, as my father, who is no longer alive." Karolinka's letter was returned to her in August 1947, so she stuck it in her diary - it never reached the addressee.
[21]

Some letters had happier, although still long journeys. Marian Kurzawski, then a cadet in the Airman School in Heliopolis told us this story:- "… A Sergeant would come in the morning, give us the post, then ask: who wants a letter to an unknown soldier? I was already receiving letters from my mother and sister in India, but I liked to correspond, so I took two – one from the Polish girl in Africa, the other, by funny coincidence, from Mita Turowicz in India, who was a friend of my sister Alina. During our correspondence, one of Mita's letters, written on a handmade Christmas card and signed also by Alina, instead of my school in Egypt went to the military hospital in Scotland where my father, Jan Kurzawski, received it. At that time he had no knowledge of the whereabouts of his family so that unexpected letter was happy news indeed".

What this correspondence meant for the lonely soldiers, separated from their families and friends, can be seen from the letter of the second of Karolinka's correspondents, Stefan Cyraniuk, written from England in 1947: - "I am grateful that you are not forgetting me. If it was not for you, I would have nobody to write to or to receive letters from...When you hear more from your mother in Poland or sister in America, let me know. Because I have no contact with the wide world, and I like to know how people live there".[22] How moving are those words of an elderly man, expecting news of the world from a child...

These letters gave a lot of satisfaction to both sides; some lasting friendships were cemented and even a few marriages, when the letter writers met after the war.

Competitions – There were many of them, on different levels, on different subjects, aiming to bring excitement into the rather monotonous life in the settlement and spur us toward greater efforts. The very first I remember was for an essay in Polish about the town or village from which we came. It was organised by the Polish Ministry of Education in London, for all Polish Schools in Africa, India, Palestine. In February 1945 all Delegates distributed the conditions of the competition and in November 1945 *"Polak w Indiach"* No. 21 (55) published the results. From the 108 essays received from India, Jury selected 9.

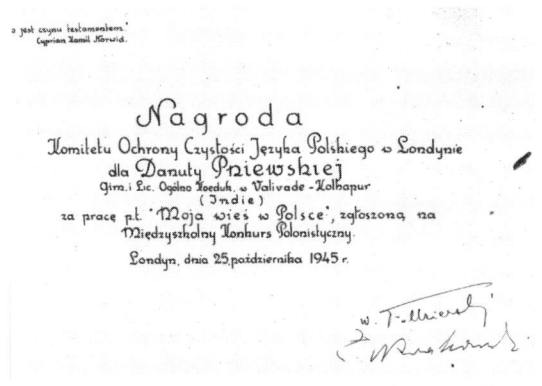

Prize certificate

Group I – Waldemar Rawicki, 4th Form, Primary School, Karachi
Group II – Adam Mickiewicz 1st Form, Grammar School, Karachi
Maria Lipczyk, 2nd Form, Grammar School, Karachi
Jan Siedlecki, 2nd Form, Grammar School, Valivade
Group III – Irena Rabik, 4th Form, Grammar School, Karachi
Danuta Pniewska, 4th Form, Grammar School, Valivade
Estella Czekierska, 1st Form, Liceum, Valivade
Janina Juzwin, 1st Form, Liceum, Valivade
Iwona Rutkiewicz, 7th Form, Panchgani

The prizes were beautiful albums, which some of us keep to this day.

Probably the last competition was for an essay in English, organised by Mr. Nielsen, the representative of IRO. The prize-giving took place on 27.11.1947. From the 110 essays in three age groups the jury selected ones submitted by Irena Piotrowicz, Władysław Radoń, Janina Tyska, Witold Boroński and Zofia Zawidzka.

The Choir with its Conductor Mr. Katkiewioz and the soloist I. Zobkówna

The School Choir attached to the M. Curie-Sklodowska Grammar School and Lyceum, came into existence at the beginning of the school year 1943/44, Its choirmaster was Henryk Katkiewicz. On his recall to the army it was taken over by Mrs. Figuła and finally by one of the more gifted pupils, Irena Zobek. Czesia Naplocha, Staszka Miluska, Wanda Rubczewska and Irena Zobek were its most prominent members and soloists. At first the membership was compulsory, later it was limited to 60 volunteers, mainly girls. The extensive repertoire consisted mostly of religious, patriotic and folk songs. The Choir, accompanied by Mr. Katkiewicz or Mr. M. Rosenthal, took part in most concerts, shows, school masses and other functions in Valivade.

THE TEACHING STAFF

Our teachers came from different parts of Poland, which until 1918 had been occupied by three invaders, and each, to a certain degree retained some characteristics specific to that region. They were educated in various teaching establishments, gained practice in different environments, and lived through very different, but always difficult and harrowing events during the first years of the WWII. Yet they were united by the common aim – to give their pupils as much education as possible in those very unusual and arduous conditions. Most of them were professional teachers with some pre-war experience in Poland. There were also some who did not have time to gain that experience, or perhaps even had not finished their training when war broke out, but who brought to their chosen profession an instinctive feeling of how to deal best with their charges. There was also a small group of well meaning amateurs, who knew their subject but had a problem sharing it with the pupils and dealing with discipline. For their pupils – although on the whole eager to learn and make up for the lost years - were like all children, always ready to take a chance for mischief.

Reading through various available documents, we have come across a few disparaging statements from English and Indian officials, and - in the worst case - from the representative of the unrecognised by us communist regime in Poland, a certain Mrs. Burakiewicz, questioning the qualifications of our teachers. From the list of the staff, prepared by Inspector Żerebecki on 19th March1947 we can confirm that 99% of Primary School teachers had at least secondary education.[23] 90% had also professional training and between two to twenty nine years of work behind them. As the secondary schools intake grew, some of the better-qualified primary school teachers were promoted to their lower grades, and were replaced by the trainee teachers. Those were recruited from the students who received a matriculation certificate, on finishing the two years of Lyceum, and were trained by the Head Teachers. In the final phase the graduates of Valivade Teacher Training College supplemented the staff.

The situation in the Secondary Schools was more difficult. Since both Nazi Germany and Soviet Russia were set on annihilating Polish intelligentsia, many Secondary School and University teachers perished in their prisons and labour camps. Some left Poland in September 1939, escaping the Germans and were now

The staffroom in 1947

abroad, or in the Army, where they were teaching in the military schools. Therefore there was a shortage of fully qualified and experienced teachers, only slightly alleviated by a few soldiers detached from their Army duties temporarily to work in Valivade schools.

A separate group consisted of the teachers of English – mainly Indians. Most of them were very dedicated and able people, but they were used to a stricter discipline in Indian schools and not experienced in dealing with the more independent European children. This occasionally led to misunderstandings.

One of the intuitive, born pedagogues was our popular teacher of History, **Anna Handerek**. Just before the outbreak of the Second World War she obtained her MA degree in History. The only teaching she did then was a compulsory job in a Belarusian village school during the Soviet occupation. Evacuated from Russia with the Polish orphanage, on arrival in Teheran she began teaching History and even, for a while, Biology, although, as she wrote in her memoirs, "my knowledge of that subject exceeded that of my pupils merely by the fact that I had the only textbook available". Later on in Ahvaz and Valivade, she taught History and Latin, two subjects she knew, liked and was able to make interesting for her pupils. Although she had no formal training, she was a wonderful teacher – made her lessons lively and was able to manage even the most unruly class. A strict disciplinarian and very demanding as a teacher, when meeting her charges in her capacity of a Guider, she was very friendly and worked with us on equal basis during the Scouting activities, in which she took active and enthusiastic part. There is more about her life in the chapter on Valivade Scouting.

Not all our teachers had that inborn talent of managing their pupils. Many stories were circulating about the two Science teachers, chemical engineers by profession, **A. Nigelszporn** and **F. Podsoński**, who found it difficult to keep discipline in the classroom, but made up for it with good humour and thorough knowledge of their subject. There is also the story of a teacher of Physics asking the class to explain an experiment (no laboratory yet). He was reading about it on the sly from the textbook, and was annoyed by the pupil, giving him wrong answers – she was also "cribbing" from the same book, but from the wrong page! Two young teachers, Aleksander Topolnicki and Janusz Wiktorowicz had a difficult life – roped in due to the shortage of staff, probably never intending to be teachers, they often found themselves helpless in front of the unruly pupils.

The majority of our teachers however were the old hands, easily combining compassion for the children struggling to make up for the years of education they had forfeited, with strict discipline. They were remarkably successful.

Michał Goławski (1904-1974), the Delegate of the Polish Ministry of Education for India, although not a member of teaching staff, was very closely connected with our schools. He attended all school and Scouting celebrations, presided over meetings, handed out prizes and made speeches. A handsome man, with distinguished looks, a good speaker and a great organiser, he enjoyed the respect of youngsters and adults. His pre-war experience, both in educational and social work, helped him to deal with tact and diplomacy during the often precarious negotiations with many organisations and individuals responsible for our education and upbringing. Before the war, as well as teaching history in the Grammar School in the county town of Białystok, he also ran an evening college *Miejski Uniwersytet Powszechny*, and from 1931 to 1939 was the head of the Education and Cultural Activities Section in Białystok County Council. During his few years in India, he changed his post several times, according to political situation, took part in most societies and was one of the few officials who worked in Bombay and Valivade till the end. On arrival in England, he found employment in the Committee for the Education of Poles and later in the British Ministry of Education, as consultant for the Polish problems, and in both those positions helped many of us to attain higher education. At the same time, with his usual enthusiasm and fervour, he engaged in many social organisations, helping to coordinate Saturday Schools for the children of Polish immigrants, editing papers and writing books.

Although respected for his phenomenal diligence and his utter devotion to the upbringing of young people, his slightly pompous demeanour, obvious enjoyment in presiding over things and his popularity with ladies, made him also a butt for some jokes. The bilingual reader may wish to refer to the Polish version of this book to read a funny poem written about him by his students in Białystok.

His Deputy, and School Inspector, **Zdzisław Żerebecki** (1896-1968) while matching him in energy and dedication, was an entirely different person. Of low stature, plump, with a round, cheerful face, hot tempered – especially during his maths lessons – he commanded respect not by his behaviour or position, but because of his intelligence and knowledge. He did not look for prestigious jobs, but put a lot of heart into whatever he did.

Born in the South-East Poland, in the working class family, thanks to his exceptional ability and diligence he obtained degree in mathematical studies at Jan Kazimierz University in Lwow, followed by pedagogical training. Before the war, he was a Headmaster of the Adam Mickiewicz Grammar School in Wilno. Under Soviet occupation, he was sentenced to 8 years deportation and hard labour. After so called "amnesty", as a Delegate of the Polish Embassy for the region of Czkalov, besides his official duties of distributing meagre supplies of cloth and food received from American welfare societies, to the crowds of needy ex-prisoners, he also engaged in helping Professor J. Czapski in trying to trace missing Polish officers (later found to be murdered in Katyń). He also helped some of the Polish ethnic minorities - mainly Jews, Belarussians and Ukrainians, regarded by the Soviet authorities as their nationals, and therefore not eligible for evacuation - by issuing them with Polish documents, for which activity he was promptly re-arrested. Released after the intervention of the British and American embassies, he received an order ... to leave USSR! The irony of that order can only be appreciated, when we realize that the way to Poland was blocked by the German Army, and a way out of Stalin's Russia - to anywhere, by any means - was the greatest dream of thousands of people, but entirely impossible to achieve for any individual!

When finally evacuated with the Polish transport, Żerebecki was entrusted with the job of organising schools, courses and training conferences in Tehran, Ahvaz, Malir, and finally Valivade. In India, as one of the few Poles with a good knowledge of English, he organised unpaid courses of that language for teachers, prepared bulletins of political news from English press and wireless, and made useful personal contacts with English and Indian officials in Kolhapur. But all the time, although burdened with two jobs, Inspector's and Deputy-delegate's of Ministry of Education, he never gave up that which was the love of his life – teaching mathematics. Here his hot temperament and inability to understand that maths is not easy for everybody, sometimes led to incidents with his students. Yet we had soon discovered that behind the shield of angry shouts and warnings, he was hiding a golden heart and sunny good humour.

On his return to Poland he joined his family and began teaching at a Grammar school in Gliwice, Silesia. (Lwów and Wilno became part of USSR so the repatriates were resettled in Western Poland.) His students nicknamed him "Bombay" and marvelled how this cosmopolitan gentleman, formerly a Headmaster, inspector and holder of many exalted positions, managed to survive in the constricted circumstances of this small, communist controlled school. But he did.

Dr. Maria Borońska (1906-1998) was born in Tarnopol as a daughter of the prominent social worker, Józef R. Schmidt. After obtaining a doctorate in Polish Philology at the Jan Kazimierz Uniwersity in Lwow, she accepted a position at the Grammar School in Tarnopol. The war and Soviet occupation broke her family life. Her husband, a reserve officer of the Polish Army, was murdered in Katyń; Maria with her 5 year old son Witek, was deported to Kazakhstan. After the "amnesty" in 1941, she was employed at the office of the Delegate of Polish Embassy. Soon the Delegate and most of his assistants were arrested by NKWD, leaving this lonely woman, burdened with a small son, in the sole charge of this difficult post. Unable to obtain any news about her husband, she made the long and dangerous journey and managed to reach Yangi Yul, where the Polish Forces were preparing to leave Russia, taking with them a limited number of civilians. To ensure that at least her son might leave this inhuman country, she placed Witek in an orphanage, but finally got herself on the same transport as well.

In Tehran she returned to teaching; and in Valivade accepted the position of Headmistress of our High School. We all remember those difficult beginnings, when the attempts to create a semi permanent teaching system were hampered by shortages of qualified teachers, books and teaching aids. But under the rule of this wise, compassionate and friendly, though very serious person, school life soon gained the orderly and enjoyable rhythm.

Since the officers murdered in Katyń had not served in the Polish Forces under the British Command, she did not qualify, as other soldiers' families, for resettlement in England. When the Valivade Camp closed, she and her son had to go to a British colony in Africa, where in Koja she resumed her job, until finally in 1950, by an invitation of some distant family, they obtained visas for the USA. There she spent the next 23 years working in a hospital. Once, when visiting her family in England, she met with her former pupils in London; she also took part in our reunions in Orchard Lake in the USA and in Toronto.

Another teacher of Polish Language and Literature in Valivade Grammar School was **Maria Czarnecka**. Here again were two excellent, but totally different personalities. The Head, Mrs. Borońska, did not like excessive use of poetic adjectives and empty slogans; her lectures on the History of Polish Literature were concise and factual; in our essays she expected concrete facts, well documented opinions. Mrs. Czarnecka however liked poetic descriptions, flowery language, enthusiastic judgments. The first Maria was demanding, but very fair and had no favourites; this second one was only interested in the clever and gifted students, ignoring those less talented. The Head, no matter how busy, always found time to listen to her students' ideas or complaints; Mrs. Czarnecka was the one who had an ear for creative ideas only.

However we forgave her all her shortcomings, because she kept us spellbound during her lectures. One of our colleagues, Szczęsna Michałowska wrote about her: -"We remember her lessons, which for many of us were the first contact with Polish literature. Deprived of books in those war years, we were listening avidly to her lectures, in which she made alive the Polish poets and writers and the heroes of their works. We can still see in our imagination the portrait of the poet, Bishop Krasicki, with the Brabant laces spilling out of his sleeves"...

The Literary Club under her patronage edited the school news-sheet, organised poetry evenings and competitions. Many plays from our classic repertoire, staged under her direction, drew enthusiastic spectators and she brought up a plethora of amateur actors and reciters.

She died before the material for this book was collected, so we don't know much about her life. Like so many of our teachers, she obtained her MA degree in Lwow. In India she was with her mother and her son Andrew, a "war child" as he was born in June 1939 and deported to Russia as a baby. In England they lived in the country, and we met her on our two first reunions.

The Indian teachers of English are described in another chapter. But the first teacher of that subject, practically from the moment of opening the Camp, was **Fanny Wray**, by most pupils nicknamed "Rejka". This very small and slim elderly woman, with a face resembling a wrinkled apple, who always stood strait like a reed, was a typical English colonial lady of the previous century. Although she lived, like us, in a simple camp accommodation, she was escorted to school by an Indian servant, who carried her basket of books. Her teaching methods were rather old-fashioned and she had some problems keeping discipline, so she often scolded us, comparing us – always unfavourably – with the English youths. But when India gained independence and she had to return to England, she obtained a job in a Polish technical school. The last few years of her life she spent in the house of Polish friends from Valivade, K. Iglikowska and I.Chmielowiec.

There were a few married couples among our teaching Staff. **Jan Latawiec**, one of the teachers relegated by the army, taught Physics and Chemistry; his wife Janina, Geography. Jan had an adventurous life – as a sixteen years old volunteer he took part in the WWI. In 1939 he was the Headmaster of the elementary school in Eastern Poland. Mobilized as an officer of reserve, he was captured by the Soviet army but escaped from the convoy to Russia. The next year he was deported with his family to Kazakhstan. On joining the Polish Army, he taught in a military school, then was transferred to work in civilian schools in Teheran, Ahvaz and Valivade. When the war ended, he and his wife were both recalled to their detachments. Janina for a while taught in the Military School for Girls in Palestine. They finally settled in the USA. Jan died in 1983, his grave is in the Polish Czestochowa in Pennsylvania.

Headteacher of the School of Rural Management, boisterous, extrovert **Mikołaj Suszyński**, was also a teacher of Biology in the Grammar School. His wife Jadwiga, very quiet and shy, taught mathematics. On leaving India they settled on a farm in the USA, but after the death of his wife, Mikołaj returned to Poland. For six years he acted as an unpaid instructor of Orchard Studies in Kortowo nr. Olsztyn. Afterwards, in a nearby village of Sprecow he started an orchard centre, which he later offered to the Convent of Carmelite Nuns in Elblag.[24]

Maria Skórzyna was born on 1.9.1901 in Żółkiew nr. Lwow, so she probably obtained her MA degree at Lwow University. We don't know much about her former life. She left Russia with her elderly mother and daughter Marysia. She taught Propaedeutics of Philosophy and Psychology in our Grammar School and was a Head of the Teacher Training College. After Valivade she spend the rest of her life in the USA.

Antonina Harasymów 6.9.1897 - Born in Jarosław in South-East of Poland, she completed educational studies in Lwow, where she met her husband. Both of them were Heads of the two elementary schools in Komarno. She was deported to Russia with her son Stanisław and her husband's nephew, Anek Cwetsch, who happened to be staying with them at the time of the deportation. She became headmistress of the primary school in Camp No.2 in Tehran, and then of No.2 School in Valivade. Not entitled to immigration to Great Britain, she and her boys went to Koja in Africa, where she was again the headmistress of the technical school. Finally they went to Western Australia. Even there she remained faithful to her vocation, though this time it was only the Polish Saturday School she was in charge of.

Wanda Kojro (Thomas) sent us her impressions of those two teachers: "…The moving spirit of the College was its Head and creator, Maria Skórzyna. All of us loved her. We could go to her with our problems and get help and advise. For many of us she was a substitute mother. Out of respect, we did not give her any nickname. But the teacher whom we feared and whose lessons we dreaded was Antonina Harasymów. It was not the person herself, but the subject she taught – methodology – that we disliked. With no handbooks available, for 7 hours a week she had to dictate concise texts, which we had to learn by heart".[25]

Zofia Chrząszczewska was the headmistress of Primary School No.1 and took part in training new teachers. One of those trainees, Zosia Evershead (Nowicka) wrote about her: - "Mrs. Chrząszczewska was a tall and well built person. She was a good disciplinarian and was treated with respect by her teachers and pupils. After my practice lessons I was often admonished for giving the children too much freedom and allowing too much noise in the classroom. She wore a beautiful ring with blue opal surrounded by small diamonds. I once mentioned that this stone is supposed to be unlucky, but she replied: "I was always lucky. It is true I have lost my husband, but that was the fate of many women during the war." That was very characteristic for her attitude to life – level-headed and peaceful."

Wanda Borzemska was a very popular teacher from the younger generation. After finishing Teacher Training College in Krakow, she began teaching in Silesia. The war broke out, when she was with her family in Rawa Ruska, from where she was deported to Russia with her mother and brother. In Valivade she began teaching in Primary School No.2 but was soon transferred to the Grammar school, where she taught Polish, Latin and History in lower forms. She was also a form mistress of the famous "male" class – the only one without girls, and she managed extremely well the unruly group of young rascals. After the war she settled in London, where she married a judge, Bolesław Dziedzic. She took very active part in the works of Polish social and cultural organisations, being in succession a teacher, headmistress and then inspector of the Polish Saturday Schools; was a co-founder of the Polish Women's Association, a head of the Office in the Department of Education and Culture in the Polish Government in Exile and for many years Chairwoman of the Polish Teachers' Association in Great Britain.

These short biographies cover merely a small fraction of the nearly one hundred teachers working in Valivade. Some of them are mentioned in the chapters on other settlements in India. All of them remain in the grateful memories of their pupils.

THE TEACHERS' ASSOCIATION

In the middle of 1944 the Teachers' Association was formed, affiliated to the Polish Teachers' Union in England. It was active in taking care of the professional rights of its members and also in the field of mutual aid. From their Management Committee's report for the year August 1945/46 we learn that it had ninety members in Valivade and Panchgani (Jamnagar did not join the Union). In that period ten meetings of the Committee and twelve general meetings took place. Part of the members' subscriptions was forwarded to the Union's Head Office in London, the remaining funds were used for local expenses and occasional help for needy members. It was the period of cut salaries and cancellation of overtime and family allowances, so teachers with large families and no help from relatives in the Army found it difficult to manage.

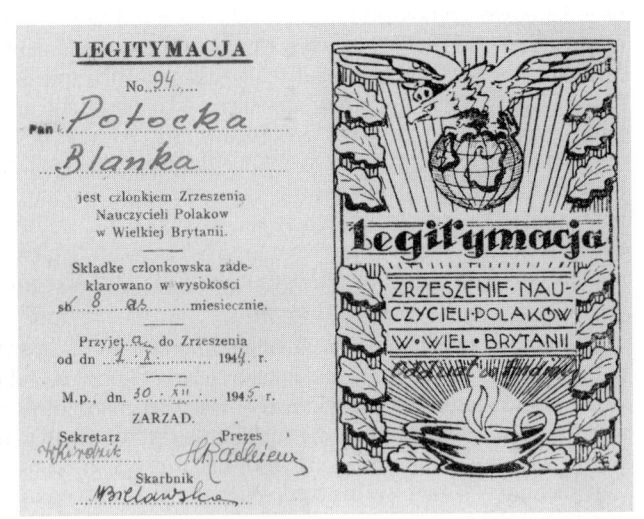

Certificate of membership

In the first years of its existence, the Association organised social and cultural events. Educational training was carried out, mainly in the form of Inspector Żerebecki's lectures on all aspects of the teaching profession. But the unstable political situation, the constant changes in institutions accepting responsibility for refugees, and the uncertain future made people more concerned with the state of their financial position. In its final years the Association had many struggles with both Polish and British Authorities, fighting for the redundancy payments for teachers leaving their jobs, overtime payments and other remunerations. Those efforts led to a heated dispute between the Association, backed by Inspector Żerebecki in Valivade and Mr. Goławski in Bombay. Goławski, at the time of winding up Delegatura's Offices, held a certain amount of unspent subsidies from the Polish Government in London, and returned them, as instructed, to the recently organised Ignacy Paderewski School Fund in Great Britain. The Association insisted that the money should have been used to settle their claims. Lengthy correspondence, first with the School Department of the Interim Committee, then with Mr. Folkierski, the minister of the officially unrecognised, but still existing in London, Polish Government in Exile and ambassador Raczyński, did not bring results. As far as we know, the redundancy payments were never received.

Henryk Katkiewicz was the Chairman of the Association for most of its existence. Even when re-called back to the Army and demobilized in England, he was in contact with his colleagues and helped them to find jobs in Polish schools in refugee camps in British Africa and in Polish schools starting up in England. He was also helping Dr. M. Borońska to deposit the archives from the Valivade schools – unfortunately we were unable to find them.[26]

POLISH PUPILS IN BRITISH SCHOOLS

As previously stated in this book, the principal aim of education and upbringing of the Polish children in India, was to prepare them for their return to Poland. But from the beginning there were people who understood that the compulsory exile in this country could give them at least one advantage – acquiring English, which was already gaining the status of an international language. One of them was Delegate Gołlawski, who himself made great efforts to improve his English and was an ardent advocate of teaching it to our youth.

The shortage of qualified teachers of English was not the only drawback to his plans. Valivade was after all a little Polish Ghetto – at school, at Scouting meetings, at home, in the streets, even in the Indian shops and bazaar, the Polish language was constantly used. (Indians are phenomenal linguists, and had quickly mastered the rudiments of our difficult language.) The only chance of learning English quickly and in depth was to send the children to English boarding schools. Since it was impossible to arrange it for everybody, only those already showing some linguistic aptitude and ability to work hard were selected. The few schools chosen were mostly convent schools, with some European teachers, programmes based on similar British schools and the examinations recognized in England. The level of teaching was quite high, there was also strict discipline and the mode of life between that of monasteries and army barracks, which in an odd way was combined with great care for bodies and souls of their pupils.

The first pupils were sent from Balachadi, girls to the convents in Karachi and Panchgani, boys to the monks in **Mont Abu**. (More about them you will find in the chapter on Balachadi.) The first group from Valivade – twenty three girls in the care of one teacher, Mrs. J.Siedmiograj – went to a convent in Sauger, but this school was found unsuitable. Larger groups found welcome at **St. Joseph's school** in Panchgani, run by the Convent of the Daughters of the Cross. Most of them went there after finishing four forms at our Grammar school, stayed there for one year and returned to Valivade to do Polish Matriculation.[27] This convent understood the needs of Polish girls and cooperated with the Polish authorities. For the girls who obtained their matriculation in Valivade, but were unable to enter Indian Universities, they opened a special course of commercial studies. And when in the final period of our stay in India the lack of financial resources became critical, they reduced the amount of fees for Polish girls.[28] The **St. Peter's Boys High School** in Panchgani also accepted some of our boys.

In 1946 our students started going to Bombay. Eleven of our matriculation holders attended eight monthly course of Book-keeping at YWCA Commercial College, another ten studied Applied Art in the **J. J. Art School**. Some of them lived in the St. Theresa Home Convent, for the rest a private hostel was organised, run by Mrs. Stefania Laskowska

St. Mary's Boys High School in Bombay run by Spanish Jesuit Fathers was a private establishment modelled on the English public schools. It had a very good reputation and high standards of education. There were excellent teachers and an extensive range of teaching aids – laboratories, gyms, libraries, even a school orchestra. This school admitted annually 200 boarders, mainly from the middle-class families and scholarship holders and another 400 day students from prosperous families. Ten of our boys aged 16-17 were accepted as boarders. They found the regime of hard study, prayer and sport rather daunting and the school food – curry, curry, curry - difficult to get used to. Three of them opted out after the first year, but seven stalwarts persisted till the matriculation. (Names under the photo.) In spite of the initial language problems, they achieved good results in examinations. And they were the mainstay of the volleyball team, a game introduced by them.

The cost of keeping the Polish students in Bombay was considerable. Although the monthly fees in YWCA Commercial College were only Rs 25, the lodging and board amounted to between Rs 90 and Rs 100, another Rs 10 were required for school equipment and with Rs 20 "pocket money" for transport etc it added up to about Rs 150 per month, nearly three times the amount of the monthly allowance we were getting. Studying in the convents was cheaper – in

St. Joseph's Convent in Panchgani and St. Mary's Boys High School in Bombay both teaching fees and boarding was given for Rs 80 per month, with no extra costs for travel and textbooks. All students had additional lesson in Polish language and Polish issues, some had extra tuition in English. They also needed extra money for holiday travel to Valivade, medical expenses and occasional help with clothing. For instance, the cost of having our students in English establishments in November 1946 was Rs 11 200 of which Rs 4 627 came from the Camp budget (66 older students at Rs 53.12 and 24 younger ones at Rs 45 monthly), the rest had to be obtained from other sources.

A. Tybulewicz, J. Kowalski, M. Dadlez, Rev. Dalton, J. Siedlecki, K. Naglik, T. Jankowski and A. Goławski

ACHIEVEMENTS

How much was achieved in less than five years (July 1943 to December 1947), under very difficult circumstances, continually changing political situation, and shortage of qualified teachers, school aids and financial support? Well, the heroic efforts and uphill struggle of our carers had remarkably good results.

Our High school (Gimnazjum and Lyceum) prepared five lots of matriculation holders – ninety eight people. Our Matriculations (Leaving Certificates) were recognised in Poland, and by some universities in the other countries (e.g. UCD in Dublin) so their holders were able to apply for Higher Education. Two Matriculations in the Teacher Training College enabled twenty nine girls to work in Polish schools in Poland and abroad, and helped some of them to get an English teaching diploma.

Our hospital training could not compare with the long training expected in British hospitals, but allowed some of our young women to work in lower grades, or have their professional training shortened. Very useful were the motor courses, even those taken in the Scouting Association, as driving licence helped in many jobs. The knowledge of English – although its level varied – especially when confirmed by the English School Certificate, helped to get a better start both in Poland and abroad.

A good example of the use of their Indian

December 1947, the last Matriculation (sitting): J. Kaśków, J. Szymańska, M. Skórzyna, M. Czarnecka and J. Kowalska

education comes from the Nowicki family. On leaving India, they settled in Africa. The eldest daughter Zosia, after finishing the High school, took a nursing course, which enabled her to work in a hospital in Mombassa. The younger daughter Danuta's diploma from Commercial College in Bombay helped her to find an interesting office job. Their brother, Zbyszek, used his knowledge of driving acquired at the Scouting course so well, that he became a Champion of African Safari Races.

From the patriotic point of view however, the greatest achievement was the upbringing of a few hundred people, loyal to their country, not ashamed of their roots and aware of their duties towards the Motherland. The fact that today – sixty years after the end of the WWII - there are still Polish churches, Polish schools, Polish Scouts and Guides, Polish newspapers, clubs and other organisations in many countries in Europe, America and Australia; that our grandchildren, although struggling with our difficult language, can use it and are interested in Polish problems; that many of them visit Poland and some even go to work there – this is a great achievement not only of our mothers, but also of the great number of teachers, priests, Scoutmasters and Guiders in India, Africa, Mexico, Lebanon and Palestine.

Translated by the Author with the help of Penny Jones

NOTES

1. KPI Na wędrownym szlaku (collected poems) - Teheran 1943 p. 46
2. IPiMS: A.19/I/14
3. Arch. KPI Bulletin No. 8 1994 s. 22
4. Arch.KPI: Album Pielgrzymka-Zjazd 1980 s.50-51
5. IPiMS: A.19/IH/10
6. IPiMS:A.19/n/16
7. IPiMS:A.19/n/16
8. IPiMS: A.23/17
9. IPiMS: A. 19/01/16
10. IPiMS: A.23/17
11. IPiMS: A.19/DI/10
12. IPiMS: A.19/0/16
13. IPiMS: A. 19/01/16
14. Pwl: year II No. 18-19 (28-29) 1944
15. Pwl: year IV No. 8 (66) 1946
16. IPiMS: A. 19/II/16
17. Pwl: year IV No. 8 (66) 1946
18. ibid
19. IPiMS: A. 19/0/16
20. Pwl: year II No. 18-19 (28-29) 1944
21. K. Bilińska Dzienniczek Karolinki p. 142-144
22. ibid: p. 91-92
23. IPiMS:A.19/III
24. Arch. KPI Bulletin No. 3 1991
25. Arch.KPI: Album Pielgrzymka-Zjazd 1980
26 IPiMS A9/Vl
27. Pwl: year IV No. 2 (60) 1946
28. IPiMS A.19/VI

LIST OF TEACHERS IN PRIMARY SCHOOLS

Abramowicz Józefat
Asłanowicz Helena
Bernatowicz Joanna
Bobolska Maria
Borzemska Wanda
Chopre Rajas
Chrząszczewska Zofia
Chylowa Anna
Derecka Maria
Dziadowicz Maria
Dzięglewska Antonina
Figuła Janina
Gaikwad Manorama
Gimzowa Maria
Górna Helena
Grużewska Zofia
Halska Helena
Harasymów Antonina
Jankowska Rypsyma
Jaworska Adela
Kamińska Kazimiera
Kamińska Zofia
Katkiewicz Jadwiga

Kawałek Ludwika
Kaźmierczak Helena
Kirdzik Wanda
Kisiel Emilia
Kowalczyk Maria
Kozakowa Maria
Krzętowska Helena
Kuchcicka Krystyna
Kuncewicz Genowefa
Kurzeja Helena
Laniewska Irma
Łaszkiewicz Maria
Maniak Antoni
Marasek Stefania
Martusewicz Helena
Masewicz Jadwiga
Matthews Anne
Matyka Józef
Mazurkiewicz Stefania
Morawska Zofia
Mróz Adela
Najdzicz Apolonia
Nowakowska Halina

Orysiuk Jan
Orzeł Janina
Pacholska Janina
Pelc Jan
Peszyńska Krystyna
Pola Waleria
Potocka Blanka
Ptakowa Janina
Radon Julianna
Rakowa Janina
Rakowska Halina
Rozwadowska Jadwiga
Rymarkiewicz Władysława
Ryżewska Anna
Sasadeusz Olga
Sawko Franciszka
Senutai Jaywantrai Dange
Skibińska Maria
Skrzatowa Anna
Sowa Katarzyna
Strzałkowska Jadwiga
Sytnik Jan
Ściborska Maria

Trella Stefania
Tyszkiewicz Waleria
Wierzbicka Maria
Wilczyńska Zofia
Woronowicz Wanda
Wronko Feliks
Wróblewska Jadwiga
Wysocka Janina
Zagórowska Zofia
Zawadzka Helena
Zielińska Anna
Zuntych Franciszek
Żabko Jadwiga
Żerebecka Irena

Trainee Teachers

Koczan Ewa
Kolischer Romualda
Leśniak Maria
Nowicka Zofia
Szwaglis Anna
Wałdoch Jadwiga

LIST OF TEACHERS IN SECONDARY SCHOOLS

Appadurai Benjamin (English)
Bielawska Maria (Librarian)
Borzemska Wanda (Polish, Latin)
Borońska Maria (Polish)
Chopre Rajas (English)
Chylowa Anna (Polish)
Czarnecka Maria (Polish)
Fr. Dallinger Leopold (Religion, Latin)
Daniel Mahrai (English)
Handerek Anna (History, Latin)
Hardy Janina (History)
Fr. Jankowski Antoni (Religious Education)
Jaworska Adela (Mathematics)
Karwowska Eugenia (Biology)
Katkiewicz Henryk (Physical Education, Music)
Kłosowska Janina (Polish)
Kościukiewicz Józef (Chemistry)
Kozula Władysław (Latin)
Latawiec Jan (Physics)
Latawiec Janina (Geography)
Łaszkiewicz Maria (Religious Education)
Łęczyński Kazimierz (Geography)
Mitro Maria (Polish)
Morris Evelyn (English)
Nigelszporn Alfred (Physics)
Ostrowicz Maria (Latin)

Pieńkowska Maria (English)
Podsoński Franciszek (Chemistry, Physics)
Proskurnicka Julia (Polish)
Przybysz Jan (Religious Education, Latin)
Sahanek Maria (Music)
Mr. Samuel (English)
Siedmiograj Jadwiga (English)
Sikorski Zdzisław (Accountancy)
Skórzyna Maria (Psychology)
Snastin Irena (Typing)
Spława-Neuman Michalina (Physical Education)
Suszyńska Jadwiga (Mathematics)
Suszyński Mikołaj (Biology)
De Souza Alice (English)
Szymańska Janina (History)
Tomanek Alfred (Physics)
Topolnicki Aleksander (Mathematics)
Walles Władysław (Physics, Mathematics)
Wiktorowicz Janusz (English)
Wilczyńska Zofia (Geography)
Wojakiewicz Helena (Mathematics)
Wray Farmy (English)
Wyspiańska Jadwiga (English)
Żerebecki Zdzisław (Mathematics)

Kowalska Joanna (Secretary)

MATRICULATION CERTIFICATES

March 1944:
- Górska Halina
- Koczan Stefania
- Kolischer Romualda
- Leśniak Maria
- Magnuszewska Irena
- Niezabytowska Janina
- Nowicka Zofia
- Sahanek Anna
- Stankiewicz Wanda
- Szwaglis Anna
- Wałdoch Jadwiga.

March 1945:
- Bień Eugenia
- Cariuk Kleopatra
- Harbuz Eliza
- Kamoda Wanda
- Klepacka Wiesława
- Krajewska Irena
- Łańcucka Anna
- Pasternak Danuta
- Sipika Janina
- Wojniłowicz Jadwiga
- Wołk Halina

External students:
- Kaśków Jan
- Ostrowski Waldemar
- Szumczyk Aleksander

October 1945:
- Adamczyk Irena
- Baławender Zofia
- Czekierska Estela
- Hajduk Irena
- Idkowiak Irena
- Juźwin Janina
- Kawałek Helena
- Kamińska Halina
- Karpińska Zofia
- Kłosowska Maria
- Kokoszko Weronika
- Królikowska Jadwiga
- Krupińska Anna
- Nowicka Maria
- Orzeł Szczęsna
- Ostrihanska Zofia
- Romanowska Bożena
- Snastin Irena
- Szafranek Halina
- Szafrańska Helena
- Waszczuk Alina
- Woyniłowicz Eleonora
- Zbyszewska Danuta

December 1945:
- Ostrowska Irena
- Tatarczuk Irena

March 1947:
- Basarab Józefa
- Dziedzic Danuta
- Górska Stanisława
- Hałaburda Irena
- Janiszewska Maria
- Klar Ryszard
- Klecki Aleksander
- Kotlicka Krystyna
- Kufera Irena
- Michalska Irena
- Morawska Barbara
- Piątkowska Alina
- Pniewska Danuta
- Sokołowska Bożena
- Studzińska Alfreda
- Suchecka Daniela
- Suszko Helena
- Trella Urszula
- Truksa Mieczysława
- Underka Teresa
- Wądołkowski Henryk
- Wiśniewska Waleria
- Zawadzka Zofia
- Zawidzka Zofia
- Żyszkowska Leokadia.
- Jankowska Janina

December 1947:
- Czerepak Stanisława
- Harbuz Bożena
- Kolkiewicz Wanda
- Loszek Danuta
- Mucha Maria
- Pacholska Anna
- Pacholski Jan
- Piotrowicz Irena
- Rubczewska Wanda
- Ryciak Maria
- Ryciak Jadwiga
- Sikona Alicja
- Surowiec Eleonora
- Szafrańska Janina
- Szelągowska Irena
- Tijewska Regina
- Tyszewicz Halina
- Wasiuk Alicja
- Woźniak Maria
- Zobek Irena

January 1948:
- Rosenthal-Helena (Szczanowska)

TEACHERS DIPLOMA

March 1947:
- Aleksandrowicz Leokadia
- Bojarska Maria
- Chyla Alicja
- Czerepak Eugenia
- Krupa Stanisława
- Kuchcicka Krystyna
- Naplocha Czesława
- Nowakowska Kazimiera
- Ostrowska Wanda
- Panek Aleksandra
- Polańska Halina
- Rolczewska Jadwiga
- Tomas Wanda
- Urbaniec Danuta
- Wojniłowicz Janina
- Zakrzewska Halina

November 1947:
- Piątkowska Alina
- Pniewska Danuta

December 1947:
- Królikowska Katarzyna
- Małaczyńska Czesława
- Masiulanis Helena
- Michalak Czesława
- Ołowiecka Stanisława
- Oszmiańska Maria
- Przytomska Helena
- Świdejko Zofia
- Topolnicka Krystyna
- Zawistowicz Wanda
- Zbróg Janina

SCHOOL AS WE REMEMBER IT
Collective Work Translated with help from Penny Jones and Adam Lewis (poems)

Danka Pniewska – My schools.

Soon after the Red Army entered Eastern Poland in September 1939, Polish schools in my town Nowogrodek started operating more or less normally. The number of pupils in secondary schools increased dramatically because the Soviet occupiers, promising the mainly Belarussian village population "equal opportunities" and "the end of exploitation by Polish lords", admitted their children without the rather stringent entry examinations, obligatory before the war. With premises not large enough for increased numbers of pupils and teaching staff depleted by the mobilisation of the army reserve, lessons had to be carried out in two shifts. The pre-war system of 12 forms – 6 years Primary School. 4 years Grammar and 2 years Lycee – was converted to the soviet "dziesieciolatka" (10 year school). The Polish Headmaster was replaced by a Russian, but many former teachers remained, at least until their turn came to be imprisoned or deported.

The first move by the new Head was to confiscate from pupils and from the library all books considered to be "politically incorrect" as we would call it today. We had to hand over our History, Religion, Polish Literature and other textbooks. Funnily enough, those books, although considered to be so damaging to our souls, were not destroyed but locked in the school's loft. When letters started arriving from Archangel and Kazakhstan from friends taken in the first two deportations in February and April 1940, most of them included requests for food, candles and books. So some of us broke into the garret and the books, forbidden to us, were sent in parcels to the Soviet Union.

In June 1941 my turn for deportation came. In the Siberian village Bożenówka five Polish families – mothers and children – were settled, to work on the collective farm, from which the majority of men were called up into the army. Between us we had just two Polish books – a volume of short stories by Rodziewiczówna, which I was reading on the night of deportation and the collective poems of Polish national poet, Adam Mickiewicz. Reading them on long autumn evenings was supplemented by recalling formerly read books and reciting from memory poems learned at school.

The Russian school in the village had only 4 classes. Most of us were too old for it, but the school teacher sometimes lent me Russian books, which - not being an eager student of Russian, during my two years in Nowogródek "dzieciciolatka" - I read with some difficulty. I started with books I already read in Polish: Andersen's Fables, Kipling's "Jungle Book" and even the Polish Communist Wanda Wasilewska's novel "The Room in the Garret"

My first Polish school in Exile was in Dzalal Abad in Uzbekistan, where we went after the so called "amnesty" to join my father whose Army Unit was stationed there. It was a very makeshift affair – our first classroom was a yard in the one of the Polish Army Quarters. A dozen or two of us sat with

School in Ahwaz, Zbyszek Dąbek last on the left

our legs in a trench, while our teacher, on a seat made from few loose bricks, tried to explain geometry problems with the help of drawings made with a stick on the sandy earth. Later we were transferred to more comfortable location – horse stables near another army unit. The senior class to which I belonged sat on the drivers' beds listening to fragments of the Polish National Epic "Pan Tadeusz", recited from memory by our teacher.

In the 3rd Civilian Camp in Tehran, Persia, my secondary school at first was in the open, with tables and benches placed in the shade of large trees, among the pomegranate bushes and over the tiny streams of cool water. When winter came a few large tents were joined together, to accommodate the pupils. Iron stoves kept the air so warm, that the snow on the tents melted and the water seeped in. The Head Teacher wanted me to go into the First Form, which I started in September 1939; I hoped for a place in the Third. After passing some sort of exam, I was allowed to join the Second Form. After two years of the Soviet school in Nowogrodek, I was top of the class in mathematics and science and even ran a maths Tuition Circle to help the less able pupils. But the history of ancient Rome and Greece, and Latin, were not taught in Soviet schools so I had a problem catching up. In this school we had blackboards and some writing materials, but still no books – a real hardship for the inveterate reader I was since my early childhood.

We arrived in Valivade Camp in India in August 1943. When helping us to unload from the train, a friend who had arrived earlier gave me wonderful news - there was a common room in the Camp and in the afternoons they were reading aloud my favourite book "The Deluge" by H. Sienkiewicz. As soon as I had helped my mother to throw our meagre belongings into the quarters allocated to us, I ran in search of that common room. They were reading volume III of the Book. I listened for an hour, standing outside the window (no seating place in the tightly packed room) and then I begged the attendant to loan me volume I. No hope – she said – every one of the few books they had was already lent out. Eventually I managed to secure volume V of the same book. Every free moment I had in the next few days I spent reading this already well known book. I read it like a drunkard after months of forced abstinence, like a traveller in Sahara desert reaching an oasis after days without water…

During the five years in Valivade our libraries grew, supplemented by precious private gifts arriving from friends in the army and later from Poland. But there were never enough books so we copied the chosen fragments into our diaries and learned the poems by heart. Years later, when visiting two friends in Poland, we have spent hours sitting on the floor of their tiny room, over the pot of broad beans and a bottle of wine (food was scarce and expensive then) reciting poems from memory or reading them from Danka's and Halina's Indian diaries… I have been a teacher in Polish Saturday Schools in London for 40 years, fighting not always successful battles to interest my pupils in Polish literature. They have never known "book starvation"…

School No. 4, class 3 -1946 with Bogdan Kmita under the pillar and Dąbek on his right

Daniela Szydło (Suchecka) – Reminiscences from the convent.

A boarding school at St. Joseph's Convent in Karachi was situated near the St. Patrick's Cathedral. It was a beautiful brick building surrounded by a large garden with a fountain and a spacious courtyard.

Our classrooms were on the ground floor. Day pupils were a majority, the boarders shared bedrooms on the first floor. Each of those rather Spartan rooms had a small enclosure, where one of the nuns slept. Absolute silence had to be kept in the mornings and evenings.

When we arrived, dressed in the khaki skirts with straps and white blouses, our shaven heads covered with short hair, hiding our meagre belongings (coarse underwear and pieces of the grey soap) in awful army iron trunks, and with practically no English language, we were the objects of curiosity to the Indian girls. Yet they tried to help us, including us in their games and trying to communicate as much as possible. Our English at first consisted of few essential polite phrases: "Yes sister! Thank you, sister!". But we worked hard and made steady progress. It took a great effort to get used to the strict discipline of the convent life: getting up at daybreak, washing and dressing in complete silence. Like ghosts we walked down without a sound to the chapel for daily mass. Sometimes one of us, under the pretence of illness, managed to skip that holy duty and catch a little more sleep, before arriving at breakfast. After the hungry time in Russia, we could eat like wolves! We cleared our plates in a hurry, hoping for the seconds. Here our dear sister Agatka – a small, elderly Indian nun, running around in the worn out sandals on her tiny feet – helped us by producing extra portions from the kitchen.

Mother Superior of the convent, sister Stanislav Kostka, showed a lot of sympathy towards us, perhaps because of her Polish convent name? (Nuns adopt names of the saints on entering the convent, and saint Stanislav Kostka was a Polish youth.) Another sister Mary Philip was a strict, demanding, but very fair person. English Literature was the most difficult subject for us; we were reading Richard II, translating Shakespeare's language into contemporary English and learning archaic verses by heart. This was an arduous task for Polish girls.

Great excitement was caused by every visit of Mr. Gruja, the Polish vice-consul, whom we all called "Tatuś" (Daddy). He brought us eagerly expected "pocket money" – welcomed, though very modest; not sufficient to buy new clothes. The worn out skirts from the Balachadi orphanage were occasionally supplemented by gifts from the American parcels.

The one event we will never forget was the descent of the swarm of locusts. The great cloud fell on the convent gardens, devastating all the laboriously raised plants. The large stone courtyard was covered with bodies of the dead insects, cleared quickly away by the flock of hungry vultures. This dreary sight will always stay in our memory.

After taking the "Junior Cambridge" exam in December 1944, some of us decided to move to Valivade. With regret we said goodbyes to dear nuns and fellow pupils. The education and upbringing we had received there was gratefully appreciated by all of us.

Hela Suszkówna – New School (fragments of the poem in the school paper)

I remember Polish school, the mother of my childhood,
(The memory weaves through my mind like a silvery thread)
Which nurtured our innocent souls, teacher great and good,
Which taught us to think and the path of truth to tread.

Now Polish school is back, the same as years before,
The Polish teacher like a father or an older brother
Strives to help us, trying to make up for
Those hard, blood-soaked years, gone forever.

We read, like in years past, the poetic art,
Now deeper understanding touches our heart
With Polish teacher, in the school that survived,
Forging strong hearts that no one can divide.

Halina Szafrańska – Green Day

The third matriculation exam was to take place in October 1945. Instead of the traditional "studniówka" (students party organised 100 days before the school leaving exam) our class, 2nd Lycee, consisting mostly of Girl Guides, decided to organise "zielony dzien". (Polish Girl Guides traditionally have one "Green Day" at their summer camp when the Guides take over the management of the camp, relegating the Leaders to the ranks.) Lessons were given by the pupils, while the teachers had to sit at the school desks. The classroom was decorated with greenery, the teachers' desk covered in flowers.

It started with the arrival of the Head Teacher to whom Wera read our proclamation in a frighteningly sonorous voice, though each letter of this text was bursting with humour. Mrs. Borońska promised to inform the teachers of our intentions. Regretfully, this text has not survived, but I did recover the song written for that occasion, which roughly translates as follows: Second Lic, second Lic, (short for "Lycee")

To matriculation only 50 days.
We don't care about teachers' wrath,
Soon the school doors will close behind us.
Let us enjoy the last school days
With laughter, happiness and noise
Let us have a happy Green Day.

Each teacher on arrival was welcomed with this song and a green leaf was pinned to his lapel.

Next period – English! Bożena made a wonderful teacher. Mr. Appadurai at first tried to run away, but once led to his place among the pupils, laughed wholeheartedly. His replies to Bożena's questions were excellent.

Before the History lesson we had closed the door, draping a carpet over the window sill. Miss Handerek, called by us "Pani Rządów Absolutnych" (Lady of Absolute Power) had to climb in. Stela conducted the lesson, Wera read a funny essay about the women's role in the World History, which ended with the words:- Man rules the world. He is ruled by woman.

Next – Psychology! This was the first of many

Sitting from the bottom: B. Romanowska, H. Szafrańska, A. Waszczuk,
I. Snastin, W. Kokoszko, A. Krupińska, E. Woyniłłowicz,
J. Królikowska, H. Szafranek, Z. Balawender, E. Czekierska,
H. Kamińska, D. Zbyszewska, Z. Ostrihanska, I. Adamczyk,
I. Idkowiak, I. Hajduk, Sz. Orzeł, H. Kawałek, J. Juźwin, M. Nowicka
I. Ostrowska, I. Tatarczuk, M. Kłosowska and Z. Karpińska

lessons of that subject in my life, long before I knew I would teach it. Mrs. Skórzyna took my place with laughter. Irka Ostrowska replied to a question about the relation between the logic and reality; Alina Waszczuk about illusions. Then came my lecture about the importance of humour in life. How could I write it – I, who treat life so seriously? Well, I suppose we all have our "Green Days" in life.

Science lesson. Ela had a lecture about astronomy. Mr. Podsoński had to gain access by cutting the web of entangled strings in the doorway, as a sign of forgiving all previous misunderstandings he had with our class. He laughed and stated, that although he did not change his opinion of our poor knowledge of his subject (chemistry), but at least he discovered we were able to think at all.

Finally – Polish Language. Szczęsna was a star, Zocha and Danka wonderful. Our form mistress Mrs. Czarnecka came accompanied by the Headmistress. They made us proud, thanking us for the pleasant surprise. Taking the group photo finished the Green Day.

Janina Niezabytowska - Feast-day wishes for Mr. Żerebecki (our School Inspector and maths teacher)

Dear Sir!
Today we're setting you a test:
To solve a function which without limits,
Ignoring all of the divisions
Continues rising without rest.

"X" has a value of eleven
And each of these is positive.
Where are all these "X's" hidden?
Do you want a clue? – here it is.

The function - a thread from which lasting feelings grew
And the eleven "X's" – the students of Lycee Class 2

Staszek Harasymów – School No. 2

Although we lived in District 1, my brother and I attended Adam Mickiewicz school No. 2, of which our mother, Antonina Harasymów was the Headmistress. Most of her pupils will probably agree with me that she was a good disciplinarian, loved history and was a very demanding teacher. She demanded good work from her pupils, but also a lot of work from herself. In spite of many years of practice, she still prepared her lessons scrupulously. In our home therefore the time spent on education took precedence over

4th Form at School No. 2 with Br. J. Orysiuk (at the back) and S. Harasymów (front row, 2nd from left)

relaxation. But we still managed to have a lot of fun with our friends.

Even during the school lessons it was possible to have some fun, especially during the English classes with young Hindu teacher, Manorama Gaikwad. She had a lovely, gentle face, large dark eyes, a long plait of black hair and a red spot on her forehead. She was always dressed in a sari, with Indian sandals on her feet. During the long break she used to go towards the toilets with a small tin of water. Its use intrigued us. Only later we came to understand it. She talked to us in English which we did not understand, so out of boredom, stupid jokes and pranks were invented. Once, annoyed by the noise and lack of attention, she told us that we had stones and potatoes in our heads.

On passing into the secondary school, I made new friends. A small group of us – "Fat" Józio Hornung, "Chrząszcz" Janek Chrząszczewski, "Śledz" Bronek Siedlecki, "Bohun" Boguś Trela and a few others formed a close group of "Black Men" who had their secrets and kept together. Fat Józio brought to school the song of the American Marines and we learned to sing it.

Andrzej Chendynski – a 7 year old boy's experiences.

After the experience of the deportation to the Soviet Union, journeys to Meshed, Tehran and Karachi, when I was sent to school no.3 in Valivade, the rules and rigours were not to my liking. Zosia Dudek, the Girl Guide who had the task of teaching me to read, found it difficult to keep me in, as I used to run away regularly. I much preferred to climb trees, swim in the river or watch films through a hole in the wall of the cinema. I satisfied my hunger by chewing sugar cane, or picking ground nuts growing in the neighbouring fields. I was fascinated by an old hermit, with very long nails, in a mysterious temple which I visited sometimes.

I liked to keep squirrels, parrots and wasps, whose nests I snatched from the bamboo mats in the empty huts. The wasps fought furiously to defend their homes and stung my face which immediately became swollen, or other parts of the body which made sitting down impossible. A good hiding ended that pursuit. As for school, one of the teachers had the idea of tying me down to my desk. Bitter tears accompanied my stammered reading of the story of "how Uncle Tom built his cabin".

Halina Babik (Rafałówna) – About the teachers and pupils

My best memories are from the 1st and 2nd year of the Secondary School, because then Damokles' sword of exams did not yet hang over our heads and there was time for play and pranks. Among the 30 pupils in class 1a were seven boys: Blumski Romek, Dąbrowski Kazik, Kołodyński Boguś, Liszka Jurek, Ostrowski Adam, Raginia Rysiek and Siedlecki Jasiek. Something was always happening in that class. I remember one day in the monsoon season we had a free period and our young rascals put on their rain capes with peaked hoods, took long bamboo sticks and formed a line on the veranda. Asked where they were going, they answered that they would convert class 1c to Christianity "with fire and sword" ("Fire and Sword" was a historical novel, avidly read by us).

On another occasion Jasiek wrote on the blackboard: If anybody denies that my Halszka is the most beautiful, I will call him to a duel. Jurek jumps from his bench and crosses out "Halszka" on the blackboard, writes "Renia" over it. At once tall and thin like a pole Jasiek and small, aggressive Jurek, with a cap crooked on his red fringe, snatch bamboo sticks and run to the playground, where watched and cheered by the whole class they carry out their duel. They look like David and Goliath.

Mrs. Skórzyna –excellent teacher and a wonderful person - taught me Latin. She made me love this subject. With Kazik Dąbrowski – the only one of the boys who shared my passion, we exchanged letters. I still cherish slips of paper with the words: Carissima mea, ego crispus vocor... On the sly we helped others during the class tests. Another helper was Renia Piątkowska, beautiful girl and solid student. She in turn helped me during the maths tests.

In higher forms Mr. Kozula taught us Latin. Classic profile, curly hair – head as if carved on a Roman medal... He made us understand Latin. Cicero was no longer some distant, ancient orator – he became a talented friendly barrister, defending his client in the Senate. When Kozula with ironic voice declared: -Quam Diu Catilina? – one wanted to be present at this trial.

Miss Wanda Borzemska with her "boys only" Form IA of the High School

When it came to reciting his verses, my dream was to equal my older colleague, Szczęsna Orzeł. But when she was entrusted with a long poem by Norwid, "Chopin's Piano", I was handed merely a very short prayer by Słowacki. Praying silently to receive some recognition for my talent, I put all my soul into that short verse. Vain hope – all I was told by our teacher was to stop making faces, when on stage.

So I tried to gain success in the school choir, but was told I sang too loudly. A successful chorister was my friend, Irka Zobkówna, who, with her beautiful voice, sung all the solo parts. She was however far from successful in maths, which was then taught by our School Inspector himself. After one of the concerts, he approached her, very moved, and declared he could not give the lowest mark for maths to such a singer.

Jadzia Wróblewska – Notes from the diary.

21.11.1946 – Today Mr. Walles said his goodbyes. He found employment outside our camp. "God heard my prayers – he said. – They are building a dam somewhere and I will pour water from one side to the other with a mug." He always liked joking and was very lenient and talkative. Today he told us, that as a small boy he has learned that the tiny wires in the electric bulbs are made of platinum, so he started collecting them. Now he collects statuettes of Indian gods, hoping they will start a museum in Poland. His little son is so used to his father collecting various things, that he brings him even nails he finds.

5.12.1946 – Dr. Tomanek replaced Mr. Wallas as a teacher of Physics. He is very stout. He says he wants to live with us in peace and that he is not so bad as he looks. For oral tests he calls us in alphabetical order, so that we can be prepared and tells us not to be nervous. We do like him! Today he sent me and Hanka K. to the hospital chemist to borrow pliers necessary for some experiment. "I have none – said the chemist, Mr. Pawlowski – I use my hand instead. Doctor has a larger hand, so his pliers will be even better". We were laughing all the way back to school.

28.01.1947 – Mr. Łęczyński always wears a tie or a bow-tie for school. Today he is wearing a green shirt, green tie and a green handkerchief. All he lacked were some green shoes and a green hat! He said he used to like our class, but likes us no longer, since we make little progress in geography. On his feast-day we gave him some flowers – he looked very smart. He was pleased with our gift and did not give us any homework. He told us that in the past he wanted to be a priest, perhaps he will still became one.

Marysia Woźniak – Chemistry during a lesson of Polish.

14.8.1946 – The Headmistress, M. Borońska, who is also our form-teacher, was giving us a lesson in Polish Literature. Silence reigned in the classroom except for Józek Ezman's voice answering her questions. Suddenly from the back of the room came a loud noise and a flare of fire. We were frightened, our teacher also paled. – What happened? – she asked. Jasiek Pacholski got up, white as paper, and explained that he had got some phosphorus, and while examining it, some of it fell on the sulphur and caused an explosion. He did not admit that he obtained the sulphur scraping a matchbox. Mrs. B called him a silly child, a rather offensive term for a young man. But only she could be so lenient, any other teacher would have thrown him out of the class!

Anna Gwiazdonik – Teacher's memories

As well as teaching History and Latin, I was also a form-mistress for one of the classes. It was a large class, over forty pupils, but very few boys: Jurek Kowalski, Jędrek Goławski, Mikołaj (Mika) Suszyński Jasiek Siedlecki. Forty young people, some of them with very interesting personalities, so the special pastoral periods were neither boring nor quiet. Sometimes the stormy and noisy discussions interfered with the Headmistress' work, as she had her office opposite my class. So one day we were evicted to the other end of the building. It did not stop the discussions, but the Headmistress could work in peace.

Teresa Kurowska – Expelled from school! (pages from the diary)

10.8.1947. - I am not expecting a good report because of this row with Mr. Wiktorowicz, when our form truanted from his English lesson in protest against him calling us names. I wrote on the blackboard: "All the dumb sheep and lambs have gone out to graze in the fields". I asked our neighbour, Miss Zosia, to go to the parents' evening, to save my Mother embarrassment. I know I shall have a bad note for "behaviour", but what mark is HE going to give me for English? He better not give me a low mark, or it would be war! I wish it was over and I knew the worst!

(Later the same day) Holy Mary! I did not expect this! I am expelled from school. Just me and Kuźmicz. Jadźka Janczewska got away with it! Mother's feisty friend, Dola, thinks it is an outrage. They are going to see Mr. Żerebecki, the School Inspector, tomorrow. I am praying hard and even went to confession to Fr. Dallinger.

11th Aug. The Inspector said that my

Class 2B with teachers Mrs. A. Ryżewska, J. Kłosowska, E. Karwowska, Miss R. Chopre and pupils T. Kurowska, G. Kunigiel, M. Bąk, L. Kuźmicz, J. Mucha, G. Chrząszcz and R. Loszek

case would be discussed at a Staff meeting. I had some hope, but found out later that a lot of other teachers were against me. Why? They all gave me top marks on my last report. What is to become of me now?

12th Aug. I heard unofficially that I was going to be suspended for three days and then transferred to Miss Borzemska's class, where there is a different teacher of English. So my prayers did help..

Halina Bąbik (Rafałówna) - Reunion

In the Polish Cultural Centre on this day
The graduates arrived in great array,
The taller and the shorter,
But all a lot older;
The slim ones and the plumper version,
With their certificates of matriculation,
Without which, my dears
They'd be out on their ears.
Once, far from our homeland exiled
They went to school amidst monkeys wild.
Knowledge they acquired as fast as they could
And were prematurely forced into adulthood.

It was hard to sit and endure schooling
As it was so very gruelling.

What is all this vocab for?
Why is it all such a chore?
When in the jungle we could swing
Like Tarzan from tree to tree we would fling.
So truants there were a few,
Some thought that dating was their due,
There was lots of fun and laughter -
Commonplace when you're a youngster;
When you are only but a teen
And the world lies before you unseen.
Anyone would want to see that world…
And that's the fate that has unfurled –
All the birds have flown the nest
But sometimes meet at such a fest,
And looking back on life recall:
SCHOOL? – not a bad place after all!

Stela Radwańska (Czekierska) - Polish girls in Bombay

Eleven of us left Valivade on the 12th of December 1945. We were lodged in Dhavbanga Flats at Pedder Rd. The whole house was crowded (you could hardly call it inhabited) by officials and their families employed by the Polish authorities in Bombay. For our living quarters we were allocated one room and two corridors. The common dining room served also as a small restaurant run by Mrs. Laskowska. The food was very frugal but we didn't have to pay for it and were receiving a small amount of money for our travel expenses and school materials.

Eight of us from Valivade and Krysia Biskupska from Bombay attended Sir J.J.School of Art. As we were only able to study in the Commercial Section of the School, the only choice we had was between the Photography, Printing, Lithography and Illustration. We were the only European students in this school and not much was demanded from us. Our contacts with teachers and other students were minimal. Only thanks to Mrs. Wanda Dynowska, also living at this place, could we meet some Hindu people, but that was on a different level.

As this was the period of great political tensions in India, the anti-British atmosphere on the street, numerous protests, demonstrations and upheavals did not encourage going out to town, so we spent most of our free time together. Polish institutions in Bombay were also beginning to change or close down. We left Bombay on 15th March 1947.

Jurek Kowalski - Polish Eagles in Bombay

The beginnings in St. Mary's Boys' High School in Bombay were very difficult. As we did not learn sufficient English in the Valivade schools, we had now to study both the language and the subjects in that language. The Jesuit discipline was stricter than the one in the army barracks. Wake up bell at 5.15a.m., cold shower at 5.20, Holy Mass at 6.00… and so on, from bell to whistle all day long, up to 10.00 p.m. This method was beneficial to our souls, since there was no time for sinful deeds or thoughts. Discipline in the classrooms, living quarters and playgrounds was enforced by reprimand, cane, or casual box on the ear with the breviary. We could leave the school on one Sunday per month – from 10 a.m. to 6 p.m. How happy we were with that one day's freedom – running to town, to the cinema, to the swimming pool (then a separate one for the whites), and to the Polish Red Cross Hospital, where we were given a lesson in Polish Contemporary Issues by Miss Janka Sułkowska, followed by a good Polish dinner.

Since we were always short of money, a way to get free travel was invented by Tadek Jankowski. He always held a 100 rupee note (equal to about £8) - an amount which in those times was sufficient to feed two people for a month. When the conductor approached us on the bus, each of us made a sign towards Tadek. He would take out that note, which the conductor was unable to accept, as he had never enough money to give him change, our bus fares being worth equivalent to 1/2 pence. He apologized and we travelled free to the end of our journey. Although the white people were not supposed to do it, we also used the crowded trams; trying not to be noticed by the white policemen, who would throw us out (there were two police forces in Bombay then, white and black).

Our Polish group worked hard and during the two years we made great progress. Albin Tybulewicz and Marek Dadlez beat the native pupils to some Prizes for the best results in the year. For young boys, living in this strange and difficult climate, on the unfamiliar diet of Indian rice curry twice a day, seven days a week, it was a great effort. But rice, like bread, never palls. There were some difficulties with the studies. We had problems in Chemistry, Physics, Commercial Maths. The History of Europe was taken in detail, but only some periods of it. Scripture was a totally unknown subject for us, it had to be learned by heart. Apart from some compulsory subjects like Mathematics, English and one Foreign Language, the rest could be taken in chosen groups, science or art. All of us were good in English Literature - Shakespeare, Sheridan, Dickens - but the English Language: spelling, idioms, style, was a nightmare.

Twice a year we went for holidays in Valivade, to see our mothers and also our girlfriends who in our absence were growing into charming young ladies. There were long walks, evening dancing to the record player, trips, communal singsongs – very proper gatherings for the young people. Sex for teenagers was not yet fashionable; holding a girl's hand, or perhaps a quick, stolen peck on her cheek was enough to make us happy. What was fashionable were long romantic letters and even longer sighs.

On leaving India our group split, settling in various countries, none returned to Poland. But each of us, in as much, as he could, tried to help in rebuilding of our ruined country, and working hard, keeping Polish traditions and upholding Catholic values, proved that our upbringing and education was not wasted.

Krysia Kuchcicka – The last pages from the diary.

4.11.1947 – Today the first group of the 2nd transport to England will leave the Camp, and the second group will follow in two days' time. Twelve girls from my dormitory in the orphanage will go. It is a sad day. After finishing Teacher Training College I worked as a teacher for two months, but many children left the school in the first transport, so I, as the youngest teacher, was discharged. But I was immediately engaged as a teacher and carer in the orphanage. Now I will miss the work with the children. I don't expect to be able to continue it in England.

Class 6 of the Primary School No. 2 with English teacher, M. Gaikwad (standing): I. Siara, M. Dżumaga, I. Kępko, I. Frąckiewicz, H. Kunigiel, A. Kurzawska, L. Bełdowski (sitting): J. Frąckiewicz, H. Koc, M. Gaikwad, A. Frączek, K. Kuczyńska, A. Francuz, W. Olesiak, A. Błach, M. Sukiennik and J. Buc

12.11.1947 – Last night we said goodbyes to my father, who together with Fr. Dallinger and 19 other men, including 3 doctors, left for Egypt. (…) Many people left our Scouting groups as well. Thinking about the approaching end of the communal life in our great Valivadian family gives me headaches.

15.12.1947 – We will leave on 19th this month. Tomorrow will be the last day at work, and it frightens me – so many partings and saying goodbyes. I was on duty today from 6 a.m. till 2 p.m. Now I am spending the evening sitting on the veranda with Danusia Dziedzic. We are sad. Danusia with her mother, sister Krystyna, her brother-in-law Janusz Wiktorowicz and their little boy Andrzejek, have no idea where they will be sent when Valivade ends its existence. Probably to Africa. I will be grateful for ever to Mr. Wiktorowicz who helped me with my English before the matriculation exam.

16.12.1947 – All day my eyes were wet. My girls were crying, we were sitting on their beds singing the Polish farewell song "…Life flies so fast "…" That was my last day of working with youngsters.

Danuta Dziedzic – From the diary of the graduate.

15.2.1947 – Matriculation exams start in a few days! I am studying hard. But it is difficult to concentrate in our Valivade blocks with matting for walls. Primus stoves hoot (supper is prepared), children cry, my neighbour's parrot is screeching loudly, and over all that noise the captain's record player booms. He has only six records which he plays again and again… And I have to study. To sort out and tidy in mind all the facts collected during the years of learning and which have to stay with me for the rest of my life – or at least till the end of the exams. I have 30 more history chapters to revise, and then Latin, Polish, Maths. I am becoming an expert on sea expansion, economic geography, conjugations, declinations, positivism, Messianism, sines and cosines – so what am I frightened of? Why am I trembling with fright, though the weather is hot and the clay tiles on our roofs emit heat.

19.3.1947 – How can I record this fact in the simplest way? Or perhaps it should be recorded in a flowery way, so it can remain in my notes and my memory with sufficient impact, emotion and pride? On 19th March 1947 the Examination Board of the Gimnazjum and Liceum in Valivade declared I have passed Matriculation. Our whole group did. So we can leave the walls of the school for ever. Yet I am already feeling that I have lost something. Something that for years was part of my life has ended for ever. School – the only link with previous camps, wherever they were. The only stable and continuous thing in our existence. Of course we were complaining about the programmes and criticized our teachers, but we liked most of them and admired them for doing their job in those difficult circumstances. The School gave us the feeling of normality. Now we are not sure what to do with ourselves. These carefree youthful years are behind us. Under this chapter of our lives I am writing the ominous word: THE END.

Valivade 1945, Form 6 of Primary School No. 4. Standing in the middle are teachers: Wanda Kirdzik, Mrs. A. Chylowa, Mrs. A. Ryżewska and Mrs. H. Kurzeja. Sitting down (amongst others): L. Makarewicz, R. Błaszczak, K. Pupa, J. Janczewska, T. Kurowska and L. Chrystowska

PHYSICAL EDUCATION AND DEVELOPMENT OF SPORT IN VALIVADE CAMP 1943-1947

by A. Błach and S. Ucinek

Physical education and its application in various forms, starting with children in playgrounds and continuing with youngsters and then with adults in competitive games, requires physical fitness and agility from the participants and maintains and improves their health.

Sporting activities can be divided into two main groups: a). individual activities and b). team games. These can be divided into subgroups. One, where the participants do not come into physical contact with their opponents, such as volleyball, netball, tennis, table tennis, badminton, track competitions, swimming, etc. And two, where the participants are in contact with the opponents, such as in football, basketball, ice hockey, rugby, boxing, etc.

Poles who were evacuated from Soviet Russia in 1942 to the Middle East - mainly to Iran, were totally exhausted by malnutrition and ravaged by dysentery, typhoid and malaria. Thousands, mainly children, died from these diseases.

Volleyball: Girls v Boys

The top priority for the Polish and British Authorities was to provide food, shelter, medicines and schools and to allow enough time for physical and mental recuperation.

By early 1943 most of the evacuated civilian population found itself accommodated in the refugee camps in India and Africa.

By then the majority of the children had regained their health and physical stamina and was able to participate in PE in schools and Scouting.

Sporting activities and specially team games have a great influence on the character building of the participants. They demand self-discipline, control of temperament and suppression of egoism. They also demand sacrifices from the individual for the benefit of the team and develop pride and the will to win.

Having in mind the educational values of sport, the management of Valivade Camp created a Committee for Organisation and Propagation of Sport (COPS) on 15.07.1943.

Its priority was to plan and build facilities for various sports and to acquire appropriate equipment such as balls, nets, shoes, boots and garments.

Mr. T. Szul was appointed head of the Committee, with a PE instructor and his assistant. All three were full time appointments, paid for by the Ministry of Education.[1]

Sports day - running R. Godlewski and Z. Nowicki

An area in front of the Administrative offices was allocated for the building of football fields, a tennis court, volleyball court, basketball court and track facilities, as well as special sand pits for long jump, high jump and pole vault jump. Areas around the school were to be used for volleyball and basketball courts.

Since at that time there was a war on in Europe (1939-1945) acquiring sporting equipment presented some difficulties. However, the British garrison in Poona generously contributed footballs and other equipment. The rest was purchased in Bombay or locally in Kolhapur.

By the beginning of July 1943, twelve courts were completed suitable for volleyball and basketball.

Then there were 24 school volleyball teams and 2 adult teams. They played 24 matches among themselves and against the Indian teams.[2]

Gymnastic facilities were erected, such as climbing ropes, ladders, swings and sand pits for the youngsters.

Mr. Henryk Katkiewicz, who as a teacher of PE in secondary schools taught the participants the basic rules of various games undoubtedly made an enormous contribution to the development of sport.

In January 1944, the Polish paper *Polak w Indiach* published his article on PE in Valivade Camp entitled "The Objectives of PE and their Educational Values".

"Let us teach our children the greatest number of good games, because they have a pronounced influence not only on physical fitness but also on the development of the intellect.

The development of each human being proceeds along a natural plan. Human, being the most advanced species on earth, enjoy a long period of babyhood and youth in order to be able to develop individual characteristics and coordinated body functions.

In conclusion about the importance of games and sport on the development of human character, let me quote one of the pedagogues in this area. 'We stop playing games, not because we are getting old, we are getting old because we stop playing games' ".

Athletics competition

Of all the games played volleyball was the most popular. It is a noble game, because the participants do not come into direct contact with the opponents. All age groups and sexes can play the game. Because the game is played and controlled by a number of rules, the physical superiority of a team does not give them the advantage. The physical fitness, intelligence and unselfishness of each player are the main assets of a winning team.

In 1944, the Ministry of Religious Affairs and Education in Bombay founded a Silver Cup for Volleyball Tournaments.

The Committee for the Development of Sport reported that in 1944 over 900 children from elementary and secondary schools could participate in games and other activities organised by this Committee.

As already mentioned the most popular games in Valivade were volleyball, football and basketball. Games like table tennis, tennis, boxing, swimming and kayaking were less popular. The track competitions had a good following.

In the beginning swimming, although popular among the boys, was forbidden by the Camp Administration on safety grounds. Panchganga river, close to the northern part of the Camp, was wide, deep, without strong currents except during the monsoon period. It was excellent for swimming. Those caught swimming had their garments confiscated by the camp guards and had to pay a fine on recovery. The swimming was unsupervised and a few of boys drowned.

High jump

In 1947 the senior Scouts under the leadership of Scoutmaster B. Pancewicz decided to build kayaks in the school woodworking shop. They were designed and built by Mr. J. Abramowicz. The project was very successful and so the Panchganga river was made officially accessible.

As previously mentioned, football was very popular and played regularly. The Camp representative team consisted of Mr. A. Maniak - coach, J. Kucharski, Dr. M. Rosenthal - team doctor, Mr. T. Szul - referee and players C. Kolendo, R. Godlewski, F. Zając, R. Grzybowski, K. Bławat, R. Blumski, K. Siara, Z. Nowicki, S. Wasiuk, W. Olesiak, A. Błach, Z. Bobolski, J. Kaśków, W. Kwiatkowski and Pietrzak.

Football Team with Dr. M. Rosenthal, J. Kucharski and T. Szul

By the year 1946 regular football matches were played with local Indian teams from Kolhapur and Miraj and were attended by a large number of local supporters.[3] Some of the Indian supporters were very aggressive and violent when their teams were losing. Most of the Indian teams played without footwear on the hard surface. They were somewhat faster but our players were better organised.

Feliks Zając reminisces: "I had the pleasure of being a member of the football team that represented Valivade Camp. Matches were frequently played with the Maharaja of Kolhapur's team consisting of his palace servants. Their goalkeeper was nicknamed by our players 'Maharaja' and he was proud of it. Many times we were allowed to walk in the Maharaja's beautiful gardens."

In June 1946 a Sports Day Competition took place. Because of the heat the games started at 3 p.m., with 30 and 60 yard relay races, 'egg and spoon' race, three legged race and sack race. The arrival of an Indian band caused a 20 minute break during which VIP's were invited for a nice afternoon tea with Polish doughnuts.

The second part of the games was very interesting and exciting for both: the spectators and competitors. The competition restarted with 'obstacle' race. The competitors in their clean garments at the starting line reappeared at the finishing line as apparitions covered in charcoal dust, grime and mud which they had to negotiate. All competitors were cheered enthusiastically by the crowd of supporters.

The 'tug-of-war' took place with the accompaniment of noisy encouragement of the onlookers who nearly jumped out of their skins in the excitement of supporting their teams.

The crowning point achieved in the four years (1943-1947) by the Committee for Organisation and Propagation of Sport, was the Sport Tournament, which took place during the first week of June 1947. The main attractions were tennis, football, volleyball and track competitions, table tennis, swimming and a tug-of-war contest. There were also games and races for the youngsters. Participation was extended to the local Indians including our Indian Camp Commandant, who took an active part in the organisation of this festival of sport. On finals day the Police orchestra from Kolhapur entertained the public and the supporters.

The Scout team won the football and volleyball finals. Their patron was Z. Peszkowski -

Scoutmaster and their Captain was Alek Błach who was presented with the Cup funded by The Ministry, which the team won for third time in succession.

Mr. A. Maniak who played Mr. Ślusarczyk won the tennis final. In the track events the winners were: 100 metres - Scout Z. Nowicki, 400 metres - Scout R. Godlewski, 1500 metres - B. Pietrzak, obstacle race - B. Strzyżewski.

Participants in each competition received prizes for 1st and 2nd place. Special prizes for outstanding achievements were presented to Lila Wasiuk, R. Godlewski and B. Strzyżewski.

Special mention must be given to Z. Nowicki, S. Ucinek, A. Błach and Pietrzak who had shown great promise as all round sportsmen. Local Indian merchants donated most of the prizes, some of which were attractive and valuable.[4]

It must be stated that the Sports Committee in Valivade Camp fully achieved its aim to provide the youth of the camp with sporting facilities. It was a pleasure to see fit, young people enjoying life and looking forward to face a better future.

Translated by A. Błach and S. Harasymów

NOTES

1. KPI: arch JAG
2. PwI: year 2, no.18 (28) 1944
3. IPiMS: C811B, page 55
4. PwI: year 5, no.8 (88) 1947

SCOUTS TAKE TO THE WATER - AT A PRICE
by J. Kowalski

Our mentor in Scouting matters, Senior Instructor Bronisław Pancewicz, rubbed hard his already extended forehead, as he had a problem to solve. The Cubs had their sing-song and games, junior Scouts enjoyed adventure trips around beautiful Indian countryside, but what to do with the Senior Scouts? They already marched up and down Kohlapur's Principality, they pedalled on hired bikes near and far, from the fortress of Chandoli to the Portuguese Goa. So what new task could he invent to keep them out of mischief? It appears, that the rubbing trick, like with Aladdin's lamp - worked well. A brilliant idea - start up a canoeing team!

Well, well he exclaimed with satisfaction. But where in this sugar-cane-and-molasses-flowing land one can find plywood, or suitable waxed canvas to build the canoes? The wood for the framework we can maybe charm out of our woodwork master, but for the other materials required, where do we turn to?

Only in Polish girl-Guides songs is every boy-Scout clumsy, when in truth (they think) they are a super-genetic breed combining brains of a genius and looks of an Apollo. And so, without much hope for success, we started to inquire locally and further afield, from individuals of upper echelons and lower castes as well, as to where we could acquire the plywood, (the term 'acquire' must be freely interpreted, as we had no funds to purchase). All attempts, like trying unsuccessfully to resolve professor Żerebecki's mathematical mysteries, lead to nowhere.

Then, as if out of the blue Indian sky, one afternoon, we were joined in a volleyball game by Doctor Bazergan, a Persian from the Polish Hospital in Bombay. Since I knew him from Iran, where the Polish Authorities leased his villa at 75, Entezan, Tehran, I asked him in Polish (he had earlier married a young Polish lady), whether he could help us to find some plywood. To my total astonishment, he said 'no problem' then in a slightly broken Polish he informed us that there was a Polish Jew who had started up a plywood factory in the middle of the Hyderabad jungle, Instantly, to a man, we shouted in jubilation 'Long live Dr. Bazergan! Long live Iran!'. He smiled graciously and responded by sending his driver to get a dozen bottles of Vimto, a drink which we liked so much but could never afford, especially when served with lots of crushed ice. Soon afterwards, three keen volunteers Henry, Wiesiek and Jurek set off on a journey into the unknown. From Valivade station to Miraj in the same Principality, there was no need for permits to travel by train and tickets were easily obtainable. However, to go any further, it presented problems, as we had to continue our journey south without tickets. Lady luck was on our side and by midnight we were sitting comfortably sharing a compartment with the British military unit., travelling all the way to Bangalore. Long live the British! This way nobody dared to ask us for our tickets or permits. In fact we were given a nice early morning army breakfast before we left the train at a small station before Hyderabad.

From there the sidings led to the adjoining parking square where we noticed lorries unloading., what looked like stacks of plywood sheets. The rain was teaming down, the monsoon in its full glory - mud up to the armpits - water going in and coming out of our Kolhapurian sandals. Our army-type capes, hardly covered us from the continuous downpour. We were totally soaked when we reached the nearest lorry, which was already unloaded. The Indian driver seeing three white faces, politely offered to take us back to the jungle factory to see the Sahib - the master. We crowded into the driver's cab - all three of us. The combination of wet clothing, the jungle heat, steamed up everything inside. We could have done with another set of windscreen wipers to work inside the cab. The track to the factory was bouncy and uncomfortable. Huge tree roots in all directions, with the soil all washed out, made it a decidedly rough ride as we were thrown from side to side. The panoramic view of the jungle was spectacular. The branches above formed a canopy with noisy monkeys playfully jumping onto the lorry and back into the branches of the tropical trees, of which I could name not even one. Inside the cab we started to argue as to who would be the spokesman for the group, as we expected to be speaking in English. As it happened there was no need for all that. The only white man in working overalls, on seeing us climbing out of the cab and reprimanding each other in Polish for being careless, shouted in complete disbelief 'Boys! where on earth have you come from into this God-forsaken hole?' All that in Polish! He had not seen a white person for the last three weeks and now there were three of them, and to top it up, all speaking his mother-tongue.

He put us up in the most comfortable accommodation reserved for visitors. We had servants for everything and we were fed like turkeys before Christmas. He took immense pride in showing us round, explaining how he had created from scratch the settlement for a few hundred people and the only plywood factory in India. Each production machine was designed from memory by himself. He taught the locals how to cast iron machine components. The lorry drivers from Hyderabad were taught as mechanics, who in turn trained others to operate the plant.

Scouts kayak with Z. Peszkowski

The finance was raised jointly by the British and the Indian Government in Delhi. This was a priority military project, as plywood was supplied to the military factories constructing gliders and light military training planes. To our great surprise, we learned, that the glue was made from the Australian imported dried bull's blood. This luxury life lasted for three memorable days during which we had to relate for him, over and again, how we managed to arrive in India, how we survived Siberia and how we found him in the jungle. Finally, he instructed his men to pack and despatch to Valivade Camp enough best plywood for at least three double-seater canoes. He prepaid our first class tickets and arranged with the train dining car that we should get a hot meal on the way home. What a man indeed! We learned later, that he had his own plywood factory in Łódź, Poland. He had escaped via Asia through China to India in 1940.

On return back to the Camp, we were heroes, or at least that is how we felt. But when the Scouting fraternity saw the plywood, they too were full of praise for us. Within the next few weeks, in a typically Indian style, with fireworks and loud festivities, the first canoe named after our troop *PIRATES* was launched on the river bank.

On the Camp's favourite walking alley for those in love, or for lonely hearts seeking companionship (pure and platonic), everybody, interested or not, had to hear our story. Unfortunately, the local Indian police also got to know it. Once a month the Indian Magistrate attended the Camp 'Court Sittings', to administer justice to the Polish D.P.'s population living there. To our horror, the interpreter, a young Polish upstart, did not help things by repeating in Polish, 'You fools! without the pass, without the ticket, you left for another Principality, how I hope the Magistrate will let you have it good and proper - hooligans!' The Magistrate in fact banged his wooden hammer with all present standing up he pronounced: 'Three days in local Camp arrest where normally Polish 'daughters of Corinth' spent their days after illegal adventures with the British troops, or ten rupees penalty paid on the same day to the court.' As usual we had no money, so under armed guard, we were sent home for our mothers to bail us out. Fortunately, we managed to sneak home through the back alleys and not go by the direct route, where everybody would have laughed their heads off seeing yesterday's heroes being marched home under guard for their mummies to get them out of trouble.

The fact, now confirmed in writing remains, that very soon the canoes graced the river's waters, with Scouts and many others enjoying the water sport. When we left India, the Indian Scout troop from the nearest village Ratnagiri, inherited the canoes.

The other painful consequence of the whole affair, was the cancellation of our miserly pocket money for one month - now that hurt a lot! To make things even worse, the long awaited film *Gone with the Wind* was screened at the Camp, with hundreds queuing up daily, but for us - no eight annas (half a rupee) - no pictures. Once again a Scout's resolve had to be put to the test. Next to the cinema, there was a huge mango tree. We climbed it not for the first time. From there, a swing on a branch and down we went straight onto the cinema's roof. There were already narrow slots carved out with pocket knives in the wooden support beams facing the screen. As in most cases nothing is perfect! Our little problem was, that when one was positioned with the head down, blood rushed to your head, but the picture was the right way up. When you looked more comfortably with the head up, unfortunately the picture was upside down. The standing joke at the time was, that the Australians see the world like that all the time but never complain. So do not be choosy and if you do not enjoy the plot, move over, there are many others to take up your slot.

POLISH SCOUTING MOVEMENT IN INDIA
by Hm. Danuta Pniewska

A FEW EXPLANATORY NOTES ABOUT POLISH SCOUTING
(before and during WW II)

Although our movement closely followed the aims and ideas of the British and the International Scouting and Guiding Movement, its internal organisation and terminology developed independently. There are a few things the readers should know, before attempting to read this chapter.

The name – Polish Scouting Association (Związek Harcerstwa Polskiego or ZHP) – covered both organisations: Polish Girl Guides and Polish Boy Scouts. Although there was a common Executive Committee called "Naczelnictwo" elected on joint conferences of Guiders and Scoutmasters, it concerned itself mainly with matters of ideology, policy and – to a certain extent, finances. Guides (Harcerki) and Scouts (Harcerze) had separate programmes and their separate Headquarters. However, during the war period the local conditions often dictated variations and a certain amount of coeducation.

The Scout law and **promise/oath** - are the same for both organisations.

The emblem – since our first Girl Guide companies were organised in 1910, before the Guiding Movement was known in Poland, our girls have never adopted the Trefoil, but use the fleur-de-lis like the Boy Scouts. The metal fleur-de-lis is worn on our headgear. In addition, we - unique in the Scouting Movement, I believe - have another emblem, invested with more emotional meaning, a special Polish Scout's and Guide's Cross, received after making the Promise and worn on the uniform. Harcerz can exchange the fleur-de-lis with fellow Scout from different country (often done on Jamborees), but he never parts with his cross.

The uniform: While the boys adopted the khaki Scouts uniform, the girls uniforms are grey.

The leaders: There are 3 levels of leadership status.

    Przewodnik - Pwd. = junior Guider/Scoutmaster
    Podharcmistrz - Phm. = 2nd class Guider/Scoutmaster
    Harcmistrz - Hm.   = 1st class Guider' Scoutmaster

Those words or abbreviations are used in front of leaders' names, rather than Sir, Mr. or Miss.

Scouts and Guides address each other, especially their leaders and the senior ones, as druh or druhna, and the shortening dh, dhna, often appears before their names.

Proficiency badges: are awarded for many skills. Advanced Proficiency Badges can be gained by Rangers and Rovers Scouts (aged 15 or over).

Grades: there are 5 levels of grades for Guides and Scouts and 3 for Brownies & Wolf Cubs.

Names: all units in the Polish Scouting and Guiding besides their registration numbers are also named, often after the famous historical figures or saints.

Sections: There were 4 sections of members in the period covered by this book: Zuch (Brownie/Wolf Cub) age 7 – 11; Harcerka/Harcerz (Guide/Scout) age 11-15; Wędrowniczka/Wędrownik (Ranger/Rover Scout) age 15 -18; and Starszy harcerz (Senior section's member) for over18. Skrzaty (Rainbow Guides/Beavers) for children aged 4 – 7 were not invented until many years later.

Polish terms are occasionally used in the following pages, where there is no equivalent English one.

INTRODUCTION

Lord Baden Powell's book 'Scouting for Boys' and the news of the new youth organisation founded by him arrived in Poland in 1910 and were met with great interest and enthusiasm. Our country was then torn between three occupying neighbours: Prussia, Russia and Austria. Only the last one permitted a modicum of freedom, when Polish organisations were concerned. So it was in Lwów, (south-east Poland, then under Austrian occupation) that the book was translated into Polish and the first Scout and Guide units organised. However, even under Prussian and Russian more prohibitive regimes, many clandestine Polish organisations existed. The ideas of Scouting were passed to them and independent patrols of Scouts and Guides started mushrooming throughout the whole country. Later on all those units combined under the common Headquarters, and formed the Polish Scouting Association – an umbrella organisation encompassing both Girl Guide and Boy Scout Associations.

Baden Powell's aim was to provide happy, healthy and helpful citizens for their countries and create a brotherhood of youth across the world. Those were exactly the same ideals of the underground organisations – working for future freedom of Poland by creating a class of strong, wise, well motivated people. But historical situation being what it was, Polish Scouting from the beginning had a very strong patriotic emphasis. Our youth not only had to serve their country, they had to fight for its independence in any way possible. When the WWI finished, bringing Poland its freedom, idea of Scouting as 'service' remained.

During the 20 years between the two World Wars the Polish Scouting movement flourished both nationally and internationally. In terms of ideology and technology it reached a high level; in competitions at international jamborees. Our woodwork, water sports and gliding skills, all earned us high recognition. Our organisation was a co-founder of the World Organisations WOSM and WAGGGS (World Assoc.of Girl Guides and Girl Scouts) and made a valuable contribution in terms of programmes and methodology. Dhna Olga Małkowska was very active in WAGGGS and a regular contributor to the Guider monthly. In 1935, according to the statistics of the International Scouting Office, the Polish Scouting Movement was the third largest in the world, after the USA and Great Britain. In Poland itself, we focussed on introducing Scouting to young people in rural areas; there were many programmes, including a literacy campaign, and we achieved the official government status of an 'organisation of special significance'.[1]

The enthusiasm and commitment shown by our young people were not even daunted by WWII. The Girl Guide Emergency Service 'Pogotowie Harcerek' was set up by 1938; it trained girls for special wartime duties. Scouts too, run similar training. Despite the upheavals of war, which sent us far and wide across the world, the work of Scouting never died and the Organisation survived.

On 9 October 1939, barely one month after the outbreak of war, dh Michał Grażyński, Chief Scout of the ZHP, convened the Chief Executive Committee in Paris[2] (at that time, Paris was the seat of the Polish Government in Exile). After the fall of France, the Committee reconvened in Scotland, where it continued under the leadership of the Chief Guide dhna Olga Małkowska; in January 1943 it moved to London.

Zbyszek Nowicki with a flag donated by The Consulate

Under the German occupation the Scouting movement in Poland went underground, operating both in smaller units as well as the major underground operations known as Szare Szeregi, Pogotowie Harcerek, Pasieka. Small Girl Guide units operated even inside two German concentration camps: Ravensbruck and Bergen-Belsen.[3]

There is little documentation about Guides or Scouts amongst the Poles forcibly deported to Russia, but there was some activity even there.[4] However, immediately after leaving that godforsaken land, Scout and Guide units started springing up both within army divisions, where older Scouts would get together in groups, and in civil settlements, where young people spontaneously set up their own Patrols and Troops, sometimes without any help from adults. And so, when I arrived at the Third Civilian Camp in Tehran in September 1942, the first person I saw at its gate was a Girl Guide wearing a grey uniform and a blue scarf. I do not remember when I joined the school; I joined the Girl Guides on 15th September.

Tehran and Ahwaz were transit camps, where Scouting activities were not made any easier by the lack of trained leaders, nonetheless the work flourished throughout their existence. Most of us arrived in India already wearing our Scout uniforms; the Scout emblem we sported on our caps had been cut out from aluminium cups.

The Beginnings

As ever, the beginnings were difficult. Those trained Leaders who survived deportations to the Soviet Union, were now in the Polish Army in the Middle East, and the majority of youngsters in their later teens were in cadet schools. Yes, we had brought our uniforms with us from Persia, but we still did not have any manuals nor equipment.

From the transit camp in Karachi (now Pakistan) which existed from 4 September 1942 until September 1945, transports of people were sent to India, Africa and Mexico; we lived from day to day. But nonetheless, some Scout and Guide units worked there, organising meetings and camp fires. It was there that the first Promise on Indian soil took place on 4th of June 1943; Phm. W. Bidakowski, the only Polish Scoutmaster in India at that time took it from the 70 girls and boys. When he was transferred to Valivade, his work was carried on by dhna Fela Parczewska, and after her by dhna Jula Proskurnicka. English Rover Scouts, who were stationed in the nearby RAF units, helped to organise activities.

Even earlier, in April 1942, the first transport of children arrived by land from Russia. First they went to Bandra (a suburb of Bombay), and later were moved to a Polish children's village in Balachadi-Jamnagar. Despite the fact that only two people in this transport had already made their Scout Promise, two Patrols were set up almost immediately. Things improved when Mrs. Janka Ptakowa arrived with the second transport. A Guide Company was set up, named after Romuald Traugutt; and then, on 15 August 1943, the second Promise ceremony in India took place.

The original team: (standing) ..., ..., J. Wojniłowicz, E. Wrzyszcz, J. Siedlecki, W. Bidakowski, I. Hajduk, ..., R. Klar, (bottom line) K. Naglik, H Szafrańska, W. Sasadeusz, ..., R. Raginia

In July 1943, the first transport of refugees arrived in the newly-established settlement in Valivade. The large number of children and teenagers necessitated opening of many schools. Phm. W. Bidakowski set about organising Scouting and Guiding. The first Council of leaders of the units which had been set up earlier in Karachi took place on 1st September 1943. It was at this meeting that the Valivade District Command was established. Within 10 days, 4 Scout Troops, 8 Guide Companies and 4 Cub and Brownie Packs had signed up.

The flow of new blood to our organisation was so great that in the course of the first 6 months of the existence of the Valivade Scouting District, there were two major Promise ceremonies: on 10th of November 1943 and 10th February 1944. Later on, the Promise ceremonies became smaller and more intimate, but to begin with they were general celebrations for the whole Polish community. The November Promise was made Patrol by Patrol (individually it would have taken too long) on the sports field, in the presence of the whole settlement. The Scout Camp Fire was then one of the few attractions available to the residents of Valivade.

On 20th November 1943, Order No. 27/43, issued by the ZHP in the East, nominated Phm. W. Bidakowski a Leader of the Valivade District, making it the third District in India (after Balachadi and Karachi). Soon after, another Scoutmaster arrived in the settlement, the Rector of the Polish Catholic Mission in India, Fr. K. Bobrowski, who took part in the Scouting activities so far as his pastoral duties allowed him.

The biggest problem was the shortage of trained leaders. By then we had made contact with Indian Scouts in Kolhapur. With their help we managed to obtain the use of a magnificent former fortress in beautiful Panhala for camps and training courses. On 16th May 1944 hundred and twenty four youngsters aged 14 - 22 gathered there for a Leaders Training Course, under the leadership of both our Scoutmasters as well as Mrs. Janka Ptakowa from Jamnagar, and our school teacher, Miss Hanka Handerek. The Course participants were Troop and Company leaders and Patrol leaders, though largely very young, who had taken on these roles without any training. The Course had to take place indoors, in a former, now abandoned maharaja's palace, for although by that time our uniforms were being made locally and

Mr. M. Goławski, the Ministry of Education representative in Bombay (who had once been a Scout himself) had obtained permission from the Command of ZHP in The East to have 600 Scout Crosses pressed locally, (the Indian Series)[5] – we still did not have any tents.

Ladies from the Zgoda Cooperative did the catering. On the first day we all fell ill; it appears they were using new metal pots which had not been blanched and were therefore toxic in some way; they should have been boiled up before use.

This camp was a sensational experience for us - various activities, camp fires, and, during the beautiful Indian nights, night watch and… ghosts. And then came a great surprise…

Arrival of the Team of Inspectors

From the very beginnings of its existence, the Headquarters of the Polish Army in the Middle East under General Anders were well aware of how soldiers' morale was affected by concern about their families. Following the evacuation of large numbers of civilians from Russia, care was taken over both their material welfare as well as their spiritual needs. Particular attention was paid to young people and children, who after years of exile and being cut off from the normal life, were in need not only of bread, but also of books, teaching, games and of leaders who would form their characters and who might identify goals for them, while they waited for return to Poland.

Many old Scouts in the army organised themselves fairly quickly. The ZHP Council in the Middle East was established in Jerusalem in October 1941. When young people from Russia started arriving in Persia, India and Africa, the name was changed to ZHP Council for the East, to include those regions as well. The ZHP Command for the East was established, and later on the Independent Scouting Department, to which the Army seconded a dozen or so Scoutmasters. Their task was to organise Scouting activities, publish a magazine *Skaut* and reprint Scouting manuals. In 1944 four teams of inspectors were set up to work in refugee settlements. Before going out into the field, the teams underwent special training in Jerusalem, setting themselves specific targets, and discussing ideological and practical issues; they even ran some experimental courses in cadet schools in Palestine.

Many years after the war, when at some social gathering the conversation turned to the work carried out by the Scout Leaders during that time, a lady said to me rather dolefully: "… it's such a pity that they had to leave the army, just as it was preparing for action…" It was not easy for our Scout Leaders to leave the army at that time, but unlike this lady, they understood that ten or twenty more dead heroes would not have changed the course of the war. But ten or twenty Scout Leaders seconded to work with young people made a positive contribution to the quality of our lives over the next few years. Thirty years later one of our Scoutmasters, then a young

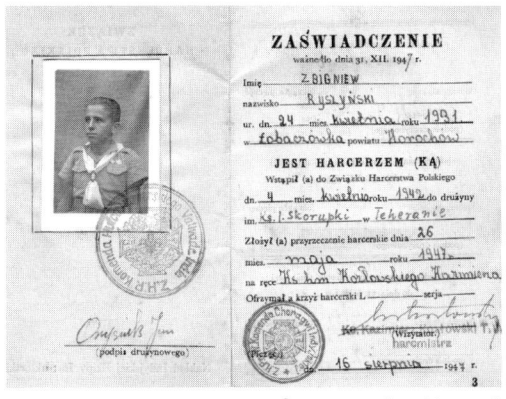

Scout membership card

lieutenant, now a prelate, Fr. Zdzisław Peszkowski, wrote to his former charges:[6]

"…Today I can readily admit that I often envied my colleagues, for the fact that they could settle their historic scores with the Germans face to face; even more, painstakingly, I counted each day I was separated from my regiment, from each battle fought - after all, that was what I had been training for…

...Today I do not regret a single moment, because together we grew and together we prepared for what we can now look back on..."

Those of us for whom Scouting was a joy, a comfort and a lesson in life in those difficult days of wanderings, are well aware of the sacrifice made by our young Scoutmasters and we are grateful.

At 8 o'clock on 11th May 1944, the Visiting Team for India sailed out from the port of Tewfik in Egypt with a convoy of naval vessels, under escort, with a barrage balloon, and arrived in Bombay on 23rd May. The team consisted of:

Cub membership card

Inspector Lieutenant Bronisław M Pancewicz, Hm. Samotny Wilk [Lone Wolf]

Deputy 2nd lieutenant Zdzisław Peszkowski, Hm. Ryś Zuch [Brave Lynx]

The Team spent the first few days in Bombay on official business and talks with Mr. E. Banasiński, Polish Consul, Mr. M. Goławski, Delegate of the Polish Ministry of Education in London, and Mr. S. Dudryk-Darlewski, Delegate of the Ministry of Work and Social Services. The last two of them - old Scouts themselves - were very sympathetic towards our movement. Although Bombay (now Mumbai) was the place where all Polish Authorities in India resided, the Scoutmasters decided to settle in Valivade, the largest Polish refugee settlement in India, so they could be in constant contact with the young people.

Five days later, on the morning of 28th of May 1944, they reported to the Valivade Camp Commandant Capt. W. Jagiełłowicz, and the same afternoon arrived in Panhala, to take over the running of the training camp for Guides and Scouts Leaders which started 12 days earlier. On the camp's staff meeting that evening the trainees were divided into three groups:

Company/Troop Leaders Course – (9 boys and 25 girls) - under Hm. B. Pancewicz; and I. Krajewska.

Brownie and Wolf Cubs Leader Course – (4 boys and 21 girls) – under Hm. Z. Peszkowski and Phm. J. Ptakowa.

Patrol Leaders Course – (27 boys, 38 girls) - under Father K. Bobrowski Hm. and Phm. W. Bidakowski.

(The predominance of girls was due to the fact that most older boys were in military cadet schools in Palestine.)

For financial reasons those courses had to finish on the 5th of June; further 2 weeks of training to be given in Valivade. The return journey to Valivade the Company Leaders made on foot (30 km!!) – their night march caused a sensation in the settlement.

The arrival of the visiting Inspectors Team gave new incentive and the Scouting Movement in Valivade exploded with a great enthusiasm and energy.

Reorganisation

Among the various tasks the Visiting Team had to undertake, was the training of the leaders, gaining the necessary equipment and finances and convincing the general public of the advantages our organisation gave to the youngsters. But the most urgent one was the reorganisation of the large and growing Polish Scouting Movement in India. They started with Valivade.

Picking out the most promising members from Panhala courses as future leaders, all existing units were divided into four groups called 'Szczep' (Tribe), consisting of the Girl Guide, Boy Scout, Brownie and Wolf Cub units, based at each of the then existing schools. Each School provided a teacher as an adult help: Miss H. Handerek, Miss W. Borzemska, br. J. Orysiuk and Mrs. Figuła helped a lot, and some of them became later full members of the Movement. In November 1944 a new school, No.4 was organised for the children and a new Szczep 5 was placed under Halina Wasilejko.

The two previously organised Districts - in Jamnagar (two Scout Troops, two Guides Companies, four Brownie and Wolf Cub Packs - 193 people in all, in charge of Phm. J. Ptakowa), and in Karachi (4 Guide Companies, 1 Scout Troop and 5 Packs of Brownies and Wolf Cubs - 243 members, led by Miss J. Proskurnicka) were taken under the Visiting Team's command in December 1944. Altogether Polish Scouting and Guiding in India in the year 1944/45 had 1334 members working in 50 units .

Two special groups Krąg Pracy and Krąg Wodzów Zuchowych (Company and Pack Leaders Councils) had a double aim: to help their members gain their own grades and proficiency badges, necessary for their advancement in the Movement's hierarchy, and at the

Pack Leaders and their 'totem poles' in Valivade

same time to continue their training as efficient leaders of the juniors. On the 24th March 1945 a Company of Senior Members called 'Flame of the Jungle' was created to accommodate girls, who after finishing High school, were too old for the Rangers, but wished to remain within the Movement. While continuing the ideology and character training, they also helped both the youth units and the Headquarters, especially in editorial work. Two other groups of Seniors were organised in October 1945 in Bombay and Panchgani, where the girls who passed their Polish Matriculation exams were sent for further education in English Institutions.

On 15th July 1945 the Headquarters of ZHP in the East terminated the existence of Visiting Teams. All Polish Scouting units in India were organised into the 'Indian Division' with B. Pancewicz as the first Division Commissioner, until his return to his army unit on 15th September 1946. Z. Peszkowski was the next Division Commissioner, and when he was in turn recalled back to the army on 10th of August 1947, our chaplain Father K. Kozłowski took his place. Despite the gradual decrease of population in our settlements, the Scouting activities lasted to the very end.

Jurek Bitschan Troop - in the middle A. Klecki, J. Orysiuk, J. Pacholski, and among others W. Olesiak, A. Błach, B. Siedlecki, Z. Kaptur J. Kucewicz and J. Chrząszczewski

The rather unsettled existence – sending some pupils to English schools outside the settlement, gradual liquidation of the Polish Refugee Camps, dispersal of people - caused many changes in organising the units and nominating their leaders. For example when there were three coeducational Districts (in Balachadi, Country Club and Valivade) Brownies and Cubs Packs belonged to them. But the great number of Packs in Valivade necessitated creation of a special post of an Assistant Commissioner ('namiestnik') who took responsibility for the programmes and activities of those units. It was held originally by Zosia Dudek, and later on by Irka Janczewska. At the end of the year 1946, after the closure of Balachadi Settlement, when practically all members of the Indian Division found themselves in Valivade, it underwent another reorganisation - separate Districts were created – two for the Guides, and one for the Scouts, while all the Brownie and Cub Packs formed a fourth one, with Danuta Pniewska as its Commissioner. More detailed description the reader may find in the Polish version of this book, while a list of leaders is available in the Appendix to this version.

METHODS AND PROGRAMMES

While the aims of Scouting remain unchanged since its origin, the methods by which these aims are achieved are constantly examined and improved, to keep up with the changes in the interests and needs of the young people. They enjoy a challenge, so they have to be given difficult tasks, completion of which will give them a sense of achievement. They feel happy associating with the young people, so we must provide young leaders. They are easily bored or disenchanted, so their upbringing must be done through interesting games and adventures, not by lectures and sermons. Trying to install in them the moral values and love of our traditions, we have to search for better, newer, more interesting ways of doing it.

We were lucky in the fact that one of our Inspectors, Hm. Peszkowski, was young, but already experienced in the work with Wolf Cubs, and trained by the famous Polish Scoutmaster, Alexander Kamiński. His elder companion, Hm. Bronisław Pancewicz, was an authority on the newly organised before the war section of Rover Scouts, and had already written a booklet *Problems of Scouting for Older Boys* printed in 1944 by the Polish Girl Guides and Boys Scouts Headquarters in Palestine.

Although many youngsters who left Russia as members of 'Junaks' (military cadets) were now in military schools in Palestine, a considerable numbers of girls and some boys over the age 15 arrived in India. So a Troop of Rover Scouts and a few Companies of Rangers ('Wędrowniczki') were formed. They wore dark green scarves and dark green shoulder strap which distinguished them from the younger members.

The basis of work with those young people was established in Poland in 1939. It consisted of: 1) Personal improvement 2) Finding one's place in the society 3) Service. What it meant in practice was character building, intellect and body training, discovering the roles they should play in their communities and social work of all kinds. The younger Guides and Scouts proficiency badges 'sprawności' were replaced by 'specjalności' – advanced badges gained by becoming cookery, health, signalling, literature or history experts, learning photography, editorial, driving or child-care skills in depth. It has to be remembered, that at that time we were still hoping to return to Poland, and we were preparing ourselves to work in small towns and villages, mainly in Eastern Poland, badly devastated by war and Soviet occupation. Work to gain those badges was undertaken by company, patrol or individual people and gained at special courses or training camps. It was later recorded in the book *'Praca Wędrowniczek i Skautów'*, (Rover Scouts and Rangers Book) - a joint effort of Hm. Z. Peszkowski and our young Guiders, published in India in 1947.

While the Lone Wolf (Hm. Z. Pancewicz) with the help of Miss H. Handerek and a few young Guiders experimented with the programmes for the senior teenagers, Hm. Z. Peszkowski – dh Ryś – concentrated on the most numerous group of our organisation, Brownies and Wolf Cubs. Two pre-war books of A. Kamiński: *'The Wolf Cubs Leaders Book'* and *'Antek Cwaniak'* were already reprinted in Palestine and were of great help. Kamiński's ideas were presented to the English Cub Leaders before the war and met with interest. They were based on the natural interests of Polish children. Rather than play at being animals – Bears, Wolfs, Monkeys etc, as described in R. Kippling's *'Jungle Book'* (there are no jungles in Poland), our kids pretend to be soldiers, firemen, nurses etc. Now some new badges were invented – for example 'Cracovian girl', 'Warsaw Girl', 'Polish Highlander', 'Knight' - which were meant to install some connection with the distant and partly forgotten motherland. When the news came about the Warsaw Uprising, a new cycle of games were invented for the badge of 'Insurgent' – as it was both topical (we were all emotionally involved with the Uprising) and adventurous (conspiracy, fighting the Germans), it met with great success.

Since we had no pre-war Brownie leaders amongst us, and the only Girl Guides Book *W Gromadzie Zuchów* (In the Brownie Pack) did not reach us until 1946, our Brownie's meetings were organised on the Wolf Cubs models shown us by our 'Brave Lynx' and his mentor Kamiński. I have used this method for the next 40 years, working with Polish Brownies in England and found it very successful.

The middle group of children, so called 'harcownicy' (age 11-14) used well established pre-war programmes and methods. All we had to do was to introduce some safety rules dictated by our exotic temporary location.

Service to God

Scouting in Poland, after the WWII underwent many turns in direction. Necessity to co-exist with the changing political climates forced it to deviate from some of the ideological principles of International Scouting, especially those referring to religion. Although the Communist regime never succeeded in diminishing the influence of the Roman Catholic Church, the state sponsored educational and social organisations were not allowed to introduce religion in their programmes.

Living outside our country, we felt compelled to guard and preserve its ideals and traditions. Our promise: ...'I will serve God and my country' was reflected in our Scouting activities. So each day at our camps started and ended with prayers in front of the little shrine, constructed by the children themselves. Special Masses and retreats were organised, discussions held for older groups and a pilgrimage to Goa was a great success.

There was even a special troop of altar boys, which nurtured several future priests and one archbishop.

In view of the above, I found it very curious when, while doing the research for this book, I came across some correspondence in which one of the priests accused our Scoutmasters of drawing away the young people from the church. It may be explained by the fact, that this particular priest was a very controversial person, difficult to cooperate with others and in the end compelled to leave India. The only reason I mention it here, is to deny categorically that anything of that sort existed. There might have been some healthy competition with the strictly religious youth organisations, but many children belonged to both. We remember with sentiment the many dawn prayers at our camps, held standing on the Panhala's precipices and the night prayers at fading campfires. And in our fond memory we keep our chaplains – the energetic and fun-loving Father Kazimierz Kozłowski, who - after leaving India for Africa - wrote lovely letters to some of us; the very sensible, matter-of-fact Father Jankowski, member of our cycling pilgrimage to Goa; and above all the wise, kind-hearted Father Dallinger, our parish priest, the spiritual leader at many of our retreats, discussions and meditations. This connection of prayers and meditations with the life in the open created strong ties with the Church, that many of us kept for the rest of our lives. Marysia Woźniak sent us a camp prayer, found in her diary:

> For You, my God and for Poland I wake up
> every morning.
> I kneel and open my lips
> To praise You, Eternal God, our Creator.
> I praise You together with everything that exists:
> With the breaking day, with the singing birds,
> With the silence surrounding us.
> Help me, Almighty God, to work towards the bright
> dawn for my country.
> The God of our fathers, you can see our thoughts,
> our dreams,
> And our hearts, that beat only for You and for Poland.

Camping

There is an old Polish Scouting song, telling young boys about adventures awaiting them at the Scout camps:

> Brother Scout, go camping, do,
> There adventure awaits you...

KOLHAPUR REGIONS

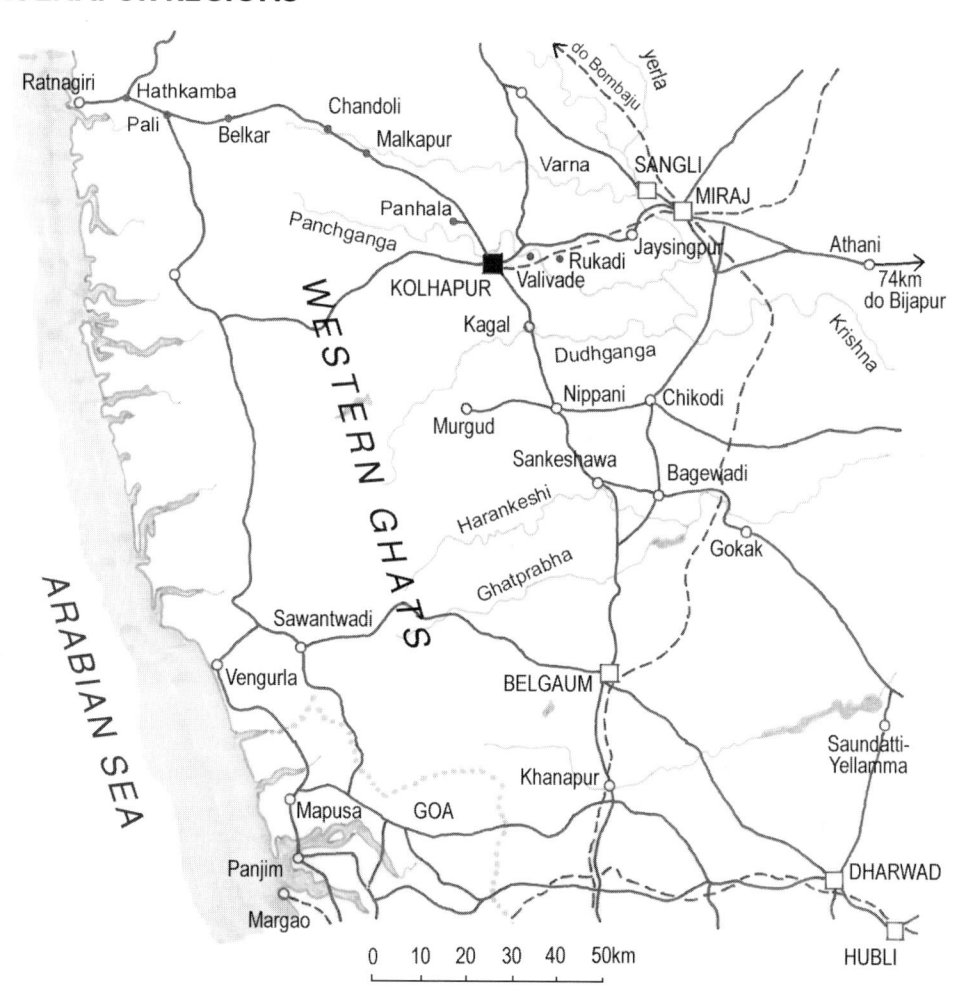

Indeed, every camp is an adventure, and our camps in India were an exotic adventure. Scorpions under your bedding, monkeys stealing bananas from your tent, the creaking floors of the abandoned palace serving as our holiday abode, green tents under huge mango trees, keeping night watch under the sky full of stars… Once even a tiger… We had to leave Poland too young to see much of the world, then came the war and deportation to Russia, and now – nominally free, but enclosed in this small Polish ghetto, with meagre social allowances not sufficient for tourists attractions – we would not be able to see anything in this beautiful country without the help of Scouting. We could only explore the places to which we could walk with knapsacks on our back and sturdy boots.

Our poor mothers, after miraculously saving us from the Soviet 'paradise' were now inclined to be overprotective, in their self-assumed duty to deliver us safely to our fathers. But we were dreaming about freedom and adventures. In our settlements, predominately peopled by women, boys felt even more constrained that girls. This was described by one of our Scouts, Staszek Harasymów:

Free time to swing on the lianas

...We were full of energy, eager for adventures... Holidays meant a Scout camp. Only there could we lead a free, happy life. Of course Scouting activities in Valivade were quite interesting, but there was no comparison with the camps.

Mine and my brother's longing for the camp was wisely used by our mother. We had to earn the right to go. –You will both go, if you are obedient, do your school work conscientiously, bring good marks on your school reports - she told us. As the holidays approached, we were making great efforts to meet her expectations. The smallest misbehaviour would result in withdrawal of this promise. But somehow, to our great joy, we always went camping. Of course with many admonitions:- ... don't drink un-boiled water, don't walk in the sun without your cask, be careful of snakes...

But we were drinking that un-boiled water and running in the scorching sun even at noon, when all reasonable natives sheltered in the shade. The heavy cork helmets – inconvenient part of our uniforms – were often conveniently 'forgotten' when going out. We were climbing the old walls of Panhala's palace, swinging on the lianas. Blissfully unaware of the danger, we were walking into the jungle with the thin bamboo stick as the only protection - and nothing happened! Well – practically nothing. There were a few unpleasant adventures, but on the whole we felt safer in that Indian jungle then, than now in London, New York or even Warsaw.

The first training camps in 1944 were attended by the future leaders, but in 1945 all our Girl Guides and Boy Scouts could go camping. In April and May (long school holidays, as dictated by Indian climate) most Troops and Companies could hold individual camps, run by their leaders, all under canvas. Only the huge Brownie and Wolf Cub Camp for 169 boys and girls took place in the old and empty Maharaja's palace, under the eye of Hm. Peszkowski, who also run the Leaders Training Course. In that year 561 young people spent 6795 camping days in Panhala, and in the opinion of the inspectors, Hm. B. Pancewicz and the Delegate of the Ministry of Education, Mr. M. Goławski, it was a very successful action.

The large number of older teenagers in Valivade made our Leaders think of other attractions, so at the end of 1945 they decided to try some rambling camps and hikes. At first this idea met with a lot of opposition from the adult population, but the youngsters were enthusiastic. Hm. Pancewicz wrote about it in the December issue of our newspaper *Polak w Indiach:*

"To wander with the tiny tent in India, see beautiful mountains, covered with a jungle, reach the ocean – so near and never seen by any of us – that would be great! And what a trial of strength of body and character it would be.

But some people oppose it. They invent a rumour: - somebody is said to have received a letter from our settlement in Africa with the news that Polish Girl Guides on a hike were attacked and eaten by wild animals or perhaps cannibals; only few of them survived."

Gossip like that frightened the parents, who forbade their children to take part in a hike. But begging and clamouring of youngsters and persuasion of the Leaders overcame the opposition. In the autumn of 1945 the first three hikes were organised. All three covered the same route: start by train or bus, then 90 km walking through Malkapur and Amba Ghat to Ratnagiri. It was not easy. The Valivade Scouting District had no car yet. Our tents, made of tarpaulin, though small were very heavy, so were the cooking utensils and provision – everything had to be carried on the few bikes, so overloaded, it was difficult to push them up the hills. The days were hot, and the nights surprisingly cold. The native people, unused to seeing white people carrying heavy loads, were plainly astonished. But the surrounding nature was beautiful, we were in high spirits and the white ribbon of the road ahead of us had magnetic draw.

The first pioneers were the Brownie and Wolf Cub Leaders, under the command of dh Ryś - Hm. Peszkowski. From 15th to 22nd October 1945 he led the twelve girls and boys to the ocean. His dog, Bill, an ugly, fat bull terrier, made it too and he took part in all the hikes that followed.

On the 22nd of October the second Hike started – twenty members of the Company Leaders Training Course under the command of Hm. B. Pancewicz and Miss Hanka Handerek. All the hikers wrote diaries, did a reconnaissance of the town of Ratnagiri and produced a map of their walk – 90 km to the scale 1 : 20 000 – a great long ribbon, later displayed at the exhibition on the 35th anniversary of Polish Scouting.

The third Hike that started on the 14th of December 1945 was made by 13 School leavers accompanied by Major L. Naimski, dh Ryś Zuch and of course Bill.

Soon afterwards, on 26th December 1945, Jan Siedlecki with Salesian Brother Jan Orysiuk led a group of 10 Boy Scouts on the first cycling trip – a 77 km. long cycle to Belgaum.

I feel compelled to categorically state here, that none of the wanderers were eaten by wild animals or kidnapped; even the scorpions and monkeys left us alone. Except for the sore feet and sun burned noses, we returned healthy, happy, with gained experience and many new friends.

Therefore next year, in October 1946, there was no opposition, when the extra large hike to Ratnagiri was organised. It was led by dh Ryś; the two groups of Guides and one of Scouts had younger captains: Lala 'Walercia' Wiśniewska, Danka Pniewska and Zenek Kaptur. Even though some participants were younger, the whole trip was easier than the previous ones, as the route was well known to the leaders. With over 50 members of the hike, we had to use larger tents, but fortunately by then our Headquarters bought an ancient lorry, which although loaded with canvas, cooking utensils and provision, could occasionally give lift to an overtired hiker or poor Bill, whose short legs and round belly were badly suited to the long march.

In the period 7th to 16th October 1946 Jurek Augustyn led twenty four Boy Scouts on the cycle trip to Bijapur.

And finally came the most ambitious cycling trip – a pilgrimage to the grave of St. Francis Xavier in Goa, which was then a Portuguese colony. In May 1947 twenty Boy Scouts were led there by Hm. Peszkowski, and accompanied by the spiritual leader Father Jankowski.

Obviously only a small number of youngsters could take part in those hikes and trips, but for the rest of them, numerous Camps and Training Courses under canvas, were organised locally.

The very ambitious plans for 1946 year, which included additional camps for adult members of KPH (Friends of Scouting Association) and for the youngsters not belonging to our organisation, very nearly met with failure, as at short notice, our permit to camp in Panhala was withdrawn. But a new camping ground was found in Chandoli, 41 km from Valivade and 6 km. from the tiny town of Malkapur. It was less convenient, but beautiful, placed on the river bank at the outskirts of a jungle.

In that year's long holidays Rover Scouts and Rangers had no ordinary camps, but could gain the Advanced Badges at the four camps run with the help of the specialists. Those were:

2nd – 20th April 1946 – Training Camp for Signalist – Commandant Barbara Morawska, Instructor St. Dudryk-Darlewski, quartermistresses J. Woźniak and K. Michalak, thirty five campers aged 16 -21.

2nd – 20th April 1946 – Training Camp for Chefs – Commandant Irka Krajewska, instructor Mrs. Maria Wasilewska, Quartermistress Danka Górska, seventeen girls aged 17-20.

22nd April to 4th June – Health Training Course, followed by additional lectures and practice in Valivade Hospital. Commandant Estela Czekierska, quartermistress Lala Wiśniewska, doctors: Feier, Finkler, Tiachow, Tajchner, Wieselberg, mgr. L. Czyński and nurses: M. Jarmułowicz, S. Sudoł, G. Maciejewska. 33 girls aged 16-21.

22nd April to 18th May 1946 – Training Camp in Topography and Cartography Commandant Hm. B. Pancewicz, Instructor W. Wallas, eleven participants. Training continued in Valivade.

KPH membership card

Signalisation course with S. Dudryk-Darlewski

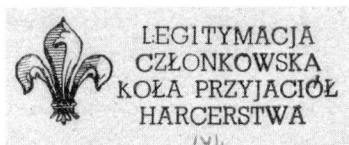

In addition twenty five Senior Boy Scouts took part in a Camp run by both Scoutmasters. Later Hm. Peszkowski ran two camps for so called 'harcownicy' (children aged 11-14) after the famous book about the Warsaw Uprising called 'Ramienie na Szaniec' – 'Stones for the Ramparts' for twenty nine boys, with the help of Jan Siedlecki, and 'Service for Others' camp for thirty seven girls with the help of Lilka Wasiuk and Joanna Chmielowska.

7th - 20th April Danka Pniewska was in charge of the Camp for thirty three Brownies. with the help of Brown Owls M. Małaczyńska, M. Wilczyńska, I. Michalska and Cz. Moniak; and from 22 April to 7 May Ela Woyniłłowicz ran a similar Camp for thirty one Wolf Cubs, with the help of Lila Wasiuk, Alek Błach, Maria Szczyrska and Irka Łosowska and two trainee leaders: Basia Morawska and Witold Olesiak. Those two camps were unusual as they were kept under canvas, which – for children under 11 - is against our rules, but there were

The Cooks' Training Course

no abandoned palaces or any other accommodation available in Chandoli.

A new initiative that year were three camps for the non-members. Thirty parents and teachers attended one from 2nd to 28th May. Another one was made by request of Mrs. Wanda Dynowska for the girls with health problems and the third one for ten students of the Health Care Course. Those camps were the only chance of a respite for many people, as there were no other possibilities available to the majority of Valivade inhabitants. No formal programme was set, but the campers could attend some of the Scouting activities and learn about our methods.

dh Z. Peszkowski, W. Dynowska and dh B. Pancewicz

And finally came the year 1947 – Although the war finished nearly two years earlier, our future was still unsure, making the atmosphere in the settlement fraught with anxiety. Some institutions were closing down; there was a shortage of finances and of people willing to help. But we did manage to have some camping in Chandoli. Danka Pniewska ran first the Brownies Camp then another one for Wolf Cubs – this time we obtained the use of an empty building. It had no doors or window panes, no bathrooms or kitchen, but at least the kids had a roof over their heads, which was as well, as the monsoon came early that year. We had also no adult cooks; meals were prepared on the camp kitchen by the girls from the Rural Management School. For washing the children and their clothes we had to use the river; all drinking water had to be carried in pails from the spring on the other side of the river (there was no bridge!) As I remember it, it was the best Wolf Cub Camp I ever had, but the Pack Leaders were so exhausted, that on the way back the younger or weaker ones fell asleep in the coach full of exited, noisy kids.

Four Boy Scout Troops had individual camps; the First Troop under Leszek Bełdowski gained the best marks – 87 and $^1/_2$ points out of 100 possible. Of the three Girl Guides camps the one under Jagoda Królikowska also attained 87 points.

The Father Skorupka's Troop, run by Jan Siedlecki and Leszek Bełdowski had a very specific character and was under the special care of the Division's Chaplain, Father K. Kozłowski. It was the brand new troop, only

Alter Boys' Camp

organised in May 1947 and all the Scouts in it were also altar boys. According to the Chaplain, they were 'the crème de la crème' and only the very special boys were admitted. Indeed, some of them were special – among them some future priests: Edward Karaś (Father Błażej, Franciscan monk) who later worked in USA and in Lithuania; Krzysztof Kozakiewicz studying for priesthood in Paris and Marian Oleś, who attained the rank of archbishop and served as Papal Nuncio in Kazakhstan and Middle Asia.

All the Ranger Guides had one joint Camp ran by Hm. Peszkowski and Phm. Handerek, while young Company Leaders were in charge of the Patrol Leaders Training Camp. Both those camps are described in the 5th book of Indian Scouting Library 'Kurs Harców i Obóz Wędrowniczek' (Scouting Course and Rangers' Camp). Once more a camp was organised for the members of The Friends of Scouting, and the long holiday finished with the Rest Camp for the Leaders.

For the Guides and Scouts those activities were more than a chance to learn some of the camping lore, gain badges and higher qualifications, get respite from school and over protective parents. It was also a source of adventures, rituals and many emotional moments.

One of those was for a few of us the admission to the exclusive 'Forest Circle' and receiving of special totem names. This ritual, which took place at the day break, after the all night's solitary vigil at a small fire, was only held twice during the 5 years we spent in India. Here are the names of the Circle's members:

1946 A. Handerek, M. Leśniak, E. Czekierska, D. Pniewska

1947 L. Bełdowski, H. Szafrańska, J. Królikowska, Z. Ostrihanska, Fr. K. Kozłowski

To conclude, I wish to stress how valuable those holiday experiences were for us. For the poor refugees, living on the meagre maintenance allowance, increased a little only if a parent was employed in the settlement, or a relative in the army sent an occasional banknote, no private excursions were possible. Nor would they be encouraged by the Settlement Authorities, especially by the English officials. The few English Guest houses were too expensive for us; the Indian ones were then 'out of bounds'.

After the hardships of deportation to Russia and the unsettled life in temporary camps, the Valivade Settlement was an oasis of stability and normality; it was a substitute home. But it had also the qualities of a small provincial town, where everyone knew everybody else and commented on everything they did. It was a tiny Polish ghetto, separated from the real world. Camping was for the younger of us the only chance of escaping the overdose of maternal care and the watchful eyes and ears of the neighbours separated only by the bamboo-mat walls. It was also a chance to see a tiny bit of this strange, exotic country, breathing the cleaner, cooler air, meeting with its fascinating nature, gaining some independence. For the older ones it was a school of leadership, of organising, taking decision, showing initiative. A school of LIFE.

Training

Training of new leaders is always important, but in our situation it was paramount. Children and young people were clamouring to join the movement. The majority of them, if they ever had a chance to enter Scouting in Poland, left it as 'Tenderfoots'. There was acute shortage of trained Leaders. The basic rule of the Scouting method is the upbringing of the young members by their slightly older companions – but those young leaders needed some preparation for their jobs. While in Tehran, Ahwaz and Karachi, some of those, who had any contact at all with Scouting in Poland, tried to organise the units, but in the more stable living conditions in India, we were able to give them proper training.

The new Team

The best place to learn Scouting methods is at a Scouting camp, and therefore most of the Training Courses were organised under canvas. Yet those were necessarily short, mainly for financial reasons, so they had to be followed up by additional sessions in Valivade. That, of course, occasionally collided with our school duties, as for majority of us even Scouting lectures were more attractive than the school lessons.

Some of the courses were intended to develop leadership abilities at all levels; others, aimed at Rover Scouts and Rangers, dealt with gaining 'speciality badges'. Those had threefold aims – gaining teaching abilities, useful in our Scouting work, giving us some idea of jobs we may be doing in our adult life and helping to fill the excess of the free time caused by the lack of other attractions, which were scarce in our small, isolated Settlement.

Our Valivade community consisted of people from different backgrounds, various levels of education, holding a variety of traditions and opinions. Not everybody understood the values of our organisation – so courses and information talks were held for adults, to gain their understanding and support.

The very first Training Course, already mentioned in the previous sections, took place in Panhala between 16th May and 5th June 1944 and was continued for two weeks in Valivade, with 2-5 hours a day of lectures, some practical work and the evening sing-songs. The completion of the course took place on 21st of June. There was a ceremony for handing out the prizes, parade of all troops, companies and packs,

2nd Class Scoutmaster Course

and in the evening our Inspectors entertained some of the former participants and invited guests at a local café. (Our two Scoutmasters were slightly better off financially than the rest of us, as being officers detached from the Polish Army, they were still receiving their army pay.) From the 30 people who finished the Company Leaders' Course, four obtained the top marks: Halina Szafrańska, Estela Czekierska, Irena Hajduk and Irena Krajewska. 25 Guides and Scouts completed the Brownies' and Wolf Cubs' Leaders' Course and top marks were given to Zofia Dudkówna and Ela Woyniłłowicz. There was also a larger Patrol Leaders' Course. As a result of that initial training, 10 Guides obtained the introductory Instructors' rank (przewodniczka). Those were:

H. Szafrańska, I. Krajewska, I. Hajduk, E. Czekierska, S. Ołowiecka (order No. 1 of 21st June1944) and Z. Balawender, H. Szczanowska, I. Idkowiak, J. Królikowska, J. Sipika (order No.2 of 30th July 1944)

Soon afterwards, between the 4th and 8th July, a four-day Information Course was held for school teachers. With the support of the Delegate of Ministry of Education and the School Inspector and with the willing attitude of the participants, this was not only useful but also a very pleasant event.

During the Scouting Inspectors' visit to Karachi from 10th August to 14th September 1944, nine Boy Scouts and forty four Girl Guides took part in the 40-hour Training for Company Leaders, while forty four teachers attended 20-hour long Information Course.

Originally the Visiting Team was expected to stay in India for six months only, so the paramount necessity was to train some local Guiders and Scoutmasters. The course for the 2nd class Instructors (Phm.) was held between 11th and 31st October 1944, again in Panhala, but this time under canvas. We were supplied with heavy army tents, suitable for eight inhabitants each. Twenty five members of the course included four teachers. It was run by Hm. B. Pancewicz, Hm. Z. Peszkowski, and Dr. M. Wysocka, while M. Kądzielawa acted as quartermaster.

The inexperience of the participants and the great extent of material to be learned in such a short time required a murderous tempo of work. Miss A. Handerek, one of the teachers, wrote in her diary on 15th of October: - For two days I found no time to write the diary. The day before yesterday the night exercises in the Morse signals did not end until 11 p.m. We send a message to the Lone Wolf: "All the wolves are now asleep, why aren't you?". It helped - he let us go to bed.

The programme of this course included:

1) Scouting techniques and skills

2) Methods of working with Brownies and Wolf Cubs, younger Guides and Scouts, Rover Scouts and Rangers.

3) Leadership, drill, issuing commands.

4) Planning the work for Districts and Division

5) Rules of the organisation

6) Bibliography – (Reviews of 11 books were required)

Twenty participants completed the course successfully, the remaining five were allowed to repeat the examination at a later date.

The Camp ended with a night walk, in full gear, to Valivade. The last moments were described in Camp's chronicle by Halina Rafał:

…"With anxiety and impatience we were awaiting the results of the Course, to be read at the final roll-call, which was supposed to take place at 4.00 p.m. Knapsacks packed, we were finishing dismantling the tents, when suddenly heavy rain fell. The only tent still standing was soon packed with wet people and their belongings. Water came under the tent's sides and its roof, heavy with water, touched our heads.

There was no roll-call. The results were read to us after supper, which was lucky for some of us, as nobody could see the faces, when unfavourable results were heard. The flag was slowly lowered from the mast for the last time. Panhala – until then so full of life – was now abandoned. At 11.00 p.m. came the command: Knapsacks on! Column form! March!

We were marching briskly. The air was full of the fragrance of unknown flowers. Full moon… I didn't feel tired, because the night was so beautiful, like the one in The Thousand Nights' Fables. The words of our songs were repeated by echo, then carried by the wind far away. Perhaps it will carry them as far as our country, perhaps they will be repeated by the wind in Polish Tatra mountains?

Past Kolhapur we stopped for an hour's rest, then marched again. At 7.00 a.m. we have reached Valivade. Our loud singing woke the inhabitants; some of them run out to see what was happening. After a few more songs, we dispersed, eager to have some rest, to gain strength for further work. Work does not frighten us, we know that we are working for Poland. Poland is our aim, towards which we march".

Those words may now sound too pathetic, but then, in that distant, fascinating, exotic country, all our thoughts were always turned towards Poland. And not only during the romantic night marches or campfires, but even on the realistic, more practical level. For example we can read in the Equipment Instructions prepared by Hm. Pancewicz on 25th Nov. 1944: "…When using or storing equipment, keep in mind saving, conservation and control… We have to strive to keep our equipment in a sufficiently good state to be taken with us for further use in Poland". Our fervent hopes of return to our motherland were not fulfilled, but the constant nagging of our Scoutmaster must have had some effect, because many years later, while camping in the Polish Scouts grounds in Wales, GB, I found there our faithful friends, old tents from India, still serving our younger generation.

And gaining that equipment was not easy. The first tents, bought just before that Training Course, arrived late and were being pitched in a great hurry and incompetently, since it was the first time we had to do it. My patrol, consisting mainly of the Brown Owls, was even less

Handing over the tents, in the middle dh Valivadecar and dh Ryś

competent than the others. We have pitched our tent in a picturesque spot, but right over a path leading from the steep hill. Before we had time to dig the rain channels around it, there came one of those sudden torrential Indian storms. The path turned into a stream, running through the centre of our tent. Some boys ran with their spades to help redirect the stream, while the rest of us tried to save our clothes, books and notes from the deluge.

Thanks to the endless efforts of our Scoutmasters, the equipment stores increased. American War Relief Service NCWC gave us Rs 10 000. Both Delegates offered some help and later so did the Committee for the Help to Refugees in India. Soon we had about 30 tents, kitchen utensils and other camping equipment, signalling tools and apparatus for topographic exercises, a typewriter and duplicator, and even two cars: Ford saloon and a light Chevrolet pick-up. For the children of deportees, who a few months earlier possessed nothing except some rags on their body, these were unheard of treasures, and looking after them taught us responsibility and economy.

Before leaving India in 1947/48, some of our tents were given to our Indian brother Scouts. Some we took with us. On every ship taking Polish refugees to England there was a group of Guides and Scouts. The appointed leader of that group was responsible for delivering the transported equipment to our companies already existing in England.

In December 1944 Advanced Course for Patrol Leaders lasted ten days and the first of the three-monthly courses of typing was initiated. Twenty-minute lessons held three times a week were attended by thirty six Rangers working toward Office Worker's Badge. (This was hardly adequate for practicing – but the typewriters were a scarce commodity in the settlement and were in great demand.)

In 1945, during the seven-week long tour of other Polish settlements, our Scoutmasters organised two more Training Courses:

From 26th January to 2nd February 1945 the Information Course for teachers took place in Balachadi nr. Jamnagar, during which twenty teachers and people from the Administration of that Settlement listened to lectures about the ideology and methods of Scouting and took part in the practical sessions as well as campfires and sing-songs organised for the youngsters. This was viewed very favourably by its participants, as confirmed by this extract from the written assessment made on the last day. ...The visit of the two Scoutmasters brought a lot of fresh air, new thoughts and beautiful moments to our isolated, small community and gave us an incentive to improve our qualifications and our approach to the work with children – wrote one person. Those words confirm once more, that not only for us, but for the whole Polish community in India, Scouting was a great help in filling inadequacies in the rather monotonous life in refugee Settlements.

The above course was just an addition to the Courses for Company Leaders, Patrol Leaders, Brownie and Wolf Cubs

Car maintanence course: B. Czaykowski, F. Herzog, W. Olesiak, A. Błach, J. Chrząszczewski and J. Leśniak

Leaders, which were the main reason for the Scoutmasters' visit. Some Rangers, who came for a holiday from a convent school in Panchgani, also took part in this training.

During the shorter visit they made to the Transit Camp in Karachi between 8th and 13th February 1945, the Scoutmasters organised conferences for parents, teachers and other adult helpers. The Course for Brownie and Wolf Cub leaders was also held.

On their return to Valivade, our unflagging Instructors started two Motorcar Courses – one for the Scouts and another for the adults. The financial help for them come from the Delegate of the Welfare Ministry, Mr. St. Dudryk-Darlewski, himself an old Scout. The shortage of petrol reached India although it was distant from the theatres of war, and motor cars were also in short supply in the Settlement, so a large part of the courses was spent at lectures and in the workshop of the 'Zgoda' Cooperative, under the care of Mr. Kurowski, where the participants learned the use of various tools and parts of the engine. Four Girl Guides and twelve Boy Scouts completed this course. The second one was run in 1946, but by then we had our own vehicles, so more practical driving was possible. One of those who finished it with merit was the future East Africa Safari Rally champion, Zbyszek Nowicki.

The third Company Leaders Course from 7th to 22nd October 1945 was three-fold: - a camp in Panhala, seven-day hike to Ratnagiri and three-day 'open camp' as a part of an Exhibition on 35th anniversary of Polish Scouting.

1946 – January and February – new year of training efforts started with Patrol Leaders Course in Balachadi. Then during the long school break, among other camps in the new camping grounds in Chandoli, four specialist camps for Rangers were organised, already described in the previous chapter.

Front row: M. Goławski (head of PCK), sister W. Łaguna (from Bombay), sister H. Kucharska (PCK - Pol. Red X) and other doctors

In 1947 Hm. Pancewicz was recalled to the Army, but the eight young Guiders newly promoted, helped Hm. Peszkowski to run the organisations. After closure of Polish Settlements in Balachadi and Karachi, the number of young Guides and Scouts in Valivade increased, so the Patrol Leaders training was a priority. Two courses were organised – one under canvas in Chandoli and another one in Valivade. Inside the Settlement there were several 'specialist' courses for the Rangers: Dr. Tomanek ran the Health Service one, Irka Snastin conducted a second typing course with additional bookkeeping practice run by Mr. Z. Sikorski. The Rangers preparing for their advance level cookery badge had some practical training, working in the kitchens of the orphanage or in the Cooperative dining rooms. The signalists and the topographers had to work alone.

In the second part of year 1947 and the beginning of 1948 the gradual liquidation of Valivade began. First transports of refugees went to Poland, England and Australia. All training action stopped - but the knowledge and experience gained in India, many of us used in the new locations for many years.

OTHER ACTIVITIES

Carrying chairs

Weekly meeting, campfires, camps and hikes did not use up all of our time and energy. Recognized as 'organisation of special significance' we had to take part in every activity of the Polish Settlements in India. So we had to sell tickets for cultural events, carry and arrange chairs for all sorts of meetings, welcome Bishops and other dignitaries visiting our Settlements, take part in various parades, patriotic celebrations and religious processions, help to run common rooms and a lot more. In February 1944 we ran a collection for the Polish War prisoners and handed Rs 599 to the Delegate in Bombay.

One of the more outstanding events was the blessing of our Banners. On the 23rd April 1946 – St. George's Day, patron saint of Scouts – the five Tribes in Valivade got beautiful green Banners. It was a solemn occasion, first a Holy Mass and the blessing, then putting in the commemorative badges by sponsors and important visitors, then the inevitable march past – the usual part of our festivities.

On the 12th of May same year a similar occasion took place in Balachadi – the Banner of the 6th Tribe being blessed in the presence of His Highness, Maharaja of Jamnagar, who made a beautiful oration ending with the words:- I will for ever remain loyal to Poland, and always be interested in the future of your country. I feel confident that Poland will regain freedom and you will return to your happy homes, to your country free from foreign aggression. (Skaut No. 8-9, 1945.)

Among the numerous patriotic festivities, occasionally a more intimate one happened. Such a happy, family occasion

Pancewicz' Wedding

for all Valivade Guides and Scouts was the wedding of the senior of our two Inspectors, Hm. Bronisław Pancewicz with Miss Janina Rymar. After a few weeks of preparations, all of us attended the Church ceremony; the reception was held in "Marna Dziupla" (the Brownie and Wolf Cub Leaders' hideout) and one of the wedding presents the young couple received, was a large tablecloth, embroidered by several Brown Owls.

Less than a year later, our 'Lone Wolf' – no longer lone – celebrated 25th anniversary of his joining the Scouting Movement. This time the celebrations took place during the holidays in Chandoli. Soon after the reveille a crowd of the campers with presents and congratulations arrived at his tent. An even happier occasion for celebration came a few months later, when a brand new 'Wolf Cub', Arthur, joined the Pancewicz family. To his Christening ceremony he was carried by young godparents: Troop Leader Leszek Bełdowski and Brown Owl Halina Strycharz, and he was given a cub scarf as one of his christening presents.

The most important Scouting event in Valivade was the 35th Anniversary of Polish Scouting. It started in the late evening of 30th October 1945 with the roll call of the Scouts killed in action in the two World Wars. Next day crowds of Valivade inhabitants gathered at the celebratory Holy Mass, followed by the inevitable march past. The Jubilee Exhibition in the local theatre, although prepared with the modest means, illustrated the achievements of the movement. The only available materials – navy blue blankets (standard issue to all refugees' households) and white paper – were used in an imaginative and creative manner, as a background to many exhibits: Brownies' and Wolf Cubs' totems, Girl Guides' and Scouts' logbooks and chronicles, handiworks and photographs. In the evening a great Jubilee camp-fire was staged at the main square of the settlement. We sat not in the usual circle, but forming the shape of Polish pre-war borders, inside which small fires were lit in memory of the towns most connected with the history of our organisation, like Warsaw, Lwów and so on. During the three days of the Jubilee an open camp was held at the outskirts of the settlement, Polish films were shown in the cinema and the last day was taken over by Brownies and Wolf Cubs, organising games and sing-songs for everybody.

Blessing of the Flags

Although each Tribe had a room in the school building and the Akelas and Brown Owls had their Marna Dziupla abode, there was no place in which the teenagers from different troops and companies could mingle. So the Wanderers Club was created. Opened on the 9th of August 1945, it occupied one set of ordinary family quarters – just two rooms. The larger one was converted into a meeting room, with tables, chairs and – a great luxury! – a few armchairs! The smaller one held a well endowed library (books and newspapers were still a luxury to us). In the tiny kitchenette tea could be made. It is hard to imagine now, what a delight it gave us, to escape from our Spartan living quarters, forget the domestic and school duties, and settle in one of those armchairs to listen to records and interesting talks, take part in discussions or simply, for a while be a member of the chosen elite, to whom all those wonderful treasures belonged.

But there was no rigid membership to this club – everybody could use it. At first it was managed by Jadzia Wojniłowicz from the Flame of the Jungle Senior Members unit, and she made everybody welcome. One of our Rangers so described the Club in the ZHP in the East Bulletin of 1st January 1947:

...."Hidden in the ordinary living block, this Club could not be found by the uninitiated. No sign board, no outside announcement... Yet all the young people know the place where Wanderers Club is. They know where to find the key to open its door, if the Club is closed. It is not surprising – the club is for the youngsters, they are its hosts. The inside is simple, but nice. The few decorations are mostly symbolic: Scout emblem, Polish eagle, map of Poland, a string of shells from Ratnagiri... but there is a real Scouting atmosphere".

Seniors' Club

Not all our actions were patriotic, emotional or entertaining. Dh Pancewicz tried to install in us the sense of resourcefulness, self sufficiency and practicality. He taught us how to look after our equipment, and how to earn the necessary finances, without which our work could not be carried out. Looking for our own, independent source of income, he organised two Scout shops, under the common name Commission for Scout Supplies. The first one was opened in Valivade in September 1945, and the second in Balachadi in February 1946. Halina Szafrańska, who managed the Valivade shop, wrote about it :-

"In some questionnaire I wrote that my interests are psychology and commerce; perhaps that was the reason I was invited to run our shop with the help of a few Guides from the Commercial School. I took it over on 4th November 1946 in the presence of Major Naimski, member of the Commission. We were selling mainly haberdashery, school materials, some fabrics and ivory figurines from Trivandrum, which were readily bought as souvenirs from India. Sometimes I brought from Bombay a few pounds of beautiful apples, imported from Kashmir, but because of a high price, I sold them singly. There were plenty of bananas, mangoes and oranges in the Indian market, but there were always people ready to pay more for an apple whose shape, taste and smell reminded them of Poland.

The supplies for the shop I bought in Bombay every two weeks or so, with the help of our Guides studying there. Mrs. Bronisława Zbyszewska did the book-keeping and helped with pricing the articles and the Rangers preparing for the Office workers' badge, helped with serving the customers and doing paper work. Our shop was open from 9.00 a.m. to 6.00 p.m. with a short lunch break. Every month I had to carry out stocktaking and write a monthly report, then I would receive my salary. The gradual liquidation of Valivade settlement started in October 1947. No longer did I go to Bombay, small supplies were brought from Kolhapur; only the ivory figurines, now eagerly purchased for souvenirs, I still had to order. Finally the shop was closed in the middle of December 1947".

That was the way our practical and sensible Commissioner tried to prepare us for the future adult life, while at the same time gain a small but constant independent income for the Scouting community.

In 1947 we were also entrusted with looking after the Farm previously belonging to the Agricultural School. Each company of Girl Guides or Boy Scouts was given a plot to cultivate under the guidance of a School Leaver Guide. Tomatoes, lettuce, papayas and fragrant tuberoses we raised, were gladly purchased by the Valivade's inhabitants.

W KRĘGU PRACY
KRÓTKI ZARYS GEOGRAFII INDII
PRACA
wędrowniczek i skautów
WIELCY MYŚLICIELE INDII
APTECZKA
NAUCZYCIEL
KURS HARCÓW i OBÓZ WĘDROWNICZY
INDIE w Walce o Wolność
Kalendarz Harcerza w Indiach 1947
GEOGRAFIA INDII
KRAJ, LUDZIE
Gospodarstwo
Czuwaj!

Motiff from Mlodzi

Publications

There is a saying that when two Poles find themselves somewhere, three political parties will be borne. I don't know whether that is true, but definitely they will start a newspaper. After the long period of intellectual starvation in the Soviet Union, all of us were longing for the printed word – so new Polish periodicals were appearing all the time. As soon, as the Delegates of Polish Government in Exile opened their offices in some of the Russian towns, they started receiving Polish papers, printed by the Army – in insufficient numbers, shared by many people, read avidly and passed to others, or even copied by hand to be sent to the less fortunate compatriots, who did not manage yet to leave the villages or forest camps.

In Tehran and later in India we had greater access to the Polish Press. The records of the School Supplies section in the Ministry of Education Delegate's office in Bombay show several titles of periodicals delivered to our Settlements. From August 1943 we were receiving *Skaut* - the monthly paper edited by the Headquarters of the Polish Scouting in the East, and some precious Scouting textbooks, reprinted in Palestine or in England. The fortnightly *Polak w Indiach* published in Bombay often printed reports of our activities; so did the Skaut, but it did not satisfy our yearnings – we needed to print our own paper.

TO PRINT – it sounds wonderful! In fact we had a few desolate typewriters and an old duplicating machine, christened 'Bazyli'. Typing articles on wax stencils was not too difficult, but scratching the illustrations with a needle was a strenuous business. So was the duplicating – many hours spent handling our ancient Bazyli, often ended in tears, when the overworked machine broke down in the middle of an urgent job. But what a lot of satisfaction this work gave to the budding Scouting journalists!

All our papers and most of the books written in India were done on this primitive machine. Some booklets we were allowed to print ourselves in the Settlement's print shop. Oh yes, the Settlement did possess a print shop, and there were some real, professional printers. They were very critical of our efforts, when some of the older Guides were sent there to learn printing and type-setting. (Our Scoutmasters believed that prospective editors should know all aspects of bringing the printed word to the reader.) I attended such a course with Danka Czech and Irka Adamczyk, members of the editing committee of our paper *Młodzi*. We were taught the now forgotten art of type-setting by hand and preparing the pages for the ancient printing machine. I am still treasuring the diploma with the overall marks 'satisfactory' – I suppose 'good' applied only to the chief printer, and 'very good' - To God?

Młodzi – that was our baby, our pride! It was a Scouting paper in so far as it was run by, and for, Girl Guides and Boy Scouts, but it had literary and social ambitions. In theory it was edited by the Senior Section members, but as there were very few of them and not always residing in Valivade, in practice everybody had to help. For example No. 25 was prepared by the Brownie and Woolf Cub Leaders, from No. 26 Danka Czech became its editor and was helped by a group of older Rangers; the last 5 issues were edited by Maria Leśniak.

Variety of subjects were undertaken: actual problems of those difficult times, scarce news from Poland, poems – our own first attempts alongside the reprints of the Polish classics (Books were still in short supply), reminiscences of past events. Now and then some gossip or funny stories from our camps, but humorists were scarce among us; the high idealistic and patriotic tones were prevailing.

The editorial in the first issue of *Młodzi*, which appeared on 24th of June 1945, stated the aims of the paper:

"...The reason for this paper's existence comes from the young people's need for expressing their thoughts and wishes. Youth has energy, willingness, strength and creativity (...) The old world, devastated by the war, is falling to pieces. To the young people will fall the duty of its rebuilding. The future will depend on us – we have to prepare for it. We have to fight with the apathy and the sluggishness of refugees' life. It is not enough to remember the past and dream of the future, talk of heroic acts and empty patriotism... We have to learn, to train, to get ourselves ready for acting, when our chance comes".

Favourable reviews in *Polak w Indiach* and letters to the editor confirm that *Młodzi* (The Young Ones) were read and appreciated not only by the youngsters. Around it a large group of enthusiasts formed, which extended its functions far outside the editing of the paper. Literary evenings were organised in the Wanderers Club, a great ball was arranged on 15th February 1947 to gain finance for the paper, and its 2nd anniversary was celebrated by a tea party and a very hot discussion.

The last issue appeared with the date 27 November 1947. The closing down Editorial signed Atom-Zuch (Marysia Leśniak, future sister Maria Benedicta, the Mother Superior of the Holy Family of Nazareth Convent in Rome) was written on board of Empire Brent ship in Bombay which was carrying the second transport of soldiers' families to England. Entitled: - Farewell to the Settlement it read:

... Usually, when a certain phase of our work is finished, past events - more or less important – come back to our minds. When we say goodbye to somebody, we remember our first meeting, the first, often very vivid impressions left by that person. And today, when preparing the last issue of our paper, I recall that unforgettable day of 'great council' in the first days of June 1945 – heated discussion about the paper's name, its graphic look – not its contents, about that we were sure from the beginning. We understood the young people's yearning for a platform, on which they could express their thoughts and wishes and we wanted to provide it.

All that is behind us – a new life opens before us. We will meet new people, new ideas... maybe they will suggest we should look for ease and convenience, drop the not always pleasant responsibilities... We have to be ready to judge them; to be able to distinguish the good ones from the bad. We have to remember that behaving badly is easy, but nothing to be proud of
...

March Past on 3rd May 1946: L. Bełdowski

Młodzi started a chain of other papers. In August 1945 the monthly *'W Kręgu Pracy'*

(Leaders Council's Bulletin) was initiated by Hm. Pancewicz, containing instructions and materials helpful to Company and Troop Leaders. A variety of subjects were covered: scouting ideology, child psychology, education. At first it carried an Information Supplement, about the actual political situation, but it was discontinued after seven issues, as a similar leaflet was issued by the Cultural Section of Camp's Administration.

Smaller circulation, but an interesting format had the quarterly paper *W Kręgu Rady* for the Brownie and Wolf Cubs Leaders, edited with the help of dh Peszkowski.

All those papers were sent to other Polish Scouting centres in Africa, Palestine, New Zealand and England.

Besides these periodicals, a small publishing company named **Indyjska Biblioteczka Harcerska** (The Polish Scouting Library in India) brought out several books and booklets, of which only some survived. The ones we were able to trace are listed here:

No.1 – *Apteczka polowa* (First Aid Field Kit) by Dr. Maria Wysocka, 31 pages, 1946

No.2 – *Apteczka dla obozów harcerskich* (First Aid for Scouting Camps) – by L. Czyński MA Pharm. 1946

No.5 – *Kurs harców I obóz wędrowniczek* (Scouting Course and Rangers' Camp) – 71 pages - 1947

No.6 – *Krótki zarys geografii Indii* (Geography of India in a Nut-shell) by A.Dudryk-Darlewski - 24 pages with 6 photos and a map of India – 1947

No.7 – *Praca Skautów and Wędrowniczek* (The work with Rangers and Rover Scouts) – 221 pages, 1947

The last two positions were actually PRINTED by youngsters in the camp's printing works. All the previous efforts were, like our periodicals, done on a duplicating machine. Poor quality of paper available to us then, makes the few surviving copies hard to read, but they are kept as relics of our hard work.

In addition, there were three other interesting publications,

Editorial board: A. Handerek, D. Pniewska, H. Szafrańska, M. Leśniak, Z. Ostrihanska, J. Królikowska, E. Czekierska, Fr.. K. Kozłowski, Hm. Z. Peszkowski

a) A small folding album of photos representing Valivade Settlement. The first edition of 420 albums made in September 1945 was sold so fast, it had to be reprinted a year later.

b) Scout's Diary 1947 – printed by Shree Laxmi Narayan Press in Bombay, which included some short but useful information about Scouting, Poland, and Polish War Effort.

c) Two postal stamps value 1 ½ As.

In the present day, when even school children have a free access to computers, it is difficult to perceive the amount of effort and hard work it took our instructors to organise the above action. But the participation in editing and publishing gave many of us a lot of satisfaction. It nurtured a few future writers, giving them a chance to try their abilities. It also taught us that pen can be as useful as a gun in a fight for ideals, if you can use it well. And although our efforts may not have been a great literary achievement, they remain as a trace of our life, and our personalities.

Brother Scouts

Scouting is an International Youth Movement. When it started in England, Poland – divided among the three occupying neighbours – was non-existent on maps of Europe. But the news about the new organisation reached the town Lwów, where a young man, Andrzej Małkowski, working as a leader in the youth associations 'Eleusis' and 'Zarzewie', was given Baden Powell's book *'Scouting for Boys'* to translate. The idea of international brotherhood enchanted him and other youth leaders – and in the autumn of 1910 the first experimental troop of Polish Scouts was organised as a subsidiary to the sports organisation *'Sokół'*.

Amongst the Indian Scouts: L. Bełdowski, Z. Nowicki, S. Ucinek, D. Pniewska, J. Orysiuk, Z. Balawender, Fr.. K. Kozłowski, Hm. Z. Peszkowski, A. Handerek, Z. Ostrihanska, E. Czekierska and M. Leśniak

In 1913, at the first Jamboree in Birmingham, the thirty four Polish boys marched under the Polish flag. The Occupiers objected – but Baden Powell, who earlier met and liked Małkowski, was adamant. They were Scouts, they were Polish – they had the right to participate as such.

During the twenty years between the two world wars Polish Scoutmasters and Guiders, especially Olga Małkowska, Andrzej's widow, took active part in organising the International Bureaus.

Fervent believers in that international brotherhood, we found it hard to accept that there were first and second class brothers. Those of us who learned sufficient English, read with dismay that Scouts in British India were not allowed to use 2 m. bamboo poles, an essential part of English Scouts' uniform, because in the eyes of Imperial officials, a bamboo in the hands of an Indian, was considered to be a weapon. British authorities in our refugee settlements were very helpful when arranging meetings with the English Scouts in Karachi, but were not so pleased, when we wanted similar contacts with the Indians. It is easier to understand it now – India was pressing for independence, the situation was fraught with anxiety and even the Polish Authorities were not encouraging us to fraternize with local people. In February 1943 Polish ambassador Poniński warned consul Banasiński in Bombay against allowing Polish emigrants …to manifest tactless pro-Indian sentiments … show solidarity, even if only by word, with the anti-British opposition which is harming the Allied war effort and therefore delaying the victory over Germany, for which our country is eagerly waiting. (The Indian Congress opposed the use of Indian soldiers in the war with Germany.)

But those political arguments left us cold. Baden-Powell taught us that all Scouts were brothers, so we managed to get in touch with the local organisation and kept friendly contacts for the whole period of our stay in India. The popular Scoutmaster in Kolhapur, Mr. Valivadecar, often organised meetings in the town, and also visited us in Valivade, sometimes bringing his own 'family troop' of several children, all dressed in Scout uniforms. Some time later contact was also made with the teacher's college in Rukadi, where the headmaster and many students were Scouts. We met for common games, parades and camp-fires. The main problem was the lack of a common language – Indian Scouts used English with some difficulty, their Guides practically didn't, and our English was not very fluent either. But we managed to communicate quite well.

Our situation of 'white, non-English' sometimes caused funny incidents. Once dh Pancewicz took several company leaders on a coach trip to Malvan, a small fishermen's village on the Indian Ocean. It was March 1946 – a period of intensive striving for India's independence. In every village we were passing, Gandhi's supporters held meetings. Our driver

Some of the Leaders with Indian friends in Bijapur: E. Woyniłłowicz, A. Handerek, I. Piotrowicz, I. Hajduk, I. Adamczyk, M. Leśniak, D. Czech and D. Pniewska

kept abandoning the coach and running to the meeting, but despite our entreats, he would not take us with him, thinking it would be dangerous. But on one occasion he asked us whether we would give a lift to some people who wanted to join another meeting in the next village. There was some room in the coach, so we agreed. Dozens of youngish men filled the coach and even hung on the outside steps. For a while they looked at us in silence, then a more adventurous one shouted: "English, go home!"- others joined him. We had nothing against it – we were waiting eagerly for the occupiers to leave our own country – so we had joined in the chorus. Consternation, dismay – then frantic efforts to explain in English, Polish and Marathi ... From the meeting in the next village our new friends brought us souvenirs – a slip of orange-white-green material with the Gandhist' emblem: the wheel of a spinning loom, symbol of Mahatma's ideas: nonviolent opposition and home industry. Wearing those emblems for the rest of the trip, we became objects of interest and curiosity. But we were ordered to take them off before entering Valivade – our Commissioner was afraid they might give a heart attack to the Camp's Authorities.

On the 9th of August 1947 we had a large camp-fire with the Indian Scouts from Kolhapur and Rukadi, as it was the day on which the first after-war Jamboree opened in France. The Jamboree to which Polish Scouting was not invited. (ZHP in Poland, under communist regime of our eastern neighbours, was not a member of WOSM; the ZHP in Exile was not recognized by them.)

15th of August was a happier occasion – India finally gained Independence. On the eve of this solemn day we were celebrating with our happy brothers in Rukadi; but on the very day they joined us for the great ceremony in Valivade. They understood that our happiness could not be complete, as confirmed by the many entries in our journals.

Before leaving India, we handed some of our equipment to the local Scouts. Fifty years later, when visiting Kolhapur with a group of friends for the unveiling of our monument in Mahavir Gardens, I was showing some old photographs to the journalists. One of them noticed Mr. Valivadecar in one of the pictures. – Look – he shouted, pointing at his neighbour – he is here!. I looked – indeed, there he stood, looking not a year older than 50 years ago! Of course, it was Mr. Valivadecar junior, whom we must have seen as a baby-Scout visiting us with his late father. And when visiting our beloved Panhala, we came across a training camp for Indian Guiders. This time there were no barriers, we could speak and sing together!

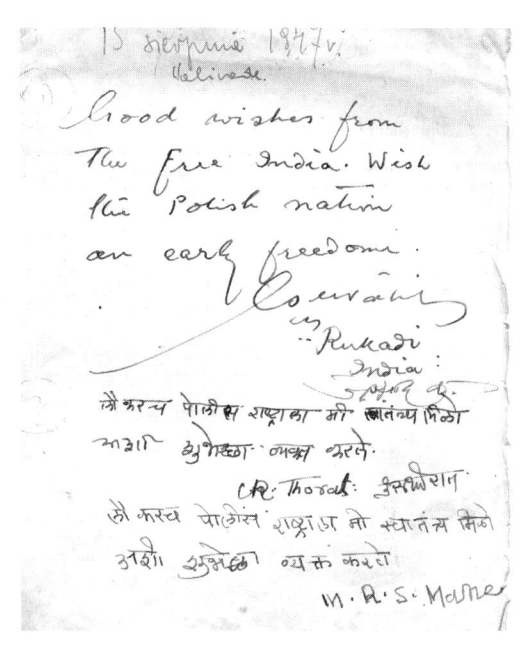

OUR LEADERS

Phm. Witold Bidakowski was the first qualified Polish Scoutmaster in India. As an invalid, unable to serve in the army, he dedicated his time, energy and knowledge to serving the Polish children. He organised Scouting units first in Persia (Iran), later in the transit camps Country Club and Malir in India, and finally in Valivade, where in the first few months, he organised single handed a coeducational Scouting and Guiding District. By ZHP in the East Order No. 27/43 of 20th September 1943, he was nominated the District Commissioner. Unfortunately his contacts with this august body were not very cordial; they resented his drive for independence and lack of subordination. [7] As a result, all the contacts with the Command in Palestine went through the Delegate of the Ministry of Education, Mr. M. Goławski.

After the arrival of the Visiting Team, Mr. Bidakowski gradually decreased his involvement in Scouting activities. Finally, in July 1944 he resigned from his function and left Valivade for Jamnagar. In both settlements he worked in various different Committees, e.g. Parish Committee in Valivade. After the war he settled in Great Britain, worked in a factory.

He did not return to the Scouting Movement.

Father Kazimierz Bobrowski Hm., in spite of his many duties as the head of the Polish Catholic Mission for India, often found time to help us in the first, difficult period of organising Valivade District, We remember him best from the first camp in Panhala. His Scouting totem name was Black Lion and he had a large repertoire of jolly songs. He was another controversial person – well liked and popular, but difficult to fit in the framework of the organisation. After leaving India for USA he did not resume his contacts with Polish Scouting.

Mrs. Janka Ptakowa was the first Guider to get her Polish leadership credentials in India.

She was given the Phm. Diploma by the ZHP in the East Order 31, dated 10 January 1944. You will find more about this charming and very popular Guider, in the chapter on Balachadi, where she did invaluable work organising the first Scouting units and acting as a sort of collective mother to dozens of Polish orphans. When the orphanage moved to Valivade, her special bond with those children continued, but she also helped them to integrate with the population of that larger, and to them rather strange community.

Young leaders: - After the Instructors' Training Course organised by the Visiting Team in October 1944, the following young Guiders received the Phm. grade of Leadership: Z. Balawender, E. Czekierska, Z. Ostrihanska, H. Szafrańska, (ZHP in East Order No.1 -2.3.1046) and A. Handerek, M. Janiszewska, E. Woyniłłowicz (ZHP in East Order No.2 29.11.1946)

Father Kazimierz Kozłowski, S. J. arrived in Valivade on 25th October 1946. Previously engaged as a Polish Army Chaplain and a District Commissioner in The Polish Cadet School in Palestine, he was sent to India to help our overworked priests. An experienced Scoutmaster, he was invaluable to our community. Besides his pastoral duties and the teaching job, he managed to find time to act not only as the Chaplain for our Scouting units, but also as an active Instructor and Leader, accompanying us to camps, conferences and training courses. When the other two Scoutmasters were recalled to the Army, he was left to carry on the Scouting work with the remnants of the community. After the closure of Valivade, he settled in Africa as a missionary.

The people mentioned above are all gratefully remembered by their charges. Some of the others deserve a fuller mention.

Hm., Bronisław Pancewicz - Druh Bronek - 'The Lone Wolf' - was born in Warsaw on 2nd February 1907. He joined the 40th Cyprian Godebski Troop on 17th April 1921 and on the 15th October same year made his Promise. And as he promised, for the next 62 years of his life he served God, Poland and other people. From his earliest years he tried to organise others and be useful: he helped his sisters with their homework, looked after the family pets, and even when camping with his Troop, he found time to visit his family at their summer country retreat and install the wireless aerial, to enable the whole village to listen to the radio.

He was a Patrol Leader and a Troop Leader in Warsaw, then as a member of the County Executive Committee in Łódz, was responsible for the work with village troops and the programmes for the Rover Scouts. He took part in many camps, hikes, training courses and was a member of the Polish contingent at the Jamboree in Netherlands in 1938.

He studied Lacteal (Dairy) Sciences, but also finished the military college. Like most of us, he was arrested, deported to the Soviet Union, and after release, joined the Polish Army in Buzułuk as a Lieutenant. When the army left Russia, he was detached to the ZHP in the East HQ as a programme maker for older Scouts.

On arrival in India, besides his administrative duties: organising the scattered units, finding finances for equipment, negotiating with English and Polish authorities - he concentrated mainly on the programmes for senior Guides, of which there were many.

At that time, when compared with his Deputy – the romantic, young, full of adventurous plans 'Brave Lynx' – he appeared to some of us too 'down to earth'. But when I met him some years later in England, as a mature Guider, I could fully appreciate his understanding of young people, absolute faithfulness and sincerity, when dealing with various problems, and deep commitment to the Scouting movement. He also possessed common sense, rather unusual among some of our idealistic, but impractical dreamers.

That does not mean he was not romantic – in his own way. He was convinced that sooner or later, we will be able to return to free Poland and tried to prepare us for that. He held an exalted vision of a Polish woman – patriotic, maternal and loyal - and was searching for such a partner for himself. It was not a long search. Shortly after their arrival in Valivade he noticed his future wife in the settlement's dining room. –"Look – he said to his colleague – that slim, blond girl, is she not the type from Rodziewiczówna's novel?" (Rodziewiczówna was a well known romantic novelist.) Not so long later, we were organising a huge Scouting wedding for the pair.

After the demobilization and settlement in England, Pancewicz, together with some friends, bought a large Cobalden Farm in Connington, Cambridgeshire and started hard work of the farmer. His slim Rodziewiczówna's lady turned into a hard working farmer's wife and tried to combine the duties of land girl, mother of three children and the hostess to many Scouting events taking place on their farm. After years of striving to make the farm profitable, it was leased out and dh Bronek took not much more lucrative, but physically easier job, of a school teacher in Peterborough. Till the end of his life he was a member of the Polish Scouts Abroad HQ, attended various training courses and conferences and wrote manuals and books, among others *How the Rover Scouts Work*, published in 1980 and *Polish Scouting in India* in 1977. Death interrupted his work on the last project: *Polish Scouting in Africa*. He died on 19th March 1983. A small group of his former charges followed his coffin on that wet March day.

Monsignor Zdzisław Peszkowski, Hm. - Druh Ryś, - 'Lynx' - was born in Sanok on 23rd August 1918. At school - as he told us - he was not a very studious pupil, because there were so many other things that interested him more. One of them was Scouting, especially the Cub Scouts. Under the guidance of the famous Cub Instructor, Alexander Kamiński, he specialised in the work with youngest section of our Movement. So dedicated to this work was he, that even when attending the Military Officers College, he organised a Wolf Cub Pack for the children of the staff.

In 1939 he joined the Jan Sobieski's 20th Regiment of Cavalry in Rzeszów. On the 20th of September together with other officers he was taken captive by the Soviet forces and imprisoned in Kozielsk. His captivity in Kozielsk he remembers with sentiment – in the midst of very hard conditions he met wonderful people among his co-prisoners; many older officers whose conversations and clandestinely organised lectures broadened his mind. When he was transferred with a small group of officers to another camp in Grazowiec, he was unaware that he would never see his former colleagues again. Despite the Geneva Convention they were murdered in the mass massacre of Polish officers in the Katyń Forest. The first news of that horrendous crime reached him in Iraq, where he was already serving in the Krechowiecki's regiment. The memory of those tragic events never left him.

When the Council of ZHP in the East was formed, Z. Peszkowski was detached from the Army to became the Head of the Wolf Cub and Brownie Section. He was sent as a visiting Instructor to Tehran, Esfahan and Nazareth. In May 1944 he was dispatched to India as a member of one of the 4 Visiting Teams sent to help the Scouting movement in civilian camps. Before the Teams left Middle East, their members had a camp fire and organised so called 'Forest Cirle' - an elite group of Scoutmasters, at which they adopted 'Forest names' – his was 'Brave Lynx', which suited him well, lynx – 'ryś' in Polish - being a very agile, rare animal still living in Polish forests. Even now, though he is an elderly and noble prelate, many of his former charges still call him 'Ryś', not knowing his real name.

The Visiting Team was a godsend for the children and young people robbed of years of normal childhood. Druh Ryś – young, handsome, full of life and energy, with many wonderful though sometimes risky plans and projects, often frightened our mothers and not always agreed with the more conservative members of the Settlement's Authorities – but brought the element of variety and adventure to our rather monotonous life. And together with his older and more practical companion, the Lone Wolf, they taught us many things, implanted many ideals and bound us into a brotherhood that survived many years and great distances.

When the difficult time of decision came, dh Peszkowski – like many Poles – decided not to return to Communist run Poland. For a while he studied history at the Oxford University, then decided that he would be better able to serve Polish youth by becoming a priest. After completing his studies at the Polish Seminary in Orchard Lake, USA and being ordained as a priest, he also obtained his MA in Polish Studies at PUNO (the Polish University in London) and remained in USA as a lecturer in the SS Cyril & Methodius Seminary and the St. Mary's College in Orchard Lake.

In spite of many pastoral and academic duties, he always found time for Scouting; he held the position of the Chief Chaplain to the Association of Polish Girl Guides and Boy Scouts Abroad. Based in Warsaw, although officially retired, he was still very active, mainly in the sphere of publication. His dream of becoming a resident priest in the sanctuary of Katyń did not materialize, due to Russia's obstinacy in admitting the massacre, but he was untiring in reminding the world of this heinous crime, and of all the suffering many people had to endure at the hands of Communists in Russia.

Hm. Anna Gwiazdonik (Handerek) – was born 12th February 1916 in Jasło. She gained MA degree in History at the Jagiellonian University in Krakow. WWII interrupted her work for Doctors degree and simultaneous studies of sociology. Deported to the Soviet Union with her brother's family, she worked hard to help them survive.

After her brother's death, she managed to get a job in a Polish orphanage, to which she took the eldest of her nephews, Staś. With the orphanage they finally reached Tehran, where Staś attended kindergarten while his aunt obtained a job in a secondary school in the Civilian Camp No.1.

Then India – in Valivade they could finally lead a more or less normal life. She was teaching History – the subject she liked and knew well. Still young, and of a very happy disposition, she easily found common language with her pupils.

Her great adventure – as she called it – was Scouting. She discovered it late in life, when sent by Educational Authority as an adult helper to our first camp. She found it fascinating and easily let the visiting Instructors persuade her to become a member. On the 8th October 1944 she made her Promise, a few days later, she attended the Instructors' Training Camp together with her pupils. She received her Phm. diploma on 29th November 1946. She held many functions in the changing structures of Valivade Scouting, always willing to lend a hand, where necessary.

She was so happy, good humoured and full of life, that only few of us knew how the years of deportation and hard work impaired her health. In spite of numerous attacks of malaria, grave heart condition and a great load of duties at school and at home, she always found time for her Guides and Scouts. When reading her diaries, it is difficult to believe how much work she could squeeze in the 24 hours. She was always with us – at hikes and camps, meetings, campfires, night games, and other activities. She helped print *Młodzi* on the ancient duplicating machine, and to decorate Wanderers Club. She bargained with the Indian Contractor about our food supplies, carried the heavy tents, spent hours over our meals cooked in the camp kitchens. After all that, she arrived at school, well prepared for her lectures. She was a very demanding teacher. And there was also Staś – the child requiring a lot of care and love. He and his best friend, Zbyszek Karaś, had to be taken with her to all those Scouting adventures. They formed the famous 'Patrol 19' – a cause of many laughs and a lot of anxiety. Only once she had to leave him behind, the hike to Ratnagiri being too demanding for the legs of a nine year old boy. Left with dh Ryś, he cried on the first day, but afterwards they managed quite well. And there was Bill – Ryś' dog, who also had to be looked after, whenever his owner disappeared from Valivade…

Staś, now a retired lawyer, wrote a poem about his aunt's problems with bringing up a young boy:

> "I hated women, the girls in my class,
> Called them names, pushed them around,
> Would not let them enter the classroom.
> Many talks with my teacher had aunt Hanka,
> Afterwards she would threaten me
> - I will put you into the reformatory…

Staś Handerek and Bill with H.Wasilejko

Of course those threats were not serious. But Staś' mother at the end of the war managed to return from Russia to Poland and she wanted her child back. He was sent to her with the first transport of repatriates. His loving aunt decided to follow and on the 12th February 1948, all those who had not yet left, turned up at the Valivade station to bid her farewell.

In September Hanka started a teaching job in Jordanów, South of Poland. At first it was fine, then with the Communist party overseeing the education, the problems started. From the constraints in the classroom, she found relief in the work with Scouts and Guides, of whom there were several units in Jordanów. She married another teacher, her parents came to share their little house; and Staś returned to his beloved aunt. No remedial school was required for him – he turned into a studious chap; became a lawyer, as a hobby he collects all sorts of memorabilia.

Hanka never forgot her 'Scouting adventure' – kept correspondence with many of her Indian pupils, came to some of our Reunions, gladly received our visits. Her death on the 4th of January 2004 saddened many of her old and new friends.

CONCLUSION

Polish Scouting and Guiding Movement in wartime India played a great role in our lives, not only because we had no access to attractions and entertainments available to young people in normal times, but also because it was the arena on which we could prove ourselves, achieve something, make friends. When we look into our old diaries, under each date we find some note about an event or happening. I hope that recording some of them here will give the reader an idea about the atmosphere of those days, the thoughts and feelings of young people, thrown far away from their country, families and friends, uncertain of their future and still able to find pleasure and reassurance in common efforts and joyful games. In the following pages you will find the same events described by the participants, in fragments from their diaries and letters.

I wish to finish this chapter with grateful thanks to our Leaders and Instructors, whose efforts and hard work, not only created a semblance of normality in the abnormal conditions of our life, but also installed in us ideals and principles that allowed us to enter adult life with assurance and sincerity. The Editor of *Młodzi* wrote in its final issue:

The Scout and Guide Law should be our main sign-post in future life, Those who live and act according to this law, are our brothers and sisters. We will help each other in difficulties and fight together for justice, fairness and freedom.

Of course many of us left the Movement. Some came back as adult helpers with their children and grandchildren. Others remained active, leading the youth units in Poland, Canada, USA, Australia or Great Britain. All of us remained faithful to the ideals of our Scouting Promise.

NOTES
1. Statute of ZHP. Monitor Polski No. 92 20.IV.1936
2. Harcerki w ZHP – Hm.. W. Seweryn Spławska. GKH-ek poza Krajem London 1993 – p.115
3. ibid p.224-226
4. ibid p.112-114 and ZHP na Wschodzie – Hm. L. Kliszewicz.. H.K.H. (Harcerska Komisja Historyczna) London 1992 p.10-11
5. Harcerstwo w Indiach – Hm. B. Pancewicz. H.K.H. London 1977 p.14
6. ibid p.116
7. ZHP na Wschodzie – Hm. L. Kliszewicz. p.20

ENGRAVED IN OUR MEMORY…
(Excerpts from diaries, contemporary newspapers, etc)
translated with the help of Marta Paluch

Before setting off for Africa, India, Iran and Palestine, members of the four Teams of Inspectors met for a conference in Jerusalem to agree their programme and methodology. One of them, Hm. Dr. W Szyryński, a young psychologist, proposed the introduction of Scouting diaries. Counselling, post-traumatic consultations and psychotherapy, so fashionable today, were not yet known, but there was an awareness that the tragic war experiences of the young people could have caused psychological damage. The aim of the journals was to 'loosen the tongues' of the victims of deportation and allow them to unload their stresses and inhibitions. Our Scout leaders were very committed to enforcing the writing of these diaries. I can't say whether and how much it helped us; reading them now I notice that we rather avoided memories of Russia. But the diaries became a source of valuable information for this book.

Writing the Diaries

- Oh this diary!!! How haphazardly it was kept by the 12-14 years old boy. Dozens of meaningless entries made, just to be left in peace by the troop leaders, Zbyszek Nowicki and Jasiek Siedlecki. What a pity that I didn't think of producing a rubber stamp with words to the effect: "I got up, said my prayers, went to school"… etc. I would have saved plenty of time, that could have been used for playing rounders or other games. Today I regret that so many wonderful things have passed unrecorded, and cannot be now recovered, as our memories are defective and fade with time… – *Leszek Trzaska*

Archery badge

I started my Scouting adventure late in life, in India, in May 1944 when the Education Committee sent me to a camp as a guardian. I gained a reputation as a strict disciplinarian when I found a pair of dirty socks under the mattress of Anielka, the deputy patrol leader, during an inspection of the patrols' bedrooms (that was before we had tents). She however professed to be delighted because "…she didn't know where they'd disappeared to." I started as a guardian, but got interested and decided to enter the ranks of students of the esoteric Scouting knowledge. On 8th October 1944 I made the Girl Guide's Promise in front of Lone Wolf and left for Panhala for the Guide Leaders' Course, which I attended with some of my pupils. And so started something which has lasted till today - if not in action, then at least in my heart. – It was then I adopted the Scouting habit of keeping the diary. Several thick copybooks are still in my possession. - *Anna Gwiazdonik (Handerek) MA*

Keeping a diary was compulsory and now and then the 'authorities' checked them. For us - Brownie and Cub Pack Leaders - the authority was druh Ryś-Zuch. He assured us that he didn't read them but was just checking that we kept writing them. Being a sceptic by nature, I put my comments about the authorities, which were not necessarily all favourable, in big brackets and then wrote in the margin: STRICTLY PRIVATE AND CONFIDENTIAL, thus ensuring that these comments would reach their target. Just like Leszek (see above) I regret that my diary was short of facts. Instead, it was full of philosophical reflections, poetic descriptions and lamentations about my inadequacies. But every now and then I find in it a few sentences which bring a flood of memories: the death of gen. Sikorski, the Jamboree in France to which Polish Scouts were not admitted, the end of the war – the wind of history penetrating the outpourings of a teenager. – *Danuta Pniewska*

Campfires and Rites

Valivade 3.12.44. – The sky is covered by thick clouds through which the light of the moon barely penetrates. The wind whistles in the bamboos and rustles the leaves of the giant mango trees. In a quiet little ravine a few slight figures in grey uniforms are building a cone of sticks for a fire. A match is struck… a flame licks the splinters and dry grass and climbs higher. The fire burns… Songs, happy memories and comments on the future work of the troop mingle with the crackle of the flames. *The Młody Las* (Young Forest) Company's Leader speaks:

- This is the first campfire of our patrol leaders' group, a group that will lead the work of our company. Today we will form the secret circle of the Young Forest and celebrate our forest christening. From now on there will be no Krysia, Zosia, Halina or Irka in our midst. In their place we will have Snowdrop - the first harbinger of the Polish spring, Edelweiss – conqueror of cloud-capped summits, Firefly – bewitching light of midsummer nights, modest but so charming Wood Violet; Spark will light the fire of work and love in our own environment, Will-o'-the-Wisp will warn people of danger, Wild Rose will sow joy and Cornflower is a symbol of our constant thoughts of our homeland.

The old names, written on cards are thrown into the fire. The grey figures kneel for prayer. Young hands join to form a sisterly circle. Night comes… God is near… The moon, a milky ball, lingers behind the net of clouds. The shapes of the houses in the settlement greet us as we approach. Tomorrow we start a new year of Scouting work in the Young Forest company. – *Helena Szafrańska*

Valivade 2 Oct 1945 – Today is the anniversary of the defeat of the Warsaw Uprising. In the afternoon we cleared up around the symbolic cenotaph of the insurgents killed in action. It looks lovely – the tomb is tall, with a cross made of thorny wood in the middle, with the symbols of Polish Underground on both sides; the Scout emblem at the back and lighted torches on either side. We assembled at seven and brought paraffin lamps. The ceremony was short but beautiful. We stood in a rectangle with banners around the tomb. Father Dallinger sang the prayers, Father Jankowski spoke, followed by druh Ryś. His speech was short but good. He told us about a scene from the Uprising when a wounded Scout comes to his Troop Leader and asks – "Do I have to die? I want to live." I don't remember everything but it was very moving and Druh Ryś spoke with feeling and asked: "what are we living for? Think about it. They gave their lives for Poland and what are we giving?" He spoke so well that I wanted to cry. His words were very real. It's difficult to give an answer to that question: how should Scouts and Guides live their lives? To live not only for pleasure but to have an aim in life that we are striving for; to live so that each day is a new victory… – *Jadwiga Wróblewska*

Panhala 25 Oct 1946 – The Elephants' Enclosure. It's midnight. I feel so strange… As I am writing this, I can hear my loud heartbeat, while all around is peace and quiet… About two hours ago druh Ryś told me to spend the night alone by the fire. – "Tomorrow you will be admitted to the Forest Ring."- he said. My first reaction, apart from surprise was fear. I wanted to say - "I don't want to, I won't go." But I went. And now I don't know what I feel more: this fear of something new, the anxiety that maybe I do not deserve to be here – or the strong desire to be admitted to this prestigious Circle… I feel trapped, tending my feeble fire, encircled by the four stone walls… We were told stories of prisoners and traitors being trampled to death by elephants in this enclosure… There is a road nearby and the voices of passing Indians sound rather eerie and interrupt my thoughts. I'm supposed to be thinking about life – what is life? I think it is the path to God. No – rather several paths, because people go to Him by many paths. Sometimes they don't know where they're going or they take the wrong path. Sometimes they're going in the right direction but the road is too hard for them. We have to live our lives not only to follow our path and reach our goal but also to help others to reach this goal. Our priest said that you can't give away your happiness or your salvation to another person but I think that perhaps you could do even that. But how can you help others if you don't know anything, if you trip at every step… What do I know? What use am I to others? I'm also worried that I know so little about the Forest Ring and that I don't have much of a forest soul… - *Danka Pniewska*

Valivade 10 Aug 1947 – Yesterday there was a campfire for the whole Division and the Indian Scouts who came to visit us. The campfire celebrated three events: 1) it was lit at the same time as a similar fire at the Jamboree in France. 2) It glowed few days before Indian independence would glow. 3) It was a farewell from us and our brother Indian Scouts for druh Ryś. He is about to leave India. **Janka Jankowska**

Valivade 23 Aug 1947 – Today there was a farewell campfire for Rover Scouts and Ranger Guides because druh Ryś is leaving on Friday. I would like to see him again sometime. It was so pleasant at the fireside. There was a long talk... druh Ryś spoke about the terrible, tragic situation in the world and in our country... We finished the evening by the Warsaw Insurgents' Cenotaph; a heavy rain was falling but we stood holding hands. It was both solemn and pleasant although water ran down our faces. – *Jadwiga Wróblewska*

CAMPS IN PANHALA

Finally my brother and I got out from under the protective wings of my mother and landed on our first Scout camp in Panhala. We were fascinated by this delightful place – the old fort on the summit of an immense hill. It was partly in ruins but a lot of defensive walls, gates and fortifications, huge granaries, old palaces and a cemetery remained. Panhala dominated the surrounding valley. There are many legends linked to the fort. One of them is about the heroic maharajah, Shivaji, who fought for the freedom of his country against the invaders. Besieged in Panhala by the enemy, he escaped by lowering himself from the window of his castle on a rope of turbans tied together, to gather reinforcements in the valley and win back the fort. This story fired our imagination and encouraged us to courageous and hazardous deeds.

Jumping between gate posts

The mornings in Panhala were amazing. At sunrise we stood at the edge of the fortifications and looked down into the vast valley brushed with the light of the sun's rays. In our morning prayers we worshiped the Creator of these marvels. Before breakfast we had PE, but this was no ordinary PE. Part of it took place on trees – their branches stretched out almost horizontally above the ground and under them huge roots protruded from the earth. The aim was to walk, crawl, or move, sitting along the branch for several metres without spilling over onto the roots below. Or there was PE in the Elephants' Enclosure. This was a square area surrounded by a two metre high wall with two entrances. There were no gates but there were two angular pilasters at the entrance with pyramid shaped tops. The aim was to get round the enclosure, jump from one pyramid to the other at the entrance and then to grab the top of the wall so as not to fall. This required courage and was risky. Another exercise we did as part of this 'Monkey PE', was walking on top of the old battlement walls. We had to do this stepping sideways along a narrow ledge, leaning back into the wall. If our mothers had seen us doing this they would have fainted. Nobody was forced to take part in these exercises and there was no serious accident. Overcoming fear and the sense of being responsible for your own fate developed our personalities and built our confidence in our own strength.

We also had lots of field activities, drill, alerts and night games, working towards grades and of course campfires. We learned to love the Scout songs, we enjoyed the performances but we also willingly listened to the fireside talks which stimulated our patriotism and belief in Scouting ideals and encouraged us to work on building our characters. After the talks we would join hands in a circle of young people whose hearts were devoted to God and the motherland. Fireflies accompanied us to our tents. – *Staszek Harasymów*

Panhala 12 Oct 1944 – Instructors' Training Course - The first 'serious' day of the camp. After mornings prayers we had PE with the inevitable jumping onto walls, (druh Ryś's speciality). I didn't do too well at that, nor at swinging on trees. Today our patrol is on duty. The results are poor so far. The campfire wouldn't light, Lone Wolf was furious, but we deal with it all with humour.

20 Oct 1944 – There is less and less time. Yesterday I had to practise being a Camp Leader of the boy's camp. Luckily I was with Jurek Augustyn, so we just about managed. Another week and a half to the end of the course, with an exam at the end. It's been a long time - five years - since I last studied for an exam, or took one.

24 Oct 1944 – We started the planned 'adventure week', but so far the only adventure has been the weather. Yesterday the rain was unbelievable and a river flowed through the tent of 'Duty' patrol, which had been pitched across the path leading from the hill, so the girls had to move to the meeting tent. Our patrol got wet, but we were not flooded. – *Hanka Handerek*

Panhala 5 May 1945 – The holidays have started! Yesterday I spent half the day arguing with the contractor and went to bed at 3 a.m. Today we have the Ranger Guides' game. In fact these last days have been all big games.

29 May 1945 – In the last three days before the camp started, I have done some of the hardest work in my life. Now we are 'resting' in Panhala, which means that I spend half the day among the pots and pans and the other half on discussions, lectures and the campfire. Last night we walked to the other Panhala and I scratched my legs really badly… But it was a really pleasant trip. We lit our campfire on the hill and druh Bronek talked about the book: *Chronicles from Narocz*. The night was lit with a moon and the fireflies are already here. – *Anna Handerek*

Panhala 10 May 1945 - Camp of 'Izabella Czartoryska's 3rd Guide Troop - (Guardian dhna H Handerek, camp leader Freda Studzińska, deputy Lala Studzińska, quartermistress Janka Jankowska) - We reached our destination at 5 p.m. The troop immediately got down to pitching the tents. I took over the equipment from the previous quartermistress and then Lala and I had to help to set up the camp because most of our Guides were young and weak. At 7 p.m. the tents were up and after supper the camp went to sleep. In the leaders' tent, we sat down to do the books. But the enemy was watchful and as soon as the lamp was lit, the attack started. At first we tried to defend our position. Our weapons were Stasio's shoes (the guardian's small nephew), drops of paraffin sprinkled by Dhna Hanka and soapy water used by Freda. But there were only five of us while the enemy marched in columns, battalions, regiments… Our endeavours were too weak against the stings of the ants, for it was they who had organised this "Swedish Invasion" as Staś called it (after the well known Polish historical novel). In the face of superior forces, we had to abandon our position. Stubborn Staś stayed and while we were pegging out a second tent, he was shouting, with a shoe in his hand, "I won't abandon my castle, I will fight to the end." Three of us were putting up the tent, laughing our heads off. It was 11 p.m. Freda had to go and reassure the girls, apologising on behalf of the command, who, instead of setting a good example, were screaming and roaring in the middle of the night. At one o'clock sleep closed our tired eyelids. (Girl Guide loves nature, but it appears

Accross the pond

that nature does not always love a Guide) – *Janka Jankowska*

20 Oct 1946 - Leaders Council's Camp. - I didn't really feel like going to this camp, but dhna Hanka Handerek said that if I don't turn up at the departure point with my rucksack, she would come herself to pack me. There was no right of appeal. I have many beautiful memories from Panhala, from the camps of our Guide troop, but now I'm worried. What will happen if I am assigned to a patrol with girls that I don't really know?

Druh Ryś is already waiting at the site with the Boy Scouts. Assembly, report… What joy - I'm in a patrol with Hanka Ostrihanska and Lilka Wasiuk. We quickly put up our tent, get organised, then it's free time and swimming. After swimming, a rosary service in front of our simple field shrine, which is for us the most fantastic temple. I am sure the Lord God prefers the columns of young Scouts praying in the open to the most opulent temples – ours are the temples of pure hearts loving the great God.

After supper we have the first campfire in the Elephant Enclosure. This is the start of further work during the camp – we get activities and assignments to complete: climbing Zbaraż and Beresteczko Hills (Polish names given to the hills by our Scouts).

We wake at dawn - the sky above Beresteczko is covered by wispy clouds. Then it becomes pink, light red, brilliant. Suddenly, amidst the crimson patch, appears the powerful shield of the sun. How wonderful to say morning prayers standing with the whole troop on the edge of the precipice. Reluctantly we return to the camp. – *Marysia Woźniak*

CAMPS IN CHANDOLI

This year we put our tents up not in Panhala but in a new place, Chandoli. A river ran beside the site but nobody knew its name. Why did we need to know the name when we thought of it as the Black Vistula. And above the river rose the hills and everyone said 'Beskidy'. And that's why everyone loved them. Only that palm tree… She charmed us with her light green braids and seduced us with her graceful silhouette. And nobody could say 'fir' because clearly this was not a fir tree. She spoiled the enchantment of the Beskidy and the Black Vistula.

Life thrives under the trees. To get to know this life it is not enough to look at the forest ornaments – the ingenious monsters and animals made from strangely twisted branches – it's not enough to sigh by the shrine decorated with flowers or to praise the perfect order. All this is only a small part of camp life behind which hides a greater task, a more serious goal.

At the Health Training Camp a large group of girls listens to the doctor's lecture with notebooks in hand. These are our future nurses – the successful completion of this course and a placement in the hospital will allow them to start work. We will go for lunch to the Cooks Camp. The lunch is excellent but in order to gain the specialisation badge, apart from the activities and lectures at the training camp, they will have two weeks experience here in Chandoli, in other camps, where they will no longer be supervised

Camp's Gateway

by instructors and they will have to plan, prepare and work out the cost of the meals all by themselves.

Participants of the Surveying course are just leaving for field activities armed with poles, levels, a surveying chain and a leveller. They are going to survey a small hill near the camp. Late into the night we'll see lights in their tents – there's no time during the day for drawings and writing up lecture notes. Work everywhere – but is there no time for fun and rest? Of course there is – there are sports and activities: archery, swimming and of course the campfires. Campfires in which Scouts and Guides see themselves, the reflections of their souls. Are they like embers? or sparks? or maybe just smoke? The call for night silence brings the rest. The Beskidy rise darkly in the distance, the Black Vistula rustles… And only the palm, proud, bewitching and bold seems to whisper, 'India, India.' It doesn't matter that Poland is far… it is for her that work thrives here and for her that our hearts beat. We will return. And we will light our campfires in the real Beskidy by the real Black Vistula. – *D.C. From The Pole in India newspaper, 1946*

Surveying Patrol in Chandoli: J. Kossowski (on the left)

Rice and Bees in Chandoli

We were preparing for the Woodcraft proficiency badge. I was assigned the privileged role of a cook. Feeling the weight of this responsibility I couldn't allow the patrol to die of hunger. I wanted to impress them, I had to gain their respect, so I thought up an amazing rice dish. But I had to start with the basics. A pot, some water, then add the rice; better a lot of it so that no one goes hungry. What happened then, cannot be explained in human words. A live thing which couldn't be controlled - and in the middle, me, a poor little Scout with a big spoon. A hill of rice, a mountain of rice, a rice volcano, a rice cyclone and me at the eye of the storm… Not a hero, but a crushed and humiliated mite.

Another adventure in Chandoli could have ended with even worse consequences. Two troops of Boy Scouts made a trip into the jungle with full kit. There was a stream that fell in a waterfall of about 40 or 50 metres, forming a little lake. We set up our bivouac by this waterfall. Around us the cliff walls were hung with dozens of wild bee swarms. A Scout loves nature but will not scorn honey. So many honeycombs within easy reach, could this opportunity be wasted? The jungle heroes quickly took action. A string of stones flew in the direction of the honeycombs. In an instant the view changed beyond recognition. It became dark and there was a buzz… Some sensible person gave a command: 'Hide under the blankets!' If it hadn't been for those blankets I don't know if anyone would have survived to tell the tale. – *Leszek Trzaska*

The Three Feathers Badge in Chandoli

Chandoli lies on the edge of the jungle which covers several hills and valleys. It was wilder here than in Panhala with the jungle creating a slightly menacing atmosphere. It was said that black panthers lived there. Our camp was sited on a clearing near the river. At that time I was a member of the Third Boy Scout Troop named after Jurek Bitschan. Our Troop Leader was druh Jerzy Liszka. Nearby were the camps of the First and Second Troops. We competed in the organisation and running of the camps. We built an observation tower, a fence with two gates, two field kitchens, an earth table and in front of each tent was the coat of arms of each patrol, racks for the mess-tins and sticks on which we recorded the numbers of good deeds. Of course we also had a beautiful shrine, based on a Scout Cross laid out of pebbles.

There were many opportunities for gaining various Scout proficiency badges but our ambition was to gain the coveted THREE FEATHERS badge. The criteria for gaining this badge were difficult and hazardous. The regulations demanded that we spend 24 hours in hiding away from the camp, without speaking, and eating only what we could find or hunt. Because of the proximity of the jungle we were allowed to go in pairs, but we had to be at least 10 steps apart the whole time. We were also not allowed to eat unknown berries because previously one Scout had eaten lots of some fruit from the jungle and became so constipated that apparently he had to sit in the stream to soften the obstruction. So we each got a slice of bread and a tin of sardines, three matches and some antiseptic. Each of us also had a knife, our triangular Scout scarf, a waterproof cape, a bottle of water and a rucksack.

My partner was Witold Łukaszewski, known as Łukasz. My own nickname was 'Spiritual Rose' because I wore a medal in the shape of a rose with a picture of the Holy Mary on it. We agreed that we would hide in the jungle and that in the night we would light a fire to keep away the wild animals.

Suspension bridge, Chandoli

In the early morning, after attending mass, we set off in pairs. Once outside the camp we had to avoid being seen by anyone. As we went, we kept our eyes peeled and listened carefully, communicating only with signs. The nearer we got to the jungle the less likely we were to meet another person. We tried to remember the lie of the land so that we wouldn't get lost on our way back. The jungle was damp and steamy and you could smell the rotting leaves. Birds cried noisily high overhead but at ground level, in the mysterious semi-darkness, the jungle seemed less charming and more menacing. We didn't come across any monkeys.

Late in the afternoon we came out onto a ridge where we decided to stay the night. Having devoured our meagre provisions and drunk the water, we started to gather dry wood for a fire. It started to drizzle. Afraid that if we waited the wood would all get wet, we decided to light the fire right then. The first match went out in a sudden gust of wind, the second was damp. We shielded the third one carefully, but it also went out and with it went our hope of a fire. What should we do? We decided to sleep on the trees. Conscientiously keeping the required distance between us, we found two trees about 10 metres apart, with wide branches that you could half sit and half lie on. Night falls quickly in the jungle. I cleaned the branch with my knife, put down the blanket and covered myself with the waterproof cape. I kept my knife in my hand as this would serve me to defend myself. The birds quietened down, but there were lots of rustling and cracking sounds. The loneliness and hunger brought various thoughts to mind. What will happen if a panther shows up? The feeling of fear grew. Why did I insist on doing the Three Feathers? Why did I come to Chandoli? Is Łukasz thinking the same things?

Finally tiredness got the upper hand. Comforted with a prayer, I fell asleep. In the night I was woken by rain. While adjusting my cover, I dropped my knife, but I didn't climb down to get it. I still dozed a little until the first light of dawn woke the forest birds who started again to make a great racket. Morning prayer was a thanksgiving. We joyfully set off towards the camp – whole, healthy and very hungry. The last difficulty was to approach the camp without being seen. And there we met almost the whole troop, with everybody telling their adventures. We attacked breakfast like wolves.

Not everybody got the Three Feathers badge, but those who didn't achieve it, got the Woodcraft badge as compensation. But the greatest reward are the recollections of our Scouting life which are carved in out memory forever. – *Staszek Harasymów*

There was authentic jungle around us, with wild animals, cobras, boa constrictors and other dangers. Most of the Boy Scouts dreamed of gaining the Three Feathers badge but how could we send these youngsters alone into the jungle for 24 hours? They only had forked bamboo sticks as protection against snakes. Waiting for them impatiently, I sent a prayer to God for their safe return.

The first expedition into the jungle ended in a failure because there was an alarm call. A cow fell into a deep ditch and everybody ran to help and so ended the silence and solitude. The Scouts tried to pull the cow out with their belts. They didn't succeed – just as well, as it was a holy cow and had been left in the forest to finish its life. After the rescue we had to organise a thorough wash. And the Three Feathers trial had to start again from scratch. – *Z. Peszkowski (from the book Droga do kapłaństwa – Road to the Priesthood)*

On the way for proficency badges

Chandoli 24 May 1946. We're in the jungle. We're preparing for the Woodcraft badge. I really wanted to do the Three Feathers but they wouldn't allow me because I'll only be fifteen in three months' time. How unfair! I so dreamed about those Feathers. On our way I wanted to cry (although I rarely cry, hardly ever.) We built a shelter to protect us against the rain, a shrine and a field kitchen. As my two best mates, Irka Kudła and Jadźka Janczewska are always full of good humour, we had a fun campfire at night. – *Teresa Kurowska*

Chandoli 17 April 1946 We mustn't forget this important day - the 25th anniversary of druh Bronek's work in the Scouting movement. The celebration took place in the morning. At 6 a.m. everyone was in the boys' camp – everyone meaning the Signal Corps, the Cooks, Brownies and Cubs and the Rover Scouts Troop. We arranged the hand made, jungle style camp furniture in front of the tent (a present from the camp participants) Behind this stood the wall of Scouts and Guides, while the Brownies and Cubs came with a cake on which 25 candles burned. Many little hands held flowers. Reveille played on trumpets with accompanying drums woke the subject of these celebrations. When he emerged from his tent, the Brownies and Cubs sang a song, their Camp Leader Danka P formally congratulated him and several gifts were presented, including an album in the shape of an oak leaf with greetings from all the troops in the Valivade area. In the evening at a campfire druh Bronek talked about his Scouting life. – *Janka Jankowska*

A Story About a Rooster

It was during a camp in Chandoli. Dr. J. Tiachow was at the camp with us, we just called him 'Doktorek.' A good hearted man, he was always smiling and full of life, perhaps a little eccentric, and although much older, he behaved like one of us. Everybody liked and respected him. This Doktorek had a rooster, yes - a rooster, with a big red crest and a beautiful coloured tail. The rooster, tied by the leg, proudly paraded with Doktorek and sometimes crowed.

The 'Three Musketeers' of the camp – Jurek Kowalski, Heniek Wądołkowski and I, decided to steal the rooster and eat it. Now with hindsight I can see that slaughtering the doctor's bird was not a very nice idea. We grabbed the rooster from in front of the doctor's tent and dived for the jungle. We had a pan, salt and potatoes which was good, but what next? Who was going to cut off the poor birds head?

I said: - "Heniek, you do it!" But he replied: - "Are you crazy? This was your idea. Let Jurek hold it and you give it the chop." And so the argument continues while the rooster walks about, scratches the ground and has no idea that its life is at stake. In the end Jurek says: - "Let's draw lots. Whoever draws the short straw is the executioner". Fine. We pull. Damn! I got the short one. I look at the rooster and he moves his head and clearly winks at me. Heniek says: - "What's up Olek, are you scared? Come on, you lost." I look at the unfortunate rooster again. What the hell! I can't touch it. I just got fond of it, that's all.

In the camp a tragedy erupts. Doktorek is running around shouting "They've stolen my rooster, the rooster is gone, maybe somebody has eaten it." And there we still were holding the rooster although he got away with his life. We're hungry as hell. We had to wait until the campfire finished. We heard "Night is nigh…" being sung, then the lights went out. We picked up the rooster, because the scoundrel had fallen asleep and around midnight we left it at Doktorek's tent.

At five in the morning the rooster crowed loudly. Doktorek wept tears of joy and us? – we felt foolish but glad in our hearts that we didn't have the courage to kill him. Doktorek never found out how close his rooster had come to being eaten. – *Olek Klecki*

A 'Court Martial' at the Camp.

During our last summer in India, in May 1947, at the request of our chaplain, Leszek Bełdowski and I organised a special a camp for Scouts who were also serving as altar boys. Two incidents from that camp stuck in my memory.

Soon after the arrival, when the tents were being erected I made it clear that around each of them a channel has to be dug, as a safeguard against the monsoon rain. Sure enough, with the first downpour not only were the tents flooded, but some even collapsed due to slack ropes. So, when I found the frightened boys praying, I told them that God helps those who help themselves – and they had to erect the tents again.

The other incident concerns cheating. A night watch had to be kept to safeguard our provisions against any animals of the jungle, and also as part of the boys' training. Once I was woken up much too early in the morning, only to discover that my wrist watch, which I displayed outside the tent (for the benefit of those on night duty) had been tampered with. Naturally I enquired who did it and just as naturally nobody would own up.

HQ of the Alter Boys' camp: J. Siedlecki and L. Bełdowski

So Leszek and I announced that there would have to be a 'court martial' and having ourselves draped in bed sheets (to add solemnity to the occasion) we declared that the whole troop will be punished by taking cod liver capsules after meals! (These were given to us as an necessary food supplement but were hated by the boys.)

I don't remember if it passed without tears and I wonder, whether H.E. the Archbishop Marian Oleś remembers that camp in which he participated as an altar boy. – *Jasiek Siedlecki*

EXPEDITIONS

First hike to Ratnagiri – Brownie and Cub Leaders' Group 15 – 22 October 1945

15 Oct 1945 – Finally, the long awaited first hike! At six o'clock we left for Kolhapur by train. The boys went ahead on bicycles with our provisions and were already waiting on the bridge. From there we set off together. The rucksacks were heavy, mine nearly impossible to carry. In the evening it poured with rain and we all got soaked. We found somewhere to stay the night. Karol forced us to take quinine. I slept very little, I heard that some Indians came and demanded money but I don't know what for. I'm glad we already had some adventures on the first day. The more adventures we have, the more interesting the trip will be.

16 Oct 1945 – near Panhala we met up with the members of the Troop Leaders' Course who brought tents for us. Lone Wolf laughed at us for taking such a lot of supplies. We will see who has the last laugh. Druh Ryś is coming with us, but he said that he will only act as an observer during the whole trip. After breakfast we went off in different directions to get to know the area. Hidden in high grass in the shade of a spreading fig tree I read The Imitation of Christ. 'Mimoza' found me in my hideout and we talked about faith. At sunset we continued our journey. After walking for three hours, I was so tired that I was falling asleep on my feet. The same was true of my partner with whom I was carrying a tent on a pole. We were so tired that we didn't pitch the tents but slept on them. In the night we were woken by the rain. It was pouring down. The water got under the tents and we were drenched through. Only druh Ryś had put up his little tent and now he tipped out the contents of his rucksack handing out dry clothes and towels. With difficulty we managed to make some tea, a couple of spoonfuls each to help the quinine down. Again some rather fierce looking Indians, armed with bamboo sticks, turned up and stayed with us till morning. But the most important part that night was played by Bill. That 'disgusting dog' suddenly became 'darling Bill.' The friendly dog warmed us like a heater; we passed him around and this saved us from catching cold. – *'Black Halina' (Strycharz)*

17 Oct 1945 – After the rain the going was good, it wasn't too hot. When we got to the river we set up a bivouac to dry out the contents of our rucksacks and the tents; our uniforms had already dried on us. I cooked lunch with Marysia L. It was the start of the hike when the dry provisions were still plentiful. Soon the wonderful smell of cabbage soup woke the sleeping company. In the early evening we resumed our march with good speed and set up camp at the next river. This time we conscientiously pitched the tents but just to spite us, there was no sign of rain. – *'Little Elephant' (Czesia Moniak)*

18 Oct 1945 - Reveille at six, it's still dark but they tell us to pack up the tents. Brr… it's cold! Hot tea and a slab of bread gave us the strength for the next stage of the hike. The surroundings are beautiful… In the morning we complained about the cold, now it's the sun… We can see Malkapur. We promised ourselves that we would visit this town and maybe we can buy something to eat. There is indeed plenty to see in this fine city – two kiosks with hot 'chai,' a bus stop and a few barber's shops. But the landscape is enchanting – lots of flowers and ferns. The miles pass, each one is meant to be the last. Finally we find a suitable place for a bivouac; siesta and cooking lunch. After afternoon tea we set off swiftly as we want to see the famous Amba as soon as possible. Another disappointment: just two kiosks, though one has an electric light. But three or four miles on is the beautiful Amba Ghat where we bivouac. Forest-covered hills – the jungle starts here. – *'Mimoza' (Marysia Małaczyńska)*

19 Oct 1945 – The fifth day of the hike. In Amba we crossed the boundary of Kolhapur and we're now in the principality of Ratnagiri. We walk towards the jungle with the song:- "to the jungle, to the jungle, au, au, au…" Somebody spotted beautifully coloured fruit decorating the bushes like glass baubles on a Christmas tree. Another noticed a butterfly with bright wings at least 15cm across. There were ferns, some as big as trees. Mimoza got so tangled in the creepers, that Witek had to cut her free with his knife. For lunch we had barley soup made with corned beef. For second course more corned beef. In fact there's a lot of beef around. Jurek, who said everything tasted good, named a nearby hill, St. Beef Hill. Behind that were the Hunger Peaks and nearer the Barley Soup River. – *Black Halina*

2nd Hike to Ratnagiri – Troop Leaders' Training Course – 22-28 October 1945

22 Oct – We're travelling by coach to Malkapur from where we will start our hike. It starts to rain. The horizon is covered with a veil of thick cloud. We are singing the wanderers' hymn:

On the shoreline of the Arabian Sea at Ratnagiri

"Choć Biedy Dwie..." (In Spite of Two Troubles.) The first trouble is already here, the rain. In Malkapur we form up and put on our kit in total darkness. Druh Bronek goes first then the main group of 'wanderers' and behind them the supply column, that is the boys leading bicycles laden with tents and I bring up the rear. We're off. The drizzle stops but the ground is soft under foot. Mikołaj keeps falling off his bike. Soon we find out what the second trouble is: rucksacks, rucksacks, rucksacks! Finally we reach Amba and Amba Ghat. At one in the morning we throw off our rucksacks and start setting up camp. – *dhna Hanka Handerek*

25 Oct – We passed the village of Kardravi and stopped in the village of Wanichi. The people here are strange, they walk around half naked, the older men have shaved heads with just the handful of hair at the top of their heads braided into a small plait. They looked at us with great curiosity and when we found one who could speak English it turned out that they didn't know anything about us. Kolhapur is too far away, 63 miles. A small Indian boy brought some wood and half a cucumber. When we gave him two annas he brought another cucumber. In Pali we stopped at a building of the American Catholic Mission. The house reminded me of a Polish manor house with its columns, porch and a well-tended garden. An old, kindly Indian man looks after it. We found more people who could speak English. They did everything they could to make us comfortable. They received this crowd of white people with surprise and they observed us with curiosity. Generally wherever we show up, we cause a stir. – *Janka Jankowska*

25 Oct – We're resting, we're resting and I'm also resting. I'm pleased not to be cooking. Frying those cutlets yesterday in the light of a candle did me in.

27 Oct – Ratnagiri at last. Bivouac by the sea. The sea is lovely, blue, shining silver in the sun with white crested waves and white sails. But the shore is not like ours – palms and dark sand. The best thing is to sit and listen to the sound of the waves. – *H.H.*

3rd Hike – School Leavers – 14-23 November 45

Valivade 13 Nov - We're leaving tomorrow. Halina and Jagoda, who are in charge of the food, are doing the shopping and packing provisions. At 4p.m. briefing with druh Bronek. The route is calculated almost to the minute and precisely to the metre. Druh Bronek is impossible with his precision!

14 Nov – On the bus we sing a little and we wonder how the days ahead will go. The hike is a kind of walking camp, which requires a higher level of Scouting skills. 9 days of better or worse shared adventures… hopefully we'll find a way of working together to solve the problems that affect us all. We get off the bus two miles outside Malkapur. We fix the provisions and two of the tents to bicycles and we carry the other two tents. I carry one tent with Major Naimski. The walking is good but our rucksacks get heavier and heavier because it's raining.

16 Nov – Yesterday we divided up the responsibilities. Zosia Ostrihanska will be

The school leavers on the hike

druh Ryś's deputy. Every day two girls are in charge of the food, another pair draw a sketch of the route and the rest push the bicycles with the provisions. Everyday a different pair prepare a topic and discussion for the campfire. There are a lot of things we have to talk through now that we're so 'grown up' and besides nearly all of us are Company Leaders. Today we sent the provisions by bus with Zosia B. and we're travelling light because the rucksacks are on the bikes. Having walked 11 miles, had lunch and done our washing, we're waiting for Zosia. After supper we set off. This is the hardest part of the walk, uphill all the way. Zocha and I take one bike, she's leading, I'm pushing. We struggle to push that bicycle up each gradient. Sweat pours down our backs and arms and streams down our faces. We eat the rest of the chocolate. Bliss! The front of the group is well ahead while the tail end is dragged out to God knows where. We're half dead. But then we see the first bike and Ryś. We've arrived. Everyone dumps their kit and bicycle and throws themselves on the grass. We set up camp on a little clearing on the hillside. Everybody is sleeping, only the cooks are finishing their bookkeeping and arranging the provisions. In the forest the monkeys giggle and shout while jackals wander over the hillside, howling and crying with human voices.

17 Nov – Halina is unable to walk fast, stays behind with Irka S. and Zocha O. who are drawing a plan of the route. Our faithful dog, Bill, keeps them company. When they reached the river near Pali, poor Bill suddenly came alive and was tearing down the stream like crazy. Zosia Karpińska, otherwise known as 'Baby', has got a new nickname: 'Motor Baby', because for the second day now she has taken a bike, loaded it up unbelievably, leaving only the saddle empty. We see her sturdy figure pushing that bike uphill at a crazy pace. Then she disappears… we meet after five miles where she asks if she should take somebody on the bike because she gets bored waiting for us on her own. Nobody can keep up with Hanka who moves her legs so fast in her short pink shorts that we always see her two bends ahead in the road. The Major is also unbeatable. He doesn't follow the rules of the hike. He doesn't rest every 5 miles but just races along as though he'd lost two thirds of his years. The bus from Kolhapur has brought provisions: sausage, beef, oranges, nuts but the driver didn't want to unload it all, so he continued on his way and is supposed to be coming back tomorrow. We're worried about those provisions.

18 Nov – Sunday. We're camped in Kuwar Bhana. There's supposed to be lots of snakes here so Raphael (druh Ryś' Indian 'boy') advised us to put bowls of milk around the tents.

19 Nov - Ratnagiri. We set up camp among the palms on the shore. We go into the sea as far as we can and sing a Polish Scout hymn: - "All that is ours we will give to Poland". We have reached the goal of our hike. After supper we discussed the menu for the next day: fish! I don't know how we moved on from fish to psychology, matters relating to the Valivade settlement, the political situation and the panic caused by contradictory information. At the campfire we discussed our Scouting magazines. Now we speak without hesitation. We have achieved another aim of the hike: becoming a team.

22 Nov - The last campfire. We talked about our impressions of the hike – they're positive. Major Naimski said his piece with humour. Only now he admitted that he hadn't known if he would be able to keep up with us (but he was a fantastic pal!) After the campfire we went to say our farewells to the sea …Druh Ryś had an attack of malaria and is shivering. He took quinine but we think this is not enough so in spite of his protests we're making tea in the night.

23 Nov– The flag is lowered slowly. We sing the national anthem and take a last look at the sea. – *Halina Szafrańska and Stela Czekierska*

Bicycle Trip to Belgaum. 26 – 31 December 1945

'Nothing will deter the knights.' This was the answer for all setbacks. And there were many of them: too little time, lack of a guardian, lack of permission, even a lack of funds… But the stubbornness and determination of the 'Sun Lunatics' overcame all the problems. They stuck with it and on 26th December 1945 at 3:45 p.m. they set off from District HQ with a tearful send off from the staff. We left with 12 bicycles under the leadership of our guardian, the well-known cyclist, Brother J. Orysiuk and our equally renowned captain, myself. The bicycles resembled tanks, laden and heavy, with fierce riders. In spite of these fierce faces, I knew that everyone's spirit was smiling and their faces were just expressing the anticipation of cycle breakdowns. In less than half an hour our muscles reminded us of their existence in rather negative terms. So we greeted every milestone on the road with joy as we were meant to reach Nipani that day.

Ticking off the milestones didn't help, it was still a long way. In addition the 'skillfully' attached baggage became unattached. Things kept going wrong. It got dark but there was still no sign of Nipani. We didn't even come across any water. Where were we to stop for the night? And thinking that if we continued at this pace we may not reach our destination on time, we decided to ride by night. But we soon bear the consequences of this decision with Chrząszcz's 'derailment', which reminds us that we need to ride more carefully. (Chrząszcz = cockchafer = nickname of Jan Chrząszczewski). I put this into practice by riding full pelt down a hill without lights. I have to admit I was a bit scared. At last there's water! After travelling 19 miles in 3 hours we pitch the tents. Duty patrol B – Chrząszcz, Oleś and Śledź brew the tea - o shame… on a primus stove. After supper - prayers, before which our guardian gave us a pep talk about friendship during the trip. After prayers the whole company readily went to bed, only patrol D and C took turns to keep watch. Three lonely tents in the open country were testimony to the will of those twelve who with the idea of 'get to know yourself and the world' set off on a cycling trip with the aim of life experience, brotherhood, resilience and further knowledge of India.

Jurek Krzysztoń in Bijapur

'A Scout considers everyone a neighbour and every Scout a brother.' A beautiful idea but will it be put into practice during these five days? It was not fulfilled on the first day, what about the others? Will they realize of their own accord or will they need to be persuaded? **- *Jan Siedlecki (from the trip's chronicle)***

4th Hike to Ratnagiri –Rover Scouts and Ranger Guides – 7-16 October 1946

7 Oct – We assemble at the church at six in the morning. From here we start the 'Outward Bound!' expedition. My rucksack is heavy, I don't know how I'll carry it, but a lot of the food will go into my stomach so it will get lighter. After church we went to the symbolic tomb of the Warsaw Insurgents. Druh Ryś, who's leading the expedition, said a few words. If we encounter any difficulties or if it's heavy going we, are to return in our minds to this tomb and remind ourselves how they suffered and this will give us new strength. It's true. In difficult moments I always think about how Jesus suffered and it helps me.

The train was waiting for us. We organised a real marathon run to catch it. The carriages were packed like sardines in a tin, but somehow we pushed our way on, only Ela was left hanging on the step with one foot. At Kolhapur station we were divided into three groups and we travelled by cars to Chandoli. Here there was swimming and food. Our group, with Lalka Wiśniewska as our leader, set off first. On the way we saw a viper about two metres long which crossed our path. Our rucksack straps dug into our shoulders so we used our Scout scarves to pad them. *– Jadwiga Wróblewska*

8 Oct – Reveille at 4:30a.m. It's completely dark as we are in the hills. We set off at 6 o'clock. At two we stopped in Sakhara by the river where some of our Guides nearly drowned, so Druh Ryś' advised that the girls let down their plaits, so that they could be easily rescued, proved valuable. Whenever it was necessary, three groups of boys instantly jumped into the water in three different directions. After a while Stasio W. was pulling dhna Jadzia by her plait while Franio G. dragged Hela 'Hare' who was shouting something incomprehensible. After lunch the patrols went to reconnoitre the area. Two new songs were also composed: "Along Unknown White Roads" and "The Rover Scouts Troop". – *Ranger Guide (from the trip's chronicle)*

D. Pniewska, Ryś-Zuch, W. Wiśniewska and Z. Kaptur

11 Oct – We marched through Ratnagiri in formation with pomp and circumstance. The town stretches out over one and a half miles. It's a bit cleaner than our Kolhapur. When we reached the sea, we took off our shoes to follow the tradition of walking into the sea and wetting the wreath of shells that we had brought back from the last hike. We pitched the tents among the palm trees. Our patrol cooked lunch. As there are a lot of false rumours about our (i.e. the Boy Scouts') cooking abilities, I have to write about this in detail. Lunch was to be beetroot soup and pancakes. We poured the water all at once into the pancake batter so we had trouble dissolving all the lumps. But everybody, including our dog Bill enjoyed them. But the girls made a pudding which came out horrible. It was so sticky that poor Bill's mouth got stuck and we had to prise his jaws open with a stick so that he could loosen his noble face. So now all objective observers can decide who are the better cooks. **Rover Scout *(from the trip's chronicle)***

13 Oct – Sunday. We march to church in columns four abreast. There are few Catholics in Ratnagiri. The little church is on a hill hidden by ancient trees. Small but great in itself. How modest and yet how rich. The faithful, all Indians, made a great impression on me. Like the first Christians – deep in prayer, concentrating, full of faith. We sang in Polish.

14 Oct – This is the penultimate day of the hike. Reveille at 6:30a.m. Before breakfast ALARM CALL! – in full kit. After five minutes the patrols are climbing the hill to reach the fort on the summit. Two patrols stopped right by the lighthouse. Down below the two remaining patrols are sending a message using disks. Oh panic! Not everyone remembers their Morse code. The message reads 'Whoever returns first, will get the most pudding.' Tadzik was the first back and got an extra helping of pudding with jam. This time it was good. Even Bill enjoyed it. Before lunch we had a chance to swim that everybody had been waiting for, but how! Druh Ryś, with a towel on his head, had us clambering into pyramids and dancing in the water. We decided to give a picture of the Black Madonna (copy of the famous picture of Holy Mary, Mother of God in the shrine in Częstochowa, Poland. Editor's note) to the local church. Frycek (Freda Oszmiańska) will organise this. Druh Ryś in his last campfire yarn said: "It's important that the sound of the sea should speak to us only of the Polish Baltic, that the shade of the palms should seem the shade of linden trees, that the life we are living now should be lived only for Poland". – *(from the trip's chronicle)*

Pilgrimage to St. Francis Xavier's Tomb in Goa – 1 – 15 May 1947 Rover Scouts Troop and 5th Boy Scouts Troop from Valivade.

6 May – I got up at four in the morning to get to mass on time and take holy communion. The cyclists left at daybreak while druh Ryś, Father Jankowski and I left by car about midday. The car broke down almost immediately, just outside Kolhapur. Our cyclists were riding fast. By the time we caught up with them they had done 40 miles in four and a half hours, a good start. The smallest Scout was so exhausted that they were pulling him with ropes. I got on a bike and did six miles in a very strong wind. We cook supper by a river and after the moon rises we cycle on. The road is beautiful, the wind has dropped, we're surrounded by forest, the moon shines with a bright silver light. Exactly at midnight we reach the bridge, seven miles from Belgaum, that is about halfway to Goa. We sleep on the tent stretched out on the ground and cover ourselves with waterproof capes.

7 May– the 2nd day of the pilgrimage. We were up before dawn. We did seven miles in record time but it took a long time to find the Salesian Fathers in Belgaum. We refreshed ourselves with ice cream (a great attraction) and lunch (very tough meat). In the afternoon the boys rode off while druh Ryś and I stayed until the evening looking for petrol. On the way we had a puncture, but luckily at low speed… We hit Khanapur at nine in the evening; the boys led us to the home of a friendly Englishwoman.

8 May – Khanapur-Londa-Anmode (British side) - Portuguese customs. We get up at first light and are in the mission church before sunrise. It's small and poor, because of the poverty of the local population and it is served by only one priest from Goa. Returning through the streets of the waking town, we see pictures of saints and crosses on the walls of the houses. Nearly the whole population is Christian. Even here you can feel the influence of Catholic, Portuguese Goa. Niusiek is ill so I cycle in his place. We stretched out in a long snaky line. We did 15 miles to Londa and then turn towards the Portuguese Goa frontier. Again two bikes break down, Godlewski's and mine… The road goes up now, it is in bad condition with potholes and stones and finally, glory be, we reach asphalt. We stopped at a sign saying GOA PORTUGUESA, PANJIM 70km. So now it's kilometres, not miles and it reminds me of Poland. We race down the asphalt road, you can smell burning rubber as we brake. At a height of over 1000ft we stop to look at the amazing view. The steep hills are covered by dense green jungle. The trees crowd together with a mass of jumbled creepers, branches and shrubs, above us piles of black boulders. We feel like we're hanging between heaven and earth! We race on, maintaining gaps between us for safety. For the moment everything is going well. Suddenly… I jump off the bike at full speed and manage to stop the old bone shaker just before the precipice. It happened in a split second. I load the bike onto the roof of the car and we carry on. We stop in the heart of the jungle. It's a real, powerful Indian jungle here. In comparison with this, Chandoli is just a little wood.

9 May – Fourth day of the trip. Portuguese customs post – Panjim (New Goa) 58 km. We stop 15 km before Panjim to get changed and have a wash because we are going to be met outside Old Goa by a local youth organisation. They wear quite nice uniforms with knee high boots. There is also a youth inspector for the whole of Goa with them. We race on together and we soon reach the church where St. Francis Xavier, the great apostle of India, is buried. In Panjim we stop at the villa of a Pole, Mr. Kronenberg.

10 May – Fifth day of the trip. Panjim. Mass at dawn at the Salesian Fathers. There are a few of them. They came here less than a year ago and with no funds set up a big mission station named St. John Bosko with a chapel, classrooms, library and a string of workshops. The Salesians offer a helping hand to the most marginalised members of society and those living in dire poverty. We offered them a picture of Black Madonna that we had brought from Valivade. The Father Superior of the mission, a pleasant Italian with a long beard and a constant laugh, gave us a

beautiful sermon. He talked about Poland, about us, about our pilgrimage with such feeling that everyone had tears in their eyes.

11 May Panjim – Panjim is very European and quite lovely with clean wide streets and tidy houses drowning in the green of palms. It reminds me so much of Poland. This impression is reinforced by the roadside shrines and crosses. But I am even more reminded of my country by the people: pleasant, helpful, kind. It's wonderful to swim in the sea but better still to sail on a boat, slowly pulling in and letting out the ropes to catch the wind and follow a route. I am jealous of one thing – their happiness. Because they are happy while we...

All the participants in the Pilgrimage

12 May – We are in the city of churches and ruins in the Old Goa. We have reached our goal. We attend mass at the grave of St. Francis Xavier in the Basilica Born Jesus. We kneel by the small altar. Above it stands the silver tomb where the remains of the great apostle of India lie. Old Goa is imbued with the sadness and emptiness of the abandoned, lonely houses of God falling into ruin. It was once a large, beautiful, vibrant town. Lying by the sea it had wonderful palaces, gardens, houses, shops, streets and churches. But the Inquisition started the decline of the town ...then an infection hit the town, all kinds of illnesses... half the inhabitants died within a month... Nobody would remember the splendour of Old Goa if it were not for the legend and the churches.

13-14 May Panjim, Portuguese boys' camp. – It was a formal campfire with many guests. There were lots of speeches, Druh Ryś offered them a book and a pennant while they gave us 24 harmonicas and books about Lisbon. Before we managed to go to bed, we had to run and help rescue the Goans, because there was a forest fire. A small part of the jungle was on fire with a fierce bright flame. At first there was total panic. We went in among the burning palms and started to cut them down while a chain of people formed to bring water from the nearby sea. Soon the fire was out. We showed what we were made of and Druh Ryś was proud of us. Before we left, we signed each others' diaries with the Goan boys.

15 May – 10th day of the trip. Today we are saying goodbye to Panjim and Portuguese Goa. The ship SS Diparati of the Bombay Steam Navigation line is waiting for us in the harbour. It's a rather nice steamer with two funnels. Bom dia, dear Goans, maybe we will come and visit you again. In my short life I have seen many beautiful and ugly places; I have seen many people and I have lived through so much. But the most beautiful land that I have seen outside Poland is the land of St. Francis Xavier.

During our whole trip we covered 441 miles of which 150 were by sea. I cycled 155 miles. The trip lasted 14 days. But on the map of India it looks microscopic. – *Jerzy Krzysztoń*

(N.B. The seventeen year old writer of this extract rode a bicycle with one arm. He lost the other a few years earlier in a road accident in Tehran.)

BROWNIE AND CUB PACKS AND THEIR LEADERS

The pack of "Krechowiaks Ulhans," with I. Janczewska and Z. Dąbek last but one on the right

The organisation of Brownies and Cubs was never so important as it is now, in exile, when the war had deprived many children of the warmth of their home and had broken up many families. The Brownie or Cub pack, must to some extent, replace it. Realizing this we organised training – two courses for Pack Leaders, a course for Summer Camp Leaders and another one for Assistant Commissioners. Soon, like mushrooms after rain, packs of Brownies and Cubs started to appear in Valivade. Now there's more than a dozen of them. Each has already developed its own customs and traditions and its sign – the totem. In the Golden Books of the packs we can see the names of the bravest Brownies and Cubs while the ribbons on the totems show that the Brownies and Cubs have gained many badges. – *Wir (Ela Woyniłłowicz) Polak w Indiach December 1945*

Panhala 5 June 1944 – Adventure Course. It was a clear, calm night, as I stood, with full kit in the castle courtyard. I could still hear in my mind the words of Will-o'-the-Wisp (Dhna Janka Ptakowa): "The chief is calling you. Go to the well near the main gate." As I walked down the stone steps of the well I felt the cold and emptiness. But a voice reached me from above:- "Wash your eyes - so that you may see well, your ears - so that you may hear well and your brow – so that you may think well." Please God, may I always have my eyes and ears open to all that is beautiful. When I returned to Will-o'-the-Wisp, I heard the question: - "What is happiness?" I answered: - "I am happiest when I give happiness to others." - "You have thought well," she responded, sending me to the tower for further directions. There I had to examine my conscience and talk to Black Lion (Father K Bobrowski) in the crypt. Later I followed a light from the Tiger Gate and had to walk with a cup of water. It is as difficult to go through life without losing an ounce of one's honour as it is to carry this water without spilling a drop. By the dying fire I was asked to think about how my work could equal the blood and sweat of our soldiers or the despair of those who had stayed back home. In the chapel I prayed for the strength to continue my path in life. I will never forget that night and neither will any of the others who spent that night walking the dark paths of Panhala reflecting on themselves. – *Zocha Dudkowna (From the Pack Leaders' chronicle)*

19 June 1944 – The kite festival. On Sunday all the Brownies and Cubs assembled, and each

Brownie had a kite. Some of the kites were very pretty. The leaders inspected the kites and then we flew them to see whose flew the highest. Then one of our leaders came dressed as druh Ryś, and we had a sing-song. People whose kite had flown the highest received prizes. In our pack Irka Suszko's kite was the highest. *– Brownie Ada Bąk From the chronicles of the Fireflies Brownie Pack*

(The most attractive kite belonged to Wyrwidęby pack with the inscription 'Division 303')

Presentation of totems. – All the packs went to the courtyard and played for a long time. Then we stood in a square and all the leaders went inside and brought the totems. Each leader came forward and held their totem. The sixers stepped out into the middle to take the totems from the leaders. Then we practised marching. *– Brownie Zofia Sikona*

March past – When the Polish Consul arrived, all the packs came with their totems for a march past. There were a lot of people. Then the packs marched along the road one by one. Some were dressed as Red Indians, others as commandos while the Fighting Eaglets pack walked on stilts. Our pack, the Fireflies, spun golden threads from our totem and we sang our song. Everybody liked it. *– Brownie Danuta Katkiewicz*

(from the Chronicle of the Brownie and Cub Pack Leaders)

Fighting Eaglets pack walking on stilts

1 Jan 1945 – The pack leaders greeted New Year 1945 with wishes and hope and they weren't disappointed because we received the long awaited title of Brownie and Cub Pack Leader. The official ceremony was held on New Year's Eve in Panhala, at the site of our first campfires and training courses. The moon had not yet risen but thousands of stars were shining in the sky. We debated what we could compare them to. 'Silver nails' was a bit banal. 'The shining eyes of angels'? 'The coat of night sewn with pearls,' recited Kryśka. 'They look like stars,' remarked Staszek philosophically and we couldn't disagree with him. We change the subject to reassure ourselves that the chief would soon be here. We had never before waited for him with such anxiety. He's coming… the trodden leaves crackle. In a while we will get the Wolf Cub badge… (the symbol of a qualified Brownie and Cub Pack Leader.) In the darkness of the Indian night the Pack Leaders Circle will be born.

The fire burns, songs and memories flow. Druh Ryś says in

"Wyrwidęby Pack" (1945) and their leader Cześka Moniak, with her deputy Z. Kamiński, then T. Chodorowski, Z. Sawko, A. Bąkowski, J. Celejewski, E. Pazik, S. Opioła, J. Jundziłł, Z. Ucinek, J. Birecki, L. Jutrzenka, R. Babula and T. Aniśkowicz

"Firefly Pack" and their leader Danka Pniewska

his fireside chat: - "Leading Brownies and Cubs is a privilege given to you by Poland. Have you earned it? Look into your heart. In a while, you will become a Pack Leader forever." One by one we approach the chief who pins the Wolf Cub badge we have dreamed of to our sleeves. We sit in a tight circle. No one has been left outside. How wonderful, how wonderful that all of us are now Pack Leaders for real.
Pack Leaders Chronicles

St. Kazimir's Day

4 Mar 1946. In Wilno (now Vilnius) this day is particularly festive. Every year there is a big market in St. Kazimir's Square. People come from all over the district, bringing a range of products. This evening's campfire was dedicated to Eastern Poland and particularly Wilno. Witek played various pieces from Lwów and Wilno. Ela gave the talk. It was straightforward and interesting and I think everyone felt as if they were in Wilno looking at the fair. We returned from the campfire in silence. Everyone was deep in thoughts. (Wilno and Lwów, two old towns in Eastern Poland, after WWII were handed over to Lithuania and Ukraine) *Niusiek (Franek Herzog)*

Kite flying festival: Cubs and their leaders, Halina Strycharz, Krysia Olesiak, Idalka Rozwadowska and Marysia Małaczyńska

POLISH – INDIAN MEETINGS

31 Mar 1947. Today we went to Kolhapur for the inauguration of the new Maharajah. The procession was led by an elephant with painted trunk, ears and head; covered with a red cape. Behind him came an infantry detachment, then the police, post office workers with their bicycles, followed by the court servants and finally a second elephant with a silver throne on his back. But there was nobody seated on the throne. Then came the carriages. The Maharajah rode in the third one under a swaying umbrella with a dignitary holding the royal insignia behind him. In one of the following vehicles rode the British Resident with a bored expression, as though he'd had enough of it all. The whole town was magnificently decorated with specially constructed gates and portraits of the whole dynasty starting with Shivaji, were hanging from the walls. This Maharajah is also a descendant of the great Chhatrapati who was greatly respected by his people… The streets were filled with crowds, which the police tried to organise into columns,

leaving the centre free for the procession. With Mr. Valivadecar (The Indian Scoutmaster) at our head, we marched to our designated viewing point. – *Janka Jankowska.*

9 Aug 1947 – At 11 o'clock in the morning a group of 100 Indians attending a Scouting Course for Teachers in Rukadi, came by train to visit us. There were only five women in the group. Our old friend Mr. Valivadecar, a Scoutmaster from Kolhapur, brought them and they were also accompanied by the Principal of their College. Our guests spent two hours visiting the schools in the settlement then the Ranger Guides prepared tea in a samovar for the Indian Scouts on our Scout farm, while the staff were invited to tea and cakes at the Wanderers' Club.

For the benefit of the visitors special Scout and Cub meetings were held by the river. There were short trips in our two kayaks; an exhibition of signalling in Morse code; and a demonstration of how to pitch a tent, which was then presented to our guests. Then they went to the sports' ground where there was a football match between Indian students from Miraj and the Valivade team. The star turn of the programme was of course the campfire which was attended by all the Guides, Scouts, Brownies and Cubs. Melancholy Indian melodies mixed with lively Polish songs. Our folk dances were followed by our guests' presentation of the 'Tiger Hunt.' The talks started – in English, Polish and Marathi. Then there was the formal moment of signing the letters which we were sending to the Jamboree, opening today in France. We present our guests with red and white pennants as a souvenir. After the campfire we accompany them, singing, to the train station.
– *From W Kręgu Pracy No. 21*

Visiting Indian Scouts in Rukadi

Return visit 14 Aug 1947 - The day before India regained its freedom, we were invited to visit the Indian Scouts in Rukadi. At 2 p.m. we left en mass from the settlement. Everyone was in dress uniform with capes. We marched along the railway lines and were there in an hour. The Indian Scouts occupied large buildings surrounded by a wall. Inside the walls there were spacious grounds with a young mango grove. (This was probably the teacher training college.) On the green by the mango grove stood a tall flagpole and the Indians raised their flag to the sound of a band, singing their national anthem. We were regaled with Polish style sweet lemon tea, although they usually drink theirs with milk. There were joint photographs on the green, then Indian dancing, gymnastics and fencing. Our presentation was drill. 40 Scouts marched in the formations of a Guard of Honour Company of the Polish Army! There were also joint games: tug-of-war and Cossack and Tartar.

Evening came. More tea, then a joint campfire. We sang songs together. When we didn't know the words, we hummed. The Indian Scouts did a fantastic show for us: jumping through burning tyres and a dance with lighted torches. The commander of our hosts presented druh Ryś with two flags – the Scout flag and also the flag of the newly independent India as well as a memorial plate in the shape of a shield. We were accompanied by a crowd to the railway station. – *Staszek Harasymów*

OF EXHIBITIONS AND OTHER MATTERS

35 years of Polish Scouting – jubilee exhibition. The theatre hall in Valivade is drowning in navy blue (camp blankets were the main decorative material – ed.) On the main wall, framed by the white fleur-de-lys, under the White Eagle (the Polish emblem) there is a Polish Scouting emblem and the large figures: 1910 – 1945. National flags and the banners of our Scouts units complete the decoration. On a side wall, a cross gleams white between the columns of names of the Scouts deceased or killed during the war. On the opposite wall, there are photographs: Marshall J. Piłsudski, the patron of ZHP; Robert Baden-Powell and A. Małkowski, creator of the Polish Scouting. Below these are photos of the current leaders of the Polish Scouting Movement in the West. Further down there are rows of tables: blocks of white and navy blue. Newspapers, Polish Scouting magazines produced in exile, chronicles and workbooks of the Scout and Guide troops, maps drawn by our topographers, woodwork, and examples of handiwork made by the Brownies and Cubs. Along the last wall there are colourful totems and workbooks of the Brownie and Cub Packs. – *L.N. Polak w Indiach December 1945*

The Exhibition

23 June 1945 – We are writing, or rather printing on a duplicator, the first issue of our paper, *Młodzi* (The Young Ones). 50 copies will come out tomorrow. We will send them to various 'high ups' for their opinion. The publishers are the girls from the 'Flame of Jungle' Senior Group. Of course Hanka Sahanek, Irka Krajewsa and Stela Czekierska did most of the work. I'm waiting for my young nephew, Staszek, to go to sleep so that I can join the 'printing press' team. I wonder how our publication will be received.

1 July 1945 – We are organising the Wanderers' Club. We went to town to find out the price of armchairs – 25 rupees each!

9 Aug 1945 – The official opening of the Wanderers' Club took place to-day. All the most important people were there. We had tea, black coffee and cakes… The club looks good, it will be nice to spend time there.

4 Nov 1945 – Our paper *Młodzi* is doing well. 145 copies were printed and they all went quickly. People are getting used to the idea that The Young Ones can really be their magazine.

1 Nov 1945 – We have printed a Jubilee issue of *Młodzi*, which came out very well. Gorgeous

cover, subtle graphics, Stela's style. But yesterday night, as we were printing off the copies, we were falling asleep on our feet. The exhibition made a good impression. Nearly all our arts and crafts have been sold

4 Nov 1945 – I've been on my feet almost without a break since 7a.m. But today is the last day of the jubilee. I've worn my uniform so much that I'll be glad to put on civilian clothes tomorrow. I'd really like to go to sleep but Zosia Ostrihanska had an idea of organising a night game for her girls. I'm at the second post, somewhere far outside the settlement and since there are many participants, I'll have to sit there for hours. 21 Oct 1945 – A new duplicator machine has arrived from England by sea. Tomorrow Bronek and Zdzich will go to Bombay and bring it here!

2 Dec 1945 – The pressure's on. Yesterday I came home at 1a.m. after duplicating *Młodzi*. For the first time an issue is out late. Today there were two meetings which went on for hours; one with the Ranger Guides troop leaders and the other with the Girl Guides troop leaders and immediately after that I went to help with *Młodzi* or they'd still be at it tomorrow… Zośka is now taking over the Ranger Guides and Jula the Girl Guides. I'm left with the boys which will be a lot of work as I'll still have to keep my finger on the pulse of the whole District. There's still a lot to do, before the Scoutmasters leave for Jamnagar. I'll only get a chance to catch up on my sleep on Wednesday night and that's not even certain because it's St. Nicholas Day and my class wants to organise an evening event.

5 Dec 1945 – I have inherited Bill (Druh Ryś's dog) This morning he ran away to his owner's apartment. I found him afterwards at District Headquarters. Now he's sitting beside me and doesn't look as though he wants to leave. He's probably understood that his master has gone. – *H Handerek*

Valivade 20 Jan 1947 – Once again, like every other holidays, we're preparing for Scout camps. Up till now the Delegate's office has contributed funds for these camps but since it's been closed down (apparently we're leaving India soon) we have to raise our own funds. Druh Ryś tries all possible means because the camps must go ahead but we need at least 500 rupees. There have been lotteries, dances, evening events and collections in order to raise money. Now he's organised an exhibition about India. It sounded interesting so I went with Dzidka Malec. We met Janka Goślinowska, Bronia Trzciankowska, Julka Rudkowska, Krysia Wypijewska, Urszula Kruk and other girls there. At the exhibition druh Ryś gave a talk explaining what was on the tables. On the first table there were Hindu gods and goddesses, which he didn't talk about, but I wanted to know the names of some of these deities. On the next table were archaeological artefacts from 2000 years ago, then weapons. Then a bust of the famous leader Shivaji, whose role for his nation was similar to Kościuszko's for us. Then Kashmiri products, mainly made of sandalwood and ivory as well as the beautiful handmade tapestries and tablecloths. I thought I knew how to embroider, but there's no comparison. There were also various photograph albums and books in different languages about India and in English about Poland. Beautiful dishes, painted or carved in silver. On the tables in the middle there were

Departure for a Scouting Camp from Valivade

reptiles and insects under glass: snakes, butterflies, birds and worms. We were amazed by the huge flies with a wing span of up to 7 cm! It's a monster, not a fly, shouted someone. The exhibition was a great success. Loads of people admired it. – *Sylwia Wojtowicz.*

13 June 1947 – In the rush of daily events I haven't even written that our president Mr. W Raczkiewicz has died. There is a black band on every Scout Cross and a mourning ribbon on every left arm. I have just come back form a memorial service, organised by the Scouting movement to honour our departed President. The mood was serious, sad, even heavy. Everyone felt the seriousness of the moment and the difficult situation as well as the loss of the person who stood at the helm of our ship, sailing to it's determined goal. It was difficult to deal with such losses. And we Poles have had little luck in this war. This is the second death of this kind. And so many crosses mark the roads we have travelled. – *Janka Jankowska*

EPILOGUE

All Good Things Must Come to an End

25 Sep 1946 – We said goodbye to druh Bronek who has finished his work with us and will soon be leaving for England. I'm sad about this but I'm not sure about what exactly. Is it the Lone Wolf himself or is it the order, calm and security which I always associate with him. I just can't imagine the Indian Division working without him. – D.P.

Ruins of the harem: K.Czarnecka, M.Wilczynska, ..., ..., I.Michalska, L.Wasiuk, E.Woyniłłowicz and B.Czaykowski

8 April 1947 – I'm going soon, but at the moment I can't really believe that I may never see again the people that I was so happy with. I hope however that everything will end well and that all of you will also return Home. I'm a bit afraid of this journey into the unknown. I know it's a crazy decision but whatever happens to me I will let you know. – *Zocha Dudkówna* (written into a friend's journal before leaving, without her family, on the first transport back to Poland)

29 Aug 1947 – Druh Ryś left today. The last few days have been so taken up with formal farewells and getting him ready for departure that the fact that he was actually leaving us didn't seem real. It was only today when we returned from Miraj that we saw how empty Valivade was without him. Yesterday we had the farewell meeting with all the Brownies and Cubs of the district. Druh Ryś said goodbye to them very warmly. Then we visited the Indian Scouts in Kolpahur. It was very pleasant. They are very warm and kind to us. In the evening Ryś came straight from the Brownies and Cubs sing-song to the *Młodzi's* office and together we printed one page. And today at five in the morning we had a final meeting of Brownie and Cub Pack Leaders. The last six candidates got their nominations as Pack

Leader and we sang for the last time our hymn… The Pack Leaders accompanied druh Ryś to Rukadi and the instructors travelled with him as far as Miraj. – *D.P.*

Panhala 31 Dec 1947 – This will probably be the last trip organised by the Division HQ Some of us travelled by train and then bus, others by car. The Boy Scouts and Girl Guides are welcoming in the New Year in Panhala. The rest of the people are sitting in Valivade on half-packed baggage. Half of our members are no longer here, and all schools will be closed from tomorrow.

Valivade Halt -14 Jan 1948 – It's us who should be waiting here for the departure of a transport to England but it's been cancelled again. Instead those who are being repatriated to Poland are leaving: druhna Halina Szafrańska, 'Blue Lotus' – pleasant, calm and direct; dhna Zosia Ostrihanska 'Pensive Flame' – very hard-working and thoughtful; dhna Hanka Handerek (Handerzyca) – I'll always remember her happy laughter and shouts, her unrelenting work for the Scouting movement to the cost of her own health. She will always be a model for me. She could take on so many responsibilities without complaining about the amount of work, always cheerful, full of enthusiasm for work and life. She liked to nag at one, but never did it without a good reason. I am writing these lines about the people who are leaving to recognise the work they did here in Valivade and to express my sorrow that they are going to Poland.

17 Jan 1948 – So they've left for Poland. We stood in a double row behind the station. All the Scouts and Guides of the Division, yet so few of us. In Valivade everything is packed. There are no books, no films, no money either…

28 Jan 1948 – Tomorrow the 4th transport to Great Britain is leaving with Father Kozłowski.

12 Feb 1948 – On the request of the Association of Poles in India, our Scouts and Guides travelled to Kolhapur to take part in the ceremonies to mark the end of the mourning period for Mahatma Gandhi. Everything went smoothly. We were already in Kolhapur at 7.20 in the morning but the procession with the handful of Gandhi's ashes left the station at 10 o'clock. There were elephants, camels, horses, the army, the Maharajah's personal guards, two orchestras, and then a beautiful carriage, covered with flowers, pulled by six horses. The carriage was surrounded by the Kolhapur cavalry and behind came the youth organisations, then us – Polish Guides and Scouts and a delegation from the Valivade Settlement, followed by crowds and crowds of people. The ashes were brought in a copper urn and placed in the carriage. We reached the river where there were speeches by Indian dignitaries, their priest and an English bishop. The ashes were scattered in the river to the accompaniment of sorrowful singing. – *Jan Siedlecki*

P.S. Mahatma Gandhi was killed by an assassin's bullet on 30th January1948. According to Hindu tradition, a symbolic tomb stands in the cemetery in new Delhi in the place where he was cremated but his ashes were dispersed across the whole country and scattered in many rivers.

'The Last Mohican,' Jasiek Siedlecki, travelled to England on the last transport on 22nd February1948. The remaining 'survivors' left India on 1st March1948 by ship to Mombassa in East Africa, from where they continued their journeys in different directions.

APPENDIX TO ZHP IN INDIA

Valivade District's original complement - Order No.1 - 15th October 1943

I. Skorupka Troop – leader Jan Siedlecki

J. Bitschan Troop – leader Kazimierz Naglik

Zawisza Czarny Troop – leader Eugeniusz Wrzyszcz

I. Paderewski Troop – leader Ryszard Klar

A. Chrzanowska Company – leader Irena Krajewska

T. Kościuszko Company – leader Irena Hajdukówna

M. Konopnicka Company – leader Helena Szafrańska

E. Plater Company – leader Krystyna Inczykówna

Second E. Plater Company – leader Zofia Kukiełko

Queen Jadwiga Company – leader Genowefa Borowiak

gen. W. Sikorski Company – leader drużynowa Rafalina Lech

Second M. Konopnicka Company – leader Jadwiga Puchalska

Brownie Pack "Elfs" – Brown Owl Łucja Ostrowska

Brownie Pack "Sun" – Brown Owl Zofia Dudkówna

Brownie and Cub Pack "Lions" – leader Wanda Kwiatkowska

N.B., Some Companies came to Valivade already organised in transit Camps, hence duplicated names occurred.

Valivade District after reorganisation - July 1944

1st Tribe (Grammar School) - total membership 302. Tribe's Chief - Irena Hajduk. School's Liaison Adult Helper - Miss Anna Handerek.

M. Kopernik Troop (36 Rover Scouts) – leader Aleksander Klecki

gen. W. Sikorski Troop (30 Rover Scouts) – leader Jan Siedlecki

Temporarily unnamed Company (47 Ranger Guides) – Irena Hajduk

T. Zan Company (38 Ranger Guides) – leader Irena Krajewska

E. Orzeszkowa Company (35 Ranger Guides) – leader Barbara Morawska

Queen Jadwiga Company (41 Ranger Guides) – leader Estela Czekierska

M. Konopnicka Company (from Oct.44) – leader Zofia Ostrihanska

Queen Dąbrówka Company (37 Girl Guides) – leader Stanisława Ołowiecka

Z. Chrzanowska Company (37 Girl Guides) – leader Zofia Balawender

2nd Tribe (Primary School No 1) - total membership 151. Tribe's Chief - Jadwiga Wojniłowicz. School's Liaison Adult Helper - Miss Wanda Borzemska.

Zawisza Czarny Troop (32 Boy Scouts) – leader Eugeniusz Wrzyszcz

gen. J. Bem Company (22 Girl Guides) – leader Jadwiga Wojniłowicz

Queen Kinga Company (42 Girl Guides) – leader Jadwiga Nowicka

Wolf Cub Pack (28 boys) – Akela Zofia Dudek

Brownie Pack (21 girls) – Brown Owl Wanda Kwiatkowska

3rd Tribe (Primary School No 2) - total membership 172. Tribe's Chief - Helena Szafrańska. School's Liaison Adult Helper - Br. Jan Orysiuk.

Jurek BitschanTroop (30 Boy Scouts) – leader Jan Pacholski

M. Curie-Skłodowskia Company (40 Girl Guides) – leader Helena Szafrańska

Queen Jadwiga Company (40 Girl Guides) – leader Maria Janiszewska

1st Wolf Cub Pack (16 boys) – Akela Alicja Wasiuk

2nd Wolf Cub Pack (16 boys) – Akela Krystyna Olesiak

1st Brownie Pack (15 girls) – Brown Owl Danuta Pniewska

2nd Brownie Pack (15 girls) – Brown Owl Irena Michalska

4th Tribe (Primary School No 3 and School of Rural Management) - total membership 188. Tribe's Chief - Eleonora Woyniłłowicz. School's Liaison Adult Helper - Mrs. Figuła

E. Plater Company (40 Ranger Guide) – leader Helena Szczanowska

I. Paderewski Troop (36 Boy Scouts) – leader Jerzy Augustyn

M. Konopnickiej (60 Girl Guides) – leader Jadwiga Królikowska

1st Wolf Cub Pack (18 boys) – Akela Czesława Moniak

2nd Wolf Cub Pack (16 boys) – Akela Halina Strycharz

1st Brownie Pack (18 girls) – Brown Owl Eleonora Woyniłłowicz

2nd Brownie Pack (15 girls) – Brown Owl Wanda Wizimirska

5th Tribe (Primary School No 4) was created on 7.11.1944. Tribe's Chief – Halina Wasilejko an independent Company of 18 Ranger Guides in Panchgani also belonged to Valivade District.

Members of the first Hike to Ratnagiri (15-22 October1945):- Hm. Zdzisław Peszkowski, Alojzy Błach, Jerzy Dobrostański, Zofia Dudek, Karol Huppert, Maria Leśniak, Maria Małaczyńska, Czesława Moniak, Witold Olesiak, Halina Rafał, Stanisław Skrzat, Halina Strycharz, Maria Szczyrska and Bill the dog.

Members of the 2nd Hike to Ratnagiri (22 -30 October 1945):- Hm. Bronisław Pancewicz, Miss Anna Handerek, Roman Blumski, Stanisława Bratkowska. Joanna Chmielowska, Maria Ganczar, Danuta Górska, Helena Grzybowska, Alicja Janiszewska, Maria Janiszewska, Janina Jankowska, Wanda Kolkiewicz, Henryka Kucewicz, Jerzy Kucewicz, Zbyszek Nowicki, Zofia Rygiel, Maria Sowa, Leonarda Studzińska, Zofia Surdyka, Mikołaj Suszyński.

Members of the 3rd Hike to Ratnagiri (14-22 December 1945):- Hm. Z. Peszkowski, major L. Naimski, Zofia Balawender, Stela Czekierska, Irena Hajduk, Irena Idkowiak, Zofia Karpińska, Irena Krajewska, Jagoda Królikowska, Zofia Ostrihanska, Hanka Sahanek, Irena Snastin, Halina Szafranek, Helena Szafrańska, Eleonora Woyniłłowicz.

Cycling trip to Belgaum (December 1945): - Jan Siedlecki, br. Jan Orysiuk, Leszek Bedowski, Jan Chrząszczewski, Jerzy Dobrostański, Jan Jabłoński, Gienek Oleś, Michał Przybył, Władysław Siatka, Michał Sibiński, Kazimierz Woźniak, Witold Jańczyk.

October 1946 - large Hike to Ratnagiri 3 groups

Hm. Z. Peszkowski
Zenon Kaptur
Stanisław Kaszuba
Jan Chrząszczewski
Ryszard Godlewski
Stanisław Wasiuk
Janusz Leśniak
Franciszek Gawęda
Stefan Myśliwiec
Janusz Kossowski
Tadeusz Janiszewski
Stanisław Ucinek
Karol Siara
Ryszard Michalski
Czesław Cwajna
Stanisław Hajdukiewicz
Aleksander Jerzykowski
Rafał (Hinduski 'boy')
Bill (the dog)

Danuta Pniewska
Alicja Wasiuk
Irena Kufera
Maria Czartowska
Władysława Delikowska
Janina Goślinowska
Agnieszka Huszcza
Genowefa Sawicka
Krystyna Haura
Danuta Polak
Wanda Kaszuba
Wiktoria Pipało
Danuta Postek
Cecylia Lisiecka
Halina Tyszewicz
Czesława Małaczyńska
Anna Ostrihanska
Helena Siwek
Teresa Kochańska

Waleria Wiśniewska
Janina Zbróg
Danuta Plich
Alicja Romanowska
Rafalina Lech
Halina Wasilejko
Elwira Piotrowicz
Janina Gałuszewska
Jadwiga Wróblewska
Elżbieta Rykowska
Waleria Pałka
Helena Lachowska
Helena Kitras
Czesława Kwater
Irena Zobek
Wanda Laskowska
Freda Oszmiańska
Janina Mocarska

Members of the Phm. Training Course (October 1944): - Irena Adamczyk, Jerzy Augustyn, Zofia Balawender, Estela Czekierska, Zofia Dudek, Irena Hajduk, Anna Handerek, Tadeusz Herzog, Maria Janiszewska, Jagoda Królikowska, Irena Michalska, Jan Orysiuk, Zofia Ostrichańska, Danuta Pniewska, Julia Proskurnicka, Stanisław Przybyłowski, Janina Ptakowa, Halina Rafał, Jan Siedlecki, Alfreda Studzińska, Halina Szafrankówna, Halina Szafrańska, Halina Wasilejko, Waleria Wiśniewska, Eleonora Woyniłłowicz.

The first motorcar course (May 1945) was completed by the following: - Emilia Balawender, Czesiek Cwajna, Eugeniusz Dybczak, Antoni Francuz, Ryszard Godlewski, Stanisław Hajdukiewicz, Stanisław Kaszuba, Bronisława Kawecka, Ludmiła Kędzior, Władysław Kopiec, Tadeusz Kozłowski, Wojciech Kwiatkowski, Jerzy Liszka, Jan Pacholski, Stanisław Ucinek, Waleria Wiśniewska.

III Company Leaders Course – (October 1945): - Roman Blumski, Stanisława Bratkowska, Halina Chmielowska, Joanna Chmielowska, Jan Chrząszczewski, Jadwiga Frąckiewicz, Maria Ganczar, Danuta Górska, Helena Grzybowska, Janina Haniewicz, Alicja Janiszewska, Janina Jankowska, Wanda Kolkiewicz, Jerzy Krzysztoń, Henryka Kucewicz, Jerzy Kucewicz, Irena Kufera, Romuald Liszka, Krystyna Michalak, Zbigniew Nowicki, Danuta Postek, Danuta Raczyńska, Zofia Rygiel, Anna Skrzypek, Maria Sowa, Leonarda Studzińska, Daniela Suchecka, Zofia Surdyka, Helena Suszko.

EVERYDAY LIFE IN THE CAMP
(Collective Reminiscences)

Regina Kowalewska: Our stay in India gave me respite after our harrowing experiences in Russia. There was a homely atmosphere in the Camp which helped the healing process of regaining our physical and mental health. For those who had lost their parents, brothers or sisters the scars would remain for the rest of their lives but minor wounds began to heal. New friendships, understanding teachers, Scout camps, plays, folk dances and choir-practices provided a normal (as far as the circumstances permitted) childhood and adolescence.

Renia Kuszell (Jagiełłowicz) - daughter of the First Camp Commandant describes the arrival of the vanguard group in Valivade:

Advance group with Capt. Jagiełłowicz to 'organise' the Camp

I arrived in the Camp on 8th June 1943 with my parents and a group of 21 people. We travelled by train from Karachi to Poona, then to Kolhapur near which the Camp was being built. The journey was interesting and absorbed each member of the group in a different way, therefore it is not surprising that it was some time before my father noticed the absence of one member of our group, a handyman capable of performing various different tasks. At the next stop my father looked for him but to no avail - he disappeared from the face of the earth, in spite of the fact that the Indian police and Polish authorities were notified.

School No.1 (still standing in 1994)

It was several days later that we saw our lost compatriot walking slowly up to our verandah one afternoon, dragging a fat pig on a thick rope. Apparently as we stopped during our journey he spotted a market and decided to acquire some stock for the new holding (as he understood it, coming from a peasant family). My father asked him how he managed to find us, 'I kept saying: me Polonus, camp Poland. Those Indians are not stupid - a clever nation', he concluded.

Leszek Trzaska: When in July 1943 our train stopped at Valivade Halt, which seemed to be in the middle of nowhere, a British officer who was in charge of unloading our luggage and admonishing the Indian porters by shouting at them and often using his swagger-stick, seemed very cruel when I noticed that the porters were spitting blood. But British imperialism and their attitude to the natives were well known, so it was not surprising! It was only much later when I realized that what I had witnessed was the Indians chewing betel leaves which result in the whole mouth turning red.

Wiktor Styburski described thus the general frame of mind of the population of the Camp in a report to the Office of Social Welfare in the Autumn of 1943:

The Camp is situated in a pleasant area and offers the inhabitants a decent standard of living, so a good atmosphere prevails. Possession of their own accommodation and small gardens gives a semblance of normality and women busy themselves with housework.

Polish administration, schools, the theatre, libraries, playing fields, their own police, fire brigade, a church reminiscent of Polish village churches, various organisations - all remind the inhabitants of their old country and help them to forget that they are far away from it.

One of the main problems is channelling the energy of the teenage group, predominantly female, in the right direction - to sport, social and cultural activities.

There is some disquiet concerning social welfare payments. Until recently, families whose husbands or fathers had perished in Russia or were killed in action at the start of the war, had their payments stopped after leaving Iran and arriving in India. Another dissatisfied group are those wives whose allowance is reduced by 10% because they receive some help from their husbands in the army. There are many considerations why this practice should be stopped and concern has been expressed to the Government in Delhi about it but so far to no avail.

The fact that there are many different social classes thrown together in close proximity does not pose problems. Initial difficulties were overcome by involving wider groups in social and cultural life.

A Typical Day in Valivade *by Alicja Kisielnicka, a visitor to the Camp*
(reprinted from *Polak w Indiach* 1.10.1943)

It is an early start in Valivade because there is so much to do each day. As soon as it gets light, the narrow streets bordered by flower beds come to life. Mysterious flames flicker in the road. It is the housewives lighting charcoal in the iron stoves which have to be started outside before being taken indoors so that breakfast can be cooked. Children must not be late for school nor grown-ups for work.

Children from the Orphanage are walking from their communal dining area. Granny Veronica is returning from morning Mass.

Soon the streets are filled with noisy groups of children. I follow them. They are discussing yesterday's production of Snow White. They haven't all seen it. But Józia knows for sure that it is going to be repeated again, so that all the children can see it and stocky Władek has heard that the Indians would like it performed in town in the local cinema. The children wish it were true.

We approach the hospital. Quiet! We must not disturb the sick. Near the outpatients' clinic there is a large group of people mainly waiting to have their dressings changed. As a rule about 250 patients are seen to.

I approach the primary school no. 1 & 2. One group of children have their lessons in the morning, the other in the afternoon. Soon, when the new school building is finished they will all have lessons just in the morning. I ask the head teacher about attendance. She says it is exceptionally good. Children don't want to miss lessons, as they have no textbooks and it is rather difficult to rely on somebody else's notes. Also maybe after missing so much schooling in Russia, they really appreciate being able to attend a Polish school and being taught in Polish? The bell announces the start of lessons. They say their prayers, then bend their heads over the exercise books.

I also notice that lack of solid walls separating classrooms is a real nuisance. But textbooks and other teaching materials are becoming more plentiful, though exercise books are still scarce. Work of dedicated school teachers, especially in the early stages when there was an acute shortage of textbooks, maps, or any other teaching materials, constitutes a remarkable chapter in our war time history.

Next I inspect the grammar school. It is possible to explore classrooms during break. Walls are often decorated with folk motifs. On the notice board there is a school magazine, notices about choir practice, folk dancing, Scout meetings. I can hear a music lesson in progress.

Further on there is block 29 which houses weaving, embroidery and woodwork workshops. They make theatre costumes, fire brigade uniforms, dress dolls in national and regional costumes.

After lunch I manage to observe more activities. There are 4 sports fields. Some youngsters are playing volleyball. Elsewhere Scouts are marching and singing. I look in on a literacy class for grown-ups. Outside the library I can hear a strong voice reading aloud to a group of engrossed listeners a story by B. Prus. Some of them are brushing away tears. I stop and listen for some time. I vow to obtain more books for those avid listeners.

After the reading some people join the evening service in the chapel, *Hail Mary, full of grace...* It is evening and the end of the day approaches.

One Day in the Life of Valivade Camp: *by Halina Strycharz*

My mother's voice calling my name wakes me up but I pretend to be still asleep. 'Come on, time to get up' - I mutter something incomprehensible in reply, which means "All right, in a minute'... I open my eyes and emerge from under the mosquito-net which offers protection not just from mosquitoes but other creatures like lizards or small snakes likely to fall from the rafters at night, as our rooms have no ceilings - just wooden rafters covered with tiles.

I enter our mini kitchen/washroom and disturb our night visitor - a mongoose. It never comes during the day, which is spent on looking for snakes. Our neighbour had a frightening experience when she found a poisonous snake - *naja-naja* attracted by the scent of fresh meat which she carelessly left in a bag on the floor. Luckily for her a 15-year old neighbour's son managed to kill it with the aid of a fire-hook. Meat has to be hidden cunningly from tawny wild cats which are huge and aggressive. Other foods like bread, butter submerged in cold water, sugar, jams, fruit are kept in tins or pots high up on the shelves. Water is kept in an earthenware pot sunk into the ground, covered tightly - an Indian way of keeping it cool in a tropical climate. In the kitchenette there is an iron stove, a bucket for slops and a stool with a washing bowl on top. There is a drowned rat in the bucket. Rats have appeared recently and have become very bold. Of all the creatures that cohabit with us I fear and detest them most. Bamboo matting separates our kitchenette from its twin on our neighbour's side. We can hear noises in our neighbour's flat through the walls made of matting. They say that the walls have ears and everybody knows their neighbour's business.

After washing myself I pay a visit to the latrines a few hundred metres away. Next I change the dressings on my legs since I suffer from running tropical sores, deep, festering for months.

Dzień dobry (good day), a young Indian boy, Dylu, greets me in Polish. He does odd jobs in the Camp like tidying the place, gardening and makes a little extra by running errands for disabled people. He usually leaves his bundle with us and today he has brought us some roasted peanuts as a gift. He speaks quite good Polish and understands a lot. In spite of all those good qualities he is in my mother's bad books. We know his wife, a hard-working young woman, so it was a big shock when he introduced a new wife whom he bought for Rs 200.

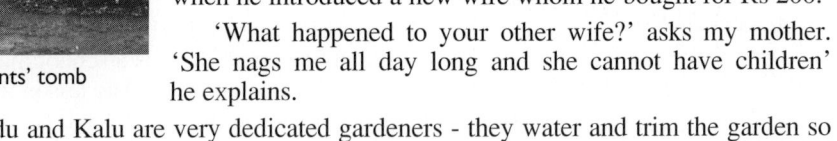

'What happened to your other wife?' asks my mother. 'She nags me all day long and she cannot have children' he explains.

Symbolic insurgents' tomb

Dylu, Pandu and Kalu are very dedicated gardeners - they water and trim the garden so that the trees are always green and there is an abundance of fragrant flowers, a variety of shrubs with multicoloured leaves, araucarias, palms, banana plants. Even during the greatest heat waves the garden looks fresh.

I am now ready to leave through the verandah, the walls of which are formed by creeping greenery growing in abundance and providing welcome shade from strong sunlight, wind and dust. The view from my terrace includes the garden, showers, waterworks, the pool, a watchtower and the blocks of District 1 of our Camp. The Indian women who gather near the waterworks are slim and very straight under the weight of linen baskets which they carry on their heads. They have a peculiar way of washing linen by hitting it against the stones and it requires a special skill to do it in such a way that the soap suds do not splash all over the place. The sight of them reminds me that it is high time to arrange with my friend Asia the time for doing our mothers' washing as that is our way of earning pocket money for ice cream and cinema tickets.

On the way to Mass I pass the main promenade of our Camp - empty now but crowded in the evenings. Mass is said by our beloved Fr. Dallinger. I pray fervently and after church, work out a bit, then rush home to snatch breakfast, school books and run to school.

After school one of my duties is to fetch a take-away lunch from a neighbour who provides them. I look round suspiciously at some vultures flying low as they often attack knocking out the utensils from our hands and devouring our dinner. I hold the pots close to my chest with both hands and try to ignore the fact that the birds hit me with their wings. My legs are shaking and my heart beats fast but I manage to bring my load to safety. I don't like hot lunches but my mother forces me to eat some. I prefer cold salads and fruit followed by cake and cold grain coffee which we usually have on Sundays. After washing up it is time for a siesta as the heat becomes unbearable. I submerge a large sheet in water and spread it over a large table in the centre of the room. Water drips from it onto the floor mats and my sister and I lie under the table as this is the coolest place in the house. My mother prefers to wrap a wet sheet round herself and lie on the bed. It gives her temporary coolness but when she wakes up she will be covered in sweat.

Tonga and water tower

It is just as well that I do not have to go out, as at this time of day it is compulsory to wear helmets to protect us from the ferocity of the sun and one can be fined for not complying if caught by the guards. I use the time to plan a meeting of my troop of Cubs called *Warszawiacy,* made up of boys from the Orphanage. Some of them arrive much earlier than the appointed time, so I offer them lemonade, sit them on the verandah with some preparatory tasks for later on and manage to get to the communal showers to freshen up. When the rest of the troop gather we march towards the river but the waters of *Panchganga* look muddy and uninviting. There is a herd of water-buffalo grazing nearby, so we give them a wide berth as they can be quite frightening. We play at trailing and tracking till sunset. Everybody cooperated today so we are marching back singing enthusiastically.

Another shower, some washing and ironing of personal items of clothing and homework by the light of an oil lamp. Out of habit I peer into the corners to see if any spiders, small snakes or scorpions are lurking about although recently there seem to be less of them around. Latin, maths, Polish, geography, English. That's the lot. Now I reach for my diary.

Vultures flying low

Before taking stock of the day just gone by I turn back the pages and stop by the letter from the 'unknown soldier' which I stuck in there. There is a charcoal drawing of *Monte Cassino* with the words of the song about the red poppies growing on the ruins... My eyes fill with tears. Many of those young soldier-heroes are really my contemporaries, just as in the Warsaw Uprising, where children younger than I were fighting. How I envy them! How do we compare with them? We are trying to overcome our weaknesses, do exercises to obtain physical fitness and prove our patriotism - but that is not IT.

Many of the girls in the Camp have now their 'unknown soldiers' since we all wrote letters in our Polish lessons to soldiers fighting in Italy and received answers from them. They are not unknown any more - Tadek, Rysiek, Bogdan and we even know what they look like from the snapshots sent. Some girls think that they are in love. My mother is convinced that I am with mine as his photo holds a prominent place on my dressing table propped against a flower-vase. Others grieve when a letter with a black border arrives. I wonder if we will ever meet them after the war? I know that if I ever fall in love it will be with a brave soldier. I turn more pages of my diary and stop by an account of the camp-fire when we sang many songs expressing our home-sickness. My favourite one is the one which compares us to autumn leaves being blown about by the winds. Sometimes we sing humorous songs usually written by Danka P.. After completing today's entry in the diary I go outside onto the terrace and inspect the starlit sky, thinking about my father. I last saw him as he left for the front at a railway station in Poland with the 12th Regiment of Podolian Uhlans. And the last memory of my grandparents is of them following the cattle train carrying their only daughter and grand-daughters into the unknown in the direction of Soviet Russia. Will I ever see them again? The clock strikes 2 a.m.. Time for bed.

The Post Office *by Wiesia Klepacka*

The post office building was situated in District No.1 of the camp. The post played a very important part in our lives as it was the only link with our fathers, husbands, brothers and sons fighting in the army. It was a source of sadness caused by war's casualties and of joy when we heard from our nearest and dearest.

A Bombay to Kolhapur train stopped at 8 a.m. daily at Valivade Halt station to unload the sacks filled with the mail for the Poles. The Indian postmen collected them. Official correspondence was taken to the Camp offices, that destined for the Orphanage separated and the ordinary inhabitants gathered by the post office building, where the Indian Postmaster Mr. Salokhe read out the names of the addressees in faultless Polish. He learnt the language very quickly. We could also communicate in Polish with some of the postmen. One of the boys, Antek Francuz, befriended a postman called Gavidron Jordou and wrote about him in his diary. After the post had been distributed women gathered in groups sharing their news with each other. If you missed the morning distribution you could call later on in the day and just ask: 'anything for me today?' You didn't even have to give your name - our clever postmaster would recognize your voice. He was pleased with a large post and worried if there were only a few letters, promising that the next day things would improve.

After the battle of *Monte Cassino* there was much sad news and the number of widows and orphans increased.

There was a box attached to the post office building for posting our own letters. During the war most of our correspondence was directed to the Army Postal Services. Some went to Great Britain or to the USA, others to Switzerland to the International Red Cross in search of missing families. After the end of hostilities in 1945 we started writing to Poland and to USSR. A lot of people sent parcels to their families in Poland. These included fabrics, shoes, tinned food, sweets. Some of those parcels never reached the addressees or there were items missing. In order to prevent theft people would send odd shoes in one parcel and the complementary ones some time later. They would also add some dollar bills for the censor.

Leszek Trzaska remembers that his stamp collecting craze started at that time. He and some of the other boys would hang around the post office building for hours begging the recipients of letters with foreign stamps for handouts. By now mail from all corners of the world reached Valivade.

Internal Circulars *by Krysia Kuchcicka*

As we had no phones there were many notices which had to be circulated round the Camp concerning the Guides, the Literary Circle, the Legion of Mary, geographic and nature societies - I was always busy. One evening my mother had had enough. 'These circulars are thrown in through the door, through the window and if we had a chimney they would probably come through there as well! What about your homework? You are always going to some meeting or other when not staying in hospital after a bout of malaria. Your school work is bound to suffer!'

I tried to point out to her that I was always learning something new when I attended those meetings that annoyed her so. My father unexpectedly took my side and said 'leave her alone - her marks are good enough', but privately warned me that I should make more effort to improve my marks.

Shops and Markets
compiled from material sent by: H. Bąbik, A. Chmielowska, W. Kleszko, I. Krawczyk, L. Trzaska, J. Zygiel.

When the first group of the inhabitants of Valivade Camp arrived at their destination, only a few of the blocks were ready for habitation and one or two food shops were open, the rest of the traders moved around the inhabited part of the Camp selling their wares from baskets carried on top of their heads. However by the end of the year there was quite a sizeable Indian market situated on the peripheries of the Camp, near the main road and even a few Polish stalls, mainly butchers. There was a hairdresser, a tea-shop, souvenir stall, a photographer, a place which had bicycles for hire. There was a variety of fabrics for sale so that you could make your own dresses or have them made to order in the Camp sewing workshop. You could buy toys, sweets, etc. Hand-made sandals could be obtained in the market but in order to buy manufactured casual shoes it was necessary to travel to Kolhapur to the Bata shoe shop.

Silver bracelet

There were two shops selling leather handbags, wallets, ivory animal figurines - especially elephants, silver bracelets with engraved emblems of the town of Kolhapur, Polish Eagle and silver signet rings - a must for the Camp dandy.

You could buy a variety of fruit like juicy mangoes, papayas and bananas in the market. Of other food products at first sugar and butter were rationed so we had to use molasses for sweetening drinks. Bread, tea, coffee, flour, salt, pepper, cooking-oil and meat were all available.

Paraffin oil for the lamps and charcoal for our stoves and irons was bought from the main contractor, Mr. Pardeshi. Leszek T. remembers that the boys found another use for the paraffin: since carbon paper was not available they would soak a page from an exercise book in paraffin to make it transparent, which enabled them to copy maps from the geography atlas accurately. The downside of this invention was the smell of petrol which lingered for a few days but it eventually evaporated. Also the erasers, which were very hard, when soaked in paraffin became soft and spongy.

Food store

All kinds of miracle healers moved around the market advertising their services. Ear-mending consisted of a tiny tube being inserted into your ear and the healer pronouncing that there was a stone inside. You could even hear it grinding, but for a small price of 2 annas you could have it removed and see the object the size of a pea allegedly extracted from your ear.

An old bearded holy man Misavay, decked with a multitude of medallions, accompanied by his grandson, used to croon: 'Misavay Asierawa, Madja Jezusa'. He received generous alms.

Later on, this whole shopping centre moved to a building originally meant for the baths, but not used for that purpose. Some enterprising inhabitants opened all kinds of stalls. You could get delicious cakes, cold meats, as well as beautiful fabrics and embroidery materials. Some women, after attending needlework classes and purchasing a sewing machine would make dresses or Scout uniforms. There were no ready to wear suits but there was a man who could make you a shirt or a pair of shorts the same day. One did not need much clothing in a tropical climate.

Mr. Wróblewski made shoes to measure, but Mr. Zawistowicz, previously employed on the railways, could only manage repairs. A cosmetic salon provided skin care with the aid of various creams and at Mr. Skrzydlewski's hair salon one could get a permanent wave. There was also the photographic shop of

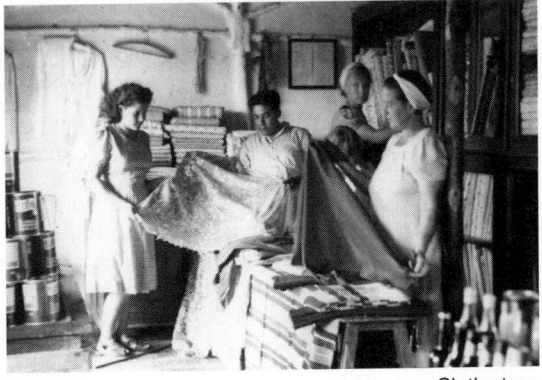

Cloth store

Messrs Pitura & Zajkowski as well as freelance photographers Klimsiak and Bachrynowski.

Opposite the main entrance to the Camp Mr. Szustak had a cafe with most excellent cakes, where one could meet friends. Mr. Tysko was selling 'poteen', a home made vodka from bananas.

Although we did most of our everyday shopping in this market, for more significant purchases we travelled to Kolhapur either by tonga (a two-wheeled cart) or by train. Those who wanted to make their living quarters more comfortable were buying coconut matting, Kashmir tapestries and curtains. Some enterprising individuals like Mrs. Wilczyńska, who had a draper's shop, travelled even further afield to Bombay or Poona for her purchases.

There were masses of flowers in the town but none with stems, just the heads as if plucked by little children. That's because the Indians use them for garlands worn round their necks. Yet somehow we came to an understanding and soon it was possible to purchase bouquets of flowers outside the Camp gates, at market stalls or even from girls carrying them in baskets on their heads. Most popular were roses, hibiscuses, tuberoses. The florists soon remembered the dates of most popular feast-days (celebrated like birthdays are in England): 15th May - Zofia, 15th August - Maria and knew that there would be a greater than usual demand for flowers. They provided for both cultures: garlands and head-dresses as well as bouquets and nosegays.

What Did Our Mothers Cook?

The first problem was to learn the knack of lighting the fire in the stove; a task which had to be done outside. You had to fan the flame or blow through a hollow bamboo stick (which could also be used as a rolling pin) till it was well established. We were issued with aluminium pots well suited to the stoves heated by charcoal.

Our mothers cooked Polish dishes familiar to them even though some commonplace products like potatoes or beef were not available. They cooked vegetable or tomato soups, stuffed cabbage leaves, *pierogi (ravioli - Polish style)*, pancakes. Some of us, except the pupils educated in English schools, had never tasted curry in all the five years spent in India. The mothers even managed to bake cakes on those one-ring stoves by putting them inside a pot with a cover and placing some hot charcoal on top.

Some ladies provided take-away meals. One of them specialised in tripe, another cooked meals for the school teachers.

Sigris stove and Mrs. L. Guziewicz

Foodstuffs

Fresh white bread and rolls were brought daily to the Camp from a bakery in Kolhapur and sold at reasonable prices. As a rule there was always enough bread except on one occasion when there was a shortage lasting two days, during which time long queues formed and people jostled each other. Some claimed that the crisis was caused for propaganda purposes in order to photograph these 'bread riots' and show how badly off Poles in India were doing.

Wheat flour was sold by travelling salesmen and was rather scarce. It was easier to buy maize flour.

Cereals. Rice was always available, sometimes sago or oats.

Fresh milk was fetched to the doorstep by Indian women for their regular customers. It was necessary to boil it in order to kill off TB bacteria and avoid getting 'Maltese Fever' which could waste you for months. It must have been milk obtained from water-buffalo. Powder or condensed Nestle's milk was also available.

Eggs like milk were fetched to the doorstep by Indians.

Fats. Butter looked very white, like dripping. Other fats we could obtain were *Marvo* and *Dalda* in tins. There was also palm cooking oil.

Meat. At the official contractor's butcher's there was rather expensive mutton, goat meat or very red water-buffalo meat for sale. An Indian surrounded by flies used to sell some pork surreptitiously outside the Camp gates. Later on, when Polish butchers opened their stalls, they sold pork and sausages. They must have been doing well as one of them, Mr. Markisz bought his son Wiktor a white racing bicycle for Rs 230 which was the envy of all the boys in the Camp. There was no chicken. There was some tinned meat but it was supposed to contain horse meat. Those who tried it said it tasted very good.

The most easily available goat meat was very tough; you could chew it all day long. In response to all the complaints Mr. Jagiełłowicz promised to obtain permission to buy beef. It was not an easy task as the cows in India are sacred, but he managed it somehow and beef was brought in. Enormous queues formed but people were promised more supplies in future. Meat purchases had to be carried home very carefully as vultures tried to snatch them.

Vegetables. These were: carrots, cabbages, turnips, lettuces, tomatoes, onions, garlic, tiny potatoes - (the size of nuts) or sweet bulbous tropical ones, sorrel. You could also buy tins of beans, peas, corn.

Fruit. All kinds of fruits were available. The most popular were oranges, lemons, limes, bananas, mangoes, papayas, pomegranates, pineapples, guavas, grapes. Apples were very rare and puny - the size of a ping-pong ball.

Drinks. We mainly drank tea, sometimes cocoa. Home-made lemonade made from squeezed lemon juice with added sugar was very popular. It was also possible to buy soda water, orangeade and a drink called *Vimto*.

There were water tablets which were tasteless yet they disinfected the water, so it was possible to drink it without boiling it first. There was no running water in our blocks so a lot of families employed an Indian who used a yoke for carrying water buckets. He was generally referred to as 'mister' (possibly from an Indian word 'bheesti' - water carrier).

Sweets were multicoloured globes, the size of a walnut, which would last a full hour. There was also chewing gum. The most popular however were 'makagigi' - nuts stuck together with chewy caramel.

'Bheesti' - water carrier

Spices were plentiful: pepper, cloves, cinnamon and various Indian varieties

The Laundry

The laundry was near the baths. We were issued with cakes of red soap smelling of disinfectant. Washing powders were also available. Those people who did their own washing dried it on their verandahs. It was not expensive to hire an Indian woman to do your washing provided you did not mind having your buttons smashed, as they would beat the washing against the stones. Some boys washed their clothes in the river not bothering to dry them. The hot sun dried them in minutes.

The mosquito nets which protected us from malaria-carrying mosquitoes and could provide us with sanctuary from the outside world, had to be washed separately.

The Street Advertising *by S. Harasymów*

One of the peculiarities of Valivade Camp was the street advertising, utilizing audio-visual techniques. It was carried out in the main and side streets, or in the lanes between the living quarters, so as to get closest to the potential customers. The street advertisements usually appeared early in the afternoon, and their frequency depended on the weather and the type of goods or services offered. The loudest of them were the ads of the picture shows in the local cinema. Most of the films shown were in English. Their titles were translated into Polish, then sign-written in colour on double-sided billboards. They were quite large and heavy, and were carted or carried on special yokes by the Indians, accompanied by a group of musicians drumming and squealing on their reed pipes, loud enough to awaken the dead.

More frequently than films, Indian women advertised their goods and services. They specialized in applying a coat of cow-dung to the clay floors of our quarters. Clay floors in a hot climate dry up quickly and become very dusty. A mixture of cow-dung and clay stabilizes the floor surface and provides longer wear. The women also offered to wash linen. Dressed in saris, perfectly upright and carrying a wide metal bowl filled with the precious dung on their heads, they usually walked along the verandahs of our quarters and yelled their message in pidgin Polish, making many Poles laugh. It sounded something like this:

'Washing, daubing for you. Fresh shit, lots shit.'

In the tropical Indian climate, cold lemonade and ice cream were very popular. The lemonade was sold in glass bottles with specially shaped necks to retain a rubber seal and a glass ball, instead of a cork. The pressure of gas inside the bottle kept the glass ball tight against the rubber seal. Pressing the ball opened the bottle. Indians produced this lemonade on small and simple manual machines. It was then cooled in ice packs. But the ice cream was produced in a Polish-owned cafe and was really delicious. Both of these products were sold by door to door salesmen, who sang the message in pidgin Polish to an Indian tune. It was something like this:

'So cold, good lemonade. Lots gas, lots juice. So cold lemonade very good'.

And then they yelled 'Warsaw ice cream, Cracow ice cream'.

To the story of the vocal street advertising in Valivade, I must also add the Polish kids who sold our Polish weekly paper printed in India. Needless to say, they were just as loud but had no difficulties with the language.

ENTERTAINMENT

The Cinema in Valivade *by L. Trzaska*

As a rule films were changed every two days and there were two shows each day. In order to find out whether a film was worth watching, one of the boys was chosen to see the first show of the day and report back. There were two kinds of films as far as we were concerned: those with a lot of fighting, shooting, horse-chases which were worth seeing and the other kind fit just for girls because they were full of love scenes, kissing and the like, and nobody got killed.

Cinema in the camp

Adventure films especially those with Tarzan, provoked us to try out our own strength following the screen heroes. It is a miracle that we did not end up in wheelchairs, because even though we could climb trees in an ape-like fashion, we did not possess much common sense.

When Torches and Tomahawks *by S. Harasymów*

For us teenagers the cinema in Valivade Camp was a great attraction. It stimulated our imagination and was also a source of ideas for our fun and games. The films were mainly American and each was shown for 2 or 3 days, 7 days a week. Our knowledge of English then was minimal, so we opted for quick-action films and short dialogues. The most popular were those of the Wild West or of European history, full of sword fights and fencing duels. Other favourites were Tarzan films and some comedies. During the years of our deportation and subsequent wanderings from place to place, we were deprived of such entertainment. Now was the time to make up for the losses, to the extent we could afford. The film shows were not for free. The cheaper front stalls in the cinema were separated from the back stalls by a not very high partition. As soon as the lights went out, and the film was about to start, one could hear a rumble on the wooden floor caused by the kids jumping over the barrier. There were others who watched the films through small holes drilled in the asbestos lined walls of the cinema. But they were usually chased away by the security guards. One of them, an old man, often said, that the film shows were not worth the money.

We were of a different opinion and whenever we could, we attended the cinema in droves. Some films were based on European history and we could comfortably relate to them. The actors were usually engaged in fencing duels, which we enjoyed very much. To own a sword or any cold steel weapon was beyond our dreams. But we imitated the fights with bamboo sticks. One of our idols was Zorro. His characteristic signature appeared on our exercise books, school seats, tables and blackboards. In our staged stick duels there were no fatalities but many cuts and bruises.

The cowboy films were also popular with the teenagers. Whoever missed such a film, listened to the stories told by those who had seen the picture. The actors were identified in a descriptive manner, i.e. the one with the moustache, the one in the black hat or the one on the white horse. We imitated the cowboys in our own way. We could not even dream of riding a horse but the toy guns and the second belt for a holster were attainable. The guns were whittled from wood and the belts with holsters were made from any type of strap. We organised cowboy games, set our own rules and formed bands of robbers. The aim of the game was to rob the hostile band of all their guns. The trick was to approach the enemy unnoticed within 10 steps, point the gun at him and be the first to shout, 'Shut up'. The cowboy taken by surprise had to forfeit one of his, say, three guns. The ideal places for these games were the rows of partly abandoned communal laundry and bathroom buildings.

The first colour film screened in Valivade was a Wild West film entitled, 'When torches and tomahawks bring shivers of fear'. An exciting story depicting battles between the American Cavalry and the Red Indians. In one of the scenes the Indians attacked an American wooden fort, enclosed with a palisade. Despite very consistent gunfire by the Cavalry, the Indians managed to set the fort alight with blazing arrows. It was a spectacular sight against the night sky. The young picture-goers did not wait long to recreate the scene. The next evening bows, arrows, cotton wool, kerosene and matches were ready. It is worth remembering that the whole Valivade Camp was constructed of timber and bamboo mats. Luckily the roofs were covered with clay tiles. When a fireman on duty noticed from his observation tower the flying blazing arrows, he sounded the alarm. The 'Red Indians' of Valivade suddenly disappeared and the hazardous game was not repeated again.

Censorship of Films

There was a Committee of four, including the Headmistress of our grammar school, who were obliged to watch every new show in order to decide whether the film was suitable for the youngsters.

License to Ride a Bicycle - *Stach Harasymów*

The present day problems of road safety in our cities were also tackled over half a century ago in our Valivade Camp of nearly 5,000 inhabitants comprising mainly women and children. There were only two or three cars. Even the two-wheeled carts drawn by bullocks or the single horse drawn tongas were not frequently seen on the streets inside the Camp. They were, however, present on the old road to Kolhapur. The streets themselves were of much lower standard than those of today. The only street with a compacted surface in Valivade camp was approximately one kilometre long, connecting the hospital and the central shopping area with the old Kolhapur road just outside the Camp. This old road was best suited for two-wheeled vehicles capable of crossing muddy pools of water during the monsoon season. However, we loved the road because of the rows of old trees growing on both sides. Their crowns were huge, touching each other, creating a shady green tunnel.

Cyclists: Danka Zbyszewska, Irka Adamczyk, Zosia Ostrihanska and Zosia Karpińska

So what was the problem with road safety, and how did they try to solve it? I did not mention before, a mechanical vehicle - the bicycle, and its popularity in India. In the forties, they were present almost everywhere. Not many people could own one, but many could afford to hire a bike. They were used as a cheap means of transport. In the marketplace, outside our camp, there were several bike hire businesses, well patronized by the Polish youth. It was not easy to get a few annas from mothers for a bike ride. But once the money was in hand, a race to a hiring place was on. On arrival, the best available machine was grabbed. Sometimes it was worth waiting for the dream bike with a bell, mud guards or a set of new brakes. Some machines were in a very poor state of repair. One could loose a lot of money hiring a defective bike, because for every part damaged, there was an extra charge. A puncture, a bent pedal or a buckled rim, attracted a stiff fee.

The bikes could be hired for half an hour, an hour or even for the day. But who could be so extravagant? Even a 30 minute bike hire was a great joy, like showing off to the friends a hands off the handlebar ride, gliding along the shady old Kolhapur road, or swiftly crossing the narrow pathways through the fields of golden Indian millet, green peanuts or sugar cane. When there were no annas in the pocket, the best thing to do was to spot some bike riders and yell to them, 'Hey, let me have a ride, just once around the block'.

As the bicycles were on the increase the road safety problem grew. A lot of kids were learning to ride. The bikes were often too big for them, so the ladies' bikes were used and when they were not available, the kids still tried to ride the men's bikes with one leg under the cross bar, which was not easy. The beginners had no idea about traffic rules. The more aggressive riders forced their own right of way. Those who had learned to ride a bike tried to go faster, taking unnecessary risks. No wonder the number of accidents increased. I do not remember any broken limbs but there was one fatality as a result of a collision between a bike and a truck. A solution to the road safety problem had to be found.

Someone from the Administration or the Social Welfare offices in the Camp came up with a proposal to introduce a license to ride a bicycle. The idea was accepted by the authorities and soon put into practice. They set aside part of our sporting grounds for the learners or for those who wanted to improve their bike riding skills. They also set the examination dates. Each candidate who enrolled for the exams received a set of road traffic rules to be learnt by heart. The theoretical part of the examination was relatively easy, but the practical part was not. It was carried out on the sports grounds and usually witnessed by a crowd of gaping onlookers, ready to laugh at any mistake or clumsiness by the rider.

C. Zając recalls the following stages of the test: first you had to ride along the corridor formed by tables lying on their sides without touching them, then cross a ravine over a shaky footbridge riding very slowly and by contrast - very fast.

Those who passed the test obtained a license which had to be shown on demand to the Camp security guards.

One unlicensed rider, Gienek Bąk, was stopped by the guards and detained until his mother was contacted and came to rescue him.

He remembers the shame of it to this day.

Dances *by Teresa Glazer*

There were a few wind-up gramophones around and some 78 rpm records which could be borrowed for special occasions to organise a dance in one's private abode. A few hours before the event the floor had to be freshly spread with the cow-dung mixture and allowed to harden and dry. Some half a dozen girls would gather and a few boys and move to the rhythm of the record, keeping an appropriate distance between the partners. There was a very dedicated girl, claims Janek Ch., who used to teach very patiently, out of the goodness of her heart, any of the uninitiated boys and girls to dance, but nobody can recall her name.

I remember organising one such event in our place. My two best friends Jagoda Janczewska

Marek Dadlez, Gienia Gruszewska, Wanda Rubczewska, Zuzia Marcinkiewicz, Kazik Naglik, Irka Michalska, Albin Tybulewicz, Andrzej Goławski, Lilka Wasiuk, Irka Zobek and Rysiek Kiersnowski - (Dances...)

and Irka Kudła had their own boyfriends but it was necessary to bring a third boy for me, so they commandeered a shy boy Jasio and frog-marched him to the 'party'. There was not much choice of records so we played the same tunes again and again. I remember clearly one of them: 'You belong to my heart, now and forever'.

Tree Climbing *by Teresa Glazer*

It is not unusual for boys to like climbing trees but in Valivade it was not just adventurous boys who favoured this past-time. The road to Kolhapur was lined with huge banyan trees with massive flexible branches, which if they touched the ground, took root. They provided refuge from the heat. It was possible to sit hidden in the branches and read a book or do some embroidery, which was a popular way among girls of making presents of our own handiwork for our mothers. There were some patterns in circulation for cushion-covers or doilies which were copied and embroidered in secret in order to have a surprise present. None of us had any pocket money at our disposal and if we needed anything, mother had to provide the funds and told what they were for.

I remember one occasion when I hid in the tallest branches I could reach, embroidering furiously in order to finish for the next day and a man with a Polish-English dictionary stopped under the tree trying to learn some new English words: Trousers - *spodnie,* shirt - *koszula* He talked aloud to himself not

On the tree: M. Leśniak, H. Souszko, Z. Dudek, A. Handerek, Cz. Moniak, F. Herzog and K. Czarnecka

realizing that anyone could hear him. I did not want to startle him and decided to wait till he goes but the call of nature was stronger so I had to jump down. The man gaped in disbelief. Feeling terribly embarrassed about overhearing his monologue, I just ran as fast as I could.

Romances *by Teresa Glazer*

To the youth of today who know all about sex and start relationships very early, our shy approaches to the opposite sex must look incredible.

Older teenagers would go to the cinema together, holding hands or go swimming or walking and then talk for hours outside the girl's home till mother gave a sign that it was time to end the conversation. To kiss a girl meant a peck on the cheek.

Some of those early friendships survived the test of time and there were several marriages when they met later in England, Canada or Australia. One pair of teenage sweethearts got separated, married other partners, but when they became widowed and met up recently, they married and are very devoted to each other.

Irka Kudła, Tadek Kozłowski and Jagoda Janczewska

Beautiful Jadzia G. married one of the few young men not in the army because of disability.

There was not just a shortage of young men but even boys in school were outnumbered by the girls, so boys often pretended to several girls that each was the chosen one. Older Guide leaders secretly fancied our handsome Scoutmaster Ryś, but he did not favour any of them, was just very professional in keeping all the youngsters fully engaged in Scouting exercises to keep them out of mischief.

There was a lot secret heartbreak when the time for transports leaving the Camp came and he or she had to leave earlier than the chosen one. Irka Z. remembers that after her Wiesiek M. said goodbye, she found a beautiful bracelet left among her school books, too late to even thank him for it. Jasiek S. received a letter from Baśka S. (with whom he once shared a night journey by coach to Panchgani), which he was supposed to open after she left, only to find out that she wrote in it 'When will you pluck up enough courage to kiss me?'

The younger teenagers did not even walk in pairs but in groups and might exchange a few saucy remarks in passing.

My biggest excitement was when, still in the last year of my primary school, one of the naughty twins in my class, Staszek, would walk with me after school to exchange a reading book, because my father sent me copies of all the Polish classics printed in the Middle East and I had a sizeable library of some 150 books, all stamped 'belongs to Teresa Kurowska' and numbered. In my diaries from that time he is just referred to as 'No.3'. No.2 was not very memorable. No.1 had been an altar boy in Karachi, responsible for me attending all kinds of church services for the wrong reasons. That 'romance' started when I portrayed a clumsy Scout at one of our camp-fires and afterwards they folded me in a blanket and sent me rolling down a hill. The most popular meeting place were the swings where there were always a lot of other people. No tête-à-têtes.

NATURE

The Wet Monsoon Season *by Stach Harasymów*

I am looking at an old photograph taken from the fire brigade's observation tower in a northwesterly direction. I can see clearly our M. Skłodowska-Curie High School and further out the roofs of rows and rows of terraced barracks, a few big trees on the outskirts of our camp and the flood waters of Panchganga river. Here and there are some emerging islands. The flood waters reach the distant hills on the misty horizon. One can mistake these waters for ravaging floods. On the contrary, these are the waters of the life-giving monsoon rains, considered by Indians as blessings from Vishnu, Shiva and Brahma. All this is quite obvious for the former inhabitants of Valivade Camp. We all remember the tower, the high school buildings, the terra-cotta roof tiles, the surrounding fields of sugar cane and other crops, clumps of trees and the waters of Panchganga river, in which we were not allowed to swim.

We also remember Panchganga in the dry season. It was then contained in the ancient riverbed 40 to 60 meters wide. A simple and primitive dam helped to retain enough water to irrigate the vast sugar cane fields. A walk to the dam was associated with fishing or illegal swimming. On the flat bank of the river one could come across a cremation ritual of a human body. It was not a pretty sight. Although the cadavers were covered over with firewood, sometimes during the cremation a limb would stretch and be exposed to view. A stench of burning flash hung in the air. We would then move away to find another fishing spot. In the muddy riverbed we used to catch a very tasty yellow coloured fish. Apart from a simple fishing rod or a hand line used during the day, we invented another method for fishing at night. A long cord was pulled across the river. It had several short lines with baited hooks each. The ends of the cord were anchored and hidden under water, and then secretly marked on the riverbank. The next morning the cord was found and pulled out with a catch.

During the wet season fishing by our methods was simply impossible. The flood waters spread far and wide into the fields, creating shallows and muddy pools unsuitable for fishing. The main stream remained in the middle of the riverbed but we had no boats. So one year we built a kayak in a woodwork class. It took a while before we found a suitable canvas as a substitute for the marine plywood, not available during the war. The monsoon gave us the opportunity of canoeing far and wide over the flooded fields, but getting close to the main stream was very dangerous. The whirlpools in the fast-flowing river could be fatal for the kayak and its crew.

But let us get back to the start of the monsoon season. A draught always preceded it. All grass dried up. All streets and lanes in the camp became dusty. Every gust of wind would raise a cloud of dust and quite frequently a whirlwind would whip off not only the leaves, but also the roof tiles. I remember doing my homework on the verandah, seated at a table, when suddenly a whirlwind snatched away my exercise and textbooks, and covered me with dust. Hearsay had it that the devil caused whirlwinds and if one could hit its centre with a knife, blood would appear on the blade. I never managed to verify whether this was true or not.

The monsoon rains usually started in a particular way. It always rained at a set time, say at 5 p.m. every day, for a few days. Then it rained more frequently and at varying intensity. The whole region was eventually covered with heavily laden, dark grey, swirling clouds. In the early evening we had to light our hurricane lamps, but it was much harder to ignite the moist charcoal in our small stoves to cook our meals. In the morning we ran to school in our rain capes, covering our books and papers, so they would not get wet. During the school breaks we played on the wide verandahs, which protected the bamboo mat walls and us from the rain. However, the rain did not interrupt our Scouting activities, but instead of bonfires we had the popular 'sing song' gatherings at a fireplace. We never lacked enthusiasm or energy to sing Scouting songs, to practice various knots or Morse code, to play many indoor games and generally to have a good time. During our leisure time after school and in between the rains, we played a game called 'Lots', on a patch of wet clay ground. A circle of around 2 metres in diameter was clearly marked and equally divided between the number of players. Then we took turns to strike a knife into the neighbour's lot. The position of the blade gave the direction for the division. To claim the part of the newly divided lot the player had to strike it 3 times with the knife. If the strike was unsuccessful the knife was passed to the next player. The object of the game was to win for oneself as much of the area of the circle as possible.

The monsoon weather limited our bike rides. But during breaks in the weather it was a great pleasure to cycle along the Rukadi Kolhapur road, through the green tunnel created by the crowns of the old trees with hanging roots growing from their branches. In the wet season these were swollen and light in colour. They looked like white beards. All around us, the fields and pastures were green, as if the whole of the flora had put on a fresh, succulent and shiny garment. Even the flower-beds running alongside our verandahs were transformed into colourful carpets. The soil was soaking wet and spring was in the air. With every spring there was a new feeling of hope. For the Indians, the hope of a bountiful harvest, to evade hunger, and for us, the hope of a prompt return to our beloved Poland.

Flora and Fauna *by Danka Pniewska*

Born in the country, I was always interested in plants, so it came to me as a surprise, when reading our diaries, how little there is in them about the Indian nature. If landscapes are mentioned, only the features reminding us of Poland seem to matter; fruit is compared in derogatory terms to our apples and pears.

I wrote poems about Polish weeping willows, beech trees, pine trees, or bird cherries. Yet there was so much beauty around us After the monsoon washed away the dust, plants seemed to grow in front of our eyes covering the earth with stunning greenery and multi-coloured, fiery flowers. We managed to grow banana trees, papaya, mango, in the narrow borders outside our dwellings.

In the part of the Camp, not yet populated, grew a huge "sacred tree", which provided a kind of bower made up of hanging lianas and over ground roots, in which it was possible to

Road to Kolhapur (1998)

hide. Similar enormous trees lined the road leading to Kolhapur, our main venue for walks. In the scorching weather, we looked for shade provided by trees, but one had to be careful as some, like a spiky acacia whose leaves hosted tiny caterpillars, which stung and caused blisters had to be avoided. Others, like branchy mangoes provided not only welcome shade, but sumptuous fruit, the smell and taste of which is unlike anything found in European markets.

One of the most beautiful shrubs was hibiscus with dark shiny leaves and flat flowers in strong colours with a mass of yellow stalks in the centre. Butterflies were drawn to them only to be captured by canny little monkeys, who ate them sandwiched between flowers. Equally stunning was the "jungle flame" with brown bare branches which exploded once a year in April in a multitude of velvety flowers resembling a flame in shape and colour. A branch of those in an Indian vase in the middle of a table, changed a humble abode into an enchanted palatial room.

There were also ground nuts and fields of sugar cane and Indian corn (dzugara), which Indian women ground between stones and baked corn-cakes on primitive fires. Some roads were lined with spiky cacti and there also grew date and coconut palms.

Outside the Maharaja's palace in Panhala we came across some exotic shrubs with multi-coloured leaves of intricate stem designs on them.

Our teachers had no time or materials to teach us about Indian nature, its fascinating history, ancient crafts, because they were using pre-war textbooks and stuck to Polish themes.

There were few wild animals on the Decan plateau. Monkeys, cobras and scorpions were everyday occurrences. Only once, during a visit to Panhala preparing ground for camping, when we stepped into an Indian tea-house and saw some men with guns, we were told that a dangerous tiger was spotted in the neighbourhood. However, thanks to the precautions we took, like sleeping with our helmets on (following a discussion whether a tiger starts devouring you from the head or the feet), we were spared.

The most memorable were fascinating fire-flies, the whirling clouds of which we watched in awe and wonder.

ECCENTRIC CHARACTERS

In Valivade we had a mixture of people from all parts of Poland, from all social classes, different ethnic groups and unconventional individuals. The most mysterious personality was Ćwiek, the tall, dark-skinned King of the Gypsies.

Another colourful character was Radziwoniuk who collected specimens of all Indian snakes, lizards, scorpions, beetles and preserved them in jars or dried them. He had two barracks in which to do his experiments and planned to take his specimens back home to Poland after the end of the war. He tried to become immune to poisonous snake-bites. Many years later in the Polish mountains one of the boys who knew him in Valivade met him again. M. Radziwoniuk caught snakes for the zoo, living in the forest in the wild all through the summer, telling stories of his knowledge acquired from the Indian snake-charmers about plants which made poisonous snake bites harmless. However his expertise was not sufficient to save him when bitten by a snake because he would have died had he not been rushed to hospital by a helicopter.

Then there was Mr. A. Bojko, who was hero-worshiped by boys because he told them incredible stories of his exploits as a pilot. He might have really been a pilot some time in the past, before he became concussed and confused.

Newcomers to our Camp would often suffer from shock when they came face to face with Adolf Hitler's double. It was Mr. Ignacy Kasprowicz who worked as an accountant, however his hair style, his moustache and his whole bearing were identical with that of the German Füehrer. He was generally known as 'our Hitler'. Those who were with him at the time of his landing in England after the end of the war tell the story of the reaction of those standing on the shore with great humour. Nobody knows what happened to him later.

Camp café: J. Pacak, M. Małek and A. Sahanek

Jagoda Lempke remembers her neighbour in the Camp Mr. Edward Szustek owner of a Camp café, not so much as an eccentric but rather as a very kind-hearted character. She had lost her father in Russia so Mr. Szustek helped the family whenever he could. She had a standing invitation to visit his café, where the perfect cream slices, fruit tartlets and buns held pride of place in the window, but the slightly damaged cakes were hers. Mr. Szustek also helped to make her wishes come true when it came to nudging Santa Claus. He once took her and her playmate Andrzej to Kolhapur in his car and asked them what they would like to have? 'Football, handball' they chanted simultaneously. He bought them their gifts without much ado. He always helped those who needed it without being obvious about it.

Leszek Trzaska claims that 11-12 years old retained more vivid details of the Camp life then the grown-ups. We all suffer from the same India-nostalgia syndrome and I am glad that modern medicine has not discovered a remedy for it yet. However, whereas the older teenagers were going through their first romantic traumas we were full of mischief, building Tarzan-like dwelling-places in the tree-tops and looking for adventure. I chide myself for not keeping a proper diary as we were encouraged to do by our Scout masters. The thought of my mother or a Scout master reading it was very disconcerting. Actions which were considered heroic by our contemporaries might appear scandalous to our elders.

One incident will haunt me to the end of my days. One of our mates, Formankiewicz, was a very weak swimmer. Our best swimming adventure was the fight against the current when the dam on the river Panchganga was opened. The difference of water levels before and after the dam created a whirl of foaming water too strong to control. It was fun to jump in and be carried by the current to a place where it slowed down so one could swim to the shore. Formankiewicz was frightened to dive in and hesitated a long while but sarcastic remarks by his mates made him jump against his better judgement. It was his last swim - his body was found some distance away after a few days.

Krystyna Szczucińska:

We lived in District No.1 near the market place. I best remember the flower stall with lots of pink bougainvilleas and other colourful flowers which my Grandmother often bought and kept under the table on the floor so they would last longer. Our relations with the Indians were more than satisfactory thanks to her. As water had to be fetched from some distance away, she employed an Indian called Shanakar for the job. After he filled two earthenware containers and all the other possible vessels she would treat him to tea. To mark all Indian and Polish holidays he would bring a garland of tuberoses and put it round her neck saying 'mamusza' (pidgin Polish for mother, often used by Indians in our Camp). Of all the Camp events I remember best the celebrations of national holidays, which made me feel patriotic. Whenever I hear the hymns *Boże coś Polskę* or *O Panie któryś jest na niebie* I am reminded of a warm night in Valivade when we all sang them with such feeling standing under the starry skies. This memory brings tears to my eyes.

We often had to be inoculated against infectious diseases, so to bribe us my mother promised to buy my brother and me some ice cream or cream cakes. I would sometimes squeeze the cream into my mouth and throw away the pastry surreptitiously so that my mother would not notice because after our experience in Russia we were not allowed to waste any food.

I remember most vividly the monsoon and the downpour of rain rather than the heat in India. After a storm the streets would resemble fast-flowing rivers in a matter of minutes. Once I witnessed a flaming globe descending among the houses, then, when it was about a metre away from the earth it rose up again. At the time I did not realize what I had witnessed but years later I read about a rare phenomenon known as ball-lightning which it obviously was. After the storm we would go for a walk to witness the ravages caused by it: huge trees torn from the ground with their roots lying across the railway line and marvel at the rapid growth of all kinds of flowers and plants. I remember very vividly the walks with my mother: either very early in the morning or late at night by the light of the moon or just with the aid of a torch.

During certain seasons of the year the road to Kolhapur was covered with an inch thick carpet of dark rose coloured petals, which the trees lining the road were shedding. One could feel the coolness of the petals treading with feet clad in Indian sandals, but had to be careful in case they hid a scorpion or a snake.

THE CHRISTMAS SEASON

B. Korodziejowski - 2nd Officer on m/s Batory:
(a circular of Merchant Navy Association in London for 1944)

It was customary for our Christmas Eve supper to be eaten at a communal table, the Captain, Officers and the rest of the crew sitting all together. There would be a small bag filled with nuts, raisins, figs and sweets placed by the side of each plate.

Boatswain Szynarowski and shipwright Pawlarczyk had a great idea - that the usual delicacies should be bought earlier this year and delivered to the children in Valivade Camp. Having obtained the Captain's permission and everybody's agreement I travelled with them to the Camp. I shall never forget the excitement and delight of the children

1944 Carol singers: R. Blumski, M. Suszyński, ..., J. Liszka, J.Siedlecki, ..., ..., when we arrived. The Camp Commandant Mr. Jagiełłowicz was a marvellous man. During our visit one of the crew, Stefański, got engaged. At his wedding two more chaps got engaged. Who knows where it would have ended if the fleet's exercises had not been interrupted?

Wiesia Kleszko:

Even though there was no snow nor frosty nights like in Poland, during the Christmas Season every effort was made to continue the traditions and seasonal festivities. The most important of those was the celebration of 'Vigilia' (Christmas Eve supper). It used to be a day of fasting and supper, the only meal of the day, consisted of special dishes, without meat. It was not easy in Valivade to obtain food for the traditional dishes like herring, fish, 'barszcz' (beetroot soup), 'pierogi' (pastry filled with mushrooms) or poppy seed cake

Before eating, white wafer ('opłatek'), would be shared with all the members of the family whilst greetings were exchanged. Thousands of letters from the army united the families. Exotic miniature trees stood in for fir trees under which presents used to be placed and distributed before Midnight Mass, which in Valivade was said in the open air under the starry skies. A brightly lit Christmas tree stood in the square near the church.

Festivities during the Christmas season never started before *Vigilia* but then lasted till 2nd of February. Carol singers often knocked on the door in the evening singing the familiar words of the well known carols. At the end of the Christmas Season there was a carol concert in the cinema hall.

Family Life *by Anna Gwiazdonik (Handerek)*

There were no proper families in India - just mothers with children or children in the Orphanage. Fathers were fighting at the front or had died in Russia. Our journey since the start of the war was dotted with unmarked graves.

Besides a lot of mothers and children there were some aunts and nephews, a few grand-dads and, because we had our own flats as opposed to communal living in previous places we had stayed in like Teheran, Ahwaz, Country Club, there was a semblance of family life.

Fathers were sorely missed, especially by older boys. When they were little, women who looked after their needs were enough, but later they really needed masculine company. That is

S. Miluska's wedding by proxy - Jurek Kowalski as substitute groom

why they looked up to their Cub or Scout leaders and those in turn to the two Scout masters sent from the army, Lt. B. Pancewicz and Lt. Z. Peszkowski.

What about the affairs of the heart? There were a few marriages between older girls and the sailors from *m/s Batory*, mixed Indian-Polish and even one Chino-Polish but these were rare events. There was one marriage where the groom was in England and his bride in Valivade and one of our boys, Jurek Kowalski, stood in for him. The one traditional wedding best remembered was between one of the Scout masters and a girl Guide.

Soldiers on Leave

After the end of the war a few lucky husbands managed to get leave from the army in the Middle East and visited their families in Valivade. The son of one of them, Adolf Kołodziej, later published a book *(Ich Życie i Sny - Dzieje Prawdziwe)* about his father's journey to India and his reunion with the family after so many years of separation.

The Last Days *by Irena Chmielowcowa*

In the glare of strong sunlight the empty Camp looked like a ghost-town. Dogs lying in front of their previous homes would raise their heads with sad eyes and howl from time to time. There were a few lucky ones which found a home with a friendly Indian family, like Mr. Jadhaw's, an employee in the Camp. He adopted Miss Klepacka's puppy.

The rest waited in vain for the return of their owners and were beginning to look like skeletons. In the end Mrs. Button who was in charge took pity on them and ordered them to be put down. Fr. Antoni Jankowski, a great animal lover, fed the ones that were left as best he could, mostly on sausage from the shop of Mr. Hajduga. The shopkeeper's wife commented on the fact that the priest got through so much sausage each day. She gossiped to her cronies, 'He only just bought a kilo and a half, an hour later comes again asking if I have anything cheaper than this sausage.'

I once caught him in the act. He asked me not to tell anyone, but I did tell Mrs. Hajduga since she suspected him of gluttony and after that she always gave him more than he was paying for.

We were no longer under the wing of the British Empire but were looked after by the international organisations UNRRA and later IRO created to care for the refugees. Why did they call us refugees? Who was a refugee? We never wanted to leave our country but were dragged by force from our homes and deported to the Soviet Union.

Translated by Teresa Glazer

AN OUTLINE OF POLISH - INDIAN CONTACTS
by Wiesław Stypuła

The early Polish-Indian contacts date back to the Renaissance.[1] They were initiated by sporadic journeys to India undertaken by Polish merchants. There was also Polish participation in the military expeditions organised by the western powers as well as in the missionary work in western India. Later the Polish commercial expeditions to India became more frequent. For example in 1729, two vessels under Polish colours were stopped in the Ganges waters by English and Dutch ships. The owners of the vessels apparently produced all the necessary documents validated by Polish authorities.[2]

There was an ever-growing demand in Poland for a deeper knowledge about India. In 1776 an interesting book, *Historia Indyi Wschodnich (The History of East India)* by T. Podlecki was published. In his book the author covered the history of the discovery of the sea route to India, the European expansion of colonialism there and detailed information about coffee, tea and sugar production.[3]

In the 18th century, Poland was partitioned and lost its independence, but the Poles' interest in India did not diminish. In 1820 in Warsaw, a famous Polish historian Joachim Lelewel published a remarkable book, *Dzieje starożytne Indii (The History of Ancient India)*, where he points out that Europeans also have a lot to learn from India.

In Poland, Indian culture was further popularised through the romantic orientalism present in the rich Polish literature of the 19th and 20th century.[4]

The regaining of independence in 1918 facilitated more direct channels of contact between Poland and India. The interest in Indian culture and art can be gauged by the fact, that Indian studies were opened in three universities - Cracow, Lvov and Warsaw. Dr. Hiranmoy Ghoshal was a lecturer of Bengali at Warsaw University. Between the World Wars, A. Gawroński, S. Stasiak, H. Willman-Grabowska, E. Staszkiewicz and Prof. Schayer were among the outstanding scholars of Indian culture. In the same period, many publications about India appeared on the market. Direct visits by the Poles to that country increased. Some of them joined the independence movement of Mahatma Gandhi, who granted Wanda Dynowska and Maurycy Frydman Indian names - *Uma Devi* and *Bharatananda* respectively, in recognition of their commitment and achievements. Among their many achievements, in the quest for mutual recognition of the two peoples, was the opening of the Indo-Polish Library.

In 1936 a *Friends of India Society* was established at Warsaw University where Prof. Schayer became its first president. Three years later, a Polish-Indian Cultural Society was formed at the University of Calcutta and the distinguished philosopher, writer and Nobel Prize laureate, Rabindranath Tagore, was its honorary president. Dr. Servepalli Radhakrishnan, later the President of India, played a major role in the Society.[5] Dr. Maryla Falk, professor at the local university, was the honorary secretary.

Apart from the cultural ties between the two countries, the commercial activities also intensified, reaching a yearly turnover of 100 million zlotys.

Other mutual contacts occurred during the Second World War, in truly dramatic circumstances, which are well covered elsewhere in this book.

NOTES

1. Władysław Góralski Geneza i początki stosunków Polsko-Indyjskich (Genesis and the Beginnings of the Polish Indian Relations). Oriental review, 1(141), 1987, pages 3-7
2. Historia Dyplomacji Polskiej (History of Polish Diplomacy), PWN 1982, t. II, page 407
3. Tadeusz K. Podlecki Historia Indyi Wschodnich skrócona (Abridged History of East India). 1776, page 94. See also Polski Słownik Biograficzny (Polish Biographical Dictionary), vol. 27, pages 117 - 121
4. Eugeniusz Słuszkiewicz Indie, Studies in Poland, The Indo-Asian Culture April 1959, vol. VII, no. 4, pages 412 - 422
5. India and Poland, In commemoration of 150th Anniversary of the 3rd May Constitution (Calcutta), 1941, page 6

OUR CONTACTS WITH THE INDIANS
by Jerzy Kowalski

Et quorum pars parva fui... and of which I was a small part.

Considering this topic, I decided to assume a form of a 'pyramid' where the office for the Ministry of Social Welfare in India was the pinnacle and the multitude of 'average' Poles, its broad base. For this reason I will refer to the extracts of reports written by this office to the Polish Government in Exile in London, dated May 1943:

"...Relations between the local Indian Authorities and our refugees, with regard to the care provided, are very favourable; they are full of understanding of our needs... The Indian society is also friendly towards us. Our railway transports from Iran to India and from Karachi to Jamnagar were always welcomed and cordially greeted... The Indian Government's stand is as follows: it will not and cannot provide any better living conditions for the refugees, than those provided for its own citizens, Indian or British. In conclusion the claims for our needs, which surpass the framework of the budget, are being met with a definite rejection"...

August 1943. "Delhi considers itself to be the depository for the Polish Government with regards to taking care and full responsibility for our refugees in India. *(Polish)* Delegates should only act as consultants, with a limited scope of intervention in all aspects of the refugees' lives... Our relations with the Authorities in Delhi are excellent and I will not allow them to deteriorate, even if this will temporarily harm our refugees... Since Minister Stańczyk's visit our relations have markedly worsened. It does not mean that we are at war with the Government. On the contrary, our relations are good, but the stand, which Delhi maintains makes it difficult for us to realize our aims."

It probably means that J. Stańczyk failed to settle the differences between his Ministry of Social Welfare and the British Authorities in Delhi.

To illustrate the attitudes of the Indian upper class towards the Polish refugees living in India I have chosen two opposite views written in a letter to the editor of *The Times of India*, just after the war.

"In your *Daily* of the 17th of July, the author of the letter signed 'Labourer', states that Poles in India are kept in idleness and in 'comfort', when England suffers a shortage of labour. Also, that they don't feel like working after the long period of inactivity. They are unwelcome guests. They should be sent out into society, where they can be useful."

The second view is more favourable. "Because I had the opportunity to learn about the refugees' lot in India, I feel obliged to explain the situation of the Poles, who were accepted here as guests. The Indian Government didn't encourage them to seek employment outside the camp. Before leaving the camp, one had to obtain a permit, even when moving to Panchgani for health reasons.

The majority of men in the camp are invalids or old, even so, if they had the chance, they would be happy to work. Among them there are qualified engineers, artists, tradesmen and weavers. Why not put their talents to good use?

Nothing was done to employ Polish women in the military supporting services, where they could have done a lot of good work. Many women are qualified milliners and many can sew well. Many could find employment with private firms, government or army offices and storerooms. An American army camp in Karachi employed many Polish girls in the offices as typists. The British and Indian army could do the same.

Are 58 rupees per month enough for a 'comfortable living,' according to 'Labourer'? Is he aware that the money must cover all expenses for food and clothing?

(-) A. B. Edmunds, Poona, 28th of July 1945."

Wanda Dynowska wrote in *Polak w Indiach (Poles in India)* in January 1946:

"...Our refugees have been living here for almost three years and know about India - I must say with regret - as little as if they arrived only yesterday. I found no satisfactory answer to the question why is it so? Are they so absorbed in their own worries and sorrows that they can't turn their attention to the reality around them? Is their home sickness paralysing their desire to get to know the way of life of another nation and its culture, so different from the European?

A man can be wise, holy or creative, yet poor. He can also be rich, live in luxury and possess products of the latest technology, yet be a philistine with no spiritual aspirations and even have the instincts of a wild animal. We may often jump to the wrong conclusions about the Indian village and the standard of the peasant living in desperate misery, unless we get to know about his family life and his relation to his hamlet, his artistic talents, sensitivity, the scope of his imagination and his innate goodness.

Casting 'golden threads' of mutual understanding and sympathy over the abyss dividing the nations and races will never be wasted, because the Brotherhood of Mankind is a fact of Nature, just like our common desires, longings and ideals."

What our Indian teachers thought of us? (*Polak w Indiach,* 18.10.1947)

Here are excerpts from a farewell speech to the Polish teaching staff, given by Mr. A. Samuel, a teacher of English, on behalf of his colleagues, at the end of their employment in the Camp:

... "Looking back at the time spent in your school, I consider it to be the happiest of my life... I got to know your life, your customs and habits, your expectations and I have found in them much grace and beauty. I would like to point out one of your qualities:

Before you came here you suffered much. You live in a foreign land, cut off from your beautiful country, families and friends. And yet you appear to enjoy life in these humble conditions, offered to you by God... If you know how to be happy, in spite of what you have been through, you have discovered the secret of happiness. St. Paul wrote his happiest letter in the Roman prison, because his heart found relief in the Spring of Happiness - in Jesus Christ. I assume that your joy flows from the same Spring of Happiness in Jesus, the Son of the Blessed Virgin Mary, who is worshiped in your beautiful wayside chapel in the Camp, as well as in your hearts.

I wish you a great deal of happiness. I know that Poland will regain her freedom, as India did after a long period of dependence. But you will be free soon. The Nation which discovered the secret of happiness, possesses the power to reclaim its independence."

Apart from one English lady, Fanny Wray, among the teaching staff of the English language we had a few Indians. Mr. Benjamin Appadurai was one of them. He was the longest serving high school teacher, who also taught privately. W. Kleszko (Klepacka) wrote about him in the album *The Young in Valivade 1975*:

"... The Indian from Madras had a similar status to ours. He and his family came over from Singapore to Madras for a holiday. Meanwhile Singapore fell and his return home to his teaching job was postponed until the end of the war. He accepted the position of an English teacher, together with living quarters, in Valivade Camp.

... Mr. Appadurai wore European garments. He was tall, cultured, composed and very patient with his students, - determined to get results. During his private lessons he made his 'victim' sweat, but the lesson was learned. I remember him with gratitude because, apart from teaching us the difficult language, he inspired self-confidence and the belief that we can succeed.

His son and daughter 5 and 7 years old respectively, soon learned the Polish language from their playmates and spoke it in front of their parents who did not understand it. Their native tongue was Tamil but they were also learning English.

Mrs. Appadurai was tiny and timid, wearing beautiful saris. Sometimes she discussed culinary topics with us. Although cooking matters were quite unfamiliar to us then, we were enthusiastic about practicing English in conversation. Our descriptions of Polish goodies were just as foreign to her, as were the Indian and Chinese dishes to us.

After the war Mr. Appadurai returned to Singapore to the position of inspector in the Department of Education. He wrote several letters to us about himself and his family. His children were slowly forgetting the Polish language, which had made such a great impression on their peers."

Of interest are letters written by Mr. Appadurai's children, addressed to the secretary of our Association. Here are a few excerpts:

"... It was so nice, after 50 years, to renew contacts with the people who had played such a great part in our lives. My sister Sushila and I learned your language quickly and we used it in front of our parents, who didn't speak Polish. We got acquainted with many Polish families, who invited us to their homes for tasty meals, especially, the Polish sausages - like *krakowska, wiejska* and *kabanosy,* which were our favourites. When I arrived in London in 1966 and bought some *krakowska,* I brought it home and unwrapped it, the smell of it reminded me of Valivade.

... I still keep old photographs in our family album. In one of them, there is our Polish friend *Helena* dressed in a sari. I also remember *Jadzia* and *Henia* who treated us to the meals. *Śmigus*, the water dousing on Easter Monday remains in my memory. I could not understand why my father was so annoyed when I poured some water on him.

... I also remember a scene from Valivade, when there was a shortage of water, and my father was standing at a small and nearly empty reservoir, drawing water with a bucket on a rope and filling other empty buckets for the waiting Polish women...

(-) David Appadurai

His sister Sushila Cherian wrote a letter in January 1995. Here are some excerpts:

"... Unfortunately I don't remember much from that period because my parents sent me to school in Bangalore. The only Polish words that I remember are : *dzień dobry, tak i nie (good morning, yes and no.)* I do remember a small Polish girl who stayed with us for a few days, while her mother was in hospital. As she sat at the table and faced a plate of rice and *dhal,* she didn't know how to eat with her fingers. Half way through the meal, she went and washed her hands."

Fixing the tower of Babel

In 1950, two years after the closing down of Valivade Camp, Dula Bazergan (Góral), the wife of the doctor in charge of the Polish Red Cross Hospital in Bombay, witnessed an amusing incident showing a small trace of our stay in India. When she was waiting at the Kolhapur railway station for her husband, she overheard a strange conversation between two Indian coolies. She moved a little closer to hear better. Indeed, they were talking in colloquial Polish. It turned out, that they had both worked in Valivade Camp and Polish was the mutual language in which they could communicate. Their native languages were *Gujarati* and *Konkani.*

On 11th November 1979 an article was published in the *Sunday Standard* in Bombay about a village in Maharashtra, where three otherwise unremarkable inhabitants: Dadu Lokhande, Maruti Bhosle and Sadku Gavalt can surprise a visitor by breaking into a conversation among themselves in Polish. Some of the other villagers, their postmaster among them, speak this language too, even though they know no English, a language they come across in India much more. Their knowledge of Polish dates back to the time when they had been employed in Valivade Camp.

Even after we left India - *by Gizela Nowakowska (Kopiec)*

Mr. L. Uberoi was a wealthy textile merchant and owned a shop in Kolhapur. That's where I met him before leaving for England. My brother and I were looking for a woollen fabric.

This man was very sympathetic towards us Poles and interested in our future. He asked me to write to him from England and so I did. Mr. Uberoi replied and to my surprise began sending us parcels of various fabrics. Clothing in England was at the time still rationed. We pleaded with him to stop sending them but to no avail. His reply was, "I am your brother, please ask me for whatever you need."

He invited us to India. Years went by and our correspondence continued. After his death, his son Ravi writes to us to this day. We befriended the whole of his family. When he came to England on business, he was our guest.

A monument to commemorate our stay in India was unveiled in Kolhapur in 1998. Ravi Uberoi sent us the local papers covering the event, so that we could refresh memories of our youth spent in Valivade.

The Polish Exhibition and Dancing in Kolhapur - *by W. Klepacka (Kleszko)*
(Polak w Indiach, December 1945)

The organisers of the *Diwali* Holiday festivities in Kolhapur invited Poles from Valivade to participate in the various shows, games, dancing and exhibitions. The event resembled a carnival.

A special stand was reserved for the Polish Camp exhibits, and right from the beginning it was besieged by visitors. The Polish exhibition made a really good impression on the visitors from the region. Pictures, posters and illustrations portrayed the beauty of our country, its cultural heritage and Polish participation in the war effort. Our dolls, dressed in regional costumes, looked very attractive. But the greatest interest was shown in the rich collection of embroidered and handicraft products supplied by our workshops *Zgoda* and by individual exhibitors. There were tablecloths, kilims, serviettes, cushions, bed linen, dresses, knitwear and leatherwear.

The children surrounded a scaled down model of a ladder-wagon pulled by a pair of fine horses and carrying a wedding party, dressed in regional costumes, leaving the church for the reception at home, in the Cracow district. The furnished home also looked realistic, with a stork's nest on the roof.

Some visitors were adventurous enough to taste Polish cakes produced by the *Zgoda* bakery.

On the first day (14.11.1945) of the festivities, the Indian Organising Committee invited a Polish Dancing Group to perform at the Kolhapur Theatre. The performance included ballroom dancing in the first part and folk dancing in the second. The theatre was filled with Indian and European VIPs. The Group won a prize, for the performance, a beautiful cup, which was later presented to the dancers, by the Resident of the Kolhapur Principality at his residence.

The performances of school children in Bombay *(Camp Chronicle)*

On the 30th of March 1944 a theatre troupe with *The Eastern Fairy Tale* written by A. Kisielnicka and a folk dance assembly, choreographed by T. Pawłowska, left Valivade for Bombay. Two teachers, the director of the assembly and pianist M. Sahankowa, went with them. They are expected back before Easter.

The visit of foreign guests to Valivade *(Camp Chronicle)*

On the 27th of February 1944 our Camp was visited by the following guests: representatives of the British Government in Kolhapur, the British Army, the Government of the Principality of Kolhapur, the British Authorities, the American Mission and many others representing the Indian upper class in Kolhapur. The guests visited our exhibition, were offered afternoon tea and walked round the Camp.

In the evening, a concert of Polish music was organised for them. After the English introduction, the programme included the works of Chopin, Paderewski and Wieniawski, played by M. Sahankowa and I. Kaliszkowa - piano, and H. Katkiewicz - violin. T. Pawłowska sang two songs, one composed by Chopin, the other by Rutkowski. Afterwards the school children performed two regional dances from Cracow and the Tatra Mountains and the youngest pair W. Zychówna and R. Rydel, a folk dance from Kujawy. The dancers received warm applause.

Young Maharaja with his sister and carers in the camp, accompanied by Jagiełłowicz family and Z. Łopiński

A visit of the Indian students from a school in Kolhapur - *by W. Kleszko (Klepacka)*

On Wednesday the 8th of September, the students from the High School for Girls in Kolhapur visited our Valivade Camp. The Headmistress and her teaching staff accompanied them. They were greeted with the Scout motto "Be prepared" by our youth, gathered in front of the Camp's Administration Office. The girls replied with their traditional greeting, by putting their hands together and they initiated some games.

After some refreshments, offered by our Girl Guides, all entered the theatre hall. The Indian Headmistress directed a few cordial words to the young audience and invited Polish students to visit her High School. Our youngsters gave a stage performance of several Polish national dances, followed by the High School choir and the first act of the musical play *Snow White*. The Indian guests joined in with their beautiful flute music and rhythmic dancing, in which hand movements were truly admired.

The Commandant of our Camp thanked the guests for coming over and expressed the hope that this visit would bring closer, mutual relations between the young people.

A visit to the Maharaja's Palace in Kolhapur - *by Halina Strycharz*

From what I read, or the stories I listened to about the Maharajas' palaces I imagined them to be wonderful, very rich, exotic, pertaining to the Indian culture and art, like palaces from a fairy tale. At last the day came to visit the Maharani's Palace in Kolhapur.

It was a misty morning after the monsoon rains. We walked from the railway station admiring the beautiful flowering trees, rows of white and pink oleanders and other bushes in bloom. The excitement rose when the slim towers of the palace appeared through the misty air. And then, an exotic clock chime sounded from the tower. It was an unforgettable moment. As we got nearer, the palace appeared to us in its full grandeur, but the nearby huts and poor children in rags were in sharp contrast to the visible wealth of the Maharaja.

The New Palace in Kolhapur

We stopped at the guarded gate and, looking through the metal fencing, we were stunned by the beauty of the garden, its fantastically cut hedges and colourful flowerbeds. We noticed some prisoners with chains working in the garden and sacred cows moving about freely. The elevation of the palace was decorated with carvings, columns, arcades and cloisters.

However, when I entered the palace, I felt cheated. Walking from room to room, instead of Indian splendour, I found the decor to be very much European, and not to my taste, with plenty of reds, velvets, porcelain figurines and stuffed animals. I admit, I felt strange in the presence of the tigers, black bears and huge bullocks, which looked so life-like. Finally we were admitted into the Throne Room, where the stained glass windows, some mosaics and a large painting of a maharaja were very impressive. The visit ended there but I left with a feeling of disappointment.

Visit to an Indian temple - *by Sylwia Korczyńska (Wójtowicz)*

South of our camp, about a kilometre past the railway line, on a gentle slope of a hillock there is a small temple devoted to the goddess Saraswati. The most beautiful of all, Saraswati is the goddess of wisdom and learning as well as the patroness of fine arts, music and literature.

The temple, with thick blackened stone walls, resembled a large tomb, rather than a place of worship. There was no trace of any carvings or maintenance of the walls. The rocky hillock, covered with yellowed grass and weeds, did not add to the temple's beauty or solemnity, but rather created a mood of sad neglect.

Pushed in, the thick wooden door creaked on its hinges. The small, low entry forced us to bow our heads. Observing the local custom, we removed our footwear and entered in silence and with respect.

Our eyes, unaccustomed to darkness, could see nothing. The stone walls didn't let in any daylight or the summer heat. It was dark and cool inside. Welcome bell ringing greeted us. The air was filled with the fragrance of various herbs. In a while we noticed to our left a small burning fire. A feeling of awe prevailed inside the temple.

After a while, to our surprise, our eyes began to recognise details of the interior, which did not correspond to the temple's drab external appearance. In the centre of the front wall, slightly forward, there was a small altar with a lighted fire, and on the right a heap of shortly chopped branches. Then in front of us, we caught a glimpse of an Indian woman. At the sound of our entry, she suddenly turned around and looked at us with fear and disbelief.

Our troop leader gave us a hand signal to keep quiet.

Bronek Siedlecki, Janek Chrząszczewski, Maria Siedlecka and Zofia Grużewska

The woman continued with her offering and we just stood silently waiting for the end of her prayers. Shortly, she stood up, lifted a container standing beside her and poured something into a hollowed stone. This was the offering she had brought with her. Then she moved towards the altar, picked up a few branches, placed them on the fire and sat on the step next to it. She waited until a flame appeared. The offering was accepted. Before leaving the temple, the woman bowed low and took another curious look at us.

Little flames lit the temple and filled the air with a fresh fragrance. Now we were all alone, so we could freely inspect the interior.

It was quite a large room with rounded corners and about three metres high. There were no windows. The only illumination was from the offering fire and an oil lamp on the left side of the altar where, in a small recess, there was a figurine of Saraswati. The four-armed goddess, seated on the wings of a swan, held in her hand a book, a small wreath, a jug and a *vina* (musical instrument). In front of the figurine was an oil lamp, floating on water in a hollowed stone set a little above the altar.

Beside her was a smaller figurine, representing Lakshmi, the goddess of happiness and prosperity, rising from a lotus flower and holding in her hands a sea shell and a lotus flower. Near the exit, Indra, the god of war and weather, was seated on his beautiful elephant. On the other side of the temple, in the right hand corner, above the floor, was a square, smooth-finished stone container, where earlier the Indian woman had put her offering.

I looked inside. At the bottom of the container I saw a white bowl and a ready to eat meal. I also noticed, on a table near by, more offerings - a few rounds of flat bread, some sweets, a handful of coins and a withered flower. A few steps further on was a figurine of Parwati, the goddess of kindness and goodness, who sat with her elephant-headed son, Ganesha, on her knees. She is one of the most adored goddesses in India and has the power to transform herself into two other persons - Durge - the goddess-warrior riding on a lion and the terrible Kali, bringing ill fortunes, wars and plagues. Further on nearer the exit Chandra, the god of the moon, sat on his cart pulled by impalas. On both sides of the temple, standing against the walls, were more figurines representing other lesser or greater gods.

Peace and silence, cleanliness and order, fragrance and the unending chiming of the bell left me with deep and pleasant recollections.

The exhibition of Indian arts and crafts *(Camp Chronicle 1946)*

The exhibition was organised by the junior students of the Commercial High School (in Valivade) to illustrate various Indian religions, to display hand crafted articles in brass, bronze, clay, paintings and woven products. The exhibition was well patronized and was extended by a few days.

A page from Teresa Glazer's (Kurowska's) Girl Guide Diary
16.7.1947, Saturday

Fragment of the exhibition

Our task was to do a sociocultural survey of the town of Kolhapur. It looked like a difficult undertaking considering our language difficulties. We started from the inspection of the park, which looked clean and pleasant. Next we inspected the hospital.

We were given some addresses of the Scouts willing to help us: one was Shi Pruvee Sivagi, Vidalaya. We asked a passer-by in the street in Scout uniform for directions and he offered to take us there. Unfortunately when we got there the place was shut. We then asked for the address of Valivadekar, a leader of the Indian Scouts we had met. We went to his house, but he was out. However his wife invited us in. The room was very clean, but nearly empty: a sort of trunk, an alcove in which there was an altar for the gods, and a rug. Our guide spread the rug on the floor and we all sat on it. We interviewed him for about an hour. He told us that:

There were about 100,000 inhabitants in Kolhapur, 25% of the male population and 75% of females were illiterate. The only youth organisations he knew were the Scouts and some para-military groups. Political parties were: the Congress Party, the Socialists, Communists and others. There were some sports clubs like: the Tennis Club, the Cricket Club, Billiards. There were some 40 primary schools (7 forms) and 8 secondary schools as well as a University with three faculties: Mathematics, the Arts, and Economics. Children start school at the age of three, so there are no nursery schools. School is not compulsory, but in future it should be.

Water for the town comes from two sources: a lake and the river Panchganga. There are six cinemas in the town, one large theatre and several smaller ones.

Our Scout escorted us to the railway station, where we thanked him for his help and said goodbye.

In the Ram Gopal School *by Hanka Dytrych (Sahanek)*

In 1938, Aleksander Janta-Pełczyński brought to Poland a young Indian dancer Ram Gopal. Warsaw raved about his performance and enthusiastic reviews appeared in the papers written, among others, by Prof. Tadeusz Zieliński. I remember my parents telling me about him. I was then a student at the Sisters of Nazareth Boarding School in Rabka.

When I performed the Polish national dances, with a group of girls from Valivade Camp, at the Dance Festival in Bombay, Wanda Dynowska, a friend of Ram Gopal, brought him to us. Wanda asked me to dance in front of him. Later he said, "If you should ever wish to learn the classical Indian dances, I shall teach you."

***

After matriculation, I enrolled at the Commercial Art College in Bombay. Thanks to W. Dynowska, and the financial help from the Indo-Polish Society, I was concurrently taking lessons in Kathaku (the northern style danced at the Great Mogul courts), from a private teacher. During the school holidays spent in Valivade, I received a letter from Wanda. She wrote that she had seen Ram and that he was about to start, with his dance ensemble, a great tour of India. He promised to take me along as a debutante in Kathaku, as well as a student, so that during the tour I could gain a lot of stage experience. I have kept this letter to this day. With my mother's approval I left everything and went to Madras, where the tour was about to begin.

The Ram Gopal Ensemble consisted of 13 dancers, the full orchestra and teachers specialising in the four classical dances. We also carried a great theatrical wardrobe - trunks of costumes, among which were the famous, 'crowns' set with semi precious stones, designed by Ram. I was asked to share the journey and training with a young Brahmin lady, Sohan, who became my dear friend.

The work was very exhausting. The tour included many towns from Madras to Lahore and New Delhi. We often travelled by night and had to practice in the morning for several hours under the watchful eye of our Guru. The performances were in the evening. We arrived in New Delhi a few days before the New Year of 1947. On the great gala evening we danced in front of Nehru and the Viceroy's cortege. Ram took a few of us to Nehru's residence. Nehru told us, I recall that we would be cultural ambassadors of India during Ram's planned tour of England. Nehru took an interest in me, being the only European - a Polish girl in Ram's ensemble. I also remember that he took me by the arm and led me to a big hall, where his family and English guests were gathered. We celebrated the New Year's Eve at the American Embassy, among the cream of society in New Delhi. The Indian ladies were dressed in beautiful saris, the Europeans in ballroom gowns and the English military in full dress.

On our return to Bangalore practice intensified in preparation for the planned English tour. Ram's family home was old and very spacious with a front porch, just like our Polish country residences, and in a garden setting. There was also a tennis court and a separate villa, where some members of our ensemble, the orchestra and the teachers were accommodated. Sohan and I lived in two-room quarters on the ground floor of the main building. I lived next to and was under the care of Ram's sister Jessie, a charming elderly lady, who dressed in Burmese clothes. (Ram's mother was Burmese and his father, a lawyer, belonged to the Kshatriya caste - the knights of Rajputana.)

Every day, early in the morning, the Guru of Kathak came to us. We were a little afraid of him; he was 80 and very demanding. Sitting on mats, Sohan and I trained the *ambinaja* (facial expressions of moods in strict accordance with set movement of eyes, eyebrows, lips and neck) and the *mudry* (symbolic gestures of palms and fingers). *Ambinaja* and *mudry* tell the story portrayed in the dance, e.g. the adventure of Krishna and Radha.

After a shower, we went to the dining room and had breakfast with Ram's whole family. Next we moved to a small building in the garden called the Studio. We practiced there, with a group of girls under the guidance of our Guru, the complete dance, i.e. *ambinaja* and *mudry*, synchronized with the movements of body and legs, which were banded around the ankles with strings of bells maintaining the rhythm. Ram didn't teach us, but he appeared in the Studio to strictly correct even the most minimal of mistakes. He often criticized but seldom praised. I remember that one of my companions, Leila, cried her eyes out after his visits. One day, in our closest circle, Shameen said, 'Do you see how proudly Ram looks at Hanka?' This was my greatest praise and reward for my work.

Our free afternoons were spent on the tennis courts, reading, or on excursions, and in the evenings Ram took us to the cinema. I befriended two of Ram's nieces, Santesh and Susheila - we were inseparable. To this day I keep their letters written to me after I left Bangalore. Jess made sure that I wouldn't neglect my piano practice. Sometimes Ram invited us to his apartment. He lived in the right wing of the house on the first floor. I remember my emotion when I saw, on a wall in one of his rooms, a large picture of Our Lady of Częstochowa and a small lamp lit in front of it.

In these very fragmentary memoirs it is difficult to name all of my Indian friends, but the closest of them were, Shevanti, a Burmese from Bombay, an excellent dancer, with the most beautiful plait that I ever saw. Rajeshwar, who abandoned his legal profession for dancing. Leila, with wonderful arms and palms, was the daughter of a well-known family of Congressmen. Natu, was a dancer from Gujarat, who every day placed fragrant buds of flowers on the threshold of my room. Shameem, a Muslim from Lahore, was Ram's stage manager. He was a poet, who often read me his poetry - in Urdu! Both of Ram's sisters, Jessie and Goodu, were my chaperones. They often spoke about their late mother, who had been the centre of love for the whole family and about young Ram, whose decision to devote himself to dancing upset his family so much, that the only support he had, for a long time, was from his sister Jessie. There was also an old servant-cook Gulab, mentioned by Janta in her book, *The Indian Memoirs*. He used to knock on my door and in a secretive voice whisper, 'Miss Hanka I have fresh *chapati* in the kitchen.'

Unfortunately, my refugee status required a lot of effort to obtain a visa to visit England. On Ram's request, the application was sent to New Delhi. The documents came too late. In 1947, in the Port of Bombay I bid farewell to Ram and his whole ensemble leaving for England. Our cordial contacts remained - for years, but my love for the beauty of Classical Indian Dance will remain - for life.

Maharaja's high tea for the Commandant's family - *by Rena Kuszell (Jagiełłowicz)*

We arrived at the Maharaja's palace in Kolhapur late in the afternoon, as requested, and were greeted by a dignitary at the gate. The hall we entered was spacious and cool, with an intricate mosaic floor. Apart from one grassed and wooded corner, occupied by tigers, the rest of the room was empty. I stopped terrified, until our guide explained "The tigers are stuffed." I felt angry with myself for being scared, yet on closer inspection I admired this life-like group of animals.

The Dowager Maharani with the young, only a few years old, Maharaja and his sister were waiting for us in the palace. After passing through several rooms, with tapestry-covered walls and polished-marble floors, we entered the reception foyer, where we met our hosts. According to Indian custom, the greetings were without handshakes. The room was filled with soft furniture, finished in fabric and leather. Our conversation was held partly in German and English, helped by an interpreter. High tea was served in the adjacent room on a huge table supported on the tusks of three elephants. The top was covered with a beautiful white tablecloth, decorated with a floral design in silver embroidery. The refreshments served were rather of a European type - small sandwiches and something like an English Christmas cake. Two waiters poured tea from silver pots into glasses standing on delicate silver receptacles with handles. It was a real pleasure to be in such an elegant environment.

His Highness the Maharaja was about seven years old, slim of build, with big dark eyes, which seemed to look a little down on the world. He was well trained to become the future ruler of the Kolhapur Principality. His manners were perfect, and the answers brief and to the point. He had been a baby when his father died and his uncle took over the reins. I was sorry for the child probably being bored with us, although he didn't show it, and kept a straight face. The Maharani, on the other hand, was very talkative and appeared to be interested in the fate of Poland. The conversation went on until my mother mentioned her parrot Jasio, which she had left behind in Poland. Then the Maharani suggested a visit to her private zoo. The children left with their governess and we followed Her Highness. The sun was low and the garden seemed flooded with green, red and golden colours. It was cool and the breeze carried the sweet fragrance of the exotic flowers. We reached a meadow, sparsely overgrown with trees, where we saw a few peacocks and one of them gracefully showed us his fully-opened tail. Next, we stopped at a large aviary with a variety of parrots, which made quite a racket. Most of them were crested and they looked like a beautiful bouquet of colourful feathers. The parrots were well looked after. 'I still prefer my Jasio', whispered my mother.

We moved along to the camels, some of them standing and some lying down, chewing grass. There were 12 of them. They belonged to the army and participated in parades. Further on a good-sized lake glistened in the setting sun. This was the elephant reserve. There were three adults and one baby. The biggest of them stood in the lake up to his belly and using his trunk poured water all over himself. Two others were on the bank and the baby elephant was rolling in the mud. They seemed to be very happy. The elephants played a major role in the Indian ceremonies and parades. They were, on those occasions, draped with richly embroidered, mainly red and gold covering of floral and oriental patterns, which were executed in silver or golden threads and glittering sequins.

Our walk through the zoo ended when we stopped at a long building with a few windows on each side. The Maharani herself opened the door and revealed an unexpected scene. Along each of the two opposite walls there were six wooden beds and on each of them sat a cheetah tied to a hook driven into the wall, yet leaving some freedom of movement. They all turned their heads towards us. Her Highness, pleased with our delighted reaction invited us in, assuring us that the animals were domesticated and behaved almost like house cats. My parents followed our host and I followed them in. I concentrated all my attention on the cheetahs' behaviour, just in case I had to make a quick retreat to the door yet I love all animals, including wild ones. All of the twelve cheetahs participated in parades. They were walked on both sides of the elephants. The cheetahs were blindfolded to prevent them from being startled, and were held on leashes by their Indian keepers. Today I was honoured to see the cheetahs' eyes.

The sun was almost behind the horizon. The cool of the evening and twilight began to set in creating a feeling of mystery. We were delighted with the afternoon and the Maharani was also in great spirits. Her Highness walked us back to our car and waved goodbye from the steps of her palace.

My impressions from the adoption ceremony of the Maharaja of Kolhapur
- from the diary of Janka Zygiel (Jankowska)

I must admit that the adoption ceremony of the Maharaja in Kolhapur was less magnificent, than similar ceremonies I saw in wealthier southern states. Nevertheless, it reflected the full splendour of the Principality.

An elephant ambling majestically led the parade. He was covered with a red cloth and his head, ears and trunk were painted. Following him was a detachment of infantry, then a police unit, postal workers on bicycles and the court servants. Then another elephant came with an empty silver throne attached to its back. Now the carriages appeared. There were a few of them. The Maharaja was seated under a shimmering umbrella in the third coach. Behind him sat a dignitary holding the royal insignia. Opposite His Highness, there were two other dignitaries, totally absorbed in conversation. Other coaches followed. In one of them rode the Resident, who looked quite bored! After the carriages, I noticed a group of marching men. They were in uniform and carried swords in ornamental sheaths resting on their shoulders. I think they represented the highest cast - the noblemen.

The whole town was beautifully decorated for the occasion. We saw several triumphal arches on our way there and in the town proper. Sometimes corridors were formed with temporary walls, where portraits of the whole dynasty were displayed, starting with Shivaji - for this Maharaja is related to the great Chhatrapati, who was greatly respected by his people.

Further up the streets, and especially on the main street, the crowds were thick. The police

The new Maharaja - June 1947

tried to form them into orderly columns, so that the parade could move on in the middle. Led by Scoutmaster Valivadekar, we marched to our observation point. The town was exceptionally clean because the gods sent rain, which had washed down all dirt. Even today a watering truck sprinkled the Kolhapurian asphalt.

When the parade had passed our observation point (it was at the Swastika shop), we almost ran to the railway station to catch a train back to Valivade.

The Maharaja's coronation - *from the diary of a Scout, 1.06.1947*

Maharaja Devas, adopted at the end of March 1947, was crowned as Regent of Kolhapur on the 1st and 2nd of June the same year.

On Sunday, in the afternoon, the Maharaja of Kolhapur Principality - Chhatrapati Shahaji II, was solemnly transferred from the biggest temple in Kolhapur to his new palace.

This was a colourful procession. There were marching warriors dressed in costumes from the Shivaji times, modern soldiers, police and two bands, one typically eastern and the other a contemporary one.

The other participants were, the Supreme Commander of the Army riding on a horse with special insignia, and other generals and dignitaries, all dressed in special colourful costumes intended for this ceremony.

The most enchanting section of the procession was the one with elephants, all ablaze in gold and scarlet, dedicated to the gods.

The Maharaja himself sat in a silver howdah, with a three-domed canopy, on top of an elephant, which was adorned similar to the others. A precious diadem was clearly visible on the Maharaja's headdress *(pugerie)* brought from the northern states of India. Behind him sat the oldest member of the court, holding the insignia of the Maharaja of Kolhapur. The newly crowned ruler greeted his people with a friendly smile and waved his hand. The three courtiers assisting him held a type of a standard and stood on suspended steps at half height of the elephant. A guest - the Maharaja from the North, riding a horse, followed him, together with the other dignitaries in coaches. Closing the procession were two troopers.

Attractive to look at were the camels, decorated in vibrant but pleasant colours of red, orange and gold. They also had quite unusual, small red caps with a golden fringe and openings for the ears. Because of their pompous walk, they looked rather droll.

Through the eyes of a Guider - *by Hanka Gwiazdonik (Handerek)*

Our contacts with India, where we found refuge for over four years, were various: contacts with the land, with nature and with the people. As for the people, they were our neighbours from the Valivade village, those from Kolhapur, Panhala Rukadi, Chandoli, Malkapur and some from Bombay. With them we had everyday, sporadic contact but there were also those planned by *Uma Devi* - our priceless Wanda Dynowska, which gave us practical and theoretical means of getting to know the Indian world around us.

The closest Indians in Valivade were the Contractor from Kolhapur, who owned several shops in the Camp, fruit and vegetable vendors in the market place on the outskirts of the Camp, also the manual workers in the Camp from the nearby Valivade village, and all the other cleaners, laundry workers male and female, carriers of water, milk, ice cream etc.

The contractor Pardeshi was a wealthy businessman who, as time went by, built a big cinema hall with seats rising in tiers and a stage, so that besides film shows, live theatrical performances could be held there.

Pardeshi knew English well, but the uneducated Indians learned the difficult Polish language surprisingly quickly. We couldn't speak a word in Marathi, Hindi or Urdu, while they spoke more and more words in Polish. The Scoutmaster Ryś, had an Indian boy, who was our interpreter outside the camp.

Sometimes embarrassing situations occurred. Women and children were in the overwhelming majority in our camp; so the Indians called every woman 'mummy' *(mamusia)*, a word applicable to mothers only.

I had a maid called Aya and a laundry man, who would pick up a bundle of dirty linen and a bar of soap and after a few days returned everything snow white and ironed, without any invoices or receipts. Aya could be safely left alone at home, without fear that something would disappear. The Indians didn't steal, although they were poor, and when they found something, they would return it to the owner.

We had very good relations with the people I mentioned, including the traders at the market place and even some merchants in Kolhapur.

Our boy Scouts and girl Guides had frequent contacts with the Indian Scouts. Soon after the opening of the Camp in October 1943, such contacts resulted in jointly organised games and exercises. In Kolhapur in January 1944, we participated in a diploma presentation ceremony to the Scout instructors and a decoration of the Scout troop leaders, with years of service badges. These Indian Scouts helped us to find and get permission to use the wonderful terrain in Panhala for our training and camping grounds. They visited our training camps, participated in the camp fires and the night exercises of the troop leaders' course.

On the day of the 35th Anniversary of the Polish Scout Movement we entertained a group of the Indian Teachers' Course students involved with the Scouting organisation, and they invited us to their place in Rukadi. It was a pleasant occasion for the exchange of banners, group photographs and almost circus-like artistic entertainment, as there were leaps through blazing hoops etc.

In the closing stages of our Camp, the Indian Scouts received from us a complete set of furniture, which belonged to the *Klub Włóczęgów (Tramps Club)* and one tent for 8 persons, with a double roof.

The Indian Scoutmaster - Valivadekar, stood out as our best friend, who arranged the majority of our joint meetings.

When our Scoutmaster Ryś - Zuch was leaving India, the Indian Scouts organised a farewell tea party. There were a few speeches and a beautiful, heraldic *fleur-de-lis (Scout emblem)* made out of tuberose and lotus flowers. On the day of his departure they gathered at the Rukadi railway station and Valivadekar handed Ryś a magnificent turban, as a souvenir of his stay on Indian soil. The farewell garlands of flowers, placed around the neck, were long to be remembered.

Farewell to Ryś (Valivadekar on the left)

The participation in our friends' observance of holidays was also an advantage. We took part in parades and marched past the Maharaja. The greatest of all the Indian holidays was certainly the Day of Independence, on 15th August 1947.

Living in India we felt almost as if we were in our own home. We embraced the wonderful world around us, which reciprocated with good will, understanding and even with its heart.

Our Indian hosts and neighbours - *by Stanisław Harasymów*
(Excerpt from an article, 'The Sea of Dark Heads')

We travelled to Kolhapur mainly by train. Being 'white' we were instructed not to take a third class compartment, so our choice was the 'inter' class, because the second and first classes were too expensive for us. Apartheid was the law of the day. The system was acceptable to Indians as they, for centuries, were divided into castes, although some resentment towards British rule existed. However, we viewed apartheid as an unjust social system.

On arrival at the Kolhapur railway station we always had to face very insistent beggars, asking for *baksheesh*. They would follow us even when we hired a tonga. In this town a white man was rather a rare specimen on the street. Many Kolhapurians and country folk looked at us with curiosity. Sometimes whole groups followed us to observe our every move. After a while they got used to us and we accepted their behaviour and habits. For example, the streets had no pavements, so the roadway was filled with crowds of pedestrians, bicycles, sacred cows, carts pulled by bullocks, horse drawn tongas and a few motor cars and buses. It did not

Jains Temple in Kolhapur

offend us to see Indians chewing betel leaves with the areca-nut parings and spitting freely on the ground. Or during the sugar cane harvest, when they chewed the cane and spat out the white pulp, which covered the whole roadway.

In the town centre, there were a few shops selling textile fabrics. They looked quite different to shops I remembered in Poland. They had no counters and the floors were covered with something like a quilt. This is where the merchants and clients were seated. Their footwear had to be left at the entrance. The rolls of cloth were stacked on wide shelves against the walls. The customer would point out the rolls he wanted to see, and then the merchant would pull them out and unroll them on the quilt-covered floor. It was customary for the merchant to treat his customers to a tasty cup of tea with milk and sugar, to create a pleasant atmosphere, before the bargaining commenced.

I remember only one little street in Kolhapur with pavements and they were very narrow. The street itself was narrow and gently curved, connecting the town centre with the bazaar-square. We used to call it Jewellers' and Cobblers' Street. The jewellery shops were small and concentrated in one section only, leaving the other to the footwear stores. These were also small and selling mainly Indian type sandals, except the Bata store, which stocked European shoes. The jewellery stores were well stocked with items such as silver and gold bangles, ear or nose rings, a variety of signets with precious stones, wrist watches, small figurines representing Hindu gods, various utensils and bibelots. The owners and shop assistants were very polite and treated everyone with respect. We usually visited Kolhapur on Saturday afternoons and Sundays, but during the school holidays we would go to town on Fridays, to watch a colourful parade of richly decorated elephants carrying Hindu dignitaries, followed by guards of honour in Indian traditional uniforms and musicians making a lot of noise. There were also similar religious processions. In Kolhapur we attended their cinemas, showing Indian films only. We got to like their somewhat strange, sonorous and rhythmic music and songs, which were an integral part of all the films. The romantic stories, courting and love scenes were aesthetically presented and I don't remember any rude or violent pictures. We were also astonished at the Indian architecture, stone relief carvings, sometimes very delicate and centuries old, especially in the temples or palaces. The carvings often depicted mythological stories and beliefs.

Laxmi Temple in Kolhapur

Our stay in India will never be forgotten. Many dates, faces, names and events are now a little blurred, but what really remains in my mind and my heart, is a deep sympathy for this mysterious country, where we found so much goodwill, sincerity and understanding. The Indian culture, beliefs and their fate are now much closer to me and I have no doubt they will remain so.

A reflection dated March 1947 - *from the diary of Janina Mineyko*

We had heard a great deal about the Indian magic spells, mysteries and fairy tales. In our childhood dreams we had imagined a distant and unknown land of yogis and fakirs, in true rainbow colours. Now that we have all these wonders around us, I wish we could ask such a yogi to recreate, even for a moment, a vision of our Polish linden trees buzzing with bees and a boulevard of maple trees with a carpet of autumn leaves in red and gold.

The Indian bazaar - *by Alicja Kisielnicka*

The Indians from our neighbourhood, anxious to make a profit, spontaneously set up a bazaar for the Poles, just outside the Camp. This market place was in competition with the Camp's main supplier, called the Contractor, and the prices were generally lower.

It soon became a meeting place for the housewives, going there for a chat, to see what was new and to haggle a little over the prices, even when no purchase was made. There were so many interesting conversations at the fruit and vegetables stalls! The old Indian textile merchant patiently unfolded bales of cottons and silks pointed out by the clients. All bargaining was carried out in Polish. Similarly, all the signboards on the stalls and booths were in Polish.

Housewives seldom carried their shopping themselves as there were scores of young Indian boys eager to offer their services in order to make enough money to buy white Polish bread and take it home. In most households Indians were given some food for various services, as it was evident that a lot of them lived in dire poverty.

The Indian police, together with the Polish security guards, were responsible for order and hygiene at the bazaar.

My meeting with Gandhi - *by Eliza M. Krawczyk (Harbuz)*

I worked in the Polish Rest Centre in Panchgani as a teacher and a nurse among the Polish children threatened by tuberculosis, and undergoing convalescent hospital treatment. One day we found out that Gandhi had arrived in Panchgani for relaxation and to restore his health, weakened by one of his consecutive hunger strikes.

In Panchgani at that time we had a number of young people who had previously attended the lectures about India given by Wanda Dynowska, when she lived for a while in Valivade. She was on friendly terms with Gandhi and talked a lot about him and his great mission. On learning that this Living Legend was near us, we decided to visit him. On the way there we purchased the most beautiful garland of flowers to greet him in accordance with Indian custom.

We trembled with emotion as we stood in front of the house where Gandhi was living. The house was small, with a verandah running around it and surrounded with trees. A beautiful white goat was tied up to one of the trees.

A girl, who turned out to be Gandhi's granddaughter, said that Mahatma would come out shortly. In a while a small and frail looking figure appeared in the doorway. The Living Legend was dressed in a white *dhoti* (a cotton garment instead of trousers) sharply contrasting with his dark skin, sun burned and dried up by the long lasting fast. Gandhi, leaning on his walking stick, came forward to greet us in the Indian way - hands together - and invited us on to his verandah. We stepped onto the verandah almost on our toes, completely overwhelmed. In front of us stood this small, old Man, emanating such power, that he seemed to be a giant.

Gandhi sat down on the spread out mats and asked us to do the same. A person from our group presented him with the garland of flowers, and someone else said a few words by way of greeting. I was so thrilled with the excitement of being in the presence of this great man who was shaping the future of India that everything else escaped my attention.

From behind his round spectacles we saw these smiling eyes full of goodwill. His eyes looked young in contrast to his tired face and frail body dressed all in white. Finally he spoke up in a quiet and somehow tired voice, which gained strength as he carried on with the speech. He talked about his friendly feelings towards the Poles and Poland and lamented over the tragedy of the Polish nation. He said that his fellow countrymen and we share the same love for our homeland and desire for freedom, the greatest treasure of all. There is no such sacrifice that is not worth giving for the good of the homeland, not even the sacrifice of life. He also admitted that in the struggle with a foe, *satyagraha* (a struggle without the use of violence and hatred) is not always effective, because the conditions are not always suitable, but he warned about hatred, which is a destructive force leading only to disaster. He recalled Christ's teaching about love for fellow men, about forgiving those who harm us and His teaching that our fellow man means not only our friend but also our foe. It is easy to forgive our friend, but to forgive one's enemy is a greater achievement. When we showed our surprise that Gandhi knew the New Testament, he smiled and said that among all the other holy books he also owned the Bible and drew from it the strength and understanding of the human soul.

Gandhi's face showed signs of weariness. Several times already, his granddaughter had appeared in the doorway looking at him with deep concern. Just before saying farewell to us, Gandhi said that he always remembers in his prayers Poland and Poles scattered around the world and wished us a speedy return to our country, to work and live there. We left in silence, fully aware of the significance of this meeting for us.

The recollection of this meeting was strongly revived when my former school friend from Valivade and I saw Richard Attenborough's film *Gandhi*. The film made a great impression on me and recalled memories of my youth, the days not entirely without worries, but full of unforgettable experiences and encounters. I had an urge to shout, so everyone could hear me, 'I had the honour to meet this man and talk with him. This was a great Man.'

An unusual mission - *by Janina Mineyko (Niezabytowska)*

The year is 1945 - the monsoon season. I am about to leave with a secret mission as an emissary of Wanda Dynowska to meet – Mahatma Gandhi.

I don't know why she chose me to deliver this important letter unless it was to avoid the censorship imposed by the British on all contacts with Gandhi. Mahatma was Wanda's close friend. She shared his ideas and was constantly in contact with him. I am overwhelmed with the importance of this mission, a little terrified about my lonely journey, but also honoured that I was the chosen one.

Boarding the night train from Valivade, Wanda and some of her friends bid me farewell. The rain is pouring down. In rubber boots and wearing my rain cape I am clutching a small borrowed old suitcase, packed with my clothes as if I were going away on holiday. I had a third class ticket, so I enter a carriage full of peasants with stacks of bundles - but not for long. To see a young European girl sitting in a third class compartment was, in those days, unheard of, so some wealthy Indian ladies from the first class invite me to move to their carriage, where I doze off for the night. Arriving in Poona, in the early hours of the morning, I continue my journey by bus to the Hill Station Panchgani, where Gandhi spent a few months every year presiding over prayers every evening.

The road to Panchgani winds upwards in serpentines, a rocky wall on one side and a precipice on the other. Chipped rocks, pushed by the wind and rain, fall in front and behind the creaking old bus, filled with passengers with bags and one goat.

In Panchgani, I enter the Polish Centre, managed by K. Łęczyński, where I am to stay and from there I am to go and join Mahatma in evening prayers. I am to hand him a book, *All for Freedom* written by Wanda, with a letter of real importance hidden inside it.

Cordially welcomed by K. Łęczyński and his mother and keeping secret the true reason for my coming, I am looking for ways and means of finding the meeting place with Mahatma Gandhi.

To my great joy, I find unexpected help from my former school friend from Teheran - Irka T., who works in Łęczyński's office and knows her way around. In the evening, Irka and I go secretly to the green valley surrounded with hills slowly filling up with those taking part in evening prayers. There are a few rows of chairs for the Europeans. We take a seat on the end of a row. I nervously clutch my book.

They begin to sing some Vedas and finally, Gandhi appears, from behind the hill, resting on the arm of a young woman - a family member. He is dressed in white, walks slowly; he is not as gaunt as often described, but is full of dignity!

I spring to my feet from the chair, step forward and hand him the book, explaining in English that it is from *Uma Devi* (Wanda Dynowska). Gandhi thanks me with a smile, asks whether I am Polish and then requests my presence tomorrow at his house to pick up an answer. Back in my seat I can still see his unusually bright eyes and his friendly and benevolent smile.

Unfortunately, the next morning at breakfast, K. Łęczyński barges in from his office, infuriated after the visit from the English secret police who had come to question him as to who was the girl, what was the book that was handed over to Gandhi and where did it come from? He demands to know what this is all about and why I am involving him with the police. I am ruining his good relations with the English Authorities, etc., etc. 'I will not allow you to attend any further meetings and I suggest you leave Panchgani immediately' he commands. Crestfallen, I board the bus back to Poona.

Heart broken and with the unopened suitcase I am on my way to Valivade. I am sorry for failing to deliver an answer to Wanda's letter, thus disappointing her, and for missing out on the second, probably more interesting meeting.

I go straight to Wanda ready for an unpleasant talk. Instead I find a smile and words, 'Oh, my child don't worry. It's important that my letter reached him and he will take care of the answer.' With this 'absolution' I return to reality, not being fully aware how historical was my encounter with Mahatma Gandhi.

The Scoutmaster Z. Peszkowski:

Thanks to Wanda Dynowska I met Gandhi four times. Shortly before my departure from India, I talked with him for the last time, in the place where he was later assassinated. He knew a lot about Poland. He said to me, 'Your history is so difficult. There must always be bloodshed.' He said this almost with reproach. My answer was that our enemies are after our blood. They want to destroy us. They don't recognise our nation's right of existence. He answered, that he understood this and added, to my disbelief, that Moscow will not spare the lives of the 'seventeen' - this referred to the arrested representatives of the Polish Underground

Government. The treacherous trial was then in progress. The representatives were invited by the Polish communist regime for talks, with full knowledge of the Allies. Instead of talks they were arrested and sent to Moscow.

Our farewell was cordial. 'Take with you my best wishes for Poland and your fellow countrymen', said Gandhi at the end. I assured him that we love India and we wished them the desired and blessed freedom. Shortly before my departure, on the 15th of August 1947, we solemnly celebrated the great moment for our Indian hosts - the restoration of their independence.

Polish participation in welcoming Indian Independence - *by Alicja Kisielnicka*
(Polak w Indiach 23.08.1947)

The Polish refugees not only witnessed the welcoming of Indian independence, but also participated in all the celebrations here on the 15th August. In the Polish Valivade Camp the Indians are only a small minority. In spite of this, the celebrations organised by the Indian Commandant of the Camp, Lt. Col. Bhalla, had a communal character because, behind the small Indian group, there stood the whole Polish community with their Commandant at the forefront. All the schools, the Scout organisation, the representatives of the Church, all Polish organisations and the Camp's residents participated.

The celebrations started in front of the Camp's Administration offices by hoisting the flag of Independent India and singing the Indian national anthem. The three band flag, orange, green and white with a dark blue symbolic sign of the *chakra* in the centre, was raised triumphantly. However, the Polish flag was raised up the mast with some difficulty. Sighing with weariness some Polish onlookers saw this as a symbol of our present political reality. Probably because of that, the Polish national anthem sounded a little quieter and sadder.

During the parade across the Camp the crowd thickened as more Poles joined in. It is worth emphasising that it wasn't only curiosity that drew people into the street. The Polish people's hearts were filled with joy because of the Indian independence and they wanted to demonstrate their feelings by sharing the celebrations with the Indians.

Liberty has a magnetic force of attraction. Who else would have been drawn more to these manifestations of liberty, than we, refugees from our own country which was not free?

When the proceedings moved to the local cinema, the hall was crowded with Poles, but the Indians took the front rows and the stage.

The first to speak was the Indian Commandant of the Camp, who in a few words emphasised the happiness which his country experiences today and thanked the Polish participants in the celebrations. He wished them a free Poland in the near future and a safe return to their homes in Poland from which they had been wrenched away. In turn, the Polish Commandant Michał Gołbawski expressed his best wishes in the name of all Poles. When he spoke about the servitude and

The Indians treat the Poles to a lunch

violence now reigning in Poland, one of the enlightened Indians raised his arm and cried out, 'Poland must be free!' Other Indians took up the cry and the Poles applauded, trying to hide their emotion.

For this sincere response to our situation, the Polish side came up with a delicate and thoughtful response. A tall, fair-haired, blue-eyed Polish boy - Antolik, dressed in the costume from the Cracow region, stepped on stage and sang an Indian song. He sang the way the Indians sing. In the same melancholy, mysterious, difficult to grasp rhythm, with the same oriental swinging motion. He sang beautifully. It was a real surprise and our Indian friends were not only amazed by it, but also visibly touched.

The Polish part of the programme also included regional dances, and in the Indian part were songs and speeches in English and Marathi. Not all the speeches were translated, especially those in Marathi, but they were all brimming with the joy of freedom and were shared and applauded by the audience. Every time the word 'Poland' emerged from a wave of indistinguishable sounds, there were more bravos and cheers. One has to admit that all the speakers paid respect to the Polish cause and emphasised the right of the Polish nation to self-determination.

In the afternoon, the second part of the programme provided more entertainment in the form of sporting competitions, games and dancing. The flares of the fireworks display lit the evening sky, writing colourful signs of joy long into the night.

On this great occasion of Indian Independence, the Polish Commandant issued an address in the name of the Polish community and handed it over to the Indian Commandant to be delivered to the Central Authorities in India. The statement was artistically decorated with the Indian and Polish flags and motifs, and read as follows:

"The Poles from the refugees' Camp Valivade of the Kolhapur State, join to celebrate the establishment of the INDEPENDENT INDIA. Being victims of this World War, we the Polish refugees will always remember the hospitality and the care, which has been given to us by the Nation and the Government of India. We hope that for us too the day will come, when our Fatherland will be free."

The Polish Association in India sent two telegrams with wishes to the Prime Minister of India - Pandit Nehru and to the Minister for Internal Affairs - Sardar Vallabhbhai Patel. The wishes stated, "Please accept these cordial wishes and congratulations from the Poles grateful for the shelter and hospitality in India. Long live Independent India - the New Hope for oppressed nations!"

The Indian Independence Day - *from the diary of Sister Jadwiga Wróblewska*

Naturally, I began the day in church. We assembled at the Scout Headquarters and then went to the railway station to welcome the Indian Scouts. They arrived with an orchestra, which played right through the flag hoisting ceremony. We marched behind the Commandant's esteemed family. Leading the parade was a boy carrying a board with portraits of Nehru, Gandhi

Raising the Indian flag

and Subachandra *(the Army Chief)* and the fourth portrait had some symbolic meaning. There were pictures of the crucified Christ, with Gandhi on the map of India at the base. There was also a map of the world. The Scout band, the Commandant's family, our Girl Guides and Scout troops, then the Indian Scouts, the Contractor's work force and crowds of Poles, all followed them. There was much jostling.

At the Administration Centre three flags were hoisted up onto masts, those of India, Poland and State of Kolhapur. There was singing of songs and anthems, the orchestra was playing and a three double-barrelled shotgun salute was fired.

From there we moved on to the bazaar, the Contractor's shopping area, the joinery workshops and finally to the vicinity of our cinema. The Camp Commandant, with a whistle in his mouth, gave directions to the parade and occasionally used his fist to bring to order one or other of his sons. His wife and his poor grandmother were both sweating profusely. However, everything proceeded according to plan.

At 10 a.m. we reached the cinema area, where the orchestra concluded their music with such a lively waltz and we found ourselves swaying to the rhythm. The parade ended there and we entered the cinema hall. There were many speeches and signing of a historical document by the Camp Authorities. At the end, a dignitary from the town, who spoke in English, talked about India's role in rebuilding peace and declared that work would continue to bring peace and freedom to others. God grant that it be so. May God bless them all!

VALIVADE CAMP TALKIES.
Indian Independence Day
15th AUGUST 1947.
FREE SHOW
9 P.M.

THE REACTIONS TO GANDHI'S DEATH

Mahatma Gandhi's Death - *from the diary of Janka Zygiel (Jankowska)*

Friday, 30.01.1948. Shocking and dreadful news spread all over India today. Gandhi was murdered. The three words tell the whole story and each one is so strong and so cruel. To appreciate this, one has to know who this Man was for India.

To think today, that one of his fellow countrymen killed him - it's horrible. At first I couldn't believe it, but soon everyone accepted it.

I learned the news at a Scout meeting - we all froze in our tracks.

The unrest after Gandhi's death - *from the diary of Bożena Barowicz (Harbuz)*

01.2.1948. The unrest in Kolhapur continued for the second day. The reason for it was the bold move by the leader of Brahmin men (the assassin came from this caste), who arranged a feast in Panhala to rejoice in Gandhi's death. He considered this a happy day. The Brahmin party was soon discovered by the Hindus and after finding the culprits they went on a rampage of burning and slaughtering. All day yesterday Brahmin properties were burning and blood was flowing. A few of them hid in our Camp and one of them came to us and told me all this news.

Today the town is under martial law. The army stepped in and no one is allowed to leave his home under threat of death.

There are still some fires burning; we can see the smoke. From time to time the Hindus appear in our Camp. Our 'guest', hidden behind the beds, is panic stricken. What will be our fate if he is found here? They are real savages. If all the villages join in the rampage, our Camp will be burnt to cinders.

Just a while ago I learned that the leader of the Brahmin men was the former Prime minister of the State of Kolhapur - the father of my Indian girlfriends who visited us.

The Hindus went to burn the surrounding villages. The village of Walure is only one and a half kilometres away from our Camp.

02.2.1948. It is a little quieter in the town. I don't know if the hunger strike taken by a Minister, who decided to starve to death unless the rampage stops, or the general hunger affecting the Kolhapurians, brought the warring parties to the negotiating table. This, however, does not stop the rebels from robbing and setting fire to the surrounding properties. We are on a volcano, which can erupt at any moment.

04.2.1948. The unrest continues, in spite of martial law. The fires are spreading, as well as the killings and atrocities. At night we can see the glow of fires. The situation is worsening. The unrest extends to neighbouring towns, where it is even worse than in Kolhapur, so they say.

This night our 'guest' left us.

An Unfortunate Bonfire - *from the diary of Jan Siedlecki*

1.02.1948. Soon after Gandhi's assassination three Polish airmen visited the Camp. They wanted to meet the Scouts and have a sing-song by the camp-fire. After clearing it with Father Jankowski I agreed to organise a camp-fire on Saturday, 31st January since they were due to leave the Camp the following day. Later, Father changed his mind and advised to cancel the meeting or at least make it a very quiet affair.

However, the visitors were in high spirits, full of laughter and... slightly inebriated. There was a stream of jokes, then each combatant told us about his own experiences - things, which you normally do not read in the papers. In the end we made our way quietly to the camp. I went to see the Priest to apologise for the singing, but he explained that he was worried on our behalf, as it was rumoured that the Indians from the neighbouring villages were planning to march on Kolhapur.

Trouble started the next day when the Indian police came to the camp to investigate the meaning of the singing and dancing by the camp-fire. Father Jankowski explained that that was the way we expressed our sorrow and they seemed to accept it. But the Camp gossips blew the whole affair out of all proportion! I was labelled a trouble maker, a Communist, and it was said that the Camp would be burnt because of me. There was already a shortage of bread and meat, and things were going to get worse. We could see the smoke rising from burning villages. My mother was afraid the fanatics might want to drown me in the river!

Gandhi's ashes in Kolhapur - Recollection - *by Stanisław Harasymów*

News of the assassination of India's spiritual and political Leader shocked the nation. His policy of passive resistance, together with his political strength and determination, brought forward the liberation of India from British rule. We learned of Gandhi's death around 6.00 p.m. on the 30th of January 1948. In accordance with Hindu custom, his body was cremated on a funeral pyre and his ashes placed in several urns to be distributed all over India and emptied into rivers, as a symbol of his boundless devotion to his nation's cause. He always believed in humanity as a brotherhood of nations, and he proved it with his life.

Mahatma Gandhi's ashes were brought to Kolhapur by train. At the station, a funeral procession was assembled ready to accompany the urn on its way to the Panchganga river. A spot in front of the station was reserved for the Polish Scouts. We got there long before the arrival of the ashes. We stood in rows together with lots of Indian students and other chosen guests. A huge crowd waited alongside the route of the funeral procession. The prevailing feeling was that of deep mourning.

At last the ashes arrived and we all moved forward. There were government, civil and religious dignitaries, army and police units in colourful uniforms, as well as parading elephants. We joined the solemn march and soon found ourselves surrounded by the huge crowd of mourners, all moving towards the river. On one of the wider streets, which sloped gently down, we could cast our eyes over the sea of human heads and appreciate the immensity of the crowd. The funeral cortege finally stopped, the crowd thickened and stood in silence. We were too far away to hear the speeches or to witness the scattering of Gandhi's ashes into the Panchganga River. But I will never forget the countless numbers of people who, by their presence, paid their last respects to the great Man of our times.

From my observations - *by Wiesia Kleszko (Klepacka)*

For us, who arrived in this exotic country renowned for its Maharajas' wealth, finding as we did such poverty here was quite a shock. Our reaction was to take pity on the poor and try to help. Our relationship with the ethnic Indians was entirely different from that of the English. They subjugated the subcontinent, reigned over it and looked down on the Indians as if they were inferior to them. In fact they were wrong and by doing so, they discredited themselves. The English were far from tolerant to others, even in the field of culture.

Our neighbours

I feel that the relations between Poles and Indians were based on an equal footing. No one even dreamed of humiliating the Indians. We knew little about their history and culture. The worst belief was that the Indians were pagans. This was the fault of the Polish upbringing where, according to the religious instructions, all non-Christians were regarded as such. That's why, some people condemned

Irrigation wells outside the camp

Wanda Dynowska for practising Hinduism while also praying in the church. Thanks to the wise stand taken by Fr. Dallinger in this matter, they began to change their mind. Her lectures, given in 1944 to high school students, opened their eyes to the riches of Indian history and culture.

There were no recorded incidents of beatings of the Indians employed in our households, for work carelessly done or for disobedience. This cannot be said of the English, obviously not all of them. In the second half of 1943, my nursing friends and I witnessed many things while working in a 50-bed hospital in Laxmi Villa outside Kolhapur. We had an English matron who supposedly had some Indian blood. The lady, who was over 50, was in charge of all nursing and domestic staff. She was more than hard on the cleaners and once she gave the old Bapu several blows. Our English then was very poor, so we went with our complaint to the Chief Medical Officer Dr. Rosenbaum - a German Jew. He listened to our indignation and although he wasn't surprised he shared our feelings. He also made us aware of the fact that unfortunately such misbehaviour among the English and even the Indians takes place. We asked Dr. Rosenbaum to tell the matron to stop this practice during our stay in the hospital. We also found understanding with the domestic staff, concerning the problem about the tea breaks, i.e. to keep them within the prescribed time. Our work with the two Indian sisters (midwives) went well; however we didn't socialize with them, because of the language barrier.

Our appearance in India was rather embarrassing for the English. I came to this conclusion a few years later. We were 'whites', the Indians were regarded as 'blacks', but we were as poor, as church mice! No Englishman would have lived in bamboo-mat walled dwellings as we were living! Even the interned Germans in the Kashmir camps lived in masonry buildings and their monthly allowances were higher than ours because they were 'whites'.

Suddenly, the Indians discovered that not all 'whites' were English rulers. Thus we began to look at each other more closely and got to know each other a little better - but unfortunately not well enough.

In time, there were a few mixed marriages between the Polish girls and the Indian boys. The girls were young and the boys were older and employed in their chosen professions. One of the girls was from the orphanage and the other two from family homes, where they lived with their mothers and siblings.

Even the poorest Indians employed by the Poles cried when the transports were leaving and unemployment was spreading at the closing down of the Camp.

Krysia Kuchcicka wrote in her diary dated 17.12.1947, "We have a real 'comedy' with our ayah. She wants to go to Bombay with us. We gave her a few things that we are leaving behind, but 'no Bombay' said my mother. She cried. She sat on the verandah near the door, covered her face with her sari and cried all day long."

In retrospect, I think that the Polish Authorities in Bombay should have organised more hikes and excursions for us, the young ones, to get to know India better. We were expected to travel in a manner suitable for white people which we couldn't afford. We left India full of sympathy towards the Indians. We had lived through their Independence Day - it had brought us some sad reflections, but no resentment, as every nation has the right to self-determination.

The Examination of Conscience - *by Zofia Ostrihanska*
(Girl Guide monthly, issue no. 25, December 1947)

Soon, the last ship with the Polish refugees will leave the port of Bombay. Now is the time to examine our conscience covering the period we have spent in India and to ask ourselves - what are we taking away to Poland and for Poland? Was our time here wasted? Did our indifference obscure matters which ought to be of interest to young inquisitive minds?

In the majority of cases our conscience isn't quite clear. Our youth showed little interest in the Indian sub-continent. For the most part, knowledge about India was minimal, although attempts were made to stimulate curiosity and increase this knowledge. However, not many took advantage of the talks given by Wanda Dynowska. Only a small group participated in the tour of Southern India. Only a few read the books, partly because of ignorance of the English language, and partly due to lack of interest. It is no exaggeration to say that our time was wasted in this regard. We had four long years in this Camp, but we kept our eyes closed to what was happening in the country of our refuge.

If at least our understanding of India and its people and the ideas they represent has increased after the time spent here - all is not lost or is it? - Everyone can answer for himself, bidding India good-bye.

Resume: *by J. Kowalski*

It may appear that we didn't take full advantage of the fantastic chance, and for the majority of us the only chance, to get to know this beautiful sub-continent - India.

A complete lack of funds, the language barrier and problems in obtaining the necessary approvals from the British Authorities to travel, partly explain our fate. Furthermore, India for us was merely a haven in our long journey to Poland. Our Church, School and Scouting made sure that we wouldn't forget where we were going. We wrote about our homeland in the school compositions, we listened and told stories at the Scout bonfires about it, and the youngsters drew Polish landscapes. This was the main aim of our educators.

But as we look closer at the 'chance', judging from the many written recollections and excerpts from diaries, we can sense a great friendship and sympathy for the Indians, our sensitivity to the beauty of their country, respect for their beliefs and our participation in their meetings and ceremonies. We rejoiced when they regained their independence, and shared their grief when Gandhi was murdered. These sentiments are quite obvious and almost tangible. How our lives were influenced by such philosophies as passive resistance and stoicism in suffering we will never fully appreciate. They were, however, a major enriching factor of our characters, during our formative years.

Translated by Stanisław and Wanda Harasymów

MAMU
by Zofia Zawidzka

Twice a week,
early in the morning,
she brought
sweet, rich buffalo milk.
Then she sat
on the threshold of our dwelling
for hours on end.
Thus our silent friendship grew.
Sometimes
her face was alive
with her family news.
Big news.
The crop was good.
Another marriage
was coming.
A new baby was born.
Then she would walk away.
Straight and graceful
with a large milk pot
balanced on her head.
We called her mamu,
out of respect.
Then one day I had news to tell.
- Mamu, we are leaving India.
Soon. We are going to London.
She did not reply
pondering my words in silence.
- Is London as big as Kolhapur?
Bigger, much bigger...

Silence. And then
- Is there a market place?
Yes, mamu, there is a market place.
Mamu was silent
for a long time
When she looked at me again
Tears glistened in her eyes.
- Stay with us - she said -
Don't go...
- We can't. We have to go...
Silence again.
- Stay with us - she said at last -
I will give you half of my land...
Come and see... I did go to see
her fields of sugar cane,
her spotless hut,
her daughters,
the newborn baby.
I tasted her delicious sweetmeats.
- This is mine - she said pointing
in a sweeping gesture of her hand
to lush fields of sugar cane -
Stay with us...
How could I explain to her? How?
How could I tell her that
She offered me more than land.
She shared her heart.

The Gold Medal

On November 2003 a Gold Medal of "the Protection of National Heritage" was conferred on Col. Vijaysinh Gaikwad (Retd.) by the Ambassador of the Republic of Poland. The ceremony was held in the Main Hall of the Municipal Offices of the town in the presence of many notables, some of whom remembered the Polish community 1943 – 1948. Among them was Wanda Kashikar (Nowicka) with her family, the only inhabitant of the Polish presence alive in Kolhapur.

Maharaja Shahu Chhatrapati, Ambassador HE Dr. Krzysztof Majka, Col. V. Gaikwad, Marek Moron, Polish Consul in Mumbai and Mantrao Katwre

The Golden Jubilee

Wanda Kashikar (Nowicka) received in May 2005 a Medallion designed to commemorate the Golden Jubilee of Diplomatic Relations between Poland and India. On this occasion, the Polish Ambassador, Dr. K. Majka, wrote: "The contribution you made... in furthering the ties of friendship between our two nations... is highly appreciable and valuable."

Then in April 2007, she also received "the Siberian Cross" from the Polish Consul Jan Bylinski.

by Jan Siedlecki

Wanda with the Polish Ambassador, her husband Vassant (in front) and in the background their son Ashok with wife Shama and their children... plus other guests

A TOUR OF SOUTHERN INDIA, 1946
by Irena Dziewulak (Adamczyk)

This excursion to Southern India was quite unique, in our quest for knowledge about the country. Although our Scout camps, hikes and excursions gave us a chance to get to know a small part of this exotic land, but not until Wanda Dynowska's arrival in Valivade did we get a better chance to discover India.

Wanda Dynowska *(Uma Devi)* had a deep knowledge of this country. She collaborated with Gandhi and had good contacts here. She shared her knowledge with us in a series of lectures. These lectures about India, its variety, culture and religion fascinated us and intensified our desire to know it better. To a great extent it was her personal charm and energy, which made our trip possible.

Our group consisted of W. Dynowska, Z. Wilczyńska (a teacher) and 20 teenage girls plus 3 boys.

Apart from sightseeing and learning about India, we were also prepared to spread awareness about Poland through our dances and songs. The cost of our trip was 100 rupees per person, but we had to raise the additional funds by means of our performances during the journey.

Intensive preparations began. Our mothers worked on the costumes. We rehearsed dances to the music of two accordions. Finally we departed on the 7th of October 1946. Our adventure had begun and was to last for a month during the school holidays.

The whole tour covered about 1,850 miles. Transport varied, depending on the terrain, by train 3rd class (Europeans at that time travelled only in the 1st or 2nd class) but usually in a separate carriage, by coach, by car, and even by *bangi* - carts pulled by bullocks, where the roads were really poor.

Looking through the carriage windows, the landscape appeared gentle, rich in the greenery of cultivated fields, palm groves and exotic trees. In the distance could be seen a low mountain range and large rocky outcrops. Among them some temples; their tower gates resembling pyramids with truncated tops, so characteristic for Southern India. They are called *gopuras* or *vimans*. We passed villages. Women, dressed in colourful saris, walk ramrod-straight under heavy burdens carried on their heads. The men lean over their ploughs pulled by bullocks. In the passing towns we noticed factories producing textiles.

In the carriage, Wojtek's accordion accompanied our singing. We were enjoying ourselves.

The Indian food we bought at the stations was pungent and hot, the rice on palm leaves was bland, but our spirits were high.

We were fine, but the urgency to share our experiences and to reassure our families in the Camp (mainly our mothers, who were brave enough to let us take the trip) made us write the first lot of postcards, treasured to this day.

"My dearest Mama - *(wrote **Pacia** on the 8th of October)* - Our departure from Kolhapur was delayed. We changed trains in Miraj. A carriage was allocated to us; we slept right through the night. We have enough food, besides Indian food is available at every station. All of my baggage is in good shape; nothing is lost so far. Don't worry about a thing, I won't swim, besides there are no such facilities so far! Today at 10p.m. we will reach Bangalore, where we will stay for two days. The nights are warm and during the day it's even more pleasant than in Valivade - the air is fresh and we don't feel the heat. Pani Dynowska takes good care of us, so I am glad I went."

Bangalore 8th - 11th of October

In Bangalore, the Indian Scouts came to meet us and offered us three rooms in the stylish *Scout House*. During our stay, they excelled in hospitality. They proudly showed us around the town which seems to be submerged in greenery.

After the first performance of our 'troupe' we became famous. We had many invitations and the Mayor himself welcomed us.

The next day we visited the Scouts. After the official welcoming ceremony, there was dancing and singing by the Indian Cubs and Scouts (to our ears, the tunes were melodious but somewhat monotonous). Next came the speeches and some refreshments, bananas and coffee. We learned that Indian Scouting was becoming more nationalistic and in the process of reorganisation to be independent. They opened their hearts to us. Following our joint fun and games, we tried to engage in conversation (frequently using sign language); and we made entries in each other's diaries. Meanwhile Pani Dynowska tried to explain to the Scoutmaster the present situation in Poland, and the reasons why we were not going back. While this was going on we took the opportunity to admire his beautiful dark eyes!

In Bangalore we visited a school, the delightful botanical gardens full of jungle flora, and a fine sandalwood-carving workshop. We also went to see some temples. One had a coach made of silver and the other one was dedicated to the Hindu god Shiva and had a huge sculpture of a bullock *(Nandi)* carved from one piece of rock.

Janka Jankowska wrote in her diary that priests in the temples made offerings for us - they celebrated the *puja* - by mentioning 108 of Shiva's names, (during the major celebrations 1001 names are mentioned) to secure for us a safe journey and a happy return.

The journey by coach continued from the state of Mysore to the land of the Tamils. All around us were rice fields under water and stooped silhouettes of working women. Interesting statues of horses could be seen in the grass.

Tiruvannamalai 11th - 14th of October

We were entertained in the *Ashram* (the Indian centre for prayers and meditation) where lives a wise man, Bhagavan Sri Ramana Maharishi, considered holy. People of various creeds and races seek truth and God here. This is how **Irena** described it in her diary:

"The first impression is rather disappointing; a few European type houses, some with thatched roofs, a place well wooded and beggars everywhere.

The room occupied by the Maharishi is in European style. The room has a sofa with a heap of cushions in the left corner; nearby is a lamp with a shade and a radio.

The Maharishi sits on a rug on the floor near some smouldering incense. He is very old. His grey, half-smiling eyes look into a different world; the smile inspires confidence. The whole figure, upon closer acquaintance, arouses respect.

Our question about the Hindu's polytheism is answered with that *'All is One'* and all revered divinities are only symbols of characters and incarnations. It is hard to comprehend all of this and also to understand the talks presented to us by a visiting Brahmin. The stories about his religion and Hindu mythology are very interesting, but such concepts as the eternal castes, reincarnation, yoga, nirvana and the attitude towards women, are foreign to us. *'You are I'* and *'I am you'*, is not convincing. To be on the safe side, we take a 'pilgrimage' around the Arunachal Mountain from 8p.m. to 12.15a.m. This is supposed to bring about a lot of favours!"

Danka Czech wrote about the *Ashram*:

"On entering, they all prostrate themselves and pay homage to him, the Brahmins, Harijans, Buddhists, Hindus, Muslims, rich and poor. They come here from the noisy, turbulent and stirred up world, from the clamour and battles, from the toilsome life, filled with continuous struggle for a piece of bread, shelter and some rags. They come exhausted to have a rest. They come psychologically unsettled, sad and in despair to find peace. They come to find God. The *Ashram* is open to all.

We come here also - the first Polish group. We bring the joy of our young lives and our carefree smiles. Our hearts thump and our heads buzz with the adventure of our journey. The sea of thrills and emotions overflows. We wait for the new, great, rare and exciting moment. The old clock chimes the 7th hour. I know it is time for the *mantras*. My heart trembles. My God! Mantras, vedic hymns, ancient songs of our Aryan forefathers, sung by them thousands of years ago. I press hard against the wall. Crouched in my own nonentity, wretched, I wait.

The Maharishi, leaning on the cushions, seems to be drowsing. He is partly veiled by the bluish smoke from the smouldering incense. The clock is ticking away with a hollow sound, just like time which has no dimension, no face, has no meaning, yet it exists and goes on measurably forward, without postponement or slowing down. At last they begin. With a few low and repetitive tones the song is born. Still quiet, lurking, sleepy as an evening; now awakened rising up and gaining power. Half spoken, the slow wave of sound flows further and further. Suddenly a single voice arises from the crowd; it springs away from the rest and breaks into a lament, sobbing with nostalgia. The voice vibrates higher, increasingly higher and softer, exhausted from its own impulse, then weakens, until it falls with broken wings and a moan. And again the choir resounds; the flowing melody embraces us and moves away to a dormant, dim remoteness.

The Maharishi disappears, enveloped in a silvery mist. Sometimes his grey head quivering with emotion, appears for a moment. Only the clock. Just like time. No! There is no time. Time stopped. Only this one moment, in which *mantras* are sung over thousands of years, remains.

You stop at a point, which neither backs up nor moves forward, but exists. This is Eternity."

One of the aims of our trip was to visit two of the biggest temples in Southern India which were built centuries ago. The first one was the Temple of Shiva. Looking at it, it was hard to believe that when our land was covered with forests and populated by nomadic tribes, here on the Indian sub-continent people were erecting multi-storey buildings and edifices, the walls of which were decorated with intricate carvings.

Gopura

Danka Czech continues:

"As we near the temple in Tiruvannamalai, we notice from a distance four nine-storey high *gopuras* (tower gates), which together with the mighty walls, surround an area of about one square kilometre. We stop at one of the *gopuras* and looking up, we try to read the details of the carvings. At the lower level there are figures depicting Shiva's world-creating dance. In the background there are plant motifs carved with precision and symmetry. We look higher. With the multitude of smaller and bigger sculptures it is difficult to recognise even well known gods like Krishna or Lakshmi. Eventually, at the top everything merges into one mass. After removing our footwear, we proceed through the gloomy gateway, which could be compared to a tunnel. In front of us stands another tower, but very much lower and painted white. Its carvings are finer and hardly legible. We then go through the second gateway, similar to the first, pass the third wall and enter a spacious courtyard. Behind the fourth wall, in the centre of the temple's square, is a sanctuary accessible only to Brahmins.

We go down the stony steps to a pool of water where every person who wants to participate in the prayers has to wash himself. Whoever has washed himself at home, washes only his hands and face. After leaving the pool, some people purify their souls by praying and by tossing a handful of water three times behind themselves.

Then our guide leads us to a hall of a thousand columns. A thousand columns? Oh, don't talk nonsense; it's impossible - the sceptics say. We step into the mysterious darkness under the masonry vault. Around us are long rows of masonry columns, which are similar to the legendary sleeping knights. We look closer at the columns; they are fully sculptured and the once clear carvings are now worn. We move deeper into this "forest", and the air becomes humid and musty. The sceptics begin to accept the unbelievable number.

Then we enter the courtyard. A middle-sized elephant walks there and using his trunk asks for a *baksheesh* of bananas. We visit all the places of interest, like small chapels, where there are bronze figurines of various gods and painted clay animals devoted to them.

The characteristic sounds of the ritual instruments are calling for the evening *puja* (prayers)."

Our dance ensemble also performed in Tiruvannamalai. It was well received and brought some funds so necessary for the continuation of our journey.

Madras 15th - 21st of October

Participants of excursions:
Irka Adamczyk, Marysia Brink, Pacia Cariuk, Danka Czechówna, Józef Ezman, Marysia Ganczar, Irka Janczewska, Janka Jankowska, Mila Kamińska, Irka Kaziewicz, Alina Kurzawska, Janusz Kurzeja, Wojtek Kwiatkowski, Lucia Ligajówna, Hanka Nadańska, Lucia Ostrowska, Irka Piotrowicz, Danka Raczyńska, Czesia Sobol, Hela Suszkówna, Janka Szafrańska, Marysia Szczyrska, Halina Śliwińska and Jadzia Wróblewska.

From quiet *Ashram* we dropped into the hustle and bustle of the sprawling and interesting city of Madras, situated on the coast of the Indian Ocean. The film producer, Subramaniam, provided us with board and lodging in his film studios. The house was set in a beautiful garden with the inebriating scent of tuberose and creepers. We could hear oriental music coming from neighbouring buildings where the films were made. The songs were lengthy and melancholy (Indian films are of 4 - 5 hours' duration). The host and his associates were very hospitable and cordial. The conversation was often helped by gesticulation. Their ladies, just like us, could speak only a little English, but it was enough to understand each other and pleasant smiles helped a lot.

We received presents such as flowers and fruit. Meals were quite substantial. According to table ritual, only the right hand is used for eating (literally). The "unclean" left hand is only used for drinking. The meals were mainly rice with vegetables and various meat dishes with sauces, Indian bread, dumplings - often very hot (we got used to them and liked them very much), lots of fruit: bananas, mangoes, melons, coconuts and milk etc., constituted our exotic diet.

Subramaniam offered us a coach and a very kind guide, L. Krishnan, to show us the sights of the City. Pani Dynowska, with Subramaniam's help, spread the news about our ensemble and had some interviews with the press. A reporter, Sitaram Puranik, joined our group during the sightseeing. The secretary of the local college took care of selling the tickets, organised our performance at the university and a meeting with the students.

Our ensemble's show turned out well and lasted twice as long due to the enthusiastic applause. The press reviews were very positive.

Subramaniam tried to introduce us to the Indian culture of fine arts, craftsmanship and handicrafts. He organised meetings with the elite of the artistic world. He also showed us rich garments and costumes from props used in his film studios: beautiful colourful saris - often threaded with gold, wonderful jewellery, weapons, swords and daggers. We were photographed dressed in these regional Indian saris and dhotis.

He demonstrated to us two Indian dances, performed by the students of his school. The first one was a folk dance - the peacock's welcoming, and the other was about the snake charmer, portrayed with great artistry by the teacher. We were enchanted by them and applauded the dancers loudly.

The Indian dances are different in character from ours. To the tempo of harmonious musical rhythms, they express their beliefs and religious ecstasy, myths and folk legends. They recreate them all with the flowing movements of their bodies, arms and legs, where every minute gesture of the fingers, the quiver of an eyebrow or eyelashes has its ritual meaning.

The musical instruments are also different; being mainly percussion - drums, gongs and cymbals, as well as seven-string guitars, *veena* and the less complicated *sitar*, the bamboo flutes *banshri* and a specific violin *sarangi*. Our friends tried to explain and demonstrate their sound.

We visited the City, attended Holy Mass at the gothic cathedral of St. Thomas and admired the solid colonial buildings, museums, galleries, shops and the bazaar.

A recollection from Adyar *by 'Konrad'*

"It rains, but it does not worry us. We get into the car and go sightseeing in Madras. First we drive to Adyar, the biggest centre of the Theosophical Association in the world. The streets are congested with traffic and pedestrians. The excitement of the City is quite evident. It is not as quiet as some of the other towns like Bangalore or Tiruvannamalai. Everyone is in a hurry and walks with a purpose. After several minutes of driving we leave our car in front of a grand building, surrounded by giant trees and vegetation - it is the library in Adyar. As we enter the building, in the first half there are sculptures of the four greatest teachers of humanity: Christ, Buddha, Zarathustra and Mohammed, as well as symbols of all the other religions of the world - Old-Hebrew, Roman, Greek, Egyptian, modern and other long dead religions. Altogether, they make an indescribable impression.

All these religions and beliefs, which for centuries clashed with each other and still do, stand side by side in peace while above them hangs a carved sign in golden letters, *"There is no higher religion than Truth"*. After being welcomed by the President of the Theosophical Association, who is a good friend of the Poles, we proceed to the library, with its countless volumes in all the languages of the world. The huge collection ranges from folders to magnificent works. Stacked on shelves they overwhelm the visitor with the wisdom they contain. Almost all the knowledge gathered by mankind over the millennia is represented in this library. In the cabinets, tied up in bundles, are ancient scripts written on tanned palm leaves, expressing the thoughts, emotions and views of the greatest Indian writers. There is also a gilded book, the Koran, a guide for the life and prayers of over 200 million people. Apart from the works on religion and philosophy there are books on almost every aspect of modern studies. We learn that Adyar was established 60 years ago by the Theosophical Association, to unite all the religions and beliefs in "the brotherhood of all living beings". They started to gather books written by the most prominent writers in human history and created this library. They also established a dance school for the poorest of castes - Pariahs, which was considered impossible because the system didn't allow for social intercourse with persons from other castes. This school was such a success that some children from the upper castes enrolled there. It was certainly a step in the right direction against Indian social and economic inequalities. For me their motto of such, 'brotherhood' is very attractive. It would be nice to be able to call every human being, regardless of nationality and colour of skin, 'my brother'. That is the aim of the founders of Adyar and this is their unquestionable greatness.

Leaving Adyar, I thought that if there were more such centres in the world, we would not have wars, partitions, occupations, the NKVD, the Curzon Line, atom bombs and other similar calamities, which prevent us from hoping for a peaceful future."

Our impressions of Tamils in Madras, wrote **Janka**, were that they were very polite, gentle and mild. Their skin is darker and they dress in intense colours, in keeping with the warm tones of the south.

We met our former teacher from Valivade, Mr. Appadurai, who, comparing the south with other parts of India, claimed that here people were more hospitable, careful of their environment and personal hygiene.

In Madras we had another unforgettable experience - the performance of Ram Gopal (the most famous dancer in India) and his ensemble of musicians, singers and dancers.

We marvelled at the classical dances - *Bharata-Natya* (the most difficult one was performed by Ram Gopal), dramatic - *Kathakali, Kathak* and folk - *Manipury*. The souvenir programmes have been kept by us to this day. The performance lasted from 6p.m. to 10p.m. and was wonderful. The Indian dance is a very difficult one and has to be practised for years.

The beauty of Ram Gopal's dance was an inspiration to **Danka Czech**, who in poetic prose described the event:

"Immersed in gold of the setting sun, Shiva performed his divine dance. Waves of quivering light showed his slender body in marvellous motion. This motion liberated, hidden in his heart a salute full of love for the departing day.

Finally he melted away into a golden light and like a nebula continued with his dance until the curtain dropped. Oh, God! Is this a dream or am I awake?

There was loud applause. Whose dance was this, in the setting sun, Shiva's or Ram Gopal's?"

Madura 22nd - 24th of October

Together with our luggage, we occupied an attractive cloister in a courtyard surrounded by coconut palms and banana plants. There were pomegranates and flowers all around and a traditional pool of water in the middle.

Madura is a very old town with a dominating temple, surrounded with a wall. The temple is devoted to Shiva whose marriage to *Menakshi* is observed as a major holiday once a year. During such a day a few indomitable participants of our tour went to the temple in the evening hours, traditionally forbidden to women.

This is what **Hela** wrote:

"The doors open. I can no longer see the sky, only a grey masonry vault. No more fresh air of the summer evening, but stuffy air, full of smoke from smouldering incense. Wherever you look around, you see gods and goddesses, their figures, often disproportionate and muscular, expressing mainly power and might.

A key grates in the lock. Big metal doors open heavily. This is the hall of a thousand columns. Oh! Here it's completely dark. In front of us strides a guardian of the temple, carrying an ancient oil lamp. We walk slowly and quietly, looking all around. Fear, but most of all, curiosity seizes us.

Columns are everywhere, grey and dark. In the reflection of the flickering flame, they come into view one after another. Every column has some divinities sculptured on them, all terrifying in this vast hall. Their only companions are bats. They fly, fluttering their wings over our heads and give out whining sounds.

Typical interior of a temple with columns

Let's go home! The swaying light in front of us makes me focus again on the divine sculptures. What thoughts do they represent? What is the truth carved by the sculptor? They are all supposed to tell about God. But what can the people think about Him, looking at these sculptures? Perhaps, that God is all-powerful, almighty and omnipotent."

Tenkasi - Cortalem 24th - 27th of October

From Madura we continue south by train. In the compartment, sitting in front of us are women dressed in shabby saris. We look at each other - they have 'jewellery' in their ears, their ear lobes stretched to the shoulders, glittering ornaments in their noses, lips and even tongues - what do they think looking at us?

After a five hour journey we enter a hilly and green terrain - Cardamom Hills. We get off the train at a small station Tenkasi and then transfer to *bangi*. The cart ride takes us through rice fields and coconut palm groves, and terminates in Cortalem village. We are now in the hills in front of our new quarters - a medium sized house, described by **J. Szafrańska**:

"Above the gate hangs a creeper with reddish-pink flowers. In the garden, behind the house, there are many bushes with multicoloured leaves and hibiscus in bloom. Further down past the garden flows a cold water brook, where we wash ourselves with pleasure after the tiring journey. Why did we stop at Cortalem? To breathe some cool mountain air, after the heat of Madura's sun; to admire the wonderful views of fresh greenery and to hike up to the five waterfalls and lakes."

Pani Dynowska wanted to show us the village where she had previously lived. The village is quite unique; one end uses an old primitive agricultural system of cultivation, while the other end nearby has a new school of agriculture, modern housing, electricity and farm machinery, as well as irrigation.

We visited the school and the following are some of **Irena's** reflections:

"For me it was a particularly interesting visit, as I am especially concerned about social matters, which are similar in India and in Poland. The Headmistress gave us all the information. There were over thirty girl students doing a one year course for village instructors. During the year the school is self supporting. Duties are rotated fortnightly. The main aim is to train each girl (or woman with a minimum of a secondary education) to become a village leader, just like a ray of light illuminating the whole village. For this reason, the school curriculum includes sewing, weaving, spinning, rearing of poultry, growing of vegetables and market gardening, as well as geography, history and even some nursing. We saw them all at work. I was interested in the enrolment fees. The Headmistress explained that these students come from different castes and provinces, some are rich, some are poor and the fees do not really matter. Those who can, donate whatever they see fit, others who can't afford a payment are asked to forget that there is such a thing as money.

The time went by very quickly in a pleasant atmosphere. These future instructors offered us excellent coffee and during the conversation we told them about the situation in our homeland. They responded by donating over 20 rupees for children in Poland.

Returning to my social concerns, I learn to my great satisfaction that college boys are also participating in similar educational programmes in nearby villages. They organise conferences, discussions and set up programmes.

Reflecting on today's events, I think back to pre-war times and recall very similar social activities that were going on in my Homeland."

Trivandrum - Nagorcoil - Cape Comorin 28th - 30th of October

On the way to Trivandrum in Travancore State, we admire the beautiful landscapes, picturesque mountains, cascading streams and thick jungle. Mighty trees and towering palms disappear from the horizon and slowly the landscape changes into plantations of sugar-cane, coconuts, rubber, coffee, cocoa, peanuts and chillies.

In Trivundrum, the centre of ivory products, we chance upon the Maharaja's birthday and an industrial and trade exhibition showing the wealth of the State.

An excerpt from **Irena's** post card from Trivandrum on 28.10.1946:

"It is nice here, clean, with lots of sunshine and palms. A beautiful museum, art gallery and generally it is the best maintained of all the southern states. Lots of Catholics and churches. People are hospitable and kind. We feel great. Whenever they find out that we are from Poland, they look at us as if we were from outer space. The climate here is better than in Kolhapur."

On the way to Cape Comorin we had an unexpected meeting with some people from the American Salvation Army, managing a large hospital in Nagercoil. They welcomed us and extended their hospitality. We stayed there for a few days, tempted by the facilities that our 'civilisation' offers, much to Pani Dynowska's disapproval.

Next was Cape Comorin, the southernmost tip of India, where we admired the beauty of the ocean. The sunrise and sunset were short but spectacular.

Mysore - Bangalore 3rd to 9th of November

Janka Jankowska wrote:

"In my diary under the date 3.11. I wrote, we are now in Mysore. A moment ago we came back from the Krishnaraja Gardens. This place - as Janusz Kurzeja says - is a colourful fairy tale. A combination of multicoloured lights, water, fountains of various shapes, cleverly scattered bowers and miniature pavilions around a well maintained park, give an impression of a place from a different world. The nearby weir and the hydro-electric scheme, supplying electricity to the whole state of Mysore, have made it possible to create this beautiful park, which attracts tourists from the whole country and from abroad. The next two days can be compared to a live lecture in history. Reading my notes, I am surprised that we have covered so much.

Mrs. De Sousa has included in her tour the most interesting places to visit, such as the Maharaja's residence full of splendour - partly turned into a museum. We stared at the artistically carved sandalwood ceilings. We crossed doors richly inlaid with ivory, passed through the knights' hall full of antique armour and the hunters' room, where stuffed animals *(reputedly shot by the Maharaja)* looked at us blandly. In one of the rooms was a figure of a seated maharaja and a troubadour with a guitar standing beside him. The first to enter was Halinka S., who stopped halfway and asked if she could greet the Maharaja. - He looked so lifelike. This summer residence is situated on top of Chamund Hill, with beautiful views of the town below."

Gopuras - Gate towers, typical of Southern India

Excerpt from an article by 'I' in *Młodzi*:

"...the hill. We are climbing higher and higher. A cool evening breeze is beginning to bite, as our coach moves up the hill. Lamp's lights accompany us, while the stars watch over us. Look down. This is Mysore glowing with thousands of lights, almost like a second firmament.

The coach climbs to the top. Here stands a temple where Mysore's patroness reigns. She picked the highest point to share it with the clouds flowing over our heads and wrapping around a lofty tower. A gleaming altar is visible from the entrance. The priests humbly offer sacrifices and prayers asking for protection over the town. A pleasant fragrance of incense and flowers scents the air and thin trails of smoke vanish under the ceiling.

From a distance we see a palace enveloped in clouds. We are now on a terrace. A few steps lead us to a multicoloured flower garden. From here we can see the winding road and further down the township of Mysore, but the buildings are indistinguishable. Mysore appears as a sea of light.

The Maharaja uses this palace as his summer residence. It is rather modest but comfortable. We are surprised to see so many wall mirrors here. Suddenly it seems that our numbers have doubled. Lots of the same people. We nearly bang our heads against the mirrors.

The clouds are just above us. The wind is blowing. It is bitterly cold but, in a way, it feels good and so close to something out of this world, something superior and supernatural."

The highlight of the day was an invitation for a cup of tea with a princely family of Juravani. Our ensemble presented a few attractive dances, which were well received and applauded.

Finally we drive to Seringapatam - an abode of Southern India's last mighty and independent Sultan Tipu in the 18th century. This is where he triumphed and later was defeated. The dungeons are the only remains of the strategically situated fort. There, he kept imprisoned Christians, and to comfort their souls he assigned to them a priest. His residence, showing the specific Moslem architecture of this region, is well cared for, full of colourful carpets and artefacts resembling a family home. Around it is a well-maintained garden, with an abundance of fragrant bushes and southern flowers.

Voice of the Bangalore press

Excerpts from an article *Polish dancing at the town hall*, written by G. Venkatachalam, printed in the local paper *Misindia No.46* dated 17.11.1946.

"...A group of twenty Polish girls from the refugees' camp in Kolhapur is touring Southern India under the leadership of *Uma Devi (Wanda Dynowska)*.

The aim of the tour is to visit South-Indian towns and temples, and during the trip they perform their national songs and dances with great success.

...In their lovely, colourful costumes, and with smiles and songs on their lips, the Polish girls won the hearts of the Indian audience.

Their dances were full of charm and beauty. These folk dances, delighted their audience with their simplicity, lively rhythms and joyful appearance... It is worth mentioning that some similarity exists between the Polish dances and those from Southern India, i.e. *Kumni* and *Kolattem*.

With their striking costumes and their young faces without make-up, they created a very attractive spectacle.

In fact they had worked hard and in some discomfort..."

In retrospect

Looking back at the recollections and impressions from the Indian tour, certain conclusions come to mind.

Firstly, our homesickness emerges there very strongly. Beautiful Indian landscapes often remind us of our homeland; i.e. the Cardamom Hills are similar to the Carpathian Mountains, the unknown trees are acacias and even the green grass reminds us of Polish meadows.

Indian temples, their beauty and their unknown power astonished us, but our spiritual rapture we can best experience only in our own churches.

Nevertheless, the direct contact with this exotic country and its people contributed to a better understanding of their culture and tradition, so different from ours.

We found many contrasts: quiet *ashrams,* noisy film studios, villages and towns, splendour of riches and extreme poverty.

The unknown religions and beliefs, with which we came into contact, were foreign to us; i.e. Hinduism, Buddhism, Islam and organisations like the Salvation Army. They opened our eyes to the richness of human abilities and achievements.

Pani Wanda Dynowska did not apotheosize Hinduism or Buddhism - she helped us to get to know them - she opened new horizons to us, encouraging us to think independently and to respect this in others.

NOTES

The above text was based almost entirely on the articles published in the periodical *Młodzi No. 27* dated 15.03.1947, published in Valivade, as well as on the diaries and postcards written on the journey. Contemporary drawings from waxed stencils are also from the same source. The articles were often signed by pseudonyms, which are now difficult to identify.

The names of places given in the text may differ from those of today because they remain in the form of the time (e.g. Madura is now Madurai).

Translated by Stanisław and Wanda Harasymów

The same year a small group consisting of Krystyna Biskupska, Hanka Sahanek and Lt. Z. Peszkowski under the leadership of Dr. Ludwik Sternbach toured Northern India (as we did 50 years later - see chapter on "India Revisited".)

PLACES OF SETTLEMENT AFTER LEAVING INDIA

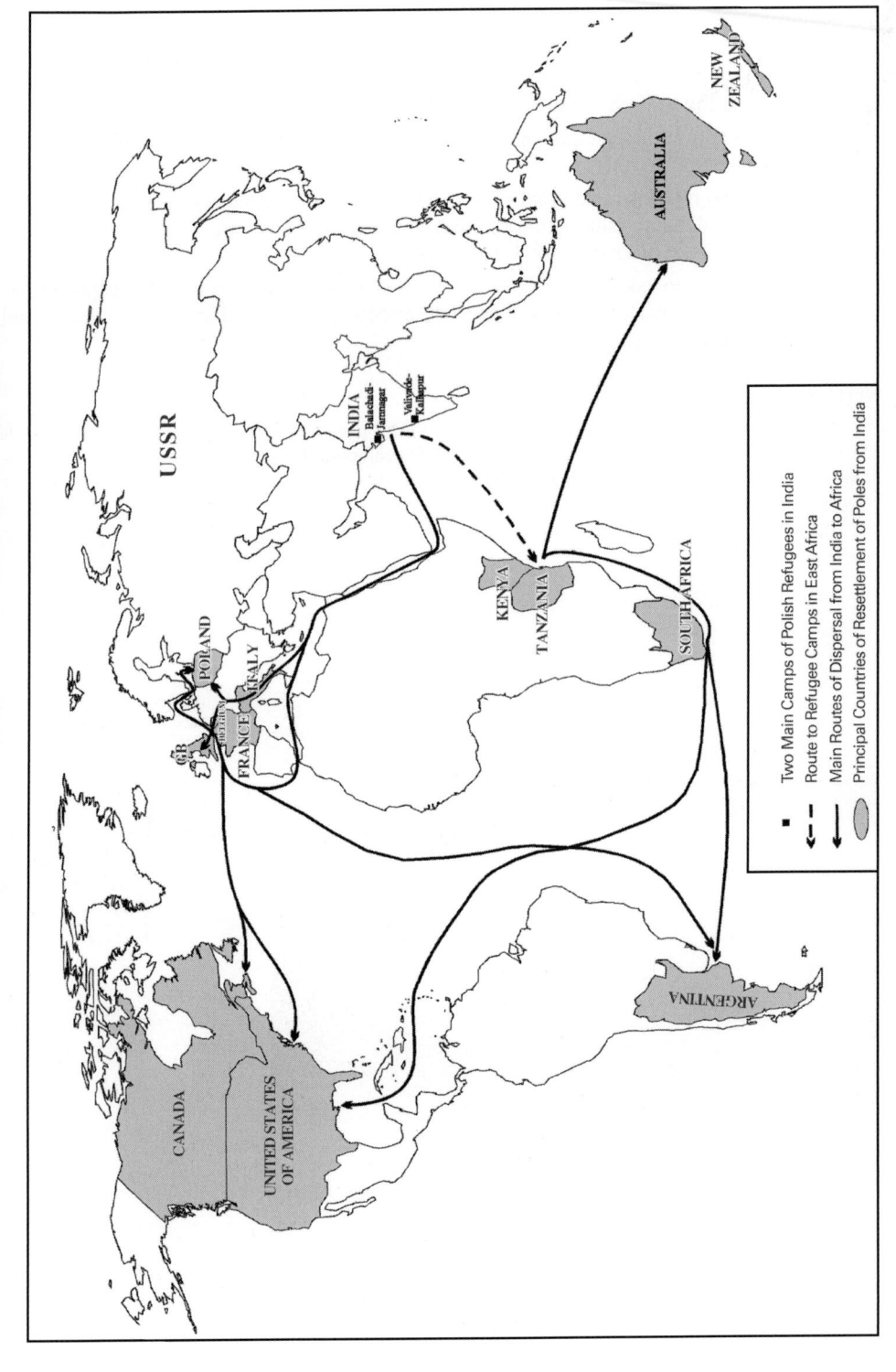

PART IV

    THE END OF THE WAR & UNRRA REGISTRATION
    REPATRIATION
    FROM EXILES TO EMIGRANTS
    PLACES OF SETTLEMENS AFTER INDIA
    FRIEDLY GATHERINGS-FORMAL ORGANISATIONS-REUNIONS
    INDIA REVISITED

THE END OF THE WAR AND REGISTRATION WITH UNRRA
by Teresa Glazer (Kurowska)

During the whole of our stay in India we awaited eagerly the ending of hostilities so that we could return to free, independent Poland. All the celebrations of our national holidays, sermons in church, campfire talks, letters written to soldiers at the front, were full of that hope.

We rejoiced in the news of Allied victories, especially those in which Polish Forces under British command participated. However, in 1943 our relations with one of the Allies, the USSR, deteriorated. In April of that year a discovery of mass graves in Katyń Forest of thousands of murdered Polish officers, prisoners of 1939 war, and a request of Polish Government-in-Exile for representatives of the International Red Cross to investigate the matter, led to the Soviets breaking off diplomatic relations with the Polish Government in London. For Great Britain and the USA Poland became an embarrassing ally, because they feared that her stance might jeopardize relations with the USSR.

Ever since the Teheran Conference of 'The Big Three' in November 1943 when Churchill's plan of attacking the Germans through the Balkans in order to control the Eastern Mediterranean had been rejected, the fate of Eastern Europe was sealed. Churchill was against leaving these territories under Soviet control, but he was outvoted by Roosevelt, who naively supported Stalin and was suspicious of British imperialism. The post war Poland's eastern frontier was to run along the Curzon Line leaving eastern Polish territories with Lvov and Wilno inside the USSR in return for lands to the North and West annexed from Germany. These decisions were not known at the time as they were kept secret.

During a conference in Moscow in October 1944 an attempt was made to reconcile the Polish Committee of National Liberation - PKWN, created from Polish Communists by Moscow, with the London Government, but it failed. On 1st January 1945 the Soviets unilaterally recognised the transformation of PKWN into a Provisional Government of the Polish Republic with Lublin as its centre.[1]

In February 1945, during the Yalta Conference, it became evident that President Roosevelt was not much interested in the fate of Central Europe; he declared that the USA intended to withdraw its armies from Europe in the near future. He was seriously ill at that time (died

6 weeks later). Churchill tried to revive talks about Poland, reminding everyone that the war had started over Poland, but he did not have much influence. It was really the United States that counted by that time.

Roosevelt was eager to have the support of the USSR in the war against Japan which had not been vanquished yet. As a reward for the enormous Soviet contribution to the defeat of Germany he was leaving Central and Eastern Europe in the sphere of their influence. The eastern frontiers of Poland were officially established along the Curzon Line, first proposed during the Versailles Settlement but rejected in 1920.

A large majority of the inhabitants of Valivade Camp came from Eastern Poland and all of us had been deportees in the Soviet Union, so how could we even consider returning to the country which had exchanged the German occupation for the Soviet one? The end of the war was near but there was no prospect of our returning to our free, independent homeland.

In June 1945 the communist Provisional Government moved from Lublin to Warsaw and on 5th July it was recognised by Great Britain and the United States. At the same time the Polish Government-in-Exile in London ceased to have their support.

What was to become of us?

As is now evident from the previously secret Foreign Office documents this painful question had been asked in London as well. Since November 1944 the Foreign Office was trying to warn the Poles, that the burden of responsibility for looking after those who found themselves living in British territories should be passed on to UNRRA (United Nations Relief and Rehabilitation Administration), an international organisation created by the United Nations for the purpose of helping people from the countries most affected by the war. Yet until such time that recognition of the Polish Government-in-Exile in London was withdrawn on 5th July 1945, all the money for financing Polish centres came from credits advanced to that Government by H. M. Government. From 6th July 1945 an entirely new set of circumstances presented itself.[2]

An Interim Treasury Committee for Polish Questions, made up of seven Poles under the leadership of Ambassador Raczyński and five British officials of the Treasury answering to Mr. W. D Allen from the Foreign Office, was set up. This body would henceforth be responsible for all monies taken from the Treasury Vote of Credit sent to the Government of India for maintenance of all essential services, but with all possible economies effected.

There were plans for winding up the Polish Consulate in Bombay in August and September 1945. Consul Litewski was to stay on as an official representative of the unofficial London Government and 14 of the former consular welfare and education staff formed a Polish Refugee Welfare Committee in India in order to maintain links between the Government of India and the Camps, oversee educational services and continue publication of the periodical *Polak w Indiach*, essential for informing the refugees, who could not read English, about world events.

The new Consulate was to be staffed by personnel sent by the Warsaw Government, but they had no jurisdiction over the refugees. The administration of the Camps was left under Capt. Webb, Principal Refugee Officer.

Even though Consul Litewski lost his diplomatic privileges, all confidential correspondence between him and the Interim Treasury Committee in London, was to travel in diplomatic bags of the Government of India.

H. H. Eggers from the Treasury in London sent a letter to R. N. Gilchrist in the India Office with a new list of salaries of the Polish employees and a confirmation that the Interim Treasury Committee had sanctioned continued payment of Polish artists and scientists.

In a letter dated 21st July 1945, Capt. Webb wrote to the Resident in Kolhapur, Col. Harvey, that it was suggested that a British Camp Commandant might be a solution to a possible split among the Poles between those who remained loyal to the London Government and any, who might be ready to recognise the Communist Government in Poland. Col. Neate seemed a suitable candidate and he officially took office on 17th October 1945. He had two deputies: Mrs. Button for Finance and Capt. Jagiełłowicz for Social Welfare. 'Relations between the Central Office in Bombay and the Government of India should remain the same as before 6th July', wrote R. N. Gilchrist from the India Office in Whitehall. Such was a temporary solution to our problems in India. A more general situation of all the Polish refugees in the world, was not clear.

During a debate in the House of Commons on 28th February 1945, Prime Minister Churchill said:

"... Finally, on this subject, His Majesty's Government recognise that the large forces of Polish troops, soldiers, sailors and airmen, now fighting gallantly, as they have fought during the whole war, under British command, owe allegiance to the Polish government in London. We have every confidence that once the new Government, more fully representative of the will of the Polish people than either the present Government in London or the Provisional Administration in Poland has been established, and recognised by the Great Powers, means will be found of overcoming these formal difficulties in the wider interest of Poland. Above all, His Majesty's Government are resolved that as many as possible of the Polish troops shall be enabled to return in due course to Poland, of their own free will, and under every safeguard, to play their part in the future life of their country.

In any event, His Majesty's Government will never forget the debt they owe to the Polish troops who have served them so valiantly, and for all those who have fought under our command I earnestly hope it may be possible to offer the citizenship and freedom of the British Empire, if they so desire. I am not able to make a declaration on that subject to-day because all matters affecting citizenship require to be discussed between this country and the Dominions, and that takes time. But so far as we are concerned we should think it an honour to have such faithful and valiant warriors dwelling among us as if they were men of our own blood."[3]

After the change of government when Labour won the election in July 1945, the official attitude towards the Polish Forces under British command remained the same, but E. Bevin, Minister of Foreign Affairs was urging them to return to Poland and, as is evident from the extracts from the following letter sent by the Under Secretary of State Paul Mason to India Office, he ordered a revision of the position of the Polish troops:

"Sir,

I am directed by Mr. Secretary Bevin to state that His Majesty's Government in the United Kingdom have had under review the position of the considerable numbers, estimated at approximately 40,000, of Polish nationals displaced by the late war who at present have found temporary asylum in countries in the Middle East, in India and in British colonial territory in Africa.

These Polish nationals were for some years maintained in the areas mentioned above at the expense of the Polish Government in exile in London. As you will be aware, with the establishment of the present Provisional Polish Government in Warsaw, the affairs of the Polish Government in London have for some time been in process of liquidation under the supervision of the Interim Treasury Committee appointed by His Majesty's Government who, as an interim measure, have assumed temporary responsibility for the continuance of financial expenditure of the displaced Polish nationals already mentioned.

His Majesty's Government assume, however, that the persons in question will in due course be repatriated to Poland. On this assumption, they have come to the conclusion that these persons would in fact qualify for relief from UNRRA, unless and until it has been finally established that their eventual repatriation is impracticable.

His Majesty's Government are aware that, under the terms of the above mentioned UNRRA is only authorised to give relief where displaced persons are necessitous and where local resources for maintaining them are inadequate or cannot be continued. On this latter point, however, the Administration are of course cognisant of the heavy financial burdens which His Majesty's Government in the United Kingdom already have to bear.

His Majesty's Government have recently been invited by Resolution No. 80 adopted at the Third Session of the Council to make a very important further contribution to UNRRA's funds. In the circumstances His Majesty's Government cannot regard it as reasonable that, in addition to making the above mentioned contribution, they should be called upon to continue to maintain displaced persons who, in their view can properly be held to come within the mandate of UNRRA. It is clear that such a situation could hardly continue indefinitely.

...the displaced Polish nationals dealt with in the present letter form the largest and most important group of United Nations displaced persons in the territories under considerations.

I am,
Sir,
Your obedient servant
(signed) Paul Mason [4]

Registering with the UNRRA

UNRRA had been created in November 1943 by the United Nations in order to help the millions of people displaced during the war by repatriating them or transporting them to their chosen places of habitation. It acts on behalf of 44 Allied Nations, including the Polish representative of the London Government. It showed an interest in us for the first time in January 1945 when the local branch in Cairo empowered its representative R. Durrant to register all displaced persons of the allied nations, in order to ascertain their numbers, transport needs, (whether they be by sea routes or land), and the final destinations.

On 13th March 1945, the Delegate, S. Darlewski stated that UNRRA needed the following information in order to register us:

1. Name
2. Marital status
3. Place of birth
4. Religion (optional)

5. Date of birth
6. Number of people in the family travelling together
7. Number of family members the person had to support
8. Father's name
9. Mother's maiden name
10. Destination to which the refugee wanted to be taken
11. Last address in Poland or the address on 1st January 1938
12. Profession
13. Other capabilities and talents
14. Languages (to be listed in order of proficiency)
15. Nationality[5]

The registration cards were to be locked up in the office until such time that the owner would be leaving the Camp, when each person would receive their own. Those who were reluctant to sign the card need not do it, but a signature would prevent any false information finding its way to the card.

By a return letter the Camp Commandant wrote to the Delegate's office asking what guarantee would the inhabitants of the Camp have against falsification of the documents, even with their signature on them? People whose birthplace happened to be on the territories assigned to the USSR by the Yalta agreements were afraid that forced repatriation to that country might be applied in their case. (We did not have the information about citizenship only applying to those who were citizens of the USSR before 1st September 1939.)[6]

On 14th March a daily bulletin no. 24, announced that a representative of the UNRRA, Mr. Durrant had arrived in the Camp and that the registration of the inhabitants would start the following day between the hours of 3p.m. and 7p.m. in the recreation room, and the day after, 16th March, from 9am to 8pm in the theatre hall. Many typists from different offices were gathered together for that purpose. One of the typists remembers: 'We sat up late at night going over the procedure. However, the following day was a complete fiasco. Only a very small group of the elderly, who did not have anyone in Gen. Anders' army, volunteered to be registered for repatriation to Poland.' People were afraid that registration with UNRRA might result in compulsory repatriation to Communist Poland.

Even though there had been assurances given by the Polish authorities in Bombay, that UNRRA was a humanitarian and not a political organisation, there was a lot of mistrust, which is reflected in the diaries of that time: 'Nobody is certain who this newcomer is. Some say he is a communist! A group of hostile women surrounded him yesterday to have a closer look and one of them poked him with a tip of her umbrella. The pros and cons of registration were discussed in school, but it was difficult to make one's mind up as different teachers expressed conflicting opinions'.

Some letters from husbands in the army warned against registration. Capt. Jagiełłowicz suggested putting off the decision for some 4-6 weeks in order to give women a chance to communicate with their husbands, but was told that Mr. Durrant was in India only for 6 weeks.

On 18th March 1945 there was a general meeting of all the inhabitants of Valivade Camp and it passed the following resolution:

1. The inhabitants of the Camp are grateful for the help offered by UNRRA.
2. They ask the Camp Commandant to make available all the information necessary to this institution's requirements from the Camp offices.
3. They ask the Consul General to intervene with the relevant authorities about adding clauses to the registration forms about political prisoners and deportees.

4. They reached a decision that they would sign the same declarations at the same time as the sovereign Polish army in the West.

5. Since a majority of the inhabitants of the Camp consists of families of soldiers fighting at the front, the choice of destination for resettlement must be reached with the Army's consent.

The resolution was presented to the Consul General.[7]

Mr. Durrant came to the conclusion that since it looked as if the Polish refugees in India would stay there for another 18 months to 2 years, UNRRA needed statistical information concerning numbers to ascertain the cost of their maintenance, rather than individual forms. During his stay in India 26 people registered a desire to return to Poland.

The cost of the upkeep of the camps after the end of the war and the reluctance of the Polish refugees to be repatriated, was a subject of correspondence between Emerson Holcomb, in charge of the repatriation section of the UNRRA in the Middle East and R. N. Gilchrist in London India Office, Whitehall. Holcomb wanted to abolish the Refugee Committee in Bombay because of their bad influence on the rest of the refugees, who, according to his opinion, would be willing to return to Poland if the government of the Polish People's Republic promised them that they could keep their land and goods, most of them being farmers. 'They would have to be given assurances, that there is no need to be afraid of Russia, that they would be transported to a Polish port, not through any territories occupied by the Russians'. Gilchrist answered that unfortunately there could be no such guarantees, as there was no part of Poland, which was not under Russian influence.[8]

Since the transfer of responsibility for the Polish refugees in India to UNRRA was to be the first step before the same happened in other territories, Polish authorities in London were anxious that a successful precedent would be established and that the Polish personnel should remain and be able to act on behalf of this organisation. In a letter dated 18th May 1946 Ambassador Raczyński in London wrote to Monsieur Litewski (no longer a consul) that overall care of the Polish refugees would remain in the British hands and that the Polish administrative personnel should stay with the exception of those officials who agitate against repatriation. He hoped that it would be possible to keep in touch with the Polish officials in Bombay, who would inform him about any new developments.[9]

The text of conditions under which UNRRA would take over the care of Polish refugees was presented to the Polish authorities in London by Sir Anthony Mayer on 30th May 1946.

The administrative costs and the upkeep of the refugees would be covered, but there was no mention of funding for the educational services, which made the Poles anxious as they considered education of the young a priority. Asked about that, Sir Anthony said that in principle schooling should be covered by UNRRA but the exact sums would be decided according to local conditions.[10]

UNRRA took over the financial responsibility for the Polish settlements in India on 1st August 1946, leaving it in the hands of the British Principal Refugee Officer, Capt. Webb.

The Organisation would pay £5 per person monthly for 5,084 refugees which would create a deficit of £6,000 a month, unless the costs were cut. On 12th October Capt. Webb proposed the following plan for cutting costs: closure of the camps in Balachadi and Panchgani and transferring the inhabitants of those settlements to Valivade as well as bringing back the pupils who were attending English schools outside the Camp. He also appealed to the people employed in the Camp, asking them to forgo their wages and work just for free accommodation, maintenance, schooling and health care. He further wrote in his appeal: 'The cost to Great Britain for all the Poles living outside their country had been £5,500,000 per month. Now this burden has been transferred to the United Nations'.[11]

The Poles agreed to the closure of Balachadi Camp; less willingly, to the closure of the Health Centre in Panchgani, but objected to any cuts in education and were not willing to work for free. Capt. Webb reported to London on 13th December that 'The Government of India asked UNRRA to raise the sum of £5 to £6 per month for the upkeep of the refugees and suggested replacing of Polish employees in the health and fire services with Indian workers, on lower wages, as well as cutting the pocket money paid to the inhabitants'.[12]

The Polish Refugee Committee in Bombay was closed in October 1946 and next month ex Consul and the majority of consular staff sailed to Australia. Only one employee of the old Ministry of Welfare, T. Lisiecki stayed on, without any official title. The only Polish institution that remained in Bombay now, was the Polish Red Cross at 15/17 Queen's Rd.

A new representative of UNRRA, Mr. Stephen arrived and held meetings with the representatives of the Association of Inhabitants of Valivade Camp, during which he gave assurances that the registration was not synonymous with repatriation and that nobody was going to be forcibly sent back. Only those, who wished to return to Poland would have their transport organised. The registration started on 31st December 1946.[13]

UNRRA looked after us till August 1947 when it transferred the responsibility for Polish refugees in India to IRO - International Refugee Organisation.

Translated by the Author

NOTES

1. J. Garliński *Polska w drugiej wojnie światowej,* 1982, p. 422-426
2. PRO: FO371, 42866, 1944
3. IOR: LP J/8/415
4. BL, IOR: WR 1265/384/48
5. JAG Archives KPI
6. Sir Carol Mather: *Aftermath of war, everyone must go home,* 1992 p. 130
7. JAG Archives
8. FO 371 57830, 1946, file 289
9. IPiMS: A18/50
10. ibid
11. ibid A73/231
12. IOR: LP J/8/415
13. PwI: year 5, no. 1, (81), 1947, p. 23

REPATRIATION
by Teresa Glazer (Kurowska)

The decision whether to return to Poland, or not, was of supreme importance for thousands of Poles scattered throughout the world from the start of World War II. All of them, irrespective of their political persuasion, planned to return to their country from the start of their life as emigres, but at the end of the war in 1945, the German occupation had been replaced by the Soviet one. The country, ravaged by the war, having lost nearly 7,000, 000 of its citizens, desperately needed workforce to rebuild it, to settle the regions of East Prussia and Silesia joined to its territory by those, who redrafted the map of Europe at Yalta, in compensation for the loss of Eastern regions incorporated into the USSR (see map on following pages). However, going back would mean accepting the lack of independence, of freedom and their country being a satellite state. There was a deep feeling of hurt and betrayal by the Allies, expressed aptly in a poem by Marian Hemar, published in *Polak w Indiach* in November 1945, called *Powrót (THE WAY HOME)* (on the next page).

It was a matter of conscience and nobody had any right to criticize those, who decided to return in spite of all the odds, nor those, who decided against it.

The problems of those times in our Valivade Camp are described well by Jagoda Lempke: "Discussion was heated - those, who had somebody in the Polish Forces under British command, or others with close family ties in Poland, knew what to do. What about the rest?"

Some of the factors, which influenced those, who decided to return were: a desire to join their families, longing for their Motherland, disillusionment with the attitude of the Allies, realization that their country needed good brains and strong hands in order to rebuild it.

A. Grubczak explains his decision by patriotic motives – a chance to return, even if not to his birthplace, (now a part of the USSR), to his own country, seemed preferable to a prospect of staying abroad, without the knowledge of any foreign languages, subjected to all kinds of humiliations as a stateless person.

Reading of the diaries written at that time, throws some light on how individual people tried to adjust to the political turmoil. H. Szafrańska wrote on 10th October 1947: "I cannot see myself as an émigré; even though I know it is not going to be easy, in my own country, I know that I can find the right place for myself."

THE WAY HOME (POWRÓT)
by Marian Hemar

For what? Long treks by night through frozen waste,
Carpathian hailstorms, Tatras blizzards faced -
snow-drifts and icy swamps ... What for?
Why those Roumanian camps, Hungarian jails -
Syrian, Libyan, Persian desert trails?
A grave on Norway's shore?
Those countless borders crossed, barren or forested;
vineyards in France or Italy where blood was shed -
who now will call to mind?

> Poles died in British skies or German clouds, aflame -
> drowned in oceans blue and green, with single aim:
> the homeward path to find.
> Should we persuade the living now to stay -
> or else advise them all to go away?
> Urge them to hurry home? How so?
> Can nobody be made to understand
> that, if Poles long to see their native land,
> They must be sure it's theirs before they go!

How can one heal the pain of exile dreams -
The bitter tears on faces that grow wan
at very thought of such returning?
How soothe the hearts of those to whom there seems
no question: home and freedom both are one -
together part of one much vaster yearning.
For, like a shattered graveyard in decay,
is how our longed-for victory looms today,
while huckster hirelings, with effrontery,
dare lecture us on sacred love of country.

(Translated by Noel Clark)

"Families were torn apart and divided by the issue of repatriation. Z. Dudek went back by herself in one of the early transports to Poland. (The rest of the family joined her later.) So did A. Janiszewska and her brother, while sister Marysia went to Australia. Many orphans from Balachadi returned. To the country of their birth went families: Bartosz, Chendyński, Czeczenik, Gromadzki, Krzysztoń, Ostrihanska, Pacholski, Rozkuszko, Skrzat, Szafrańska, Trzaska, and others. Decisions taken at that time influenced the rest of our future life. It was the time of "the migration of nations", after which the iron curtain divided us from them." (Wrote J. Lempke)

Scouts and Guides were torn between the position of Scoutmaster Ryś, who felt it was our duty to stay out as emigres and fight for Poland's independence by whatever means possible and Guider Hanka, who believed that her country needed people with vision and the more of those returned, the better a chance of winning.

In most cases the final decision whether to return or stay, depended on the individual family situation. Those whose closest family members were in Poland, often returned even though they disapproved of the imposed regime. Our close friend Mrs. Maria Kobordo with daughters

Halina and Jagoda, lost her husband in Kharkov (a victim of the Katyń forest Massacres) and the whereabouts of her only son were not known to her. Those of us who had somebody in the Polish Army under British command, could come to England, so my Father, who served in that army registered her as his married sister, to give her a chance to come here. In the meantime, however, the Red Cross gave her some information about her son in Poland and that influenced her decision to return.

The first list of 25 people, who registered to be repatriated, was sent to Mr. M. Nagar, Assistant Secretary Commonwealth Relations Dept., on 13th October 1945. Most people on that list, made it clear that their willingness to return depended on getting some answers from the representative of the Warsaw Government to questions, which concerned them. Eleven Byelorussians and Ukrainians had no reservations and definitely wished to return to Poland.[1]

In February 1946, *Polak w Indiach* informed its readers, that the Russian Foreign Secretary, Molotov, issued pronouncements attacking Gen. Anders, leader of some 100, 000 Polish soldiers used by the Allies to occupy Italy at that time, accusing him of terrorising the common soldier, who would be willing to return to Poland had it not been for hostile leadership. In fact, most of those soldiers had been deported to the USSR at the start of the war and did not need anyone else telling them what life under Communism meant – they had seen it with their own eyes. The British, remembering the Polish input during the war years, defended the Poles. However, the upkeep of the Polish Forces burdened the British taxpayer, so in March 1946, Foreign Secretary Ernest Bevin issued an appeal in the House of Commons urging them to return to their own country, stating that an agreement with the Warsaw Government regarding conditions of their return had been reached. The following day Warsaw radio announced that no new declaration concerning

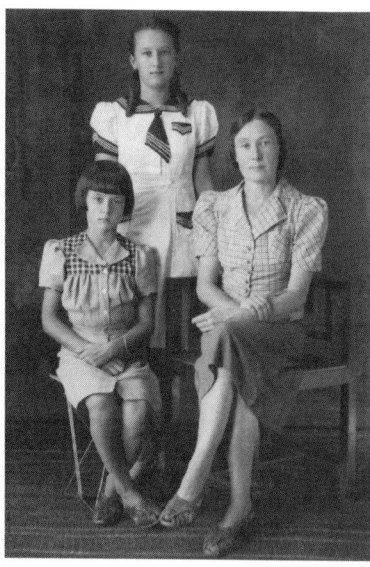

Kobordo family

Departure from Valivade

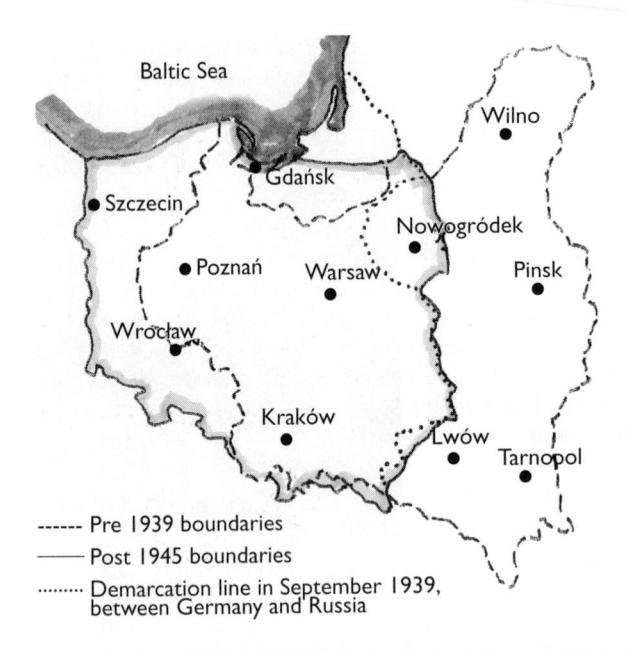

the return of the soldiers had been made. The Polish Government in London, in response to the Bevin speech, pointed out that the British Government prejudged the fate of the Polish Forces, even before decisions made at Yalta, promising free elections, had been carried out. Most of the soldiers were reluctant to return to the country ruled by authorities imposed on them, not democratically elected.

On 20th March 1946 Polish Press Agency in Edinburgh expressed the concern of the Polish soldiers, who received an anonymous leaflet, written in poor Polish, supposedly guaranteeing safety by the Warsaw authorities, but mainly threatening those who "acted against the Polish State".[2]

Map legend:
------ Pre 1939 boundaries
——— Post 1945 boundaries
.... Demarcation line in September 1939, between Germany and Russia

Fortunately, United Nations Assembly adopted Elenor Roosevelt's resolution stating that people displaced by the war, who had legitimate reasons for not wishing to return to their own country, cannot be forced to do so. The Soviets lost their attempt to deprive those people of any kind of protection.

In Valivade, people were alarmed by the news that consular representatives of the Warsaw administration in London, ordered registration of all Poles in the British Isles, except soldiers on active duty. Such registration would mean acceptance of orders from the Warsaw Government and loss of the status of a political refugee, so it was opposed.

In the Camp, a Temporary Repatriation Committee for the purpose of informing those, who were interested in repatriation, was formed in August 1946. One of the daily bulletins stated that "...the transport being currently organised by UNRRA would be the only one financed by that organisation. All future transports would have to be financed privately. The proposed land route would lead from India to Egypt, then Trieste, and an alternative sea route, from Egypt to Gdynia by boat. The luggage allowance would be 295lbs. for adults and 150lbs. for children under the age of 16.[3]

In the August edition of *Polak w Indiach* 1946, the following resolution, prompted by imminent arrival of the Warsaw repatriation mission in India, was published:

"...The declaration, undersigned by the representatives of all the organisations of Polish refugees in India and accepted unanimously by a mass meeting of all the inhabitants of Valivade-Kolhapur, stated that the Polish refugees never accepted the authority of the Warsaw administration, mistakenly called the Government of Poland. The refugees in India, together with all true Poles in Poland and throughout the world, recognise the lawful continuity of the Polish State with its head, President W. Raczkiewicz and the Coalition of Polish political parties in London, as their only democratic representatives. Hence their attitude to the repatriation mission cannot be expected to be positive."

An English translation of this declaration appeared in the Indian press : *Times of India* and *Bombay Morning Star*.

In April 1946 Repatriation Mission numbering 5 people was established with the Polish legation in Cairo.[4] They wrote to the authorities in Warsaw asking them to send an English speaking candidate for India. In November Ms. Burakiewicz*, representing Polish Legation in Cairo arrived in Valivade in order to inform the inhabitants about conditions of life in Poland and organise repatriation of those, who voluntarily wanted to return there. The inhabitants received her mistrustfully. Her visit was thus described in the *Camp Chronicle:*

"On 13th Nov.1946 Ms. Burakiewicz was met by representatives of the group waiting for repatriation at Valivade Halt on the way to Kolhapur, where she was to stay at the residency of the state of Kolhapur as a guest of Col. Harvey. Next day she was taken round the Camp by Col. Neate. Most of the inhabitants stoically ignored her. Only the people interested in returning to Poland welcomed her and their registration took place on 21st and 22nd November. A meeting of 135 people interested in repatriation, chaired by the Resident and the Camp Commandant took place on 25th November at which Ms. Burakiewicz spoke. She later gave an interview to the Kolhapur press correspondent, painting a very negative picture of the Camp and its inhabitants. The first transport to Poland was scheduled for 8th December."

In her report to the Polish legation in Cairo on 16th February 1947 she wrote that as a result of hostile propaganda in "reactionary" papers like: *Polak w Indiach.*

"...All are contra and think of living anywhere else except Poland. They are afraid of NKWD, Siberia, and do not believe that the Polish Government is really Polish, think that Russia rules over everything. They have been told that those who come from Eastern Poland, now belonging to Russia, would be transferred there under compulsion. Some are guilty of political or criminal offences dating back to their stay in the USSR and are worried about facing penalties as they are convinced of Russian rule in Poland.

...Most women are waiting for the decision of their husbands or brothers, who are still in England. They keep quoting their experiences of suffering and hunger during the deportations in the Soviet Union. Their base desire for material possessions and attempts to squeeze as much as possible out of the British, is camouflaged by ideology of martyrdom and patriotism. It is impossible to find a common language with these people.

...The person, who does us most damage on Indian subcontinent and thwarts our efforts to repatriate, is Wanda Dynowska. This lady has lived in India for a number of years, has adopted Indian religion and dress, and a name of Uma Devi. She is well regarded by both the British and the Indians, belongs to Gandhi's inner circle, knows Nehru and is friendly with a Polish Jew, Frydman, who is a member of the Congress. She visits the Camp, gives lectures on India, takes Polish children dressed in regional costumes of Cracow or Łowicz on tours of India, where their songs and dances are supposed to promote the good name of Poland. When I intervened and asked why the lady often stays in the Camp I was told that she is only engaged in cultural and educational activities.

The devil dances with beetroot
Well matched pair
Though they easily be defeated
By Baby Jesus and Mary!

*Burakiewicz - burak = beetroot

Pandit Nehru told me, that a deputation from the Camp visited him asking for permission to stay in Kolhapur. He told them that they could stay for the time being, but they should not regard India as a place of permanent settlement, as the war ended two years ago, it was time to return home, or settle wherever they would be welcome – India had enough of its own population."[5]

The first transport of 154 repatriates left Valivade on 8th December 1946 in the afternoon.

They started their journey in third class carriages at Valivade Halt and were taken late at night to Kolhapur, then to Poona and Bombay, where they went on board a ship going to Naples. From there, they were going to travel by train to Poland.

Ola Czeczenikow described the journey: "...We took a photo of the whole group before leaving Valivade. We spent Christmas at sea. On the morning of 1st January 1947 we entered the Bay of Naples, from where Mt. Vesuvius could be observed on the right and the lights of the Isle of Capri on the left. In the second half of January the rest of the group went by train to Poland, but our family had to stay in Italy because of the illness and subsequent death of my six-year old brother. After the funeral we joined a group of Poles, who were being repatriated from Africa." Ola's family were not the only people, who had to be detached from the first transport because of illness. Rena Płocka, following a recent appendicitis operation in the Red Cross hospital in Bombay, had to be rushed to an Italian hospital when her stitches burst. Her luggage and documents were left behind. She could not communicate with anyone in Polish or English. She had a lucky break when she overheard two nuns speaking in Polish. She begged them to contact her "unknown soldier" with whom she corresponded and knew that he worked for a publication called *Parada*. The "knight in shining armour" came to the rescue: traced her documents, smuggled her out of the hospital, married her in St. Peter's Basilica and later brought to England.

The Association of Poles in India collected funds for warm clothing for children returning to Poland and gave each child some money for the journey. All repatriates were equipped with medicines supplied by the Social Welfare. The second transport left on 8th April 1947.[6]

In the February edition of *Polak w Indiach* appeared an article written in English by Syt. Sitram Puranik for an Indian paper *The Mahratta* entitled "Why they do not want to return?": "They would say that Poland - the first country to oppose the armed violence of the Nazi aggression, which has not produced even a single Quisling, which suffered more terribly than any other in the war for the common cause and which contributed its full share to the success of the Allies, is not free to-day. The country which deserved to reap the rewards of her steadfastness and endurance, courage and sacrifice, has not yet recovered her freedom and sovereignty, while all the other Allies, France, Belgium, Holland and Norway have been 'liberated' and have gained their former independence, Poland has merely exchanged one slavery for another.

The Government which sits in Warsaw is not the Government of the people of Poland. It has been imposed on them by Soviet Russia with the backing of her armed force and the support of Communists who are now ruthlessly exterminating all political elements hostile to Communism. A rule of political terror, through the secret police, has been imposed on Poland.

Socially and economically the position is not better. Those who had the opportunity of making investigations have declared that Russia is now trying to make Poland her political and economic satellite. Eighty percent of the 'Polish Army' officers are Russians. Factories have been deprived of machinery. Workers have no right to strike. No civil liberty exists.

Farms are stripped off from livestock and implements and only those peasants who agree to join the Communist Party are offered any help.

Is it any wonder, that those Poles who have managed to remain outside do not go back to Poland? Have they no right to ask that their country should be free to develop her own national life in accordance with her own ideals?

Among those one hundred and fifty who decided to go, there were many who had their close relatives in Poland and who were repeatedly asked by them to return.

But there are hundreds of others who refuse to go in spite of appeals from their relatives or friends. A typical case is that of a boy of about thirteen, with a brother of nine, who was induced to return to Poland on assurance that his father was awaiting his arrival there. A letter was shown to him as coming from his father in the 'Polish army'. This boy, with a smart face and eyes full of fire, told one Madam Burakiewicz who called herself the representative of the Warsaw Government, that he was not sure that the letter came from his father. "Why should my father write type-written letter to a stranger like you? Why should he not write to me? Maybe the signature is his own, but I do not know if he really wrote the letter. I am very anxious to meet my father but not in Poland today. How can I forget the death of my mother in the labour camp in Russia, where she was lying in the street without food? If you try to take me away, I shall jump out of the train or the boat", he said.

"One often meets people who argue, "But why should India spend for these refugees?" This argument sounds very reasonable but it is based on wrong information, for there never was a time when India paid for these refugees.

Attempts are now being made to prejudice the case of these Poles by declaring that they are not prepared to go back because they are afraid of misery and hard work. The fact is that because these refugees are members of the Polish soldiers' families, they still run the risk of deportations and even deaths. Besides, their return to Poland is likely to be interpreted as tacit acceptance of the present (Communist) Warsaw Government to which they are opposed.

What can Indians do in this matter? Indians can take more informed interest in the life and culture, literature, music and art of the Poles. They will find on closer study, many things in common with the Poles, particularly the outlook on life, which is so very different from the materialistic view of the West and so very akin to that of Indians."[7]

In May 1947 it became known from statistics published by the Commission of IRO that the Poles were the largest group (335,000) amongst other nationals, who decided to return to their Motherland, even though they knew that Poland was not free and democratic. After a time it became obvious that the naive belief in the possibility of another war against the USSR was not realistic and that life of a political émigré fighting for human rights and Poland's independence would not be easy.[8]

On 17th May the third transport composed mainly of families of military settlers and agricultural workers, 17 children from the orphanage and some single elderly people – 197 in all, left.[9]

In 1947 on the average about 75 letters from Poland reached the Camp. Most were very cautious, reporting family news, but some teenagers courageously described the Soviet influence in all aspects of life and openly stated their regret of the decision to return.[10]

The 4th transport of 53 people took away some significant personalities: Inspector Z. Żerebecki, Head of the Orphanage, F. Zwierzchowska, ex Camp Commandant R. Dusza. They left Bombay on 2nd July.[11]

The official propaganda in Poland tried to create a rift between those, who refused to return, painting them as people, who were derailed from the right path, and the rest of the nation. In fact most Poles felt and thought alike, but had to adapt to the grim reality.

Halina Szafrańska described the transport, which left on 17th January 1948: "In Bombay we boarded a large transport ship *Georgic* carrying English and American soldiers returning home. We crossed the Red Sea, and reached Port Said, where 40 Polish soldiers and some 1,000 British, joined us. We disembarked in Naples and transferred to a train. We exchanged cigarettes brought from India for oranges and apples. On the way to Rome the ravages of the recent war were very noticeable. In Rome the Polish Consul visited us and spoke about the difficult conditions of life in Poland and advised us what to buy in Italy to bring with us.

On 4th February we saw a Polish train waiting for us. All the notices were in Polish! But the sight of the White Eagle, an emblem of Poland, without the crown was a shock. We reached the Polish border on 10th February. Above the gates of the transit camp we read "YOUR MOTHERLAND WELCOMES YOU", but the inhabitants of Koźle, where the camp was situated, expressed a surprise that we should have chosen to return from abroad. We had to have various inoculations and a fortnight's quarantine. A journalist writing for the *Workers' Tribune* came to visit us on 14th February and asked questions about where we came from".

The diary of Leszek Trzaska describes the journey of the last group of repatriates: "We left Valivade on 22nd Feb.1948 and boarded a troop-ship General M. B. Stuart. We sailed to Mombasa, where some of the inhabitants of Valivade, who were not returning to Poland, landed, and others, from various African camps, joined us. We crossed the Suez Canal and reached Genoa on 21st March. Here the transport was divided into two groups: those returning to Poland and the other group going to Germany and further destinations. Those of us, who were travelling to Poland left Genoa on 27th March by a Polish train. We crossed the border at Międzylesie and reached the repatriation centre, from where people were to travel to different parts of Poland".

Landing permit

Altogether only an insignificant percentage of the inhabitants of Valivade decided to return, not more than 473 people.[12] The majority chose the difficult role of political emigres, believing that they can better serve their country by taking every opportunity to voice the opinion that there was no truly independent Poland.

NOTES
1. IOC:LPJ/8/414
2. arch. KPI - Documents on Return of Poles to Poland, 1946
3. IPiMS: C 811 B
4. AAN: Sygn 417
5. Ibid:
6. IPiMS: C811 B
7. PwI, year 5, No.2 (82), 1947, p.34 -36
8. PwI: year 5, No.4 (84), p.2
9. PwI, year 5, No.4 (84), p.6.
10. PwI, year 5 No.8 (88),1947 p.6
11. PwI, year 5, No.11(91)1947, p.5
12. PwI, year 6, No.1 1948, p. 3

FROM EXILES TO EMIGRANTS
by Teresa Glazer (Kurowska)

Great Britain became the centre of post World War II immigration for the Polish exiles: it was the seat of the legal Polish Government, established in accordance with the April 1935 constitution, thousands of soldiers from Gen. Anders' Second Corps, settled there. In June 1946 demobilisation of the Polish Forces started and a Resettlement Corps (PKPR) was established for 159 000 of those who refused to go back to communist Poland. Ten thousand of them, under the age of thirty, could join the British army and the others were to be trained in various skills. An agreement of the trade unions was obtained, as there was a shortage of workforce at that time. Former soldiers lived in camps and tried hard to learn English.

Military personnel, who had been seconded for special duties from the Army, had to report to England in order to undergo the process of demobilisation. One of those was Lieut. Z. Peszkowski, who left Valivade on 29th Sept. 1947 as a leader of a group of soldiers.

"In 1947 the House of Commons passed a Polish Resettlement Act, which gave the Polish army families the same rights as those of the British. This paved the way for transports of Poles from India to Great Britain. Before the end of 1947 some 17 000 members of soldiers' families were to arrive from India and Africa".[1]

Finding suitable means of transport for the families became the main problem. In Valivade at the end of August 1947, the first transport 960 strong, made up of wives and children was being organised. They were to be provided with warm clothing and rainproof capes. They left on 6th Sept. travelling first to Bombay by train, then sailing on the Empire Brent. One of the participants described the journey for *Polak w Indiach:*

"The train journey was quite comfortable. Transferring the sick in Poona to a Bombay train was a bit tricky, but the English transport leader managed it very well, carrying some patients himself. The ship is very comfortable : 4, 8, 10, or 16- people cabins have spring bunks, hot water, mirrors. There is a common room, a room with toys for children, club rooms on the top deck. The sick are in the care of a doctor and nurses. Food is tasty and plentiful. Father Pluta makes announcements through the loudspeaker and tells us the menu choices each day. The dining room shines with cleanliness and sparkling cutlery. It would be nice if the next transport could travel in similar comfortable conditions. Before we left port, thirty people went on a sightseeing tour of Bombay."[2] For many this was the first opportunity to do this, even though we stayed in India for several years. Zosia Balawender wrote in her diary: "They travelled by coach and tried to see as much as possible in the short time available. We passed the University, the Opera House, Theosophical Library, Polish Red Cross. By the "Tower of Silence", we were told that the adherents of an ancient Persian religion, Parsees, leave the bodies of their dead there to be picked by vultures, as they are against polluting earth, fire or water, which are sacred. *'The Hanging Gardens'* do not actually hang, but are on the ground, and there is a huge reservoir of natural water under them. Besides gorgeous flowers, there are trees and shrubs shaped into animal and human forms. In the museum exponents of Indian culture go back several thousand years before Christ. There are bronze objects, pottery figures of their gods, fabrics, seals, swords, articles carved in ivory. We passed the *'Gate of India'* and visited the cathedral." She was in charge of a large group of 143 Scouts and Guides during the journey. Irena Kępa described their tasks in her diary: "Next day after our arrival, when the second group of passengers came from Valivade, the Guides were used to take the new passengers to their cabins and to look after the children. They managed to do this efficiently and in two hours' time, everyone was settled. All the Scouts and Guides were divided according to age into four sections, each with a different leader. The programme included English lessons, keeping watch in the dining hall, hospital and club, in order to prevent disorder. There were games, singing, fireside chats, discussions. Scouts wanted to learn the marine way of life, so the Captain suggested learning about radar, cartography, finding out the depth of the water, handling a life-boat and washing the decks. They liked it all, except the last item."

Other diaries tell us about the ship's route. Marysia Kokoszko wrote: "On 15th Sept. we crossed the Suez Canal. Next day we stopped in Port Said at 2pm. It was a memorable day, as we were visited be General Wiatr accompanied by our Scoutmaster, Z. Peszkowski. The General was greeted with a bouquet of red roses by the Guides, as he was known for his support of Scouting. He signed our Chronicle and spoke to us about the aims of the emigres and said that the fight for Poland was not yet over. Wished us safe journey and we cheered him loudly."

Gen. Wiatr and Lieut. Z. Pasakowski visit our ship at Port Said

Small boats brought local produce to the ship. Leather handbags with Egyptian motifs were very popular. We left the port at 5p.m. sailing into the Mediterranean Sea. We crossed the Straits of Gibraltar on 21st and entered the Atlantic Ocean, which was rough and cold".

Another entry, in Z. Balawender's diary, describes the farewell evening." The Officers of the ship's crew were presented with gifts such as inscribed books; there was singing and folk dancing. The Captain of the Empire Brent said that he had never before transported such a well disciplined group as ours."

Letters sent to Valivade from England warned people getting ready for the next transport that they should avail themselves of warm clothing as, after passing Gibraltar the temperature suddenly dropped and many passengers of Empire Brent caught colds, since they did not possess jumpers, stockings or warm coats. The ship arrived in Southampton on 26th Sept. at 10.30 p.m. Landing started the following day. Heavy luggage was submitted to the Customs and passengers were only allowed to keep light bags. Customs officers inquired about arms, alcohol, cigarettes, carpets, woollen or silk cloth. They checked some items at random.

The new arrivals in England were placed in a transit camp, in a wooded area, Possingworth Park, Cross in Hand, Sussex. Family reunions were very moving – many fathers could hardly recognise their children, after many years of separation.[3]

Especially poignant was the tragedy of Leszek Bełdowski's family, as the father died whilst mother and son were on the way to join him. Other families were disappointed that soon after greeting their men-folk, they were separated again as it took 4-5 weeks before all the formalities were completed and a proper reunion could take place. In the transit camp they lived in prefabs, known as "barrels of laughs" because of their shape, furnished with iron beds and stoves. The sudden change of climate from the tropical to especially harsh winter of 1947, was very hard.

Ist transport to UK: J. Kowalski. Z. Marcinkiewicz, M. Dadlez and E. Grużewska

After the departure of the first transport, made up of the close families of soldiers in the Second Corps, it was not clear who was entitled to travel to the British Isles and who was not. The lot of married children over the age of 21 and of army widows, whose husbands had died at the start of the war or in the USSR, was uncertain. There was a list in Commandant's office of several hundred widows, who were entitled and many in exactly the same position, were left out. Different sources of information varied on the subject.[4]

The second transport of 972 people left the Camp in early November and boarded the same ship, Empire Brent, which had carried the first transport. All the remaining wives and children of the members in the Resettlement Corps have now gone, as well and some mothers and more distant family members. Among those still remaining in the Camp, some were preparing for the third transport, others faced an uncertain future. Often families were split: married sisters, aunts etc. were left behind.[5]

Letters sent from Port Said reported disgraceful behaviour of some individuals, who stole tableware from the dining room, so that handbags had to be searched on leaving the room and brought shame on the rest of the passengers. Some young hooligans forced the Captain to introduce military discipline. One letter sent to *Polak w Indiach* on 6th December suggested that in future a list of people suspected of antisocial behaviour should be handed to the authorities before the next transport left.

Yet things couldn't have been that bad, because another passenger on this journey, Danka Pniewska found only positive entries in her diary: of pleasant indoor fireside gatherings with the participation of the crew, a fantastic duet of polka danced by Halina Bąbik and Witek Olesiak, and the birth of a baby, which pleased the Captain no end; a new British citizen of Polish ancestry.

This transport docked in Liverpool on 28th November and was welcomed by our Scoutmasters, Z. Peszkowski and B. Pancewicz. There was some trouble with M. and J. Leśniak's luggage, as they wrapped some memorabilia of Scouting camps in India into tents and the customs officers were rather suspicious of it, told them to unpack and examined it very thoroughly. All new arrivals were taken to a transit camp in Darlingworth nr. Cirencester, Glos. They experienced the first frost for five years. Danka's present from her father, an RAF leather, fur-lined jacket became very useful and was widely borrowed by those, who had to fetch coal for the iron stoves.

The last official gathering of Federation of Poles in India (sitting) A. Kisielnicka, Prof. J. Szymańska, Mjr. F. Kłosowicz, Mrs. M. Button, Capt. Nielsen, M. Goławski, Z. Kiełbińska, W. Melnarowicz (standing) M. Chmielowiec, O. Grabianka, Z. Sikorski, W. Oszmiański, K. Łęczyński and Cz. Polechowicz

In the second half of November, a representative of the Inspectorate of PKPR and of the War Office, Mjr F. Kłoskowicz, arrived in Valivade in order to correct the mistakes concerning all the people, who were entitled to travel to Britain within the 19 categories described by the War Office on 8th July 1947. "On Sunday, 23rd Nov. there was a meeting of all the inhabitants of the Camp in the local cinema, during which Mjr F. Kłoskowicz repeated the assurance made by Gen. Anders, that he would not forget any Pole, who had been rescued from the Soviet Union."[6]

The Major stayed on for ten days in the Camp and managed to find out about the schools, the cultural life, workshops. His entry in the Camp Chronicle on 29th Nov.1947 stated that he found a tiny piece of Poland inhabited by true Polish patriots in this faraway part of the world. He collected the data of all the widows and orphans in order to present them at the War Office. After the lists for future transports were compiled it turned out that about 400 people did not qualify to be admitted to Great Britain. Jan Siedlecki's family was in that number. Entries in his diary show confusion, worry about the uncertain future and changes of plans for travel to the USA, Australia, nostalgia for the old country, countered by reasons for refusal to return to Poland even if his Mother would be willing. All this before his final exams in his school in Bombay.

In the meantime, 280 people, who found sponsors, left on individual contracts for Canada and the USA. An Australian immigration officer arrived in the Camp trying to engage young men 16-40 years old for hydro-electrical works in Tasmania, but he was not very successful; only ten men and ten women, volunteered for hospital work. Australian Government also showed an interest in looking after a group of orphans, who were going to be looked after by Catholic organisations, but the project fell through, because the immigration officer could not provide any reassurance that those orphans would not be handed over, in case the Polish communist government claimed them.

Marysia Shannon and her husband were in the group travelling to Australia. She described their journey:" We sailed from Bombay in an Australian ship 'Manoora', previously used for transporting the armed forces during the war, therefore rather primitive: no individual cabins, but large dormitories. Most passengers were English or Anglo-Indian, so there are language difficulties. Thanks to my school in Karachi, I managed to communicate in English. In the evenings dances and other social events were held. Australian films showed spacious cities, sandy beaches, healthy, sun-tanned children running about the green gardens. We were filled with hope for the future and felt gratitude to the country offering us sanctuary. We docked in Freemantle, a port in Western Australia, near Perth. They put us up temporarily at the Seamen's Club, which seemed very luxurious after the barracks in Valivade and the rough ship. It was 15th August (Polish national holiday); there were flowers and wine. My first purchase on Australian soil was a vase for those flowers. We would have to look for a place to live in and for work. The start of an independent life was dawning!."

The third transport for England was being organised at the start of December 1947, originally for 1000 passengers, but the ship Ormond could only take 375. They left the Camp on 19th Dec. and sailed from Bombay on 21st. They would have to celebrate Christmas at sea.[7]

Krysia Kuchcicka described Christmas Eve in her diary: "We gathered on the deck before supper and our priest made a very moving sermon. When we started breaking the wafer, the English passengers were curious and we had to explain the tradition. After supper there was music and some people started dancing. However, when some Polish girls joined them, it was condemned in our group. Midnight Mass was said on the top deck in the first class salon filled to the full with our people as well as some English families. We sang our carols and the sound was carried to the stars far over the Arabian Sea.

….We docked at Tilbury on 8th Jan. The Captain thanked our group for being model passengers. England seemed wet and cold. We were taken by train to a transit camp in Daglingworth. Here our Scoutmaster, Z. Peszkowski came to meet us. He gathered all the Guides and organised a campfire. It was very sad compared with our camp-fires in India. We were cold and I thought that many of us would never meet again…."

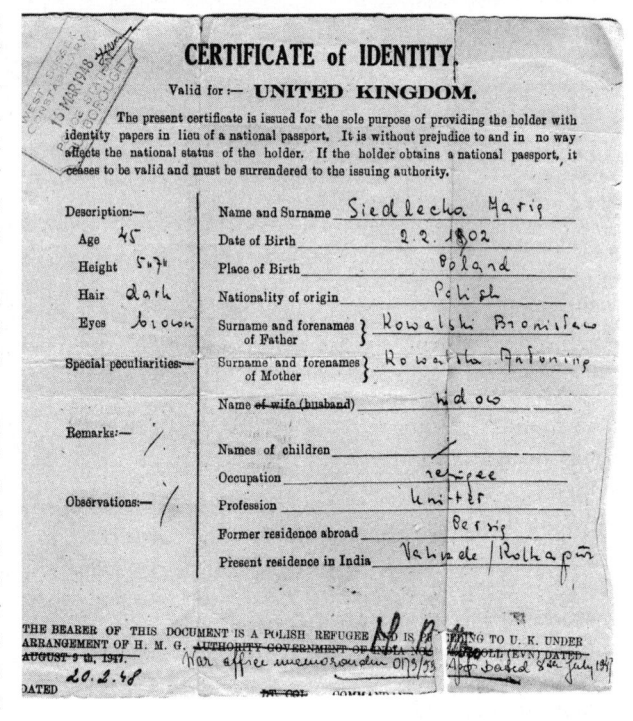

The last transport to Britain left on 21st Feb. 1948. We know from Jan Siedlecki's diary that the young people sang uncontrollably during the train journey all the way to Poona, and mothers were nervous, as among their number there were 100 widows whose status as army families was in question, as their husbands fell in battle in Poland in 1939, like Jan's father, or died during their exile in the Soviet Union, like J. Chrząszczewski's father, a judge and reservist in the army, before they had a chance to join the Polish army under British command. Even when they reached Bombay, it was not certain that they would board the 'Asturias', bound for Southampton. A firm stand of Mrs. Button, the Camp Commandant at that time, helped them, as she refused to have them back in the Camp, so they were allowed to board the ship with the rest of the passengers. They sailed at 19.30 on 23rd Feb. When the ship was sailing through the Straits of Gibraltar, they honoured by a minute's silence the memory of General Sikorski, who had died there in an air crash in July 1943.

On 10th March the 'Asturias' was stopped outside Southampton, as two cases of smallpox were suspected; however, after a medical inspection they were allowed to dock in Southampton on 11th March and were taken to a camp in West Chiltington in Surrey, the following day.

Bronek Siedlecki, who had a weak heart, had left earlier than the rest of his family on a so-called hospital ship carrying convalescents from battles in Malaya and Palestine. He was assigned duties such as carrying buckets of soup up spiral stairs to the top deck, before he managed to explain in broken English his heart condition. He reckoned that he would have been better off travelling with the rest of his family, especially as the person in charge of their transport was his own doctor from Valivade who knew his state of health.

After the departure of the army families, there were still 400 people left in the Camp waiting to be re-settled. Two hundred and fifty of those left in February 1948 for East Africa on an American ship General Stuart. Olek Klecki, whose father was in charge of a group of orphans, described their fate. They landed in Mombassa, where they were divided into two groups: one was sent to a camp in Tengeru, Tanzania, the other to Koja in Uganda, on the shores of Lake Victoria. Olek, in the first group, writes:

"The Tengeru camp was situated in a valley between the mountains of Kilimanjaro and Meru. Each family had their own, circular hut, like that of the natives. There was a church, schools, theatre. Polish cultural life thrived. The number of inhabitants diminished gradually as transports for England left. Our turn came in the Autumn of 1948. We sailed in the Polish ship Batory to Southampton. From there we were sent to Checkendon, a camp near Reading."

Wiesia Kleszko provided some information about the camp at Koja. Compared with Valivade the camp was much smaller and more remote from

Last transport to UK: (from left) E. Oles, H. Wądołkowski, R. Blumski, W. Rubczewska, S. Wasiuk, J. Siedlecki, A. Tybulewicz and A. Wasiuk

the nearest town. The post only arrived two or three times a week. However, the climate was less dry and therefore better for the complexion. Africa was very green; pineapples and bananas grew in abundance; whole branches of bananas would be bought by the yard and then picked at home. The camp was closed in 1950, after most of the inhabitants left for Australia, some for England.

Renia Nilon and her husband Bronek arrived in Mombassa with the other passengers from India, but instead of going to a camp, they joined a transport for Europe going to an international camp Villachen in Austria. As Bronek spoke several languages, he was employed in the office of I R O - the International Refugee Organisation as a translator for consular officials, who came to choose refugees for settlement in their own countries. Soon Renia and Bronek were chosen too and granted a New Zealand visa. They sailed on the Dundale Bay to Wellington in June 1949.

In Valivade in 1948, still left was a group of 150 people made up of the elderly, pregnant women and mothers with small babies. Mr. Nielsen, representative of I.R.O., tried to get their agreement for repatriation but without much success. Eventually Lebanon, one of the few countries, which still recognised the Polish Government in Exile, agreed to accept those people. They left the Camp at the end of April and reached Beirut on 20th May. Mrs. Chmielowiec described their arrival there:

"We were divided into groups and distributed throughout the neighbouring towns and villages. The biggest group of Poles already settled in Lebanon, lived in a mountain town of Ghazir. We were pleasantly surprised that we were to live in charming houses available for rent, surrounded by gardens with exotic fig, lemon, olive trees. Paradise! We received a monthly allowance to cover rent and food. It was not much, but sufficient to live on. Most people added to their funds by a small income from sewing, knitting, baking cakes for sale. In the Arab kitchens there were tiled alcoves for spirit stoves only, but it was possible to bake with the aid of special cake-tins.

We liked living in Lebanon, a country renown for providing a venue for relaxation for millionaires. We had a chance to witness great wealth as well as poverty, but the contrast was not as striking as it had been in India. There were two universities in Beirut: a French and an American one. Some Poles could be found among their students; either released from the army to enable them to finish their studies interrupted by the war, or those who recently matriculated in the Cadet schools. Leszek Słowikowski from Valivade gained a place at the American University, while his mother found a catering job at the Polish Red Cross in Beirut. Some Poles found permanent employment and the right to settle for good in the country. Several pretty girls married rich Arabs."

One lady, E. Huntington (Duszyńska) travelled to Lebanon independently, on a merchant ship, which carried only six passengers, because she wanted to stop in Palestine to visit her son in a Cadet School. When she eventually arrived in Lebanon, she was refused the allowance, because it looked as if she had independent means, which was not the case. Luckily she managed to find a secretarial job at the Brazilian Consulate, owing to her knowledge of English and French.

We know from Mrs. I. Chmielowiec's account that "After two years of life in Lebanon, the group from Valivade was granted the right to travel to the United Kingdom within the framework of the action of uniting families. Now married daughters, grown-up sons, cousins, aunts and grannies, could all join their families already living in the British Isles.

We sailed into a foggy port of Hull in August 1950 and were sent to a camp in the north of England. In front of the camp head office was spread a figure of a huge white eagle made up of sea shells and pebbles. Along the main road there were sign-posts stating the distance in kilometres from Wilno, Lvov-

It signified that the inhabitants of this camp came from Eastern Poland.

We were starting our life as political emigres."

NOTES

1. J. Wróbel: *Zeszyt Historyczny I*, 1996, pp. 115, 116.
2. PwI: year 5, no.21 (101), 1947, p.5.
3. Ibid: year 5, no.25 (105), 1947, p.3.
4. Ibid: year 5, no.29 (109), 1947, p.1.
5. Ibid: year 5, no.28/29 (108/109), 1947, pp.3, 4.
6. The Polish Institute and Sikorski Museum: C 811 c.
7. Ibid: year 5, nos.34/35 (114/115), p.7

PLACES OF SETTLEMENT AFTER LEAVING INDIA
collective work

In this chapter we are trying to establish what happened to the inhabitants of Valivade after leaving the Camp: their conditions of living, ability to find work, which suited them. What became of those, who left India as children, did they get a chance to continue their studies if they wished to do so?

We know that many individuals in that group achieved remarkable successes in their chosen professions, all contributed greatly to the communities in which they found themselves, overcoming considerable difficulties in adjusting to the new reality. What kind of community it was, depended on the choice their families made at the end of the war, which displaced them from their homes. Some, because of family ties, or patriotic obligations, decided to return to Poland in spite of the imposed communist regime and the fact that for many now their pre-war homes were within the Soviet Union. Others, a great majority, demonstrated their anti-Communist feelings and a desire to serve the cause of free Poland, by remaining in the West, where without the knowledge of the language, they had to start life afresh in difficult circumstances.

GREAT BRITAIN - *by Teresa Glazer (Kurowska)*

The Polish Government in Exile, with W. Raczkiewicz as President and General Sikorski as Premier, originally formed in Paris at the end of September 1939, moved to London in June 1940 after the fall of France. Their aim was preservation of legality (according to the April 1935 Polish Constitution) of the authority of the Polish State in the free world and continuation of the fight against the Germans. The Anglo-Polish Agreement of 5th August 1940 formed the basis of the formation and training of Polish Forces, which later took part in all the different theatres of war.

Even though at the end of the war official recognition of the members of London Government had been withdrawn on 5th July 1945, they were allowed to keep their offices and look after the Polish Forces transferred from Italy in 1947 to the British Isles, later joined by their families brought from India and Africa.

According to the statistics published in the book, *Polacy w W. Brytanii*, written by B. Czaykowski and B. Sulik, there were around 135,000 Poles in the British Isles after the Second World War.[1] Later, some of them emigrated to other countries.

During the first years after the war the Polish emigrants in Great Britain formed a nation in exile with their government, military leadership, the press, clergy, research institutions. In later years, after the death of President Raczkiewicz in 1947 a split of the leadership into two rival camps hindered action for Polish independence and alienated the younger generation from taking part in political life of the emigres. The split resulted from the fact that President Raczkiewicz nominated August Zaleski as his successor without consulting his Premier, nor any representatives of political parties, as he should have done according to the Paris Agreement of 30th November 1939 concerning the continuity of the authority of the Head of State. Some people accepted A. Zaleski as the new President, others saw him as an usurper.[2]

In spite of the split, the main aims of the emigres: rejection of the Communist dictatorship, looking after the insignia of authority of the free Polish State until such time that it would be possible to pass them on to the government freely and democratically elected, were common to all. These aims would be realized half a century later, when the last president of the Government-in-Exile, R. Kaczorowski, took back to Poland the symbols of the continuity of free Polish State and presented them on 22nd December 1990 to the first democratically elected President of Poland, Lech Wałęsa.

Transfer of the Presidential Insignia (courtesy of J. Englert)

The attitude of the British, who had previously shown their appreciation of the Polish Forces' contribution in all theatres of war, especially the fighter pilots in the RAF, who helped to win the Battle of Britain, has changed for the worse after the war ended. Of all the combatants, only the Poles, who fought under the British command, were excluded from the Victory Parade in June 1946, because of the controversy, which Poles were to be represented – those in London or Warsaw? The Allies did not wish to antagonize Stalin. Only the 303 squadron was invited, but it declined, as the invitation was nor extended to other Army and Navy units. Forgotten was the fact that by the end of the war, Poland was the fourth largest contributor to the Allied effort in Europe, after the Soviet Union, the USA and Great Britain with its Commonwealth.[3]

The left-wing press was openly hostile and Foreign Secretary, E. Bevin, urged the Poles to return to their own country. Yet we did not believe any promises of free elections and had no wish to accept communist rule. Permission to stay in this, alien to us, country, was considered as the lesser of two evils, because what we really wanted was to be able to return to free Poland – a wish impossible to fulfil because of the betrayal of Britain and the USA eager to appease Stalin.

Most people initially stayed in hostels, which had served as army camps or hospitals during the war, living in Nissen huts. It was a continuation of war-time communal life. Gradually in the 1950s some people moved to lodgings in towns, or bought family homes in very difficult circumstances, having to take in lodgers in order to pay their mortgages. Some tried individual farming, or joined agricultural co-ops. One such experiment, *The Lark Ltd.*, run by ex army officers, (our Scout Master B. Pancewicz among them), without any previous experience of working the land, was not very successful and collapsed after a few years.

Nissen huts - 'barrels of laughter'

Many, afraid to take on the responsibility for their own lives stayed on in the hostels much longer than the British authorities anticipated.

Creation of PKPR (Polish Retraining, Resettlement Corps) was supposed to help soldiers adjust to civilian life. However, because of the lack of English, or qualifications recognised in this country, only menial jobs like washing up dishes in restaurants or work in factories, were on offer. It was hard, especially for the officers, who had been used to issuing commands and being addressed as "Sir" to switch to answering to their anglicized version of their first name and being treated like halfwits. In order to retain their identity, they met in Polish clubs, filled the auditoria of Polish theatres, attended national anniversary celebrations. They organised themselves quite well: there was a Polish daily newspaper (the only daily published in a foreign language in this country), the Sikorski Institute collected valuable archive material. With very few exceptions, such as those, who were mentally or physically sick as a result of concentration camps, they were not a burden on social services.

Teenagers and young people worked very hard in order to obtain qualifications, which the generation of their parents lacked.

A Committee for the Education of Poles in Great Britain was established in April 1947 and it supervised primary, secondary education as well distribution of grants for further education till September 1954. Several secondary boarding schools were organised: Grammar schools for girls at Stowell Park nr. Cheltenham and Grendon Hall, Grammar school for boys in Bottisham nr. Cambridge, Technical School for boys at Lilford and a Secondary Modern for boys at Diddington. At first these schools followed a pre-war curriculum preparing them for a Polish matriculation. This, however, would not give them a chance of higher education in GB.[4]

An experimental course for 155 young soldiers and Cadets, aged 17-25, as well as 56 girls 17-22 years old from Women's Voluntary Services, was started at a co-ed Joseph Conrad Secondary school at Haydon Park in Dorset following the University of London matriculation curriculum, from February 1948 to December 1949. It achieved 70% success in the exams and this encouraged the other 3 grammar schools to follow its example: 117 pupils obtained "General School Certificate", 32 "Matriculation."[5]

In the years 1947-1960 some 9000 students, including those attending the Polish University College, obtained grants for higher education. They were not always free to choose the nature of their studies; most were directed towards technical subjects, economics or teaching.[6] I was one of them. Along with many girls from Valivade I went to the I. Paderewski grammar school in Stowell Park near Cheltenham, Gloucestershire. Fellow third year students there were Irka Kudła, Gienia Kunigiel, Irka Pawlak, and others. Initially, we used Polish textbooks, while learning English intensively. Our Polish teachers' English was no better than ours. We only had a few English language staff. We were entered, together with some of our teachers, for the "Cambridge Certificate", which consisted of 3 parts: translation, precis, and oral. At the first attempt, the headmistress, Mrs. Felińska, Mr. Bryl, our Latin master and I, passed 2 parts of the exam, but had to re-sit the precis part. We all succeeded at the second attempt!

In the 4th year we were split into two groups: science and humanities, and began to prepare for the General School Certificate in English. Because a new history teacher, Mr. H. Nowacki could speak English well and made the subject very interesting, I chose humanities. I belonged to the first group who took exams in English. Since all the examinations, except foreign languages, were written, a foreign accent did not matter and I managed to get good results. We took Polish as a foreign language. Mr. Pietrkiewicz from the School of Slavonic Languages usually asked us to recite a poem in Polish, or describe a picture, which seemed very easy to us. While waiting for the results, we prepared for the Polish matriculation exam in Polish literature and history. Subjects already passed for the School Certificate, such as mathematics or Latin, did not have to be taken again.

Teresa's family

My education in England was rather typical of that of many girls from Valivade. As there was a shortage of teachers, I was given a grant and went to Stockwell College, which was part of the University of London Institute of Education. After I graduated, I asked for my grant to be extended to enable me to study history at Southampton University, as I wanted to teach that subject. Even though I used to get good grades for my essays and could read and write English well, my foreign accent remained. During the first teaching practice, I must have looked and sounded a comic figure. I gesticulate a lot.

Living near London, I spent every weekend with Polish people, attending many Polish clubs, dances or cabarets. It was not until I shared digs with two English girls in Portsmouth, while studying history, that one of them, Anne Carmichael, explained England to me and introduced me to reading in English for pleasure.

Later I taught history at all levels for 33 years in various secondary schools, Sixth Form College, and became Head of History Department in a Catholic Comprehensive school, St. Theresa's in London. I married an ex-Polish army officer, Bolek, and our daughter, Ewa, is bilingual.

Kazia Skorupińska followed a similar route, except that she had difficulty getting a grant to Southampton Training College, as her father had died in the USSR and grants were usually only awarded to the families of soldiers, who had fought in the Polish Forces under British command. Eventually she did get a grant through the intervention of her friend's father.

She writes: "I was the only foreigner in my year. English fellow students were very helpful. Our College Principal spent half an hour every day giving me elocution lessons. I had a particular problem pronouncing "th" and had to practise it. I still retained my accent, but during my teaching practice, unexpectedly it turned out to be useful, as children listening to my unusual pronunciation, did not play up. However, in my first job, which was in a London East-End school, I encountered new difficulties: I could not understand the Cockney accent. After 10 years, I moved to a different school, nearer to where I lived and stayed there until my retirement. I chose to teach young children, as with them one can instantly see the results of one's work. Teaching gave me a lot of pleasure and I found it rewarding."

Kazia

Zosia Durant (Baranowska), who also matriculated in Stowell Park and was also sent to Teacher Training College, managed to have a more varied career. After teaching for only a few years in Sheffield, she travelled the world, teaching in Uganda and New Zealand. After returning to England in 1970, she became a probation officer. In 1991 she obtained her MA at East London Polytechnic, on the strength of her thesis about under-age offenders in the English and Polish systems, suggested to her during Anglo-Polish exchanges in 1988-9.

Danuta Croft (Ryżewska) after leaving Stowell Park, studied at Plymouth College of Art. She obtained a National Diploma in Art and Design (Oil Painting and Textile Design) She married a Polish army officer M. Skalski and had two daughters with him. Unfortunately he died and left her a widow at 34 years of age. She worked for 17 years as a display Artist in Plymouth Centre and taught Art in St. Boniface College for boys. In 1977 she married Arthur Croft CPO, who encouraged her pure art. She still paints and displays her work in the Art Frame Gallery, Tavistock. She is listed in "Who is who in Art", Hilmarton Manor Press.

Croft family

Her Oxford educated, historian grandson, Dr. Matt Kelly, a published author, is currently writing a book about the experiences of Poles deported to Russia during the 1939-45 war as told by one family.

Eugenia Maresch (Polnik) left India for England when she was eleven. Educated at Polish and English schools, studied physics and worked in Medical profession. Years later almost entirely devoted her time to social and cultural pursuits and turned into historical researcher and a publicist. For many years she administered the Polish Library in London and presently is an active member of the Council of several Polish Institutions, including the Archival Heritage based in Warsaw. A member of the Anglo-Polish Historical Committee established in 2000 with the full support of the Prime Ministers of both countries to report on close Intelligence co-operation between the British and the Poles during the Second World War. In 2005 awarded the order of Polonia Restituta.

Eugenia

Children of primary school age, like my brother, Andrew Kurowski, and Wanda Kuraś (Frąckiewicz), who were sent to English primary schools, learnt to speak English properly. Wanda later attended a private Catholic grammar school at Pitsford, run by the nuns of the order of Holy Family of Nazareth, where Sister Benedict (M. Leśniak) and Sister Jadwiga (W.Delikowska) from Valivade, worked for many years. Wanda herself became a teacher and taught mathematics in various secondary schools, until her retirement. Andrew also became a teacher with a reputation as a strict disciplinarian and became headmaster of St. Austin's R.C. school for boys in Charlton.

In families, where both parents were Polish, children grew up bilingual. Wherever larger groups of Poles settled, there would be a Polish parish and a Saturday school established to teach children their language, history, and culture. With mixed marriages, where a mother was English, children usually spoke only English. Very few Polish girls married Englishmen; most of them wed Polish ex-combatants. The husbands had to work during the day in order to support their families and study at evening classes to obtain qualifications recognised in this country.

Janka Pająk (Haniewicz), who settled in Cambridge, writes: "My husband found it hard to find work at first, as they said he was overqualified for manual jobs. Eventually he was employed in a chemical laboratory, where practice helped him gain technical qualifications." She herself worked in an accounts office, which prepared her for her role as an excellent treasurer of our Association.

Some of our Polish Red Cross nurses found work in military hospitals on arrival in England, but without a diploma of a 3-year nursing school, they could only be employed as auxiliaries in British hospitals. This is what M. Jarmułowicz did in a Nottingham hospital. Sister E. Maciejewska, who decided to do a nursing course, only had to do two years, as her Polish qualifications and years of practice were taken into account. Her knowledge of Russian as well as Polish led to her employment in a centre for refugees from Eastern Europe. Sister S. Sudoł was employed in a lab in a London hospital, as she could produce a certificate in both English and Polish of her qualifications gained in India.

A group of younger nurses, among them I. Adamczyk, E. Bień, H. Górska, Z. Karpińska, E. Woyniłłowicz, enrolled in nursing schools and obtained qualifications, Górska with distinction. After working for some years as nurses they gained the status of ward or theatre Sisters, which in an English establishment, was no mean achievement. I. Idkowiak was given a grant to study medicine, but after her marriage she abandoned her studies and became a draughtsman.

Janka and her brother

Private firms which did not discriminate against foreigners employed girls who, owing to courses attended in Bombay or Valivade, could type and knew some English. Thus D. Pasternak worked for Dunlop's as a shorthand typist. D. Nowicka worked for an insurance company in Guildford, where she reached a position of Assistant Manager, K. Cariuk found office work in Derby. The Secretary of our Association, W. Kleszko, worked for many years for Rank Organisation; this prepared her well for becoming the mainstay of our organisation. Ala Walczowska (Król) was accepted at Pittmans to do a secretarial course, and she had very good results.

Before joining a seminary in Orchard Lake, USA, our Scoutmaster in India Lieut. Z. Peszkowski, studied at Oxford and encouraged **Leszek Bełdowski** to continue his studies. Leszek settled with his mother in a small village of Comrie in Perthshire, Scotland, where his father had rented a cottage before his death. He started work in a garage and it was only due to the intervention of our Scoutmaster, that he enrolled at the N. Copernicus grammar school and matriculated. He later studied history at Leicester University, followed by library studies in London and worked for the next 30 years in the library of Leicester University as its Deputy Head. He was very active in various Polish academic institutions like the Historical Association, the Sikorski and Piłsudski Institutes, Polonia Aid Foundation and others.

Leszek

Danka Pniewska writes about herself: "Encouraged by my parents and our Scoutmaster, I tried to enrol at university, but it was rather difficult as English soldiers whose studies had been interrupted by the war had a priority. Then I discovered through my Scout contacts, that a Catholic university in Dublin recognised Polish matriculation so I went to Ireland in the Autumn of 1949. I studied Philosophy for three years and obtained my BA.

In the meantime my parents moved from the camp in Oulton Park in Cheshire to London, where father found work in a restaurant and my mother did some sewing. I could not find any work in which my degree would be of any use, so I worked in bookkeeping for 10 years. I then applied for a job with the Civil Service, but had to sit an entrance exam as neither my Polish matriculation, nor my Irish diploma counted for much. I was offered a job on the lowest rung and had to climb up slowly for the next 25 years until my retirement. I was awarded an MBE, which gave me a chance to shake Her Majesty's hand. I was always more interested in my social work than the professional one; I taught in the Polish Saturday school and took active part in the Guide movement. More recently, my involvement in the activities of our Indian Association, for which I edit a bulletin, (the main link between all Association members) twice a year, takes up a lot of my time".

Danka with Haneczka Slowikowska

Bogdan Czaykowski, before leaving for Canada, studied history in Dublin, then Polish literature at London University with professor J. Pietrkiewicz. He was an active member of the Association of Polish students in exile. In the 1950s he made his name as a poet, publishing in Merkuriusz Polski and Kultura - a Paris cultural magazine. In 1957 a collection of his poems, *Trzciny Czcionek* was published. He belonged to the experimental theatre Pro Arte and became a literary editor of *Kontynenty*, where a "dialogue about language" concerning the dilemma of a poet writing in a foreign country, was conducted. Bogdan felt that he did not belong to his homeland as it was then, nor to the society in which he had settled and described this condition as that of "fish landed on sands."[7]

Another poet, Jerzy Sito, returned to Poland despite the restrictions on artistic freedom.

Bogdan

Joanna Chmielowska's story illustrates the difficulties in obtaining a grant if you chose a subject that did not belong to one of those categories recommended by the Committee for the Education of Poles. Joanna writes: "I was one of the last students at Stowell Park Grammar school to sit the Polish matriculation examination in 1949. After that the school changed over to the English system. Even before I had a certificate in my hand, I started looking for a place in an art school, as I was always keen on drawing and hoped to have a career doing something which I liked. I was accepted by the Cambridgeshire Technical College and School of Art, where I met Stella Czekierska from Valivade, who was in her third year. Even though my family moved from Ludford Magna in Lincolnshire to Mepal, a camp closer to Cambridge, I had a 20 mile bus journey to and from college daily. I had no grant during the first year of my studies, but the Committee must have been moved by my determination, as I was awarded a grant for the next 3 years. My diploma in 1953 entitled me to illustrate books, but I never did that. My first and only job was with More O'Ferrall Outdoor Advertising, where I worked for the next 35 years.

Joanna

Aleksander Klecki studied at the Polish University College (PUC) in London, obtaining a degree in architecture (RAST). As an architect he has many important achievements: with Sir Frederick Gibbert, work on London Heathrow Airport, with Louis De Soisson, the Brighton Marina; first prize for the Housing Estate in Kent, City of London's "Office of the Year" award. He won many national and international competitions. He has also distinguished himself in sculpture and stained glass. His stained glass windows were exhibited at the Royal Academy of Art in London and published in *La Revue Modern* in Paris. Other noteworthy works are: Katyń Memorial in Bristol, the main altar mural with the figure of Christ the King in Newcastle and bronze murals in Watford. Among the Polish community he is best known for the work he did on the interior of St. Andrew Bobola's church with its stained glass windows dedicated to various units of the Polish Forces in the Second World War, and its sculptures. The latter was widely publicised in the architectural and national press as well as being captured on film by Rank organisation series *"Look at Life"*.

Boys from Valivade, who attended St. Mary's High School in Bombay, and sat the Cambridge matriculation examination in English, had no difficulty entering higher education establishments. The following three belong to this group.

Stained glass window in memory of Gen. W. Anders at St. Andrew Bobola Church - London

Jan Siedlecki writes: "Soon after arrival here in 1948, I managed to obtain a grant and a place at Leicester College of Art to study architecture. The next five years were full of hope acquiring a profession, which would give me a chance to participate in the rebuilding of the post–war world, even if not my own country. I graduated in 1953 and my first job was in the bombed-out city of Coventry. It was time for building a career and starting a family. I married Barbara, a graphic designer, whom I met in College and we moved to London. In 1961 at last we bought our own, modern house and the next year our twins were born. After obtaining a British passport, I went to visit Poland for the first time. Shortly afterwards. I joined an Anglo-Polish firm Inskip & Wilczynski where I became a partner and worked for the next 20 years.

For relaxation I began diving with London no. 1 Branch, which enabled me to film underwater wonders and gave me unforgettable experiences. Then I started a BS–AC (British Sub-Aqua Club) Wreck Register and in 5 years we compiled a collection of 250 wrecks around these shores. But nothing gave me more pleasure than an article by a Belgian journalist, in which he said that it needed a foreigner to initiate such a project.

Jan on a diving site

After retirement, I devoted my time to our Association, organising trips to India, building the monument in Kolhapur, and recently the publication of this book in Polish and now its English translation.

Jerzy Kowalski in his own words: "I arrived in England in 1948. Four years later I received a National Diploma from Blackburn Technical College, where I studied textile technology. My first job was in Manchester, where I married a girl I knew in India, Zuzia Marcinkiewicz. In 1953 our son Andrew was born and I obtained a permanent job in Loughborough. After 11 years of steady progress I reached the position of an instructor programming the modern textile machinery. I was later moved to the Export section, initially for Eastern Europe, later the whole world. For the next quarter of a century a suitcase, an aeroplane and hotels were my mode of life. I got to know and I befriended people from such different countries as Switzerland and China, Nigeria, the Arab states. In the last 10 years before my retirement in 1994 I was employed in a managerial capacity modernising the knitting machinery industry, also specialising in the planning and execution of complex international turnkey projects."

Jerzy (2nd left) on air in 1970's recalls India's hospitality 1943-1948

In 1994 Jerzy visited a hospital in Minsk, where he saw victims of the Chernobyl disaster. He is a member of a committee which brings groups of children over to England for recuperative holidays and organises help for those who suffered most in the disaster.

Albin Tybulewicz is one of the few Poles listed in Who's Who. A physicist, he has edited and translated (from Russian into English) scientific periodicals and books. In 1990 he was awarded the Natthorst prize for scientific translation by the International Federation of Translators. He is a co-founder of the Institute of Translation and Interpreting, the first British professional organisation in this field.

From 1980-84 he and his wife, Tuliola, headed the charity Food for Poland. During this period the charity sent a total of 175, lorry loads of food (valued at £4 million) to their homeland. This food aid was financed by the Polish-American Congress in the USA, the European Commission in Brussels, the British public and the Polish community in Great Britain.

Another charitable organisation with which some of our "Indians" have been actively involved, is the Medical Aid for Poland Fund (founded in 1981), which helped the people of Poland during their difficult time under martial law. Between 1981 and 1996, the charity dispatched a total of 334 lorries carrying medical equipment and medicines worth several million pounds. The charity continues to aid the acutely needy clinics to this day. This aid is financed by Poles resident in Great Britain and their British friends.

Albin with his "Natthorst" prize

Stach Ucinek, after leaving the Polish Boys' School at Riddlesworth, worked for a time in a factory, but soon decided to become self-employed. He changed his business every 10 years: first he drove around the Polish camps selling Polish food, then he opened a Delicatessen, in the next decade, a factory producing handbags, suitcases . In the meantime he met Jadzia through a national Folk Dance group, married and had two children a daughter and a son. The last 15 years he spent organising transports of parcels to Poland in the North of England, Dar-Trans.

Stach

Jan Chrząszczewski (JohnYoung): "On our arrival in England we were greeted by the most severe winter the country had experienced in years - the winter of 1947/8. After the heat of the Indian climate and without the appropriate winter clothing, we suffered the cold acutely. Living in a camp near Cirencester in Nissen huts, (made of corrugated iron), with one coal burning stove per hut, we shivered non-stop. This is my first memory of this country.

After several unsuccessful attempts to join the RAF, I decided to continue my education in a Polish school in Riddlesworth (Norfolk), where most of the students were either ex-servicemen or cadets. This school was later transferred to Beccles (Suffolk) and eventually to Bottisham

Jan

near Cambridge. After passing both Polish and English matriculation, I was awarded a grant to study chemistry at Woolwich Polytechnic. I obtained work in the North of England in a rubber factory, where for the next twelve years or so I must have occupied most of the executive positions, finishing as Managing Director.

In 1973, together with a colleague, we opened a factory producing plastic foam. It ran for four years, employing 100 people, and its annual turnover was £10 million. Later we started another firm, a consultancy, which advised various suppliers, particularly to the Automotive industry, about producing the required goods, sales and how to increase turnover and profit in the light of cut-throat competition.

I am now practically retired, which enables me to devote more time arranging text and photographs on a computer for the publication of our book.

After years of spelling my Polish name over the phone, (which could take up to 10 minutes) I was still receiving letters with my name mis-spelt. In an attempt at making life easier, I started using my Christian name Jan (pronounced Yan). Correspondence then started arriving addressed to Young. In the end I gave up and became "John Young".

Even though **Bronek Siedlecki** passed both the English and Polish matriculation in Bottisham. After leaving school he worked in a factory for a year, studying landscape at evening classes. After a year, he obtained a grant and a place at Reading University, where he graduated as a Lanscape Architect. In 1956 was elected Associate of the Institute of Lanscape Architects and in 1972, Fellow of this Institute. He worked for the London County Council Parks Department, creating green spaces in the bombed-out areas of East London.

In 1956 he took British nationality. Up until that point he, like the rest of us "Indians", had a so-called "travel – document", which enabled him to travel to any country other than Poland. British passport allowed him to visit Poland. In order to visit your own homeland, you had to change your nationality.

A three year spell at the Corby New Town, where he married his French wife Marie-Therese, was followed by work the North Riding County Council as a Senior Planning Assistant looking after the Yorkshire Dales and North Yorkshire Moors National Parks.

Bronek

He took "time out" in Zambia, with his wife and daughter Veronique, living in Lusaka and working on numerous government projects all over this fascinating, exotic country.

Upon his return to the UK he joined the Ministry of Public Works Department, which enabled him to visit the FO and Ministry of Defence sites in Cyprus, Zaire and Cameroons. But the principal client were the Land Forces in the UK with their barracks, firing ranges in many territories: from the Isle of Wight to the Outer Hebrides.

After 18 years with the Ministry, he took early retirement to the South of France, where he bought a ruined sheepfold situated among the vines, pine woods, and now spends his time making it habitable and cosy.

Janusz Kossowski also matriculated in Bottisham and later studied mechanical engineering at Woolwich Polytechnic. He joined Fords as a graduate trainee, which led to permanent employment.

Alek Błach, another Bottisham pupil, could not get a grant for further education, so he started work in a garage, and later in a rubber factory. His love of sport helped to improve his situation: he used to represent the school in the volleyball and basketball teams, and could play table-tennis and badminton. Over badminton games he got to know senior factory personnel who managed to get him a job in the laboratory as a junior assistant and he enrolled on a three year day-release course at National College of Rubber Technology in North London. He obtained a diploma and in time was promoted to the position of Chief Chemist of the factory, followed by the appointment to Senior Rubber Technologist of the 7 factories in the group.

Alek

Outside of work, he joined the Polish Academic Sports Club, which at that time had the top volleyball team in England. He subsequently passed the Volleyball Referees' test (Grade 1). In 1991 was awarded the Golden Badge for promoting Polish sports activities in Great Britain.

After his marriage to an Irishwoman and starting a family, he lost touch with the Polish community for the next 35 years, until 1993, when a heart attack placed him in hospital. This period of forced inactivity gave him an opportunity to reflect. He discovered a desire to return to his roots: Polish friends, religion, culture. He moved back to London, to St. Anthony's Court in Balham, where he is an "unofficial gardener." He also participates in the activities of our Committee of "Poles in India."

Karol Huppert found work in a Polish factory producing leather goods and shoes in Millom, Cumberland. After the company closed down, he found similar work in London. Courses at evening classes helped him to gain the position of Technical Designer - product engineer.

A number of boys, among them **Gienek Wrzyszcz**, **Tadeusz Wawrzynowicz**, who enlisted to join the naval college in England, left Valivade in January 1945. They spent some time in Bombay with some British sailors and airmen, who taught them to talk like "real men", and where they were given their uniforms. Their journey to Britain by sea involved them navigating the Mediterranean Sea in total darkness to avoid enemy submarines.

Karol

The Polish Merchant Navy College in Landywood, near Walsall in England was created by the Ministry of Navigation and Seafaring of the Polish Government–in-Exile in 1945 under the leadership of Capt. Borhart. The 400 students came from Valivade, Isfahan, Kenya, Uganda, Palestine, Egypt, German hard-labour camps, as well as from Maquis in France. Subjects taught, besides general knowledge, were: navigation and seafaring technology. Gienek Wrzyszcz graduated as a Second Officer, but his first job was as an ordinary seaman for £7 a month. Later he was promoted to coxswain and spent a total of 25 years sailing the seas. The school was later moved to Lilford and in 1949 transformed into a technical college.

Cadets (in the middle): A. Ostrowski, (below right) T. Wawrzynowicz

Tadeusz Wawrzynowicz never became a sailor. After leaving school, he obtained some City & Guilds qualifications and worked as a draughtsman for a petrol company on North Sea oil rigs, then in Norway. So was the education in the Naval College of any use to him? He thinks, yes. It taught him good discipline, social skills; how to play bridge, (which turned out to be very useful during his stay abroad) and started life-long friendships.

Wacław Wróblewski also attended the technical college at Lilford, where he played violin in the school orchestra. He later formed his own band, in which he himself played the saxophone, and they toured all the clubs in north west England. In 1967 he started a company making machinery, and during his sales trips to industrial centres, often had to explain the circumstances that had led to his living in this country. In the end he decided to buy all the copies of a publication by J. Żaba *For your Freedom and Ours*, because it explained the matter well and used it instead of having to give a talk on the subject.

Gienek

Bogusław Wróblewski, Wacław's brother, is a well-known Orthopaedic surgeon in Wrightington, near Wigan. On one of his lecture tours round the world, he found himself in Bombay, where he was asked if there was anywhere he wished to visit, before the end of his trip. He named Kolhapur and Valivade. Having explained the reasons for selecting these places, his wish was granted.

Ryszard Grzybowski, born to a family of military settlers in Poland's Eastern Marches, is now chairman of an organisation formed by their descendants in 1983 in England, to publicise the achievements, and tragedies of their parents. Since his arrival in this country in 1947, he followed a successful career as technical design director in the textile industry.

Ryszard

Elwira Stechley (Piotrowicz) after leaving school in Stowell Park, studied music. In 1949 she organised a dance group which demonstrated Polish Folk dances for Polish and English audiences. She joined the Operatic Society and Varsovia choir, where she sang solo parts. Her husband was the leader of Vistula orchestra. Their son, Janusz, became the first Pole to win an Honorary Music Scholarship for Eton. After a distinguished career as a concert pianist, he now conducts orchestras all round the world.

Between the years 1976 and 1988 Elvira had a shop selling antique jewellery, silver and porcelain in Ascot. In the meantime, she gained a diploma in Beauty Therapy, but practised only on selected clients.

Irena Świrska (Kudła) is another person who, besides her professional training and work as Staff Nurse, studied music, joined a choir and a dance group which performed for both Polish and English audiences in the Midlands.

Irena as 'pani Dulska'

Marriage and children interrupted her artistic career. She was widowed after nine years and had to bring up five children on her own. She made sure that they all had a good education. Her daughter Halina distinguished herself by winning Saga fur design awards, which secured her a job as a designer with the well-known London furrier Philip Hockney. After the children grew up, Irena had more time for social work among the Polish community in Birmingham. She joined an amateur theatre group which toured the Midlands giving performances much praised in the press. Her most successful part was that of Mrs. Dulska in a much loved comedy *"Moralność pani Dulskiej"*.

Halina Bąbik (Rafał), famous in Valivade for her witty writing, settled in Leicester, where she took part in many performances of the Polish amateur theatre; she is best known for her role as *"Ciotka Albinowa"*.

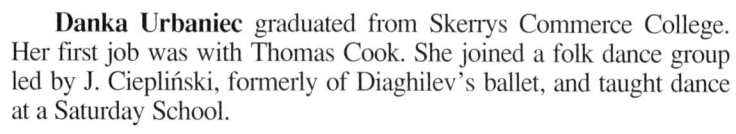

Danka Urbaniec graduated from Skerrys Commerce College. Her first job was with Thomas Cook. She joined a folk dance group led by J. Ciepliński, formerly of Diaghilev's ballet, and taught dance at a Saturday School.

After meeting Sue Rider, who was helping the casualties of war, particularly Poles, Danka left her job and went to Germany, where she worked without a salary. Her job involved visiting the sick, lonely, homeless former prisoners of concentration and labour camps, who still lived in refugee camps, years after the end of the war, unable to work and lead independent lives because of their traumatic war experiences. She commuted between England and Germany. She later helped out in the Cavendish House convalescent home and worked with Joyce Pearce in Ockenden Venture, bringing in children from Germany to be educated in boarding schools. Sue Ryder in her book *And the Morrow is Theirs*, praises Danka for her organisational skills and for her assistance in setting up the first Sue Ryder charity shops, later familiar on our high streets.

Halina

Danka

Many of our friends from Valivade, besides looking after their families and working, devoted time to social activities and continue to do so in their retirement. All over England, wherever a large group of Poles settled, Saturday schools were established so that Polish children could learn their language, literature, history and become involved in cultural activities, such as country dancing, choral singing and the Scouting movement. I have only been able to include detailed information about "Indians" who responded to the editorial committee's request for biographies when we started collecting materials for our book, but I personally know that Idalka Mahorowska (Rozwadowska), Lala Tutak (Masiulanis), Halina Naks (Karakułko), Marysia Sieradzan (Kokoszko), Danka Raczyńska in London and Marysia Wylot (Woźniak) in High Wycombe, have taught for many years in the Polish Saturday schools. Marysia W. also trains Guiders in Buckinghamshire as she had vowed in Valivade, that she would remain a Guide all her life and she is keeping her promise.

Iza Wolf (Nieczykowska), Karol Huppert and Ala Walczowska (Król) have done voluntary work at the Sikorski Institute for many years, Joanna Chmielowska at the POSK library and others help in many charitable and social organisations throughout the British Isles.

Janka Małkowska (Zbróg) often acted as a translator in court in Manchester, whenever a case involved Polish people.

Looking back over the last fifty years of our life in Great Britain, the following observations come to mind. Even though my generation (now 60 to 80 years of age) and our children are well assimilated into the communities in which we live, most of us have British nationality, we are nevertheless, very much aware of our Polish roots. Even the generation of our children, born here, when asked whether they feel to be British or Polish, after consideration, usually admit to the latter. The best test comes during international football matches or the Olympic Games; they invariably support the Polish teams. In the post-communist era, we can now visit our homeland, but we often feel ill at ease with the young generation of our countrymen brought up under the communist regime imposed on them by force. They have a new vocabulary, a different sense of values. Unrealistically, most of us pine for the Poland of our childhood and find it hard to adjust to reality, like *Fish Stranded on the Sands*, as B. Czaykowski put it.

NOTES:

1) B. Czaykowski and B. Sulik *Polacy w Wielkiej Brytanii*, 1961, p15 (lines 2,3,4, p.627, no 2)

2) *Materiały do Dziejów Uchodźctwa Niepodległościowego*, 1866,vol.3, p.39

3) *For Your Freedom and Ours*, by A.Olsen & S.Cloud, p.6

4) Kol. 417, The Sikorski Institute

5) H.Staszewski, *Na pamiątkę - Szkoła im. J. Konrada*, 1973, p5-6

6) B. Czaykowski and B. Sulik, 'Polacy w W. Brytanii', 1961, p. 523

7) Interview in 'Kultura', No. 7, 1966, p. 85

POLAND
by Jagoda Lempke (Kobordo)

Building a New Home.

Looking back at events that happened years ago and now in possession of certain historical knowledge, I realize, that having returned to Poland we did not quite understand the full situation. It was a broad area of human experience, sometimes beautiful, sometime shameful, yet it was a part of our shared national history.

To get acquainted with the experiences of those who returned to Poland, questionnaires were sent to 100 individuals – 57 responded. It has to be understood that the questionnaires were sent to a group of people depleted in numbers since our return. Many of our friends have now passed away and it is difficult to know if their experiences were similar to those who answered the questionnaires.

The decision to return to Poland was motivated, according to the majority of respondents (36), by the desire to unite with their families. Uncertain future prospects if remaining outside Poland persuaded 14 people and nostalgia influenced the decision of 7 others. The majority of respondents (49) returned from India and 8 from England and Africa. Their return route led through Bombay, Mombasa, Naples, Rome, sometimes Venice, Genoa, Austria, Prague, Dziedzice or Koźle-Kędzierzyn. Unreliable statistics make it impossible to establish accurate dates of their return. From the questionnaires it appears that most returned from Valivade either in May 1947 or February 1948. One of the last to return was Ala Janiszewska who arrived from England on the 21st May 1949.

It transpires that 50 returnees did not regret going back to their homeland, 5 did regret, and 2 had no say in the matter as decisions were made by their parents or guardians. The majority of us settled down in the Repossessed Territories in Wrocław, Szczecin, Warmia and Masuria and a few in Łódź, Cracow and Warsaw.

Return to Poland appeared to us generally as a very difficult undertaking. The first contact with Poland was the sight of a devastated and ruined country, in need of rebuilding. Warsaw lay in ruins. (American aid for post-war Europe according to Marshall Plan in the years 1948-52 was not allowed in the countries of Eastern and Central Europe because of the pressure from the USSR.) The Repossessed Territories were being resettled, but there was a lack of workers, particularly educated people, as the Polish middle class had been decimated. The first contacts with the locals showed their openness and readiness to help, but also sometimes mistrust, even unfriendliness towards strangers, nervousness and tension. It was so different from the experience of friendliness and warmth in Valivade.

At that time a "new social and political order" was being established in Poland. It became necessary to accept one's lot and the hard reality - to seek a means of livelihood, attain knowledge, complete studies, find love, establish families and to live with the awareness, that after a day of hard work we can fall asleep with the conviction of having performed useful and honest work.

One of the questions asked in the survey was if the repatriated encountered any repression. Responses to the question differed. A total of 22 replied in the negative, while expressing surprise that such a question was asked at all. The 29 people who answered positively understood repression as the deliberate difficulties created for them at schools and in admittance to higher education, in obtaining jobs, or being assigned punishing jobs and finally being harassed by the Security Service. Włodek Kosciów states, that he was arrested and spent three months in prison for refusing to work for the Security Services and to spy on people returning from the West. The majority of the respondents reported less drastic experiences. Anyone applying for a job or admittance to studies had to answer a questionnaire containing personal details including questions relating to relatives and war experiences.

Typical is the experience described by Halina Strycharz: "I remember an amusing experience when preparing my Curriculum Vitae, which I had to amend a number of times. Initially I wrote that I was deported to Siberia. The document was returned, with advice that I alter that sentence. I changed it to say that I was transported to the Soviet Union. That was not good enough either. Finally I wrote, that as a result of war action, I found myself in the territory of the Soviet Union. The experiences of others were probably similar. There are amongst us people whose "inappropriate" life stories hindered them in obtaining a job or gaining admittance to studies.

We all met with the ubiquitous ideological indoctrination. We returned to Poland with a certain understanding of the political situation, knowledge of history learned at school and our own war experiences. Our well-defined understanding of good and evil was now being confronted at school and work with an unceasing flow of completely different ideas. We were told that others were heroes, not the persons we perceived as such, that historical truth was quite different to what we believed it to be, that white was black and black was white. Under the pressure of those differing views it was necessary to find your own position and to hold your own opinions. Circles of new friends, new relationships, teachers and professors helped in dealing with this problem.

Many met with persuasion and pressure to join organisations they had no wish to join. Lech Trzaska describes one such situation. "I was enrolled into the ZMP (Association of Polish Youth) in circumstances characteristic of the 'voluntary' nature of the procedure. All school exits were locked, except the one where ZMP activist sat at a table. Only those who enrolled could leave. Others stayed until they joined as well. The last batch of students left in the evening, all of them as new members of ZMP". Our everyday decisions were in some way involved with politics more often than was the case with of our friends in the West. The decision not to join an organisation, not to take part in voting, not to participate in parades, marches or celebrations, was regarded as declaration of reactionary and hostile views. These days we view our early experiences without emotion, from the perspective of many years of life in Poland, sharing with others everyday problems, struggles and experiences, moments both painful and happy. Our experiences in Poland were diverse. In comparison with our friends abroad, more of us had opportunity to complete our studies. Admission to studies was relatively easy (except for a few returning from India who met difficulties because of "politically unacceptable" information in their personal questionnaire), study was free, and students did not have to overcome language barriers. From amongst the respondents to the questionnaire, 28 achieved higher education. They were to become teachers, lawyers, biologists, journalists, engineers, scientists, doctors, inventors and other professionals. **Zbyszek Bartosz** because of his specialist knowledge of topography was allowed to finish the Military Academy (Akademia Sztabu Generalnego), do post graduate studies on Military Geography and attain the rank of the colonel and a managerial position in the Army, even though his father had been in Gen. Anders' Army in the West, which at that time had been a deterrent to promotion. This however, is not a full list of personal achievements.

When one thinks about all our friends who returned to Poland, there are amongst them individuals who did not attain any significant professional achievements. They are the people who founded families and gathered around them a circle of friends for whom they became the support, the help and the guide in life.

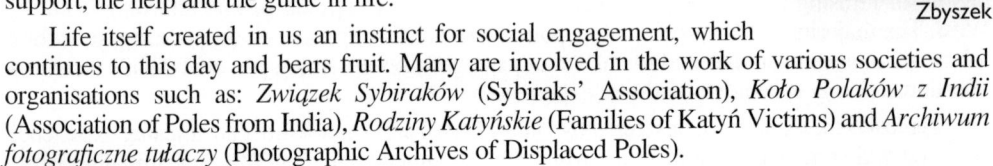

Zbyszek

Life itself created in us an instinct for social engagement, which continues to this day and bears fruit. Many are involved in the work of various societies and organisations such as: *Związek Sybiraków* (Sybiraks' Association), *Koło Polaków z Indii* (Association of Poles from India), *Rodziny Katyńskie* (Families of Katyń Victims) and *Archiwum fotograficzne tułaczy* (Photographic Archives of Displaced Poles).

From the analysis of the questionnaire, it transpires, that in our group people pursue many different hobbies such as: touring, collection of Indian memorabilia, sport, literature, history, wood carving, philately, yachting, woodwork, English language and literature, Scouting, collecting, antique collecting, sinology, music, theatre, motor cars, interior decoration and garden design, gardening, ornithology, herb science, fishing, mushrooming, dancing, bridge, photography, travelling, model plane building, geography and needlework. Of course, workaholics have no time for anything!

B. Rozkuszko, J. Lempke and J. Szczawiński

Achievements

A number of our friends can claim literary attainment. The late Jerzy Krzysztoń, who died in 1982, entered Polish literature as prose writer, playwright and publicist.

A poet Jerzy S. Sito, published a number of books of his collected poems, under titles: *Wiozę swój czas na ośle*, *Zdjęcia z koła*, *Ucieczka do Egiptu* (Escape to Egypt). He has also translated English poets. Other respondents to the questioner list their published works:

Teresa Achmatowicz published literary sketches in *Czytelnik*.

Zbigniew Bartosz accounts for many works in the field of geodesy and topography.

Andrzej Chendyński co-authored treatise on Polish chemical industry, as well as being an author of expert economic documentation.

Anna Ostrihanska-Kajak, an ecologist, still publishes works relating to environment protection.

Felicja Szpak-Ławniczek has prepared expert textbooks for English language study in the field of physical education and recreation.

Zofia Ostrihanska wrote extensively about juvenile delinquency.

Jan Pacholski is a well-known inventor of textile machinery, holder of 45 Polish and foreign patents. He has an entry in *Encyklopedia odkryć i wynalazków* (Encyclopedia of discoveries and inventions) - published by Wiedza Powszechna) and *Kto jest kim w Polsce* (Who is who in Poland).

Wiesław Stypuła has published on the subjects of water technology and flood prevention, as well as two books about his stay in India: *W Gościnie u Maharzdży (Maharaja's Guests)* and *we Wszystkie Strony Świata (Dispersed Throughout the World)*.

Helena Szafrańska published 22 papers on the theory and practice of pedagogics. Amongst her works was a 1984 publication by PWN of *Wpływ wychowawcy klasy na postawy ideowe dorastającej młodzieży* (Teachers influence on ideological attitudes of adolescents). She also wrote for *Wychowanie Obywatelskie i Harcerstwo* (Civic Upbringing and Scouting) and contributed to collective works published by the Higher School of Pedagogics and Teachers Training Institute in Szczecin.

Janka Szafrańska, Helena's sister, obtained a diploma in plastic arts application in the textile industry. She has designed dress fabrics and arranged factory stands at the Poznań Trade Fair. She also painted.

The above details do not constitute, as mentioned before, the full record of achievements of those who returned from India. I think that each one of us, through work, application of knowledge and personal ability, served an honest cause and contributed towards the growth of a common good of the country.

Sursum Corda

Studying the completed questionnaires I experienced a growing feeling of pride at the amount of dignity and patriotism they displayed. Those were heroic times, demanding heroism, and we were equal to these demands, everyone in his, or her, own way. Living in those interesting times we witnessed history in the making and paid a high price for it.

On our return to Poland, our greatest problem was lack of housing. A prolonged wait for a home, sometimes lasting years, while living in cramped lodgings, was ruining our nerves. We were greatly affected by shortages of provisions, queues and great difficulty in buying anything. There were ration cards for food, footwear and petrol and passport restrictions applied. There were many negatives but we can not discount some positives.

There was no visible unemployment and a well-developed system of social care took Poles from infancy, through kindergartens and schools up to the tertiary education. Access to medical care was assured, with free or heavily discounted medicine. The system of railway fare discounts was well established, while access to holiday resorts was cheap and easy.

W. Stypuła, S. Rumińska, H. Szafrńska, Cz. Krygiel, Z. Bartosz, F. Herzog and O. Szwacińska

In discussing our difficult living conditions,

we have to mention the role played by our friends from abroad in helping us to deal with them. Many of us received parcels from them, which were of real assistance as well as an expression of lasting friendship. A bond was maintained between friends from India who lived in close proximity to each other in Poland. This was accompanied by a willingness to help each other, as exemplified by medical assistance given by Bronka Rozkuszko in resolving particularly severe health problems.

The sum total of our experiences are contained in the evaluations and opinions expressed in the returned questionnaires. I do not wish to quote all the replies, though they all deserve a mention, but considering that the expressed thoughts and feelings are often repeated, I will only choose a representative few.

"It was a difficult period viewed from the point of material wellbeing; during my studies I often suffered from hunger, I had to take difficult decisions and make difficult choices. I do not regret making them and there was nothing to be ashamed of."

"My place was in Poland, the country for which my father fought in the Polish army during the First World War."

"At times I used to have moments of doubt, when I thought that returning to Poland had not been such a good decision. But those were moments of weakness. Basically, I do not regret my decision. I have completed my studies and I like my professional work."

"My place is in Poland – as there is only one Poland on the map of the world."

"I consider that Poland ought to be the main centre of my activity. After my return, I was met with ungrudging kindness and help. Thanks to professors, who were not interested in my political inclinations (I did not belong to any organisations), I was able to study and to develop my interests. I did not personally experience, or hear from others about any oppression encountered by those who returned from India."

"In Valivade I was an altar boy and a Scout. My desire was to join a Missionary College in Madras but my father did not agree. I lost seven siblings in Siberia and my father was against my remaining in India."

"I returned, because I was a patriot and loved my country, even if it was not completely independent."

"We went back to join our mother, whom we longed to see. In Tehran we buried our four year old sister, a fact we kept secret from our mother, as only three of us reached India."

"I regret my decision to return. Earning low wages, I battled against a continuous need, living on the verge of poverty. Nevertheless I laboured in my own country. Here I was needed."

"My education was 'extended'. I passed my university entry exam, but was not accepted due to the 'lack of university places'. I appealed to President Bierut. The University Rector passed my case on to the military authorities and I was called up to the labour battalions to work in mines in Śląsk."

"I do not regret returning. We did not desire to go to Africa, but chose to go back to Poland. I live amongst Poles and am glad of having played a small part in rebuilding the extensively war damaged city of Wrocław. I brought up my children to be good and honest people."

"Notwithstanding a difficult start in life and low standard of living, I believe that a Pole's place is in his native country."

"It is not possible to express opinion on the correctness of our choice. No one could predict the fate of our family if we stayed outside Poland. In Poland we had relations who gave us spiritual support."

"We had visas to enter the USA or Great Britain, yet we chose to return to Poland.

We suffered living conditions, that often bordered on poverty. But these shortcomings were recompensed by the love of the family, human kindness and clear consciences."

"From Valivade I wrote to my father: 'My Beloved Daddy, we know that we shall face hardships, but we would rather just eat potatoes with you, than bananas and oranges out here'."

"I am grateful to my friend from India, who stayed in the West and, throughout the many years of crisis, helped me by sending parcels."

"I do not regret my return to Poland. I met a wonderful woman who is now my wife. I could have left Poland at any time, as I was a sailor and my ship called at many ports."

"We wanted to return to father, who had served with the Polish Underground. Now I am free of nostalgia; I am amongst my own, living a quiet autumn of my life."

Opinions and evaluations display many shades. From the analysis of the questionnaire, it transpires, that in our group people pursue many different hobbies. They are characterised by deep reflection, thoughtfulness, pride, dignity and the conviction that we have carried out a great deal of useful work.

Perhaps it can be illustrated in a verse written by Karol Wojtyła:

It is necessary that each one carry as much as possible -

And that each one carries it as far as possible –

After that – it is God's business not man's.

Edited by Zofia Ostrihanska and translated by B & M Trella

NOTES.

My work is based mainly on the questionnaires, but I was also helped by materials in following publications: *Lapidarium II* by Ryszard Kapuściński and *Rozproszeni po świecie* (Scattered throughout the world) by E. & J. Wróbel.

INDIVIDUAL REMINISCENCES

Difficult Beginnings *by Anna Kajak (Ostrihanska)*

Our decision to return to Poland was taken without too much hesitation. We had no one in the Polish army in the West, our relatives were in Poland and we considered that our place was there too. It was winter 1947/48. Sailing from Bombay, we sang carols aboard our ship *Georgic*. Our first contact with Poland took place in Italy, in Rome, where waiting for us was a Polish Red Cross train. Clean, neat and comfortable, it made a good impression on us. Our life in Poland began in a transit camp in Koźle where we underwent quarantine.

Our closest relatives lived in the Śląsk town of Bielsko where my grandparents resided before the war and where I spent my early childhood. Our first unpleasant impression occurred when we had to change trains at the Katowice railway station. While handling the heavy trunks containing all our possessions, we were rudely abused by a young man who did not like us blocking the entrance but did not even think of helping women struggling with the heavy loads.

Arrival at Bielsko, a cordial welcome from relatives and then the start of a prosaic life. The housing situation turns out to be disastrous. People wait for years for the housing bureau to allot them living quarters. My married uncle lives in an allotted room, part of a beautiful house, but to reach the kitchen or bathroom they have to cross two rooms occupied by the main tenants. They find this situation embarrassing, despite the fact that the other tenants are highly cultured people. The uncle's wife occupies a room in a house divided between three families. The main tenant, unhappy with the situation, tries to make life unpleasant for the others. When she goes out she takes the bath plug with her so that others cannot use the bath. My aunt has a strong, but fitting, nickname for her. We lodge with our cousin who has an apartment in his suburban house. We are not comfortable with this situation as we see ourselves as intruders.

We don't know which way to turn. Taking the advice of her relatives, mother decides to look for work in Warsaw where we lived before the war and also have some relatives. With the widespread shortage of workers it is not difficult to find employment. However the housing situation is worse than elsewhere. Many people are heading for Warsaw while the city is in ruins. Mother finds accommodation with her cousin. The house, which belongs to the Ministry of Finance, is occupied by two families but relations between them are friendly and pleasant. There exists the atmosphere of a pre-war home. Mother sleeps on a folding bed in the kitchen. My sister and I are stay with an aunt who manages a millinery. We have to leave the house early before the modistes start their work and come back after they finish.

We are seeking the allocation of our own apartment but it is a very difficult task. My greatest desire is to have our own place. With hope and envy I look at new houses being built. Finally, after a year of trying and with some backing, we get a room in a three-room apartment. It is located in Brzeska Street, in the suburb of Praga near the well-known Różycki bazaar. The size of the longed for room is 12 sq. m. It contains an iron stove, which serves both as a heater and a cooking range. The state of shared facilities is absolutely disgusting. A bathroom with an old, chipped bathtub and a gas heater that does not work; the toilet is not much better; the kitchen only used for fetching water. Other residents are an elderly man, who owns the

Ostrihanska family

place, his mistress, who has a stall in the nearby bazaar and his wife with two daughters. Shared facilities cause arguments and disagreements, no one wants to clean them. Such a situation is characteristic of most of the shared houses. In such conditions we live for seven years until my marriage, when, thanks to the generosity and courage of our boss, my husband and I get a room at our workplace. It is not strictly legal; the reason given is that we have to look after some experiments, but everyone knows it is not true. The building's administrators frown on our staying there. We have to virtually hide our presence and sneak through the passages in the evenings. After another year we get our first real home, but again not quite legally. Our colleague, who plans to leave for Israel, registers us as living in his apartment. Ostensibly he leaves to visit his aunt. Under pretence of going only on a short trip, he doesn't cancel his registration as occupier of the apartment. The apartment belongs to our employer, The Polish Academy of Science. Since we have no formal allocation for the apartment, the thought of being evicted is our constant fear for many years.

During the first years after the war there were no difficulties with provision of food. In Poland we had adequate supplies during a period when most European countries were experiencing malnutrition and rationing of many products. There were a variety of popular dinners served in restaurants. We could dine at high-class spots, like *Bristol* or *Polonia* in Warsaw, where we used to go for excellent and inexpensive dinners. I do not recall how long such a system lasted, none the less I took advantage of it during my studies.

It is worth mentioning a network of milk bars that was established during those years. They are a disappearing institution now, only surviving in a few places. They served vegetarian food, mainly dairy based, reminding one of home cooking and they were cheap. We often ate there while living away from home.

Living in Brzeska Street, we had no baking oven. When baking was needed, we used to place prepared pastry on steel trays and take them, tagged, to a bakery in the morning. The baked pastry was ready to be picked up in the afternoon.

The most important matter for us youngsters was the 'how and where' to find further education. My secondary school level reached in India was one year before matriculating. I realized that the standard of science and mathematics taught in India was much lower than in Warsaw secondary schools, leaving gaps difficult to fill. To top it off, my uncle thought that upkeep of our family should not depend only on our mother, but that I should also take a job. Convinced that my further education is essential, I faced the eventuality of studying in schools for working people. In hindsight it was a bad decision. I began working for the newspaper *Express Wieczorny* writing addresses in the dispatch department. I went to work with some trepidation, uncertain of my acceptance by others. My apprehension was justified, as I did not fit in well in the company of my new colleagues. There, for the first time, I met with discussions about alcohol drinking. Stories about drinking bouts were the main conversation topic and various occasions at work were celebrated with alcohol. I found it very difficult to take part in all this. Fortunately, I only stayed in this job for a few months, as it soon became obvious that working and studying for matriculation exams is impossible. The greatest benefit of working for the newspaper was that I was able to obtain free and excellent seats to theatre performances.

My high school class presented a good example of conditions prevailing at the school. My teachers were not of the best quality, often unqualified. They were mostly part time teachers supplementing salaries earned at their main employment or their pensions. I was particularly appalled at the study of history. Our study, being based on a book about the times of the Piast and Jagiellonian Dynasties, was full of details about dynastic and aristocratic connections and other trivia, giving us no chance of advancing to the later times. I found mathematics hard to follow, as in my previous studies I had not come across the concepts of 'integration' and 'differentiation' that were essential to my study. Only in Polish and English did I feel up to the standard. At that time religious study was still a part of the curriculum. I recall a priest who taught us religion hinting that he was against the current system and that we ought to feel the same way. However, we were not swayed by his suggestions, as he did not back them up with any arguments.

There were a number of distinct groups amongst the students. There was the 'Golden Youth': children of privileged parents, talented, certain of matriculating from this school. They were mostly interested in other matters and did not put much effort into study. There were a number of students who were forced to work because of their living conditions. They fought fiercely in an attempt to prevent the school's standards rising too high and wanted it to be exclusively for working students. Others strived to obtain both high marks and to leave school with a favourable opinion as an assurance of access to higher education. Membership of the ZMP, the first step to Communist Party membership, served towards that end. Some of us were just ordinary people who kept their beliefs, such as religious sympathies, to themselves. To me, having spent time in the Soviet Union, joining the ZMP was out of the question. I had seen too much at close range and I knew. Nonetheless I thought that events taking place in Poland were something entirely different. It seemed to me that the system in Poland depended exclusively on the calibre of its people and leaders and what happened in Russia only had a minor influence.

I thought that many beneficial changes took place in Poland after the war. Nationalisation of factories and an agrarian reform seemed to us as a great achievement. Similarly, the access of village youth to schools and the widespread migration from the country to town and city also seemed to be an achievement. It took time to notice the negative side of the changes and, gradually, our subjugation to Russia became obvious.

I think that, at least in my line of studies, the entrance exam results had much more weight than membership of organisations or parentage. The standard of teaching, not always sufficiently high, was often a problem. Persons studying in England or the USA on scholarships were gaining much more solid foundations than in our schools. We were experiencing a lack of qualified teaching staff, shortage of textbooks and inadequate laboratory facilities. Amongst our professorial staff were many outstanding teachers, but also a bunch of utter mediocrities.

Early Recollections *by Bronka Rozkuszko*

We arrived in Poland through Zebrzydowice on the 10th February 1948, exactly to a day eight years after deportation to Russia in February 1940.

My parents took advantage of the first opportunity to settle in Dolny Śląsk (Lower Silesia), close to some pre-war friends, transferred from the territories of our former home, which are now on the Soviet side of the Polish-Soviet border.

Our initial accommodation was in a flour mill. While staying there, I was suspicious of our fellow lodgers, who appeared to be hiding out and then slowly disappearing. Later we moved to a modest village hut with an attached plot of land. My parents felt happy, living without the fear of being deported to Russia, of dying from starvation. They liked living among people resettled from the territories, now under Russian rule.

We, the three teenage daughters, realized that our parents had no idea what to do with us. They held no high ambitions regarding our futures. I had completed five grades of high school and my certificate from the last class had a negative grade for behaviour (arguing with my maths teacher).

I heard from Hanka Ostrihanska, that in Warsaw they had a special preparatory course for entry to tertiary studies without matriculation. I travelled to Warsaw, lodged an application for admittance to the course, enclosing a certificate of completion of grade 4 high school and (oh, what naivety!) a reference from the Polish Scouting organisation in India. I was accepted, possibly my peasant background being the deciding factor. The course lasted a year. The student body was very diverse in respect of age, level of preparation and background. Thanks to what I learned in Valivade school, I had no problems with the study except for the subjects of Marxism and the history of The United Communist Party of Bolsheviks, but one can learn anything. Our professors were excellent, mostly former teachers of the well known Stefan Batory High School, which was closed as reactionary. On completion of the course and passing the final exam, I was admitted to the tertiary study without having to sit an entrance exam.

While attending the course I met Marysia S. She was older than I, experienced, had lived through the war in Poland and was married to a musician who played first violin in the National Philharmonic Orchestra. She is an unusual person, kind and talented, easily establishing contacts, admired by those who come across her. She is in a class of her own. Our friendship endures to this day. She now lives in the USA and works as a psychiatrist.

All course attendants joined the ZMP. Marysia looked at it as a kind of 'immunisation' and also joined. I did not and nobody really tried to force me to join. Both, Marysia and I were admitted to Academy of Medicine in Warsaw.

I lived in a Students' House, under rather difficult conditions. Permanently hungry and without money, I was loath to ask my parents for assistance. Marysia's home was the only place where I could assuage my hunger. All through the studies we worked like mad. There were no textbooks, so we continuously spent time in the Medical Circle. We sat for the exams in the first term – as Marysia used to say: 'I hate that work so much, that it is better to have it behind me'. I lived somewhat in the shadow of Marysia, in a way she looked after me. Attendance at lectures was compulsory and student rolls were checked. I often used to miss lectures. I got away with it, because Marysia took notes for me and a kind group leader used to mark me down as present.

Most of the 400 students in our year belonged to the ZMP but I was one of the few so called 'not organised', who did not. Instead, I was actively involved in helping students with learning difficulties. There was also a program to teach illiterate persons in which I took part as a teacher. Another activity in which I participated was removal of rubble left after the destruction wreaked on Warsaw during the war. However, it didn't take me long to realize that the whole endeavour was a propaganda exercise, a senseless shifting of bricks from one spot to another.

A separate issue were the May Day parades. Attendance was strictly enforced, there were assemblies and roll calls. I don't know if I attended even two of them. Later on I gave up attending altogether, realizing that the strict discipline was applied only to ZMP members. There existed an active group of ZMP members that we called the 'red cavalry', who controlled the whole course. There were instances of expulsion from studies, harassment of professors (pre-war cadre) and searches in Students' Houses. We knew very well who was behind it. It needs to be said however, that it took place just after the war. The young people involved came mainly from small towns and villages, having not yet been demoralised by our system and the majority of them believed in socialism in its eastern version. I must confess that I was not a very inquisitive person, probably not quite realizing what was happening around me.

I engrossed myself in study, often hungry and poorly dressed (as were most of the others), and wearing torn stockings which needed some ingenuity to make them wearable.

I completed my studies at the Academy of Medicine in 1954 and was one of the first to receive a certificate of completion. When I passed the last exam, I embraced the first person I met, shouting: 'I am now a doctor'. There existed a system of allocation to medical positions determined by a commission, in which the ZMP played a large part. Permanent positions in clinics were, naturally, given to ZMP members and appointments were not based on their individual ability. There existed a belief that research work was superior and other medical practice was spurned. During my studies I belonged to a society of neurological studies. A ZMP activist watched over each of these societies. Our watchdog was a primitive dullard, who later became a professor with one of the clinics.

This was the period when Lysenko's pseudo-scientific biological theory was being taught. This produced a generation of scientists ignorant in the field of genetics. Let me quote a joke from that time: 'a result of crossing an apple tree with a dog, was, that the apple tree barked when anyone picked its apples and it was self-watering'.

I applied for and received a scholarship to specialise in neurology for a two year assignment in a run down hospital in Wola. It was a truly squalid place, still partly occupied by Soviet soldiers, but staffed by an excellent medical team including wonderful Janina Morawiecka. We were very poorly paid, so young doctors worked 24 hours every second day to increase their income. It was extremely hard work, but I learned a great deal. Friendships established at that time are still alive and social contacts still maintained.

Scholarship payments were so low that they could not possibly cover the living expenses. To throw some light on the financial conditions under which doctors existed in those times, let me give an example. When patients were being discharged from a hospital, they usually gave their doctor a gift of chocolate or flowers, as an expression of gratitude. Some of my colleagues used to pass those gifts back to shops for resale.

My problem of accommodation was solved, thanks to my friends, by renting a room in a dilapidated pre-war villa set in park-like grounds near Warsaw. My 'room' was a corner of a large hall, which also served as a walk-through for others. It felt like living in a railway station. The landlords were pleasant and kind towards me, but somewhat insensitive. When the senior of the family died, they laid his body out in my hall, where we both slept; he for eternity and I just on my settee.

After two years I passed exams to the second level of specialisation in neurology. The year was 1956, the famous 1956, while I was sitting in my corner studying like mad. Having passed my specialisation exam, I lost my position in the Wola hospital. Fortunately, with the new relaxation of the political constraints, the system of position allocation came to an end and they forgot about me. A new hospital was established in a former communist party school building in Stępińska Street. A former Wola hospital doctor became its medical director and offered me a position.

The hospital had a well run neurological ward, supervised by the late Dr. Maria Filipowicz, a person of high principles and learning. I spent 20 years working in this hospital, mostly as a deputy ward-supervising doctor. There I also obtained the second level of specialisation. The work was hard, with a large number of 24-hour shifts. Apart from the hospital position I also had two additional jobs. Due to very low pay I had to find some additional means to live. Lack of proper accommodation was a continuing problem. I learned of the existence of a Medical Academy housing cooperative, which was building new apartments at 79 Złota Street. I got in touch with them. The president of the cooperative, a pharmacist, remains my good friend to this day. The financial arrangements were favourable, consisting of monthly payments with 20 years of matching government credit. I had my own apartment!

Then came my great love. Alas, it was a great mistake, yet it gave me my daughter Ania. I had to bring her up alone. It was a demanding time of my life. During this period I lost both my parents who were living in Rembertów at that time. I now exchanged my apartment for a larger one. Working all day at a number of places, I needed to have someone to look after Ania.

After 20 years employment in the Czerniakowska Street hospital, I decided to leave. Being offered the position of the retiring Dr. Filipowicz prompted my decision. I felt that the position would not suit me, as I prefer to be responsible only for myself. I like my type of work and I like my patients. I transferred to a Psychiatric Hospital, where I had worked previously as a consultant, and I am still working there.

I feel that never in my life have I done anything that was contrary to my basic personality. Even my 'wild decisions', when looked at closely, I knew, were acceptable to me. I retained my trust in people (some call it gullibility), I like them and try to help them, if it is at all possible. In summary, it was not an easy life and I would not wish to begin it again. My greatest joy and achievement is my daughter Ania. People valued me for my integrity and liked me for that touch of madness inherent in me.

Now something about my sisters. The younger Janka (Kluszczyńska), doubtlessly most intelligent and gifted of us all, was prevented from undertaking tertiary studies in geography because of politically unacceptable detail in her 'curriculum vitae'. While in a high school she participated in a school strike. Having completed a draughtsman's course conducted by professor Nigelszpurn in Valivade, she started working as a draughtsman in a project bureau. She married an architect work colleague who only recently died. She has two children and four grandchildren.

The elder sister Tosia (Rainczuk) completed high school to the so-called 'minor matriculation' level and worked as a bookkeeper. She has two children and three grandchildren.

Jerzy (Jurek) Krzysztoń *by Halina Krzysztoń*

Born in Lublin on 23rd March 1931. As a child he moved to Grodno with his family. Following the Soviet invasion of Poland on the 17th September 1939 his father, solicitor Franciszek Krzysztoń, was arrested on the 6th October 1939 and taken to Minsk prison never to be heard of again. Jurek, his mother, brother and aunt were deported to Kazakhstan on the 13th April 1940. His own, his family's and friends' experiences of those times are described by Jurek in his two books: *Wielbłąd na stepie* (Camel on a steppe) and his next book *Krzyż Południa* (Southern Cross) which deal with their departure from the Soviet Union to Tehran. There was going to be a third book on the final stay in India. Alas, his premature death prevented the completion of this trilogy of WWII personal experiences. Notwithstanding the fact that since the publication of both these books, there is now extensive literature on the subject, his two books are still being read and republished. The National Library lists them as a recommended reading for young people.

Thanks to the well-known and already extensively described action by Gen. Anders, Jurek with his family found himself amongst those saved from starvation and death in Soviet captivity. 'We stood on the Persian soil on the 15th August 1942, Feast of The Assumption of The Blessed Virgin Mary', he wrote later in his diary and that day remained as an especially memorable day in his life. In June 1943 he wrote: 'Arrived in India, stayed in a transit camp in Karachi, three months later reached Valivade, a place where we could rest and start living somewhat more like human beings'. India - which he got to know through many organised Scout trips or his own forays in the country - made an enormous and never forgotten impression on Jurek. Its magnificent architecture, literature and history dazzled him. On the other hand the sight of misery, hunger and sickness, a frightening contrast between an enormous wealth and an absolute depth of human despair, depressed him. It is all contained in his diary written in the years 1945-47 and these same experiences are echoed in his first book written in 1953, under a significant title: *Opowiadania indyjskie* (Indian Stories).

Sadly and irretrievably, the five-year stay in India comes to an end, an event described by Jurek on the 31st December 1947: "We say goodbye to Valivade and Kolhapur (…) In Bombay we board a quite large and fine looking American ship *General Stewart* (…) We depart on the 27th February (…) On the 8th.March we come within sight of Africa and Mombasa. The train journeys through an enchanting region – charming country. We arrive in the Polish Settlement Koja on the banks of Lake Victoria".

Eight months later his mother decides to return to Poland together with Jurek and his brother Janusz. In their native city of Lublin, Jurek matriculates in 1949 and commences studies at the Lublin Catholic University. After graduating in English and Polish studies, he moves to Warsaw in search of work. From 1960 he works in Polish Radio, initially as an editor and later as a director of the radio drama section. He also works for the monthly *"Więz"* (Bonds), whose founder and chief editor was Tadeusz Mazowiecki. The following years will abound in a great deal of new writing, which despite difficult encounters with censorship, would contribute to the enrichment of Jurek's literary achievements. Jurek received a number of awards: W. Pietrzak award for *Opowiadania indyjskie*, Pen Club's award for *Skok do Eldorado* (A Leap into Eldorado), Brother Albert's award for *Wielbłąd na stepie* and twice a readers' award for *Obłęd* (Madness). He also earned several awards for his radio dramas. His book about the Warsaw Uprising, *Kamienne niebo* (Stony Sky) has been made into a film. He was also a valued translator of Anglo-American prose. Jurek died in Warsaw on 16th May 1982, following a long and serious illness. His literary achievements became a permanent part of the Polish post-war literature.

AFRICA
by Zofia Evershed (Nowicka)

From the beginning of 1948 Valivade was gradually becoming deserted and depressing. No. 1 School, where I taught had closed and the remaining pupils and I joined the No. 3. School. As we already knew that we, together with those returning to Poland and a group that was going to Germany, would be transported to Koja Settlement in Uganda, lessons were performed in a robotic manner.

Africa? Perhaps we should go back to Poland? But there was nobody and nothing to return to. Perhaps if we waited, the situation there might change. But in the meantime there was no other choice; Africa it has to be. We dearly wanted to go to England with the families of servicemen, where our authorities and government was. But it was not to be.

In February 1948 we said goodbye to Valivade and sailed on an American ship, *General M. B. Steward*. This was the last chance to talk with the Valivadeans - Mrs. Tetmajer and her daughter Krysia, who were returning to Poland, to Kraków; brother Orysiuk, who was going to Germany but was hopeful of getting to England later on. Wiesia Klepacka and I discussed our situation a lot - she was also hopeful of getting to England. Dr. Borońska travelled with us, but she was in a reflective mood and kept herself to herself.

As we neared the coast of Africa, Mombasa came into view. Seeing the green land, full of coconut palms, the bay with white sandy beaches, on the walls of an ancient fort and the city spreading out on an island, I was filled with a sense of pleasure. When we docked, a local representative of IRO appeared, a handsome Egyptian lawyer named Mr. Bahari. Apart from arranging our disembarkation, he was also looking for a secretary as his Polish-American one was in hospital and would not resume her work. My sister, Dzidka, applied for the position. "What family do you have? I can keep here only persons able to work." - "My sister is a teacher." - "What can I do with a teacher?" - "But she has also completed a nursing course." "Good, I'll employ her in the hospital." - "My brother aged 18, is a high school student, but he can drive." - "Good, he will be a transport officer."- Mr. Bahari did not ask about our mother. The four of us held a conference - we were afraid of going deep into Africa, to the jungle, as news coming from there was not encouraging. Perhaps from Mombasa it will be easier to go somewhere else. This was to be our first separation from our friends and acquaintances. Were we doing the right thing staying in Mombasa? Only the future would tell. Those going to Uganda boarded a train; a journey of 2 to 3 days awaited them. We stayed one more day aboard the ship.

At long last our family was sent to a transit camp - English Point Camp. It was empty but the barracks soon filled with people leaving Africa for other parts of the world. The hospital itself contained 16 beds and a dispensary. The staff consisted of Dr. Czyżewicz and two nurses.

I became the third one. Every few weeks transports would arrive, then the hospital would fill up with patients - great numbers of people suffering from malaria and many with tropical ulcers.

A transport of families of Polish servicemen arrived from Koja in transit to England. Mother observed the women and remarked - "Just as well we did not go there, look at their burnt and damaged skin. We did not look like that in Valivade!"

With one of the transports a nurse arrived and the doctor engaged her in the hospital. More fastidious than the three of us, she began with a thorough clean up of the dispensary. When she moved the heavy dispensary cupboard, the head of a cobra appeared. We all screamed, the doctor ran in with a cane and fought with the cobra. We wondered how long it had been there near the cupboard while we worked, unaware of its presence.

Once a week the doctor held a clinic for African camp workers. Our task was to dress ulcers and other similar wounds. The dispensary contained a great number of medicines - gifts from America - enough for people in the camp and the African workers. But when it came to penicillin, it was only available in the pharmacies for cash. I began to learn Swahili and was able to say – "one tablet in the morning, one at noon and one in the evening."

After 8 months' stay in Mombasa we received official news that we could have the right of permanent stay in Kenya, with one proviso - that we obtain a steady job. Mombasa transit camp was closing having served its purpose. Return to Poland was out of the question and as there were no offers of settlement anywhere else, the only thing was to remain as migrants. I was the first who left the camp to go to Nairobi to work in a private hospital. There, from the position of an acting sister, I was demoted to a student nurse with wages of five pounds a month plus board. It was hard for me to get used to the new situation and I cried a lot at night. I suffered a lot of teasing - "Zofia you are educated but cannot make a bed". Nevertheless, I was given a lot of responsible work like attending to surgical dressings and assisting the doctors. Our patients were all white, mostly English but also some Italians, Yugoslavs and Poles. I managed well in English but telephone conversations frightened me as some were difficult to understand. After some months Irka Zobek came to work in Bydand Nursing Home and we shared a room. By now I had progressed from five to ten pounds a month and Irka was put under my charge. Being only a nursing aide, she had no inkling of nursing but was a good worker with a happy disposition. She also had a horror of dead bodies.

In the Bydand Nursing Home I nursed professor Nigelszpurn from Valivade. He suffered from tick-typhus. The ticks had many victims. Those who owned cats or dogs had to continuously clean their muzzles and ears to rid them of these revolting black, blood filled, big ticks, as large as garden peas. I have also nursed the famous Battle of Britain Chief Air Marshall Sir Hugh Dowding. He came for a holiday and a visit to his relatives in Kenya, but the Nairobi altitude was bad for his heart. That elderly gentleman liked to chat with me, which gave me a respite from the continuous running about. He talked about Polish airman and his admiration for them. Apparently he had nieces who married Poles.

After a few more months I said goodbye to nursing for ever - the physical work was too much for me. In the meantime Mother, Dzidka and Zbyszek came to Nairobi. Mother worked as a nanny for an English family, Zbyszek in a garage and Dzidka in an office. Dzidka and Zbyszek stayed in the Gloucester Hotel, a small hotel run by Armenians that was full of Poles from the old Polish Delegation in East Africa. Almost all Polish women worked in sewing workshops and stores in the English army camp. Every day a lorry arrived in the morning to pick them up and then dropped them off in the evening. Only Nusia Czyżewska worked in the Nairobi BBC as she not only spoke perfect English but also French. I too joined this Gloucester group and with the help of Dzidka found work in a firm importing suitcases, china and biscuits and exporting coffee. I did the estimates. With a wage of £30 a month, the cost of hotel being £12.50, life was improving and my confidence grew. The food here was cheap whilst in England ration cards were still in use. The shops were full of good fabrics and, as the ready-made dresses were very expensive, I bought myself a sewing machine. 'Nairobi', it was then said , 'is the Paris of the East'. Masses of colourful flowers were sold in front of Hotel Stanley. This is where Poles met for coffee or a glass of lemonade after mass on Sunday. The climate was wonderful, the days hot, the nights cool.

One day we found out that a transport of Poles from Koja would be passing through. Quite late at night all of us went to the railway station. Among the arrivals were our acquaintances from Valivade, among them Mrs. Marten with whom I talked for a long time. She and her son Wojtek were on their way to Australia. Mrs. Marten was very depressed, because her married daughter Krysia was remaining in Uganda. Every one had a different story to relate. Families were being separated and many were apprehensive about the future.

On the 3rd of May, the Polish community celebrated Polish National Day with Polish folk dances and songs in the centre of Nairobi. Father Wargowski directed the choir. On another occasion, major Królikowski arranged a session on Radio Nairobi in which he, Hanka Prochowska and I took part.

On the outskirts of Nairobi lived a group of Polish tradesmen employed by the Public Works Department. One evening a week I travelled there to teach English to the women and on another evening, Dzidka taught the men. Some years later I met one of the women, who said that thanks to me she could, when widowed, earn her living as a saleswoman. It gave me great pleasure to hear her words.

One Sunday I met Janka Niezabytowska. Janka worked on a farm that also had dog kennels. She was in her element looking after the dogs. By this time Dzidka, had bought herself an old, but still drivable car. We visited Janka on the farm and after seeing her situation there, we decided that she must come to Nairobi as there was no future on an isolated farm. In Nairobi she and her mother could at least go to church. Dzidka, who achieved some standing in the accounts department of a large firm, Dalgety & Co., recommended Janka for a vacant position. Soon both mother and daughter joined us in the Gloucester Hotel. As there were a number of Polish women working in that firm, my future husband used to jokingly refer to the company as Dalgety & Polka Ltd (Polka means Polish woman). A few days before her departure to America, Mrs. Borońska and her son Witek, now a grown boy, paid us a visit at the Gloucester Hotel.

There were many Polish-English marriages. In 1951 I married an Englishman who worked in the Treasury Department. A few months later Dzidka married Dr. Czyżewicz. My life once again was distanced from the Polish community, but I subscribed to *Wiadomości* (Polish Literary News). My husband, who began to learn Polish, copied for me recipes from a loaned Polish cookbook. Two years later he was posted to Mombasa, where Irka Zobek and her Scottish husband lived. Irka was in seventh heaven when my husband managed to get her a job in the Treasury Department. It was very difficult for Europeans to find work in Mombasa as many Indian people, whose wages were lower, waited and applied for every vacant job, especially office positions. As my mother stayed with us, I was able to return to work as bookkeeper for the African Mercantile Company when my son was 11 months old.

My husband, who served in the East African High Commission, was entitled to six months paid holidays in England every three years. On his return he was always assigned to a different place so we lived in Nairobi, Mombasa, Kampala, Eldoret and again in Nairobi. In 1954 I went to England for the first time. My Valivade dream came true, but under different circumstances.

After 4 months' stay in England we returned to Africa, this time to Kampala. Uganda did not pass me by. I remember the Ugandan people with pleasure, but not the climate. You have to live through the frightening thunderstorms, their ferocity probably influenced by Lake Victoria, which is only 25 miles away. An added attraction were minor earthquakes - three during our stay in Kampala. In Kenya and Uganda, nationality did not play a role. More important was the skin colour. Europeans kept together and, as there were not many of them in Uganda, they all knew each other.

One day in Kampala I fell into conversation with an English woman. "A Polish woman came from England, she is a beauty" enthused the elderly lady. A few days later in a shop I saw a familiar face – "Stella, is that you?" – Yes it was Stella Radwańska (Czekierska). Her husband, a cartographer, was employed in mapping Uganda.

I must mention that Dzidka's husband, apart from being a doctor, was also a painter. His main interest was the African countryside, which he painted in watercolours, pastels and oils. Old Mombasa Town and seaside scenery were also the subjects of his paintings. He did portraits as well. An exhibition of his paintings was held in Nairobi. When Princess Margaret visited Nairobi in 1957, she received a painting of the Kenyan bush, one of his works, as a present from Kenya.

Other Poles are also worthy of mention. The one most outstanding and at the same time most humble, was the monk Józef Nowicki. He arrived in Kenya from the region of Poznań with a group of Carmelites, the so-called 'White Fathers'. They brought with them seedlings of Arabian coffee that suited well the red soil of Kenya and became that country's main export commodity. Apart from proclaiming Christianity, the 'White Fathers' also taught the Kenyan people practical skills and trades. Brother Nowicki was a master builder. He educated hundreds of masons and carpenters. Apart from the church in Mombasa, he built all the other Catholic churches in Kenya. When he died, advanced in years, Kenya honoured him with a magnificent funeral. I learned about his contributions to Kenya from the Kenyan press.

Zbyszek receiving his Safari trophy

In Eldoret I met Krysia Marten, who brought her son to a boarding school. Krysia lived somewhere in the bush and had had enough of it. She and her husband were planning to go to Australia to join her mother and brother there.

Life in East Africa was monotonous but there was a yearly attraction – a car rally known as the 'Coronation Safari' as the first rally was held in 1953 to celebrate Queen Elizabeth's coronation. This rally achieved fame all over the world. From that year onwards every Easter everybody sat glued to the radio or waited at sections of its 3,000 miles track. My brother Zbyszek took part in the rally from its inception, at first in his own car, later in the Peugeot team car with their mechanics. As he always came in the first 10, Peugeot cars received good publicity and the firm became famous. The high point of the rally was the year 1961 when, from the hundred cars that started only seven finished. Zbyszek came first. The seven were given the nickname the 'Unsinkable Seven'. That year Easter was very wet and the roads in all of East Africa were flooded with the drivers having to negotiate deep mud without sinking in it. Kenya by this time was independent. Jomo Kenyatta was its president and it was he who presented the winners with their trophies. Zbyszek repeated his triumph in 1963.

With the independence of Kenya most of the overseas officials lost their positions and left the country. My husband was in that group. By then Dzidka was widowed. She managed to get a position as a private secretary to the vice president of Kenya, Mr. Arap Moi, who, after Jomo Kenyatta's death became the next president. In 1964 we left Kenya and sailed for England. Kwaheri Kenya – goodbye Kenya. You were good to me.

***

Zbyszek Nowicki. The Nowicki sisters and their mother left for England but Zbyszek stayed in Kenya. At first he worked for the Peugeot car firm, later, while in his retirement, he switched to tractors and became the chief director of Fiat Tractors, part of the Lornho group. He is known as Nicki Noviki, 'Grandad Safari', as he took part in all the car rallies. Zbyszek donated his winning cups to the Museum of Sport in Warsaw.

Ludka Jakutowicz (Zawadowska) left India with her mother for Koja in Uganda. In 1950 her mother married Czesław Polechowicz. Fr. Kozłowski arranged for him a managerial position on a Jesuit farm in Northern Rhodesia. Later they lived in Salisbury (now Harare, Zimbabwe) where Ludka married an architect from a Polish settlement in Africa and they settled in Cape Town, in South Africa.

AUSTRALIA
by Urszula Paszkowska (Trella)

When we landed in Australia in 1950 its population was merely 7 million, of which approximately half lived in large cities. Fresh in the minds of Australians were the advances of the Japanese army, which had invaded Indonesia and parts of New Guinea and had bombed the northern Australian town of Darwin. If it was not for the victory of the American fleet in the Coral Sea, the danger to this country would have been extreme. An increase of the population, through immigration, was therefore one of the aims of the Australian Government, but Poles were not favoured in the early post-war years. Preference was given to the so-called Balts, that is, Estonians, Latvians and Lithuanians, as well as Dutch and even Germans.

The first small group of Polish immigrants consisted of nineteen adults, who came here in 1947 from a Polish settlement in India. Shortly after, a group of Polish demobilised soldiers arrived. They were accepted here, because a number of them had served alongside Australian soldiers defending the besieged Tobruk. These former Polish soldiers were sent to Tasmania to build dams and work on large hydro-electric power projects. They found themselves quite isolated in the bush, but in spite of this they later formed a well organised and vibrant group, which gained the recognition and respect of the local population. A number of these former soldiers married Australian women.

Our group, which arrived in the port of Fremantle from East Africa on the 14th of February 1950 consisted of 1,179 persons (some were former inhabitants of the Valivade Camp). It was different from other immigrants, as it was homogeneous and consisted mainly of women and children. We were told later, that most hope was placed on the children becoming future loyal citizens of Australia. Adults were also well received, especially the ones who knew some English and were able to do physical work.

Australia had not been affected by the war, but it was mainly an agricultural country. Industrial development started taking place after the arrival of the new post-war migrant workforce. New hydroelectric schemes were created, such as the large Snowy Mountains project and others in Tasmania and Victoria. A very successful car industry was developed in Australia commencing with the Holden, which proved very popular. Furthermore, Australia also developed an agricultural machinery production capability. The arrival of a large number of immigrants

Australian group

changed Australia not only industrially, but brought changes in the whole structure of social and cultural life. Melbourne and Sydney probably had a more cosmopolitan character. In contrast Perth was a city almost deserted on Sundays. All shops and restaurants were closed, there were no venues where one could drop in to meet friends, or have some tea. As for the coffee it was not available even during the week, as only liquid Bushells was on the market, but sadly did not resemble the real one. Sports fields, bars and picture theatres were the only venues, where one could meet friends. However, bars closed in Western Australia at 9.00 p.m. (in Victoria 6.00 p.m.) and were closed all day Sunday. Women could not be served in public bars, they were only allowed to drink in saloon bars or in the beer gardens, where they could meet with men.

Even though Perth had a beautiful theatre building, designed, it was said by a Polish architect, it was only used occasionally by guest artists. At that time, local artists had to travel to Europe and perform there first in order to gain recognition in Australia. The same applied to doctors, who had to specialise in England. There was a university in Perth, the only free one in Australia, thanks to a large bequest but it lacked a school of medicine.

The local population was friendly and in spite of some prejudice rather kindly disposed towards immigrants and therefore helpful. There was a large demand for workers particularly in the countryside. Wages were good especially for men. Manual workers could earn more that an office clerk or even a University lecturer. It was extremely difficult to obtain recognition of Middle or Eastern European diplomas. Medical doctors so qualified could not even dream of practising in Australia. There was even a case of a doctor working as an orderly in a hospital where medical students were learning from a book written by him. Engineers fared somewhat better, but it depended on local demand. Some immigrants managed to get employment in the offices, but generally they were not welcomed there. Officially the immigration ministry gave introductions to employ immigrants in hard physical work so as not to antagonise the local population. On entry to Australia, everyone received a document classifying every man as a labourer and every woman as a domestic. An official in the transit camp in Bonegilla in Victoria addressing large groups of immigrants advised them to burn old documents. Other officials instructed them to forget their past, previous work and even their native tongues.

A teenager from our group was employed in a factory, where he was obliged to work shifts. He requested the employment service to allow him to take a job in another factory where he would have free evenings, allowing him to take up part time study, only to be told that he had come to Australia not to study, but to work. It was however, not a whim of one person, but official instructions, which are now long forgotten. In spite of this attitude, some of our young men and women attained further education. It was facilitated by evening lectures at colleges, which could be attended after work.

From our 'Indians' let me mention **Stach Harasymów** who obtained a diploma of architecture, my brother **Bogusław Trella** received in the early sixties a diploma in electrical engineering. **Janusz Kurzeja** after a period of factory work completed teachers' training college, continued his university studies and obtained his PhD. He was a principal of a secondary school for a number of years. His sister Zosia was received together with other seven Polish girls at the boarding school of a secondary Catholic college in Perth, where fees were minimal and only required, when their mothers obtained work. Here admittance was thanks to the personal interest and support of the archbishop of Perth, reverend Edmund Prendiville, after his visit in a transit camp in Northam. Zosia commenced university studies after matriculation, which she interrupted to marry Dr. Andrzej Skarbek, who obtained his medical degree in Melbourne. Zosia returned to her studies, when her children were independent and obtained a degree of BSc at Melbourne University specialising in genetics and psychology. She now works as a psychologist at the Commonwealth Rehabilitation Services.

Anek Cwetsch studied accountancy and obtained a responsible position in the large firm of Elders.

Ryszard Pawłowski commenced mechanical engineering studies at evening classes. On moving to Melbourne in 1957 he, obtained work as a draughtsman, in a firm specialising in fire protection projects. His brother Henryk, undertook evening studies and subsequently worked as a commercial artist in various advertising firms in Perth.

B. Trella working on a fishing vessel "Villaret"

Thanks to her experience in Uganda, Regina Tijewska was able to obtain work as a typist. After her marriage, she helped her husband in running a travel agency that also provided parcel and money transfer services to Poland.

Ewa Pacak on conclusion of her studies at a training college in Perth worked as a teacher. She married Jurek Gruszka, who came here from East Africa. He enlisted in the Australian Army after serving out his two year contract as a physical worker. On obtaining confirmation, that his

Polish matriculation certificate obtained in a Polish High School in Tanganyika was recognised by Cambridge University as binding in all the countries of the British Commonwealth, he was able to graduate as an officer. He completed the school of cartography with distinction. In the Gibson Desert in Western Australia he discovered a fresh water lake which was officially given his name in 1962. Following his posting to New Guinea, where Ewa worked as a teacher, he returned to Australia, where he finished his military career as a colonel. Eventually they settled in Adelaide with their two daughters and Ewa's mother.

Janina Huszczo did a typing and stenography course in Perth and worked in an office. She married a former Polish Home Army (AK) soldier who worked as a technical officer in the Commonwealth Serum Laboratories. They settled with Janina's mother in Melbourne. As a mature student she enrolled at Melbourne University to obtain a degree in Sociology and Philosophy. She was also a Secretary of the Polish Association. Her brother Jan enlisted in the Australian Navy in 1955, where he served for 20 years, taking part in the Malaysian confrontation with Indonesia and convoys to Vietnam during Australia's engagement there. He undertook various studies including the power of command and a managerial course and ended his career as Chief Petty Officer. He married an Australian girl, settled in Sydney and raised three sons and a daughter.

Jan Huszczo

Their sister Agnieszka joined a religious order in South Africa in 1949. Realizing that religious life was not suitable for her she left the convent after 18 months of novitiate and found herself in Durban without money, family or friends. She found employment in an infectious diseases hospital, where she worked as a nursing aid for 6 months. Afterwards she commenced nursing training. On completion of her training she worked in an infectious diseases hospital in Johannesburg. Later she undertook a midwifery course. Agnieszka left South Africa for Rhodesia and worked in Bulawayo for 2 years in the emergency surgical ward of a hospital. During a visit to her family in Melbourne in 1959 she decided to stay in Australia. She worked here in an oncology hospital, then joined the RAAF as a registered nurse at a rank of a section officer. During her posting in Queensland she met and married an air force flight lieutenant, Ronald Crimmins, who later served in Vietnam as a liaison officer between the Australian and American forces. He was promoted to the rank of wing commander and had several command postings in Australia. Sadly he died at the age of 48. Agnieszka settled down in Brisbane. She still continues working in the nursing profession. She works with the intellectually disabled. Her main duties are administration and training of carers for them. She has a daughter and two sons.

Zdzisław Krawczyk, after finishing his secondary school in Perth, enlisted in the Australian Air Force and later worked as a pilot for Quantas airline. He was in charge of the flight that landed at Okęcie in Warsaw with one of the first Polish groups of tourists after 1956. It created quite an interest in Poland. He settled in Sydney.

Bogdan Harbuz, after moving to Melbourne, worked in telecommunications and took an active interest in Polish social life.

Jurek Dobrostański, after a three month stay in Northam, moved to Melbourne with his mother and younger brother to join their relative Mrs. Maria Bobin, formerly Janas. The Dobrostańskis chose a lengthy train journey, rather than an expensive air flight and arrived tired but safe whilst the plane which they would have taken crashed and all aboard were killed. In Melbourne the whole family worked in the Westinghouse factory assembling telephones and transformers as part of their two year contract. Jurek wanted to study, but university fees were too high. He undertook some technical studies and obtained work as a technician in a telephone exchange. He became interested in filmmaking and with an Australian friend produced advertising and documentary films. During the Olympic Games in Melbourne in 1956, Jurek in his role as a technician with the Australian Telecommunication Authority was attached to the Polish reporters' group and sent commentaries and reports to Poland. Afterwards he received an offer from the Polish Government of a scholarship in the Polish film School. His answer was typical of Jurek. He thanked them politely, but stated that he cannot accept the offer, as he had never contributed to the Polish treasury.

Jurek won fame when he photographed Cardinal Wojtyła with a kangaroo during the Eucharistic Congress in Melbourne in 1973. On the cardinal's ascension to the papacy, the photograph became quite popular and was reproduced in many newspapers and journals including the *Times*. He also contributed articles to the *Polish Weekly* in Melbourne and for a period to *Kultura Monthly* of Paris where he wrote columns of the Australian Chronicle. He also produced and read the news for the local Polish language radio station. Soon after the Olympic Games Jurek commenced studies at the University of Melbourne in the field of commerce and export trade. He later worked in two commercial firms and finally in the Wool Corporation, as a market researcher. On his sudden death in 1990, the flag on their headquarters flew at half-mast as a sign of respect.

Urszula Paszkowska (Trella) and Jurek Dobrostański

Jurek's mother Janina worked from 1955 at the *Polish Catholic Weekly* later named *Polish Weekly*. Before the war she had been a theatre actress and she continued her work in the *Polish Theatre* in Australia, formed and managed drama groups, establishing and taking part in various productions. Their home was extremely friendly and welcoming especially to young people, who usually gathered there during weekends. All the former inhabitants of Valivade found their home a place of great hospitality where the hostess often provided temporary accommodation, not disclosing the fact to her guests that she had to pay for their lodging. Tadeusz, the younger son of the family transported guests to and from the train station. He started work in 1952 in the field of industrial photography and later conducted the department of clinical and criminal photography at the University of Melbourne for 34 years.

After a six month stay in the transit camp near Northam, where she worked as a nurse in its hospital, **Wiesia Wojtaszewicz** came to Melbourne, with her mother, to meet and later to marry her pen friend and fiancé Mirek Paszkiewicz, with whom she became acquainted at the Scouts and Girl Guides meeting in Tehran in 1942. They were both very active in voluntary social field in Melbourne especially in Scouting. Wiesia was for a number of years the chief commissioner of the Polish Girl Guides in Australia. She initiated educational courses for future Girl Guide leaders.

My daughter finished one of them and was later active in the movement.

In 1949 **Lala Rosenthal (Szczanowska)** arrived from England with her husband Max. Lala has written about their experiences: "The decision to go to Australia was taken while we were still in India and was achieved when on 11th of October 1949 we landed in the port of Melbourne. We arrived on the Italian ship *Toscana* from Genoa, after a 6 week voyage. We hoped that my husband would be able to continue his practice as a dentist. Unfortunately his Viennese diploma was not recognised here and he had to work at the General Motors factory loading trucks with coal. Luckily it did not last long. I have to emphasise that his co-workers were mostly doctors and solicitors, who found themselves in a similar situation. Later he obtained employment in a medical store, where at least he could smell the medicines.

At first I worked in clothing factories, later in the office of a business college and eventually as a bookkeeper until my retirement. We took an active part in social life, and were members of the *Polish Cultural and Artistic Club*. My husband participated in the Polish theatre. At first we found it extremely difficult to rent a flat, as Australians were reluctant to let them to foreigners."

Bożena Romanowska also found herself in Australia. She completed her studies soon after arriving from England and found employment teaching in secondary schools.

The **Dudryk-Darlewski** family settled in Melbourne. Their son, Stanisław a former Delegate of the Polish Welfare Ministry in Bombay, died shortly after arriving from India. Mrs. Dudryk-Darlewski survived both her son and her husband and lived in Melbourne for many years.

The seven members of the **Wierzbiński** family came from England in 1947 to join one of the daughters, Regina Mazajczyk, who had married a Polish merchant seaman while still in India. Another daughter Maria, married Mr. Piórkowski, a well-known lemonade producer in Valivade. A third daughter Nela married Leon Woźny in Melbourne, where they both took an active interest in Polish social activities.

Another Polish ex-seaman residing in Melbourne, Mr. Kazimierz Skoczek, was married to **Maria Burzyńska** from Valivade. All of them were frequent guests of Mrs. Dobrostański's house.

Irena Nowicka with her husband Witold Janson emigrated from England to Perth in the 1960's and later moved to Melbourne. Witek worked as a mechanical engineer for the firm of Ericsson. Sadly he died young. Irena was for years in charge of midwifery section of a hospital until her retirement in 1994.

Edward Bielski resided in Melbourne with his family. He was a former ward of the Valivade Orphanage, which he later left to stay with his older sister Pelagia, who worked at the Valivade hospital. Entitled to join his ex-serviceman brother in England he refused to go, not wanting to become a burden to his brother. On the liquidation of the Valivade Camp, he left for Lebanon. His sister in the meantime married her friend from the orphanage, Zygmunt Kowałko, who joined the Polish Merchant Navy and served on the *MV Batory*. Pelagia, as a mother of two small children in 1949 was unable to sign the two year contract required by the Australian Authorities. The sixteen year old Edward signed the contract and together with his sister's family he arrived in Australia. His first employment was with the firm of McKenzie and Holland a division of Westinghouse. Eventually his brother joined him in Australia from England. Edward tried various jobs and during a brief economic crises, in 1952, managed to convince a glazier to take him on as an apprentice, stating that he would soon learn the trade. He was true to his word, eventually establishing his own well prospering glazing firm. His three daughters and a son attended Polish language classes, joined Polish Scouting and the Polish dance group *'Polonez'*. Later his eldest daughter Jadzia coached the youngest members of *Polonez* for a period of 15 years. Her three sons also joined *Polonez* and were members of the Polish Scouts. Edek died in November 2001 and his funeral was attended by a large number of people.

Jadzia Ryciak-Solka-Krajewska, who came to Australia from Lebanon in 1950, lives in Sydney. She was in the last group of 49 persons who left Valivade. Soon after her arrival in Sydney she commenced a fashion and designing course, in a private academy which was run by a French couple. On its completion she set up her own small dress making and fashion boutique. She was assisted by her mother and her sister Halina, who arrived a little later. From the beginning Jadzia undertook intensive social work. She was motivated, as she says, by her patriotic upbringing and the whole atmosphere of Valivade. Jadzia was co-founder of the Polish Ladies Association, and co-founder of the first Polish Women's Federation in Australia and New Zealand, as well as president of the Polish Perpetual Fund in Australia. She was also a founder of the Polish Sibiraks Association in New South Wales and one of the sponsors of an artistic and cultural festival, *Polart*, established 25 years ago and staged at three-yearly intervals in different State Capitals.

Stefan Ślusarczyk arrived in Perth with his mother from Valivade in August 1947. He finished his studies and taught in Secondary schools. He married an Australian girl.

Marysia Shannon (Janiszewska) together with her husband Józef, a former member of Carpathian Brigade and the 'Desert Rats', arrived in Perth in 1947. They were part of a group of women and men from India who were early arrivals in Australia. The Shannons lived in Perth for a number of years. Once their children went to school, Marysia took up studies and completed a secretarial course, which enabled her to be employed as and office worker.

In the same group of Poles from India were Mrs. Szpadowska and her daughter Irena who, upon meeting some demobilised Polish soldiers travelling to Tasmania, decided to head for the same place themselves. Eventually they both married Polish ex-servicemen.

Mrs. Krystyna Chociej, who had worked as an interpreter for the British Censorship Office in Bombay, obtained work in St. John's Hospital laboratory in Perth, following recognition of her degree from Lwów University. In 1950 she married Mr. Bolesław Singler and moved to Melbourne. During the war Mr. Singler served with the Carpathian Brigade and took part in campaigns in North Africa, (including the siege of Tobruk) and Italy (where he participated in the taking of Monte Cassino). In Melbourne Mrs. Singler worked as an accountant. They were both well known and respected philanthropists. They supported the *Polish Polcul Foundation*, which every year grants awards to individuals in Poland for outstanding literary and scientific achievements, and rewards persons who promote ethnic and religious tolerance and work for socially disadvantaged people. They also supported the Foundation of Polish Studies at Macquarie University at Sydney, Polish University in London, Catholic University in Lublin in Poland and a number of other organisations, especially in former Eastern Poland with emphasis on children's welfare. For her charitable work, Mrs. Singler was awarded medals by the Polish Government in exile and later by the Polish President Lech Wałęsa.

Jadzia Wróblewska joined the order of Resurrection Sisters in England and was later sent to South Australia, where for a number of years she was a member of the examination board of foreign languages, as well as a teacher of languages in secondary schools. She published a Polish reader *Polish Language in colour* for the beginners. She also taught Polish language classes and took an active part in the Polish Girl Guide movement.

Going back to our immigration of 1950, I must point out that teachers with a good knowledge of English could find work in this field soon after arrival, due to a shortages of teachers.

Mr. Aleksander Topolnicki was soon employed as a maths teacher. A number of other young Poles from East Africa, continued their studies after finishing teacher training college and eventually obtained responsible and prestigious positions.

I was allowed, to commence nursing training at the Royal Perth Hospital after a year of work in a geriatric hospital in Perth. Three years later I obtained a nursing certificate and moved to Melbourne where I received my Midwifery Certificate after another year of training. I settled in Melbourne, got married and had two children. I continued working first in the operating theatre of the Eye and Ear Hospital and later in the paediatric wards of a large teaching hospital. On retirement 12 years ago I took up duties on the committee of Polish Siberaks Association in Victoria. A large part of our work involves charitable causes. My husband is a well-known author of several historical books and contributed to the Polish emigre press.

Mrs. Jadzia Chołąckiewicz-Szebert lived in Northam Western Australia, where for 27 years she worked in the local hospital. Her Red Cross nursing course in Tehran and a long period of work in Valivade and Koja hospital were not considered sufficient to qualify her as a hospital sister, but she was appreciated and liked by her co-workers.

I would like to mention the type of work performed by our young boys on arrival in Australia as part of their two year contract. My brother and the Pawłowski brothers worked in a factory that produced wire and wire netting. Wojtek Marten was sent to work in the country where he became a road plant operator for Dalwallinue Shire. Apart from his official job, he also worked in a local garage and later contracted to operate a school bus. A keen sportsman, Wojtek became involved in local sporting activities. He played Australian Rules football and for years captained the local team. He married a local farmer's daughter, Winnie. Over the years they owned roadhouses, farms and orchards and established tourist facilities on their property. They prospered, thanks to their initiative, hard work and perseverance. Wojtek maintains contact with his former Valivade friends living in Perth.

Stach Harasymów and Anek Cwetsch worked on augmenting the capacity of the Mundering water reservoir near Perth, from which water was pumped via a 560 km pipeline to the Kalgoorlie Goldfields. He became actively involved in the Polish social and cultural life. In the early seventies he designed the club premises and playing fields for the Cracovia (Polish) soccer club and edited its bulletins. In the eighties he was a secretary of the Australian Fund of Solidarity with Poland. Later together with his wife they undertook work with the Polish Radio Committee preparing and broadcasting radio programs. He is an active member of the Polish Siberaks Association in Western Australia.

My brother, **Bogusław Trella** completed his part time studies in Melbourne in the early sixties and subsequently worked as an electrical engineer for the State Electricity Commission. He joined the Polish Technical and Professional Association in Victoria,

S. Białkowski, R. & H. Pawłowski and S. Harasymów

where at times he served on the committee. Following his retirement, he was elected to the Federal Council of Polish Association in Australia, where he was responsible for organising financial help for Poles living in the former Soviet Union. For a short time he served as an acting treasurer of the Federal Council.

Our mothers were not required to sign the two year contract if they had reached the age of forty nine, but they had to have a guarantor, usually their older children, who pledged to look after their financial needs. Though not obliged to work, the majority found employment in institutions such as schools, hospitals, hotels and offices where they worked as cleaners, tea ladies or kitchen help. No one was ashamed of such physical work. The pay and treatment were good and in some cases a mother's employment allowed her children to continue their studies.

While we were still in the transit camp, a Polish priest arrived from Germany, where he had been interned in a concentration camp. Later two more priests of similar background joined him. To enter Australia they had to sign a two year contact as well, but were soon released from it and given the opportunity to carry out their priestly duties, not only in the camps but also in one of the churches in Perth.

During our first year in Western Australia the Polish Association was established and a fund was started to buy our own club house, which was eventually purchased in 1952. It was an ordinary family home, but after some alterations became quite suitable for meetings and even social functions including dances.

A Polish weekly *Echo* began appearing in Perth. Its publisher Mr. Tabaczyński married a Valivade girl, Gina Tijewska. We also received from Melbourne *Tygodnik Katolicki* (Catholic Weekly) which contained a lot of practical information for new arrivals.

New marriages were taking place between new immigrants usually within their own communities, but there were also some Polish-Australian marriages. Polish language classes were organised as well as choirs, national dance groups, sports clubs and a Scouting movement. Polish ex-servicemen formed their own association.

The aim of the Australian immigration policy was a gradual integration and assimilation of a large number of post war foreign arrivals. A special organisation was even established known as "Good Neighbours Council" which was to facilitate this process.

Officially we were referred to as "New Australians", but commonly offensive words like 'foreigners', 'wogs', 'Balts', 'refos' and similar, continued to be used for a long time.

Official government policy regarding immigrants was radically changed in the early seventies. It was due in a large measure to the efforts of Professor Jerzy Zubrzycki a Polish sociologist, who later became the founder professor of sociology at the National University of Canberra. He submitted a number of reports to the federal government showing the negative aspects of the policy of the assimilation of immigrants. With the backing of other eminent Australians, he was able to convince the government of the undesirable effects on migrant families and on the mental health of single migrants, of rapid assimilation policies. Under such policies, serious divisions began to appear within immigrant families between parents and children. The children, considering themselves to be more or less Australian, were losing contact with their elders and with their cultural heritage, often feeling ashamed of their ethnic background. This estrangement from their parents' community often led to resentment and character flaws, causing behaviour that at times necessitated police intervention.

A new policy, known as multiculturalism, was created and adopted by successive federal governments and supported by the ethnic communities. Now government not only encourage the preservation of the languages and customs of the countries of origin of new settlers, but actually provide financial support for their preservation.

Teaching of ethnic languages, is now a part of the school curriculum. Accommodation for such classes is now provided and the Education Ministries pay teachers. Examination results from these studies are now counted towards the final score when applying for entry into the tertiary institutions.

The numbers of students from non-English speaking backgrounds has increased considerably with half of the students in medicine and law having non Anglo-Saxon names.

The introduction of the multicultural policy, led to the establishment of the Special Broadcasting Service (S.B.S.), which provides radio programs in 68 ethnic languages throughout the Country. The television section of S.B.S. broadcasts in all Capital Cities and caters primarily for the needs of ethnic and indigenous communities, but is also valued by the wider Australian community because of the uniqueness of its programs and their high standard.

The spiritual needs of the Polish Catholic community are well served by an adequate number of Polish priests and churches (often financed and built by Poles) in all states.

Our children have integrated well into Australian Society. There are doctors, solicitors, pilots, engineers, chemists, diplomats, businessmen, journalists, film makers, teachers, and academics of Polish descent. Up till now however, we have not achieved any success in political life. Descendants of Greek, Italian and Lebanese immigrants serve as ministers in state and federal governments. Vietnamese have achieved positions in state and local governments though they are much later arrivals in Australia.

Wojtek Marten and Bogusław Trella aboard USAT "General WC Langfitt" on their way to Australia

The 40th anniversary of our arrival in Australia from East Africa aboard the *General W. C. Langfitt*, was celebrated by members of the "General Langfitt Group", both in Perth and in Melbourne. Numerically smaller, the Melbourne group attracted visitors from other States and even from overseas for the celebration. Commemorative plaques were unveiled on Fremantle Dock, our port of landing in 1950, and at Tobruk House in Canberra. Politicians representing federal, state and local governments attended the unveiling ceremonies.

Following the anniversary celebrations, our Melbourne members convinced that our history was unique in post-war Australian immigration, applied to the Federal Government for a grant to have it officially recorded. Our application was successful and we were granted $32,000 for research into our background and settlement in Australia. The results of interviews and archival research by the historian Marion Allbrook were published in 1995 under the title *General Langfitt Story*. The book is now out of print, but can be accessed on the Internet.

In writing I have used material from my own experience and interviews with the following persons:

- E. Bielski,- M. and T. Dobrostański, - S. Harasymów, - I. Janson (Nowicka), - W. Paszkiewicz (Wojtasiewicz), - R. Pawłowski, - J. Pienkoś (Huszczo), - B. Singler, - Z. Skarbek (Kurzeja), - J. S. Krajewska (Ryciak), - H. Rosenthal (Szczanowska), - B. Trella, - N. Woźny (Wierzbińska).

I also found helpful the following books:

- E.F. Kunz's *Displaced Persons: Callwell's New Australians* published by the National

University Press 1988; (Sydney) and *The intruders: Refugee Doctors in Australia* published by the National University Press 1977; (Canberra)

- Memoirs of F Ostrowski *The Road and the Passer-by* published in 1992 by Roman Migocki and Wojtek Ihnatowicz (Sydney) and

- *The Monument of Polish – Australian Brotherhood in Arms* by Tadeusz Kempa published in Hobart, Tasmania, in 1984 and

- Articles published in *Tygodnik Polski* (Polish Weekly) No 12/48 and No 49/91 page 9 and 13.

CANADA
by Maria Solecka (Kołodziej)

Most Poles from the refugee camps in India, who settled in Canada after World War II, were family members of soldiers from the Polish Second Corps and First Armoured Division in the Allied armies. After demobilization, most families had first reunited in England and Scotland, but many decided to move on and settle in other parts of the world. The determining factor in their decisions was the hope of better prospects for the future. Those who emigrated to Canada, settled mainly in the province of Ontario, some in Quebec, British Columbia, Alberta or Calgary; fewer in Saskatchewan and Manitoba, and none in the eastern provinces. With some exceptions, most live in large cities: Toronto, Ottawa, Montreal, Vancouver, Edmonton, Regina and Winnipeg.

I still remember my first impression of Canada, a feeling of more freedom and less restraint than in England. The first wave of Polish immigrants, who settled in Canada at the end of the nineteenth century, had already established various organisations and associations, had built churches, published Polish newspapers and owned various enterprises and stores. And yet, our beginnings in Canada were not easy. The Canadian Government did not help newcomers at the time of our immigration in the 1950s. Grateful for being allowed into this country, we shaped and improved our lot entirely on our own.

The Canadian group

Maria Solecka, Mostrowska and Trybuś in Toronto 1987

Depending on our different ways of arriving in Canada, we can be divided into three general groups. The largest group was made up of families who arrived on their own initiative. As a rule, they already had someone in Canada with whom they had kept in touch. On arrival they briefly stayed with their friends, or in a hotel, and immediately began looking for employment and a place to live. The second group of arrivals were the families of people who had been recruited by various Canadian firms or British overseas branches. Among those was the family of **Maria Ostrowska (Wypijewska)**, whose husband was employed by Massey Ferguson, and the family of **Czesia Krygiel (Moniak)**, whose husband was employed by Ontario Hydro. The third group consisted of families joining their brothers or sons (young, single veterans from the Polish Second Corps) who had arrived in Canada on two-year work contracts on farms and in forestry. Among those who came to join their brothers were: **Lila Fischer (Wasiuk)**, **Janka Godwood (Kitras)**, **Hela Łomnicka (Kitras)** and **Kazia Burdzy (Krzyżaniak)**.

Much has been written in the publications of the Association of Polish Combatants about the situation of these demobilized soldiers from the Italian campaign who had won the final battle for the German stronghold at Monte Cassino. These men found it hard to live with the bitter disappointment felt at the turn of events which deprived their country of freedom, for which they had fought alongside the Allies. The unfortunate circumstances of their arrival in Canada, and their exhausting work for minimum pay, were described in detail by Edward Sołtys and Benedykt Heydenkorn in their book *Trwanie w Walce* (Persistence in Struggle). The authors recounted some of the incidents arising from the harsh treatment of these young war veterans by the farmers who were used to the free labour of German prisoners of war. "When a large group of them arrived in Lethbridge (Alberta), their train was halted before reaching the railway station and surrounded by guards, who had previously served in a camp for German POWs. Nobody was allowed to approach the train. Later the Poles were taken to the, by then, vacant POW camp and they were not even allowed to leave it, till later after some interventions. The newly arrived Poles were treated as a replacement for German POWs.; a fact which was not acknowledged publicly."

I had the opportunity to hear about the difficult beginnings of these demobilized soldiers who had arrived in Canada on farm-work contracts, from one of them, Mr. S. Kochan, who visited me in Toronto. The feelings of humiliation and sorrow have troubled him for half a century. Exasperated, Mr. Kochan recalled how a farmer's wife had been comparing him in a disparaging way to Hans, the German prisoner of war, and how he had tried to defend himself in broken English: 'Me, Polish veteran!'

It was a well known fact that not all demobilized soldiers were treated equally in Canada. New immigrants were not entitled to the same benefits as other Allied veterans who lived in Canada before World War II. They only became entitled to these benefits after 10 years residence in Canada

There were approximately 4,000 Polish veterans from Italy who had immigrated to Canada after World War II. In the course of time, as their living conditions improved, they became fond of this country and adopted it as their second homeland.

A popular Polish saying states that there is nothing bad that cannot be turned into good.

Eventually, the needs of the diverse ethnic communities in Canada were addressed, and, with the establishment of the Ministry of Multiculturalism, discrimination of any kind was discouraged. Help is now readily available to immigrants taking their first steps in Canadian society.

Most women among the Poles from refugee camps in India, who arrived in Canada after the war, were young married women, seeking immediate employment in an effort to help their husbands in establishing life in a new country. In England, due to the language difficulties, many of them had worked in factories, in spite of having completed or being close to completion of Polish High School in India. Upon arrival in Canada, with no previous work experience, they generally accepted the first job available. I myself had arrived in Toronto on a Saturday, in June 1952, and on the following Monday I began my work as a seamstress in a factory.

As a rule, those who became employed right away had their mothers or, in some cases, their fathers helping them full-time in taking care of small children and housework. Those who did not have such help, usually stayed at home until their children were older, and only then resumed further education or joined the workforce.

According to our recent mini-survey, some were employed in banking from the beginning. Among them were: **Irena Jager (Michalska)**, **Krysia Rytwińska (Wypijewska)**, **Janka Wojniłowicz (Jackiewicz)**, **Dzidka Chełmecka (Sobol)**, **Czesia Krygiel** and **Wanda Truksa (Kaszuba)**. Wanda later achieved the status of a Fellow of the Institute of Canadian Bankers. **Janka Karczuga (Morska)** became employed in banking after completing a secretarial course. **Marysia Kiellerman (Szuber)** attended a commercial school.

Some of those who had at first worked in factories, improved their lot in later years. Among them were: **Oleńka Hałko (Burek)**, Lila Fischer, a bank teller for many years and **Marysia Solecka**, who was employed at the International Division of the Toronto Dominion Bank. Some were employed in nursing. Among them were **Lodzia Wrońska (Moroz)** and **Aniela Różycka (Ołowiecka)**.

Stasia Ołowiecka, her sister Janka and **Ziuta Czerwińska (Bednarska)**, were employed in clerical work; Ziuta in the civil service of the Federal government. Kazia Burdzy, **Stasia Przybyłowska (Krupa)** and **Krysia Tomaszewicz (Kuchcicka)**, were employed in clerical capacity in large department stores.

Those who had business inclinations became self-employed. Stasia Krukowska (Bratkowska), had a hairdressing salon in Hamilton, and **Kazia Faruniarz (Postek)** and her husband, ran a grocery store. **Jadzia Zawadzińska (Wojniłowicz)** and her husband, started by purchasing a rental house and later grocery store. After selling the grocery store they bought a summer resort, which they operated for 25 years. During the winter months, they both held jobs in Toronto, Jadzia in clerical work.

Gienek Dybczak, in addition to his work at Ontario Hydro, performed the duties of an organist at St. Casimir's Church in Toronto for forty years

Some pursued higher education and professional careers. **Leszek Truksa** had arrived in Canada as a research scientist on contract with FCL, and subsequently enrolled at the Department of Chemical Engineering at the University of Waterloo. After his thesis on chemical reactors, he obtained his MSc degree, and then a PhD. Presently, Leszek is president of I-T Inc.

Danuta Polak became a medical doctor, practising her profession in Toronto.

Well-known to us were the achievements of **Danuta Bieńkowska (Czech)**, who obtained her PhD in Polish literature, and in the last years of her life was employed as a lecturer at the Department of Slavonic Studies at the University of Toronto. Danuta also wrote articles for the Polish press, and poetry in Polish and English. After her early and tragic death on a cable railcar during a skiing holiday in Norway in 1974, a collection of her poetry and prose, *Między Brzegami* (Between the Shores) was published at the initiative of the Polish Canadian Research Institute.

Janina Radalus (Tabaczyńska), had obtained her 'Cambridge Papers' in England, and in Canada studied psychology and languages.

Janina Wadoń (Łochowska) studied English literature at the University of Toronto, and subsequently was employed as a translator-analyst at the R.C.M.P. division of intelligence service (during the years of Communist rule in Poland). She also translated articles of Polish writer W. Gombrowicz, and still continues to translate.

Most of the above information about education and work experience concentrates mainly on those who live in Toronto and its vicinity. It could probably apply as well to others who settled in different parts of Canada, but only some of them keep in touch.

Wadoń family in 1970, Janina in the middle

Bogdan Czaykowski, a well-known poet, translator and critic of Polish literature, was employed as a lecturer and later, in the years 1974-97, as Head of the Department of Slavonic Studies at the University of British Columbia in Vancouver. He recently published the masterfully edited *Anthology of Polish Poetry Abroad, 1939-1999*.

Bożena Heczko (Sito), made a forty-year career for herself in Montreal at the National Film Board of Canada in Montreal, where, through the process of learning on the job, she became an animator, filmmaker, and finally a director. After directing a couple of documentary films: Pictures *Out of my Life* and *Laugh Lines* (one of them shot in the Canadian Arctic), she returned to animated films, among which her best were: *A Special Letter* and *Children Speak*.

Zosia Zawidzka had first gained experience in the clinical laboratories of hospitals in Montreal and Ottawa and later was employed for 26 years in the laboratories of the Sir Frederick Banting Research Centre, where she authored and co-authored many publications in comparative haematology and toxicology. Zosia took early retirement to enable her to devote more time to her work in various organisations defending Christian values, the preservation of wildlife and the environment. She is a Benedictine Oblate of Christ the King Convent, a co-founder of the Committee of Relief for Polish Missions (1974) and chairperson of a team of editors of the Hyacinth Mission Quarterly. The Committee began its activity by establishing contact with two missions in Africa and a leper care centre in India. Currently it helps 200 centres in 33 countries. Financial aid sent to the Missions up to and including year 2000, amounted to $700,000 CDN. For her dedication in the service of the Church, Zosia has been distinguished with the Papal Cross - Pro Ecclesia et Pontifice. In her book of poetry, *Czarne bzy* (Black Lilacs) published in Canada in 1995, the prevailing themes are philosophical and spiritual contemplations about God, eternity and nature. Some of her poems, translated into English, form a part of an anthology of Canadian poetry: *Symbiosis - an Intellectual Anthology of Poetry*.

Although most of us have retired from employment by now, we still try to be useful members of the communities in which we live. Indeed, the moral principles implanted in us in our Polish schools in India, have inspired us throughout our lives to participate in social, cultural and charitable work wherever we lived.

Janina Gładuń (Sułkowska) was very active in the work of the Polish community in Canada - the Canadian Polonia. Before moving to Toronto, she taught at the Polish school in St. Catherines, and for twelve years performed the duties of headmistress. She was an active member of the Association of Polish Teachers in Canada, editor of the Teachers' Bulletin, and chairperson on the board of editors who prepared text-books for Polish schools in Canada. She was also editor and co-author of the collective work Polska Wczoraj i Dziś (Poland Yesterday and Today). For her work Mrs. Gładuń was awarded a silver and gold Medal of Honour by the Canadian Polish Congress, a Silver Cross of Merit by the Government of the Polish Republic, and also a Volunteer Service Award.

Among those who took an active part in volunteer work at the Polish Combatants Association Centre in Toronto were Zuzia Wacyk (Gac), Dzidka Chełmecka (Sobol) and Lila Fischer. Zuzia and Dzidka also participated in the work of the Polish charitable organisation, known as 'Opieka Społeczna' (Social Welfare). The volunteers of the Opieka Społeczna have been collecting, packing and sending used clothing to the needy people in Poland for many decades.

Wanda Truksa (Kaszuba), **Czesia Krygiel** and **Stasia Rumińska (Jundziłł)**, have been more recently active in various Polish organisations and voluntary work, including raising funds for Polish-Canadian children and organising church bazaars. Wanda and Czesia received awards for their participation in the charitable work of the Marie Curie-Skłodowska Foundation, which had been established by a group of women from the first wave of Polish immigrants.

Basia Charuba (Morawska) and Stasia Kunicka, presently Sister Maria Alfonza, help in the care of seniors in Polish parishes: Basia in Ottawa, and Stasia at the Copernicus Lodge in Toronto. Stasia also taught in Polish schools at St. Casimir's Parish.

Oleńka Hałko (Burek) and her husband, Leszek, were one of the families who privately sponsored the first refugees from Poland after the December 1981 imposition of martial law by the Soviet controlled Polish Communist government in response to the Solidarity workers' movement for free trade unions, freedom to strike, free press, etc.. In Polish publications, and more importantly in the Canadian press, we often come across the name of Leszek Hłasko, safeguarding the good name of Poland by rectifying false or misleading information.

Janina Wadoń, was actively involved in the life of the Canadian community on Toronto Island, where she and her family lived for 27 years. Among other things, she volunteered in the long-term care of a disabled, bedridden member of the community, and took part in the political campaign to save the island homes from expropriation.

Zosia Stohandel (Balawender) has been known among the Canadian Polonia for her involvement in the Polish Boy Scouts and Girl Guide Association. Having arrived in Canada as an experienced Guider, she became the chief Guide leader of the Polish Girl-Guide Group in Canada, as well as the leader of the Girl-Guide Troop 'Watra', and an organiser of Scout camps. Together with her husband, Zosia edited Wici, a publication of Polish Scouting in Canada. Aside from Scouting, she has been active in the Canadian Polish Congress.

Also involved as leaders in Polish Scouting in Canada were Stasia Ołowiecka in Ontario and **Janina Zygiel (Jankowska)**, in Edmonton.

Polish Scouting in Canada has established the base for its summer activities near the oldest Polish parish in Wilno, Ontario, in the midst of the Barry's Bay region, known as Kaszuby. The area is populated by the fourth generation of Polish Kaszubs, who emigrated to Canada in the second half of the nineteen century. It is a heavily forested terrain, interspersed with rolling hills and many lakes - an excellent natural environment for summer camps or cottages. It was explored

D. Pniewska, J. Zygiel, Z. Stohandel and S. Ołowiecka

and chosen as the site for Polish Scouting in 1951, by the members of one of the Senior Scouting Groups, known as Krąg Tatry. In 1952 Krąg Tatry organised the first gathering and conference of Polish Senior Scouting in Canada, on one of the Kaszub farms, in the vicinity of Wilno. Among the participants of this mini-jamboree were the newly arrived in Canada Scoutmasters and instructors, including **Zosia Stohandel**. In 1953 some of the land at Kaszuby was acquired as real estate property for the Order of Franciscans, and since then some of it has been rented to Polish Scouting annually for summer camps. Soon after, more land was purchased by the Polish Scouting Association. In both cases, the large lots were bought either from the Kaszub farmers or Crown Land. The land for the Franciscans was acquired by one of its priests, Father Rafał Grzondziel, with the intent of establishing a Catholic Youth Centre; which he duly built with the volunteer help of Kaszub farmers, Krąg Tatry, and Polonia. Father Grzondziel - a former army chaplain and Scoutmaster from the Polish Second Corps - played an important role at Kaszuby as spiritual leader of Polish Scouting. But the pioneer in recruiting, organising and leading Polish youth and children in the earliest Polish Scouting movement in Canada (1951-1953) were the experienced Scoutmasters and instructors of Senior Scouting, among them **Zosia Stohandel** and members of Krąg Tatry.[1] The membership in Polish Scouting in Canada has substantially increased after the arrival of post-Solidarity immigration in the early 1980s. The Senior Scouting Group Tatry changed the nature of its activities with the passing, and has become more of a senior social group, bound by the Scouting ideology and lasting friendship. A number of Poles from India are among its more recent members.

A popular song refers to Poles abroad as "dry leaves scattered around the world", but somehow there have always been ways of gathering these "leaves", so that they would not disperse too far. From the beginning of our life in Canada, we were recognizing familiar faces, exchanging news about friends from the past, and making contacts. I still remember these unexpected and surprising meetings in churches, at dances, and in the street. Our reunions of the Association of Poles in India, which are organised every two years, give us an excellent opportunity to rekindle old friendships. One of the earliest was held in Toronto in 1978.

The years pass so fast now - bringing with them memories of the past. I feel that by now we can not expect all of our aspirations and dreams to come true, but rather face the realities of life, keep on improving our lot, and enjoy each day. And I believe that most Poles from India who live in Canada, share my view that we have never regretted our decision to settle in this country - the most democratic country in the world. As if to offset the trauma of our forced exile in the past, the good Lord has allowed us to draw joy from the plentiful blessings of life in our adopted homeland.

Translated and edited by Janina Wadoń (Łochowska)

NOTES:

1) Brief summary, edited and translated from J. Grodecki's *"Krąg Tatry - Historia"*

USA
by Irena Metelica (Hajduk)

Our departure for the USA had a special meaning for me, as it was the first independent travel in my life. There was no involvement of UNRRA, no registration, official lists, transport arrangements or organised groups and no transit camps. We travelled on our own, no one was interested in us.

I need to mention that I am describing exclusively our own experiences after arrival in the USA. Ex-servicemen, who came to the USA following signing of a special law by President Truman, travelled individually or in groups and their experiences differed substantially from ours.

Our ship *Ile de France* reached New York on the 5th March 1951. From New York we went by train to Chicago. We were dressed in clothes suited to the English weather, while here it was beautiful and warm. My husband's friend Henio met us at the Union Station wearing a grey summer suit. The temperature was above 90°F. This lovely weather lasted only three days and then changed to an intense cold. The winds blowing from Lake Michigan were the worst. Now we understood why Chicago is known as the "Windy City".

In England we left a circle of close friends and we missed them greatly. Henio was married to an Italian girl, a professional teacher, who had not yet learned English. Whenever we met, our husbands talked about their heroic days in Italy while we communicated by sign language and a few Latin, Italian or English words.

Our Henio had a modest apartment and a four month old baby so we stayed with their friends for a few days. Next, with some help from an American neighbour, we rented a "kitchenette apartment". It was a large room with carpets and lounge furniture. One door led to a fully equipped kitchen, while the other door, on opening, would release a hidden folding bed. This suited us perfectly, as we had no furniture of our own.

On Saturday mornings we could hear vacuum cleaners being used by some young people cleaning stairways. Later we learned that they were the children of our landlord who were students at Chicago universities. In Europe it would be considered unusual for the children of an owner of thirty apartments to be helping with the cleaning. It turned out that Mr. and Mrs. Furman spoke excellent Polish and had lived in Chicago for 40 years. We then realized that their English sounding name, Furman, was of Polish origin, derived from a word for "coachman".

A few days later my husband got a job as a draftsman but it turned out that the firm was going to be closed for a two week holiday. Taking into account our situation, my husband's boss offered him a job painting fences around the building during that period. And so it happened that he and a Polish

The Chicago group

Army Major, who arrived from Germany, worked very happily together getting a wonderful suntan. Seeing his suntan others wondered how we could afford a holiday in Florida. The job lasted only a short time, but the Major remained our friend for many years. My husband's next job was in a former machine-gun factory that had been converted to the production of printing machines.

After spending a couple of lonely weeks at home I ventured 'downtown' and, map in hand, found the labour agency. Within hours I was employed in a bank's loan section. My new boss was a demobilised American officer, who during the war fought alongside the Poles. He was very friendly and promised every necessary help. My immediate supervisor was an English woman married to an American pilot.

In 1952 a Congressional Commission investigating the case of the Katyń massacre arrived in Chicago. With the permission of my boss, I attended the investigation and, quite unexpectedly, became one of the witnesses. I finished the day with an appearance on television. Next day there were long articles in the press. I stood in the train, seeing my big picture in the paper, but none of the readers recognized or took any notice of me, that's how short lived my fame was. The Katyń case is always very close to my heart as it was there that I lost my father.

As a result of the newspaper articles, **Irena Krajewska**, a former Girl-Guide leader, now living in Chicago got in touch with me.

We began to travel to the Northern side of Chicago where the whole Polish community congregated. Today the district is known as 'Polanowo'. The Circle of Self-Help, founded by Polish refugees from Germany who arrived some years before us, was very active. They felt more at home than we did, but because of language difficulties, they preferred the Polish district. Very often they worked in Polish enterprises, a situation not very conducive to learning English. The Association of Polish Veterans was already in existence, as was the well-organised Polish Scouts movement.

From the outset, our emigration had, due to our economic situation, contacts with the old Polish community. The old community came here during WWI or even earlier. They asked us from which 'guberniya' - an administrative unit of territory occupied by one of the three foreign powers, which ruled over the partitioned Poland at the time when they left home. They could not quite understand that our position as political immigrants, particularly of the ex-servicemen, was different from their own. Greater misunderstandings occurred within the private sphere, e.g. between the landlord and the lodger. But the differences were soon erased. Our organisations amalgamated with "The Congress of American Poles" and "Polish National Association" in Chicago.

Our first care was for unity amongst the very large Polish group. The first united action was the 3rd May Parade, beautiful, enormous and colourful. Over the years our children and veterans took part in the parade, but now, whoever still has enough strength, attends.

The end of the fifties was very difficult. Many firms closed due to the change of production from war materials to consumer articles. Many people lost their jobs; the first in line were newcomers. But it did not last long. Soon people from our immigrants, started to buy homes, cars and began looking for better jobs. We kept up contacts with the Polish Community, had many friends, but among them was no one from India.

On leaving England we bade farewell to all our acquaintances by placing a few words in a Polish newspaper. As a result we received a letter from **Jagoda Królikowska** from Syracuse, NY. At last a kindred soul was found. We visited her in 1957. Her whole family was there. There were also a number of people from Valivade and the family of **Prof. Suszyński** lived nearby. Polish ex-servicemen continued to arrive in Chicago. Our boys of conscription age, although they did not possess American citizenship, were enlisted in the American Army and fought in Korea. One young man refused to respond to the call up papers into the American army and as a result, there was a lot of antagonism and unpleasantness towards Poles and other ethnic nationals.

The situation in Poland was not promising and after five years most of us took up American citizenship. It often helped in obtaining a better job. But as far as studies were concerned, the situation was very difficult. Fees were very high and the possibility of obtaining a scholarship was minimal. But slowly, studying at night, some completed their studies. They paid the fees themselves or were partly subsidised by firms. My husband was one of them.

After a year my mother arrived from England. I worked for a large insurance firm, which covered my mother's medical expenses when she was very ill in the sixties. In our situation the medical cover was very helpful, as the cost of medical treatment was very high. At that time there was no medical cover for the retired or old people in America. Medical care then was very good, which cannot be said of the present state of things.

Children were growing up. Polish Saturday schools became active as well as the Polish Scout camps. Very active and helpful in the Scouting movement were **Czesław** and **Wanda Kojro** – our Wanda Tomas from Valivade.

At that time our family lived through a very interesting time. My husband worked in a government firm designing 'guided missiles'. After checking all our private documents and investigating all our friends and acquaintances in England, we were put under 'protection'. After our visits to friends, the FBI used to appear on their doorstep although we never saw anyone following us. When, in 1961, my husband's mother died in Poland, he was refused permission to travel there. Alas, the job ended when the firm moved to Philadelphia, but we did not want to. My husband soon found another position in which, as a vice president, he remained until his retirement.

Because of my husband's frequent official travels we moved to a suburb near O'Hare airport. I began working four hours a day for a firm which had very good conditions for working mothers. If it was necessary, I could take my girls with me to work. I worked there for twenty years and took early retirement when in a position of a chief accountant. I kept in touch with the firm until it came under Japanese ownership.

Our Association of Poles from India in Chicago was founded in 1980 through the initiative of **Lonia Bogdanowicz**, **Marysia Janiszewska (Shannon)** and myself. Its character was social. At first there was great interest and we enjoyed good attendances. It transpired that most of the young people who attended were young boys who had come with Fr. Bobrowski and had been placed in schools in Orchard Lake, Michigan State. Not many of them became priests, but they finished their education and today enjoy a good life style. **Fr. Błażej Karaś** OFM, our school friend from India, works among the homeless and alcoholics.

In our Valivade group the majority were girls who married ex-servicemen. We used to all meet once a year, but see each other occasionally during the many Polish shows and pageants.

I imagine every one of the 'Indians' knows of 'druh Ryś' (now **Monsignor Peszkowski**), who studied and lectured for many years at the Orchard Lake Seminary near Detroit. **Dr. Maria Borońska**, our School Principal in Valivade, found herself in Detroit. Her Polish philology doctorate was of no use in finding work in her profession. She worked at the Ford Hospital, first as a Nurse's -Aid, and later as a laboratory assistant. After some time she was sent on a haematology course, which she finished with excellent results. The hospital had a valuable worker for the next 23 years. Dr. Borońska died on 3rd Oct. 1998.

Living in Chicago we lead a double life. From different parts of the city we, like birds, flock together to take part in the Polish community life. Afterwards we return to our American nests.

Now most of us are retired. As long as we have strength, we visit Poland, travel and look after our grandchildren. Our life is spent within families, socially with friends and we delight in each encounter.

THE OTHER "INDIANS" WHO SETTLED IN THE STATES WRITE:

Sister Nora-Marie (Honorata Syberyjska) who entered a Bernardine convent:

"I belong to a group of 50 girls, who left India in March 1946 and, at the beginning of 1947, found ourselves at a convent of Bernardine nuns. At first almost half of us chose convent life but with time, only 11 remained. The majority of us were educated as teachers or hospital workers. I worked 44 years as a teacher, 4 of them in Liberia, West Africa. I have been working for the past three years in a parish as a 'Christian Service Co-ordinator'. It is a job similar to a social worker, but adapted to parish needs. I am always studying. I am now almost 69 years old, but as long as we can work, we do not retire.

Present convent life has changed radically from the convent life we entered into. The very strict rules, which now appear to me to be impracticable, gave way to a life so free, that it is difficult to believe. The greatest changes occurred in vows of poverty. Before, we worked for ten cents or for nothing and depended on charity for the existence of the congregation. No nun could keep the smallest donation for herself. Even when travelling, if we found ourselves in some difficulty, we had to beg someone for ten cents to make a telephone call. Now we receive $75 a month for our personal needs, which does not include food and medicine, and even in some cases, we can ask to keep the charitable donation.

We also have a choice of what we wear: we can wear a traditional habit or lay clothes. The rules for contacts with family have also changed. Previously it was permitted to visit one's family only once every three years but now we can visit every year, even twice a year, if the family covers the cost of travel. Because my family lives overseas, I could not see them at all. Now I can visit them once every three years.

As I have no contact with Polish language, our Association's bulletin which I receive, is extremely important to me."

Eugeniusz Bąk:

"A number of Valivade "Indians" settled in various parts of the United States, some in Cleveland Ohio. They became active in Polish organisations, championing Polish causes. The most notable was Pani Janina Ptak, a teacher and Scout activist in India. She continued to teach the Polish youth and together with her husband, was involved in their activities.

Eugeniusz Bąk, after finishing his studies, worked for an international chemical company as an executive and upon retirement became a co-founder of the Polish American Cultural Centre. He wrote a book about his experiences during the war "Life's Journey", published by the Columbia University Press.

Eugeniusz and his wife

Cleveland became a home for other Indians, notably **Alina Czernec (Bąk)**, who is very active in the Cultural Centre and other youth groups, **Karolina Krawczyk (Bąk)**, **Anna Nowak (Bąk)**, **Wiktoria Zimnicka (Pipalo)**, **Helena Różycka (Klimczyk)**, **Regina** and **Jerzy Stolarczyk**, and **Albin** and **Jadwiga Czechowicz**.

Wanda Kojro (Tomas) sent recently some information about her family, who arrived in Detroit in Dec.1951 and about many other Indians, who settled in the USA. She worked for a time at Henry Ford Hospital together with Mrs. Borońska. She later moved to Chicago where she met **Danka Ostrowska (Dziedzic)** and her sister **Krystyna Wiktorowicz**, both married with children. Danka and another friend from Valivade, **Oleńka Środulska (Panek)** became godmothers to Wanda's twins born in 1954.

Mrs. Skórzyna, our teacher in Valivade, arrived in Detroit from Africa in the late 1950s and worked in the Detroit Library for a time, but after suffering a stroke, was moved to a nursing home in Florida by her doctor daughter, where she died.

" I met many more girls from Valivade at various Veterans' Reunions, as most of us had married ex-soldiers from Gen. Anders' 2nd Corps. Some of the friends I was reunited with at these gatherings were: **Urszula Szatan (Korol)**, **Cecylja Ropa (Jajko)**, **Irena Szwaglis (Siara)** and her husband **Witek**, **Gutka Piechuta (Kwiatek)** whom I hardly recognised, as I knew her as a little girl and she was now a tall, beautiful young lady.

Marysia Shannon (Janiszewska) arrived in Chicago from Australia and started looking for friends from India. Once she invited **Helcię Wapiennik (Tomasiewicz)**, who had married in England, then left for Argentina, but after several years moved to the state of Connecticut in the USA to join the rest of the family. Helcia visited me several times, despite the fact that we live over 1000 miles apart, because she loves to fly. My children belonged to the Polish Scouting organisations in Chicago. I myself joined the Friends of the Polish Youth Organisation (KPH) and held several different positions, ending with the Presidency, which I held for several years. It was through this volunteer work with the Scouts, that I met Irenę Metelica (Hajduk), who started the (Chicago Indian Association). At our first reunion in 1981 I met more people from Valivade: **Lala Russ (Szymel)**, **Basia Firley (Sokołowska)**, the **Malec** sisters **Danka** and **Dzidka** and their brother **Leszek**, **Marysia Wypijewska's** brother **Dennis**, **Ryszrd Godlewski**, **Irka Swiderska**, **Maryla Kurowska (Synowiec)**, **Helena Suszko**, **Waleria Chentoryska (Sciber)** and her sister **Lonia Bogdanowicz**, **Czesia Wolf (Kosmala)** and her sister **Amelia**, (their mother attended all our reunions despite being over 90 years old).

Dennis Wypijewski and his wife **Marysia** were very helpful in distributing the Polish edition of our book in their neighbourhood

Our Association organised a beautiful banquet for our 20th anniversary, which was attended by over 300 people. Soon after it was dissolved; both Lonia and Irena, who acted as presidents have died. We still have our Secretary, **Kazia Bargiełowska (Mickiewicz)**, whom we call if we need any information. Some of our ladies still meet once a month in a restaurant for lunch and to talk, but as we are getting older, travelling becomes more difficult.

After 45 years in Chicago, and now a widow, I moved to Rockford, Illinos, 70 miles away to be close to my daughter and her family. Here I met yet another friend from high school in Valivade, **Teresa Domańska (Konopko)**. She and her husband **Mieczysław** turned out to be very helpful neighbours.

Time never seemed to pass so fast as it does now. Is it because I am always busy... or am I starting to get old?"

Dyzio in US army uniform

ARGENTINA
by Mieczysława Popławska (Truksa)

Having left India we arrived in Great Britain. At the outset, in Liverpool, we were welcomed by a penetrating cold. The refugee camp, then in the process of establishment, did not have heating or any other necessary comforts. Even when the situation improved, we sorely missed our time spent in India, even the heat and the monsoonal rains.

What predisposed us to a further emigration were the unpleasant climate, the monotonous life and work, and the arrogance of the staff at the Labour Exchange. Emigration to Canada required £2,000 in capital and questions on the application form such as 'Can you plough?' and 'Can you milk?' were not very encouraging. Australia, although warm and affluent, at the outset presented immigrants with various formal difficulties. In the end the choice was Argentina – a country of vast expanse of arable soil and varied climate, from subtropical to temperate and whose Latin culture was closer to our own.

In 1951, following my husband's demobilisation, we left for Argentina. The three week sea journey on the comfortable English ship *Andes* was a well deserved holiday after three years spent labouring in the misty Isles. Sailing south we experienced the climatic changes and the differences between the ports. From cold stony Cherbourg to a sunny Lisbon and then to the unbelievably beautiful tropical Rio de Janeiro. Nearing the port of Buenos Aires we saw a flat land from which arose an unending expanse of suburban buildings. My husband's friends, who arrived here earlier, helped us in the first days of our arrival in that huge city of 11 million people.

President Peron then governed Argentina. In his two terms of office Argentina changed from a single rural economy to a rural-industrial one. During these years a large number of immigrants from Europe, mostly Italians, arrived in Argentina. The existing Polish community, numbering 70,000, increased by 18,000. In the climate of expanding industry, Polish engineers and technicians had no problem in obtaining work. The Polish firm Adelfia, which had input into the electrification of Argentina, deserves a special mention.

In those days banks were advancing loans on easy terms for the building of private houses, starting businesses or purchase of plant and machinery. There was plenty of work available and qualifications were not asked for. On that basis my husband, together with a Polish journalist and a Polish economist worked for two years as self-employed roof constructors and carpenters. I was employed as a decorator in a Polish owned factory producing home-wares. In time, with the advance of plastic production, we borrowed money and opened our own factory where, until 1982 we produced small plastic articles and artificial jewellery. After the fall of Peron the economy gradually went down. A free market and the dumping of overseas goods paralysed the local economy and forced many factories and workshops, including our own, to close. Following his retirement, my husband worked on a casual basis as a travelling salesman. During those years many Polish people left Argentina, bound mainly for the USA and Canada and some went to Australia. Some, of advanced years, returned to England.

From the outset, the post-war Polish immigration invigorated the local Polish community life. The previously moribund Federation of Polish Associations, an umbrella for various Polish organisations in Argentina, moved into its own magnificent building in the centre of Buenos Aires. Its official forum is the weekly *Głos Polski*. The issue *Niezależny Kurier Polski*, to which my husband and I contributed, ran for 19 years. In *Kurier*, apart from endeavouring to give honest information about events in Poland, we also supported the building of millennium schools in the Western Regions of Poland, the return of the Wawel treasures to Poland and the reconstruction of the Royal Castle in Warsaw. The two great achievements of the local Polish community were the establishment of the Ignacy Domeyko library and the Polish Club in which lectures and social events are held. Through the initiative of Jan Kobylanski the organisation USOPAL (which embraces all Polish organisations in Latin America from Mexico to Argentina) came into existence.

BELGIUM

Gustaw Pasternak who settled in Waterloo, Belgium wrote about himself:

"We left Valivade in the middle of December, 1947. We travelled from Bombay to London aboard the Orient Line ship ss *Ormonde*. In the middle of January 1948, after a very interesting month's journey across the Indian Ocean, the Red Sea, the Mediterranean and the Atlantic, we landed in Tilbury, England. After a short stay in the Melton Mowbray camp, we moved to France in March 1948 to the town of Le Mans, where our father found himself following his imprisonment by the Germans in Wilno and a period of forced labour on the Atlantic Wall. Father died a year after our arrival. In spite of a difficult situation, I finished technical college in Le Mans.

In 1956 I commenced studies in Strasbourg (ENSAIS), which I completed in 1960 specialising in electronics. I commenced my professional career in the oil industry in Hassi-Messaoud (French Sahara), then I worked on the design and building of offshore drilling platforms. For 15 years I was an independent consultant to oil firms, mainly in the North Sea and the Persian Gulf.

In 1987, because of my work, we moved from Versailles to Waterloo. Soon after the move I had to interrupt my work because of chemically induced illness."

FRANCE
Rev. Roman Podhorodecki (Society of Christ)

Roman finished his first year of high-school in Balachadi, then with eight other boys, was sent for further study to the St. Mary's High School in Mount Abu, run by Christian Brothers from Ireland.

In 1944 he returned to his family in Valivade and entered the third year of high school. When, at the beginning of 1945, the Polish Naval School was opened in England, Roman, together with other boys, applied. He also put his name on a list of boys for the Polish Seminary in Orchard Lake in USA. Both groups of boys waited for transport in Bombay. The Consul General, Mr. Banasiński, tried to persuade Roman and three other boys to choose between the two such diverse study directions. But they made up their minds, that they would go with the first group that departs. The Naval School won.

In England they studied two and half years, graduating as third officers in 1947. Roman sailed around the world till 1950 but it was not his intention to permanently remain a sailor. Upon his return to England he lived with his mother in Fairford Camp where he worked in the local electricity generating board.

In the camp's common room he happened upon a leaflet inviting boys with matriculation certificates to study at the Polish Seminary in Paris. As his work in the powerhouse has just ended, he decided to go to Paris. When his mother asked "What for?" he answered "I haven't been there yet and have heard that Parisian women are the most beautiful." But he took with him all his school certificates and documents. On his way to the Seminary a 'Parisian girl' proposed to show him Paris, but he refused, saying he was on his way to become a priest. The rector admitted him straightaway. The date was 28th June 1953.

After three years the rector suggested a pause in study. Roman returned to England and worked at Harrods for two years. But he never lost his desire to become a priest and following his contact with the Order of the Society of Christ (inaugurated by Cardinal Hlond after WWI for pastoral care of Polish emigrants), he returned to Paris to complete his studies at his own expense. For the next three years he prepared 30 Polish immigrant lads for matriculation in the Roubaix school, near Lille, teaching religion, Polish and English.

In September 1961 he completed his novitiate and took his vows. His fourth year theology study was completed in the Catholic Institute in Paris. He was ordained by Bishop André Parenty of Boulogne on 26th December 1963. His first parish was in Bruay near Lille. In 1968 he bought the Tour de Lambre tower, a ruin dating back to 1503, which he renovated and called it 'his castle'. But before he completed the renovation he was sent to Aulnay-sous-Bois, where he spent the next 10 years.

Father Roman writes "…At that time my parish territorially was larger than Paris. There I managed to get a house from some nuns in return for a promise to have it refurbished every 2 years. I stayed in that parish for 10 years. I used to travel to 28 different places where Poles lived. During that time I ruined my heart, which to this day is defective, but it also toughened me, as there were groups of troublesome communists of different sorts, as well as many good people.

I returned to Bruay in 1978. The Order of the Society of Christ, numbering 27, is under the authority of the Polish Catholic Mission in Paris. Our aim is to maintain Polish culture among the Polish immigrants, recognising that there is now a fifth generation of Frenchmen of Polish descent whose ancestors came here from western and central districts of Poland between the years 1921-25. Apart from them, there are so-called Westphalians, who owned up to their Polish ethnicity - in spite of their German speech - and to whom the French gave better contracts and better working conditions. These people suffered during the WWII, but there were also incidents of co-operation with Germans. These individuals had to leave after the war. The 1921-25 emigration had the support of the Polish Government, which guaranteed them a Polish priest, school and parish. The year 1993 was the 30th anniversary of my priestly work."

ITALY

Two Valivade girls, who took Holy Orders, found themselves in Rome. **Marysia Leśniak**, now Sister Benedykta, joined the Sisters of Nazareth in Pitsford, England, in 1950 and was assigned to a school just being established. Transferred to the Sisters of Nazareth motherhouse in Rome, she has lived there for many years, lately as Mother Superior. She also works at St. Peter's Basilica, helping pilgrims from all parts of the world, among them 'Polish Indians'.

Sister **Irena Piotrowicz** went on a pilgrimage from England to Rome, where on the 4th September 1950 she joined the Order of Resurrection Sisters. Mother Superior noted Irena's great intellectual potential and sent her to study at a University in Rome. She obtained a masters degree in theology and later diplomas in sacral music and management of novitiate. Between 1968 and 1973 she was in charge of the Novitiate. In 1975 she was nominated the legal representative of the Order in Italy. She also assisted the general Curia, carrying out translations into Italian language. She died suddenly of a heart attack on the 28th June 1994.

Writing about the late Sister Irena in the December 1994 *Biuletyn*, Irena Grunwald-Nowakowska said: "I met her in 1975 during my visit to Rome. I was amazed by her profound knowledge of the history of art, her particular sensitivity to the unique value of each work of art and its meaning set against the background of its times. Her deep knowledge and uniquely sublime way of thinking, testified to her great intellect. Seeking logic and harmony, she reacted with impatience and with disapproval to anything, which in her opinion, was destroying that harmony. Having once expressed her disapproval, she would not carry on with further arguments. During her lectures (Sister Irena was also a teacher and in 1975 was appointed schoolmistress), she was calm, composed and with understanding answered all questions."

Marysia Moro (Łańcucka) went from India to the Koja settlement in Uganda. While in Uganda, she met her future husband, an Italian . After they were married, they spent a further 16 years in Africa because of her husband's work. From Africa they moved to Pakistan, near Karachi, known to her from war times. They used to visit Italy as tourists during vacations. While spending a few days in Rome in 1952, Marysia tossed a coin into the Di Trevi fountain, which, according to a common belief, foretells a return to Rome. And indeed, in 1968, they came back and settled in Rome, where Marysia, now widowed, still lives.

CENTRAL ASIA
(According to the information in the bulletin KPI, Nos. 4 & 10)

His Grace Archbishop Marian Oleś, 'our Indian', was nominated in 1994 papal nuncio for central Asia and Kazakhstan.

The archbishop, who arrived in England from Valivade, finished his high school in England and then studied at the Papal University in Rome where, in 1961, he took holy orders. Next he attended the Lateran University, where he received a doctorate in canon law, and the Papal Academy of Diplomacy. Later on he served in the nunciatures in Ecuador, Indonesia and Portugal.

He accepted his nomination as nuncio for Central Asia reluctantly as, in his opinion, the position needed a younger man. Nevertheless, he found great joy and satisfaction in it. There are about half a million declared Catholics in Central Asia, and possibly the same number of those who are still afraid to own up to their faith. There are Slavs, (among them many Poles), Germans and Koreans, all fervent Catholics, thirsty for religious and sacramental life. The archbishop, when in Samarkand, visited the tomb of Tamerlan (Timur), the 15th century murderer of Christians in Asia, to let him know: we are back!

Inauguration of Arch. M. Oleś at St. Peter's Basilica 6 Jan.1988

In spite of great difficulties including the lack of priests and church buildings, the archbishop was full of hope. He planned to build churches, schools, orphanages and old people's homes.

The greatest achievement of his apostolic work was organising a Papal visit to Kazakhstan, a place, where so many Poles had suffered.

His last position was in Slovenia and Macedonia in the years 2001-2002, when he had to resign his post for health reasons. He died in Poland on 25th May 2005. All the 'Indians' are proud of the fact that he grew up amongst us.

INDIA

A number of Valivade girls married Indian men and settled in India.

Seventeen years old **Wanda Nowicka** from the Orphanage worked as a nurse in a hospital, where she met a medical student, Vasant Kashikar, whose family lived in Kolhapur. They became engaged despite opposition from the British Administration. The Orphanage supervisors had no objections. Vasant's family made secret preparations for an Indian style wedding. Wanda left Valivade on a hired bicycle, to be met by her fiancée's sisters waiting for her. The wedding took place and when on the next day Wanda presented the wedding certificate to the Camp Administration, they had no choice but to accept it. Wanda found herself in a family belonging to the Brahmin cast, whose rules forbid non-Brahmins access to the kitchen. Throughout the first years of marriage Wanda had to conform to this custom. Not until her husband established his own business and they moved to Bombay, was she able to free herself from her mother in law's influence. Theirs is a happy marriage and they have a number of sons. Wanda is a member of the "Association of Poles in India" while Vasanta is active in "The Indian Polish Friendship Society" and took part in discussions with the city officials regarding placement of a Polish commemorative monument in Kolhapur.

Irena Afzil Kahn (Winnicka) married a Pakistani and lived in Karachi (Bulletin 29, p.25)

Roma Biegalska married an RAF pilot, R.H. Chawdry and lived in Jamnagar for some time, then in Kanpur, where her daughter Urszula Farrah was born. Subsequently the daughter applied for a Polish passport in 2003. She visited her mother in England and stayed there for some time, becoming famous for her catering for British Airways, supplying them with 'Roma mushrooms'. She divorced her first husband and married R. Lall, with whom she still lives in Moosoorie.

A number of other Polish-Indian marriages did not endure the test of time.

Wanda Kashikar

This chapter was compiled and edited by Teresa Glazer and translated by B. and M. Trella (with the exception of Great Britain, Canada and Australia)

FRIENDLY GATHERINGS, FORMAL ORGANISATION AND REUNIONS
by Kazimiera Skorupińska (Czarnecka)

After the war only a handful of us returned to Poland, the rest were scattered all over the world. Growing up, studying, starting families, battling with everyday problems took all our energies and concentration. Time was passing.

The five years spent in India bonded us all together with very strong ties. The memories of those friendships, made so long ago in school and Scouting, under the starry Indian skies, survived the test of time. A desire to rekindle them became stronger. The 'Indians', as we call ourselves, started rallying together.

THE FIRST INFORMAL GATHERINGS

One of the first to organise a reunion were members of the **Gen. W. Sikorski Orphanage from Valivade in London in 1954**. The meeting was arranged by Stefania Zawerbna (Kowalczyk) and Józef Zawadzki. It took place in the Polish Catholic Mission at Devonia Road the oldest Polish church in London since 1930. There were present 60 members, among them, the last principal Mr. K. Łęczyński and Mrs. O. Sasadeusz - Head of the Primary School of the Orphanage. Two years later they organised a dinner- dance at Ladbrooke Grove Baths in London.

First meeting: London 1954

The first meeting of all *Indians* who could join took place in **London in 1971.** It coincided with a visit from Poland of our former teacher, Hanka Gwiazdonik (Handerek). Some learned of the meeting from the Polish Daily paper, others by private correspondence. There were representatives from USA and Canada. On the eve of the meeting, the *Indians* gathered at Szczęsna Michałowska's (Orzeł) house, and were trying to recognise each other amid laughter and shouts of joy. There was no talk of the present - we were again in Valivade, we were young and carefree. The evening came to an end all too soon.

Hanka Gwiazdonik (Handerek) at the reception

The reunion proper started with the Mass at the Polish Club in Balham followed by lunch. During the lunch speeches by our former teachers: Mr. M. Goławski, H. Gwiazdonik and M. Czarnecka, made us thoughtful. We are now grateful for their advice, careful education and example they set. We are proud that we kept faith bestowed on us.

The reunion was met with such enthusiasm and pleasure that we decided there and then to continue the meetings as often as possible.

The second meeting in **London in 1973** on the 25th anniversary of our departure from Valivade. It was better organised and attended than the first. This time we met in the Church of the Sacred Heart in Wimbledon. The Mass was celebrated by Fr. J. Przybysz and Fr. Z. Peszkowski (both from Valivade).

After the Mass we gathered in the church hall for coffee, reading greetings, messages, speeches and photographs.

In the evening there was a dinner-dance at the White Eagle Club in Balham. In the happy, carefree atmosphere the reunion came to the end. It was good to be together. That year the first album *The Young in Valivade* was issued. Though the formal reunion was over, the *Indians* from abroad were entertained in private houses for a few more days. A desire to be in close contact with each other led to further meetings, excursions, picnics etc., in the USA, Canada, England and Poland.

At one of these meetings an idea of having a reunion in Toronto came into being. An organising Committee under the leadership of Krystyna Tomaszewicz (Kuchcicka), prepared the agenda and sent out notices. Replies came mostly from Canada, USA and some from England. It was to take place in **August 1978 in Toronto.**

The first morning of the reunion was spent in happy, somewhat emotional atmosphere, getting to know each other all over again. The official part of the reunion was the banquet and the ball in the Club of SPK (Society of Polish Combatants). During the banquet Zosia Stohandel (Balawender), read greetings and introduced the honorary guests, among them the former Headmistress of our grammar school, Dr. M. Borońska. Those present at the banquet were entertained by Basia Charuba (daughter of the *Indian* Barbara Charuba-Morawska).

At Częstochowa

Sunday Mass was celebrated by Fr. Z. Peszkowski, our former Scout master in Valivade. After a sumptuous lunch the 'Kominek', a kind of camp-fire entertainment, but indoors, concluded official reunion. On Monday the 'Indians' from abroad were taken sightseeing in Toronto, Ontario and to Niagara Falls.

Next came a memorable pilgrimage in **Poland in Częstochowa in July 1980** organised by Rev. Fr. Z. Peszkowski and H. Gwiazdonik. It all began at Jasna Góra. There were representatives from the USA, Canada, England and a great number of 'Indians' from Poland. L. Jankowska

(Żyszkowska) reminisces: 'the reunions in England and Canada were youthful, happy and full of laughter, but the Pilgrimage to the Sanctuary of Our Lady of Częstochowa had deeper connotations. It was a spiritual experience. The vigil at the altar of the miraculous icon of Mary Mother of God, where for hundred of years millions of compatriots knelt and prayed with the Kings and Queens of Poland, was unique and unforgettable'.

The visit to the ancient City of Cracow and a meeting with Cardinal Macharski was a lesson in Polish history. The climax of our Pilgrimage was an audience with the Primate of Poland, Cardinal S. Wyszyński.

During the Toronto meeting there were a few people from Jamnagar but they felt outnumbered by crowds of *Indians* from Valivade. Franek Herzog conceived an idea of organising a reunion of former inhabitants of Balachadi near Jamnagar camp. It took three years for the idea to ripen. In April 1981 with the help of Sr. Jacinta (Respondowska) and Halina Prestarz (Hutkiewicz), preparations began. The meeting eventually took place in **August 1981 at Alvering College, Reading, PA in the USA**. The guests of honour were: Fr. F. Pluta, Mrs. J. Ptakowa, Mrs. W. Tyszkiewicz and Sr. Alfonsa - former teachers and carers at the orphanage. Stefan Bukowski, the only representative from Poland, wrote: 'We greeted each other, after 35 years of separation, like a long lost family. Happiness and a deep feeling of friendship abounded. Two days passed too quickly. The exchanged promises of future meetings eased our sadness at parting'.

In July 1987 a reunion was held at **Orchard Lake, Michigan, USA** in which 150 'Indians' mainly from Canada and the USA, but also some from England and Poland participated. The guest of honour was Dr. M. Borońska, former Headmistress of the Grammar School in Valivade. Thanks to Rev. Fr. Z. Peszkowski we had an opportunity to visit the Polish Seminary at Orchard Lake, where some of the Polish boys from India studied. We acquainted ourselves with its interesting history and archives. We also admired mementos and relics of the Second Polish Division from the World War II.

The reunion in Rome in May 1989 was, according to general opinion, the best so far. It lasted the whole week from 20th - 27th May. We stayed in the Polish Pilgrim's House, founded by subscriptions from Poles in the USA and the rest of the world. The friendly welcome made our lively group feel at home. The quiet house echoed with our singing and laughter, shocking the Administration and other pilgrims. However, soon they got used to us, and joined in our celebrations. Best remembered, was the celebration commemorating the 35th Anniversary of Priesthood of Prelate Z. Peszkowski and the 25th of Prelate M. Jagosz, director of John Paul II House for Pilgrims. Short extracts from their lives were read, greetings and flowers, followed by singing and reminiscences of days in Valivade.

Meeting with the Holy Father - Rome 1989

The most memorable were the audiences with John Paul II. First, in the private apartments for 'Indians' from Canada and USA. The general audience in St. Peter's Square with people from all over the World. The second private audience in the Vatican gardens for the 'Indians' from England, with the Mass celebrated by John Paul II. We presented Holy Father with an icon of Our Lady of Ostra Brama carved by A. Klecki.

Lastly a moving visit to Monte Cassino, after which Halina Bąbik (Rafał) wrote the following poem:

> I bowed to the sons of Poland
> Who lie here at Monte Cassino
> At the foot of a famous monastery
> And I asked myself WHY
> Why didn't they fall under the Polish sky?
> Where their mothers and sisters
> Could bring flowers to their graves
> Instead of crossing state after state
> Anniversary days to celebrate
> Look up at the monastery on the top
> Read the inscription on the block
> And question the merciful God
> Why did they have to take this road?
> Why so many of Poland's best
> Amid red poppies came to rest?

Of all the battles of World War II, the battle of Monte Cassino has a special significance for the Polish people. The Allied advance on Rome in 1944 was held up at a point where the main road was dominated by the German fire from an impregnable position in the rocks of a mountain with an ancient monastery on top - Monte Cassino. There had been three unsuccessful attacks by the French, British, Indian, New Zealand troops with heavy losses earlier in the year.

In the fourth battle carried out in May 1944 the Second Polish Corps 45,000 strong, commanded by General W. Anders took part in the assault in which 1,100 guns targeted Cassino. After several fierce attacks, on 18th May the Poles placed their flag on top of the ruins of the monastery. Soon after the Union Jack was flown next to it.

In a fortnight of fighting the Poles lost 281 officers and 3,503 other ranks. In the war cemetery which now stands on the slopes of the hill known as Point 593, there is a poignant inscription:

> We Polish soldiers
> For our freedom and yours
> Have given our souls to God
> Our bodies to the soil of Italy
> And our hearts to Poland.

A song about the *Red Poppies on Monte Cassino* became a sort of second national anthem during the communist years in

Poland when it was not allowed to openly give credit to the Polish forces which fought in the West, under British command.

The reunion in Rome had been organised by Danka Pniewska from London without any back-up from the territory where it was to take place, as there were only two nuns and one married 'Indian' in Rome. It brought into focus a need for an organisation with its own funds, sharing of functions and responsibilities.

SETTING UP OF AN ASSOCIATION

Although the idea to create a formal, worldwide organisation was first mooted after our reunion in 1971, most of us were then too preoccupied with our individual lives and careers to consider it. After the first reunion in London, Szczęsna Michałowska with a small group of supporters urged us to form an association, but the majority was reluctant. Up to now, casual, ad hoc called meetings relied on goodwill of energetic individuals. However with the passage of years we had more time and a stronger urge to belong to a group speaking the same language, no matter in which part of the world we lived.

The first to form a **'Circle of Indians' in 1981**, with regular meetings and a chair person were 80 people living in **Chicago, USA.**

In Poland those who as children lived in Balachadi near Jamnagar, formed the **Jamnagar Club**. In the first years after their return to Poland, there was no time for meetings, social gatherings were frowned upon and in most cases even dangerous. Poland then was under the Communist regime. As the years passed, Stefan Bukowski and Wiesław Stypuła initiated a meeting of former friends from Balachadi orphanage living in Warsaw. Soon the word spread and friends scattered all over Poland, joined them. It was time to legalize their meetings. The organisers called on a non-political Polish-Indian Society and formed, within it, the Jamnagar Club, under the leadership of Wiesław Stypuła. The Club was able to act as an independent unit. Their aims were: to acquaint the Polish community with the historical facts of the exiles in India during World War II, to collect documents and mementos, gather information about other exiles in the Polish settlements in India. In 1980 the members of Jamnagar Club, took part in Częstochowa Reunion. After the reunion their publicity intensified. There were interviews on radio and television, followed by a series of articles in the Press. In November 1983, the first well attended reunion of Jamnagar Club was organised in Warsaw. During the reunion plans were made for future activities - a visit to India, to list and renovate graves there, to fund and erect a commemorative plaque in Balachadi.

It was not until 1990, when most of us had retired, that the circumstances seemed more appropriate. Those of us living in Great Britain took steps to establish an umbrella organisation uniting all *Indians* living on different continents. A provisional Committee was elected, notifications were sent to *Indians* in Australia, Argentina, Canada, England, Poland and the USA. The replies came pouring in. There were 119 applications for membership, many letters commending our venture, others offering help and assistance.

The first General Meeting was held in April 1991 under the chairmanship of I. Mahorowska (Rozwadowska) and most of the original members of the first Committee remained in office: J. Siedlecki as Chairman, W. Kleszko and D. Szydło as Secretaries, J. Pająk as Treasurer, J. Pancewicz - Mutual Aid, L. Bełdowski as Archivist, D. Pniewska as Editor of the Bulletin.

It was agreed that we should be known as "Association of Poles in India 1942-1948" and apart from social gatherings, excursions and bulletins we should provide mutual help to our members. We also decided to start collecting materials for an archive to enable us to publish a book about our experiences. To keep in touch with all members of our Association a newsletter in a form of a bulletin would be published twice a year. To finance these activities an annual subscription would be required. Various social events should be self supporting.

With the Headquarters in London, the Association has branches in Poland, Canada, USA and Australia - 450 members altogether, dispersed throughout the world. By general acclaim the Patrons were to be Dr. M. Borońska, Mrs. A. Gwiazdonik, Fr. Z. Peszkowski and Fr. J. Przybysz. (All now deceased.)

REUNIONS

The first reunion in **Warsaw in July 1992** was very special, because we met in free Poland after 50 years of domination by the Communist Regime. There were members from Australia, Belgium, Canada, England, Italy, Poland and the USA.

The Holy Mass opened the proceedings. The Chairman of the Association in Poland, Jurek Szczawiński, welcomed the invited guests among them the Indian Ambassador. After short speeches came the reports: 'Balachadi and Valivade' by W. Stypuła, 'Odyssey of the Deported' by J. Lampke and 'Indians in the World' by D. Pniewska and L. Bełdowski, followed by a concert of Indian music.

In the evening the camp-fire in Szczęśliwiecki Park, where the atmosphere was steamy, nearly tropical, dark starry sky and brightly burning fire took us wistfully back to India. We felt it deeply, it made us glad to be together again. The second day was devoted to sightseeing: The Old Town, the Royal Palace, Łazienki Park with the statue of Chopin and St. John's Cathedral. Tired but happy of being together again we said our farewells.

May 1994: Fawley Court (nr. Henley) UK

After the last reunion we decided to meet every two years, because the time passes quickly and we are not getting any younger. Fawley Court, once a boys' school, now Pilgrims House, run by Marian Fathers, situated in a beautiful park on the bank of the river Thames, was an ideal place for the Reunion.

After the official Reunion, sightseeing in London: Greenwich Pier (Cutty Sark)

The pre-reunion evening began with a glass of wine and singing accompanied by W. Stetchley on the accordion. Saturday brought in invited guests and families of members. The Reunion as always began with the Mass in the small church, founded by Prince Radziwiłł, in the grounds of Fawley Court. At the official opening, Chairman Idalka Mahorowska, welcomed all assembled, among them Prelate S. Świerczyński, Rector of the Polish Mission in London and the Representatives of the Polish Social Organisations. Then there were short reports of the 'Indian' activities in different countries, followed by a recital, called 'Our Roads' which took us through Russia, Persia, Balachadi and Valivade in poetry and extracts from a book *Krzyż Południa* written by our friend from Valivade J. Krzysztoń.

After lunch we toured an exhibition of photographs collected by J. Siedlecki, and held a seminar organised by T. Glazer and L. Bełdowski about the proposed edition of our book.

On Sunday, during the Mass, we presented the Marian Fathers with an icon of Our Lady, painted by H. Klecka, specially for the Reunion.

There followed a thoughtful hour of the poetry recitation given by the poet Zofia Zawidzka from Canada. The 'Kominek' prepared by the 'Indians', from Poland, with songs, poetry and anecdotes about the life in Poland and abroad concluded the official Reunion.

September 1996: Kraków

Zbyszek Bartosz the Chairman of the 'Indians' in Poland, welcomed the guests and introduced them to a short history of our life in Balachadi and Valivade.

One of the first speakers was Ambassador of India, Shashi Tripati, a charming lady in a red sari who began in Polish 'Brothers and Sisters', which met with a loud applause. Then she said a few words about the Polish-Indian cultural relations, stressing the fact, that India always supported the oppressed without prejudice of their origin or religion. She expressed the admiration for Poles and ended - 'I am proud to call you *Indians*'.

Other speeches followed no less complimentary. The usual campfire evening, with sausages and beer, prepared by the soldiers, concluded the first day. The second day, was set aside for sightseeing, a coach-load went to Wieliczka, the old salt mine, turned into a museum, others full of enthusiasm, braved the rain to see the sights of Kraków. In the evening there was a visit to a cabaret 'Jama Michalikowa'. On Sunday we had an unbelievable treat: A Holy Mass in Wawel Cathedral, where the Polish Kings were crowned. Then a visit to the Crypt, containing the remains of Kings and of great men of Poland. After lunch there was the official ending to our meeting and last embraces and final farewells.

August 1998: Wasilków (nr. Białystok)

Wasilków, 6 km from Białystok, situated on the river Surpaśl, was chosen for our Reunion. After the Mass, Zbyszek Bartosz officially greeted the invited guests; the First Secretary of the Embassy of the Indian Republic, Mr. Subash C. Vohra, prof. A. Stelmachowski, prof. M. K. Byrski, the former ambassador to India. Special welcome was given to S. Polak and K. Matwiejczyk from Australia, who for the first time came to our reunion, and to Poland since the end of the World War II. Next - the speeches. The First Secretary of the Indian Embassy read a letter from the Ambassador in which he said ...'we always treated you as citizens of our Country, you play an important part in Polish-Indian relations, you are our ambassadors in the countries you inhabit'... Prof. Stelmachowski in his speech stressed - 'that it rarely happens for the people to retain the spirit of unity and friendship for so many years in spite of living in so many Continents'. He encouraged us to bring our children and grandchildren to the Reunions. There were more friendly and encouraging speeches.

In the afternoon, we celebrated the 80th birthday of Prelate Peszkowski and assisted in

At the entrance to the Bison Reserve

the planting of an oak tree sapling in the grounds of the hotel. The evening brought traditional campfire entertainment with singing accompanied by the local musicians. We listened to the interesting life story of Fr. Roman Podhorodecki, from the *Orphanage to Priesthood*. Prof. Byrski talked about his contacts with the language and culture of India. The next day there was a trip to Białowieża, the primeval forest with the only bisons surviving in Europe. The last evening was spent reminiscing in the hotel coffee house. On the last day after sightseeing in Białystok, Z. Bartosz officially brought the Reunion to the end, and announced that the next meeting will be in Warsaw in the year 2000.

May 2000: Międzeszyn (Warsaw)

The reunion 2000 was organised at a conference centre in Miedzeszyn, near Warsaw. The facilities were excellent, friendly atmosphere, Polish food resembling home cooking. Besides large groups of members from the UK (31), Canada (16), Poland (51), USA (5), there were 3 people from Australia, one from France, one from Italy and a very unusual visitor from South Africa.

Staszek Harasymów wrote about the most lasting memories of this reunion for the December edition of our bulletin: 'The joy of meeting old friends from Valivade, amazement at their memory of those times spent in India. Slides and talks by Raj Patel and J. Siedlecki about Kolhapur and Balachadi as well as re-enactment of an episode from the book *Ramayana* by the pupils of Jam Saheb High School in Warsaw brought those times back to life'.

Zbyszek Bartosz wrote about the naming of a school after '*their*' Maharaja, Jam Saheb Digvijaysinhji. When asked during their stay in his state, over 50 years ago, how could they repay his kindness to the Polish children, the Maharaja of Jamnagar said jokingly that maybe some time in future they could name a street in Warsaw after him. They decided that not many people bother to find out who the person after whom their street was named was? However, if they name a school after him, the children who were always his special concern, will know about their patron.

There was a solemn ceremony on 20th June 2002 attended by the Indian Ambassador Mr. Nalim Surie, representatives of our Association from Canada, USA and Poland when a high school in Warsaw was named after him.

June 2002: Sobieszewo (nr. Gdańsk)

The venue was Sobieszewo on a wooded island 15 km from Gdańsk, accessible by a pontoon bridge from the mainland. The bridge broke down just before the arrival of our coach so we had to leave our luggage in the coach and walk 4 km to the hotel. Some of our colleagues who arrived a day early by car drove small groups in their vehicles but the rest started singing old marching songs remembered from our Valivade days and plod on. A journalist from programme II of the Polish Radio, Hanna Maria Giza, who came from Warsaw to report on our reunion was impressed by our attitude. She reported to her listeners: 'They just got off the coach and started walking, like they did getting out of Russia during the war'. She interviewed people about their experiences in the USSR, in India and compiled a programme which was later broadcast on 17th September - the tragic anniversary of the date when the Red Army crossed the Polish borders, stabbing the Polish army fighting the Germans in the back.

There were some 18 people who came to one of our reunions for the first time.

Another new feature was the presence of 7 young people, sons and daughters of our *Indians*. Janek Young's 3 daughters were in Poland for the first time. They wrote to our bulletin no.25: "The whole experience of coming to Poland was fascinating, a real mixture. Yes, there are signs of poverty and struggle, especially when contrasted with life in England. But the abiding memory one takes away is the pride and love everyone feels for their country, the depth of people's knowledge and love of their history, religion and land."

The conference was very well organised from start to finish. We sometimes struggled to participate as fully as we wanted to, with no Polish, but the warmth and helpfulness of everyone there meant we still felt very much part of the whole thing. It was a privilege to be able to feel we could become a small part of this wonderful group." Signed Nina, Tessa and Sally.

After the official end of the conference there was a trip organised to Toruń, Gniezno - the cradle of the Polish nation. In Toruń those who took part in the trip were invited by the President of the City for a cruise down the river Vistula, with all the places of historical interest clearly visible.

Sightseeing in Gdańsk (Janek & 2 of his daughters, sat front left)

Some of our Canadian *Indians* who belong to 'Polish Canadian Children Support Group' visited two children's homes: in Toruń and Piława Górna which they help to finance.

Another radio programme for the Pomorze and Kujawy region about us was broadcast on

12th August after Z. Pająk interviewed some of our *Indians*.

During a discussion where to organise the next reunion several venues were proposed, but in the end it was decided that it would again be in Poland. In the south-west this time.

May 2004: Polanica Zdrój (nr. Kłodzko)

A well-known spa in South –Western Poland, near the Czech border, at the foot of the Sudetan mountains was a very good choice for our meeting. Our base was the Nasz Dom hotel, with all amenities for a successful sojourn. There were 19 people, who came to the reunion for the first time and we had the pleasure of the company of our younger generation of children and cousins of the old guard, like Bożenka Pająk, Ewa Glazer, Maryla Zdzienicka, Tomek Konieczny, who captured the best moments of our reunion on film.

There were trips organised to local places of interest, and a walk through the forest to a statue of a bear, near a spring. A legend proclaims that in this place, long time ago, a forester was injured by a bear. After being washed in the waters of the spring, his wounds healed surprisingly quickly. Hence the spa.

Monument to the 'bear'

One outing took us across the Czech border to the *Adrspasskie Skaly*, which were really spectacular.

Some people from our group visited the local grammar school, where a history teacher introduced them as "living history".

They were asked to tell the children about their deportations to the Soviet Union, their stay in India during the Second World War, and settlement in Great Britain, Canada, USA, Italy, after the war ended.

Discussing a possible venue for the next reunion in two years' time, Rome was mentioned, but the majority of members prefer a location in Poland, not only for emotional reasons, but also because it has the most convenient and reasonably priced conference centres, sanatoria. Zbyszek Bartosz and his team put a lot of effort into organising these events and we are very grateful to them.

After the official programme ended, 37 people set out by coach on a trip to Vienna. They visited the Vienna Opera House, the castle at Schonbrunn with all its memorabilia of the Habsburg dynasty, especially the last of them, Franz Joseph, who ruled for 60 years over his vast Empire, St.

Klodzko

Stephen's Cathedral, and tasted Viennese coffee with strudel.

They also visited Kahlenberg on the outskirts of Vienna, where in the 17th century, a Polish King Jan Sobieski, won a great victory over the Turks. Polish Husaria (cavalry clad in armour with wings) stopped Kara Muatafa's army from conquering Europe.

A little church – museum, where Mass had been celebrated before the start of the battle, stood there, with the beautiful background of the Alps and river Danube.

27th May to 3rd June 2006: Nałęczów (nr. Lubin)

This time we gathered in Nałęczów, another spa town, full of interesting museums, palaces, a quaint wooden church, buildings in different ornamental architectural styles, and an enormous park.

For nearly two hundred years this health resort has attracted famous Polish writers like H. Sienkiewicz, B. Prus, and others. The ambiance of this place aided their creativity.

The reunion was well attended (148 people) including some children and grandchildren of our members. The "Energetyk", where we resided, was bursting at the seams.

On Monday 29th May, after Mass celebrated by our chaplain Fr. Z. Peszkowski, the chairman, Zbyszek Bartosz, opened the proceedings by welcoming the invited guests, among whom was Mr.Vinay Kumoca, 2nd Secretary of the Indian Embassy in Poland. In his speech, Zbyszek stressed that the younger generation was our hope for the future. "We trust that they will respect and foster the history of their parents and grandparents, so that the fate of their predecessors would not be forgotten."

The guests were given a short information leaflet about our past history between 1939 to 2006, and were invited to say a few words to the assembled 'Indians'. After the speeches, the local School of Music, produced some musical entertainment.

Łyczakowski Cemetery

Before the festive lunch, there was time to visit a photographic exhibition arranged by A. Chendyński. Some photos were of pre-war childhood, others of our time in Valivade, or Balachadi and the trip to India in 2005. In the evening we had a get together to reminisce and catch up on the latest events in our lives.

As always, during each reunion, sightseeing was a must. Every two years we get a chance to discover different regions of Poland. This time it was the district of Lublin. The town itself dates back to the medieval times and is connected with the historic "Union of Lublin", when in 1569 the Kingdom of Poland accepted the Grand Duchy of Lithuania as an equal partner. We toured the old town with its varied architecture and the 13th century walled castle with a beautiful chapel. Next on the list was Czrtoryskis' palace at Puławy, where time had stood still and we could glimpse into the past life of that great family. Nearby, an old village of Kozłówka kept a windmill and smithy in good working order, as if waiting for the owner's return. Last of all was Kazimierz Dolny, situated on the river Vistula. We even cruised along the river, but the constant rain somewhat marred our enjoyment.

After the end of the official reunion, a trip was organised to Lwów, a once beloved Polish town, now in the Ukraine. We toured the ornate opera building, visited the Łyczakowski cemetery with the Panteon of its youthful defenders against the Bolsheviks in 1920. Next came Krzemieniec with Queen Bona's castle and home of J. Słowacki, a great romantic poet. We continued on to places made famous by H. Sienkiewicz's Trilogy: Zbaraż, Złoczów, Spirz an Wisniowiec.

Tired, but happy, we promised to meet again in two years' time.

18th – 26th May 2008: Waplewo (nr. Olsztynek)

This time the reunion was organised in the Recreation Centre in Waplewo, Warmia-Mazury in the Lake district of Poland.

As usual, we had a chance to visit places of interest in the area:

We sailed on the Elbląg – Ostróda Canal, which joins the lakes, where, instead of passing through locks, the boat was hoisted onto the rails, in order to reach different levels of water. This unique mechanical devise, designed by a local engineer (Jacob G. Steenke), opened in 1870, is apparently the only one of its kind in the world.

We celebrated the feast of Corpus Christi in a traditional way at the shrine of Our Lady in Sacred Lipka. There was a procession of the congregation

On the canal

in the market place, where the four altars were decked with flowers and greenery. The singing of hymns was very moving.

Next day we visited Grunwald, the site and museum of a historic battle, where a Polish king, Władysław Jagiełło won a great victory over the Tutonic Knights in 1410. The description of the battle by a local guide was so vivid, that we could almost imagine we were there when it happened.

Although we enjoyed the Reunion, there was a touch of sadness prevailing, because our Druh "Ryś", (Rev. Fr. Z. Peszkowski) was no longer with us, since he died a few months previously. He was sorely missed.

Entrance to Recreation Centre in Waplewo

With his passing and a new Chairman of the Association in Poland, Andrzej Chendyński, who organised this reunion, a New Era began.

During the final assembly, we agreed to meet again in Poland in 2010. The choice of venue was left to the organisers.

There will be other meetings and reunions for as long as we live. We need each other. We feel comfortable together. We understand each other. We grew from the same roots and lived through the same experiences. We are glad that God deemed to give us more time to enjoy each other and remember those who passed into Eternity.

The wet bonfire: singing in the rain

Translated by Kazimiera Skorupińska (Czarnecka)

INDIA REVISITED
collective work

EARLY ENCOUNTERS *by Jerzy (George) Kowalski*

I left India in 1948 and any threads of friendship with my colleagues from the Jesuit School in Bombay were severed for a number of years. Only when I became a representative of a textile machinery firm did I start travelling abroad. First to Eastern Europe, then the Middle East in the sixties and eventually to the Indian Continent in the seventies.

I was pleased to be going back to the country of my relatively carefree youth when somebody else was making decisions on my behalf and steering the course of my life. It was all different now for not only did I have to think for myself, but also for others that depend on me.

As we were approaching Karachi I became excited nearly as much as when landing in Warsaw after an absence of 30 years. I saw the dry river bed at the Country Club and the village of Malir, and I knew I was 'home'.

I came with the British commercial delegation, which was met at the airport by the Embassy officials and representatives of the Pakistan Chamber of Commerce. All very proper and correct, but just to one side a young Pakistani was waving a placard with my name on it and telling me that his father, Abdul Razzak, knew me from Bombay, years ago and that we should go straight to his house, as they were all awaiting me. With a certain amount of diplomacy I had to explain that I had a hotel booked and must stay with my group, but I would see them later that evening.

I met up with the most warm welcome and was provided with a chauffeur driven car and an interpreter (despite the fact that the majority of Pakistanis speak excellent English). I was not allowed to spend any of my own money, which was quite embarrassing and before departure I was given silk for my wife, sandals for my son, handbags and wallets of beautiful soft leather - there was no end to it. We have also agreed to work together, bringing the 'Raza' firm to the forefront of Asiatic trade after only 5 years. It was not only for me but for Britain and Pakistan, those early friendships bore fruit.

Whilst in Karachi I went to St. Joseph's Church, which my wife Zuza Marcinkiewicz attended. There I met one of the nuns who remembered well the Polish girls and showed me a doll in a faded national costume, which she received from her grateful pupils.

The next surprise was when meeting a wealthy manufacturer in his house, I mentioned I had been here before and from behind the screen came an elderly Oswald family patriarch who, although retired, still liked to keep in touch. He said he remembered a military parade on St. George's day in 1943, when the Polish boys, 13-14 years old were marching behind the British Army. As soon as they passed the main stand where the band was playing, they broke into their own 'mazurka' type song. He recalled how smart the boys looked in their freshly pressed uniforms and pith helmets, with red and white scarves round their necks. I admitted to being in the front row with Richard Godlewski and Władek Kopiec who initiated the singing. Apparently this made news at the local cinemas for some weeks to come... And so the business meeting was transformed into a friendly gathering after which we kept in touch for a long time.

During the dinner at the High Commissioner's Residence I met W. B. Eden, brother of our ex-prime minister, who knew my uncle, a Polish pilot in the RAF, stationed at Newark during the war. We parted with the traditional 'thumbs-up' pilot sign. After that our party flew to Bombay, where everything was as I remembered it from 1948. Now my room was in the new extension to the Taj Mahal hotel, which was originally designed by an Italian architect, who committed suicide when it was built back to front, opposite the Gate of India.

During our stay, talks were taking place regarding the delivery of jet fighters to India and someone with an Indian connection was needed... Somehow I was chosen to speak in Bombay Chamber of Commerce. There I began by thanking India for giving us shelter during WWII, where we not only had a roof over our heads, but I also received an education, here in Bombay... Then I continued to explain that having gained considerable experience in the textile field I came to sell machinery, which would help to modernise this particular industry.

I do not know whether it was because of my radio or TV interview, but on return to the hotel at least 20 people were wanting to see me after all those years. They were Hindus and Parsees (one was even from London) with their wives and children - the whole families, as well as dozens of telephone messages. The most surprising was one in Polish, from a relative of Mr. Pardeshi, who was a supply contractor to our Camp in Valivade. The next day his son came to take me to his elderly father, who spoke some Polish and still remembered us and my uncle, the school inspector, Mr. Żerebecki. Although inconvenient at the time, I was glad to go, for as it often happens with me, the heart had an upper hand.

After this first return visit to India, our business prospered in Bombay, Bangalore, Delhi and mostly in Ludhiana (Punjab). Up to my retirement the Indian trade was the most pleasant one. Many of my contacts would not let me stay in the hotels, inviting me instead to their private residences, with swimming pools and tennis courts, all the things the big money can provide.

I became most friendly with an Indian family from Puri. They took me in their private plane to many interesting places like Kashmir, Katmandu and even Lahore in Pakistan. Naturally my house in England was always at their disposal. Their sons, after their studies adopted some of my business philosophy and a sense of humour. To many of the Punjabis I have become 'uncle George'.

On my last visit to Teheran, literally in the days when the Shah fled the country, I mentioned to our agent there, that if things were to turn up for the worse to send their teenage son Babak to England. After a few weeks, the young Iranian turned up in our factory, but soon became very ill. Remembering with my wife how we came in 1942 to Persia from the Soviet Union, and how the Persians gave the Polish children clothing and fruit - we decided to take him into our home where he stayed until he was well enough to enroll at Loughborough College. His mother came to see him as soon as the Ayatollah Khomeni permitted.

For as the good book says "whatever good you do here on earth God will repay you double in heaven"...

THE JAMNAGAR CLUB EXCURSION IN 1986 by Wiesław Stypuła

This trip was organised by me with the help of Stefan Bukowski who was also the treasurer and Jurek Tomaszek the interpreter. There were five more members of the Club who were also original inhabitants of the Polish Camp in Balachadi, with two of their children plus two others. The enterprise proved to be a great success.

The main purpose of the trip was to visit the site of the former camp, where the new SAINIK Military School is now situated. They made contact with the school authorities and were hosted by Mr. Jaghubal Tanny, meeting a few old employees of the Camp and some of their representatives. Two former doctors employed by the Camp were also present including Dr. Ashani, who had spent sleepless nights by the beds of sick Polish children in the Hospital. He could not hold back the tears, repeating 'my children, have returned'. The wise Dr. Joshi stood to attention, his eyes wet with tears, saying in Polish 'I welcome you back to Jamnagar' whilst presenting his own translation into Gujarati of the famous poem *Ode to Youth* by A. Mickiewicz.

(Standing at the back): S. Bukowski, J. Tomaszek, Mayor, J. Bielecki, S. Jasiński, (In the middle): W. Stypuła, J. Truchanowicz (Piotrowska), J. Leszczyński, A. Grubczak, (Front row): A. Stypuła and A. Bukowska

Another pleasant episode was the inclusion of the story of the Polish Camp into the history of the Sainik Cadet School by its authorities.

Later the group visited the graves of departed colleagues who were buried in the now disused cemetery in Jamnagar. On our return to Poland, a collection was organised from the club members for the refurbishment of the head stones by local craftsmen.

The next undertaking was the erection of a commemorative plaque on the site of our camp. The plaque measuring 5' 3" x 8' 0" and weighing nearly 2000 lbs was designed by a sculptor Z. Korpalski. The project was managed by me and J. Leszczyński. Cast in bronze, it depicted an Indian woman with a child in her arms, taking care of a Polish child at her feet. It had a Hindu and Polish inscription, including the words: "BE PRAISED THE FARAWAY LAND, THE FRIENDLY LAND, THE GOOD LAND..." The

W. Stypuła, Maharaja's son and S. Bukowski

unveiling took place in 1989 in the presence of the most worthy personality remaining from that era, Madame Kira Banasińska, widow of the former Polish Consul and Jam Saheb Shatrushanysinhji, the son of the late Maharaj. The Jamnagar Club was represented by the author and Stefan Bielecki.

(This Club later amalgamated with the Association.)

TOURING INDIA IN 1994 *by Idalia Mahorowska*

When India received us as refugees some 50 years ago, we had no chance of touring or sightseeing the country. To make up for it, the Vice-chairman of our Association Jan Siedlecki, in conjunction with the London based tour operator, Trans Indus, organised a sightseeing tour to the country of our childhood.

Under the direction of our courier, Davinder S. Wazir, we started in Delhi admiring the new and old, like Qutb Minar with its non-rusting Iron Pillar, the huge Jama Masjid Mosque, which can accommodate over 20000 of the faithful. We paid respect to the Gandhi memorial ground with its abundance of flowers in Samadhi Park and were somewhat overwhelmed by the masses of people and streets full of bullock carts, cars, buses, scooters and rickshaws.

In Varanasi (the old Benares) we greeted the sunrise on the Ganges with leafboat lamps and watched the people come to pray and bathe in the sacred river. In nearby Sarnath we visited the golden Buddha in the park and walked round the silk workshops, where the children help weave the fine gold in the cloth.

Later in Khajuraho, we saw the erotic sculptured walls of its temples. After visiting the abandoned forts of Orchha and Gwalior, we reached Agra to admire the famous Taj Mahal, the pinnacle of Mogul architecture and purportedly one of the eight wonders of the world. Its walls patterned with precious stones, remain in our memory. Whilst there, we visited Fathepur Sikri, the capital of the Moghul Akbar, abandoned after only a few years.

At Sariska, we experienced the cold winter nights in the Maharaja's hunting lodge. Before daybreak we drove in search of a tiger, but all we found were his footprints in the ground. However there were plenty of monkeys and spotted deer by the watering hole.

On the way to Jaipur, we stopped by a village school. The actual building was quite small and the children were taking lessons in the open air, in the courtyard. This reminded us of Tehran when, in a similar manner, we were attempting to catch up with our schooling interrupted by the war. Here it seemed as if the pupils were all boys and the only girl was the headmaster's daughter.

In Jaipur we arrived at the Amber fort on elephants in truly Indian fashion and later went sightseeing in the Pink City spread below the fort. Driving through the Aravalli Hills we stopped to see the famous Jain temples of Rankaphur, finally arriving at the charming city of Udaipur situated amongst the lakes. Here we stayed at the Maharaja's former hunting lodge, where the animals gathered at

At the Amber Palace: A. Frank, I. Wolff, B. Hicks, B. Siedlecka, L. Delaney, Davinder Wazir, I. & T. Mahorowska, L. Chrystowska, S. & J. Ucinek, A. & J. Brzęczek, E. & G. Maresch, M. Krasnodębska, K. Kozieł, A. & T. Tybulewicz, J. Zawadzińska, L. Bełdowski and E. Stechley

dawn and dusk. Some of us stayed in the tents used for hunting parties.

Finally we reached cosmopolitan Bombay, where we had to say goodbye to our friendly guide Davinder. The city streets were full of traffic, noisy, hot and dusty. Even more so than we remembered from before. Here we were warmly welcomed with cold champagne by Dr. Majka at the Polish Consulate and traditional garlands around our necks. We met up with some members of the Indo-Polish Friendship Association (Amity). Among them was our friend of old, Wanda Nowicka from Valivade, who married Vassant Kashikar and remained in India.

From there we went by train to Kolhapur, becoming quite excited when we saw VALIVADE HALT sign. At the station we were met by Mr. M. D. Bhosale, representing the Collector and at the Shalini Palace Hotel, Kashikar family were awaiting us. And so began the most emotional part of our return journey, retracing our footsteps of long gone days. The next day, on the way to the cemetery we stopped at the Jesuit school of St. Xavier's to look at the commemorative tablet provided by the Polish Council for the Protection of Monuments for Struggle and Freedom, bearing an inscription composed by our colleague from Valivade, Jurek Krzysztoń: *"In memory of 70 Poles who on their journey back home died on Indian soil 1943-1948, Valivade, Kolhapur"*. The sight of the cemetery however was really depressing. The animals and children from the surrounding slums have access through the gaps in the ruined boundary wall... We found it difficult to identify the graves in the undergrowth, let alone read the names on headstones. Some graves had subsided into the waterlogged ground. In 1986 the same Council had built a cenotaph with the names of all the Poles buried there, but that also required renovation.

Later on the same day, excited and curious, we travelled to Valivade. What we saw was not 'our' Valivade... (See later page in this chapter.)

In the evening we attended a reception at the residence of Ajit Kumar Jain I. A. S., the Collector, where we met a few of the old guard from the SUPPLY SYNDICATE. We were given tea and cucumber sandwiches in the best British tradition, served by servants in white gloves. It was not the first time that we encountered echoes of India's colonial past such as buildings and students in public school uniforms. Although the guides frequently made some caustic remarks about the English past masters, the footprints of the colonial past were still discernible. Apart from the Collector and his family we also met some other people connected with the former Valivade Camp.

On the last day we went to the old fort of Panhala, the scene of our Scout Camps. Now it has become a local tourist resort, with new hotels, bungalows and eating places. At long last, an all night journey back to Bombay, to pack the suitcases with souvenirs and newly acquired 'treasures' from India. Full of emotional impressions, we returned to England, contemplating our next journey to India.

THE POLISH EAGLE IN KOLHAPUR *by Danuta Pniewska*

When in 1994 we ended our trip to India in Kolhapur, we discovered that the local authorities had scant knowledge that we were in fact revisiting the country which was our 'home' for five years during WWII. Luckily amongst the invited guests at the Collector's reception, there were a few, who not only remembered us, but were actively involved in our Camp affairs. On this occasion, it was Col. Vijay Gaikwad that proposed erecting an obelisk to commemorate our stay in Kolhapur, which we eagerly accepted.

It soon became obvious that it would have to be negotiated at intergovernmental level. The Polish Consul in Bombay, Dr. K. Majka, Mr. V. Kashikar who married our Wanda Nowicka and members of 'Amity', were actively engaged in promoting the idea, but it soon transpired that the initial designs were too ambitious for our budget.

Eventually in 1997 we had no choice but to leave it in the hands of our own vice-chairman, the architect, Jan Siedlecki, in England, who managed to have his design executed with active help from the Colonel, the

At the unveiling of the monument (from left): Paras B. Oswal (the constructor), HH Shahu Chhatrapati (Maharaja of Kolhapur), Dr. Krzysztof Dębnicki (Chargé d'Affaires), Col. Vijay Gaikwad, Jan K. Siedlecki (Vice President of the Association)

On the terrace of the new Palace (from left) Sambhaji's wife, Shahaji II's Dowager, K. Kozieł, Dr. K. Dębnicki, K. Czajka, E. Stechley, A. Stanisławska, Maharaja Shahu, J. Siedlecki, Dr. H. Pyz Hermeet Singh, J. Łotyczewska, Z. Durant, G. Kunigiel, B. Siedlecka, Col. V. Gaikwad, D. Pniewska, T. Makles, H. Ball and L. Bełdowski

originator of the idea and the new Polish Consul Mr. Ireneusz Makles. Soon the right place was found in Mahavir Gardens and the approval of Kolhapur Municipal Corporation obtained. The contractor (Puja Builders) was appointed to build the pillar fashioned in the form of an early Indian column (as seen in the Laxmi temple of Kolhapur) topped by the Polish Eagle, copied from the regimental colours displayed in the Sikorski Museum in London and procured for us by our colleague Karol Huppert. The monument was clad in red granite with an inscription in Marathi, Polish and English which reads: *"In the years 1943-1948, thanks to the hospitality of Kolhapur State, 5000 Polish refugees found shelter in Valivade Camp. Dispersed throughout the world, we remember India with heartfelt gratitude. On the 50th anniversary of our departure: Association of Poles in India, 1998."*

The monument was financed by the subscription of our members with additional funds provided by some Polish firms in India. Time was limited as the 50th anniversary of our departure from India was fast approaching. To the last, we were not certain whether we shall meet the deadline and on arrival in Kolhapur the day before the unveiling, we still were not sure if the project was completed. The monument however was erected, but without the Eagle...

At the same time we were invited to Valivade by its Sarpanch Grampanchayat, Mr. Amasaheb S. Kusale, where we were cordially welcomed and entertained at the sugar cane factory/workshop and for tea at his house. All the time however we were concerned about our Eagle... Back at the hotel we met charge d'affaires Dr. K. Dębnicki from the Polish Embassy and the Consul Mr. Makles and his wife, who gave us the good news that 'the Eagle has landed'.

The next day at 10 a.m., on 3rd February 1998, we arrived at the gates of the Gardens to be met by a small crowd of onlookers. A police band and a military one in colourful Scottish tartan shawls were tuning their instruments. A red carpet was laid to the mound on top of which stood the monument with our Eagle spreading its wings. Under an awning rows of invited guests and dignitaries were seated. We were elated, for as our history teacher and girl Guide leader Mrs. A. Gwiazdonik (Handerek) wrote: '...this monument is a part of all of us'.

The presiding officer Mr. Sebastian Fernandes, from the Polish Consulate, called the principal guests and speakers to the front as the ceremony was about to start. Our vice-chairman welcomed the guests and outlined the history of the monument, thanking all those who contributed to its installation. The speeches in English, our common language were short. Dr. Dębnicki talked of the friendly relations between our two countries and thanked India for playing host to the Polish Refugees. H. H. Shahu Chhatrapati, Maharaj of Kolhapur said that the War had brought our two nations together and called the monument a symbol of 'good' over 'evil'. He emphasised our common difficulties, the joy of India's Independence in 1947 and now the Polish rejection of Communism.

After the inaugural speeches, the Maharaja, together with the Polish charge d'affaires and our vice-chairman assisted by Col. Vijay Gaikwad and the Contractor Mr. Paras B. Oswal performed the unveiling ceremony - whilst the Police Band faultlessly rendered the Polish National Anthem, followed by the Maharashtra Anthem played by the Military Band..

The Jesuit Fathers from St. Xavier's High School with lay nuns, led the hymn singing and prayers, after which Fr. Mario Fernandes S. J. consecrated the monument.

The Consul then read telegrams from well wishers: The Polish Council for War Graves, the Polish Consul in Toronto and members of our very active Branch there. This was followed by three more speeches: Mrs. Krystyna Kozieł recalled life in the camp fifty years ago. Whether it was her blond hair or her words, she struck a chord with the audience. Then our Delegation cheered as Mr. Shumrao Tuksam Gaikwad, (who worked in the Camp) unexpectedly addressed us with a few words in Polish, but what really provoked the warmest appreciation was an impromptu short speech in Hindi, spoken by our guest Dr. Helena Pyz, who runs the Social and Leprosy Rehabilitation Centre in Raipur, Madhya Pradesh.

After the formal ceremony we entertained a multitude of our guests and friends with their children at a garden tea party in the Park. We met up with a son of Mr. Valivadekar, the friendly Scoutmaster who worked with us in the past. The Kashikar family were there and the sons of Mr. B. B. Bage, the Camp photographer. At the same time we were endeavouring to answer numerous questions and conduct interviews with local and national press and television reporters.

We spent the rest of the day in friendly informal gatherings. First we were treated to a traditional Indian lunch of thali by Messrs Oswal and Padwal of Pooja Builders. Then later in the afternoon we were invited for tea at the Maharaja's palace, part of which is now a splendid hunting museum. On the first floor we had very tasty rice with sultanas and met up with the dowager Maharani who was there in 1947.

The grand finale of the day was a party in the garden of their home, given by Colonel Gaikwad, who officiated at the bar and his charming wife Pryia, who prepared excellent and tasty dishes.. The celebrations continued well into the night singing Polish, English and Marathi songs and we found it hard to part company...

The next day we revisited the Jesuit High School and the cemetery where we lit candles and prayed for our 'dear departed'. Then we began negotiations regarding refurbishment of the graves. After visiting Panhala fort, reminiscent of our early Scouting days, we went South to explore other regions of India, which we could not afford to see 50 years ago, but as Rudyard Kipling would say - 'that's another story'.

AN EXCURSION TO THE SOUTH *by Jan K. Siedlecki*

After unveiling of the monument in Kolhapur we went to Bijapur, the capital of the old Moslem empire in the Deccan, where 50 years ago we were trekking as Scouts and Girl Guides.

From there we turned South into the heartland of the Chaluka Kings (VI-IX centuries) one of the earliest of the mighty Hindu dynasties, whose buildings in the villages of Aihole, Pattadakal and Badami were forerunners of the great temples of Madurai. It is Badami however that was the biggest and the most famous of the three with its cave temples carved in the rock face of its hills and ravines.

Further south in the fertile and irrigated countryside covered in huge volcanic rock boulders, we admired the vast ruined city of Hampi, from the Vijayanagar empire (1336-1565) now a World Heritage site. According to a contemporary Portuguese traveller, the city equalled Rome.

From there we went via Bangalore (with its Tipu palace) and Madras, finally stopping to rest amongst the famous monolithic temples sculptured out of rock, in the beautiful seaside village of Mahabalipuram, famous for its sculpture school and stone carvings. Naturally we also visited Kanchipuram, one of the seven Hindu holy towns, residence of 'math' (a kind of Hindu pope) and renowned for silk production. Memorable also were trips to the crocodile conservation centre in the village of Vadannameli and the unforgettable walled temples of the Pallava kings in Tirrukalukkundram.

Thus we ended our journey, making up for the time we lived in India, but did not see it...

PRESENT DAY IMPRESSIONS OF VALIVADE *by Krystyna Kozieł*

In 1994 and 1998 when in Kolhapur, we visited our old refugee Camp. Beautiful, green Valivade was unrecognisable. Our tidy squares full of vegetation and flower beds alongside the barracks have disappeared. The barrack verandas and the church are no more. All that remained of those days is the old post box and the ruins of the post office.

After our departure in 1947/48 the camp was taken over by the Indian refugees from the province of Sind, which became part of Pakistan after the Partition. Our camp which was originally planned for 3 years has lasted 50. The new inhabitants who are enterprising and hard working, neglected the greenery which was surrounding us. They have widened the barracks by moving the inner walls to the edge of the veranda and rendered the masonry. Some people built upwards through the existing tiled roofs and those that could afford it built new villas.

End wall of a barrack

Our beautiful tree lined avenues had also disappeared and the settlement, now called GANDHINAGAR extends to the other side of the railway line, but the old name remains - VALIVADE HALT.

We persisted in tracing signs of our old existence, trying to recognise the much changed and altered barrack accommodation. Someone managed to find an old school, others found their living quarters because the old numbers were still visible on the masonry gable ends. We found the square that was in front of the church, but no church.

My old barrack no. 154 was still there, but the part we lived in was now a two storey brick house.

We obtained permission to tour the newly built replacement hospital. It was very clean and the staff impressed us. We were invited in and the layout of rooms was the same as before, but the walls were masonry and plastered. There were electric fans in the ceiling, but the

New villa - part of the old barrack

cleanliness of the interior contrasted sadly with the outside. Some of us remembered when we worked there.

During our visit to the settlement we encountered a few older residents who could still say 'dzień dobry' and 'dobra mamusia' ('good day' and 'good mother'.)

The young ones did not know anything about us and enquired about the purpose of our visit. Later at a reception given by the village authorities we tried to explain our presence to the youngsters in the audience.

I also wanted to see other parts of the 'camp' and even reach the river, but suddenly we were surrounded by school children all wanting my autograph. Never in my whole life did I sign my name in so many exercise books, on so many scraps of paper and even on the back of hands... Eventually I had to run away to catch our coach.

We were leaving Valivade, perhaps for the last time. Soon there will be a new town here and any signs of our existence will disappear. In the meantime other 'Polish Indians' (as we are sometimes called) will revisit the old places and write their reminiscences in the 'Bulletin' published by the 'Association of Poles from India'. In spite of the changes, our beloved Valivade will live in our hearts and memory.

Translated by Jan K. Siedlecki

MAHARAJA OF KOLHAPUR SON'S WEDDING *by Jan K. Siedlecki*

Over 50 years ago standing in the street crowd to witness the enthronement of the new Maharaj of Kolhapur, Shehaji II who succeeded an adopted child which we saw in 1944 in Valivade. I never imagined having the privilege to attend the wedding of his great grandson, Malojiraje Chhatrapati and Soubhagyakankshini Dhawalshereeraje. Even though the title of 'Maharaj' was officially abolished in August 1947, "ours" keeps the old tradition alive.

Now we came face to face with the whole distinguished family. There was the present Maharaj Shahu Chhatrapati (the son of Shahji II eldest daughter) and his very handsome brother (that my wife wanted to be photographed with) and their father, looking very much like a Polish nobleman, also Sambhaji, the brother of the bridegroom. Even the venerable widow of Shahaji II was there, as well as our great friend from Maharaja's retinue Col. Vijaysinh Gaikwad (Retd.) with his charming wife Priya. All in their finest traditional attire of yore, holding swords wrapped in silk scarves, wearing long coats and pugerie on their heads and ladies' Saree's dripping with gold.

Unfortunately the Polish Government was meagerly represented, for the Ambassador M. Mroziewicz and the Consul I. Makles were both incapacitated in hospitals and only Actg.

Jan & Barbara Siedlecki with Col.V. Gaikwad under the portrait of Shaji II

Commercial Counsellor put in a brief appearance. So I felt somewhat elevated "representing" Poland.

The marriage ceremonies lasted for several days, starting with Welcoming Party, which was followed the next day by the Gentlemen's Gathering (Tila Samarambh) in the morning and Ladies Gathering (Bride's then Bridegroom's Haldi) in the afternoon. The actual Marriage (Mangalashtaka) took place on the auspicious day of Saturday 11th December 1999 in front of 6500 guests. The farewell Party followed on Sunday at the New Palace in Kolhapur, where all the celebrations and ceremonies were held.

The whole occasion was like a fairy story from Shaharezade 1001 nights, colourful guests, exotic music, gun salutes and fireworks display, only the elephant was missing (prominent before in 1947) for the Groom arrived in a classical cabriolet. I can attest to all this for we were there representing the Association and had "wine and mead" (actually whiskey and soda) as the Polish saying goes...

THE THIRD VISIT TO KOLHAPUR/VALIVADE *by Andrzej Chendyński*

In Feb. 2005 a trip to India was organised from Poland. Apart from the 17 inhabitants of the Polish Refugee Camps, it included half a dozen young people of the new generation and friends. After landing in Goa we soon transferred to Kolhapur, where we met with a warm welcome from Col.Vijaysinh Gaikwad, his wife Priya, Wanda Kashikar (Nowicka), her husband Vassant and their numerous family, journalists and local inhabitants.

However, we could not wait to get to Gandhinagar, as our Valivade is now known. We went there the next morning. Once there, we headed straight for the railway "stop", which has retained its name Valivade The local Indians associate this name with the Poles. The hill, which we remembered as barren, inhabited only by an old hermit, is now covered with green fields and palm tree groves. The little temple that used to dominate the landscape is no longer visible. The road behind the railway station , that runs to Kolhapur, lined with trees in our days there, is now a built-up area. Of our Valivade Camp only a few blocks have survived. In a year or two, they will all disappear. We therefore liked the idea of the Mayor, Mrs. Poonam I. Parnamadani, that a monument or a commemorative plaque should be erected there, or some fragment of the Camp should be preserved, as suggested by Anuradha Bhattacharjee, a journalist from Delhi, accompanying us.

At the end of our morning visit, we went to the Kolhapur cemetery, where 77 people from Valivade are buried. We prayed for their souls: May they rest in peace.

In the afternoon we went to an official meeting with the people of Kolhapur. Again the meeting was cordial, Indian style, in the Town Hall, filled to the last seat. The meeting was addressed by: the Polish Consul in Bombay, Marek Moron, Maharaja Shahu Chhatrapati, Col. Gaikwad and other dignitaries. They recalled our stay in Valivade and stressed the necessity of maintaining ties between Indian and Polish people. On behalf of our group I expressed thanks for the hospitality, I spoke about our suffering during World War II, the tragic deportations of the Polish people to the Soviet Union, which became the grave of so many of them. I also recalled the five happy years, 1943-1948, which we spent in Valivade, and how both, the Indians and Poles had celebrated the 15th Aug. 1947, when India regained her independence.

The celebration continued in the Mahavir Garden, which hosts two monuments, one, designed by our Jan Siedlecki and founded by us in 1998 as a token of our gratitude to India, and the other, funded by the Indians, in memory of the fighters for Indian independence. Assisted by soldiers in parade uniforms and a military band, we laid our wreaths, Danka Pniewska at the Polish monument, I myself at the Indian one. After the official part was over, the meeting turned into a picnic. We were surrounded by a crowd of curious local people all the time. In the evening we were received by Col. Gaikwad in his residence.

The most poignant, however, was our reunion with the river – the scene of many of our youthful adventures. All the boys were thinking about it, and felt that something was missing. The girls were not in on it. We had to go back to Valivade once more to find "our" river. We picked up an Indian boy, who pointed us in the right direction. We had to leave the coach and continue on foot. Indian women carrying baskets on their heads, filled with their washing gave us a clue that we must be close. Suddenly, there it was down in the valley, and the dam as firm as ever. We were close to tears, but tried to hide our emotions. We remembered vividly our carefree, boyhood days, before we scattered to different parts of the world. The journalist,

Anuradha, who accompanied us, asked me "how do you feel?", but I was unable to utter a word. Nobody wanted to talk. I moved away to be alone with my Panchganga river and her dam... All those years ago, when I was growing up, I did not even know her name...

We returned to the village and were soon surrounded by children, who wanted to invite us to their school. As we entered the school yard, 300 voices sprang into song to welcome us. They were sitting in rows on the verandas, class after class. We stood in the middle of the yard. What a surprise! They did not quite understand what we said in English, but I remembered a song in Marathi about "God's greatest love", and when I rendered it, I received a loud applause.

Soon afterwards, we were approached by some old Indians, who still remembered us after 60 years! They were recalling some Polish words for: ja krawiec, ja szewc, ja woda nosic, (me tailor, me cobbler, me water carrier). What an encounter! A young member of our party, Haneczka Słowikowska, summed it up: "It was worth visiting India just for that!".

We were bid farewell first by the Maharaja's family, then by many Indians at the railway station. We left that friendly place for Bombay, where we paid respects to the tomb of Kira Banasińska, our war-time benefactress.

Later, we were hosted by the Polish Consul, Marek Moroń. It was a pleasant surprise to see Col. Gaikwad and his wife at the party. They must have travelled by car all the way from Kolhapur, in order to see us off and decorate men with the insignia of the Regiment of Kolhapur Infantry, and women - with bracelets. In return, we handed the Gaikwads albums about us and about Poland.

The rest of our trip was very interesting – each day different, full of tourist attractions, which can be found described in full in tourist guides and our route marked on maps: Varanasi-Kajuraho-Orcha-Gwalior-Agra-Jajpur-Amber-Delhi.

Our trip ended in Delhi, where Mr. Krzysztof Majka, the Polish Ambassador, received us in his residence exceptionally warmly and thanked us for making Polish – Indian ties even closer.

Chapter translated by Jan Siedlecki

LIST OF ABBREVIATIONS
Some of them stand for Polish words

AAN	New Archives in Warsaw	MSZ	Ministry of Foreign Affairs
AD	Anno Domini	MWRiOP	Ministry of Religious Affairs and Education
AH	Anno Hegirae-Hidzra, Journey of Mohammed from Mecca to Medina in 622 AD. This date is the start of the Muslim Calendar	NCWC	National Catholic Welfare Conference
		NIK	National Audit Office
APOL	Polish Archives in Orchard Lake Mich. USA	NKWD	National Commissariat of Internal Affairs 1934-1943. Russian Political (Secret) Police
BA	Bachelor of Arts	ONZ	UN - United Nations
BPL	Polish Library in London	PCK	Polish Red Cross
BL.OIOC	British Library Oriental and India Office Collections	PCM	Polish Catholic Mission
		PES	Polish Evacuation Staff
CIE	Companion of the Order of the Indian Empire	PMK	Polish Catholic Mission for England and Wales
CPWD	Central Public Works Department	PRC	(PKPR) Polish Resettlement Corps
DIU	Part of Combined Territory of Goa, Dahan & Diu	PRL	Polish Peoples Republic
FBI	Federal Bureau of Investigation	PRO	Public Records Office - London
FO	Foreign Office	PSWK	Polish Women's Auxiliary Force
GCIE	Grand Command of (the Order of) the Indian Empire	PSZ	Polish Army
		PUC	Polish University College, London 1947-1953
GCSI	Knight Grand Commander of the Star of India	PWD	Public Works Department
GCVO	Grand Cross of the Victorian Order	PWN	Polish Academic Publications
GHQ	General Headquarters	QMG	Quartermaster General
GUS	Statistical Headquarters	RKKA	Russian Workers Peasant Red Army 1919 - 1946
ICS	Indian Civil Service		
IPiMS	Polish Institute and Sikorski Museum in London	RKO	Cultural Section
		RAF	Royal Air Force
IOR	India Office Records	RAAF	Royal Australian Air Force
IRO	International Refugee Organisation	RP	Republic of Poland
ITC	Interim Treasury Committee for Polish Questions	SGGW	The Main Agricultural School
		SHAEF	Supreme Headquarters. Allied Expeditionary Force
KDH	Commission for Scout Supplies	SPKP	WRS - War Relief Services
KPH	Friends of Scouting Association	SWIATPOL	World Association of Expat Poles
KPI	Archives of Polish Association in India	UN	UNO - United Nations
KU	Refugee Council	UNRRA	United Nations Relief and Rehabilitation Administration
JAG	Archive of the Camp Commandant (Jagiellowicz)		
MASc	Master of Applied Science	WRS-NCWC	War Relief Services
MATSc	Master of Applied and Technical Science	YMCA	Young Men's Christian Association
		ZHP	Polish Scouts' Association
MD	Medical Doctor	ZHPkgK	Polish Scouts Association Outside Poland
MERRA	Middle East Relief and Refugee Administration		
		ZMP	Polish Youth Association
MON	Ministry of National Defence	ZSSR	USSR; UNION of Soviet Socialist Republics
MPiOS	Ministry of Works and Social Welfare		

GLOSSARY

ABINAJA	Moods displayed with facial expressions	GUPIS	Name given to shepherdesses admiring Krishna
ADAJAR	Name bridge, river and district in Madras, current name of the town is Chennai	GURU	Spiritual teacher
		HAMAL	A carrier
		HARIJAN	Untouchable
AHIMSA	Doctrine against the use of force in Buddhism, Hinduism and Jaism	HILL STATION	Places with a cool climate, situated in high regions, over 1500m, where families of British civil servants and army officers were sent during the hot seasons
AYAH	Nursemaid. In valivade the name was used for a maidservant		
ANNA	Indian coin worth 1/16 of a rupee		
ASHRAM	Centre of prayer and meditation	JAINISM	Religion started between VI and V century BC by a sage Vardhaman
BAKSHEESH	Bribe, tip, gift		
BANSHRI	Bamboo flute		
BEGUM	A lady, Indian honorary title given to widows and wives of princes in Mogul northern India	JAGGERY	Unrefined cane sugar
		JAM	Hereditary title of princes
		JEEVODAJA	Dawn of life, name given to a leprosy healing centre
BHANGI/ METHAR	Sweeper from the cast of untouchables	JINA	7 string instrument
		JOWAUR/JOWAREE	Type of oats
BHEESTI	Water carrier	JUGARA	Type of grain
BRAHMA	Creator of the universe (see Trimurti)	KASTRA	Cast of Rajputan knights
		KATHAK	Dancing style in Mogul courts
BRAHMIN	The highest cast member from the four traditional social classes	KOLHOZ	Collective farm in the USSR
		KOMANDARM	Commander of the red army (USSR)
CRORE	100 lakh, 10 million		
CHARPOY	Indian bed		
CHAPPATI	Indian flat bread	KRESY WSCHODNIE	Lands on the eastern borders of Poland
CHAPRASSI	Servant messenger		
CHHATRAPATI	Lord of Baldahim, Sivaji gave himself this title during 1674 coronation, from which time the title is given to maharajas of Kolhapur	KUKRI	Short Indian dagger
		LAGIER	Soviet concentration camp
		LAKH	100,000 rupees
		LAKSHMI	Wealth goddess, the incarnation of beauty, wife of Vishnu
CHOWKIDAR	Night porter		
DALDA & MARVO	Commercial names for plant cooking oils	MAHARAJA	Great ruler, king
		MAHARASTRO	Large kingdom, currently one of the most developed states in north western India
DHAL	Lentils		
DHOTI	Mens white cotton clothes, several meters long and over a metre wide		
		MAHARINI	Great queen, wife of maharaja
		MAHATMA	Title used for ascetic people, mystics, philosophers, title given to M. K. Ghandi
DIVALI, DIPALI	Hindu festival of light		
DURBAR	Princedom government, also a mens public meeting in the court of maharaja		
		MAIDA	White flour
		MANTRA	Vide text, prayer, magic
GANESHA	God of luck and wisdom, son of Shiva	MARATHI	Indoarian language in Maharastra
		MARVO	(see Dalda)
GHATS	East and west mountain ranges of Dekan	MEHTAR	(see Bhangi)
		MESSERSCHMIT	German aeroplane
GOPURA	Square tower build over a temple gate in southern India	METRANI	Woman cleaner

MILE	Mile = 1.609 KM
MOLASSES	Syrup made from sugar cane
MONSOON	Period of rains
MUDRY	Symbolic use of hands (palm and fingers)
MUKHTYAR	Helper
NAJA NAJA	Indian cobra
NANDI/NANDIN	White bull of Shiva
NAVAB/NABAB/NABOB	Noble title given by the British to the Muslims in Mogul empire
PAYTAN	Sandal
PARIAH	In southern India a man who does not belong to any cast, man without any rights
PARSEE	An adherent of Zaroastrianism, descendant of those who fled from Persia to India in the 7th-8th century
POLITICAL AGENT	Official of Indian national administration representing viceroys, second in command in smaller princedoms
POSIOŁEK	Settlement in the USSR
PUJA	Prayer and gift offer
RAJ	Kingdom, British rule in India 1858 - 1947
RAJA/RAJAH	Ruler, king, prince, noble title given to Hindus by the British
RESIDENT	Viceroy, representative in the courts of more important princedoms (states)
RUPEE	Indian money, in 1940 equal to 16 annas and 13.25 rupees to the pound sterling
SADHU	Saint sage, ascetic man
SAHIB/SAHEB	Title by which all Europeans are addressed
SARANGI	3 string instrument of Arab origin
SARASWATI	Goddess of knowledge, art and music
SARI	Ladies gown made from one piece of fabric
SHIVA	Destroyer (see Trimurti)
SHRI	Housewife title, often used and repeated as a sign of respect
SITAR	7 string musical instrument
SOWCHOZ	National collective farm in the USSR
SWAGGER STICK	Short cane (baton) carried by British officers
TONGA	Two wheel cart
TRIMURTI	Triad of Indian Gods including; Brahma Vishnu and Shiva
VAKIL	Representative, lawyer
VALIVADE HALT	Valivade railway station
VEDA	Knowledge - name of oldest Indian texts, believed to have been inspired by Gods
VIMTO	Juice from raspberries, black currants and grapes
VISHNU	Protector of existence
WALONKI	Cotton and felt high boots worn in Russia

LIST OF INDO POLISH LIBRARY PUBLICATIONS 1939 -1990
Compiled by Eugenia Maresch

Explanatory Notes

a) Lines 6 - 15 Refer to the Anthology of Indian Ballads
b) Lines 30 - 32 by Bhavagad Gita – Songs of God
c) Lines 108 - 117 by Krishnamurti Jiddu – Meditations of Human Life
d) Lines 133, 134, 135, 158, 159 Refer to Teachings by Shri Ramana Maharishi

1. **Ali, S.R.**: Russia, Poland and India. Bombay, Indo-Polish Library, [1944].
2. **All for freedom**. The Warsaw Epic. Opr. Umadevi [W.Dynowska]. Swatantrapur, Aundh, wyd. M. Frydman dla Indo-Polish Library, 1946. Praca zbiorowa z przedmową Gandhiego, autorzy: prof.O. Halecki, M. Kukiel, M. Kuncewiczowa, Świętosławski, Z. Nowakowski, S. Stroński, A. Cwojdziński, M. Brzeska, W. Dynowska, S. Zahorska i inni. W tekście 58 dokumentów,125 zdjęć, okładka biało-czerwona z herbem Warszawy.
3. **Andrzejewski, Jerzy:** Rakh aur hire. [Popiół i diament]. Tłum.na Hindi Raghuvir Sahay. New Delhi: Sahitya Akad, 1978.
4. **Anstruther, Fay Carmichael.:** Poland's Part in the War. Bombay, Indo-Polish Library, 1944. Przedruk z wyd. I, Glasgow, 1941 z przedmową gen. Mariana Kukiela.
5. **Antologia pieśni indyjskiej** wszystkich wieków i prowincji w 7 tomach. Przekł.i opr. W. Dynowska. Przedmowa Anirwan Swami. Mistycyzm Indii. T.1. sanskryt. Adyar:Biblioteka Polsko-Indyjska, 1950.
6. **Antologia pieśni indyjskiej**. Przekł.i opr. W. Dynowska. T.2. tamil. Adyar, Bibl.Pol.-Ind., 1951.
7. **Antologia pieśni indyjskiej**. Przekł. i opr. W. Dynowska.T.3. hindi. Madras, Bibl.Pol.-Ind., 1952.
8. **Antologia pieśni indyjskiej**. Przekł. i opr. W. Dynowska. T.4. gudżerati. Madras, Bibl.Pol.-Ind., 1955.
9. **Antologia pieśni indyjskiej**. Przekł. i opr. W. Dynowska. [T.5]. marati. Madras, 1956, Bibl.Pol.- Ind., 1956.
10. **Antologia pieśni indyjskiej**. Przekł. i opr. W. Dynowska. T.1. sanskryt. II wyd. [Madras], Bibl. Pol.-Ind.1959.
11. **Antologia pieśni indyjskiej**. Przekł.i opr. W. Dynowska. II wyd.T.2. tamil. Madras, Bibl.Pol.-Ind., 1958.
12. **Antologia pieśni indyjskiej**. Przekł. i opr. W. Dynowska. II wyd. T.3. hindi. [Madras], Bibl.Pol.- Ind., 1959.
13. **Antologia pieśni indyjskiej**. Przekł. i opr. W. Dynowska. II wyd.T.4. gudżerati. Madras, Bibl.Pol. Ind.,1960. Wyjątki z pism Gandhiego.
14. **Antologia pieśni indyjskiej** wszystkich wieków i prowincji w 7 tomach. Przekł. i opr. W. Dynowska. II wyd. T.5. marati Wielcy święci Maharasztry. Wstęp, mistycy chrześcijańscy i hinduscy. Madras, Bibl.Pol.-Ind., 1960.
15. **Antologia pieśni indyjskiej**. Przekł. i opr. W. Dynowska. Część I. T.6. Poeci i Pieśniarze Bengalu. Madras, Bibl Pol.-Ind., 1964.
16. **Anujan, O.M.**: Purvvayuroppil oru samskarika paryatanam.- ottayam. Nakładem Autora, 1972. Dotyczy Polski.
17. **Arundale, G.S.**: Duch młodości. Everest. Joga. Przekł. W. Dynowska. Madras, Bibl.Pol.-Ind., 1960.
18. **Bala, Suman**: Joseph Conrad's fiction, a study in existential humanism. New Delhi, Intellectual Publishing House, 1990.
19. **Banasińska, Kira** : Autobiography of Ms Kira Banasińska. Mumbay, Modhu Kotak & Co., 1997.
20. **Bandurski, Wł. ks. Biskup** : O wewnętrznym odrodzeniu narodu. Valivade, nakład i druk SPKP., 1947. Przedruk kazania wygłoszonego w Katedrze Lwowskiej.
21. **Bannerji, A. K.**: Sziwa, hinduskie pojęcie Boga. Przekł. W. Dynowska. Bombaj, [Bibl. Pol.-Ind.,[1948].
22. **Baranek, F.M.**: Czechoslovak-Polish Relations. Batanagar, Czechosłowackie Towarzystwo w Kalkucie, Bombaju, Sekunderybadzie i Lahore, wydane na fundusz pomocy polskim dzieciom, 1942.
23. **Besant, Annie** : Wstęp do dziejów Indii. Przekł. W. Dynowska. [Bombaj], Bibl.Pol.-Ind.,[1948].
24. **Besant, Annie** : Zagadnienie dobra i zła czyli Dharma. Przekł. W. Dynowska. Adyar, 1950, Bibl.Pol.-Ind., 1950. Trzy odczyty.
25. **Besant, Annie** : Zagadnienie dobra i zła czyli Dharma. Przekł. W. Dynowska.II wyd. Madras, Bibl.Pol.Ind., 1956.
26. **Besant, Annie i Jinarajadasa, C**.: Prawo przyczyny i skutku, czyli jak kierować swym przeznaczeniem. Karma. Przekł. W. Dynowska. Madras, Bibl.Pol.-Ind., 1952.
27. **Besant, Annie i Jinarajadasa, C.**: Prawo przyczyny i skutku, Karma. Przekł. W. Dynowska, Madras, Bibl.Pol.-Ind., 1960. Wydanie II.
28. **Betley, Jan Andrzej** : An early 19th Century traveller in India. Indica vol.15, Heras Institute of Indian History and Culture, Bombay, 1978. Dotyczy Wł. Małachowskiego.
29. **Bhagavad Gita. [Mahabharata]**. Pieśń Pana. Przekł. W. Dynowska. Svatantrapur, Bibl.Pol.-Ind., 1947. Zawiera wstęp Sir Sarwapalle Radha Krishnan, przedmowa Umashankar Joshi.Tłumaczenia IV księgi Mahabharaty i objaśnienia terminów sankryckich.
30. **Bhagavad Gita**. Pieśń Pana. Przekł. W. Dynowska. Madras, Bibl.Pol.-Ind., 1956. Wydanie II.
31. **Bhagavad Gita**. Pieśń Pana. Przekł. W. Dynowska. [Madras], Bibl.Pol.-Ind.,[1960]. Wydanie III.
32. **Bhagavad Gita**. Pieśń Pana. Przekł. W. Dynowska. Bombaj, Bibl.Pol.-Ind., 1972. Z przedmową Radhakrishnan Sarvepalli, Joshi Umashankar: Tajemnica najwyższej harmonii oraz Gandhi. Wydanie IV.
33. **Bharatanandra [Frydman Maurycy] i Umadevi [Wanda Dynowska]**: Dwugłos z Indii. Bombaj, Bibl.Pol.Ind., 1945. Zawiera własne poezje autorów oraz tłumaczenia poezji hinduskiej.

34. **Bławatska, H.P. [Blavatskaia, E. P.]**: Klucz do teozofii. Przekł. W. Dynowska. Madras, Nakł. "Ludziom Dobrej Woli" 1954.
35. **Bławatska, H.P. [Blavatskaia, E. P.]**: Nauka Tajemna. Przekł. W. Dynowska. Madras, Nakł."Ludziom Dobrej Woli" 1957.
36. **Boswell, Alexander, Bruce:** The Eastern Boundaries of Poland. Bombay, Indo-Polish Library, 1944. Przedruk.
37. **Bragdon, Claude:** Joga dla Ciebie czytelniku. Przekł. W. Dynowska. Madras, Bibl.Pol.-Ind., 1955.
38. **Bragdon, Claude**: Joga dla Ciebie czytelniku. Przekł. W. Dynowska. Bombaj, Bibl. Pol.-Ind., 1970. Wyd. III.
39. **Carus, Paul**: Nauka Buddhy. Ze starych ksiąg. Przekł. W. Dynowska. Madras,Bibl.Pol.-Ind., 1962.
40. **Carus, Paul**: Nauka Buddhy. Ze starych ksiąg. Przekł. W. Dynowska. Madras, Bibl.Pol.-Ind., 1969.
41. Certain and dubious. **Modern Polish poetry.** Antologia poezji polskiej. Tłumaczenie Reszelewski Zdzisław i Simms Norman. Calcutta, Writers Workshop Saffronbird Book, 1980. Autorzy między innymi: St. Barańczak, Krzysztof Gąsiorowski, Zbigniew Herbert, Tadeusz Kubiak, Anatol Stern, Jacek Trznadel, Józef Wittlin, Czesław Miłosz, Wiktor Woroszylski, Adam Zagajewski.
42. **Chatterjee, S.P.**: Poland and its Frontiers. Calcutta, Calcutta Geographical Society. 1939.
43. **Curie Eve**: Madam Kuri. Tłum. z ang. Kalpana Ray. Calcutta, Radical, 1962.
44. **Czapski, Józef**: The Mystery of Katyń. [Bombay], Indo.-Pol.Lib., [1946]. Przedruk
45. **Cześć Marii.** Księga Sodalicji Mariańskich w Indiach. Valivade, Polska Misja Katolicka, 1947.
46. **Czyński, L.**: Apteczka dla obozów harcerskich. Valivade, Indyjska Biblioteka Harcerska, 1946.
47. **Czytanki Polskie.** Na klasę III szkoły powszechnej. Karachi, Delegatura Min.WRiOP.,[1944].
48. **Czytanki Polskie.** Na klasę IV szkoły powszechnej. Karachi, Delegatura Min.WRiOP.,[1944].
49. **Czytanki Polskie.** Na klasę V szkoły powszechnej. Karachi, Delegatura Min.WRiOP.,[1944].
50. **Czytanki Polskie.** Na klasę VI szkoły powszechnej. Karachi, Delegatura Min. W.R.i O.P.,[1944].
51. **Dangerfield, Elma**: Deportees. Bombay, Indo-Polish Library, 1945. Przedruk.
52. **Dasa, N.K.**: Krótka monografia o Polsce. [Bombay], Bibl. Pol.-Ind.,[1945]. Broszura w języku hindi.
53. **Dharma.** Przeznaczenie, dobro i zło. Przekł. W.Dynowska. Madras, Bibl.Pol.-Ind., 1961.
54. **Dhopeswarkar, Atmarama i Dynowska, Wanda**.: O nauce Krishnamurtiego. Madras, Bibl. Pol.-Ind.,1955. Na okł. tytuł: Dwa głosy o nowej nauce. Zawiera Nauki i Rady Krishnamurtiego, referat wygłoszonya Kongresie Filozoficznym.
55. **Dollan, Patrick J.**: Socialists and Poland. Bombay, Indo-Polish Library, [1945].Przedruk.
56. **Dudryk - Darlewsk**i, Antoni : Geografia Indii - Kraj, Ludzie, Gospodarstwo. Bangalore, Bibl. Pol.-Ind.,1948.
57. **Dudryk - Darlewsk**i, Antoni : Krótki zarys geografii Indii. Valivade, Komenda Chorągwi Ind. ZHP.,1947.
58. **Dynowska, Wanda** : Z pielgrzymką hinduską w głąb Himalajów. Bombaj, Bibl.Pol.-Ind.,1944.
59. **Dynowska, Wanda** : The Heart of a Nation. Bombay, Indo-Polish Library, [1945].
60. **Dynowska, Wanda** : Ideals of Polish History. [Bombay], Indo-Polish Library, [1945].
61. **Dynowska, Wanda** : Underground Poland. Bombay, Indo-Polish Library, [1945]
62. **Dynowska, Wanda** : Indie w walce o wolność. Aundh, wyd. M. Frydman dla Bibl.Pol.-Ind.,1947. Broszura zawiera wiersz "Vande Mataram" - cześć Tobie Matko.
63. **Dynowska, Wanda** : Razem pod wiatr. Wiersze indyjskie; Pożegnanie Polski; Z rozmów ze sobą. Bangalore, Bibl. Pol.-Ind.,1948.
64. **Dynowska, Wanda** : Pożegnanie Polski. Z rozmów ze sobą. Bangalore, Bibl.Pol.-Ind.,1948.
65. **Dynowska, Wanda** : Wiersze indyjskie. [Bombaj]. [Bibl.Pol.-Ind.], 1962.
66. **Dynowska, Wanda** : Pielgrzymka hinduska w głąb Himalajów oraz Kaszmiru. Madras, Bibl. Pol.-Ind., II wydanie, 1959.
67. **Dynowska W**. Jinarajadasa, Curuppullage : O przyrodzie i sztuce. Madras, Bibl.Pol.-Ind.,1961.
68. **Dynowska, Wanda** : Czy tylko raz żyjemy na ziemi? Rzecz o reinkarnacji. Wedle danych Wschodu i Zachodu. Madras, Bibl. Pol.-Ind.,1962.
69. **Events and personalities of Polish history**. Bombay, Indo-Polish Library, 1944. Przedruk z Torunia 1936.
70. **Ewangelia według św. Marka**. Przedruk, nakładem Lady Dow. Karachi, 1943.
71. **Ewangelia Hinduizmu**. Przekł. W. Dynowska. [Bombaj], Bibl. Pol.-Ind.,[1945].
72. **Falk, Maryla, dr** : Król Himalajów. [Bombaj], Bibl.Pol.-Ind.,[1944].
73. **Falski, Marian** : Elementarz cz.1. Karachi, Delegatura Min.WRiOP.,1944.
74. **Falski, Marian** : Elementarz cz.1. Karachi, Delegatura Min.WRiOP.,1946.
75. **F.E.**: The Soviet Occupation of Poland 1939-1941. Bombay, wydawca Maurycy Frydman, Aundh Publishing Trust dla Bibl.Pol.-Ind.,1945. Przedruk z broszury Free Europe.
76. **Fifteenth August** - its meaning for India and the World. Bombay, Bil.Pol.-Ind.,1947. Przedruk.
77. **Frydman, Maurycy [Bharatanandra]**: Zbiór wierszy. [Bombay], Bibl.Pol.-Ind.,[1948].
78. **Ghose, Aurobindo Shri**: Pramacierz i jej postacie oraz światła na drodze jogi Przekł. W. Dynowska. Madras, Bibl.Pol.-Ind.,1958.
79. **Ghose, Aurobindo Shri** : Joga i co w niej pomaga. Przekł. W. Dynowska. Madras, Bibl.Pol.-Ind.,1962.
80. **Gibran, Kahli**l : Prorok. Przekł. W. Dynowska. Madras, Bibl.Pol.-Ind.,1954.
81. **Gibran, Kahli**l: Jezus, Syn człowieczy. Jego słowa i czyny zapisane i opowiedziane przez tych, którzy Go znali. Przekł. W. Dynowska. Madras, Bibl.Pol.-Ind.,1956.

82. **Grabowski, Zbigniew**: Twenty years of Polish Independence. Bombay, Wydawca M.Frydman Bibl.Pol.Ind. dla Aundh Publishing Trust, 1945. Przedruk.
83. **Grabski, Stanisław**: The Polish - Russian frontier. Bombay, wyd. M.Frydman dla Bibl.Pol.-Ind.,[1944]. Przedruk.
84. **The Heart of a Nation**. Bombay, Indo-Polish Library, [1945]. Przedruk.
85. **Henderson, Horace Wright** : The Polish Conspiracy ?. Bombay, Bibl.Pol.- Ind.,[1945]. Przedruk.
86. **Henderson, Horace Wright** : Polish - Soviet Relations 1917-1945. [An outline of Polish - Soviet relations]. Bombay, Bibl.Pol. Ind.,[1945]. Przedruk.
87. **Herbert, Jan**: Wielcy Myśliciele Indii Współczesnych. Tłum. H. Witkowska. Svatandrapur Aundh, Bibl.Pol.-Ind.,1945. Przedruk z 1938.
88. **Homarin Irakaciyam**. Tłum. na jęz. tamil. S. Somasundaram. Madras, New Century, 1970. Autorzy utworów: St. Lem, Konrad Fiałkowski, Andrzej Czechowski.
89. **In the Depths of Soviet Russia**. Bombay, wyd. M.Frydman dla Indo-Polish Library, [1945]. Wspomnienia młodej nauczycielki z zesłania do Rosji 1939-1941.
90. **India and Poland**. Calcutta, International Federation of Culture, 1941. Praca zbiorowa: Rabindranath Tagore, Sir Sarvapalli Radhakrishnan, Pramatha Nath Banerjea, Suniti Kumar Chatterjee, Shahid Suhrawardy, Benoy Kumar Sarkar, Kalidas Nag oraz Maryla Falk. Publikacja zawiera fragmenty przekładów przez Marylę Falk na jęz. hindi poematów: Adama Mickiewicza "Dziady", Juliusza Słowackiego "Król Duch", Zygmunta Krasińskiego "Przedświt".
91. **Indology of Poland**. rozprawa w "Annals of the Bhandarkar Oriental Research Institute", vol XXIV.
92. **Jałowiecki-MacDonald, Mieczysław i Barski J** : Free Poland. Bombay, wyd. M.Frydman dla Bibl.Pol. Ind.,[1945]. Przedruk z Free Europe.
93. **Jarosz, Włodzimierz i Kargol Adolf** : Opowiadania z dziejów ojczystych, cz.I i II. dla 5 i 6 kl., Karachi, Min.WRiOP.,[1944].
94. **Jasińska, Magdalena** : O samopoznaniu i psychice intergralnej. Bombay, Indo-Polish Library, 1975. [Nadbitka: Moralność i społeczeństwo. Księga jubileuszowa dla Marii Ossowskiej, Warszawa 1969]. Dotyczy nauki Jiddu Krishnamurtiego.
95. **Jinarajadasa, Curuppumllage** : Człowiek we wszechświecie, według okultyzmu. T i-2, Przekł. W. Dynowska. Madras, Bibl.Pol.-Ind.,1957.
96. **Jinarajadasa, Curuppumllage**: Prawo ofiary. W imię jego. Nauka serca. Przekł. W. Dynowska. Madras, Bibl.Pol.-Ind.,1956.
97. **Jinarajadasa, Curuppumllage**: Prawo ofiary. W imię jego. Nauka serca. Przekł. W. Dynowska. Madras, Wydanie II, 1959.
98. **Jinarajadasa, Curuppumllage** : O przyrodzie i sztuce. Przekł. W. Dynowska. Madras, Bibl.Pol.-Ind.,1961.
99. **Jodłowski, Stanisław** : Gramatyka polska dla klasy VI szkoły powszechnej. Karachi Delegatura Min.WRiOP.,1943.
100. **Jordan, Peter [pseud.], Lutosławski, Aleksander, Tadeusz**: First to Fight. Bombay, Bibl.Pol.-Ind.,1944. Przedruk.
101. **Kalendarz Harcerza w Indiach 1947.** Bombaj: Biblioteka Harcerska, 1947.
102. **Kantak, Kamil**: Dzieje uchodźców polskich w Libanie 1943-1950. Przedruk "Cedr i Orzeł", Bejrut. Madras, Wyd. W. Dynowska [Bibl.Pol.-Ind.], 1955.
103. **Katechizm Religii Katolickiej.** Valivade, Wydawca SPKP, 1947.
104. **Kinvig, R. H.**: Poland. Wyd. University of Calcutta, [n.d.]
105. **Klemensiewicz, Zenon**: Język polski dla klasy V szkoły powszechnej. Karachi, Delegatura Min. WRiOP, 1943.
106. **Kochanowski, Jan**: Gypsy studies.New Delhi: International Academy of Indian Culture, 1963. Dotyczy polskich cyganów.
107. **Kot, Stanisław**: Five centuries of Polish Learning. Bombay, Indo-Polish Library, 1944. Przedruk z Blackwell.
108. **Krishnamurti, Jiddu** : Nowe podejście do życia. Tłum.W. Dynowska. Bangalore[Bibl.Pol.-Ind.], 1948 Bez znaków polskich.
109. **Krishnamurti, Jiddu** : Nowe podejście do życia. Tłum.W. Dynowska. Bombay, Bibl.Pol.-Ind.,1975.
110. **Krishnamurti, Jiddu** : O Polsce i Finlandii. Przekł. W. Dynowska na jęz. Tamil. Madras, Bibl.Pol.-Ind.,1959.
111. **Krishnamurti, Jiddu** : Uwagi o ludziach i życiu. Przekł. W. Dynowska. Madras, Bibl.Pol.-Ind.,1968.
112. **Krishnamurti, Jiddu** : Dogłębna przemiana człowieka jako jedyne wyjście z obecnego chaosu. Z przemówień w Londynie w 1953 [Przekł. W. Dynowska]. Madras, Bibl.Pol.-Ind.,1954.
113. **Krishnamurti, Jiddu** : Przemiana człowieka. Przekł.z ang. W. Dynowska. Bombaj, Bibl.Pol.-Ind.,1969.
114. **Krishnamurti, Jiddu**: Przemiana człowieka. Przekł. z ang. W. Dynowska, Bombaj,Bibl.Pol.-Ind.,1975. Wyd. II.
115. **Krishnamurti, Jiddu** : Uwagi o ludziach i życiu. Przekł. W. Dynowska. Bombay, Bibl.Pol.-Ind.,1970. Wyd.II skrócone.
116. **Krishnamurti, Jiddu** : Ku wyzwoleniu. Przekł. W. Dynowska, wybór przemówień T.1. 1928-1948, T.2. 1931-1934, [Bombay], Bibl.Pol.-Ind.,1950.
117. **Krishnamurti, Jiddu** : Ku wyzwoleniu. Przekł. W. Dynowska. II wydanie. [n.m], Bibl.Pol.-Ind.,1969.
118. **Kukliński, Antoni** : Contributions of regional planning and development, Mysore Institute of Development Studies, 1971.
119. **Kurs harców i obóz wędrowniczek.** Valivade, Praca zbiorowa pod redakcją Z. Peszkowskiego, Komendy Chorągwi Indyjskiej ZHPpgk., 1947.
120. **Leadbeater, Charles Webster**: Człowiek wczoraj...jutro. Przekł. W.Dynowska. [Bombaj], Bibl.Pol.-Ind.,1970.
121. **Leitgeber, Bolesław** : East and West in man's perrenial quest. Calcutta, A Writers Workshop Publication, 1978. Przedruk.
122. **Leeuw, Jacobus Johannes** : Bogowie na wygnaniu. Zmora zła. Przekł. W. Dynowska. Madras, Bibl.Pol. Ind.,1959.
123. **Lies, Trials, Atomic Bomb**. Praca zbiorowa : St. Mackiewicz, F.A. Voigt, S. Stroński. [Bombay], Indo-Polish Library, [1945]. Przedruk.

124. **Malinowski, W.R.**: Towards Polish Russian Understanding. [Bombay], Bibl.Pol.-Ind.,[1944]. Przedruk.
125. **Mały Modlitewnik**. Karachi, Wyd.Ks.A. Jankowski [SPKP], 1944.
126. **Matuszewski, Ignacy** : What Poland Wants. [Bombay], Indo-Polish Library, [1944]. Przedruk.
127. **Mickiewicz, Adam**: [Róża Polska]. Częściowy przekł. Sonetów Krymskich na język Hindi przez Umshanker Joshi. Bombay, Bibl.Pol.-Ind.,1944.
128. **Miedzińska, Janina** : The protection of women workers and minors in Poland. Tłum. May Bamford. Bombay, Bibl.Pol.-Ind.,1945. Przedruk z wyd. londyńskiego 1941.
129. **Miłosz, Czesław**: The Issa valley. [Dolina Issy]. Tłum. Louis Iribarne. Calcutta, Rupa, 1982.
130. **Misra, Amulyakrsna** : Myadam Kyuri. Bhubaneswar, Orisa State Bureau of Text, Book, 1978.
131. **Modlitewnik Uchodźczy**. Valivade, Wyd. War Relief Service [SPKP], 1947.
132. **Mukhopadhyay, Kanak**: Ekti samajtantrik dese kayekdin. Calcutta, Pachimbanga Ganatantrik Mahila Samity, 1984. Dotyczy społeczeństwa polskiego.
133. **Nauka Shri Ramana Maharishi**. Przekł. W. Dynowska, Madras, Bibl.Pol.-Ind.,1957.
134. **Nauka Szhi Ramana Maharish**i. Przekł. W. Dynowska. Madras, Bibl.Pol.-Ind.,1959.
135. **Nauka Shri Ramana Maharishi**. Przekł. W. Dynowska. Madras, Bibl.Pol.-Ind.,1959.
136. **Newman, Bernard**: The People of Poland. Bombay, Indo-Polish Library, 1945. Przedruk.
137. **Newman, Bernard** : The People of Poland. Bombay, Indo-Polish Library, 1945.Tłum. na jęz. hindi.
138. **Niranjana, Tejaswini i Reszewski, Zdzisław**: Eppathaidu Polish kavitegalu. Antologia 75 polskich współczesnych poematów tłum. na Kannada. Bangalore, Kathaa Saahitya, 1978.
139. **O'Koński, Alwin.E.**: America on Poland. Bombay, Indo-Polish Library, 1945. Przedruk.
140. **O'Koński, Alwin, E.**: The Moscow Trial. [Bombay], Indo-Polish Library, [1945]. Przedruk.
141. **Omkar** : Medytacja o sobie. Tłum.z ang. W.Dynowska. Bombay, Bibl.Pol.Ind.,1973.
142. **Omkar** : Medytacja o sobie. Tłum.z ang. W.Dynowska. Bombay, Bibl.Pol.Ind.,1974.
143. **Paderewski, Ignacy** : Chopin. [Bombay], Bibl.Pol.-Ind., [1945]. Przedruk.
144. **Palestyna Ziemia święta**. Valivade, Przewodnik po wystawie, wyd.Krąg wodzów zuchowych, 1944.
145. **Peace? a symposium**. [Bombay], Indo-Polish Library, [1945]. Praca zbiorowa pisarzy europejskich i amerykańskich: Don Levine, Roggers, H.W.Henderson, Colen, Brogan.
146. **Plain Facts about Poland**. Broszura. [Bibl.Pol.-Ind.,Bombay, 1945].
147. **Podręcznik do nauki zecersko-drukarskiej**. Opracował Franciszek Andrzejewski. Valivade, Drukarnia szkolna SPKP, 1947.
148. **Podstawy Hinduskiej Kultury,** z różnych autorów. Przekł. W.Dynowska. T.1. Madras, Bibl.Pol.-Ind.,1964. Zawiera: Coomaraswami Ananda, Banerji, R. Tagore i inni.
149. **Poland**. Opr. Zdzisław Tomczyk. Tłum. z ang. na Bengali Kamal Gupta. Calcutta, wyd. Consulate of the Polish Peoples Republic, 1969.
150. **Polish Exhibition Catalogue.** Bombay, Min.Pracy i Opieki Społecznej, 1944.
151. **Polish-Soviet Relations 1917-1939**. Facts and Documents. Bombay, 1944. Przedruk.
152. **Polish Poetry**. Opr. W. Dynowska. Bombay, Indo-Polish Library, [1945].
153. **Polish Short Stories**. Opr. Umadevi [W. Dynowska]. Swatantrapur Aundh, wyd. M. Frydman dla Indo-Polish Library, 1946. Utwory: J. Weyssenhoffa, M. Konopnickiej, S. Żeromskiego, K.P.Tetmajera, J. Pietrkiewicza, H. Naglerowej i innych.
154. **Ponikowska, M.L. i Jurkowa M.**: Polish youth yesterday, today and tomorrow. Bombay, Bibl.Pol.-Ind.,1945. Przedruk z poprzednich wyd.z 1942.
155. **Praca Wędrowniczek i Skautów**. Praca zbiorowa pod red. Z. Peszkowskiego. Valivade, Komenda Chorągwi Indyjskiej, ZHP na Wschodzie, 1947. Praca zbiorowa w 3 częściach: Z. Peszkowski, H. Szafranek, A. Handerek, ks. K. Kozłowski, Z. Ostrihanska, M. Leśniak, I. Adamczyk, J. Snastin, E. Woyniłłowicz, E. Czekierska, H. Suszko, D. Czech, D. Pniewska.
156. **Prawo ofiary.** Opr. częściowo W. Dynowska według Annie Besant i C. Jinaradajasa. W imię Jego. W. Dynowska: Nauka serca [B.m.w.], Bibl.Pol.-Ind., 1956.
157. **Preston, Elizabeth** : Historia stworzenia i historia człowieka według Nauki tajemnej. Bławatskiej. Przekł W. Dynowska. Madras, wyd. "Ludziom Dobrej Woli", 1956.
158. **Ramana Maharish**i, **Bhagavan Shri**: Nauka Szri Ramana Mahariszi. Przekł. W. Dynowska. Madras, Bibl.Pol.-Ind.,1959. Zawiera: Sat-Wida, Upadesza Saram, Hymny do Arunadali.
159. **Ramana Maharishi, Bhagavan Shr**i: Nauka Szri Ramana Mahariszi. Przekł. W. Dynowska i M. Frydman. Bombay Bibl.Pol.-Ind.,1969. Wybór utworów.
160. **Rawicz, Sławomir i Downing, Roland**: Mala nisatalac pahije. Tłum. z ang. Srikanta Lagu. Pune, Rajahamsa Prakashan, 1984. Oryg. tyt. The long walk.
161. **Resurrecturis. to Them Who Will Rise Again 1.IX.1939-1.IX.1940**. Bombay, Polish Relief Committee, 1940. Numer specjalny do czasopisma Polish Relief Work.
162. **Rose, William J. prof.**: The Growth of Polish Democracy. Bombay, Bibl.Pol.-Ind.,[1944]. Przedruk.
163. **Różewicz, Tadeusz** : Goci [Wyszedł z domu]. Tłum.z ang. na Marati Sadananda Santaram Rege. Bombay, 1974.

164. **Różne głosy o nowej nauce**. Praca zbiorowa: Rao Sandżiwa, Ewelina K., M. Frydman, Francis de Miomandre, Dżajakar, M. Payne. Oprac. W. Dynowska. Madras, [Bibl.Pol.-Ind.], 1957.
165. **The Scarlet Muse**. An anthology of Polish poems. Opr. W. Dynowska. Bombay, Wydawca i red. Harishandra Bhatt, 1945. Autorzy utworów: J. Kochanowski, A. Mickiewicz, A. Fredro, K. Norwid, K. Wierzyński i inni.
166. **Sienkiewicz, Henryk:** W pustyni i w puszczy. Karachi, Delgatura Min.WRiOP, 1944.Ilustr. S. Norblina.
167. **Sienkiewicz, Henryk**: Quo Vadis. Tłum. na Hindi Sekhar. New Delhi, 1969.
168. **Skolimowski, Henryk**: Technology and human destiny. Madras, Madras University, 1983.
169. **Socialists and the Polish Cause**. Praca zbiorowa: M.R.Masani, Philip Murray, Robert Watt, David Dubiński. Swatantrapur Aundh, wyd. M.Frydman dla Indo-PolishLibrary, 1945. Zawiera cytaty Lenina, Marxa, Liebknechta, Trockiego.
170. **Souvenir Book**. Książka pamiątkowa z Międzynarodowej Wystawy Kultury. Bombaj, wyd. Komitet Wystawy Klubu Rotarystów, 1945.
171. **Souvenir of the Memorial Meeting** organised by Indo-Polish Association to celebrate the 400 years of Nicolas Copernicus 1473-1543. Opracowała dr Maryla Falk w jęz. ang. Calcutta, wyd. Indo-Polish Association 1944.
172. **Sternbach, Ludwik:** Archaic and ancient Indian terracottas. Bombay, Druk S.A. Bliss, Examiner Press, 1941. Dotyczy kolekcji Konsula Generalnego Eugeniusza Banasińskiego.
173. **Sternbach, Ludwik:** A sociological study of the forms of marriage in ancient India. Annals of the Bhandharkar Oriental Research Institute vol.22, 1942. Odczyt.
174. **Sternbach, Ludwik:** Juridical studies in ancient Indian law. The Raksasa-Vivaha and the Paisaca-Vivaha. New Indian Antiquary vol.6, 1943. Odczyt.
175. **Sternbach, Ludwik**: The harmonising of law with the requirements of economic conditions according to the ancient Indian Dharmasastras, Arthasastras and Grhyasutras. [Indie, 1943]. Odczyt.
176. **Sternbach, Ludwik:** Juridical studies in ancient Indian law; Reciprocal responsibility for debts contracted by married people. The Annals of the Bhandarkar Oriental Research Institute vol 24, Poona, 1944. Odczyt.
177. **Sternbach, Ludwik**: Legal relations between employers and employees in ancient India. The Poona Orientalist vol 8, Poona, 1944. Odczyt.
178. **Sternbach, Ludwik**: India as known to medieaval Europe. Journal of the Annamalai University. 1944. Odczyt.
179. **Sternbach, Ludwik**: Some forms of marriage in ancient India. Journal of the Annamalai University, [Bombaj], 1944. Odczyt.
180. **Sternbach, Ludwik**: Vesya - synonyms and aphorisms. Bharatiya Vidya, vol.IV. Bombay, 1945. Odczyt.
181. **Sternbach, Ludwik**: India as described by Mediaeval European travellers. Bharatiya Vidya, vol.VII. Bombay, 1946. Odczyt.
182. **Sternbach, Ludwik** : Juridical Aspects of the Gandharva Form of Marriage. The Poona Orientalist, vol.X.[Bombay], 1946. Odczyt.
183. **Sternbach, Ludwik** : Juridical Studies in Ancient Indian Law. Bharatiya Vidya, vol.VII. Bombay, 1946. Odczyt.
184. **Strassburger, Henryk** : The core of a Continent. Bombay, 1944, Indo-Polish Library.
185. **Stroński, Stanisław** : The Atlantic Charter. Swatantrapur Aundh, wyd. M.Frydman dla Bibl.Pol.-Ind.,1945.
186. **Super, Paul** : Elements of Polish Culture. Bombay, Indo-Polish Library, 1944. Przedruk z Baltic Pocket Library.
187. **Super, Paul** : Events and personalities in Polish history. Bombay, Indo-Polish Library, 1944. Przedruk z publikacji z 1936.
188. **Święto pieśni Tamilnadu**. Antologia hinduskiej poezji religijnej. Przekład W. Dynowska. Bombay, Bibl.Pol.-Ind., [1944].
189. **Symptoms of Life, Symptoms of Love**. Antologia poematów współczesnych. Przekład i redagowanie Z. Reszelewski i N. Simms. Calcutta, Writers Workshop, 1980. Autorzy utworów: U. Kozioł, K. Iłłakowiczówna, M. Pawlikowska-Jasnorzewska, W. Szymborska, M. Buczkówna, A. Pogonowska, E. Lipska, M. Bocian.
190. **Tagore, Rabindranath** : Sadhana. Tłum. W. Dynowska. Madras, Bibl.Pol.-Ind.,1960.
191. **Themerson, Stefan** : Była gdzieś taka wieś. Bombaj, Min.WRiOP., 1946. Przedruk z książeczki dla dzieci wydrukowanej w Warszawie.
192. **Theosophist**. Czasopismo w jęz. ang. vol.LXIII poświęcone Polsce. Madras, Adyar, 1942.
193. **Thomas, Vellilamtatam**: Despair, hope and bliss. Kottayam, Oriental Institute Publications, 1980. Dotyczy wypowiedzi papieża Jana Pawła II.
194. **Tiruvalluvar:** Tiru - Kural. Arcydzieło tamilskiej literatury, 1 wiek przed Chryst. Przekład W.Dynowska. Madras, Bibl.Pol.-Ind.,1958.
195. **Tokarczyk, Roman**: Some remarks on the contemporary political thought.Indian Journal of Politics, vol 10, 1976.
196. **Trzy drogowskazy**. Dla tych którzy szukają ducha. Przekład W.Dynowska. Madras, BIbl.Pol.-Ind.,1955.
197. **Trzy drogowskazy**. Dla tych którzy szukają ducha. Przekład W. Dynowska. Madras,Bibl.Pol.-Ind.,1960.
198. **Tyabji, Raihanah**: Serce Gopi - Pasterki. Poemat w przekładzie W.Dynowskiej. Bangalore, Bibl.Pol.-Ind.,1948.
199. **Vatsya, Santaram**: Meri Kyuri. Delhi, Jnan Bharati, 1971. Dotyczy Marii Curie-Skłodowskiej.
200. **Valivade**. Album pamiątkowy. Valivade, Związek Harcerstwa Polskiego na Wschodzie, 1945.
201. **Valivade**. Album pamiątkowy. Valivade, Związek Harcerstwa Polskiego na Wschodzie, 1946.
202. **Voigt, Fritz August**: Poland, Russia and Great Britain. Bombay, Indo-Polish Library, [1944]. Przedruk.
203. **Voigt, Fritz August**: The Polish Question. Bombay, Indo-Polish Library, [1944]. Przedruk.

204. **W.R.**: History of Poland. Bombay, Indo-Polish Library, [1944]. Przedruk.
205. **Warsaw, the martyr city**. [Bombay], Indo-Polish Library, [1945]. Przedruk.
206. **Welcome to Goa**, Pope John Paul II. Souvenir book. Goa Coord. Centre, 1986.
207. **Weyers W.J.**: Poland and Russia. Bombay, Indo-Polish Library, [1944]. Przedruk.
208. **Wielhorski, Władysław**: The Polish Eastern Provinces. Bombay, Indo-Polish Library, [1945]. Przedruk.
209. **Wysocka, M.dr**: Apteczka polowa. Valivade, SPKP, 1946.
210. **The Winter Maidens and other short stories**. Zbiór nowel polskich w opracowaniu W. Dynowskiej. Bombay, wyd. M. Frydman dla Indo-Polish Library, 1947. Utwór Zimowej Panny ze Skalnego Podhala K. Tetmajera, inni autorzy: P. Chojnowski, W. Reymont, Jan Karski, J. Meissner.
211. **Wianuszek drogocenny o Dharmie Buddhy wśród ptaków**. Ludowa pieśń tybetańska Przekład W. Dynowska. 1967.
212. **Zajączkowska, Anna**: The Underground Struggle. Bombay, Bibl.Pol.-Ind., [1945]. Przedruk.
213. **Zaleska, Zofia**: The Welfare of Mothers and Children in Poland. Bombay, Indo-Polish Library, [1945]. Przedruk.
214. **Zeltech, A.**: Inside Poland. Bombay, Indo-Polish Library, 1945. Przedruk. Zawiera 3 części: From inside Poland; The story of Maria Morska; Alexander Erlich speaks of his father.
215. **Żerebecki, Zdzisław**: Nauczyciel - szkice o zawodzie nauczycielskim. Valivade, Nakładem drukarni szkolnej, 1947.

PERIODICALS

1. **Biuletyn Amerykańskiej Służby Pomocy Katolickiej Polakom (SPKP)**. [Bombay], 1946, Dyrekcja War Relief Services (NCWR). Czasopismo.
2. **Biuletyn Wewnętrzny Zarządu Centralnego Zjednoczenia Polaków w Indiach.** Valivade, 1946, Zjednoczenie Polaków w Indiach. Czasopismo.
3. **Głos Osiedla** - codzienny biuletyn na powielaczu. Wydawca Polski Komitet Opieki nad Uchodźcami w Valivade, 1946.
4. **Informacja Prasowa**. Tygodnik informacyjny na powielaczu wydawany w Valivade [1947].
5. **Młodzi**. Czasopismo na powielaczu. Valivade, 1947, Wydawca Krąg Starszoharcerski Płomień Dżungli.
6. **Na Etapie**. Gazetka szkolna, wydawca Koło literackie przy gimn. w Malir i Valivade, 1943.
7. **Polak w Indiach**. Czasopismo. Wydawca Min.Pracy i Opieki Społecznej od 1943-1945, Bombaj. Od No. 50-117, 1945-1948 wydawcą Zjednoczenie Polaków w Indiach, Valivade.
8. **Polish News**. Czasopismo w jęz. ang. Bombay, 1942. Wydawca Zjednoczenie Polaków w Indiach.
9. **Polish Relief Work**. Czasopismo w jęz.ang. Bombay, 1939, Komitet Pomocy Polakom.
10. **Słoniątko Indyjskie**. Dodatek dla dzieci, wydawany przez Polaka w Indiach. Bombay Min.WRiOP, 1944-1947. Red. Janina Sułkowska, ilust. Krystyna Biskupska.
11. **W Kręgu Pracy**. Czasopismo harcerskie na powielaczu. Wyd.Komenda Chorągwi Indyjskiej w Valivade.
12. **W Kręgu Wodzów**. Czasopismo harcerskie. Wyd. Krąg Wodzów Zuchowych w Valivade.

INDEX OF NAMES IN THE BOOK SECOND WORLD WAR STORY OF POLES IN INDIA 1942-1948

The index may not be completely accurate, because the spelling of some names vary
in individual documents and texts of different authors

Abramowicz Józefat 285, 302, 303, 313, 330 , 347

Achmatowicz Teresa 520

Adamczak Wojciech 207, 213

Adamczyk/Dziewulak Irena 225, 331, 335, 376, 380, 414, 427, 466, 470, 509

Adamek Bronisława 234, 240

Adamek Maria 07, 213

Alberti Zofia 303

Albol Aleksander

Albrecht Stanisława

Aleksandrowicz Leokadia 331

Alfonsa Maria Sr 563

Alina Sr. 318

Allan S. 146, 147, 148, 152, 154

Allen W. D. 481

Amery L. S. 40

Anders Gen. 296

Anders Władysław xi, 9, 11, 19, 20, 26, 53

Andrijewska Zofia 279

Andrzejewski Franciszek 594

"Anielka"/Wawrzyńczyk 387

Antolik 458

Antolik Maria 200

Antoszewicz Maria 279

Appadurai Benjamin 297, 330, 441

Appadurai/Cherian Sushila 442

Appadurai David 442

Ashani Kirit 95, 100, 576

Atkinson Col. 55

Augustyn Jerzy 290, 363, 390, 413, 414

Babis Teresa Zofia 279

Babula Roman 405

Bachrynowski 207, 423

Baden-Powell Robert 352, 397, 408

Badura Hania 248

Bage B.B. v, 581

Bagińska Zofia 191

Bahadur Khan 198

Bahari 530

Balawender/Brzozowska Mila vi, 28, 414

Balawender/Stohandel Zofia 331, 335, 368, 382, 379, 412, 413, 414, 497, 548, 549, 561

Baliński A. 39

Ball/Kunigiel Helena 580

Bałaban Andrzej 7, 8, 12, 19, 20

Bałaban Łucja 251

Banaji Dr. 62

Banasińska Kira 48, 52, 54, 60, 61, 64, 66, 74, 75, 76, 81, 82, 84, 92, 100, 155, 183, 189, 192, 198, 577, 587, 591

Banasiński Eugeniusz 20, 40, 46, 47, 48, 49, 50, 63, 64, 70, 74, 77, 161, 173, 175, 171, 182, 191, 198, 212, 241, 295, 356, 379, 556

Banbuła Waldemar 279

Baniowski Stanisław 279

Baran Stanisława 234

Baranek F.M. 51, 591

Baranowski Franciszek 191

Bargiełowska/Mickiewicz Kazimiera 234, 554

Barowicz/Harbuz Bożena 331, 459

Bartosz Zbigniew 93, 96, 488, 520, 521, 567, 568, 570, 571

Basarab Józefa 331

Batis Karol 318

Batogowski Marian 267

Bazergan Jalal 61, 62, 348, 349

Bazergan/Góral Dula 442

Bąbik/Rafałówna Halina 337, 340, 421, 498

Bąk Ada 405

Bąk Eugeniusz 428, 553

Bąk Marian 339

Bąkowski Adam 405

Bednarska Józefa 546

Belbot Agata 251

Bełdowski Leszek vi, x, 33, 165, 342, 365, 377, 379, 395, 396, 566, 578, 580

Benal Ludwik 205, 231

Benal/Golenia Paulina 234

Berch Marian vi, 53, 54, 55, 170

Bereźnicki Mikołaj 206

Beria Ławrientij 7, 9

Bernatowicz Joanna 304, 330

Besant Annie 45, 591, 594

Bevin Ernest 482, 489, 490, 505

Bezdel Ewalda (Wala) 224, 234

Bhagavan Sri Ramana Maharishi 468, 594

Bhalla D.S. 188, 196, 457

Bhatt Harishandra 46, 595

Bhattacharjee Anuradha 585

Bidakowski Władysław 185, 204

Bidakowski Witold 184, 190, 207, 246, 266, 304, 353, 354, 356, 381

Bielawska Maria 310, 330

Bielecka Kazimiera 191

Bielecki Jan 576

Bielska/Kowałko Pelagia 234

Bielski Edward 539, 543

Bień Eugenia 238, 331, 509

Bieńkowska/Czech Danuta 546

Bierońska vel Biedrońska Józefa,

Bierut Bolesław 295, 522

Bilimoria H. 62

Bilińska Karolina 318, 329

Bill (dog) 363, 385, 396, 399, 401, 409, 413, 414

Birar Antoni 281, 285, 290, 291

Birecki Jan 405

Biskupska/Iglikowska Krystyna 56, 57, 285, 340, 596

Blumska Maria 191

Blumski Romuald 225, 285, 337, 347, 413, 414, 435, 501

Błach Alojzy vii, 308, 342, 344, 347, 348, 358, 364, 370, 413, 515

Błach M. 231

Błachowa Maria 234

Błaszczak Rysiek 343

Błażej Edward Karaś Fr. 265, 273, 366, 552

Bober-Bobrowski Kazimierz Fr. 55, 62, 260, 261, 263, 381, 382

Bobin Maria 537

Bobolska Maria 302, 303, 330

Bobolski Z. 437

Bodura Anna 279

Bodura Zofia 191

Boekwad Maharaja 89

Bogdanowicz/Ścibek Lonia 552, 554

Bogdańska Renata 27

Bojarska Maria 308, 331

Bojko Aleksander 433

Borońska M. 138, 247, 301, 306, 323, 326, 330, 335, 339, 530,532,552, 554, 561, 563, 566

Boroński Witold 319

Borowiak Genowefa 412

Borucki Gwido 27

Borzemska/Dziedzic Wanda 302, 325, 330, 340, 338, 357, 412

Bozman G.S. 180

Bożek M. 93, 96

Brady Gen. 155

Bratkowska Janina 191

Bratkowska Stanisława 413, 414, 546

Brażuk Jadwiga 184

Brindley Pamela 141

Brink Maria 470

Bronowicz Jadwiga 251

Bronowicka Zofia 191

Brunnee Barbara Dr. 158, 159

Bruner Halina 55

Brycki Bolesław 279

Bryl Mieczysław 506

Brzezińska Anna 281

Brzęczek Andrzej 578

Brzęczek Jadwiga 578

Buc Aniela 279

Buc Jarosław 342

Budnik Lucjan 187

Budny 66

Bukowska Ala 576

Bukowski Stefan 94, 287, 563, 656, 576

Burakiewicz Maria 320, 491, 493

Burdzy Fredek 120

Burdzy/Krzyżaniak Kazimiera 545, 546

Burek/Hałko Ola 546, 548

Burek Teresa 9

Burrows L.R. 154

Button Mabel 184, 185, 190, 194, 196, 198, 217, 218, 220, 301,437, 482, 499, 501

Byrski M.K. 567, 568

Cadogan Alexander George 20, 65

Cariuk Kleopatra 281, 285, 331, 470, 509

Carrington C.E. 30, 34

Cazalet 41

Celejewski Józef 405

Chałubiński Tytus 130

Chamberlain Neville 5

Charuba/Morawska Barbara 548, 561

Charuba Basia 561

Chełmecka/Sobol Dzidka 470, 546

Chendyński Andrzej vii, 258, 337, 488

Chesson John 130

Chmielowcowa/Świątkowska Irena 57, 437

Chmielowska Aniela 421

Chmielowska Halina 291, 414

Chmielowska Joanna (Jaśka) v, 155, 291, 293, 364, 413, 414, 511, 517

Chmielowska Zofia 234, 279

Chociej Krystyna 152, 540

Chodorowski Tadeusz 405

Chojno Wiktor 184, 190, 596

Chojnowska Kazimiera 619

Chomczenowska Zofia 251

Chomko Konstanty 191

Chopre Rajas 330, 331

Chronowska Janina 228, 231, 234

Chronowska Julia Zofia 279

Chrystowska Halina 150, 184, 191

Chrząszczewska Zofia 302, 303, 325, 330

Chrząszczewski/Young Jan v, 337, 358, 370, 400, 413, 414, 445, 501, 513, 514

Churchill Winston 13, 41, 63, 65, 282, 480, 481, 482

Chyla Alicja 308, 331

Chylowa Anna 303, 304, 330, 343

Cichocka Jadwiga 251

Ciechanowicz Mikołaj 279

Ciepliński Jan 517

Citron Edwin 60

Clarke Geoffrey 48, 82, 94, 96, 126

Clarke Catherine 48, 82, 94

Condie J.D. 177, 179

Cooper R. and S. 62

Cortesi N. 63

Craen Olga 137

Cripps Stafford 40

Cwajna Czesław 308, 414

Cwetsch Franciszek (Anek) 138, 325, 536, 541

Cyraniuk Stefan 319

Czachór Wanda 324

Czajka Kazimierz 580

Czajka Maria 279

Czapski Józef 322, 592

Czarnecka/Skorupińska Kazimiera 410, 429, 560, 573

Czarnecka Maria 291, 307, 316, 323, 328, 330, 336, 561

Czarny Józef 279

Czartowska Maria 414

Czaykowski Bogdan 93, 108, 287, 370, 410, 504, 510, 518, 547

Czeczeników Olga 492

Czekaj Ignacy 207

Czekańska/Miklaszewska Grażyna 135, 228

Czekierska/Radwańska Estela 319, 331, 335, 340, 364, 365, 368, 378, 379, 382, 399, 408, 412, 413, 414, 511, 533, 594

Czerepak Eugenia 331

Czerepak Stanisława 331

Czernek Madzia 150

Czerniawska Bronisława 287

Czerwińska/Bednarska Ziuta 545

Czogało Wanda 62, 66

Czyżewska Nusia 531

Ćwiek/Kwiek 433

Ćwirko-Godycka/Banasińska Kira 46

Da Albuquerque Alfonso 270

Da Cunha F.C. 133, 135

Dacz Irena 251

Dadlez Marek 328, 341, 429, 498

Da Gama Gaspar 271

Da Gama Vasco 271

Dajek Jan 53, 71, 279

Dallinger Leopold Fr. 62, 156, 157, 184, 190, 225, 247, 256, 261, 262, 265, 266, 267, 280, 302, 302, 330, 339, 342, 360, 388, 419, 462

Dalton H. 328

Daman Mrs. 224

Damany J. 62

Daniel Mahrai 350

Dashmukh vel Deshmukh G.B. 198, 216, 218

Davinder Wazir 577, 578

Dąbek Maria 312, 332, 333, 404

Dąbrowska Julia 184, 185, 187

Dąbrowski Kazik 337

Dedena 111, 112

Delaney Lorna 578

Delikowska Władysława/Sr. Jadwiga 414, 508

Derecka Maria 330

Desai L.R. 301

De Soisson Louis 511

De Souza Alice 141, 142, 330

Dembińska Janina 234

Dębnicki Krzysztof 579, 580, 581

Dhawalshereeraje Subhagyakanshini 584

Digvijaysinhji patrz. Jam Saheb 69, 70, 78, 82, 94, 104, 106, 110, 120, 123, 125, 127, 168, 190, 198

Dingelage Biddy von 141

Dobolewicz Władysław 279

Dobolewicz Władysława 132

Dobrostańska Janina 93, 106, 108, 123, 126, 184, 281, 283, 287, 289, 290, 291

Dobrostański Jerzy 413, 537, 538

Dobrostański Tadeusz 91, 123, 126, 287, 543

Doering Henryk 261, 265, 266, 284

Dragosz Zofia 191

Dubash Mrs. 82, 150

Dubicka Franciszka 145

Dubowik Zofia 279

Duda Antoni 234

Dudek/Mościcka) Zofia 14, 285, 337, 358, 412, 413, 414, 429, 488

Dudko Wanda 234

Dudryk-Darlewski Antoni 378

Dudryk-Darlewski Stanisław 52, 53, 55, 64, 188, 190, 197, 267, 356, 363, 364, 371, 539

Durant/Baranowska Zofia 508, 580

Durrant Robert 483, 484, 485

Dusza Roman 184, 190, 220, 281, 493

Dybczak Eugeniusz 414, 546

Dylu 418

Dymicki Jan 191

Dynowska Wanda/Uma Devi 45, 46, 47, 51, 58, 59, 60, 236, 260, 267, 283, 289, 340, 365, 438, 440, 447, 451, 454, 455, 456, 462, 463, 466, 467, 470, 473, 475, 476, 477, 491, 591, 592, 593, 594, 595

Dytrych/Sahanek Hanka 281, 289, 290, 291, 316, 408, 413, 434, 447, 477

Dyżurko Michał 594

Dziadowicz Maria 330

Dziadowicz Stanisław 147

Dziadura Maria 279

Dziedzic Danuta 331, 342, 554

Dziedzic Bolesław 325

Dziewulak/Adamczyk Irena 466, 597

Dzięglewska Antonina 137, 330

Dzikowski Józef 290

Dzierżek Adam 184

Dziubaty Jan 279

Dżumaga Maria 342

Eden Antony 9, 42, 65, 575

Eggers H.H. 482

Evershed/Nowicka Zofia vii, 530

Ezman Józef 470, 621

Falk Maryla 592

Feier Józef 621

Fernandes Mario 581

Fernandes Sebastian 581

Filipowicz Maria 621

Finkler Gustaw 149, 229, 231, 232, 364, 621

Fischer/Wasiuk Alicja 545, 546, 548

Flecker Edyta 621

Folkierski Władysław 55, 326

Forbes Brig. 194

Formankiewicz Władysław 279, 434, 621

Francuz Antoni 342, 414, 420

Frąckiewicz Irena 342, 621

Frąckiewicz Jadwiga 342, 414, 621

Frąckiewicz/Kuraś Wanda 621

Frączek Antonina 621

Frer Hartley 130

Fujarczuk Helena 621

Furman Mr. & Mrs. 550

Frydel Radosław 291, 621

Frydman Maurycy/Bharatananda 45, 56, 58, 60, 438, 591, 592, 593, 594, 595, 596, 621

Gaikwad Khanderao B. 190

Gaikwad Manorama 330, 337, 342, 405, 439, 445

Gaikwad Priya 584, 585

Gaikwad Shumrao 581

Gaikwad Vijay 465, 579, 580, 581, 584, 585, 586, 587

Ganczar Maria 413, 470

Gandhi Mahatma 17, 45, 56, 143, 380, 411, 438, 454, 455, 456, 457, 458, 459, 460, 461, 463, 466, 491, 577, 591

Gaweł Władysław 191

Gawęda Franciszek 414

Gawlina Józef Ep./Arch. 63, 64, 94, 260, 263, 275, 299

Gawron Loda 135

Gawroń Zbigniewa 62

Gemma, Sr. 140, 141, 142

Giza Hanna Maria 569

Gębski Andrzej 308

Ghoshal Hirranmoy 438

Gavalt Sadka 442

Gilchrist R.N. 40, 52, 482, 485

Gimza Maria 303, 330

Glazer Ewa 570

Glazer/Kurowska Teresa v, vi, vii, 21, 28, 343, 345, 428, 429, 430, 437, 446, 480, 487, 496, 504, 559, 567

Gładuń/Sułkowska Janina 56, 57, 341, 548

Głębicka Helena 234

Głodek Franciszka 114

Godlewski Adam Sylwester 279

Godlewska Danuta Halina 279

Godlewski Józef 279

Godlewski Ryszard 345, 347, 348, 402, 414, 554, 575

Godwood/Kitras Janka 545

Golenia/Benal Paulina 231, 234

Goławska Maria 291, 316, 317

Goławski Andrzej 328, 339, 429

Goławski Michał 53, 55, 56, 60, 190, 197, 236, 247, 256, 267, 297, 299, 304, 321, 326, 327, 355, 356, 362, 371, 381, 499, 561

Gopal Ram 45, 52, 447, 472

Goślinowska Eugenia 62, 222, 234

Goślinowska Janina 409, 414

Goślinowska Katarzyna 231

Goshal Hiranmani 53

Góral/Bazergan Jadwiga 62, 442

Górna Helena 330

Górska Czesia 222

Górska Danuta 364, 414

Górska Halina 62, 331, 509

Górska Maria 207

Górska Stanisława 331

Górska Wanda 190

Grabianka Felicja 190

Grabianka Olgierd 184, 189, 190, 192, 266, 499

Grabowski Zbigniew 593

Gray A.G. 47

Grażyński Michał 351

Greczyło Danuta 234

Grobel Lucyna 207

Grochocka Janina 56

Grochola Zofia 251

Gromadzka Henryka 184, 281

Grubczak Alojzy 487, 576

Gruja J. 54, 334

Grula Czesia 91

Gruszka/Pacak Ewa 208

Gruszka Jerzy 536

Gruszewska Genia 429

Grużewska Zofia 181, 249, 266, 330, 445, 498

Gryzel Franciszka 251

Grządziel Rafał 549

Grzybowska Helena 414

Grzybowski Henryk 248, 279

Grzybowski Ryszard 347, 516

Gulab 196, 448

Gulczyński Czesław 53, 190

Gune 185

Gurgul Janina 285

Gurgul Józef 184, 191

Gutkowski Kazimierz 251, 291

Gutowski Roman 96,

Guziewicz Leokadia 423

Gwiazdonik/Handerek Anna 306, 307, 309, 312, 321, 330, 335, 339, 257, 363, 366, 368, 378, 379, 380, 384, 390, 391, 397, 409, 411, 412, 414, 436, 451, 561, 562

Gwieździński B. 312

Gwóźdź Leokadia 279

Haczewska Elżbieta 185, 191

Hadała Henryk 74, 100

Hajduga Mr. and Mrs. 437

Hajduk/Metelica Irena 236, 238, 331, 335, 354, 368, 380, 412, 413, 414, 550, 554

Hajdukiewicz Stanisław 414

Hajdul Halina 185, 191, 283

Hajnowa Halina 281

Halgerson H.C. 275

Haller Gen. 18

Halska Helena 330

Hałaburda Irena 331

Hałko/Burek Ola 546, 548

Handerek/Gwiazdonik Anna 306, 307, 309, 312, 321, 330, 335, 354, 357, 359, 363, 366, 368, 378, 379, 380, 382, 384, 387, 390, 391,398, 409, 411, 412, 413, 414, 429, 436, 451, 561, 581, 594

Handerek Stanisław 385

Haniewicz/Pająk Janina 414, 509

Haracz Genowefa 62, 66

Harasymów Antonina 300, 303, 308, 325, 330, 336

Harasymów Stanisław v, 130, 137, 138, 171, 233, 235, 238, 274, 336, 348, 361, 389, 394, 408, 425, 426, 427, 431, 452, 461, 464, 477, 536, 541, 543, 568

Harasymów Wanda v, 171, 233 , 238, 464, 477

Harbuz/Krawczyk Eliza 135, 145, 285, 331,454

Harbuz/Barowicz Bożena 331, 459

Harbuz Bogdan 537

Hardy Janina 317, 330

Harvey C.W.L. 50, 64, 198, 213, 218, 482, 491

Haura Krystyna 414

Helen Mary Sr. 141

Hemar Marian 51, 487, 488

Henderson H. W. 593, 594

Herzog Franciszek 370, 406, 429, 521, 563

Herzog Tadeusz 132, 290, 414

Heydenkorn Benedykt 545

Hicks Betty 578

Hill Donald Mrs. 78

Hitler Adolf xi, 3, 4, 5, 8, 45, 108, 434

"Hitler"/Kasprowicz I. 185, 200, 204, 434

Hlond August 274, 577

Holcomb Emerson 485

Holland Sr. 158

Hopkinson Col. 53

Hornung Józio 337

Horohna S. Dr. 62

Hryczyszyn Helena 234, 248

Hudyga Danuta 279

Hume A.O. 31

Humphrys Francis 41

Humphrys/Kisiówna Katarzyna 61, 248

Huntington/Duszyńska Eugenia 502

Huppert Karol 413, 515, 517, 580

Huszczo/Pieńkoś Jasia 543

Huszczo Janek 537

Huszczo Janina 537

Idkowiak/Haniewicz Irena 142, 236, 237, 238, 331, 335, 368, 413, 509

Iglikowska/Biskupska Krystyna 56, 57, 285, 291, 340, 596, 477

Ignatowicz Józefa 191

Ingle N.D. 190

Iwanejko Katarzyna 279

Jabłoński Jan 413

Jacinta Sr. see Respondowska Ella 563

Jackiewicz/Wojniłowicz Janina 308, 544

Jacoby H. 133

Jadziewicz Jan 191, 279

Jager/Michalska Irena 331, 364, 410, 413, 414, 429, 546

Jagielnicki Zygmunt Fr. 156, 157

Jagiełłowicz Maria 563, 190

Jagiełłowicz/Kuszell Teresa 415, 448

Jagiełłowicz Władysław 50, 155, 160, 177, 179, 180, 183, 184, 190, 226, 267, 356, 415, 436

Jagosz Michał 563

Jagus J.O. 79

Jakubik Władysław 279

Jakutowicz/Zawadowska Ludka 534

Jam Saheb Digvijaysinhji 69, 70, 78, 82, 94, 104, 106, 120, 123, 125, 240, 264, 287, 568

Janas Maria 92, 537

Janczewska Irena 358, 404, 470

Janczewska Jadwiga 339, 343, 395, 428, 430

Janiszewska Alicja 413, 414, 488, 518

Janiszewska/Shannon Maria 331, 382, 413, 414, 500, 540, 552, 554

Janiszewski Tadeusz 414, 488

Jankowska/Zygiel Janina 197, 317, 388, 391, 395, 397, 407, 410, 414, 450, 467, 470, 473, 548

Jankowska/Żyszkowska Leokadia 562

Jankowska Rypsyma 201, 285, 302, 330

Jankowski Antoni Fr. 56, 62, 63, 143, 149, 161, 200, 203, 232, 263, 270, 363, 402, 437, 460, 594

Jankowski Tadeusz 285, 328, 341

Jankowski Józef 279

Janowski Bronisław 205, 315

Janta-Pełczyński Aleksander 45, 447

Januszajtis 18

Jańczyk Witold 413

Jarmułowicz Melania 234, 364, 509

Jarosz Bolesław 113

Jasiński Stanisław 576

Jaworska Adela 330

Jerzykowska Janina 184, 185, 187, 191

Jerzykowski Aleksander 414

Jessie and Goodu (Gopal) 447, 448

Jędrychowska Halina 184, 281

Jędrzejewska Regina 62

Jędrzejewska Oktawia 234

Jinarajadas C. 591, 592, 593

Jodłowski Marian 279

Jolly Gordon 101

Jordou Gawidron 420

Joshi vel Johsi Anant vel Ananti 95, 100, 127, 576

Joshi Umashanker 591, 594

Józefczyk Stanisława 191

Jundziłł Józef 502

Juralewicz/Sztela Maria vi, 242

Jurecka/Bilińska 318, 319

Jurczyńska Olga 234

Jutrzenka Antoni 279

Jutrzenka Leon 405

Juźwin Jadwiga 314

Juźwin Janina 319, 331, 335

Kacera Mikołaj 56, 236,

Kahn/Winnicka Irena 692

Kaiser Józefa Barbara 370

Kaiser Maria 291, 372

Kaiser Mieczysław 369

Kajak/Ostrihanska Anna vii, 521, 523, 524, 528,

Kalinowska Czesława 319

Kalinowska Eufrozyna 257, 326

Kalisz 148

Kaliszek Irena 376, 390, 547, 567

Kalawajtis Regina 369

Kalawaitys Stanisław 422

Kamińska Mila 303, 470

Kamińska Zofia 325, 330

Kamiński Zygmunt 405

Kamoda Wanda 331, 432

Kaptur senior 536

Kaptur Stella 236, 278, 315

Kaptur Zenon 358, 457, 465, 466, 500

Kapuścińska Maria 200

Karasiewicz Kazimiera 281, 308

Karczuga/Morska Janka 546

Kardasiński Antoni 204

Karpińska Zofia/"Bebi" 331, 335, 399, 413, 427, 509

Karwowska Eugenia 307, 330, 339

Kashikar Wanda 465, 559, 578, 581, 585

Kashikar Vasant 465, 559, 578, 579, 581, 585

Kashikar Ashok 465, 581, 585

Kashikar Shama 465, 581, 585

Kasprowicz Ignacy 185, 200, 204, 434

Kaszuba Stanisław 285, 414

Kaszuba/Truksa Wanda 414, 546, 548

Kaśków Izabela Stanisława 328

Kaśków Jan 285

Katkiewicz Danuta 405

Katkiewicz Henryk 285, 307, 308, 316, 320, 326, 330, 345, 443

Katkiewicz Jadwiga 302, 330

Katkiewicz Marta Ewa 279

Kawałek Helena 331

Kawałek Ludwika 330

Kawecka Bronisława 414

Kaziewicz Irka 470

Kądzielawa Maria 368

Kenyatta Jomo 533

Kernberg Krystyna 292

Kędzior Ludmiła 414

Kępa Irena 497

Kępko Irena 342

Khan Bahadur 187, 198

Khare N.B. 180

Kiellerman/Szuber Maria 546

Kiełbińska Zofia 143, 499

Kiersnowski Ryszard 429

Kijanowska Maria 191

Kirchner Zofia 234

Kirdzik Wanda 330, 343

Kisiel Emilia 330

Kisielnicka Alicja 56, 57, 158, 161, 191, 198, 202, 205, 262, 281, 283, 288, 416, 443, 454, 457,

Kisiówna/Humphrys Katarzyna 61, 248

Kitras/Godwood Janka 545

Kitras Helena 414, 545

Kittur R.A. 190, 217

Klar Ryszard 331, 412, 354

Klar Mrs. 202

Kleeberg Gen. 5

Klecki Aleksander senior 217, 245, 249, 251

Klecki Aleksander junior-Olek 155, 286, 290, 316, 317, 331, 358, 395, 412, 501, 511, 564

Klecka Halina 567

Klepacka/Kleszko Wiesława v, vi, 61, 130, 155, 207, 223, 265, 270, 318, 421, 436, 441, 442, 444, 461, 501, 509, 509, 565

Klepacki Józef 200, 207, 285,

Klimowiecka Genowefa 234

Klimsiak 425

Klimsiak Mr. 207

Kluszczyńska Janina 528

Kłoskowicz F. Mjr 499

Kłosowska Janina 330, 339

Kłosowska Maria 145, 331, 335

Knaplund P. 34

Kobordo Halina 489

Kobordo/Lempke) Jagoda vii , 434, 487, 488, 489, 518

Kobordo Maria 488, 489

Kobuś vel Kobuz Wł. 61, 66

Kobylański Jan 556

Koc Halina 372

Kochanowska Eugenia 251

Kochańska Teresa 414

Koczan Stefania (sen.) 331

Koczan Stefania Ewa (jun.) 285, 330

Koczy Leon 60

Kojder Helena 236, 237, 238

Kojro/Tomas Wanda 325, 552, 553

Kokociński Antoni 234

Kokoszko/Sieradzan Marysia 497, 517

Kokoszko Weronika 331, 335

Kolendo Czesław 347

Kolischer Romualda 331

Kolkiewicz Wanda 414

Kołodziej Adolf 437

Kołodziej/Solecka Maria vii, 6, 19, 544, 545, 546, 548, 570

Konarski Stanisław Dr. 61, 71, 72, 83

Konieczny Tomek 570

Konopko Teresa 554

Kopeć Franciszka 234

Kopiec/Nowakowska Gizela 442

Kopiec Władysław 308, 414

Kordaś Zygmunt 94

Korczyńska/Wójtowicz Sylwia 445

Korodziejowski Bohdan 435

Korpalski Zygfryd 576

Korzeniowska Eleonora 145

Korzeniowska Eugenia 286

Korzeniowska Urszula 145

Korzeniowski Hieronim 314

Kossowska Janina 184, 300

Kossowski Janusz 392, 414, 515

Kostecki Piotr 279

Kościukiewicz J. 232

Kościukiewicz Józef 232. 330

Kot Mila 132

Kot Stanisław 9, 10, 48, 53, 66, 593

Kotlarczyk Amelia 146

Kotlarczyk Melania 60

Kotlarz Genowefa 248

Kotlicka Jadwiga 281, 282

Kotlicka Krystyna 331

Kowal Piotr 279

Kowalczyk Maria 303, 330

Kowalczyk/Zawerbna Stefania 560

Kowalewski Czesław 265

Kowalewska Kazimiera 187, 190, 277

Kowalewska/Przyrodzka Regina 415

Kowalec Zofia 287

Kowalska Katarzyna 198

Kowalska Joanna 306, 307, 328, 330

Kowalski Jerzy vii, 285, 339, 340, 348, 395 436, 437, 439, 463, 498, 512, 574

Kowałko Zygmunt 539

Kozakiewicz Krzysztof 366

Kozielska Hilda 53

Koziełł/Nieczykowska Krystyna vii, 578, 580, 583

Koziełkowski Leon Dr. 157, 158. 224, 285

Kozińska Maria 53

Kozłowski W. 290

Kozłowski Kazimierz Fr. 260, 263, 273, 274, 299, 357, 360, 365, 366, 382, 411, 534, 594

Kozłowski Rev. 64

Kozłowski Tadeusz 414

Kozula Mr. 338

Kozula Władysław 330

Krajewska Karolina 232, 233, 234

Krajewska Irena 290, 331, 356, 364, 365, 368, 412, 413, 551

Krajewska Stanisława 540, 543

Krajewska Wincentyna 207, 312, 314

Krasnodębska Maria 578

Krawczyk/Harbuz Eliza 454

Krishnamurti 591

Krishnan L. 470

Kronenberg Mr. 271, 402

Król/Walczowska Alicja vi, 132, 133, 136, 138, 509, 517

Król Józef 265

Królikowska Barbara 331

Królikowska/Morrison Jagoda 413, 414, 550

Królikowska Katarzyna 331

Królikowska Stanisława 200

Królikowski 532

Kruk Krystyna Maria 279

Kruk Urszula 409

Krukowska/Bratkowska Stasia 546

Krupa Stanisława 308, 331

Krupińska Anna 203

Kruszyńska Danuta 335

Krygiel/Moniak Czesława 521, 545, 546, 548, 570

Krzesiński Andrzej 46

Krzętowska Helena 330

Krzysztoń/Bełdowska Halina vii, 403, 529

Krzysztoń 488

Krzysztoń Franciszek 529

Krzysztoń Jerzy vii, 251, 281, 400, 403, 414, 520, 529, 567, 578

Kucewicz Henryka 413, 414

Kucewicz Jerzy 358, 413,

Kucharska Helena 234, 371

Kucharski Marian 347

Kucharski Józef 291

Kuchcicka/Tomasiewicz Krystyna 330

Kuchcicka Wanda 251

Kuchcicki Władysław 285

Kuczyńska Krystyna 342

Kudlicka Olga 234

Kudła Irena/Swirska 430, 506, 516

Kufera Irena 331, 414

Kukiel M. 591

Kukiełko Zofia 412

Kumoca Vinay 571

Kuncewicz Genowefa 330, 506

Kunicka Stasia 548

Kunigiel Genia 339, 506

Knigiel Helena 597

Kupczyńska Teofila 234

Kuraś/Frąckiewicz Wanda 508

Kurkowski Adam 279

Kurkowski Waldemar Mikołaj 279

Kurowska/Glazer Teresa v, vi, vii, 21, 28, 343, 345, 428, 429, 430, 437, 446, 480, 487, 496, 504, 559, 567

Kurowska Jadwiga 21 ,22 ,177, 510, 533

Kurowski Andrzej 22, 150, 181, 508

Kurowska Maryla 554

Kurzawska Alina 308, 342, 470

Kurzawski Jan 318,

Kurzawski Marian 318

Kurzeja Helena 303, 343

Kurzeja Janusz 285, 470, 474, 536, 542

Kusale Annasaheb S. 580

Kuszell/Jagiełłowicz Teresa 415, 448

Kuźmicz Lucjan 339

Kwater Czesława 414

Kwiatkowska Maria 312

Kwiatkowska Wanda 412

Kwiatkowska Zofia 279

Kwiatkowski Wojciech 347, 414, 470

Kwiecień Marcin 191

Lachowska Helena 414

Laniewska Irma 302, 330

Laskowska Stefania 185, 327, 340

Laskowska Wanda 414

Latawiec Eugenia 184, 191

Latawiec Jan 310, 324, 330

Latawiec Janina 189, 307, 330

Latawiec Joanna 279

Latawiec Marcin 207, 279

Latawiec W. 291

Lech Aniela 251

Lech Rafalina 412, 414

Leila 448

Lempke/Kobordo Jagoda 434, 487, 488, 518, 520

Leszczyński Jerzy 576

Leśniak Janusz 370

Leśniak Maria/Sr. Benedykta 302, 378, 379, 380, 429

Lewett H. 146, 147

Lichodziejewski Czesław 90

Ligaj Łucja 470

Linlithgow 30, 47

Lipczyk Maria 319

Lipiński Andrzej 200

Lipska Teodora 595

Lisiecka Cecylia 414

Lisiecki Tadeusz 46, 71, 74, 77, 241, 486

Liszka Jerzy 285, 337, 392, 414, 435

Litawska/Czaputowa Luiza 57

Litewska 190

Litewski 37, 46, 64, 93, 96, 102, 141, 190, 299, 301, 316, 481, 482, 485

Lode Maria 250, 312

Loszek Danuta 331

Loszek/Tomaszewska Romualda 292, 339

Lotarewicz Władysław 251, 290

Loveday Mrs. 224

Ludberga Sr. 141, 142

Łaguna Wanda 61, 135, 371

Łańcucka Anna 331

Łaszkiewicz Maria 330

Ławniczek/Szpak Felicja 521

Ławniczek Stanisław 206

Łempicki 143

Łęczyńska Wanda 145, 414

Łęczyński Kazimierz 134, 145, 249, 259, 330

Łomnicka/Kitras Helena 545

Łopiński Zygmunt 53, 184, 190, 443

Łosowska Irena 308, 364

Łossowska Mieczysława 233

Łoszowska Antonina 251

Łoś Romualda 234

Łotyczewska/Kubis Agnieszka (Jagoda) 580

Łoziński Karol 25

Łozińska Irena 26

Łukasiewicz Juliusz 53

Łukaszewski Witold 393

Macharski Franciszek 563

Maciejewska Eugenia 231, 232, 233, 364, 509

Mackiewicz Józef 593

Magnuszewska Irena 184, 187, 191, 236, 238, 331

Magor E.W.M. 198, 218

Mahorowska/Rozwadowska Idalia vii, 547, 565, 567, 577, 578

Mahorowska Teresa 578

Majewska Maria 191

Majka Krzysztof 465, 578, 579, 587

Major A. 62

Majski Iwan 8, 9

Makles Ireneusz 580, 584

Makles Tania 580

Malcharek Adela 62, 66, 236, 238

Malec Dzidka 409, 554

Małachowska Helena 190, 191, 267, 414

Małaczyńska Maria 406

Małaczyńska Stanisława 53

Małaczyński I. 53

Małek Mieczysław 434

Małkowska Olga 352, 353, 379

Małkowska/Zbróg Janina 251, 331, 414, 517

Małkowski Andrzej 379

Mamnicka/Orzechowska Teresa vi, 140

Mancini/Sr Clemenza 276

Maniak Antoni 93, 106, 109, 110, 111, 112, 113, 114, 118, 330, 347, 348

Marasek Stefania 330

Marchewka Józef 191

Marcinkiewicz Zuzanna 291, 308, 429, 498, 512, 574

Marczyńska Stefania 191

Maresch/Polnik Eugenia 39, 508, 578, 591

Maresch Grażyna 578

Margaret Clair Sr. 141

Markisz vel Marisz Józef 424

Markisz Wiktor 424

Marlewski 39, 40, 65

Marshall Narry 94, 95, 127

Marten Krystyna 532, 533

Marten Wojtek 541, 543

Martusewicz Helena 285, 330

Maruti 281, 442

Mary Alban Sr. 141

Mary Haldin Sr. 141

Masewicz Jadwiga 105, 330

Masina A. 62

Masiulanis Antonina 279

Masiulanis/Tutak Helena 199, 331, 517

Masiulanis Nadzieja 279

Masiulanis Pelagia 234

Masiulanis Piotr 200, 202, 207

Mason 40, 49, 66, 482, 483

Massani M.R. 34, 45

Materek Jadwiga 234

Matthews Anne 330

Matulewicz Wiesław 285

Matwiejczyk Karol 567

Matyka Józef 330, 593

Mazajczyk Walenty 539

Mazajczyk/Wierzbińska Regina 539

Mazowiecki Tadeusz 530

Mazur Stanisław 119

Mazurek Franciszka 279

Mazurkiewicz Stefania 330

Mehta 111
Melnarowicz Władysława 184, 499
Metelica/Hajduk Irena 236, 550, 554
Mędrala Andrzej 279
Michalak Czesława 331
Michalak Krystyna 363, 414
Michalak Stanisława 191
Michalska Aleksandra 234
Michalska Danuta 279
Michalska/Jager Irena 381, 364, 410, 413, 414, 429, 546
Michalska Janina 281
Michalski Ryszard 414
Mickiewicz Adam 286
Mickiewicz Leokadia 234
Mieczkowska/Przychodzeń Jadwiga 241, 242
Miklaszewska-Czekańska Grażyna 135, 228
Mikulicka Władysława 145
Mikulicki Józef 191
Mikuszewski Leonard 66, 285
Milker Aleksander 135
Miluska Stanisława 137, 320, 436
Mineyko/Niezabytowska Janina 286, 454, 455
Miranda S. 61
Misiur Jadwiga 132
Mistry Mr. and Mrs. 236, 237, 238
Misuno Władysław 191
Mitro Maria 135, 330
Mocarska Janina 414
Moi Arap 534
Mołdzyński Jan 150
Moniak/Krygiel Czesława 364, 397, 405, 413, 439, 545
Mordak Freda 287
Morawiecka Janina 527

Morawska/Charuba Barbara 331, 363, 364, 412, 561
Morawska Zofia 330
Morris Evelyn 330
Moroz/Wrońska Lodzia 546
Mościcki Ignacy 5
Mooney E. 275
Moos F. 62
Mrozowa Anna 60, 75
Mróz Adela 60, 330
Mucha Janina 339
Mucha Maria 331
Mückowa Janina 285
Mularczyk Lidia 234
Myśliwiec Stefan 414

Naglik Kazimierz 633
Naimski Ludwik 633
Najdzicz Apolonia 330
Narkiewicz Felicja 291
Natu 448
Nawój Michał 633
Nawój Janina 633
Nehru Pandit 447, 458, 491, 492
Nieczykowska Maria 150, 153, 633
Nieczykowska/Wolff Izabella 150, 517, 633
Nieczykowska/Kozieł Krystyna 633
Niedźwiedzka Helena 633
Niedźwiedzka Stanisława 633
Nielsen 319, 499, 502
Nigelszporn Alfred 330, 633
Niezabytowska/Mineyko Janina 286, 290, 291, 300, 331, 336, 455, 532, 633
Nilon Bronek 502
Nilon/Piątkowska Renia 502
Norblin Stefan vi, 52, 67, 68

Noronham S. 62
Nottman Jim 248
Nowacki Henryk 507
Nowakowa 224
Nowakowska Czesława 633
Nowakowska Gizela 442
Nowakowska Halina 330, 633
Nowakowska/Grunwald Irena 558, 633
Nowakowska Kazimiera 308, 331, 633
Nowakowska Sabina 633
Nowakowski Jan 279, 591
Nowicka Maria 331, 335, 633
Nowicka/Jansen Irena 539, 543
Nowicka Jadwiga/Sr. Reginata 412, 633
Nowicka Józefa 633
Nowicka/Czyżewicz Dzidka 509
Nowicka/Evershed Zofia 276, 290, 291, 302, 325, 329, 330, 331, 530, 633
Nowicka/Kashikar Wanda 198, 465, 669, 578, 579, 585, 633
Nowicki Jan 633
Nowicki Józef 266, 583, 633

Nowicki Zbyszek 225, 308, 329, 345, 347, 348, 353, 371, 379, 387, 413, 414, 534, 633
Nowosiadły Józef 633
Nowosielska Alicja 633
Nowosielska Lucyna 633
Nowosielska Józefa 633
Nykiel Katarzyna 633
Nykiel/Kelley Stefania 633

O'Boyle Rev. 63
Odlanicka-Poczobut Zofia 285
Olesiak Krystyna 406, 413

Olesiak Witold 342, 347, 364, 370, 413, 498

Oleś Gienek 501

Oleś Marian Ep. 396, 558

Olszańska Aleksandra 89

Olszewski A. 128

Opioła Stanisław 405

Opolska Anna 53

Ordonówna/Tyszkiewicz Hanka vi, 52, 72, 77, 78, 105, 131, 132

Orysiuk Jan Br. 265, 266, 274, 275, 285, 302, 330, 336, 357, 358, 363, 379, 400, 413, 414, 530

Orzechowska Maria 279

Orzechowska/Mamnicka Teresa 137, 140, 145

Orzeł/Michałowska Szczęsna 290, 316, 331, 335, 338, 561

Orzeł Janina 330

Ostaszewska Maria 251

Ostrihanska Anna/Kajak 391, 414, 521, 526

Ostrihanska Olga 147, 521

Ostrihanska Zofia 378, 379, 382, 398, 409, 412, 427, 463, 521, 523, 524, 594

Ostrowska/Dziedzic Danka 342, 554

Ostrowska Irena 331, 335, 366

Ostrowska/Wypijewska Maria 545

Ostrowska Łucja 412, 470

Ostrowska Wanda 304, 316, 331

Ostrowski F. 544

Ostrowski Waldemar 184, 499

Oswald Family 575

Oswal Paras B. 579, 581

Otto Magdalena 279

Pacak/Gruszka Ewa 138, 536

Pacak Jan 135, 136, 137, 157, 201, 204, 207-208, 265, 285, 434

Pacak Urszula 136, 139, 142, 143

Pacholska Anna 331

Pacholska Janina 330

Pacholski Jan 155, 285, 331, 339, 358, 413 414, 488, 521

Paderewski Ignacy 70, 287, 299 326, 412, 413, 443, 506, 594

Pająk Bożenka 570

Pająk Z. 570

Pająk/Haniewicz Janina 183, 509, 565

Palin S/Lt. 146

Paliwoda Julia 279

Pancewicz Bronisław 123, 128, 277, 312, 315, 347, 348, 356, 357, 358, 359, 362, 363, 364, 365, 368, 369, 371, 372, 373, 374, 378, 380, 382, 383, 386, 413, 437, 499, 505

Pancewicz/ Rymar Janina 281, 373, 565

Panek/Środulska Aleksandra 308, 331, 554

Parczewska Felicja 353

Pardeshi Shankarlal M. 213, 217, 218, 220, 288, 422, 451, 575

Parenty André Ep. 557

Parfińska 414

Parzych Ryszard 279

Pasternak Danuta 331, 509

Pasternak Gustaw 556

Paszkiewicz Mirosław 538

Paszkiewicz/Wojtasiewicz Wiesława 543

Paszkowska/Trella Urszula vii, 534, 538

Patel Jamnadas 62, 75

Patel Raj 568

Patel Sardar Vallabhbhai 458

Paulikowa Irena 286, 291

Pawlak Irena 506

Pawlarczyk 435

Pawłowski 338

Pazik Edward 405

Pearce Joyce 517

Pelc Jan 207, 330

Peron Juan Domingo 555

Perry E.W. 174, 180, 218

Peszkowski Zdzisław (Ryś Zuch, Brave Lynx) v, vi, xi, 123, 257, 290, 347, 349, 355, 356, 357, 358, 359, 362, 363, 364, 365, 366, 368, 369, 371, 378, 379, 382, 383, 384, 387, 401, 413, 414, 437, 451, 452, 456, 477, 496, 497, 499, 500, 509, 552, 561, 562, 563, 566, 567, 571, 593, 594

Peszyńska/Tetmajer Krystyna 310, 330

Philip Mary Sr. 334

Piasecki Leon 44

Piątkowska Alina 331

Piątkowska/Nilon Renia 338

Pienkoś/Huszczo Jasia 543

Pieślak Tomasz 279

Pietrkiewicz J. 507, 510, 594

Pietrulewicz F. 184

Pietrzak B. 347, 348

Pietrzak W. 530

Piłsudski Józef 18, 67, 509

Piórkowska Emilia 234

Piórkowska Jadwiga 205

Piórkowski Henryk 539

Piotrowicz Irena Sr. 319, 331, 380, 470, 557

Piotrowicz Józef 251

Piotrowicz/Stechley Elwira 414, 516, 578, 580

Piotrowska Filipina 234

Piotrowska/Truchanowicz Jadwiga 576

Pipało Wiktoria 553

Piskorski Stefan 191

Pitura 207, 423

Pitura Wojciech 184, 200

Platta Jan 279

Pluta Franciszek Fr. 62, 71, 73, 76, 77, 82, 92, 93, 95, 96, 97, 100, 102, 106, 107, 114, 116, 117, 118, 121, 124, 128, 264, 276, 277, 496, 563

Pniewska Danuta v, vi, vii, 24, 292, 319, 331, 332, 351, 358, 363, 364, 365, 366, 378, 379, 380, 387, 388, 401, 406, 413, 414, 432, 498, 510, 549, 565, 566, 579, 580, 586, 594

Pniewska Jadwiga 231, 234

Pobereźniczenko Tadeusz 207

Poczobut-Odlanicka Zofia 285

Podsoński Franciszek 192, 307, 321, 330, 336

Poklewski Family 46

Pokrzywa Janusz 94

Polechowicz Czesław 204, 310, 311, 312, 499, 534

Polnik/Maresch Eugenia vi, 39, 509

Pool A. 76

Popławska/Truksa Mieczysława vii, 555

Postek Danuta 414

Postek/Faruniarz Kazia 546

Potocka Blanka 157, 302, 303, 330

Power Ada 224

Prendiville Edmund 536

Prestarz/Rutkiewicz Halina 562

Preston Elizabeth 594

Preston T. H. 42, 43, 65

Prochowska Hanka 532

Proskurnicka Julia 330, 353, 357, 414

Przybył Michał 413

Przybyłowska/Krupa Stanisława 546

Przybyłowski Stanisław 414

Przybysz Jan Fr. 184, 189, 247, 262, 266, 274, 299, 330, 561, 566

Przychodzeń Mieczkowska Jadwiga 242

Przytomska Helena 331

Ptakowa Janina 92, 114, 123, 330, 354, 356, 357, 381, 404, 414, 563

Puchalska Antonina 191

Puchalska Jadwiga 412

Puk Janina 132

Puller A. 76

Pupa Krystyna 343

Puranik Sitaram 470, 492

Pyz Helena 580, 581

Rabik Irena 319

Raczkiewicz Władysław 5, 160, 295, 296, 410, 490, 504, 505

Raczyńska Danuta 470

Raczyński Edward 39, 481

Radalus/Tabaczyńska Janina 547

Radhakrishnan Servepali 439, 591, 593

Radwańska/Czekierska Estela 300, 408, 412, 413, 414, 511, 533, 594

Radziwonik vel Radziwoniuk Mikołaj 433

Rafał/Bąbik Halina 337, 340, 421, 498, 517, 564

Raginia Ryszard 337, 354

Raińczuk/Rozkuszko Tosia 488, 529

Rajeshwar 448

Rakowska Halina 330

Ramish 234

Randall A.W.G. 40

Rawicki Waldemar 319

Rayman Władysław 56

Razzak Abdul 574

Respondowska Ela/Sr Jacinta 287, 563

Rishi S.N. 184

Roberts Frank K. 40, 41, 65

Roberts Thomas Arch. 47, 61, 63, 77, 78, 103, 117, 139, 266, 267

Rokicka Dobrosława 285

Rolczewska Jadwiga 308, 331

Romaniuk 207

Romanowska Alicja 414

Romanowska Bogumiła 234

Romanowska Bożena 316, 331, 335, 539

Rommel Erwin 160

Roosevelt Eleonora 490

Roosevelt F.D. 42, 63, 282, 480, 481

Rosada Zygmunt 54, 147, 152, 154

Rosenbaum Edmund 223, 224, 226, 462

Rosenthal Erika 233, 238

Rosenthal Maksymilian 226, 227, 320, 347

Rosenthal/Szczanowska Helena 331, 539, 543

Ross Aleksander 11, 13, 14, 20, 42, 241

Rozkuszko Bronisława vii, 488, 520, 522, 526

Rozwadowska/Mahorowska Idalia vii, 406, 517, 565

Rozwadowska Jadwiga 330

Rozwadowska Zofia 77, 97, 106

Różański Marian 106

Rubczewska Wanda 277, 320, 331, 429, 501

Rubinsztein Józef 102

Rudkowska Julka 409

Rupina 258

Ruszczyc Wanda 75

Rutkiewicz Iwona 140, 141, 143, 145, 319

Rutkowska Halina 287

Rycerz Halina 287

Rycerz/Kopota Maria 308

Ryciak Anna 234

Ryciak/Solka Jadwiga 331, 540, 543

Ryciak Maria 331

Rydel Radosław 443

Ryder Sue 517

Rygiel Zofia 413, 414

Rykowska Elżbieta 414

Rymar/Pancewicz Janina 281, 373

Rymarkiewicz Władysława 251, 330

Rytlewska Irena 251

Rytwińska/Wypijewska Krystyna 409, 545, 546

Sadri N.N. 198

Sahanek/Dytrych Anna 281, 289, 290, 291, 316, 331, 408, 413, 447, 477

Sahanek Maria 330, 434

Saheb Rao 216, 218, 221

Salokhe Mr. 420

Samotny Wilk/Pancewicz B. 356

Samuel A. 330, 440

Santesh 448

Sapieha Eustachy 61

Saplis Zofia 184, 300

Sarnowiec Franciszek 57, 77

Sasadeusz Olga 242, 245, 246, 249, 250, 258, 303, 330, 560

Sasadeusz Witold 354

Sawicka Genowefa 414

Sawko Franciszka 330

Sawko Zygmunt 405

Schayer 438, 439

Searles Edward 248

Seect Hans von 3, 5

Senutai Jaywantrai Dange 330

Serednicka Karolina 191

Serocińska Helena 234

Serwacki Hieronim 54

Shahaji Chhatrapati 169, 450

Shahu Chhatrapati 168, 169, 465, 579, 580, 581, 584, 586,

Shivaji/Siwadżi III, IV & V Chhatrapati 165, 168, 169, 195, 406, 450, 465, 579, 581, 584, 586, 589

Shameem 448

Shannon/Janiszewska Maria 500, 540, 552, 554

Shephard Gillian 251

Siara Karol 308, 347, 414

Siara Irena 342, 554

Siatka Władysław 413

Sidoryk Tadeusz 94, 500

Sieczko Jan 193, 279,

Siedlecka Barbara v, 578, 580

Siedlecka Maria 445

Siedlecki Bronisław 337, 358, 445, 501, 514

Siedlecki Jan K. 37, 50, 67, 129, 165, 173, 183, 192, 199, 209, 215, 285, 319, 328, 339, 354, 363, 364, 365, 387, 396, 400, 411, 412, 413, 414, 435, 460, 465, 499, 500, 501, 512, 565, 567, 568, 577, 579, 580, 582, 584, 586

Siedmiograj Jadwiga 327, 330

Siedmiograj Wanda 285

Sieradzan/Kokoszko Maria 517

Siewierska Jadwiga 62, 66

Sikona Alicja 331

Sikona Zofia 405

Sikorski Zdzisław 190, 200, 307, 308, 309, 314, 330, 371, 387, 499

Sikorski Władysław x, 5, 8, 9, 11, 13, 25, 39, 41, 42, 51, 53, 69, 160, 242, 254, 259, 282, 283, 303, 501, 504

Sikorskij 25

Singh Hermeet 580

Singh Jaswant 101

Singh Umaid 67

Singler Bolesław 540

Sipika Janina 145, 331, 368

Sito Bożena 106, 108, 287, 547

Sito Jerzy 510, 520

Siwek/Wydro Helena 414

Siwek Jadwiga 308

Skarbek Andrzej 536

Skarbek-Peretiatkowicz Hanna 44, 46

Skarbek/Kurzeja Zofia 543

Skarżeńska Rozalia 107

Skibińska Maria 330

Skoczek Casimir 539

Skomorowski Antoni 283, 288, 290

Skorupińska/Czarnecka Kazia vii, 507, 560

Skórzyna Maria 93, 104, 105, 307, 308, 309, 324, 325, 328, 330, 336, 337, 554

Skrzat Stanisław 413

Skrzatowa Anna vi, 27, 285, 302, 330

Skrzeczkowska Helena 184

Skrzydlewski Franciszek 207, 315, 422

Skrzypek Anna 414

Skrzypek Bronisława 234

Skrzypek Leon, Teodor 200, 204, 283, 285

Słowikowska/Woyniłłowicz Eleonora vi, 280

Słowikowska Haneczka 510, 587

Słowikowski Leszek 502

Słuszkiewicz Eugeniusz 439

Smith Conran 74

Smuts Jan Christian 241

Snastin Irena 330, 331, 335, 371, 413

Snastin Lidia 234

Sobol Czesława 470

Socha Maria 251

Sohan 447, 448

Sokołowska Bożena 331

Sokołowska Jadwiga Barbara 554

Solecka/Kołodziej Maria vii, 6, 8, 544, 546

Sołowiej Kazimierz 622

Sołtys Edward 545

Sowa Katarzyna 330

Sowa Maria 413, 414

Spława-Neuman Michalina 309, 330

Stalin Józef 5, 9, 10, 11, 13, 39, 42, 49, 53, 63, 108, 282, 322, 480, 505

Stanislav Kostka Sr. 274, 334, 436

Stanisław Brat 104, 117

Stanisławska Antonina 580

Stanisławski Sławek 124

Stańczyk Jan 39, 49, 52, 53, 101, 134, 160, 174, 180, 183, 192, 197, 211, 212, 439

Stankiewicz Anna 233, 234

Stankiewicz Wanda 281, 291, 331

Staruszkiewicz Andrzej 370, 372

Staruszkiewicz Franciszek 369

Staruszkiewicz Katarzyna 370

Staruszkiewicz Krystyna Jadwiga 370

Stasiak Stefan 438

Staszkiewicz Eugeniusz 438

Stechley/Piotrowicz Elwira 516, 578, 580

Stefański 436

Stella Sr. 367

Stella... 150

Stelmach Magdalena 145

Stelmachowski A. 567

Stenzówna Joasia 64

Stephen 486

Sternbach Ludwik 57, 58, 477

Sternbach Leon 51

Stohandel/Balawender Zofia 548, 549, 561

Strycharz Antonina 191

Strycharz/Wyczałkowska Halina 296, 373, 396, 406, 413, 417, 444, 519

Strzałkowska Jadwiga 330

Strzyżewski Bronisław 348

Studzińska Alfreda 317, 331, 390, 414

Studzińska Leonarda 413, 414

Styburski Wiktor 16, 43, 49, 52, 53, 55, 63, 101, 134, 175, 178, 189, 197, 199, 211, 416

Styczyńska Irena 92, 116, 291

Stypuła Agusia 576

Stypuła Wiesław vi, vii, 69, 94, 101, 287, 438, 521, 565, 566, 576

Subramaniam 470

Suchecka Alina 137, 145

Suchecka/Szydło Daniela 331, 334, 414

Suchocka Jadwiga 233

Sudoł/Ryszkowska Stefania 232, 233, 364, 509

Sudopłatow 6

Sukiennik Mieczysław 342

Sulik Bolesław 504

Sulimirski Tadeusz 301

Sułkowska/Gładuń Janina 56, 57, 341, 546

Sułkowski Jan 54, 204

Surdyka Zofia 413, 414

Surowiec Eleonora 331

Susheila 448

Suszko Helena 331, 334, 414, 470, 554

Suszko Irena 405

Suszyńska Jadwiga 330

Suszyński Mikołaj Sr. 285, 310, 311, 317, 324, 330, 551

Suszyński Mikołaj Jr. 339, 413, 435,

Syberyjska Honorata/Sr. Nora-Marie 308, 553

Synowiec/Tobis Stanisława 241

Sytnik Jan 135, 330

Szabłowska Wiktoria 234

Szafranek Halina 142, 331, 335

Szafrańska Janina 331, 473, 521

Szafrańska Helena (Halina) 331, 335, 354, 366, 368, 374, 378, 382, 388, 399, 411, 412, 413, 414, 470, 487, 494, 521

Szambiar Irena Janina 370

Szanakar 535

Szarejko Anna 202, 285

Szarejko Józef 285, 313

Szarejko Zygmunt Andrzej 370

Szatkowska Irena 54

Szczanowska/Rosenthal Helena 331, 368, 413, 539, 543

Szczanowski Stanisław 285

Szczawińska Stanisława 251

Szczawiński Jerzy 295, 520, 566

Szczepańska Władysława 234

Szczęsnowicz Wiktor 191

Szczucińska Eleonora 184, 190

Szczucińska/Przednowek Krystyna 434

Szczurowski Bogusław 226, 290

Szczypek Stanisław 191

Szczyrska Maria 285, 316, 364, 413, 470

Szebert/Chołąckiewicz Jadwiga 541
Szelągowska Irena 331
Szemis Wirginia 251
Szewczyk Aleksandra 234
Szołkowska Barbara 141, 143, 145
Szołomińska Leokadia 369
Szpadowska Aleksandra 234, 540
Szpak/Ławniczek Felicja 521
Sztengel Helena 251
Sztrom Helena 291
Szul Tadeusz 190, 345, 347
Szumczyk Aleksander 331
Szustek vel Szostak Edward 207, 423, 424
Szwaglis Anna 290, 303, 330, 331, 554
Szwajnoch Józef 312, 313
Szydło/Suchecka Daniela 331, 334, 414
Szyk Helena 251
Szymańska Janina 285, 330
Szymańska Józefa 518
Szymarowski czy Szynarowski Roman 453
Szymel Cecylia 226, 227, 234
Szyryński W. 386
Szyszkin Anna 233

Ścibek/Bogdanowicz Lonia 552
Ściborska Maria 302, 330
Śliwińska Halina 470
Śliwińska Stefania 53, 60
Ślusarczyk Stefan 240
Ślusarczyk 348
Świątek Maria 234
Świątkowska/Chmielowcowa Irena 57, 157, 158, 285, 286, 291
Świdejko Zofia 331
Świerczyński Stanisław 567

Świergoń Antoni 205, 207, 266
Świeżawska Maria 137

Tabaczyńska Łucja 145
Tabaczyńska Janina 547
Tagore Rabindranath 44, 47, 439, 593, 594, 595
Tajchner Marcus 233, 364
Tarasiewicz Aleksandra 234
Tarasiewicz Stefan 153
Tarnogórska Jadwiga 72, 75, 93, 98, 105
Tatarczuk Irena 145, 331, 335
Templeton 75
Terlecki Andrzej 147
Tetmajerówna/Peszyńska Krystyna 594, 596
Tetmajerowa Anna 288, 289, 530
Tiachow Jerzy 148, 233, 290, 364, 395
Tijewska Regina 331, 536, 542
Tijewski Bronisław 184, 190, 193, 267
Tipu 476
Tkaczyk Franciszek 207
Tobianka Artur 191
Tomanek Alfred 227, 232, 330, 338, 371
Tomas/Kojro Wanda 325, 552, 553
Tomaszewicz/Kuchcicka Krystyna 546, 561
Tomaszek Jerzy 576
Tomaszewska Helena 152
Tomaszewska/Loszek Romualda 292, 339
Tomaszewska Stanisława 191
Topolnicka Krystyna 331
Topolnicka Jadwiga 285
Topolnicka Janina 251

Topolnicki Aleksander 251, 321, 330, 541
Topolski Feliks 52
Trella Bogusław v, 250, 523, 536, 541, 543, 559
Trella Stefania 330
Trella Urszula 331, 534, 538
Tripati Shashi 567
Truchanowicz/Piotrowska Jadwiga 576
Truksa Leszek 308, 546
Truksa/Popławska Mieczysława 331, 555
Truksa/Kaszuba Wanda 546, 548
Trzaska Leszek 387, 392, 416, 421, 426, 434, 488, 494, 519
Trzciankowska/Wrotniak Bronisława 409
Tubielewicz Ludwika 279
Turowicz Leontyna 184, 191
Turowicz Mita 318
Tutak/Masiulanis Helena 199, 517
Twarowska Bożena 304
Tybulewicz Albin 328, 341, 429, 501, 513, 578
Tybulewicz Tula 578
Tybura Zofia 224
Tyska Janina 319
Tyski Karol 191
Tysko... 207, 423
Tyszewicz Halina 331, 414
Tyszkiewicz/Ordonówna Hanka 131
Tyszkiewicz Michał 72
Tyszkiewicz Waleria 92, 107, 330, 563

Uberoi L. 442
Uberoi Ravi 442
Ucinek Jadwiga 513

Ucinek Stanisław 308, 344, 348, 379, 513

Ucinek Zbigniew 405, 414

Uma Devi/Dynowska Wanda 438, 451, 456, 466, 476, 491

Underka Teresa 331

Urban 90

Urbaniec Danuta 308, 331, 517

Valivadekar 446, 450, 452, 581

Valivadekar Jr. 561

Van Damme 81

Venkatachalam G. 476

Vere Hodge Barbara 18, 41

Vohra Subash C. 567

Walczak Władysława 185, 279

Walczowska/Król Alicja 131, 138, 509, 517

Walenia Antoni 279

Walker E.A. 40, 47

Walles Władysław 185, 310, 330, 338

Wałdoch Franciszek 184, 191

Wałdoch Jadwiga 145, 330, 331

Wałęsa Lech 505, 540

Warawa Anna 191

Wargowski 532

Wasilejko Halina 357, 385, 413, 414

Wasilewska Irena 239, 240, 242

Wasilewska Maria 310, 311, 332, 364

Wasiuk/Fischer Alicja 331, 348, 364, 391, 410, 413, 414, 439, 501, 545

Wasiuk Stanisław 347, 414, 501

Waszczuk Alina 330, 335, 336

Waters H. 63

Wavel Lord 159

Wawrzynowicz Leon 184, 185

Wawrzynowicz Maria 137, 145

Wawrzynowicz Tadeusz 515, 516

Wawrzyńczyk Leokadia 184, 185

Wazir Davinder 577, 578

Wądołkowski Henryk 331

Wcisło Stanisława 234

Webb Archibald W.T. 40, 43, 48, 49, 50, 51, 52, 53, 54, 55, 64, 65, 66, 70, 76, 81, 94, 117, 129, 174, 175, 117, 178, 179, 181, 182, 183, 188, 193, 194, 195, 196, 198, 211, 213, 214, 216, 218, 221, 243, 482, 485, 486

Weindling Halina 145

Wera/Kokoszko Weronika 335

Werner Aleksander v

Wesołowska Jadwiga 191

Węgrzyn Józef 191, 279

Węgrzyn Leon 497, 592

Wiatr J. 497, 592

Widmańska Maria 61, 62, 66, 224

Wieniawski Ignacy 310, 443

Wierzbicka Maria 136, 330

Wierzbińska/Mazajczyk Regina 539

Wierzchowska Felicja 249, 251

Wieselberg Samuel 135, 233, 364

Wiktorowicz Janusz 321, 330, 339, 342

Wiktorowicz Krystyna 285, 554

Wilczewski Tadeusz 190

Wilczyńska Zofia 285, 330, 466

Wilczyńska Maria 191, 364, 410, 423

Wilczyńska Marysia 364

Wilczyński Antoni 191

Wilczyński P. 207

Willman-Grabowska Helena 46, 438

Winnicka Aniela 559

Wiśniewski Andrzej 279

Wirth Maria 184, 191

Wiśniewska Waleria 331, 363, 364, 400, 401, 414

Witek zob.Olesiak Witold 342, 347, 358, 364, 370, 406, 413, 498

Wizimirska Wanda 413

Wlizło-Wilińska Aniela 279

Wojakiewicz Helena 330

Wojakowska Stefania 145

Wojciechowska Elżbieta 207

Wojciechowska Rozalia 61, 66

Wojewódka Bogumiła 141, 143, 145

Wojniłowicz/Zawadzińska Jadwiga 546, 578

Wojniłowicz/Jackiewicz Janina 546

Wojtasiewicz/Paszkiewicz Wiesława 538, 543

Wojtyła Karol 523, 538

Wolff/Nieczykowska Iza 150, 153, 517

Wolniewicz Maria 251

Woronowicz Wanda 92, 330

Woyniłłowicz/Słowikowska Eleonora 280

Woźny/Wierzbińska Nela 539, 543

Wójcicki Stanisław 279

Wójtowicz /Korczyńska Sylwia 410, 445

Wray Fanny 307, 324, 330, 441

Wright Leslie 151

Wronko Feliks 92, 330

Wrońska/Moroz Lodzia 546

Wróblewska/Rozwadowska Jadwiga 330

Wróblewski Bogusław 516

Wróblewski M. 304

Wróblewski Mr. 422

Wróblewski Wacław 516

Wrzyszcz Eugeniusz 354, 412, 515

Wycisło Alojzy 63

Wyczałkowska/Strycharz Halina 296, 373, 406, 413, 417, 444, 519

Wylot/Woźniak Maria 248, 517

Wypijewska/Rytwińska Krystyna 409, 546, 554

Wypijewska/Ostrowska Maria 545

Wysocka Janina 330

Wysocka Maria 158, 233, 368, 370, 596

Wyspiańska Jadwiga 330

Wyszyński Stefan 563

Wyszyński Andrzej 71

Young/Chrząszczewski Jan v, 337, 358 370, 400, 413, 414, 445, 501, 513,

Young Nina 569

Young Sally v, 569

Young/Webster Tessa 569

Yule George 31

Zabajo 271

Zagórowska Zofia 330

Zagórska Irena 234

Zając Gen. 43

Zając Czesław 428

Zając Feliks 206, 312, 347

Zajkowski 207, 423

Zaleski August 44, 505

Zaleski Michał 44

Zalewski Józef 54

Zanoziński Jan 57, 64

Zator Helena 234

Zawadowska/Jakutowicz Ludmiła 532

Zawadowska Waleria 135, 234

Zawadzińska/Wojniłowicz Jadwiga 354, 331, 374, 374, 412, 546, 578

Zawadzka Helena 330

Zawadzka Zofia 331

Zawadzki Józef 569

Zawerbna/Kowalczyk Stefania 560

Zawidzka Zofia vi, 29, 260, 272, 319, 331, 464, 547, 567

Zawistowicz Konstanty 207, 422

Zawistowicz Wanda 331

Zawojska Bronisława 185

Zbróg/Małkowska Janina 251, 331, 414, 517

Zbyszewska Bronisława 191, 312, 374

Zbyszewska Danuta 331, 335, 427

Zdzienicka Marylka 570

Ziarkiewicz Józef 191

Zieliński Tadeusz 447

Zielińska Anna 330

Zieliński Marian 318

Zimińska Eugenia 184

Ziubrzycki Bronisław 207

Zobek Irena 320, 331, 414, 429, 531, 532

Zubrzycki Jerzy 542

Zubrzycki Stanisław 190

Zuntych Franciszek 330

Zychowicz/Wawrzyńczyk Aniela 387

Zychówna Władzia 443

Zygiel/Jankowska Janina 421, 459, 548, 549, 470, 475

Żabko Jadwiga 330

Żarnower Michał 228

Żelichowska Lena 52, 67

Żelichowska Renia 150, 156

Żerdzicki Zygmunt 46

Żerebecka Irena 330

Żerebecki Zdzisław 306, 309, 320, 322, 326, 330, 336, 339, 348, 493, 575, 596

Żmigrodzki Antoni 72

Żogal Felicja 191

Żołądkiewicz Stanisława 184, 187

Żyszkowska/Jankowska Leokadia 331, 563

LIST OF POLISH REFUGEES RESIDING IN INDIA IN THE YEARS 1942-1948
Compiled by the Ministry of Works and Social Welfare in Bombay

The original list (numbers 1-3121), dated 15-11-1943, was followed be three supplementary ones: first, (Nos. 3122-3605); next dated 31-01-1944, (Nos. 3606-4075); and the last one, made on 1st Nov.1944 (Nos. 4075-4775). As the lists were incomplete, some names were added after verification, but those are without the Ministry index numbers. For the purpose of this book, names have been arranged in alphabetical order, containing dates of birth and the index number only. The full lists with additional information of place of birth, names of parents, last address in Poland and place of domicile in India are deposited at the Polish Institute and Sikorski Museum in London and in the Association's Archives.

L.p. Surname	Date of Birth
1 Abramowicz Józefat	27.08.1908
4078 Abramska Józefa	3.01.1904
4080 Abramska Zofia	17.02.1930
4079 Abramska Wanda	11.05.1936
4076 Abramska Helena	27.04.1928
4077 Abramski Józef	4.07.1939
3 Adamczak Kamila	17.08.1929
4 Adamczak Stefania	14.08.1910
5 Adamczak Wojciech	9.04.1900
2 Adamczak Eugeniusz	6.11.1926
6 Adamczyk Anna	07.1911
7 Adamczyk Anna	31.03.1898
8 Adamczyk Teresa	12.10.1909
9 Adamczyk Wojciech	28.04.1881
4081 Adamczyk Maria	14.08.1902
0082 Adamczyk-Pająk Irena	27.06.1926
11 Adamek Eleonora	15.02.1922
12 Adamek Eugeniusz	30.03.1933
10 Adamek Bronisława	26.07.1902
13 Adamek Joanna	20.08.1926
14 Adamek Maria	21.02.1915
15 Adamek Władysława	24.04.1898
16 Adamowska Eugenia	24.07.1909
18 Adamska Janina	26.01.1928
17 Adamska Antonina	14.06.1907
4083 Adamska Rozalia	4.09.1903
19 Adamski Eugeniusz	6.11.1932
20 Adamski Włodzimierz	15.07.1936
3123 Ajzen Dawid	15.12.1911
3122 Albel Aleksander	2.01.1925
22 Alberti Zofia	5.11.1905
21 Alberti Maria	8.06.1882
24 Aleksandrowicz Anna	22.07.1902
23 Aleksandrowicz Leokadia	22.07.1926
25 Aleksandrowicz Bogusława	5.09.1935
26 Aleksandrowicz Irena	1.09.1928
27 Aleksandrowicz Ryszard	9.09.1930
4084 Aleszczyk Anna	8.09.1910
4085 Aleszczyk Irena	9.01.1936
29 Allerhand Irena	28.10.1922
30 Allerhand Ludwik	17.09.1889
28 Allerhand Ernestyna	22.02.1867
32 Ambroziak Felicja	13.03.1931
31 Ambroziak Aleksandra	20.09.1904
33 Ambroziak Leokadia	28.12.1930
34 Ambroziak Sabina	10.09.1937
35 Ambroziak Stefan	13.09.1935
37 Andrejaszek Maria	15.08.1899
36 Andrejaszek Aniela	1.03.1928
38 Andrejaszek Stanisława	18.08.1930

L.p. Surname	Date of Birth
3124 Andrejuk Trofim	8.10.1897
39 Andrijewska Zofia	20.02.1893
41 Andrzejewska Maria	8.09.1916
40 Andrzejewska Helena	15.10.1885
42 Anecka Bronisława	20.08.1908
43 Anichwer Anna	25.01.1901
44 Anichwer Dawid	23.08.1886
45 Anichwer Piotr	7.06.1931
4088 Aniołkowska Karolina	15.06.1878
4087 Aniołkowska Janina	15.06.1904
4086 Aniołkowska Alicja	8.01.1912
3606 Aniśkowicz Olga	13.04.1912
3607 Aniśkowicz Tadeusz	13.03.1938
3608 Antczak Maria	1932
47 Antolik Maria	15.10.1901
46 Antolik Bogdan	9.10.1931
4090 Antonowicz Franciszka	16.01.1906
4089 Antonowicz Antonina	4.04.1925
48 Antoszewicz Maria	1887
49 Arciszewska Aleksandra	8.07.1908
50 Arciszewska Genowefa	10.07.1924
51 Arciszewska Irena	26.12.1932
52 Arciszewski Tadeusz	15.09.1934
3125 Arfa Brajna	28.08.1917
3126 Arfa Fajwel	6.01.1913
3127 Aronsohn Ludwik	22.04.1895
53 Artuciowicz Jadwiga	15.07.1927
3610 Asłanowicz Ludwik	4.01.1928
3609 Asłanowicz Helena	25.08.1907
4091 Audykowska Maria	2.01.1896
3128 Augustowski Stanisław	29.05.1891
55 Augustyn Maria	12.09.1935
54 Augustyn Jerzy	21.01.1927
56 Augustyńska Maria	15.03.1935
4094 Awdziejczyk Janina	25.05.1916
4093 Awdziejczyk Irena	10.04.1937

4092 Awdziejczyk Edward	5.11.1939
57 Azarko Jadwiga	24.06.1923
58 Azarko Maria	20.08.1888
59 Azarko Maria	12.02.1933
4095 Babicka Zofia	1.01.1891
3613 Babula Józef	8.03.1933
3612 Babula Antoni	8.06.1938
3614 Babula Roman	5.02.1935
3611 Babula Anna	5.05.1912
3616 Bachrynowska Waleria	9.08.1914
3615 Bachrynowska Bronisława	4.05.1936
3617 Bachrynowski Zdzisław	10.02.1942
60 Baczyńska Katarzyna	17.06.1892

L.p. Surname	Date of Birth
4096 Baczyńska Olimpia	25.02.1870
4097 Badowska Anna	11.10.1896
61 Badyńska Helena	03.1902
3129 Bagan Jadwiga	25.09.1914
62 Bagińska Zofia	30.11.1910
63 Bakun Antonina	13.06.1904
64 Bakun Irena	22.04.1938
67 Balawender Zofia	20.01.1925
65 Balawender Emilia	10.02.1927
66 Balawender Marta	29.01.1903
3618 Balewicz Elżbieta	15.06.1906
3619 Balewicz Stanisława	6.04.1928
3621 Bałaban Łucja	7.12.1898
3620 Bałaban Andrzej	10.09.1933
68 Bambuła Aniela	31.05.1937
70 Bambuła Waldemar	17.09.1933
69 Bambuła Leokadia	20.12.1905
71 Banas Maria	22.03.1894
72 Banas Stefania	18.09.1920
Banaś Bronisława	20.02.1905
Banaś Irena	27.12.1938
4099 Banaś Stanisława	28.01.1914
4098 Banaś Andrzej	27.12.1942
78 Bancarz Stefania	10.09.1906
77 Bancarz Eugeniusz	18.05.1930
73 Baniowska Helena	21.05.1907
74 Baniowska Janina	22.03.1933
75 Baniowski Józef	21.06.1929
76 Baniowski Stanisław	5.05.1935

80	Baran Maria	1932	107	Bąk Adela	30.03.1935	124	Biduń Eugenia	25.12.1907
79	Baran Anastazja	27.12.1930	108	Bąk Marian	15.07.1930	126	Biedrzyńska Zofia	24.05.1911
82	Baran Stanisława	9.12.1924	3629	Bąk Genowefa	13.07.1936	125	Biedrzyńska Urszula	08.04.1939
81	Baran Olga	25.08.1913	3630	Bąk Stanisława	25.01.1928	127	Biedul Sławomir	1933
4100	Baran Michał	17.06.1943	3628	Bąk Czesław	15.05.1931	3643	Biedul Józef	11.08.1931
83	Baranek Anna	1921	3627	Bąk Adela	1933	3642	Biedul Anna	26.07.1906
84	Baranek Maria	1900	3632	Bąkowska Marianna	18.08.1905	3641	Biedul Andrzej	25.04.1938
4102	Baranek Maria	17.05.1907	3631	Bąkowski Adam	31.08.1934	4127	Bieganowska Michalina	11.12.1885
4101	Baranek Emilia	16.11.1930	3633	Bąkowski Mieczysław	12.05.1937	4129	Bielawska Teresa	18.10.1936
88	Baranowska Rozalia	14.08.1902	3634	Bąkowski Władysław	13.03.1930	4128	Bielawska Maria	21.01.1913
85	Baranowska Alberta	15.08.1910	109	Bednarczyk Danuta	21.03.1943	129	Bielecka Barbara	1935
89	Baranowska Zofia	15.05.1934	110	Bednarczyk Helena	11.11.1932	133	Bielecka Kazimiera	24.03.1925
4104	Baranowska Olga	1891	111	Bednarczyk Ksawera	24.11.1918	130	Bielecka Irena	4.01.1932
87	Baranowski Kazimierz	1931	112	Bednarczyk Ludwik	1.01.1939	132	Bielecka Janina	14.04.1938
90	Baranowski Zygmunt	1936		Bednarska Józefa		134	Bielecka Krystyna	24.09.1923
86	Baranowski Julian	1929		Bednarski Stanisław		135	Bielecka Stefania	10.05.1895
4103	Baranowski Franciszek	8.12.1874	113	Bełda Helena	31.05.1928	4130	Bielecka Bronisława	29.04.1929
3622	Bargiełowska Dorota	6.03.1906	114	Bełdowska Janina	31.12.1898	4132	Bielecka Katarzyna	8.12.1898
3623	Bargiełowska Kazimiera	27.02.1924	115	Bełdowski Leszek	1.07.1929	4131	Bielecka Emilia	10.02.1926
91	Bartosz Czesław	1938	4114	Bełzko Maria	17.07.1904	128	Bielecki Adam	16.03.1936
92	Bartosz Janina	1.08.1930	4112	Bełzko Czesława	9.05.1932	131	Bielecki Jan	05.1934
93	Bartosz Zbigniew	22.02.1935	4113	Bełzko Jadwiga	17.07.1928	4133	Bieleń Franciszek	17.10.1913
4107	Bartosz Krystyna	4.04.1935	4118	Bena Julia	18.02.1888	137	Bielińska Kazimiera	28.04.1932
4105	Bartosz Andrzej	29.11.1938	4117	Bena Helena	22.02.1922	136	Bielińska Irena	16.03.1930
4106	Bartosz Bronisława	24.12.1909	4115	Bena Feliks-Marian	29.07.1943	141	Bielska Pelagia	23.08.1927
4109	Bartosz Teresa	12.10.1941	4119	Bena Maria	22.04.1925	139	Bielska Emilia	17.08.1938
4108	Bartosz Liliana	12.01.1932	4120	Bena Otylia	22.03.1920	142	Bielska Stefania	6.01.1917
94	Bartoszewicz Halina	24.08.1918	4121	Bena Zbigniew	6.05.1936	138	Bielski Edward	1932
95	Bartoszewicz Irena	5.10.1938	4116	Bena Franciszek	2.12.1883	140	Bielski Julian	2.02.1899
96	Bartoszewicz Weronika	27.01.1879	3132	Benal Wiktoria	31.03.1889	145	Bień Aniela	28.07.1904
98	Bartyzel Edward	28.09.1937	3130	Benal Ludwik	7.01.1886	144	Bień Aleksander	30.06.1929
97	Bartyzel Aniela	28.10.1915	3131	Benal Paulina	7.01.1921	146	Bień Eugenia	17.12.1923
101	Baryła Franciszka	27.12.1916	116	Berch Marian	6.02.1897	147	Bień Franciszka	20.07.1880
100	Baryluk Katarzyna	07.1879	4124	Bereznicka Maria	5.10.1928	148	Bień Piotr	20.06.1875
99	Baryluk Jan	15.03.1872	4122	Bereznicka Aleksandra	15.08.1923	3644	Bień Antonina	5.05.1912
3625	Baryluk Michał	24.12.1926	4123	Bereznicki Karol	15.10.1932	143	Bieniarz Helena	28.08.1928
3624	Baryluk Antonina	10.03.1901	4125	Bereznicki Michał	14.05.1874	3645	Bieńkowska Leokadia	19.07.1927
3626	Baryluk Stefania	22.07.1932	3636	Bereźnicka Karolina	5.06.1905	3136	Biernacka Zofia	26.11.1910
104	Basarab Józefa	20.03.1926	3637	Bereźnicki Mikołaj	11.01.1900	3646	Bierońska Józefa	5.05.1927
103	Basarab Janina	14.04.1943	3638	Bereźnicki Włodzimierz	7.08.1930	149	Bieroński Tadeusz	18.11.1928
102	Basarab Anna	14.02.1903	3635	Bereźnicki Józef	10.07.1931	150	Bil Aleksander	27.04.1931
4111	Bator Józef	19.03.1897	4126	Bernatowicz Joanna	24.12.1888	151	Bil Stanisława	1929
4110	Bator Anna	22.06.1905	3639	Bernsztein Renata	16.07.1921	153	Bilińska Antonina	1935
	Bąbik Józefa	1892	3134	Beszkiewicz Józef	14.03.1891	154	Bilińska Karolina	1934
	Bąbik Alina	1924	3133	Beszkiewicz Aniela	15.04.1901	152	Bilińska Aniela	15.09.1927
	Bąbik Irena	1925	117	Bezdel Maria	3.01.1929	3647	Bilińska Adolfina	6.01.1884
105	Bączyk Alicja	7.04.1932	118	Bezdel Ewalda	8.05.1922	3648	Birecka Emilia	4.11.1901
106	Bączyk Henryk	23.02.1927	119	Bezdel Stanisława	20.11.1900	3650	Birecki Zygmunt	30.11.1930
	Bąk Alina	28.10.1938	3135	Białek Tadeusz	12.04.1908	3649	Birecki Jan	9.03.1933
	Bąk Anna	1935	3640	Białouś Waleria	9.12.1887	3137	Birońska Elżbieta	5.04.1886
	Bąk Eugeniusz	18.07.1933	121	Bidakowska Ludmiła	28.04.1908	156	Biskupska Waleria	11.11.1893
	Bąk Helena	15.10.1915	122	Bidakowski Witold	30.06.1910	155	Biskupska Krystyna	10.01.1921
	Bąk Karolina	1913	123	Bidakowski Władysław	14.09.1877	157	Biznia Bronisława	7.10.1912
	Bąk Leszek	1941	120	Bidakowski Andrzej	22.05.1932	3138	Blacher Lejzer	13.11.1914

158	Blumska Maria	30.11.1899	196	Borek Zofia	30.05.1935	236	Buc Aniela	14.04.1890
159	Blumski Romuald	30.11.1929	4140	Borek Krzysztof	24.07.1944	237	Buc Irena	20.01.1924
161	Błach Maria	22.03.1903	199	Borkowska Irena	9.10.1935	238	Buc Jarosław	26.03.1929
160	Błach Alojzy	18.06.1929	200	Borkowska Maria	11.11.1908	4142	Buchowiecka Maria	20.05.1883
4136	Błaszczak Ryszard	5.06.1933	198	Borkowska Helena	3.05.1933	3664	Buczak Irena	6.01.1928
4134	Błaszczak Anna	26.07.1904	3659	Borkowska Ludwika	12.03.1925	3663	Buczak Eugenia	8.11.1931
4135	Błaszczak Halina	4.03.1929	3658	Borkowska Danuta	1936	3662	Buczak Emilia	9.11.1904
162	Błaszczuk Jan	23.05.1913	197	Borkowski Eugeniusz	6.10.1931	270	Budhusaim Anastazja	1.01.1927
164	Błażewicz Mieczysław	29.04.1924	3660	Borkowski Piotr	29.06.1929	271	Budhusaim Jan	15.03.1891
163	Błażewicz Józef	13.12.1927	201	Borońska Maria	19.01.1906	239	Budnik Lucjan	26.10.1888
167	Błońska Longina	15.05.1921	202	Boroński Witold	25.06.1934	245	Budzyńska Zofia	10.11.1932
165	Błońska Józefa	2.05.1902	203	Borowiak Genowefa	1.12.1926	240	Budzyńska Anna	25.12.1937
166	Błoński Leszek	19.09.1940	4141	Borowska Maria	13.03.1898	241	Budzyńska Irena	25.03.1930
3651	Bober-Bobrowski Kazimierz Fr.	22.02.1905	204	Borowski Jan	19.01.1890	242	Budzyńska Jadwiga	28.09.1934
168	Bobolska Maria	11.07.1905	3661	Borwicz Elżbieta	24.12.1864	243	Budzyńska Magdalena	22.07.1900
169	Bobolski Zbigniew	2.02.1929	205	Borysiewicz Helena	20.01.1922	244	Budzyńska Maria	4.12.1928
	Bobotek Elżbieta		207	Borzemska Wanda	2.10.1912	246	Budzyńska Zenobia	7.02.1940
	Bobotek Henryk		206	Borzemska Stanisława	7.05.1893	3666	Bujakowska Irena	17.11.1928
	Bobotek Władysław		208	Bożek Czesław	16.08.1928	3665	Bujakowska Agnieszka	21.12.1902
170	Bobrowicz Antoni	17.01.1886	210	Bożek Michał	1930	183	Bujnowska Bronisława	21.01.1928
171	Bocun Kazimierz	1929	209	Bożek Marian	1937	185	Bujnowska Zofia	22.03.1930
172	Boduch Wiesława	1.09.1927	211	Bożek Stanisław	26.02.1927	184	Bujnowski Stanisław	24.12.1934
173	Boduch Wiktoria	23.12.1886	3142	Bożek Genowefa	16.07.1919	248	Bukowski Zbigniew	1935
3653	Bodura Zofia	6.02.1925	3143	Bożek Tomasz	24.12.1877	247	Bukowski Stefan	17.10.1928
3652	Bodura Anna	7.12.1931	212	Bratkowska Felicja	1.09.1899	249	Bułakowska Anna	15.02.1881
175	Bogdanowicz Wanda	15.11.1919	213	Bratkowska Janina	17.05.1923	250	Bułakowska Helena	2.03.1918
176	Bogdanowicz Helena	22.05.1910	214	Bratkowska Stanisława	29.09.1928	251	Bułdak Adela	25.05.1920
174	Bogdanowicz Genowefa	10.12.1878	215	Braumuller Alfred	21.02.1927	253	Bułdak Władysław	17.08.1890
3140	Boguchwalska Izabella	5.10.1923	216	Brażuk Jadwiga	14.10.1907	252	Bułdak Józefa	1882
3139	Boguchwalski Walenty	26.08.1901	217	Brażuk Maria	20.01.1934	254	Bura Felicja	3.03.1907
177	Bogucki Feliks	30.10.1897	3144	Bregman Hersz	15.04.1911	258	Buras Zbigniew	3.10.1939
3141	Bogucki Stefan	19.06.1910	218	Bronik Wacław	22.02.1935	257	Buras Stefan	11.11.1906
3654	Boguniecka Genowefa	9.09.1926	219	Bronik Władysława	15.03.1928	256	Buras Józef	20.04.1931
178	Bogusławska Maria	1875	223	Bronowicka Zofia	19.03.1923	255	Buras Irena	4.10.1932
180	Bojarska Ludwika	19.05.1899	222	Bronowicka Maria	8.03.1927	4143	Buras Władysław	13.05.1909
4138	Bojarska Maria	12.12.1923	220	Bronowicka Antonina	13.06.1930	260	Burdzy Henryk	1932
4137	Bojarska Józefa	5.05.1903	221	Bronowicka Halina	13.04.1929	259	Burdzy Ferdynand	18.02.1928
179	Bojarski Bolesław	31.05.1931	224	Bronowicz Danuta	27.05.1931	262	Burek Irena	29.03.1907
4139	Bojarski Józef	8.02.1891	225	Bronowicz Jadwiga	5.03.1904	264	Burek Zbigniew	3.10.1931
181	Bojda Anna	1930	3145	Bruch Kazimierz	17.09.1899	263	Burek Teresa	22.11.1928
182	Bojko Aleksander	1.01.1921	226	Brucka Helena	15.05.1928	261	Burek Aleksandra	21.07.1927
188	Bołbot Agata	1906	3148	Bruner Janina	13.12.1931	267	Burger Julia	15.07.1891
189	Bołbot Wiera	13.03.1929	3147	Bruner Halina	6.06.1902	266	Burger Józefa	20.10.1932
186	Bolc Edward	1933	3149	Brycki Bolesław	27.03.1899	265	Burger Emilia	4.12.1926
187	Bolc Michał	1937	228	Brzezina Bronisława	18.04.1910	269	Bury Tadeusz	1931
3655	Bolc Maria	11.01.1911	230	Brzezina Jan	23.05.1899	268	Bury Eugeniusz	11.02.1927
191	Bomba Romana	8.05.1934	227	Brzezina Bolesław	5.06.1936	4144	Burzyńska Maria	13.07.1912
190	Bomba Leonarda	1936	229	Brzezina Emilia	19.10.1937	3667	Buzuł Halina	1932
3656	Borcz Stanisława	25.10.1930	231	Brzezińska Anna	2.12.1924	3668	Buzuł Jan	1935
3657	Borcz Weronika	9.03.1903	232	Brzezińska Józefa	4.03.1900	272	Bychowiec Alfred	10.06.1934
195	Borek Maria	1898	3146	Brzozowska Zofia	6.08.1905	273	Bychowiec Genowefa	19.11.1907
194	Borek Janina	7.02.1928	233	Brzozowski Bronisław	5.05.1904	274	Bychowiec Jadwiga	2.11.1878
192	Borek Apolinary	1.01.1930	234	Brzykcy Antonina	3.09.1902	275	Bychowiec Regina	8.11.1930
193	Borek Jan	1886	235	Brzykcy Franciszka	15.09.1926	276	Bychowiec Zofia	6.07.1922

277	Bystrzyc Bolesław	8.04.1897	3685	Chojnowska Stanisława	18.12.1903	4162	Citron Adela	19.03.1891
4145	Bzowa Anastazja	20.03.1890	3683	Chojnowska Irena	20.02.1938	4163	Citron Edwin	8.04.1893
4146	Bzowa Anna	11.02.1926	301	Chołąckiewicz Jadwiga	29.09.1906	334	Ciula Jadwiga	15.08.1905
4147	Bzowy Jan	5.05.1931	302	Chołąckiewicz Rozalia	30.06.1870	333	Ciula Felicja	15.10.1930
4148	Bzowy Stanisław	3.10.1929	300	Chołaj Zdzisław	16.03.1939	3166	Cmut Marta	
			299	Chołaj Stanisław	4.05.1943	3165	Cmut Józef	17.01.1906
3670	Cariuk Kleopatra	27.09.1923	297	Chołaj Edward	11.06.1933	335	Cwajna Czesław	10.01.1929
3669	Cariuk Anastazja	22.12.1884	298	Chołaj Maria	2.11.1909	336	Cwetsch Franciszek	31.08.1932
278	Cechanowicz Julia	10.04.1918	303	Chomczenowska Antonina	20.12.1928	4164	Cynkin Helena	19.05.1889
279	Cechanowicz Mikołaj	7.05.1883	304	Chomczenowska Zofia	15.08.1907	3167	Cynowicz Hersz-żelik	24.03.1903
3672	Celejewska Józefa	4.07.1902	4155	Chomicki Korneliusz	14.09.1881	3168	Cywinger Mordechaj	14.05.1913
4149	Celejewska Maria	2.02.1944	306	Chomin Janina	8.03.1904	337	Czabanowska Stefania	2.09.1895
3673	Celejewski Stefan	15.08.1893	305	Chomko Konstanty	25.03.1892	338	Czachor Krystyna	1930
3671	Celejewski Józef	6.02.1935	307	Chowaniec Janina	29.08.1899	339	Czachor Tadeusz	1931
282	Celtner Zofia	15.05.1923	308	Chożempa Józef	1936	340	Czachor Bronisława	29.11.1919
281	Celtner Paulina	20.12.1894	311	Chrol Maria	6.04.1930	341	Czachor Wanda	15.05.1920
280	Celtner Helena	1.01.1932	310	Chrol Halina	7.06.1933	343	Czajka Ignacy	18.03.1931
3150	Chajłowicz Józef	1.05.1920	309	Chrol Antonina	11.1889	344	Czajka Kazimierz	13.11.1936
3151	Charlab Chaim	3.11.1920	312	Chrol Wanda	10.02.1928	345	Czajka Maria	1893
283	Chatys Petronela	30.05.1892	313	Chronowska Janina	28.08.1919	346	Czajka Michał	27.10.1930
284	Chendyński Andrzej	30.08.1936	314	Chronowska Julia	13.10.1882	342	Czajka Antonina	4.03.1928
3152	Chłopecka Janina	1933	315	Chróścicka Stanisława	8.04.1930	348	Czajkowska Zofia	17.01.1901
3153	Chmielewska Irmina	1.09.1921	317	Chruściel Stanisława	10.02.1931	347	Czajkowska Julia	16.12.1912
285	Chmielowiec Michał	19.10.1918	316	Chruściel Franciszka	30.09.1927	3169	Czajkowski Alojzy	3.06.1897
286	Chmielowska Zofia	25.03.1894	4157	Chrystowska Helena	22.08.1932	4165	Czapa Antoni	30.05.1894
3678	Chmielowska Joanna	3.10.1928	4156	Chrystowska Halina	9.02.1896	4166	Czapa Maria	28.12.1893
3676	Chmielowska Halina	24.02.1927	320	Chrząszcz Stefania	15.06.1927	350	Czarnecka Czesława	20.12.1920
3675	Chmielowska Aniela	24.10.1903	318	Chrząszcz Anna	1.10.1892	351	Czarnecka Leontyna	24.04.1926
287	Chmielowski Eugeniusz	5.03.1929	319	Chrząszcz Jan	24.08.1894	352	Czarnecka Maria	10.03.1906
3677	Chmielowski Jerzy	17.11.1930	4158	Chrząszcz Genowefa	15.05.1930	353	Czarnecka Maria	11.09.1909
290	Chocha Tatiana	1894	322	Chrząszczewska Zofia	22.02.1902	354	Czarnecka Sabina	17.12.1923
288	Chocha Anna	1922	321	Chrząszczewski Jan	1.06.1931	355	Czarnecka Stanisława	28.08.1887
289	Chocha Józef	15.07.1885	3159	Chudzik Bolesław	28.10.1938	356	Czarnecka Teresa	24.09.1933
3154	Chochłuń Katarzyna	20.02.1919	3160	Chudzik Maria	28.02.1910	357	Czarnecka Wacława	10.08.1931
4150	Chociej Krystyna	26.07.1904	3162	Chudzio Janina	3.04.1926		Czarnecka Anna	22.12.1902
3156	Choczner Amalia	25.10.1915	3163	Chudzio Ludmiła	27.05.1929		Czarnecka Kazimiera	24.09.1929
3155	Choczner Hirsz-Lejb	30.11.1904	4159	Chyla Alicja	23.07.1926	359	Czarnecki Władysław	5.11.1928
291	Chodkiewicz Eudokja	15.04.1904	4160	Chyla Anna	10.12.1897	360	Czarnecki Zdzisław	25.08.1935
292	Chodkiewicz Genowefa	1.02.1923	4161	Chyla Zofia	19.03.1930	361	Czarnecki Zenon	10.08.1928
4153	Chodor Zofia	10.05.1902	323	Ciastoń Franciszka	1896	358	Czarnecki Andrzej	22.06.1939
4152	Chodor Stanisław	24.04.1892	3161	Ciążyńska Czesława	24.05.1901	363	Czarnota Katarzyna	20.04.1929
4151	Chodor Helena	1.09.1927	325	Cichocka Jadwiga	14.05.1930	362	Czarnota Katarzyna	24.11.1887
4154	Chodorowska Eleonora	21.02.1913	324	Cichocka Jadwiga	1926	364	Czarny Józef	28.03.1888
3680	Chodorowska Petronela	25.03.1904	326	Cichocka Rozalia	13.07.1897	365	Czartowska Irena	21.04.1925
3682	Chodorowska Wanda	27.06.1929	3164	Ciemochowska Felicja	15.05.1919	366	Czartowska Maria	8.10.1900
3679	Chodorowska Leokadia	12.01.1934	328	Cieplik Lesław	18.10.1930	367	Czartowska Maria	8.10.1929
3157	Chodorowski Maks	20.08.1917	327	Cieplik Helena	18.10.1892	349	Czaykowski Bogdan	10.02.1932
3681	Chodorowski Tadeusz	6.01.1936	331	Ciruk Renisław	29.08.1933	369	Czech Janina	25.10.1925
3158	Chojnacki Kazimierz	1.01.1908	332	Ciruk Tadeusz	20.01.1933	368	Czech Anna	18.07.1899
295	Chojno Mirosław	16.12.1930	330	Ciruk Józefa	22.02.1908	4167	Czech Danuta	7.12.1927
296	Chojno Wiktor		329	Ciruk Jadwiga	24.10.1930	4168	Czech Maria	9.02.1897
294	Chojno Melania	24.12.1898	3688	Cisiewicz Maria	10.09.1926	4169	Czechowicz Albin	2.10.1901
293	Chojno Leokadia	23.08.1929	3687	Cisiewicz Janina	12.04.1935	4170	Czechowicz Jadwiga	30.01.1907
3684	Chojnowska Kazimiera	27.05.1927	3686	Cisiewicz Anna	15.01.1925	4171	Czeczeników Gabriel	25.03.1901

4173	Czeczeników Olga	16.12.1925	393	Czynczyk Kazimierz	1930	3183	Derecka Urszula	20.10.1930
4174	Czeczeników Sergiusz	31.07.1940	394	Czynczyk Tadeusz	1933	426	Derecki Wacław	1.09.1936
4176	Czeczeników Włodzimierz	27.10.1937	395	Czynczyk Zofia	1937	3184	Derecki Jan	20.10.1930
4175	Czeczeników Teodor	16.09.1930	4193	Czyński Józef-Ludomir	3.08.1886	3185	Deręgowski Leon	30.12.1906
4172	Czeczeników Mikołaj	7.11.1932	397	Czyruk Katarzyna	2.01.1938	430	Dereń Mieczysław	11.1928
4177	Czeczeników Zenaida	6.05.1906	396	Czyruk Florian	20.11.1878	429	Dereń Maria	22.10.1926
	Czeczeników Krystyna	17.02.1945	398	Czyruk Ksenia	28.01.1888	431	Dereń Władysław	1931
371	Czekaj Ignacy	17.12.1896	399	Czyruk Maria	1.03.1936	427	Derencz Eligiusz	22.09.1930
370	Czekaj Bronisława	5.06.1930	400	Czyruk Matrona	12.11.1912	428	Derencz Wiesław	22.09.1932
372	Czekaj Kazimiera	10.06.1941	4195	Czyż Bogusława	3.04.1943	433	Derkacz Zofia	22.08.1903
373	Czekaj Maria	18.08.1908	4194	Czyż Anna	8.09.1915	432	Derkacz Kazimierz	18.10.1934
3689	Czekańska Bogumiła	13.10.1932	401	Czyżewska Leokadia	2.03.1927	434	Derzurko Michał	12.12.1898
3690	Czekańska Grażyna	26.06.1906				3186	Deutsch Walter	31.05.1898
3691	Czekański Józef	20.05.1935	3174	Ćwiczyńska Anna	8.08.1922	435	Dębczak Józefa	14.04.1892
375	Czekierska Wanda	13.07.1890	3175	Ćwiczyńska Dominika	4.08.1896	414	Diageńczuk Tadeusz	10.12.1929
374	Czekierska Estela	30.10.1925				3187	Diamant Samuel	14.04.1900
3170	Czepukojć Zuzanna	22.04.1922	402	Dacz Aniela	24.06.1896	436	Dobolewicz Apolonia	11.12.1925
4183	Czerepak Stanisława	28.12.1927	403	Dacz Alicja	10.01.1925	437	Dobolewicz Leokadia	13.11.1930
4178	Czerepak Bronisław	1.01.1931	404	Dacz Irena	20.10.1923	438	Dobolewicz Marianna	17.02.1908
4179	Czerepak Eugenia	8.03.1925	3176	Dajek Jan	30.06.1891	439	Dobolewicz Władysława	13.09.1934
4180	Czerepak Jan	17.03.1898	405	Dallinger Leopold Fr.	24.10.1884	440	Dobolewicz Władysława	6.03.1928
4181	Czerepak Janina	10.06.1933	406	Dawid Lechosław	1.04.1932	442	Dobosz Kamila	14.06.1906
4182	Czerepak Maria	28.04.1897	4197	Dąbek Zbigniew	7.10.1936	443	Dobosz Tadeusz	17.03.1933
377	Czerepowicka Józefa	20.07.1893	4196	Dąbek Maria	27.10.1907	441	Dobosz Czesława	20.08.1927
376	Czerepowicka Jadwiga	2.10.1928	408	Dąbrowska Julia	5.09.1917	444	Dobrostańska Janina	16.09.1903
379	Czerepowicki Wacław	12.10.1926	407	Dąbrowska Anna	4.02.1911	446	Dobrostański Tadeusz	17.03.1933
378	Czerepowicki Czesław	12.04.1931	3694	Dąbrowska Teresa	5.05.1939	445	Dobrostański Jerzy	3.03.1930
4185	Czerkas Kazimierz	13.02.1931	3177	Dąbrowska Alicja	23.05.1941	447	Dobrowolska Genowefa	3.01.1933
4186	Czerkas Krystyna	10.10.1928	3693	Dąbrowska Izabella	24.10.1936	448	Dobrowolska Irena	17.09.1939
4184	Czerkas Franciszek	21.01.1933	3178	Dąbrowska Maria	2.02.1919	449	Dobrowolska Zofia	20.12.1912
	Czerkawska Helena	7.06.1900	3692	Dąbrowska Helena	3.08.1909	451	Dobrowolski Mieczysław	20.03.1930
	Czerkawska Krystyna	6.12.1932	412	Dąbrowski Romuald	7.07.1939	450	Dobrowolski Edward	10.03.1938
381	Czerniawska Wanda	21.01.1917	409	Dąbrowski Edward	1.03.1938	453	Dokurno Krystyna	13.03.1933
4187	Czerniawska Bronisława	10.02.1930	411	Dąbrowski Kazimierz	21.08.1928	454	Dokurno Romuald	20.09.1931
380	Czerniawski Antoni	23.04.1939	410	Dąbrowski Józef	29.07.1929	452	Dokurno Karolina	23.09.1937
383	Czerniejewska Henryka	27.02.1936	413	Dąbrowski Stanisław	1932	455	Dokurno Stanisława	1898
384	Czerniejewska Janina	9.08.1926	4198	Dąbrowski Władysław	12.02.1916	456	Dokurno Szczepan	25.12.1929
382	Czerniejewska Adela	15.11.1900	3179	Dąbska Maria	28.05.1909	4201	Doliński Zygmunt	23.03.1885
385	Czernik Anastazja	1880	416	Dederska Lubomira	12.03.1912	3188	Domanowicz Hersz	23.04.1912
386	Czernik Maria	29.08.1921	415	Dederska Aniela	8.02.	458	Domańska Teresa	10.04.1891
387	Czernik Sergiusz	1930	417	Dederski Edward	28.02.1935	457	Domańska Czesława	4.03.1930
388	Czernik Walentyna	20.05.1927	3180	Dehler Augustyn	2.09.1888	3189	Domańska Stefania	28.10.1896
390	Czerniowska Zofia	23.04.1906	419	Dejnowska Maria	12.02.1891	460	Door Irena	23.04.1931
389	Czerniowska Krystyna	5.09.1930	418	Dejnowska Jadwiga	21.03.1929	459	Door Anastazja	24.06.1891
3171	Czerski Czesław	21.08.1900	421	Delikowska Władysława	20.12.1927	461	Door Jadwiga	13.04.1922
4188	Czeszejko Anna	11.02.1897	420	Delikowska Salomea	26.05.1882	462	Dorosz Bożena	14.05.1930
4189	Czeszejko Stefania	2.02.1926	422	Dembczak Helena	1932	464	Dowgiałło Genowefa	20.06.1923
4190	Czochańska Wiesława	7.01.1939	423	Dembczak Irena	1934	465	Dowgiałło Janina	7.09.1927
3172	Czogało Wanda	13.06.1919	4199	Dembińska Janina	17.05.1915	463	Dowgiałło Anna	1.05.1899
391	Czubryt Anna	18.03.1914	4200	Dembiński Zbigniew	20.01.1936	466	Dragosz Helena	15.05.1930
3173	Czubryt Józef	6.04.1937	3181	Derczański Zoruch	7.09.1905	467	Dragosz Zofia	25.03.1921
4191	Czwarnos Irena	11.03.1928	425	Derecka Stefania	7.02.1904	469	Drałus Józef	19.03.1930
4192	Czwarnos Stanisława	1.11.1908	424	Derecka Maria	15.02.1931	470	Drałus Maria	12.05.1903
392	Czynczyk Eugenia	1938	3182	Derecka Maria	22.11.1894	471	Drałus Stanisław	28.09.1928

#	Name	Date
468	Drałus Helena	22.11.1934
4202	Draus Józefa	13.11.1927
4203	Draus Maria	10.01.1931
4204	Draus Wanda	20.07.1932
4206	Drążek Helena	18.08.1925
4205	Drążek Antonia	13.11.1899
472	Dreja Janina	15.12.1929
473	Dreja Zofia	24.07.1927
4207	Dreja Stefania	2.08.1930
475	Drimmer Leon	21.02.1926
476	Drimmer Tauba	21.03.1904
474	Drimmer Jakub	14.05.1941
478	Drobik Maria	25.07.1925
477	Drobik Anna	14.12.1902
479	Drozd Józef	10.07.1888
480	Drozd Katarzyna	17.07.1888
482	Drozdalska Danuta	12.05.1929
481	Drozdalska Aniela	25.05.1896
484	Drzewiecka Petronela	1881
483	Drzewiecka Marianna	7.04.1903
485	Dubicka Floriana	2.02.1929
486	Dubicka Franciszka	3.12.1907
487	Dubicka Lidia	26.11.1934
489	Dubicki Józef	1934
488	Dubicki Henryk	28.04.1932
491	Dubiel Stanisława	17.12.1926
490	Dubiel Anna	11.05.1904
492	Dubis Czesława	3.09.1936
493	Dubis Filomena	22.02.1902
494	Dubis Marian	21.06.1926
495	Dubowik Zofia	1.01.1871
3696	Dubrawska Zofia	15.05.1898
3695	Dubrawski Feliks	2.04.1897
4208	Duda Antoni	18.05.1908
497	Dudek Irena	24.10.1929
498	Dudek Maria	7.04.1907
496	Dudek Barbara	20.08.1932
499	Dudek Zofia	17.02.1927
500	Dudek Zdzisława	28.04.1928
501	Dudek Helena	1930
502	Dudek Józef	1928
503	Dudek Stanisława	1932
505	Dudko Wanda	14.10.1913
504	Dudko Maria	14.11.1940
3697	Dudryk-Darlewska Anna	16.02.1890
3698	Dudryk-Darlewski Antoni	25.01.1880
3192	Dudryk-Darlewski Stanisław	14.04.1911
3191	Duduk Józef	22.12.1899
3190	Duduk Anna	12.09.1916
3194	Dudzik Maria	
3193	Dudzik Leonard	28.07.1905
509	During Krystyna	6.04.1929
510	During Stefania	17.01.1895
508	Duszyńska Teresa	2.02.1929
507	Duszyńska Maria	1938
4210	Duszyńska Eugenia	13.09.1910
4209	Duszyński Aleksander	1.11.1897
3699	Dybczak Eugeniusz	23.07.1928
3700	Dybczak Sylwia	31.12.1903
4211	Dymicki Jan	10.11.1912
511	Dymska Paulina	25.05.1920
513	Dymurska Felicja	11.11.1928
512	Dymurska Anna	22.12.1926
3195	Dynowska Wanda	30.06.1888
514	Dysiewicz Aniela	26.10.1890
516	Dziadura Katarzyna	24.11.1898
517	Dziadura Rozalia	20.03.1932
515	Dziadura Eugenia	18.02.1926
518	Dziedzic Kazimiera	19.09.1910
519	Dziedzic Otylia	17.03.1932
520	Dziedzic Wiktoria	15.07.1930
524	Dzięgielewska Bożenna	3.06.1939
523	Dzięgielewska Antonina	17.01.1906
3702	Dzięgielewski Stanisław	17.10.1897
4212	Dzierżek Adam	16.04.1891
521	Dzieszuk Helena	1876
522	Dziewiątkowski Józef	25.02.1908
3701	Dziewięcka Apolonia	3.03.1914
4213	Dzioba Antoni	6.07.1932
4214	Dzioba Albina	29.06.1906
526	Dźumaga Maria	3.09.1927
525	Dźumaga Anna	26.07.1907
527	Ehrlich Edmund	8.11.1928
3196	Eilenberg Chejwet	14.07.1907
3197	Eisner Chinka	24.04.1906
528	Ejsak Helena	20.11.1910
529	Ekert Danuta	27.09.1927
530	Ekert Zofia	17.04.1895
3198	Estkowska Elżbieta	19.07.1907
4215	Ezman Irena	4.03.1929
4216	Ezman Józef	23.08.1924
4217	Ezman Leokadia	5.05.1882
3199	Fajtlowicz Jakub	23.07.1910
532	Fałdrowicz Helena	22.06.1912
533	Fałdrowicz Roman	23.12.1897
534	Fałdrowicz Maria	5.11.1935
531	Fałdrowicz Bogusław	5.11.1938
3200	Falk Maria	26.04.1906
4219	Falkowska Leokadia	23.08.1925
4218	Falkowska Anna	10.11.1900
4220	Feier Józef-Wilhelm	11.11.1905
535	Felter Aleksandra	15.12.1907
536	Felter Celina	24.01.1936
537	Felter Jadwiga	12.12.1930
543	Feń Weronika	7.09.1924
539	Feń Barbara	4.12.1890
540	Feń Helena	21.03.1920
541	Feń Lidia	21.11.1914
542	Feń Teodory	7.01.1885
538	Feń Antoni	21.06.1940
3202	Fenigstein Flora	
3201	Fenigstein Grzegorz	14.08.1902
3204	Feuer Antonina	26.04.1914
3203	Feuer Ignacy	29.12.1913
3205	Figoń Maria	6.01.1901
3703	Figuła Janina	20.01.1908
545	Fijał Ludwika	1902
546	Fijał Stanisława	10.09.1926
544	Fijał Bazyli	20.02.1894
547	Filipowicz Helena	15.04.1920
548	Filipowicz Maria	1.10.1909
	Filipowicz Stefania	9.11.1911
	Filipowicz Stefania	26.07.1931
4221	Filippoto Paweł	3.11.1884
4222	Filozof Helena	3.11.1885
4223	Filozof Jan	2.05.1884
550	Fin Janina	17.07.1930
549	Fin Genowefa	8.09.1927
3206	Finke Leon	8.09.1877
3207	Finkel Mojsiej	13.08.1910
4224	Finkler Gustaw-Bernard	25.08.1904
551	Firko Wanda	10.06.1926
3208	Flancreich Natan	5.11.1910
552	Flecker Edyta	20.04.1902
4225	Flis Edward	20.02.1906
554	Formankiewicz Władysław	15.03.1930
553	Formankiewicz Maria	15.03.1931
555	Formankiewicz Zofia	21.04.1895
556	Forysiak Franciszka	28.12.1903
557	Francus Antoni	8.09.1929
558	Francus Bronisława	30.05.1922
561	Francus Olga	28.10.1926
560	Francus Ludmiła	16.11.1898
559	Francus Eugenia	23.02.1925
3209	Frankenstajn Gerszon	5.03.1900
564	Frąckiewicz Jadwiga	7.12.1928
563	Frąckiewicz Irena	24.12.1929
562	Frąckiewicz Felicja	24.04.1910
565	Frąckiewicz Wanda	5.10.1939
570	Frączek Stanisława	3.05.1930
571	Frączek Teresa	10.06.1935
568	Frączek Jan	12.11.1931
567	Frączek Czesław	12.06.1933
566	Frączek Antonina	30.01.1928
569	Frączek Maria	3.11.1905
3704	Fride Sabina	23.10.1921
3210	Frider Jakub	18.07.1916
3212	Friedman Simon	24.08.1916
3211	Friszberg Fiszel	8.10.1920
572	Frydel Wanda	1935

3705	Frydel Janina	30.01.1910	3709	Gąsiorek Helena	2.03.1927	629	Głowaczewska Katarzyna	1934
3706	Frydel Radosław	23.12.1930	3223	Gąsiorowicz Anita-Anna		630	Głowaczewski Stanisław	1932
3215	Frydman Mojsze	23.03.1909	3221	Gąsiorowicz Maria	6.09.1898	631	Głuszczak Helena	1934
3214	Frydman Maurycy	20.10.1901	3222	Gąsiorowicz Stefan-Jerzy		4243	Gmiter Barbara	10.06.1915
3216	Frydman Pesla	20.12.1917	601	Gąska Karolina	1930	632	Gnatek Kazimierz	26.02.1886
3213	Frydman Boruch	18.04.1910	602	Gąsowska Wiktoria	8.02.1931	4253	Gnyp Olga	5.05.1931
574	Fujarczuk Karol	10.06.1932	3710	Gąsowska Stanisława	1930	4251	Gnyp Katarzyna	14.09.1927
573	Fujarczuk Helena	15.08.1898	4230	Gąsowska Anna	10.02.1919	4252	Gnyp Maria	5.09.1929
			4231	Gąsowski Stanisław	6.08.1942	4250	Gnyp Helena	3.03.1933
	Gac Kazimierz	1874	603	Gdyra Ludwika	27.06.1890	4246	Godawa Wanda	10.07.1926
	Gac Helena	1875	3714	Gębska Zofia	27.05.1905	4245	Godawa Franciszka	7.10.1905
	Gac Helena	01.05.1932	3711	Gębski Andrzej	20.10.1930	4244	Godawa Bolesław	16.08.1932
	Gac Honorata	19.04.1906	3713	Gębski Stanisław	9.01.1933	644	Godlewska Weronika	20.01.1900
	Gac Józefa	08.03.1930	3712	Gębski Czesław	27.07.1934	634	Godlewska Antonina	1866
	Gac Zuzanna	24.11.1926	4233	Giezek Stefania	18.02.1930	635	Godlewska Irena	16.10.1931
3707	Gajewska Anna	9.06.1900	4232	Giezek Helena	24.05.1903	636	Godlewska Janina	20.04.1902
4227	Gajewska Helena	6.07.1913	604	Gil Zofia	8.03.1921	643	Godlewska Stanisława	5.05.1902
4226	Gajewski Aleksander	29.01.1934	605	Gil Maria	11.11.1882	641	Godlewska Krystyna	10.06.1933
575	Gajkiewicz Helena	1.10.1911	606	Gimiter Barbara	10.06.1915	4247	Godlewska Ewa-Wanda	1.07.1943
4229	Gajlikowska Zofia	15.05.1916	608	Gimza Zofia	23.10.1930	640	Godlewski Justyn	17.11.1895
4228	Gajlikowski Lech	2.03.1942	607	Gimza Maria	10.12.1901	639	Godlewski Leon	17.04.1935
576	Galanek Józef	05.1933	3224	Ginzberg Maks	5.09.1900	633	Godlewski Antoni	16.11.1895
578	Gałka Stanisława	13.11.1926	610	Giryń Wacław	1936	637	Godlewski Józef	1868
579	Gałka Zofia	8.05.1889	609	Giryń Eugenia	1936	638	Godlewski Józef	20.10.1934
577	Gallas Jadwiga	29.09.1892	3226	Gitein Małka-Perla	27.01.1912	642	Godlewski Ryszard	20.04.1928
580	Gałuc Anna	5.09.1926	3225	Gitein Łazar	5.04.1904	645	Godlewski Witold	4.10.1933
	Gamoń Maria		613	Głąb Zofia	6.07.1923	646	Godycki-Ćwirko Jan	1.05.1886
	Gamoń Danuta		612	Gładkowska Stanisława	8.10.1930	4248	Goldberg Adam-Jan	17.04.1907
	Gamoń Mieczysław		611	Gładkowska Antonina	28.05.1895	648	Goleniewska Wiktoria	10.06.1907
581	Gancarz Stanisława	10.06.1926	4235	Głębicka Helena	1.04.1876	647	Goleniewski Ryszard	29.09.1929
582	Ganczar Józefa	8.12.1905	3227	Glezer Mowsza	26.12.1918	3715	Golinowska Anna	8.12.1927
583	Ganczar Kazimierz	28.10.1928	4234	Gliwa Józef	18.02.1901	3716	Golinowska Helena	11.02.1925
584	Ganczar Maria	2.05.1926	615	Głodek Jerzy	2.03.1935	652	Goławska Zofia	1880
586	Garbacka Tekla	23.09.1907	614	Głodek Franciszka	26.10.1910	650	Goławska Maria	24.05.1901
585	Garbacki Lech	3.06.1942	4237	Głodowska Zofia	10.02.1898	649	Goławski Andrzej	20.04.1930
587	Garbicz Emilia	15.05.1895	4236	Głodowska Maria	8.09.1925	651	Goławski Michał	17.05.1905
3217	Garboliński Stanisław	28.09.1919	617	Głogowska Czesława	17.09.1931	658	Gołębiowska Teresa	16.12.1938
3218	Gargulińska Józefa	28.06.1940	618	Głogowska Janina	13.04.1930	656	Gołębiowska Maria	18.05.1902
3220	Gargulińska Maria	13.06.1914	616	Głogowska Antonina	24.12.1909	654	Gołębiowska Antonina	15.06.1910
3219	Garguliński Bronisław	28.11.1933	4239	Głogowska Anna	22.06.1886	655	Gołębiowska Czesława	1.04.1934
589	Garkut Franciszka	10.02.1879	4240	Głogowska Irena	30.05.1933	657	Gołębiowska Maria	18.05.1924
588	Garkut Danuta	1932	620	Głogowski Mieczysław	13.04.1934	3717	Gołębiowska Janina	4.04.1901
590	Garkut Józefa	2.02.1912	619	Głogowski Józef	10.09.1898	653	Gołębiowski Alfred	18.06.1926
591	Gaudyn Marian	1929	4238	Głogowski Andrzej	22.10.1882	659	Gołuszewska Janina	24.10.1928
592	Gaudyn Stanisław	1.11.1927	621	Głowacka Antonina	12.02.1905	660	Gołuszewska Teofila	23.04.1901
594	Gaweł Zofia	24.12.1932	623	Głowacka Halina	20.07.1940	662	Gomulczak Rozalia	9.08.1902
593	Gaweł Władysława	30.12.1926	625	Głowacka Maria	8.10.1904	663	Gomulczak Władysław	27.06.1931
597	Gawęda Karolina	7.10.1912	4241	Głowacka Maria	21.11.1907	664	Gomulczak Zofia	14.10.1927
598	Gawęda Krystyna	9.07.1933	4242	Głowacka Zofia	27.10.1932	661	Gomułczak Lucyna	26.09.1938
595	Gawęda Franciszek	15.06.1928	624	Głowacki Jerzy	4.06.1930	666	Gomułka Bolesław	4.02.1932
596	Gawęda Franciszka	4.10.1900	627	Głowacki Romuald	25.08.1931	667	Gomułka Janina	6.07.1921
599	Gawlik Barbara	10.05.1895	626	Głowacki Roman	18.03.1936	668	Gomułka Maria	6.10.1913
3708	Gawroń Zbigniewa	14.12.1922	622	Głowacki Bronisław	18.10.1934	665	Gomułka Aniela	8.10.1926
600	Gąsienica Aniela	8.09.1875	628	Głowacki Waldemar	2.10.1928	3721	Gończyński Franciszek	30.09.1905

3718 Gondek Janina	2.08.1933
3720 Gondek Natalia	12.12.1910
3719 Gondek Józef	18.03.1932
669 Gorgul Anna	26.07.1896
670 Gorgul Helena	20.04.1928
671 Gorgul Zofia	15.09.1932
672 Gorzelnik Czesława	1.11.1928
673 Goślinowska Janina	16.02.1931
675 Goślinowska Katarzyna	25.03.1909
3228 Goślinowska Eugenia	3.09.1913
674 Goślinowski Jarosław	21.01.1934
3724 Gospodarek Łucja	13.12.1936
3723 Gospodarek Helena	2.03.1905
3722 Gospodarek Irena	5.08.1942
3229 Goworczyk Rachmil	5.12.1914
676 Góra Maria	20.03.1880
3230 Góra Edward	19.06.1903
677 Góral Jadwiga	13.07.1922
681 Górka Waldemar	12.06.1934
680 Górka Maria	20.01.1905
678 Górka Krystyna	10.11.1936
679 Górka Łucja	12.06.1932
684 Górniak Tadeusz	17.07.1938
682 Górniak Janina	8.07.1931
683 Górniak Julia	3.05.1907
685 Górska Anna	28.07.1929
686 Górska Czesława	1935
690 Górska Jadwiga	22.11.1913
688 Górska Elżbieta	7.11.1893
687 Górska Danuta	18.10.1926
689 Górska Halina	27.12.1922
3725 Górska Wanda	15.11.1912
4249 Górski Krzysztof Wacław	2.08.1944
691 Grabianka Felicja	1.01.1907
692 Grabianka Janusz	6.06.1942
693 Grabianka Olgierd	19.01.1903
695 Grabowska Helena	8.05.1933
696 Grabowska Irena	30.12.1930
697 Grabowska Jadwiga	15.09.1925
701 Grabowska Olga	4.01.1896
699 Grabowska Kazimiera	8.11.1930
694 Grabowska Czesława	5.01.1928
700 Grabowski Kazimierz	7.12.1931
698 Grabowski Jerzy	28.12.1939
703 Gracz Stanisława	1923
702 Gracz Jadwiga	3.06.1929
705 Greczyło Danuta	1921
704 Greczyło Alicja	1924
706 Griessgraber Jerzy	1937
707 Griessgraber Stanisława	21.07.1930
3231 Grinberg Mojsze	24.02.1913
3232 Grinberg Sara	5.08.1914
709 Grobel Lucyna	30.06.1926
710 Grobel Rozalia	20.06.1905
708 Grobel Helena	30.03.1925
4254 Grobelny Konstanty	30.05.1880
712 Groblicka Maria	2.03.1902
711 Groblicka Alicja	18.12.1927
713 Groblicki Tadeusz	9.06.1929
3726 Grochocka Janina	20.02.1904
715 Grochola Zuzanna	13.10.1931
714 Grochola Zofia	4.04.1905
717 Grochowska Maria	30.03.1937
716 Grochowska Benedykta	11.05.1914
3728 Groele Julia	11.11.1905
3727 Groele Helena	28.12.1928
718 Gromadzka Helena	10.03.1927
719 Gromadzka Henryka	7.03.1925
720 Gromadzka Józefa	25.12.1900
721 Gromadzka Maria	13.08.1923
724 Gromadzka Zofia	22.02.1931
722 Gromadzki Mieczysław	16.11.1936
723 Gromadzki Wacław	28.09.1933
725 Groń Anna	5.01.1881
3233 Gronek Feliksa	7.06.1913
3235 Gross Suita-Klara	1911
3234 Gross Samuel	1900
727 Grubczak Czesława	27.05.1926
726 Grubczak Alojzy	4.04.1930
3236 Grubiński Wacław	01.1883
3238 Grudzień Stanisława	16.10.1895
3237 Grudzień Maria	25.03.1917
728 Grula Anna	5.01.1927
729 Grula Czesława	20.01.1940
730 Grula Daniela	8.01.1935
731 Grula Krystyna	11.03.1937
732 Grula Maria	3.09.1907
733 Grula Stanisława	28.09.1929
734 Grula Zofia	20.09.1932
736 Gruszka Kazimierz	22.02.1938
737 Gruszka Mieczysław	20.06.1932
738 Gruszka Stefania	20.09.1930
735 Gruszka Anastazja	16.09.1910
739 Grużewska Zofia	1892
741 Grycuk Natalia	14.02.1886
740 Grycuk Maria	17.09.1923
742 Gryglich Jadwiga	28.02.1927
743 Gryglik Zdzisław	1932
3239 Grynberg Chaskiel	16.05.1897
744 Grynbiat Mordko	15.01.1920
3240 Gryngauz Izrael	22.10.1907
3241 Gryngauz Maria-Ewelina	
3729 Gryzel Franciszka	2.03.1898
3730 Grzebieniak Helena	28.07.1930
3731 Grzebieniak Józefa	8.07.1927
745 Grzelecka Kazimiera	25.11.1898
3242 Grześkowiak Eugenia	23.02.1910
3243 Grześkowiak Wojciech	7.02.1938
747 Grzeszuk Bronisława	7.09.1895
748 Grzeszuk Jan	22.06.1928
749 Grzeszuk Maria	17.04.1926
746 Grzeszuk Antoni	17.04.1926
750 Grzeszuk Piotr	15.08.1936
751 Grzonkowska Józefa	10.05.1899
752 Grzonkowski Marian	3.02.1931
754 Grzyb Kazimierz	1929
753 Grzyb Józef	1930
755 Grzybowska Helena	5.08.1927
756 Grzybowski Henryk	15.05.1931
757 Grzybowski Ryszard	7.08.1929
3244 Guberman Efroim	24.05.1910
3245 Guberman Sara-Szyma	
3247 Gudes Szymiel	1881
3246 Gudes Daniel	2.11.1914
758 Gulczyński Czesław	7.07.1900
760 Gurgul Józef	14.07.1898
761 Gurgul Kazimierz	1.03.1928
762 Gurgul Magdalena	22.07.1899
759 Gurgul Janina	25.11.1925
763 Gutkowska Anastazja	8.05.1896
764 Gutkowska Janina	30.01.1926
765 Gutkowska Stefania	2.09.1930
766 Gutkowska Weronika	3.11.1924
4255 Gutkowski Franciszek	6.05.1889
Gutkowski Tadeusz	
767 Gutowski Roman	19.04.1935
768 Guziewicz Franciszek	20.05.1929
769 Guziewicz Helena	5.06.1931
770 Guziewicz Jadwiga	19.08.1927
771 Guziewicz Kazimiera	27.07.1925
772 Guziewicz Leokadia	22.01.1903
774 Guzikowska Jadwiga	1937
773 Guzikowska Bronisława	1932
776 Gwiazda Piotr	1937
775 Gwiazda Anna	1932
777 Gwóźdź Czesława	17.10.1926
778 Gwóźdź Leokadia	5.01.1921
779 Haczewska Elżbieta	7.07.1900
780 Hajda Franciszek	13.03.1900
781 Hajduk Irena	15.01.1926
782 Hajduk Janina	15.05.1896
784 Hajdukiewicz Janina	12.07.1915
785 Hajdukiewicz Józef	1931
786 Hajdukiewicz Maria	1932
787 Hajdukiewicz Melania	7.06.1923
788 Hajdukiewicz Roman	02.1929
789 Hajdukiewicz Stanisław	4.03.1928
783 Hajdukiewicz Janina	2.02.1925
790 Hajdul Alina	20.03.1916
791 Hajdul Halina	10.07.1939
793 Hajzyk Irena	19.07.1922

794	Hajzyk Jadwiga	13.08.1927	834	Hnat Aniela	10.04.1896	3259	Igielski Chaim	5.06.1909
795	Hajzyk Jan	20.09.1933	3252	Hochberg Szmul	12.07.1920	869	Ignatowicz Aleksandra	9.05.1903
796	Hajzyk Stanisława	4.04.1894	3254	Hochenberg Meri		870	Ignatowicz Anna	7.10.1932
792	Hajzyk Gustaw	21.04.1887	3255	Hochenberg Mojsze		871	Ignatowicz Feliks	29.03.1929
3733	Halska Krystyna	17.02.1935	3256	Hochenberg Janina		872	Ignatowicz Józefa	19.11.1925
3732	Halska Helena	21.03.1912	3253	Hochenberg Abram	10.05.1890	873	Ignatowicz Leokadia	17.06.1928
797	Hałaburda Irena	24.03.1929	4259	Hochfeld Fryderyka	4.10.1912	874	Ignatowicz Olga	1.01.1903
798	Hałaburda Olga	10.07.1901	836	Hochhauser Irena	10.09.1929	875	Ignatowicz Rajmund	3.03.1934
800	Handerek Stanisław	12.11.1936	835	Hochhauser Antonina	8.08.1899	876	Ignatowicz Stanisław	30.05.1934
799	Handerek Anna	12.02.1916	837	Hochhauser Teodor	9.05.1929	877	Ignatowicz Wacław	13.12.1931
802	Hanebach Helena	1.02.1928	839	Hofbauer Wanda	24.01.1911	879	Inczyk Michalina	10.07.1897
801	Hanebach Eugenia	9.02.1926	838	Hofbauer Jerzy	8.08.1934	880	Inczyk Wincenty	6.05.1890
803	Hanebach Janina	8.12.1924	841	Hołownia Józef	26.06.1870	878	Inczyk Krystyna	28.07.1926
805	Haniewicz Joanna	20.05.1886	842	Hołownia Helena	27.05.1915	4263	Inglot Eugenia	15.12.1913
804	Haniewicz Janina	1.04.1927	840	Hołownia Anna	1.11.1888	4264	Inglot Stanisław	5.05.1936
807	Hara Rozalia	1929	843	Hołownia Kazimierz	4.04.1891	4265	Inwalska Stanisława	31.03.1916
806	Hara Janina	1935	844	Hołownia Zofia	15.05.1914	4266	Inwalski Zbigniew	2.01.1937
3250	Haracz Pelagia	26.02.1896	846	Hołub Halina	1.04.1931	3260	Iseppi Antoni	6.02.1907
3248	Haracz Genowefa	11.04.1925	847	Hołub Lucyna	1.01.1921	4267	Iskra Celina	23.09.1928
3249	Haracz Lidia	27.02.1931	848	Hołub Zofia	15.05.1904	4269	Iskra Zofia	2.02.1904
808	Harasymów Antonina	6.08.1897	845	Hołub Danuta	6.02.1936	4268	Iskra Marian	22.09.1930
809	Harasymów Stanisław	6.02.1932	849	Horbenkowska Daniela	19.03.1877	881	Iskrzyńska Ludwika	10.08.1888
811	Harbuz Bożena	31.12.1926	4260	Hornung Antonina	17.01.1905	3261	Issak Józef	22.12.1920
812	Harbuz Eliza	24.04.1924	4261	Hornung Józef	22.11.1930	3262	Issler Auschel	1.09.1911
813	Harbuz Maria	11.10.1896	851	Horoch Leon	9.02.1943	3263	Itison Morduch	2.07.1892
810	Harbuz Bogdan	1932	850	Horoch Halina	14.12.1914	883	Iwanejko Katarzyna	3.03.1898
4256	Hardy Janina	15.06.1909	853	Horwat Stanisława	7.06.1934	882	Iwanejko Daniel	9.07.1931
4257	Hardy Maria	14.08.1883	852	Horwat Franciszka	2.02.1902	884	Iwanejko Maria	3.03.1924
4258	Hardy Maria	26.08.1934	3738	Hrycyszyn Mirosław	10.12.1930	885	Iwanejko Michał	10.12.1929
814	Hartman Alfred	2.02.1935	3739	Hrycyszyn Stanisław	18.07.1929	886	Iwonek Maria	1934
815	Hartman Irena	23.07.1924	3737	Hrycyszyn Helena	2.09.1924	888	Izbicka Janina	14.07.1929
816	Hartman Maria	26.04.1899	854	Hryniewicz Anastazja	8.12.1900	889	Izbicka Łucja	12.08.1930
817	Hartman Pelagia	16.10.1927	855	Hryniewicz Mikołaj	8.08.1930	887	Izbicka Danuta	10.10.1932
818	Hartman Ryszard	25.05.1937	4262	Hubena Helena	1909	890	Izbicka Stanisława	14.07.1906
819	Hartman Tadeusz	6.02.1930	856	Hubicka Antonina	18.12.1898			
3735	Hartman Jerzy	8.12.1891	3741	Hudyga Danuta	1934	891	Jabłonka Zofia	5.05.1881
3736	Hartman Magdalena	4.06.1935	3740	Hudyga Czesława	1936	892	Jabłonowska Emilia	30.10.1903
3734	Hartman Irena	8.09.1897		Huppert Zofia Julia	15.03.1897	894	Jabłońska Danuta	30.09.1941
3674	Haśko Irena	1936		Huppert Karol	01.07.1928	893	Jabłońska Adela	24.12.1916
821	Haura Stanisław	24.12.1935	857	Hurko Jadwiga	7.11.1901	3742	Jabłońska Jadwiga	1.01.1927
822	Haura Stanisława	29.08.1926	859	Husarz Mieczysław	1932	895	Jabłoński Julian	20.06.1930
820	Haura Krystyna	21.01.1930	858	Husarz Ferdynand	1934	3743	Jabłoński Jan	8.03.1929
824	Heger Maria	25.03.1925	860	Huszcza Agnieszka	21.01.1931	897	Jachimowicz Stefania	21.06.1928
823	Heger Antoni	3.03.1916	861	Huszcza Jan	27.03.1935	896	Jachimowicz Natalia	1935
826	Hendel Stanisława	12.08.1927	862	Huszcza Janina	2.09.1932	3264	Jadziewicz Jan	27.08.1899
825	Hendel Barbara	19.05.1903	863	Huszcza Weronika	29.05.1905	898	Jagielska Amelia	1898
827	Herus Bronisława	18.07.1922	865	Hutnik Eugenia	6.10.1935	899	Jagielska Romualda	18.08.1907
828	Herus Genowefa	26.07.1931	866	Hutnik Helena	14.01.1908	900	Jagielski Stanisław	31.01.1930
829	Herus Józef	4.08.1937	864	Hutnik Anna	24.08.1938	907	Jagiełło Zofia	19.03.1924
830	Herus Karolina	7.10.1902				905	Jagiełło Tomasz	10.09.1880
831	Herus Wanda	26.07.1928	3257	Ickowicz Abram	13.07.1905	906	Jagiełło Wanda	18.02.1930
833	Herzog Tadeusz	27.08.1926	3258	Ickowicz Estera		901	Jagiełło Czesława	8.11.1927
832	Herzog Franciszek	28.04.1931	868	Idkowiak Irena	26.03.1927	902	Jagiełło Dominik	4.08.1934
3251	Hiliński Eugeniusz	19.09.1906	867	Idkowiak Feliksa	14.04.1907	903	Jagiełło Maria	15.09.1931

904	Jagiełło Tekla	18.02.1890	943	Janosz Zbigniew	1938	983	Jaworski Edmund	10.04.1941
908	Jagiełłowicz Maria	2.07.1898	944	Januchta Jan	17.08.1897	3747	Jaworski Wacław	13.09.1935
909	Jagiełłowicz Teresa	16.10.1926	946	Janusz Bogumiła	11.07.1936	4282	Jaworski Romuald	8.02.1877
910	Jagiełłowicz Władysław	12.12.1895	947	Janusz Józefa	12.02.1926	985	Jaźwińska Apolonia	1.01.1892
3268	Jagłom Jakub		948	Janusz Mieczysław	12.03.1928	988	Jaźwińska Maria	8.09.1932
3269	Jagłom Mozes	7.07.1893	949	Janusz Zdzisław	8.07.1929	987	Jaźwińska Leokadia	10.11.1907
3267	Jagłom Anna		945	Janusz Anna	28.10.1903	4283	Jaźwińska Bronisława	10.07.1887
3265	Jagłom Boruch	15.08.1895	950	Janusz Zofia	24.04.1897	986	Jaźwiński Gustaw	25.02.1929
3266	Jagłom Esfir		952	Januszczak Zofia	15.06.1912	989	Jeleński Aleksander	17.02.1897
912	Jagodzińska Stefania	1.01.1897	951	Januszczak Stanisława	21.01.1935	990	Jermak Władysław	30.08.1927
911	Jagodziński Franciszek	12.02.1890	4278	Jarmołowicz Amelia	1.07.1913	992	Jerzykowska Janina	1.04.1902
914	Jajko Jan	1934	4279	Jarmołowicz Grażyna	15.09.1936	991	Jerzykowski Aleksander	13.12.1931
915	Jajko Maria	5.01.1912	4280	Jaros Stefania	29.08.1929	994	Jewtuch Maria	10.05.1926
913	Jajko Cecylia	25.10.1931	954	Jarosz Jerzy	10.02.1927	993	Jewtuch Anastazja	10.11.1901
917	Jakielaszek Karolina	1914	955	Jarosz Maria	27.07.1919	4286	Jezierska Teresa	27.01.1938
916	Jakielaszek Aniela	1892	953	Jarosz Bolesław	7.06.1931	4285	Jezierska Stanisława	3.05.1896
	Jakieła Janina	14.09.1930	956	Jarosz Stanisław	1932	4284	Jezierski Andrzej	20.05.1939
	Jakieła Eugenia	15.05.1932	957	Jarosz Wacław	1935	996	Jeziorska Stanisława	25.03.1932
4270	Jakubas Franciszek	20.02.1905	959	Jarzębska Jadwiga	16.10.1926	995	Jeziorska Jadwiga	21.12.1926
4271	Jakubas Janina	8.07.1931	960	Jarzębska Wiktoria	10.03.1925	997	Jeziorski Zygmunt	3.01.1930
4272	Jakubas Paulina	29.06.1900	958	Jarzębska Emilia	26.06.1904	3748	Jędrychowska Halina	11.01.1916
918	Jakubik Władysław	1.01.1874	962	Jasiewicz Janina	1929	4288	Jędrzejczak Stanisław	14.05.1930
919	Jakubowska Kazimiera	20.12.1915	961	Jasiewicz Helena	2.06.1902	4287	Jędrzejczak Irena	16.11.1923
4273	Jałowiecki Michał	25.01.1913	963	Jasiewicz Kazimierz	4.03.1934	4289	Jędrzejczak Waldemar	25.10.1933
920	Janas Marianna	15.08.1913	964	Jasiewicz Wanda	1910	998	Jędrzejczyk Barbara	19.09.1933
4276	Janczewska Maria	14.04.1899	967	Jasińska Janina	1.05.1934	999	Jędrzejczyk Benedykt	1934
4274	Janczewska Irena	12.10.1926	968	Jasiński Stanisław	3.05.1931	1000	Jędrzejewska Oktawia	7.06.1911
4275	Janczewska Jadwiga	15.07.1930	965	Jasiukiewicz Aleksandra	8.04.1905	1001	Jędrzejewska Regina	26.08.1926
922	Janczyk Romualda	25.03.1927	966	Jasiukiewicz Janina	16.08.1928	1002	Jodłowska Józefa	26.02.1902
923	Janczyk Witold	4.06.1930		Jaśko Tadeusz	1926	1003	Jodłowska Leonarda	26.02.1924
921	Janczyk Maria	1931		Jaśko Teresa	1929	1004	Jodłowski Marian	12.04.1929
924	Janicka Jadwiga	15.10.1900		Jaśko Zofia	1930	3276	Jordan Rozalia	
925	Janicka Leokadia	4.05.1929		Jaśko Zdzisława	1933	3275	Jordan Marian	10.02.1905
926	Janicki Zbigniew	15.05.1931	979	Jaśkowiak Maria	24.08.1894	1006	Jortner Maria	22.07.1902
929	Janiszewska Maria	1926	982	Jaśkowiec Franciszka	2.01.1933	1007	Jortner Michał	23.05.1895
927	Janiszewska Alicja	1.01.1928	980	Jaśkowiec Antonina	13.06.1900	1005	Jortner Juliusz	3.03.1936
928	Janiszewski Lech	13.04.1934	981	Jaśkowiec Bronisława	1.10.1926	3277	Jortner Ignacy	15.08.1896
930	Janiszewski Tadeusz	28.05.1928	973	Jastrzębska Maria	19.07.1926	3278	Jortner Ludwika	
931	Jankiewicz Waldemar	18.09.1928	971	Jastrzębska Konstancja	15.04.1905	1008	Józefczyk Henryk	17.08.1938
932	Jankowska Felicja	14.06.1905	970	Jastrzębska Genowefa	4.05.1925	1009	Józefczyk Stanisława	25.02.1921
937	Jankowska Karolina	15.04.1897	975	Jastrzębski Ryszard	1937	1010	Józefczyk Tadeusz	28.08.1928
934	Jankowska Janina	25.05.1925	969	Jastrzębski Bolesław	7.02.1932	3279	Jóźwowiak Lucyna	1.10.1918
935	Jankowska Józefa	12.04.1915	974	Jastrzębski Mieczysław	6.12.1936	3749	Jundziłł Alojza	10.04.1906
938	Jankowska Rypsyma	11.12.1890	972	Jastrzębski Konstanty	10.02.1900	3751	Jundziłł Józef	20.02.1934
3745	Jankowska Janina	24.12.1923	976	Jastrzębski Stanisław	1932	3752	Jundziłł Stanisława	3.07.1930
3744	Jankowska Bronisława	10.01.1882	3271	Jastrzębski Zbigniew	15.09.1910	3750	Jundziłł Jadwiga	7.07.1932
3270	Jankowski Antoni, Fr.	13.06.1914	978	Jaszczuk Kazimiera	13.04.1933	1011	Jurczyńska Olga	17.06.1890
933	Jankowski Franciszek	13.10.1900	977	Jaszczuk Helena	6.04.1931	1012	Jurek Bronisława	4.07.1931
939	Jankowski Stanisław	8.05.1937	3272	Jaworowska Irena	27.04.1901	1013	Jurek Franciszka	12.07.1912
940	Jankowski Tadeusz	4.09.1928	3274	Jaworowski Waldemar	17.10.1929	1014	Jurek Jan	15.02.1930
941	Jankowski Zbigniew	19.03.1935	3273	Jaworowski Teofil	28.01.1928	1015	Jurek Mieczysław	21.09.1930
936	Jankowski Józef	19.03.1903	984	Jaworska Nadzieja	10.04.1911	1016	Jurek Stefania	18.12.1933
4277	Jankowski Wacław	17.12.1902	4281	Jaworska Anna	16.07.1885	1017	Jurek Zbigniew	18.09.1941
942	Janosz Edward	1936	3746	Jaworska Adela	13.11.1907	1018	Jurek Zofia	15.04.1912

1020 Jurkiewicz Zofia	12.09.1901	
1019 Jurkiewicz Edmund	12.11.1930	
1021 Jurkojć Jan	19.01.1930	
1022 Juszkiewicz Waleria	23.12.1894	
3756 Jutrzenka Józefa	12.04.1882	
3753 Jutrzenka Antoni	24.02.1879	
3757 Jutrzenka Leon	8.07.1934	
3754 Jutrzenka Czesława	20.12.1911	
3755 Jutrzenka Halina	18.01.1942	
3758 Jutrzenka Mirosław	6.07.1936	
1023 Juzwin Jadwiga	31.10.1897	
1024 Juzwin Janina	10.02.1925	
1026 Kacpura Marian	1937	
1027 Kacpura Stanisława	1936	
1025 Kacpura Bolesław	1928	
1028 Kaczyńska Aleksandra	2.02.1886	
1029 Kaczyński Aleksander	15.07.1928	
1031 Kaftan Domicela	2.05.1929	
1030 Kaftan Aniela	30.05.1905	
1032 Kaftan Helena	22.11.1926	
1033 Kaftan Janina	27.01.1928	
3281 Kahan Zygmunt	22.10.1912	
3280 Kahan Aleksander	9.05.1909	
1034 Kajdan Katarzyna	15.01.1874	
1035 Kajder Jan	12.01.1932	
3308 Kajman Izydor	21.08.1904	
1036 Kajzer Mieczysław	30.09.1913	
1037 Kakowska Józefa	10.03.1888	
1038 Kaleta Stanisława	20.04.1925	
3759 Kaleta Genowefa	26.08.1930	
3760 Kaleta Wincenty	1935	
1039 Kalicka Anna	10.08.1907	
1040 Kalicka Emilia	8.04.1926	
1041 Kalicki Jan	11.10.1929	
3761 Kalicki Piotr	29.06.1930	
1043 Kalinowska Eufrozyma	05.1890	
1042 Kalinowska Czesława	2.07.1925	
3282 Kalińska Zofia	12.06.1913	
1044 Kaliszek Irena	1.11.1898	
3283 Kallir Karol	18.03.1898	
4292 Kalwaitys Regina	14.09.1927	
4291 Kalwaitys Bronisława	14.03.1924	
4290 Kalwaitys Anna	24.11.1901	
4293 Kalwaitys Stanisław	12.12.1930	
3284 Kamieńkowski Chaim	16.05.1913	
1057 Kamilski Zygmunt	20.05.1929	
1045 Kamińska Czesława	28.11.1926	
1048 Kamińska Helena	4.04.1933	
1049 Kamińska Katarzyna	14.05.1902	
1050 Kamińska Kazimiera	3.01.1911	
1051 Kamińska Regina	10.06.1896	
1052 Kamińska Zofia	14.08.1904	
1053 Kamińska Zofia	4.07.1927	

1046 Kamińska Emilia	18.05.1927	
1047 Kamińska Halina	22.05.1925	
4294 Kamińska Emilia	17.07.1928	
4296 Kamińska Zofia	27.06.1901	
1056 Kamiński Jan	20.07.1938	
1054 Kamiński Andrzej	24.01.1935	
1055 Kamiński Jan	30.11.1890	
4295 Kamiński Mieczysław	3.01.1930	
3285 Kamiński Wacław	15.04.1892	
4297 Kamoda Anna	28.09.1895	
4298 Kamoda Emilia	28.11.1922	
4299 Kamoda Wanda	30.10.1924	
1059 Kania Julian	11.04.1936	
1060 Kania Michalina	11.10.1893	
1061 Kania Stanisława	29.09.1935	
1058 Kania Halina	10.10.1928	
3762 Kaniecka Kamila	11.06.1912	
3763 Kaniecki Zenon	21.06.1936	
1062 Kapała Franciszek	20.05.1928	
1063 Kapała Genowefa	1930	
1064 Kapała Rozalia	10.10.1925	
1065 Kapała Stanisław	1932	
3286 Kapłan Izrael	7.05.1904	
3287 Kapłański Szolem	28.10.1918	
1067 Kaptur Jerzy	18.02.1935	
1068 Kaptur Zenon	8.09.1928	
1066 Kaptur Helena	15.05.1902	
1069 Kapuścińska Maria	22.01.1888	
3288 Kapusta Jankiel	1.12.1914	
1070 Karakułko Halina	2.02.1927	
1071 Karakułko Jadwiga	18.03.1900	
1078 Karaś Roman	19.01.1932	
1073 Karaś Edward	5.06.1930	
1074 Karaś Irena	29.09.1909	
1075 Karaś Józefa	31.01.1929	
1076 Karaś Paulina	24.12.1906	
1077 Karaś Paulina	25.09.1918	
1072 Karaś Adam	9.06.1934	
1079 Karaś Stanisława	14.02.1926	
1080 Karaś Stefania	28.10.1924	
1081 Karaś Zbigniew	29.04.1938	
1083 Karasiewicz Kazimiera	18.12.1920	
1082 Karasiewicz Jerzy	18.01.1939	
1084 Karasiewicz Stanisława	24.05.1899	
1086 Karczewska Kazimiera	29.06.1908	
1087 Karczewska Maria	8.12.1928	
1085 Karczewska Alfreda	8.05.1935	
1088 Karczewski Jan	20.06.1896	
1089 Karczyńska Danuta	1936	
4300 Kardasińska Adela	8.12.1924	
4303 Kardasińska Stanisława	8.05.1900	
4302 Kardasińska Danuta	3.08.1937	
4304 Kardasiński Stanisław	1.05.1930	
4301 Kardasiński Antoni	3.06.1932	

3289 Karkut Mieczysław	1935	
3290 Karkut Zygmunt	1932	
3291 Karp Falk	15.08.1919	
3764 Karpińska Danuta	18.05.1914	
3766 Karpińska Jadwiga	17.05.1939	
3765 Karpińska Izabela	15.04.1934	
4307 Karpińska Zofia	26.02.1926	
4306 Karpińska Wasa	3.09.1906	
3768 Karpiński Władysław	25.09.1941	
4305 Karpiński Ryszard	8.05.1936	
3767 Karpiński Jan-Józef	27.12.1909	
3769 Karwacki Michał	8.12.1921	
1090 Karwowska Eugenia	20.05.1910	
1091 Karwowski Wiesław	7.07.1937	
4309 Kaskiewicz Maria	22.08.1905	
4308 Kaskiewicz Janusz	28.06.1936	
1103 Kaśków Jan	18.12.1921	
3293 Kasperska Stanisława	30.01.1928	
3292 Kasperska Janina	1935	
1092 Kasprowicz Ignacy	11.11.1891	
1095 Kasprzyńska Wanda	28.08.1936	
1093 Kasprzyńska Józefa	6.03.1905	
1094 Kasprzyńska Paulina	15.11.1915	
1096 Kasprzyński Tadeusz	25.05.1935	
1099 Kaszuba Maria	13.05.1905	
1100 Kaszuba Stanisław	6.02.1928	
1097 Kaszuba Jadwiga	4.09.1943	
1102 Kaszuba Zygfryd	25.02.1932	
1098 Kaszuba Leokadia	8.08.1925	
1101 Kaszuba Wanda	13.03.1930	
1105 Katkiewicz Henryk	6.09.1898	
1104 Katkiewicz Danuta	4.07.1934	
1106 Katkiewicz Jadwiga	25.10.1905	
1107 Katkiewicz Marta	10.10.1939	
3295 Katzenell Małgorzata		
3294 Katzenell Fryderyk	25.03.1907	
1109 Kawa Irena	1.03.1926	
1108 Kawa Edward	1937	
4310 Kawa Maria	8.12.1876	
3296 Kawa Jakub	19.07.1898	
3773 Kawałek Stefania	1.07.1930	
4311 Kawałek Ludwika	11.06.1922	
3772 Kawałek Krystyna	29.09.1933	
3771 Kawałek Katarzyna	7.11.1898	
3770 Kawałek Helena	1.04.1924	
1111 Kawałko Zygmunt	5.03.1927	
1110 Kawałko Marian	1930	
1112 Kawczyńska Danuta	1936	
1114 Kawecka Ludmiła	23.12.1898	
1115 Kawecka Maria	1.02.1930	
1113 Kawecka Bronisława	23.02.1925	
3297 Kazała Anna	25.07.1912	
3298 Kazała Henryk	1.04.1935	
3299 Kazibutowski Janusz	3.04.1908	

4313	Kaziewicz Irena	9.11.1929	1151	Kinach Ludmiła	27.05.1933	1178	Kłosowski Marian	25.03.1888
4312	Kaziewicz Bolesław	30.04.1943	3306	Kincel Zbigniew	18.06.1930	1179	Kłosowski Stefan	1932
4314	Kaziewicz Stanisława	17.11.1904	3305	Kincel Anna	15.03.1900	3313	Kmieć Bronisław	3.07.1930
3774	Kazimierow Helena	7.07.1936	3307	Kincel Zenon	7.04.1932	3314	Kmieć Feliks	14.01.1935
3775	Kazimierow Stanisław	8.12.1927	4321	Kirchner Zofia	24.05.1886	3315	Kmieć Maria	25.11.1902
1116	Kaźmierczak Helena	1903	4320	Kirchner Jerzy	11.10.1935	1181	Kmiotek Genowefa	20.10.1930
1117	Kaźmierczak Jerzy	9.10.1932	4322	Kirdzik Maria	5.01.1890	1182	Kmiotek Janina	6.08.1905
4316	Kądziela Maria	21.09.1914	4323	Kirdzik Wanda	24.04.1920	1180	Kmiotek Anna	15.05.1912
4315	Kądziela Krzysztof	13.05.1936	1153	Kirkiłło-Stacewicz Adela	1887	1183	Kmiotek Józefa	4.12.1933
1123	Kempa Stanisław	28.01.1930	4324	Kirkiłło-Stacewicz Julian	5.03.1870	1184	Kmiotek Kazimiera	15.10.1935
1124	Kempa Stanisława	1936	1154	Kisiel Ludwika	8.09.1894	4335	Kmita Cecylia	7.11.1910
1121	Kempa Janina	1933	4325	Kisiel Anna	26.03.1938	4334	Kmita Bohdan	7.03.1937
1120	Kempa Jan	8.01.1929	4326	Kisiel Emilia	11.06.1903	4336	Knapik Helena	10.04.1900
1122	Kempa Kazimiera	1938	4327	Kisiel Kazimierz	8.09.1940	4337	Knapik Michalina	10.05.1928
3300	Kerszenbaum Aron	14.12.1911	1155	Kisielnicka Alicja	10.10.1898	4338	Knapik Stanisława	10.11.1923
3778	Kersztyn Marianna	13.11.1886	1156	Kiszyńska Maria	26.05.1906	3788	Kniażewska Łucja	12.05.1898
3777	Kersztyn Maria	13.08.1922	3783	Kiś Maria	1933	3789	Kniażewska Wanda	30.07.1927
3776	Kersztyn Genowefa	15.05.1925	3781	Kiś Jan	1930	1186	Knieja Stanisława	15.03.1919
3780	Kersztyn Zofia	28.01.1929	3782	Kiś Katarzyna	1926	1185	Knieja Irena	1.12.1937
3779	Kersztyn Piotr	8.01.1882	3784	Kiś Piotr	1932	3316	Knoff Czesław	10.12.1883
3301	Kesselhut Herman	10.02.1903	1158	Kitras Janina	14.07.1926	3317	Knoff Wanda	
1125	Keżun Józef	15.05.1885	1157	Kitras Helena	1.09.1928	3320	Kobelska Maria	13.01.1899
1127	Kędzior Helena	30.07.1900	4329	Kiwalle Wanda	1.01.1908	3319	Kobelska Halina	4.03.1921
1126	Kędzior Ludmiła	26.06.1927	4328	Kiwalle Maria	21.11.1934	3318	Kobelski Bolesław	12.06.1893
3302	Kędzior Helena	27.11.1925	1160	Klar Ryszard	5.07.1927	1188	Kobordo Jadwiga	14.01.1936
1128	Kępka Maria	2.02.1932	1159	Klar Anna	2.04.1907	1187	Kobordo Halina	14.02.1929
1129	Kępka Stanisława	27.04.1929	3787	Klecka Maria	15.03.1899	1189	Kobordo Maria	31.12.1903
1130	Kępka Stefania	8.08.1907	3786	Klecki Aleksander	28.02.1893	3790	Koboś Eugeniusz	17.05.1933
1131	Kępka Wanda	27.07.1927	3785	Klecki Aleksander	26.01.1928	3791	Koboś Marian	1.01.1935
1133	Kępko Maria	18.05.1895	3310	Kleinberg Salomea		3792	Kobuz Władysława	26.08.1927
1132	Kępko Irena	12.04.1930	3309	Kleinberg Maurycy	3.03.1897	1191	Kobyra Genowefa	5.05.1930
1134	Kęs Helena	22.01.1927	1161	Klepacka Hildegarda	26.09.1886	1192	Kobyra Helena	20.09.1922
3303	Kichler Juliusz	5.09.1897	1162	Klepacka Wiesława	26.01.1922	1193	Kobyra Maria	8.11.1898
1136	Kiefer Jan	13.02.1893	1163	Klepacki Józef	31.12.1880	1190	Kobyra Aniela	11.1928
1137	Kiefer Zofia	18.02.1927	4330	Klimczuk Helena	10.06.1929	1194	Koc Halina	15.01.1931
1135	Kiefer Antonina	20.01.1900	4331	Klimczuk Maria	31.03.1921	1195	Koc Maria	22.07.1908
4317	Kielan Anna	11.11.1895	3311	Klimczyk Władysław	24.08.1893	1197	Kocaj Kazimiera	1938
4318	Kielan Maria	16.07.1928	4332	Klimowiecka Genowefa	2.01.1899	1196	Kocaj Adam	1936
3304	Kiełbińska Zofia	20.02.1908	3312	Klimsiak Aleksander	12.06.1921	3794	Kochanowska Eugenia	9.05.1923
1138	Kierenia Anna	10.08.1904	1164	Kloss Maria	1931	3793	Kochanowska Antonina	27.11.1903
1139	Kierenia Kazimierz	29.11.1934	1166	Kluka Stanisław	3.10.1937	3795	Kochanowska Wanda	31.09.1925
1141	Kijanowska Maria	16.03.1902	1167	Kluka Stefania	28.04.1914	1199	Kochańska Teresa	28.12.1928
1142	Kijanowska Urszula	22.03.1928	1165	Kluka Jerzy	1.02.1939	1198	Kochańska Maria	28.08.1930
1143	Kijanowska Zofia	15.10.1907	4333	Kłoczkowska Jadwiga	14.11.1895	4339	Kochman Maria	17.10.1914
1140	Kijanowska Ewa	7.02.1928	1168	Kłopotowska Halina	10.02.1929	4340	Kocińska Bronisława	16.07.1908
1144	Kijanowski Czesław	1932	1169	Kłopotowska Mirosława	1932	1201	Koczan Stefania	5.05.1924
1145	Kilian Janina	1.05.1939	1170	Kłos Danuta	1.01.1927	1200	Koczan Stefania	21.08.1907
1146	Kilian Józefa	1937	1171	Kłos Irena	27.02.1928	3321	Koczorowska Milica	17.10.1915
1147	Kilian Julia	6.05.1927	1172	Kłosińska Zofia	14.05.1906	4341	Kodrębska Helena	3.03.1879
1148	Kilian Michalina	1.04.1925	1173	Kłosowska Franciszka	18.09.1926	3796	Kogut Józefa	17.06.1927
1149	Kilian Władysław	1931	1176	Kłosowska Maria	3.11.1924	3322	Kohn Regina	25.07.1918
1150	Kilian Zbigniew	6.05.1939	1175	Kłosowska Łucja	1935	1203	Kokocińska Wanda	22.03.1890
4319	Kilińska Antonina	15.01.1920	1174	Kłosowska Janina	14.12.1897	1202	Kokociński Antoni	3.06.1885
1152	Kinach Wiktoria	16.04.1913	1177	Kłosowski Apoloniusz	1933	1204	Kokoszko Anastazja	10.11.1897

1205	Kokoszko Irena	6.08.1929	1246	Kopeć Eugeniusz	29.12.1929	1286	Korżenko Wiktoria	28.07.1927
1206	Kokoszko Krystyna	1927	1247	Kopeć Franciszka	17.09.1904	1282	Korżenko Aniela	4.04.1925
1207	Kokoszko Bronisława	30.01.1900	1248	Kopeć Helena	6.12.1927	1288	Kosałka Zofia	5.02.1929
1208	Kokoszko Halina	7.03.1936	1249	Kopeć Maria	18.06.1895	1287	Kosałka Maria	10.08.1894
1209	Kokoszko Maria	10.07.1927	1245	Kopeć Edward	2.01.1932	1289	Kosiba Danuta	23.08.1929
1210	Kokoszko Weronika	12.12.1925	1250	Koper Jan	12.07.1929	1303	Kosiński-Rawicz Tadeusz	27.10.1935
3798	Kolendo Olga	28.09.1912	1255	Kopiec Władysław	15.11.1928	4355	Kosior Maria	3.06.1929
3797	Kolendo Janina	28.03.1934	1252	Kopiec Helena	1904	1291	Kosmala Anna	1.01.1906
	Kolendo Czesław	20.07.1920	1253	Kopiec Józef	17.09.1928	1290	Kosmala Amalia	16.02.1928
1212	Kolischer Zofia	6.08.1889	1254	Kopiec Maria	25.12.1893	1292	Kosmala Czesława	28.08.1932
1211	Kolischer Romualda	24.02.1923	1251	Kopiec Genowefa	10.10.1927	1293	Kossowska Janina	16.08.1889
1214	Kolkiewicz Leszek	2.10.1928	1256	Koprowska Antonina	1877	1294	Kossowska Janina	5.11.1905
1215	Kolkiewicz Jadwiga	13.09.1932	1257	Koprowski Jan	3.01.1876	1295	Kossowski Janusz	14.03.1932
1213	Kolkiewicz Józefa	22.02.1901	4346	Korab-Gutkowska Władysława	25.10.1918	1297	Kosteczko Józef	22.03.1929
1216	Kolkiewicz Wanda	17.03.1927	4345	Korab-Gutkowski Kazimierz	1.08.1910	1296	Kosteczko Jan	29.11.1897
3799	Kołakowska Eleonora	5.10.1929	1259	Kordas Natalia	26.07.1935	1298	Kostuś Helena	17.08.1928
3800	Kołakowska Franciszka	3.12.1903	1258	Kordas Apolonia	1926	1299	Kosz Teodor	1897
4342	Kołkowska Helena	1.09.1903	1260	Kordas Helena	1924	3331	Koszer Abe-Pejsach	14.04.1898
4343	Kołkowska Zofia	12.05.1927	1261	Kordas Janina	6.06.1927	1300	Kościów Włodzimierz	1.09.1927
1218	Kołodyńska Stefania	24.12.1904	1262	Kordas Zygmunt	26.08.1929	1302	Kościukiewicz Józef	22.09.1892
1217	Kołodyńska Jadwiga	23.09.1929	4347	Korepta Wanda	23.03.1925	1301	Kościukiewicz Anna	28.02.1920
1219	Kołodyński Bogusław	5.04.1934	3328	Korn Alfreda		3803	Kościukiewicz Stanisław	6.11.1943
4344	Kołodyński Zdzisław	16.05.1930	3327	Korn Hersz	15.07.1905	1304	Kot Emilia	5.07.1931
1221	Kołodziej Maria	13.07.1927	3329	Korn Lejb	23.11.1907	1305	Kot Zbigniew	5.10.1929
1220	Kołodziej Maria	23.02.1915	3330	Korngold Jerzy	15.07.1919	1307	Kotlarczyk Danuta	27.06.1933
1222	Kołodziej Maria	1934	1264	Korol Mieczysław	1935	1308	Kotlarczyk Zbigniew	8.06.1930
1223	Kołodziej Stefania	1904	1265	Korol Urszula	15.07.1927	1306	Kotlarczyk Amelia	16.02.1908
1225	Komarnicka Maria	17.05.1900	1263	Korol Janina	1933	1309	Kotlarz Czesława	20.04.1930
1224	Komarnicki Jerzy	12.03.1936	1267	Korolewicz Leonarda	3.03.1931	1310	Kotlarz Genowefa	26.10.1926
1226	Komiago Florian	1934	1266	Korolewicz Genowefa	24.03.1929	1311	Kotlarz Wiesław	1936
1227	Komikiewicz Władysław	1932	1269	Korotka Jadwiga	13.03.1904	3332	Kotler Michel	1914
3323	Konarski Stanisław	14.07.1912	1268	Korotka Anna	22.11.1928	1313	Kotlicka Krystyna	10.10.1927
1229	Konieczna Janina	27.12.1927	1270	Korotki Jan	1931	1312	Kotlicka Jadwiga	2.02.1907
1228	Konieczna Genowefa	20.07.1929	1271	Korotki Stanisław	1933	1314	Kotlicki Tadeusz	2.04.1929
1230	Konieczna Ludwika	17.05.1905	1272	Korotki Władysław	10.06.1906	3804	Kotlińska Sabina	10.09.1928
1232	Konieczny Stanisław	13.03.1931	4352	Korus Stanisława	24.09.1924	3805	Kotlińska Stanisława	2.04.1925
1231	Konieczny Jan	25.05.1898	4348	Korus Irena	9.03.1933	1315	Kowal Maria	12.12.1896
3324	Konopka Jadwiga	25.08.1903	4350	Korus Justyna	18.07.1895	1316	Kowal Piotr	1.04.1926
1233	Konopko Stanisława	11.11.1903	4349	Korus Józefa	6.07.1928	1318	Kowalczyk Maria	2.07.1904
1235	Konopko Witold	17.07.1935	4351	Korus Maria	30.11.1926	1319	Kowalczyk Maria	18.07.1901
1234	Konopko Teresa	24.08.1926	1274	Korzeniewicz Władysława	1932	1320	Kowalczyk Olga	17.02.1933
1238	Kończak Henryka	22.09.1929	1273	Korzeniewicz Grzegorz	16.08.1914	1321	Kowalczyk Stefania	15.07.1927
1236	Kończak Andrzej	18.01.1938	1275	Korzeniewska Jadwiga	20.10.1880	1317	Kowalczyk Irena	10.06.1936
1237	Kończak Florentyna	17.02.1927	1279	Korzeniowska Urszula	25.01.1928	3807	Kowalczyk Stefan	27.04.1928
3325	Kończakowska Antonina	13.06.1896	1278	Korzeniowska Maria	25.03.1887	3806	Kowalczyk Bronisława	28.11.1925
3326	Kończakowska Kazimiera	4.03.1925	1276	Korzeniowska Eleonora	23.04.1926	3808	Kowalczyk Teresa	1928
1240	Kopcio Janina	17.12.1931	4353	Korzeniowska Anna	9.11.1896	1322	Kowalec Leokadia	12.12.1929
1241	Kopcio Józefa	11.11.1927	4354	Korzeniowska Teresa	22.06.1929	1327	Kowalewska Kazimiera	1922
1239	Kopcio Aniela	12.05.1893	1277	Korzeniowski Hieronim	30.09.1879	1325	Kowalewska Halina	14.02.1928
1242	Kopcio Katarzyna	10.11.1918	1280	Korzennik Ruta	6.05.1928	1326	Kowalewska Józefa	28.02.1897
1243	Kopcio Kazimiera	9.06.1937	1281	Korzon Wincenty	24.05.1895	1329	Kowalewska Teresa	15.01.1936
1244	Kopcio Weronika	17.09.1925	1283	Korżenko Feliks	26.04.1929	1324	Kowalewski Edward	10.03.1930
3802	Kopciowska Józefa	1.10.1926	1284	Korżenko Maria	1.01.1901	1323	Kowalewski Czesław	28.02.1897
3801	Kopciowska Anna	8.02.1898	1285	Korżenko Teresa	8.08.1937	1328	Kowalewski Marian	1938

1330	Kowalik Waleria	8.02.1911	1362	Krasnowska Salomea	1900	3826	Krukowicz Weronika	22.06.1922
3809	Kowalik Jan	7.01.1904	1361	Krasowska Leonarda	1.11.1920	3824	Krukowicz Eugenia	25.02.1935
1335	Kowalska Zofia	15.02.1929	1363	Kraszewski Norbert	5.06.1929	3827	Krupa Anna	26.03.1920
1333	Kowalska Joanna	21.11.1905	1365	Krawczuk Fenia	16.05.1922	3828	Krupa Zofia	9.07.1916
1334	Kowalska Katarzyna	26.07.1925	1366	Krawczuk Helena	1892	4371	Krupa Aleksandra	8.09.1897
3810	Kowalska Gabriela	23.02.1906	1367	Krawczuk Konon	15.05.1902	4372	Krupa Stanisława	8.09.1926
3813	Kowalska Halina	14.08.1942	1368	Krawczuk Mikołaj	13.05.1932	4373	Krupa Stanisław	29.01.1929
3811	Kowalska Halina	23.08.1930	1369	Krawczuk Teodora	18.10.1924	1391	Krupińska Anna	30.11.1924
3812	Kowalska Halina	22.05.1907	1371	Krawczyk Franciszek	6.09.1910	4375	Kruszyńska Helena	4.08.1904
1331	Kowalski Eugeniusz	1932	1372	Krawczyk Teofil	09.1931	4374	Kruszyńska Danuta	18.11.1934
1332	Kowalski Jerzy	13.01.1929	1370	Krawczyk Anna	1.09.1927	4376	Kruszyński Zygmunt	25.12.1928
3814	Kowalski Józef	10.12.1928	4361	Krawczyk Helena	7.10.1902	1392	Krysiuk Antoni	16.04.1888
3815	Kowalski Mikołaj	1930	4362	Krawczyk Zdzisław	6.12.1936	4377	Krzeszczucki Władysław	4.10.1894
1336	Kowol Franciszek	23.01.1899	3334	Krawiec Judka	8.02.1911	3829	Krzętowska Helena	26.03.1902
1338	Kozak Jerzy	30.10.1932	3335	Krawiecka Anna	15.05.1925	1394	Krzykowiak Janina	5.11.1918
1339	Kozak Maria	16.07.1902	3336	Krawiecka Paulina	25.12.1924	1393	Krzykowiak Irena	20.09.1939
1337	Kozak Janina	5.10.1938	3337	Krawiecka Bronisława	25.07.1888		Krzykowska Helena	8.06.1928
1340	Kozak Marian	13.08.1943	1374	Kreczmańska Jadwiga	1932		Krzykowska Stefania	1.11.1895
1341	Kozak Marta	16.09.1917	1373	Kreczmański Bolesław	19.06.1928		Krzykowska Zofia	24.09.1916
4356	Kozak Marian	13.08.1943	3338	Kremnitzer Stanisław	4.01.1910	4379	Krzysztoń Jerzy	22.03.1930
	Kozak Mieczysław		3339	Kremnitzer Celina		4380	Krzysztoń Janusz	22.12.1935
3333	Kozarski Stefan	12.12.1908	3340	Krischer Beniamin	23.09.1900	4378	Krzysztoń Janina	5.06.1910
1342	Kozdraś Józef	12.1870	3342	Kronenberg Chaja		4381	Krzywiecka Halina	12.07.1902
	Kozera Wiesława		3341	Kronenberg Abram	12.09.1912	1396	Krzyżaniak Józefa	17.08.1905
	Kozera Barbara		1376	Król Helena	09.1933	1395	Krzyżaniak Edward	27.07.1930
	Kozera Jadwiga		1377	Król Jadwiga	19.08.1932	1397	Krzyżaniak Kazimiera	27.02.1928
	Kozera Danuta	1928	1378	Król Józef	27.03.1921	1398	Krzyżanowska Kazimiera	28.03.1914
1343	Kozielska Hildegarda	5.03.1917	1375	Król Alicja	26.09.1927	4382	Krzyżanowska Ludwika	25.08.1870
1345	Kozina Stanisława	24.04.1919	1379	Król Józefa	28.12.1924	4383	Książek Elżbieta	19.11.1902
1344	Kozina Aniela	9.01.1934	1380	Król Kazimierz	1927	4384	Książek Emilia	15.07.1925
1346	Koziołkowski Leon	3.08.1890	1381	Król Lech	24.10.1937	4385	Książek Zdzisława	10.03.1931
1348	Kozłowska Janina	1.01.1931	1382	Król Natalia	24.02.1913	1400	Kubica Ludomira	25.05.1933
1349	Kozłowska Maria	23.09.1903	4364	Król Anna-Barbara	19.12.1943	1401	Kubica Maria	14.12.1910
1347	Kozłowska Helena	5.11.1893	4363	Król Andrzej	4.03.1930	1399	Kubica Jarosław	6.03.1939
3816	Kozłowska Antonina	7.02.1905	4368	Król Natalia	6.09.1935	1402	Kubieniec Danuta	26.05.1934
	Kozłowski Kazimierz Fr.	15.07.1902	4366	Król Katarzyna	15.04.1897	1403	Kubieniec Janina	28.08.1909
1350	Kozłowski Tadeusz	19.03.1928	4367	Król Maria	25.04.1925	1404	Kubieniec Stanisława	19.03.1937
4359	Kozula Władysław	26.08.1902	4365	Król Jan	5.01.1931	1406	Kubik Jan	13.08.1928
4357	Kozula Helena	26.06.1929	4369	Król Olga	4.02.1927	1407	Kubik Kazimierz	12.02.1891
4358	Kozula Józefa	19.03.1904	1384	Królik Leokadia	16.12.1928	1408	Kubik Witold	7.05.1930
3818	Kożuch Julia	5.10.1924	1383	Królik Hilary	12.01.1930	1409	Kubik Zofia	12.12.1900
3817	Kożuch Anna	25.07.1926	1386	Królikowska Barbara	15.12.1900	1405	Kubik Alfreda	6.06.1926
1353	Krajewska Konstancja	8.09.1904	1387	Królikowska Barbara	25.04.1932	1410	Kubińska Agnieszka	19.01.1909
1352	Krajewska Irena	14.02.1924	1388	Królikowska Jadwiga	13.12.1927	3830	Kubis Agnieszka	22.09.1928
1359	Krajewska Zuzanna	27.01.1932	1385	Królikowska Anna	5.03.1924	3831	Kubis Eliza	30.10.1934
1354	Krajewska Leokadia	9.12.1900	1389	Królikowska Katarzyna	15.08.1927	3832	Kubis Ireneusz	25.11.1931
1355	Krajewska Ludgarda	16.11.1920	1390	Królikowska Stanisława	10.10.1909	3833	Kubis Teofila	1907
1357	Krajewska Stanisława	29.11.1927	3819	Krótkowa Janina	6.03.1906	1411	Kubszta Andrzej	1.11.1888
1358	Krajewska Wincentyna	3.06.1904	3820	Kruk Urszula	6.12.1928	1412	Kucera Mikołaj	15.11.1899
4360	Krajewska Karolina	7.08.1899	3821	Kruk Zofia	23.04.1906	1414	Kucewicz Jadwiga	4.12.1905
1351	Krajewski Eugeniusz	26.03.1935	4370	Kruk Krystyna	12.10.1944	1413	Kucewicz Henryka	7.01.1927
1356	Krajewski Romuald	3.12.1929	3823	Krukowicz Antoni	10.06.1932	1415	Kucewicz Jerzy	1.05.1929
1364	Kraśnik Anna	14.07.1931	3822	Krukowicz Aleksandra	10.05.1901	1417	Kucharska Czesława	1935
1360	Krasnowska Eugenia	1922	3825	Krukowicz Janina	15.08.1939	1418	Kucharska Felicja	30.05.1927

627

1419	Kucharska Helena	8.01.1909	4394	Kuncewicz Krystyna	5.09.1938	4405	Kwiatkowska Bogusława	26.07.1887
1420	Kucharska Karolina	4.04.1931	1460	Kunicka Stanisława	8.05.1929	4407	Kwiatkowska Maria	12.03.1909
1416	Kucharska Barbara	8.10.1930	1459	Kunicki Alfons	1935	4408	Kwiatkowski Wojciech	3.08.1930
4386	Kucharska Czesława	9.11.1922	1462	Kunigiel Helena	3.03.1928	4406	Kwiatkowski Kazimierz	22.07.1922
3343	Kucharska Stefania	28.03.1922	1463	Kunigiel Maria	10.11.1900	3839	Kwiatkowski Antoni-R.	21.09.1943
1421	Kucharski Zdzisław	1933	1461	Kunigiel Genowefa	12.04.1931	1488	Kwiecień Marcin	15.02.1887
4387	Kucharski Marian-Jerzy	30.01.1944	1464	Kunigiel Stanisława	13.11.1927	1490	Kwiecińska Irena	27.09.1931
1423	Kuchcicka Janina	20.10.1928	1465	Kunik Zofia	1934	1489	Kwiecińska Józefa	9.03.1900
1424	Kuchcicka Krystyna	7.09.1925	3348	Kunik Ela	15.11.1918	1491	Kwiecińska Janina	3.12.1927
1425	Kuchcicka Wanda	1909	4395	Kupczyńska Teofila	2.11.1898	3355	Kwit Ludwika	25.12.1904
1422	Kuchcicka Emanuela	15.06.1930	3349	Kupferman Leopold	7.07.1912			
4388	Kuczewski Bolesław	5.08.1936	4396	Kupszta Andrzej	1.09.1888	1492	Lach Alojzy	8.06.1933
1426	Kuczyńska Apolonia	1.07.1926	3834	Kurek Zofia	15.06.1892	1495	Lach Leokadia	28.03.1930
1427	Kuczyńska Eugenia	12.01.1908	1466	Kuriata Wacława	28.09.1926	1493	Lach Anna	1912
1428	Kuczyńska Krystyna	15.01.1928	1467	Kurkowski Adam	7.08.1896	1494	Lach Helena	28.08.1928
1429	Kuczyńska Longina	9.03.1925	3350	Kuropatwa Leokadia	11.12.1911	1496	Lachewicz Alicja	30.09.1938
1430	Kuczyńska Natalia	15.07.1936	4400	Kurowska Teresa	23.08.1932	1498	Lachowska Zofia	01.1929
1432	Kuczyńska Zofia	16.10.1930	4398	Kurowska Ewa J.	17.11.1910	1497	Lachowska Helena	20.01.1926
1431	Kuczyński Tadeusz	30.09.1933	4397	Kurowski Andrzej	6.11.1937	3356	Landau Eleonora	26.09.1870
1434	Kudelska Nadzieja	10.10.1910	4399	Kurowski Marian	16.07.1894	3357	Langsam Elias-Aleksander	4.03.1915
1435	Kudelska Regina	29.11.1934	3351	Kuryj Michał	3.12.1887	4410	Laniewska Irma	6.10.1891
1433	Kudelska Laurencja	13.08.1933	1469	Kurzawska Regina	2.05.1907	1501	Laskowska Stefania	16.09.1899
4389	Kudła Irena	22.02.1931	1468	Kurzawska Alina	1929	1503	Laskowska Wanda	8.06.1927
4391	Kudła Stanisława	8.05.1908	4403	Kurzeja Zofia	11.08.1936	1500	Laskowska Irena	21.07.1933
4390	Kudła Jan	15.05.1932	4401	Kurzeja Helena	19.07.1906	1499	Laskowska Anna	17.06.1931
1437	Kudlicka Olga	4.10.1901	4402	Kurzeja Janusz	20.05.1931	1504	Laskowska Zofia	29.10.1029
1436	Kudlicki Bohdan	21.03.1921	1470	Kustra Ewa	9.11.1889	4411	Laskowska Honorata	13.04.1884
3346	Kudryl Stefania	7.05.1913	1472	Kuszel Antonina	5.05.1904	1502	Laskowski Tadeusz	7.04.1938
3345	Kudryl Józef	24.10.1934	1471	Kuszel Antoni	5.05.1930	1506	Latawiec Eugenia	2.02.1904
3344	Kudryl Genowefa	7.11.1932	1474	Kutereba Bronisław	4.11.1932	1508	Latawiec Janina	3.06.1909
1438	Kufera Irena	20.10.1926	1473	Kutereba Anna	11.11.1929	1509	Latawiec Joanna	21.01.1883
1439	Kufera Lucyna	19.06.1928	1475	Kuźmicz Józefa	15.09.1896	1510	Latawiec Marcin	10.11.1876
1440	Kufera Stanisława	6.01.1903	1476	Kuźmicz Leonard	7.09.1930	1507	Latawiec Jan	23.12.1902
4392	Kujawińska Józefa	10.07.1898	1477	Kuźmicz Leonarda	6.11.1928	1505	Latawiec Andrzej	27.01.1935
1442	Kujawska Zofia	1899	1478	Kuźmicz Lucjan	9.09.1932	1511	Latek Tadeusz	1931
1441	Kujawska Halina	1932	1479	Kuźmicz Stanisława	26.06.1934	3359	Laufer Chana	
1444	Kukiel Eliasz	1.09.1937	1480	Kuźniar Katarzyna	14.10.1896	3358	Laufer Jakub-Rubin	27.01.1905
1445	Kukiel Jan	3.07.1923	3835	Kuźniar Franciszek	19.07.1906	1517	Lech Rafalina	19.10.1926
1446	Kukiel Maria	11.06.1932	3354	Kuźnik Weronika	10.01.1905	1518	Lech Zofia	29.11.1926
1443	Kukiel Anastazja	1905	3352	Kuźnik Daniel	20.07.1932	1512	Lech Aniela	1911
1447	Kukiełka Władysława	17.11.1928	3353	Kuźnik Regina	2.05.1930	1516	Lech Katarzyna	23.11.1903
1448	Kukiełka Zofia	7.11.1926	3838	Kwapisz Tadeusz	15.03.1940	1513	Lech Czesława	4.03.1935
1449	Kulak Eugenia	1936	3836	Kwapisz Anna	29.05.1913	1514	Lech Jan	4.03.1932
1450	Kulawa Pelagia	1879	3837	Kwapisz Bożenna	23.01.1936	1515	Lech Janina	8.03.1930
3347	Kulesza Aleksander	10.01.1905	1481	Kwater Czesława	9.11.1927	1519	Lecko Irena	16.07.1932
1453	Kuligowska Rozalia	12.09.1884	1483	Kwiatek Wiktor	1.01.1928	1520	Lecko Olga	10.11.1910
1452	Kuligowska Helena	29.06.1929	1484	Kwiatek Zofia	5.04.1907	1521	Legendziewicz Józef	18.08.1934
1451	Kuligowski Antoni	14.06.1887	1482	Kwiatek Gustawa	31.07.1931	1522	Legendziewicz Stefania	10.09.1915
1454	Kulik Aniela	27.03.1932	1486	Kwiatkowska Wanda	8.09.1926	3360	Lejzerowicz Beniamin	3.02.1919
1455	Kułak Danuta	1936	1485	Kwiatkowska Teresa	1932	3361	Lejzerowicz Józef	3.03.1915
1456	Kułak Halina	25.08.1931	1487	Kwiatkowska Zofia	1935	4412	Lemańczyk Jadwiga	12.03.1892
1458	Kumpicki Kazimierz	1935	3840	Kwiatkowska Maria	28.01.1907	3841	Lendnau Maria	11.03.1927
1457	Kumpicki Bolesław	1935	4404	Kwiatkowska Anna	29.01.1932	1526	Leniewicz Luba	4.09.1921
4393	Kuncewicz Genowefa	15.10.1910	4409	Kwiatkowska Zofia	1928	1527	Leniewicz Stefania	11.11.1909

1525	Leniewicz Jerzy	4.10.1942	3370	Lipiński Nochem	28.12.1908	1596	Ławińska Janina	18.02.1930
1524	Leniewicz Halina	24.04.1938	1565	Lipska Bronisława	1.08.1902	1595	Ławińska Anna	16.03.1927
1523	Leniewicz Aniela	3.05.1933	3371	Lipska Teodora	14.04.1913	1597	Ławińska Maria	18.07.1917
1528	Lesisz Zygmunt	25.01.1926	4416	Lipska Kazimiera	19.04.1899	1598	Ławniczek Felicja	8.05.1926
3842	Leszczar Adam	3.12.1935	1566	Lipski Jerzy	22.08.1937	1600	Ławniczek Wiktoria	15.05.1905
3844	Leszczar Karolina	20.01.1929	3372	Lipszyc Boruch	7.04.1921	1599	Ławniczek Stanisław	1.01.1897
3843	Leszczar Feliks	12.08.1930	3373	Lipszyc Moszek	14.02.1918	1602	Ławrynowicz Jadwiga	29.06.1909
1531	Leszczyńska Bronisława	16.07.1921	1567	Lipucka Bogusława	1936	1601	Ławrynowicz Edward	15.10.1931
1532	Leszczyńska Eleonora	2.06.1933	1568	Lis Maria	8.10.1930	1603	Ławrynowicz Wanda	21.05.1933
1533	Leszczyńska Jadwiga	10.11.1929	4418	Lis Barbara-Stanisława	3.12.1886	3380	Łączna Feliksa	29.06.1898
1530	Leszczyńska Antonina	7.12.1897	1570	Lisiecka Lidia-Teresa	4.10.1943	4422	Łęczyński Kazimierz	10.06.1912
1536	Leszczyńska Weronika	12.05.1907	1569	Lisiecka Halina	21.06.1926	4423	Łęczyńska Wanda	12.10.1890
1535	Leszczyńska Stanisława	29.11.1939	3846	Lisiecka Alodia	17.09.1927	1605	Łobuczek Stanisław	18.05.1929
1534	Leszczyński Jerzy	24.04.1930	3845	Lisiecka Cecylia	26.09.1929	1604	Łobuczek Janina	18.11.1932
1537	Leszczyński Witold	2.01.1937	4419	Lisik Danuta	9.05.1932	1606	Łochowska Janina	6.05.1929
1538	Leszczyński Zbigniew	1.06.1928	4420	Lisik Helena	30.09.1905	1607	Łochowska Rozalia	30.08.1930
1529	Leszczyński Alojzy	7.10.1931	1571	Listek Bronisława	1875	4425	Łojko Michał	10.08.1887
1539	Leszkiewicz Mikołaj	10.06.1926	1572	Liszka Helena	8.02.1904	4426	Łojko Urszula	15.08.1892
4414	Leszkowicz Helena	11.04.1915	1573	Liszka Romuald	12.11.1928	4424	Łojko Irena	15.12.1927
4413	Leszkowicz Danuta	20.01.1939	3374	Litawska Luiza-Maria	11.08.1908	1608	Łomaska Stanisława	15.11.1915
4415	Leszkowicz Józef	22.02.1897	3375	Litawski Odo-Józef	18.11.1910	1610	Łopatowska Wanda	5.05.1926
1541	Leśniak Maria	20.08.1925	3847	Litwińczuk Maria	12.05.1915	1609	Łopatowska Janina	11.04.1928
1540	Leśniak Janusz	1.11.1929	3848	Litwińczuk Teresa	11.10.1938	1611	Łopiński Zygmunt	20.04.1889
1543	Leśniowska Zofia	4.06.1933	1574	Lode Maria	10.05.1928	1612	Łopuć Elżbieta	25.11.1914
1542	Leśniowska Katarzyna	15.05.1899	1575	Loszek Danuta	19.06.1928	1613	Łopuszyńska Jadwiga	4.11.1930
3362	Leuschner Wacław	1.06.1911	1576	Loszek Janina	24.12.1904	1620	Łoś Romualda	9.08.1925
1544	Lew Józef	1932	1577	Loszek Romualda	12.02.1932	1619	Łoś Marian	8.01.1930
1545	Lew Stefania	1930	4421	Lotarewicz Władysław	27.06.1914	1618	Łoś Joanna	29.10.1927
1546	Lew Zofia	7.05.1926	3376	Luksenberg Abram	17.11.1904	1617	Łoś Jadwiga	12.05.1927
1547	Lewandowska Julia	20.09.1897	1579	Luzar Wiktor	1930	1621	Łoś Zofia	1934
3363	Lewi Józef-Chaim	9.05.1919	1578	Luzar Stanisława	25.11.1927	1616	Łoś Irena	1933
1550	Lewszuk Jan	15.03.1933	1580	Lwowska Bronisława	27.10.1913	1614	Łosoś Jerzy	17.08.1937
1552	Lewszuk Michał	18.06.1926	1581	Lwowska Julia	1885	1615	Łosoś Władysława	9.04.1915
1551	Lewszuk Maria	13.10.1925				3853	Łosoś Zbigniew	12.12.1943
1549	Lewszuk Antonina	1931	1583	Łaguna Jan	20.08.1938	4428	Łosowska Mieczysława	1.01.1911
1548	Lewszuk Antoni	1937	1584	Łaguna Wanda	24.12.1910	4427	Łosowski Andrzej	23.02.1943
1553	Libera Jadwiga	20.02.1929	1582	Łaguna Ewa	22.09.1935	4429	Łossowska Antonina	13.06.1904
1555	Libera Zofia	3.07.1924	3377	Łanienter Szaja	26.10.1910	4430	Łossowska Irena	23.02.1930
1554	Libera Klara	11.01.1895	1589	Łańcucka Teresa	21.04.1935	1623	Łozdowska Stanisława	27.07.1917
1557	Lichodziejewska Ewa	11.12.1904	1586	Łańcucka Helena	8.11.1901	1622	Łozdowski Maciej	4.03.1870
1556	Lichodziejewski Czesław	11.09.1928	1587	Łańcucka Irena	26.10.1928	1624	Łuba Aleksandra	31.07.1920
3365	Lichtenstejn Abram	26.11.1902	1588	Łańcucka Maria	12.03.1930	4432	Łubina Halina	5.11.1938
3366	Lichtiger Jeszaja	15.03.1915	1585	Łańcucka Anna	15.11.1924	4433	Łubina Maria	7.04.1908
3367	Lifschutz Szymon	4.03.1905	3849	Łapiński Edward	2.02.1899	4431	Łubina Grażyna	6.04.1937
1559	Ligaj Łucja	13.12.1924	3378	Łapiński Edward	2.01.1920	3854	Ługiewicz Sławomira	23.05.1922
1560	Ligaj Maria	8.09.1927	3379	Łaski Roman	10.12.1914	1625	Łukaszewicz Eugenia	22.08.1901
1558	Ligaj Andrzej	1935	3851	Łaszcz Mieczysław	1930	1626	Łukaszewicz Józef	21.01.1928
3368	Lindenberger Edmund	30.07.1899	3852	Łaszcz Stefania	1932	4434	Łukaszewicz Jadwiga	22.02.1912
3369	Linderberger Elżbieta		3850	Łaszcz Janina	28.11.1927	4435	Łukaszewicz Jerzy	25.09.1942
4417	Lipczyc Kazimiera	19.12.1890	1590	Łaszkiewicz Maria	21.07.1877	3855	Łukaszewska Balbina	31.03.1909
1564	Lipińska Władysława	5.01.1932	1591	Łatanowska Eugenia	25.11.1897	3856	Łukaszewski Witold	17.03.1932
1563	Lipińska Janina	25.04.1909	1592	Łatanowska Małgorzata	23.11.1937	1627	Łukjaniec Helena	7.07.1903
1562	Lipińska Eugenia	4.07.1923	1594	Łatkowska Teofila	4.02.1895	1629	Łukjaniec Teodozja	24.11.1923
1561	Lipiński Andrzej	5.11.1909	1593	Łatkowski Jan	1929	1628	Łukjaniec Teodor	24.02.1934

4436 Łukowska Danuta	12.02.1931
4437 Łukowska Helena	22.05.1895
3385 Łużna Stanisława	30.10.1924
3381 Łużna Maria	30.07.1927
3383 Łużna Janina	30.04.1930
3382 Łużna Eugenia	22.12.1902
810 Łużna Bronisława	20.11.1934
3163 Łyżniak Kazimiera	15.07.1922
1631 Łyżniak Stanisława	1883
1634 Machaj Janina	7.07.1932
1632 Machaj Adela	15.07.1904
1633 Machaj Edward	25.06.1930
1637 Maciak Stefania	2.06.1896
1636 Maciak Matylda	4.04.1925
1635 Maciak Helena	12.12.1922
1639 Maciejewska Eugenia	21.11.1905
1638 Maciejewski Bogusław	9.08.1930
1732 Mączakowska Jarosława	19.12.1928
1640 Magnuszewska Anna	15.05.1890
1641 Magnuszewska Irena	4.10.1922
1645 Magryś Stanisława	1.01.1935
1644 Magryś Stanisława	3.05.1900
1643 Magryś Maria	25.10.1927
1642 Magryś Janina	2.02.1929
4438 Magryś Stanisław	2.02.1929
1647 Majewska Maria	12.06.1915
1646 Majewski Bogdan	19.05.1938
1648 Majka Kazimiera	19.03.1909
1649 Mak Zbigniew	22.07.1926
4442 Makarewicz Natalia	12.02.1929
4443 Makarewicz Stefania	22.06.1902
4441 Makarewicz Lubomir	21.02.1931
4440 Makarewicz Jadwiga	24.08.1924
4439 Makarewicz Henryka	19.01.1926
1650 Makaruk Rozalia	4.08.1888
3858 Maksymów Paraska	12.02.1927
3857 Maksymów Józef	22.02.1929
1669 Małachowska Helena	5.08.1914
1668 Małachowska Helena	18.07.1874
1671 Małaczyńska Maria	2.08.1929
1670 Małaczyńska Czesława	1.04.1927
1673 Małaczyńska Stanisława	2.11.1895
1672 Małaczyński Mieczysław	4.11.1890
1654 Malarz Zofia	20.08.1927
1651 Malarz Anna	23.08.1905
1653 Malarz Michał	1.01.1930
1652 Malarz Jan	8.09.1935
4446 Malcharek Eugenia	3.10.1878
4444 Malcharek Adela	15.01.1914
4445 Malcharek Barbara	22.02.1939
1657 Malec Leszek	29.06.1931
1658 Malec Rozalia	13.03.1900
1656 Malec Hermina	29.11.1928
1655 Malec Danuta	13.03.1926
1674 Małek Mieczysław	8.07.1885
1659 Malenczuk Maria	5.06.1910
4447 Malewska Jadwiga	29.01.1916
1664 Malinowska Jadwiga	24.04.1886
1663 Malinowska Irena	13.05.1931
1660 Malinowska Aleksandra	10.10.1927
1661 Malinowska Antonina	20.11.1908
1665 Malinowska Józefa	8.07.1932
1662 Malinowska Bronisława	8.04.1908
3387 Malinowska Blanka	
1666 Malinowski Józef	13.05.1937
1667 Malinowski Ryszard	21.03.1930
3386 Malinowski Leon	20.02.1907
3388 Małowicki Josel	10.05.1922
3859 Maniak Antoni	20.05.1911
1675 Marasek Stefania	3.12.1902
1676 Marchewa Janina	12.12.1927
1677 Marchewka Józef	14.02.1900
4448 Marchewka Bronisław	15.05.1932
1678 Marcińczak Józefa	9.11.1926
3860 Marcinkiewicz Roland	26.01.1931
3861 Marcinkiewicz Zuzanna	11.02.1927
1679 Marczak Emilia	30.10.1901
4449 Marczewska Sabina	9.09.1927
4451 Marczewska Władysława	25.05.1896
4450 Marczewski Władysław	10.12.1889
3862 Marczuk Tekla	24.07.1924
1680 Marczyńska Stefania	27.12.1903
3863 Markiewicz Matylda	19.02.1908
1684 Markisz Nadzieja	1896
1685 Markisz Wiktor	1.10.1931
1682 Markisz Józef	6.02.1891
1681 Markisz Feliksa	1.05.1934
1683 Markisz Janina	10.04.1929
3390 Maron Władysława	12.03.1895
3389 Maron Krystyna	24.01.1922
1689 Marten Wojciech	7.01.1931
1687 Marten Krystyna	6.04.1929
1688 Marten Wincenta	9.10.1900
3391 Martusewicz Helena	13.03.1907
3392 Martusewicz Krystyna	23.11.1930
1692 Martyka Wiesław	14.02.1940
1691 Martyka Romualda	3.05.1930
1690 Martyka Leokadia	25.10.1909
1694 Martynowicz Józef	27.02.1927
1693 Martynowicz Jan	24.11.1928
1695 Maruniak Zofia	15.03.1905
1698 Marzec Tadeusz	1931
1696 Marzec Daniela	10.03.1931
1697 Marzec Stanisława	10.10.1907
1709 Maścianica Weronika	14.11.1905
1700 Masewicz Jadwiga	12.12.1910
1699 Masewicz Izabela	24.12.1935
1704 Masiulanis Konstancja	11.02.1903
1705 Masiulanis Nadzieja	10.11.1889
1706 Masiulanis Pelagia	23.03.1904
1702 Masiulanis Halina	9.06.1938
1708 Masiulanis Ryszard	29.05.1934
1701 Masiulanis Antonina	17.11.1865
1703 Masiulanis Helena	14.09.1925
1707 Masiulanis Piotr	24.10.1889
3393 Masłowski Roman	24.12.1921
4452 Maszniew Piotr	6.09.1892
3397 Matczak Wacław	17.03.1931
3396 Matczak Józefa	15.03.1905
1710 Materek Jadwiga	17.10.1901
1713 Matias Teresa	17.02.1934
1712 Matias Malwina	12.1892
1711 Matias Janina	17.02.1934
3394 Matkowski Marian	1916
1686 Mattych Eleonora	10.01.1880
1714 Matulewicz Sabina	26.01.1910
1715 Matulewicz Wiesław	3.06.1928
Matuszczyk Wilhelmina	1872
4453 Matuszek Joanna	20.11.1925
1716 Matwes Gabryela	7.01.1919
1719 Matwiejczyk Jan	8.11.1930
1717 Matwiejczyk Antoni	1935
1721 Matwiejczyk Karol	1934
1722 Matwiejczyk Maria	1936
1723 Matwiejczyk Stefan	25.11.1929
1718 Matwiejczyk Jadwiga	15.06.1902
1720 Matwiejczyk Janina	5.04.1927
3395 Matwijów Jan	25.12.1914
1724 Matysiak Maria	12.03.1909
4454 Matysiak Henryk	31.07.1943
1728 Mazur Magdalena	1939
1727 Mazur Kazimiera	1930
1726 Mazur Jan	1933
1725 Mazur Jan	27.12.1919
3398 Mazur Kazimierz	4.03.1907
1729 Mazurek Franciszka	10.04.1931
1730 Mazurek Janina	5.02.1913
1731 Mazurek Wanda	22.01.1932
4457 Mazurek Paulina	28.06.1930
4458 Mazurek Weronika	7.10.1925
4455 Mazurek Aniela	11.03.1890
4456 Mazurek Franciszka	11.03.1916
3399 Mazurkiewicz Stefania	26.11.1911
1751 Mediuch Maria	20.05.1898
1750 Mediuch Czesława	17.11.1934
1749 Mediuch Bronisław	22.04.1928
1733 Melnarowicz Władysława	11.03.1912
3400 Melodysta Leyla	3.01.1909
3402 Mendelsohn Nachman	12.11.1919
3401 Mendelsohn Manes	21.11.1894
3403 Mendzylewski Szyja	8.08.1903

1734	Mianowska Teresa	24.11.1929	1773	Misiewicz Paraskowia	4.10.1897	1821	Możejko Maria	10.03.1906
1736	Michalak Stanisława	22.02.1922	3866	Misiewicz Stanisława	22.08.1913	1819	Możejko Helena	28.07.1929
1735	Michalak Krystyna	6.09.1925	4312	Misiewicz Stanisław	3.04.1908	1823	Możejko Stanisława	16.08.1926
1739	Michalska Danuta	8.11.1928	1774	Misiur Jadwiga	15.05.1930	1818	Możejko Bronisława	17.09.1930
1741	Michalska Irena	8.03.1926	1775	Misuno Włodzimierz	22.02.1918	1820	Możejko Janina	1.06.1929
1743	Michalska Krystyna	25.09.1926	4313	Miś Jan	4.01.1909	1822	Możejko Paulina	6.06.1902
1737	Michalska Aleksandra	20.08.1903	1776	Miśkowicz Franciszka	16.07.1897	1827	Mroczek Zbigniew	1936
1740	Michalska Franciszka	6.02.1904	1777	Mitro Maria	17.07.1905	1825	Mroczek Regina	10.08.1929
3404	Michalska Janina	23.11.1911		Mizera Tekla	24.07.1907	1824	Mroczek Danuta	1939
1745	Michalski Zdzisław	1930		Mizera Genowefa	12.03.1934	1826	Mroczek Romualda	1932
1738	Michalski Andrzej	27.01.1937	1778	Mleko Zofia	28.08.1904	1829	Mróz Jerzy	16.06.1936
1742	Michalski Kazimierz	25.02.1928	1782	Mocarska Janina	3.07.1929	1828	Mróz Anna	26.05.1909
1744	Michalski Ryszard	1.03.1930	1780	Mocarska Irena	7.09.1928	1831	Mucha Janina	10.03.1930
3405	Michaluk Roman	3.06.1915	1779	Mocarska Bronisława	15.01.1900	1830	Mucha Anastazja	10.11.1908
1747	Michniak Felicja	2.05.1928	1781	Mocarska Jadwiga	15.12.1926	1832	Mucha Maria	3.02.1927
1748	Michniak Krzysztofa	6.03.1930	1783	Moch Bolesław	1936	1833	Muchowska Józefa	20.10.1894
1746	Michniak Bogumiła	27.05.1934	4314	Modzylewski Zdzisław	6.07.1897	1835	Muchowska Maria	22.07.1923
4459	Mickiewicz Leokadia	9.12.1911	1785	Molendo Janina	26.02.1928	1834	Muchowska Leokadia	4.06.1930
	Mickiewicz Adam		1784	Molendo Anna	9.12.1889	3868	Muck Janina	16.05.1887
3864	Mickowski Antoni	12.03.1893	1786	Moniak Czesława	24.10.1928	1849	Mueller Janina	23.10.1912
1752	Mierzejewski Kazimierz	1934	1787	Moniak Ryszard	18.11.1932	1848	Mueller Irena	17.07.1938
1753	Miętus Józef	17.04.1910	1791	Morawska Julia	20.03.1897	1836	Mularczyk Lidia	24.10.1917
4308	Migas Kazimiera	25.04.1939	1792	Morawska Kazimiera	1932	1839	Multan Michalina	3.01.1893
3406	Migas Apolonia	6.02.1923	1790	Morawska Janina	8.04.1927	1838	Multan Józef	3.01.1930
3407	Migas Władysława	20.06.1898	1794	Morawska Zofia	15.05.1899	1837	Multan Janina	3.01.1933
4460	Migas	1.10.1944	1789	Morawska Danuta	10.10.1933	1841	Murat Kazimierz	25.07.1932
	Mikołajewicz (matka)		1788	Morawska Barbara	27.01.1926	1840	Murat Andrzej	10.04.1938
	Mikołajewicz Halina		1793	Morawski Władysław	28.08.1896	1842	Murat Weronika	9.03.1902
1757	Mikulicka Wiktoria	24.05.1894	1796	Mordak Kazimierz	15.05.1936	1843	Murias Józef	10.03.1929
1758	Mikulicka Władysława	8.09.1926	1797	Mordak Lucyna	1934	3867	Musiał Katarzyna	14.08.1900
1756	Mikulicka Marianna	2.02.1933	1795	Mordak Alfreda	1932	1844	Musialik Irena	3.12.1924
1755	Mikulicka Józefa	8.09.1921	4464	Mordasewicz Mieczysław	18.10.1913	1845	Musialik Wiktoria	1.01.1903
1754	Mikulicki Józef	25.07.1888	1799	Moroz Stanisława	25.12.1902	4467	Muszyńska Maria	24.06.1870
4461	Mikuszewski Leonard-Józef	6.11.1897	1800	Moroz Teresa	21.07.1933	1847	Muter Stefania	13.03.1900
1760	Milczarska Stefania	1932	1798	Moroz Leokadia	13.12.1928	1846	Muter Łucja	21.12.1927
1761	Milczarska Władysława	5.12.1925	4466	Morska Janina	26.06.1929	1850	Myćka Józefa	12.02.1915
1759	Milczarski Piotr	24.08.1930	4465	Morska Aleksandra	10.03.1904	4469	Myślińska Olga	3.01.1928
1764	Miłek Henryk	17.06.1933	1804	Morys Stefania	16.07.1931	4468	Myślińska Jadwiga	10.09.1902
1766	Miłek Waleria	29.07.1942	1801	Morys Emilia	25.05.1902	1850	Mysza Teresa	21.04.1926
1763	Miłek Helena	16.10.1916	1802	Morys Kazimiera	25.06.1927			
1762	Miłek Anna	15.03.1898	1803	Morys Maria	25.07.1937	1852	Nabierzko Franciszek	1937
1765	Miłek Maria	8.09.1926	1806	Mosiewicz Piotr	14.03.1936	4315	Nabożna Maria	18.05.1918
1768	Miłosz Janina	30.04.1930	1805	Mosiewicz Aleksandra	18.01.1927	4471	Nadańska Józefa	25.01.1888
1769	Miłosz Regina	20.12.1928	1807	Mosiewicz Weronika	1934	4470	Nadańska Anna	26.07.1927
1767	Miłosz Jadwiga	19.08.1896	1808	Moskal Tadeusz	1931	1853	Nadborska Helena	14.01.1907
3865	Miluć Natalia	20.01.1928	1812	Moskalenko Teresa	18.04.1930		Nadel Anna	
4462	Miluć Eugenia	15.08.1931	1811	Moskalenko Danuta	20.10.1936	3417	Nadel Anna	
4463	Miluć Władysław	22.10.1899	1809	Moskalenko Anna	23.11.1927	3416	Nadel Henryk	6.01.1904
4309	Minc Abram	2.09.1906	1810	Moskalenko Cezaria	27.01.1909	1855	Naglik Kazimierz	4.03.1928
4311	Minc Rafał	20.04.1919	1813	Moss Wacława	1936	1856	Naglik Stanisława	8.05.1991
4310	Minc Aida		1814	Moss Władysława	28.04.1931	1854	Naglik Cecylia	22.11.1914
1771	Misiewicz Józef	1933	1815	Motłoch Sylwester	1937	1857	Nagrodzka Eugenia	1937
1770	Misiewicz Anna	1929	1816	Mozolewska Maria	15.05.1894	1858	Nagrodzki Wacław	24.04.1927
1772	Misiewicz Maria	15.07.1927	1817	Mozolewska Wanda	22.06.1926	3418	Naida Michał	20.10.1900
						3419	Naida Irena	

3869	Naimski Ludwik	28.02.1894	4477	Nowak Bronisława	26.06.1928	1929	Okoń Henryka	16.05.1928
1860	Najdzianowicz Teresa	09.1930	1891	Nowakowska Czesława	5.05.1915	1930	Olbrecht Janina	3.01.1931
1859	Najdzianowicz Apolonia	09.1900	4480	Nowakowska Halina	10.03.1922	1931	Olbrycht Stanisława	7.05.1931
1862	Najdzisz Barbara	13.06.1935	4482	Nowakowska Kazimiera	16.09.1924	1932	Olczyk Stefan	27.02.1927
1861	Najdzisz Apolonia	27.03.1909	4483	Nowakowska Sabina	10.05.1891	1933	Olechnowicz Dominika	1872
4473	Naplocha Czesława	15.12.1926	4481	Nowakowski Jan	24.06.1882	4492	Olechnowicz Feliksa	2.03.1898
4474	Naplocha Jadwiga	15.10.1880	1895	Nowicka Jadwiga	6.04.1928	4493	Olechnowicz Maria	27.12.1925
4472	Naplocha Adam	15.04.1876	1893	Nowicka Jadwiga	7.09.1904	1934	Olejnik Halina	13.08.1929
1864	Narczyk Czesław	10.12.1929	1892	Nowicka Irena	12.08.1928	1942	Oleś Marian	8.12.1936
1863	Narczyk Bolesław	1932	1898	Nowicka Józefa	05.1932	1943	Oleś Teresa	8.05.1932
1866	Narolska Danuta	2.10.1935	1899	Nowicka Maria	22.07.1899	1940	Oleś Eugeniusz	8.04.1930
1865	Narolska Aniela	11.01.1934	1900	Nowicka Maria	8.09.1902	1941	Oleś Franciszka	18.12.1898
1867	Narolska Mieczysława	15.08.1917	1894	Nowicka Jadwiga	16.01.1926	1937	Olesiak Witold	5.01.1930
1868	Naściuszonek Bronisław	12.12.1898	1902	Nowicka Zofia	22.11.1923	1935	Olesiak Janina	7.06.1904
3420	Natanowicz Mojżesz	29.05.1916	3875	Nowicka Wanda	6.06.1927	1936	Olesiak Krystyna	17.06.1925
1869	Nawój Janina	19.02.1925	3874	Nowicka Anna	7.08.1928	1939	Oleszczuk Irena	9.01.1936
1871	Nawój Michał	22.05.1889	1901	Nowicki Zbigniew	9.10.1929	1938	Oleszczuk Anna	8.09.1910
1870	Nawój Maria	10.04.1887	1897	Nowicki Józef	24.03.1929	1944	Olewiński Stanisław	25.01.1909
1872	Nawrocka Helena	28.10.1874	1896	Nowicki Jan	1873	3877	Ołowiecka Aniela	1.12.1929
3421	Nazarkiewicz Janina	23.05.1919	1903	Nowik Jan	24.03.1903	3879	Ołowiecka Ludwika	1.07.1924
1873	Nerka Władysław	29.07.1929	1904	Nowosiadła Anna	10.04.1930	3878	Ołowiecka Janina	13.02.1928
4475	Neuman Janina	7.07.1917	1905	Nowosiadły Józef	3.08.1885	3880	Ołowiecka Stanisława	28.10.1926
1874	Nicpoń Władysław	25.04.1902	1908	Nowosielska Lucyna	14.06.1924	3876	Ołowiecka Agata	5.02.1902
	Nieczykowska Maria	27.10.1906	1907	Nowosielska Józefa	21.03.1893	3427	Olszański Krzysztof	
	Nieczykowska Krystyna	26.02.1930	1906	Nowosielska Alicja	12.01.1928	1945	Olszewska Jadwiga	20.09.1898
	Nieczykowska Izabella	2.08.1927	4485	Nowosielska Halina	9.08.1927	4494	Opelt Bogusław	29.09.1930
1875	Niedziółko Aleksander	20.11.1909	4487	Nowosielska Zofia	26.10.1902	4495	Opelt Jadwiga	3.09.1933
1876	Niedźwiedzka Helena	9.03.1929	4484	Nowosielska Danuta	13.03.1929	4496	Opelt Jadwiga	4.04.1909
1877	Niedźwiedzka Stanisława	28.01.1928	4486	Nowosielski Marian	31.12.1933	3881	Opioła Aniela	1.01.1904
1878	Niemczyk Janina	23.01.1927	1909	Nykiel Bronisław	12.10.1935	3882	Opioła Stanisław	3.01.1934
1880	Niezabytowska Józefa	15.10.1892	4489	Nykiel Karolina	3.08.1892	3883	Opioła Tadeusz	5.05.1939
1879	Niezabytowska Janina	15.04.1923	4490	Nykiel Stefania	6.01.1927	3884	Opioła Teresa	13.10.1930
4476	Nigelszporn Alfred	21.02.1893	4488	Nykiel Janina	8.12.1931	3885	Opioła Zofia	1.01.1929
1881	Nikiel Zofia	23.04.1901				1946	Opolska Anna	12.10.1927
1882	Nikiforowska Antonina	10.01.1919	1913	Obłój Tadeusz	28.08.1931	1947	Opolska Ewa	13.10.1905
3422	Nikołajewicz Antonina	11.05.1931	1911	Obłój Edward	28.04.1935	1948	Orendecki Władysław	10.11.1931
3423	Nikołajewicz Halina	17.11.1935	1910	Obłój Bernarda	28.02.1939	3430	Orlańska Maria	22.11.1902
3424	Nikołajewicz Maria	13.02.1909	1912	Obłój Stanisława	11.11.1911	3428	Orlańska Leokadia	3.06.1932
3871	Nizielska Lucyna	20.06.1936	1914	Obłój Władysław	14.07.1932	3429	Orlański Jerzy	6.07.1927
3870	Nizielski Jerzy	20.01.1939	4491	Obłój Mieczysław-Zygmunt	17.05.1944	1949	Orlicka Eliza	9.06.1939
1883	Noculak Genowefa	16.10.1901	1915	Obolewicz Zofia	5.08.1885	1951	Orlicka Janina	29.08.1913
1884	Nojek Maria	13.04.1888	1919	Obuchowicz Kazimierz	6.01.1926	1950	Orlicki Eugeniusz	18.05.1939
3426	Norblin Helena		1920	Obuchowicz Maria	6.03.1936	4497	Orsicz Maria	8.09.1891
3425	Norblin Stefan	29.06.1892	1918	Obuchowicz Janina	5.08.1932	1954	Orysiuk Jan	16.06.1915
1886	Nosowicz Barbara	17.08.1936	1917	Obuchowicz Jadwiga	23.04.1906	1953	Orysiuk Helena	3.05.1884
1885	Nosowicz Adam	17.09.1928	1916	Obuchowicz Emilia	23.05.1930	1952	Orysiuk Bartłomiej	12.10.1886
1887	Nosowicz Małgorzata	14.03.1903	1921	Obwarzanek Genowefa	2.01.1924	1955	Orzech Aniela	15.08.1900
1889	Nowak Anna	19.07.1903	1922	Obwarzanek Stefania	27.08.1923	1956	Orzech Julia	9.01.1930
1888	Nowak Albina	16.02.1929	1923	Ochrym Romana	24.12.1934	1960	Orzechowska Maria	22.12.1882
1890	Nowak Bronisław	1.11.1892	1924	Ochrym Rozalia	5.01.1887	1957	Orzechowska Jadwiga	30.05.1928
3872	Nowak Henryka	1932	1925	Ochrym Stefania	21.03.1928	1959	Orzechowska Józefa	19.03.1900
3873	Nowak Zofia	23.11.1926	1926	Ogibiński Marian	15.08.1900	1962	Orzechowska Teresa	1.06.1926
4478	Nowak Henryka	27.01.1938	1928	Okołotowicz Weronika	9.06.1901	1963	Orzechowska Wanda	16.09.1926
4479	Nowak Janina	5.11.1926	1927	Okołotowicz Henryk	9.12.1936	1958	Orzechowski Janusz	20.11.1932

4498	Orzechowski Dyonizy	12.05.1889	4511	Owczarek Kazimierz	18.05.1904	3445	Paszyc Aleksy	9.08.1912
1966	Orzeł Radosława	3.02.1927	4510	Owczarek Janina	6.05.1907		Pateluch Helena	20.06.1928
1967	Orzeł Szczęsna	26.10.1924	4509	Owczarek Halina	6.05.1935		Pateluch Maria	
1964	Orzeł Franciszka	3.03.1891					Pateluch Pola	25.07.1927
1965	Orzeł Ludomir	13.11.1932	1988	Pabian Franciszek	1931	4520	Patoń Apolonia	10.07.1890
3432	Orzeł Michał	7.12.1933	1991	Pacak Urszula	6.01.1910	2018	Pawlak Maria	5.03.1932
3888	Orzeł Władysław	14.07.1943	1989	Pacak Ewa	5.05.1936	3902	Pawlak Aniela	25.05.1933
3887	Orzeł Roman	14.07.1938	1990	Pacak Jan	11.11.1900	3903	Pawlak Irena	13.04.1930
3886	Orzeł Janina	8.06.1913	1992	Pacek Eugeniusz	26.10.1930	2019	Pawliczek Ludwika	24.08.1900
3433	Orzeł Stanisława	6.12.1910	1995	Pacek Zygmunt	1937	2020	Pawlik Julia	6.01.1888
3431	Orzeł Jan	2.07.1936	1993	Pacek Tadeusz	1935	2021	Pawlikowska Krystyna	1937
1970	Osińska Weronika	9.01.1908	1994	Pacek Władysława	06.1932	2022	Pawlikowska Zofia	13.10.1927
1968	Osiński Janusz	1.03.1937	1996	Pacholska Anna	1.08.1927	2025	Pawłowska Maria	15.08.1910
1969	Osiński Leszek	9.09.1931	3897	Pacholska Janina	28.09.1897	2027	Pawłowska Tatiana	15.01.1906
1971	Osipowicz Franciszka	16.10.1926	3896	Pacholski Jan	15.02.1928	2023	Pawłowska Bronisława	28.11.1935
1972	Osipowicz Stanisława	15.04.1930	1997	Pachucki Franciszek	1932	4521	Pawłowska Jadwiga	6.01.1899
3434	Osnos Józef	25.06.1904	1998	Pajączek Bolesław	1934	2026	Pawłowski Ryszard	7.08.1932
3435	Osnos Maria		2000	Pajor Mieczysław	1933	2024	Pawłowski Henryk	24.08.1933
3889	Ostapiuk Maria	1930	2008	Pałasz Teresa	23.11.1931	4522	Pawłowski Józef	24.04.1887
3436	Ostapiuk Bronisław	17.06.1930	2007	Pałasz Regina	27.12.1929	3906	Pazik Jadwiga	1.02.1937
3437	Ostapiuk Leokadia	19.04.1928	2003	Pałasz Ewa	8.05.1908	3905	Pazik Edward	6.11.1931
3438	Ostapiuk Waleria	17.11.1897	2004	Pałasz Honorata	24.09.1926	3904	Pazik Bolesława	1.11.1906
1973	Ostaszewska Maria	25.03.1888	2005	Pałasz Jadwiga	27.12.1927	2028	Pelc Anna	18.07.1896
1974	Ostolski Jerzy	9.12.1931	2006	Pałasz Janina	24.06.1938	2030	Pelc Jan	6.01.1892
4501	Ostrihańska Zofia	22.02.1926	1999	Palczewski Stefan	1933	2031	Pelc Jan	18.07.1891
4500	Ostrihańska Olga	10.12.1895	2002	Paluch Stanisław	15.10.1933	2032	Pelc Krystyna	24.11.1926
4499	Ostrihańska Anna	25.09.1929	2001	Paluch Bronisława	1938	2033	Pelc Michalina	25.09.1932
1975	Ostromęcka Zofia	17.09.1888	3440	Pałys Mieczysław	14.12.1920	2034	Pelc Tadeusz	27.10.1927
1978	Ostrowska Leokadia	16.10.1893	3439	Pałys Halina	28.12.1923	2035	Pelc Teresa	8.06.1919
1977	Ostrowska Janina	30.08.1932	4513	Pałys	8.07.1944	2036	Pelc Wanda	21.07.1933
1979	Ostrowska Longina	20.01.1901	4514	Panek Aleksandra	3.03.1927	2037	Pelc Zofia	15.05.1905
1980	Ostrowska Łucja	3.03.1928		Panek Zofia	15.01.1931	2029	Pelc Bronisław	25.06.1929
1981	Ostrowska Maria	16.07.1894	4516	Panek Mieczysław	10.08.1933	3907	Peszyńska Krystyna	11.07.1911
1982	Ostrowska Melania	6.01.1885	4515	Panek Maria	19.09.1894	4524	Peszyńska Zofia	16.08.1899
1983	Ostrowska Olga	15.11.1907	4517	Panek Władysław	17.04.1894	4523	Peszyński Władysław-Zbigniew	20.01.1944
1985	Ostrowska Wanda	26.04.1925	2009	Parafińska Stanisława	12.06.1914	2038	Pianko Janina	25.04.1915
3890	Ostrowska Anna	14.08.1898	3442	Parczewska Feliksa	17.04.1918	2041	Piątkowska Olga	8.04.1895
3891	Ostrowska Irena	28.08.1923	3441	Parczewska Ewa	21.05.1879	2042	Piątkowska Regina	29.07.1928
4502	Ostrowska Janina	7.07.1923	3443	Parczewski Rajmund	23.01.1879	2043	Piątkowska Zofia	3.06.1907
4503	Ostrowska Maria	16.07.1894	2011	Pasierbska Karolina	7.02.1882	2040	Piątkowska Alina	8.02.1927
1986	Ostrowski Wiesław	15.02.1935	2010	Pasierbska Bernarda	25.02.1927	3908	Piątkowska Maria, Ewa,	10.11.1907
1987	Ostrowski Zbigniew	13.09.1931	2012	Pasternak Gustaw	10.03.1936	2039	Piaucha Jerzy	1933
1984	Ostrowski Piotr	3.12.1936	2013	Pasternak Jadwiga	19.09.1903	2044	Piechowicz Kazimierz	1930
1976	Ostrowski Adam	24.12.1926	4518	Pasternak Danuta	1.05.1922	2065	Pięciorak Emilia	23.04.1912
3892	Ostrowski Waldemar	11.12.1925	4519	Pasternak Klementyna	5.05.1888	2066	Pięciorak Józefa	5.03.1885
4506	Oszmiańska Maria	23.01.1924	2014	Pastuła Leokadia	8.02.1930	3911	Pieczonka Władysława	1935
4507	Oszmiańska Rozalia	27.08.1898	3898	Paszkiewicz Ezechiela	28.10.1931	3912	Pieczonka Zofia	14.05.1930
4504	Oszmiańska Alfreda	2.05.1926	3899	Paszkiewicz Marcjanna	1933	3909	Pieczonka Helena	28.12.1928
4505	Oszmiański Czesław	13.09.1930	3900	Paszkoska Halina	28.11.1914	3910	Pieczonka Kazimiera	12.09.1926
4508	Oszmiański Wawrzyniec	8.08.1892	3444	Paszkowska Jadwiga	19.08.1900	2045	Piekarski Edward	11.11.1928
3895	Otto Mieczysław	15.06.1935	2015	Paszkowski Piotr	1934	2046	Piekarski Stanisław	1929
3894	Otto Magdalena	15.08.1914	2016	Pasznicka Julia	31.03.1916	2049	Pielka Leokadia	22.10.1927
3893	Otto Janina	6.06.1938	2017	Pasznicki Zygmunt	12.10.1936	2048	Pielka Kazimiera	11.05.1921
4512	Owczarek Ryszard	4.11.1936	3901	Paszoska Maria-Danuta	1.04.1937	2050	Pielka Władysława	10.02.1928

2047 Pielka Janina	22.06.1924
2052 Pieńczak Wiktoria	22.02.1899
2051 Pieniążek Leona	28.11.1928
3447 Pieślak Michał	23.06.1915
2053 Piestrak Adam	1928
2055 Piestrak Wanda	22.06.1920
2054 Piestrak Janina	20.12.1928
3914 Pietkiewicz Irena	7.03.1937
3913 Pietkiewicz Czesław	1.11.1931
3915 Pietkiewicz Ludwika	9.01.1900
2067 Piętko Ryszard	1932
2056 Pietroń Irena	21.08.1932
2058 Pietrukowicz Mikołaj	23.08.1935
2057 Pietrukowicz Anna	1.10.1909
2059 Pietrukowicz Sergiusz	30.09.1932
4525 Pietrulewicz Franciszka	26.01.1912
2061 Pietruszko Witold	8.09.1932
2060 Pietruszko Regina	15.02.1929
Pietryka Maria	15.8.1934
2063 Pietrzykowska Maria	8.05.1931
2062 Pietrzykowski Łucjan	1934
2064 Pietrzykowski Zdzisław	23.09.1927
2068 Pigmistrzańska Anna	18.09.1896
Pilarz Antonina	4.12.1885
Pilarz Władysława	25.09.1924
Pilarz Julia	19.01.1927
3450 Pilipszyn Stanisława	7.01.1937
3448 Pilipszyn Antonina	17.06.1909
3449 Pilipszyn Franciszek	9.03.1932
2098 Pink Wacław	6.07.1930
2097 Pink Maria	2.08.1942
2096 Pink Kazimiera	15.09.1905
2095 Pink Jan	8.03.1935
2094 Pink Jadwiga	30.12.1934
2084 Piórkowska Maria	6.03.1938
2083 Piórkowska Jadwiga	15.10.1913
2081 Piórkowska Emilia	10.04.1917
2085 Piórkowski Stanisław	2.01.1936
2082 Piórkowski Henryk	25.04.1912
3451 Piórkowski Jan	20.06.1918
4529 Piotrowicz Pelagia	2.02.1897
4527 Piotrowicz Irena	22.05.1927
4528 Piotrowicz Józef	2.02.1881
4526 Piotrowicz Elwira	1.08.1938
2078 Piotrowska Stanisława	23.03.1927
2080 Piotrowska Zofia	29.12.1905
2069 Piotrowska Alina	6.11.1929
2077 Piotrowska Leokadia	1934
2076 Piotrowska Izabela	4.01.1935
2075 Piotrowska Franciszka	30.09.1905
2071 Piotrowska Bronisława	13.04.1929
2072 Piotrowska Celina	24.07.1925
2070 Piotrowska Barbara	22.10.1930
2074 Piotrowska Filipina	22.09.1898
4530 Piotrowska Danuta	18.03.1934
4531 Piotrowska Jadwiga	12.09.1912
4532 Piotrowska Ludwika	11.04.1924
2073 Piotrowski Czesław	16.04.1929
2079 Piotrowski Wiesław	23.07.1931
2086 Pipała Wiktoria	23.12.1928
3446 Pipes-Meisner Eugeniusz	28.09.1909
4533 Pisarczuk Józefa	15.03.1872
2087 Pisarewicz Czesław	15.10.1930
2088 Piskorski Stefan	18.07.1899
4534 Piskozub Stanisława	26.10.1896
2089 Piss Zdzisława	1.10.1928
2090 Pitera Danuta	23.02.1930
2091 Pitura Maria	2.02.1913
2093 Pitura Wojciech	4.04.1911
2092 Pitura Tadeusz	29.03.1932
4535 Pitura Zdzisław	31.05.1944
2099 Piwowar Janina	2.04.1937
3454 Piwowar Maria	23.11.1926
3455 Piwowar Zofia	3.05.1922
3453 Piwowar Julia	6.12.1932
3452 Piwowar Anna	2.04.1935
3456 Piwowarski Zdzisław	13.08.1921
3918 Platta Stanisława	20.10.1928
3916 Platta Emilia	1.02.1942
3919 Platta Stefania	9.03.1903
3917 Platta Jan	15.07.1899
3457 Plewińska Jadwiga	24.10.1930
3458 Plewińska Kunegunda	6.01.1898
2100 Plich Danuta	26.03.1928
2103 Plucińska Teresa	26.05.1925
2101 Pluciński Andrzej	3.03.1927
2102 Pluciński Józef	25.12.1928
3459 Pluta Janina	1917
2104 Pluta Franciszek Fr.	24.12.1905
Pławińska Irena	19.02.1923
Pławińska Klara	
3920 Płocica Anna	8.05.1926
3921 Płocica Julia	28.02.1928
3922 Płocica Tomasz	1930
3923 Płocka Regina	30.03.1926
3924 Płocka Waleria	30.11.1908
3925 Płocki Zbigniew	12.11.1935
3931 Płonka Teofila	12.05.1925
3927 Płonka Genowefa	28.01.1929
3930 Płonka Michał	1933
3929 Płonka Maria	1936
3926 Płonka Albina	1931
3928 Płonka Łucja	1937
2105 Płusa Jan	1931
2107 Pniewska Jadwiga	12.12.1905
2106 Pniewska Danuta	2.01.1926
2108 Poberezniczenko Tadeusz	1.12.1918
2109 Poczobut-Odlanicka Zofia	15.01.1902
2112 Podhorecka Zofia	1.01.1901
2110 Podhorodecki Roman	19.07.1926
2111 Podhorodecki Stefan	13.10.1931
3460 Podlewska Maria	25.03.1901
3461 Podlewski Michał	11.02.1890
3462 Podsońska Zofia	6.10.1922
3932 Podsoński Franciszek	4.10.1884
2113 Pokrzywa Emilia	13.09.1906
2114 Pokrzywa Janusz	22.07.1932
2116 Pol Józefa	20.04.1902
2117 Pol Leon	20.06.1897
2118 Pol Tadeusz	25.09.1930
2115 Pol Irena	20.10.1933
Pola Danuta	27.03.1932
Pola Halina	23.07.1941
Pola Konrad	26.11.1934
Pola Waleria	8.03.1908
2119 Polak Danuta	1.04.1931
2120 Polak Irena	12.12.1933
2121 Polak Janina	4.01.1909
2122 Polak Stanisław	29.06.1930
3933 Polak Barbara	11.04.1936
3935 Polak Weronika	10.06.1915
3934 Polak Janusz	15.10.1943
3936 Polakiewicz Czesław	1932
2123 Polańska Halina	20.09.1926
3938 Polechowicz Czesław	20.07.1903
3937 Polechowicz Bogusława	5.05.1933
2124 Polek Jerzy	1938
2126 Polikowska Halina	23.12.1929
2127 Polikowska Leokadia	13.06.1931
2125 Polikowska Anna	18.05.1904
2129 Polnik Antonina	12.07.1902
2128 Polnik Aniela	14.07.1925
2130 Polnik Eugenia	6.10.1935
2132 Popławska Franciszka	15.02.1886
2131 Popławska Anastazja	13.11.1930
2134 Porębna Władysława	1934
2133 Porębny Kazimierz	1936
4536 Porębska Wiktoria	6.03.1922
3463 Posłuszny Marian	22.10.1884
3464 Posłuszny Kazimierz	
2135 Postek Danuta	20.02.1930
2136 Postek Kazimiera	17.04.1926
2137 Postek Zofia	8.02.1902
3941 Potentas Zdzisława	12.12.1928
3940 Potentas Maria	20.07.1891
3939 Potentas Irena	25.04.1925
2138 Potocka Blanka	19.11.1907
2139 Potocki Janusz	21.12.1938
2141 Potrząsaj Halina	29.11.1926
2140 Potrząsaj Anna	1928
2142 Potrząsaj Oktawia	1931
4537 Poturaj Aleksander	1.02.1910

4541	Półchłopek Stefania	15.01.1936	2177	Puk Zbigniew	4.03.1934	2209	Ramotowska Bolesława	23.12.1908
4538	Półchłopek Henryka	20.07.1923	2178	Pukacki Marian	30.11.1894	2210	Ramotowska Celina	29.10.1930
4539	Półchłopek Jan	18.01.1931	2180	Pułkowska Janina	22.06.1925	2212	Ramotowski Tadeusz	28.05.1928
4540	Półchłopek Stanisław	15.08.1929	2179	Pułkowska Henryka	5.03.1902	2208	Ramotowski Antoni	12.06.1861
4542	Półchłopek Władysława	17.05.1926	4548	Pupa Krystyna	9.05.1932	2213	Raś Maria	1.11.1901
3466	Półtorak Józefa	25.08.1925	4547	Pupa Eugeniusz	17.12.1930	2214	Rebeczko Felicja	1936
3467	Półtorak Stefania	29.09.1929	4549	Pupa Zofia	17.12.1907	2215	Rebeczko Genowefa	29.06.1929
3465	Półtorak Aniela	4.06.1918	2182	Putro Benigna	8.02.1934	2216	Rebeczko Józef	28.08.1934
2143	Praczyk Maria	8.08.1900	2181	Putro Anna	24.07.1935	2217	Rebeczko Michał	19.04.1932
3943	Preisner Maria	15.02.1902	2183	Putro Helena	24.11.1913	4555	Rebeczko Maria	2.07.1909
3942	Preisner Janina	15.04.1922	2184	Pytasz Ignacy	7.04.1881	4556	Recht Ernest	1.04.1907
2144	Preiss Zofia	25.09.1897	3472	Pytlak Józefa	10.01.1928	3480	Regina Włodzimierz	22.11.1913
2146	Pronko Maria	20.05.1910	3471	Pytlak Bronisława	1.08.1925	2219	Reich Józefa	11.12.1891
2147	Pronko Maria	10.03.1918	3470	Pytlak Aniela	6.12.1898	2218	Reich Emilia	26.09.1930
2145	Pronko Helena	6.08.1935				3482	Reich Karolina	
2148	Przechodny Józefa	10.03.1929	3473	Raab Izrael	30.05.1900	3481	Reich Samuel	21.12.1894
2149	Przechodny Karolina	12.04.1894	2186	Raba Ryszard	12.01.1938	3484	Reichenbaum Sara	
2150	Przechodny Mikołaj	11.04.1888	2185	Raba Marian	13.04.1934	3483	Reichenbaum Erwin	8.07.1903
2152	Przełęska Marta	20.03.1934	2187	Rabiarz Henryka	16.02.1927	4557	Reid Krystyna	2.10.1924
2151	Przełęska Janina	3.01.1911	2188	Rabiarz Józef	1933	2230	Rękawek Krystyna	13.08.1927
2153	Przełęski Stanisław	7.05.1931	2189	Rabiarz Stanisław	10.04.1931	2229	Rękawek Janusz	20.06.1929
2154	Przybył Jadwiga	31.07.1926	3475	Rabinowicz Gutel	25.06.1887	2231	Rękawek Maria	22.07.1903
3944	Przybył Michał	14.08.1928	3476	Rabinowicz Tanchum	13.12.1917	2221	Rembisz Czesława	3.11.1909
	Przybyło Helena		3474	Rabinowicz Chana		2220	Rembisz Aniela	21.01.1936
	Przybyło Andrzej		3477	Rachsztajn Szmul	10.07.1921	2222	Rembisz Eugeniusz	6.06.1930
2155	Przybyłowski Stanisław	28.01.1926	3478	Rachsztajn Moszek	4.09.1916	2224	Respondowska Janina	25.06.1905
3945	Przybysz Jan Fr.	23.01.1909	4550	Raczyńska Danuta	25.05.1926	2223	Respondowska Eulalia	23.11.1931
3469	Przybyszewicz Rozalia		4551	Raczyńska Eleonora	18.12.1903	2225	Respondowska Otylia	27.10.1933
3468	Przybyszewicz Józef	17.01.1897	4553	Radkowska Stefania	5.01.1910	2226	Reszkowska Anna	26.07.1936
4543	Przybyszewska Danuta	30.04.1944	4552	Radkowska Barbara	4.02.1926	2227	Reszkowska Waleria	24.07.1909
4544	Przybyszewska Janina	28.03.1918	3946	Radoń Maria	2.11.1927	2228	Reszkowski Władysław	21.10.1943
2156	Przychodzeń Jadwiga	8.09.1929		Radoń Julianna	27.06.1913	3950	Reszyńska Julia-Maria	1.01.1906
2157	Przychodzka Regina	8.10.1908		Radoń Maria	2.08.1943	3949	Reszyńska Jadwiga	24.02.1933
2158	Przyrodzka Bolesława	1927	2191	Radymska Józefa	12.05.1906	3948	Reszyńska Felicja	24.12.1930
2159	Przyrocka Regina	1929	2192	Radymska Stanisława	11.07.1931	3951	Reszyński Stanisław	21.08.1940
2161	Przytocka Wanda	25.01.1907	2193	Radymski Tadeusz	30.08.1933	3952	Reszyński Zbigniew	24.04.1931
2160	Przytocka Irena	28.02.1928	2190	Radymski Jan	20.12.1906	3953	Reyman Władysław	23.04.1907
2162	Przytocki Jakub	13.09.1930	3947	Radziwonik Mikołaj	20.11.1919	2232	Ringler Helena	14.02.1908
2163	Przytomska Helena	14.03.1927	2194	Radziwonka Tadeusz	1930	2233	Robak Anna	12.08.1908
2164	Ptak Janina	15.03.1912	2196	Rafał Jadwiga	16.09.1930	3488	Rocniak Maria	15.08.1890
4545	Ptaszyńska Anna	16.01.1875	2197	Rafał Janusz	4.12.1931	3489	Rocniak Zofia	6.08.1925
2166	Puchalska Danuta	20.01.1924	2198	Rafał Wanda	20.04.1906	3487	Rocniak Jan	15.06.1888
2167	Puchalska Jadwiga	26.02.1926	2195	Rafał Halina	1.01.1926	3486	Rocniak Czesław	15.02.1930
2168	Puchalska Jolanta	29.10.1930	2199	Raginia Franciszka	12.06.1900	3485	Rocniak Anna	24.04.1928
2165	Puchalska Antonina	13.06.1896	2200	Raginia Mirosława	12.12.1931	2234	Rogacz Maria	13.04.1914
4546	Puchalska Helena	15.11.1930	2201	Raginia Rudolf	31.12.1934	3955	Rogalla Hieronim	11.09.1939
2169	Pucia Józef	24.10.1935	2202	Raginia Ryszard	7.04.1928	3954	Rogalla Franciszka	19.02.1908
2170	Pucia Katarzyna	1938	2203	Rajska Helena	2.03.1904	2236	Rogoża Nadzieja	15.08.1900
2171	Pucia Maria	15.08.1922	3479	Rajski Tadeusz	24.08.1937	2235	Rogoża Józef	10.04.1934
2172	Pucia Zofia	16.08.1930	2205	Rak Zofia	15.02.1908	2238	Rokicka Dobrosława	13.01.1903
2174	Puk Janina	24.10.1936	2204	Rak Teresa	29.08.1937	2239	Rokicka Genowefa	21.08.1908
2173	Puk Henryk	1938	2206	Rakowska Halina	4.04.1909	2240	Rokicka Grażyna	30.03.1929
2175	Puk Kazimiera	1931	2207	Rakowski Lechosław	27.08.1943	2237	Rokicka Adela	12.05.1932
2176	Puk Maria	25.08.1928	2211	Ramotowska Regina	24.05.1932	2241	Rokicka Irena	18.02.1934

2242 Rokicki Leon	5.02.1933
2244 Rolczewska Jadwiga	8.10.1925
2243 Rolczewska Agnieszka	1.01.1874
3491 Roman Jadwiga	
3490 Roman Jerzy	5.09.1891
2246 Romanowska Bogumiła	1930
2248 Romanowska Wacława	1937
2245 Romanowska Alicja	6.01.1929
3957 Romanowska Bożena	24.09.1922
3956 Romanowska Anna	6.02.1898
2247 Romanowski Leopold	1939
3958 Romejko Ryszard	30.05.1928
3959 Romejko Zofia	11.07.1923
3960 Rosada Zygmunt	23.04.1899
3492 Rosenberg Elżbieta	14.07.1902
2249 Rosenthal Maksymilian	19.08.1902
4559 Roszkowska Helena	30.04.1900
4558 Roszkowska Agnieszka	31.07.1930
3493 Rotter Salo	3.10.1907
2251 Rowińska Stanisława	8.08.1931
2250 Rowińska Anna	10.11.1887
4560 Rowińska Helena	07.1912
4561 Rowiński Tadeusz	23.02.1935
3495 Rozenbach Maria	
3496 Rozenbach Elżbieta	
3494 Rozenbach Ludwik	25.08.1895
Rozkuszko Janina	1930
Rozkuszko Józefa	1898
Rozkuszko Antonina	5.11.1926
Rozkuszko Bronisława	14.09.1928
Rozkuszko Stanisław	28.11.1896
2252 Rozwadowska Zofia	15.11.1907
4563 Rozwadowska Idalia	21.06.1927
4562 Rozwadowski Jan	27.01.1884
Rożańska Krystyna	12.07.1936
Rożańska Maria	05.07.1908
Rożański Marian	2.06.1930
2254 Rubczewska Klementyna	23.11.1907
2253 Rubczewska Elżbieta	20.08.1931
2255 Rubczewska Lucyna	6.07.1940
2256 Rubczewska Wanda	19.07.1928
3498 Rubinek Izrael	30.08.1899
3497 Rubinek Chil	26.11.1895
3499 Rubinowicz Zawel	19.04.1920
4564 Rubinsztejn Józef	12.04.1894
2257 Rudka Władysław	1936
2259 Rudkowska Julia	19.11.1930
2260 Rudkowska Natalia	20.06.1907
2258 Rudkowska Halina	7.10.1933
2261 Rudkowska Olga	12.03.1928
2262 Rudolf Józefa	1921
3500 Rudrof Zofia	25.05.1916
2263 Rudzewicz Marian	1930
2264 Rudzik Wojciech	5.02.1929
2265 Ruebenbauer Zofia	4.07.1883
2266 Rupar Anna	26.04.1874
2267 Rusiecka Anna	1904
2268 Rusiecka Irena	27.06.1926
2270 Rusiecka Maria	29.01.1888
2271 Rusiecki Leon	14.03.1930
2272 Rusiecki Zygmunt	1935
2269 Rusiecki Jerzy	30.06.1935
2273 Rusinek Leokadia	6.04.1934
2276 Ruszczak Bazyli	1930
2275 Ruszczak Anastazja	1904
3501 Ruszczak Anna	5.05.1904
3502 Ruszczak Józef	1.08.1888
4565 Ruszczak Jan	11.05.1944
2277 Ruszczyc Wanda	24.05.1918
3503 Rutenberg Samuel	29.05.1898
3505 Rutenberg Jerzy	
3504 Rutenberg Szejna	
2278 Rutkiewicz Halina	14.07.1932
2279 Rutkiewicz Iwona	23.05.1927
2280 Rutkiewicz Maria	6.12.1904
2283 Rutkowska Wiktoria	11.04.1884
2281 Rutkowski Jan	10.12.1923
2282 Rutkowski Stefan	12.07.1927
2284 Rybakowicz Franciszka	2.04.1887
2285 Rybakowicz Regina	14.08.1923
4566 Rybicka Anna	15.05.1904
4567 Rybicka Emilia	23.12.1926
4568 Rybicka Eugenia	1.12.1937
4569 Rybicka Stanisława	15.06.1930
2286 Rycak Anna	9.10.1925
2287 Rycak Franciszek	1931
2288 Rycak Rozalia	24.04.1928
2289 Rycerz Helena	10.10.1929
2290 Rycerz Maria	5.11.1925
4572 Rychlińska Stanisława	15.11.1901
4570 Rychlińska Irena	10.03.1928
4571 Rychliński Ryszard	4.01.1932
3506 Rychter Abram	21.08.1919
2291 Ryciak Halina	22.01.1927
2292 Ryciak Jadwiga	2.09.1925
2293 Ryciak Leokadia	24.09.1903
2294 Rydel Genowefa	31.05.1926
2295 Rydel Irena	6.01.1929
2296 Rydza Piotr	1929
2297 Rygiel Janina	14.12.1920
2298 Rygiel Kazimiera	28.04.1929
2299 Rygiel Teresa	3.08.1932
2300 Rygiel Zofia	1926
Rykowska Elżbieta	19.09.1926
2301 Rymar Janina	14.07.1923
2302 Rymar Józefa	19.03.1929
4573 Rymarkiewicz Władysława	29.11.1884
2303 Rymarska Stanisława	20.10.1929
2304 Ryszewska Anna	26.07.1899
Ryszyńska Julia	1906
Ryszyńska Felicja	1932
Ryszyńska Jadwiga	1933
Ryszyński Zbigniew	1931
Ryszyński Stanisław	1940
4575 Rytelewska Janina	18.07.1931
4574 Rytelewska Jadwiga	14.01.1936
2305 Rytlewska Irena	18.01.1927
3507 Ryżewska Olga	26.02.1907
Ryżewska Anna	6.11.1903
Ryżewska Wanda	26.04.1928
Ryżewska Maria	15.06.1932
2306 Rządzińska Irena	16.09.1924
2310 Sadowska Regina	7.01.1933
2307 Sadowska Helena	1.02.1929
2308 Sadowska Jadwiga	1906
2309 Sadowski Jan	12.05.1936
2311 Sahanek Anna	29.08.1924
2312 Sahanek Maria	16.07.1893
2313 Sajdak Helena	11.09.1905
2314 Sajdak Janina	1.11.1924
2316 Sałata Jerzy	21.03.1930
2317 Sałata Romualda	1933
2315 Salmonowicz Maria	24.06.1906
3961 Samocka Janina	8.04.1927
2318 Sanocki Czesław	1931
2319 Saplis Zofia	15.07.1899
3508 Sarnowiec Franciszek	13.02.1892
2320 Sasadeusz Olga	10.07.1897
2321 Sasadeusz Witold	24.05.1928
2325 Sawicka Gabriela	12.04.1928
2322 Sawicka Antonina	19.03.1908
2323 Sawicka Bogusława	16.12.1933
2333 Sawicka Wanda	18.06.1935
2332 Sawicka Regina	20.01.1932
2326 Sawicka Józefa	19.03.1897
2327 Sawicka Józefa	19.09.1929
2328 Sawicka Krystyna	9.05.1934
2330 Sawicka Marianna	27.09.1911
4576 Sawicka Barbara	15.08.1924
4577 Sawicka Stefania	26.12.1900
2331 Sawicki Otton	10.10.1934
2329 Sawicki Marian	6.10.1943
2324 Sawicki Bolesław	13.11.1931
2334 Sawicki Wiesław	1.01.1939
2335 Sawicz Helena	16.03.1916
2336 Sawicz Marian	1935
2337 Sawicz Weronika	27.03.1872
3964 Sawko Wanda	4.04.1933
3962 Sawko Felicjan	17.05.1937
3963 Sawko Franciszka	14.02.1906
3965 Sawko Zygmunt	18.09.1935

2339	Scazighino Roger	20.07.1935	2369	Sikona Halina	30.11.1925	3979	Smal Bolesław	14.06.1914
2338	Scazighino Feliks	3.12.1933	2370	Sikona Zofia	14.04.1935	3980	Smal Janina	20.12.1921
3509	Schonbrenner Stefan	5.11.1900	2371	Sikora Genowefa	3.04.1930	3981	Smal Tadeusz	1930
3510	Selzer Markus	5.12.1909	3969	Sikorski Zdzisław	18.04.1913	2406	Smalewska Józefa	21.02.1865
3511	Selzer Kaete		2372	Silaus Stanisław	21.01.1929	2407	Smalewska Maria	16.01.1903
2340	Semak Stefania	18.12.1894	2373	Silber Erwin	6.01.1917	2410	Smoczyńska Halina	5.05.1936
2341	Sendziuk Karol	1936	2374	Simińska Regina	1930	2409	Smoczyńska Genowefa	12.04.1904
3512	Serdeczna Maria	6.12.1927	3970	Simińska Irena	30.09.1927	2408	Smoczyńska Danuta	4.06.1938
4579	Sereda Bronisław	2.10.1932	3971	Simiński Jan	3.05.1937	3982	Smolag Maria	2.02.1902
4580	Sereda Ewa	6.05.1912	3972	Simiński Zenon	5.12.1935	3983	Smoter Aniela	21.09.1910
2344	Serednicka Maria	6.08.1882	2375	Sioma Józef	10.11.1900	3524	Smutek Julian	20.02.1923
2343	Serednicka Karolina	20.07.1919	2377	Siostrzykowska Olga	20.08.1903	2413	Snastyń Ludwika	8.05.1888
2342	Serednicki Franciszek	10.10.1939	2376	Siostrzykowska Helena	20.10.1927	2414	Snastyń Mieczysław	30.03.1929
2345	Seretna Aniela	6.03.1892	2381	Sipika Leokadia	9.02.1933	2412	Snastyń Lidia	6.02.1916
2346	Seretna Anna	25.04.1924	2379	Sipika Julia	10.03.1901	2411	Snastyń Irena	24.10.1924
2347	Seretna Stefania	1932	2378	Sipika Janina	10.08.1922	2415	Sobecka Emilia	22.04.1928
2348	Serko Sergiusz	15.09.1926	2382	Sipika Maria	2.07.1929	2416	Sobiech Stefania	8.09.1922
3513	Serocińska Helena	3.02.1907	2380	Sipika Kazimierz	5.02.1928	2420	Sobocińska Genowefa	3.01.1930
2350	Serwacki Hieronim	6.07.1887	2383	Siring Izabella	12.04.1933	2418	Sobocińska Apolonia	25.06.1923
3515	Sężoł Łucja	6.06.1931	2384	Siring Maria	15.08.1906	2419	Sobocińska Ewa	24.12.1892
3514	Sężoł Eleonora	6.01.1906	2385	Sitko Kazimiera	1.09.1928	2417	Sobociński Andrzej	22.11.1880
2354	Siara Stefania	17.04.1900		Sito Bożena	8.08.1932	4589	Sobol Julia	7.07.1900
2352	Siara Karol	28.10.1929		Sito Franciszka	29.01.1900	4590	Sobol Zdzisława	24.12.1928
2353	Siara Katarzyna	5.11.1875		Sito Jerzy	8.11.1934	4588	Sobol Czesława	23.09.1927
2351	Siara Irena	9.12.1930	2387	Siwek Jadwiga	31.10.1926	2423	Sobolewska Zofia	8.09.1894
2356	Siatka Władysław	1930	2386	Siwek Helena	17.07.1928	2422	Sobolewska Sabina	17.10.1930
2355	Siatka Anna	30.12.1926	2390	Skarzeńska Rozalia	4.10.1902	3985	Sobolewska Irena	8.05.1931
3521	Siberpfenig Zachariasz	23.11.1902	2389	Skarzeńska Maria	8.09.1929	3986	Sobolewska Lidia	28.07.1928
2357	Sibińska Bożena	21.03.1927	2388	Skarzeński Józef	1933	3987	Sobolewska Malwina	19.04.1905
2358	Sibiński Witold	1.11.1928	3973	Skibińska Anna	2.05.1938	3984	Sobolewska Daniela	17.01.1927
2359	Sidoryk Michał	3.10.1928	3975	Skibińska Maria	23.01.1905	2421	Sobolewski Kazimierz	17.03.1892
2360	Sidoryk Tadeusz	15.01.1929	3974	Skibiński Jerzy	2.04.1936	3988	Sobolewski Zygmunt	19.04.1938
2361	Sieczka Jan	15.03.1892	3976	Skomorowski Antoni	17.01.1897	3989	Socha Maria	4.12.1926
2364	Siedlecka Maria	2.02.1902	2392	Skóra Maria	1.09.1901	2424	Sokołowska Bożena	27.07.1927
3517	Siedlecka Irena	9.03.1918	2393	Skóra Maria	19.10.1930	2425	Sokołowska Maria	1.11.1902
3516	Siedlecka Felicja	21.11.1888	2391	Skowroński Kazimierz	19.03.1930	2426	Sokołowski Mieczysław	6.03.1923
2363	Siedlecki Jan	11.03.1928	2394	Skrobot Józef	15.10.1905	2427	Solecka Danuta	21.05.1938
2362	Siedlecki Bronisław	19.07.1930	2396	Skrzat Stanisław	23.05.1930	3525	Solecka Stefania	19.04.1911
2365	Siedler Konstantyna	5.09.	2395	Skrzat Anna	26.07.1907	3990	Sołoducha Leokadia	22.07.1924
3519	Siedmiograj Jadwiga	10.12.1912	2397	Skrzat Tadeusz	13.07.1936	3991	Sołoducha Pelagia	18.10.1885
3520	Siedmiograj Wanda	2.02.1870	2399	Skrzeczkowska Helena	7.06.1912	2428	Sołtan Jan	1941
3518	Siedmiograj Barbara	24.04.1939	2398	Skrzeczkowska Barbara	4.03.1939	2429	Sołtan Józef	1929
3966	Sielewicz Halina	15.01.1932	4586	Skrzypecka Antonina-Wanda	1.07.1943	4591	Sołtan Maria	2.09.1925
3967	Sielewicz Janina	6.03.1910	2400	Skrzypecki Adam	23.10.1915	4593	Sołtan Rozalia	27.08.1907
3968	Sielewicz Witold	17.09.1937	2401	Skrzypek Anna	24.06.1929	4592	Sołtan Romualda	15.04.1936
4581	Sienkowska Anastazja	15.05.1906	2402	Skrzypek Józefa	24.10.1927	2430	Sołtys Jan	1872
4582	Sienkowska Jadwiga	13.08.1926	3522	Skrzypek Maria	29.11.1896	2431	Soroko Aleksander	1.03.1892
4583	Sienkowska Narcyza	11.04.1935	3977	Skrzypek Bronisława	21.09.1923	3527	Sosnowska Maria	14.06.1905
4584	Sienkowski Piotr	2.02.1904	3523	Sławatycka Marianna	8.11.1903	3526	Sosnowska Emilia	10.08.1880
2349	Sierocińska Aleksandra	27.02.1933	4587	Słodkowska Leokadia	13.12.1871	2433	Sowa Weronika	1930
2366	Sierociuch Krystyna	25.08.1925	2403	Słucki Teodor	9.05.1899	2432	Sowa Maria	29.01.1928
4585	Siewierska Jadwiga	23.05.1917	2405	Sługocka Stanisława	25.12.1931	3992	Sowa Katarzyna	20.12.1908
2367	Sikona Alicja	30.11.1925	2404	Sługocka Bronisława	2.02.1902	3993	Sowa Ryszard	1.01.1938
2368	Sikona Emilia	30.04.1894	3978	Smal Aniela	1887	2434	Sówka Aleksandra	10.10.1914

2435 Sówka Marianna	15.03.1880	4614 Stelmaszczyk Aniela	10.03.1905	2507 Suchocka Stefania	17.07.1936
4014 Spałek Bolesław	1936	2462 Stelmaszyk Magdalena	20.05.1893	2508 Suchocka Stefania	1932
4595 Spława-Neyman Michalina	1.10.1914	2463 Stepaniuk Anastazja	10.03.1904	2504 Suchocka Anna	11.11.1907
4594 Spława-Neyman Aleksander	14.09.1936	2464 Stępniewska Leokadia	11.10.1883	2506 Suchocka Sława-Maria	27.07.1939
4596 Spława-Neyman Walery	4.02.1935	3995 Sterlińska Anna	24.07.1926	2505 Suchocka Jadwiga	21.11.1910
2437 Sroka Mieczysław	1930	3534 Sterna Janina	14.02.1940	2509 Suchocka Teresa	10.05.1938
2436 Sroka Józefa	8.09.1902	3536 Sterna Władysław	15.03.1931	2511 Sudnik Genowefa	19.03.1926
4598 Sroka Helena	19.03.1923	3535 Sterna Maria	20.08.1912	2514 Sudnik Zenon	14.12.1929
4597 Sroka Bolesława	20.10.1927	3537 Sternbach Edward	3.01.1874	2513 Sudnik Waleria	20.11.1898
4600 Sroka Kazimierz	4.09.1933	3538 Sternbach Klara		2512 Sudnik Tadeusz	4.11.1938
4599 Sroka Józefa	10.04.1925	3539 Sternbach Ludwik	12.12.1909	2510 Sudnik Franciszek	10.12.1932
2438 Stachoń Cecylia	13.09.1904	3540 Sternlicht Hugo		2516 Sudoł Antoni	1873
2439 Stachyra Helena	2.02.1906	2466 Stolarska Maria	2.02.1904	2517 Sudoł Stefania	2.03.1919
2440 Stachyra Stanisław	2.11.1901	2465 Stolarski Janusz	20.08.1935	2515 Sudoł Anna	1887
2441 Stala Agnieszka	30.08.1931	3996 Stoncel Maria	11.11.1919	2518 Sukiennik Cecylia	15.01.1933
2443 Stala Józefa	2.11.1912	2467 Stopa Stanisław	1931	2519 Sukiennik Maria	24.01.1898
2442 Stala Barbara	21.01.1934	2469 Strachowska Janina	8.10.1928	2520 Sukiennik Maria	10.01.1930
4606 Stanisławska Regina	26.08.1924	2470 Strachowska Julia	10.06.1904	2521 Sukiennik Mieczysław	22.05.1928
4603 Stanisławska Maria	3.09.1919	2471 Strachowski Roman	15.03.1930	2522 Sułek Anna	19.10.1929
4602 Stanisławska Józefa	4.09.1902	2468 Strachowski Edmund	30.06.1932	2524 Sułkowska Janina	14.08.1914
4607 Stanisławska Stanisława	14.07.1932	2473 Strelau Jadwiga	12.10.1929	2526 Sułkowska Stefania	23.02.1901
4601 Stanisławska Janina	26.09.1928	2472 Strelau Franciszka	1934	2527 Sułkowska Teresa	15.10.1936
4605 Stanisławski Mirosław	15.07.1939	2474 Strelau Zuzanna	8.02.1928	2528 Sułkowski Witold	30.08.1934
4604 Stanisławski Mieczysław	4.03.1934	2477 Strojkowska Stanisława	28.12.1903	2525 Sułkowski Józef	25.03.1932
2446 Stankiewicz Stanisława	31.03.1888	2478 Strojkowska Zofia	22.05.1936	2523 Sułkowski Jan	16.05.1887
2445 Stankiewicz Julia	22.05.1877	2476 Strojkowska Danuta	11.11.1931	2530 Surdyka Zofia	14.07.1927
2447 Stankiewicz Wanda	24.02.1922	2475 Strojkowska Aleksandra	13.01.1927	2529 Surdyka Teodora	17.09.1931
2444 Stankiewicz Anna	17.07.1920	2480 Strupczewska Jadwiga	19.01.1931	2531 Surman Antoni	17.11.1937
2450 Stanko Maria	17.03.1913	2479 Strupczewska Czesława	1895	2532 Surman Genowefa	24.09.1915
2448 Stanko Bogumiła	20.04.1939	2482 Struś Czesława	1930	2533 Surman Józefa	5.04.1934
2451 Stanko Zdzisława	30.08.1934	2484 Struś Stanisław	1936	2534 Surman Ludwika	16.03.1934
2449 Stanko Czesława	15.07.1930	2483 Struś Katarzyna	22.09.1905	2535 Surowicz Zbigniew	14.12.1927
2453 Starczewska Rozalia	25.08.1931	2481 Strusik Janina	24.05.1927	2537 Surowiec Leopold	26.07.1928
2454 Starczewski Walenty	1935	4615 Strutyńska Stanisława	27.09.1891	2536 Surowiec Eleonora	25.12.1926
2452 Starczewski Michał	1934	2485 Strycharz Antonina	25.07.1909	2538 Surowiec Maria	15.05.1898
3994 Staruszkiewicz Franciszek	7.07.1917	2487 Strycharz Janina	16.06.1932	4617 Suszko Mikołaj	6.11.1899
4608 Staruszkiewicz Krystyna	2.10.1944	2486 Strycharz Halina	5.09.1929	2629 Suszko Helena	6.10.1926
2455 Staszczak Anna	13.08.1901	2488 Stryjska Sabina	8.12.1922	2630 Suszko Irena	15.07.1924
2456 Staszczak Łucja	30.11.1928	2489 Strzyżewski Bronisław	1929	2631 Suszko Piotr	26.11.1930
2457 Staszczak Maria	27.05.1915	2492 Studzińska Malwina	20.03.1901	2632 Suszko Stanisława	02.02.1902
3531 Statter Herman	31.08.1888	2490 Studzińska Alfreda	4.06.1925	2539 Suszyńska Aleksandra	4.11.1932
3530 Statter Małgorzata		2491 Studzińska Leonarda	20.03.1927	2542 Suszyńska Maria	7.11.1934
3529 Statter Alfred	22.07.1912	2493 Studzińska Maria	8.12.1925	2541 Suszyńska Jadwiga	7.07.1930
2458 Stawicka Maria	26.01.1904	2494 Styburski Wiktor	7.05.1902	2540 Suszyńska Jadwiga	2.01.1902
4609 Stec Zofia	10.02.1915	2496 Styczyńska Irena	12.12.1912	2544 Suszyński Mikołaj	30.03.1929
2459 Steckiewicz Stanisława	24.05.1892	2495 Styczyńska Ewa	14.08.1939	4618 Suszyński Bogdan	25.05.1944
2460 Stefanowicz Eugeniusz	1932	2497 Stypuła Wiesław	18.02.1931	2543 Suszyński-Ihnatowicz Mikołaj	19.12.1903
4610 Stefanowicz Aniela	15.08.1926	2498 Sucharzewska Anna	5.12.1929	2545 Suwała Genowefa	28.11.1929
4611 Stefanowicz Antonina	16.02.1901	2499 Sucharzewska Helena	27.12.1902	4619 Syberyjska Anna	2.02.1903
4612 Stefanowicz Zofia	11.07.1927	2500 Sucharzewska Jadwiga	11.11.1932	4620 Syberyjska Honorata	21.03.1926
3532 Stefański Marian	17.11.1909	2502 Suchecka Daniela	17.04.1925	2548 Sydor Tekla	17.08.1912
4613 Stefański Tadeusz	21.09.1944	2501 Suchecka Alicja	21.01.1928	2547 Sydor Michał	25.12.1936
3533 Steinbach Gizela	24.01.1914	2503 Suchecki Zbigniew	14.08.1929	2546 Sydor Eugenia	16.02.1933
2461 Stelmaszczuk Władysława	1930	4616 Suchecki Stanisław	15.11.1896	3997 Sylin Aleksander	6.05.1890

2550	Sypuła Maria	8.08.1906	4628	Szczurowski Bogusław	1.01.1925	3548	Szpiro Kopel	22.02.1904
2549	Sypuła Franciszek	1.02.1936	2583	Szczypek Stanisław	29.04.1898	3549	Szpiro Debora	
3998	Syroka Władysław	7.07.1885	2584	Szczyrska Gabriela	20.06.1902	2614	Szpitun Serafina	8.04.1914
2551	Sytnik Jan	15.05.1892	2586	Szczyrska Maria	22.12.1928	2613	Szpitun Ryszard	2.01.1936
4621	Szablewska Cecylia	30.01.1878	2585	Szczyrski Jan	12.02.1931	3528	Szprung Joachim	23.01.1893
4622	Szablewski Jerzy	29.03.1910	4629	Szeląg Anna	1.09.1939	4016	Szpyrka Janina	15.07.1934
3999	Szablicka Joanna	11.07.1937	4630	Szeląg Maria	2.02.1905	4017	Szpyrka Tadeusz	25.07.1930
4000	Szablicka Wiktoria	17.10.1917	2589	Szelągowska Wanda	18.09.1927	4015	Szpyrka Ewa	25.07.1888
2552	Szabunia Cezaria	28.01.1905	2588	Szelągowska Stanisława	2.02.1908	4018	Szretter Zofia	14.03.1918
2553	Szadbej Elżbieta	24.02.1888	2587	Szelągowska Danuta	4.12.1930	4019	Sztela Maria	20.12.1930
2554	Szafnicka Józefa	12.10.1893	3544	Szelechow Teresa	11.04.1913	4020	Sztela Władysława	20.11.1927
2555	Szafran Jadwiga	27.06.1901	3543	Szelechow Mikołaj	9.06.1904	2616	Sztengel Wiktor	17.11.1940
2557	Szafranek Helena	5.02.1898	2591	Szemis Tadeusz	30.05.1937	2615	Sztengel Helena	17.06.1912
2556	Szafranek Halina	23.04.1925	2590	Szemis Józefa	14.01.1906	3550	Sztrauch Berek	10.07.1901
2559	Szafrańska Halina	22.10.1924	4011	Szemis Wirginia	15.11.1919	3551	Sztybrych Jadwiga	17.12.1908
2560	Szafrańska Janina	4.09.1926	4009	Szemis Janina	2.05.1912	2619	Szuber Wiktoria	13.06.1902
2558	Szafrańska Emilia	5.04.1896	4010	Szemis Luba	15.10.1894	2617	Szuber Kazimierz	2.09.1934
2561	Szagidewicz Ewa	20.09.1911	2592	Szenbir Józef	15.05.1883	2618	Szuber Maria	20.08.1932
4003	Szajowska Zofia	27.01.1910		Szeptycki Zbigniew		4636	Szuberla Józefa	13.10.1923
4001	Szajowska Janina	2.04.1940		Szeptycka Stefania	09.06.1907	2620	Szubert Czesława	3.10.1929
4002	Szajowski Krzysztof	30.01.1936		Szeptycka Janina	08.02.1937	2621	Szubert Mieczysław	1932
2562	Szałajko Tadeusz	11.07.1928		Szeptycki Zbigniew	01.12.1934	4637	Szubert Danuta	4.08.1931
2564	Szamborska Janina	29.01.1929	3545	Szerc Anna	18.12.1911	4638	Szubert Helena	4.12.1927
2565	Szamborska Zofia	6.01.1906	2593	Szerszenowicz Janina	1938	2622	Szufla Stanisław	1.03.1897
2563	Szamborski Edward	13.12.1936	2594	Szerszenowicz Wanda	1937	2624	Szul Zuzanna	11.08.1922
3541	Szapiro Mowsza	7.05.1911	2595	Szewczuk Aleksandra	20.03.1886	2623	Szul Tadeusz	12.06.1915
4623	Szarejko Anna	26.08.1912	2599	Szewczyk Mieczysław	1930	3552	Szul Zdzisław	22.11.1943
4624	Szarejko Janina	28.04.1926	2598	Szewczyk Maria	1.05.1932	4021	Szulc Walentyna	15.08.1907
4625	Szarejko Józef	15.10.1900	2597	Szewczyk Janina	10.02.1924	4022	Szumczyk Aleksander	19.09.1916
2566	Szaruga Erazm	17.03.1929	2600	Szewczyk Stanisława	5.06.1900	4023	Szumlańska Czesława	10.09.1904
4006	Szczanowska Zofia	24.08.1897	2601	Szewczyk Stanisława	4.05.1929	2626	Szuprowicz Jadwiga	13.07.1926
4004	Szczanowska Helena	6.10.1924	2596	Szewczyk Jan	16.06.1934	2625	Szuprowicz Feliksa	13.07.1903
4005	Szczanowski Stanisław	18.09.1893	2604	Szlachta Wiktoria	9.05.1900	2627	Szustek Edward	30.06.1898
4627	Szczawińska Stanisława	20.02.1898	2602	Szlachta Antoni	5.07.1930	2628	Szustowska Anna	18.07.1894
4626	Szczawiński Jerzy	15.05.1933	2603	Szlachta Felicja	12.02.1928	4639	Szutkowska Irena	11.10.1916
2573	Szczech Genowefa	1928	4634	Szlamka Krystyna	4.04.1933	3554	Szuttenbach Stefania	1.07.1904
2567	Szczepaniak Maria	26.06.1907	4632	Szlamka Janina	23.04.1937	3553	Szuttenbach Halina	5.02.1923
2568	Szczepańska Janina	22.06.1922	4631	Szlamka Barbara-Lucyna	4.12.1943	2633	Szwaglis Anna	20.06.1898
2569	Szczepańska Zuzanna	11.08.1896	4635	Szlamka Maria	8.10.1911	2634	Szwaglis Anna	29.11.1923
2570	Szczepańska Zuzanna	22.09.1925	4633	Szlamka Józef	4.08.1935	2635	Szwarcewicz Grażyna	20.01.1939
3542	Szczepańska Maria	15.10.1910	2605	Szmigielska Józefa	1936	2636	Szwarcewicz Halina	1929
4007	Szczepańska Anna	1930	2677	Szniger Jan	11.05.1869	2637	Szwarcewicz Maria	20.06.1905
4008	Szczepańska Władysława	10.07.1924	2676	Szniger Henryk	28.07.1931	2638	Szwarcewicz Zyta	4.06.1926
2571	Szczerbicka Agata	24.08.1887	2606	Szołkowska Barbara	21.05.1927	2639	Szyk Helena	30.03.1910
2572	Szczerbicki Tadeusz	19.02.1930	2607	Szołomicka Leokadia	19.01.1917	2640	Szyk Marian	29.09.1934
2574	Szczęsnowicz Wiktor	21.05.1889	3546	Szostak Danuta	10.02.1932	2641	Szyk Zofia	11.02.1892
2575	Szczęsnowicz Zofia	10.06.1908	3547	Szostak Helena	8.05.1926	2643	Szykier Jerzy	1928
2576	Szczucińska Eleonora	13.04.1909	2608	Szostakowska Jadwiga	15.10.1880	2644	Szykier Stella	14.03.1923
2578	Szczucińska Krystyna	20.06.1938	2609	Szot Marian	2.12.1932	2642	Szykier Fryda	21.03.1897
2577	Szczuciński Janusz	20.06.1936	4012	Szpadowska Aleksandra	26.11.1910	2646	Szyłak Longina	1934
2579	Szczur Adam	1934	4013	Szpadowska Irena	24.01.1930	2647	Szyłak Narcyz	6.06.1936
2580	Szczur Franciszek	1937	2611	Szpan Eugeniusz	22.04.1928	2645	Szyłak Gertruda	5.09.1929
2581	Szczur Helena	1927	2612	Szpan Jadwiga	17.11.1899	2655	Szymańska Kornela	25.10.1939
2582	Szczur Maria	20.08.1925	2610	Szpan Alicja	7.03.1924	2654	Szymańska Karolina	26.09.1910

2653	Szymańska Janina	27.09.1912	2678	Świątkowska Irena	12.07.1918	2714	Tomas Maria	26.01.1886
2652	Szymańska Franciszka	15.08.1930	4028	Świda Janina	19.10.1919	2718	Tomasiewicz Władysława	2.09.1902
2651	Szymańska Emilia	7.02.1929	4029	Świda Krystyna	4.12.1938	2716	Tomasiewicz Helena	1.10.1924
2656	Szymańska Stanisława	8.05.1931	4658	Świder Monika	11.12.1925	2717	Tomasiewicz Janina	10.02.1926
2649	Szymańska Czesława	15.09.1928	2679	Świerdzewska Genowefa	15.06.1922	4664	Tomasiewicz Kazimierz	2.10.1902
4641	Szymańska Józefa	19.10.1916	2681	Świergoń Marianna	21.01.1919	2719	Tomaszewska Krystyna	8.05.1932
2650	Szymański Edward	25.05.1940	2682	Świergoń Zofia	15.05.1878	2720	Tomaszewska Stanisława	7.11.1910
2648	Szymański Bogusław	1.09.1937	2680	Świergoń Antoni	8.05.1874	2721	Tomaszewski Leszek	5.07.1936
4640	Szymański Edmund-Jan	24.09.1942	2683	Świeżawska Maria	16.05.1902	2723	Tomczak Józefa	24.02.1906
4024	Szymborska Aleksandra	19.09.1910	2685	Świstak Jan	28.01.1882	2722	Tomczak Henryk	1.01.1935
4025	Szymborska Janina	13.01.1936	2684	Świstak Anna	15.05.1892	2724	Tomczak Tadeusz	27.10.1937
2657	Szymborski Adam	1929				2726	Tomolonis Stanisława	9.05.1929
2658	Szymel Anna	5.05.1891	2686	Tabaczyńska Łucja	14.05.1904	2725	Tomolonis Jadwiga	15.04.1936
2659	Szymel Bogusława	15.05.1930	2687	Tabaczyńska Janina	12.04.1929	2728	Topolnicka Krystyna	1.09.1927
2660	Szymel Cecylia	22.11.1901	2688	Tabaczyńska Irena	13.07.1930	2727	Topolnicka Jadwiga	16.03.1888
2662	Szymel Julia	16.02.1876	2689	Tabor Czesław	3.05.1938	4666	Topolnicka Janina	23.03.1923
2661	Szymel Helena	16.06.1907	2690	Tabor Wanda	11.03.1899	4665	Topolnicki Aleksander	17.08.1921
2664	Szypnicka Danuta	8.01.1930	4659	Tajchner Markus	14.01.1893	2730	Trawińska Halina	13.04.1936
2663	Szypnicki Bogdan	7.04.1932	3559	Tajkef Lejzer	31.08.1903	2729	Trawińska Antonina	14.12.1911
2665	Szypnicki Waldemar	27.10.1930	2691	Taramina Maria	1930	4033	Trella Bogusław	20.03.1932
4645	Szysz Nadzieja	15.03.1930	2692	Taramina Stefania	01.1907	4034	Trella Stefania-Józefa	17.06.1899
4642	Szysz Aleksy	6.10.1885	2693	Tarasiewicz Aleksandra	3.07.1899	4035	Trella Urszula	20.09.1926
4646	Szysz Stefania	1885	2694	Tarasiewicz Aleksander	2.03.1935	2731	Trębacz Jerzy	1935
4643	Szysz Eugeniusz	20.02.1933	2696	Tarnogórska Jadwiga	26.12.1904	4667	Trębacz Ludmiła	27.01.1915
4644	Szysz Mikołaj	20.04.1920	2695	Tarsiewicz Maria	27.03.1931	4668	Trochimowicz Wanda	5.03.1926
4647	Szyszkin Anna	22.02.1886	2697	Tatarczuk Irena	24.12.1924	3564	Trojanowska Anna	30.08.1898
4648	Szyszkin Anna	17.08.1915	2698	Tatur Remigiusz	11.09.1933	3565	Trojanowski Jan	8.09.1886
4650	Szyszko Irena	2.01.1916	4660	Tebinka Artur	26.10.1883	2736	Truksa Romana	27.07.1927
4651	Szyszko Krystyna	9.01.1935	3562	Teichler Blima		2732	Truksa Janusz	21.03.1934
4649	Szyszko Bohdan	2.01.1939	3563	Teichler Natan		2733	Truksa Lesław	19.03.1929
			3561	Teichler Jakub	26.09.1902	2734	Truksa Maria	14.02.1900
2667	Ścibek Leontyna	9.06.1934	3560	Tejkef Nelly		2735	Truksa Mieczysława	2.01.1925
2666	Ścibek Jadwiga	15.10.1901	2699	Tełowska Antonina	12.10.1907	2737	Truksa Zofia	9.04.1931
2668	Ścibek Waleria	4.04.1932	2700	Tełowski Bogdan	17.12.1937	2738	Trzaska Bronisław	23.12.1936
4578	Ścibek Zygmunt	20.12.1893	2702	Terlecka Wiktoria	24.12.1903	2741	Trzaska Lidia	13.03.1940
2669	Ściborska Irena	4.03.1928	2701	Terlecka Jadwiga	15.10.1928	2739	Trzaska Jadwiga	12.10.1905
2670	Ściborska Maria	6.02.1902	2703	Terlecki Teodozjusz	1.01.1879	2740	Trzaska Lech	17.03.1934
2671	Ściborski Roman	18.04.1938	2704	Tetkowska Aleksandra	1880	2744	Trzciankowska Stefania	25.09.1930
2672	Śliwińska Olga	17.04.1922	4030	Tetmajer Anna	1.02.1874	2742	Trzciankowska Bronisława	25.02.1929
2673	Śliwińska Stefania	3.03.1907	2706	Tęcza Maria	1.01.1928	2743	Trzciankowska Katarzyna	29.10.1903
4653	Śliwińska Halina	12.04.1930	2705	Tęcza Katarzyna	23.04.1904	4669	Trześniowska Emilia	20.08.1908
4652	Śliwińska Antonina	13.06.1906	4661	Tiachow Jerzy	14.10.1899	4670	Trześniowski Jan	14.04.1936
4654	Śliwiński Tadeusz	23.09.1931	2707	Tijewska Lidia	9.08.1898	2764	Tucholska Elżbieta	8.02.1927
3556	Ślusarczyk Stefan	22.08.1929	2708	Tijewska Regina	13.08.1927	2765	Tucholska Józefa	14.03.1892
3555	Ślusarczyk Aniela	7.08.1904	2709	Tijewski Bronisław	22.10.1888	4671	Tukanowicz Zofia	25.01.1896
4657	Ślusarczyk Salomea	4.11.1886	2710	Tkaczek Franciszek	25.01.1909	2745	Tuliszka Stefania	24.05.1893
4655	Ślusarczyk Józefa	17.06.1924	4662	Tłumacz Agnieszka	20.01.1903	2746	Tuliszka Tadeusz	12.12.1932
4656	Ślusarczyk Ludwika	8.01.1928	2713	Todryk Michalina	1896	2747	Tuliszka Zygfryd	18.06.1928
3558	Śmigielska Janina	12.07.1932	2711	Todryk Bolesław	15.05.1885	2748	Tumanow Weronika	4.05.1931
3557	Śmigielska Helena	25.05.1930	2712	Todryk Bolesława	20.06.1937	2749	Turczyńska Eufemia	7.03.1906
2674	Śniadkowski Kazimierz	1933	4663	Tomanek Alfred	4.05.1900	2750	Turczyński Wacław	6.11.1936
2675	Śniadkowski Ryszard	1936	4032	Tomaniak Julia	16.09.1894	2751	Turczyński Zdzisław	20.02.1934
4027	Świątek Maria	11.05.1924	4031	Tomaniak Janina	22.12.1929	2753	Turek Helena	24.02.1924
4026	Świątek Genowefa	13.12.1929	2715	Tomas Wanda	18.03.1924	2754	Turek Regina	17.08.1896

2752 Turek Bolesław	10.03.1931
2756 Turowicz Leontyna	1.11.1899
2755 Turowicz Janina	8.03.1929
2757 Turowska Zofia	19.08.1928
2759 Turska Lidia	8.09.1902
2758 Turska Julia	1.11.1927
2760 Turski Mirosław	1.01.1936
2761 Twardowska Jadwiga	30.10.1921
4673 Twarowska Janina-Wanda	30.08.1905
4672 Twarowska Bożena	15.05.1934
Tworogal Danuta	26.10.1930
Tworogal Stanisława	08.12.1906
Tworogal Zbigniew	26.09.1935
4675 Tybulewicz Elżbieta	19.11.1904
4674 Tybulewicz Albin	1.03.1929
4676 Tybulewicz Oktawian	20.11.1931
2762 Tybura Marek	20.10.1935
2763 Tybura Zofia	9.05.1907
2766 Tymicka Krystyna	1938
2767 Tymosiuk Helena	1906
2769 Tyska Janina	9.07.1935
2768 Tyska Gabriela	18.03.1896
2770 Tyski Karol	1.01.1891
Tyszczuk Wiktoria	1934
Tyszczuk Teresa	
4037 Tyszewicz Józefa	1.03.1899
4036 Tyszewicz Halina	22.06.1928
2771 Tyszkiewicz Waleria	18.10.1911
2772 Tyszko Walentyna	29.09.1912
2773 Ubysz Eleonora	07.1934
4038 Ucinek Bronisława	5.01.1908
4039 Ucinek Stanisław	22.02.1929
4040 Ucinek Zbigniew	1.08.1933
2774 Underka Teresa	11.07.1925
2775 Underka Zofia	11.02.1928
2777 Uniewska Rozalia	14.07.1910
2776 Uniewski Czesław	25.01.1936
2778 Uniewski Tadeusz	19.05.1934
3566 Urbach Dawid	30.04.1911
2782 Urban Stanisław	15.12.1933
2779 Urban Bronisława	25.11.1910
2780 Urban Edward	28.09.1928
2781 Urban Leokadia	19.09.1929
2783 Urban Stefania	3.05.1935
4677 Urban Krystyna	17.07.1943
4678 Urbaniec Eugenia	22.01.1902
4679 Urbaniec Danuta-Anna	15.03.1926
4680 Urbaniec Ryszard-Janusz	7.02.1932
2785 Urbanowska Halina	12.05.1931
2784 Urbanowska Barbara	9.05.1940
2786 Urbanowska Janina	8.05.1901
2787 Urbanowski Kazimierz	16.10.1935
2788 Uruska Anna	4.09.1929

3568 Uścinowicz Maria	20.03.1900
3567 Uścinowicz Józef	14.08.1891
2791 Uścińska Stanisława	15.10.1905
2789 Uścińska Jadwiga	15.01.1932
2790 Uściński Janusz	15.08.1939
4041 Utzig Maria	25.05.1920
4042 Utzig Marian	25.10.1941
4043 Utzig Wanda	10.02.1940
3569 Wachsmacher Henryk	3.07.1904
2792 Walak Alojzy	1932
4047 Walak Weronika	29.09.1903
4045 Walak Marian	15.02.1936
4044 Walak Krystyna	18.05.1930
4046 Walak Stanisława	24.11.1931
2794 Walas Stanisław	1927
2793 Walas Emilia	1933
2795 Walasik Czesława	14.05.1926
2797 Walawender Józef	26.02.1928
2796 Walawender Antoni	1930
2799 Walczak Władysława	3.06.1903
2798 Walczak Danuta	17.06.1929
2808 Wałdoch Ryszard	21.05.1932
2806 Wałdoch Franciszek	30.11.1897
2805 Wałdoch Barbara	22.04.1940
2807 Wałdoch Jadwiga	17.03.1924
3574 Wałdoch Maria	4.03.1902
2800 Walek Felicja	1934
4682 Walenia Maria	3.12.1919
4681 Walenia Agnieszka	24.11.1875
2801 Walerian Leokadia	1935
3571 Walisko Jerzy	26.12.1942
3570 Walisko Eryk	27.06.1912
3572 Walisko Romualda	2.02.1915
2810 Wałkuska Władysława	26.12.1888
2809 Wałkuska Czesława	29.09.1924
2804 Walles Zofia	15.09.1911
2802 Walles Krzysztof	20.02.1939
2803 Walles Władysław	12.03.1905
3573 Walles Ryszard	5.11.1943
2814 Waniuk Tatiana	1924
2813 Waniuk Maria	1929
2812 Waniuk Andrzej	1934
2811 Waniuk Anastazja	1876
4048 Waniuk Maria	1936
2815 Warchoł Aleksandra	30.11.1926
2816 Warchoł Józefa	9.11.1929
4683 Warenik Elżbieta	1.05.1932
4684 Warenik Irena	15.06.1938
4685 Warenik Maria	15.02.1927
4686 Warenik Zofia	25.12.1903
4049 Warwara Anna	23.05.1927
2817 Wasilejko Halina	21.11.1926
2818 Wasilewska Grażyna	1.01.1933

2819 Wasilewska Iwona	29.03.1934
2820 Wasilewska Maria	12.10.1909
4687 Wasilewska Natalia	29.10.1906
2823 Wasiuk Stanisław	15.05.1930
2821 Wasiuk Alicja	12.02.1928
2822 Wasiuk Maria	11.11.1894
2824 Wasiukiewicz Bolesława	12.10.1906
2825 Waszczuk Alina	11.10.1923
2826 Waszczuk Maria	9.03.1892
4688 Waszczuk Alina	18.10.1935
4689 Waszczuk Bronisława	14.06.1930
4690 Waszczuk Helena	18.07.1933
4692 Waszczuk Maria	15.03.1932
4693 Waszczuk Wanda	18.09.1929
4691 Waszczuyk Katarzyna	2.11.1906
2827 Waszkiewicz Jan	15.10.1931
2834 Wawrzyńczyk Aniela	13.11.1931
2835 Wawrzyńczyk Leokadia	15.11.1922
2836 Wawrzyńczyk Ludwika	3.09.1879
2828 Wawrzyniak Stanisław	27.10.1903
2830 Wawrzynowicz Krystyna	1.05.1931
2829 Wawrzynowicz Aniela	31.05.1897
2833 Wawrzynowicz Tadeusz	3.07.1927
2832 Wawrzynowicz Maria	8.01.1925
2831 Wawrzynowicz Leon	7.11.1896
4050 Wąchała Łucja	5.12.1880
2837 Wądołkowska Genowefa	7.04.1906
2839 Wądołkowska Jadwiga	1.07.1931
2838 Wądołkowski Henryk	10.03.1926
2840 Wądołkowski Zbigniew	8.12.1928
3576 Wąs Tomasz	13.12.1895
3575 Wąs Anna	15.05.1916
3577 Wąsik Władysław	5.02.1921
2841 Wąsowska Eugenia	25.05.1921
2843 Wąsowska Katarzyna	25.11.1875
2844 Wąsowska Kazimiera	16.01.1918
2842 Wąsowski Jerzy	23.04.1943
2845 Wcisło Nina	5.11.1903
2846 Wcisło Stanisława	17.07.1923
2847 Wehrstein Anna	26.11.1880
3578 Weinres Guido	7.09.1919
3579 Weitz Kalman	24.10.1877
2848 Wereszczaka Aniela	21.11.1901
2849 Wereszczaka Irena	29.01.1931
2850 Werner Helena	3.04.1924
2851 Weron Zbigniew	1932
4694 Wesoła Janina	3.12.1933
2855 Wesołowska Jadwiga	17.05.1922
2856 Wesołowska Małgorzata	14.02.1881
2854 Wesołowska Helena	6.04.1892
2852 Wesołowska Antonina	11.11.1911
2853 Wesołowska Franciszka	5.12.1933
4695 Wesoły Bolesław	5.12.1930
4696 Weyndling Eleonora	18.12.1882

4697 Weyndling Jadwiga	25.10.1923
2857 Wędrogowska Józefa	13.03.1912
2858 Węglarz Czesław	2.01.1924
4051 Węglarz Władysława	25.09.1927
2859 Węgorzewska Helena	11.09.1886
2860 Węgrzyn Leon	30.04.1913
2861 Wiczkowska Wanda	29.05.1883
2862 Widmańska Maria	4.12.1894
3580 Wiecha Chaim	20.09.1917
2866 Wieczorek Wiesława	2.01.1925
2864 Wieczorek Irena	1932
2863 Wieczorek Helena	10.12.1899
2865 Wieczorek Jadwiga	1.08.1914
4699 Wielgosz Krystyna	21.04.1937
4698 Wielgosz Józef	17.03.1943
4700 Wielgosz Maria	15.08.1912
4701 Wielopolska Danuta	6.07.1943
4702 Wielopolska Stanisława	31.12.1913
2871 Wierzbicka Wiesława	1934
2870 Wierzbicka Maria	15.08.1896
2868 Wierzbicka Janina	7.06.1929
2867 Wierzbicka Aldona	2.01.1931
2869 Wierzbicka Maria	1903
2875 Wierzbińska Leokadia	7.12.1931
2874 Wierzbińska Kazimiera	28.02.1934
2873 Wierzbińska Jadwiga	28.10.1901
2878 Wierzbińska Regina	21.10.1926
2872 Wierzbińska Aniela	1.08.1928
2877 Wierzbińska Maria	7.07.1924
2879 Wierzbiński Wiesław	2.11.1942
2876 Wierzbiński Longin	30.09.1930
2880 Wierzbowska Anna	13.12.1927
4703 Wierzchowska Feliksa	1.07.1910
4704 Wierzchowski Zbigniew	6.07.1932
4705 Wieselberg Samuel	25.12.1900
2881 Więcek Barbara	11.02.1934
2882 Więcek Krystyna	18.07.1936
2883 Więcek Maria	24.04.1908
4052 Więckowicz Maria	22.01.1919
2885 Więckowska Maria	10.08.1907
2884 Więckowska Łucja	10.11.1937
4706 Więcław Tatjana	16.11.1908
2887 Wilczek Barbara	29.10.1943
2886 Wilczek Aleksandra	6.11.1912
2888 Wilczek Tadeusz	17.07.1938
4053 Wilczewski Tadeusz	23.01.1889
2891 Wilczyńska Zofia	28.01.1900
2890 Wilczyńska Maria	1.01.1930
2889 Wilczyński Antoni	15.05.1886
4054 Wilińska Maria	7.10.1915
4707 Wilkosz Anna	21.11.1925
4708 Wilkosz Józef	28.03.1928
4709 Wilkosz Mirosław	30.07.1933
4710 Wilkosz Zbigniew	4.12.1935
2893 Wilusz Paraska	5.06.1902
2892 Wilusz Maria	15.11.1930
2894 Wincenciak Maria	8.12.1885
2899 Winnicka Teresa	24.06.1930
2895 Winnicka Aniela	4.01.1900
2896 Winnicka Irena	25.03.1928
2897 Winnicka Jadwiga	15.10.1926
2898 Winnicki Napoleon	17.05.1931
2900 Winogrodzka Janina	10.07.1904
4055 Wirth Maria	3.07.1908
3581 Wistreich Artur	28.04.1890
2901 Wiszowata Bogumiła	22.02.1933
2902 Wiszowata Waleria	13.03.1901
2904 Wiśniewska Henryka	10.12.1936
2905 Wiśniewska Izabela	10.09.1936
2907 Wiśniewska Józefa	19.03.1902
2903 Wiśniewska Barbara	19.02.1938
Wiśniewski Leon	19.02.1938
2912 Wiśniewska Waleria	6.06.1926
2909 Wiśniewska Koletta	15.08.1897
2908 Wiśniewska Julia	30.07.1910
4056 Wiśniewska Wanda	18.01.1920
3582 Wiśniewska Julia	22.05.1885
2906 Wiśniewski Jerzy	1934
2911 Wiśniewski Stanisław	4.06.1902
2910 Wiśniewski Leon	19.02.1937
2915 Witaszek Zdzisław	29.03.1929
2913 Witaszek Józef	25.02.1935
2914 Witaszek Lucyna	8.12.1926
3583 Witko Maria	16.08.1901
4057 Witoszyńska Janina	23.10.1887
2918 Wizimirska Katarzyna	8.02.1906
2916 Wizimirska Danuta	5.12.1935
2917 Wizimirska Janina	27.05.1928
2919 Wizimirska Wanda	8.10.1926
2920 Wizimirska Zofia	4.04.1930
4711 Wlizło-Wilińska Aniela	17.06.1877
2921 Włodkowska Janina	6.07.1936
2922 Włodkowski Stanisław	9.01.1929
4714 Wojakiewicz Marian	20.10.1939
4715 Wojakiewicz Teresa	5.10.1937
4713 Wojakiewicz Helena	8.06.1905
4712 Wojakiewicz Bogdan	1.06.1932
4058 Wojakowska Stefania	25.11.1881
2970 Wójcicka Maria	6.12.1897
2971 Wójcicki Stanisław	22.02.1896
2924 Wojciechowska Genowefa	1926
2925 Wojciechowska Rozalia	3.12.1927
2923 Wojciechowska Emilia	7.12.1904
4716 Wojciechowska Emilia	4.10.1944
2927 Wojciechowski Wiktor	3.03.1889
2926 Wojciechowski Stanisław	8.06.1930
2978 Wójcik Julia	1928
2928 Wojewoda Leonia	9.11.1912
2229 Wojewoda Maria	26.02.1937
2931 Wojewódka Franciszek	1937
2932 Wojewódka Kazimierz	6.09.1936
2933 Wojewódka Krystyna	11.03.1930
2930 Wojewódka Bogumiła	28.01.1928
2935 Wojniłowicz Jadwiga	1897
2936 Wojniłowicz Jadwiga	26.01.1924
2937 Wojniłowicz Janina	26.07.1928
2939 Wojtasiewicz Wiesława	16.03.1927
2938 Wojtasiewicz Apolonia	6.02.1888
4717 Wojtkowska Maria	1905
4718 Wojtkowski Stanisław	13.04.1931
2941 Wojtowicz Bolesław	1936
2940 Wojtowicz Anastazja	15.04.1904
4721 Wojtowicz Tadeusz	8.08.1931
3584 Wojtowicz Krystyna	12.11.1943
4720 Wojtowicz Jan	28.09.1932
2942 Wojtulewicz Julia	28.05.1890
2982 Wójtowicz Franciszka	1.03.1890
2989 Wójtowicz Sylwia	18.11.1929
2987 Wójtowicz Lidia	31.01.1921
2986 Wójtowicz Józefa	2.12.1929
2983 Wójtowicz Jan	18.06.1932
2984 Wójtowicz Joanna	15.04.1939
2981 Wójtowicz Feliksa	26.01.1924
2988 Wójtowicz Maria	3.05.1936
2979 Wójtowicz Aniela	13.08.1930
2980 Wójtowicz Feliksa	23.10.1904
2985 Wójtowicz Józefa	24.06.1928
4725 Wójtowicz Antonina	10.08.1902
2943 Wolak Agnieszka	20.04.1893
2944 Woldański Marian	1931
2946 Wolniewicz Maria	8.11.1902
2945 Wolniewicz Klara	28.02.1924
4722 Wolski Józef	30.09.1886
2947 Wołczyński Robert	2.01.1932
2948 Wołk Halina	23.04.1925
2951 Wołk-Lewanowicz Sergiusz	1869
2949 Wołk-Lewanowicz Aleksandra	24.01.1900
2950 Wołk-Lewanowicz Amalia	1870
4723 Wołkowska Maria	1.02.1890
2952 Wołodźko Stefan	21.01.1896
1961 Wołodźko Maria	15.05.1918
4724 Wołodźko Kazimierz	9.09.1944
2954 Wołoszczuk Wanda	1930
2953 Wołoszczuk Stanisława	22.04.1903
2955 Wołoszyn Romuald	1932
2957 Wołożyńska Leonia	11.04.1905
2956 Wołożyńska Jadwiga	1.04.1898
2958 Wołożyńska Maria	15.12.1864
2959 Wołożyński Sylwester	31.12.1887
2960 Wołujewicz Salomea	1900
2962 Woronowicz Wanda	4.04.1907
2961 Woronowicz Krystyna	10.07.1936

2963	Worotyńska Melania	17.04.1906	3022	Wysokińska Irena	22.09.1933	4745	Zaleśny Józef	17.01.1929
2964	Worotyńska Regina	17.12.1925	3023	Wysokińska Krystyna	22.10.1929	4744	Zaleśny Edward	25.04.1936
2965	Worotyński Witold	15.12.1928	3021	Wysokińska Celina	3.06.1927	4746	Zaleśny Stanisław	17.01.1929
2968	Wortman Genowefa	3.11.1902	3024	Wysokiński Roman	4.08.1877	3054	Zalewska Aleksandra	24.12.1904
2967	Wortman Anna	3.02.1937	3020	Wysokiński Bogdan	21.02.1936	3057	Zalewska Maria	8.07.1937
2966	Wortman Andrzej	14.09.1935	4732	Wyspiańska Jadwiga	3.02.1911	3056	Zalewska Jadwiga	4.11.1934
2969	Woszczyńska Stanisława	1934	4733	Wyspiańska Sabina	17.02.1888	3058	Zalewska Stefania	22.08.1894
2934	Woyniłłowicz Eleonora	31.01.1924	4734	Wyspiański Stanisław	26.09.1942	3059	Zalewski Józef	14.02.1885
2977	Woźniak Stanisława	22.04.1906	3026	Wysznacka Maria	21.11.1888	3055	Zalewski Florian	29.12.1928
2976	Woźniak Maria	25.06.1927	3028	Wyszyński Witold	1932	3060	Zalewski Wacław	6.08.1931
2975	Woźniak Kazimierz	20.09.1929	3027	Wyszyński Jan	1929	3592	Zalewski Józef	3.03.1898
2973	Woźniak Jadwiga	13.07.1927				3061	Zalot Albina	26.02.1886
2974	Woźniak Kazimiera	15.06.1930	3029	Zabrzeska Adela	28.05.1929	4060	Zaniewska Helena	1892
2972	Woźniak Franciszek	4.10.1921	3031	Zabrzeska Leokadia	15.01.1930	2274	Zaremba Stefania	1.01.1912
2990	Wronko Feliks	27.05.1902	3032	Zabrzeska Zofia	8.10.1925	4748	Zaremba Tadeusz	1.09.1944
2995	Wróbel Leokadia	2.02.1921	3030	Zabrzeska Czesława	15.08.1927	4747	Zaremba Józef	25.07.1912
2991	Wróbel Edward	3.03.1936	3033	Zabrzeski Zygmunt	1930	4061	Zarzycka Emilia	3.03.1928
2992	Wróbel Franciszek	2.08.1937	3034	Zacharczyk Rozalia	26.03.1897	4063	Zarzycki Lucjan	18.05.1931
2994	Wróbel Kazimiera	1.01.1930	3035	Zacharkiewicz Ewa	15.08.1914	4062	Zarzycki Jan	8.02.1930
2993	Wróbel Józef	1.03.1931	3036	Zagórowska Zofia	6.10.1903	3062	Zarzycki Mikołaj	22.05.1901
2997	Wróblewska Jadwiga	12.07.1907	3037	Zagórska Irena	15.09.1912	3064	Zasowska Anna	7.12.1907
2996	Wróblewska Irena	31.10.1929	3040	Zając Feliks	23.03.1928	3063	Zasowska Alodia	30.06.1927
4728	Wróblewska Jadwiga	8.09.1928	3039	Zając Czesława	31.05.1935	3065	Zasowska Halina	9.10.1929
4726	Wróblewska Anna	13.07.1909	3045	Zając Piotr	26.03.1888	4064	Zastawna Maria	18.04.1905
2998	Wróblewski Marian	17.01.1935	3044	Zając Maria	18.04.1901	3067	Zator Ludwika	3.01.1902
3585	Wróblewski Alfons	5.12.1905	3042	Zając Katarzyna	26.03.1888	3066	Zator Helena	18.05.1923
4727	Wróblewski Bogusław	10.05.1934	3043	Zając Kazimierz	1937	3068	Zator Maria	17.06.1929
4729	Wróblewski Wacław	28.05.1932	3041	Zając Jan	5.05.1929	3070	Zawadowska Waleria	22.02.1917
3001	Wruszczak Sławomir	1.01.1935	3038	Zając Czesław	26.11.1930	3069	Zawadowska Ludmiła	22.06.1936
2999	Wruszczak Danuta	28.03.1936	4738	Zając Regina	12.05.1932	4067	Zawadzka Maria	2.07.1927
3002	Wruszczak Stefania	10.03.1912	4735	Zając Helena	18.10.1926	4066	Zawadzka Krystyna	1937
3003	Wruszczak Trofim	10.02.1887	4736	Zając Kazimierz	3.08.1935	3072	Zawadzka Zofia	5.02.1927
3000	Wruszczak Lubomir	14.01.1933	4737	Zając Maria	27.09.1923	4068	Zawadzka Zofia	9.10.1932
3005	Wrzyszcz Lubomir	22.08.1933		Zając Bolesława	1909	4749	Zawadzka Helena	20.12.1888
3006	Wrzyszcz Stefania	2.03.1905		Zając Wanda	1927	4065	Zawadzki Józef	7.04.1931
3004	Wrzyszcz Eugeniusz	20.05.1928		Zając Zdzisław	1936	3593	Zawadzki Wojciech	16.04.1894
4730	Wszoł Antoni	9.06.1907	4740	Zajączkowska Olga	23.12.1905	3071	Zawadzki Leon	19.01.1914
4731	Wszoł Katarzyna	20.04.1889	4739	Zajączkowska Jadwiga	10.08.1940		Zawidzka Zofia	26.06.1926
3007	Wujek Leokadia	12.03.1928	3046	Zajkowska Julianna	19.10.1912		Zawidzka Aniela	13.11.1902
3012	Wypijewska Maria	1.12.1924	4059	Zajkowski Jerzy-Józef	22.06.1919		Zawidzki Tadeusz	7.06.1934
3010	Wypijewska Helena	13.05.1901	3590	Zakrzewska Jadwiga	29.03.1927	3076	Zawiestowicz Zofia	1883
3008	Wypijewska Albina	28.08.1933	3588	Zakrzewska Danuta	7.08.1937	3073	Zawiestowicz Helena	1909
3011	Wypijewska Krystyna	9.10.1929	3589	Zakrzewska Genowefa	2.12.1900	3074	Zawiestowicz Konstanty	17.01.1879
3009	Wypijewski Dyonizy	9.12.1930	3047	Zakrzewska Halina	4.02.1924	3075	Zawiestowicz Wanda	6.08.1925
3586	Wyrobiec Antonina	7.07.1904	3591	Zakrzewski Piotr	19.10.1931	4750	Zawojska Bronisława	27.12.1900
3587	Wysocka Maria	15.08.1913	3051	Zaleska Maria	1885	4069	Ząbek Helena	25.07.1909
3013	Wysocka Alicja	1934	3049	Zaleska Barbara	4.12.1918	3594	Zbieranowska Danuta	15.06.1931
3015	Wysocka Paulina	30.10.1907	3048	Zaleska Aniela	10.02.1882	3595	Zbieranowski Ryszard	3.04.1933
3016	Wysocka Romualda	28.02.1934	3052	Zaleska Wanda	10.01.1940	3596	Zbieranowski Zygmunt	19.01.1928
3019	Wysocka Władysława	1918	3053	Zaleski Wincenty	15.08.1877	3597	Zbilut Helena	11.05.1882
3014	Wysocka Danuta	4.05.1937	3050	Zaleski Leszek	10.05.1938	3077	Zbróg Janina	2.07.1929
3017	Wysocki Stanisław	12.05.1936	4742	Zaleśna Franciszka	26.06.1927	3079	Zbyrad Janina	6.05.1925
3018	Wysocki Wilhelm	28.05.1931	4741	Zaleśna Anna	5.03.1931	3078	Zbyrad Bronisława	18.11.1904
3025	Wysokińska Stanisława	15.02.1903	4743	Zaleśna Maria	25.05.1926	4752	Zbyszewska Bronisława	9.06.1901

4753	Zbyszewska Danuta	14.10.1924	4073	Zubrzycka Wanda	11.02.1911	3107	Żarów Janina	20.08.1928
3080	Zdancewicz Jadwiga	14.09.1924	4071	Zubrzycki Robert	29.06.1938	3108	Żawryd Wanda	15.03.1895
3081	Zdrochecki Andrzej	1937	4072	Zubrzycki Stanisław	28.10.1890	3109	Żebrowska Józefa	15.01.1893
4754	Zdrójkowska Aniela	2.02.1897	3099	Zwodzińska Janina	18.04.1922	4771	Żelechowska Adela	1.11.1914
3598	Zellerkraut Mendel	15.05.1898	3102	Zych Stanisława	15.10.1903	4772	Żelechowska Teresa	2.10.1939
3082	Zerko Jan	18.06.1888	3101	Zych Pelagia	23.03.1929	3110	Żelisko-Żelska Bronisława	15.05.1897
3083	Zglinicka Maria	17.12.1913	3100	Zych Genowefa	21.12.1927	3111	Żelisko-Żelska Kazimiera	19.12.1928
3085	Ziarkiewicz Wiktoria	22.08.1897	4757	Zych Władysława	2.01.1932	4773	Żerebecka Irena	28.06.1906
3084	Ziarkiewicz Józef	18.04.1899		Zychowicz Danuta		3112	Żerebecki Zdzisław	1.01.1896
4755	Ziarnicka Stefania	13.01.1909		Zychowicz Wanda		3098	Żogał Felicja	17.08.1923
3086	Zielińska Anna	10.07.1911	4760	Zygmunt Ludwika	15.05.1878	3113	Żołądkiewicz Ludwik	6.01.1932
3087	Zielińska Stanisława	13.03.1940	4759	Zygmunt Katarzyna	9.01.1918	3114	Żołądkiewicz Stanisława	18.07.1912
3088	Zielski Roman	18.06.1929	4758	Zygmunt Eugeniusz	4.11.1936	3115	Żołądkiewicz Wiesława	15.03.1935
3089	Ziemba Helena	3.03.1929	3602	Zylbersztajn Wolf	6.05.1915	3116	Żołądziejewska Antonina	8.02.1914
3599	Zientek Teresa	27.10.1937				3117	Żółtańska Teresa	1883
4756	Zientek Teresa	24.07.1929	3105	Żaba Alina	16.12.1888	4074	Żukowska Danuta	5.05.1928
3091	Zimińska Kazimiera	26.03.1927	3106	Żaba Danuta	14.03.1927	4075	Żukowska Kazimiera	25.03.1921
3090	Zimińska Bronisława	1.01.1895	4761	Żabko Jadwiga	13.08.1907	3603	Żurek Tadeusz	28.01.1941
4070	Zimińska Eugenia	13.04.1917	4762	Żabko Ryszard	2.08.1931	3604	Żurek Wanda	16.07.1919
3092	Zimmermann Janina	17.06.1912	4764	Żak Irena	26.03.1932	3605	Żurowska Stefania	26.12.1902
3093	Zimmermann Mirosława	19.10.1934	4763	Żak Anatol	3.07.1934	4774	Żygadło Maria	6.08.1893
3094	Ziubrzycka Antonina	10.03.1878	4765	Żak Józefa	24.03.1927	3104	Żyszkowska Stefania	2.02.1895
3095	Ziubrzycki Bronisław	30.07.1905	4766	Żak Helena	29.08.1929	3103	Żyszkowska Leokadia	20.01.1925
3601	Znojko Ludmiła	22.03.1927	4767	Żak Maria	28.11.1905	3118	Żywółt Anatoli	7.01.1880
3600	Znojko Izabella	27.03.1930	4768	Żak Maria	9.04.1925	3121	Żywółt Olga	1903
3096	Zobek Irena	6.07.1927	4769	Żak Władysław	4.11.1896	3119	Żywółt Eugeniusz	5.11.1927
3097	Zobek Paulina	2.07.1900	4770	Żarnower Michał	20.07.1899	3120	Żywółt Maria	25.02.1929